Twentieth-Century Literary Criticism

Topics Volume

Guide to Gale Literary Criticism Series

When you need to review criticism of literary works, these are the Gale series to use:

If the author's death date is:	You should turn to:

After Dec. 31, 1959
(or author is still living)

CONTEMPORARY LITERARY CRITICISM

for example: Jorge Luis Borges, Anthony Burgess, Ernest Hemingway, Iris Murdoch

1900 through 1959

TWENTIETH-CENTURY LITERARY CRITICISM

for example: Willa Cather, F. Scott Fitzgerald, Henry James, Mark Twain, Virginia Woolf

1800 through 1899

NINETEENTH-CENTURY LITERATURE CRITICISM

for example: Fyodor Dostoevsky, Nathaniel Hawthorne, George Sand, William Wordsworth

1400 through 1799

LITERATURE CRITICISM FROM 1400 TO 1800
(excluding Shakespeare)

for example: Anne Bradstreet, Alexander Pope, François Rabelais, Phillis Wheatley

SHAKESPEAREAN CRITICISM

Shakespeare's plays and poetry

Antiquity through 1399

CLASSICAL AND MEDIEVAL LITERATURE CRITICISM

for example: Dante, Homer, Plato, Sophocles, Vergil

Gale also publishes related criticism series:

CHILDREN'S LITERATURE REVIEW

This series covers authors of all eras who have written for the preschool through high school audience.

SHORT STORY CRITICISM

This series covers the major short fiction writers of all nationalities and periods of literary history.

POETRY CRITICISM

This series covers poets of all nationalities, movements, and periods of literary history.

DRAMA CRITICISM

This series covers playwrights of all nationalities and periods of literary history.

BLACK LITERATURE CRITICISM

This three-volume set presents criticism of works by major black writers of the past two hundred years.

WORLD LITERATURE CRITICISM, 1500 TO THE PRESENT

This six-volume set provides excerpts from criticism on 225 authors from the Renaissance to the present.

ISSN 0276-8178

Volume 34

Twentieth-Century Literary Criticism

Topics Volume

**Excerpts from Criticism of Various Topics
in Twentieth-Century Literature, including Literary
and Critical Movements, Prominent Themes and
Genres, Anniversary Celebrations, and Surveys
of National Literatures**

Paula Kepos
Editor

Marie Lazzari
Thomas Ligotti
Joann Prosyniuk
Laurie Sherman
Associate Editors

 Gale Research Inc. • *DETROIT* • *WASHINGTON, D.C.* • *LONDON*

STAFF

Paula Kepos, *Editor*

Marie Lazzari, Thomas Ligotti, Joann Prosyniuk, Laurie Sherman, *Associate Editors*

Susan Windisch Brown, Michelle L. McClellan, Debra A. Wells, *Assistant Editors*

Jeanne A. Gough, *Permissions & Production Manager*
Linda M. Pugliese, *Production Supervisor*
Jennifer E. Gale, Suzanne Powers, Maureen A. Puhl, Lee Ann Welsh, *Editorial Associates*
Donna Craft, Christine A. Galbraith, David G. Oblender, Linda M. Ross, *Editorial Assistants*

Victoria B. Cariappa, *Research Supervisor*
Karen D. Kaus, Eric Priehs, Maureen Richards, Mary D. Wise, *Editorial Associates*
H. Nelson Fields, Rogene M. Fisher, Judy Gale, Filomena Sgambati, *Editorial Assistants*

Sandra C. Davis, *Permissions Supervisor (Text)*
H. Diane Cooper, Kathy Grell, Josephine M. Keene, Kimberly F. Smilay, *Permissions Associates*
Maria L. Franklin, Lisa M. Lantz, Camille P. Robinson, Shalice Shah, Denise M. Singleton,
Permissions Assistants

Patricia A. Seefelt, *Permissions Supervisor (Pictures)*
Margaret A. Chamberlain, *Permissions Associate*
Pamela A. Hayes, Lillian Quickley, *Permissions Assistants*

Mary Beth Trimper, *Production Manager*
Marilyn Jackman, *External Production Assistant*

Arthur Chartow, *Art Director*
Nicholas Jakubiak, C. J. Jonik, *Keyliners*

Laura Bryant, *Production Supervisor*
Louise Gagne', *Internal Production Associate*
Kelly Krust, Sharana Wier, *Internal Production Assistants*

∞™ This book is printed on acid-free paper that meets the minimum requirements of American National Standard for Information Sciences— Permanence Paper for Printed Library Materials, ANSI Z39.48-1984.

Library of Congress Catalog Card Number 76-46132
ISBN 0-8103-2416-4
ISSN 0276-8178

Printed in the United States of America

Published simultaneously in the United Kingdom
by Gale Research International Limited
(An affiliated company of Gale Research Inc.)

10 9 8 7 6 5 4 3 2

Contents

Preface vii

Acknowledgments xi

Authors to Be Featured in Forthcoming Volumes xv

New Criticism

World War I Literature

Preface

Since its inception more than ten years ago, *Twentieth-Century Literary Criticism* has been purchased and used by nearly 10,000 school, public, and college or university libraries. With this edition—volume 34 in the series—*TCLC* has covered over 500 authors, representing 56 nationalities, and more than 25,000 titles. No other reference source has surveyed the critical response to twentieth-century authors and literature as thoroughly as *TCLC*. In the words of one reviewer, "there is nothing comparable available." *TCLC* "is a gold mine of information—dates, pseudonyms, biographical information, and criticism from books and periodicals—which many libraries would have difficulty assembling on their own."

TCLC is a companion series to Gale's *Contemporary Literary Criticism*, which reprints commentary on current writing. Because of the different periods under consideration (*CLC* considers authors who were still living after 1959), there is no duplication of material between *CLC* and *TCLC*. For additional information about *CLC* and Gale's other criticism titles, users should consult the Guide to Gale Literary Criticism Series preceding the title page in this volume.

Scope of the Series

TCLC is designed to serve as an introduction for students and advanced readers to authors who died between 1900 and 1960, and to the most significant interpretations of these authors' works. The great poets, novelists, short story writers, playwrights, and philosophers of this period are frequently studied in high school and college literature courses. In organizing and excerpting the vast amount of critical material written on these authors, *TCLC* helps students develop valuable insight into literary history, promotes a better understanding of the texts, and sparks ideas for papers and assignments. Each entry in *TCLC* presents a comprehensive survey of the author's career or an individual work of literature and provides the user a multiplicity of interepretations and assessments. Such a variety allows students to pursue their own interests; furthermore, it fosters an awareness that literature is dynamic and responsive to many different opinions.

Topics Volumes

Every fourth volume of *TCLC* is devoted to literary topics that cannot be covered under the author approach used in the rest of the series. Such topics include literary movements, prominent themes in twentieth-century literature, literary reaction to political and historical events, significant eras in literary history, prominent literary anniversaries, and the literatures of cultures that are often overlooked by English-speaking readers. *TCLC* 34, for example, examines the following five topics: the Bloomsbury Group, a circle of English writers, thinkers, and artists whose works are among the most important of the twentieth century; the German Expressionists, whose subordination of representation to emotional experience greatly influenced the development of modern art and literature; the American Muckrakers, a group of investigative journalists whose exposés instigated many government, labor, and health care reforms in the first decade of the twentieth century; the New Criticism, a movement that revolutionized literary criticism in the United States; and the literature of World War I, a conflict that conclusively changed the nature of modern combat and inspired an impassioned literary response. Entries in Topics volumes are generally restricted to the period between 1900 to 1959, and do not duplicate criticism from *CLC*.

Organization of the Book

Each subject entry in a Topics volume consists of the following elements: an introduction, a list of representative works, excerpts of criticism (each preceded by an annotation and followed by a bibliographic citation), a list of further reading on the topic, and numerous illustrations.

- The *introduction* briefly defines the subject of the entry and provides social and historical background information important to an understanding of the criticism.

- The list of *representative works* identifies writings by authors associated with the subject. Arranged chronologically by date of first book publication, the list also indicates the genre of each work. In the case of foreign authors with both foreign-language publications and English translations, the title and date of the first English-language edition are given in brackets. Unless otherwise indicated, dramas are dated by first performance, not first publication.

- The *criticism* is arranged thematically. Entries commonly begin with general surveys of the subject or essays providing historical background information, followed by essays that develop particular aspects of the topic. For example, the entry devoted to German Expressionism begins with excerpts detailing the history and major figures of the movement and examining aesthetic principles advanced by its leading theorists. These are followed by sections devoted to Expressionist drama, poetry, film, painting, and music. The entry concludes with an essay evaluating the philosophical convictions and political goals of Expressionist writers. Each section has a separate title heading and is identified with a page number in the table of contents.

   The critic's name is given at the beginning of each piece of criticism; anonymous essays are headed by the title of the journal in which they appeared. Many critical essays in *TCLC* contain translated material. Unless otherwise noted, translations within brackets are by the editors; translations within parentheses are by the critic. Publication information (such as publisher names and book prices) and parenthetical numerical references (such as footnotes or page and line references to specific editions of works) have been deleted at the editors' discretion to provide smoother reading of the text.

- Critical essays are prefaced by *annotations* providing the reader with information about both the critic and the criticism that follows. Included are the critic's reputation, individual approach to literary criticism, and particular expertise in the subject under discussion. Also noted are the relative importance of a work of criticism, the scope of the excerpt, and the growth of critical controversy or changes in critical trends regarding the subject. In some cases, these notes cross-reference the work of critics who discuss each other's commentary.

- A complete *bibliographic citation* designed to facilitate location of the original essay or book follows each piece of criticism.

- The bibliography of *further reading* appearing at the end of each subject entry lists further secondary sources on the subject, in some cases including essays for which the editors could not obtain reprint rights, and anthologies of primary sources.

- *Illustrations* throughout the entry include portraits of the authors under discussion; reproductions of important manuscript pages, magazine covers, dust jackets, movie stills, artwork, and maps; and photographs of people, places, and events important to the topic.

Cumulative Indexes

Each volume of *TCLC*, including the Topics volumes, contains a cumulative author index listing all authors who have appeared in the following Gale series: *Contemporary Literary Criticism, Twentieth-Century Literary Criticism, Nineteenth-Century Literature Criticism, Literature Criticism from 1400 to 1800,* and *Classical and Medieval Literature Criticism.* Topic entries devoted to a single author, such as the entry on James Joyce's *Ulysses* in *TCLC* 26, are listed in this index. Also included are cross-references to the Gale series *Short Story Criticism, Children's Literature Review, Authors in the News, Contemporary Authors, Contemporary Authors Autobiography Series, Dictionary of Literary Biography, Concise Dictionary of American Literary Biography, Something about the Author, Something about the Author Autobiography Series,* and *Yesterday's Authors of Books for Children.* Useful for locating authors within the various series, this index is particularly valuable for those authors who are identified with a certain period but who, because of their death dates, are placed in another, or for those authors whose careers span two periods. For example, F. Scott Fitzgerald is found in *TCLC,* yet a writer often associated with him, Ernest Hemingway, is found in *CLC.*

Beginning with *TCLC* 34, each volume in Gale's Literary Criticism Series will include a cumulative topic index, which lists all literary topics treated in *NCLC* Topics volumes, *TCLC* Topics volumes, and the *CLC* Yearbook.

Each *TCLC* Topics volume also includes a cumulative nationality index which lists all authors who have appeared in regular *TCLC* volumes, arranged alphabetically under their respective nationalities, as well as Topics volume entries devoted to particular national literatures.

Titles discussed in the Topics volume entries are not included in the *TCLC* cumulative title index.

Suggestions Are Welcome

In response to suggestions, several features have been added to *TCLC* since the series began, including annotations to excerpted criticism, a cumulative index to authors in all Gale literary criticism series, entries devoted to criticism on a single work by a major author, more extensive illustrations, and a title index listing all literary works discussed in the series since its inception.

Readers who wish to suggest authors or topics to appear in future volumes, or who have other suggestions, are cordially invited to write the editors or call our toll-free number: 1-800-347-GALE.

Acknowledgments

The editors wish to thank the copyright holders of the excerpted criticism included in this volume, the permissions managers of many book and publishing companies for assisting us in securing reprint rights, and Anthony Bogucki for assistance with copyright research. We are also grateful to the staffs of the Detroit Public Library, the Library of Congress, the University of Detroit Library, the University of Michigan Library, and the Wayne State University Library for making their resources available to us. Following is a list of the copyright holders who have granted us permission to reprint material in this volume of *TCLC*. Every effort has been made to trace copyright, but if omissions have been made, please let us know.

COPYRIGHTED EXCERPTS IN *TCLC*, VOLUME 34, WERE REPRINTED FROM THE FOLLOWING PERIODICALS:

Bucknell Review, Winter, 1966. Reprinted by permission of Associated University Presses.—*Critical Inquiry,* v. 2, Autumn, 1975 for "The Poetics of Surrender: An Exposition and Critique of New Critical Poets" by Richard Strier; v. 4, Summer, 1978 for "The New Criticism: Pro and Contra" by Rene Wellek; v. 6, Winter, 1979 for "Bloomsbury and 'The Vulgar Passions' " by Quentin Bell; v. 5, Spring, 1979 for "Critical Response: New Criticism Once More" by Gerald Graff. Copyright © 1975, 1978, 1979 by The University of Chicago. All reprinted by permission of the publisher and the respective authors.—*Criticism,* v. IX, Winter, 1967 for "Expressionism: Style or 'Weltanschauung'?" by Ulrich Weisstein. Copyright, 1967, Wayne State University Press. Reprinted by permission of the publisher and the author.—*The Drama Review,* v. 19, September, 1975 for "German Expressionist Acting" by Mel Gordon. Copyright © 1975, *The Drama Review.* Reprinted by permission of The MIT Press, Cambridge, MA and the author.—*English Literature in Transition: 1880-1920,* v. 12, 1969 for "G. E. Moore and the Bloomsbury Group" by Donald J. Watt. Copyright © 1969 *English Literature in Transition: 1880-1920.* Reprinted by permission of the publisher and the author.—*English Studies in Canada,* v. V, Spring, 1979 for "Revolt and the Ideal in Bloomsbury" by Linda Hutcheon. © Association of Canadian University Teachers of English 1979. Reprinted by permission of the publisher and the author.—*Essays by Divers Hands,* n.s. v. XXXVI, 1970 for "A Military Historian's View of the Great War" by Correlli Barnett. © the author 1970. Reprinted by permission of the author.—*European Studies Review,* v. I, April, 1971. Copyright © 1971 SAGE Publications Ltd. Reprinted by permission of the publisher.—*The Georgia Review,* v. XXIV, Spring, 1970. Copyright, 1970, by the University of Georgia. Reprinted by permission of the publisher.—*German Life & Letters,* v. XX, 1966-67. Reprinted by permission of the publisher.—*The German Quarterly,* v. XL, March, 1967. Copyright © 1967 by the American Association of Teachers of German. Reprinted by permission of the publisher.—*The Historian,* v. XLVII, November, 1984. Copyright 1984 by Phi Alpha Theta. Reprinted by permission of the publisher.—*Journal of the History of Ideas,* v. XXV, April-June, 1964. Copyright 1964, Journal of the History of Ideas, Inc. Reprinted by permission of the publisher.—*Journalism History,* v. 10, Spring & Summer, 1983 for " 'The Jungle' and Its Effects" by William Parmenter. Copyright © 1983 by CSUN Foundation. All rights reserved. Reprinted by permission of the author.—*The Literary Criterion,* v. XVII, 1982. Reprinted by permission of the publisher.—*The Massachusetts Review,* v. XXI, Spring, 1980. © 1980. Reprinted from *The Massachusetts Review,* The Massachusetts Review, Inc. by permission.—*Mid-America: An Historical Review,* v. 46, April, 1964. © Loyola University 1964. Reprinted by permission of the publisher.—*Midway,* v. 9, Autumn, 1968 for "The Bloomsbury Group" by Carolyn G. Heilbrun. © 1968 by The University of Chicago. Reprinted by permission of The University of Chicago Press and the author.—*MLN,* v. 97, December, 1982. © copyright 1982 by The Johns Hopkins University Press. All rights reserved. Reprinted by permission of the publisher.—*The New Republic,* v. 175, October 2, 1976. © 1976 The New Republic, Inc. Reprinted by permission of *The New Republic.*—*The New York Review of Books,* v. XXII, April 17, 1975. Copyright © 1975 Nyrev, Inc. Reprinted with permission from *The New York Review of Books.*—*The New York Times Magazine,* February 25, 1962. Copyright © 1962 by The New York Times Company. Reprinted by permission of the publisher.—*San Jose Studies,* v. V, February, 1979 for " 'The Hogarth Letters': Bloomsbury Writers on Art and Politics" by Selma Meyerowitz. © San Jose University Foundation, 1979. Reprinted by permission of the publisher and the author.—*The Sewanee Review,* v. LXXXVII, Fall, 1979. © 1979 by The University of the South. Reprinted by permission of the editor of *The Sewanee Review.*

COPYRIGHTED EXCERPTS IN *TCLC*, VOLUME 34, WERE REPRINTED FROM THE FOLLOWING BOOKS:

Bannister, Robert C., Jr. From "Race Relations and the Muckrakers," in *Muckraking: Past, Present and Future.* Edited by John M. Harrison and Harry H. Stein. Pennsylvania State University Press, 1973. Copyright © 1973, The Pennsylvania State University Press, University Press, PA. All rights reserved. Reprinted by permission of the publisher.—Bell, Quentin. From *Bloomsbury.* Weidenfeld & Nicholson, 1968. © 1968 by Quentin Bell. Reprinted by permission of the publisher.—Benn, Gottfried. From "The Confessions of an Expressionist," in *Voices of German*

Authors to Be Featured in Forthcoming Volumes

Sholom Aleichem (Ukrainian-born Yiddish short story writer) Sholom Aleichem was one of the founders and most important writers of Yiddish literature, noted for his humorous, often poignant portrayals of Jewish life in rural Russia.

Bertolt Brecht (German dramatist)—Ranked among the most influential modern playwrights, Brecht is recognized in particular for his creation of the "epic" dramatic style, in which elements such as plot and characterization are subordinated to intellectual concerns. *TCLC* will devote an entry to his play *Mutter Courage und ihre Kinder (Mother Courage and Her Children),* which is regarded as one of Brecht's most effective expositions of his concern for the fate of the virtuous individual in a corrupt society.

Benedetto Croce (Italian philosopher and critic)—Considered the most influential literary critic of the twentieth century, Croce developed aesthetic theories that became central tenets of modern arts criticism while establishing important critical approaches to the works of such authors as William Shakespeare, Johann Wolfgang von Goethe, and Pierre Corneille.

Theodore Dreiser (American novelist)—A prominent American exponent of literary Naturalism and one of America's foremost novelists, Dreiser was the author of works commended for their powerful characterizations and strong ideological convictions.

John Gould Fletcher (American poet)—Fletcher was an innovative poet and major contributor to the development of Imagism, an influential early twentieth-century movement dedicated to replacing traditional poetics with freer rhythms and a more concise use of language.

André Gide (French novelist and critic)—Although credited with introducing the techniques of Modernism to the French novel, Gide is more highly esteemed for the autobiographical honesty and perspicacity of his work, which depicts the moral development of a modern intellectual. *TCLC* will devote an entry to *Les faux monnayeurs (The Counterfeiters),* Gide's most ambitious and stylistically sophisticated novel.

James Joyce (Irish novelist and short story writer)—The most prominent writer of the first half of the twentieth century, Joyce was the author of virtuoso experiments in prose which redefined both the limits of language and the form of the modern novel. *TCLC* will devote an entry to his only short story collection, *Dubliners,* which is regarded as a landmark in the development of the genre.

Sinclair Lewis (American novelist)—One of the foremost American novelists of the 1920s and 30s, Lewis wrote some of the most effective satires in American literature. *TCLC* will devote an entry to his novel *Babbitt,* a scathing portrait of vulgar materialism and spiritual bankruptcy in American business.

Desmond MacCarthy (English critic)—A member of the influential Bloomsbury circle, MacCarthy was among the most prominent literary and dramatic critics of his time, praised for the great erudition and objectivity of his evaluations.

Thomas Mann (German novelist)—Mann is credited with reclaiming for the German novel an international stature it had not enjoyed since the time of the Romantics. *TCLC* will devote an entry to his novel *Buddenbrooks,* a masterpiece of Realism which depicts the rise and fall of a wealthy Hanseatic family.

Stanislaw Przybyszewski (Polish dramatist and novelist)— Enormously popular during his lifetime, Przybyszewski remains well known for his romantic, often mystical, dramas and for his frank autobiographical writings.

Italo Svevo (Italian novelist)—Svevo's novels, which demonstrate the influence of the psychoanalytic theories of Sigmund Freud, earned him a reputation as one of the most original and influential authors in modern Italian literature.

Algernon Swinburne (English poet)—Controversial during his lifetime for his powerfully sensual verse, Swinburne is today recognized as one of the most talented lyric poets of the late-Victorian period.

Marina Tsvetaeva (Russian poet)—Tsvetaeva's Modernist experiments with poetic rhythms and syntax are considered a unique and important contribution to Russian literature.

Mark Twain (American novelist)—Considered the father of modern American literature, Twain combined moral and social satire, adventure, and humor to create such perennially popular works as *The Adventures of Tom Sawyer* and *The Adventures of Huckleberry Finn. TCLC* will devote an entry to the novel *A Connecticut Yankee in King Arthur's Court,* in which Twain satirized romantic idealizations of medieval life such as those presented in Sir Thomas Malory's *Morte d'Arthur.*

Emile Zola (French novelist)—Zola was the founder and principal theorist of Naturalism, one of the most influential literary movements in modern literature. His twenty-volume series *Les Rougon-Macquart* is a monument of Naturalist fiction and served as a model for late nineteenth-century novelists seeking a more candid and accurate representation of human life.

The Bloomsbury Group

INTRODUCTION

The Bloomsbury Group was a circle of English artists and intellectuals that gathered around the novelist Virginia Woolf and her sister Vanessa Bell early in the twentieth century. Although the membership of the group has been variously defined, and in fact remains a matter of some dispute, commentators agree that at the very least it included writers E. M. Forster and Lytton Strachey, critics Desmond MacCarthy, Clive Bell, and Leonard Woolf, painters Duncan Grant and Roger Fry, and economist John Maynard Keynes. Broader definitions include friends, acquaintances, relatives, and lovers of the core members, yet it has been argued that such definitions are based solely on social relations and do not take into account the shared attitudes and aesthetic commitments that differentiate Bloomsbury members from other intellectuals of the period. Most commentators therefore confine their discussions of the Bloomsbury Group to the ten individuals mentioned above, who are often referred to collectively as "Old Bloomsbury."

In her memoir of "Old Bloomsbury," Virginia Woolf dates the group's inception to the year 1904, when she, Vanessa, and their brothers Thoby and Adrian Stephen moved into a house in Gordon Square, in the Bloomsbury district of London, following the death of their father, the eminent literary critic Leslie Stephen. Thoby had recently graduated from Cambridge, and his university friends frequently visited him at his new home. Gradually, these gatherings became a regular forum for lively philosophical discussions, while friendships and love affairs developed between various participants, forming a complex network of relationships that served to increase the solidarity of the group as a whole. Although the group's members were also unified by their liberal political views and their advocacy of Modernist art, critics note they cannot be considered a movement in the traditional sense, since they developed no single philosophical or aesthetic doctrine. The Bloomsbury Group is instead viewed as a collection of highly talented individuals whose passionate commitment to free thought and free speech created a supportive, stimulating atmosphere that fostered the independent intellectual development of the various members.

Most commentators, including Woolf herself, suggest that the demise of the Bloomsbury Group coincided with the outbreak of the First World War in 1914. After that date, geographical separation and the deaths of key members combined with the increasing personal and professional commitments of other members to disperse the original group. Friendships remained, and various members continued to interact on both personal and professional levels, yet Bloomsbury ceased to function as an intellectual community. However, the contributions to twentieth-century art and thought made by members of the group—most notably the Modernist novels of Virginia Woolf, the anticolonialist novels of Forster, the liberal economic theories of Keynes, and the progressive aesthetic ideas of Fry—have extended the influence of the Bloomsbury ethos and created a lasting legacy.

REPRESENTATIVE WORKS BY BLOOMSBURY WRITERS

Bell, Clive
  Art (criticism) 1914
  Peace at Once (pamphlet) 1915
  On British Freedom (pamphlet) 1923
  Civilization: An Essay (nonfiction) 1928
  Old Friends: Personal Recollections (essays) 1956
Forster, E[dward] M[organ]
  Where Angels Fear to Tread (novel) 1905
  The Longest Journey (novel) 1907
  A Room with a View (novel) 1908
  Howards End (novel) 1910
  A Passage to India (novel) 1924
  Aspects of the Novel (criticism) 1927
  Two Cheers for Democracy (essays) 1951
  Maurice (novel) 1971
Fry, Roger
  Vision and Design (criticism) 1920
  Transformations (criticism) 1926
Keynes, John Maynard
  The Economic Consequences of the Peace (essay) 1919
  Treatise on Probability (philosophy) 1921
  Two Memoirs (essays) 1949
  The Collected Writings. 30 vols. (essays and letters) 1971-83
Strachey, [Giles] Lytton
  Landmarks in French Literature (criticism) 1912
  Eminent Victorians: Cardinal Manning, Florence Nightingale, Dr. Arnold, General Gordon (biography) 1918
  Queen Victoria (biography) 1921
  Elizabeth and Essex: A Tragic History (biography) 1928
  Portraits in Miniature, and Other Essays (essays) 1931
  Characters and Commentaries (criticism) 1933
  The Collected Works of Lytton Strachey. 6 vols. (biographies, history, and criticism) 1948
Woolf, Leonard
  International Government (pamphlet) 1916
  Essays on Literature, History, Politics, Etc. (essays) 1927
  Sowing: An Autobiography of the Years 1880-1904 (autobiography) 1960
  Growing: An Autobiography of the Years 1904-1911 (autobiography) 1961
  Beginning Again: An Autobiography of the Years 1911-1918 (autobiography) 1964
  Downhill All the Way: An Autobiography of the Years 1919-1939 (autobiography) 1967
Woolf, Virginia
  The Voyage Out (novel) 1915
  Night and Day (novel) 1919
  Jacob's Room (novel) 1922
  Mr. Bennet and Mrs. Brown (criticism) 1924
  The Common Reader (essays) 1925
  Mrs. Dalloway (novel) 1925

To the Lighthouse (novel) 1927
Orlando: A Biography (novel) 1928
A Room of One's Own (essay) 1929
The Waves (novel) 1931
Three Guineas (essays) 1938
Roger Fry (biography) 1940
The Letters of Virginia Woolf. 6 vols. (letters) 1975-80
Moments of Being (autobiographical essays) 1978
The Diary of Virginia Woolf. 5 vols. (diaries) 1978-84

HISTORY AND MAJOR FIGURES

J. K. JOHNSTONE

[*In the following excerpt, Johnstone introduces the central figures in Bloomsbury and traces the early development of the group.*]

"Bloomsbury" is the name of the close group of friends who began to meet about 1906 and included, among others, John Maynard Keynes, Lytton Strachey, Virginia and Leonard Woolf, Vanessa and Clive Bell, Duncan Grant, E. M. Forster, and Roger Fry. The term was applied derisively to the group before the First World War, because their hostesses, Virginia and Vanessa Stephen (who became Virginia Woolf and Vanessa Bell), lived in the London district of Bloomsbury.

"Bloomsbury" meant a number of things—snobbish, "highbrow," "arty," "Bohemian"—all rolled into one word. It was intended to smack, all at once, of the British Museum, of untidy art studios, of an exclusive, "unconventional" life, of pale aesthetes who met to read esoteric papers in some ivory tower.

This derisive epithet had, of course, a grain of truth in it. Bloomsbury was "arty" in that its members believed art to be the most important thing in the world, the highest expression to which man has attained. What is more, they practised this belief. They infused new life into the novel, the biography, and art criticism; and they have made important contributions to British painting. But they were not exclusively "arty." They have made contributions at least equally important to economics and to international affairs.

They were, in a sense, "high-brows" too. Their approach to problems was intellectual. They were fastidious and highly civilized; yet their life was, no doubt, rather "Bohemian"—the one probably demanded the other. But they were not snobs. Certainly they did not wish to keep the good things of life, among which they believed the creation and appreciation of works of art to be the best, to themselves. Rather, they did a great deal to publicize and popularize art, and it is largely to them that we owe the Arts Council. Their political beliefs ranged from Liberal on the Bloomsbury right to Socialist on the Bloomsbury left. Their religious beliefs, in so far as they can be said, as a group, to have had any, were non-Christian. (pp. ix-x)

"Bloomsbury" began shortly after the death of Sir Leslie Stephen in 1904. Stephen, with other eminent Victorians, had, by his bold thinking, helped to prepare the way for Bloomsbury. It was ironic, though in the nature of things, that Stephen's death should have been required before the way was finally clear.

Leslie Stephen's life, which neatly straddled Victoria's reign (he was born in 1832), was an epitome of a facet of the intellectual life of that era. He was brought up by Evangelical parents in the faith of the Established Church; he went to Cambridge, and in good time received a Fellowship from his college and entered Holy Orders. But after eight years of the life of a Cambridge don, his reading caused him to question the teachings of his Church. As a result, he resigned his Tutorship and before long withdrew from Cambridge to take up a literary career in London, to become editor of *The Cornhill Magazine,* and to begin the *Dictionary of National Biography.* He was a friend of many of the writers and intellectual leaders of his time; his masters were Mill, Darwin, and Huxley; he explained and defended his position as an agnostic.

As a father, Leslie Stephen gave his children a training which he had not had. They *began* to think, as it were, at the point that he had reached when he left Cambridge, and, freed from the Articles of the Church, began to follow the bent of his own mind. If they were given a religion at all, it must have been one that maintained the value of human relationships. "Though [Leslie Stephen] was an agnostic," says his daughter Virginia, "nobody believed more profoundly in the worth of human relationships." And she tells us more of her father:

> The relations between parents and children to-day have a freedom that would have been impossible with my father. He expected a certain standard of behaviour, even of ceremony in family life. Yet if freedom means the right to think one's own thoughts and to follow one's own pursuits, then no one respected and indeed insisted upon freedom more completely than he did. His sons, with the exception of the Army and Navy, should follow whatever professions they chose; his daughters, though he cared little enough for the higher education of women, should have the same liberty.

And so his daughter Vanessa was allowed to paint, and Virginia read anything she would in his library at the age of fifteen.

Leslie Stephen's influence upon his daughters was strong. Their mother, Stephen's second wife, died suddenly in 1895 when Vanessa was sixteen and Virginia thirteen. The two girls were educated at home, and for a time after their mother's death Stephen was their schoolmaster. He was not suited to the task, and had to give it up, for he could not adapt himself to the formal teaching of young, undeveloped minds. His informal teaching was more successful. Each evening, for an hour and a half, he would recite poetry or read fiction to his children. Scott's novels were the most popular and were all read through. There were also times when Stephen, like some of the fathers and elderly gentlemen that Virginia was later to create in her novels, was preoccupied with his thoughts; but "when, suddenly opening his bright blue eyes, and rousing himself from what had seemed complete abstraction, he gave his opinion, it was difficult to disregard it," Virginia tells us. She gives us other glimpses of her parent: "Sometimes with one word—but his one word was accompanied by a gesture of the hand—he would dispose of the tissue of exaggerations which his own sobriety seemed to provoke." But he was capable of his own exaggerations. He sometimes cast himself in a tragic rôle, and a small incident which caused him discomfort might assume extraordinary proportions in his mind. Often the girls were left to themselves while Stephen worked in his study. "As [my father] wrote he smoked a short clay pipe, and he scattered books [around his low rocking chair] in a circle. The thud of a book dropped on the floor could be heard in the room beneath."

In 1902 Stephen's health broke down, and he became more dependent upon his daughters, on whom the responsibilities of housekeeping had fallen. He suffered from internal cancer, and was an invalid until his death in 1904. It was perhaps memories of this period, of the secluded life in her parental home, and of the forceful parent who must often have dominated the girl, that prompted Virginia in later years to write bitterly against the conception of the daughter as, as she calls it, "The Angel in the House," who is to stay at home, sacrificing herself to others, while the sons go up to university and out into the world. At any rate, Leslie Stephen's death was necessary to Vanessa's and Virginia's freedom, though it was he who had taught them to demand freedom and, once gained, to put it to use.

After their father's death Virginia and Vanessa left his home, at 22 Hyde Park Gate, to set up house with their brothers, Thoby and Adrian, at 46 Gordon Square, Bloomsbury. The duties of Hyde Park Gate were left behind; they had a remarkable degree of freedom for young women of their generation, and the opportunity, since they were financially independent, to make of their lives what they chose.

Virginia chose to write; Vanessa to paint; and both of them made new friends. Thoby Stephen had been to Cambridge, and his University friends came to his new home. This was Thoby's one contribution to Bloomsbury, but it was a vital one. He was handsome, charming, and admired; among the friends that he brought to Gordon Square and introduced to his sisters were some of the most gifted and original young men of his generation. He had little more than introduced them when he died of typhoid fever in 1906, while on holiday in Greece with his brother and sisters.

One of Thoby's best friends was Clive Bell, that "gay and amiable dog," as Maynard Keynes has called him. Bell was enamoured of the visual arts; he believed aesthetic experience to be "the end of existence"; but he was also, in these days at least, "concerned for the fate of humanity," and he planned, in one of those dreams of youth that are never realized, to write a "*magnum opus,* a book to deal with nothing less than every significant aspect of our age, a book to be called *The New Renaissance.*" Though not a deep or original thinker, his conversation and writing were spirited, and he was often acute enough to express an idea more clearly than its originator had succeeded in doing—a gift which is too useful to be belittled. Above all, he had a sense of humour, and this, as he himself has said, is "one of the qualities that most clearly distinguish a civilized man from a savage . . . ; and . . . is in the last analysis nothing but a highly developed sense of values."

Clive Bell married Vanessa Stephen a few months after Thoby's death, in 1907. To allow the newly-married couple to live at 46 Gordon Square, Virginia and Adrian moved to 29 Fitzroy Square, nearby. Around these four a group of young, talented intellectuals, who were all interested in art, began to form. Duncan Grant, a neighbor and close friend of the Stephens and Bells, describes the gatherings at Fitzroy Square:

> [Adrian's] study on the ground floor had the air of being much lived in. It was to this room that [Virginia's and Adrian's] friends came on Thursday evenings—a continuation of those evenings which began in Gordon Square before Thoby died and before Vanessa married. It was there that what has since been called "Bloomsbury" for good or ill came into being.
>
> About ten o'clock in the evening people used to appear and continue to come at intervals till twelve o'clock at night, and it was seldom that the last guest left before two or three in the morning. Whisky, buns and cocoa were the diet, and people talked to each other. If someone had lit a pipe he would sometimes hold out the lighted match to Hans the dog, who would snap at it and put it out. Conversation; that was all. Yet many people made a habit of coming, and few who did so will forget those evenings.
>
> Among those who constantly came in early days were Charles Sanger, Theodore Llewelyn Davies, Desmond MacCarthy, Charles Tennyson, Hilton Young (now Lord Kennet), Lytton Strachey.
>
> It was certainly not a "salon." Virginia Stephen in those days was not at all the sort of hostess required for such a thing. She appeared very shy and probably was so, and never addressed the company. She would listen to certain arguments and occasionally speak, but her conversation was mainly directed to someone next to her. Her brother's Cambridge friends she knew well by this time, but I think there was always something a little aloof and even a little fierce in her manner to most men at the time I am speaking of. . . .
>
> I do not think that her new existence had "become alive" to Virginia's imagination in those first years. She gave the impression of being so intensely receptive to any experience new to her, and so intensely interested in facts that she had not come across before, that time was necessary to give it a meaning as a whole. It took the years to complete her vision of it.

The quiet life at Hyde Park Gate must inevitably have continued to have its effect upon Virginia Stephen, and there was, as well, the shadow of mental illness, which had manifested itself for a time in 1905. But if these evenings of conversation and discussion with young people were a new experience for her, they were not new to Lytton Strachey and his Cambridge friends.

Strachey and several others of the Cambridge men who came to Fitzroy Square had been members of the Cambridge "Society" which was begun by F. D. Maurice, Tennyson, and Hallam in the 1820s, whose members came to be known as "Apostles," and whose affairs were supposed to be kept secret. The Apostles were a select group. Their numbers were small—sometimes as few as six undergraduates were included. New members were chosen with extreme care. As a result, and due in some measure too, no doubt, to the nature of the Society itself, many of Cambridge's most distinguished men have been Apostles. All of them, from Tennyson and Dean Merivale, to Henry Sidgwick and to Maynard Keynes, are unanimous in their affection for the Society and in their testimony to the value they attach to the rôle it played in their lives. The Society was the centre of Cambridge life for its members. They were seldom apart. They dined in one another's rooms; they went on boating parties and on vacations together; and, above all, they talked. Once a week, on Saturday evenings, they met to read and discuss a paper that one of them had written. Sidgwick tells us of the spirit of the Society and of these discussions:

> I can only describe it as the spirit of the pursuit of truth with absolute devotion and unreserve by a group of intimate friends, who were perfectly frank with each other, and indulged in any amount of humorous sarcasm and playful banter, and yet each respects the other, and when he discourses tries to learn from him and see what he sees. Absolute candour was the only duty that the tradition of the society enforced.

This spirit and tradition endured throughout the years in the Society and were brought from Cambridge to Bloomsbury.

Lytton Strachey and his friend Maynard Keynes were two of the most prominent undergraduate members of the Society in the first years of the present century. In appearance they could scarcely have been more dissimilar. Sir Max Beerbohm has described Strachey as he saw him, several years later, in 1912: "an emaciated face of ivory whiteness, above a long square-cut auburn beard, and below a head of very long sleek dark brown hair. The nose was nothing if not aquiline, and Nature had chiselled it with great delicacy. The eyes, behind a pair of gold-rimmed spectacles, eyes of an inquirer and a cogitator, were large and brown and luminous." And this face and head surmounted a very tall, very thin body, so loosely knit that it appeared disjointed. Keynes was much more solidly built than his friend. His easy air of physical relaxation made him appear athletic in contrast to Strachey, whose body, when in repose, seemed entirely beyond his control. Keynes's eyes, piercing, yet reflective, were set beneath overshadowing brows. A decisive nose led to a neat moustache that fully covered his upper lip. His lower lip was full; his chin receded slightly; his head was set forward on his shoulders. Keynes looked poised, ready to give his attention at once to any problem that might confront him. His whole appearance, though not handsome, was urbane. His voice, one may be sure, was suave. Strachey's voice "went into a high pitch on the emphatic termination of a sentence."

But Keynes and Strachey had enough in common. They were also different enough to complement one another. They both came from solid Victorian homes to which they owed a debt at least as great as Virginia and Vanessa Stephen owed to theirs. Keynes's father was a Cambridge don and official; Strachey's father a great Indian administrator. Both Strachey and Keynes were gay, and each had a sharp sense of humour. Deep in both, well masked, perhaps, were passionate natures. They were very interested in human relations, and, as their letters to one another testify, they spent a good deal of time in character analysis. What was X really like? Why had he done such and such? And in what subtle ways did his character reveal itself? They gained practical experience in this sort of character-study, no doubt, as they scouted the undergraduates for new members for the Society. They were both intellectual. Keynes exercised his mind in logic and mathematics, and soon interested himself in political economy. Strachey was more active in his study of history than in these sciences, but they met on common ground in their interests in philosophy and in literature. They had fine minds, and, inevitably and rightly, they were aware that they had, and trusted their

own abilities. They intended to revalue things for themselves, and in making their judgments they did not hesitate—and this was in part an outcome of their love of character analysis—to criticize their predecessors or to ridicule those in authority. But it would be wrong to think of them as revolutionaries in the intellectual world. They stood squarely within a tradition, and they carried that tradition a step or two farther. To do that it is necessary to diverge somewhat from the past in order to keep the essential continuity. Keynes and Strachey did not want to burn down the Victorian house; they wanted to sweep out some trash, move in some new furniture, and rearrange the rooms.

The Society was the centre of their intellectual life. It gave them an opportunity to discuss and mature their ideas; and, although their Apostolic friends were sharp enough critics, Strachey and Keynes could develop their ideas more boldly within such a circle than they could have done elsewhere. The Society gave them shelter, and the feeling of security and superiority that the closed, exclusive brotherhood always generates among its members. And in the Society they found, as well, a philosopher, G. E. Moore, who seemed to them to have swept out the materialist, utilitarian, and moral trash of the Victorians, and to have formulated a logical, idealist philosophy based upon premises that the twentieth century could accept. "The influence," says Keynes, "was not only overwhelming; but it was the extreme opposite of what Strachey used to call *funeste;* it was exciting, exhilarating, the beginning of a renaissance, the opening of a new heaven on a new earth, we were the forerunners of a new dispensation, we were not afraid of anything." It was the same feeling, no doubt, that caused Clive Bell to plan his *magnum opus, The New Renaissance.*

And this was the feeling that came to Bloomsbury to enliven the hitherto quiet lives of Vanessa and Virginia Stephen. Strachey soon found, at Fitzroy and Gordon Squares, the centre that he had found in the Society. Bloomsbury was never quite as important to Keynes as to Strachey, if only because the profession of economics, which Keynes adopted, took him into a wider, busier world, less related to Bloomsbury than Strachey's profession of letters. But Keynes was important to Bloomsbury, particularly perhaps, during its first ten or fifteen years, as a friend who could give authoritative advice on almost any matter. In 1908 he took up a Fellowship at his college, King's, in Cambridge; but he kept rooms in London with his friend Duncan Grant so that he might come regularly to London and to Bloomsbury.

Duncan Grant, whom we have already met briefly as a Bloomsbury neighbour of Virginia and Adrian Stephen, was a cousin of Lytton Strachey. He was brought up partly in the Strachey household, while his family were in India. Lady Strachey encouraged his aptitude for painting and persuaded his parents to allow him to take up painting as a profession. After Keynes's undergraduate years Duncan Grant became his best friend, and remained so throughout Keynes's life. Grant was conscientiously devoted to painting, but his interests were not narrow, and to any discussion he brought intelligence and the level-headed outlook of the craftsman who works with material things and knows their limitations.

Interest in the creation and appreciation of paintings became a dominant characteristic of Bloomsbury. Lytton Strachey and Clive Bell, who had championed the visual arts at Cambridge and had aroused Keynes's lively interest, retained their enthusiasm. Clive Bell wrote on art and became a well-known critic. Vanessa Bell and Duncan Grant painted together. . . . There was scarcely anyone in the group who did not have a lively interest in the visual arts; and the leader in this interest was Roger Fry.

Roger Fry matured late. Unlike Strachey and Keynes, who as undergraduates seemed already to be in possession of powers that only required development to become the powers of great men, Roger Fry was not able until middle age to control and direct the abilities that made him a great art critic. But in middle age he had many of the finest qualities of youth— qualities that are even more lovable, because they are rarer, in a man than in a boy.

Fry was fifteen years or so the senior of most of the other members of Bloomsbury. He was born in 1866 to rather austere Quaker parents, and he was brought up, of course, in the Quaker faith. His father, Sir Edward Fry, was a judge. After an unhappy, tortured existence at a private school, Roger went to a public school at Clifton, where the years were dull and monotonous, relieved only by the friendship of John Ellis McTaggart, a fellow schoolboy who was later to become a famous Cambridge philosopher. It was not until he came up to Cambridge and entered King's College to read for the science tripos that Roger Fry discovered that life could really be a very pleasant affair.

Fry's Cambridge was the Cambridge of the youthful McTaggart, Goldsworthy Lowes Dickinson, and Nathaniel Wedd. It is best epitomized for us in E. M. Forster, another Bloomsbury associate and member of the Society. . . . Forster came up to Cambridge in 1897, twelve years later than Fry; but the spirit that Fry knew still endured; and Forster, much more, for example, than Maynard Keynes, who entered King's in 1902, seems to belong to the last century. McTaggart was at Trinity, Dickinson and Wedd were Fellows of King's College, when Forster was an undergraduate. "Wedd," Forster says, "taught me classics and it is to him . . . more than to anyone that I owe such awakening as has befallen me. It is through him that I can best imagine the honesty and fervour of fifty years back. Wedd was then cynical, aggressive, Mephistophelian, wore a red tie, blasphemed, and taught Dickinson how to swear too—always a desirable accomplishment for a high-minded young don, though fewer steps need be taken about it now." It is indicative of Dickinson's character, as well as of the times, that he had to be taught to swear and yet was willing to learn. One cannot imagine that he was a very adept student of the art. "He was," Forster agrees with Dickinson's former bedmaker at Cambridge, "the best man who ever lived." His creed is perhaps expressed best in his *Letters from John Chinaman:* "To feel, and in order to feel to express, or at least to understand the expression of all that is lovely in Nature, of all that is poignant and sensitive in man, is to us in itself a sufficient end." He believed that the pursuit of this ideal was becoming more and more difficult throughout the world, because the modern governments and industrialists of the West were spreading "ugliness, meanness, and insincerity." He looked longingly to Ancient Greece, where he believed that the real had been close to the ideal; but at the same time he worked, in the "League of Nations Society," to bring the League of Nations into being. And with Wedd and others he founded a magazine, *The Independent Review,* which Forster, who was a contributor, tells us was "not so much a Liberal review as an appeal to Liberalism from the Left to be its better self." In his broad Liberalism Dickinson differed from his friend McTaggart, a traditionalist who became more and more reactionary as he

grew older. But he could agree with McTaggart that the human relation of love (in its broadest sense) is the best thing we can know, and he shared McTaggart's faith in reason while trying, like McTaggart, to gain knowledge in other, more intuitive ways. In these beliefs of Dickinson's, Forster, who became an intimate friend, concurred with few reservations. Through Forster and Roger Fry, at least, Dickinson had his effect upon Bloomsbury.

Dickinson, Wedd, and McTaggart were Fry's close friends at Cambridge; Dickinson the most intimate. They were all four members of the Society; they rowed and holidayed together; their philosopher in these early days was, of course, McTaggart. Cambridge, Forster says in his biography of Dickinson, "acquired a magic quality. Body and spirit, reason and emotion, work and play, architecture and scenery, laughter and seriousness, life and art—these pairs which are elsewhere contrasted were there fused into one. People and books reinforced one another, intelligence joined hands with affection, speculation became a passion, and discussion was made profound by love." Like the hero of one of Forster's novels, Roger Fry found at Cambridge that "his boyhood had been but a dusty corridor that led to the spacious halls of youth."

Fry graduated in 1888 with a first-class degree. His father saw prospects of a brilliant scientific career for him; but Roger had become so interested in art as to think it his "only possible job." He compromised with his father by staying at Cambridge for a few more terms in order to study painting and anatomy, while trying, half-heartedly and unsuccessfully, for a Fellowship. Sir Edward was bitterly disappointed, and Roger was for years sensitive to the fact that his father regarded him as a failure. Their relationship, though a break between them was never threatened, was made the more difficult because at Cambridge Roger's religious faith had slipped from him.

Cambridge and its spacious halls were left behind. The next decade or so Roger Fry spent learning his art: studying in Italy and France, painting at home. In December 1896 he married Helen Coombe, a fellow art student; and there followed one of those rare, perfectly complete periods that came now and then in a life that had enough anxieties and disappointments. But in the spring of 1898 Helen Fry became mentally ill, afflicted with, as it was later learned, an incurable thickening of the skull.

Money was badly needed, and Fry, whose painting had not brought him success, set out to earn it by writing and lecturing on art. He was at once successful. He loved art enough to choose it as his "only possible job" when that choice was a very difficult one to make; and he had found art to be the one thing of real value that time and life's misfortunes could not destroy. He wished, for he was nothing if not sympathetic, generous, and sociable, to share that discovery and his love of art with others. He would stand before a picture (and his sensibility was great), submitting himself to his sensations. Then, in a tentative, unassuming style that seemed to take his listeners or readers on a quest with him, and with a voice, if he was lecturing, that another great lecturer, Bernard Shaw, believed was worth listening to for its own sake, he would try to describe his feelings and convey them to his audience. Finally—for had he not been a fellow Apostle of McTaggart and Dickinson?—he would subject his feelings to a rigorous intellectual examination in an attempt to learn what, in the painting, had caused them. He had found his vocation (though he continued his practice of painting and considered it of more importance than criticism), and he became famous.

Meanwhile there were respites in Helen Fry's illness, intervals when she and Roger thought that they could plan life together once more, and that the disease which they fought might be beaten. There were two children. In 1905 Fry was appointed Director of the Metropolitan Museum in New York; and he had to spend two or three months of each of the next five years in America. His hopes were to be disappointed there too, for he could not agree with the President of the Museum, Pierpont Morgan, and he left his position in 1910. In the same year Helen Fry entered an asylum, where she remained until her death in 1937.

It was in 1910 that Roger Fry became a member of the Bloomsbury family. He looked, Virginia Woolf tells us, much older than his age of forty-four; but he was about to begin the most important and, if one may speak so without too great danger of paradox, the most youthful phase of his career. To the consternation of the English public, he introduced them in November 1910, by means of an exhibition which he called "Manet and the Post-Impressionists," to the new movement in French art. The public were aghast or thrown into fits of laughter before the paintings of such men as Cézanne, Van Gogh, Matisse, and Picasso; some of them believed that Fry was out to dupe and to swindle them, and many were indignant. But there were others, a small number and most of them young, who were inspired by the Post-Impressionist paintings. Bloomsbury was foremost among this group. Its painters were enthralled by the pictures; its writers and thinkers by Fry's explanation of why these pictures were great works of art. There was a new feeling of excitement in Bloomsbury, and it was liveliest in Roger Fry himself. "I feel," he wrote to an art critic, "that I . . . have an altogether new sense of confidence and determination which I shall stick to as long as it will last." He believed, as Maynard Keynes and Clive Bell had believed ten years earlier, that the world was about to witness a renaissance. He arranged a second Post-Impressionist Exhibition in the autumn of 1912. In July 1913 he opened the Omega Workshops in Fitzroy Square, where he employed young artists to design textiles, furniture, and other household articles. He hoped to improve interior design and decoration, and to give artists an opportunity to make a living that would leave them free to paint as they wished.

Shortly after the first Post-Impressionist Exhibition, Leonard Woolf, who had been an Apostle at the same time as Lytton Strachey and Maynard Keynes, returned to London after seven years in Ceylon in the Civil Service. In 1912 he married Virginia Stephen. Woolf was a student of history; he had had practical experience in government in Ceylon; and he was convinced that socialism is the only answer to the world's problems. In a group that leaned, if anything, to the left side of centre, he was the only member who was solidly leftist—though if we use that term we should remember that he envisioned the introduction of socialism as a step forward in the progress of civilization, not as a revolution or break with the past. And he carried the Bloomsbury trait of respect for reason to its furthest extent. In an unfinished work, *After the Deluge,* he attempts to give an account of "the communal psychology which developed between the French Revolution and 1914 and ended in the war." He believes that the communal psychology of the First World War and of the Treaty of Versailles should be investigated as well, and that, after these investigations are complete, the historian should be able to "place" the war in the past history of the human race and in relation to the future. He would then be better equipped to do his job, which should be, Woolf believes, to tell men what will happen if they move in certain directions. But Woolf was not occupied only with such broad, historical matters. He was also concerned with more immediate affairs, such as colonial administration, social welfare at home, and the establishment of the League of Nations, for which he worked, with Lowes Dickinson, in the League of Nations Society. And in 1917 he and Virginia Woolf founded the Hogarth Press—at first a hand-press that they operated themselves—to publish work, whether didactic or purely artistic, which contained new ideas.

Leonard Woolf brought these social and political interests into Virginia's life, and he shared with her an interest in literature. He respected and encouraged her talents as a writer, while introducing her to a world less fastidious, more concerned with the basic needs of life, than she had met before. He helped her to satisfy, one may imagine, both her desire to explore her mind in solitude and to commune with others—an ambivalent desire that we all share, but which was intense in Virginia Woolf, perhaps because of her vivid awareness of two worlds, "one flowing in wide sweeps overhead, the other tip-tapping circumscribed upon the pavement." And thanks to his care and vigilance she had less to fear from attacks of mental illness. As the years passed, the shy, aloof, rather fierce girl, who had listened to her brother's friends in Fitzroy Square, became, in the words of T. S. Eliot, "the centre . . . of the literary life of London." According to another witness, she was, among people whose company is a delight, in a class apart.

Virginia Woolf's development owed much to Bloomsbury, as well as to her married life. As an artist or as an individual she could scarcely have found a more suitable milieu than she did in this society of equals, who had a similar background, who had few worldly pretensions, and who, although each member was an individual with a distinctive contribution to make to the group, had common interests and shared a point of view. All Bloomsbury believed in reason, and this belief was leavened or balanced by sensitiveness and a love of beauty. Every one in Bloomsbury was interested, directly or indirectly, in the production of works of art; and no one, with Leonard Woolf and Maynard Keynes in the group, could be unaware of contemporary social and political problems. This awareness did not mean, however, that Bloomsbury thought it necessary to mix art and politics. Bloomsbury was gay; it was sceptical; it was polite. Friendship was the basis of the society; friendship had drawn its members together; and Bloomsbury depended on a family feeling for its continued existence. Friendship made possible a frank exchange of views, which, Bloomsbury found, enlarged the individual. For this, conversation was necessary; and because Bloomsbury loved beauty, and found conversation to be of great value, conversation became an art in its midst and was more important than it had been, perhaps, since the days of Dr. Johnson. Bloomsbury was a society in which the artist could test his ideas, develop his personality, and perfect his art. It was not unlike the society that Virginia Woolf, in her biography of Roger Fry, says Roger Fry envisioned shortly before the First World War:

> At last, he felt . . . a time was at hand when a real
> society was possible. It was to be a society of people
> of moderate means, a society based upon the old

Cambridge ideal of truth and free speaking, but alive, as Cambridge had never been, to the importance of the arts. It was possible in France; why not in England? No art could flourish without such a background. The young English artist tended to become illiterate, narrow-minded and self-centered with disastrous effects upon his work, failing any society where, among the amenities of civilization, ideas were discussed in common and he was accepted as an equal.

Bloomsbury gave its artists the advantage of a society of this sort. In its sheltered, invigorating climate they gained strength and confidence. They felt that the world was about to experience a new renaissance, and, what is more, that they were to be leaders in the reawakening. They had not long enjoyed this feeling when "suddenly, like a chasm in a smooth road," as Virginia Woolf describes it, "the war came." Maynard Keynes was plunged into the business of financing the war, and then into what he found to be the chicanery at Versailles. Leonard Woolf and Lowes Dickinson began to investigate the causes of the war and to work for peace. E. M. Forster served as a non-combatant in Egypt. Duncan Grant, Vanessa Bell, Virginia Woolf, and Lytton Strachey continued to write and paint as best they could. Life, art, the amenities of civilization were threatened; and security was scarcely regained in the two feverish decades that followed the war and preceded the second catastrophe. But Bloomsbury had formed its values in a calmer era and recalled happier days. It remembered when there had been more time for long, leisurely evenings of conversation; it remembered listening to G. E. Moore as he expounded an idealist philosophy at Cambridge; it remembered boating parties and summer days when all the good things of life seemed to have coalesced; and it remembered, rather ruefully, no doubt, its belief that a golden age was about to dawn. It had to change some of its conceptions, but it was more certain than ever before that art was necessary to civilization; and it carried this belief into the troubled years that lay ahead. (pp. 3-19)

J. K. Johnstone, in his The Bloomsbury Group: A Study of E. M. Forster, Lytton Strachey, Virginia Woolf, and Their Circle, *1954. Reprint by Octagon Books, 1978, 383 p.*

VIRGINIA WOOLF

[*In the following excerpt, Woolf offers her memories of the beginnings of the Bloomsbury Group. Bracketed material in this excerpt was added by Jeanne Schulkind, the editor of the volume in which the essay first appeared.*]

When one sees it today, Gordon Square is not one of the most romantic of the Bloomsbury squares. It has neither the distinction of Fitzroy Square nor the majesty of Mecklenburgh Square. It is prosperous middle class and thoroughly mid-Victorian. But I can assure you that in October 1904 it was the most beautiful, the most exciting, the most romantic place in the world. To begin with it was astonishing to stand at the drawing room window and look into all those trees; the tree which shoots its branches up into the air and lets them fall in a shower; the tree which glistens after rain like the body of a seal—instead of looking at old Mrs. Redgrave washing her neck across the way. The light and the air after the rich red gloom of Hyde Park Gate were a revelation. Things one had never seen in the darkness there—Watts pictures, Dutch cabinets, blue china—shone out for the first

time in the drawing room at Gordon Square. After the muffled silence of Hyde Park Gate the roar of traffic was positively alarming. Odd characters, sinister, strange, prowled and slunk past our windows. But what was even more exhilarating was the extraordinary increase of space. At Hyde Park Gate one had only a bedroom in which to read or see one's friends. Here Vanessa and I each had a sitting room; there was a large double drawing room; and a study on the ground floor. To make it all newer and fresher, the house had been completely done up. Needless to say the Watts-Venetian tradition of red plush and black paint had been reversed; we had entered the Sargent-Furse era; white and green chintzes were everywhere; and instead of Morris wall-papers with their intricate patterns we decorated our walls with washes of plain distemper. We were full of experiments and reforms. We were going to do without table napkins, we were to have [large supplies of] Bromo instead; we were going to paint, to write; to have coffee after dinner instead of tea at nine o'clock. Everything was going to be new; everything was going to be different. Everything was on trial.

We were, it appears, extremely social. For some months in the winter of 1904-05 I kept a diary from which I find that we were for ever lunching and dining out and loitering about the book shops—"Bloomsbury is ever so much more interesting than Kensington," I wrote—or going to a concert or visiting a picture gallery and coming home to find the drawing room full of the oddest collections of people.

Cousin Henry Prinsep, Miss Millais, Ozzie Dickinson and Victor Marshall all came this afternoon and stayed late, so that we had only just time to rush off to a Mr. Rutter's lecture on Impressionism at the Grafton Gallery. . . . Lady Hylton, V. Dickinson and E. Coltman came to tea. We lunched with the Shaw Stewarts and met an art critic called Nicholls. Sir Hugh seemed nice but there isn't much in him. . . . I lunched with the Protheroes and met the Bertrand Russells. It was very amusing. Thoby and I dined with the Cecils and went on to the St. Loe Stracheys where we knew a great many people. . . . I called for Nessa and Thoby at Mrs. Flower's and we went on to a dance at the Hobhouses'. Nessa was in a state of great misery today waiting for Mr. Tonks who came at one to criticise her pictures. He is a man with a cold bony face, prominent eyes and a look of serenity and boredom. Meg Booth and Sir Fred Pollock came to tea. . . .

So it goes on; but among all these short records of parties, of how the chintzes came home and how we went to the Zoo and how we went to *Peter Pan*, there are a few entries which bear on Bloomsbury. On Thursday March 2nd 1905 Violet Dickinson brought a clergyman's wife to tea and Sydney-Turner and Strachey came after dinner and we talked till twelve. On Wednesday the 8th of March: "Margaret sent round her new motor car this afternoon and we took Violet to pay a series of calls, but we, of course, forgot our cards. Then I went on to the Waterloo Road and lectured (a class of working men and women) on the Greek Myths. Home and found Bell, and we talked about the nature of good till almost one!"

On the 16th [of] March Miss Power and Miss Malone dined with us. Sydney-Turner and Gerald came in after dinner—the first of our Thursday evenings. On the 23rd [of] March nine people came to our evening and stayed till one.

A few days later I went to Spain, and the duty which I laid

on myself of recording every sight and sound, every wave and hill, sickened me with diary writing so that I stopped—with this last entry: May the 11th—"Our evening: gay Bell, D. MacCarthy and Gerald—who shocked the cultured."

So my diary ends just as it might have become interesting. Yet I think it is clear even in this brief record in which every sort of doing is piled up higgledy-piggledy that these few meetings of Bloomsbury in its infancy differed from the rest. These are the only occasions when I do not merely say I had met so and so and thought him longfaced like Reginald Smith or pompous like Moorsom, or quite easy to get on with, but nothing much in him, like Sir Hugh Shaw Stewart. I say we talked to Strachey and Sydney-Turner. I add with a note of exclamation that we talked with Bell about the nature of good till one! And I did not use notes of exclamation often—and once more indeed—when I say that I smoked a cigarette with Beatrice Thynne!

These Thursday evening parties were, as far as I am concerned, the germ from which sprang all that has since come to be called—in newspapers, in novels, in Germany, in France—even, I daresay, in Turkey and Timbuktu—by the name of Bloomsbury. They deserve to be recorded and described. Yet how difficult—how impossible. Talk—even the talk which had such tremendous results upon the lives and characters of the two Miss Stephens—even talk of this interest and importance is as elusive as smoke. It flies up the chimney and is gone.

In the first place it is not true to say that when the door opened and with a curious hesitation and self-effacement Turner or Strachey glided in—that they were complete strangers to us. We had met them—and Bell, Woolf, Hilton Young and others—in Cambridge at May Week before my father died. But what was of much greater importance, we had heard of them from Thoby. Thoby possessed a great power of romanticizing his friends. Even when he was a little boy at a private school there was always some astonishing fellow, whose amazing character and exploits he would describe hour after hour when he came home for the holidays. These stories had the greatest fascination for me. I thought about Pilkington or Sidney Irwin or the Woolly Bear whom I never saw in the flesh as if they were characters in Shakespeare. I made up stories about them myself. It was a kind of saga that went on year after year. And now just as I had heard of Radcliffe, Stuart, or whoever it might be, I began to hear of Bell, Strachey, Turner, Woolf. We talked of them by the hour, rambling about the country or sitting over the fire in my bedroom.

"There's an astonishing fellow called Bell," Thoby would begin directly he came back. "He's a sort of mixture between Shelley and a sporting country squire."

At this of course I pricked up my ears and began to ask endless questions. We were walking over a moor somewhere, I remember. I got a fantastic impression that this man Bell was a kind of Sun God—with straw in his hair. He was an [illegible] of innocence and enthusiasm. Bell had never opened a book till he came to Cambridge, Thoby said. Then he suddenly discovered Shelley and Keats and went nearly mad with excitement. He did nothing but spout poetry and write poetry. Yet he was a perfect horseman—a gift which Thoby enormously admired—and kept two or three hunters up at Cambridge.

"And is Bell a great poet?" I asked.

No, Thoby wouldn't go so far as to say that; but it was quite on the cards that Strachey was. And so we discussed Strachey—or "the Strache," as Thoby called him. Strachey at once became as singular, as fascinating as Bell. But it was in quite a different way. "The Strache" was the essence of culture. In fact I think his culture a little alarmed Thoby. He had French pictures in his rooms. He had a passion for Pope. He was exotic, extreme in every way—Thoby described him—so long, so thin that his thigh was no thicker than Thoby's arm. Once he burst into Thoby's rooms, cried out, "Do you hear the music of the spheres?" and fell in a faint. Once in the midst of a dead silence, he piped up—and Thoby could imitate his voice perfectly—"Let's all write Sonnets to Robertson." He was a prodigy of wit. Even the tutors and the dons would come and listen to him. "Whatever they give you, Strachey," Dr. Jackson had said when Strachey was in for some examination, "It won't be good enough." And then Thoby, leaving me enormously impressed and rather dazed, would switch off to tell me about another astonishing fellow—a man who trembled perpetually all over. He was as eccentric, as remarkable in his way as Bell and Strachey in theirs. He was a Jew. When I asked why he trembled, Thoby somehow made me feel that it was part of his nature—he was so violent, so savage; he so despised the whole human race. "And after all," Thoby said, "it is a pretty feeble affair, isn't it?" Nobody was much good after twenty-five, he said. But most people, I gathered, rather rubbed along, and came to terms with things. Woolf did not and Thoby thought it sublime. One night he dreamt he was throttling a man and he dreamt with such violence that when he woke up he had pulled his own thumb out of joint. I was of course inspired with the deepest interest in that violent trembling misanthropic Jew who had already shaken his fist at civilisation and was about to disappear into the tropics so that we should none of us ever see him again. And then perhaps the talk got upon Sydney-Turner. According to Thoby, Sydney-Turner was an absolute prodigy of learning. He had the whole of Greek literature by heart. There was practically nothing in any language that was any good that he had not read. He was very silent and thin and odd. He never came out by day. But late at night if he saw one's lamp burning he would come and tap at the window like a moth. At about three in the morning he would begin to talk. His talk was then of astonishing brilliance. When later I complained to Thoby that I had met Turner and had not found him brilliant Thoby severely supposed that by brilliance I meant wit; he on the contrary meant truth. Sydney-Turner was the most brilliant talker he knew because he always spoke the truth.

Naturally then, when the bell rang and these astonishing fellows came in, Vanessa and I were in a twitter of excitement. It was late at night; the room was full of smoke; buns, coffee and whiskey were strewn about; we were not wearing white satin or seed-pearls; we were not dressed at all. Thoby went to open the door; in came Sydney-Turner; in came Bell; in came Strachey.

They came in hesitatingly, self-effacingly, and folded themselves up quietly [in] the corners of sofas. For a long time they said nothing. None of our old conversational openings seemed to do. Vanessa and Thoby and Clive, if Clive were there—for Clive was always ready to sacrifice himself in the cause of talk—would start different subjects. But they were almost always answered in the negative. "No," was the most frequent replay. "No, I haven't seen it"; "No, I haven't been there." Or simply, "I don't know." The conversation languished in a way that would have been impossible in the drawing room at Hyde Park Gate. Yet the silence was difficult, not dull. It seemed as if the standard of what was worth saying had risen so high that it was better not to break it unworthily. We sat and looked at the ground. Then at last Vanessa, having said perhaps that she had been to some picture show, incautiously used the word "beauty." At that, one of the young men would lift his head slowly and say, "It depends what you mean by beauty." At once all our ears were pricked. It was as if the bull had at last been turned into the ring.

The bull might be "beauty," might be "good," might be "reality." Whatever it was, it was some abstract question that now drew out all our forces. Never have I listened so intently to each step and half-step in an argument. Never have I been at such pains to sharpen and launch my own little dart. And then what joy it was when one's contribution was accepted. No praise has pleased me more than Saxon's saying—and was not Saxon infallible after all?—that he thought I had argued my case very cleverly. And what strange cases those were! I remember trying to persuade Hawtrey that there is such a thing as atmosphere in literature. Hawtrey challenged me to prove it by pointing out in any book any one word which had this quality apart from its meaning. I went and fetched *Diana of the Crossways*. The argument, whether it was about atmosphere or the nature of truth, was always tossed into the middle of the party. Now Hawtrey would say something; now Vanessa; now Saxon; now Clive; now Thoby. It filled me with wonder to watch those who were finally left in the argument piling stone upon stone, cautiously, accurately, long after it had completely soared above my sight. But if one could not say anything, one could listen. One had glimpses of something miraculous happening high up in the air. Often we would still be sitting in a circle at two or three in the morning. Still Saxon would be taking his pipe from his mouth as if to speak, and putting it back again without having spoken. At last, rumpling his hair back, he would pronounce very shortly some absolutely final summing up. The marvellous edifice was complete, one could stumble off to bed feeling that something very important had happened. It had been proved that beauty was—or beauty was not—for I have never been quite sure which—part of a picture.

From such discussions Vanessa and I got probably much the same pleasure that undergraduates get when they meet friends of their own for the first time. In the world of the Booths and the Maxses we were not asked to use our brains much. Here we used nothing else. And part of the charm of those Thursday evenings was that they were astonishingly abstract. It was not only that Moore's book had set us all discussing philosophy, art, religion; it was that the atmosphere—if in spite of Hawtrey I may use that word—was abstract in the extreme. The young men I have named had no "manners" in the Hyde Park Gate sense. They criticised our arguments as severely as their own. They never seemed to notice how we were dressed or if we were nice looking or not. All that tremendous encumbrance of appearance and behaviour which George had piled upon our first years vanished completely. One had no longer to endure that terrible inquisition after a party—and be told, "You looked lovely." Or, "You did look plain." Or, "You must really learn to do your hair." Or, "Do try not to look so bored when you dance." Or, "You did make a conquest," or, "You *were* a failure." All this seemed to have no meaning or existence in the world of Bell, Strachey, Hawtrey and Sydney-Turner. In that world the only comment as we stretched ourselves after our guests had gone, was, "I must say you made your point rather well"; "I think you were talking rather through your hat." It was an immense simplification. And for my part it went deeper than this. The atmosphere of Hyde Park Gate had been full of love and marriage. George's engagement to Flora Russell, Stella's to Jack Hills, Gerald's innumerable flirtations were all discussed either in private or openly with the greatest interest. Vanessa was already supposed to have attracted Austen Chamberlain. My Aunt Mary Fisher, poking about as usual in nooks and corners, had discovered that there were six drawings of him in Vanessa's sketchbook and [had] come to her own conclusions. George rather suspected that Charles Trevelyan was in love with her. But at Gordon Square love was never mentioned. Love had no existence. So lightly was it treated that for years I believed that Desmond had married an old Miss Cornish, aged about sixty, with snow-white hair. One never took the trouble to find out. It seemed incredible that any of these young men should want to marry us or that we should want to marry them. Secretly I felt that marriage was a very low down affair, but that if one practised it, one practised it—it is a serious confession I know—with young men who had been in the Eton Eleven and dressed for dinner. When I looked round the room at 46 I thought—if you will excuse me for saying so—that I had never seen young men so dingy, so lacking in physical splendour as Thoby's friends. Kitty Maxse who came in once or twice sighed afterwards, "I've no doubt they're very nice but, oh darling, how awful they do look!" Henry James, on seeing Lytton and Saxon at Rye, exclaimed to Mrs. Prothero, "Deplorable! Deplorable! How could Vanessa and Virginia have picked up such friends? How could Leslie's daughters have taken up with young men like that?" But it was precisely this lack of physical splendour, this shabbiness! that was in my eyes a proof of their superiority. More than that, it was, in some obscure way, reassuring; for it meant that things could go on like this, in abstract argument, without dressing for dinner, and never revert to the ways, which I had come to think so distasteful, at Hyde Park Gate.

I was wrong. One afternoon that first summer Vanessa said to Adrian and me and I watched her, stretching her arms above her head with a gesture that was at once reluctant and yielding, in the great looking-glass as she said it—"Of course, I can see that we shall all marry. It's bound to happen"—and as she said it I could feel a horrible necessity impending over us; a fate would descend and snatch us apart just as we had achieved freedom and happiness. She, I felt, was already aware of some claim, some need which I resented and tried to ignore. A few weeks later indeed Clive proposed to her. "Yes," said Thoby grimly when I murmured something to him very shyly about Clive's proposal, "That's the worst of Thursday evenings!" And her marriage in the beginning of 1907 was in fact the end of them. With that, the first chapter of Old Bloomsbury came to an end. It had been very austere, very exciting, of immense importance. A small concentrated world dwelling inside the much larger and looser world of dances and dinners had come into existence. It had already begun to colour that world and still I think colours the much more gregarious Bloomsbury which succeeded it.

But it could not have gone on. Even if Vanessa had not married, even if Thoby had lived, change was inevitable. We could not have gone on discussing the nature of beauty in the abstract for ever. The young men, as we used to call them, were changing from the general to the particular. They had ceased to be Mr. Turner, Mr. Strachey, Mr. Bell. They had become Saxon, Lytton, Clive. Then too one was beginning to criticise, to distinguish, to compare. Those old flamboyant portraits were being revised. One could see that Walter Lamb whom Thoby had compared to a Greek boy playing a flute in a vineyard was in fact rather bald, and rather dull; one could wish that Saxon could be induced either to go or to say something perhaps that was not strictly true; one could even doubt, when *Euphrosyne* was published, whether as many of the poems in that famous book were sure of immortality as Thoby made out. But there was something else that made for a change though I at least did not know what it was. Perhaps if I read you a passage from another diary which I kept intermittently for a month or two in the year 1909 you will guess what it was. I am describing a tea-party in James Strachey's rooms at Cambridge.

"His rooms," I wrote,

> though they are lodgings, are discreet and dim. French pastels hang upon the walls and there are cases of old books. The three young men—Norton, Brooke and James Strachey—sat in deep chairs; and gazed with soft intent eyes into the fire. Mr. Norton knew that he must talk; he and I talked laboriously. The others were silent. I should like to account for this silence, but time presses and I am puzzled. For the truth is that these young men are evidently respectable; they are not only able but their views seem to me honest and simple. They lack all padding; so that one has convictions to disagree with if one disagrees. Yet we had nothing to say to each other and I was conscious that not only my remarks but my presence was criticised. They wished for the truth and doubted if I could speak it or be it. I thought this courageous of them but unsympathetic. I admired the atmosphere—was it more?—and felt in some respects at ease in it. Yet why should intellect and character be so barren? It seems as if the highest efforts of the most intelligent people produce a negative result; one cannot honestly be anything.

There is a great change there from what I should have written two or three years earlier. In part, of course, the change was due to circumstances; I lived alone with Adrian now in Fitzroy Square; and we were the most incompatible of people. We drove each other perpetually into frenzies of irritation or into the depths of gloom. We still went to a great many parties: but the combination of the two worlds which I think was so [illegible] was far more difficult. I could not reconcile the two. True, we still had Thursday evenings as before. But they were always strained and often ended in dismal failure. Adrian stalked off to his room, I to mine, in complete silence. But there was more in it than that. What it was I was not altogether certain. I knew theoretically, from books, much more than I knew practically from life. I knew that there were buggers in Plato's Greece; I suspected—it was not a question one could just ask Thoby—that there were buggers in Dr. Butler's Trinity [College], Cambridge; but it never occurred to me that there were buggers even now in the Stephens' sitting room at Gordon Square. It never struck me that the abstractness, the simplicity which had been so great a relief after Hyde Park Gate were largely due to the fact that the majority of the young men who came there were not attracted by young women. I did not realize that love, far from being a thing they never mentioned, was in fact a thing which they seldom ceased to discuss. Now I had begun to be puzzled. Those long sittings, those long silences, those long argu-

ments—they still went on in Fitzroy Square as they had done in Gordon Square. But now I found them of the most perplexing nature. They still excited me much more than any men I met with in the outer world of dinners and dances—and yet I was, dared I say it or think it even?—intolerably bored. Why, I asked, had we nothing to say to each other? Why were the most gifted of people also the most barren? Why were the most stimulating of friendships also the most deadening? Why was it all so negative? Why did these young men make one feel that one could not honestly be anything? The answer to all my questions was, obviously—as you will have guessed—that there was no physical attraction between us.

The society of buggers has many advantages—if you are a woman. It is simple, it is honest, it makes one feel, as I noted, in some respects at one's ease. But it has this drawback—with buggers one cannot, as nurses say, show off. Something is always suppressed, held down. Yet this showing off, which is not copulating, necessarily, nor altogether being in love, is one of the great delights, one of the chief necessities of life. Only then does all effort cease; one ceases to be honest, one ceases to be clever. One fizzes up into some absurd delightful effervescence of soda water or champagne through which one sees the world tinged with all the colours of the rainbow. It is significant of what I had come to desire that I went straight—on almost the next page of my diary indeed—from the dim and discreet rooms of James Strachey at Cambridge to dine with Lady Ottoline Morrell at Bedford Square. Her rooms, I noted without drawing any inferences, seemed to me instantly full of "lustre and illusion."

So one changed. But these changes of mine were part of a much bigger change. The headquarters of Bloomsbury have always been in Gordon Square. Now that Vanessa and Clive were married, now that Clive had shocked the Maxses, the Booths, the Cecils, the Protheroes, irretrievably, now that the house was done up once more, now that they were giving little parties with their beautiful brown table linen and their lovely eighteenth-century silver, Bloomsbury rapidly lost the monastic character it had had in Chapter One; the character of Chapter Two was superficially at least to be very different.

Another scene has always lived in my memory—I do not know if I invented it or not—as the best illustration of Bloomsbury Chapter Two. It was a spring evening. Vanessa and I were sitting in the drawing room. The drawing room had greatly changed its character since 1904. The Sargent-Furse age was over. The age of Augustus John was dawning. His "Pyramus" filled one entire wall. The Watts' portraits of my father and my mother were hung downstairs if they were hung at all. Clive had hidden all the match boxes because their blue and yellow swore with the prevailing colour scheme. At any moment Clive might come in and he and I should being to argue—amicably, impersonally at first; soon we should be hurling abuse at each other and pacing up and down the room. Vanessa sat silent and did something mysterious with her needle or her scissors. I talked, egotistically, excitedly, about my own affairs no doubt. Suddenly the door opened and the long and sinister figure of Mr. Lytton Strachey stood on the threshold. He pointed his finger at a stain on Vanessa's white dress.

"Semen?" he said.

Can one really say it? I thought and we burst out laughing. With that one word all barriers of reticence and reserve went down. A flood of the sacred fluid seemed to overwhelm us. Sex permeated our conversation. The word bugger was never far from our lips. We discussed copulation with the same excitement and openness that we had discussed the nature of good. It is strange to think how reticent, how reserved we had been and for how long. It seems a marvel now that so late as the year 1908 or 9 Clive had blushed and I had blushed too when I asked him to let me pass to go to the lavatory on the French Express. I never dreamt of asking Vanessa to tell me what happened on her wedding night. Thoby and Adrian would have died rather than discuss the love affairs of undergraduates. When all intellectual questions had been debated so freely, sex was ignored. Now a flood of light poured in upon that department too. We had known everything but we had never talked. Now we talked of nothing else. We listened with rapt interest to the love affairs of the buggers. We followed the ups and downs of their chequered histories; Vanessa sympathetically; I—had I not written in 1905, women are so much more amusing than men—frivolously, laughingly. "Norton tells me," Vanessa would say, "that James is in utter despair. Rupert has been twice to bed with Hobhouse" and I would cap her stories with some equally thrilling piece of gossip; about a divine undergraduate with a head like a Greek God—but alas his teeth were bad—called George Mallory.

All this had the result that the old sentimental views of marriage in which we were brought up were revolutionized. I should be sorry to tell you how old I was before I saw that there is nothing shocking in a man's having a mistress, or in a woman's being one. Perhaps the fidelity of our parents was not the only or inevitably the highest form of married life. Perhaps indeed that fidelity was not so strict as one had supposed. "Of course Kitty Maxse has two or three lovers," said Clive—Kitty Maxse, the chaste, the exquisite, the devoted! Again, the whole aspect of life was changed.

So there was now nothing that one could not say, nothing that one could not do, at 46 Gordon Square. It was, I think, a great advance in civilisation. It may be true that the loves of buggers are not—at least if one is of the other persuasion—of enthralling interest or paramount importance. But the fact that they can be mentioned openly leads to the fact that no one minds if they are practised privately. Thus many customs and beliefs were revised. Indeed the future of Bloomsbury was to prove that many variations can be played on the theme of sex, and with such happy results that my father himself might have hesitated before he thundered out the one word which he thought fit to apply to a bugger or an adulterer; which was Blackguard!

Here I come to a question which I must leave to some other memoir writer to discuss—that is to say, if we take it for granted that Bloomsbury exists, what are the qualities that admit one to it, what are the qualities that expel one from it? Now at any rate between 1910 and 1914 many new members were admitted. It must have been in 1910 I suppose that Clive one evening rushed upstairs in a state of the highest excitement. He had just had one of the most interesting conversations of his life. It was with Roger Fry. They had been discussing the theory of art for hours. He thought Roger Fry the most interesting person he had met since Cambridge days. So Roger appeared. He appeared, I seem to think, in a large ulster coat, every pocket of which was stuffed with a book, a paint box or something intriguing; special tips which he had bought from a little man in a back street; he had canvases under his arms; his hair flew; his eyes glowed. He had more

The house at 46 Gordon Square where the Bloomsbury Group first gathered.

knowledge and experience than the rest of us put together. [His mind seemed hooked on to life] by an extraordinary number of attachments. We started talking about *Marie-Claire.* And at once we were all launched into a terrific argument about literature; adjectives? associations? overtones? We had down Milton; we re-read Wordsworth. We had to think the whole thing over again. The old skeleton arguments of primitive Bloomsbury about art and beauty put on flesh and blood. There was always some new idea afoot; always some new picture standing on a chair to be looked at, some new poet fished out from obscurity and stood in the light of day. Odd people wandered through 46; Rothenstein, Sickert, Yeats, Tonks—Tonks who could, I suppose, make Vanessa miserable no more. And sometimes one began to meet a queer faun-like figure, hitching his clothes up, blinking his eyes, stumbling oddly over the long words in his sentences. A year or two before, Adrian and I had been standing in front of a certain gold and black picture in the Louvre when a voice said: "Are you Adrian Stephen? I'm Duncan Grant." Duncan now began to haunt the purlieus of Bloomsbury. How he lived I do not know. He was penniless. Uncle Trevor indeed said he was mad. He lived in a studio in Fitzroy Square with an old drunken charwoman called Filmer and a clergyman who frightened girls in the street by making faces at them. Duncan was on the best of terms with both. He was rigged out by his friends in clothes which seemed always to be falling to the floor. He borrowed old china from us to paint; and my father's old trousers to go to parties in. He broke the china and he ruined the trousers by jumping into the Cam to rescue a child who was swept into the river by the rope of Walter Lamb's barge, the "Aholibah." Our cook Sophie called him "that Mr. Grant" and complained that he had been taking things again as if he were a rat in her larder. But she succumbed to his charm. He seemed to be vaguely tossing about in the breeze; but he always alighted exactly where he meant to.

And once at least Morgan [E. M. Forster] flitted through Bloomsbury lodging for a moment in Fitzroy Square on his way even then to catch a train. He carried, I think, the same black bag with the same brass label on it that is now in the hall outside at this moment. I felt as if a butterfly—by preference a pale blue butterfly—had settled on the sofa; if one raised a finger or made a movement the butterfly would be off. He talked of Italy and the Working Men's College. And I listened—with the deepest curiosity, for he was the only novelist I knew—except Henry James and George Meredith; the only one anyhow who wrote about people like ourselves. But I was too much afraid of raising my hand and making the butterfly fly away to say much. I used to watch him from behind a hedge as he flitted through Gordon Square, erratic, irregular, with his bag, on his way to catch a train.

These, with Maynard—very truculent, I felt, very formidable, like a portrait of Tolstoy as a young man to look at, able to rend any argument that came his way with a blow of his paw, yet concealing, as the novelists say, a kind and even simple heart under that immensely impressive armour of intellect—and Norton; Norton who was the essence of all I meant by Cambridge; so able; so honest; so ugly; so dry; Norton with whom I spent a whole night once talking and with whom I went at dawn to Covent Garden, whom I still see in memory scowling in his pince-nez—yellow and severe against a bank of roses and carnations—these I think were the chief figures in Bloomsbury before the war.

But here again it becomes necessary to ask—where does Bloomsbury end? What is Bloomsbury? Does it for instance include Bedford Square? Before the war, I think we should most of us have said "Yes." When the history of Bloomsbury is written—and what better subject could there be for Lytton's next book?—there will have to be a chapter, even if it is only in the appendix, devoted to Ottoline. Her first appearance among us was, I think, in 1908 or 9. I find from my diary that I dined with her on March the 30th 1909—I think for the first time. But a few weeks before this, she had swooped down upon one of my own Thursday evenings with Philip, Augustus John and Dorelia in tow: she had written the next morning to ask me to give her the names and addresses of all "my wonderful friends." This was followed by an invitation to come to Bedford Square any Thursday about ten o'clock and bring any one I liked. I took Rupert Brooke. Soon we were all swept into that extraordinary whirlpool where such odd sticks and straws were brought momentarily together. There was Augustus John, very sinister in a black stock and a velvet coat; Winston Churchill, very rubicund, all gold lace and medals, on his way to Buckingham Palace; Raymond Asquith crackling with epigrams; Francis Dodd telling me most graphically how he and Aunt Susie had killed bugs: she held the lamp; he a basin of paraffin; bugs crossed the ceiling in an incessant stream. There was Lord Henry Bentinck at one end of the sofa and perhaps Nina Lamb at the other. There was Philip fresh from the House of Commons humming and hawing on the hearth-rug. There was Gilbert Cannan who was said to be in love with Ottoline. There was Bertie Russell, whom she was said to be in love with. Above all, there was Ottoline herself.

"Lady Ottoline," I wrote in my diary,

> is a great lady who has become discontented with her own class and is trying to find what she wants among artists and writers. For this reason, as if they were inspired with something divine, she approaches them in a definite way and they see her as a disembodied spirit escaping from her world into one where she can never take root. She is remarkable to look at if not beautiful. Like most passive people she is very careful and elaborate in her surroundings. She takes the utmost pains to set off her beauty as though it were some rare object picked up in a dusky Florentine back street. It always seems possible that the rich American women who finger her Persian cloak and call it "very good" may go on to finger her face and call it a fine work in the late renaissance style; the brow and eyes magnificent, the chin perhaps restored. The pallor of her cheeks, the way she has of drawing back her head and looking at you blankly gives her the appearance of a marble Medusa. She is curiously passive.

And then I go on to exclaim rather rhapsodically that the whole place was full of "lustre and illusion."

When indeed one remembers that drawing room full of people, the pale yellows and pinks of the brocades, the Italian chairs, the Persian rugs, the embroideries, the tassels, the scent, the pomegranates, the pugs, the pot-pourri and Ottoline bearing down upon one from afar in her white shawl with the great scarlet flowers on it and sweeping one away out of the large room and the crowd into a little room with her alone, where she plied one with questions that were so intimate and so intense, about life and one's friends, and made one sign one's name in a little scented book—it was only last week that I signed my name in another little scented book in Gower Street—I think my excitement may be excused.

Indeed lustre and illusion tinged Bloomsbury during those last years before the war. We were not so austere; we were not so exalted. There were quarrels and intrigues. Ottoline may have been a Medusa; but she was not a passive Medusa. She had a great gift for drawing people under. Even Middleton Murry, it is said, was pulled down by her among the vegetables at Garsington. And by this time we were far from drab. Thursday evenings with their silences and their arguments were a thing of the past. Their place was taken by parties of a very different sort. The Post-Impressionist movement had cast—not its shadow—but its bunch of variegated lights upon us. We bought poinsettias made of scarlet plush; we made dresses of the printed cotton that is specially loved by negroes; we dressed ourselves up as Gauguin pictures and careered round Crosby Hall. Mrs. Whitehead was scandalized. She said that Vanessa and I were practically naked. My mother's ghost was invoked once more—by Violet Dickinson—to deplore the fact that I had taken a house in Brunswick Square and had asked young men to share it. George Duckworth came all the way from Charles Street to beg Vanessa to make me give up the idea and was not comforted perhaps when she replied that after all the Foundling Hospital was handy. Stories began to circulate about parties at which we all undressed in public. Logan Pearsall Smith told Ethel Sands that he knew for a fact that Maynard had copulated with Vanessa on a sofa in the middle of the drawing room. It was a heartless, immoral, cynical society it was said; we were abandoned women and our friends were the most worthless of young men.

Yet in spite of Logan, in spite of Mrs. Whitehead, in spite of Vanessa and Maynard and what they did on the sofa at Brunswick Square, Old Bloomsbury still survives. If you seek a proof—look around. (pp. 162-79)

> *Virginia Woolf, " 'Old Bloomsbury'," in her* Moments of Being: Unpublished Autobiographical Writings, *edited by Jeanne Schulkind, Harcourt Brace Jovanovich, 1976, pp. 157-79.*

DEFINITIONS

S. P. ROSENBAUM

[*Rosenbaum is a Canadian critic and editor. In the following excerpt, he seeks a definition of the nature of the Bloomsbury Group.*]

The Bloomsbury Group was a collectivity of friends and relations who knew and loved one another for a period of time extending over two generations. Because friendships—especially those that developed out of their shared education at Cambridge—were the original and enduring bonds of the Group, Bloomsbury is a difficult entity to define. Polemical misrepresentations of the Group's membership or purposes and essentialist definitions that have futilely sought commonly held beliefs of the Group have resulted from time to time in denials of the Group's existence. I have tried to show in *The Bloomsbury Group: A Collection of Memoirs, Commen-*

tary, and Criticism how the Group described themselves and were seen by their contemporaries. It is fairly clear now that the problems of defining Bloomsbury have as much to do with preconceptions about the nature of artistic or intellectual groups as with the elusive character of the Bloomsbury Group itself.

Bloomsbury was closer to being a modern movement than a traditional school, although neither term applies to it very accurately. G. E. Moore and Roger Fry profoundly affected the Group's thought and art but they were not its masters. No doctrine was taught in Bloomsbury. "We had no common theory, system, or principles which we wanted to convert the world to," Leonard Woolf asserted in the clearest account of Bloomsbury that has been written by one of its members [his *Beginning Again;* see excerpt below]. Because Bloomsbury was not a school of writers, artists, or intellectuals, the term "circle" that is sometimes used to identify the Group is too restrictive, as is the term "set," which applies essentially to social relations. The looser notion of "group" seems more accurate. Bloomsbury's associations included philosophical, artistic, literary, political, economic and moral affinities in addition to their friendships, but the affinities accompanied the friendships rather than the other way round. As a cultural group Bloomsbury has been described as a fraction by association with, rather than in programmatic opposition to, the English upper middle class. But like an avant-garde movement Bloomsbury sometimes defined itself in terms of opposition to various cultural establishments or to other avant-garde movements; it also rejoiced in change and experiment and sought an artistic, intellectual and familial milieu—but not in the Victorian family way. Virginia Woolf's writing can be difficult, yet no one in Bloomsbury practised the "linguistic hermeticism" that often characterises avant-garde writing. A belief in the common reader underlies Bloomsbury's prose. Nor did the Group maintain any little magazines, as avant-garde movements appear to do. Bloomsbury could be said to have a press, but it published little of E. M. Forster's work, none of Lytton Strachey's, and many of the Hogarth authors had nothing at all to do with Bloomsbury.

The difficulty of mapping a network of friendships is another reason why Bloomsbury is difficult to define. Friends of the friends were not necessarily members of the Group. It was not obvious from the outside who belonged, and this allowed their enemies to associate all sorts of unlikely people with Bloomsbury. The Group's easiest defence was simply to deny their existence as a group. With the publication of Bloomsbury biographies and autobiographies the membership of Bloomsbury along with the complex nature of their associations became clear. Other difficulties in defining the people in Bloomsbury have to do with the "marriage and death and division" that Swinburne, an early favourite poet of Bloomsbury's, says "make barren our lives." The membership of the Group altered somewhat with marriages of one kind or another, with the coming of the younger generation, and with the dying of the older. Perhaps the simplest way of identifying the members of the Bloomsbury Group is to look at the Memoir Club that was founded in 1920 to commemorate—ironically and otherwise—Old Bloomsbury. Whether the Group came together in Cambridge undergraduate discussion societies or during the early years of the new century in that district of West Central London from which the Group took its name, the papers of the Memoir Club and other autobiographies of the members agreed that Old Bloomsbury ended with the First World War.

Originating in shared past experiences, the Memoir Club provided a continuing basis for the New Bloomsbury that lasted more or less through the Second World War. The last meeting was in 1956. According to Leonard Woolf the initial members of the Memoir Club, in addition to himself and his wife, were Vanessa and Clive Bell, Lytton Strachey, John Maynard Keynes, Duncan Grant, Roger Fry, E. M. Forster, Saxon Sydney-Turner, Adrian Stephen, and Desmond and Mary MacCarthy. There is room for qualification and disagreement in this as in all Bloomsbury lists, but for the purposes of literary history the only writer missing from Leonard Woolf's list who was intimately associated with Bloomsbury is David Garnett, and he did not become involved with Bloomsbury until the First World War.

It is worth emphasising that Leonard Woolf's list includes a very important writer who is sometimes left out of Bloomsbury accounts because he was not closely involved with the Group during its Edwardian years. For purposes of literary if not personal history, E. M. Forster is crucial to Bloomsbury. His novels and essays influentially embodied Bloomsbury values, and his achievements were of considerable significance for Virginia and Leonard Woolf as well as for Lytton Strachey and Desmond MacCarthy. Forster's significance together with Bloomsbury's is sometimes ignored by feminist interpretations of Virginia Woolf that emphasise the influence of other women upon her. But Virginia Woolf herself was quite clear on the importance of a group for an artist's development. In a public dispute with Desmond MacCarthy over the intellectual status of women, she argued that among the necessary conditions for a Shakespeare was "that he shall have had predecessors in his art, shall make one of a group where art is freely discussed and practised, and shall himself have the utmost of freedom of action and experience." The women artists such as Vita Sackville-West or Ethel Smyth that Virginia Woolf knew outside the Bloomsbury Group did not give her such an opportunity. And of course within the Group was the most important woman in her life, her sister the artist—matriarch Vanessa Bell.

Other writers of the younger generation who became closely associated with Bloomsbury in various ways, and therefore also have some place in its later literary history during the Georgian years and into the 1930s include James and Marjorie Strachey, Arthur Waley, Francis Birrell, Gerald Brenan, Raymond Mortimer, F. L. Lucas, John Lehmann and, of course, Julian and Quentin Bell. But it should be noted that some writers who had a close relationship with one or two people in Bloomsbury were not considered to be members by the Group or themselves, despite what the writers of reviews or surveys sometimes say. The Sitwells were not Bloomsbury, though polemical outsiders lumped them together. Vita Sackville-West and her husband Harold Nicolson were closer, but neither their Hogarth Press books, which interested Bloomsbury, nor Virginia's affair with Vita should obscure the considerable differences in class, education and values between them and Bloomsbury. The relations of Bertrand Russell and T. S. Eliot with Bloomsbury are again different. Russell's philosophy and social criticism, Eliot's poetry and literary criticism influenced Bloomsbury deeply; both were at times good friends with various members, but neither was associated throughout his career in the manner of intimate friendship that characterises Bloomsbury's relations. Then there is Lady Ottoline Morrell—always a special case, but she was not really a writer; of her Virginia Woolf remarked [in an essay collected in her *Moments of Being;* see excerpt above] that when

the history of Bloomsbury came to be written (she thought it would be a good subject for Strachey's next book) a chapter or at least an appendix would have to be devoted to her.

"Division" in Bloomsbury has sometimes affected definitions of the Group. Because, as Leonard Woolf said, they had no commonly held theory, system or principles, it has been assumed that there was no intellectual basis for the Group. Such an assumption has been reinforced by the unsparing criticism that the members had directed at one another's life and work. This mutual criticism, along with the mutual admiration that the Group is often accused of, is among the most important kinds of interconnection a literary history needs to trace in Bloomsbury's writings. As for the lack of common ideas, Leonard Woolf himself also wrote in a passage cited above that "the colour of our minds and thought had been given to us by the climate of Cambridge and Moore's philosophy." This colour changed at least its hue when Bloomsbury encountered in Edwardian London the political climate of suffragism, socialism, pacifism, and the aesthetic climate of post-impressionism. None of these can be considered a defining characteristic of Bloomsbury, but this does not mean that Bloomsbury fails to manifest a clear similarity of convictions about philosophy, art and society. There is, in Wittgenstein's metaphor, a family resemblance between members of the Bloomsbury Group that appears not in their common features but in their overlapping and crisscrossing similarities. A literary history of the Bloomsbury Group needs to trace this family resemblance in their writings.

Another philosophical comparison that can clarify the nature of the Bloomsbury Group is G. E. Moore's notion of an organic whole. For Moore it is a whole that bears no regular relation to the sum of its parts. Moore applied his idea to the assessment of value, but it is relevant to Bloomsbury's writings: they have a value as a whole for Bloomsbury's literary history that has no regular relation to their intrinsic value as works of literature. Leonard Woolf's novels, for instance, or Desmond MacCarthy's reviews are not among the monuments of English fiction or criticism, but in the literary history of Old Bloomsbury they are invaluable. (pp. 3-7)

The nature of the Bloomsbury Group is truly remarkable only in one aspect. There are innumerable groups without leaders or goals, that are based on friendship and whose membership is not easily defined. Here, for example, is a description of a group in a novel talked about in Cambridge at the beginning of Bloomsbury's history: "Oh yes; not a formal association nor a secret society—still less a 'dangerous gang' or an organization for any definite end. We're simply a collection of natural affinities . . ." (Henry James, *The Awkward Age*). What makes the Bloomsbury Group more than simply a collection of affinities is the work they achieved. Their lives are best understood, finally, as they are enacted in and through their work. (p. 7)

S. P. Rosenbaum, in his Victorian Bloomsbury: The Early Literary History of the Bloomsbury Group, *Vol. 1, Macmillan Press, 1987, 316 p.*

LEONARD WOOLF

[*In the following excerpt from his autobiography, Woolf provides a definition of "Old Bloomsbury" and presents his view of its essential character.*]

What came to be called Bloomsbury by the outside world

never existed in the form given to it by the outside world. For "Bloomsbury" was and is currently used as a term—usually of abuse—applied to a largely imaginary group of persons with largely imaginary objects and characteristics. I was a member of this group and I was also one of a small number of persons who did in fact eventually form a kind of group of friends living in or around that district of London legitimately called Bloomsbury. The term Bloomsbury can legitimately be applied to this group. . . . Bloomsbury, in this sense, did not exist in 1911 when I returned from Ceylon; it came into existence in the three years 1912 to 1914. We did ourselves use the term of ourselves before it was used by the outside world, for in the 1920's and 1930's, when our own younger generation were growing up and marrying and some of our generation were already dying, we used to talk of "Old Bloomsbury," meaning the original members of our group of friends who between 1911 and 1914 came to live in or around Bloomsbury.

Old Bloomsbury consisted of the following people: The three Stephens: Vanessa, married to Clive Bell, Virginia, who married Leonard Woolf, and Adrian, who married Karin Costello; Lytton Strachey; Clive Bell; Leonard Woolf; Maynard Keynes; Duncan Grant; E. M. Forster . . .; Saxon Sydney-Turner; Roger Fry. Desmond MacCarthy and his wife Molly, though they actually lived in Chelsea, were always regarded by us as members of Old Bloomsbury. In the 1920's and 1930's, when Old Bloomsbury narrowed and widened into a newer Bloomsbury, it lost through death Lytton and Roger and added to its numbers Julian, Quentin, and Angelica Bell, and David (Bunny) Garnett, who married Angelica. (pp. 21-2)

We were and always remained primarily and fundamentally a group of friends. Our roots and the roots of our friendship were in the University of Cambridge. Of the 13 persons mentioned above three are women and ten men; of the ten men nine had been at Cambridge, and all of us, except Roger, had been more or less contemporaries at Trinity and King's and were intimate friends before I went to Ceylon.

There is another point. In the first volume of my autobiography, in dealing with my years at Cambridge, I said that it was "necessary here to say something about the Society—The Apostles—because of the immense importance it had for us, its influence upon our minds, our friendships, our lives." Of the ten men of Old Bloomsbury only Clive, Adrian and Duncan were not Apostles. Of the other seven of us, Desmond, Morgan [E. M. Forster], Lytton, Saxon, Maynard, and I, all overlapped more or less at Cambridge and had already grown into a peculiar intimacy there as active members of the Society. I tried in *Sowing* to give some idea of the character of G. E. Moore and of his tremendous intellectual (and also emotional) influence upon us and upon the Society of those days. The main things which Moore instilled deep into our minds and characters were his peculiar passion for truth, for clarity and common sense, and a passionate belief in certain values. I have said that Moore's influence upon us was lifelong. How profound it was is shown by what Maynard Keynes wrote in his book *Two Memoirs*. What Moore and his *Principia Ethica* gave to us as young men and what we 60 years ago embraced with the violence and optimism of youth Maynard calls a religion and he is affectionately critical of its and our adolescent one-sidedness and absurdities. But as a final summing up he writes

It seems to me looking back that this religion of

ours was a very good one to grow up under. It remains nearer the truth than any other that I know, with less irrelevant extraneous matter and nothing to be ashamed of; though it is a comfort today to be able to discard with a good conscience the calculus and the mensuration and the duty to know *exactly* what one means and feels. It was a purer, sweeter air by far than Freud cum Marx. It is still my religion under the surface.

That is the point: under the surface all six of us, Desmond, Lytton, Saxon, Morgan, Maynard, and I, had been permanently inoculated with Moore and Moorism; and even Roger, who was seven years older than Moore and highly critical of his philosophy, continually proved by his criticism of Moorism that he was "under the surface" a Moorist. Through us and through *Principia Ethica* the four others, Vanessa and Virginia, Clive and Duncan, were deeply affected by the astringent influence of Moore and the purification of that divinely cathartic question which echoed through the Cambridge Courts of my youth as it had 2300 years before echoed through the streets of Socratic Athens: "What do you mean by that?" Artistically the purification can, I think, be traced in the clarity, light, absence of humbug in Virginia's literary style and perhaps in Vanessa's painting. They have the quality noted by Maynard in Moorism, the getting rid of "irrelevant extraneous matter."

There have often been groups of people, writers and artists, who were not only friends, but were consciously united by a common doctrine and object, or purpose artistic or social. The utilitarians, the Lake poets, the French impressionists, the English Pre-Raphaelites were groups of this kind. Our group was quite different. Its basis was friendship, which in some cases developed into love and marriage. The colour of our minds and thought had been given to us by the climate of Cambridge and Moore's philosophy, much as the climate of England gives one colour to the face of an Englishman while the climate of India gives a quite different colour to the face of a Tamil. But we had no common theory, system, or principles which we wanted to convert the world to; we were not proselytizers, missionaries, crusaders, or even propagandists. It is true that Maynard produced the system or theory of Keynsian economics which has had a great effect upon the theory and practice of economics, finance, and politics; and that Roger, Vanessa, Duncan, and Clive played important parts, as painters or critics, in what came to be known as the Post-Impressionist Movement. But Maynard's crusade for Keynsian economics against the orthodoxy of the Banks and academic economists, and Roger's crusade for post-impressionism and "significant form" against the orthodoxy of academic "representational" painters and aestheticians were just as purely individual as Virginia's writing of *The Waves*—they had nothing to do with any group. For there was no more a communal connection between Roger's "Critical and Speculative Essays on Art," Maynard's *The General Theory of Employment, Interest and Money*, and Virginia's *Orlando* than there was between Bentham's *Theory of Legislation*, Hazlitt's *Principal Picture Galleries in England*, and Byron's *Don Juan*. (pp. 23-6)

Leonard Woolf, "London and Marriage, 1911 and 1912," in his Beginning Again: An Autobiography of the Years 1911 to 1918, *Harcourt Brace Jovanovich, 1963, pp. 15-83.*

CLIVE BELL

[In the following excerpt, Bell provides a brief history of the Bloomsbury Group in an attempt to counter the charge that they exerted a stultifying influence on English art and letters.]

The name [Bloomsbury] was first applied to a set of friends by Lady MacCarthy—Mrs. Desmond MacCarthy as she then was—in a letter: she calls them "the Bloomsberries." The term, as she used it, had a purely topographical import; and the letter, which doubtless could be found at the bottom of one of five or six tin boxes, must have been written in 1910 or 1911. But the story begins earlier. It begins . . . in October 1899, when five freshmen went up to Trinity—Cambridge, of course—and suddenly becoming intimate, as freshmen will, founded a society as freshmen almost invariably do. It was a "reading society" which met in my rooms in the New Court on Saturdays at midnight, and here are the names of the five original members: Lytton Strachey, Sydney-Turner, Leonard Woolf, Thoby Stephen, Clive Bell. After he had gone down, and after the death of his father, Thoby Stephen lived at 46 Gordon Square, Bloomsbury, with his brother Adrian and his two sisters Vanessa (later Vanessa Bell) and Virginia (later Virginia Woolf). These two beautiful, gifted and completely independent young women, with a house of their own, became the centre of a circle of which Thoby's Cambridge friends were what perhaps I may call the spokes. And when, in 1907, the elder married, the circle was not broken but enlarged; for Virginia, with her surviving brother Adrian, took a house in nearby Fitzroy Square: thus, instead of one *salon*—if that be the word—there were two *salons*. If ever such an entity as "Bloomsbury" existed, these sisters, with their houses in Gordon and Fitzroy Squares, were at the heart of it. But did such an entity exist?

All one can say truthfully is this. A dozen friends—I will try to name them presently—between 1904 and 1914 saw a great deal of each other. They differed widely, as I shall tell, in opinions, tastes and preoccupations. But they liked, though they sharply criticised, each other, and they liked being together. I suppose one might say they were "in sympathy." Can a dozen individuals so loosely connected be called a group? It is not for me to decide. Anyhow the first World War disintegrated this group, if group it were, and when the friends came together again inevitably things had changed. Old friends brought with them new and younger acquaintances. Differences of opinion and taste, always wide, became wider. Close relationships with people quite outside the old circle sprang up. Sympathy remained. But whatever cohesion there may have been among those who saw so much of each other in Gordon Square and Fitzroy Square, among Lady MacCarthy's "Bloomsberries" that is, by 1918 had been lost. That was the end of "old Bloomsbury."

Now I will try to name these friends. There were the surviving members of the Midnight Society. Thoby Stephen had died in the late autumn of 1906: Leonard Woolf was in Ceylon between 1904 and 1911: remained in Bloomsbury Lytton Strachey (who, in fact, lived in Hampstead), Saxon Sydney-Turner, Clive Bell. There were the two ladies. Add to these Duncan Grant, Roger Fry, Maynard Keynes, H. T. J. Norton and perhaps Gerald Shove, and I believe you will have completed the list of those of the elder generation who have been called "Bloomsbury." Certainly Desmond and Molly MacCarthy and Morgan Forster were close and affectionate friends, but I doubt whether any one of them has yet been branded with the fatal name. So much for the old gang.

As I have said, after the war a few men of a younger generation became intimate with most of us. I will do my best to name these, too; but as the new association was even looser than the old, the classification will be even less precise. First and foremost come David Garnett and Francis Birrell, both of whom we—by "we" I mean the old Bloomsberries—had known and liked before 1914. Immediately after the war, by a stroke of good luck, I made the acquaintance of Raymond Mortimer; and about the same time Lytton Strachey, lecturing at Oxford, met Ralph Patridge. I do not know who discovered Stephen Tomlin: but I remember well how Keynes brought Sebastian Sprott and F. L. Lucas from Cambridge to stay at a house in Sussex shared by him with my wife, myself and Duncan Grant. I think it may have been through Francis Birrell that we came to know a brilliant girl from Newnham, Frances Marshall (later Mrs. Ralph Partridge).

Now whether all or most of the people I have named are the people publicists have in mind when they speak of "Bloomsbury" is not clear. In fact that is one of the questions I am asking. But from words let fall in broadcasts and articles I infer a tendency to lump together the two generations and call the lump "Bloomsbury." We can be sure of nothing till the journalists and broadcasters and the high authorities too have favoured us with their lists. I have given mine; and so doing have given what help I can and set a good example. I have named the friends who were intimate before 1914 and have added the names of those, or at any rate most of those, who became friends of *all* these friends later. Naturally, with time and space at their familiar task, the bonds of sympathy loosened—though I think they seldom snapped—and so the friends of "the twenties" were even less like a group than the friends of the pre-war period. That, as I have said, has not prevented some critics lumping them all together, and calling the combination or compound, which it seems exhaled a mephitic influence over the twenties, "Bloomsbury." It is impossible, I repeat, to know whom, precisely, they have in mind; but, assuming their list to be something like mine, again I put the question: What had these friends in common that was peculiar to these friends?

Not much, I believe you will agree, if you will be so kind as to read my chapter to the end. For beyond mutual liking they had precious little in common, and in mutual liking there is nothing peculiar. Yes, they did like each other; also they shared a taste for discussion in pursuit of truth and a contempt for conventional ways of thinking and feeling—contempt for conventional morals if you will. Does it not strike you that as much could be said of many collections of young or youngish people in many ages and many lands? For my part, I find nothing distinctive here. Ah, say the pundits, but there was G. E. Moore the Cambridge philosopher; Moore was the all-pervading, the binding influence; "Moorism" is the peculiarity the Bloomsberries have in common. I should think there was G. E. Moore; also the influence of his *Principia Ethica* on some of us was immense—on some but not on all, nor perhaps on most. Four of us certainly were freed by Moore from the spell of an ugly doctrine in which we had been reared: he delivered us from Utilitarianism. What is more, you can discover easily enough traces of Moorist ethics in the writings of Strachey and Keynes and, I suppose, in mine. But not all these friends were Moorists. Roger Fry, for instance, whose authority was quite as great as that of Lytton Strachey was definitely anti-Moorist. So, in a later generation, was Frances Marshall who, beside being a beauty and an accomplished ballroom dancer, was a philosopher. Assuredly Raymond Mortimer, Ralph Partridge and Stephen Tomlin—all three Oxford men—were not devout believers in *Principia Ethica;* while F. L. Lucas, who in those "twenties" may well have heard himself called "Bloomsbury," at that time called himself a Hedonist. I doubt whether either of the Miss Stephens gave much thought to the all important distinction between "Good on the whole" and "Good as a whole." Also it must be remembered that Bertrand Russell, though no one has ever called him "Bloomsbury," appeared to be a friend and was certainly an influence.

Lytton Strachey, I have agreed, was a Moorist. Of him I have written at some length elsewhere and have said that, being a great character, amongst very young men he was inevitably a power. But at Cambridge, and later among his cronies in London, his influence was literary for the most part. He inclined our undergraduate taste away from contemporary realism towards the Elizabethans and the eighteenth century. But when, about 1910, Roger Fry and I became fascinated by what was being written in France he did not share our enthusiasm. Quite the contrary: and as for contemporary painting, Lytton, who had a liking, a literary liking, for the visual arts, thought that we were downright silly about Matisse and Picasso, and on occasions said so. It begins to look—does it not?—as though this thing called "Bloomsbury" was not precisely homogeneous. Maynard Keynes, whose effect on economic theory was, I understand, immense, bore no sway whatever amongst his friends in the West Central district. They liked him for his cleverness, his wit, the extraordinary ingenuity with which he defended what they often considered absurd opinions, and his affectionate nature. They disliked other things. He had very little natural feeling for the arts; though he learnt to write admirably lucid prose, and, under the spell of Duncan Grant, cultivated a taste for pictures and made an interesting collection. Said Lytton once: "What's wrong with Pozzo"—a pet name for Maynard which Maynard particularly disliked—"is that he has no aesthetic sense." Perhaps Lytton was unjust; but with perfect justice he might have said the same of Norton. On the other hand, Pozzo and Norton might have said of some of their dearest friends that what was wrong with them was that they were incapable of wrestling with abstractions. You see we were not so much alike after all.

I have done my best to name those people who certainly were friends and of whom some at any rate have often been called "Bloomsbury." I have suggested that the people in my list held few, if any, opinions and preferences in common which were not held by hundreds of their intelligent contemporaries: I emphasise the words "in common." Wherefore, if my list be correct, it would seem to follow that there can be no such thing as "the Bloomsbury doctrine" or "the Bloomsbury point of view." But is my list correct? It should be. And yet I cannot help wondering sometimes whether the journalists and broadcasters who write and talk about Bloomsbury have not in mind some totally different set of people. There are critics and expositors, for instance that leader-writer in *The Times Literary Supplement,* who describe Bloomsbury as a little gang or clique which despises all that is old and venerable and extols to the skies, without discrimination, the latest thing whatever that thing may be—the latest in art or letters or politics or morals. Also, according to this school of critics, the writers of Bloomsbury delight in a private and cryptic language, unintelligible to the common reader, while mocking at whatever is clear and comprehensible. Now who are these crabbed and wilfully obscure writers who despise all

that is old? Surely not those reputed pillars of Bloomsbury, Lytton Strachey, Roger Fry, Maynard Keynes, David Garnett? I beseech the *Supplement* to give us the names.

There are other critics, of whom I know as little as they appear to know of the reputed pillars of Bloomsbury, who hold a clean contrary opinion. I write from hearsay; but I am told there are brisk young fellows, authorities on the "twenties," whose distressing accents are sometimes heard on the wireless by those who can stand that sort of thing, who explain that in "the twenties" there still existed in England a gang or group which for years had devoted itself to stifling, or trying to stifle, at birth every vital movement that came to life. Oddly enough this gang, too, goes by the name of Bloomsbury. Now who can these baby-killers have been? Obviously not Roger Fry who introduced the modern movement in French painting to the British public, nor Maynard Keynes, who, I understand, revolutionised economics. Nor does it seem likely that the critics are thinking of Lytton Strachey who, far from being reactionary, went out of his way to help the cause of Women's Suffrage when that cause was reckoned a dangerous fad, or of Leonard Woolf who was a Fabian long before British socialism had become what the Americans call a racket. Whom can these castigators of "Bloomsbury" have in mind? Clearly not Virginia Woolf who invented what amounts almost to a new prose form; nor, I hope, certain critics who, long before 1920, had appreciated and defended the then disconcerting works of Picasso and T. S. Eliot.

Once more I cry aloud: Who were the members of Bloomsbury? For what did they stand? In the interests of history, if common decency means nothing to them, I beseech the Bloomsbury-baiters to answer my questions; for unless they speak out and speak quickly social historians will have to make what they can of wildly conflicting fancies and statements which contradict known facts. Thus, disheartened by the impossibility of discovering opinions and tastes common and peculiar to those people who by one authority or another have been described as "Bloomsbury," the more acute may well be led to surmise that Bloomsbury was neither a chapel nor a clique but merely a collection of individuals each with his or her own views and likings. When to this perplexity is added the discovery that no two witnesses agree on a definition of the "Bloomsbury doctrine," historians are bound to wonder whether there ever was such a thing. At last they may come to doubt whether "Bloomsbury" ever existed. And did it? (pp. 129-37)

Clive Bell, "Bloomsbury," in his Old Friends: Personal Recollections, *Chatto & Windus, 1956, pp. 126-37.*

INFLUENCES

S. P. ROSENBAUM

[In the following excerpt, Rosenbaum examines the dominant religious, philosophical, and aesthetic influences on Bloomsbury thought.]

Bloomsbury was born and bred Victorian. The rational and visionary significance of the Group's writing has its origins in Victorian family, school and university experience. The Group's literary history begins with this experience, particularly as it is reflected in their autobiographical texts. But the Group's Victorian upbringing and education were moulded by certain intellectual attitudes that need to be described first, and here intellectual and literary history are not easily separable. Bloomsbury's writings in all their forms are related in important ways to Victorian beliefs about religion, philosophy, politics and art. Therefore the literary history of Bloomsbury is, among other things, the story of how their writings transmuted these beliefs into modern convictions about ultimate reality, knowledge, society and value. Of course there were other crucial sources, in French, Russian, American and especially eighteenth- and early-nineteenth-century English culture—sources which obviously influenced Victorian culture too—but in the literary history of Bloomsbury it is Victorian evangelicalism, utilitarianism, liberalism and aestheticism out of which the Group's habits of thought and feeling grow.

None of these terms is very precise. All need considerable qualification before they can be used to describe the strands of religious, philosophical, political and artistic thought that constitute Bloomsbury's intellectual backgrounds.

"Our religion," wrote John Maynard Keynes in the celebrated memoir of his early beliefs, "closely followed the English puritan tradition of being chiefly concerned with the salvation of our own souls." By religion Keynes meant "one's attitude towards oneself and the ultimate," as distinguished from morals, which had to do with "one's attitude towards the outside world and the intermediate." This distinction is an important and controversial one in Bloomsbury's history; it shows just how far Bloomsbury moved from its Victorian origins. The English puritan tradition was certainly present in Keynes's own background, for his grandfather had been a minister in Bunyan's church. The puritan tradition in which Keynes locates Bloomsbury is essentially evangelical puritanism. But, in its extended sense, the tradition can also be applied to the Hebraism of Bloomsbury's most puritanical member, Leonard Woolf. But Bloomsbury's puritan context is most manifest in two remarkable religious groups to which a number of Bloomsbury's ancestors belonged: the Clapham Sect and the Society of Friends.

Both E. M. Forster and Virginia Woolf had great-grandfathers who were active members of that early-nineteenth-century upper-middle-class collectivity of reforming Anglican evangelicals whose undying achievement was the abolition of slavery in the British Empire, and whose revolutionary methods of organising social dissent through their writings and public meetings were radically influential. Forster's description of Clapham [in his *Marianne Thornton*] could almost serve as a definition of Bloomsbury: "It was not a closed sainthood, there were no entry tests, no esoteric hush-hush, but the members of it shared so many interests that they hung together, and lived as near to each other as they could." Forster was critical of Clapham because it did not go on to interest itself in the abolition of industrial slavery and because its religious impulses were more moral than mystical. Again this helps to define the distance between Clapham and Bloomsbury.

The evangelical character of the Clapham Sect was an essential aspect of its influence. [In his *Victorian England: Portrait of an Age*] G. M. Young has well described the Victorian heritage of evangelicalism in words that illuminate its relation to Bloomsbury:

> On one of its sides, Victorian history is the story of the English mind employing the energy imparted by Evangelical conviction to rid itself of the restraints which Evangelicalism had laid on the senses and the intellect; on amusement, enjoyment, art; on curiosity, on criticism, on science.

In Bloomsbury this riddance was continued, as the Group divested itself of the restraints that the Victorians had maintained on religious, ethical, political and artistic ideas. Among the characteristics of the Group that they appear to have inherited from their evangelical forebears, however, were outspoken truth-telling, social nonconformity, a quest for moral and aesthetic salvation, self-reliance on intuitive ideals, and a contempt for luxury.

The Quakers, with their legacy of the inner light, pacifism, simplicity, asceticism, nonconformity, a strong sense of group identity and perhaps also a sense of persecution, were present in Bloomsbury's religious background through the family of Roger Fry. After G. E. Moore (whose mother had been a Quaker), Fry was the most important influence on Bloomsbury's early intellectual development, and the intuitive formalism, the pacifism, the group feeling and the mysticism of various members of Bloomsbury suggest connections with Quakerism, though Fry himself was not a believer or an observer. But Fry's relatives were not the only Victorian Quakers among the families of Bloomsbury. The sister of that puritan agnostic Leslie Stephen was a widely read Quaker author at the end of the nineteenth century. (Women were allowed to be more prominent and effective among Quakers than in Clapham.) The subtitle of one of Caroline Emelia Stephen's books, "Thoughts on the Central Radiance," could describe the mystical meditations in some of Virginia Woolf's fiction. Her aunt called her religious belief "rational mysticism," a phrase that fits the mystical experiences in her niece's novels and in Forster's as well. But there were also fundamental differences here: Caroline Emelia Stephen's mysticism is introvertive, arising from an inner light, whereas the sources of the visionary moments that Mrs. Dalloway, Mrs. Ramsay, and even Mrs. Moore experience are extrovertive, coming from external nature.

For all the significance of evangelicalism in the intellectual origins of Bloomsbury, it must not be forgotten that they sought a secular salvation. Almost all the members were not just Victorian agnostics, like a number of their fathers and mothers, but modern atheists. It has been suggested [by Noël Annan in his *Leslie Stephen: The Godless Victorian*] that Bloomsbury rejected the evangelical notion of original sin for an eighteenth-century faith in reason and the perfectibility of man. But we do not have to return to the eighteenth century for the ethical antecedents of Bloomsbury's transformation of evangelical puritanism. They are clearly present in the nineteenth-century utilitarianism that Bloomsbury adapted.

The importance of utilitarianism in the philosophical backgrounds of the Bloomsbury Group has generally been overlooked. Bentham and his followers formed a group very different from the Clapham Sect or the Society of Friends, yet it was a group whose ideas did more than either of them to form the minds of Bloomsbury. For readers of English literature the writings of Dickens and Carlyle have often discredited one of the most influential, liberating modern moral theories. The utilitarian ethical environment which the

Keyneses, the Stephens and the Stracheys grew up in was created not so much by Bentham's hedonistic calculus as by John Stuart Mill's reconciliation of the values of Bentham's thought with those of Wordsworth and Coleridge. Leslie Stephen and John Neville Keynes were utilitarian philosophers. And Moore's *Principia Ethica* together with his later *Ethics* are works of moral philosophy belonging to the utilitarian tradition, though they also owe something to the Victorian intuitional moralists. Moore, John Neville Keynes and the Cambridge Apostles were all strongly influenced by Henry Sidgwick, whose achievement as an ethical thinker may be second only to Mill's in the Victorian period. Through the work of Mill, Sidgwick, Stephen, Keynes and finally Moore, the rationality of utilitarianism—its valuing of common sense and clarity, its eschewing of metaphysics and mysticism—became part of Bloomsbury's way of thought.

Yet utilitarianism in Bloomsbury underwent a transformation almost as extensive as its evangelicalism. It was the utilitarianism, in fact, that fundamentally changed the evangelicalism. Bloomsbury retained one of the two basic tenets of Victorian utilitarianism but not the other. Moore called one of his chapters in *Ethics* "Results the Test of Right and Wrong," and this concisely summarises what has been called the "consequentialism" that Moore and Bloomsbury retained from utilitarianism. "Consequentialism" is a more exact, if inelegant, term than "utilitarianism" to describe Bloomsbury's nineteenth-century ethical heritage. But Moore and his disciples were all agreed in rejecting Bentham's calculus of pleasure and pain. In place of the hedonistic ends of Bentham's and Mill's ethics, Moore substituted a plurality of goods together with an intuitional concept of good as an indefinable property. This, of course, affected utilitarian calculations: good as an indefinable rather than a hedonistic property does not lend itself in the same way to calculations of the greatest good for the greatest number.

Bloomsbury's consequentialism is rooted in the essential distinction of *Principia Ethica* between good as a means and good as an end in itself. The distinction is engrained in the Group's thinking and writing. With it Strachey and others were able to reduce those large Victorian notions of duty and virtue to their proper size as matters having to do with the right means to good ends. And Virginia Woolf would use the distinction to argue in her feminist criticism that value in women's work must not be confined to the instrumental; as she wrote at the end of *A Room of One's Own*, "Do not dream of influencing other people, I would say, if I knew how to make it sound exalted. Think of things in themselves." The language here and elsewhere in Bloomsbury is paradoxically Kantian; the distinction between means to ends and ends in themselves turns finally into one between appearance and reality.

The presence of words relating to means and ends in the titles of various Bloomsbury works, sometimes expressed in metaphors of travel, shows how significant Moore's means–ends analysis of ethics was for Bloomsbury's work. Think of *The Longest Journey, Howards End, Landmarks in French Literature, The Voyage Out, The Economic Consequences of the Peace, A Passage to India, To the Lighthouse, Landmarks in Nineteenth-Century Painting* or *The Journey Not the Arrival Matters.* The basic distinction in *Principia Ethica* between instrumental and intrinsic value is probably more important for an understanding of Bloomsbury's ethics than the book's Ideals of aesthetic enjoyments and personal relations.

Keynes thought Bloomsbury forsook Moore's ethical means for his ends, but Leonard Woolf and others have effectively denied this. Keynes was nevertheless right when he pointed to the presence of neo-Platonism in Moore's thought and in Bloomsbury's. The only philosophical tradition comparable to utilitarianism in the intellectual backgrounds of Bloomsbury is Platonism. (Virginia Woolf's godfather James Russell Lowell described Emerson as a "Plotinus Montaigne"; Moore as interpreted by Bloomsbury might be described as a Platonic Mill.) The centre of value in Bloomsbury's literary texts is ultimately an intuitive awareness of an unanalysable good. And this good brought back into Bloomsbury's ethics something of the mysticism, if not the metaphysics, that the Group's utilitarianism excluded.

The contemplative life that Bloomsbury so valued was not particularly admired in the active ethics of the utilitarians. This brings us to the Victorian sources of Bloomsbury's political convictions. But before sketching them it is important to note that there was an essential epistemological dimension to the philosophical sources of Bloomsbury's ethics. Utilitarianism often combined with an empirical philosophy of mind from which Bloomsbury's ideas about the nature of consciousness are descended. The philosophical Realism of G. E. Moore and Bertrand Russell rejected British and German (but not necessarily Greek) Idealism and substantially changed the theory of knowledge of Mill and others. Bloomsbury's epistemological assumptions were derived from this philosophical Realism, with its dualistic analyses of perception into acts and objects of consciousness. Forster is clearly a philosophical Realist in his fiction. In the writings of Virginia Woolf the representation of states of mind and their shifting sense- and self-perceptions belong to a tradition of philosophical psychology that focused on the associations of sense-experience. It is a tradition that connects, among others, Locke, Hume, Mill and William James—a tradition evident in Virginia Woolf's so-called stream-of-consciousness techniques and with links to continental phenomenology. This philosophical context also helped to make Freud's psychology more available to Bloomsbury.

The importance of Bloomsbury's utilitarianism has not been much remarked upon, perhaps because it has been considered part of the Group's liberalism—and everyone knows that Bloomsbury was liberal. Liberalism is a political and economic philosophy often accompanied by utilitarian ethics. Its intellectual spirit has been well described in various essays by Bloomsbury's most famous liberal, John Maynard Keynes. His account, for example, of the intellectual tradition of Malthus's work is also an account of the liberal background of Bloomsbury's work:

> It is profoundly in the English tradition of humane science—in that tradition of Scotch and English thought, in which there has been, I think, an extraordinary continuity of *feeling,* if I may so express it, from the eighteenth century to the present time—the tradition which is suggested by the names of Locke, Hume, Adam Smith, Paley, Bentham, Darwin, and Mill, a tradition marked by a love of truth and a most noble lucidity, by a prosaic sanity free from sentiment or metaphysic, and by an immense disinterestedness and public spirit. There is a continuity in these writings, not only of feeling, but of actual matter.

The continuity of feeling and matter in liberalism, as distinct from utilitarianism, centres around the values and requirements of individualism, but here the political and economic aspects of liberalism can become confused. The rational individualism of political liberalism consorts with economic philosophies ranging from *laissez-faire* capitalism to socialism. In trying to identify which strain of liberalism affected the formation of Bloomsbury's political convictions, the best touchstone again is the work of John Stuart Mill. Bloomsbury came to change Mill's liberalism almost as much as its inherited Victorian religious and philosophical beliefs. The direction of the change was socialist rather than conservative, though not Marxist. Keynes again illustrates this development of Bloomsbury's liberalism; in 1926 he succinctly defined "the political problem of mankind" as having "to combine three things: economic efficiency, social justice, and individual liberty."

That ideal combination was the basis for Leonard Woolf's, Lytton Strachey's and E. M. Forster's condemnations of the imperialism that nineteenth-century liberalism had helped to foster. Strachey and Forster also used liberal assumptions to argue for a *laissez-faire* sexuality. And in the writings of Virginia Woolf the two come together in her recurrent exposure of sexual imperialism. Virginia Woolf's feminism is liberal in origin. It is not a coincidence that the most influential feminist work written is still probably John Stuart Mill's *The Subjection of Women*. But in her awareness that the liberty of the individual must be protected from the encroachments of patriarchal institutions, be they families or armies, Virginia Woolf is also a very modern feminist.

Mill's liberalism influenced Bloomsbury not only because he applied the principles of individual liberty and critical toleration more widely than any other liberal thinker, but also because he recognised some of the emotional and imaginative shortcomings of nineteenth-century utilitarianism and liberalism. The liberal tradition's continuity of feeling that Keynes honours also produced philistinism. Individual liberty was a means, not an end in itself, and the inadequacy of liberalism's ends is a Bloomsbury theme that goes back to Matthew Arnold as well as Mill. Arnold does not belong to Keynes's tradition of humane science, yet he is a significant Victorian influence on Bloomsbury, though not as important as Mill.

In Bloomsbury, Arnold's as well as Mill's criticisms of liberalism are most apparent in the fiction and criticism of E. M. Forster. Liberal democracy, said Forster . . . [in the title essay of his *Two Cheers for Democracy*], deserved two cheers because its values were various and because it allowed criticism; only love got three cheers, and it was a private as well as an artistic, but not a political, state. Forster is Arnoldian in his realisation of the lack of coherence and fraternity in liberalism that so bothered such unliberal critics of Mill as Carlyle and that other Stephen, Sir James Fitzjames Stephen. For Forster and Bloomsbury, social cohesion lay not in patriarchies but in tolerant cooperation, personal relations and aesthetic experience. Art, said Forster in another famous essay, was "the one orderly product which our muddling race has produced." The title of that essay was "Art for Art's Sake," and this brings us to the last of the Victorian backgrounds of Bloomsbury's intellectual assumptions.

Aestheticism requires even more explanation and qualification than evangelicalism, utilitarianism or liberalism in the intellectual origins of Bloomsbury. Yet no other term conveniently sums up the nineteenth century's concern with the value of art, a concern so important in the development of the

Group. It has been widely assumed that Bloomsbury's view of art as an autonomous activity of very great potential value was basically a modern extension of the *fin-de-siècle* aestheticism of Walter Pater in particular, but also of Swinburne, Wilde, Whistler, Symonds, Beerbohm and other English aesthetes. There are certainly important connections between the writing of these men and Bloomsbury, but there were other, equally influential sources, which Bloomsbury transformed as thoroughly as they modified their religious, philosophical and political inheritance.

Bloomsbury's aestheticism, like so many aspects of modernism, is Romantic in origin, of course. The formalistic, autotelic aesthetics of Roger Fry and Clive Bell go back to Kant's *Critique of Judgement,* which separated disinterested aesthetic experience from the exigencies of practical and pure reasons. Bell's influential doctrine of significant form also clearly owes something not just to Moore's ethics but also to Plato's theory of forms: the significant form of a work of art is an indefinable, intuited Platonic idea behind the representational surface. In the later nineteenth century the direct and indirect sources of Bloomsbury's ideas about art appear to be principally French. The Group's admiration of French culture's devotion to art is summarised by Lytton Strachey at the end of his first book, *Landmarks of French Literature:*

> The one high principle which, through so many generations, has guided like a star the writers of France is the principle of deliberation, of intention, of a conscious search for ordered beauty; an unwavering, an indomitable pursuit of the endless glories of art.

Even more influential on Bloomsbury's aestheticism than French literature was French painting. The close association of the arts of writing and painting is one of the primary characteristics of the Bloomsbury Group. In Virginia Woolf's work, though not in Forster's, art approached the condition of painting rather than, as Pater thought, of music. When Virginia Woolf stated in her modernist manifesto "Mr. Bennett and Mrs. Brown" that "on or about December, 1910, human character changed," and therefore the novel changed, she was alluding with that very specific dating to Roger Fry's first post-impressionist exhibition. Virginia Woolf's impressionism has been widely noted, but it has not been sufficiently recognised that her mature work was post-impressionist in being both visionary and designed.

The source usually given for Virginia Woolf's impressionism is Walter Pater's *The Rennaissance.* His emphasis on knowing one's impression as it really is, on living for moments of aesthetic ecstasy, has illuminated her work for many readers. Pater's great accomplishment, along with Swinburne's and the Pre-Raphaelites', has been described as the purifying of Ruskin's aesthetics by ridding it of moral bias. This aesthetic purification was continued by Bloomsbury, but it is an oversimplification to locate the origins of the Group's artistic convictions only or even mainly in the work of Pater and other English aesthetes. Bloomsbury's aesthetics developed out of puritan, utilitarian Cambridge rather than Anglo-/Roman Catholic Idealist Oxford. Pater's sceptical, even solipsistic, epistemology, and the Idealist implications of Wilde's theory that nature imitates art were refuted for Bloomsbury by the common-sense philosophical realism of Moore, which gave to Bloomsbury's aesthetics a solidly logical underpinning. It is true that Moore's ethics resembles Pater's aesthetics in several respects: both relied upon an intuitional ideal, valued aesthetic experience for its own sake, thought of that experience primarily in terms of perception, and were unconcerned with its temporal dimensions. But there is a crucial difference between Pater's aesthetic attitude and Moore's—a difference that clearly limits the aestheticism of Pater and others for Bloomsbury.

Moore's Ideal in *Principia Ethica* was twofold not single: personal relations were at least as important as aesthetic experience—and love was more important. In Bloomsbury's aesthetics, therefore, love was not subsumed under art. In his memoir on his early beliefs Keynes wrote that he and his friends at Cambridge had sterilised human experience by classifying it as aesthetic experience. There is little conformation of this in Bloomsbury's Cambridge writings; still, Keynes reveals here how aware later Bloomsbury was of the dangers of aestheticism. Forster in his fiction and essays is vigilantly critical of the aestheticising of love that characterised the undeveloped heart of a certain kind of English man or woman. Yet, Forster, Strachey and, in her different way, Virginia Woolf clearly do continue the aesthetes' use of their art as a weapon of social revolt against the sexual authoritarianism of their time. Sex and art were combined in the martyrdom of Oscar Wilde, and the lesson was not lost on Bloomsbury.

The use of the moment in the novels of Forster and Virginia Woolf is also quite different from the Paterian moment in the conclusion to *The Renaissance*. Its function, when ecstatic, is not simply an end in itself but also a means to the enhancement of ordinary daily experience for Bloomsbury. And sometimes in Bloomsbury's novels the structured moments of vision were desolating. ("Moments of Vision" was a phrase Virginia Woolf took from a poet much admired in Bloomsbury, Thomas Hardy.) Yet there is a difference in tone, mood and style between Bloomsbury's texts and those of the Victorian aesthetes. Traces of *Weltschmerz* can be found in Strachey's or Leonard Woolf's writings, but Bloomsbury's pessimism is tougher, more modern, than the tender-minded religious glooms of Pater or Swinburne. "Modern literature," wrote Virginia Woolf in 1927, "which had grown a little sultry and scented with Oscar Wilde and Walter Pater, revived instantly from her nineteenth-century languor when Samuel Butler and Bernard Shaw began to burn their feathers and apply their salts to her nose." There is, however, a kinship between the well-made essays of Strachey, Forster, Bell, Keynes, MacCarthy and Virginia Woolf and those not just of Macaulay, Arnold and Stephen, but of Pater, Wilde and especially Beerbohm too. But the greatest writer of prose at the end of the nineteenth century in England was Henry James. His relationship to French and Victorian aestheticism is, like everything else about him, complex. If one is looking for anxieties of influence among the novelists and critics of the Bloomsbury Group, he is surely a most important precursor. James's moral aestheticism is finally the best clue, in both its achievements and its limitations, to Bloomsbury's literary aestheticism.

Even so, the influence of Victorian aestheticism on the Group's ideas about the purpose and value of art cannot truthfully be reduced to the influence of one writer. Roger Fry, the chief source of Bloomsbury's aesthetics, studied painting in Italy and France in the 1890s and knew such aesthetes as John Addington Symonds. The ideas of William Morris were also influential on his development, as the Omega Workshops disclose, and behind Morris is the com-

plex influence of Ruskin, which impinges on Bloomsbury in a number of places, the last being the Group's enthusiasm for Proust. Virginia Woolf's father had an anaesthetised aesthetic sense, but through her mother she was connected to the world of the Pre-Raphaelites. And in her own relationships she associated with the families of Victorian aesthetes: Pater's sister began teaching her Greek, and Symonds's daughter may have been her first love.

In *Art* Clive Bell thanked both the aesthetes and the French impressionists for awakening the aesthetic conscience dormant since before the Renaissance. They both taught that the significance of a work of art lay in itself and not in the external world. Unlike Fry, Bell did not believe this significance held true for literary works of art because words had meanings that paint did not. Fry argued for the unity of the arts, and thought the first fruitful work in aesthetics had been done by Tolstoy. For all the perversity of *What Is Art?*, its expressive, emotive, socially aware aesthetics permanently influenced Bloomsbury's aesthetics. Fry and Bell agreed, however, with the utterly un-Tolstoyan literary formalism expressed by A. C. Bradley in his 1901 inaugural lecture as the Oxford Professor of Poetry. "Poetry for Poetry's Sake" is perhaps the best statement of the transformation that Victorian aestheticism underwent in the literary history of Bloomsbury. In some respects Bradley was a latter-day representative of the Oxford aesthetic tradition; his brother was the famous Oxford Idealist, and the lecture cites Arnold and Pater in the course of its argument. But that argument contains an analysis of art for art's sake that carefully qualifies it. Bradley distinguishes between two meanings of the phrase: art as an end in itself, and art as "the whole or supreme end of human life." Forster made the same distinction nearly half a century later and joined Bradley in upholding the first and completely rejecting the second. Here is the most basic difference in doctrine between Bloomsbury and the aesthetes. Bradley does not talk about love, but it was love that ultimately restricted the role of art in Bloomsbury. Bradley went on in his lecture to analyse what he called heresies of separable form and content, arguing that in evaluating poetry the recognition of both aspects, as he called them, are necessary, "So that what you apprehend may be called indifferently an expressed meaning or a significant form." It is interesting, in the light of how this last phrase became famous as a formalist theory of painting, that it was first used as a description of literature.

> Every man naturally exaggerates the share of his education due to himself. He fancies he has made a wonderful improvement upon his father's views, perhaps by reversing the improvement made by the father on the grandfather's. He does not see, what is plain enough to a more distant generation, that in reality each generation is most closely bound to its nearest predecessors.
>
> [Leslie Stephen]

The religious, philosophical, political and artistic backgrounds of Bloomsbury's convictions can be resolved into four very general traditions of Western thought. The ultimate origins of the Group's religious ideas were Protestant, not Catholic. Empiricism rather than rationalism was their primary philosophical tradition. They were democratic not authoritarian in their fundamental political assumptions. And they were more romantic than classical in their basic aesthetic attitudes.

The usefulness of such generalising is to be found in the outline this chapter offers of how these traditions descended to Bloomsbury through the Victorian period. Leslie Stephen's observations on the influence of the previous generation apply to the generation that succeeded his own. Bloomsbury was closely bound by its inherited evangelicalism, utilitarianism, liberalism and aestheticism, though each of these intellectual traditions was transformed in the Group's development. They modified Victorian evangelicalism with atheism and utilitarianism with Platonism; their liberalism was qualified by pacifism and their aestheticism by love. To understand the intellectual backgrounds of Bloomsbury, it is essential to recognise each of these different traditions as well as the changes that were made in them.

But it is even more important to be aware of how the evangelical, utilitarian, liberal and aesthetic origins interacted in Bloomsbury—of how it is possible to speak, for example, of the evangelicalism of liberals or the aestheticism of utilitarians. The strongest claim that can be made for the significance of Bloomsbury's intellectual sources is that the ignoring of any one of them will affect our understanding of the others and therefore of the whole that the intellectual origins of Bloomsbury's literary history comprise. (pp. 21-34)

S. P. Rosenbaum, in his Victorian Bloomsbury: The Early Literary History of the Bloomsbury Group, Vol. 1, *Macmillan Press, 1987, 316 p.*

DONALD J. WATT

[*In the following excerpt, Watt examines the influence of G. E. Moore's thought and personality on members of the Bloomsbury Group.*]

> Mrs. Sidney Webb once said to me: "I have known most of the distinguished men of my time, but I have never yet met a great man." I had admiration and affection for Beatrice Webb, but when, in her cold and beautiful voice, she pronounced one of these inexorable Sinaic judgments . . . I used to feel that in one moment I should be submerged in despair and desolation, that I was a miserable fly crawling painfully up the Webbs' window to be swotted, long before I reached the top, by their merciless commonsense. But sometimes the fly gave a dying kick, and on this occasion, I said: "I suppose you don't know G. E. Moore." No, she said, she did not know G. E. Moore, though she knew, of course, whom I meant, and the question of human greatness having been settled, we passed to another question. . . . George [Edward] Moore was a great man, the only great man whom I have ever met or known in the world of ordinary, real life
>
> [Leonard Woolf, in his *Sowing: An Autobiography of the Years 1880 to 1904*].

Leonard Woolf's recollection of his encounter with Mrs. Webb, recorded almost sixty years after his introduction to G. E. Moore, signifies the often unqualified admiration of several members of the original Bloomsbury Group for Moore's mind and personality. The characteristics of Moore's personality and the implications of some of the thoughts expressed in his *Principia Ethica* (1903) generated a vital excitement within a large segment of the Group because they seemed to provide philosophical strength for Bloomsbury's most seminal convictions. Today, the figure and intellect of G. E. Moore offer a significant clue to the beliefs of some of

Bloomsbury's more important and influential writers. I shall try to describe Moore's effect on the Bloomsbury Group by examining his personal and intellectual impact on a selection of its members.

To begin with, Leonard Woolf's portrait of Moore conveys tellingly the sincerity and intensity of that personality which so deeply impressed the Bloomsbury circle. Woolf calls Moore's mind "Socratic," noting that Moore's simplicity and integrity were attractive to the young men of Cambridge in a way similar to that in which the young Athenians were drawn to Socrates: "Plato in the *Symposium* shows us a kind of cosmic absurdity in the monumental simplicity of Socrates; and such different people as Alcibiades, Aristophanes, and Agathon 'rag' him about it and laugh at him gently and affectionately. There was the same kind of divine absurdity in Moore." Nonetheless, Moore had a pure and intense passion for truth which could alarm a new colleague. Woolf relates the tension he experienced in Moore's presence in the early weeks of their friendship:

> When I first got to know him, the immensely high standards of thought and conduct which he seemed silently to demand of an intimate, the feeling that one should not say anything unless the thing was both true and worth saying . . . tinged one's wish to see him with some anxiety, and I know that standing at the door of his room, before knocking and going in, I often took a deep breath just as one does on a cool day before one dives into the cold green sea. For a young man it was a formidable, an alarming experience, but like the plunge into the cold sea, once one had nerved oneself to take it, extraordinarily exhilarating.

Woolf concedes that the tension relaxed under the influence of time, intimacy and affection, but he claims that the fact that it never entirely disappeared was, perhaps, a proof of that greatness which distinguished Moore from other people. Woolf goes on to point out that Moore displayed the same intensity and understanding in singing a Beethoven melody as in discussing a philosophical issue: "He played the Waldstein sonata or sang 'Ich grolle nicht' with the same passion with which he pursued truth; when the last note died away, he would sit absolutely still, his hands resting on the keys, and the sweat streaming down his face." Although Moore was hardly noted for his wit, he could react vigorously to the sometimes untoward humor of others, especially that of Desmond MacCarthy. Woolf recalls that Moore laughed with the same passion with which he spoke or sang. One of Woolf's favorite scenes was, he confides, "Desmond standing in front of a fireplace telling a long, fantastic story in his gentle voice and Moore lying back on a sofa or deep in an armchair, his pipe, as usual, out, shaking from head to foot in a long paroxysm of laughter."

Woolf punctuates his study of Moore by contrasting him to Bertrand Russell. At Trinity in 1902-1903, says Woolf, Russell would frequently come to Moore's rooms in order to discuss some difficult problem in the writing of his *Principles of Mathematics*. The differences between the two minds were striking. Russell's mind was quick, his conversation scintillating with wit, a kind of puckish humor flickering through his thought. Like the greatest of chess players, Russell could see "in a flash six moves ahead of the ordinary player." Moore, on the contrary, "pursued truth with the tenacity of a bulldog." His conversation did not scintillate, nor was his mind as supple and quick as Russell's: "To listen to an argument between the two was like watching a race between the hare and the tortoise. Quite often the tortoise won—and that, of course, was why Russell's thought had been so deeply influenced by Moore. . . ." The tortoise was, evidently, a tenacious competitor who possessed a remarkable combination of clarity, integrity and passion.

Woolf prints two of Moore's letters to him in which Moore suggests the painful slowness and meticulosity with which he composed. Moore began his articles over and over again with agonizing care because he sought so consistently both something *worth* saying and an adequate *means of expressing* his subject. Concerning the paper on "Hume's Philosophy," which was reprinted later in his *Philosophical Studies* (1922), Moore wrote to Woolf:

> *All* this year I have been trying to write an article on Hume for MacCarthy's *New Quarterly,* and nothing is done yet, though I've begun it over and over again. . . . Sometimes I seem to see how I could do it; very often I feel as if I can't or won't try; and, when I do try, I almost always seem to lose the thread. . . .

The finished article, when finally published, was a clear, concise and coherent essay on a major problem in theories of knowledge. Woolf's admiration for Moore's "tortoise" tenacity proved to be, at least in this instance, quite justifiable.

Moore's cogent arguments for common-sense realism seemed especially to delight George Lytton Strachey. Further, both Woolf and Roy F. Harrod, the biographer of John Maynard Keynes, comment on Moore's alert appreciation of Strachey's mobile witticisms. Harrod observes: "When Strachey made one of his subtle, perhaps cynical, perhaps shocking, utterances, the flavour of which even his clever undergraduate friends did not at first appreciate at its full value, Moore was seen to be shaking with laughter." During the autumn of 1905 Moore read his paper on "The Nature and Reality of Objects of Perception" to the Aristotelian Society. On January 2, 1906, Strachey wrote to Keynes with some excitement:

> Who d'you think—talking of intellects—has been here half to-day? Moore. He was really splendid. We talked about the Society and his Aristotelian paper from 2:30 to 4:30. . . . On the question of secondary qualities, etc. he was quite superb. He had used an argument in his paper about hens and eggs which Hawtrey said was "too simple." It was, that in order to know that hens laid eggs, *someone* must have seen both a hen and an egg. Hawtrey denied this—because the fact that hens laid eggs determined your mental state, and therefore you could infer it from your mental state. Moore said he could only say such things because his head was full of philosophical notions. Quite magnificent! I was with him heart and soul.

Moore's reply to Hawtrey forecasts his contributions to commonsense realism in later essays such as "A Defence of Common Sense" and "Proof of an External World." Strachey, in all probability, was attracted to Moore's stolid rejection of philosophical cant. Strachey had a zest for new and bold ideas, for honest controversy, for a style based on economy rather than encomia. Too, as his later critical and biographical prose intimates, Strachey was indebted to Moore's insistence that the thinker's first step was to formulate clear questions in order to make it possible to formulate clear answers.

Not so incidentally, Moore's careful intense use of language coincided with Bloomsbury's revaluation of what is (perhaps too readily) dismissed as Victorian vagueness and obscurity. For example, Moore's very style, in both his conversation and his writing, impressed Keynes greatly. [In his *Two Memoirs*] Keynes reminisces that, under the stern influence of Moore's method, the phrase "What *exactly* do you mean?" was most frequently on their lips: "If it appeared under cross-examination that you did not mean *exactly* anything, you lay under a strong suspicion of meaning nothing whatever." Keynes reacted enthusiastically to Moore's chapter on "The Ideal" in the *Principia Ethica:* "I know no equal to it in literature since Plato, and it is better than Plato because it is quite free from fancy. It conveys the beauty of the literalness of Moore's mind, the pure and passionate intensity of his vision, unfanciful and undressed up." Keynes told Harrod that he thought Moore had carried the use of ordinary speech as far as it would ever be possible to carry it in conveying clear meaning. As Harrod observes, Moore's style is characterized by twists and turns and elaborate convolutions of phrase, with plentiful use of italics, by which he succeeds in conveying thought which is clear, distilled, purified, in its very quintessence expressed so that it is impossible to mistake his meaning. The precise effect of Moore's style on Bloomsbury is difficult to estimate accurately, but his desire for closely molded sentences and lucid analyses of intricate issues, his dogged pursuit of a reality that was both beyond the perceiver and yet apprehensible, are at least somewhat analogous to the stylistic experiments of Virginia Woolf and, to a lesser degree, E. M. Forster—experiments directed toward a grasp of complex external events in a moment of clear and credible perception.

At any rate, Moore's greatest impact on the Bloomsbury Group was achieved by the 1903 publication of his *Principia Ethica.* The *Principia Ethica* stimulated a profound, almost Messianic reaction among key members of the Bloomsbury circle. As J. K. Johnstone points out [in *The Bloomsbury Group,* excerpted above], it is the book from which Helen Ambrose, the stabilizing force in Virginia Woolf's first novel, *The Voyage Out,* derives her practical wisdom. It is the book which John Maynard Keynes lauds as "a stupendous and entrancing work, *the greatest* on the subject." It is the book which prompted Lytton Strachey to write a vigorously enthusiastic letter to Moore to celebrate the arrival of the Age of Reason:

> I think your book has not only wrecked and shattered all writers on Ethics from Aristotle and Christ to Herbert Spencer and Mr. Bradley, it has not only laid the true foundations of Ethics, it has not only left all modern philosophy bafouée—these seem to me small achievements compared to the establishment of that Method which shines like a sword between the lines. It is the scientific method deliberately applied, for the first time, to Reasoning. . . . The truth, there can be no doubt, is really now on the march. I date from Oct. 1903 the beginning of the Age of Reason.

Like Keynes, Strachey could compare Moore only with Plato, and, at that, Strachey wrote Leonard Woolf that, next to the *Principia Ethica,* Plato comes out but "tolerably well."

Moore's leading contention in the *Principia Ethica* is that the essential concern of Ethics is intrinsic good, not human conduct: "The peculiarity of Ethics is not that it investigates assertions about human conduct, but that it investigates assertions about that property of things which is denoted by the term 'good,' and the converse property denoted by the term 'bad'." Moore poses two basic questions which he hopes to illuminate:

> I have tried to show exactly what it is that we ask about a thing, when we ask whether it ought to exist for its own sake, is good in itself or has intrinsic value; and exactly what it is that we ask about an action, when we ask whether we ought to do it, whether it is a right action or a duty.

Moore insists that the latter question is a matter of Practical Ethics. Ethics asks "What ought to be?" Practical Ethics asks "What ought we to do?" Accordingly, questions about conduct and duties "can only be answered by showing the relation of the actions in question, as *causes* or *necessary conditions,* to what is good in itself."

The primary question, then, is "What things are goods or ends in themselves?" In the concluding, most influential chapter of the book, "The Ideal," Moore calls this "the fundamental question of Ethics." In order to obtain a correct answer to the question "What is good in itself?" we must consider, claims Moore, what value things would have if they existed absolutely in isolation:

> Indeed, once the meaning of the question is clearly understood, the answer to it, in its main outlines, appears to be so obvious, that it runs the risk of seeming to be a platitude. By far the most valuable things, which we know or can imagine, are certain states of consciousness, which may be roughly described as the pleasures of human intercourse and the enjoyment of beautiful objects. No one, probably, who has asked himself the question, has ever doubted that personal affection and the appreciation of what is beautiful in Art or Nature, are good in themselves; nor, if we consider strictly what things are worth having *purely for their own sakes,* does it appear probable that any one will think that anything else has *nearly* so great a value as the things which are included under these two heads.

Moore's judgment can be condemned as unfounded intuitionism or applauded as a common-sense recognition of self-evident truths. Whatever the case may be, Moore holds, in the end, that "personal affections and aesthetic enjoyments include *all* the greatest, and *by far* the greatest, goods we can imagine."

Moore's conclusions buttressed the operative principles of the secretive Midnight Society at Cambridge to which Strachey, Bell, and Leonard Woolf belonged. The Cambridge Apostles, whose origins extend back to the early days of Tennyson and Arthur Hallam, emphasized close personal affections among their colleagues, careful selection of new members, and free exchange of new ideas within its zealously guarded confines. Here, too, Moore's figure was influential because, as Harrod tells us, new members were often brought before him for inspection.

But the most significant reaction inspired by Moore's arguments emerged from the notion that art is in itself one of the greatest goods imaginable. The *Principia Ethica* was like a new book of revelation, a Bloomsbury *Bible,* on the basis of which the creation and appreciation of works of art was hailed as literally a new religion. "To grasp this intimate exhilaration entirely," writes an anonymous commentator for the *London Times Literary Supplement* ["The Air of Bloomsbury," 20 August 1954] "it is essential to remember how

close nearly all members of the group were to Victorian forbears . . . by whom the arts would have been considered chiefly as a means to a fuller and better life of service." Moore's proclamation of aesthetic enjoyment as an intrinsic good was to his young friends an authoritative source for a reaffirmation of art as a respectable *end in itself.* Moore's incisive argument severed aesthetics from received views of morality and, for several Bloomsbury thinkers, insured the future autonomy of art.

Clive Bell and Roger Fry were among the foremost of aestheticians to explore the consequences of Moore's thesis. Although Bell, in *Old Friends,* calls Fry "definitely anti-Moorist," Fry did conceive and advocate largely a theory of aesthetics which complements Moore's 1903 approach to ethics; and, although Bell and Fry disagree in many particulars, their responses to the central issue of aesthetics are similar. Bell, in his 1913 statement on stylistic theory, *Art,* refers reverently to the *Principia Ethica:* "I have no mind by attempting to reproduce his [Moore's] dialectic to incur the merited ridicule of those familiar with the *Principia Ethica* or to spoil the pleasure of those who will be wise enough to run out this very minute and order a masterpiece with which they happen to be unacquainted." Instead, Bell accepts Moore's reading of aesthetic enjoyment as an intrinsic good and sets forth his own view of the source of art's value. "The starting-point for all systems of aesthetics," says Bell, "must be the personal experience of a peculiar emotion. The objects that provoke this emotion we call works of art. All sensitive people agree that there is a peculiar emotion provoked by works of art." Bell names this the aesthetic emotion and urges that "if we can discover some quality common and peculiar to all the objects that provoke it, we shall have solved what I take to be the central problem of aesthetics." Bell asks, perhaps echoing Moore's questioning method itself, "What is this quality?" What quality is shared by all objects that provoke our aesthetic emotions?" Only one answer seems possible, according to Bell. In all the diverse achievements in art—the windows at Chartres, Mexican sculpture, the masterpieces of Poussin, Piero della Francesca, and Cezanne, to name a few—lines and colors combine in a particular way, "certain forms and relations of forms, stir our aesthetic emotions. These relations and combinations of lines and colours, these aesthetically moving forms, I call 'Significant Form'; and 'Significant Form' is the one quality common to all works of visual art."

Bell goes on ecstatically to pronounce that art is a religion: "It is an expression of and a means to states of mind as holy as any that men are capable of experiencing; and it is towards art that modern minds turn, not only for the most perfect expression of transcendent emotion, but for an inspiration by which to live." Bell finds that art is the one religion which "will never for long be fettered in dogmas" because it is "always shaping its form to fit the spirit." Art, for Bell, becomes "the most universal and the most permanent of all forms of religious expression, because the significance of formal combinations can be appreciated as well by one race and one age as by another, and because that significance is as independent as mathematical truth of human vicissitudes." As with Keynes and Strachey, so with Bell, Moore's liberation of aesthetic pleasure from the bondage of social utilitarianism seemed to herald the dawn of a promising new age.

In "An Essay in Aesthetics" (1909), which Bell lauds as "the most helpful contribution to the science since the days of

Kant," Roger Fry grapples less boldly with the problem of justification for art. Fry rejects the popular notion that imitation is the sole purpose of the graphic arts. He declares that "the graphic arts are the expression of the imaginative life rather than a copy of actual life." Arguing against Tolstoy's position in "What is Art?" Fry submits: "We must therefore give up the attempt to judge the work of art by its reaction on life, and consider it as an expression of emotions regarded as ends in themselves." Thus, in his preface to a catalogue for the second Post-Impressionist Exhibition at the Grafton Galleries in 1912, Fry defends painters like Picasso and Matisse against charges of violating the representational aim of art:

> Now, these artists do not seek to give what can, after all, be but a pale reflex of actual appearance, but to arouse the conviction of a new and definite reality. They do not seek to imitate form, but to create form; not to imitate life, but to find an equivalent for life.

Like Bell, Fry urges the value of aesthetic emotion as an end in itself and, if he disagrees with Bell's extreme claims for Significant Form, he does nonetheless feel that form is the most essential quality for the work of art.

Virginia Woolf develops Moore's apparent celebration of the artist into her own views on the role of the novelist. In her crusading *A Room of One's Own* Woolf contends that "good books are desirable and that good writers, even if they show every variety of human depravity, are still good human beings." "Thus," she advises, "when I ask you to write more books I am urging you to do what will be for your good and for the good of the world at large." Woolf next tries to evoke her concept of reality and to suggest the writer's intimate relationship with it:

> What is meant by "reality"? It would seem to be something very erratic, very undependable—now to be found in a dusty road, now in a scrap of newspaper in the street, now a daffodil in the sun. It lights up a group in a room and stamps some casual saying. It overwhelms one walking home beneath the stars and makes the silent world more real than the world of speech—and then there it is again in an omnibus in the uproar of Piccadilly. Sometimes, too, it seems to dwell in shapes too far away for us to discern what their nature is. But whatever it touches, it fixes and makes permanent. This is what remains over when the skin of the day has been cast into the hedge; that is what is left of past time and of our loves and hates. Now the writer, as I think, has the chance to live more than other people in the presence of this reality. It is his business to find it and collect it and communicate it to the rest of us.

In her essay on "Modern Fiction" Woolf argues that "any method is right, every method is right, that expresses what we wish to express, if we are writers." She suggests that life is a luminous halo, "a semi-transparent envelope surrounding us from the beginning of consciousness to the end." The novelist's task, then, becomes to convey this elusive inner halo with as little outside interference as possible, a goal which stresses the value of the novel as pure art, as a good or end in itself. Woolf's concept of the novelist's independence seems to coincide with Fry's feeling that works of art should be autonomous, "completely self-consistent, self-supporting, and self-contained—constructions which do not stand for something else, but appear to have ultimate value and in that sense to be real." And Woolf's novels, using Fry's phrase describing the Post-Impressionists, seek "to arouse the conviction of a new and definite reality."

Many of the essays by E. M. Forster in *Two Cheers for Democracy* seem to be expressions of Bloomsbury's values, but the article entitled "Art for Art's Sake" is especially significant because of Forster's reasons for his belief in the autonomy of art. Forster admits from the outset that a belief in art for art's sake does not necessarily mean that only art matters: "No one can spend his or her life entirely in the creation or the appreciation of masterpieces. Man lives, and ought to live, in a complex world, full of conflicting claims, and if we simplified them down into the esthetic he would be sterilised." A work of art, however, does form a world of its own, does live in and for itself: "A work of art—whatever else it may be—is a self-contained entity, with a life of its own imposed on it by its creator. It has internal order. It may have external form. That is how we recognise it." The internal order of art interests Forster considerably. We all agree, he proposes, that a work of art is a unique product. But Forster wishes to probe further; he wants to know the reason for art's autonomy. Forster asks why art is unique, and decides:

> It is unique not because it is clever or noble or beautiful or enlightened or original or sincere or idealistic or useful or educational—it may embody any of those qualities—but because it is the only material object in the universe which may possess internal harmony. All the others have been pressed into shape from outside, and when their mold is removed they collapse. The work of art stands up by itself, and nothing else does. . . . It is the one orderly product which our muddling race has produced.

Forster sees works of art as the sole objects in the material universe which possess inner order, and this, he concludes, is why, although he does not believe that only art matters, he does believe in art for art's sake.

Forster's credo is at once an expression and a modification of Moore's description of intrinsic good. As Michael Holroyd's chapter, "Bloomsbury: The Legend and the Myth," [in his *Lytton Strachey: A Critical Biography*] suggests, local and specific influences of the *Principia Ethica* are not always easy to prove irrefutably. And yet Moore's invitation to his colleagues to examine potential justifications for regarding the aesthetic emotion as an end in itself surely contributed to Bloomsbury's widespread faith in the singular quality of art. Moore's book strengthened a notable portion of the Bloomsbury Group in their revolt against the notion of art as a mere means, and the impact of this revolt in the history of modern British literature is perhaps broadly comparable to the impact in philosophy of the reaction against F. H. Bradley by Russell and Moore himself.

The revolutionary implications of the *Principia Ethica*, though, apparently reached beyond aesthetics. In his chapter on "Ethics in Relation to Conduct" Moore outlines his position on human actions. He submits that the most that Ethics can do "is to show that certain actions, possible by volition, *generally* produce better or worse total results than any possible alternative." If we give the name of "duty" to these actions, Moore continues,

> it may be possible to prove that a few of the commonest rules of duty are true, but *only* in certain conditions of society, which may be more or less universally presented in history; and such a proof

is only possible *in some cases* without a correct judgment of what things are good or bad in themselves—a judgment which has never yet been offered by ethical writers.

At this point Moore is, in effect, offering his own foundation for Practical Ethics. For, as we have seen, he will go on in the next chapter, "The Ideal," to present his judgment of things good or bad in themselves. Here, Moore concludes with a key statement on conduct:

> With regard to actions of which the *general* utility is thus proved, the individual should *always* perform them; but in other cases, where rules are commonly offered, he should rather judge of the probable results in his particular case, guided by a correct conception of what things are intrinsically good or bad.

In his insistence on the close dependence of Practical Ethics on intrinsic good, Moore seems to emphasize the integrity of the individual conscience in a social climate wherein moral rules cannot often be proven to comprise absolute truth.

The significance of Moore's stance on Ethics in relation to conduct is easily overlooked. Holroyd speaks of "the puritanical element in Moore's teaching" and Keynes claims that the Cambridge intellectuals set aside that part of the *Principia Ethica* "which discussed the duty of the individual to obey general rules." But the force of Moore's conclusion would seem to be that only a very few common rules of duty are valid—and even these rules can be proven "*only*" in certain conditions of society" and only "*in some cases* without a correct judgment of what things are good or bad in themselves." The identification of intrinsic goods is, for Moore, of primary importance in Ethics. It follows that that person who possesses a firm understanding of real intrinsic values should, to a large extent, be allowed to make his own decisions about duty. Moore, like Russell, engages in a tough analytical interrogation of traditional systems and doggedly elbows muddle and irrelevance out of his report. Moore carefully avoids a relativistic interpretation of duty but, similarly, he refuses to believe that universal propositions with duty as predicate can ever be demonstrably proven. In a word, Moore's argument constitutes an intensive scrutiny of moral absolutism; it constitutes a withering inquiry into what Bloomsbury would regard as Victorian platitudes.

The ramifications of Moore's argument may not have escaped Lytton Strachey. Holroyd states that Strachey "turned his back on ethics in relation to conduct," but in his October 11, 1903 letter to Moore, cited by Holroyd, Strachey writes that the last two chapters of the *Principia Ethica* "interested me most, as they were newer to me than the rest." As Holroyd declares, Moore was "the prophet of that divine companionship for which he [Strachey] so urgently longed. Above all else *Principia Ethica* spelt out one word to Lytton: *friendship.*" Strachey probably read Moore's announcement of personal affection as an intrinsic good in a way Moore never intended. But Moore's advice that individual conscience has priority in the absence of proven social norms quite possibly steadied Strachey in his need for personal conviction, and the *Principia Ethica,* to a considerable degree, provided him with a basis for that quality of detachment which he so fully cherished.

Excerpts from the autobiographical writings of Keynes and Leonard Woolf are helpful in assessing Moore's influence on the ethical thinking of early Bloomsbury. Keynes's exuberance highlights that fervor at Cambridge which spread impulsively as a result of Moore's stimulus. Keynes avows that Moore's influence "was not only overwhelming; but it was the extreme opposite of what Strachey used to call *funeste;* it was exciting, exhilarating, the beginning of a renaissance, the opening of a new heaven on a new earth. We were the forerunners of a new dispensation, we were not afraid of anything." Keynes calls the New Testament "a handbook for politicians" by comparison with Moore's chapter on "The Ideal." Keynes notes in his memoir, "Early Beliefs," that the Cambridge intellectuals were meliorists who believed that they could be safely released from conventional restraints and traditional standards; Wittgenstein pronounced with justice that they lacked reverence for everything and everyone. Looking backward, Keynes says their religion "was a purer, sweeter air by far than Freud cum Marx" and confides, "It is still my religion under the surface."

To return to *Sowing,* however, Leonard Woolf's commentary indicates that Moore's personal influence was quite substantial. In doing so, Woolf modifies what he feels is a rather radical interpretation of Moore's effect by Keynes. Like Desmond MacCarthy, Woolf objects to the idea that Bloomsbury engaged in moral frivolity. A main point in Keynes's memoir is that Moore propounded both a religion and a system of morals in his book, and that the Cambridge group accepted his religion but discarded his morals:

> We entirely repudiated a personal liability on us to obey general rules. We claimed the right to judge every individual case on its merits, and the wisdom, experience and self-control to do so successfully. . . . We repudiated entirely customary morals, conventions and traditional wisdom. We were, that is to say, in the strict sense of the term, immoralists . . . we recognised no moral obligation on us, no inner sanction, to conform or to obey. Before heaven we claimed to be our own judge in our own case.

Woolf protests that Keynes's estimate is "a distorted picture . . . of the influence of his [Moore's] philosophy and character upon us when we were young men up at Cambridge in the years 1901 to 1904." Woolf insists "we were not 'immoralists' . . . he and we were fascinated by questions of what was right and wrong, and what one *ought* to do. We followed him closely in this as in other parts of his doctrine and argued interminably about the consequences of one's actions, both in actual and imaginary situations."

Curiously enough, the opposing views of Keynes and Woolf suggest the polar reactions of modern opinion to the problem of challenging tradition. Both Keynes and Woolf admit Moore's close questioning of traditional systems, but Keynes emphasizes a resulting sense of freedom, while Woolf underscores an intensified need for responsibility. Woolf's rejoinder seems especially sound, for he stresses that the Cambridge intellectuals were most involved with Moore through conversation and argument. In this, C. D. Broad's remarks on Moore [in his preface to Moore's *Philosophical Papers*] are helpful:

> Though his published works are all absolutely first-rate contributions to philosophy, his influence on English philosophic thought was out of all proportion to his comparatively small literary output. It was by his lectures, his discussion-classes, his constant and illuminating contributions to discussion at the Cambridge Moral Science Club and the Aristo-

telian Society, and his private conversations with his colleagues and pupils that he mainly produced his effects on the thought of his time.

Possibly, Woolf's revaluation of Keynes's estimate is quite salutary. As William Van O'Connor observes in response to Keynes's memoir [in "Towards a History of Bloomsbury" in his *Backgrounds of Modern Literature*], "Perhaps it is fairer to say that they were not indifferent to morality but opposed to those forms of morality that become weapons in philistine hands." Woolf's objections readjust our perspective on Moore's influence by reminding us that Bloomsbury had not only the *Principia Ethica* as a stimulating manifesto, but also its author as a modifying consultant.

Moore's overall effect on the Bloomsbury Group extended beyond his *Principia Ethica*. Although the book was the most singular source of Moore's influence, his personality apparently exerted considerable force within the circle itself. Plainly, it is no difficult matter to snipe at either Moore's 1903 views of ethics or the Bloomsbury extension of them into aesthetics. Moore's position is vulnerable to charges of narrowness and incompleteness. As J. K. Johnstone advises, Moore's ethics, from a layman's point of view, appear academic and cloistered, omissive of many other states of mind of great value, such as the satisfaction derived from a task well done or the contemplation of a just and well-ordered community. Conversely, Bloomsbury's often doctrinal attitude towards art is susceptible to objections that it leads to cultural mysticism and critical dogmatism. But Moore's personality may have tempered some initial Bloomsbury inclinations toward extreme artistic mysticism. Broad submits that Moore was fundamentally "a man of simple tastes and character, absolutely devoid of all affectation, pose and flummery." Leonard Woolf verifies this when he calls Moore a "silly." The term is by no means pejorative; it stems from Tolstoy (a writer thoroughly admired by Bloomsbury), who proposed that a profound simplicity is characteristic of the finest human beings. The quality of such an earnest simplicity may seem absurd to ordinary, practical men, but it is a quality which eliminates in the personality affectation, egotism and hypocrisy. In this sense, Keynes's use of the word "immoralists" in connection with Moore is perhaps not quite accurate. Moore's abiding impact on the Bloomsbury Group was surely that of an invigorating tonic, but his modest personality and unassuming mind could hardly have prompted that anarchic licence which Keynes's description appears to suggest. Moore's personal influence, as Woolf's testimony plainly indicates, was a sobering and maturing one. It was an influence potent enough to move Lytton Strachey, as it did Leonard Woolf, to declare later in his career that of all the notable people he had met throughout his life, Moore was the only one who impressed him as being unquestionably great. In fine, Moore was at once an inspiration and a challenge to several members of Bloomsbury—an inspiration in his bold analysis of values in support of their highest ideals, a challenge in his steadying personal example. (pp. 119-31)

Donald J. Watt, "G. E. Moore and the Bloomsbury Group," in English Literature in Transition: 1880-1920, *Vol. 12, No. 2, 1969, pp. 119-34.*

BLOOMSBURY THOUGHT

QUENTIN BELL

[*The son of Clive and Vanessa Bell, Quentin Bell is a noted art critic and the author of numerous books and articles concerning the Bloomsbury Group, of which he is sometimes considered a member. In the following excerpt, he identifies rationality as the unifying principle of the social, political, and aesthetic beliefs of members of the Bloomsbury Group.*]

Imagine a great highway up which walks a heterogeneous crowd—the British Intellectuals. There is in that great concourse a little group of people who talk eagerly together, it is but one of many similar groups and sometimes groups seem to merge. Figures move in towards the centre and move away again to walk elsewhere; some are silent, some are loquacious. When the great ambling procession begins to march in time to a military band, the part to which we devote our attention falls out of step; this makes it, for a time, conspicuous, and yet even so it is not perfectly definable. There are other groups which also become noticeably civilian; moreover, martial music is an infectious thing, and it is hard to say who is and who is not walking to its rhythms. Then, at a later stage, the group suddenly becomes enlarged. Everyone seems to be joining it, so that it is no longer a group, it has become a crowd. It dissolves, the original members disappear, and it is gone.

The image is sufficiently banal but I can find none better to convey the amorphous character of my subject.

What then had this group in common apart from the fact that it was talking? Perhaps this in itself may be a distinction, for there are groups that do not talk, they shout and yell and come to blows. Bloomsbury did none of these things. Despite tremendous differences of opinion, it talked. Indeed it did more, it talked on the whole reasonably, it talked as friends may talk together, with all the licence and all the affection of friendship. It believed, in fact, in pacific and rational discussion.

Now there is nothing remarkable about this; most of us behave quietly and carry on rational conversations. But we also do other things: we create works of art and perform acts of worship, we make love and we make war, we yell and we come to blows.

Bloomsbury sometimes did these things, too, and in fact we all live our lives upon two contradictory principles, that of reason and that of unreason. We come, as best we may, to a synthesis of opposites; the peculiar thing about Bloomsbury was the nature of its dialectic.

A creative artist in modern society can hardly be unaware of the charms of unreason. He is, by the nature of his employment, so very much more dependent upon intuition than upon ratiocination. Art in our time—I am thinking of the visual arts in particular—has broken free from any pretence of utility. The artist is bound by no rational programme, no reasonable dependence upon mimesis; his images are made in accordance with unbiddable inner necessities, they are such stuff as dreams are made on and are judged in accordance with an aesthetic which is of its nature dogmatic and impervious to reason. While this is obviously true of the musical and visual arts, in literature, where a certain tincture of thought may be apprehended, the sway of the unreasoning emotions, the "thinking in the blood" that makes for heroism, passion, chastity, and nearly all the strong emotions that are the very stuff of tragedy, can be overwhelmingly powerful.

The irrational has an even stronger pull, in that it is so often a communal phenomenon. He who thinks much is perforce a lonely man, whereas the great unreasoning emotions of mankind bring us into a glorious brotherhood with our kind. We feel (I quote from [Wyndham Lewis's *Hitler,* 1931]) "the love and understanding of blood brothers, of one culture, children of the same traditions, whose deepest social interests, when all is said and done, are one: that is the only sane and realistic journey in the midst of a disintegrating world. That, as I interpret it, is the national socialist doctrine of *Blutsgefühl.*"

These words were written at a time when it was still possible for a partial observer to ignore the uglier side of National Socialism. They may serve to remind us that the Janus-face of Social Love is Social Hatred; it is hard to create a God without also creating a Devil.

In the year 1900 the world had not seen what a modern nation could do when it put its trust in *Blutsgefühl,* but it was obvious enough that if men were to surrender to the voice of authority, to yield to the strong irrational demands of religion, or nationalism, or sexual superstition, hatred no less than love would be the result. The hatred of Christian for Christian, of nation for nation, the blind unreasoning hatred that had hounded Oscar Wilde or killed Socrates, these were all communal emotions that resulted from irrationality. The sleep of reason engenders monsters, the monsters of violence. It was therefore absolutely necessary, if charity were to survive in the world, that reason should be continually awake.

This I think was the assumption that determined Bloomsbury's attitude and gave a distinctive tone to its art and to its conversation.

No one today could for one moment suppose that the irrational forces in life, the love of death and of violence, were not present in the world, or that they do not lie somewhere within each of us, but whereas to some of us they are not merely immanent but something to be embraced and accepted with joy, connected as they are with so many great spiritual experiences, for Bloomsbury they were something to be chained, muzzled and as far as possible suppressed. The great interest of Bloomsbury lies in the consistency, the thoroughness and, despite almost impossible difficulties, the success with which this was done.

The first great step was to transfer nineteenth-century scepticism from the cosmic to the personal field. The rejection of dogmatic morality meant that the traditional sanctions of social hatred were removed. G. E. Moore's limpid intellectual honesty remained and with it a morality which excluded, or very nearly excluded, aggressive violence. As Maynard Keynes says:

> The New Testament is a handbook for politicians compared with the unworldliness of Moore's chapter on the "Ideal." Indeed there is, in *Principia Ethica,* a certain remoteness from the hurly-burly of everyday life, which, I suspect, results from the extraordinarily sheltered and optimistic society that was to be found in Cambridge at the beginning of the century, and this mild emotional climate was, I apprehend, an indispensable prerequisite for a society which attempted to lead a completely non-aggressive existence.

"We repudiated"—I am again quoting from Maynard Keynes—"all versions of the doctrine of original sin, of there being insane and irrational springs of wickedness in most men." Now this may be true, but if it is true it is surprising. It may be true, because the human mind is capable of such extraordinary feats of inconsistency, but if one considers the novels of E. M. Forster, which are deeply involved in this very question, I find it hard to believe that his contemporaries completely ignored the menace of the irrational.

Death and violence walk hand in hand through these novels; the goblins walk over the universe and although they are driven away, we know that they are still there; children are killed, young men are struck down with swords, blind hatred and blind prejudice are never far away. Where Forster differs from his friends and is not, to my mind, altogether Bloomsbury, is in his essentially reverent and optimistic attitude. His reverence is, to be sure, evasive and half veiled. But it is there all right, in the woods of Hertfordshire or the caves of Marabar; there is something that escapes his reasoning and I can just imagine him buying a rather small dim candle to burn before the altar of some rather unpopular saint—something that Lytton Strachey, for instance, could never have done.

Ethically however he seems to me altogether on the same side as Bloomsbury: conscious, deeply conscious of the dark irrational side of life but absolutely convinced of the necessity of holding fast to reason, charity and good sense.

Bloomsbury may or may not have appreciated the role of "the insane and irrational springs of wickedness" that seem so close to the surface of life in *Howards End,* but must it not have seen them gushing forth in cascades of derisive laughter or in torrents of abuse in the Grafton Gallery Exhibition?

The public reaction to Gauguin, Cézanne and van Gogh was not founded upon any process of reasoning. The public laughed or was angry because it did not understand, and also, I think, because it *did* understand. People could hardly have been so angry, would hardly have reiterated, again and again, the charge of indecency (this hardly seems credible when we think of Cézanne's still lives) or of anarchism, unless they had become aware of some profoundly disturbing, some quite positive emotion in that which they so much hated and were later, with equal unreason, so greatly to love.

Now at first sight it would appear that when faced by such obstinate and furious aesthetic convictions reason would be powerless, and indeed speechless. Speechless she was not. Both Clive Bell and Roger Fry had plenty to say about art between 1910 and 1914. They would most willingly argue with anyone who would listen to them, and while Clive Bell elaborated his theory of significant form, Roger Fry was explaining, persuading, reasoning in talk and conversation, and in letters to the press. Here, Fry seems to be arguing a purely intellectual case. His method is to find common ground and then proceed by a process of enquiry: We both agree in liking A but you do not like B. What then is the difference between A and B? It turns out of course to be something very insubstantial and the opponent is in a perfectly nice and entirely rational way flattered. Such is the method of his argument: he refuses to be dogmatic and he refuses to be angry. He appeals continually to reason.

There was a certain element of deception here, not, I think, of conscious deception. Up to a point Roger Fry's arguments were fair enough, but at a certain point a mixture of charm and what, for lack of a better word I would call "overwhelm-

A Max Beerbohm caricature of Roger Fry (left) and Clive Bell.

He saw in this art, with its abstract and rhythmic sense of ornament and color and its mystic power, an affirmation of his own anti-classical art. He was one of the first artists to protest against the relegation of primitive art objects to anthropological museums, where they were still exhibited as scientific specimens. His own "blood and soil" mystique made him an early proponent of the indigenous art of all peoples.

In fact, of course, the tendency of the Bloomsbury art critics was to look away from content altogether. It is a tendency better exemplified by Clive Bell than by Roger Fry; neither of them in fact held it with complete consistency. But undoubtedly the main tendency of their writings between, say, 1910 and 1925 is in the direction of a purely formalist attitude. The aesthetic emotion is, or at least can be and probably should be, something of almost virgin purity, a matter of harmonious relationships, of calculated patterning, entirely removed from the emotive feelings; and these, when they do occur in works of art, are not only irrelevant and "literary" but productive of that vulgarity, sentimentality and rhetoric which is the besetting sin of nineteenth-century art. Indeed it is the existence of that kind of "Salon Art" which, I fancy, prompted these rather hazardous generalisations. The sentimentality of Raphael and Correggio, the violence of Goya and Breughel, are not reproved but dismissed as irrelevant, or at least inessential.

Something of the same attitude may, I think, be traced in the actual paintings of the group. Bloomsbury finds its masters amongst the Apollonian rather than the Dionysiac painters, turning to Piero della Francesca rather than Michelangelo, Poussin rather than Bernini, Constable rather than Turner. Amongst the Post-Impressionists it looks to van Gogh and to Gauguin but above all to Cézanne.

Cézanne, whose genius is large enough to be interpreted in many ways, is used as a guide to architectonic solidity, to the careful ordering and redisposition of nature. He is not used as the Vorticists and the Germans use him, as a provider of anguished angularities, violent, emphatic, exclamatory drawing and dynamic chaos.

The insistence that art be removed from life, that painting should aspire to the condition of music, which may certainly be deduced from the writings of Clive Bell and Roger Fry, would, one might have thought, have been translated in practice into pure abstraction, but apart from a few brief essays made before 1914 Bloomsbury painting remains anchored to the visible world. For this there was an important psychological reason: the Bloomsbury painters were, I think, intensely interested in content.

Vanessa Bell continued to the last to paint landscapes and still lives, girls, children and flowers, which to me at all events seem to be replete with psychological interest, while at the same time firmly denying that the story of a picture had any importance whatsoever. Duncan Grant has always been rather less positive in his statements; his lyrical inventions are equally if not more suggestive of a highly literary mood. And the mood, which may also be observed in the work of Roger Fry, is again one of passion firmly controlled by reason, sensual enjoyment regulated by the needs of serenity.

Looking at Duncan Grant's *Lemon Gatherers* in the Tate and considering its quietly lyrical quality, the calm precision of its design, its tacit sensuality, who could doubt that in 1914

ingness" would clinch the victory. His friends knew this to their cost, for when Roger started some really March hare, some business of black boxes, dark stars, thaumaturgic parascientific nonsense for which he had a strong though inconsistent affection, his force of character, his air of sweet reasonableness and scientific integrity, was such that he could convince himself and his friends of the truth of whatever chimerical bee might for the moment have flown into his bonnet.

The excellence of Seurat, Cézanne and Poussin were not, in my opinion at all events, chimerical nonsense, but Fry made his hearers believe in those excellencies, made them feel them by means of a method of argument which had the purest air of scientific objectivity, in a field in which, ultimately, science has no authority. Roger Fry is concerned not only to present a "fair argument" but to argue about fair things. By this I mean that he does not readily allude to the esoteric or mysterious side of art but talks rather about sensual and easily demonstrable characteristics. His attitude to primitive art is revealing: confronted by Negro sculpture he is amazed by its plastic freedom, its "three-dimensionalness," the intelligence with which the negro translates the forms of nature, his exquisite taste in the handling of material. Only in one brief allusive phrase does he touch on the magical purposes of these articles. Compare this with the attitude of Emil Nolde, as reported by [biographer Peter Selz]:

he would be a conscientious objector? The answer of course is that anyone could doubt it and that paintings do not have such clear diagnostic value as that, but I let the sentence stand because, overstatement though it is, it conveys a certain measure of truth. Bloomsbury painting, like Bloomsbury writing and Bloomsbury politics, is pacific even when it is not pacifist. It is by no means unconscious of violence, but it reacts against it either by deliberately avoiding it, or by criticism and mockery, or by trying to find a formula to contain it.

On the whole the painters shrink from violence. Roger Fry attempts to explain art in other terms; for him violence was something stupid and irrational, a means to pain when clearly pleasure is the end of life. Lytton Strachey and Maynard Keynes both fight it with ridicule, Clive Bell veers between ridicule and evasion, Virginia Woolf finds its origin in the relationship of the sexes and seeks its cure in their fusion. All turn to reason as the one possible guide in human affairs precisely because the forces of violence lie within even the best-intentioned men. As Clive Bell wrote [in *On British Freedom*], "those were not naturally cruel men who burnt heretics for not agreeing with them, and witches for being vaguely disquieting, they were simply men who refused to submit prejudice to reason."

Even those who would declare that faith is in some sort a higher thing than reason would, probably, agree that there is a good deal to be said for this view—in theory. The difficulty, as anyone who surveys the world from Birmingham, Alabama to Salisbury, Rhodesia, and back again by way of Saigon, will know is that when it comes to a struggle between reason and violence reason nearly always takes a beating.

And yet this is not the whole picture. Reason does win victories and Bloomsbury has helped to win them. This paradoxically is one of the things that makes us undervalue its achievements. It would be quite easy to compile an anthology of Bloomsbury's pronouncements on prudery, sexual persecution and censorship, which would command the assent of nearly all literate people at the present day and would, for that reason, be rather dull; the audacities of one age become the platitudes of the next.

But in its larger effort, the effort to live a life of rational and pacific freedom, to sacrifice the heroic virtues in order to avoid the heroic vices, Bloomsbury was attempting something which, to the next generation, seemed unthinkable. It could only have been thought of by people in a favoured social position at a particularly favourable moment in the history of England. It could be maintained, but only just maintained, between the years 1914 and 1918 because in that war it was still possible for an intelligent man or woman to be neutral. (pp. 103-17)

With the advent of Fascism, Bloomsbury was confronted by a quarrel in which, believing what they believed, neutrality was impossible. The old pacifism had become irrelevant and the group as a group ceased to exist. (p. 118)

Quentin Bell, in his Bloomsbury, *1968. Reprint by Basic Books Inc., Publishers, 1969, 126 p.*

IRVIN EHRENPREIS

[*An American critic and scholar, Ehrenpreis was noted in particular for his writings on eighteenth-century English literature and modern American poetry. In the following excerpt, he summarizes the social and philosophical principles of the Bloomsbury Group and examines the expression of those principles in the fiction of E. M. Forster and Virgina Woolf.*]

Bloomsbury is a part of west-central London that includes the British Museum, University College, and the Slade School of Art; so it peculiarly suits intellectual temperaments. Once fashionable, it had declined by the turn of our century into a region of boarding houses and private hotels. Here the children of Sir Leslie Stephen chose to settle after their father's death, abandoning the far more respectable address where he had darkened their youth with his years of invalidism. A number of friends and acquaintances soon came to live near by, but only the intimates of the two daughters and their husbands are identified as the "Bloomsbury Group." (p. 9)

Stephen's youngest daughter, given to manic-depressive cycles, became the novelist Virginia Woolf. Her more stable and even more beautiful elder sister became the painter Vanessa Bell. Both married: Virginia to Leonard Woolf, who combined sanity with intellectual brilliance; Vanessa to Clive Bell, remarkable as a sportsman, philanderer, and critic of art. Among the closest friends of the couples were three men of genius who had had a triangular love affair with one another: the writer Lytton Strachey, the economist Maynard Keynes, and the painter Duncan Grant. From an older generation the group adopted Roger Fry, the most influential art critic of the age; and one of their enduring fringe benefits was E. M. Forster.

If we call these people and those who kept in touch with them "Bloomsbury," how far can we go in defining what they stood for? For rough bearings we can use other well-mapped territories: the London of Eliot and Pound, the England of Lawrence, the Ireland of Yeats. These men were attracted by the mysterious power of the irrational in human nature, and they did not underestimate it. The Bloomsbury direction points elsewhere, away from what Lawrence drove at when he condemned self-consciousness. It points away from what held Lawrence when he described Mussolini as one of the few examples of true leadership. While Lawrence yearned for the "fierce singleness" of the "old, hardy, indomitable male," Virginia Woolf jeered at the "unmitigated masculinity" of Rome under fascism. Like a resurrection of Sir Leslie's brother Fitzjames Stephen, Lawrence warned civilization against decadence: "One realises, with horror, that the race of men is almost extinct in Europe. . . . Nothing left but the herd-proletariat and the herd-equality mongrelism, and the wistful poisonous self-sacrificial cultured soul." Bloomsbury had grown up with full access to that belvedere, and had moved away.

The mysteries of the earth, of the body, of love, easily survived in Bloomsbury. The mysteries of church and state, of money and sex, did not. In these departments reticence seemed opposed to health. Think of the Schlegel household in Forster's novel *Howards End*—so like the Stephen children on their own. Here when Margaret Schlegel has an ill-bred young clerk to tea for the first time she thinks nothing of asking him (for his own good) how much money he has. Or think of that true occasion when Lytton Strachey read the history of a day in his life to a group of Bloomsbury friends. Here he cheerfully described his efforts to make a rendezvous with a postman, the failure of the scheme, and the attempt to console himself with the arms of David Garnett: "We kissed a great deal and I was happy."

So much honesty and pursuit of truth may rise to larger doses than we can get down. But before we primly shut our mouths, we might think about political implications, and consider the national alternatives to exhibitionism. Which governments fuss the most about sexual decencies; which discourage visitors from poking into remote corners? Secretiveness, we have learned, commonly means there is something to hide.

Large doses of reality can only be compounded in an air of extreme tolerance; and this of course is quintessentially the atmosphere of Bloomsbury. In its origin the air started from undergraduate friendships made at Cambridge and maintained in London, where they reached into other connections. It started from the teachings of the Cambridge philosopher G. E. Moore.

Moore's philosophy combines several distinct elements: a methodical insistence that one analyze and carefully define one's meanings ("What *exactly* do you mean?"); an acceptance of commonly followed rules of practical morality—don't kill, don't steal, etc. ("Always conform to rules which are both generally useful and generally practised"); but above all, a definition of the ultimate, intrinsic goods of this life as "states of mind" focused on love and friendship, beauty in nature and art, and the search for true knowledge.

A feature of these states of mind is, I think, their fragility. Moore described them as complex but organic wholes in which different parts must work together: the individual subject, his correct appreciation of the person communed with or the thing contemplated, and his feeling of the appropriate emotion. It is obvious that any of these can easily change; and as soon as that happens, the state of mind must vanish. Beethoven's Fifth Symphony is an example Moore employs: he doubts there can be any value in even the "proper emotion" if the listener does not accompany this with some "consciousness, either of the notes, or of the melodic and harmonic relations between them"—i.e., of the exact qualities that make up the beauty of the sound.

As it happens, Forster in *Howards End* gives several pages to a performance of Beethoven's Fifth, with Helen Schlegel listening. We quickly discover that this English Antigone appreciates the melodic and harmonic relations between the notes; but while she undergoes plenty of emotions, we may doubt that they are appropriate. Once the organic whole is broken by the close of the finale, she leaves the concert hall without waiting to hear Brahms. The state of mind has no cause to last any longer.

A loving state of mind would have little more endurance; for duration has no share in these organic unities, and every element of love constantly shifts. Moore made deliberate attacks on Christian ethics, chastity, love of God, the idea of heaven. But if devotion and chastity have no use apart from the rest of an organic whole, matrimony can hardly defend itself. Moore found it easy to imagine a civilization in which conjugal jealousy and parental affection were abnormal. Perhaps some of his tenets are among the reasons that the sexual patterns of Bloomsbury were so intricate.

Keynes once pointed out the dangers that "Moorism" might lead to. In the frame of such principles, he said, social reform and political action were never ends in themselves. "We repudiated entirely customary morals, conventions and tradition-

al wisdom; . . . we repudiated all versions of the doctrine of original sin, of there being insane and irrational springs of wickedness in most men." With time, he said, the pure doctrines deteriorated. "Concentration on moments of communion between a pair of lovers got thoroughly mixed up with the, once rejected, pleasure. The pattern of life would sometimes become no better than a succession of permutations of short sharp superficial 'intrigues,' as we called them."

Leonard Woolf took issue with Keynes. He protested that his circle of friends at Cambridge had worried a great deal about political and social action, and indeed about right conduct generally, but that they thought ridicule was a fair weapon to turn against obscurantism. He admitted the air of arrogance and flippancy but linked it to the most serious intellectual idealism—a confidence that the new generation, by fresh methods, would correct the errors of the old. It was, according to Woolf, during the decade after these men left Cambridge that their skepticism coarsened, their devotion to friendship, the mind, and the arts was colored by easier enjoyments, and that their questioning of authority became an excuse for self-indulgence.

Today anyone who studies the products of Bloomsbury will find they fairly quiver with social and political meanings. Putting aside the obvious relevance of Keynes's and Leonard Woolf's writings or the whole plan of the Omega Workshops, even putting aside explicit statements in the essays of Strachey, Forster, and Virginia Woolf, one still meets the inescapable implications of the novels: feminism, antimilitarism, anti-imperialism, a passion for civil liberties, for the rights of the poorest Englishmen. *Howards End* and *A Passage to India* rest on prophetic insights into national destiny.

We may now give these themes some literary associations. Moore taught that when, as often happens, a man must choose among several good courses and there is no commonly accepted rule of practical morality to guide him, he should prefer what he strongly desires, what concerns him directly, and what he can get fast. A man should reject greater goods that he cannot appreciate, extended beneficence that he may not persist in, and those goods he would have to wait a long time for.

In Forster's novel *The Longest Journey* Gerald puts off his marriage to the girl he loves until financial prudence would recommend it. Gerald dies in a football match while his fiancée watches. Rickie, in the same story, must choose between following an impulse of compassion for one of his pupils and suppressing the impulse for the benefit of the whole school. He suppresses the impulse and injures both the boy and the school. Stephen puts down his weak desire to work in Scotland and yields to a strong desire to visit his native county; he is rewarded with a legacy.

If we set Forster aside for Virginia Woolf, we should remember the fragility and immediacy of states of mind; for she composed her best novels out of immediate sensations that convey quickly changing states of mind, the best of which are contemplations and communions. In the autobiographical novel *To the Lighthouse* Mrs. Ramsay (a portrait of Mrs. Stephen) watches Mr. Ramsay (a portrait of Sir Leslie) reading at the end of the day, and then looks out the window while he—as she very well knows—turns his head to watch her, to think how beautiful she is, and to wish she would say she loves him. Mrs. Ramsay then turns back:

> And as she looked at him she began to smile, for

though she had not said a word, he knew, of course
he knew, that she loved him. He could not deny it.
And smiling she looked out of the window and said
(thinking to herself, Nothing on earth can equal
this happiness)—"Yes, you were right. . . ."

This passage ends the long first part of the novel and produces its highest moment.

Such parallels are too simple. The relation between art and intellectual history is not in fact so plain. It would be absurd to say that G. E. Moore and the Bloomsbury direction led to the novels of Forster and Woolf, the paintings of Vanessa Bell and Duncan Grant, the art criticism of Clive Bell and Roger Fry, the biographical essays of Lytton Strachey, or the autobiography of Leonard Woolf. England at the death of Victoria, about to start dividing itself from the empire, was poised for efflorescence as nations are when imperial energies suddenly concentrate themselves in a drifting capital. The talents that had governed colonies, purified religion, and abolished slavery were now drawn into the labors of the imagination.

Civilization would have made its leap without Bloomsbury. The novelists would still have had the examples of Austen, Meredith, and James to show the way. The painters would have known postimpressionism without Roger Fry. But it would be fair to say that Bloomsbury represented a magnificent English variation of the movement in philosophy and the arts that transformed European culture during the first third of our century, and that the Bloomsbury direction, with its playfulness, tolerance, and honesty, its respect for human ties, its suspicion of authority, connects us to the greatest humanists, Rabelais, More, and especially Erasmus. (pp. 9-10)

Irvin Ehrenpreis, "Bloomsbury Variations," in The New York Review of Books, Vol. XXII, No. 6, April 17, 1975, pp. 9-12.

BEREL LANG

[*Lang is an American critic and scholar. In the following essay, he analyzes the role of intuition in the ethical philosophy of G. E. Moore, the aesthetic philosophy of Roger Fry, and the probability theory of John Maynard Keynes.*]

If—as some of its "members" have asserted—the Bloomsbury Group did not exist, it would have to be invented. Even should we choose to ignore the compelling historical evidence of its activities, conceptual affinities in the work of many of the figures usually connected with it would identify an unusually cohesive intellectual coterie among whom a single idea frequently circulated and reappeared in a variety of forms. The concept of intuitive knowledge is an example of such an idea, worth noting both because of the consequent influence of the formulations given it by Bloomsbury and because of the clear example it offers of movement in the history of ideas. More specifically: the present essay claims that the concepts of intuition applied by G. E. Moore to ethical knowledge, by J. M. Keynes in his consideration of probability theory, and by Roger Fry to the analysis of aesthetic form are linked to each other both structurally and historically; and that the details of this "isomorphism" provide a revealing insight into the personality and intellect of the figures concerned and of the "group" they form.

The rôle of intuitive knowledge in Moore's critique of ethical judgment follows from his definition of the term "good." That term, Moore writes in his attack on the Naturalistic Fal-

lacy, cannot be reduced, as the Utilitarian writers claimed it could, to simpler, "natural" terms like pleasure or happiness, if only because we can further and meaningfully ask whether *those* properties are good. Rather, Moore suggests [in his *Principia Ethica*], we find in ethical judgments that the objects or activities evaluated possess a characteristic which is simple or "unanalysable"—irreducible and non-natural—not located in space or time. Natural properties may also be unanalysable; but they are set in physical contexts, and their existence is open to public inspection or manipulation in a way which, Moore asserts, distinguishes them from the elements of ethical perception. Since we can (or claim that we can) identify "good" objects and activities, and since that identification differs in certain respects from the apprehension of natural properties, a special or at least a special *form* of cognitive relation is apparently implied.

Moore's conception of intuitive knowledge thus describes a direct, unmediated relation, not reasoned (if by that term we refer to the steps of a syllogistic progression), and self-evident. It contrasts with non-intuitive knowledge most patently in the last of these characteristics which suggests that external criteria or instruments of verification are irrelevant. Discursive argument retains a place in ethical investigation: only through a controlled and dialectical process can we determine the course of action to be followed in a given situation. But this process is contingent on a prior, nondiscursive one which directly determines the locus of goodness. All judgments of what is good "may be taken as self-evident premises . . . no reason can be given for them." In some way—here Moore invokes his analogy between the perception of what is good and the perception of colors—we establish immediate contact with the property, knowing it as surely and as objectively as we know any of the "natural" aspects of the objective world.

What power or faculty structures this intuitive process, and whether and how conflicting claims of intuitive knowledge can be adjudicated were issues which caused Moore considerable difficulty; but they are of less immediate concern to us than are the characteristics of the intuitive relation and the fact that the latter was to reappear in almost identical form in contexts quite different from the one for which Moore originally intended it. Moore anticipates these ramifications, for instance in the last chapter of the *Principia,* when he bases a definition of beauty on his analysis of ethics. The sections in the *Principia* which are concerned with translating intuitions of the good into statements of ethical obligation, furthermore, obliquely suggest a connection between intuitive knowledge and estimates of probability. But Moore's comments are abbreviated in both instances, and the relevance of the concept of intuition to the contrasting schemata of probability and aesthetic form becomes quite explicit only with its appearance in the work of Keynes and Fry.

[In his *Treatise on Probability*] Keynes introduces his theory of probability by distinguishing several modes of knowledge. There is a difference, he suggests, between "indirect" knowledge which is the product of argument or inference, and "direct" knowledge which is the more immediate result of "contemplating the objects of acquaintance." The knowledge involved in both of these categories is knowledge of propositions, and thus, both represent relatively high levels of abstraction. Logically prior to them, however, is a phase hinted at in the definition of direct knowledge by the reference to "objects of acquaintance." In "direct acquaintance," the

A portrait of Clive Bell by Roger Fry.

sensa which provide the content for direct and indirect knowledge are determined. Thus, the judgment of a flower as yellow is an example of indirect knowledge; and the proposition "yellow is a color" is a conclusion of direct knowledge. The sensum yellow itself, however, emerges in the earlier process of direct acquaintance. It is with this point that Keynes effects the transition between his epistemology and his theory of probability—by proposing that acquaintance with the probability relation between two propositions is of the same nature as direct acquaintance with the color sensum. "We pass from a knowledge of the proposition *a* to a knowledge about the proposition *b* by perceiving a logical relation between them. With this logical relation we have direct acquaintance."

Keynes thus far does not make use of the term "intuition," and when he does, he identifies it with the mental power which controls direct acquaintance rather than with either the act itself or its consequences. But even allowing for this discrepancy, the similarity between Keynes' analysis of probability determination and Moore's of ethical knowledge (even to the example of color by which they indicate what the product of intuition is *like*), is clear. For both figures, what is realized in the intuitive process is unanalysable, for both, the perception involved is direct, i.e., unmediated by categories; and for both, discourse concerned with other, related questions—for Moore, in assessing ethical obligation, for Keynes, in applying predictions to specific situations—though itself requiring extra-intuitive elements, is contingent on the original intuition.

Fry's analysis of "aesthetic vision" adheres closely to the schematism employed by Moore and Keynes. It originates

with his claim [in his *Transformations*] that the various moments of aesthetic experience are defined by a single recurrent characteristic. This can only be the case, Fry reasons, if the work of art possesses some correspondingly objective and distinctive characteristic. He names this property "plasticity"; and his description of the process in which "plasticity" is apprehended fixes the analogy in his position to the conceptions of intuition in the other theories described.

Ordinary perception, Fry suggests, is moved by a variety of sensations, objects, and events; it is directed by its practical design and origin beyond the initial stimuli. A discursive chain emerges in this process which the perceiver follows from cause to consequence to a further point at which the consequence reappears as cause. In aesthetic vision, on the other hand, we have "a very fair *a priori* case for the existence . . . of a special orientation of the consciousness, and above all, a special focussing of the attention, since the act of aesthetic apprehension implies an attentive passivity to the effect of sensations apprehended in their relations." The elements which contribute to (but do not define) plasticity, e.g., rhythm, mass, light, cohere in a distinctive pattern, and their apprehension presupposes a correspondingly distinctive state or "orientation" of consciousness. Aesthetic vision thus depends on a perceptual relationship which defies the usual, mediated rules of perception. Where the latter is uniformly responsive to the external ends served by the relation, the former is satisfied by the intrinsic quality of linear balance and harmony. And this is the case because of a property within the work. The terms of the analogy in the work of Moore and Keynes are thus repeated. The perception of plasticity is direct; peripheral references and categories of analysis are excluded; and although the "natural" elements which contribute to the effect of plasticity can be enumerated, the sum of their relations is greater than that of the individual parts and is itself irreducible.

The same structural similarity visible in the conceptions of intuition proposed by Moore, Keynes, and Fry is further evident both in the theories of knowledge criticized by them and in the criticism to which their own positions have in turn been subjected. Moore's most persistent dispute, it was noted above, is with attempts to reduce the property "good" into other, natural properties. A second version of ethical judgment attacked by Moore is that which identifies judgments of value with expressions of personal preference or interest. Moore takes issue with the former position on grounds which have already been remarked; the second position (which Moore considers in a less sophisticated form than its recent "emotivist" or "non-cognitivist" variants) is rejected on the basis of what remains for Moore a decisive principle of philosophical analysis: it does not reflect what he *thinks* he is doing—i.e., speaking about an objective property—when he makes an ethical judgment or when he argues about ethical value.

The criticism by Keynes and Fry of alternative positions to their own follows the pattern of Moore's work. Thus Keynes, reviewing earlier versions of probability theory, belabors both the "classical" theory of the Port Royal Logic and the "empiricist" reaction to it of Ellis and Venn. The latter theory, which attempts to take account of Hume's critique of causality, reduces statements of probability to a proportion based on the number of instances in which a given property has been exhibited. Keynes rejects the underlying assumption of this analysis that the probability relation is no more than a summary of past events: " . . . Where our experience is incomplete, we cannot hope to derive from it judgments of probability without the aid either of intuition or of some further a priori principle." It will be noted that he criticizes here the "emotivist" as well as the "naturalistic" position. Not only has the empiricist tradition in probability theory been mistaken in its attempt to resolve statements of probability into summaries of historical ratios, but variations of it have mistakenly attempted to ground judgments of probability on degrees of personal expectation. For Keynes, no less than for Moore, it is important to recognize that the property uncovered by intuition is objective in character.

Fry's critique of the systematic alternatives to his position is less well developed than Moore's or Keynes', but the tendencies he means to combat are unmistakable. Almost from the beginning of his career, Fry was involved in controversy with what he called the "psychologistic" reading of art in which aesthetic significance was related to the ideas or objects represented by the art work. Aesthetic value, for Fry, needs to be both rendered and appreciated quite independently of such "natural" elements: " . . . Pictures in which representation subserves poetical or dramatic ends are not simply works of art, but are in fact cases of the mixture of two distinct and separate arts . . . the art of illustration and the art of plastic volumes. . . ." The art of illustration conceives of beauty as a function of concepts or representative forms, and succeeds only, for Fry, in missing the Significant Form of art which remains beside the point of any such naturalistic elements. Fry does not argue so explicitly with the emotivist position (although, for other reasons, he criticizes I. A. Richards who applied that doctrine in aesthetics); but Fry's attitude, in light of his efforts to get art viewers to see what *was* there, as opposed to what they *thought* was there (e.g., in his defense of African art and of the post-Impressionists), can hardly be doubted.

The parallels in their criticism of other theories ironically but not surprisingly foreshadow the unity of critical attack which has been directed against the conceptions of intuition described by Moore, Keynes, and Fry. One objection directed against the systems of each of the three criticizes the manner in which the intuitive knowledge they describe is acquired. The process is characteristically different from that which we ordinarily think of as culminating in knowledge—and the questions concerning the nature of this process have suggested that the proposal of a special cognitive relation, with its implication of a special criterion of verification, must raise at least as many difficulties as it is likely to resolve. The objection is raised, moreover, that the process of intuition does not adequately account for the judgments supposedly derived from it. So, for instance, [in "Fallacies in Moral Philosophy," *Mind* 58 (1949)] Hampshire rejects the intuitionist criticism of ethical naturalism, describing *its* fallacy as "the inference from the fact that moral or practical judgment cannot be logically derived from statements of fact that they cannot be based on, or established exclusively by reference to, beliefs about matters of fact." Because the property intuited cannot be *fully* translated into other properties does not mean, as the intuitionist position maintains, that it is absolutely apart from them. Indeed, Hampshire suggests, to take the latter position, in the case of ethics, is to misrepresent what ethics is about. And analogous comments have criticized Fry and Keynes: the significance of art need not be "entirely other" than the significance of ordinary experience, even if it is difficult or perhaps impossible to reduce the former to the latter; and an

analogous claim has been made concerning assertions of the intuitive character of probability relations.

The character of the historical, as distinct from the formal or systematic relationship between Moore and Keynes is suggested in a statement from one of Keynes' *Two Memoirs:* "I went up to Cambridge at Michaelmas 1902, and Moore's *Principia Ethica* came out at the end of my first year. . . . Its effect on us, and the talk which preceded and followed it, dominated, and perhaps still dominate, everything else." The memoir in which this appears was written in 1938, but Keynes' reminiscence is supported by the evidence of letters contemporary with the period he describes. He writes, for instance, to his friend Swithinbank (7 October 1903): "I have just been reading Moore's *Principia Ethica,* which has been out a few days—a stupendous and entrancing work, the greatest on the subject." The interchange between Keynes and Moore, we know furthermore, was personal as well as literary. In 1903, Keynes became a member of the Apostles, the undergraduate discussion society at Cambridge which in a short span of time around the turn of the century included among its members Whitehead, Russell, Fry, McTaggart, G. Lowes Dickinson, and G. E. Moore, who, as a fellow of Trinity College, was able to maintain an interest in the affairs of the Society well after his own undergraduate days.

Considerable evidence is available concerning the contact between the two men, especially in the Cambridge years and shortly thereafter; and Keynes, in the preface to the *Treatise* is careful to acknowledge the influence of Moore's thought on that work. There appear to be no statements by either man specifically attesting to the translation of the concept of intuition from one's work to that of the other; even if such statements existed, however, they could not be accepted unequivocally, and thus, perhaps, the historical side of the present thesis need not admit to greater uncertainty than would any other claim concerning intellectual origins or influence. So [R. F.] Harrod, considering Keynes' intellectual development, feels able to conclude that "there was one point [in the *Treatise*] on which Moore's influence was of quite paramount importance. Basic to all the arguments of the *Treatise* is Keynes' view that probability should be regarded as an indefinable concept. There can be no doubt that his confidence that it was legitimate to treat a concept of this kind as indefinable was due to the respectability with which Moore had endowed such treatment of a fundamental concept."

The case is weaker with respect to the relations between Fry and the other two; at least the influence which those relations exerted on his work, if only because of the difference in age between him and them, is less overt. The thesis argued here, however, is not of specific translation from one writer to another, but of a context in which such passage would have the opportunity to take place. And there is ample evidence of such opportunity in the case of Fry's work. His friendships with G. Lowes Dickinson, with Virginia Woolf, whose Bloomsbury home gave its name to the Group, and with Clive Bell, whose writings on aesthetics bear such a close resemblance to those of Fry, serve to support this claim. And even Fry's sometimes caustic comments on the Group (the "last of the Victorians," he once called them) reflects as much his acceptance of their mood as any dissociation from it.

Both its formal and historical evolution, then, seem to point to the ambience and recurrence of the single concept of intuition within the boundaries of Bloomsbury; and one would like, in recognizing the phenomenon, to be able to explain it.

The Victorian background is undoubtedly relevant—an England which lived in the most comfortable of all possible worlds, envisaging in its peculiar synthesis of utilitarianism and Anglican theology the solution of any problem which might arise in social theory, religion, art, or even science. Using this fulcrum, it had stood its ground successively before the Industrial Revolution, the growth of empire, and *The Origin of Species*. And with such an inheritance, the course followed by a new and highly articulate generation, bred on the one hand in the security of tradition, and looking forward, on the other hand, to a future whose outline was still dim enough to encourage the excitement of anticipation, might have been predicted.

Numerous impressions of the response stimulated by this background fall into a single pattern. D. H. Lawrence reacted intensely against those of the Group whom he met, who had, he complained, "no reverence, not a crumb or grain of reverence."—and the phrase, although reflecting Lawrence's bent for exclamation, is echoed by other writers both within and without the group in such a way as to suggest that it ought to be taken seriously. Keynes cites Wittgenstein's comment that he (Keynes) and his friends "lacked reverence for everything and everyone," and Keynes himself, even in retrospect, disagrees with Lawrence and Wittgenstein in *evaluating* the trait rather than on the question of its persistence: "We entirely repudiated a personal liability on us to obey general rules. We claimed the right to judge every individual case on its merits, and the wisdom, experience, and self-control to do so successfully." "[This religion of ours] remains nearer the truth than any other that I know. . . ."

It would be easy to push this impressionistic description too far, and in a sense, as an explanation, it needs to be explained itself. But the phrase "lack of reverence" is suggestive. The Victorian morality weighed heavily and cut not at all deeply; the Utilitarian calculus was, as it must be, offensive to a sensibility of the beautiful and the good. [In her *Orlando*] Virginia Woolf describes the results as she writes of the "climate" of the then-new century: "The damp struck within. Men felt the chill in their hearts; the damp in their minds. In a desperate effort to smuggle their feelings into some sort of warmth one subterfuge was tried after another. Love, birth, death were all swaddled in a variety of fine phrases."

Such was the background, then, of Bloomsbury—if only as Bloomsbury saw it; and even allowing for the condensation of such generalizations and the limitations of what might seem a "pendulum" philosophy of history, it seems reasonable to view Bloomsbury as a response to the inertia of these forces which on several levels confronted it. Its setting had, by and large, refused to concede the authenticity of questions of ethics and art. The tradition, moreover, even so far as it did consider those questions, had been honored not for its persuasiveness or originality, but because it had the weight of tradition. The reaction against such a setting would almost inevitably require a conceptual scheme—such as that articulated in the concept of intuition—which allowed to values an incorrigible reality of their own, one that lay within the responsibility and power of each individual to discover for himself.

The perspective influencing the above remarks is, of course, a eulogistic one. Viewed less kindly, the same concept of intuitive knowledge must recall the criticism most frequently directed against Bloomsbury. A doctrine which asserts for any field of knowledge that one either sees the truth or one

doesn't, and that whether one does or not depends on a native faculty of sorts—implying that the writer who recognizes *this* fact of course possesses such a faculty—fairly asks to be charged with the intellectual snobbery and assumed sense of privilege which characterized, in many cases at least, the lives and works of many of the Bloomsbury figures. Such an afterthought, however, is perhaps an inevitable counterpoise to the representation of intuition as an emancipator from the grip of a constrictive tradition. Neither comment, of course, is in itself either a justification or condemnation of the concept. And even if, as seems to be the case, more can be said for the latter assessment than for the former, interest will remain in the phenomenon generating this divided response—both substantively and for the prospect it offers for tracing the ambience of an idea. (pp. 295-302)

Berel Lang, "Intuition in Bloomsbury," in Journal of the History of Ideas, *Vol. XXV, No. 2, April-June, 1964, pp. 295-302.*

CAROLYN G. HEILBRUN

[*An American novelist and critic, Heilbrun is the author of* Toward a Recognition of Androgyny *(1973) and* Reinventing Womanhood *(1979), which are regarded as major contributions to feminist literature. In the following essay, which was originally published in 1968, she discusses the unconventionality of Bloomsbury thought as a reaction against Victorian sex-role stereotypes and social standards.*]

It is tempting to begin by pointing out how like [the members of the Bloomsbury group] were, when young, to the rebellious youth of today. "Is there no possibility," Strachey asked in a speech to the Apostles at Cambridge, "of a breakup so general and so complete that the entire reorganization of society would be a necessary sequence? Personally, I welcome every endeavour, conscious or unconscious, to bring about such an end. I welcome thieves, I welcome murderers, above all I welcome anarchists. I prefer anarchy to the Chinese Empire. For out of anarchy good may come, out of the Chinese Empire nothing."

No longer as young as that, the members of the Bloomsbury group and men like Bertrand Russell, then closely associated with it, were almost the only people in England to fight against the patriotic butchery of World War I, and the nationalistic fervor which accompanied it. Even the usually iconoclastic Wells called the war an affair of honor, not of reason. D. H. Lawrence, who hated the war, nonetheless wrote: "I am mad with rage myself. I would like to kill a million Germans—two millions." Meanwhile Strachey, whose long locks and golden pirate earrings had already scandalized several English country towns, went to his trial as a conscientious objector (though bad health quite precluded his serving in even the most desperate army) rigged in an outfit designed to infuriate the self-righteous court and preceded by his brother carrying an air cushion for him to sit upon. As Maynard Keynes was to write years later, "our beliefs influenced our behaviour, a characteristic of the young which it is easy for the middle-aged to forget." Through the war Keynes had believed that "it was for the individual to decide whether the question at issue was worth killing and dying for."

This sounds quite up-to-date, yet Bloomsbury nevertheless arouses profound hostility in the young. Considerable animus was expressed to me this past year by a seminar at Columbia to which I lightly exposed the Bloomsbury group. The spokesman for the general contempt felt by the seminar was a very bright young Englishman who tried heroically to enunciate the reasons for his loathing. Having accused them all of being shrill, arty, escapist, aristocratic, and insufficiently talented (was *Mrs. Dalloway*, after all, as great a book as *Ulysses?*) he finally attacked them, with passion, for being, many of them, homosexual. This truly astonished me, for he was at that time engaged in a study of another Englishman, greatly admired by both of us, who is also homosexual. "That," my student announced, "is different. He admits it." Ignoring the fact that he had not "admitted" it in any document I had read, I pointed to the evidence in Holroyd's biography of Strachey's eagerness to "admit it." "Oh, well," my young Englishman said, "the truth is I just can't bear them." I approved the bluntness of this statement, and sensed in it an honorable challenge.

Those who have defended Bloomsbury have been members of the group, or friends of its members, and have tried, with a plaintiveness not unmixed with humor, to set the record straight. Quentin Bell's . . . study of Bloomsbury [excerpted above] is certainly the most measured, and successful, example of this. Bloomsbury, Bell has said, was prepared to sacrifice the heroic virtues in order to avoid the heroic vices, among which violence was the chief. They recognized reason as always and unquestionably superior to unleashed violence, but they are notable not because they honored reason but because they came as near as any group of people has to allowing it sway in their lives.

Holroyd records that Strachey, like his friends, refused to accede any rights or claims to jealousy. This is not easy—it is certainly less easy than the violent expression of jealousy—but it did lead to humane and sophisticated relationships. However irregular their lives by conventional standards—for they believed that where passion, lovemaking should follow—they held, through the fluctuations of passion, to the sacredness of friendship. If attacks were launched on them by inconstant friends, they outraged their opponents by refusing to fight back. For themselves, they regretted not the attack but the lost friendship. "How wretched all those quarrels and fatigues are," Strachey wrote. "Such opportunities for delightful intercourse ruined by sheer absurdities! It is too stupid. 'My children, love one another'—didn't Somebody, once upon a time, say that?"

It is ironic that though scorning Christianity as identical with its institutions, the group should carry about them some aura of the Gospels. Commenting on *Principia Ethica,* Keynes said, "the New Testament is a handbook for politicians compared with the unworldliness of Moore's chapter on 'The Ideal,'" and he noted, concerning his friends, that "of beauty, and knowledge, and truth and love, love came a long way first." It is not altogether clear that Bloomsbury's encompassing definition of love was less holy than that of the churches, but such a statement would have shocked them if anything could. Strachey was amused, during the war, to hear himself echoing, in his pacifism, the words of Jesus. Imagine, he wrote, finding oneself on the same side as that fellow. Never inclined to grapple, as their parents had, with the arduous demands of agnosticism, they shed religion as easily as convention and with as little regret.

The ascendancy of reason which excludes violence but not passion was possible to the Bloomsbury group, I believe, because within it, perhaps for the first time, masculinity was infused, actually merged, with femininity. I have avoided the word feminism, with its inevitable odor of militancy. Nothing could have been further from the quality I wish to identify as uniquely a part of Bloomsbury, although several of Strachey's sisters were, in fact, militant fighters for women's rights. Rather, Bloomsbury insisted on rejecting the Victorian stereotypes of masculine and feminine in favor of an androgynous ideal. Indeed, the very model of Victorian manhood was Sir Leslie Stephen himself, the father of Bloomsbury's Virginia Woolf and Vanessa Bell. There was as yet no Freudianism to deter Sir Leslie's intrepid masculinity, with its outspoken admiration of the virile, and its horror of the effeminate.

Sir Leslie's attitude toward women was one of benevolent despotism, and toward his daughters a despotism, encouraged by self-pity, which was often less than benevolent. From this masculinity the Bloomsbury group, homosexual or not, were consciously to detach themselves. It is the quality about them, apparently, most difficult of appreciation, at least by Americans in recent times. So broad-minded and liberal an imagination as Lionel Trilling's, for example, cannot encompass a world in which the "sacred" fathers and mothers, manliness and womanliness, are not always and forever absolutely distinguishable. It is perhaps because men like F. R. Leavis and Trilling so admired Lawrence as opposed to Bloomsbury that they were unable to perceive in Lawrence's masculine chauvinism a peculiarly virulent homosexual jealousy which, rather than any confrontation with Bloomsbury ideas, was, as Bell clearly shows, the cause of his violent antagonism toward some members of the group. "Ottoline," Lawrence said, in a statement typical of him, "has moved men's imaginations and that's perhaps the most a woman can do." It would not have occurred to any member of the Bloomsbury group to make so Victorian a statement.

When one has mentioned the androgynous nature of the group—a factor which must not, of course, be confused with the homosexuality of many of its members—one has, perhaps, identified at once its most threatening and most distinguishing characteristic. Their celebration of the feminine principle is connected with their pacifism, as well as with the particular quality of their individual geniuses and their openness before new concepts of art. It is not possible to examine the Edwardian period without recognizing that the new literary forms—created by Joyce and Lawrence and James, as well as by members of the Bloomsbury group— were in direct opposition to the world of Kipling, Galsworthy, Wells, and Bennett, whose views Virginia Woolf identified as unremittingly masculine: "The emotions with which these books are permeated are to a woman incomprehensible. One blushes . . . as if one had been caught eavesdropping at some purely masculine orgy." There is probably no question but that the wave of hostility toward Virginia Woolf which followed her death had its origin exactly in such an observation. We have been in, and are now perhaps just leaving, an age of manliness.

Have I enunciated a contradiction? The Bloomsbury group, I have said, extolled reason above violence, finding in the use of reason one of man's ideals. Yet at the same time they eschewed the purely masculine virtues of which, surely, reason is the chief. But while reason is an ideal of masculinity, convention and the violent defense of convention have been, in fact, its practice. Any reader of Strachey's essay on Florence Nightingale, for example, must soon discover that the masculine defenders of the status quo in the Crimean War could scarcely be said, by any standard, to have had reason on their side. Later, Miss Nightingale herself, defending the medical principles she had discovered in the Crimea, did not, when applying them to different climates, have reason on her side either. Reason, in fact, belongs exclusively, to neither sex. Strachey saw this when he accused Thomas Arnold of having tried to institutionalize the masculine virtues in the modern public school by placing them fatally beyond the reach of civilized feminine influence.

The young men of Cambridge, friends and students of G. E. Moore, who were the original nucleus of what was to become the Bloomsbury group, could never in fact have succeeded in forming so liberated a circle had it not been for the two young women, sisters of Thoby Stephen, whom he introduced to his friends. Certainly, without these young women the group would not so successfully have achieved its almost total rejection of conventional sexual taboos. Quentin Bell has said that "there had never before been a moral adventure of this kind in which women were on a completely equal footing with men." What is important is not that they had equal "rights," whatever that phrase can possibly be taken to mean, but that they were considered equally valuable as human beings.

There had been every expectation that Vanessa and Virginia Stephen would live the ordinary lives of two beautiful, well-born young ladies. That they did not do so is only partly attributable to the fact that they were extraordinarily talented, one a genius. It was rather that with their contemporaries, particularly their brothers, they found the possibility of a different life, and that their father, old when they were born, died when they were young enough to achieve a beginning. Many are shocked to read in Virginia Woolf's diary the statement that, had her father lived, his life would have ended hers. Yet it is a simple statement of truth. The two beautiful young ladies did not, in any case, succeed in society, nor did they care for the proper, eligible young men, though every one of their brothers' friends fell in love with them, even those not by nature seekers of the love of women. Vanessa Stephen, with a reputation for sitting up all night talking to young men (which she did) and for attending balls "improperly" clad (which she did also) has recorded the moment when she was "cut" by someone she had known well and felt, with enormous relief, that she need never bother with such people again.

Rupert Brooke is an example of a contemporary of the Bloomsbury group who, going another way, achieved his apotheosis of manliness. "This mixing of the sexes is all wrong," he enunciated; "male is male and female is female . . . manliness is the one hope of the world." He was to welcome war, to write its slickest patriotic poems, to sneer at "half-men" and "all the little emptiness of love." Hassall's biography sadly demonstrates that, in a real sense, he had ended his life before it ended. But one remembers that when he had asked Virginia Stephen to swim with him, she had doffed her clothes to do so, and was able to report that his legs were *not* bowed, and that when he had asked her for the brightest thing she knew, she had said immediately: sunlight upon a leaf. The young men of Cambridge who did not go on to glorify war had found in the drawing rooms of Gordon Square that, as Duncan Grant has said, "they could be shocked by the boldness and skepticism of two young women."

"What a pity one can't now and then change sexes," Lytton Strachey wrote to Clive Bell. Outspokenly homosexual with-

in his own circle and wishing that one could write frankly about English sexual habits as Malinowski had about the sexual life of the Trobriand islanders (but, Strachey knew, one would have to publish it in New Guinea), he feared no diminution of the masculinity he admired by his celebration of feminine virtues, such as the ability to write good letters. Those who honor the Bloomsbury group are unable to agree with Anthony Burgess, typical of his generation of writers in America and England, who boasts that he is frightened of submitting himself to a woman author and who must castigate Ivy Compton-Burnett as a "big sexless nemistic force," and George Eliot as a wholly successful "male impersonator." Perhaps those under thirty, now so busy casting off the artificial signs of sexual difference, will be less tempted than their elders have been to reassume the Victorian terror of women and pride in heterosexuality.

With the publication of Holroyd's life of Strachey [excerpted below], the fact of English homosexuality can finally be faced up to. In the past it has been made the basis for much nasty comment—for example by a critic in *Scrutiny* who wrote of Strachey that "incapable of creation in life or in literature, his writings were a substitute for both"—but it was rarely a subject for serious discussion. Goronwy Rees, in *Encounter,* has complained of the failure of anyone, up to now, honestly to confront the matter. Certainly the most culpable here is Sir Roy Harrod, whose biography of Keynes, brilliant in many ways, would not have been so widely mentioned as a practice in hagiography had not Harrod not only ignored Keynes's homosexuality but flatly denied, in his preface, that he had withheld anything whatsoever of importance about his hero. (Written earlier, E. M. Forster's *Goldsworthy Lowes Dickinson* does not commit this fault, but then Dickinson did not have a mother living at the time of the biography's publication.) Whether Englishmen are peculiarly homosexual because of the English public school and university system, which isolates young men from women through the years of adolescence and young adulthood, is uncertain, but Noël Annan has suggested this, and Freud himself recognized the contribution of social factors to the development of homosexuality. In fact, many artistic men *are* homosexual, and perhaps we ought to take a hint from Bloomsbury and cease to regard this phenomenon as mysteriously and fundamentally threatening.

If Virginia and Vanessa Stephen tolerated homosexuality in their friends largely because they knew the rigidly masculine world of their father would never have done so, that fact does not bring into question the extraordinary sympathy which existed between the members of the group, of whatever sexual inclination. Leonard Woolf has criticized Holroyd for taking with appalling seriousness all of Strachey's loud, youthful lamentations about love, which were never as serious as Holroyd seems to think. But when, in the second volume, Strachey has found his name and his identity, the shrill dramatizations of homosexual infatuation give way to the moving expressions of love as genuine as it was unconventional. The love between Strachey and Carrington, for example, however "abnormal," surely triumphs over all but the most bigoted objections to remind us that love, after all, is love, and scarce enough. "It is only," Forster writes in *Howards End,* "that people are far more different than is pretended. All over the world men and women are worrying because they cannot develop as they are supposed to develop. Here and there they have the matter out, and it comforts them. . . . It is part of the battle against sameness. Difference—eternal differences, planted by God in a single family, so that there will always be colour."

When Julian Bell, the son of Clive and Vanessa, described the environment of his boyhood: "Leisure without great wealth; people intent to follow mind, feeling and sense where they might lead," it must have been in the awareness of what envy such a description can arouse. "Orchard trees run wild," he writes, describing Charleston, his family's home and one of the meeting places of Bloomsbury:

> West wind and rain, winters of holding mud,
> Wood fires in blue-bright frost and tingling blood,
> All brought to the sharp senses of a child.

It required money, of course, and Bloomsbury did not underestimate the value of money. But they had far less of it than is generally supposed, and they never cared for money in itself. Holroyd has demonstrated that for Strachey, the money he made from his biographies represented opportunities to share pleasure with his friends. John Lehmann, who himself came from a wealthy home, has described Charleston in the twenties: "The half-finished canvases of Duncan Grant, or Julian's mother Vanessa, or his brother Quentin piled carelessly in the studios, and the doors and fireplaces of the old farmhouse transformed by decorations of fruit and flowers and opulent nudes by the same hands, the low square tables made of tiles fired in Roger Fry's Omega workshops, and the harmony created all through the house by the free, brightly coloured post-impressionist style one encountered in everything. . . . [All] seemed to suggest how easily life could be restored to a paradise of the senses if one simply ignored the conventions that still gripped one in the most absurd ways, clinging from a past that had been superseded in the minds of people of clear intelligence and unspoilt imagination." Charleston, where Clive Bell wrote *Civilization* and Keynes *The Economic Consequences of the Peace,* still strikes one in the same way. I visited the place one afternoon because I wanted to buy a self-portrait of Duncan Grant, and the sense of life being lived rather than endured still clung about it. Can one describe Charleston by saying that it had been created, not copied, and that no thought had been taken of propriety?

Virginia Stephen had been brought up to observe the proprieties: when she set up housekeeping with her brother in Bloomsbury, and Lady Strachey came to call, the dog Hans made a mess on the hearth rug and neither lady mentioned it. Yet soon Virginia was to take part in the now legendary Dreadnought Hoax, in which she, her brother, and their friends, disguised as Abyssinians, were piped aboard the admiral's flagship. Questions were later asked in Parliament. But fun was always to be made of any institution, new or old, which attracted pomposity. They all had an enormous sense of fun about everything. When Virginia Stephen accepted Leonard Woolf's proposal of marriage, Strachey wrote to a friend: "She hoped that everyone would be thunderstruck. Duncan alone came up to her expectations—he fell right over on the floor when she told him: and of course really he had been told all about it by Adrian before." For a short time Strachey was prepared to think of airplanes as exciting: "As I was returning from my walk in the afternoon," he wrote to a friend, "an aeroplane was seen to be gyrating round the house, three times it circled about us, getting lower and lower every time. Intense excitement! The farm hands, various females, Olive and her mother, all the cats, and myself, rushed towards it. . . . Finally the machine came down in a field ex-

actly opposite the lodge gates at the end of the avenue. There I found it—a group of rustics lined up at a respectful distance. I took it upon myself to approach—but in a moment perceived that the adventure would end in a fizzle. No divine Icarus met my view. Only a too red and stolid officer together with a too pale and stolid mechanic. They had lost their way. I told them where they were, asked them to tea which they luckily refused, and off they went. It *might* have been so marvelous." Everything is here of the Bloomsbury manner likely to make F. R. Leavis wake screaming in the night. But how much else is there beneath the mockery, not least of all the prophetic insight into what dreary and deadly paths the planes would carry us. Some years later a future admiral of the fleet invited Lytton to fly with him. Strachey declared that "he was the wrong *shape* for flying and that his beard presented a hazard that was likely to foul the controls." Bloomsbury would never do, or not do anything, except from kindness, unless it chose.

Clive Bell and his son Julian happened to enjoy hunting: they hunted. Although Clive Bell was an important art critic as well as a scholar of Latin and Greek, he was, it is said, "as good company in brushing room and butts as he was in the National Gallery or the Tate." None of them bothered with proper clothes; as Virginia Woolf said, an intellectual dresses well, or badly, but never correctly. And one of Forster's characters wrote over his wardrobe the motto: "Mistrust all enterprises that require new clothes."

Unquestionably, their greatest gift was for conversation, on all the ponderous and frivolous subjects in the world. They remind us of the inevitable conjoining of gaiety and kindness. The listener was essential to the speaker: "Don't you feel," Virginia Woolf said after Strachey had died, "there are things one would like to say and never will say now?" Whether or not it was the influence of Moore, with his famous: "What exactly do you mean by that?" or the remarkable degree to which they were all gifted which gives one such a strong sense of conversation as the apotheosis of human communication, certainly they must have believed that what one says is not more important than how one says it. We are convinced, somewhere in the depths of our beings, that cleverness and insincerity are inextricably combined. It is frequently forgotten of the wittiest of epigrammatists, Oscar Wilde, that he was, until his imprisonment, the kindest of men. Bludgeons are infrequently wielded by the frivolous, and conversational wit is not the handmaiden of cruelty. No member of the Bloomsbury group was ever nasty in public. True, as Strachey wrote of Walpole: "It is impossible to quarrel with one's friends unless one likes them; and it is impossible to like some people very much without disliking other people a good deal." But if Strachey himself sulked when bored, Clive Bell, John Russell has told us, was "ready to talk about anything: and however feebly the ball might be put up, he would always give of his best. 'Yes,' he would say after some notorious *mauvaise langue* had been to see him, 'he spoke a good deal of ill of all of us, but I must say I found him very agreeable.' " Virginia Woolf regretted that all criticism of living authors could not be spoken to them "over wine-glasses and coffee cups late at night, flashed out on the spur of the moment by people passing who have no time to finish their sentences. . . ."

"I do not know," Auden wrote some years ago, "how Virginia Woolf is thought of by the younger literary generation; I do know that by my own, even in the palmiest days of social consciousness, she was admired and loved much more than she realized." Auden must now, one supposes, know how Virginia Woolf is considered by a younger generation: has any important writer, a quarter century after his death, ever been the object of so much cruel yet meaningless vituperation? It is almost as though the present world needs, somehow, to protect itself against her charms. It would be neither fruitful nor enlightening to enumerate the many diatribes against her; one can only hope that the recent blundering account of her essays on the front page of the *New York Times Book Review* may be the nadir. I wonder, not why she is so widely disliked—for reputations, like investments, fluctuate—but why there exists so crying a need to flay her in public. Partly, perhaps, because her husband, in deciding to publish those sections of her diary which deal with her writing, inevitably published the passages in which she was most strained; partly because she was, as T. S. Eliot wrote, the center, not merely of a group "but of the literary life of London. Her position was due to a concurrence of qualities and circumstances which never happened before, and which I do not think will ever happen again . . . with the death of Virginia Woolf, a whole pattern of culture is broken." Partly it is that uniting, within her works, the feminine and masculine vision, and in portraying, moreover, what Stephen Spender has called her knowledge of "how it felt to be alone, unique, isolated," she presented a vision of itself which the world is not, at present, prepared to contemplate. Most writers, if they are honest, Auden suggests, will recognize themselves in her remarks: "When Desmond praises 'East Coker' and I am jealous, I walk over the marsh saying I am I." But how many wish to experience with her what Auden calls "the Dark Night," when "reality seemed malignant—the old treadmill of feeling, of going on and on and on, for no reason . . . contempt for my lack of intellectual power, reading Wells without understanding . . . ; buying clothes; Rodmell spoilt; all England spoilt; terror at night of things generally wrong in the universe." This is the side of her which has been thrust at us, and for many it is unbearable, particularly since she does not lay the blame for her despair on governments, or interviewers, or the distortions of public judgments. She accepts the despair as her personal burden, and yet functions, completing her ninth novel before she takes her life.

Yet for those who remember her—and it is the saddest of ironies—the memory is of gaiety. "What made her," Rose Macauley asked, "the most enchanting company in the world?" Those who have loved a suicide are fated to remember what in her was most alive. "She was herself," Vita Sackville-West said, "never anybody else at second hand . . . the enormous sense of fun she had, the rollicking enjoyment she got out of easy things." "I don't feel Bloomsbury," Virginia Woolf once said to a friend, "do you feel Marylebone?" William Plomer reminds us how unrecluse-like her life had been: Virginia as a young girl, going in a cab to a ball at a great house; Virginia learning Greek with Clara Pater, the sister of Walter; Virginia printing books and tying parcels for the Hogarth Press; Virginia laughing with her nephews; Virginia asking the Nicolson boys about their day ("What happened this morning? Well, after breakfast . . . No, no, no. Start at the beginning. What woke you up? The Sun. What sort of sun?" and she would hand back glittering, Nigel Nicolson wrote, what they had imparted so dully); Virginia "sitting up all night in a Balkan hotel reading the *Christian Science Monitor* to cheat the bugs"; Virginia witnessing a murder under her window in Euboea; "Virginia continuing to play bowls at Rodmell during the Battle of Britain, with Spit-

fires and Messerschmitts fighting, swooping and crashing round her"; Virginia writing her extraordinary letters to friends and to other people because they were sick or lonely or disappointed.

"Virginia was a wonderful raconteur," David Garnett writes: "she saw everyone, herself included, with detachment. . . . But alas, while I was living at Charleston, I almost deliberately avoided having a friendship with Virginia, for it would have been impossible without confidences and in the home circle she had the reputation as a mischief-maker. . . . Thus it was only later on that I became on terms of close friendship with Virginia and then our friendship grew steadily until . . . my hair was streaked with gray. . . . By then she had for me long ceased to be a possible mischief-maker and became the very opposite—a woman on whose sympathy and understanding I could rely when I most needed support." A reputation for mischief-making, however, is more adhesive than a reputation for friendship. Clive Bell, to suggest her vivacity, remembered "spending some dark, uneasy, winter days during the first war in the depth of the country with Lytton Strachey. After lunch, as we watched the rain pour down and premature darkness roll up, he said, in his searching personal way, 'Loves apart, whom would you most like to see coming up the drive?' I hesitated a moment, and he supplied the answer: 'Virginia, of course.' "

Certainly there hang over her memory vague questions about her sexuality. It is impossible to pin them down. There have been widely scattered intimations similar to Holroyd's, who, giving no source, speaks of her as "shying hysterically away from sexual intercourse." Lytton Strachey remarked of *To the Lighthouse* that "she rules out copulation," an interesting statement about a novel of which the heroine has eight children. Whatever the truth—and the world takes as swift revenge on childless married women as on spinsters—it was perhaps inevitable that her reaction against the aggressive masculinity of the Victorian world should be interpreted as a fear of manhood. Mrs. Leavis sneered at her for having no cradle to rock. But one may choose to remember that when Freud, who had greatly admired the works of Lytton Strachey, met Virginia Woolf he presented her with a flower. I have always thought it an act of gallantry and wisdom.

As a woman, I know that Virginia Woolf has uniquely presented some part of the female sensibility: its pain, its impotent awareness, its struggle to be free of the littleness of life, its deep distrust of political parties and the state. She understood creation: Auden mentions a passage in *The Waves* as the best description of the creative process he knows. Stuart Hampshire has explained why her work has been smothered by "nervous polemics. Her elegant play with language seems to have aroused a sense of social grievance among critics, because her tone and style were taken to be a return to the genteel tradition of *belles lettres.*" Still, Hampshire reminds us, she contributed on one occasion to the *Daily Worker.*

"But," my English student said to me, "she was mad." True, I pointed to Trilling's brilliant essay on the madness of the artist in which he declares that, while we may all be ill, the artist alone finds health in the work he completes. Her style, like that of all Bloomsbury, was never to be in a hurry. She took seven years to finish her first novel, which none of her friends thought an extraordinary length of time, and she never wrote more than three hours a day. Yet she completed seventeen books, and essays and stories enough for six posthumous ones, and, it must not be forgotten, cooked dinners

("And now with some pleasure I find that it's seven; and must cook dinner. Haddock and sausage meat."), set type, talked to friends, traveled, walked with a dog over the downs and by the river.

What astonishes one most about the whole group, perhaps, is how much they accomplished. They had become friends before any of them had done more than learn brilliantly to talk to one another. Yet Keynes became the outstanding economist of his age and ours. Roger Fry and Bell, in their artistic theories, particularly that of significant form, had a profound effect, and also introduced the post-impressionists to an outraged England. The Hogarth Press, under Woolf's direction, became one of the most impressive of publishing houses; Lytton Strachey changed forever the possibilities of biographical art. Forster, if not, as Spender has called him, the greatest novelist of his generation, is certainly one of the most important. Leonard Woolf was a writer, editor, and active socialist. Vanessa Bell and Duncan Grant were impressive portraitists, as a visit to the Tate will testify, and they were able still, in the thirties, to shock the bourgeoisie, specifically, as Stansky and Abrahams explain, "the directors of the Cunard Line, who commissioned Grant to decorate a room on the *Queen Mary* and then having seen the work, decided nervously that it would not do." Finally, of course, there is Virginia Woolf, a novelist of genius each of whose works was a new experiment in the technique of fiction. Strachey might have been thinking of the Bloomsbury group when he praised the salon of Julie de Lespinasse: "If one were privileged to go there often, one found there what one found nowhere else—a sense of freedom and intimacy which was the outcome of real equality, a real understanding, a real friendship such as have existed, before or since, in few societies indeed." But surely neither the members of that salon, nor of any other, produced so much work, or so greatly transformed the culture of their country, or represented, along the spectrum of intellectual interests, so wide a range.

A word must be said about G. E. Moore, the Cambridge philosopher, whose *Principia Ethica* has mistakenly been credited with providing the entire ethos of Bloomsbury. J. K. Johnstone's book [excerpted above], the only one so far devoted to the group, was written, necessarily, with too little information available; suspecting ritual, Johnstone sought the dogma to explain it. Quentin Bell's [*Bloomsbury,* excerpted above] indicates that, in fact, the group, while admiring Moore's work, used it as justification for its own already held convictions; Keynes's memoir, carefully read, can be seen to admit that the *Principia* provided an expost philosophical justification for immoralism, in Gide's meaning of the word.

What is of more immediate interest about Moore is the sort of man he was: brilliant, gentle, generous of heart, and virtuous. His influence on English philosophic thought was, as C. D. Broad has said, out of all proportion to his comparatively small literary output. It was by his discussions, his conversations, mainly with students, that his influence was felt. He never lectured but that he held a discussion class, and a point raised there, Braithwaite tells us, would make him revise in his next lecture what he had previously said. He never took a sabbatical leave, and anyone interested in knowing what Moore was thinking could always find him at Cambridge. His lectures were never the same from year to year, which left him little time for publication, and his most brilliant thoughts were kept for conversation with his pupils. Is there, today, a comment to be made? Except to say, with

Peguy, that "a great philosophy isn't one against which there is nothing to say, but one which has said something."

The men and women of Bloomsbury were extraordinarily accomplished both in their individual lives and works and in the life of love and friendship they shared. As Brenan said of Strachey, they were "almost indecently lacking in ordinariness," but they did not wish to persuade the world to share their eccentricities, nor to respond other than good-humoredly to its sneers. They were civilized even if, as Virginia Woolf remarked of Clive Bell's book on that subject, civilization turns out to be a lunch party at 50 Gordon Square. Civilization is capable of worse things, and usually achieves them. (pp. 71-85)

Carolyn G. Heilbrun, "The Bloomsbury Group," in Midway, *Vol. 9, No. 2, Autumn, 1968, pp. 71-85.*

BLOOMSBURY PROSE

SELMA MEYEROWITZ

[*In the following excerpt, Meyerowitz discusses the aesthetic, social, and political ideas manifested in* The Hogarth Letters, *a collection of essays written in part by Bloomsbury members.*]

The Hogarth Press provides important insights into Bloomsbury thought and art. Leonard and Virginia Woolf began the Press in 1916 as a hobby, but it soon developed a serious purpose: to publish works by new writers that commercial and more conservative publishing houses would reject. Since Hogarth was not concerned about the popularity of its publications, it ventured into experimental or controversial material. In the 1920s and 1930s, for example, Hogarth published several pamphlet series with distinctly political and social commentary. If a single volume can indicate the philosophy toward art, literature, and politics of both the Hogarth Press and the Bloomsbury Group, it may well be *The Hogarth Letters.* This collection of eleven letter-essays written in 1931 and 1932 reflects the major concerns of Bloomsbury members: social and political affairs are represented by essays on imperialism, the state of the church, disarmament and British politics, and the psychology of fascism; the arts are discussed in essays on poetry, the novel, and painting.

The letter-essay is particularly appropriate considering the social climate of the early 1930s. The rise of fascism caused extreme social change and developments in international politics which threatened traditional forms of self-expression and communication. As individual rights were being destroyed by totalitarian governments, the need to assert one's personal voice became important. The letter-essay emphasizes the individual voice and interpersonal communication through its one-to-one relationship between writer and reader. Because it directly reveals the writer's unique personality, the letter-essay is essentially dramatic and psychological, yet its form also creates a structure of intellectual debate which clarifies thought and merges personal expression with social commentary.

World War I had an enormous impact on Bloomsbury as it did on Europe. Leonard Woolf described the pre-World War

I era as a period of social progress during which the hope developed that man might become permanently civilized. But the outbreak of war, the resurgence of brutality, and the use of scientific advances for destructive purposes shattered social optimism and indicated how modern man had relapsed into barbarism. Bloomsbury was thoroughly anti-war, but more importantly, its members realized that it was not sufficient to condemn war; one had to work toward a system of preventing war. During the post-World War I period, the key political issues were disarmament, international government, and imperialism. The League of Nations grew out of the belief that a formal body for international government was necessary to prevent the recurrence of war. Bloomsbury supported this approach to world peace. In 1922, when Leonard Woolf stood for Parliament as a candidate of the Labour Party, the foreign affairs section of his platform supported the League of Nations. Woolf's recognition of the importance of an international system of laws to regulate relations between nations had developed earlier, and in 1916, he published *International Government,* a study for the Fabian Society. Further, a list of Hogarth Press publications reveals several works on the League of Nations, suggesting Bloomsbury's commitment to international peace.

In *The Hogarth Letters,* the issues of disarmament and international government are addressed by Viscount Cecil. Directing his comments to the British politician Brownjohn in "A Letter to a Member of Parliament on Disarmament," Cecil argues that disarmament is a central concern of the British public. Although he recognizes that internal affairs, such as unemployment, the state of industry, tariffs, and taxation, are important to the British electorate, Cecil emphasizes that foreign affairs are crucial to the British economy because it is still tied up with "payments for past wars and preparations for wars in the future." War would threaten the economic survival of Britain, since the nation is dependent upon other countries for both food supply and industrial raw materials. Peace is also essential because of Britain's relationship to its Empire. Commonwealth countries are asserting nationhood; the unity of the Empire, already in a precarious state, would be further strained by international war, and Britain might be left without the support of its Empire nations.

Cecil urges Brownjohn to respond to public opinion and support international government. He cites newspaper commentary and mass demonstrations as indicating the general public's view of war as "a mad and evil thing." He claims that the public favors the League of Nations as a means of preventing international disaster. Yet, Cecil notes, British politicians continue to ignore the strong public support for preventing war. As a result, the electorate is beginning to consider party issues "stale and narrow"; the political candidate who indicates concern with international peace and has constructive ideas for preventing war would find a wide base of popular support.

Cecil also addresses himself to the shaky status of the League. He points out that huge expenditures on armaments negate the League's main function and make its moral authority seem a farce. The crucial point about disarmament is that it is not "feasible unless it is universal, and no one nation unaided can achieve it." The League was based on the concept that mutual assistance against aggression would protect nations from external threats without compelling increases in armaments. Military aggression would be an international crime, for which each nation would accept responsibility and express condemnation.

Cecil's comment on imperialism and its relation to international peace, British politics, and economic survival is reiterated by other Bloomsbury writers. Leonard Woolf had been a civil servant in Ceylon where he grew to dislike imperialism and its destructive effect on native culture. Woolf considered the liberation of the colonies and the dissolution of the British Empire as a key problem of the post-World War I period. Similarly, in *The Hogarth Letters,* E. M. Forster comments upon the destructive cultural influences of imperialistic domination. Forster's correspondent in "A Letter to Madan Blanchard" was a member of an East India Company ship which was shipwrecked in the Pelew Islands in 1783. According to the captain's journals, Blanchard decided to stay on the islands; his refusal to return to England is for Forster a rebellion against constricting cultural conventions at home. But Forster considers the Pelew Prince, Lee Boo, who returns to England with the ship as a more serious aspect of imperialism. A pawn in the imperialists' plans, the Prince is to be educated in England and sent back to rule the islands as an Englishman would. When Lee Boo dies of smallpox, Forster sees his death as a comment on the incompatability of cultures which imperialism provokes, as well as a symbol of the islands' independence from colonial rule.

Bloomsbury understood that international government and the end of imperialism would not ensure the end of international conflict. Leonard Woolf, for example, was fascinated by the concept of communal psychology, which he defines as those beliefs and desires held by individuals forming classes or nations. Communal psychology is based on social standards of value which can cause communal actions. Woolf analyzed the history of civilization in terms of a recurring struggle between the forces of civilization—reason, freedom, democracy and communal altruism—and the forces of barbarism—unreason, intolerance and tyranny. The rise of fascism in the late 1920's symbolized for Woolf a turn toward the communal psychology of barbarism. Woolf believed that fascist ideology was based on the lowest standards of value, specifically fear, hatred, greed and aggression—qualities more appropriate to the criminal element of society than to its political leaders. Like Leonard Woolf, E. M. Forster was appalled by the dehumanization of culture caused by fascism. He saw a terrifying empty look in the faces of the Nazi young and commented that "you cannot go on destroying lives and living processes without destroying your own life." Both Woolf and Forster considered political beliefs to be an indication of social and personal ideals.

In *The Hogarth Letters,* Louis Golding's "A Letter to Adolf Hitler" is an anti-fascist statement which indicates Bloomsbury's reaction to fascist ideology. Golding considers Hitler to be the most notorious of contemporary anti-semites. He parallels the anti-semitism of Hitler's youth with that of the young boys in his Lancashire infant school who considered Jews to be Christ killers and with that of the adolescent mill-hands in whom anti-semitism was more venomous because "life in so few years had become so much bitterer for them. They wondered . . . why . . . and they blamed this alien, palpable race thrust down in their midst." Later, at Oxford, Golding observed another example of anti-semitism in young gentlemen who uttered "scurrilities concerning Jews in general." The Great War with its social idealism seemed to hold out the promise of an end to persecution of the Jews, but it merely suspended the hostility temporarily. After the war, a "fury of Jew-hatred" broke out, which Golding regarded as "a product in the defeated countries of the psychology of defeat."

For Golding, social expressions of anti-semitism are not as significant as archetypal anti-semitism, an elusive, continuing hatred that would exist even if there were no motivating causes. Archetypal anti-semitism cannot be eradicated, for it is a phenomenon of human existence rather than a product of social circumstances. It reflects man's continuing inclination toward the forces of barbarism which oppose the impulses of civilization.

Although Bloomsbury was very concerned with political and international events, it also attacked social institutions and conventions, as "A Letter from a Black Sheep" by Francis Birrell indicates. Addressed to his cousins in England from his home in France, Birrell attacks both the middle-class Englishman's philistinism, commenting "I know you never cared about poetry," and love of English countryside, which he describes as "stupid little hills and commonplace copses." After a visit to his cousins, he adds insult to injury by writing, "I thought you were the stuffiest set of provincial fools I'd ever met in my life, frightfully sweet and all that, but unimaginative beyond words." Even more an object of Birrell's scorn is the way English society is bogged down in sterile traditions and class-consciousness. To Birrell, each Englishman is in competition with his neighbor for the status of gentleman, and thereby participates in a meaningless snobbery, "aping a social system, which no longer has any real existence." Birrell also attacks the public schools for creating elitism and self-satisfaction, while actually contributing to a mingling of "the territorial aristocracy with the commercial middle-class [that] has produced a hybrid which lacks the better qualities of each."

Birrell does not find it surprising that England no longer leads the world as it did through the eighteenth century. English society is hopelessly provincial; it is not open to foreign influences; it is unable to set standards because it is "so damned antiquated . . . so badly educated." Also lacking is the social and personal freedom which exists elsewhere. Birrell maintains that censors, official and unofficial, are stifling all creative instincts. He measures the conservatism and repression of English culture by the fact that young English people "live like exiles in their own country and are always flying abroad to get a breath of fresh air." Like these young Britishers, Birrell is an exile in France because he finds English society too restricting.

Middle-class conventions and institutions are not the only subjects of social criticism in *The Hogarth Letters.* "A Letter to an Archbishop" by J. C. Hardwick, a priest, criticizes the Church, not its ideology, but its relation to society. Religious irreverence was part of Bloomsbury's intellectual rebellion against restricting social conventions, and although Hardwick was not a member of Bloomsbury, his analysis of the role of the Church suggests the nature of Bloomsbury's rejection of religion. Hardwick observes that the Church had an important place in society during the Victorian period: "the social position of the beneficed clergy was high, the British public was behind them, and there was no shortage of men or money." A stable social structure and shared social beliefs reinforced church doctrines. Yet the fall of the Church from its position of "cultural pilot" was inevitable because it failed to develop new ideas to counteract changes in society: the in-

creasing materialism and technology; the Education Act of 1902 (which secularized religion by giving rise to a new type of middle-class child who was materialist, utilitarian, and anti-religious); the new Press and its worldliness and nationalism; and social welfare programs, which influenced individuals to look to the state rather than to the Church.

During the Great War, the Church enjoyed a temporary resurgence of popularity, but Hardwick points out that the war produced "mental penury"—four years of catch-words, slogans, and misguided idealism. Again, the Church failed to meet changes in social and economic conditions with intellectual advances. This failure constitutes for Hardwick the "religious and mental debility" that is destroying the Church. The Church can "no longer originate and create; it can only repeat and copy"; it is conservative and hostile to new forms of expression. Hardwick condemns this death-ridden state and comments, "all genuine religion, like all genuine art, is kept alive by change. . . . to be afraid of change is to be afraid of life." The salvation of the Church lies in the hands of creative individuals; however, young men are rejecting the Church because they know it is not a place for intellectual freedom and creativity. As Hardwick appeals to the Archbishop to reorganize and rejuvenate the Church, he echoes both Bloomsbury's rejection of dead social conventions and its belief that intellect and creativity must regenerate social institutions.

Bloomsbury's attention to national and international political issues and to social institutions is related to its concern with the arts. Indeed, Bloomsbury recognized that social and economic conditions affect the artist and that art forms respond to changes in social and personal experience. Virginia Woolf emphasizes this point in her essay "The Leaning Tower," as she examines the post-World War I situation of the writer. Before August 1914, society's structure was stable and the artist's tower, symbolizing his elevated position in society because of middle-class birth and expensive education, was secure. After 1914, the tower was no longer stable because World War I threatened both the organization of individual societies and the foundations of civilization. Thus, Woolf comments, writers and artists could no longer avoid taking a political stand about changes in the social environment.

Virginia Woolf is clearly sympathetic to the challenges the new generation of artists faces. In *The Hogarth Letters,* her well-known essay "A Letter to a Young Poet," addressed to John Lehmann, focuses on the plight of contemporary poetry. The mass reading audience of 1931 demands literature that is exciting and amusing, and the poet cannot disregard his audience. He must maintain contact with "life," but he must not cater solely to the tastes of the mass audience. He must not become submerged in the actual and the colloquial which fail to stimulate imagination or provide a fusion between reality and imagination. Also, the poet must not become obsessed with himself. He must find a relationship between the self, which for Woolf is "the central reality," and the world outside. Through the power of rhythm, an element basic to all forms of life, the poet may find a unified vision of "the relation between things that seem incompatible yet have a mysterious affinity." Woolf urges experimentation as a means of rejuvenating the state of poetry, discovering the poetic voice that can express contemporary experience, and maintaining a relationship to the long tradition of past poets.

Peter Quennell's "A Letter to Mrs. Virginia Woolf" provides an interesting parallel to Woolf's comments on contemporary

A portrait of Virginia Woolf by Vanessa Bell.

poetry. Quennell recognizes that the artist is a "creature of his social and political setting," that practical politics and the state of society affect the artist's thought and work. Yet Quennell does not attribute the difficulties of the contemporary poet to an insensitive public or an unstable social structure. Instead, he sees poetry as growing narrower in its scope. Compared to ancient times, when the poet was at the center of all learning and expression, the contemporary poet has a much smaller terrain. As new genres developed, poetry lost several elements: the religious, dramatic, narrative, and philosophic. Quennell nevertheless sees an important function for poetry, a function that no other literary genre can fulfill: the expression of emotion with "a crystalline sense of words" and, thus, the discovery of authentic, expressive language. Like Virginia Woolf, Quennell argues that the poet must find a balance between the inner self and the outer world, a continuity of tradition combining the poetry of the past with a new poetry appropriate for the society in which he lives.

The comments about poetry by Woolf and Quennell are similar to Virginia Woolf's discussion of developments in the novel. Her essay *Mr. Bennett and Mrs. Brown* is a literary manifesto which argues that changes in society and personal relationships during the early years of the twentieth century have necessitated a new approach to the novel. She rejects the materialist approach to character and experience of the Edwardian novelists, particularly Arnold Bennett, John Galsworthy, and H. G. Wells. Seemingly, she would disagree with Hugh Walpole's argument in "A Letter to a Modern Novel-

ist," which essentially supports the Edwardian approach to literary conventions. Both Walpole and Woolf examine, however, the dilemma of the contemporary writer and the problems of developing craft while maintaining a meaningful relationship to the audience.

Walpole addresses his letter to a nephew who has solicited his uncle's opinion on his first novel. Walpole finds the work lacking the qualities of strong writing and uses Anthony Trollope's novel *Barchester Towers* as a standard of comparison. Trollope presents all human passions, from which the plot develops; thus, the social conflict over the church, which is the center of *Barchester Towers,* also reveals human nature in relation to multiple social and personal contexts. Trollope draws the reader into the work through characters which Walpole describes as those "great normal figures that triumph through the world's literature" and exist beyond the literary work. In contrast to Trollope, the modern novelist (according to Walpole) creates characters who are a minority and thus "foreign" to two-thirds of his readers. Further, the influence of Henry James has caused the modern novelist to feel that his work should represent, rather than state, the theme. Thus, the modern novelist does not allow his reader to enter into the work by giving him full information as Trollope does, but instead, turns his reader into an observer who watches the writer investigate his material and shape his work. Walpole objects to any tendency to alienate the reader, and he proclaims the importance of moral values, urging the new generation of novelists to expand their art and solidify their relationship to the reader by generating moral themes.

Like the literary artists of Bloomsbury, the visual artists were preoccupied with changes in society and the way these changes affected their art forms. An especially important influence on Bloomsbury was the First Post-Impressionist Exhibit in 1910, organized by Roger Fry. The English public reacted strongly against the new style in painting, but Bloomsbury's art critics and painters—Fry, Clive Bell, Vanessa Bell, and Duncan Grant—supported the new movement. In "A Letter on the French Pictures," Raymond Mortimer's comments on the visual arts and Impressionist painting reveal Bloomsbury's attitude toward art.

From a Bloomsbury address, Mortimer directs his letter to friends in the country who have entertained him in typically gracious upper-middle-class style and have promised to meet him at The French Exhibition. He is skeptical whether they will benefit from the exhibit unless they can recognize the revolutionary nature of the paintings. Mortimer points out that this exhibit should cause a reorganization of the viewer's perceptions; one should leave "a changed person, or rather with changed eyes," ready to see the world anew. Like Clive Bell and Roger Fry, Mortimer believes an important relationship exists between the painter and his audience:

> All art is a collaboration between the artist and his audience, he is sending you messages, so that you must keep your eyes open . . . and use your imagination to reconstruct what is going on in his mind. It is fatal to be passive, and to take it for granted that the picture is what it is.

Although Mortimer credits his correspondent Harriet with aesthetic taste, he asserts that she does not use her eyes, but instead relies on intelligence, or academic and historical standards of judgment. He urges her to approach The French Exhibit with sense response only and, like the artist who sees everything new, to develop a new mode of seeing. For Mortimer, the Impressionists are particularly important because they capture the appearance of things most truthfully; they do not state all the facts, just as we do not observe all the details when we look at something. Their mode of representation is implicit rather than explicit and thus stimulates imagination.

Through their diversity of subject matter and point of view, the eleven letter-essays published in the Hogarth Letter Series are striking examples of social, literary, and artistic opinion in England during the early 1930s. These essays also indicate that those concerns which preoccupied Bloomsbury writers and artists affected English society as a whole. Virginia Woolf's image of the artist in a leaning tower being influenced by social, economic, and political forces reasserts Bloomsbury's focus on the relationship between social experience and literature and graphic art. Although part of the established upper-middle class through birth and education, Bloomsbury was critical of social and political institutions. Believing that man's intellectual freedom and the survival of the arts are related to these institutions, Bloomsbury argued that if institutions deny freedom and fulfillment to individuals, they should be changed. The social upheaval of the 1930s made Europe, including Bloomsbury, aware that social values and conventions and political ideology could threaten individual and social survival. *The Hogarth Letters* reveal that Bloomsbury writers used literature, and especially the Hogarth Press, to express their political consciousness and their views on the role of art and literature in society. (pp. 77-85)

Selma Meyerowitz, *"'The Hogarth Letters':*
Bloomsbury Writers on Art and Politics," in San
Jose Studies, *Vol. V, No. 1, February, 1979, pp. 76-*
85.

P. N. FURBANK

[Furbank is an English critic, editor, and the author of critical biographies of Samuel Butler, E. M. Forster, and Italo Svevo. In the following excerpt, he identifies some significant characteristics of Bloomsbury prose.]

When, in writing about the Brownings, Virginia Woolf takes as her hero a spaniel, and when, to write about Keats, Forster assumes the standpoint of his unscrupulous guardian Mr. Abbey (not even naming the poet till the last paragraph), we recognise a likeness and say to ourselves, here is a "Bloomsbury" trick, here is "Bloomsbury" writing. How shall we define the quality? Perhaps, "cultivated perversity"? In neither writer is the trick or invention a pointless whimsicality; and Forster's essay, though it verges on overplayfulness, makes its point, a novelist's point, very brilliantly. Nevertheless, this obliqueness and teasing refusal of the high road is a distinctively Bloomsbury trait. Indeed, come to think of it, such a devious approach to hallowed subjects is central to Bloomsbury's appointed task, the dismantling of Victorianism. It is the technique prescribed by Lytton Strachey in the Preface to *Eminent Victorians:*

> It is not by the direct method of a scrupulous narration that the explorer of the past can hope to depict that singular epoch. If he is wise, he will adopt a subtler strategy. He will attack his subject in unexpected places; he will fall upon the flank, or the rear; he will shoot a sudden, revealing searchlight into obscure recesses, hitherto undivined. He will row out over that great ocean of material, and

lower down into it, here and there, a little bucket. . . .

Bloomsbury writing, to speak more generally, aims at a beautiful amusingness. It is not the implacable, systematic spoofing of Max Beerbohm, which has shades in it still of art-for-art's sake and the nineties; it is not the tragic lightness of Ronald Firbank, which lies closer to "modernism." It is a more enjoying, more sociable lightness; there is a holiday feeling about it, as there is about Bloomsbury painting. "Amusing" it must however, inexorably, be. Leonard Woolf recalled once, in a paper to the Memoir Club:

> Just as one hesitated in Moore's rooms in Cambridge to say anything amusing which was not also profound and true, so in Bloomsbury one hesitated to say anything true or profound unless it was also amusing.

In its prose, as in its conversation, Bloomsbury followed the jets, the freaks, the vagaries of the mind; it prized spontaneity—the bubble blown, the fantasy constructed, upon the instant. Bloomsbury prose-style says, "Having thrown off corsets and crinolines, see how very nimbly I can move."

As for "perversity," the word of course cannot but have its sexual overtones. What Virginia Woolf is conveying in the hero/heroine of *Orlando,* what David Garnett is conveying in *Lady into Fox,* is some message about homosexuality and feminism. "If it is possible for a husband to remain in *rapport* with a wife even after she has become a fox, then how much easier the task of an ordinary husband—yet the Victorians failed in it"; such is the message, or part of the message, of David Garnett's neo-Victorian fable. And in *Orlando,* of course, such thoughts become more explicit. These are light jokes about a theme—the need to understand and enter into the other sex's experience—which almost constituted modernity, and which received directer treatment in *Women in Love* and *The Waste Land.* (Edward Carpenter thought that the "Uranian," being supposedly especially adept in such understanding, might be Nietzsche's true Superman.)

The lightness was Bloomsbury's chosen instrument, as it was sometimes its weakness. And Forster's lightness of touch—the informality, the cattiness, the demure and deflating good sense—can be thought of as "feminine." Equally that mixture in him (so disconcerting) of lightness and earnestness can, if you like, be thought of as a reconciling of "feminine" and "masculine" qualities. But one does not need to think of this in biographical terms. The *Zeitgeist* recommended such a reconciling. Modernism and anti-Victorianism lay precisely in that direction, the assumption or resumption of feminine characteristics by men.

Let me now quote the opening of an essay I much admire, Forster's "A Letter to Madan Blanchard":

> | *April, 1931* | The London Library,
St. James's Square,
London. |
>
> MY DEAR MADAN,—
>
> Captain Wilson keeps telling me about you, and I feel I should like to write you a line. I shall send it by air mail to Paris, but from Paris to Genoa in a pre-war express. At Genoa the confusion will begin. Owing to the infancy of Mussolini the steampacket will not start on time, and will frequently put in for repairs. So slow is the progress that the Suez Canal may close before it can be opened, and

my letter be constrained to cross Egypt by the over-land route. Suez is full of white sails. One of them, tacking southwards, will make India at last, another bring tidings of Napoleonic wars on a following breeze. Smaller boats, duskier crews. Brighter dawns? Quieter nights anyhow. The world is unwinding. What of Macao, where no news follows at all? What of the final transhipment? The last little vessel scarcely moves as she touches the Pelews, the waves scarcely break, just one tiny ripple survives to float my envelope into your hand. As the tide turns, I reach you. You open my letter a hundred and fifty years before it is written, and you read the words "My Dear Madan."

Here, I would say, we have the quintessence of Bloomsbury prose. And how close in some ways it is to Virginia Woolf (who indeed published the essay as a Hogarth Press pamphlet in 1931). As an invention (and it is a lovely invention) this prose enactment of the unwinding of time and history could so easily, one feels, have found its place in *Orlando*. In texture and tone, though, it is not quite Virginia Woolf, and is indeed pure Forster. How characteristic is that progression: "Suez is full of white sails. One of them, tacking southwards, will make India at last. . . ." Forster, as often, surprises by his sense of reality. We read "full of white sails" lazily, as piece of conventional scene-painting, and then, with a tiny jolt, we are reminded of the function of sails. How typical, and admirable, again is: "Smaller boats, duskier crews. Brighter dawns? Quieter nights anyhow. The world is unwinding." Prose could hardly be more nimble and disencumbered or more rich in *nuances*. And then, with what beauty, what "amusingness" raised to high art, the sentences lengthen again and mime in their arrangement the turning of a tide.

This kind of prose is somewhat out of fashion, for good and for bad reasons. It was even, in a sense, out of fashion at the time that it was written. For Woolf and Forster (like Yeats) had a "style"; and it was characteristic of serious artists in the 1920s to have gone beyond "style," to practice a hundred styles and no style, to create a new style for each work. But if Woolf and Forster had a style, they had one with a difference. Forster's ease and informality gave him a quite new flexibility. In his novels he is in a sense more Victorian than the Victorians in that he is always conversing with the reader, buttonholing him, telling him what to think. The difference is, he is better at it than they. Or rather that, whilst they did it only some of the time, he is doing it all the time: it is always the one voice, though endlessly modified, and we notice no hiatus or change of gear in passing from light witticism to compelling eloquence. As for Virginia Woolf, we feel the existence of a style which is her very self, the expression of her inmost being; and in her novels the deeper she delves into her characters, the more they speak with this voice and begin to sound like herself. But she is far from always using this voice. She also plays with "style," in an extravagant way. *Orlando* is full of rather unplaceable games with style, which you cannot call "parody" or "pastiche." Sometimes it even falls into concealed doggerel. And altogether it represents a curious new attitude to "style," peculiar to its author. We may think, too, of Lytton Strachey. One tends to assume that he had, very unmistakably, a "style," but this may be an over-simplification. In looking through *Lady Ottoline's Album,* the collection of Ottoline Morrell's snapshots published in 1977, it struck me how Augustus John always looked exactly like himself, whereas Lytton Strachey looked like all sorts of different people: he would look hunnish, like Count von X of the Prussian Foreign Office; or aspiring, like the young Robert Elsmere; or exotic and criminal, like Fagin. The impression agrees with what Max Beerbohm said, very perceptively, in his 1943 Rede Lecture on Strachey:

> His manner is infinitely flexible, in accord to every variation of whatever his theme may be. Consider the differences between his ways of writing about Lord Melbourne, Lord Palmerston, Mr. Disraeli, and Mr. Gladstone. His manner seems to bring us into the very presence of these widely disparate Premiers. Note the mellow and leisurely benignity of the cadences in which he writes of Lord Melbourne—"the autumn rose" as he called him. Note the sharp brisk straightforward buoyancy of the writing whenever Lord Palmerston appears; and the elaborate Oriental richness of manner when Mr. Disraeli is on the scene.

The "Madan Blanchard" passage leads me to my second theme, Forster's prose not in its "Bloomsbury" aspect but in its own right. One of the things that one notices about Forster's prose is that he always "realises" or follows through his metaphors. Having said that, like a rat, he has deserted the ship of fiction, he continues "and *swum* towards biography." This fidelity to his metaphors is one source of his wit—as when, speaking in "Ibsen the Romantic" of the influence of mountains upon Ibsen and Wordsworth, he writes: "Wordsworth fell into the residential fallacy; he continued to look at his gods direct, and to pin with decreasing success his precepts to the flanks of Helvellyn." (The final clause is almost a Beerbohm cartoon.) This same fidelity also rewards him with thoughts of extreme originality, as when, in "Forrest Reid," he writes:

> He [Reid's hero Denis Bracknell] has reached squalor through beauty. It is as if, in the world beyond daily life, there was no moral full-stop: it is as if the scale of ecstasy might there rise until it has traversed the entire circle of its dial, and, passing the zero, indicate a state far lower than that from which it started.

Indeed this characteristic leads us to the heart of Forster's beliefs. He trusted metaphor to lead him where it would because he believed "things" contained the truth, albeit a truth probably very different from men's presuppositions. Though a rationalist and a humanist, he was neither a materialist nor a solipsist. Schoolmasters and men of good will, he wrote once (in "The Game of Life") were keen to tell us what Life is. "Once started on the subject of Life they lose all diffidence, because to them it is ethical. They love discussing what we ought to be instead of what we have to face—reams about conduct and nothing about those agitating apparitions that rise from the ground, or fall from the sky." He refused to assign those "agitating apparitions" to any traditional category—such, for instance, as "the supernatural." For him the truth about them was that they could come in any form, and in any context—in the visible scene or in human relationships, in the bed or the temple or at the tea-table. Accordingly, though he gave them a large role in all his writing, he assigned them only the status of an "as if." He wrote often *as if* inanimate things had wills and purposes of their own. At the end of *Where Angels Fear to Tread* it is as if the train deliberately shakes Phillip towards Miss Abbott and then away from her. At the end of *A Passage to India* it is as if the horses, the earth, the temple, the tank and the jail want to part Fielding and Aziz. He restricted such notions to metaphor; they pervade *A Passage to India;* and they have the force that they do because of his habitual respect for, and faithfulness in "realising," metaphors.

And a further aspect may be perceived to his respect for "the truth of things." He was, as his scene-descriptions show, fascinated by topography. And, by extension, he looked at human life itself in a topographical fashion. He was a master of *angle*. There was such-and-such a fact, such-and-such a truth, that one could see, in any situation, and others that were concealed by the lie of the land. Of course, one could change one's viewpoint. . . . Nothing is more striking in his masterpiece *A Passage to India* than the continual, and sometimes dizzying, shift of viewpoint, so that at one moment we are *tête-à-tête* with his characters, and the next moment viewing them from the ends of the universe. (pp. 161-66)

> *P. N. Furbank, "Forster and 'Bloomsbury' Prose," in* E. M. Forster, a Human Exploration: Centenary Essays, *edited by G. K. Das and John Beer, New York University Press, 1979, pp. 161-66.*

LINDA HUTCHEON

[*In the following excerpt, Hutcheon discusses the views of human sexuality expressed in the fiction of Bloomsbury writers.*]

One good justification for a study of revolt and the ideal in the sex and art of Bloomsbury—at a time when feminism and homosexuality are current issues—can be found in the public response to members of the Bloomsbury group during their own lifetimes. Although the aim of their contemporaries' criticism ran the gamut from class to personality, from financial status to ideology, the major emphasis seems to have rested upon their art and their sexual mores. At first the relationship between these two points of attack seems rather startling, given the relative lack of explicit sex in the published works of E. M. Forster, Lytton Strachey, and Virginia Woolf—the three major writers of the group. Their books were never banned, as were those of D. H. Lawrence or Radclyffe Hall, yet critics such as Roy Campbell attacked them as both artists *and* as "sexless folk whose sexes intersect."

In *The Georgiad,* Campbell set out, among other things, to parody Virginia Woolf's *Orlando* with his own Androgyno, a "joint Hermaphrodite-of-letters," complete with long blue stockings and a sexual metamorphosis. His multi-directional satire seems to be directed against Vita Sackville-West and also Woolf's androgynous literary creation, since he specifically calls his creature a "new Orlando" speaking with a "Bloomsbury accent." However, the homosexuality of Bloomsbury in general also comes under attack:

> Both sexes rampantly dispute the field
> And at alternate moments gain or yield.
> This was no neuter of a doubtful gender,
> But both in him attained their fullest splendour,
> Unlike our modern homos who are neither
> He could be homosexual with either.

- - - - -

> Taking his pleasure in and out of season,
> He gave for his perversity no reason.

L. H. Myers took a similar stand against the homosexual artist in the "Pleasance of Art" section of *Prince Jali.* His Daniyal, who would seem to be a satirical portrait of Lytton Strachey, spends his day squeezing young boys and writing sav-agely ironic portraits of "famous characters in religious history" (*à la Eminent Victorians*)—portraits which only serve to reveal the mocker's own inadequacies. To Myers's hero, Jali, such efforts are "spiteful, tasteless and pretentious." The homosexuality together with the art were seen by Myers as deliberate attempts to outrage moral and literary conventions: "the pleasure which the Camp took in regarding itself as scandalous was actually the chief source of its inspiration, its principal well-spring of energy."

Was Bloomsbury compulsively exhibitionistic or consciously revolutionary? Myers raises questions that had already come to the fore during the trial of Oscar Wilde, with "the love that dare not speak its name." What are the motives of those who are unconventional in their art or in their sexual proclivities? Was Wilde a social rebel? How closely linked are art and sex? To E. M. Forster they were intricately connected because of the inhibiting English social code. Citing the "ridiculous cases" of the suppression of *The Well of Loneliness, The Rainbow, Ulysses,* and *Boy,* he wrote [in "Liberty in England," in *Abinger Harvest*]: "I want greater freedom for writers, both as creators and as critics. In England, more than elsewhere, their creative work is hampered because they can't write freely about sex, and I want it recognized that sex is a subject for serious treatment and also for comic treatment."

Yet the enemies of Bloomsbury remained deaf and blind, but not at all dumb. In his 1954 introduction to *The Apes of God,* Wyndham Lewis deplored the "wave of male perversion among the young" in the 1920s. He saw that it was revolutionary in intensity but, characteristically, failed to understand that it was against people like himself that the revolt was directed. Strachey and Forster—both homosexuals—would certainly have resented their sexual tendency being labeled a "nasty pathological oddity." They probably would have resented as well Lewis's condescending approbation of sentimental friendships between adult males—with no penal consequences. Lewis apparently felt strongly that all decent men would *want* to impose such restraints on "pathological perverts." Indeed, in 1967, Lord Arran still found the opponents of his Sexual Offences Bill prophesying the fall of England on sexual grounds, on the model of Greece and Rome. In the Terminal Note to *Maurice,* Forster's posthumously published homosexual novel, the author wrote that any change in law would merely mean a shift in public opinion from "ignorance and terror to familiarity and contempt." That seems the truer prophecy.

It appears to be an historically validated fact that if an artist is a recognized homosexual, his work will first be judged by non-aesthetic criteria. Wilde's name had to be obliterated from posters of *The Importance of Being Earnest* before the public would attend the performances. Publishers refused "The Portrait of Mr. W. H." only when Wilde's trial seemed to be going poorly. The "unconscious deceit" or "muddle-headedness" that Forster condemned in his "Notes on the English Character," triumphed over autonomous literary judgment. Was this sexual/aesthetic hypocrisy not enough to make artists contemplate revolt?

Similarly, perhaps, was not the narrow heterosexual perspective of the age enough to make homosexuals revolt? D. H. Lawrence wrote: "*the* problem of today, the establishment of a new relation, is the readjustment of the old one, between men and women." In *Maurice* we get the fullest critical portrait of this heterosexual chauvinism. Mr. Ducie's "All's right in the world. Male and Female," Dr. Barry's view of homosexuality as an "evil hallucination," Mr. Borenius's desire to see all "sexual irregularities" punished severely—all these tend to prove Forster's contention that England had "always been disinclined to accept human nature." The "outlaws," those who indulge in the "unspeakable vice of the Greeks," are finally forced out of society. Forster deliberately gave the novel a happy ending, however; unlike *The Well of Loneliness, Maurice* ends with the united lovers. As Forster ironically suggested: "If it had ended unhappily, with a lad dangling from a noose or with a suicidal pact, all would be well, for there is no pornography or seduction of minors. But the lovers get away unpunished and consequently recommend crime." For this reason the book remained in manuscript for fifty-eight years, and those homosexual short pieces only saw print a few years ago in *The Life to Come and Other Stories.*

In the light of such social pressures, seemingly insignificant comments take on new suggestiveness. In *Aspects of the Novel* Forster wrote that the inner lives of characters must be presented in fiction (although they are never known in real life): "even if they are imperfect or unreal, they do not contain any secrets, whereas our friends do and must, mutual secrecy being one of the conditions of life upon this globe." Homosexuality demands secrecy; fiction does not.

Forster was no doubt very aware of what homosexuality could contribute to art: he saw and appreciated Diaghilev, Nijinsky, Strachey, and many others. Homosexuality, although no doubt intensified by the educational system of the upper classes which physically and intellectually separated males and females, was a credible social phenomenon in Europe at the time. Perhaps, however, another way of accounting for this is that the Victorian heterosexual standards of value were finally being challenged. In other words, maybe homosexuality was less a congenital public school disease than a deliberate form of anti-Victorian revolt. And the revolution was against not only this sexual snobbery, but also the social position of women that prevented even a true heterosexual love between two equals. In 1898 Strachey wrote: "I think it is too much that one cannot speak to a member of 'the sex' without being looked upon askance by somebody or other. If only people were more sensible on this point, half the so called immorality would come to an end at once." His biographer, Michael Holroyd, claims that Strachey spasmodically experienced some attraction to women—to Carrington, Ottoline Morrell, Nina Hamnett, Katherine Mansfield, Vanessa Bell—but that his intense childhood love for his mother always restrained him. It seems wisest at this point, however, to let lie the matter of particular psychological reasons for homosexuality: the literature itself of Bloomsbury is rich with less hypothetical material for such a study.

Whatever the individual or social reasons for this revolt, it seems evident that Bloomsbury did want to lead the way to a change in educated public opinion on sexual mores. After all, the times were changing. Virginia Woolf wrote to Vita Sackville-West: "I will tell you about Anna Karenina and the predominance of sexual love in nineteenth century fiction, and its growing unreality to us who have no real condemnation in our hearts any longer for adultery as such."

Yet many felt differently and revolutionaries were still needed to combat the hostility of society. Although never published during his lifetime, *Maurice* was E. M. Forster's self-consciously rebellious tract against the exclusiveness of that Victorian heterosexual love that "ignored the reproductive and digestive functions." As Noel Annan suggests in his re-

view of the novel: "When Forster describes Maurice and Clive in love, we feel he is observing them with an intruding sympathy, believing that he has to excuse them, although the theme of the book is that they need no excusing." Unlike Wilde, neither Maurice nor his creator ever married. They were not bisexual; nor were they ever hypocrites. Neither was attracted to homosexuality as a "sin," or solely for its shock value.

Yet is not some concept of the fascination of moral disobedience probably at the heart of all rebellions against moral codes which are considered absurd? In his biography of Goldsworth Lowes Dickinson, Forster discusses his mentor's impatience as a child with "current rules of conduct," and his deliberate disobeying of his parents. Dickinson wrote: "I emerged from it ultimately as a rebel, and at bottom have been so all my life." His homosexuality, subtly yet definitely suggested in the biography, could perhaps be yet another form of this revolt. But the rebellion was a concealed one: Virginia Woolf wrote to Roger Fry in 1921 that Dickinson had written a "dialogue upon homosexuality which he won't publish, for fear of the effect upon parents who might send their sons to Kings: and he is writing his autobiography which he won't publish for the same reason. So you see what dominates English literature is the parents of the young men who might be sent to Kings."

Could rebellion, then, be seen as a motive power behind Strachey's homosexuality as well? Perhaps. "The Trinity Diary—November 1902," a dialogue with G. Trevelyan about the love of men, would intimate this. However, his letters do suggest a desire to shock people and a need for attention as equally strong conscious forces.

There are therefore obvious qualifications that must be made on the claim for a revolutionary intent among Bloomsbury writers. Perhaps revolt was not the *primary* reason for insistence upon homosexual love for Strachey and Forster. Undoubtedly, given the restrictive social code, one was a rebel, a challenge to society by one's very existence as a homosexual. However, as an explanation of the phenomenon, revolt does not fully take into account the intellectual nature of Bloomsbury. These writers were not primarily social activists, although they obviously cannot be criticized for being unaware of, or uninterested in, social issues. Must we look elsewhere for the intellectual and ideological reasons for this sexual rebellion?

Once again, an enemy of Bloomsbury leads us to a possible answer. In *The Georgiad* once again Roy Campbell mockingly wrote:

> For, sure enough, his love was Humbert's kind,
> Though not, like it, Platonic, of the mind,
> Yet it extended out of time and space
> To all the members of the human race—

Despite the irony, he has placed his finger exactly on one of the major concerns of Bloomsbury: love and human relations *in general.* Society thwarts the intimate relationships of individuals—by its trivial conventions, its moral strictures—regardless of sex. Marriage cannot be a truly loving union of equals when the woman is relegated to the role of "the Angel in the House." When Mrs. Thornbury in *The Voyage Out* declaims: "You men! Where would you be if it weren't for women!", the sardonic Ridley Ambrose replies: "Read the *Symposium.*"

Virginia Woolf preferred intimate friendship with women because it was possible to achieve "a relationship so secret and private compared with relations with men," as she wrote to Vita Sackville-West. Her nephew, Quentin Bell, writes in his biography of her affection for this, her Sapphist friend: "There may have been—on balance I think that there probably was—some caressing, some bedding together. But whatever may have occurred between them of this nature, I doubt very much whether it was of a kind to excite Virginia or to satisfy Vita. As far as Virginia's life is concerned the point is of no great importance; what was, to her, important was the extent to which she was emotionally involved, the degree to which she was in love." Love was not seen as an emotion which was limited, as society claimed, by the barrier of sex. It was a question of *human* relations.

As Campbell suggested, the origins of this particular "justification" for homosexuality are Platonic. In the *Symposium* those males who love men are said to be the most noble, yet "do not act thus from any want of shame, but because they are valiant and manly, and have a manly countenance, and they embrace that which is like them." Heterosexual relations are seen as common, and indeed more devotion is expected in homosexual love, since it is the more spiritual. Plato's dialogue continues: "Evil is the vulgar lover who loves the body rather than the soul." Heterosexuals are pregnant in the body only, but homosexuals have souls which are pregnant. The latter do not waste creative energy on having children: their offspring are wisdom and virtue. The link between homosexuality and the products of creative energy first appeared to Lytton Strachey through his love for the painter Duncan Grant: "I am filled with . . . joy,—not by the consummation of my own poor pleasure . . . but by the sudden knowledge that he too was moved. . . . For the first time, I loved his soul. In the future when we meet, I want to be worthy . . . of what I am feeling now. I want our intercourse to be unmarred by the weaknesses that I know are mine too often . . . let us be occupied with the cleansing aspirations of our art as much as with each other and with ourselves." Strachey had discovered the *Symposium* during a boyhood infatuation: "I may be sinning, but I am doing so in the company of Shakespeare and Greece."

This Platonic desire for an ideal love would seem to have been a common concern among Cambridge intellectuals—even before *Principia Ethica*. According to Goldie Dickinson, the philosopher McTaggart believed that "in the relation of love we come into the closest contact we can attain with Reality; for the Reality is an eternally perfect harmony of pure spirits united by love." Dickinson himself wrote that "there is no good like friendship; which indeed may be termed love; which love, it seems to me, is the one thing to be cherished if there is to be any purport in life; cherished as the fundament of one's conduct and opinions—much deeper and more important than they." The idealized Hellenistic homosexuality of his *The Greek View of Life* perhaps influenced his young friend, E. M. Forster.

In that review of *Maurice,* Noel Annan claims that Forster saw sex as an attribute of love, but by no means the most important one. Like Plato, he expected devotion and affection from his relationships: "indeed because children, coquetry and the impediments of social conventions were absent from homosexual love, he expected more from it than from heterosexual love." Nevertheless the world conspires against homosexual lovers. In an early novel, Forster writes: "Dutiful sons,

loving husbands, responsible fathers—these are what [Nature] wants, and if we are friends it must be in our spare time. Abram and Sarai were sorrowful, yet their seed became as the sand of the sea, and distracts the politics of Europe at this moment. But a few verses of poetry is all that survives of David and Jonathan." Rickie, in *The Longest Journey,* may desire "the marriage of true minds," but like Fielding and Aziz in the later *A Passage to India,* he realizes that the time and the place for such an ideal and demanding male love have not yet come in the modern world. As Forster wrote in *Howards End:* "When men like us, it is for our better qualities, and however tender their liking, we dare not be unworthy of it, or they will quickly let us go."

For Forster, love was "harmonious, immense"—regardless of the sex of the lovers. In *Maurice* he tried to show how homosexual love could also unite the "brutal and the ideal," "athletic" and platonic love, lust and sentimentality. Alec and Maurice must "live outside class, without relations or money; they must work and stick to each other till death. But England belonged to them. That, besides companionship, was their reward. Her air and sky were theirs, not the timorous millions' who own stuffy little boxes, but never their own souls." As Furbank notes in his introduction to the novel, if there is any "perversion" in the matter, it is the perversity of a society which insanely denies part of the human heritage. Homosexual love was a revolt against this denial, but it was also an ideal.

Plato, McTaggart, Dickinson and, we might add, Edward Carpenter, seem to have been the mentors behind Forster's belief in love as the consummate experience of life. Strachey reached a similar conclusion by way of the *Symposium* and G. E. Moore's *Principia Ethica*. In his famous chapter on the "Ideal," Moore claimed: "By far the most valuable things which we know or can imagine, are certain states of consciousness, which may be roughly described as the pleasures of human intercourse and the enjoyment of beautiful objects." States of consciousness are not determined by the sex of the possessor, it would seem; nor do "human intercourse" and personal affection imply any heterosexual limitations. Indeed given Victorian social constrictions, they might almost be said to preclude heterosexual love. Strachey's early letters to Keynes point to his awareness of this irony. Holroyd claims that Lytton felt "the superiority of homosexuality to the humdrum heterosexual relationship lay in the greater degree of sympathy and the more absolute dual-unity which it could command. Between opposite sexes there must always be some latent residue of doubt, ignorance, perplexity; so often intelligence was matched with stupidity, talent paired off with mediocrity."

In Strachey's later relationships, it was the intensity of his state of mind, not of his passion, that acted as the ultimate criterion for evaluating his love. Indeed, what Moore called the "mental qualities" often seemed to be uppermost in Strachey's mind during his love affairs. Holroyd makes much of Strachey's aversion to physical lust, his fetishes and his fantasies, but tends to underplay the importance of the philosophic quest for an ideal love. Bertrand Russell, ironically, seems to have comprehended the seriousness of this search in his criticism of Strachey, who he felt had perverted Moore's doctrines so as to condone and exalt his own homosexuality. It is important to keep in mind Strachey's belief that society continually prevented the realization of real love even between members of *opposite* sexes—a belief shared by Forster in *Howards End.*

If revolt alone seemed inadequate as an explanation of Bloomsbury homosexuality, so does this idea of an ideal love. However, *together,* these two theories take into account the emotional needs, the philosophic search for truth and the reaction against social convention—the three elements that seem to have given men like Strachey and Forster the strength to accept and to believe in their homosexuality, despite the attacks of the critics of Bloomsbury. These two possible explanations are reflected in the tone of the recently published short pieces by Forster. It ranges from somber idealism in the name of honour and truth and love (often in stories set in another time—"The Life to Come"—or in an isolating location—"The Other Boat") to ironic, even facetious cuts at heterosexual chauvinism ("What Does It Matter? A Morality").

It is interesting to note that *Maurice* was the only full-scale literary study of overt homosexuality done by any Bloomsbury member and that it was not published until 1971. Yet, as we have seen, criticism of Bloomsbury art was often founded on sexual grounds. Critics seemed unwilling to allow art any autonomy from life, when something in life (the subject matter of art seemingly) outraged them.

There *are* homosexual characters in the fiction of Virginia Woolf and E. M. Forster, but they are usually minor and their sexual proclivities are rarely explicit. They hardly merit the critics' moral wrath. Does Mr. Carmichael in *To the Lighthouse* love Andrew Ramsay? We know that he used to take the boy to his room to "show him things," and that he lost all interest in life after Andrew's death; but does this make him a homosexual? Is the question even relevant, much less interesting? In other of Woolf's novels we suspect homosexuality in certain male characters because they are fictive portraits of Lytton Strachey. With the publication of Holroyd's biography and Carrington's letters we are better equipped to see parallels between Strachey and the fictional characters.

Strachey himself wrote a few humorous pieces on homosexual themes: "The Unfortunate Lovers" or "Truth Will Out," written in 1913, and in the same year, "Ermyntrude and Esmeralda." This latter piece of privately circulated "pornography" is interesting because the young Esmeralda sees the love of her brother, Godfrey, and his Oxford tutor, Mr. Mapleton, as natural and innocent. Her father, however, banishes the tutor and exiles his son to Germany. For his part, Godfrey (relates Esmeralda) "did not think he'd done anything wicked at all, and it seems the Greeks used to do it, too—at least the Athenians, who were the best of the Greeks. . . . And he said that Mr. Mapleton agreed with everything he's said, and, in fact, he had told him most of it; and as for Papa, he said he was a silly old man and he expected he'd done just the same himself when he was a boy at school but that he'd forgotten all about it." When the young girl asks the visiting cleric, a school friend of her father, what love is, he replies that it is "the purification and the sanctification of something," *unless* its object is a member of the same sex. Although Socrates was a homosexual, the Dean says, "it was one of the mysteries of Providence that the highest and the lowest sometimes met in the same person, and that the Greeks had not had the benefits of the teaching of Our Lord." Needless to say the Dean is horrified by her notion that he had loved her father when they were boys. His overreaction,

however, suggests the truth of her unwitting accusation. It is perhaps a sign of Strachey's confidence in his homosexuality that he can joke about Plato and the serious motives seen above—revolt and the search for the ideal.

This is the very portrait of him we find as Risley in *Maurice.* Just as Strachey acted as a challenge to Forster, so Risley dares Maurice, in so many words, to caper with him on the phallic mountain, leaving behind "the Valley of the Shadow of Life." "Dark, tall, and affected," Risley is always "at play, but seriously." This seriousness is what Wyndham Lewis, for one, failed to comprehend in Strachey. His broad satire of him in *The Apes of God* as Matthew Plunkett, a homosexual feasting on "Eminent Victorian giants," trying to be "normal" by seducing the boyish Betty Bligh (Carrington), is rather crude.

When Strachey appears in Virginia Woolf's fiction, the portrait is usually sympathetic, but rarely without some irony. The arrogant, intelligent St. John Hirst in *The Voyage Out* does not like young women—on intellectual as well as physical grounds—but is careful to try to be fair, asking Rachel whether the lack of "mind" in women is due to lack of training, or "native incapacity." In *Jacob's Room* Strachey appears as "Bonamy who couldn't love a woman and never read a foolish book." Bonamy's "peculiar disposition" as one of the "men of that temperament" makes his love for Jacob deeper than his heterosexual friend could ever understand. He is the "dark horse," left alone to mourn Jacob's death. Strachey was aware himself of the link Woolf had made for him with this fictional character. He once wrote to her: "Of course, you're very romantic—which alarms me slightly—I am such a Bonamy."

He was also a Neville. Although the brilliant mind of this character in *The Waves* likely belongs to another Bloomsbury bisexual, John Maynard Keynes, Neville's delicate health, his revolt against religion, his obsession with his physical unattractiveness, and his habit of reading French novels, are decidedly Strachey's. Neville's one-sided love for the handsome, if rather stolid, Percival recalls the "absurd and violent passions" of Strachey's youth. Neville is perhaps the most significant homosexual character in Virginia Woolf's fiction. He is, however, only one of seven equally important characters in the novel, and Hirst and Bonamy place second to Terence, Rachel, and Jacob.

The same holds true for Forster's work. Except for the posthumously published short stories and *Maurice,* the novels are about asexual friendships between members of the same sex: Rickie and Ansell, Mrs. Wilcox and Margaret, Fielding and Aziz. Admittedly, many of the marriages in his fiction are less successful than these other relationships: Gino and Lilia (*Where Angels Fear to Tread*), Rickie and Agnes, Rickie's own parents (*The Longest Journey*), Leonard and Jacky Bast (*Howards End*), the British couples and, potentially, Adela and Ronny (*A Passage to India*). In Forster's last novel, the friendship of Aziz and Fielding must combat great odds merely to exist. As in *The Longest Journey,* the world conspires against them. It is not only culture, or even politics, and that prevents an ideal relationship, despite their mutual affection. At the end of the novel their horses bump together, they embrace, but the horses, the earth refuse them their wish—"not yet" and "not there."

Is there a suggestion of homosexuality in their love? Perhaps, but Forster was subtle and above all cautious. Even D. H.

Lawrence was much more explicit, yet the attacks made on him were directed against his concepts and portrayal of heterosexual love. Birkin, in *Women in Love,* says: "I believe in the additional perfect relationship between man and man—additional to marriage." To be safe, Lawrence had him repeat and explain that "additional." He made no claim to the rebellious courage of idealistic confidence in the value of male love that one finds in Strachey and Forster. Implicit in Birkin's remark, however, is the one potential drawback that Forster perceived. In *Maurice* he wrote: "the thought that he was sterile weighed on the young man with a sudden shame. His mother or Mrs. Durham might lack mind or heart, but they had done visible work; they had handed on the torch their sons would tread out." Although the suburban Maurice may be condemned to sterility, Forster, like Plato's ideal lovers, sought his immortality in the products of his creative energy—his art.

It is perhaps wise to recall at this point once again that Forster, like Woolf, was not primarily a "homosexual" novelist. In Woolf's fiction we find Rachel and Terence, Katherine and Ralph, the Dalloways, the Ramsays, and many more traditional couples. On the other hand, marriage is never the final word in human relations. There should be free room for all the other variations on the theme of love—in fiction, at least.

One of these variations is the true friendship of women, and its sexual aspect, lesbianism. The same would seem to hold true here as in our investigation of male homosexuality: there are elements of revolt against society and of a search for an ideal love that knows no barriers. We have already seen that Virginia Woolf preferred the friendship of women because it permitted greater intimacy. Whatever the relationship with Vita Sackville-West, it seems likely that it was more an affair of the heart, than of the body. Woolf remained childless for medical and psychological reasons. Like Plato's lovers she too then had to choose to assert her immortality in more spiritual ways. For her too this meant through her art. She admitted to an "insatiable desire to write something before I die," and once referred to her novels as her "offspring."

In her fiction, love between women is often seen as the ideal relationship. Clarissa Dalloway's love for Sally Seton remains, even after her marriage, the most significant and potent emotion in her life: "The strange thing, on looking back, was the purity, the integrity, of her feeling for Sally. It was not like one's feeling for a man. It was completely disinterested, and besides it had a quality which could only exist between women." Indeed, the most sexual moment in the novel is that of the "consummation" of their love: "Then came the most exquisite moment of her whole life passing a stone urn with flowers in it. Sally stopped; picked a flower; kissed her on the lips. The whole world might have turned upside down! The others disappeared; there she was alone with Sally." Yet Clarissa hates Miss Kilman, her daughter's presumed "seducer," "the woman who had crept in to steal and defile." She tells herself: "it might be only a phase . . . such as all girls go through. It might be falling in love." She never consciously connects Elizabeth and her teacher with herself and Sally. The ugly, poor, but educated Miss Kilman rarely had opportunities to meet the opposite sex; instead her energies and passions are directed towards her lovely student.

A somewhat more subtle version of this same love appears in *To the Lighthouse.* Lily Briscoe, the spinster painter, resists the male force of Mr. Ramsay, considers marriage a "degradation," and love "tedious, puerile, and inhumane." But it can also be "beautiful and necessary" if the right object is found. Lily "had much ado to control her impulse to fling herself (thank Heaven she had always resisted so far) at Mrs. Ramsay's knee and say to her—but what could one say to her? 'I'm in love with you?' "

If Lily speaks out for love between women as an ideal union, Orlando pleads for it as a rebellion against unnatural social conventions. After "his" sex change "As all Orlando's loves had been women, now, through the culpable laggardry of the human frame to adapt itself to convention, though she herself was a woman, it was still a woman she loved; and if the consciousness of being of the same sex had any effect at all, it was to quicken and deepen those feelings which she had as a man." Despite expert male opinion, states Orlando's "biographer," women *do* enjoy each other's company. So true is this that our androgynous heroine manages to enjoy her relations with women quite as much as those with men.

Never in her fiction, even while attacking social convention, did Virginia Woolf become strident or chauvinistic, as did Radclyffe Hall in *The Well of Loneliness*—a heavily Freudian novel about a lesbian named Stephen. Not one of Woolf's heroines even has the strident anti-male tone of Lawrence's Winifred Inger (*The Rainbow*): "As if I would be betrayed by him, lend him my body as an instrument for his idea . . . they are all impotent, they can't take a woman." His man-hater is, naturally, a member of the Women's Movement. As if that were not damning enough, Lawrence finally has to marry her off to the effeminate Tom Brangwen: "He looked at the athletic, seemingly fearless girl, and he detected in her a kinship with his own dark corruption." Similarly, in *The Fox,* the masculine March is made to respond to the "old spell of the fox" in Henry, who wants to submerge her identity in his.

At least Lily Briscoe has her independence, her memories of love, and her art; these are worth as much to her as Mrs. Dalloway means to her husband, and indeed more than Isa means to hers (in *Between the Acts*). Lily's love, like Clarissa's, is one that operates silently, outside the conventions of heterosexual marriage. It is an ideal emotion, like that of Moore and Dickinson, Strachey and Forster, Bonamy and Maurice. In Bloomsbury fiction the question of sexual mores is never totally in the limelight (except in *Maurice* of course), nor is it ever totally absent. As Maynard Keynes wrote in "My Early Beliefs," in Bloomsbury "one's prime objects in life were love, the creation and enjoyment of aesthetic experience," and the pursuit of truth. But, love did come first. If they discussed in their art the affection between members of the same sex, as well as marital love, it was perhaps because—given the current social conventions—it was one way of calling attention to the need to see human relations in a broader perspective. They actually wrote no essays or tracts on the subject: their subtle vehicles were their works of art and their lives.

We have already witnessed the critics' scornful response to this plea for a less narrow sexual outlook. The position of the homosexual artist in this society, however, was really little different from that of the female artist: they both exist but must one really acknowledge their worth as human beings or writers? As Keynes remarked in his address, "Am I a Liberal?", these problems indicated that certain changes were absolutely imperative: "Birth Control and the use of Contraceptives, Marriage Laws, the treatment of sexual offences and abnormalities, the economic position of women, the economic position of the family,—in all these matters the existing state of the law and of orthodoxy is still Mediaeval—altogether out of touch with civilized opinion and civilized practice and with what individuals, educated and uneducated alike, say to one another in private."

Only after 1919 were the professions opened to women; in education opportunities were slim—there was no female equivalent to "Arthur's Education Fund." In *Three Guineas,* Virginia Woolf wrote that the daughters of educated men formed a class unto themselves, an "anonymous and secret Society of Outsiders"—not unlike homosexuals. She knew that independence of mind depended upon independence of income, but she wanted none of the possessiveness, jealousy, pugnacity, and greed of the public world of men. Her ideal was perforce catholic: "As a woman, I have no country. As a woman I want no country. As a woman my country is the whole world." As Cassandra says in "A Society," once a woman learns to read, "there's only one thing you can teach her to believe in—and that is herself."

Virginia Woolf was no militant feminist, however. A woman could have a profession, like Peggy, the doctor in *The Years,* but perhaps it was not desirable to grow pugnacious like men and go to prison for one's suffragist convictions, like Rose. In many of her essays ("Two Women," "Ellen Terry," and others), Woolf expressed a special concern for the woman as artist. In *A Room of One's Own,* she asserted that a woman must have money and a room of her own if she is to write fiction. The room here is a symbol of independent consciousness, as well as of privacy and protection from the hostility of society. Money would mean an end to her subservience to the male world. She need never alter her values in deference to masculine opinion. Art depends on intellectual freedom, which in turn depends on these material things. Otherwise we are left with "the unpublished works of women, written by the fireside in pale profusion," as she wrote in *Jacob's Room.*

As a woman novelist, Woolf was very concerned about finding a workable relationship between her art and her femininity. Perhaps her solution was dictated by her temperament; perhaps, like Vita Sackville-West and Carrington, she felt she had to struggle for recognition more than a man. Whatever the reason, her answer to the problem took the form of a Platonic theory of the androgynous artist. As we have seen, Roy Campbell chose this aspect as a starting point for his satire in *The Georgiad.* He could not separate, however, this from the sexual theme; he remained blind to the androgyn as a literary concept.

For Woolf, as for Coleridge, the great mind was androgynous. In "The Patron and the Crocus," she wrote: "if you can forget your sex altogether . . . so much the better; a writer has none." Shakespeare's mind was truly androgynous, she claimed in *A Room of One's Own:* it remains "resonant and porous . . . it transmits emotion without impediment . . . it is naturally creative, incandescent, and undivided." Except for Proust, all male writers of her time, she felt, were writing with only the male sides of their minds. As in married love, "some collaboration has to take place in the mind between the woman and the man before the art of creation can be accomplished. Some marriages of opposites has to be consummated."

In *To the Lighthouse,* then, Lily Briscoe had her mystic vision of Mrs. Ramsay, and immediately "She wanted him," Mr. Ramsay. She united the male and the female principles, adding the phallic black stroke to the purple triangle, Mr. Ramsay's lighthouse goal to Mrs. Ramsay's "wedgeshaped core of darkness." Charles Tansley may have felt in the novel that "Women can't paint, women can't write," but Lily's painting and Virginia Woolf's novel were completed in the same moment: the goal could be reached.

Orlando is Woolf's fullest study of the androgynous mind (and body) of the poet. The same concerns as we discovered above are present here too: "Different though the sexes are, they intermix. In every human being a vacillation from one sex to another takes place." Orlando's poem, "The Oak Tree," is the literary record of this union and vacillation. In *The Waves,* the writer Bernard says: "But joined 'to the sensibility of a woman' (I am here quoting my own biographer) 'Bernard possessed the logical sobriety of a man'."

Finally in the last—and unrevised—novel Virginia Woolf wrote before her death, we have a woman writer figure—Miss LaTrobe. It is rather disconcerting, however, to discover that she is a defeated writer of country pageants who, despite her superior literary vision of unity, is driven to drink for solace and even inspiration. Did Woolf's ideal begin to fail her now that her youthful rebellious spirit had been somewhat quelled by age, illness and two wars? Miss LaTrobe is "an outcast," like the homosexual William Dodge and the unhappily married Isa. She is the "slave of her audience," she laments. The tone of the novel is somewhat bitter.

In Woolf's response to this challenge to social convention (Miss LaTrobe is also a lesbian), there is little of the satiric confidence of Strachey's "Ermyntrude and Esmeralda" or the defiant revolt of Forster's lovers in the Greenwood. A different note has been struck. Isa, the unhappily married woman, feels she has known the homosexual William for years: "Weren't they, though, conspirators, seekers after hidden faces?" Are these hidden faces those of ideal lovers? Do such lovers exist—in either sex? Or do they forever remain hidden? These are some of the questions the last Bloomsbury novels—so separated in time—leave us with. Are we to believe that it is only for the young to rebel or to seek an ideal of personal affection, outside social restrictions, if necessary? Perhaps these issues do look different at 59, after two major wars and the rise of Hitler. However tempting, there is no cause to speculate that Woolf's suicide was brought on by any such realization. And yet, the tonal change in her work is there.

On his deathbed Lytton Strachey lamented not having married Carrington. Forster felt that his revolutionary social novel, *Maurice,* was publishable, "but worth it?" and he never wrote another piece of fiction after *A Passage to India.* Before his death he confided to his diary: "I should have been a more famous writer if I had written or rather published more, but sex has prevented the latter." In the last Bloomsbury novels, the land that says "No—not yet" and those "hidden faces" suggest the very intimate connection of sex and art. Novels end; human relations remain unconsummated. Is there also an intimation of defeat, a realization of the impossibility of reconciling the individual consciousness with current social convention, even in fiction? The Greenwood exists no more—or not yet. After the 1914 war Forster felt this. During the next one, it became increasingly clear to Virginia Woolf. The fighter planes do buzz over the pageant in her last novel. And *Maurice,* we recall, was dedicated to "A Happier Year." (pp. 78-92)

Linda Hutcheon, "Revolt and the Ideal in Blooms-

A sketch of E.M. Forster by Roger Fry.

bury," in English Studies in Canada, *Vol. V, No. 1, Spring, 1979, pp. 78-93.*

BLOOMSBURY AND LITERARY CRITICISM

PAUL BLOOMFIELD

[*In the following excerpt, Bloomfield discusses the principles applied in literary criticism by members of the Bloomsbury Group.*]

Literary criticism was chiefly represented in Bloomsbury by Lytton Strachey and Virginia Woolf, who in the special circumstances were under obligations to George Moore, a Cambridge philosopher and critic of morals (most of the men had been at Cambridge); to Roger Fry, a critic of the plastic arts; to Clive Bell, a critic of painting and of the arts of living—in which he was reputed to be something of a connoisseur. This is not the whole story. If you have a set of talented people who know one another intimately and see one another constantly, you expect them to owe their friends more than the stimulus of particular theories. There is a ferment of ideas, which encourages each in his own bent, while at the same time mutual reactions and concessions bring into existence an ethos. So it was that the topographical name "Bloomsbury" legitimately got a new significance.

Now in a memoir that Keynes wrote in 1938 he made what appears to be a rather surprising statement about the attitude of Bloomsbury in the early, formative days. "We were not aware," he said, "that civilization was a thin and precarious crust erected by the will and personality of a very few, and only maintained by rules and conventions skilfully put across and guilefully maintained. We had no respect for traditional wisdom or the restraints of custom. We lacked reverence, as Lawrence observed . . . for everything and everybody." What they *did* have, Keynes goes on to say, and he makes it responsible for a kind of superficiality which he alleges he shared with the others, was a complacent belief that human beings are by nature rational. They ignored "certain powerful and valuable springs of feeling." They were also too individualistic, not so much in overrating personal character as in underrating the power of those impulses which affect "the order and pattern of life amongst communities, and the emotion they inspire." The Freudian sun was about to come up: strange that in Bloomsbury it should have been so dark before dawn.

One has a suspicion that Keynes was saying too much. After all, young people with a disposition to reasonableness always examine traditional values before they accept them. If they are brilliantly clever their criticism will almost certainly be severe, partly because—in their impatience to be unshackled—they want to revenge themselves a little on the older generation, for *being* the older generation, and, if these were impressive, then for *being* impressive. The Bloomsbury ancestors were most impressive.

To go back for a moment to the memoir. "As the years wore on towards 1914," Keynes wrote, "the falsity of our view of man's heart became, as it now seems to me, more obvious; and there was, too, some falling away from the original doctrine." But the falsity of the view was already more obvious to some of the others—then. We can say, on the evidence, that they were picking up some anthropology and psychology more quickly than Keynes allowed. For the ball had opened, and Bloomsbury criticism had made its bow, with the appearance in 1912 of a small book in which the unreasonableness of exclusive rationality was acknowledged in the plainest words. Lytton Strachey's *Landmarks in French Literature* begins: "When the French nation gradually came into existence among the ruins of the Roman civilization in Gaul, a new language was at the same time slowly evolving." It is a model book, with not a flat sentence or trace of flagging zeal, and in it some of the features of the Bloomsbury tradition are already visible. Respect for tradition *tout court* is clearly one of them; we could not have a warmer celebration of gradual coming into existence and of slow evolving. And in Chapter Five, writing of Voltaire—his hero then and ever after—there is Strachey actually shaking his head over the archrationalist's immunity from those emotional states of mind "which go to create the highest forms of poetry, music and art"; and he says "this was certainly a great weakness in him—a great limitation of spirit."

Five years later Strachey was famous—and infamous. *Eminent Victorians* had come out in 1918. The admirable life of Queen Victoria followed in 1921. For three later books of criticism it could be claimed that many of the essays in them were works of art. The last, *Characters and Commentaries,* was published in 1933, the year after Strachey's death at the early age of fifty-two.

To many of us who do not share Strachey's outlook his prose is a delight. The total effect of almost every one of his essays strikes me as characteristic, of a piece, and memorable. He is inspired by reason without being tainted by the recurrent heresy which consists in reason, that is to say reason's self-appointed champions, denying the existence of *what-is-given* when this apparently cannot be reconciled with its—reason's—own logic. He writes movingly of life and of death. (pp. 161-63)

" 'To see the object as in itself it really is,' has been justly said to be the aim of all true criticism whatever; and in aesthetic criticism the first step towards seeing one's object as it really is, is to know one's own impression as it really is. . . ." This is Pater speaking, and it follows from what he says that a good deal depends on the sensibility of whoever is receiving the impression.

The eminent Bloomsbury aesthetician, Roger Fry, while recognizing that unusual—and measurable, why not?—sensitivity was indispensable to a critic (of prose and poetry as well as of the visual arts), trusted to certain inherent qualities in the "object" for keeping the critical balance dressed. They were the qualities peculiar to any art, the beauties not in the eye of the beholder, which give the art its power of evoking "aesthetic emotion." In prose and verse the objective element is presumably style.

The most deliberate literary stylist in Bloomsbury was David Garnett—not *ipso facto* the most careful writer. How far he was influenced by Fry I should not venture to guess, but he composed his remarkable books on an aesthetic principle. He suppressed the pervasive narrator, the intrusive moralist, the whisperer between the lines. He aimed at a kind of consistency by trying to let his stories tell themselves. D. H. Lawrence, who hated this impersonal manner, may have been thinking of Garnett, and of the early Joyce of *Dubliners,* when he described such writing (he did so in the preface of one of his Verga translations) as no less "conceited" than wrong-headed.

What then were the objects on which Strachey and Mrs. Woolf relied for counterweighing *their* subjectivism, the lightning-conductors for their flashes of perception? Shall we find them being guided by Fry's theory or Garnett's practice (improbable, as he was a good deal their junior)? A picture should perhaps be pictorial, and a bronze should have bronziness; but need style be stylish? An immense amount of uninhibited, awkward and stilted writing—as in Dickens, Browning, Hardy—has added up to great literature. Let us hear Pater again. He says: "What is important is not that the critic should possess a correct abstract definition of beauty for the intellect, but a certain kind of temperament, the power of being deeply moved by the presence of beautiful objects."

Though at first it sounds as if the question were being begged—sensibility is all—we are really a little further on. For the beginning of Pater's sentence contains the important admission that a general aesthetic principle applicable to *whatever carries conviction* has never been discovered, and is never likely to be. The next writer of genius who comes along carrying conviction will also bring with him a licence to break what rules he feels he must. It happens that David Garnett was brilliantly successful. Would even his warmest admirer have expected everyone in future to try to write in the same way? Mrs. Woolf, for one, was not doing so, nor did she do so later. In short, to discover the controls of Strachey's and Mrs. Woolf's sensibilities—and allowing for the great differences between them—we have to look to no "abstract defini-tion" of anything, but to the conditions which fostered the Bloomsbury ethos. And the only reasonable method of judging whether N or M is in the Bloomsbury tradition is to understand that ethos and to consider to what extent N or M shares it.

Our fundamental axiom must be that the members of the Bloomsbury coterie sprang almost one and all from the great effective bourgeoisie of the last century, England's serious-minded and powerful liberalizing professional middle class. Many Stephens and their blood relations had been eminent public servants; the Stracheys had distinguished themselves particularly in India. The Garnetts showed hereditary ability too, and Roger Fry belonged to the philanthropic Quaker cousinhood into which Elizabeth Gurney had married—Mrs. Fry the prison reformer, that is to say. It is brash if we speak of the "bourgeois virtues" to include ironically what we really think of as bourgeois vices, for instance immoderate conventionality. Legalism and *mesquinerie* or pettiness are bourgeois failings, and so is hypocrisy over sex; but not all bourgeois have had these at any time. The educated middle class are the middle way people, and their middlingness, like their regularity and habits of hard work, is a virtue born perhaps of necessity, but none the less a virtue: the same necessity would have broken ancestors of less tough fibre and scattered their seed to the winds. If history is going to be a success it will be by civilization becoming stabilized on an upper-middle-class level.

In past centuries it did not enter literate people's heads to doubt that there was such a thing as excellence. Though there have always been the familiar jealousies and backscratchings, better and worse in literary performance were assumed to be referable to "eternal standards." There was no *class* jealousy: if the poor scholar or poet excelled, he did so according to those standards and was welcome to his laurels. As late as the eighteenth century William Blake, who was not a socialite, declared us all contemporaries *vis-à-vis* excellence. "The ages are all equal," he said, "but genius is always above the age." With the qualifications one has to make if one knows some history Hazlitt believed the same, though he was a radical: so did Pater, who was not; so did Strachey and Mrs. Woolf congruously with their upper-middle-class Bloomsbury ethos. (pp. 169-72)

Keynes has told us that he became aware that "civilization was a thin and precarious crust erected by the will and personality of a very few"; how long had it been before the eyes of the rest of the coterie were opened? Freud's essay on "The Disillusionment of War"—about the thinness and precariousness of that crust—was written in 1915, and must have reached Lytton Strachey's psychologist brother James at the earliest possible moment. In her second novel, *Night and Day* (1919) Mrs. Woolf showed she knew something about the links of blood and tradition which hold civilization together. The coterie's reaction against unsympathetic father-figures was nothing like as important as their sense that it was *only congruous* to be identified with traditions of intellectual integrity and respect for talent. In relation to society they were good upper-middle-class; and though not Christians they were After-Christians; and they had no use for the *pari passu* heresy.

A reaction against the parents there was, of course. Though there may be, and I believe there is, a Oneness underlying the appearance of multiplicity, it is vain for determinism to insist on a kind of consolidated motive in everything that has motion. An artistic coterie, like a Communist Party, segregates itself and takes a line. Segregated impulses and conflicts are the bricks of the structure that may or may not have been blue-printed before the beginning of years. Bloomsbury amended the parental complex of congruities and was Bloomsbury, something now fairly far removed from the Clapham of the Quaker and Evangelical ancestors. Some of the differences were a matter of a shifting of emphasis only.

At any rate there were at least these three principles underlying Bloomsbury literary criticism: that personality and merit must be respected, that "in all ages there have been some excellent workmen and some excellent work done" (Pater yet again), and that it is a religious duty to preserve the freedom of thought to be sceptical. To give the *Zeitgeist* priority over these assumptions would have seemed to the coterie at best a confession of immaturity, at worst callowness or a mark of inferior natural endowments. The spirit of the age can be a traitor. There is no inevitable progress, by dialectical materialist or other kinds of eventfulness, and since man refuses to stay still—usually preferring almost any commotion to serenity—he may as likely as not be found moving in the wrong direction. (pp. 172-74)

Paul Bloomfield, "The Bloomsbury Tradition in English Literary Criticism," in The Craft Letters in England, *edited by John Lehmann, 1956. Reprint by Houghton Mifflin Company, 1957, pp. 160-82.*

BLOOMSBURY POLITICAL IDEALS

QUENTIN BELL

[*In the following excerpt, Bell examines the ways in which the determination to reject the emotional appeal of such ideals as nationalism and female purity shaped the social and political attitudes expressed by Bloomsbury writers and influenced their responses to current events in the early twentieth century.*]

Bloomsbury, it is agreed, was very much concerned with the arts. But aesthetically it has two rather different characters. The Bloomsbury painters—Roger Fry, Vanessa Bell, and Duncan Grant—follow very much the sort of careers that one would expect of artists born at the end of the nineteenth century. They set out in that tradition of modified impressionism which flourished in England under the leadership of Whistler and the New English Art Club; they are deeply affected first by the fauves and then by cubism and around the year 1914 they make experiments in pure abstraction. Like the great majority of their contemporaries they abandon abstract form and, from about 1919, return to a style which has something in common with impressionism and something that derives from the British art of a much earlier generation. The writers are much more conservative and never so deeply committed to "modernism"—for the most part they remain indifferent to the literary adventures of Eliot and Pound, Joyce and Gertrude Stein.

There is another way of expressing this difference, and it will, I think, help us to understand the character of the group (in so far as it had a literary character). When they were shown to a bewildered public, the earlier works of Grant and Bell

and Fry could only have appealed to a small minority. In this sense they were elitist. The only one of the writers whose manner was incomprehensible at the time of publication was Virginia Woolf, and this was true only of a part of her work; the Bloomsbury writers were therefore in a large measure demotic.

In our century we have seen the very strange phenomenon of engaged art, propaganda indeed, which has been hidden from the public in the obscurity of a modern idiom. Picasso's *Guernica* is an obvious example.

Nevertheless it remains true that when an author has an argument which he wants to be generally understood he is likely to look for a language more generally accessible than that of *Useful Knowledge* or *Finnegans Wake*. The prose of Lytton Strachey, Maynard Keynes, E. M. Forster, Leonard Woolf, Clive Bell, and Desmond MacCarthy is understandable by almost anyone who knows English, even though it may sometimes contain fairly abstruse allusions; the same is true of Virginia Woolf in her reviews, her polemics, and the great majority of her novels.

The mere recital of these names should be sufficient to remind us that Bloomsbury produced authors who were not primarily or not wholly concerned with aesthetic but with social problems and indeed that there were some whom we should hardly think of as "literary artists" but rather as social theorists who made use of language.

Obvious though this may seem, the idea takes some people by surprise. Another image of Bloomsbury has become established in the public mind. In this image we perceive a society largely devoted either to the creation or to the contemplation of works of art and having no other end in life than aesthetic delight and the pleasures of human intercourse, a society in no way concerned with the machinery of government or the mobilization of opinion. The view is fairly widespread and indeed one of the charms of this subject would appear to derive from the nostalgic image of figures such as Strachey and Virginia Woolf exquisitely doing nothing. It is an image which students in particular seem to find wonderfully attractive. The picture is false—for one thing there simply wasn't the cash for that kind of decorative inactivity. Those who remember the apparently inexhaustible activity of Keynes and Fry, of Leonard, and indeed of Virginia Woolf when she had her health, will find it hard to think of Bloomsbury as the abode of dolce far niente ["sweet idleness"], nor can any place at which painters are seriously at work be anything of the kind. Nevertheless there is a scintilla of truth in the image. There were those in Bloomsbury who, even if they couldn't usually achieve it, would thoroughly have enjoyed a life of cultured idleness, and, more importantly from the point of view of this essay, there was a certain political vagueness in Bloomsbury which distinguishes it from a later generation, that of Rupert Brooke and the Neo-Pagans which was in a much more considered way political.

In his dedication to *Civilization* dated April 1927, Clive Bell writes to Virginia Woolf:

> Its conception dates from our nonage. You remember, Virginia, we were mostly socialists in those days. We were concerned for the fate of humanity. And from that concern sprang first the idea, then the rough draft, of what was to be, of course, my *magnum opus*.

Just who was included in that "we" it would be hard to say nor can one decide with any certainty what is meant by "mostly." Although Clive Bell was himself politically active with the Liberals and Virginia with the Suffrage movement, it is not easy, trying to look at Bloomsbury as a whole, to arrive at a description of its politics before 1914.

The nearest that I can come to it, taking my own definition of the group as a basis, is to offer the following propositions: They would have rejected the idea that the capitalist system was sacred. They were opposed to what they would have called "jingoism," that is, extreme nationalism and imperialism. On the whole they welcomed the social reforms of the then Liberal government. On the whole they felt that woman should have the vote. They had no particular affection for the hereditary Upper House or the union with Ireland. In all this they might be classed as liberal or radical, but they were also libertarian in that they felt that government had no right to punish immorality when it took a form which did not injure others, as for instance in the case of homosexuals. This distinguished their liberalism sharply from the political liberalism of the day but only in theory, for their libertarianism would not have been regarded as practical politics, except in the matter of temperance legislation, where Bloomsbury would, I imagine, have been in sympathy rather with the Conservatives than with their opponents—the issue was hardly allowed to appear in public.

Except in this matter—which was to some extent bipartisan—Bloomsbury may be thought of as being distinctly left of centre. Speaking as one who many years later found himself in much the same position, I should say that they didn't get much fun out of it. It is true that the Miss Stephens heard the news of the 1905 election in the company of George and Gerald Duckworth and enjoyed themselves hugely (partly I fear because the Liberal triumph pained their half brothers), but in general I doubt whether they took a lively interest in either the political or the industrial struggle. The high words and fury engendered by the first post-impressionist exhibition were of much greater interest to them than was the constitutional crisis of the same year. It is hardly astonishing, for after all their political attitudes were based upon the view that politics should as far as possible be a matter of human convenience and common sense. Intense emotion was in such a business foolish and dangerous, and it was the use of emotive ideas and emotive language which, in their opinion, were the very stuff of reactionary politics. In 1913 the red bogey was already a well-worn political prop, so too the Union Jack. The Home, Female Purity, and Moral Cleanliness were also handy for those who felt it better to feel than to think; when once they or any one of them had been invoked argument became unnecessary, and the speaker felt justified in saying: "This is a matter concerning which there can be no argument." In Bloomsbury it was generally felt that there can be no such matters; they discussed or attempted to discuss everything and felt that nothing ought to be taboo. Given such a premise, it might be possible to use reason in the management of public affairs. In 1913 it was possible to be optimistic (and therefore complacent) about the possibility of rational government. The forces of unreason had taken a severe beating in France and again in South Africa. Was it altogether ridiculous to suppose that the new forces of organized labour would grow so powerful and so urgent in their demands that the governing classes would see the unwisdom of placing guns in their hands? I suppose it was.

I was brought up to think of the war years as the years of National Insanity; it was thus that my parents saw it; but the most forcible account of that nationwide lunacy has been provided by Bernard Shaw in the preface to *Heartbreak House*. It had been a time when the yahoos were in power, when the windows of Swiss shops with German names were smashed, when any atrocity story was believed so long as it was the Germans who were atrocious, when in the law courts there was no justice for the alien or the pacifist, when hideous cruelties were inflicted upon conscientious objectors, when all constitutional guarantees of liberty and well-being were set aside, when not only the basest elements of the lumpen proletariat but highly educated men behaved like savages.

> The Christian priest joining in the war dance without even throwing off his cassock first, and the respectable school governor expelling the German professor with insult and bodily violence, and declaring that no English child should ever again be taught the language of Luther and Goethe, were kept in countenance by the most impudent repudiations of every decency of civilization and every lesson of political experience on the part of the very persons who, as university professors, historians, philosophers, and men of science, were the accredited custodians of culture. . . . when it came to frantic denunciations of German chemistry, German biology, German poetry, German music, German literature, German philosophy, and even German engineering, as malignant abominations standing towards British and French chemistry and so forth in the relation of heaven to hell, it was clear that the utterers of such barbarous ravings had never really understood or cared for the arts and sciences they professed and were profaning. . . .

This was the dark side of the religion of nationalism; there was another side, an heroic and even a charitable side, and to this I shall return. But the wave of popular emotion which overwhelmed the nation was what we learnt of and what our parents remembered. Nor did it take much imagination to understand that it took a high degree of courage in that dark period not simply to oppose the war—which manifestly was blasphemy—but to treat it in a rational spirit. It is not therefore without some family pride that I record that, whereas the whole of Bloomsbury kept its sanity at that time, my father was the first publicly to challenge the prevailing faith.

He has not come very well out of the spate of revelations and publications of the past few years; his relationship with Virginia Woolf was not much to his credit nor indeed to hers, and he, who admired and respected so many women, is, no doubt for that very reason, the bête noire of militant womanhood today. To this I must add that in his later writings there is much that I could have wished unwritten. Let us then put something in the other side of the balance: in the very first days of the war he tried to make his attitude public in a letter to the press and in 1915 he published a pamphlet: *Peace at Once,* an appeal for an end to the fighting before the cost of victory or indeed of any kind of settlement became too horribly great. Needless to say the pamphlet was condemned to be burned. Some of the predictions, some of the economics that he advanced were of doubtful validity, but with painful realism he saw through the shallow optimism of liberal militarists such as Wells and Gilbert Murray with their slogan that this was a war to end war.

> We want a peace that will end not war, but *this* war. The agreement that will end all war may follow. I

hope it will, but I am not sanguine. This war will be ended by a treaty not unlike other treaties, drawn up after a deal of that particular kind of lying and cheating which is called diplomacy. That is the only kind of peace obtainable at present. Some day the people of Europe may be ready for a real international agreement. They will have to make that for themselves. But this war must be ended by the people who made it—the diplomats.

Europe failed to get the kind of peace for which Clive Bell had hoped, and the treaty imposed by Lloyd George, Wilson, and Clemenceau was even worse than he had feared. Again a voice was raised in Bloomsbury, and this time it was at least heard.

In [an] article in the *Times Literary Supplement,* Professor Skidelsky has commented on Maynard Keynes' attitude towards the Versailles Treaty and has examined the view, that one has often heard expressed, that his attack upon that settlement was analytic, clinical and cold, and for this reason politically impotent. "Far from being an ice cold logician, or someone moved solely by abstract ideas of justice, Keynes was an emotional person strongly influenced by personal affections." Speaking as one who knows nothing of economics and only a little of those political matters which Keynes also claimed as his province but as one who did know Maynard, I should say that this is true. Ultimately he felt policy must be founded upon a respect for values, but the values themselves will be obscured unless we start from a wholly rational point of departure.

Here in the *Economic Consequences of the Peace,* Keynes reminds his readers of these decencies which, in the stress of war, they had forgotten.

> I cannot leave this subject as though its just treatment wholly depended either on our own pledges or on economic facts. The policy of reducing Germany to servitude for a generation, of degrading the lives of millions of human beings, and of depriving a whole nation of happiness should be abhorrent and detestable,—abhorrent and detestable, even if it were possible, even if it enriched ourselves, even if it did not sow the decay of the whole civilised life of Europe. Some preach it in the name of Justice. In the great events of man's history, in the unwinding of the complex fate of nations, Justice is not so simple. And if it were, nations are not authorised, by religion or by natural morals, to visit on the children of their enemies the misdoings of parents or of rulers.

That needed to be said even though politically speaking it was an unpopular thing to say. The appalling fact was that at that moment there was, apart from a small and politically impotent minority on the extreme left, nobody else in England who was ready to say the same thing.

Harrod, in his biography of Keynes, says that given his subject's upbringing and environment it was

> utterly unthinkable that he should take any other view. He reminded English readers of what was bred in their bones. . . . high minded Cambridge . . . the sage thinkers of refined feeling who were his immediate seniors, Whitehead, Trevelyan, Goldie Dickinson, all this world would accept the precept of magnanimity without question. There is no need in this connection to cite G. E. Moore and his Bloomsbury disciples, who may have carried

their idealism to unpractical extremes. Men of culture, in Cambridge, in London, throughout Britain, whose thoughts were conditioned by the reading of Shakespeare and other great masters, men rooted too, even when agnostic, in the ethics of Christianity, thought alike on this matter.

Nor was this all. The politicians were moved by the same noble impulse, as for instance:

> Asquith, Edward Grey, Robert Cecil and other eminent statesmen; from across the sea we had the imperial contributions which, if not specifically British, were derived from the same cultural roots—those of Botha and of Smuts. . . . We may go further and say that this mode of thought was not the exclusive property of deep thinkers or eminent statesmen, but was characteristic of the ordinary British citizen. It was part of the British way of life. History illustrates it.

Harrod does us proud; but it has to be admitted that the really excellent principles which had been bred in our bones were not, in the year 1919, very evident elsewhere. Even in the combination room of Kings the voice of magnanimity was faint—elsewhere it was mute. Harrod explains this strange silence by referring to the vulgarization of British public life, the fact that party politics, and therefore political instruction, was in abeyance, and further that women had been given the vote. Be this as it may, the fact remains that, if we were magnanimous by nature, we had for the time forgotten it. "What was peculiar about Keynes," concludes Harrod, "was that he kept his head in the maelstrom, and voiced the sentiments of the civilisation to which he belonged."

I am not sure what Harrod had in mind when he spoke of the "idealism" of the Bloomsbury followers of Moore, but certainly in their attitude to the war they seem to have adopted a fairly large variety of opinions ranging from that of Leonard Woolf and of Maynard himself who were ready to shoulder what we may figuratively call "a musket" to that of Duncan Grant and Gerald Shove who attempted as far as possible to avoid any kind of aggressive action. They cannot be said to have shared a common philosophy but they did share a common attitude; they refused to accept what I have called "the religion of war"; as Harrod puts it they kept their heads in the maelstrom, and in this Maynard was thoroughly Bloomsbury, he could not share those unreasoning emotions which he himself was later to call "the vulgar passions."

When one rereads the *Economic Consequences,* and how well it still does read, even now when it has retreated so far into the background of history, one cannot fail to notice how Maynard in his attitude and even in the cadences of his prose seems to have *Eminent Victorians* in mind.

One of those choice remarks about Bloomsbury which I treasure comes from the pen of my learned colleague Dr. Christopher Campos of the University of Sussex. "All the works of Bloomsbury," he said, "were about the past." For Bloomsbury read Strachey or the statement becomes too fatuous to be considered; but with this radical emendation, although inaccurate, it is not entirely untruthful. *Eminent Victorians* is political only in its implications. Strachey is indeed at war with the forces of unreason. He attacks popular mythology, the larger than life heroes and heroines: the lady with the lamp, the hero of Khartoum, the great leaders of religion and public school education. Where a politician would have examined the forces which made these great personages what they were, he extracts them from their environment, as an entomologist might with his forceps remove an insect from a flower, twists them and turns them, describes their peculiarities, and, with something between a smile and a sigh, sets them down again. He brings no doctrine to his study but he does bring a gentle power of ridicule which was, in its effect, political and which was enormously welcome to a nation which, in the summer of 1918, was sick and tired of heroics. He avoids the maelstrom and he does so by choosing his subjects in the past.

It is partly for this reason, partly because his prose was, when all is said and done, enormously alive, that Strachey was so acceptable and so popular with all save a few die-hards who cherished our national myths, but it is this also which makes him the least political of these Bloomsbury figures: he laughs at but finally avoids the vulgar passions.

At the opposite end of the spectrum stands Leonard Woolf, a great part of whose incredibly industrious life was devoted to the day-to-day business of politics, who did not disdain the common every-day business of keeping a ward Labour party alive, and who at the same time undertook the education of the British Labour party, a party which, because it was so closely connected with the trade unions, tended to be parochial and largely unaware of the problems of international and imperial policy.

There is a poetry of politics and a prose. The poetry, if you like that kind of thing, is sufficiently exhilarating and may show us the vulgar passions in a not unpalatable form. There are banners and songs, demonstrations and, most seductive, and as I suspect most dangerous, of all, the experience of addressing a large and enthusiastic meeting, a vast and happy crowd which throws back applause and agreement at the speaker so that he feels for a movement magnified by their support and affection. Politics offer a kind of vast ideological agape in which ten thousand people love you because you love what they love and you are all comrades together. That overwhelming experience, made perhaps even more intoxicating when there is opposition to be overcome, was never sought by Leonard Woolf or I think by any other Bloomsbury character. Leonard went for the prosaic side, the side where things are actually done and where the intellect can play its proper part.

But how prosaic it is: Mr. A, Mr. B, Mr. C, and the chairman sit on hard chairs around a hard table in a small and ugly room while Mr. D, rising on a point of order, observes that if the chair will consult standing orders paragraph 8, clause 4, section F/ii, little (e), he will discover—what, it hardly seems to matter, for Mr. A is trying to make his pipe draw, Mr. B is picking his nose, Mr. C is drawing naked women on his blotter, and the chair is having the greatest difficulty in keeping its eyes open. The ability to deal with the prose of politics day after day, year in year out and yet to remain a humane and decent person with a clear sense of the ultimate ends of politics is something rare and wholly admirable; we must have such people if there is to be any hope for us, and Leonard was one of them. At the end of his life in a moment of bitterness he doubted whether he had achieved anything in all his years of labour. On the face of it, his doubt seems understandable; but there is another side to the matter.

Consider this: Leonard started as a severe imperial administrator doing unpopular things and doing them remorselessly, never seeking popularity. When such a man returns after

many years to the old seat of proconsular power, a power now taken by the natives, there is no reason why he should be received with any special kindness. Leonard was welcomed almost as a hero. It is not often that an empire smells so fragrant when it is dead. The reason lies surely in those hours of committee work in London.

That committee work certainly achieved more than Clive Bell's pamphlet of 1915; whether it achieved more than his second pamphlet *On British Freedom* is another matter. At the time this appeal for what we now call a permissive society seemed to have done nothing, and now it is forgotten, nor is it at all likely to be revived, for there is hardly a word in it with which anybody under the age of eighty—apart from a few professional prudes—would be likely to disagree. Then it was too controversial to be accepted, today it is trite. I would like to notice one point in this attack upon British puritanism; it is also an attack or rather an appeal to those who were far from being puritans, those who indulged in what were regarded as the manly vices but who drew the line and drew it savagely in the case of those whose vices were in their eyes unnatural. He speaks with feeling because he could so easily have been one of that majority; many of his friends were homosexuals, but from the idea of homosexual lust he recoiled with deep disgust. Here again it was a matter of rising superior to the vulgar passions, of letting reason direct conscience and invoke fair play.

> With what face . . . can we employ the whole force of the State, while we sit there drinking and smoking and gambling, against two wretches who are doing us no harm but are occupying themselves in a way which seems to them perfectly natural and to us revolting? For very shame we should leave them alone, even were liberty not in question. But liberty is in question. Liberty is not the right of you or me to live as we please; it is the right of everyone to live as he or she pleases provided he or she does not interfere too violently with other people's security and well-being.

Clive Bell knew well enough that his only hope was to win over the great mildly vicious majority, if once they could be argued into a state of tolerant neutrality, the witch hunters and kill-joys would in the end be defeated, as has indeed happened. Whether his forgotten pamphlet did anything to hasten the day of liberation one cannot say. Certainly he knew no such dramatic success as that which Morgan Forster was to achieve in his struggle with British imperialism. Forster, because he was a great novelist, wielded a far more deadly weapon, and his influence was immense. I feel no doubt at all in using that word.

The weakness of the British Empire lay always in the fact that although the machinery of empire rested upon military power, that machinery was itself, in the long view, dependant upon the will of an elected assembly. For a very long time the necessary majority was always there, because British imperialism derived support from both the reformers and the conservatives in Parliament. Conservative sentiment was inspired by the quite simple feeling that, to use Churchill's words, "what we have we hold"; it was enormously reinforced by the liberal view that the British Raj was something honest, incorruptible, benevolent, and efficient. India, in this view, was something not wholly unlike the tidy, well-regulated society which the Webbs had imagined. But it was necessary for those who believed this to suppose that the servants of empire were almost unnaturally intelligent and virtuous; the colonial servant had to be idealized. This idealization was made possible by writers as different as Fitzjames Stephen (Virginia's uncle) and Rudyard Kipling; they gave a convincing picture of the wise, noble, fair-minded white man doing his duty under appalling difficulties and providing government which, even if they didn't like it, the Indians ought to like, it being so very good for them. What opposition there was in the metropolis came from sentimentalists, cranks, and professional revolutionaries, the Mrs. Besants and their like, who were more interested in a kind of religious belief in liberation than in effective government and who could easily be contained both at home and in India by the solid majority of both main political parties.

What Forster did was to destroy the myth on which the theory of the benevolent Raj was built and at the same time to make English people understand the psychological impossibility of building benevolence upon compulsion. His white men ceased to be heroic figures and became ordinary, not particularly virtuous people whom one knew well enough in their native surroundings; his Indians were equally real, and because of this one understood that even the impartial white demigod of fiction with all his divine attributes would, to an educated Indian, have been a quite intolerable person simply because he was imposed by force. The disastrous effects of imperial rule become clear when we see that an Indian and an Englishman may be so well attuned that they could love each other, were it not for the Raj. It is not a matter of idealizing the Indians, their faults are not unnoticed; neither is it a matter of denigrating the British, they are seen, often, in an attractive light. It is once again a matter of going beyond the vulgar passions of both sides, of seeing what people really are like and what a political dispensation can do to them.

As the force of this was born in upon one, as one became convinced of its truth, one began to apprehend India in a new way and without the old comfortable mythology. It began to seem necessary and inevitable that India should rule herself.

I suppose it would have happened anyway; Britain in India like France in Indo-China had to withdraw after the vicissitudes and catastrophes of the years 1939-45, but one can imagine a longer and more exhausting struggle, some kind of foolish rearguard action with its heavy price of misery and bitterness, had it not been for the settled conviction of educated opinion in this country that the imperial cause was hopeless and at bottom indefensible. That conviction was made by many people in many ways but above all, I would suggest, by the genius of Forster. Whether in the scales of history he, who is so large a measure decided the fate of a subcontinent inhabited by many millions of people and at the same time pointed the way to an equally momentous abdication in Africa, is to be accounted a weightier figure than he whose thought has directed the economies of the West for the past quarter of a century I do not know, nor am I qualified to offer an opinion concerning the arguments which are now advanced in opposition to Keynesian economics; even if I were, the political reckoning would still defeat my powers of calculation. But of this I am sure, if anyone had been willing twenty years ago to make any such calculation or indeed to allow at all that Bloomsbury had been one of the political seminaries of the modern world, no one would have seen Virginia Woolf as a maker of political ideologies comparable with the great anti-imperialist or the prophet of deficit budgeting.

In his Rede Lecture, given in the year of Virginia Woolf's death, Forster was inclined to be dismissive. "In my judge-

ment there is something old-fashioned about this extreme Feminism [dear Morgan you little knew to what extremities it might go]; it dates back to her suffragette youth of the 1910's. . . ." He concludes, however, characteristically enough: "The best judges of her Feminism are neither elderly men nor even elderly women, but young women. If they, the students at Fernham, think that it expresses an instant grievance, they are right."

Well, the students at Fernham and indeed those of a great number of other places have in recent years taken Mr. Forster at his word. They do indeed think that Virginia's writings express an instant grievance, and he at least would think that they were right. It now almost begins to look as though in this catalogue of *la littérature engagée*, Virginia stands on a hitherto unexpected level of political importance certainly with her husband, her brother-in-law, and her old friend Lytton, perhaps with Keynes and with Forster, for although the destiny of imperialism and the right management of money are no doubt matters of grave import, here we have a cause in which the rights of one half of the human race is involved and with it the happiness of all.

Virginia's life was not devoted to the cause of feminism; she had other interests and specifically feminist writings form but a small part of her total oeuvre. I suppose that it may also be said that she has in some measure been posthumously enlisted in the ranks, and certainly she might have been puzzled, perhaps a little dismayed, by some of the things that are now done and said in her name. Nevertheless, it was a matter about which she felt passionately. Ever since the time when her brothers were expensively educated at Cambridge while she was left with her sister to do the honours of the tea-table at 22 Hyde Park Gate, she had felt a sense of burning injustice. She was ready in the battle of the suffrage to work humbly in the most prosaic of political occupations and, when the occasion offered, she was delighted to express her views in print.

I have already published my own views on *A Room of One's Own* and said how fair and reasonable an argument it seems to me, how well-presented and how skilfully, how invincibly she marshalls her arguments. Here I need only note, once again, how well she exhibits the Bloomsbury habit of rational thought combined with moral purpose. How, by keeping her head above the maelstrom, she makes her argument with good sense and good humour and perceives the way in which in both sexes' injustice breeds passionate unreason and a descent to the vulgar passions. Women must not only defeat the anger in men but must do so by defeating their own anger; she uses the argument with special reference to the art of the novelist, but it is sound political advice well worth applying to other fields of activity if politics is to be the art not simply of violence but of persuasion.

A Room of One's Own was published in 1929, its successor *Three Guineas* was published almost ten years later, and those ten years had been years of disaster. Throughout the great part of the world the greatest of the vulgar passions, nationalism, was again on the move, advancing from triumph to triumph in Manchuria, in Abyssinia, in Spain, in Central Europe; the uniformed bully was in control, driving the defeated liberals and internationalists before him with irresistible force. The whole climate of the world was changed, aggression had again and again been rewarded, and for those who opposed fascism and imperialism the choice was between surrender and war.

Under these circumstances it was not easy to write a book as playful in tone and as subtly strong as *A Room of One's Own*. One should also add that while this book was being written, its author was still suffering from the terrible strain involved in finishing *The Years* and also from a more private and personal tragedy.

Three Guineas contains much that is wise and true, much that is well argued, and, as one would expect, much excellent writing; but in some ways it is a saddening and an exasperating production and, in the view of many people, the majority I should imagine, by no means so beautifully convincing a polemic as *A Room of One's Own*. There is something forced, something unsatisfactory about the argument which robs it of the power of convincing us. The crucial difficulty as I felt, and as I think a great many other people also felt at the time, was that a perfectly good and sound argument concerning the rights and wrongs of women was involved with an extremely unconvincing argument concerning the causes of war. The connection could only be made by assuming that men, on the whole, wanted war while women, on the whole, did not. Therefore, if women could be given greater political power their innate pacifism would ensure peace. That the great majority of men and women in England at that time feared war and longed for peace but that eventually, if forced to choose between war and capitulation, we should reluctantly opt for war is a possibility which Virginia does not examine.

The proposition that "to fight has always been the man's habit, not the woman's. . . . Obviously there is for you some glory, some necessity, some satisfaction in fighting which we have never felt or enjoyed" surely contains some measure of truth; but it is a truth which, as that ardent feminist Lady Rhondda observed in a letter which she wrote to Virginia, needs to be qualified.

> I hope it may be really true that there is an inherent difference between men and women in the matter of combativeness. If there really is and if we could get the power we might really help. But in my own heart we find, it seems to me, such echoes of the pride, vanity and combativeness I ever see in men that I don't need to have it explained. I know. Still it's true we don't do the actual killing.

But alas, if one is looking for the possible benefits of giving women political power, is this preference for slaughter by proxy so very important an advantage? History, and indeed quite recent history, suggests that feminine rulers are no more reluctant than their brother politicians to use war as an instrument of policy.

So far as one can see there is no very marked difference in the political behaviour of the sexes in this matter. There are hawks and there are doves of both sexes, and I should have thought that this was certainly the case in England in 1936. The trouble at that time was one which afflicted us all; it was to know whether one ought to be a hawk or a dove.

To understand something of the horror of our situation at that time it is useful to remember the allusions which Virginia makes to photographs, photographs which were published in England by the Spanish government showing ruined houses and slaughtered children. At that time we were less used to such things than we have since become. I remember them well, the rows of little doll-like victims with beautiful staring dead eyes and fearfully torn bodies. With fine honesty Virginia reminds us more than once of these sad little corpses. Her

correspondent, a dove who, so far as one can infer, had remained true to his plumage, was of course horrified, so was Virginia. What was he to do about it? "You, of course, could once more take up arms—in Spain, as before in France—in defence of peace. But that presumably is a method that having tried you have rejected."

Here indeed was our dilemma. We had grown up in the aftermath of the First World War and we felt that we knew all about that fraud, that "war to end war"; we knew also how the atrocity story could be exploited. We had sworn that we would never be fooled again, as our fathers had been fooled, those who went out to fight for "Brave Little Belgium." The moral was clear: the people of Madrid must be left to their fate. But, if we did come to that conclusion it was one which no man or woman who hated fascism and all that fascism stood for could take without deep sorrows and some shame.

What Virginia wanted us to do was never made completely clear. To the person who saw General Franco as the aggressor she had indeed little to offer. Women should be given equal opportunities with men, they should be enabled to live on equal terms with men, they should, if they wished to, be allowed to become parsons, and the daughters of educated men should refuse to accept academic honours. All this was, one agreed, admirable in its way. It might eventually in some distant future make wars rather less likely but, even if the necessary legislative measures could have been undertaken overnight, would they have brought a grain of comfort to the people of Madrid?

The militant attitude, that which Virginia describes as being typical of the male sex, the attitude of those who rejoiced in the opportunity to fight for "our splendid empire" was now strangely modified. In this view it appeared that those photographs were mere propaganda. Franco was a great Christian gentleman, he represented all that was pure, noble, and religious in Spain, his enemies were reds and deserved to be exterminated; or, even if it were allowed that there were aspects of the fascist regimes in Germany and elsewhere which were distasteful, even if a few children did get in the way of the bombs, still, it was the lesser evil; Hitler stood between us and bolshevism, and it was right that he should be appeased. Thus the hawks turned into a species of dove even though there were a few who, like Winston Churchill, remained hawkish in the old tradition and urged resistance to aggression if not for the sake of the Spanish Republic at least in the national and imperial interest. These, the patriots of the right, the Churchills, the Edens, did indeed correspond more or less with Virginia's image of the bloodthirsty belligerent male twisting his moustache and fingering his scabbard. But those others, those sad and serious men who could not turn their eyes from the appeal of bombed Madrid, who had been ardent pacifists preaching until the eleventh hour, indeed nearly until it was too late, the need for disarmament, for treaty revision, for colonial home rule but who reluctantly and with many inward doubts shouldered a rifle telling themselves that this was a different kind of war; they were not nationalists, Hun eaters or jingoes—incidentally, one of the first of them to fall was a woman.

Looking for an example of the masculine attitude to war Virginia finds it in the words of a young man who served in 1914: "Thank God, we are off in an hour. Such a magnificent regiment! Such men, such horses! Within ten days I hope Francis and I will be riding side by side straight at the Germans."

How it dates! And how in 1938 it already dated; the innocent optimistic ferocity of the young cavalry officer seemed as much a thing from the distant past as was his horse. We knew at least that war was not going to be like that. Nor did it seem likely that biographers would say of the young men who volunteered for the International Brigade: "From the first hour he had been supremely happy, for he had found his true calling."

But here in fairness to Virginia we must pause. As a general rule the youth of England did not go into the war against fascism rejoicing, but there were exceptions. In any conflict there are likely to be a few pacifists who discover, when it comes to the point, that they have an appetite for war. By a curious fatality Virginia found herself confronted by just such a one in the person of her nephew Julian Bell.

In him the revolution of feeling had been very complete. Starting his political life as an out-and-out pacifist, a member of the No More War movement which condemned violence in any circumstances, he found fierce opposition and a fierce delight in meeting it, until finally he could write, with carefree illogicality, "I believe that the war-resistance movements of my generation will in the end succeed in putting down war—by force if necessary." This intellectual *volte-face* has been well described by Peter Stansky and William Abrahams in their admirable book, *Journey to the Frontier*. It need not detain us; here let it suffice that as early as 1934 he was writing to "B": "I hope I shall spend at least a part of my life—even the last part—on battlefields."

His wish was granted. For a few hectic but not unhappy weeks he saw the realities of war and, even though not in uniform, joined in the battle for Brunete on the Madrid front and here he was killed.

To Virginia this all seemed a senseless horror; she saw the effect of her nephew's death upon her sister, and for her it would have been made no less senseless by the fact that she knew a great deal of Julian's opinions before he left for Spain and more of them when the Hogarth Press published a memorial volume of his writings.

Already, in July 1937, shortly after his death she wrote:

> I suppose its a fever in the blood of the younger
> generation which we can't possibly understand. I
> have never known anyone of my generation have
> that feeling about a war. We were all C.O.'s in the
> Great war [here her memory played her false]. And
> though I understand that this is a "cause," can be
> called the cause of liberty & so on, still my natural
> reaction is to fight intellectually. . . . The moment
> force is used, it becomes meaningless & unreal to
> me.

I do not know what answer she would have given to Julian's remark, "I cannot let other people do my fighting for me," but that she knew that she was dealing with what she considered—and I suppose rightly considered—a typically masculine emotion is clear enough and certainly helps us to understand the generalizations in *Three Guineas*.

These painful and too personal details of old sorrows shall not be prolonged, but they should be mentioned because they do help us to understand the conditions under which the book was written. In her diary (3 June 1938), she said, "I was always thinking of Julian when I wrote," and I have no doubt that she was, and if Julian had been a rather different kind of person, if he had said "I hate war utterly but I hate fascism so much that I cannot avoid it; I go unwillingly to the slaughter," then *Three Guineas* might have been a rather different kind of book. But this was not his attitude, his attitude was: "war is inevitable let us therefore learn the art of war and let us acquire the military virtues."

It is, in my opinion, the fault of *Three Guineas* that this really rather idiosyncratic attitude is generalized as "the fever in the blood of the younger generation," but under the circumstances this seems to me a much more pardonable error than it would be if there had been no hideous private tragedy always in the writer's consciousness.

As I see it, the historic role of literary Bloomsbury was to act as a sort of check or antibody continually attacking the proponents of the vulgar passions in the body politic whenever these menaced the traditional values of liberal England. In a democracy and perhaps in any modern state there is always a danger that men seeking power will rely upon the feelings rather than the intelligence of the masses. Such appeals to the vulgar passions represent a continual danger; fight on till the Huns are smashed, squeeze Germany until the pips squeak, woman's place is in the home, stamp out dirty unnatural vice, keep the black man in his place—exhortations of this kind can be terribly effective. Against them, or most of them, one may oppose the arguments of the Sermon on the Mount: love your enemies, all men are brothers. This Bloomsbury did not do; it had no use either for the hero or for the saint. In its polemics it appeals to good sense and good feeling and relies upon the belief that ultimately the reasoned argument will prevail.

Such an attitude is bound to be highly unpopular, particularly at a time when passions are running high; it is made more so by the fact that it condemns not only the excesses of popular passion but its virtues; the religion of war is not all bad and not wholly absurd—there are certain generous, benevolent impulses which find expression in a nation at war, and the mere feeling of national solidarity has its own magic. To reject, to deride, all the manifestations of violent nationalism in time of war may be reasonable, but it is an unsympathetic stance. Thus the achievements of Bloomsbury, in so far as it made any immediate impact, were mostly confined to the nineteen-twenties and early nineteen-thirties when the political temperature was sufficiently low for a criticism of the vulgar passions to be tolerable, and, even so, much that Bloomsbury advocated had to wait for realization until another war had been fought.

The run up to that war and the war itself were things quite unlike the sudden explosion of 1914. Briefly the situation was that the people of England, like the people of France, did not at all want a war; their passions were not at all engaged. The Germans on the other hand were perfectly ready, morally and materially speaking, to fight. The solution of our difficulty was an inglorious one, the monster called for blood, we fed him our friends until at last France herself was overrun. At that point the vulgar passions did indeed erupt in England, and the nation was united in its determination to resist the aggressor. In all this Bloomsbury's role was perforce negative; in the earlier phases of the process it was not passion but apathy and anxiety which dominated the nation's emotions; in the final phase, although our government did many foolish things and some things that were immoral, the part of the vulgar passions was positive rather than negative. Bloomsbury, which now barely existed, had no part to play.

Three Guineas was written at that point when the nation was still a deeply uncomfortable spectator of events. Like Clive Bell, Virginia Woolf made a reckless but temporary excursion into extreme pacifism and continued to defy, but at the same time to misread, the anxieties of a bewildered people and to write as though she had to rebuke the passions of 1914. Under the circumstances her essay could hardly fail to be a political irrelevance.

But it would be wrong to end on that note. In the last months of her life Virginia made two important political statements: "The Leaning Tower" and "Thoughts on Peace in an Air Raid." I have not time to discuss these works at length but I think that anyone who is willing to do so will be struck by the absence of that painful desire to see in war a manifestation of purely masculine faults and at the same time will observe that she is now at last in harmony with the passions that then possessed the nation. Passions, which, though in the truest sense vulgar, she could now find sympathetic and true. (pp. 239-56)

> Quentin Bell, "Bloomsbury and 'the Vulgar Passions'," in Critical Inquiry, Vol. 6, No. 2, Winter, 1979, pp. 239-56.

THE RESPONSE TO BLOOMSBURY

MICHAEL HOLROYD

[*Holroyd is an English novelist, critic, and biographer who is best known for his two-volume study of the life of Lytton Strachey. In the following excerpt from that work, he examines two widespread misinterpretations of the nature of the Bloomsbury Group.*]

About 1910 or 1911, Molly MacCarthy, the wife of Desmond MacCarthy, in the course of a letter to Frank Swinnerton, described the Stephen family and their associates as "Bloomsberries." The word caught on, and it was not long before Arnold Bennett and other writers outside this tiny oligarchy were referring to Virginia Woolf, as she had then become, as "the Queen of Bloomsbury." The phrase, used mostly in a derogatory sense, was intended to convey a meaning similar to "highbrow," the leader of a semi-precious, brittle form of mock-Hellenic culture, encased in a Gallic frame. But, as Vanessa Bell pointed out in a paper entitled "Old Bloomsbury," the original circle, which had started to meet in 1904 and broke up at the beginning of the war, had really ceased to exist several years before the term became fashionable, and other people inherited its name and reputation.

In the years that followed, two divergent fables of Bloomsbury arose and were given wide controversial publicity. Though opposite in many respects, both fostered one common and fundamental fallacy—that the Bloomsbury Group was a strategically planned and predetermined literary movement, starting in about 1905 and continuing on with various alterations in membership and in emphasis of sacred doctrine until the early 1930s. In much authoritative French, German and Russian criticism of early twentieth-century literature in England, the Bloomsbury myths were, and still are, strongest, perhaps because the individuals involved are less well known. Yet even in England numerous essays and theses have been produced which imply or state categorically that the work of Clive and Vanessa Bell, David Garnett, Duncan Grant, Maynard Keynes, Leonard and Virginia Woolf, E. M. Forster, Lytton Strachey and several others, shares an identical system of aesthetics, the same philosophy and values, all of which stem from *Principia Ethica* and that unsuspecting innocent, G. E. Moore.

Despite their superficial contradictions, the twin concepts of Bloomsbury were closely related to each other, and seem to have taken root from a variety of human motives. Those contemporary writers who were not admitted to the select band thought they saw in it a dangerous organic unity which it did not really possess. Others disliked these eminent late-Victorians for their socially secure antecedents and inherited financial independence. And for still others again, Bloomsbury represented a new exclusive movement, an avant-garde fashion of superior, voluntary ostracism from life—"life" so often meaning a mixture of politics and cricket. At the same time, the more obscure rank and file on the fringe of the set lent currency to this damaging mystique so as to attract unto themselves a reflected glory from the luminaries of W.C.1. Then more recently, studious literary critics, who appear to comprehend next to nothing of the isolated way in which a work of art is evolved, have prolonged the legend to a point where it threatens to become established tradition. With the result that now, what had initially been useful as a quick, rough-and-ready term of classification to the journalist, has been built up into a very real obstacle in the labours of the literary historian and biographer.

The two imaginary Bloomsburies are in amusing disaccord. For many years the Press notices which this largely fictious coterie drew were unfavourable. An over-serious, self-important Bohemia, Bloomsbury was said to be composed of highly pretentious, ill-mannered dilettanti, who derived a masochistic excitement from casting themselves in the role of supersensitive martyrs to the coarse insensitivity of the barbarian world of twentieth-century London. Arrogant, squeamish pedagogues, their desire to take in people whom they affected to consider their antipodean inferiors in every way belied their assumption of conceit. It was all a sham. Their pseudo-Greek culture, their overriding contempt for the less well educated, at whose head they placed D. H. Lawrence, their insularity and the uncertain grimaces, mock-frivolity and infantile practical hanky-panky which passed among them for humour, were in fact outlets of a rigid and reactionary class system such as, perhaps, only England could boast of. Under their wincing, spinsterish mannerisms these world-shunners were immensely, ruthlessly ambitious. They possessed, however, little potent imagination and to attain their aims they formulated a set of restricting artistic rules which had the effect of substituting phoney aestheticism for genuine creative talent. Exclusive not by virtue of any extraordinary ability, but mainly through a supercilious, studiously cultivated priggism, they were too clever by half to perform ordinary services on behalf of the community, yet too "arty" and unreliable to find places in the universities where they might otherwise have been usefully employed.

Strange rites, sinister rituals and unmentionable initiation ceremonies were soon attributed to those who tended the dark flower of Bloomsbury. Beside this exotic growth, the green carnation was a very pallid cosmetic. According to the pugilistic poet Roy Campbell, the Bloomsbury equivalent to shaking hands was a pinch on the bottom accompanied by a mouse-like squeak—a salutation that does not appear to have varied with the sexes. Yet in spite of many such emphatically sub-normal and heterologous characteristics, no one seemed able to agree as to who precisely made up this queer tribal faction. Everyone, of course, knew the chieftains—Lytton Strachey, Virginia Woolf, Clive Bell and so on—but after them, as Osbert Sitwell put it, there "followed a sub-rout of high-mathematicians and low-psychologists, a tangle of lesser painters and writers." Taking a census of these lesser breeds was no easy matter since, as another wit explained, "all the couples were triangles and lived in squares." Free speech, of course, abounded. They held forth in the mixed company of their late-night cocoa parties with the greatest freedom about sexual generalities, but, in the words of E. M. Forster, "would have shrunk from the empirical freedom which results from a little beer." According to Frank Swinnerton, Strachey's level of free speech was somewhat in advance of that of the others, and he dangled before them "the charms of lasciviousness, the filth of Petronius, the romance of the Arabian Nights." Love, too, so the rumour went, was uninhibitedly free; and yet there seemed little enough ebullience:

> Here verse and thought and love are free;
> Great God! Give me captivity.

despairingly cried E. W. Fordham in the *New Statesman*. Second to no one in the violence of his hostility towards Bloomsbury was Percy Wyndham Lewis, who depicted it as a select and snobbish club comprising a disarray of catty, envious and shabby potentates, collectively bent upon getting the better of himself. Making a cultural stronghold of the Victorian hinterland where they resided, these freakish monsters of his imagination had managed to set up a *societification* of art, substituting money for talent as the qualification for membership. Private means, he explained, was the almost invariable rule. "In their discouragement of too much unconservative originality they are very strong. The tone of 'society' (of a spurious donnish social elegance) prevails among them. . . . All are 'geniuses' before whose creations the other members of the Club, in an invariable ritual, must swoon with appreciation." There was another rather curious way in which they differed—namely in their dress. "For whereas the new Bohemian is generally as 'mondain' and smart, if a little fantastic, as he or she can be, this little phalanstery of *apes of god* went the length of actually dressing the part of the penniless 'genius'." They presented, Lewis affirmed, a curious spectacle of a group of financially secure men and women, "drifting and moping about in the untidiest fashion."

And then, of course, there was the Bloomsbury voice, an appendage of the Strachey clan—"bringing to one's mind," Wyndham Lewis commented, "the sounds associated with spasms of a rough Channel passage"—which further cut off this abominable company of citizen-intellectuals from the commonplaces of burgess life. Modelled on the infectious Strachey falsetto—in whom it was doubtless the result of some unfortunate malformation—this rare dialect was taken up and soon spread from Cambridge to Bloomsbury and thence to the outlying regions of Firle and Garsington. "The tones would convey with supreme efficiency the requisite degree of paradoxical interest, surprise, incredulity," observed Osbert Sitwell; "in actual sound, analysed, they were unemphatic, save when emphasis was not to be expected; then there would be a sudden sticky stress, high where you would have presumed low, and the whole spoken sentence would

run, as it were, at different speeds and on different gears, and contain a deal of expert but apparently meaningless syncopation." By this manner of communication, Osbert Sitwell continues, were the true adherents to the cult of Bloomsbury to be recognized. "The adoption by an individual of the correct tones was equivalent, I apprehend, to an outward sign of conversion, a public declaration of faith, like giving the Hitler salute or wearing a green turban."

The great exemplars of Bloomsbury remained for a long time unrecognized by the general public, who are always indifferent to such cliques and juntas unless they are represented as having other than artistic significance. But in the First World War, the Bloomsbury Group was advertised as a left-wing pressure organization which aimed at taking over the Labour Party and establishing an intellectual dictatorship that had little or nothing in common with the ordinary working man. It was hinted darkly that they had built up a sinister hold over the Press, though no one, it seems, thought of asking why, with such a powerful underground network of public relations, they were not depicted by journalists in a rather more attractive light. In the latter part of the war, when most of Bloomsbury came out as agricultural pacifists and rustic conscientious objectors, hostility towards them greatly intensified, and ardent-eyed patriots, who had hitherto dismissed the group as a bunch of harmless prigs, now pointed with alarm to the explosive danger, in the very centre of London, of an obviously militant pro-German force. During the twenties, this hysterical enmity abated: some critics, feeling themselves prematurely outdated, still poured out derision, but many more expressed admiration qualified only by envy. *Queen Victoria,* for example, was greeted with almost universal approbation, and from America Hugh Walpole reported that Lytton Strachey was worshipped, "the God of the moment everywhere."

Probably the chief cause for aversion still felt by some outsiders was the overblown approbation which members of the élite exchanged among themselves in books, and reviews—the most notorious example being Clive Bell's *Te Deum* sung in joint praise of Duncan Grant and Vanessa Bell, which was especially interesting in the light of these artists' very close relationship. But for the most part this reciprocal, closed-shop admiration was greatly exaggerated by outsiders. For in England, where the creative artist is regarded as an antisocial delinquent, writers and painters inevitably turn to one another for the warmth and reassurance with which to lighten their unenviable task, and dispel the cold climate of alien indifference that envelops them. This sympathy—often rather hypocritical and amply compensated for by the adverse criticism expressed to third parties—which members of Bloomsbury extended to one another was interpreted by the less favoured as a peculiarly unhealthy, almost incestuous outbreak of mutual patronage and self-admiration—a view which was neatly summed up in Roy Campbell's narcissistic epigram, "Home Thoughts on Bloomsbury":

> Of all the clever people round me here
> I most delight in me—
> Mine is the only voice I hear,
> And mine the only face I see.

The other popular and complementary version of Bloomsbury may be briefly defined as a counter-interpretation of the same abstract assumptions. The group is said to have comprised an alert and original band of men and women whose splendidly unfashionable and undemocratic enlightenment

Vanessa Bell.

proved too strong for our universities and too idiosyncratic for our uncultured society. The much derided Bloomsbury voice, believed to symbolize in some mysterious way all that the movement stood for, came naturally to Lytton Strachey in whom it was so delightful that it charmed everyone and soon spread equally naturally to his friends. Occasionally it might be put on a little to tease—for there was perpetual gaiety in Bloomsbury—and sometimes, by the sly cadence of a single word—"*Really?*" or "Extra*ord*inary!"—an outsider's truism was horribly crushed—for Bloomsbury could never gladly suffer fools. But there was more to it than this. By certain bold inflections of emphasis, they could induce rather conventional people, who would have resented direct opposition, to question and revalue their long-cherished principles.

During the war, the Bloomsberries were said to have displayed marked moral courage by resisting the attractions of armed combat, and by persisting in their rational aversion to senseless avoidable slaughter. In a time of crass barbarism they alone retained their sanity. When an angry old pullover-knitting lady asked an elegant young man-about-Bloomsbury whether he wasn't ashamed to be seen out of uniform while other young men were fighting for civilization, the reply was confident and characteristic: "Madam, *I* am the civilization they are fighting for." That their united pacifism was practical and common-sense, not cowardly, was proved in the Second World War—a very different affair involving different points of Moorish ethics—when many of them came out as staunch and active patriots. In the opinion of many, including Roy Harrod and Rosamond Lehmann, Strachey also

might have come out strongly in favour of war in 1939 had he been alive. David Garnett is more assured and surprising in his suppositions. "Lytton was maturing and developing," he wrote.

> The rise of Hitler, the abominations carried out in Germany before the war and in almost all countries of Europe and Asia during it, the legacy of evil that the Germans have left behind them in France, would have been to him what the Calas affair was to Voltaire.

> Lytton, if he had lived, would have spoken for mankind on Auschwitz, Hiroshima, the nuclear bomb and torture in France with a clarity and force with which the political leaders of the world would have had to reckon. He could not have been neglected as Russell and Forster are.

In between these wars we are to picture Strachey and other brave Bloomsbury spirits with their copies of *Principia Ethica* debating how best to translate its message into the various realms of art, economics, literature (subdivided into fiction and non-fiction), painting and politics. All members chose or were allocated particular fields in which to work, and spent the remainder of their careers running this specialized school for higher philosophical propaganda.

Such, in essence, is the view of Bloomsbury projected recently, in particular by J. K. Johnstone in his closely reasoned study, *The Bloomsbury Group* [see excerpt above]. Treating the individual differences between the novels of Virginia Woolf and E. M. Forster, the biographies and essays of Lytton Strachey, and the aesthetic criticism of Roger Fry as being merely superficial variations on a generic pattern, he set out to discover some basic agreement between their work and the ethical pronouncements of G. E. Moore. And in the Conclusion at the end of his book, the author recapitulates his findings.

> There is [he declares] a common respect for things of the spirit; a belief that the inner life of the soul is much more important than the outer life of action or the outer world of material things; an admiration for the individual and for the virtues of courage, tolerance and honesty; a desire that man shall be whole and express himself emotionally as well as intellectually; a love of truth and of beauty. And the integrity and careful composition of their books demonstrate a profound respect for art, and a conviction that form is as important to a work of art as content; that, indeed, the two are inseparable since the artist cannot express emotions and ideas adequately except in significant form.

But are these really the qualities by which we recognize the characteristic output of Bloomsbury? Surely in so far as they apply to each and every member of the group they may be said to apply equally to nearly *all* artists—a fact which perhaps explains why so many dissimilar writers working in the first part of the twentieth century, and ranging haphazardly at one time or another from William Gerhardie to F. R. Leavis (who hold nothing in common except their complete independence from the clan) have quite erroneously been classified in print by various ill-informed critics as "typical Bloomsbury." Besides which, not all Bloomsbury did hold these values. A number of them, being devout atheists, cherished little respect for the inner, immortal life of the soul. And if this inner life was counted so very much more important than the life of action, why was it that Strachey chose two queens, a general and a dynamic woman of action as subjects for his biographies? The all-embracing importance which he himself certainly attached to significant form was by no means shared by all the others—Desmond MacCarthy, for example, whom Johnstone mentions as another member of the sect.

Some attempt to interweave these two fables of Bloomsbury into a convincing, comprehensive pattern has been made by the poet Stephen Spender. In setting about this he has been obliged to treat as indivisible "Old Bloomsbury" and the new-look Bloomsbury of the 1920s. The plausibility of his version springs from the literary skill with which it is presented and from his wisdom in not regarding Bloomsbury as a proselytizing body, but simply as a tendency. To qualify for membership, Spender explains, one had to be agnostic, responsive to French impressionist and post-impressionist painting, and in politics a liberal with slight leanings towards socialism. The group represented "the last kick of an enlightened aristocratic tradition." Setting their standard at five hundred pounds a year and a room of one's own (in Virginia Woolf's words), they sought to entrench themselves within an impenetrable, class-conscious ring against the social revolution advancing on all sides. Their tolerant, scrupulous, cerebral flirtation with left-wing politics was an indication of the guilt which they felt at their own inborn and untouchable snobbery. In short, Stephen Spender's Bloomsbury is chiefly sociological—the symbol of a cultured, intelligent, politically naïve era, as seen by a representative of the 1930s—a less aesthetic but more serious and politically responsible decade.

In the sinking of unique differences beneath a general classification, critics have incorrectly assumed that, in matters of taste and judgement, the writers and artists whose names are linked with Bloomsbury were in accord with one another, and that they presented to the world a united if not easily definable front. The danger of seeking common trends within any set of people is that one is obliged to misrepresent, now slightly, now more drastically, the actual individual truth in order to preserve an even façade. In the case of Bloomsbury this has been particularly noticeable, for often the opinions and inclinations of its members were very far from being uniform. Leonard Woolf was always passionately interested in politics; Strachey, though he inclined to become more leftish under his brother James's persuasion during the war, was largely indifferent to political questions of the hour. Clive Bell enthused over the most abstract art; Roger Fry held aloof; while Strachey himself was even more conservative and dismissed Clive Bell's *Art*, in a letter to James Strachey, as "utter balls" (22 February 1914). Though he had learnt at Cambridge to enjoy a literary appreciation of the visual arts, Strachey considered that both Clive Bell and Roger Fry were downright silly in their highflown admiration of Matisse and the early Picasso, and he made some attempt through Vanessa Bell to discourage Duncan Grant from the post-impressionist and cubist influences under which he was falling. As for Maynard Keynes, Strachey maintained that he possessed no aesthetic sense whatever; and Clive Bell held a similar opinion of Harry Norton. Despite his tenuous friendship with E. M. Forster, who was certainly no atheist or even agnostic, Strachey found his novels quite unreadable—a view similar to that which Virginia Woolf affected to hold of his own biographies—while his aesthetic differences with Roger Fry, who injected a mood of earnest Quakerism into the group, effectively stifling the movement towards sybaritic pleasure, were, according to Gerald Brenan, enlivened by

personal antipathy. Nor had Strachey much in common with Arthur Waley whose scholarship he respected—though it does not seem to have inspired him as did the work of the non-Bloomsbury Professor Giles—but whose unremitting shyness exasperated him. Several of the so-called group he hardly knew at all! Sir Charles Tennyson, whom Duncan Grant names as one of the original intimate circle which met at Fitzroy Square, wrote to the present author: "I was fairly often in the same room with him [Strachey], but never really knew him. He was a good many years younger than me and in a more highbrow set, so that I really have nothing beyond a quite superficial and useless impression." Another critical mistake has been to assume that all Bloomsbury was nourished on Moore's ethics. The two Stephen sisters seldom if ever discussed questions of academic moral philosophy, while some later recruits to the group, Raymond Mortimer, Ralph Partridge and Roger Senhouse who were all at Oxford, and Gerald Brenan, who did not go to Cambridge, never burnt the midnight oil over the complicated pages of *Principia Ethica*. Roger Fry, whose aesthetic principles J. K. Johnstone claims were closely integrated with Moore's work, and in a sense completed it, actually dismissed *Principia Ethica* as "sheer nonsense."

According to the Freudian definition, "two or more people constitute a psychological group if they have set up the same model-object (leader) or ideals in their super-ego, or both, and consequently have identified with each other." If one accepts this conception, then clearly Bloomsbury was not strictly a group at all. But it did comprise something—an atmosphere, a mood, a culture which today can be detected in those who have inherited its tradition, Noël Annan, Quentin Bell, Kenneth Clark, Cyril Connolly and others. Although it accepted part of the Apostolic severity—a then idiosyncratic belief in good moral values, true personal relationships, free and more or less reasonable thinking and speech—it was permeated with other qualities that made it very unlike the original Cambridge Conversazione Society. Maynard Keynes and Harry Norton, two Apostles of the highest-grade intellect who belonged to Bloomsbury, were rather despised by most of the others. For Bloomsbury was deficient in purely intellectual interests, being strongly dominated by the visual arts and literature. Science was unheard of, and even music was almost absent.

Fry's influence on the whole climate of English painting was unrivalled. Many of his theories, as Kenneth Clark has written, were "assimilated by those who had never read a word of his writings . . . in so far as taste can be changed by one man, Fry changed it." Ironically, this change in taste may have been more beneficial to painters with whom he was not closely associated than to the "Bloomsbury Court Painters," Vanessa Bell and Duncan Grant. The work of Ben Nicholson, for example, approached theoretically far closer to the Bloomsbury ideal of the significant relationships of line and colour divested of all reference to life and its emotions, than that, say, of Vanessa Bell who, while proclaiming that Fry did not go far enough in his denunciation of representational art, drew inspiration for her best work from the emotional content of the places and people she knew most intimately.

Latterly neither Fry nor Clive Bell much liked the purely abstract art to which their theories so logically led. Fry was seldom interested in people, or the relation of theories to people. He relied for personal insight on the opinions of the three women he loved—Vanessa Bell, Virginia Woolf and Helen

Anrep. His influence on the work of Duncan Grant may well have been particularly inappropriate. Grant was a lyrical painter in the English tradition of Constable, a natural impressionist in his handling of paint, and a born decorator with a flair for inventive designs, for rich and original colour harmonies. His participation in the Omega Workshops gave much scope to these gifts, though the Bloomsbury insistence on amateurishness led to an almost deliberate use of nondurable materials, so that few of his delightful Omega products now survive. But in the 1920s he became a victim to "significant form," following Fry's vehement commitment to the more austere traditions of Cézanne and away from the decorative surface of Matisse and Gauguin from whom he had most to gain. Already by 1923, Fry seems to have appreciated that Formalist principles were not conducive to bringing out the best in Grant's work. With his usual honesty, he confessed to a fear that Grant's preoccupation with solid form and the third dimension was harming the expression of his rhythmic sense and exquisite taste in colour and decoration, all of which were geared most successfully to the flat surface.

Today the name of Bloomsbury is respectable—perhaps too respectable—while at the same time remaining unfashionable. Its collective reputation had declined with that of Strachey's individual status, for its present comparatively low quotation is felt by many to be due to its characteristic Stracheyesque shortcomings—in particular a fondness for exaggeration leading to distortion of truth and a fake aestheticism which was already beginning to bring the author of *Elizabeth and Essex* into some disfavour by 1930 and which has helped to prolong the usual widespread denigration after death—a recognition, David Garnett believes, of the influence he would have exerted had he lived. Of his two Cambridge idols, Lowes Dickinson had devoted his life to the task of interpreting, for the benefit of his compatriots, Plato and the Greek ideals of civilization; while G. E. Moore, in the words of Maynard Keynes, was even "better than Plato." The Apostles who immediately succeeded Moore, and who were led by Keynes and Strachey, modified these ideals, which were later transferred to Bloomsbury, making them more worldly and sophisticated. There these ideals were translated into a neo-Greek cult of friendship, donnish rather than Hellenic. In his book *Civilization: An Essay,* Clive Bell echoed a recurrent theme of Bloomsbury writers: that to be completely civilized a human being must be liberated from material cares and vexations. Indisputably the best example of such a scheme in practice was given by Plato. The Greeks, he pointed out, because they had slaves who freed the citizens from everyday chores so that they might concentrate on worthier affairs, had attained a standard of civilization that came nearer the heart's desire than was conceived possible by any other people in history. And so it should be with Bloomsbury, which took its inspiration from the Greek example. Virginia Woolf's celebrated "five hundred a year each of us and rooms of our own" is anticipated by Strachey in a letter to Duncan Grant (23 August 1909): "Good God! to have a room of one's own with a real fire and books and tea and company, and no dinner-bells and distractions, and a little time for doing something!—It's a wonderful vision, and surely worth some risks!"

Independence founded on the Hellenic model—that was what so many of them aspired to. Strachey had no very scholarly knowledge of the Greek language, but he saw in the élite at Cambridge the centre of a new and expanding civilization, sweetened by the free, venturesome flavour of ancient Greece and the sentiment of Athens. Having shed the dry Victorian

ectoderm, the world seemed solid and fruitful, and he and his friends felt convinced that fresh progress would now start up, and that they would contribute something of value to this advancement. It was this undefined, hopeful, reforming spirit of "neo-Platonism" which spread from Trinity and King's to the literary salons of London that later became recognized as the distinctive religion of Bloomsbury. "A strange thing—when you come to think of it—this love of Greek," Virginia Woolf reflected in her novel, *Jacob's Room,* "flourishing in such obscurity, distorted, discouraged, yet leaping out, all of a sudden, especially on leaving crowded rooms, or after a surfeit of print, or when the moon floats among the waves of the hills, or in hollow, sallow, fruitless London days, like a specific; a clean blade; always a miracle."

The inevitable reaction to this "civilization" came, ironically, from Cambridge itself, starting with I. A. Richards, whose *Principles of Literary Criticism* (1925) aimed at exploding the aesthetic approach to literature, and declared the concepts of "beauty" and "pure aesthetic value" to be myths. From then on literary criticism was to be led by precept rather than example, and under the new dictatorial authority, impressionistic writing lost favour. The disciples of this new "scientific" criticism were irritated by the extreme aestheticism of Bloomsbury, which, they proclaimed, accentuated strangeness and fascination at the expense of heart and conscience, and which had tended to evolve a flippant society where, to use the words of Lord David Cecil, "it is more important to be clever than good, and more important to be beautiful than to be either!"

This new wave of criticism subsequently gained in strength and reached its full impetus under the redoubtable leadership of Dr F. R. Leavis, whose dislike of Strachey—the Mephistopheles of the Bloomsbury World—rested on his antipathy to what he saw as an immature valuation of life masquerading under an air of detached irony, a ruthless sacrifice of truth for literary purpose, and a puny, irresponsible assertion of personal prejudice over serious sociological scrutiny. That divine confluence of Cambridge amenities, hymned by E. M. Forster in his Life of Goldsworthy Lowes Dickinson, was denounced by Leavis as: "Articulateness and unreality cultivated together; callowness disguised from itself in articulateness; conceit casing itself safely in a confirmed sense of sophistication; the uncertainty as to whether it is serious or not taking itself for ironic poise; who has not at some time observed the process?"

The narrowly blinkered Leavis could observe little else. His assumption that good ends could not conflict clothed him in a strait-jacket which prevented him from reaching much that was valuable in literature. To him the charmed circle of Bloomsbury and Strachey's lucid interval of prestige, both of which dominated temporarily the metropolitan centres of taste and fashion, were an unforgivable departure from the great tradition of powerful representative Cambridge men of their time—Sidgwick and Leslie Stephen, Maitland and Dr. Leavis. "Can we," he asked with rather Stracheyesque rhetoric, "imagine Sidgwick or Leslie Stephen or Maitland being influenced by, or interested in the equivalent of Lytton Strachey?" Can we imagine Dr. Leavis being so interested? And this same derisory question is, by implication, repeated again and again and again throughout his writings. For as the conviction of personal persecution thickened round his critical faculties and choked his turgid prose style, so he laid greater and greater emphasis on the inessential trappings of literature, its civic importance and tutorial status.

Despite this low grading from Downing College, many of the King's and Trinity members of Bloomsbury were undoubtedly perfect representatives of the Cambridge culture of their generation. They were passionately attached to the beauty and emotional flavour of the place, and in London looked for what most resembled it. If the Bloomsbury Group has to be treated as a homogeneous entity, then it can in no manner be dissociated from Cambridge, and all Cambridge stood for. The best features in their environment of privileged culture—the play of mind with mind on literary and other topics, and a sane and humane morality—Strachey with his sensitive intelligence and irregular deviations was well qualified to absorb and enjoy. Nor was Bloomsbury the wholly desiccated intellectual unit it is so often depicted as being, but was bound together by intense and enduring personal relationships, which for all their complexity were managed in a very civilized way. For a number of years, however, after going down from Cambridge—years of self-discontent and aimlessness—Strachey also exemplified the limitations of the over-cultivated. By a perversion of language, good taste came to mean not the taste of persons with healthy appetites, but of persons with weak digestions. The collective literary voice—described by F. L. Lucas in a letter to Irma Rantavaara as "shepherd's piping in Arcadia"—is distinctive in its thinness and its clarity. Moreover, the superhuman detachment and remoteness on which they sometimes prided themselves did sever them from the deeper sources which stem out of a raw and vulnerable contact with reality. Romantic academics and quietists, deeply allergic to the humdrum, many of them were, to use the words of E. M. Forster, full of the wine of life without having tasted the cup—the teacup—of experience.

The myths which have billowed up round the name of Bloomsbury are like voluminous clouds arising from a small central flame. For although these friends who met on Thursday evenings before the war shared no fixed and common values germinating from an original gospel, they may be said to have been permeated with similar intuitions. The keystone to these intuitions was a desire for partial independence from the parochial and pretentious fog of Victorianism. They were alike in their determined opposition to the religious and moral standards of Victorian orthodoxy; and in their work they represented more truly than anything else the culmination and ultimate refinement of the aesthetic movement. Essentially they were reformers rather than revolutionaries. Virginia Woolf's concept of a proper financial and domestic standard, no less than Strachey's Preface to *Eminent Victorians,* was a declaration of this spirit of partial independence, a wish to cut herself off from the immediate past by escaping from the family sitting-room to another, unopened wing of the same house—not to a new house or town or country.

And if they looked back to the example of ancient Greece, in the modern world they turned their eyes towards the Continent. Under the delusion that things were ordered differently in France, they made an attempt to establish on French lines a society fit for the discerning minority. "A time had come," wrote Virginia Woolf in her biography of Roger Fry,

> when a real society was possible. It was to be a society of people of moderate means, a society based on the old Cambridge ideal of truth and free speaking, but alive, as Cambridge had never been, to the im-

portance of the arts. It was possible in France; why not in England? No art could flourish without such a background. The young English artist tended to become illiterate, narrow-minded and self-centred with disastrous effects upon his work, failing any society where, among the amenities of civilization, ideas were discussed in common and he was accepted as an equal.

But Bloomsbury did not transform the naturally isolated and painful process of artistic creation. Once "Old Bloomsbury" had lost its bloom and become moribund, the new Bloomsbury Group flowered into a gayer, more pleasure-loving and fashionable clique, tripping in quicker, high-stepping time to the light fantastic twenties. But, like all rather self-conscious "modern" movements, this phase was destined, as surely as the coming of death itself, to dwindle and wither into an extinct relic in the history of artistic taste. For all their elegant and ingenious tinkerings, most of the Bloomsbury writers and artists were unable finally to sever the umbilical cord joining them to the inherited traditions of the past. Theirs was a tenuous transitory mood, largely barren and inbred, a suspension bridge that now forms our authentic link back to the solid cultural traditions of the nineteenth century. They modified, romanticized, avoided those traditions with varying degrees of success. But rather than being the real founders of a new and originally conceived civilization as Virginia Woolf supposed, they were, in the words of Roger Fry himself, "the last of the Victorians." (pp. 36-54)

> *Michael Holroyd, in his* Lytton Strachey and the Bloomsbury Group: His Work, Their Influence, *revised edition, Penguin Books, 1971, 400 p.*

NIGEL NICOLSON

[*An English critic, Nicolson is the son of Harold Nicolson and Vita Sackville-West, whose relationship he chronicled in* Portrait of a Marriage (1973). *Editor of his father's diaries and letters, Nicolson also edited the multivolume* Letters of Virginia Woolf (1975-80). *In the following excerpt from a lecture delivered at the University of Texas Virginia Woolf Centenary Celebration in 1982, he discusses the reputations of Woolf and the Bloomsbury Group in England and America, assesses the veracity of their autobiographical documents, and describes the nature of their association and its legacy.*]

[It] seems to me sad that I should need to come to Texas in order to celebrate the centenary of the birth of Virginia Woolf, since in my own country, which was also hers, there has been no comparable celebration. Last January the memory of her was not just overshadowed, but virtually obliterated, by the memory of James Joyce, who was born only a week later. There were no memorial articles about Virginia in our literary journals as there were in yours, no broadcasts, no gatherings of the faithful outside the many rooms which she could call her own, no society named in her honour as you have, no equivalent to your MLA sessions on the Bloomsbury writers or the symposium you held this summer in West Virginia. In fact, as far as I observed, there was only one reference to her in the British press, and that was a fiendish attack on Bloomsbury in *The Times,* not, as you might imagine, for their opinions and influence, their books or their paintings, but because, in the author's view, Bloomsbury consisted of a set of crashing bores.

This article was not written by some hack temporarily short of copy. It was by Bernard Levin, the most respected, humane and witty of our journalists, a man devoted to literature, music, friendship, art, good living and the charms of a metropolitan society—all things in which Bloomsbury itself delighted. But here he was, swearing a public oath that never, never would he read another line written by or about them, nor subject even his basest enemy to so unpleasant an ordeal. Nobody except myself protested, and my letter was rejected by *The Times*. I argued that, if I had written an article to expose Shakespeare as a bore, or Wagner as a bore, there would have been an outcry, not least from Levin. But everyone was as delighted by his exposure of Bloomsbury as was the crowd when the child remarked that the Emperor was stark naked. Bloomsbury is regarded in England as fair game for abuse. It can be called boring with impunity, although of all the epithets of disapproval which might be applied to it, that is the least appropriate. Why, I wondered, should this be so?

I have a nasty feeling that we have here an example of the most unattractive of our national characteristics, the dislike of the intellectual. We are mentally a lazy people. If Levin says that we needn't read *The Waves* because it is incomprehensible and dull, and that he has no intention of trying to read it himself (which gives away the fact that he has no basis for his judgement), we heave a sigh of gratitude and relief, as if we were told by a bishop that as non-believers we needn't go to church. If, further, Bloomsbury can be stigmatised as having got it all wrong, whatever "it" may be, an aesthetic theory, God, sex or the country's economy, we British will hug ourselves with joy, just as we did some twenty-five years ago when the skull of Piltdown Man, reputedly the oldest inhabitant of our islands, was exposed as the skull of a contemporary ape painted brown. The whole nation hooted with delight, as if we had collectively scored off not only the professors of anthropology but the entire educational establishment. It is much the same with Bloomsbury. Bloomsbury, as the saying goes, was too clever by half, by which we mean that they lacked common sense, were unlovable, too pleased with themselves and despised people like us. They were in fact snobs and, what was far worse in British eyes, intellectual snobs. Those of us who tried to correct this widespread but erroneous doctrine only succeeded in propagating it further. The more information we supplied, the deeper the hostility we aroused. All those letters, diaries, memories and biographies of the Bloomsbury Group and their descendants, all those exhibitions to be visited, houses to be saved, auctions to bid at, lectures to attend, made too great a demand upon the public's patience and appetite for culture. It was like an avalanche of unsolicited mail. People grew to hate the source of all this propaganda, and Bloomsbury-hating became a national sport. Of course, indirectly it was a tribute to them. The degree of hatred a person arouses is a measure of his influence, and I think it remarkable that so small a group of men and women who flourished in the early part of this century, and who are now almost without exception dead, should today cause such annoyance to millions of their countrymen who scarcely know who they were. Ask the average Briton what he knows about Virginia Woolf, and he will give you Albee. I truly believe that, if T. S. Eliot had been more closely associated with the group, he would not have become the cult symbol which he now is. But of course Eliot had little to do with Bloomsbury, and he was an American, which excuses much, even the fact that he was a supremely gifted poet.

So I come to the United States to find kindred spirits who believe with me that Bloomsbury did contribute something of which we are all beneficiaries, and that they were exciting people well worth studying today. Far more attention is given to Bloomsbury in your universities than in ours. At Cambridge, until a couple of years ago, Virginia Woolf was virtually ignored by the English Literature school. At Oxford it is a little better: she is slowly escaping the stigma of second-rateness which the Leavises managed to attach to her for two generations, but she is regarded there more as a theorist and practitioner of the novel than as a central figure in Bloomsbury or a standard-bearer for the feminist movement. But even at Oxford there is nothing faintly comparable to the interest which she arouses in America. There is much more serious work done on her here, more courses, more enthusiasm, but almost too much veneration, I suggest, for Virginia Woolf was only one member of the group, and she should not be allowed to eclipse others who are equally important in the history of ideas—Lytton Strachey, for example, Roger Fry, Vanessa Bell and Leonard Woolf.

The interest in America, it seems to me, operates on three levels.

There is first the scholarly interest, with which I have complete sympathy, the joy of finding unpublished material, the academic sparring, with footnotes as the favoured weapon, the pleasure of turning a multi-faceted glass ball this way and that in order to catch and distribute the light from a slightly new direction, and the feeling that Bloomsbury is still only two-thirds discovered, like an archaeological site in the fourth year of excavation, when its shape and outline history are known, but the potsherds and tesserae seem inexhaustible and the interpretations tantalisingly open to new conjectures. Bloomsbury, like the Old Testament, is exceptionally fertile ground for commentary and expertise, and the fun is that, unlike an archaeological site, each new generation can start all over again.

At the second level of interest is the relevance of Bloomsbury to questions which still concern us today—pacifism, feminism, socialism. While for you Bloomsbury bulks large in the development of these ideas, it is not the same in Britain. We look for our pioneers to the Fabians, the Webbs, Wells, Shaw, Marie Stopes, Ethel Smyth, Millicent Fawcett, Mrs. Pankhurst, contemporaries of Bloomsbury but not by any conceivable definition part of Bloomsbury. I shall have more to say later about their political attitudes. For the moment, I simply call attention to the danger that you may be overestimating, and we underestimating, the contribution which Bloomsbury made to social and political change. You may inadvertently be moulding these characters into your preconceived notions of them, and put into their mouths things that you wish they had said or meant, but which they didn't actually say or mean, while we may be dismissing the important things that they did say as plagiarisms or platitudes. American and British scholarship could grow apart, the British resenting that "our" Bloomsbury has been collared by America, that "our" Virginia has become your Woolf (for it often happens that what one least cherishes one is most reluctant to give away), and America resenting that we are diminishing her, or at least honouring her for the wrong reasons, fixing her like a fly-in-amber as something curious, or labelling her as mad, bad and dangerous to know. At the moment there is some trans-Atlantic suspicion of each other's motives. . . . [I hope] that this unreal controversy will soon settle down to a mid-Atlantic position on which we can all agree. Neither of our nations should try to force Bloomsbury into straitjackets of our own design. The British should not regard it as a historical incident which has little relevance to us today; America must not regard it as a phenomenon of universal significance, much as we regard the small group of men who centred around Jefferson at a time when you were right and we were wrong. You may think it strange, but the first Philadelphia Congress of 1774 means more to a pro-Bloomsbury Englishman such as I than Bloomsbury will ever mean.

At the third level, there's the fascination which these people still exert on us as individuals and in their combined lives. The discovery of their intimacies, the cat's cradle of their correspondence, the vicarious excitement which they generate in us, are pleasures familiar to all of us who have done a course in Bloomsbury. We are privileged to know more about them than any one of them knew about the others. We can catch their portraits not just in one mirror, but in a dozen mirrors set at slightly different angles. For American students, there is an extra perspective, for Bloomsbury men and women existed half a century ago at their prime and 5000 miles from Austin, so that they must appear to you like characters in a Trollope novel, half in your world and half out, recognisably human, moving in predictable ways, yet as different as Canadians are from Texans, but not so different as Texans are from, say, Japanese. Many of the social devices which we take for granted today were first practised by Bloomsbury, such as the techniques of starting or breaking off a love affair, praising a friend's book which we have much disliked without actually lying, or maintaining a triangular relationship without pain to any of the three persons involved. Bloomsbury can still teach us how to live, how to be happy, how to allocate our time. I do not regard as foolish the study of them as social beings, particularly as we are unlikely ever to know so much about an equivalent group of friends. If there is a neo-Bloomsbury Group now forming at Austin, as there may well be, I am prepared to bet that you are not documenting its origins as thoroughly as Bloomsbury did theirs.

Let us pause for a moment to examine the overflowing written and oral testimony that Bloomsbury has left behind. Is it wholly trustworthy? If we are tempted to make of them something which they were not, were they not guilty of deceiving us? Did Bloomsbury invent Bloomsbury? Just because they were so articulate, they were not entirely truthful. I do not simply mean that they told white lies, such as writing to Lady Ottoline Morrell that you loved your weekend at Garsington and were furious at being suddenly summoned home, when out of sheer boredom you had sent the telegram to yourself from the village post office. Bloomsbury were masters of the social fib. No, I mean that they were so anxious to amuse each other that they exaggerated their friends' failings and misfortunes, magnified their own small adventures, and gilded every lily so richly that there was little of the original flower left visible. One early distinction made between the Cambridge and Gordon Square phases of Bloomsbury was that at Cambridge you never said anything witty unless it was also profound, and in Bloomsbury you never said anything profound unless it was also witty. They liked to dress up their compliments as insults, their ideas as mental frolics, incidents as major dramas. In their letters they would assume attitudes familiar to their correspondents but puzzling or shocking to outsiders, use words such as "fascinating" or "deplorable" with certain values peculiar to the group. Within the Bloomsbury language there were a variety of dialects. Thus the Virginia-Leonard baby talk would have astonished Vanessa if she could have read their letters to each other, and Carrington when talking or writing to Lytton Strachey was quite a

different person from when she was with Gerald Brenan. We must be cautious before accepting it all at face value.

Bloomsbury was not exactly malicious. They simply enjoyed epistolary repartee. Let us remember that there was much more leisure then, even for active people. There were servants to cook and clean for them, no television, not many cars or telephones, little moral pressure to be constantly at work. So they had the time and inclination to write letters. It was an accepted social art. The postal services were then very rapid—a letter mailed in London before 10 a.m. would reach its address in Sussex that very evening—and so the letter was the perfect vehicle for the polished insult. It could be replied to before the writer's lips had had time to uncurl. It was like playing a game of chess by telegram. But we who are privileged to read these letters fifty years later cannot, as the recipient could, visualise the affectionate smile that accompanied the written jibe, nor hear in the witticisms a remembered and much loved tone of voice. What to them was kittenish teasing seems to us feline bitchiness; what was expressed with apparent indifference (like her family's joking references to Virginia's terrible bouts of lunacy) was a cover-up for intense concern. Bloomsbury seldom wrote intimately. If one of them wished to express undying devotion, it was suggested, rarely declared. If a letter of sympathy was required, the method was to refer to the disaster in a sentence, and then bury it under the latest gossip, as when visiting a friend in hospital you must toss the flowers on the bed and then quickly tell stories of the world outside. On their work, their writing or their art, they rarely corresponded. A Bloomsbury probationer would soon learn that the one thing you must never do to an artist is ask him what he is writing, painting, composing or acting now.

So the letters, fun to read, may give us quite a false impression of their society, which was fundamentally a serious one. They may lead us to think them frivolous and cold. Surely the diaries will rectify this? No, not entirely. For what is a diary—yours, mine, Virginia Woolf's—but a wineglass to exaggerate the sparkle of our pleasure and a sump for our despair? After keeping a diary for a few months, Byron gave it up, saying that he found that he lied to himself even more than he did to other people. Although we may assert that we write our diaries for no other eye than our own in old age, surely we would not impose this daily task upon ourselves unless we had half an eye cocked upon posterity, and we don't wish posterity to think as ill of us as we periodically think of ourselves. So we write, "The Secretary of State was amused when I told him . . . ," remembering all too vividly how the Secretary was glancing over our shoulder in search of more congenial company. Bloomsbury was quite capable of such self-deceit. We have to guess which of two versions of a conversation or incident is more likely to be true, from our knowledge of the diarists' characters, but it is a chancy business when you are dealing with such chancy people.

Even more misleading are the essays written for Bloomsbury's Memoir Club. Never has there been such self-satisfaction posing as self-criticism. I do not believe that any such club would be conceivable today. I ask you to imagine that your present special group of friends will reunite monthly for the next forty years to read to each other recollections of your time at this university, and that your children, when even they are middle-aged, will still enjoy listening to their dotard parents rambling on about the 1980s, and confessing, indeed wallowing in, the indiscretions of their youth. You wouldn't do it. But Bloomsbury did. That was how the group was kept alive for so long, and one reason why we know so much about them. But the memorialists were not on oath. They were talking to intimates who would know what was exaggerated, invented or grossly unfair, and, although they were far more honest about themselves than most of us, there is a limit. As Mark Twain once remarked, when refusing to write his autobiography, "Confession may be good for my soul, but it sure plays hell with my reputation."

But, if we dismiss as suspect the letters, the diaries, the Memoir Club, surely we can trust the memories of people who knew Bloomsbury at first hand? Certainly not. Beware the eye-witness, and even more the ear-witness. Because they have so often said that such-and-such happened, they are determined that it must have happened, and anyone who challenges their version is met with the crushing rejoinder, "But I was there and you weren't even born." We have all been guilty of making our favourite anecdotes a little brighter with each telling, and gradually establish as truth in our own minds what we once knew was an invention. For years I have told a story about a visit I paid to Monk's House in 1933 when I was sixteen (pause for some elementary mathematics). I was taken by my mother to have supper with Virginia and Leonard Woolf, and the only other people there were Maynard Keynes and his wife, the ballerina Lydia Lopokova. We sat around the fire, all except Virginia, who stood beside it, her elbow resting on the high mantelpiece in the classic pose which flatters the slender figure, and as she talked she stroked her long dark hair. The conversation rose and fell much like the flames of the logs burning in the grate. I forget its subject. But what I remember quite distinctly is that for the first time in my life I discovered in Virginia the distinction between a beautiful woman and a pretty woman, and in the easy association between the four other people something that was almost sublime. There came a moment when Virginia grew excited by the argument, began to speak a bit wildly and wave her hands about, and Leonard, observing her, rose from his chair, walked across to where she was standing, and put one hand upon her shoulder, at which, without a word of inquiry or protest, she immediately left the room with him and went upstairs. They returned some ten minutes later, and nobody asked what had happened, for all except myself knew exactly what had happened. Leonard had recognised the danger signals, and knew that, if Virginia were to continue talking so excitedly, she might trigger off another attack of madness. Later that evening, she took me up to her room, asked kindly after my life at school and gave me a copy of *Flush,* which she had just published.

Well, on occasions, if the audience looked innocent enough, I would add to this story enticing detail, but I firmly believed that, apart from these embellishments, it was a true story. Then I thought that I should check it before retelling it to you today. I went to Monk's House. The mantelpiece was far too high for any elbow to rest upon it. From a photograph, it is clear that Virginia at that period wore her hair closely shingled, and she could not have stroked it in the way that I'd described. Moreover, from her diary (which confirms that Vita brought her younger son with her), I learnt that the other people were not Keynes and Lopokova, but Duncan Grant and Vanessa Bell. At least it was true about *Flush,* for I still have the copy which she inscribed for me that evening.

I got many of the facts wrong, but I do think that I got the atmosphere right, and the relationship between these people.

This is something which the eye-witness can supply and documentation cannot. We can know all there is to know about Abraham Lincoln except what it was like to be in the same room with him. That is why I can answer with some confidence those who maintain that Virginia and Leonard did not get on, that he undermined her confidence in herself, and was indirectly responsible for her suicide. Anybody who ever saw them together will know that this is a travesty of the truth. That single gesture, when he touched her on the shoulder, was almost biblical in its tenderness. The pleasure which they all took that evening in each other's company is something which I could never have invented. I had a sudden glimpse of a society that was different from any other.

But Bloomsbury would deny it. Bloomsbury itself was responsible for the legend that Bloomsbury had never existed, that it was the invention of its enemies. The two people who were most vocal in denying its reality, Virginia and Leonard, were the same two who gave the expression widest currency. Virginia would say to an outsider such as Ethel Smyth, "Why do you call me Bloomsbury? I don't call you Chelsea," but in writing on the very same day to her nephew Julian Bell in China she speaks of Bloomsbury as a shorthand expression which needs no explanation. It was not simply a convenient term to identify a group of friends who happened to live in the same part of London; to her, it denoted a special type of mind, shared characteristics, experiences and beliefs. How can we explain why they rejected publicly a term which they constantly employed privately? I think it was because they were annoyed, as we should all be, to be labelled as belonging to a single set, like a class at school, when they all had friends and careers outside that set, and often disagreed profoundly with those within it. Also, Bloomsbury was used by its enemies in a pejorative sense, and it took some time before Bloomsbury adopted it in self-defence, much as the Conservatives in my country began to call themselves Tories, a name originally used for Irish rogues and marauders and then applied to the Conservatives by their opponents. But Bloomsbury came into general use mainly among the Woolfs and Bells. Fry, Strachey, Forster and MacCarthy rarely employed it, probably thinking it silly and self-approving. And, who, in any case, composed the group? All had different versions. For instance, Roger Fry, writing to Vanessa in 1917, gave his list but omitted Leonard Woolf and E. M. Forster, whom others would consider to be among its stars.

I need not retell the familiar story of how it all started in 1904, when a group of young men who had been friends at Cambridge moved to London and formed, with the two sisters of one of them, Thoby Stephen, the habit of meeting every Thursday evening to discuss art, literature and philosophy. In retrospect, this early period of Bloomsbury seemed its heyday, when its members shook off the habits and prejudices of their parents, and life was just one long festival of youth. The fact that the two young women, Vanessa and Virginia Stephen, were more beautiful than any girl has a right to be, and the young men plainer than any youth has the right to be, didn't matter. They were all in love, man with girl, man with man, girl with man, girl with girl, and January was permanently June. Such, at least, was the legend. But when you come to read the contemporary record, it wasn't like that at all. In 1905, Virginia thus described for Violet Dickinson a Bloomsbury party in Cornwall:

> They sit silent, absolutely silent, all the time; occa-
> sionally they escape to a corner and chuckle over
> a Latin joke. Perhaps they are falling in love with

Nessa. Who knows? It would be a silent and very learned process. However, I don't think they are robust enough to feel very much. Oh women are my line, not these inanimate creatures.

And four years later, in 1909, she writes to Vanessa, again from Cornwall, about another disastrous holiday:

Then there came Lytton, James Strachey and Frankie Birrell, Duncan Grant, Keynes, Norton, and Horace Cole [let me interpolate that this was probably the most scintillating group of young people you could assemble in one room at that time]. They sat around mostly silent, and I wished for any woman—and you would have been a miracle. I talked to Frankie and Keynes most of the time. It was desperate work, like climbing a wall perpetually.

Of course, she was exaggerating. If parties are as awful as this, you do not repeat them every week for years. They must have been more convivial, particularly if Clive Bell was present, for so infectious was his delight that it was impossible not to be happy in his company, and as they grew older they all lost the gravity of their student days. But it is true that at the start the women were stronger characters than the men.

I can just remember what it was like, because once I crept into a Bloomsbury party under my mother's skirts. The room was large, smoky and warmed more by excitement than by any artificial means. There were divans and carpets and gaudily painted walls, like a seraglio, gramophone records on trays and books everywhere. There were people sitting on the floor at other people's feet in no special order of precedence, and there was a lot of noise and laughter, high-pitched and faintly neighing, which ceased suddenly on the arrival of new people such as we. It was extremely alarming, not in the least like Monk's House. Vita Sackville-West was not entirely accepted by Bloomsbury, but she was allowed in as Virginia's friend, and we found a corner where we could sit more or less unobserved. I was given a tomato sandwich. People were jumping up all the time, reaching for a book, peering into a picture, and there was an undercurrent of competitiveness, as if everyone there had to justify their presence each time afresh. If you were under fifteen, as I was, you were left alone. But, if you were even marginally adult, you had to look after yourself, as in a medieval mêlée. It has been recorded that on one such occasion when Virginia told a particularly malicious and funny story, and the laughter had died down, she turned to a girl of eighteen and said, "Now you tell us a story."

Of course it wasn't kind. It wasn't intended to be. Bloomsbury demanded that people should be able to catch the ball when it was suddenly thrown in their direction, and if you missed you weren't asked again, and probably didn't want to be.

In this way they acquired a not undeserved reputation for exclusivity. They seemed to draw a circle around themselves. They were not only alarming, but could be gratuitously offensive. Stories began to circulate in Kensington and Chelsea, such as the reply of a Bloomsbury conscientious objector in the First World War to the question why he didn't want to fight with other young men in the defence of civilisation, "Because I am the civilisation they are fighting to defend." When an eminent composer introduced himself to Lytton Strachey with the words, "I think we met once before, Mr. Strachey, about four years ago," Strachey replied, "A very good interval," and walked on. This attitude is not one which I should commend to you as the best way to make friends and influence people. Bloomsbury would defend itself by saying that honesty is always the best policy, that it did bores good to know that they were bores, and if you have high intellectual standards you should never compromise with philistines. They were equally plain-spoken about each other. If Forster thought *Night and Day* a bad book, he told Virginia so. If she thought Fry's latest portrait of Vanessa poorly painted, she said so, to his face. Let those who accuse Bloomsbury of being a mutual-admiration society look again at the evidence, which proves the opposite. (pp. 7-18)

If it can be said that a group exists, that it has an identity, surely it must hold certain ideas in common and wish to propagate them. Although I am convinced that Bloomsbury did exist, I find it very hard to define what those ideas were, beyond saying, in the loosest sense, that the members of the group were more liberated than their predecessors, expressed themselves more frankly, treated women as equals to men and had a general respect for intellectual excellence. But that does not amount to a doctrine. Michael Holroyd has pointed out that it is quite untrue that they shared a system of aesthetics or philosophy, and that those who claim they did, "understand next to nothing of the isolated way in which a work of art is evolved." Forster's novels owe nothing to Virginia's, Strachey's theory of civilisation little to Clive Bell's. Or take Leonard's thinking on international affairs, or Keynes's on economics: in no way could it be said that either was a Bloomsbury way of thinking. There was a little more community of taste in art and music, and in a negative way they were linked by their indifference to science and religion, as well as by their pacifism in the First World War.

Ah, you might say, but what about their socialism and their feminism? I reply that it would be a bold person who described Bloomsbury as socialist in any sense that we would mean today. In *Civilisation* Bell said that to be completely civilised a human being must be liberated from material cares, like the non-slave Greeks. Therefore, there must be servants and capital and freehold property. Bloomsbury's attitude to servants was that they were necessary and their status almost unalterable. If they resigned or complained, they were exercising their undoubted rights, but it was thought disloyal and a nuisance. Women spent more time scolding and soothing their servants than if they had done the household chores themselves, and they never seemed to resent the loss of privacy which living-in servants entailed. Nor was Bloomsbury really sympathetic to the working classes. With only a slight sense of guilt, they accepted and enjoyed the economic system as they had inherited it. Bloomsbury was quite well off, and a few of them, such as Keynes and the Woolfs, made a lot of money by their own efforts. They thought the class gap unbridgeable. Virginia made a few gallant efforts, as when she lectured at Morley College and organised at Hogarth House meetings of the Women's Co-operative Guild, but her innermost feeling about the working class was that they were curiously dull. She wrote to Margaret Llewelyn Davies in October 1930, "What depresses me is that the workers seem to have taken on all the middle class respectabilities which we have faced and thrown out," and she gave examples, such as they were shocked by a woman smoking a pipe, or reading a detective novel, or admitting that she was fat though it was no fault of her own, or using the word "impure." When she voted Labour at an election, she did so without any deep commitment, for, although she approved in general of Labour's political aims, she disliked intensely the political process. She seems to have agreed with Henry Adams that "politics is the systematic organization of hatred," that oratory is the meanest of the arts, that committees and conferences never achieve anything, and that a statesman was merely a dead politican. I cannot remember a single passage in her writings, public or private, where she expresses admiration for the skills of political persuasion, even on behalf of causes in which she believed, even with Leonard beside her as an example. I hesitate to restate an opinion which has already got me into trouble, but I think I must. Virginia Woolf held strong political views, but did not possess a political mind.

We can all agree that she felt deeply about the position of women. She was not the only person in Bloomsbury to do so, but she was the most articulate. If we look into the lives and letters of other Bloomsbury women, Vanessa, Molly MacCarthy, Mary Hutchinson, Carrington, the Strachey sisters, and the Frys, we miss the note of indignation and challenge that we find in *A Room of One's Own* and *Three Guineas.* Why should this be? It was partly because Virginia was so splendid a standard-bearer that she needed no lieutenants. And partly because Bloomsbury took the women's case as self-evident. All Bloomsbury men were in favour of votes for women, all were in favour of opening the universities and professions to them, and most were husbands or intimate friends of women who had seized their opportunities and made the most of them. Keynes and Leonard Woolf did not disagree with the feminist argument in *Three Guineas,* but they thought it unnecessarily strident, an accusation which Virginia herself brought against Ethel Smyth. Bloomsbury's true claim to a medal in the battle for women's rights lies not in their polemics, apart from those of Virginia herself, but in the way they treated women among themselves. People are people of different types, they thought, and two of the types are male and female, not except biologically a distinction of great importance. This was a rare assumption at the time. (pp. 19-21)

Bloomsbury was a reality. It did exist. It is identifiable with named individuals about whom we can now know a great deal. Separately they achieved much in different fields, and collectively they expressed an attitude to life of which each of us is unconsciously an inheritor. But do not let us exaggerate that inheritance. We must leave ourselves other moulds to break. The best of their legacies is their concept of friendship. Nothing—not age, nor success, nor rivalry in art or love, nor different careers and different friends, nor separation for long periods by war, travel or occupation—ever parted these people who had first come together as young men and women. How surprised they would be if they could know that a man would be lecturing about them in Austin, Texas, nearly eighty years later, but not I think, wholly displeased that he should emphasise, above all other achievements, their gift for friendship. (p. 22)

Nigel Nicolson, "Bloomsbury: The Myth and the Reality," in Virginia Woolf and Bloomsbury: A Centenary Celebration, *edited by Jane Marcus, Macmillan Press, 1987, pp. 7-22.*

FURTHER READING

Annan, Noël. "Georgian Squares and Charmed Circles." *The Times Literary Supplement,* No. 4001 (23 November 1979): 19-20.
Review of Leon Edel's *Bloomsbury: A House of Lions* [cited below], in which Annan criticizes the "swooning prose" of what he considers an overly sympathetic portrait of the group but praises Edel's shrewd analysis of characters and his assessment of the impact of Bloomsbury's behavior on society. Annan also surveys criticism of Bloomsbury, debates the relative importance of an artist's life and work, and speculates on the place of Bloomsbury in the history of ideas.

Anscombe, Isabelle. *Omega and After: Bloomsbury and the Decorative Arts.* London: Thames and Hudson, 1981, 176 p.
Account of the Omega Workshops, a project founded by Roger Fry to involve painters in the decorative arts. Anscombe describes the importance of this project in the careers and personal lives of Vanessa Bell and Duncan Grant.

Back, Kurt W. "Clapham to Bloomsbury: Life Course Analysis of an Intellectual Aristocracy." *Biography* 5, No. 1 (Winter 1982): 38-52.
Examines the Bloomsbury Group through a combination of standard biographical approaches and "life course methods" borrowed from the social sciences. Back explores the development and maintenance of the group, analyzing the interaction between personal and social factors and the role of families in the transmission of ideas.

Bergonzi, Bernard. "The Bloomsbury Pastoral." In his *The Myth of Modernism and Twentieth Century Literature,* pp. 1-11. Brighton: Harvester Press, 1986.
Evaluates recent scholarly works on the Bloomsbury Group, suggesting that the "pull of gossip and biography remains strong, but one must somehow escape it if one is to try to understand the phenomenon or idea of Bloomsbury. . . ." Bergonzi then offers his own assessment of the continuing appeal of Bloomsbury and its place in English intellectual and cultural history.

Bobbit, Joan. "Lawrence and Bloomsbury: The Myth of a Relationship." *Essays in Literature* 1, No. 3 (September 1973): 31-43.
Claims that most accounts exaggerate the animosity between D. H. Lawrence and the Bloomsbury Group, asserting that "the Lawrence-Bloomsbury 'relationship' did not fail; it simply failed to materialize." Bobbit examines several theories regarding Lawrence's attitude toward Bloomsbury and then describes how Lawrence evaluated individual members of the group and suggests how he might have reacted to Bloomsbury's values and ideas.

Campos, Christophe. "The Salon (Bloomsbury)." In his *The View of France: From Arnold to Bloomsbury,* pp. 208-37. London: Oxford University Press, 1965.
Argues that the Bloomsbury Group idealized France as a center for literature and art but had little practical knowledge of the country.

Chapman, Robert. "The 'Enemy' versus Bloomsbury." *Adam International Review,* Nos. 364-66 (1972): 81-4.
Recounts Wyndham Lewis's critical attacks on the ideas and attitudes of the Bloomsbury Group, particularly those of Virginia Woolf.

Chase, Kathleen. "Legend and Legacy: Some Bloomsbury Diaries." *World Literature Today* 61, No. 2 (Spring 1987): 230-33.
Praises the literary qualities of Virginia Woolf's diaries and describes the historical and biographical significance of journals kept by Harold Nicolson, Katherine Mansfield, Evelyn Waugh, and others. Chase suggests that diaries should not be subjected to strict criteria for evaluation but should be judged by individual standards.

Crabtree, Derek, and Thirlwall, A. P., eds. *Keynes and the Bloomsbury Group: The Fourth Keynes Seminar Held at the University of Kent at Canterbury.* New York: Holmes & Meier, 1980, 112 p.

Includes Richard Shone's "A General Account of the Bloomsbury Group" and Raymond Williams's "The Significance of 'Bloomsbury' as a Social and Cultural Group." Shone maintains the importance of studying the members of Bloomsbury as individuals rather than as part of a homogenous group; he then describes the family background of the members, emphasizing the influence of cultural and historical context on the group's development. Williams characterizes Bloomsbury as a "fraction" of the English upper class, suggesting that while they claimed to be against its values, they nevertheless remained a part of it.

Dowling, David. "Bloomsbury Aesthetics." In his *Bloomsbury Aesthetics and the Novels of Forster and Woolf,* pp. 11-28. London: Macmillan, 1985.

Examines Bloomsbury aesthetics, particularly the art criticism of Roger Fry and Clive Bell, for insights into the literary aesthetic underlying the works of Virginia Woolf and E. M. Forster. Dowling asserts that "aspects of the ideas of Bell and Fry—significant form, psychological volume, rhythm, the aesthetic emotion—inform, in different ways, the novels of Woolf and Forster."

Edel, Leon. *Bloomsbury: A House of Lions.* Philadelphia: J. P. Lippincott Co., 1979, 288 p.

Biographical study of the Bloomsbury Group, beginning with the members' early lives and concluding when they reach middle age. Edel remarks of his study, "I resolved to seek my truths in both an episodic structure and a psychological interpretation of Bloomsbury's past."

Fassler, Barbara. "Theories of Homosexuality as Sources of Bloomsbury's Androgyny." *Signs: Journal of Women in Culture and Society* 5, No. 2 (Winter 1979): 237-51.

Outlines theories regarding the causes of homosexuality and the relationship between homosexuality and androgyny that were prevalent in the early twentieth century, suggesting that an understanding of Bloomsbury's attitudes toward these theories aids in interpreting their works.

Gadd, David. *The Loving Friends: A Portrait of Bloomsbury.* London: Hogarth Press, 1974, 209 p.

Account of the Bloomsbury Group which emphasizes the lives of its members rather than their works. Gadd states that his book "seeks to present Bloomsbury as it essentially was and thus point the way for further reading."

Henig, Suzanne. "*Ulysses* in Bloomsbury." *James Joyce Quarterly* 10, No. 2 (Winter 1973): 203-08.

Recounts the debate concerning whether the Hogarth Press would publish *Ulysses* and contends that Virginia Woolf's negative appraisal of the work was influenced by her emotional responses rather than objective evaluation. Henig concludes, "Though the Bloomsbury group stood for open-mindedness, freedom of speech and action, and a certain liberality of lifestyle, its philosophical ethic was not open-minded, free or liberal enough to embrace the publication of such a startling new work."

———. "The Bloomsbury Group and Non-Western Literature." *Journal of South Asian Literature* 10, No. 1 (Fall 1974): 73-82.

Studies Bloomsbury's role in promoting non-Western literature in the English-speaking world. Henig states that Bloomsbury advocated non-Western literature by translating and publishing the works of non-Western writers, by incorporating elements of this literature into their own works, and by influencing young Western writers to examine other literary traditions.

Himmelfarb, Gertrude. "A Genealogy of Morals: From Clapham to Bloomsbury." In her *Marriage and Morals among the Victorians,* pp. 23-49. New York: Alfred A. Knopf, 1986.

Notes an "intellectual and moral lineage" between the Clapham Sect, an influential group of Evangelicals that flourished in the early nineteenth century, and the Bloomsbury group, some of whom were descendants of members of the Clapham Sect. Himmelfarb then examines Bloomsbury's attitudes toward religion, morality, art, and personal relations.

"Commonwealth Literature and Bloomsbury: A Symposium." *The Journal of Commonwealth Literature* 18, No. 1 (1983): 79-130.

Features six articles about the interaction of Bloomsbury and Commonwealth writers. The collection includes personal recollections of E. M. Forster and H. G. Wells by Mulk Raj Anand; an examination of the manuscript of Leonard Woolf's *The Village in the Jungle* by Yasmine Gooneratne; a comparison of Katherine Mansfield's *Prelude* and Virginia Woolf's *To the Lighthouse* by Angela Smith; a discussion of the South African poets Roy Campbell and William Plomer and the Bloomsbury group by Peter Alexander; and a description of the Kikuyu writer Parmenas Mockerie, whose *An African Speaks for His People* was published by the Hogarth Press.

Kramer, Hilton. "Bloomsbury Idols." *The New Criterion* 2, No. 5 (January 1984): 1-9.

Evaluates Frances Spalding's *Vanessa Bell* and Victoria Glendinning's *Vita: The Life of V. Sackville-West,* asserting that the revival of interest in the Bloomsbury Group has been chiefly biographical and that future scholarship on the group should focus more on the members' works than on their personal lives.

Levy, Paul. "The Bloomsbury Group." In *Essays on John Maynard Keynes,* edited by Milo Keynes, pp. 60-72. London: Cambridge University Press, 1975.

An affectionate sketch of Keynes, describing in particular the development of his relationship with other members of the Bloomsbury Group.

Marcus, Jane, ed. *Virginia Woolf and Bloomsbury: A Centenary Celebration.* London: Macmillan Press, 1987, 307 p.

Collection of essays published on the centennial of Woolf's birth to "show the wealth and diversity of Woolf criticism on both sides of the Atlantic." The volume includes Nigel Nicolson's "Bloomsbury: The Myth and the Reality" [excerpted above]; Noël Annan's "Bloomsbury and the Leavises," which considers Bloomsbury and its opponents within the context of modern English intellectual history; and Michael Holroyd's "Bloomsbury and the Fabians," which compares the philosophies of the two groups.

Rantavaara, Irma. *Virginia Woolf and Bloomsbury.* Helsinki: Suomalaisen Kirjallisuuden Seuran Kirjapainon Oy, 1953, 171 p.

Study of Virginia Woolf's life and works that examines "her relation to her intimate circle of friends and the ideas they imbibed in Cambridge."

Rosenbaum, S. B. "Bloomsbury Letters." *Centrum* n.s. 1, No. 2 (Fall 1981): 113-19.

Studies the correspondence of the Bloomsbury Group to demonstrate the role of letters in literary history. Rosenbaum describes how Bloomsbury letters were intended as fictive and nonfictive and as public and private documents, notes the transitive nature of letters and the importance of the relationship between the writer and the intended audience, and emphasizes the interconnectedness of all Bloomsbury's writings regardless of genre.

———. "The First Book of Bloomsbury." *Twentieth Century Literature* 30, No. 4 (Winter 1984): 388-403.

Examines *Euphrosyne,* a collection of poems by Lytton Strachey, Leonard Woolf, Clive Bell, Saxon Sydney-Turner, and others, which was published in 1905. Rosenbaum suggests that this volume is important as the first example of "the kinds of interaction that give Bloomsbury its collective literary significance."

————, ed. *The Bloomsbury Group: A Collection of Memoirs, Commentary and Criticism.* London: Croom Helm, 1975, 444 p.

    Includes reminiscences of notable Bloomsbury participants, discussions of the works of individual members, and examinations of the numerous controversies surrounding the group.

Shone, Richard. *Bloomsbury Portraits: Vanessa Bell, Duncan Grant, and Their Circle.* Oxford: Phaidon, 1976, 272 p.

    Study of the artistic development of Vanessa Bell, Duncan Grant, and Roger Fry.

Thomson, George H. "E. M. Forster, Gerald Heard, and Bloomsbury." *English Literature in Transition* 12, No. 2 (1969): 87-91.

    Analyzes Forster's attitude toward Bloomsbury, focusing on a short sketch in which Forster called Bloomsbury "the only genuine *movement* in English civilization." Thomson maintains that Forster's attitude can be more thoroughly understood by examining how he applied Heard's theories on the relationship between intellectualism and emotionalism to the Bloomsbury Group.

"The Air of Bloomsbury." *The Times Literary Supplement,* No. 2742 (20 August 1954): 521-23.

    Positive review of *The Bloomsbury Group* by J. K. Johnstone [excerpted above], a study which focuses on the three most prominent literary figures of the group: Lytton Strachey, Virginia Woolf, and E. M. Forster.

Turnbaugh, Douglas Blair. *Duncan Grant and the Bloomsbury Group.* Secaucus, N.J.: Lyle Stuart Inc., 1987, 119 p.

    Biography that focuses on the importance of the Bloomsbury Group in Grant's artistic development.

German Expressionism

INTRODUCTION

One of the liveliest controversies in modern humanities scholarship concerns whether or not the German-speaking writers and painters who rebelled against the principles of Realism, Naturalism, and Aestheticism early in the twentieth century represent an artistic movement in the traditional sense of the word; in other words, whether or not there was such a thing as German Expressionism. While the term has been widely used to refer to the theories and products of those avant-garde artists, critics have noted great diversity in both the aesthetic and the ideological aspects of their work, and have therefore questioned their designation as a single movement. It has also been suggested that many works regarded as quintessentially Expressionist, including the paintings and graphics of Edvard Munch, the later plays of August Strindberg, and the novels of Franz Kafka, were produced by writers and artists outside the principal centers of Expressionism in Germany. Attempts to define a specific German Expressionist aesthetic have therefore yielded limited results. However, critics have identified several unifying elements in the works of those authors in question; these include the rejection of previous concepts of artistic form, the tendency to subordinate representation to emotional and visionary experience, which resulted in the creation of a highly subjective universe, and a profound disillusionment with the modern world that often led to social and political activism. As a result, the use of the term German Expressionism is accepted as useful when referring to German avant-garde art of the early twentieth century. Moreover, while critics continue to debate the specifics of Expressionist theories, they agree that those theories had an enormous impact upon the development of modern art.

REPRESENTATIVE WORKS

Barlach, Ernst
Der tote Tag (drama) [first publication] 1912
Der arme Vetter (drama) 1919
Die echten Sedemunds (drama) 1921
  [*The Genuine Sedemunds* published in *Three Plays,* 1964]
Der Findling (drama) 1922
Die Sündflut (drama) 1924
  [*The Flood* published in *Three Plays,* 1964]
Der blaue Boll (drama) 1926
  [*The Blue Boll* published in *Three Plays,* 1964]
Die gute Zeit (drama) 1929
Becher, Johannes
Der Ringende (poetry) 1911
An Europa (poetry) 1916
Verbrüderung (poetry) 1916
An Alle! (poetry) 1919
Benn, Gottfried
Morgue und andere Gedichte (poetry) 1912
Ithaka (drama) 1914

Söhne: Neue Gedichte (poetry) 1914
Gehirne (short stories) 1916
Fleisch (poetry) 1917
Spaltung (poetry) 1925
Das Unaufhörliche (poetry) 1931
Statische Gedichte (poetry) 1948
Der Ptölemäer (novellas) 1949
Fragmente: Neue Gedichte (poetry) 1951
Destillationen: Neue Gedichte (poetry) 1953
Aprèslude (poetry) 1955
Primal Vision: Selected Writings of Gottfried Benn
  (poetry, essays, dramatic sketches, novellas, and short
  stories) 1960
Brecht, Bertolt
Trommeln in der Nacht (drama) 1922
  [*Drums in the Night,* 1966]
Baal (drama) 1923
  [*Baal,* 1964]
Im Dickicht der Städte (drama) 1923
  [*In the Jungle of Cities,* 1957]
Döblin, Alfred
Die Ermordung einer Butterblume (short stories)
  1913
Die Lobensteiner reisen nach Böhmen (novellas and
  short stories) 1917
Edschmid, Kasimir
Das rasende Leben (short stories) 1915
Die sechs Mündungen (short stories) 1915
Timur (short stories) 1916
*Über den Expressionismus in der Literatur und die neue
  Dichtung* (lectures) 1919
Die achatnen Kugeln (novel) 1920
Ehrenstein, Albert
Tubutsch (prose) 1911; revised edition, 1914
  [*Tubutsch,* 1946]
Selbstmord eines Katers (prose) 1912
Briefe an Gott (prose) 1922
Mein Leid: Gedichte, 1900-1931 (poetry) 1931
Einstein, Carl
Bubuquin (novel) 1912
Die schlimme Botschaft (drama) [first publication]
  1921
Goering, Reinhard
Seeschlacht (drama) [first publication] 1917
  [*Naval Encounter* published in *Vision and
    Aftermath: Four Expressionist War Plays,* 1969]
Goll, Ivan
Der Ungestorbene (drama) [first publication] 1918
Der Unsterbliche (drama) [first publication] 1918
  [*The Immortal One* published in *An Anthology of
    German Expressionist Drama: A Prelude to the
    Absurd,* 1963]
Chaplinade (drama) [first publication] 1920
Melusine (drama) [first publication] 1922
Methusalem oder der ewige Bürger (drama) [first
  publication] 1922
  [*Methusalem, or The Eternal Bourgeois* published in
    Seven Expressionist Plays, 1968]

Hasenclever, Walter
  Der Jüngling (poetry). 1913
  Der Sohn (drama) 1916
  Antigone (drama) 1917
    [*Antigone* published in *Vision and Aftermath: Four Expressionist War Plays,* 1969]
  Menschen (drama) 1918
    [*Humanity* published in *An Anthology of German Expressionist Drama: A Prelude to the Absurd,* 1963]
Heym, Georg
  Der ewige Tag (poetry) 1911
  Umbra Vitae (poetry) 1912
  Der Dieb (short stories) 1913
  Marathon (poetry) 1914
Hoddis, Jakob van
  "Weltende" (poetry) 1911; published in journal *Die Aktion*
Kaiser, Georg
  Die Bürger von Calais (drama) 1917
    [*The Burghers of Calais* published in *Georg Kaiser: Five Plays,* 1970]
  Die Koralle (drama) 1917
    [*The Coral* published in *Georg Kaiser: Five Plays,* 1970]
  Von Morgens bis Mitternachts (drama) 1917
    [*From Morn to Midnight* published in *Georg Kaiser: Five Plays,* 1970]
  Gas, I (drama) 1918
    [*Gas I* published in *Georg Kaiser: Five Plays,* 1970]
  Gas, II (drama) 1920
    [*Gas II* published in *Georg Kaiser: Five Plays,* 1970]
Kandinsky, Wassily
  Der gelbe Klang (drama) 1956
Kokoschka, Oskar
  Mörder Hoffnung der Frauen (drama) 1907
    [*Murderer Hope of Womankind* published in *An Anthology of German Expressionist Drama: A Prelude to the Absurd,* 1963]
  Hiob (drama) 1919
    [*Job* published in *An Anthology of German Expressionist Drama: A Prelude to the Absurd,* 1963]
Kornfeld, Paul
  Die Verführung (drama) 1917
  Himmel und Hölle (drama) 1920
Lasker-Schüler, Else
  Styx (poetry) 1902
  Der siebente Tag (poetry) 1905
  Die Nächte der Tino von Bagdad (short stories) 1907
  Meine Wunder (poetry) 1911
  Der Prinz von Theben (short stories) 1914
  Die Wupper (drama) 1919
Lichtenstein, Alfred
  Gedichte und Geschichten. 2 vols. (poetry and short stories) 1919
Loerke, Oskar
  Wanderschaft (poetry) 1911
  Gedichte (poetry) 1916; also published as *Pansmusik,* 1929
  Die heimliche Stadt (poetry) 1921
  Der längste Tag (poetry) 1926
  Atem der Erde (poetry) 1930
  Der Silberdistelwald (poetry) 1934
Pinthus, Kurt, ed.

Menschheitsdämmerung (poetry) 1919
Sorge, Reinhard Johannes
  Der Bettler (drama) 1917
    [*The Beggar* (partial translation) published in *An Anthology of German Expressionist Drama: A Prelude to the Absurd,* 1963]
Stadler, Ernst
  Dichtungen. 2 vols. (poetry and prose) 1954
Sternheim, Carl
  Chronik von des zwangzigsten Jahrhunderts Beginn. 2 vols. (novellas and short stories) 1918
  Aus dem bürgerlichen Heldenleben. 2 vols. (dramas) [first publication] 1947
    [*Scenes from the Heroic Life of the Middle Classes,* 1970]
Stramm, August
  Die Heidebraut (drama) [first publication] 1914
    [*The Bride of the Moor* published in journal *Poet Lore,* 1914]
  Rudimentär (drama) 1914
  Sancta Susanna (drama) [first publication] 1914
    [*Sancta Susanna* published in journal *Poet Lore,* 1914]
  Du (poetry) 1915
  Erwachen (drama) [first publication] 1915
    [*The Awakening* published in *Seven Expressionist Plays,* 1968]
  Geschehen (drama) [first publication] 1916
  Die Menschheit (drama) [first publication] 1916
  Die Unfruchtbaren (drama) [first publication] 1916
  Tropf blut (poetry) 1919
  Twenty-Two Poems (poetry) 1969
Toller, Ernst
  Die Wandlung (drama) 1919
    [*Transfiguration* published in *Seven Plays by Ernst Toller,* 1935]
  Masse Mensch (drama) 1920
    [*Masses and Man,* 1923; also published as *Man and the Masses,* 1924]
  Gedichte der Gefangenen (poetry) 1921
  Die Maschinenstürmer (drama) 1922
    [*The Machine-Wreckers,* 1923]
  Der Deutsche Hinkemann (drama) 1923
    [*Brokenbow,* 1926; also published as *Hinkemann* in *Seven Plays by Ernst Toller,* 1935]
  Das Schwalbenbuch (poetry) 1924
    [*The Swallow-Book,* 1924]
  Hoppla, wir Leben! (drama) 1927
    [*Hoppla!,* 1928; also published as *Hoppla! Such Is Life!* in *Seven Plays by Ernst Toller,* 1935]
Trakl, Georg
  Gedichte (poetry) 1913
  Sebastian im Traum (poetry) 1915
  Die Dichtungen (poetry) 1918
  Selected Poems (poetry) 1968
  Poems (poetry and prose poems) 1973
Unruh, Fritz von
  Offiziere (drama) 1911
  Louis Ferdinand, Prinz von Preussen (drama) [first publication] 1913
  Ein Geschlecht (drama) 1918
Wedekind, Frank
  Erdgeist (drama) 1898
    [*Erdgeist: Earth Spirit,* 1914]
  Die Büchse der Pandora (drama) 1904

[*Pandora's Box,* 1918]
Frühlings Erwachen (drama) 1906
    [*The Awakening of Spring,* 1909; also published as
        Spring's Awakening in *Tragedies of Sex,* 1923]
Werfel, Franz
Der Weltfreund (poetry) 1911
Wir sind (poetry) 1913
Einander (poetry) 1915
Die Mittagsgöttin (drama) [first publication] 1919
Nicht der Mörder, der Ermordete ist schuldig (novella)
    1920
    [*Not the Murderer* published in *Twilight of a World,*
        1937]
Spiegelmensch (drama) 1921
Bocksgesang (drama) 1922
    [*Goat Song,* 1926]
Schweiger (drama) 1923

HISTORY AND MAJOR FIGURES

RENATE BENSON

[*In the following excerpt, Benson summarizes the history of the
Expressionist movement.*]

While critics still are not certain when the term "expressionism" was first used, there is a general consensus that the
movement known as Expressionism first manifested itself in
Fine Art. A convenient date to mark the birth of Expressionism is 1905 for in that year a Paris exhibition brought together such painters as Matisse, Dufy, Derain and Rouault who
were at once labelled *Les Fauves* ("The Wild Beasts") by the
dismayed public and critics alike, because of the new and unconventional ways in which these artists used colour and
form. In the same year in Dresden, Germany, a group of
painters founded *Die Brücke* ("The Bridge"); among them
were Kirchner, Schmidt-Rottluff and Heckel. These artists
saw themselves, like the Fauvists, as enemies of conventional
bourgeois art, and as prophets and creators of new values.
They sought not mimesis but expression of a new vitalist feeling, the *élan vital,* and of their personal vision of the world.
While Impressionism may be said to represent a subjective
rendering of the visible world, Expressionism is basically the
subjective expression of an inner world (vision); in representing his personal reality the artist has to free himself from all
academic rules and traditional aesthetic concepts (especially
traditional norms of beauty). The experience of the reality
must be "immediate" and "genuine"; consequently the artist's *Ego* becomes a primary element in his work. While Expressionism manifested itself in many countries, it has come
to be associated most closely with German art, literature,
music (Schönberg), architecture (Gropius and the Bauhaus)
and film (Wiene's *Das Kabinett des Dr. Caligari;* Murnau's
Nosferatu; Lang's *Metropolis*).

In 1911 *Die Brücke* moved to Berlin which by then had begun
to supplant Paris as the capital of art. In their paintings the
Brücke artists expressed ecstatically (through the use of
bright, contrasting colours and new shapes) their vision of nature (animals, flowers, the sea) and the basic primitive joys

of human nature associated especially with dance, music and
eroticism. Their many religious paintings sprung from an inherent belief in the goodness of human nature, and the Christ
figure became its ideal representative. But, as can be seen in
Kirchner's *Strassen* ("Street Scenes"), 1913-23, they also reflected in their work a progressively sinister vision of a dehu-
manised and self-destructive world.

A second Expressionist group, *Der Blaue Reiter* ("The Blue
Rider"), was founded in Munich in 1911 by Kandinsky,
Marc, Macke, Klee and Jawlensky. Their aim was to revita-
lise art by tapping its primitive origins and in doing so they
emphasised abstractionism (Kandinsky created his first abstract work in 1910); they also stressed the role of the artist
as creator bound only by an inner imperative, and they insisted on the necessity of relating the arts to each other in a common synaesthesia. Kandinsky, who outlines these ideas in his
influential treatise *Über das Geistige in der Kunst* (*On the
Spiritual in Art*), 1912, was a close friend of Schönberg, and
many of Kandinsky's paintings were called *Improvisation* or
Komposition to draw attention to the fact that he wished to
express musical dynamics through colours. Like *Die Brücke,*
Der Blaue Reiter ceased to exist when the war broke out.

In German literature van Hoddis' 1910 poem "Weltende"
("End of the World") is one of the earliest examples of Expressionism:

> The bourgeois' hat flies off his pointed head,
> the air re-echoes with a screaming sound.
> Tilers plunge from roofs and hit the ground,
> and seas are rising round the coasts (you read).
>
> The storm is here, crushed dams no longer hold,
> the savage seas come inland with a hop.
> The greater part of people have a cold.
> Off bridges everywhere the railroads drop.

The poem combines two features of early literary Expressionism: its form is dominated by a series of seemingly unconnected and random images and, secondly, it is apocalyptic in its
denunciation of the bourgeoisie and in its prophecy of imminent doom. Many of the new generation of German artists
shared this apocalypticism which arose out of what Kandinsky
called *Existentielle Angst* ("Existential Fear"); the world had
become transparent, man was naked with nothing to cling to
for support except his own *Ego.* The influence of Nietzsche,
Schopenhauer, Darwin and Freud can be traced in nearly all
these writers.

Heym's poems "Umbra Vitae," "Die Dämonen der Städte"
("The Demons of the Cities"), "Morgue," "Und die Hörner
des Sommers verstummten" ("And the Horns of the Summer
Fell Silent"), Werfel's "Fremde sind wir auf Erden alle"
("We Are All Strangers on Earth"), Trakl's "De profundis,"
"Ruh und Schweigen" ("Quiet and Silence"), Benn's
"Ikarus," Otten's story *Der Sturz aus dem Fenster* (*The Fall
from the Window*) and many others reveal a clear vision of
man's alienation and his existential fear. This feeling of imminent disaster was reinforced by the fact that the newly in-
dustrialised Germany was dominated by a military caste.
Heym's "Der Krieg" ("The War") and "Der Gott der Stadt"
("The God of the City") are among the best examples of
poems which speak prophetically of the outbreak of war and
of a society corrupted by technology.

But despite their fears, these writers were also rebels who proclaimed ecstatically that a better society was to come. "Aus Vision wird Mensch mündig" ("Vision creates Man") wrote Kaiser, and it was this vision of a new world which dominated the first and "ecstatic" phase of German literary Expressionism. Pinthus called his 1919 anthology of Expressionist poems *Menschheitsdämmerung (The Twilight of Humanity)* because the poets "felt early how man was sinking into the twilight . . . sinking into the night of obliteration . . . but he would emerge again in the clearing dawn of a new day." Their ecstatic *Schrie* ("Scream") is for "kindness, justice, comradeship, love of man for man . . ." because "the world begins in man and God is discovered as a brother." *Aufbruch* ("Departure") became the catch-word for the Expressionists' desire for transfiguration or moral regeneration. The names of many Expressionist journals similarly reflect this wish for a new beginning: *Der Sturm, Revolution, Die Aktion, Die weissen Blätter (The White Leaves)* and also Hiller's 1912 anthology, *Der Kondor (The Condor)*. Typically, these writers, led by an overwhelming desire to destroy tradition, rejected the values of the previous generation. The generation conflict, especially between father and son, as depicted in Expressionist literature is unparalled in German writing. Hasenclever's *Der Sohn,* 1914, Sorge's *Der Bettler (The Beggar),* 1912, and von Unruh's *Ein Geschlecht (A Family),* 1915-16, are prime examples of how the young writers viewed the father figure as a symbol of tyrannical authority and constraint; the murder of the father is a recurrent motif expressing symbolically their desire to liberate themselves from a stifling past. Wedekind explored this topic as early as 1891 in his *Frühling's Erwachen (Spring's Awakening).*

A major influence on the language of German Expressionism was exercised by the Futurist Marinetti who in an influential manifesto, *Technisches Manifest,* published in *Der Sturm* in 1912, laid down a number of rules designed to purify the language of bourgeois clichés. Marinetti argued that sentences should depend as far as possible on nouns and verbs and especially on the infinitive which conveyed a sense of the elasticity of experience; adjectives and adverbs were weak and should be avoided; analogies and images—especially those which were striking and unusual—should be used to relate nouns in a meaningful pattern; punctuation might be omitted and capital letters must be used much more extensively. Stramm was so impressed by Marinetti's ideas on language that he destroyed his poems written between 1902 and 1913 and began again. His Expressionist writing, although slight—two cycles of poems, five short dramas (he died in the war in 1915)—is the most abstract of the early Expressionist phase. In his plays he no longer creates characters but types—Man, Woman—who express their feelings "only in sound sequences within the rhythm of their actions." Language used this way comes to be known as *Telegrammstil* and may be illustrated by one of Stramm's poems:

Melancholy

Striding striving
living longs
shuddering standing
glances look for
dying grows
the coming
screams!
Deeply
we
dumb.

Unlike Expressionist painters and composers—the latter in-

fluenced by Schönberg's *Harmonielehre (Theory of Harmony)*—Expressionist writers did not have a clearly defined programme. In fact many of the writers of the first phase did not associate themselves with Expressionism although they were agreed on common aims: the necessity to break with tradition, the need for a new language, the renewal of mankind. Furthermore, many of these writers had no chance to develop their art. Heym, Trakl, Stadler, Stramm, Lichtenstein—now considered among the greatest poets of Expressionism—were dead before 1920, most of them killed in the war.

The second stage of German Expressionism (1917-23) is associated primarily with drama, which is probably its most coherent genre. Its theme, the possibility of man's regeneration, is developed more fully than had been done in Expressionist prose and poetry. Expressionist drama can be traced back to Wedekind (the *Lulu* dramas), Sternheim (*Die Hose*), and especially to Strindberg. His *To Damascus,* 1898, structurally and thematically anticipates many features of German Expressionist drama: the *Stationentechnik* (a non-traditional dramatic technique presenting the various stages of the protagonist's development), the transfiguration motif and the introduction of types instead of individual characters. Because this drama is based on autobiographical events it belongs to the category of the *Ich,* or *Bekenntnisdrama* ("The I," or "Confession Drama"). Sorge's *Der Bettler* follows Strindberg closely. The theme is the development of a youth (Sorge himself) into a man and his transfiguration into a better self; like Strindberg in *To Damascus* Sorge employs dream scenes in order to reflect inner experiences (the murder of the father, the death of the mother, a love-relationship with a woman whose child is from another man). Strindberg's Wanderer eventually leaves the world behind to enter a monastery; Sorge's protagonist, through his transfiguration, also turns into an outsider who in finding his *totales Ich* ("the total I") feels released from all societal bonds and responsibility. The Wanderer and the Beggar are forerunners of *Der Neue Mensch* ("the New Man"), the ideal type of German Expressionist drama, especially that of Ernst Toller and Georg Kaiser.

Because German Expressionist drama was different in its conception of man and in the language with which it treated its themes, it also evolved a distinctive Expressionist style of performance which one critic has subdivided into three general styles: (1) the *Geist* ("Spirit") *performance;* (2) the *Schrei* ("scream" or "ecstatic") *performance;* (3) the *Ich performance.* The *Geist performance,* the most abstract, may be seen "as an ultimate vision of pure expression without the conventional intervention of dramatic characters or intricate plot." Stramm's plays were most suited for this kind of performance. The *Schrei performance* can be compared "to an actual, if hazy, intense dream-state, where movement, exteriors, language, motivation, and inner logic were uniformly and bizarrely warped." The *Ich performance* resembles the *Schrei performance* but differed in that it focused upon a central character. Performances of Toller's *Die Wandlung (Transfiguration)* and *Masse Mensch (Masses and Man)* demonstrated these two styles most purely. Actors often used exaggerated gestures, masks, or mask-like make-up, to portray human types, and "ecstatic" or dynamic speech to convey a renewed or "extraordinary" state of being.

New stage techniques were also developed for Expressionist drama. The main influence came from Appia and Craig whose theoretical works *La musique et la mise en scène*

(1899) and *The Art of the Theatre* (1905) were immediately published in German. Both advocated abstract stage design with emphasis on geometrical forms and "dramatic" lighting. In a 1913 production of part of Gluck's *Orpheus und Euridike* at Hellerau, Appia designed the set which "consisted solely of steps, ramps, platform and directional lighting." The dance sequences choreographed by Jacques-Dalcroze anticipated the stylised movement which was to become an integral part of German Expressionist staging, especially in crowd scenes. Germany's most famous director, Max Reinhardt, used directional lighting in his 1917 production of Sorge's *Der Bettler*. Another influence came from Antoine's *Théâtre Libre* and the German *Stilbühne* which stressed simplicity in staging and dispensed as much as possible with props. But it was the younger generation—some of them pupils of Reinhardt—who fully developed Expressionist stage techniques. The most noteworthy among them were Falckenberg, Hellmer, Fehling, Martin and Leopold Jessner. Jessner became famous for the use he made of Appia's steps; they became known as *Jessnertreppen*—a "single flight of steps raked back from the front of the stage" (as in his 1920 production of *Richard III*). But they were more than just steps, writes a contemporary, Kenneth Macgowan: "Jessner fills his stage with steps. He seems unable to get along without them. He must have platforms, levels, walls, terraces. They are to him what screens, towering shapes, great curtains are to Gordon Craig."

When the Nazis came to power in 1933 they regarded Expressionism as degenerate and set about destroying all evidence of it (no prompt book for any major Expressionist drama production exists). It is a tragic irony, as Pinthus notes, that young German audiences after 1945 only became acquainted with Expressionism through the works of foreign writers like T. S. Eliot, Eugene O'Neill, Thornton Wilder and Tennessee Williams who themselves had been influenced so powerfully by German Expressionists. (pp. 1-9)

> *Renate Benson, in her* German Expressionist Drama: Ernst Toller and Georg Kaiser, *Macmillan Press, 1984, 179 p.*

WALTER H. SOKEL

[*Sokel is an Austrian-born American critic who specializes in the study of German Expressionism. In the following excerpt, he traces the development of the Expressionist movement.*]

Around the year 1910 a far-reaching revolution took place in western art and literature which was not unconnected to the contemporary revolutions in science. Between 1905 and 1910 Picasso and his associates developed Cubism in painting while Apollinaire and Max Jacob started a "cubist" poetry which Apollinaire later called Surrealism. In 1910 Marinetti wrote his manifesto of Futurism. T. S. Eliot began his "Prufrock" in 1910, Joyce his *Ulysses* in 1914. In 1913 Stravinsky's *Sacre du Printemps* threw its Parisian audience into an uproar. Einstein's theory of special relativity had appeared in 1905 and a few years earlier, in 1900, Freud published his *Interpretation of Dreams*. These men and others like them have revolutionized our world and changed our concepts of the universe and of the self. World War I with its aftermath was the political counterpart to this upheaval which is only now settling into a new tradition—the modern tradition. Yet shocking and upsetting as this "birth of the modern era" was for its contemporaries, it was not really new, but a culmina-

tion of developments which characterized the whole nineteenth century and had its roots in even earlier periods.

The term Expressionism designates one aspect of this modern revolution in art and literature, an aspect which between 1910 and 1925 came to particular prominence in Germany. However, its principles transcend national boundaries and form an integral part of modern literature and art. Expressionist principles inform O'Neill's *The Great God Brown;* Thornton Wilder's *Our Town* and *The Skin of Our Teeth;* the Nighttown episode in James Joyce's *Ulysses;* Elmer Rice's *The Adding Machine;* and a number of works by Sean O'Casey, Tennessee Williams, Samuel Beckett, Friedrich Dürrenmatt, and others. However, Expressionism also contains many features that date it as a German phenomenon of the World War I period.

As early as 1901 the term "Expressionism" was coined in France to distinguish Matisse and other "Indépendents" from the preceding Impressionist painters. In Germany it was first applied to groups of painters in Dresden, Berlin, and Munich who followed and developed the style of Van Gogh, Gauguin, and Munch. Soon the term also included the new poetry, drama, and narrative fiction, most of which was first published after 1910 by *avant-garde* periodicals like *Der Sturm, Die Aktion,* and *Die weissen Blätter,* and by progressive publishers like Kurt Wolff in Leipzig, who united many Expressionists in a series of books and pamphlets called *Der jüngste Tag (The Day of Judgment*). Yearbooks and anthologies likewise propagated Expressionism; most important among them was Kurt Pinthus' *Menschheitsdämmerung (Twilight of Mankind*). Its apocalyptic title was ambiguous because the German word *Dämmerung* can mean both "twilight" and "dawn." This particular ambiguity—reflecting extremes of pessimism and optimism—was to become a decisive characteristic of German Expressionism.

We must distinguish between Expressionism as a form of modern art and literature with forerunners in the Book of Revelation, Dante's *Inferno,* the paintings of Bosch, Grünewald, Rembrandt, Goya, and the poetry of Blake, and Expressionism as a peculiarly German phenomenon, which contains elements, notably the violent conflict between the generations, not to be found to the same extent in the experimental literature of other countries. The history of German literature since the 1770's has been marked by revolts of youthful poets and writers which aim not only at a new style in writing but at a new way of life as well. Expressionism is the last and most intense of these revolts. The crest of the Expressionist wave is always associated with the German revolutions of 1918 and 1919, and Expressionism was the target of Hitler's attacks upon "degenerate art" and "cultural bolshevism." On the other hand, the Nazis, members of the Expressionist generation themselves, transmuted the bizarre horror of Kafka's tales and Heym's visions into social reality. Hannah Arendt speaks of the "political expressionism" of totalitarian terror, and a Dutch investigator sees in Expressionist poetry "the shadow of nihilism" that was to thicken into the night of barbarism two decades later. Affinities between the Expressionist longing for the "total man" and the subsequent regime of the total state were pointed out as early as 1933. Günther Anders has accused Franz Kafka of subtle complicity in the creation of the totalitarian frame of mind, and Albert Camus has shed light on the connections between the sensibilities of literary "modernism" and the totalitarian imagination. The fact that Expressionism can be considered the antithesis (and principal

Title page from the catalog of a 1912 Brücke exhibit. From a woodcut by Ernst Ludwig Kirchner.

cultural victim) of Nazism as well as its forerunner and kin indicates the complexity and inner range of this movement as well as its central position in the *Geistesgeschichte* ["history of ideas"] of Central Europe. Thus Expressionism has a double interest for us. On the one hand, it is part of the great international movement of modernism in art and literature; on the other hand, it is a turbulent and vital chapter in the catastrophic history of modern Germany.

It follows from this double aspect of Expressionism that there could not be stylistic unity among the German Expressionists. Political Expressionists like Frank, Rubiner, and Toller put their message above everything else. Other Expressionists, such as Kafka, Trakl, Heym, Barlach, and Benn, put their art above everything else; they were true pioneers of modernist literature and made outstanding contributions to the international movement. Yet there were many Expressionists—Werfel, Otten, and Rubiner, for example—who hardly belonged to modernism. They merely injected revolutionary or ecstatic frenzy into basically conservative forms. Wolfgang Paulsen in his pioneering study on Expressionism, *Expressionismus und Aktivismus,* distinguished between political Activists and genuine Expressionists. But perhaps it would be even more appropriate to distinguish between Expressionists who contributed to the artistic success of the international modern movement (and there are Activists like Sternheim among them) and those who merely copied a few

devices of modernism, but remained basically old-fashioned in their form.

Such very diverse foreign authors as Walt Whitman, Tolstoy, Dostoevski, Strindberg, and Rimbaud made the greatest impact on different Expressionists. However, poets like Werfel, deeply impressed with Walt Whitman's ecstatic humanitarianism, or Rubiner, worshiping Tolstoy's radical negation of esoteric art, hardly could have accepted Rimbaud's coldly "irresponsible" *Illuminations* which in turn deeply influenced the finest poets of early Expressionism, Heym and Trakl. Yet the example of Rimbaud shows that we cannot always draw a sharp line between artistic experiment and spiritual revolt. For the Expressionists, Rimbaud's experimental poetry merged with the legend of his life. Introduced to the Germans in 1907 in a mixture of mediocre translations and fabulous hagiography, Rimbaud became a symbol for the Expressionists. Although Rimbaud repudiated his poetry when he set out to Africa to become a trader, the Expressionists saw his art and life merged in a greater unity: existence as spiritual adventure and the violent rejection of the European establishment, first in its traditional poetry, then in its traditional way of life.

Beneath its stylistic diversity there is an underlying spiritual unity in Expressionism. Kurt Pinthus in the introduction to his anthology *Twilight of Mankind* calls the common element of Expressionist poets "the intensity and radicalism of feeling, world-view, expression, form." Titles like *Twilight of Mankind, Day of Judgment,* "World's End," "Demons of the Cities," *Parricide,* and *Gas* reveal an apocalyptic extremity that gave Expressionism its distinctive note. Ludwig Meidner's paintings of tumbling cities and the Norwegian Munch's painting "The Cry," showing a scream of utter horror, correspond to Expressionist writing. Hermann Bahr, the Viennese critic, playwright, and essayist, singled out the shriek as the chief characteristic of Expressionism. Many Expressionists endeavored to give the same effect on the printed page that Munch achieved in his painting. Some writers expressed their feeling of gruesome urgency by monosyllabic outcries, furious hyperboles, and cannonades of exclamation points. Others, like Kafka with his calmly controlled nightmares or Kaiser with his dagger-thrust dialogues, expressed the same feeling with infinitely greater artistic effectiveness. (pp. 1-4)

German Expressionism sought to be two things in one: a revolution of poetic form and vision, and a reformation of human life. These two aims were hardly compatible. As a part of the stylistic revolution of modernism, Expressionism was too difficult and recherché to serve its didactic and proselytizing ambitions; as a Messianic revolt it had to be too preachy to form a genuine part of modernism. The ideal of "the new man" clashed with the ideal of "the new form," and each interfered with and diluted the other. Only the haze of Messianic enthusiasm which enveloped the movement for a brief span of time was able to conceal the basic contradiction. The moral idealism of activism and the aesthetic idealism of modernism were capable of being confused and seen as one during a few years of intoxication. Both scorned existing reality as the subject matter of art and both strove to create a new reality through abstraction. But no true symbiosis could ensue; and the rapid collapse of the chiliastic illusions brought the underlying incompatibility of the two idealisms quickly to the fore. Shortly after 1920 the two goals of Expressionism—attachment to an objective reality and free creation of a surreality—appeared distinct and irreconcilable. The ethical and the aesthetic wings of Expressionism divorced and this divorce spelled the end of the movement. Henceforth the former Expressionists were to travel on widely separate and diverging routes. Among the international best-sellers and potential Hollywood scripts of Werfel, the Communist clichés of Becher, the Nazi clichés of Johst, and the esoteric abstractions of Benn, there existed no common denominator. Nothing was left to indicate that four so radically different authors had once united in a common movement.

Yet the movement had contained the seeds of all four developments.

Werfel, Becher, Johst, and many other Expressionists, had decided to attach themselves to an objective external reality. They eschewed experimental form and returned to the most conventional and "popular" forms of writing. Werfel's spiritual anchorage became a happy and profitable blend of commercialism and Judaeo-Christian sentiments. Becher and Johst found a spiritual and material haven in the totalitarian movements. Despite the vast differences between them, these three authors (and many others like them) had found solutions to the serious writer's crisis that were alike in one fundamental respect: they decisively accepted an objective communal reality which, while it caused them to repudiate and utterly forsake formal experiment, brought them in return a spiritual shelter, a vast public, and material or social success. Millions of shopgirls from Zurich to California wept and rejoiced over Werfel's *Song of Bernadette,* while a few years later millions of East German school children learned Becher's accolades to Stalin and the proletariat by heart. The world-famous resident of Hollywood and the Communist commissar of East German literature—both former Expressionists—had moved from modernism and the experimental phase of their youth as far as it was possible to move; and in return they had succeeded in different contexts and by different means in becoming truly "popular" authors. Their abandonment of the Expressionist form, however, did not imply a complete reversal of all the tendencies that had inspired them as Expressionists; on the contrary, it constituted the fulfillment of the most basic yearnings of their Expressionist phase. Formal experiment had not been essential to their Expressionism; ethical conviction and moral faith had, and these were fully and consistently developed only in their post-Expressionist period.

Werfel's *Song of Bernadette* was the most triumphant exemplification of the view, expressed in his *Verdi,* that man achieves the truth of his existence when he lives and acts as a vessel of God. By writing a novel in a style as simple, naïve, and conventional as that of *Bernadette,* and utilizing a theme made for capturing the imagination of millions of readers, Werfel successfully emulated his ideal of the artist set forth in *Verdi.* Ironically enough, the actual composer Verdi failed to conform to the ideal of his Austrian admirer. Unlike Werfel's image of him and unlike Werfel himself, Giuseppe Verdi traveled not toward greater and greater simplicity but, on the contrary, toward ever more pronounced sophistication and complexity. *Otello* and *Falstaff,* if not close to modernism, are at any rate far removed from the facile popular style of Verdi's earlier works; they were not the kind of music to be whistled and sung by the masses in the streets. Werfel's image of Verdi (which must be carefully distinguished from the historical reality of Verdi) had been the ideal of his entire Ex-

pressionist period. It arose from his craving to be "related to man." The same ideal guided the planned "theater of the masses" of which Sorge's *Beggar* had dreamed at the outset of Expressionism. For Sorge, as for Werfel, the goal of "the new art" lay in a direction opposite to that in which the main development of modernism had taken place. The goal was the artist's liberation from his ivory tower and his communion with mankind. The kind of art capable of redeeming him from his isolation would also be a soothing solace of the unfortunate, an exhilarating uplift for the underprivileged and oppressed. Not to the connoisseurs but to the masses did these (and most) Expressionists hope to appeal. There can be little doubt that *The Song of Bernadette* achieved this Expressionist goal better than any work written in the Expressionist period. Since its aim was to stir the masses rather than to stimulate aesthetes and connoisseurs, it cannot be denied that the facile best-seller and the Hollywood movie were more suitable for communionism than the esoteric Strindbergian form in which it had originally appeared.

Those Expressionists who joined the totalitarian movements and rose in them to heights of power did not essentially betray their Expressionist past either. Not the experimental form but the ecstatic spirit of revolt had been most remarkable about Johst's Expressionist "scenario" *The Young Man.* Nazism promised a perpetuation of this ecstatic state on a nationwide and eventually universal scale. In contrast to the low-pressure bourgeois world, Nazism raised life to a feverish intensity and endowed the commonplace with a strident pitch. It eradicated the privacy of the person which Expressionism, too, had hated and despised; and it drowned isolation in an orgy of communal festivals. At the same time, it confirmed the insight of late Expressionism which had realized that the Utopianism of the activist phase had to be wedded to an existing objective reality if it was not to perish or degenerate. This context of reality was the national, racial, and linguistic community of Greater Germany which Nazism began to postulate around the same period. The confluence of late Expressionism and Nazism was consequently neither a chance happening nor a reversal of the Expressionist current but a natural denouement of basic Expressionist tendencies.

The consistent continuity between activist Expressionism and Communism is even more marked than that between late Expressionism and Nazism. Whereas Nazism was closely related to the second *Wandlung* or recoil of the Expressionists, Communism was reached by numerous Expressionists in a straight line from their first *Wandlung.* Rebellion against his nationalist-bourgeois family and background which propelled Becher to his activist Utopianism soon afterward led him to Communism; and when he joined the Communist movement in the flush of his activist period, Becher was convinced that he continued to travel toward the same goal—the universal brotherhood of the World Commune. After his decision he merely had to adhere to it inflexibly and ignore whatever discrepancies arose between activist dream and Communist reality. His road from lonely outcast and dissenter in bourgeois Germany to boss of culture in Communist East Germany appeared to Becher as a straight and logical course. The powerful rhetorics of his youthful Expressionism had to be jettisoned and changed into the hollow rhetorics of "Socialist Realism," and in this process his poetry lost whatever vigor and strength it had once possessed. But the ideology, the politico-moral content of his Expressionist poetry, which for Becher as for most Expressionists had been of far more vital relevance than the Expressionist form, had in his view simply matured; it had been freed of youthful naïveté, filled with "concrete content," tempered in "the furnace of social reality," wedded to "the truth of the class struggle." Communist actuality fulfilled Expressionist potentiality. Like Werfel, Becher could feel that he had never betrayed his Expressionist beginnings; and his final dignity and power as Communist commissar of culture probably appeared to him as the well-deserved reward of unswerving loyalty to youthful ideals and lifelong convictions. In contemplating Becher's career one wonders whether one should respect his dogged perseverance, despise his blind inflexibility, or admire his skill in self-deception.

Werfel, Johst, and Becher eliminated all traces of Expressionist form from their mature works; but they retained something of the ethical aspirations that, even in their Expressionist period, had mattered more to them than style. However, the totalitarians among them compromised the ideals they retained with the exigencies of reality until only soothing self-deception could claim these ideals as essentially unchanged. What all of them gained was success in personal terms, a mass audience, the triumph of personal integration and power in the world. What they lost was success in aesthetic terms—the permanence and long-range effectiveness of their works. None of them, not even Werfel, whose literary power far surpasses that of the rest, has achieved the rank of a classic.

Those Expressionists who refused to compromise the ideal of "the new man" achieved neither personal nor aesthetic success. In 1939, when Hitler's avalanche began to engulf all of Europe, Toller committed suicide in New York. Long before that he had been a thoroughly defeated and disillusioned man. As early as 1919, he had seen his cause kill itself at the moment of its illusory triumph. Soon afterward his creative energy was exhausted. After he had given voice to his doubts, self-defeat, disillusionment, and despair in *Man and the Masses, Hinkemann,* and *Hoppla, We Live!,* only pale ghosts of his former dramatic vitality issued from his pen.

Even more acutely than Toller, Unruh experienced premature decline from work to work. Unruh never compromised the symbiosis of ethical idealism and experimental form which had been the most salient feature of Expressionism. He refused to make concessions to the facile formulae of commercialism, or the crippling distortions of the ideal perpetuated by totalitarianism. Loyal to the symbiosis, he remained an Expressionist to the end. But his end was inglorious and pathetic. The symbiosis proved to lack the breath of life. It failed to produce viable works of art. The cancer of high-flown and nebulous oratory that had plagued Expressionism from the beginning devoured in Unruh's later works whatever substance there had been in the works of his youth. While Toller in the act of suicide acknowledged personal defeat and historical disaster in one gesture, Unruh suffered a worse tragedy by failing to acknowledge his tragedy. He survived his own significance without comprehending his fate. Unrecognized in his American exile and forgotten in his homeland, he continued to produce in all seriousness works that could no longer be taken seriously. Since he continued to combine the ethical idealism and the aesthetic-formal experimentalism of the movement, Unruh symbolized better than any of his former comrades the ultimate failure of Expressionism. The continued combination of "the new man" with "the new

form" had led to oblivion—commercial failure and aesthetic bankruptcy in one.

Utter failure or at best ephemeral success was the fate of former Expressionists who placed the ethical ideal, the gospel of moral regeneration, in the foreground. A very different kind of success came to those Expressionists who had never concerned themselves with hope for "the new man," but had developed new forms in which to express their despair. The poetry of Heym, Trakl, Stramm, and Benn, and the prose of Kafka, form that aspect of Expressionism which is alive and relevant today.

Despite his temporary flirtation with Nazism in 1933, Benn never abandoned the experimental form of his poetry; on the contrary, he developed and matured it to ever greater perfection. After the silence imposed on him by the Nazis, he emerged in the late 1940's as the most representative poet of the Expressionist generation, the only one who had remained both a great artist and faithful to himself. He became an inspiring example for the post-Hitlerite generation of German poets and very few escaped his influence. Closely related to that of Pound and Eliot, his style was helped to fashionable prestige by the decisive influence which Anglo-American literature, and especially T. S. Eliot, acquired in defeated Germany. Benn formed the powerful living link in Germany between the new Anglo-American modernism and the long-forgotten Expressionist modernism once indigenous to Germany, and he did not tire of stressing his kinship with the movement from which he had sprung. His ever-continuing and maturing productivity in post-Hitlerite Germany brought about a revival of interest in the roots of this poetry. Editions of Heym, Trakl, and Stramm appeared, and Fritz Martini's scholarly and critical study of the great poets of early Expressionism (1948) formed a milestone in the rediscovery of the movement by the country which had sought to extirpate its memory.

The most successful of all Expressionists, however, was the one least successful in his life—Franz Kafka, whose work had grown from the same soil as that of the early Expressionists Strindberg, Trakl, and Heym, and whose death in 1924 coincided with the death of the movement. Unlike Benn's, Kafka's art is not at one with the form modernism has taken in other countries. It constitutes the most distinctive gift of German Expressionism to the world. Like most Expressionist dramas, Kafka's novels and late tales are parabolic formulations of existential questions. But what distinguishes Kafka from the contemporary dramatists and constitutes his unique significance is his refusal to go beyond the formulation of questions. Kafka's parables show that nothing can be shown. They convey, not ethical doctrine and moral imperative, but fragmentariness, indeterminacy, and ambiguity as last (not ultimate) meanings to be obtained. Thereby they express the innermost truth of an age which has learned that the nature of answers is the posing of questions. (pp. 227-32)

Walter H. Sokel, in his The Writer in Extremis: Expressionism in Twentieth-Century German Literature, *Stanford University Press, 1959, 251 p.*

GOTTFRIED BENN

[*In the following excerpt, Benn, who for a brief time supported the Nazis, defends Expressionism against Nazi-era critics who decried the movement as a degenerate phase of German literature.*]

The leadership of the new Germany is extraordinarily interested in questions about art. As a matter of fact, their outstanding intellectuals are the ones who are concerned whether Barlach and Nolde can be called German, whether a heroic style is possible or necessary in literature, who should supervise the repertory of the theatre and determine concert programs, who, in a word, should make art almost daily a matter of extreme urgency for the state and the public in general. The enormous biological instinct for racial perfection which pervades the whole movement keeps this idea uppermost in their minds no matter how great external and internal political, social and pedagogical problems might be: this instinct tells them that art is the center of gravity, the focal point for the entire historical movement: art in Germany, art not as an aesthetic achievement but as a fundamental fact of metaphysical existence which will decide the future, which is the German Reich and more: the white race, its Nordic part which is Germany's offering, her voice, her call to the declining and endangered culture of the West; and for us it is another indication of what Europe until now cannot see or will not see: to what extent this movement took upon itself tremendous duties and responsibilities, burdened itself with incredible spiritual struggles, struggles which it undertakes for that whole part of the world in which Germany occupies the center.

Surely such an admirable interest in art will tolerate a small objection, something which I would like to discuss in connection with a specific problem in the arts. This overwhelming faith in a new greatness for German art is, at the moment, no less an overwhelming rejection of the style and the will to form of the last German epoch. It has become customary to call this whole period "Expressionist." Today's new faith is in absolute opposition to this previous epoch. At a large political meeting which was held a short time ago at the Sportpalast, Berlin, a meeting which was well covered by the press, the curator of the Rhine Heimatsmuseum in the presence of the ministers of the Reich characterized Expressionism in the visual arts as degenerate, anarchistic snobbism; in music he called it cultural bolshevism and the whole movement he claimed was an insult to the *Volk.* Literary Expressionism is also publicly condemned. A famous German writer has no hesitation about saying that deserters, convicts, and criminals created this milieu, that they advertised their wares with ballyhoo worthy of dishonest financiers pushing watered stock; he said that these artists were utterly corrupt and he named names, including mine.

As a matter of fact, in some histories of literature, for example Soergel's *Im Banne des Expressionismus,* I have been named, along with Heym, as a founder of German literary Expressionism; and I admit that psychologically I am in its sphere of influence and its methods (which will be discussed presently) suit my temperament; now I wish to change and since I am the only one of this dispersed and discredited group who has the honor of being a member of the new German Academy of Literature I would like to step forward once more to speak for this group. To stand up for their names, to recall their spiritual condition, and to direct attention to certain points in their defense, in the defense of a generation whose development was blighted by a war which destroyed many of them: Stramm, Stadler, Lichtenstein, Trakl, Marc, Macke, Rudi Stephan; a generation burdened by monstrous existential problems, the problems of the final generation of a world which in most respects was utterly ruined.

First of all, it must be emphasized that Expressionism was no German eccentricity and it was not a foreign conspiracy either. It was a European style. In Europe from 1910 until 1925 almost no naive—i.e., representational—art was produced, only antinaturalistic expressions. *Picasso* is a Spaniard; *Léger, Braque* are French; *Carra, Chirico,* Italians; *Archipenko, Kandinsky,* Russians; *Masereel,* Flemish; *Brancusi,* Roumanian; *Kokoschka,* Austrian; *Klee, Hofer, Belling, Poelzig, Gropius, Kirchner, Schmidt-Rottluff,* Germans; here the West was assembled and not one of those named was anything but Aryan. In music *Stravinsky* is Russian; *Bartók,* Hungarian; *Malipiero,* Italian; *Alban Berg, Křenek,* Austrian; *Honegger,* Swiss; *Hindemith,* German; and racially all are pure Europeans. In literature: *Heym, Stramm, Georg Kaiser, Edschmid, Wedekind, Sorge, Sack, Goering, Johannes R. Becher, Däubler, Stadler, Trakl, Loerke, Brecht,* pure Germans. Furthermore, *Hanns Johst* also came out of this great wave of talent. We are faced, then, by an impressive closed front of artists who, without exception, are European. The outbreak of a new style on so broad a front speaks without need for further explanation for the absolutely autochthonous, elementary directness of its forms, for a new European consciousness. By no means can it be explained as a mere rebellion against earlier styles: Naturalism or Impressionism; actually it is a new form of historical existence. An existence in the formal as well as in the human sense which is of an avowed revolutionary character; in Italy the major proponent of this new existence, *Marinetti,* advocated in his basic manifesto of 1909: "the love of danger," "on becoming accustomed to energy and bold action," "aggressiveness," "the death leap," "beautiful ideas that kill." Moreover, fascism has adopted this movement and Marinetti today is "Excellency" and president of the Roman Academy of Arts. "Adopted" is not even the right word; Futurism helped create fascism; the black shirt, the battle cry, and the war song, the Giovinezza, all derive from "Arditismus," the warlike section of Futurism.

Futurism as a style, also called Cubism and frequently designated as "Expressionism" in Germany, is greatly varied in appearance, but it is unified in its basic intention which is to shatter reality, to go to the very roots of things ruthlessly until they are no longer individually or sensuously colored or falsified or displaced in a changed and weakened form in the psychological process; but instead await in the acausal silence of the absolute ego the rare summons of the creative spirit—this style had been anticipated throughout the nineteenth century. In *Goethe* we can find countless passages which are pure Expressionism. For example, such well-known verses as these: "toothless pines chatter and the tottering skeleton, intoxicated by the last ray . . . ," etc. Here, instead of rational meaning, an emotional mood connects the different verses. No particular theme is exclusively developed, but rather feelings, magical associations of a purely transcendental sort determine relationships. The second part of *Faust* contains innumerable examples of this, as does most of Goethe's work from his old age. The same things holds true for *Kleist;* his "Penthesilea" is a dramatically ordered, versified orgy of pure emotion. There is also *Nietzsche,* his as well as Hölderlin's fragmented lyric poems are pure Expressionism: loading a word, a few words with an enormous amount of creative tension, actually it is more a matter of *taking hold of words in a state of high tension;* and then these mystically captured words become alive with a truly real and inexplicable suggestive power. In the modern period we can point to *Carl Hauptmann*'s richly expressive pieces; and we find in *Paul Fechter*'s history of literature (someone who by no means is sympathetic to Expressionism) the interesting reference to *Hermann Conradi* (1862-90), whom Fechter interprets as anticipating *Joyce, Proust,* and *Jahnn;* yes, and *Freud* too; "for Conradi, analysis is an end in itself," says Fechter, it penetrates into "inner reality." This inner reality and its direct revelation as form, that is precisely the art under discussion: we can find it already in parts of *Richard Wagner*'s absolute music; *Nietzsche* called it "his flight into primeval states." In painting, *Cézanne,* France; *Van Gogh,* Holland; *Munch,* Norway are both heralds and consummators of this style. Actually we can truthfully say that Expressionism is part of all art; but only at a certain time (namely the period which has just passed), when it springs from many men does it determine a style and an age.

I said, that in Europe between 1910 and 1925 there was hardly another style except an antinaturalistic style; there was also no reality, at most only fragments of reality. "Reality" was a capitalistic concept, "Reality," that meant real estate, industrial products, mortgages, everything which could be given a price by merchants and middlemen. "Reality," that was Darwinism, international steeplechases and everything else reserved for the privileged classes. "Reality," that was war, famine, historical humiliations, lawlessness, and naked power. Spirit had no reality. It turned to its own inner reality, its own existence, its biology, its development, its mixture of physiological and psychological forces, its own creation, its illumination. The method used to experience this, to possess this was to intensify the creative power of the spirit, like something from India; it was ecstasy, a particular kind of spiritual intoxication. And ecstasies are hardly disreputable from the ethnological point of view. Dionysos came to stolid shepherds and under his orphic spell these unhysterical mountain people were stirred to frenzy; and later *Master Eckhart* and *Jakob Böhme* had visions. Blissful encounters, old as the hills! Naturally, *Schiller, Bach,* and *Dürer* are important, these treasures, these streams of life-giving energy, but they had a different sort of existence, they derived from a different anthropological source, they had a different nature; but nature was also *here,* the nature of 1910 to 1925; yes, and more than nature was here; here we find a complete identity between the spirit and the epoch.

Reality—Europe's demonic concept: only that age, only those generations which had no doubts about it were truly fortunate; in the Middle Ages reality was first profoundly shaken when religious unity was disrupted; it has been shaken to its very foundations since 1900 with the destruction of that scientific reality which for the past 400 years had defined "reality." Since science could only destroy the old reality, people looked at the new reality within themselves and it looked back. Externally the oldest remnants of the former reality disintegrated and all that was left were relations and functions; crazy, rootless utopias; humanitarian, socialist, or pacifist wastepaper; merely so much action and business for its own sake; meaning and purpose became imaginary, formless, and ideological although a conspicuous flora and fauna of little business enterprises flourished, forever sneaking about under cover of function and concept. Nature disintegrated, history disintegrated. The old realities of space and time: merely functions of consciousness; even the most concrete powers such as state and society could no longer be understood, only business and action for its own sake—the striking remark of Ford, brilliant as a maxim for philosophy and business: *First make autos, streets will follow;* meaning: first develop needs and the means for their satisfaction will

automatically follow; first initiate activity and then it will proceed of its own accord; yes, it proceeded of its own accord, an ingenious psychology for the white race: impoverished but maniacal; undernourished but lofty-minded; with 20 marks in their pocket they gain a perspective of Sils Maria and Golgotha and buy themselves formulae for processes and functions—that was 1920-25, that was the world dedicated to decline; its business, that was functionalism ripe for the storm which then came, but previously there was only that handful of Expressionists, those believers in a new reality and an old absolute who opposed their own existence to this disintegration with an unprecedented fervor, with the asceticism of saints and in the certain knowledge that they would suffer hunger and ridicule.

This last great art movement of Europe, this last great creative tension which was so involved in an irresistible destiny that a style developed out of it, how remarkable that it should be so utterly rejected today! Basically this Expressionism was the Absolute, the antiliberal function of Spirit at the very time when corrupt scribblers threw garbage down for the nation to gobble up: fiction writers posing as epic poets with their mishmash of faded psychology and miserable bourgeois philosophy; composers of popular ditties and nightclub comics from a world of bars and low dives. In any case there was struggle, yes, a clearcut historical issue. The question with which Kant had ended one epoch in philosophy and inaugurated another 150 years ago—"How is experience possible?"—was transferred to aesthetics—*How can one create form?* The creation of form was no longer an artistic problem, it was a riddle, a mystery as to why man created art in the first place, why he needs art; what a singular experience within the sphere of European nihilism! It was nothing else but intellectualism and absolutely destructive. As a major issue it was part of that compulsion of the twentieth century, part of that obsession to make conscious the unconscious, to comprehend experience only as scientific knowledge, emotion as perception, the soul as psychology, and love as only a neurosis. It also reflected the general mania for analyzing and dissolving the primeval barriers of silent order, for individualistically attacking the physiological and organic habits developed with great effort by humanity during earlier ages, for revealing more and more of the "it" which even Goethe, Wagner, and Nietzsche mercifully covered with night and terror. But this calling of everything into question was authentic preparation, authentic experience of a new mode of existence, radical and profound; and it produced, yes even in Expressionism, the only spiritual achievement that this wretched group of liberal opportunists was capable of, that the scientist's world of pure transformation left behind, the only achievement which broke through that atmosphere of bigbusiness rationalism and took the difficult path inward to the creative depths, to the archetypes, to the myths; and attempted, in the midst of the horrible chaos of reality's destruction and the perversion of values, to strive with absolute discipline and system for a new image of man. It is all too easy now to characterize that effort as abnormal and distorted and racially alien. After all, since then the great national movement has been at work creating new realities, has completely reorganized and reconstituted the utterly degenerate classes and obviously has the moral strength to lay the foundations upon which an entirely new art can develop. But we are talking about a period when that had not yet occurred, when everything was empty, when nihilism hovered above the waters instead of the Spirit of God, when Nietzsche's words held true for an entire generation of Germans, when the only metaphysical activity which life demanded from us was art.

Art, this monstrous problem! For countless generations, Western man has been concerned about art, measured himself against it, consciously or unconsciously examined over and over again all cultural, legal, and epistemological principles in relation to its mysterious nature, its infinitely various and impenetrable existence; and now suddenly art must be exclusively Volkish in all its aspects without taking into consideration the condition of this *Volk,* whether it is declining, developing, stagnant, or furiously active. One ignored that a Volkish and anthropological loss of content had occurred which made any penetration into the material of earlier epochs impossible. Instead one violently attacked as abnormal and racially alien, anti-*Volk* an art which sought its material in its own inward life. One did not appreciate the elementary power and amazing intensity of its brilliant will to style, instead one complained about obvious difficulties by saying: it is purely subjective, unintelligible, crude; and especially: purely formalistic. These criticisms sound very paradoxical indeed coming from our contemporaries who work similarly in modern physics and have inflated their theories into such a big bag of hot air—filled with world-historical significance and exalted wisdom—that the readers of both morning and evening newspapers drool over the splitting of atoms. This monstrous science in which there are nothing but invisible concepts, ingenious abstractions; the whole thing, in Goethe's sense, a senselessly constructed world. To this theory, understood by only eight specialists, five of whom attack it, are dedicated villas, observatories, and Indian temples; however, if a poet submits to his very own experience of words, or a painter to his own love of color, it is anarchism, formalism, yes, even an insult to the *Volk!* Obviously, art must simply float through the air, free like a speck of dust, dropping down to earth outside of time, its determinants, its cultural and intellectual structures; obviously arrogant *Volk*-hating snobs are just peddling garbage. Obviously art, which is free, dare only offer to the public what has been a commonplace for twenty years in grade schools; but science which is astronomically expensive to the nation, to the provinces, to the public, to taxpayers, can fuss with its specialized humbug among widows and orphans. Certainly the new Germany will not tolerate such a paradox. Our leaders, themselves artists or artistically inclined, know too much about art and about the hybrid character of all synthetic activities not to know also that art too has a specialized aspect, and that this specialized aspect in certain critical periods must be especially active and that art's relationship to life cannot always be a matter of directly representing everyday appearances. Actually, no one, not even its opponents, dares challenge the identity of Expressionism with its period and that period's undisputed achievements and its style which was not considered alien to the *Volk:* it was the aesthetic equivalent of modern physics and its abstract interpretation of the world, the expressive parallel of non-Euclidian geometry which had abandoned the 2000-year-old classical world in favor of irreal spaces.

Actually, no other explanation is possible. Everything which has been interesting, even meaningful in European art for the past twenty years has been genetically related to Expressionism. Now we can attack this European world, and I do so with all my heart for historical and for intellectual-spiritual reasons; but we have to look the past straight in the face: here the old Europe proposed one more new style, a style brought forth by its liberal-individualistic spirit, and everything based

upon classical, romantic, and naturalistic points of view was profoundly transformed. What Expressionism might have achieved if the war and history had not interfered can only be a subject for utopian and individualistic speculation. But I am positive, and others agree with me, that all the genuine Expressionists of my generation experienced what I have experienced: precisely they out of the chaos of their life and times experienced an evolution subject to the most urgent inner necessity not given to other generations, an evolution toward a new order and new historical meaning. At this point, in reaction to the irrationalism, violence, and ecstasy which possessed us and surrounded us, an overpowering need for form and for discipline arose. It was precisely the Expressionist who most appreciated the profound objective necessity of technical matters in art, the ethos of craftsmanship, the ethics of form. He demands discipline because he was the most undisciplined; and not one of them, whether painters, composers, or poets would wish the myth to end in any other way than that Dionysos should find his final rest at the feet of the serene Delphic god.

Expressionism then was art, the last art of Europe, her last breath as everywhere a long, magnificent, aged epoch died away. An epoch with Art, now forever over and done with! The early Greeks did not have art, instead they had holy and political stone carving, odes made to order, ritualistic arrangements. It began with Aeschylos, then 2000 years of Art. Now it is all a thing of the past. What is now beginning, what is now making its first appearance is no longer art; it is more and it is less but now we can only speculate. In what follows if I say art, I am talking about a phenomenon that belongs to history.

There is, however, one legitimate criticism which can be leveled against the very essence of this last and final style—it did not assume a historical Volkish mission; it spent its last years disinterested in politics. But this unpolitical point of view was very much a part of our tradition: Goethe, Hölderlin, Rilke, George. Moreover, in our formative years, there was that grand and wonderful Germany intoxicated with its joy and freedom which did not require our attention when we painted and wrote. Then came the war and, as has been mentioned, the Expressionists took from it their share. And in those years politics meant Marxism, meant Russia, the murder of the bourgeoisie and the intellectuals, the murder of all art as "private idiocy" (Tretjakow), meant antiheroism, dialectical twaddle, and that functionalism which I have already discussed. This destructive approach was opposed by Expressionism by means (inner and outer means) which were not political, namely with a formal absolutism which excluded all chaos. A few novelists wrote political propaganda, they tried to subdue history with words and in parliamentarism they found a satisfying parallel to the wordiness of their epic prose. But the Expressionists were not interested in society small talk, they were interested in an abstract world. They made art.

Admittedly, they had no instinct for politics. And perhaps they had a shocking number of biologically defective qualities, also moral weaknesses, yes, and some had criminal tendencies, that has been demonstrated, I won't deny it. But as for such epithets like "deserters, convicts, criminals, degenerates, libertines, trash, and swindlers," the question arises as to whether or not all artists did not look like that from close up? There has been no reasonable and cultivated art since Florence, none, none which developed with full public approval and in terms of an established set of values; for centuries art has been an art of reaction and an art of genesis. Later, when an epoch comes to an end, when the race is dead and the kings are at rest, and in the entrance hall the servants lie asleep forever, when kingdoms have collapsed and even the ruins standing between the eternal seas have crumbled to dust, then in retrospect everything seems to have been beautifully ordered, as if one had only to reach up to snatch a ready-made crown, magnificent and gleaming; but all that actually was achieved through bloody struggle and terrible sacrifice, torn from the underworld and wrestled out of the shadows. Perhaps we waste too much time these days with the degenerates and refuse to recognize that here too several works and several men will survive; their expressive method has raised their spirit and the disintegrating, suffering, shattered existence of their century into those spheres of form where above ruined cities and destroyed empires only the artist can give human immortality to an epoch and a people. I believe it, and I am convinced that those whom I see coming after us will also believe it.

Never again will there be art in the sense of the past 500 years; Expressionism was its last phase; our spiritual condition simply cannot be conceived as too critical, or too final; total transformation lies ahead of us; a new race will appear in Europe. Many friends of the National Socialist [i.e., Nazi] movement are skeptical about this movement's theories of race and breeding; they claim that those ideas are too naturalistic, too materialistic—we would rather sit around the table and dream while the ravens circle about and Barbarossa's beard grows through the stone. But I say that you cannot view these matters too naturalistically, in fact, you can view them only naturalistically; propaganda affects the germ cells; the word influences the genitals, no doubt about it; nature's cruelest fact is that brain life changes the character of the germ cells, that the spirit is an active and organizing force in the evolution of life: there is unity here: what is defined politically will be developed organically.

What is defined politically will not be art but a completely new though already quite recognizable race. I have no doubt that the Ghibelline synthesis of which Evola spoke is approaching politically that moment when Odin's eagles fly to meet the eagles of the Roman legions. This eagle as a coat of arms, the crown as mythos and several great intellects as the world's spiritual inspiration. Mythologically this means: the return home of the Norse gods, white man's earth from Thule to Avalun, imperial symbols there: torches and axes, and the breeding of superior races, solar elites for a world half-Doric, half-magical. Infinite distances being filled with possibilities! Not art. Ritual around torches and fire. There were three great periods of genius for the German people: 1500, with innumerable painters in their midst, second only to those of the Mediterranean; the seventeenth and eighteenth centuries filled with music. Poetry began in the eighteenth century, it was the beginning of a long period which extended up to the present day; Expressionism was its extreme projection, a kind of *Monts Maudis*—a naked Inferno, perhaps, but still part of that great epoch. Now a pause for two or three generations and then the fourth age will begin, there are dreams and visions—it is approaching, difficult to grasp—God.

The race, there it is: in spirit and deed, transcendental realism or heroic nihilism, these marks of a tragic and individualistic era cannot be completely eradicated; but all in all this race is profoundly fortunate in comparison to us, their individuali-

ty will have balance, be more universal than Faustian. The architecture of the South, fused with the lyricism of the Northern foglands; the stature of the Atlantids, their symbols will become grand songs, oratorios in Amphitheaters, choirs of fishermen, symphonies of conch shells, in limestone halls blending with the horns of primeval hunters. Infinite distances being filled, a great style approaching.

The race, there it is: it looks back in time: *our* century, *Götterdämmerung, Ragnarökr*—"humane" and liberal times: perfunctory and vague ideas about everything; nothing is seen round and whole. Nothing clearly defined, everything ideological, evasion everywhere. But one group hammers away at the Absolute—succumbing to it yet transcending it spiritually in hard, abstract forms: image and verse and flute melody. Poor and clean, disdaining bourgeois interest in fame, in the wealth of a guzzling rabble. They live off of shadows, they make art. Yes, this tiny group in the face of the ultimate transformation of whole worlds lives art, which is to say: lives ready for death, lives sustained by Germany's devout blood. (pp. 192-203)

> *Gottfried Benn, "The Confession of an Expressionist," in* Voices of German Expressionism, *edited and translated by Victor H. Miesel, Prentice-Hall, Inc., 1970, pp. 192-203.*

AESTHETIC THEORIES

ULRICH WEISSTEIN

[*Weisstein is a German-born American critic. In the following excerpt, he examines the aesthetic and ideological principles of Expressionism. The essay from which this excerpt was taken was originally published in* Criticism *in 1967; this revised version was taken from* Expressionism as an International Literary Phenomenon: 21 Essays and a Bibliography, *edited by Weisstein.*]

[Viewed as a historical phenomenon in its totality, Expressionism cannot be properly regarded as a movement.] The term *movement,* that is to say, should be reserved for groups of contemporaries having a common goal and subscribing to a formulated program. To be sure, in painting we have *Die Brücke,* a true *Künstlergemeinschaft* ["community of artists"] until Ernst Ludwig Kirchner's chronicle met with the disapproval of his fellow painters. The *Blaue Reiter,* on the other hand, showed relatively little artistic coherence. In literature, the situation was even more chaotic; and, with the exception of the clique gathered around Herwarth Walden's periodical *Der Sturm,* programs were written and theories developed only after the fact by critics, editors, anthologists and other "outsiders."

In the introduction to his pamphlet *Über neue Prosa* (which forms part of the well-known series *Tribüne der Kunst und Zeit*), Max Krell observes that E. is a collective term used to refer to a complex of views and feelings ("Sammelwort eines Gefühlsund Anschauungskomplexes") but that the individual Expressionist prefers *Lösung* ("creative freedom" or "independence") to *Bindung* ("adherence to a common cause"). However, as Krell points out, there are the Activists, a group of writers associated with publications like *Das Ziel, Die Aktion,* and René Schickele's far less virulent *Die weissen Blätter.* The Activists, of whom Heinrich Mann was the most prominent, had specific goals and shared a *Weltanschauung,* the term being here used in the narrower, socio-political sense. Perhaps they actually were, as one writer puts it, thwarted humanists who had discovered that the world in which they lived did not measure up to the ideal glowingly painted by their teachers. (pp. 32-3)

What, however, makes it possible for us to discuss the Expressionists as a group, if there is no such thing as an Expressionist program or manifesto? And can we, in spite of the apparent incoherence of views and styles, find some common denominator for all their efforts? I think most of the writers and painters whom we now regard as Expressionists would have agreed that they were primarily concerned with capturing the essence of things rather than their external appearance. They found nothing more contemptible than the Naturalistic "slice of life" and its Impressionist variant. "Mensch werde wesentlich", the clarion call sounded by the Baroque epigrammatist Angelus Silesius, was their motto. The essence or core of things, however, can be reached only by resolutely piercing through the various layers of social, political, and psychological reality. This thrust, this plunging into depth, i.e., into a realm forbidden to the senses, presupposes a quasi-religious fervor, an urge to bring about a total *Vergeistigung* ("spiritualization") of life and art. In the works of E., man is, therefore, directly confronted with eternity. Art, for these writers and painters, was not a substitute for religion; it was religion itself. And their principal line of communication, like that of the Mystics, was not a horizontal but a vertical one. This, naturally, poses an entirely new problem of communication on the human plane.

Even before World War I, a number of critics conversant with the current trends sought to isolate certain traits in order to gain valid criteria for analyzing contemporary works of art. They did so almost invariably in terms of style, not content. For even if one concedes that certain themes—such as the father-son conflict, the struggle between duty and conviction, the *Aufbruch* ["new start"] from one mode of existence to another—occur frequently in Expressionist literature, the thematic approach is doomed to failure when it comes to judging the plastic arts or comparing poetic with pictorial works. Pinthus, who singled out "intensity" as the principal feature of E., himself succumbed to the thematic fallacy—which he rejected in theory—when arranging the contents of his anthology.

In his collection of essays *Der neue Standpunkt,* one of the first and most eloquent apologies for the new art, Theodor Däubler—the man whom Barlach seems to have used as a model for *Der blaue Boll*—lists "speed, simultaneity, and extreme intensity in the telescopic view of the world" as traits characteristic of a style which, in his as yet undifferentiated view, comprises Cubism, Futurism, and E. "When a man is hanged, he relives his entire life in a final moment" is another way in which Däubler expresses the same idea. Viewed historically, such a description would seem to be more applicable to paintings like Marc Chagall's proto-Surrealistic "I and the Village" (1917) or Gino Severini's "Dynamic Hieroglyphic of the Bal Tabarin" (1912) than to any Expressionist work, except perhaps of the type represented by Franz Marc's "Tierschicksale" ("The Fate of the Animals," 1913).

Däubler also refers to Expressionist art as that of a highly concentrated vision: "A vision seeks to manifest itself with extreme succinctness in the realm of mannered simplicity: that is E. in every style." With regard to literature, Kasimir Edschmid, another pioneer of E. in both theory and practice, claims that "the rhythmic construction of the sentences is different. They serve the same intention, the same spiritual urge which renders only the essential." The sentences "link peak with peak, are telescoped into each other, and have ceased to be connected by the buffers of logical transition or the external plaster of psychology."

An excellent illustration of this technique occurs in Kaiser's play *Von morgens bis mitternachts,* when the protagonist—a bank clerk who has absconded with a large sum of money and is now trying to reap the fruits of his *Aufbruch*—describes the effect of the climactic moment of a tandem race upon the already frenzied audience: "This is the utmost concentration of fact. Here it does the impossible. A fusion of all galleries. The utter dissolution of the individual leads to the formation of a dense core: passion." And later, when the waiter of a restaurant enters the *chambre separée* to inquire what he wants to eat, the clerk replies: "Peaks, peaks, from beginning to end. Peaks are the utmost concentrations in everything." It is this passion for intensity which explains, among other things, the telegram style of the Expressionist *Schrei-Drama,* as exemplified by Reinhard Goering's famous *Seeschlacht.* This telegram style is the very opposite of the Naturalist *Sekundenstil,* which forms the literary equivalent of the "slice of life."

Phrases such as "Höhe des Gefühls", "Spitzen des Gefühls", "Berge des Herzens" ["heights of feeling," "summits of feeling," "peaks of the spirit"] (this latter coined by Rainer Maria Rilke) abound in Expressionist literature, indicating that its mysticism is dynamic. Indeed, nothing could be further from the Expressionist than to imitate the saints in the First Duino Elegy who, experiencing levitation, "knieten, Unmögliche, weiter und achtetens nicht." ("Kept on kneeling, impossible ones, and did not heed it.") Perhaps the word most frequently uttered by Expressionist protagonists is *Aufbruch* which, untranslatable into English, suggests a complete desertion of the past, a burning of bridges, a progress beyond the point of no return. *Aufbruch* is the catchword of a generation which, following Faust's example, seeks "auf neuer Bahn den Äther zu durchdringen / Zu neuen Sphären reiner Tätigkeit" (to penetrate the ether on new paths toward new spheres of pure activity). Such an awakening may occur either in the form of a sudden, volcanic eruption or, as in the *Stationendrama* of Strindbergian provenience, in a number of stages leading to some sort of spiritual catharsis, as in the protagonist's contrived Ecce Homo pose at the end of *Von morgens bis mitternachts.*

The "Weltgefühl" which animates the Expressionist writers is captured in the titles of the numerous magazines, books, series, and anthologies issued between 1910 and 1920: *Erhebung, Anbruch, Verkündigung, Botschaft, Entfaltung, Das neue Pathos, Der jüngste Tag* ["*Exaltation,*" "*Daybreak,*" "*Annunciation,*" "*Message,*" "*Unfurling,*" "*The New Fervor,*" "*The Youngest Day*"], whereas the Activist publications carry names like *Kameraden der Menschheit* or *Gemeinschaft*["*Comrades of humanity*" or "*Community*"]. *Menschheitsdämmerung* ["*Twilight of humanity*"], patterned after Richard Wagner's *Götterdämmerung* and Nietzsche's *Götzendämmerung,* points both to the end (dusk) of an epoch and to the beginning ("dawn") of a new era. By far the most influential of these periodicals was *Der Sturm,* not only because, in its pages, literature, painting, and the graphic arts found themselves united—for that was a feature common to many publications of the time—but also because its editor, Herwarth Walden, solidified his own views on modern art by extracting a literary theory from the poems of August Stramm and by founding and supporting institutions like the *Sturmschule* and the *Sturmbühne.*

The title of my essay ["Expressionism: Style or 'Weltan-schauung'?"] must seem paradoxical to those who believe that, whether directly or indirectly, style must be a reflection of *Weltanschauung, Weltanschauung* being the sum total of intellectual views and emotional attitudes embraced by a given individual. No such paradox applies to those artistic movements which aim at reproducing tangible reality by means of imitation. If Realism, which is the most moderate and commonsensical of these movements, can be defined, with Vivian de Sola Pinto, as "that art which gives a truthful impression of actuality as it appears to the normal consciousness," then the "advance" of Naturalism or Impressionism can be measured as a deviation from that norm, as a shift of accent or change in emphasis effected by a Gustave Courbet or Claude Monet, a Paul Verlaine or Emile Zola.

Realists, Naturalists and Impressionists, in their different ways, wish to portray solely that which is visible, audible, etc., not only to themselves but to all men. They fight their pitched battles uniformly in the name of objectivity. With the Expressionists—as, by the way, also with the Surrealists—the matter is radically different. In their opinion, the function of art is not to reproduce the visible but, in Paul Klee's words ("Kunst gibt nicht das Sichtbare wieder, sondern macht sichtbar" ["Art doesn't repeat the visible, but rather makes visible"]), to make visible that which is not ordinarily revealed to the senses. "The world exists already," says Edschmid. "It would be useless to repeat it." Unlike the Surrealists, however, the Expressionists realized that before one can make the invisible visible one must experience a vision.

As Marcel Proust points out in *Du coté de chez Swann,* this externalization of the internal is natural enough to the writer, who enjoys the inestimable advantage of being able to place himself and his readers inside the characters he has created, whereas in real life we cannot intuit other people's soul states:

> A real person, profoundly as we may sympathise with him, is in a great measure perceptible only through our senses, that is to say, he remains opaque, offers a dead weight which our sensibilities have not the strength to lift . . . The novelist's happy discovery was to think of substituting for those opaque sections, impenetrable by the human spirit, their equivalent in immaterial sections, things, that is, which the spirit can assimilate to itself.

But how is the painter to accomplish a similar feat? How can he, being so closely tied to the world of ordinary sense perception, break through the shell in order to reveal what it hides from view, i.e., our inmost thoughts and feelings? The answer furnished by the Expressionists is simple: *through style;* style meaning primarily shapes and colors representing an order of things that is different from the natural one. Seen from the mimetic point of view, however, this signifies abstraction or, at least, some sort of more or less violent distortion. Unlike mere *Stilisierung* ["stylization"], as we find it, say, in Mannerism or *Art Nouveau* (*Jugendstil*), style is not constituted by a gradual, decorative abstraction from organic form, re-

sulting in a kind of arabesque. In the most radical instances of Expressionist style, the beholder, unless he prefers to ignore the artist's intentions by concentrating on formal values, is thus faced with the grim task of reuniting "abstract" compositions with their underlying *Weltanschauung.*

The arguments I have adduced are partly taken from Worringer's book *Abstraktion und Einfühlung* which, originally published in 1908, was the aesthetic Bible of E., especially of the *Blaue Reiter.* Worringer contends that the urge for abstraction (*Abstraktionsdrang*) arises on two different levels of man's spiritual evolution: (a) at the primitive stage when, numinously overwhelmed by the supernatural forces which he thinks inherent in nature, man fashions objects which, being geometric and regular, i.e., *unnatural,* give him a sense of superiority and, hence, security; and (b) at a highly sophisticated stage when the world of matter becomes indifferent, and transcendence is, once more, desired. This latter phase produces the abstract, spiritualized and highly ornamental art of the Orient.

Worringer and his British disciple T. E. Hulme—the man who laid the theoretical foundations for Vorticism—scorned the realistic stage which intervenes between a and b. They spoke contemptuously of the classical art of Greece, of the Renaissance, and of the positivistic nineteenth century. Inspiring the Expressionists, Worringer singled out the Gothic and the Baroque as the only two ages which, due to their spiritual unrest and mystical aspiration, ought to be admired by the moderns. He himself preferred the Gothic to the Baroque, because the latter, by intensifying the sensual until it became suprasensual, had chosen a devious way toward spiritualization, whereas in the Gothic cathedral man's urge toward spiritual transcendence (*Vergeistigung*) was directly embodied.

In Worringer's and Hulme's opinion, all classical art, grown out of a harmonious relationship between man and nature, signals an abdication of the will. *Kunstwollen* ("artistic volition"), however, to their mind, was the agent which assured man's ascendancy over his environment. Empathy and imitation are the cornerstones of an aesthetic formed by weaklings. They were now to be deposed, and alienation and abstraction crowned in their place.

The two leading German schools of Expressionist art may serve to illustrate the two levels of abstraction named by Worringer: the *Brücke* group representing the neoprimitive phase, and the *Blaue Reiter* the oriental. As Hermann Bahr states in his book *Expressionismus,* "Just as primitive man, frightened by nature, hides within himself, we moderns flee a civilization that devours man's soul." How the members of *Die Brücke* saved their souls was demonstrated, some years ago, by the exhibition "Das Ursprüngliche und die Moderne," which was held at the West Berlin *Akademie der Künste.* Here the primitive objects owned by the Berlin and Dresden ethnographic museums were shown side by side with the paintings and sculptures they had inspired.

Following in the footsteps of Paul Gauguin, Emil Nolde and Max Pechstein separately visited the South Sea Islands in 1913 and 1914. Both returned imbued with the "savage" spirit. Pechstein's Credo in the volume *Schöpferische Konfession* begins with exclamations like "Work! Frenzy! Crush the brain! Chew! Devour! Gulp! Squash! Blissful pains of delivery. The brush cracks and should like to pierce the canvas. Trample on the paint tubes . . . Paint! Roll in paints, wallow in chords! In the thick of chaos." At approximately the same time, Igor Stravinsky reincarnated the savage state in his *Sacre du Printemps,* and O'Neill followed suit with his drama *The Emperor Jones.*

The neo-primitives of the *Brücke* group were at their best in the graphic arts, especially in the woodcut. Wyndham Lewis found their work to be "African, in that it is sturdy, cutting through . . . to the monotonous wall of space, and intense yet hale; permeated by eternity—an atmosphere in which only the black core of life rises and is silhouetted". For him, the woodcut was "a miniature sculpture where the black nervous fluid of existence in flood forms into hard stagnant masses." What appealed to the Expressionists in this medium, as used by the German primitives of the fifteenth century, was its imperviousness to psychological finesse, as well as its harsh angularity.—In the field of sculpture, Amedeo Modigliani in France (with his Caryatids) and Gaudier-Brzeska in England came perhaps closest to reaching this Vorticist-Expressionist ideal, whereas Germany, Barlach excepted, produced no major Expressionist sculptor, even though Wilhelm Lehmbruck's elongated figures are often drawn into the discussion.

The works of several *Blaue Reiter,* on the other hand, breathe the spirit of Worringer's post-empathetic phase. Marc looked at his own art in much the same light, as is shown by his remark: "Our European urge for abstract form is nothing but our hyperconscious, superactive reaction to, and triumph over, the sentimental spirit. Primitive man, however, had not met the latter when he loved abstraction." August Macke, reaching, at least experimentally, the stage of pure abstraction in 1907, wrote to his fiancée: "Just now all my bliss derives from pure colors. Last week I placed colors side by side on a wooden board without thinking of any object, such as men or trees, as in crochetry." Kandinsky and Adolf Hoelzel—Nolde's and Willi Baumeister's teacher—broke the barrier around 1910, and Marc, with his "Fighting Forms," four years later. Of the members of *Die Brücke,* Kirchner was probably the only one to grope his way toward abstraction in his colored woodcut illustrations to Adelbert von Chamisso's *Peter Schlemihl.*

We have reached the crucial point in any discussion of E. in literature or painting; for whoever wishes to make his peace with that style has to know where to draw the line between so-called nonobjective and representational art. In statement after statement, the Expressionists professed that it was their aim to mate the abstract with the concrete, soul with body, and spirit with matter—just as the Surrealists wished to reconcile the world of dreams with that of waking, the subconscious with the conscious. Walter von Hollander, for example, calls Paul Kornfeld's drama *Die Verführung* Expressionistic in so far as, in it, the soul finds an outlet through the body. And Edschmid bluntly states: "We want the flesh, but in sharpened suprasensual pleasures."

As the chief apologist for Expressionist literature, Edschmid fought the notion that a school of pure abstraction might develop within its framework. "The urge for abstraction no longer knows any limits, no longer realizes how subtle the balance of content and creative form. Exceeding the boundaries of the sensuous, it creates pure theory." Edschmid was undoubtedly shocked by Däubler's definition of the new style as "color without a name, line without boundary," but the criterion of "rhythmically placed nouns without attributes" must have been more to his taste. Still, Edschmid must have rejected the extreme views pushed by the artists of the *Sturm*

circle: Rudolf Blümner's use of abstract word formations and Lothar Schreyer's theory of the Expressionist *Gesamtkunstwerk* ["total work of art"] composed of pure words, sounds, forms, colors, and rhythms.

Indeed, "Abstract Expressionism" is a logical absurdity unless we can somehow salvage Kandinsky's concept of art as based on the principle of inner necessity. Kandinsky himself would not have called his works abstractions, since, for him, form was always the expression of a content. Thus, as far as the underlying intentions are concerned, his Impressions, Improvisations and Compositions are polar opposites of the serene abstractions of *De Stijl* and the stark geometries of Kasimir Malevich's Suprematism.

Kandinsky's aesthetic issues from the conviction that art is a vehicle of communication between the artist and his audience. In his programmatic treatise *Über das Geistige in der Kunst* (*Concerning the Spiritual in Art*) he uses the piano to show that art is "purposive playing with the human soul." With the aid of color and form, the feelings of the beholders of his pictures are to be manipulated in such a way that "[color] is the keyboard, the eyes are the hammers, the soul is the piano with many strings, [and] the artist is the hand that plays, touching one key or another purposively, to cause vibration in the soul."

To this end all of Kandinsky's efforts were directed. Ideally, he wanted the beholder to be compelled to "wander around" in the finished picture, just as Klee, writing in *Schöpferische Konfession,* invites us to take a little journey. What Kandinsky hoped to achieve was, paradoxically enough, a sort of "empathy through abstraction." But how was this empathy to be brought about? For assuming even that one sincerely believes in the veracity of the feelings an artist claims to have channeled into his work, it is, and always will be, quite impossible to extract such feelings from their visual record on the canvas. Of course, we may rely on intuition, which found so strong an advocate in Henri Bergson. But intuition is an unreliable guide and difficult to translate into the language of ordinary logic. Thus Kandinsky's paintings after 1910, to quote Däubler's beautifully turned phrases, are "blue manifestations of a decision before their embodiment in action; Mongolianisms which mistily invade us, creating chaos through the mystical use of color or [generating] a cosmos."

Schönberg, the inventor of the "method of composition with twelve tones which are related only with one another," broke resolutely with the musical past by completing a process that had begun with Wagner's chromaticism and continued via Claude Debussy's experiments to the full emancipation of dissonance in Stravinsky's *Sacre.* Similarly, Kandinsky broke with the tradition of representational art by pushing to the limit the implications of a statement with which Vincent van Gogh, writing from Arles to his brother Theo, had announced the emancipation of pictorial dissonance:

> Because instead of trying to reproduce exactly what I have before my eyes, I use color more arbitrarily so as to express myself more forcefully. Well, let that be as a matter of theory, but I am going to give you an example of what I mean.
>
> I should like to paint the portrait of an artist friend, a man who dreams great dreams, who works as the nightingale sings, because it is his nature. He'll be a fair man. I want to put into the picture my appre-

ciation, the love that I have for him. So I paint him as he is, as faithfully as I can, to begin with.

But the picture is not finished yet. To finish it I am now going to be the arbitrary colorist. I exaggerate the fairness of the hair, I get to orange tones, chromes and pale lemon yellow.

Beyond the head, instead of painting the ordinary wall of the mean room, I paint infinity, a plain background of the richest, intensest blue that I can contrive, and by this simple combination the bright head illuminated against a rich blue background acquires a mysterious effect, like the star in the depths of an azure sky.

I do not think that the Expressionist theory of art in general, and of portrait painting in particular, has ever been more clearly articulated. The painter's statement helps to resolve the dichotomy posed by our contention that the Expressionists wanted to show the essence of things (their *Wesen*) and Herbert Read's definition of the style as one which seeks to reproduce "not the objective reality of the world, but the subjective reality of the feelings which objects and events arouse in us." For the finished product, as indicated by Van Gogh, was to embody both the sitter's personality and the artist's estimation thereof, i.e., a perfect blend of the objective (not conceived in a superficial, realistic way) and the subjective.

With the coming of E., the focus of attention was, once again, shifted from physical to human nature. Indeed, the Expressionists are among the greatest portrait painters of all time. They invariably show their sitters *en face,* never in profile, because the eyes "are the windows of the soul." It is precisely the soul, however—especially the soul in writhing anguish—which the Expressionists desired to project.

Edvard Munch, many of whose paintings are, in Däubler's words, "highly erotic but not sensual," reflects this anguish in his pictorial allegory of the Scream, which seems to illustrate Bahr's puzzling statement: "Impressionism treated the eye like an ear, E. like a mouth. The ear is dumb, and Impressionism bade the soul to be silent. The mouth is deaf, and the Expressionist cannot hear the world." Paula Modersohn-Becker's portrait of Rilke (1906) represents one of the earliest stages in the Expressionist search for the pictorial equivalent of soul states; and Kokoschka's masterful Self-Portrait of 1917 reveals the "ghost" of the painter through the enormously dilated pale blue eyes and the twisted hands that look like caterpillars. According to Edschmid, a literary parallel to this phenomenon is found in the work of Döblin, "who so fabulously permeates and irradiates the flesh with injections of spirit that the ghost (a different thing from the skeleton) becomes solely visible." Edschmid credits August Strindberg—we think of his *Ghost Sonata*—with having done the same thing in drama.

Unlike Munch, Modersohn-Becker, and Kokoschka, certain Expressionists sought to plumb the depth of the souls of animals. According to Macke, "the senses are a bridge connecting the visible and the invisible. To look at plants and animals means to feel their secret." Thus Marc, the Expressionist animal painter par excellence, sought to portray the world of beasts not as we see it but as the eagle, the horse, the cow, or the tiger see it. Every animal thus becomes, in Däubler's words, "the incarnation of its cosmic rhythm."

Moving still further down the Great Chain of Being, other Expressionists breathed a soul even into inanimate things, not

in order to reveal their inner geometry (for that was what the Cubists aimed at doing) but with the intention of demonstrating their latent dynamism. Speaking of Robert Delaunay, Däubler calls him the first Expressionist on account of his "portraits" of the Eiffel Tower. In fact, the tower is "scaffold and skeleton of the future . . . [It] is the first Expressionist . . . [it] has a soul . . . [it] is an artist . . . It is also the father of Delaunay." Thus Worringer hits the mark when, surveying E. in a retrospective essay, he credits it with having theomorphized the world in its drive for total spiritualization. Impressionism having run its course, landscape, too—in the words of Pinthus—was no longer "copied, described, glorified . . . but wholly humanized." Such an interpretation could well be placed on El Greco's View of Toledo or Van Gogh's Starry Night.

On the pictorial plane, such spiritualization is invariably manifested as distortion. Distortion of form or color is, in fact, the very hallmark of Expressionist art. But how about Expressionist literature? I believe that even in this respect a perfect parallelism exists between the two media. A few hints may suffice in the present context. The immediate forerunners of German literary E. were Frank Wedekind and Carl Sternheim, whose tools were caricature, the grotesque, and satire; in other words: techniques which invariably involve distortion. When Thomas Mann defined E. in his *Betrachtungen,* he singled out these very traits to show how totally writers like his brother Heinrich had lost touch with contemporary life and political reality.

The syntactical distortions which occur in Expressionist poetry are nowhere more prominent than in Benn's poem "Karyatide", which contains the difficult lines "Bespei die Säulensucht: toderschlagene / Greisige Hände bebten sie / Verhangenen Himmeln zu," which Hamburger renders clumsily as "Spit on this column mania: done to death / mere senile hands they trembled / towards cloud-covered heavens," and Lohner/Corman more appropriately "Spit on this passion for pillars: the death-dealing / hoary hands trembled them / to overhanging heaven."

To be sure, in the realm of language it seems particularly bold to strive for the kind of simplification and foreshortening found in the woodcuts of the *Brücke* group or the type of abstraction familiar from Kandinsky. Nevertheless, such tendencies made themselves felt in the poetry of Stramm and other, more radical exponents of *Sturm* art. Walden demanded that the poet should use words and rhythm in the same way in which the painter uses color and form, and the composer sound and rhythm. Stramm, who was not a theoretician, transformed *Dichtung* ("poetry") into *Wortkunst* ["word art"], as in the poem "Schwermut", which reads:

> Schreiten Streben
> Leben sehnt
> Schauern Stehen
> Blicke suchen
> Sterben wächst
> Das Kommen
> Schreit!
> Tief
> Stummen
> Wir.

> Striding Striving
> Life yearns
> Shuddering Standing
> Glances seek

Dying grows
The coming
Cries!
Deeply
We
Mute.

Under the aegis of Blümner, the level of pure abstraction was reached shortly afterwards in the *Lautkunst* of poems like "Ango Laina", which opens with the cryptic line "Oiaí laéla oia ssisialu" and ends with what sounds like a parody of Stramm's one-word lines: "gádse / ina / leíola / kbáo / sagór / kadó." Blümner took the matter very seriously and would have been offended had anybody told him about the curious resemblance between "Ango Laina" and certain Dadaist nonsense poems. Like the experiments with abstract rhythms which Edith Sitwell undertook in her sequence of poems *Fa-çade, Lautkunst* entails a complete breakdown of communication on the level on which language commonly operates. For how are we to extract any sort of meaning from Blümner's African-sounding word formations? Benn, who was fascinated by what he called "das südliche Wort" ["the southern word"], and who dreamed of realizing the purely formal art which Gustave Flaubert envisaged when he stood on the Acropolis, wisely refrained from putting his theory into practice. So did Ezra Pound, a great admirer of Kandinsky, who wished to rid poetry of all literary values (as Verlaine had proclaimed in his poem "Art Poétique") and who, at least in the Imagist-Vorticist phase of his career, championed an art devoid of meaning. For while the general public has, at long last, been reconciled with abstraction in the pictorial arts, abstraction in literature, or even a private, synthetic language of the kind employed in James Joyce's non-novel *Finnegans Wake,* is not likely ever to be fashionable.

As a term, E., which had been launched by the French painter Julien-Auguste Hervé in 1901, found general acceptance in 1911 when a number of German art critics applied it to the Fauvist paintings included in an exhibition of the Berlin *Sezession.* Worringer gave his blessing when, writing in *Der Sturm,* he spoke of the "Pariser Synthetisten und Expressionisten: Cézanne, Van Gogh, Matisse." No transfer to literature was attempted until several years later, probably 1914 or 1915; and as early as 1918 Edschmid spoke of literary E. as a fad embraced by a horde of imitators. Four years later, Pinthus, asked to prepare a new edition of his anthology, decided to leave *Menschheitsdämmerung* untouched. For he felt that "after the completion of this lyrical symphony, no poetry has been written that inalienably belongs to it."

Those were the years of transition from E. to *Neue Sachlichkeit* ("New Objectivity"). Soon the *Bauhaus* was to be the most influential force in the fine and applied arts, and sobriety began to reassert itself in literature and music. E. was an impulse quickly spent. The *Weltanschauung* at its root, and the style to which it gave rise, were those of youthful enthusiasts who overreached themselves or slid back into more conventional channels of expression. "Let the young", said Rudolf Kurtz in a phrase that applies to the Storm and Stress as well as to E., "stay young even to the point of catastrophe. Immaturity is the most potent yeast of history."

The title of our essay posed the question as to whether E. should be viewed primarily as a stylistic phenomenon or as a *Weltanschauung,* i.e., whether it should be judged by aesthetic or extra-aesthetic criteria. We pointed out that, luckily, its socio-political aspect can be subsumed under the term Ac-

Self-portrait by Ernst Barlach.

tivism. If, excluding this aspect, one defines the term broadly enough to include man's attitude toward himself, his fellow-beings and the world at large, one can defend the use of *Welt-anschauung* in the sense of a sharp rejection of previously embraced views on the part of an entire generation. This is what the Expressionists meant by *Aufbruch,* by their concentration on soul states, by their determination to make the invisible visible. Hence the intensity, the spiritual unrest and the emotionally charged atmosphere of their products. Indeed, one cannot imagine an Expressionist work to be conceived rationally and in cold blood. (pp. 33-44)

Ulrich Weisstein, "Expressionism: Style or 'Weltanschauung'?" in Expressionism as an International Literary Phenomenon, *edited by Ulrich Weisstein, Didier, 1973, pp. 29-44.*

WOLFGANG PAULSEN

[*Paulsen is a German-born American critic and the author of* Expressionismus und Aktivismus *(1935), a study of the Expressionist movement. In the following excerpt, he examines the relationship between form and content in German Expressionist writing.*]

There is no denying . . . that the young writers and poets who gathered in the various Expressionist circles in Berlin and elsewhere considered themselves to be "Expressionists" in the demonstrative sense of the word. For them the term denoted far more than a literary slogan; it was a battle cry.

They were Expressionists very often in the way in which some of the talented young members of later generations were Marxists, with or without having read Marx. Fifty years later, we find it difficult to enter into their revolutionary language, its aggressiveness and militancy. And yet, we would do well to consider their revolutionary intent carefully. Obviously, the terms "revolt" and "revolution" can mean very different things. Roy Allen's meticulous investigations into the Expressionist circles of Berlin have shown beyond a shadow of a doubt the exclusive concern of the young men and women gathering around the various cafes to have been with problems of aesthetics, and their original concern gave way only gradually to an awareness of the social and political reality of the day. It took a World War to jolt them out of their complacency—a complacency which we can call thoroughly "bourgeois"—and a Russian Revolution to redirect their thinking. In the course of little more than ten years, the term "Expressionism" changed from an avant-garde concept to a derogatory one denoting, and castigating, a "typically German" form of withdrawal into an aesthetic never-never-land.

If one considers these developments, Freud's dictum of the "Unbehagen in der Kultur" ["discontent with civilization"], an extraordinarily farsighted formulation at the time it was coined, comes to mind. "Discontent" seems a rather passive reaction to things, but one that might develop into protests of all kinds at any time. In this sense, the Expressionist movement was, in spite of its origins in aesthetics, no more and no less than the first signal of a much broader crisis, which would shake the Western World later in our century, a crisis which, whenever it occurs, seems to be strangely related to prosperity and physical well-being, and which seems to increase proportionally with the size of the population and the spread of the media. Within this larger framework, the young Expressionists, discontented with the cultural status quo, were clearly an ephemeral phenomenon, a minor aspect of a more fundamental upheaval. They may have failed to deal with the larger issues involved, but they nevertheless created an artistic language which would one day lend itself to the expression of such concerns. They were revolutionary in the sense that they brought about a basic change in perception and by so doing, immeasurably enriched human sensitivities. Most of the Expressionists' creations, when taken by themselves (and here we refer specifically to their literature, not to their work in the Fine Arts), may strike us as utterly naive, amateurish and often even inept, in short as "bad literature," yet coming as they did over a number of years they completely altered the artistic consciousness of their public and thereby the emotional foundations of their society. It is not accidental that the very German philistines who had reacted so violently to the Expressionists' artistic gyrations began to fill the Expressionist theatres and bought their books or their pictures.

The protectors of public order and morality, however, had already grown accustomed to such cases of insubordination, because, after all, the Expressionists only took up where the Naturalists and those that followed them, like Frank Wedekind, had left off. That is one of the reasons why literary historians have recently maintained that "die Moderne" (in the sense in which Walter Sokel used the term in his *The Writer in Extremis* [see excerpt above]) began with the rebellion of the Naturalists. Hauptmann's *Weber* and *Vor Sonnenaufgang,* therefore, can be regarded as the beginning of a new era in German literature, as Theodor Fontane realized at the time, with a sense of relief, when he had to review their

first performances in Berlin. The Expressionists, however, did not really take their cue from the Naturalists, not even from Wedekind whom they may have admired for his ideological position more than for his literary achievements, but even he cannot be said to have had a lasting influence on their writing. When the Expressionists protested, they protested against very different things. One could even argue that they were very much closer to the great formalists of the age, like Stefan George—that is, to the cultural reactionaries par excellence in the tradition of Nietzsche. With George they shared a disdain for an art that had allowed itself to be degraded by concentrating on a drab reality. If anything mattered to them it was the artist's ego which they managed to blow up to such extraordinary proportions. It is no coincidence that both Sternheim and Kaiser had come within the orbit of George's world; before he found his way to his specific form of comedy, Sternheim had written poetry echoing George's diction. But they were not the only "Expressionists" to have come along this improbable path: several years ago, Kurt Mautz demonstrated how Georg Heym's monolithic poems, some of the earliest manifestations of Expressionism in German literature, derive from parodistically-inverted George poetry. A writer can take recourse to parody to free himself from an influence that has become unbearable. It indicates the direction in which he is heading, but also the point of departure from which he has come. Parody, therefore, is, or can be, a point of convergence of the old and the new, its degree of bitterness depending in each case on the severity of the inner conflict involved. The form Carl Sternheim developed for his comedy is, in many ways, the result of a similar intellectual cross-fertilization. In his youth he had felt very much at home in the world of Neo-Romantic fantasies, peopled with conquering heroes and very submissive ladies, and when he was forced to leave his literary utopia he began attacking the middle-class morality that had placed the validity of his values in jeopardy. However, he was artist enough—undoubtedly one of the great talents of the time—to develop his own artistic means of attack, a form and a language of such ruthless precision that they bewildered friends and foes alike, leaving his ultimate intentions a matter of debate for his critics to this day. In taking this course, he fell back on what he had gained in younger years in the school of Stefan George. He could do so because, in his heart, he shared George's cultural conservatism. We have to conclude, therefore, that Sternheim's very insistence on form and its concomitant aesthetic and social values are grafted on the old tree of realistic theatre, the well-made play of the Nineteenth Century. During the first Amherst Colloquium on Modern German Literature, Andrzej Wirth showed convincingly that even Georg Kaiser's famous *Gas*-trilogy is rooted in this very same dramatic tradition, the well-made play, in which we undoubtedly have to see one of the great structural achievements in the history of Western drama.

Stepping back for a moment and taking a broad look at Expressionist writing in Germany, we are again and again surprised at how derivative was not only its underlying view of form, but also its subject matter. Perhaps we have to except only one topic that runs through much of Expressionist literature from such a broad indictment, that of pacifism. Pacifism is the one postulate which was given to the Expressionists as a present by history, and it is, therefore, historical in a positive as well as in a negative sense of the word—negative for no other reason than that historical phenomena come and go and that, even if they seem to recur, they are never the same. Pacifism in literature is in itself a mere attitude, not a philosophy, nor even a social concept. If it is carried over into everyday life, it engenders something fine and noble, a somewhat evangelistic "brotherliness." I am sure we are all for brotherliness—and these days also for sisterliness—but on a purely literary level, in the void of pure emotionalism, it is apt to become quite unbearable in a short time. Do I have to prove my point with examples? The poetry of the young Werfel could be quoted almost in its entirety. Nothing would be more absurd than to try to apply the pacifist manifestoes of the Expressionists to our own struggles toward the same end. The same is true of their social message, as far as we can speak of one. What solution does Georg Kaiser propose in all seriousness in *Gas* to free the workers from the straightjacket of industrialization? Their dispersal in the "victory gardens" (*Schrebergärten*) along the outskirts of the big cities. When this solution does not work, he blows up "the whole works." Of course, poets are under no obligation to provide us with solutions, even if they pretend to have all the answers. It is enough—and, indeed, very important—that they keep the problems before our eyes. They have rightly been called the conscience of their time. Kaiser's solution is that of the atom bomb, leading into deadly nothingness. There are those who have marvelled at his prophetic vision, seen in retrospect and from our point of view. To read Kaiser thus is to give his dramatic gesture of desperation a rational implication which it did not have. He is not the man to come to us with a warning but one who is at the end of his rope. Whenever he seems to have grappled with economic problems, and that seems to have been the case from his earliest plays on, he did so not from any deeper insight into economics than that he himself was constantly out of cash. This certainly is part of the reason why his work never experienced a genuine revival after the last war.

And yet, the "decade of Expressionism" from 1910 to 1920 was a period of fundamental changes that affected the whole national body. No matter how solipsistic the concern of its artists for aesthetics may have originally been, it still contained a revolutionary ferment, which only needed some cause to be channelled into politics. After all, these ten years not only saw a World War but also a Russian Revolution. The biographies of the editors of the two most important journals of the time, Franz Pfemfert of *Die Aktion* and Herwarth Walden of *Der Sturm,* may be indicative of the general trend that began to develop toward the end of the war and in the twenties, because both of them, in spite of their former grave differences, turned to Communism. There have been broad accusations that the Expressionists were precursors of National Socialism, as indeed some of them undoubtedly were. By and large, however, Communism—well-understood or not—was the only radical alternative they had, and those who joined Hitler in later years only prove the wisdom of the old adage that the extreme right and the extreme left tend to converge.

Although we have had to simplify the situation in several respects, it still seems rather odd that it should have been Germany which provided the most fertile soil for Expressionism in all of its many manifestations. The conditions that had to be fulfilled for its emergence—and they were eminently cultural and political in nature—were present in no other Western country. In a way, one might actually argue that it was the particular constitution of the German middle classes that produced it. The position that the young Expressionists took was, on an essentially personal level, the result of the inner conflict in their society that had opened up a gulf between the generations. This gulf reflects the unresolved dichotomy between the needs of the middle classes and the consistent denial of these needs by a state clinging desperately to the last vestiges of feudalism. If history were to follow the dictates of pure reason, the middle classes should have made common cause with their young liberators, but the good citizens had been conditioned for too long to the authoritarian principle and had indelibly incorporated it into their own way of thinking, in public life no less than in the family. By the end of the last century the all-pervading spirit of Prussian militarism had gotten complete hold of this society and had transformed it into a vast and well-functioning camp. To refresh our memory, it would help to turn to Fontane in his last years and to what he had to say about the German "Militärstaat" in the nineties. What matters is to understand how the typical German "pater familias" and the ordinary schoolteacher had been drilled (today we would call it "brainwashed") on the military training-grounds of the country, and how everyone knew on which side his bread was buttered. Peter Uwe Hohendahl has investigated this social background from the point of view of Expressionist literature. Although his data were often too meager for a well-rounded sociological study, he was still able to draw a convincing picture of historical ramifications and of the impact they had had on Expressionist writing and thinking. Actually, his findings go well beyond an exclusive concern with the Expressionists, who never gained a clear view of what was ailing them. Their reaction to the patriarchal society, in which they had grown up and which attempted to force them into its mold, remained completely emotional. We are referring, of course, to the fact that so much of Expressionist writing centered around the conflict between father and son, and less—excepting Heinrich Mann and a few others at the outer edges of Expressionism—around the problems created by these patriarchal conditions for the German school system and its vast supply of Professor Unrats. One must perhaps have lived outside of Germany long enough to perceive in the father of Hasenclever's *Sohn* the totally and tragically non-paternal qualities of this father-image, something unthinkable, it seems to me, in any other literature. But one meets this strange prototype again and again, with slight variations. Allowing a son to punch his father in the nose (but in the safe distance of fiction and poetry!) was the Expressionists' way of challenging authority and attacking the social system. On the other hand, it was largely left to the Neo-Romantics, Hermann Hesse foremost among them, to take the school-system to task for its perennial horrors, particularly for its often ruthless suppression of the gifted, the budding artists and writers who did not fit into it. The Neo-Romantics' emphasis was less on social criticism, however, than on the misery of their own youth, in which they indulged with pitiless persistence. Only in one regard did the Expressionists make common cause with the Neo-Romantics: in their insistence on the need for sexual freedom. Here again, the attack was ultimately directed against the social status quo, because sex really is a dynamic force that implicitly threatens the bourgeois demand for "law and order." Sex always has played its usual role in any society. What has changed is the degree to which it is now freely admitted and therefore allowed to be discussed publicly. For the German bourgeoisie at the end of the nineteenth century it was taboo, but the attacks against such taboos are not without their comical aspects—afterwards. Who can nowadays read Wedekind's *Frühlings Erwachen* (*Spring's Awakening*), which was the first broadside against them, without laughing in the wrong places? If Wendla cannot talk her mother into giving her the most primitive information in matters of sex education and is sent instead to the "Klapperstorch" (stork), it is high comedy for us, but our laughter is, at the same time, the worst possible indictment of a whole society. Toward the end of the last century, Wedekind had pleaded only for honesty and good mental as well as physical health, but the Expressionists went one step further (or maybe two!) and put the prostitute on a pedestal. They took their cue from Dostoevsky's *Crime and Punishment,* but placed the holy prostitute in the service of a Nietzschean "Umwertung aller Werte" (Revaluation of all Values). It is hardly possible to think of Expressionist literature without its array of prostitutes; at least that is what they are rather liberally called in Expressionist writings, although in fact it would be difficult to find one who sells herself for money, and none of them ever runs the risk of contracting syphilis. In real life, however, things looked quite differently, as the gynecologist Gottfried Benn knew when he made his statement about having seen the whole feminine side of the Expressionist generation as patients in his office. The term "Hure" as used by the Expressionists was clearly intended to shock the "Bürger" out of their wits while the freewheeling women they liked to portray were simply "emancipated women," even when stationed in brothels—as, for instance, Adrienne in Hasenclever's *Der Sohn.* Yet, the term "emancipated woman" will have to be used with great care in this context since it differs widely from the one in our own vocabulary. The female characters in Expressionist literature are merely women placed outside the social order, set into the marginal regions of the Bohème where they could live their lives undisturbed—lives, however, that were, when all is said, completely and exclusively devoted to the needs of the men who created and who surrounded them: male fantasies pure and simple. Dostoevsky's real message was completely lost on the Expressionists. The truly "liberated woman" never becomes a theme in their literature. Man remains the center of its imaginary universe in which women serve only as supporting characters, sentimentalized, glorified, but also often brutalized out of all proportion, as for instance in Kokoschka's plays. One can never be quite sure whether one is dealing with a prostitute, a madonna, or both. It follows that the Expressionists did very little to change the role of women in Germany society: they only preached what they—just as the rest of their contemporaries—were doing anyway; that is, they transposed their own life-style into literature, essentially the life-style of the emerging big city. (pp. 140-47)

At this juncture we return to our previous claims that the primary concern of Expressionism was with form and thus with aesthetics rather than with content, and that, if we except some later pacifist documents such as Hasenclever's *Antigone* and similar activist contributions, it was without any genuine social criticism. I am quite aware that I am running counter not only to popular opinion but also to what appears to be the general consensus of a goodly number of experts, most recently, Wolfgang Rothe. The crux of the problem seems to be the failure to recognize that the Expressionists' obvious delight in formal destructiveness shows a deep-seated concern for form. It is probably safe to say that at least the slightly older members of the various Expressionist groupings, among them Sternheim and Kaiser, had had previous experience with traditional literary forms before they started to attack them. In some cases, their breaking with tradition was actually not as radical as we are sometimes led to believe. Nothing could be further from the truth than to consider them iconoclasts in the old sense of the word. Today, half a century later, we can easily recognize the pioneering quality of their attitude toward language and form, and are in a better position than their contemporaries to understand to what extent they broke the ground for almost everything that is characteristic of avant-garde literature in our own days. This simple fact already justifies their insurrection in historical terms, but it does not answer our specific question regarding their attitude toward form and content. Of course, we could avoid the whole issue by summarily declaring that art's primary concern is, was, and always will be with form, or that art and a real rejection of form would be contradictions in terms. Thus, nothing was more ludicrous than the declaration of the demise of literature coming, not so long ago, from Germany. Anybody endowed with but a minimum of perceptiveness could have foreseen that its "demise" would logically be followed by a "Literature after the Death of Literature," this being the translation of the actual title of a book that appeared a few years ago on the German book market. There are, it seems, all kinds of resurrections, some more convincing than others. It also demonstrates once again the advisability of cultivating a healthy sense of humor. One should perhaps go even one step beyond speaking of the Expressionists' fascination with form, because what we are faced with in their case is more than a fascination, it is a fixation—a painful fixation, because it resulted from a tragic lack of viable alternatives contingent on their historical situation. Despite their fixation on form, however, the Expressionists were unable to create new formal structures. They dissolved "normal" language with every means available to them and could raise the pitch of their poetic diction to the point of the unbearable, but they had nothing new to offer, literally, in the way of lyrical or dramatic forms, let alone the medium of prose, where a superimposed linguistic radicalism cannot hide their use of traditional genres. Even the Naturalists were more inventive in this respect, because they at least have to their credit not only Arno Holz's "Mittelachsenvers" but also the concept of the "eternal stage." The only new form that is supposedly typical of Expressionism is the "Stationen-drama," and that was taken over directly from Strindberg.

We shall have to find a way out of this apparent dilemma, and I suggest that we do so by distinguishing between two aspects of form: between what one might call "inner" and "outer" form. In order not to get bogged down in technicalities that would only obscure the real issue, I shall assume that the distinction I propose is immediately clear, and if not, that the following examples and our brief and admittedly cursory interpretations will sufficiently clarify it. As soon as we make the suggested distinction, however, we can see that the Expressionists concentrated their energies on what we called the "inner form" of a work, while playing freely with the formal structures they had inherited. Like Rilke during the same years, they did not even hesitate to write sonnets if the spirit moved them, but they exploded them, as it were, from within. In a famous poem, Ernst Stadler described the moment of tension that results from such diverging tendencies on the one hand, and on the other from the fact that the poet is held captive in the world of form despite his declared desire to break out of it. The poem, conventional to the point of heaviness, reflects the hold tradition still had on him. He underscored the key words of the poem by placing them in the title; they have a distinctly erotic ring to them:

Form ist Wollust

Form und Riegel mußten erst zerspringen,

Welt durch aufgeschlossene Röhren dringen:
Form ist Wollust, Friede, himmlisches Genügen,
Doch mich reißt es, Ackerschollen umzupflügen.
Form will mich verschnüren und verengen,
Doch ich will mein Sein in alle Weiten drängen—
Form ist Härte ohn' Erbarmen,
Doch mich treibt es zu den Dumpfen, zu den
   Armen,
Und in grenzenlosem Michverschenken
Will mich Leben mit Erfüllung tränken.

        Ernst Stadler: *Form Is Lust*

Form and fetters had to be rent asunder,
World through opened tubes to me must thunder:
Form is lust, peace, heavenly contentment,
But still I'm drawn to plow the soil.
Form intends to bind me and restrict me,
Yet I must expand in all directions—
Form is harshness void of mercy,
Yet I'm driven to the dulled ones and impover-
   ished,
And by giving freely of myself
Life will still me with fulfillment.

Critics tend to understand this poem as tangible evidence that an old way of thinking and feeling is giving way to a new, the dusk of the one and the dawn of the other. To some extent, these critics are, of course, correct in that Stadler, as so many of his contemporaries (around 1910), had turned against the pure Formalism of the Aestheticism indulged in by the previous generation (Stefan George and Hugo von Hofmannsthal, including the French Symbolists) which had also been the gospel of Stadler's own early writing. His turn toward Expressionism related more to the content than to the form of his poetry, expressing a yearning for greater closeness to reality which, in itself, was not a particular characteristic of the Expressionist movement. In a way, one could say that he wanted it "both ways"—hence the form he used remained rather strict, if not heavy-handed, while the new content was limited to a vague message of human understanding. One notices the awkwardness with which he put into words what he considered his compassion for the "downtrodden," the "Dumpfen" and the "Armen" who had so vividly impressed him with their misery in the London East End. But who are the "Dumpfen"? The mentally dull or the inhabitants of the slums? The word is a far cry from the social concerns of the Naturalists, to wit, their "Mitleidsethos" (Ethos of pity). Stadler, a promising young professor of German literature and a member of the Alsatian upper-middle-classes, was not the man to "Ackerschollen umzupflügen" (to till the soil) a term that today has even assumed a rather sinister connotation in that it foreshadows the "Blut und Boden" (Blood and Soil) literature of the darkest time in modern German history. It is all very stiff, the words too stilted for the purpose, as in line two where the poet asserts that the world had "to press on to him through open pipes." The realm of form is alluded to in its dual nature of "Wollust" and "Härte ohn' Erbarmen" because both "Wollust" and this particular "hardness" to one's fellowman are positive and negative values at the same time, and so is "peace and heavenly satisfaction." Stadler rejects the old empty formalism but he creates for himself a new one, and it would be interesting to know where all this would have led him if he had not been killed during the first weeks of the war. We are reminded of Platen's famous lines:

    Wer die Schönheit angeschaut mit Augen,
    Ist dem Tode schon anheimgegeben,

    Wird für keinen Dienst der Erde taugen, . . .
    Denn ein Tor nur kann auf Erden hoffen,
    Zu genügen solchem Triebe.

        August von Platen, from *Tristan*

    Whoever's seen Beauty face to face,
    Is consigned to Death already,
    He's unfit for any earthly service . . .
    For no one but a fool can hope to suffice
    Such desire in his life.

Here, as there, it is the age-old joy of suffering which is the poet's lot. And the Expressionist makes no exception.

Walter Hasenclever published as late as 1913, at the age of 23, a volume of poems entitled *Der Jüngling* (*The Youth*), a word that enjoyed a strange popularity among the Expressionists (it occurs also in Lichtenstein's poem below), even though it is marked by the peculiar preciosity of the "Jugendstil" of the turn of the century. "Jugendstil" was the style of life and of art in which very many of the Expressionists had grown up and which, therefore, had left indelible marks on their work and their thinking. Hasenclever's small volume is made up of a group of short poems all having the same basic structure, which, at first sight, reminds the reader of a volume by Stefan George. The stanzas fill the pages like little squares with a visual regularity that bespeaks a keen sense of form. Yet, the individual poems vary slightly in size, consisting of between twelve and fourteen mostly iambic lines of differing length with remarkably dextrous rhymes, clearly in the tradition of Rilke and Hofmannsthal. If we examine these poems more closely, our expectations of Expressionism are put to a test. They develop thoughts that seem to be the opposite of what one would expect from an Expressionist, because they value rationality higher than irrationality, "Geist" higher than "Gefühl," old age higher than youth. Nevertheless, they also reveal a distinct tension which indicates a struggle between two forces, one inside, the other outside. We shall have to limit ourselves to a brief look at the poem:

    Ich rufe dich, Gefühl, das oft kredenzte,
    Vom Schauplatz der Amouren ab.
    Wer liebt, der rennt im Trab;
    Hinter ihm tanzt die buntgeschwänzte
    Peitsche der Angst, die Wiege und das Grab.
    Wer liebt, irrt in Gefahr. Wer liebt, der schildert
    Unwirkliches hinaus mit seinem Blut,
    Der hebt zum Rausch das Bein, der wird verwildert
    Und ein verbrannter, gelber Sommerhut.
    Denn nur wer vieles weiß, der kann sich retten,
    Der bleibt im Wehen wie im Süßen gut;
    Ihn trägt ein Flötenton in allen Betten,
    Gleich einem Spiegel, durch die Flut.

    Walter Hasenclever, from the volume *The Youth*

Back I call you, feeling, often solemnly served,
From the scene of love's affairs.
Whoever loves, must run at a trot;
Behind him dance the vivid-colored tails
Of the whip of fear, the cradle and the grave.
Whoever loves is lost in danger. Whoever loves de-
   picts
Unreal things drawn with his blood.
He shakes a leg in his delirium, he goes to seed
And becomes a burnt-out yellow summer hat.
For only he who knows a lot can save himself,
He stays on top in sun and rain;*
A flute-tone carries him in any bed,
Just like a mirror, through the flood.

(*lit., in all that hurts and that is sweet)

Before we turn to the poem itself, a brief biographical note seems to be in order: The young Hasenclever is known to have had an ungodly number of "Amouren," indeed he was so obsessed with sex that he had his closest friends deeply alarmed. His restlessness stemmed from a sense of insecurity that had its roots in his early childhood experiences. His poem is the outcry of a man who wants to save (*retten*) himself by turning to "knowledge" (*wer vieles weiß*) and in the process he vividly depicts in ever-changing metaphors the course taken by the obsessed lover. The first metaphor is that of a tournament which leads (line 3) to that of a horse race where the horse stands for the listless lover. The psychological significance of the horse does not have to be explained to a reader in the post-Freudian age. From this point on, the poem seems to become distorted by swirling metaphors, a practice typical of Expressionism. What really happens is the admission of fear (*Angst*) into the poem together with the attempt to stem it by evoking the powers of reasoning. It would be interesting to follow Hasenclever's train of thought in greater detail and to analyze his particular diction down to the "burnt yellow summer hat" that marks the last stage of wear and worthlessness to be reached by the sexually obsessed male. There is a sharp contrast in the flow of words which describe the wild chase of the lovelorn youth on one hand, and on the other, the calm of the man "who knows a lot" and, therefore, can save himself, who remains "good" in adversity (*das Wehe*), as well as in sweet happiness (*das Süße*). Love is not forsworn but it is channelled into a more moderate course, albeit still "in allen Betten" (in all beds). Again we approach the shores of "Jugendstil" with its sounds of flutes and its "flood" of life.

Whatever criticism we may have, Hasenclever's poem has its distinct qualities, and we must regret that his early poetry has been so badly neglected. It is equally true, though, that his diction may be restless, probing, even in parts tumultuous, yet it is anything but revolutionary. His poetic language can and will get louder and shriller in the course of his next few years, but it will never cast off its ties to tradition completely. When he finds his way into comedy and to the well-made play in the twenties, he will not have betrayed Expressionism and all that it stood for, but will have returned to his beginnings.

To strengthen our argument, we shall place another poem next to Hasenclever's, Alfred Lichtenstein's "Die Dämmerung," without a doubt one of the single most prominent pieces of poetry of the whole generation:

Die Dämmerung

Ein dicker Junge spielt mit einem Teich.
Der Wind hat sich in einem Baum gefangen.
Der Himmel sieht verbummelt aus und bleich,
Als wäre ihm die Schmincke ausgegangen.

Auf lange Krücken schief herabgedrückt
Und schwatzend kriechen auf dem Feld zwei
  Lahme.
Ein blonder Dichter wird vielleicht verrückt.
Ein Pferdchen stolpert über eine Dame.

An einem Fenster klebt ein fetter Mann.
Ein Jüngling [!] will ein weiches Weib besuchen.
Ein grauer Clown zieht sich die Stiefel an.
Ein Kinderwagen schreit und Hunde fluchen.

Alfred Lichtenstein, *Twilight*

A little fat boy makes a pond his toy.
The wind's got caught up in a tree.
The sky's hung over and so pale
As if its makeup had run out today

Upon tall crutches, crooked, hanging down,
Two lame men chatter crawling on the field.
A blond-haired poet may be going crazy.
A horsie stumbles o'er a lady.

A fat old man is sticking to a window.
A youth would like to go to some soft woman.
A grayish clown pulls on his boots.
A baby carriage screams and dogs go cursing.

What strikes the eye immediately is, once again, the conventional form of the four-line stanza, this time also in iambic meter but with a regularity that goes well beyond the one we found in Hasenclever's poem. Whatever dynamism it contains is even more strictly limited to what we called the "inner form." Leafing through Kurt Pinthus' anthology *Menschheitsdämmerung,* where Lichtenstein's poem as well as Stadler's "Form ist Wollust" were first printed, we will be surprised to see how many of the Expressionists used this simple device of the four-line stanza, especially, of course, Georg Heym.

Lichtenstein's poem predates Hasenclever's by almost two years. It was written and published early in 1911, and was closely patterned after Jacob van Hoddis' famous poem "Weltende." Lichtenstein's and van Hoddis' poems grew out of the daily experiences with the Expressionist circles in Berlin, lending them an authenticity that Hasenclever, who was at that time still very much an outsider, cannot claim.

If we compare "Die Dämmerung" with Hasenclever's poem, we must conclude that it has no message at all, no underlying train of thought. The series of images, following each other line by line in obsessive monotony, are supposed to evoke a larger whole, to capture the mood of twilight. One could be tempted to define the poem as a string of impressions—impressions, however, that differ from those of the Impressionists by appearing arbitrary and incoherent, the reflections of a very subjective, but also ironically detached mind. As impressions they are, however, more "correct" in the sense that they have not been subjected to the corrective memory that the observer normally applies automatically to what he sees on the basis of his experiences with objects surrounding him. They are less "correct" in comparison with ordinary impressions because they are intentionally deflected by an intellectual attitude on the part of the author. Lichtenstein has expressed himself directly on this particular problem of observation by stating that he knew very well that the man was not glued to the window, but stood behind it, and that it is not the baby carriage that screams, but the child in it. Since he can actually see only the baby carriage, he has to say that is "the baby carriage" that "screams." It would be a lyrical fallacy (*unwahr*), he claimed, if he wrote: A man stands behind a window—and he explained the other oddities of the poem in a similar manner. Clearly, his primary, if not exclusive concern was with aesthetics, and we can readily grant him that, especially on the basis of our experience with fifty years of subsequent international poetry. It would be interesting to place the poem Trakl wrote under the same title next to Lichtenstein's: in subject matter—for Trakl, the life of the insane in an institution—they differ greatly, but the poetic technique would be amazingly similar.

And here we shall rest our case. I fully realize the selective nature of the material upon which I have drawn and readily concede that there are other aspects of that intriguing phenomenon which is German Expressionism, but I would still maintain that it is form and not content which was uppermost on the mind of these poets. (pp. 148-56)

Wolfgang Paulsen, "Form and Content in German Expressionist Literature," in The Massachusetts Review, Vol. XXI, No. 1, Spring, 1980, pp. 137-56.

H. STEFAN SCHULTZ

[*In the following excerpt, Schultz identifies some aesthetic tenets of Expressionism and examines the application of those tenets in German Expressionist poetry, prose, and drama.*]

The late Gottfried Benn was asked to write an introduction for a collection to be entitled "Lyric Poetry of Expressionism," in 1955. He looked at the publisher's manuscript and found that many of the selections had nothing to do with expressionism. He questioned the term "expressionistic" when applied to some of his own verses and wondered about the inclusion of half a dozen writers. But the publisher informed him that the poems in question had been called "typically expressionistic works" by professional literary historians and essayists. The result of many weeks of reading and research, on the part of Benn and the editors of the proposed anthology, was the realization that apparently not all poets dubbed expressionistic are actually "expressive," nor were all the expressive ones representatives of the period. The collection was finally published under the title *Lyric Poetry of the Expressionistic Decade* with the tacit assumption that the public knew, as a matter of course, the ten years from 1910 to 1920 were meant. If we add "forerunners" and "stragglers" we may, with some justification, enlarge the period and arrive at two decades, from about 1905 to 1925. Yet as soon as we try to recollect the events of these twenty years, we are overwhelmed by the number and force of momentous changes. Where will we find the common denominator for an age that saw the placid peace of capitalist Europe turned into a First World War, followed by revolutions and galloping inflations? And how could we hope to press into a few pages the history of literary expressionism in Germany when Albert Soergel needed, in 1925, some eight hundred and ninety-five pages for his *Under the Spell of Expressionism?* Soergel wrote a very good book containing a wealth of material and many quotations from sources that are practically unobtainable now.

No one seems to know how and when the handy term "expressionism" was applied to the new movement. The literary arts, as usual, borrowed from the visual arts, or rather from art historians. When Wilhelm Worringer's *Abstraction and Empathy* appeared in 1908, artists of the new movement found a theoretical basis for their practice of "abstraction." Worringer showed that man's artistic purposes have not always been the same. He believed that a sympathetic relationship between man and the external world, which he called "empathy," tends toward the production of organic, naturalistic, classical works of art: art melts into nature. But there are other epochs—the primitive, the Byzantine, the late Roman, the new art of Cézanne, Van Gogh and Matisse—when man feels the need to tear the object from its natural context in the world and give it a new and absolute form—geometric or stylized.

When Hermann Bahr published his *Expressionism* in August 1914, he put the matter in a slightly different way: man possesses the physical sense of sight, a passive organ that receives impressions; the mind, to be sure, transforms them, but the result is a work of art close to nature. But man has also an inner eye capable of visions; it is the eye of the spirit that turns away from external life toward the inner life, listens to the voices of the hidden within, and believes man is not merely the echo of his world, but rather its maker ("Täter"), or at least just as strong as the world. Bahr said: "Impressionism is after all nothing but the final word of classical art, its completion and fulfillment. It tries to enhance the external vision to the highest degree and to exclude as much as possible the inner vision, it tries to weaken more and more the eye's spontaneous life, its self-activity, its will, and thus turns man into a debtor to his senses." Bahr quotes Maurice Barrès as an example of this state of man: "But I myself no longer existed, I was simply the sum of all that I saw."

It is worth noting that both Worringer and Bahr base their arguments not on artistic forms and styles as they occurred in history, but on human attitudes and faculties that, by necessity, had to produce certain artistic types. The human being comes first; the formal aspects of art are secondary. This is surprising to us who recognize the new art—be it expressionistic, futuristic, or cubistic—by its formal aspects. Yet Kandinsky wrote, in the second edition of *Der blaue Reiter* (1914) when he could look back on the two years since the inception of the group in Munich, that his primary, though unfulfilled, aim had been to show by practical example and theoretical proof that "the question of form in art was of secondary importance, that the question of art was principally one of content." Kandinsky meant by "content" "the inner element of the work, created by the vibration of the soul." The formal element was a matter for the academicians, what mattered now was a "geistige Bewegung," which is a "spiritual" rather than an "intellectual" movement in English. Kandinsky also speaks of "das geistige Leben" ("the spiritual life") and the mutual approximation and interpretation of the heretofore separate realms of the intellectual-spiritual life. The very catholicity of *Der blaue Reiter*—its content ranging from a Goethe-quotation to Pablo Picasso, from Bavarian votive pictures to the Douanier Rousseau, from Russian folk-art to Japanese pen-drawings—indicates the pluralism of forms which, at least, the Munich group found acceptable. Kandinsky said: "Matter is the pantry from which the spirit, like a cook, chooses that which is necessary in the particular case." The abstract spirit is like a white fructifying ray, it is the creator of new values. Life rejoices in the victory of the new value. But as soon as the new value is accepted by the many it becomes a barrier against tomorrow. The transformation of the new value (the fruit of freedom) into a petrified form (a wall against freedom) is the work of the "blackhand." All evolution has to destroy, once more, the barriers against freedom even though they had been created out of new values. Thus we see that not the new value is the most important thing, but the spirit revealed in this value. The absolute is not to be looked for in the form. Form is always temporal, i.e. relative, since it is no more than the temporal necessary means by which a temporal revelation is announced. Therefore, we should not make of form a god. We should not look for salvation in *one* kind of form, for every form carries the stamp of the artist's personality. Kandinsky's argumentation, with its echo of the Hegelian dialectics of history and its metaphors of "the white beam" and "the black hand," reminds us of the romantics of the early nineteenth century. The "wild men" of pre-war expressionism were a dedicated brotherhood of individualists. This is quite apparent in Franz Marc's preface to *Der blaue Reiter.* Since his remarks to my knowledge have never been translated, they may be given as further proof for the variety and pluralism in the seemingly monolithic new art.

"All that becomes can only be started on this earth." This sentence of Däubler's can stand as a motto over our whole work and intention. A fulfillment will come, at some time, in a new world, in a different existence. On earth, we can only indicate the theme. This first book is the opening chord to a new theme. Its jumping, restlessly moving manner has probably revealed to the attentive listener the sense in which it was conceived. This listener found himself in a region of sources, where, at a hundred places simultaneously, the waters pulsate, full of secrets, sing, and murmur, sometimes in a hidden way, sometimes openly. We went with the divining rod through the art of the ages and of the present. We showed only that which was alive and untouched by the compulsion of conventions. Our love was dedicated to all in art that was born of itself, lives of itself, and does not walk on the crutches of convention. We pointed at any crack in the crust of convention, since we hoped for some power underneath which some day would come to light. Many of these cracks have since been closed again, our hope was in vain; from others, however, there bubbles today already a living fountain. But this is not the only meaning of this book. The great comfort of history has forever been that nature always pushes up new energies through dead rubbish; if we were to see our task merely as one that has to point to the natural spring-time of a new generation, then we might safely leave it to the sure course of time; there would be no reason for conjuring up and calling for the spirit of a great turn of the times.

We set against great centuries a NO. We well know that by this simple NO we shall not interrupt the serious and methodical course of the sciences and of triumphant "progress." Nor do we intend to get ahead of this development, but we pursue a side-road—to the scornful astonishment of our contemporaries—which scarcely seems to be a road at all, and we say: This is the main road for the development of mankind. We know that the many cannot follow us today; the road is for them too steep and too untravelled. That some, however, want to walk with us has been the lesson of the fate of this first book which we publish once more without changes while we ourselves have already left it behind and are engaged in new work. We do not know when we shall gather for the second book. Perhaps only at a time when we shall be once again quite alone; when modernism will have stopped its attempt to industrialize the primeval forest of new ideas. Before the coming of the new book, much has to be stripped off and torn off that has clung to the movement in these years. We know that all may be lost when the beginnings of a spiritual discipline are not saved from the greed and impurity of the many. We are wrestling for pure thoughts, for a world in which pure thoughts can be and spoken without becoming impure. Only then shall we, or others who are called, be able to show the other face of the Janus-head which today is still hidden and turned away from the times.

How we admire the disciples of early Christianity because they found the strength for inner stillness in the roaring noise of that time. We pray hourly for this stillness and strive for it.

Notable is the feeling of a turning point in the history of mankind and the desire for a spiritual renewal. Marc's voice speaks gently and with a seriousness which reminds us of the German Nazarenes in Rome almost a hundred years before *Der blaue Reiter,* or of the Pre-Raphaelite Brotherhood. Others say the same thing, but in a shriller tone. The titles of magazines founded at the time tell something of the wish for the destruction of the old and outworn. A mighty storm was to cleanse the air, the young were to storm the citadels of convention, action was the watchword. In 1902, a group of Alsatian artists founded the short-lived *Der Stürmer.* Herwarth Walden started *Der Sturm* in Berlin in 1910 as a weekly for culture and the arts. *Die Aktion,* edited as a weekly by Franz Pfemfert in Berlin from 1910 to 1933, embodied in its title the call to action. So did *Die Tat,* on the conservative side, a "monthly for the future of German culture," published from 1908 to 1933, when it was forced to conform to the new tenets of the Nazis. *Das neue Pathos* from 1913 emphasized the rhetorical phrase that was to become paramount in the writings during the years of 1918 and 1919.

Der Sturm was probably the most influential periodical of the new art. It was truly an international gathering place of artists and spread the new gospel through more than 150 exhibitions in Europe and abroad. Here we read: "Expressionism is not a fashion. It is a view of the world (*Weltanschauung*); and a view by the senses, not by concepts. And at that, a view of the universe of which the earth is a part." Lothar Schreyer and Herwarth Walden speak out against the cult of personality; impressionistic portraits, for instance, are proof of the arrogance of personality. A changed world means a changed art. The changed man returns to himself. Expressionism is the intellectual movement of a time which places the inner experience above external life. But this inner experience is not personal; the artist is the involuntary (blind) servant of the "Never experienced." He announces the experience of "intuitive knowledge." "The art of the present is the message of revealed knowledge." Art is therefore a secret which to unriddle is as impossible as to solve the secrets of life, love, or god. "This apocalyptic time separates the poor people, who maintain that they know love, from those men who have love. It separates people who claim to know art from human beings who have art." We note the language of Gnosis and religious mysticism, even though the practice of Herwarth Walden, for instance, makes us doubt the "involuntary" and "visionary" nature of his production. His puns and play with words are products of the purposeful intellect rather than of inner visions compelling the writer's expression. Puns as well as dialectical contrasts result from an analysis of language. Herwarth Walden's epitaph to Franz Marc is a case in point:

The animals listened to him, and he gave them the colors of his love. / The love of his colors. How they love each other, the colors, if one does not disturb them. How the forms embrace if one does not break them. / No fire burns those who themselves are burning.

August Stramm, born in 1874, died in Russia in September, 1915, expressed the extreme theory and practice of the new movement. A Ph.D. and a high official in the postal service, Stramm composed his visions for twenty years and was turned down by every journal and publisher until Walden opened the pages of *Der Sturm* to him. Walden described

Stramm as a mere tool of his visions: words flow through him and out of him, he is the vessel for eternal flow, for the parable of art. But Stramm was writing every poem thirty, fifty, a hundred times. His letters testify to his minute deliberation over every word. Utmost concentration and ultimate simplicity are his aims. Punctuation is absent, with the exception of exclamation marks. Instead of sentences and the logic of syntax, we have erratic blocks of words strung along as "phonetic gestures." The "I" and the personal ending of the verb are frequently suppressed—Marinetti was to say in his Futurist Manifesto of 1909, "One must abolish the adjective and destroy the "I" in literature." Stramm loves infinitives: impersonal activity. This makes translation of many, or most, of his poems an impossibility, for an absolute infinitive in German has to be rendered in English by a gerund, which by its very *-ing* ending approaches the adjective. There is, in a 1914 collection of love poems entitled *Du,* a poem "Bordello" beginning: "Lights whore from the windows / Lues spreads at the door" with the line "Motherwombs yawn childrendeath." One line in this poem consists of the word *"Schamzerpört"* which a thinking and attentive type-setter changed into the more obvious *"schamzerstört,"* i.e. destroyed by shame. Stramm wrote to Walden and defended his neologism as follows:

> *"Scham"* and *"Empörung"* struggle with each other and *"Scham zerdrückt."* *Schamempört* does not express this in any way; furthermore, the characteristic of the word *empören* is in my feeling not in the *em,* which has importance only as a clue to word formation. For our feeling, the idea of *empören* is contained merely in *pören* or rather, simply and completely, in the one sound *pö.* Omit the dots over the *o* and the whole concept is ruined. This is the reason why I consider *schamzerpört* the only word that says everything.

Stramm's trick of combining shame, indignation, and the feeling of being crushed by them in one word may have parallels in Joyce's *Anna Livia Plurabelle.* But Joyce, unlike Stramm, had to call on languages other than English for many of his neologisms. Like Joyce, Stramm did not establish a "school."

While Stramm frequently reduced the lines of a poem to one word or even one syllable, Ernst Stadler wrote the longest lines in German poetry. Stadler was born in 1883 at Colmar in the Alsace. Rhodes scholar at Oxford, Professor extraordinary at Brussels, able translator of Francis Jammes, Stadler had been called to the University of Toronto when the outbreak of the war, and his death in action in October, 1914, put an end to the most promising of young poets. His "Journey at night over the Rhine-Bridge at Cologne" may serve as a sample of his poetry (it seems almost a verbal parallel to Luigi Russolo's painting "Train at full speed"). The poem was published in his *Preludes* of 1904.

> The express gropes and pushes along darkness.
> No star wants forward. The whole world only a
>   narrow nightroundrailed mine gallery,
> where at the face at times spots of blue light tear
>   open sudden horizons: fiery circle
> of spheric lamps, roofs, chimneys, steaming,
>   flowing . . . only for seconds . . .
> and again all black. As if we drove into the
>   bowels of night to our shift.

> Now lights tumble toward us . . . lost, alone without solace . . . more . . . and gather . . . and
>   thicken.
> Skeletons of gray house-fronts lie bare, in twilight
>   paling, dead—something must come . . .
>   oh, I feel it heavily
> in my brain. A tightness sings in my blood. Then
>   the ground suddenly thunders like a sea:
> We fly, uplifted, royally, through air snatched from
>   the night, high above the river. O bending of
>   millions of lights, a silent watch
> before whose lightening parade heavy the waters
>   downward roll. an endless lane, drawn up
>   as greeting at night!
> Storming like torches! Joyful! Salute of ships
>   beyond the blue sea! Starry feast!
> Swarming, a throng with bright eyes! Up to where
>   the city's last houses release their guest.
> And then the long solitudes. Naked banks.
>   Quiet. Night. Reflection. Heart-searching.
>   Communion. And fervor and zeal
> for the ultimate blessing. For the feast of creation.
>   For lust. For prayer. For the sea. For extinction.

In early expressionist poetry, traditional language and neologisms wrenched from customary syntax are to be found side by side. A violent subjectivism may go hand in hand with the desire to merge the "I" with cosmic forces, or with the common "We." A joyful ecstasy and a fervent wish for death may be joined, as in Stadler's "Night Journey."

Victor Hadwiger (1879-1911) from Prague, published in 1903 poems under the title *I am.* The theme of his poetry, however, is not "being" as much as a dissolution of the "I" in death, in love, in song, in beauty. The husk of individuality bursts: "the land grows light before me and boundless the glow / I am the brook, I am the flow, / gently the fields incline towards my course." The sentiment, if not the poetry, is like that of the young Goethe in the early 1770's. It is perhaps no accident that so many of this first expressionist generation either died before the First World War, or became its victims. Most of them were in their twenties: Georg Trakl, Reinhard Johannes Sorge, Ernst Wilhelm Lotz, Alfred Lichtenstein, to name just a few writers. Their visions of doom and destruction, of a great cataclysm, a twilight of the gods, and of mankind anticipated the coming reality.

Georg Heym drowned while skating on the Havel in 1912. He was 24 years old. He used traditional metres and rhymes with great skill; the content of his poetry shows a keen eye for the daemonic and ghoulish reality of modern life: the smoke stacks of the big cities, freight trains, slums, the poor, the blind, the sick in hospitals, the dead and dying. Heym does not accuse, he simply states: the god of the city is the red-bellied Baal to whom clouds from factories rise like incense. We are never told why the god is wrathful and furious, he just consumes, with his fists of a butcher, the city in a tremendous conflagration. Heym's "War" of 1911 is a vision which became reality only in the tremendous destructions of the Second World War. Huge cities throw themselves into the belly of the abyss, night is parched by the torch of war. That there is something inevitable and deserved about the cataclysm is barely indicated in the last line of the poem: "Pitch and fire dripping on Gomorrha."

Georg Heym.

The world's end, however, does not always come in an outward destruction, where "the smoke of the country went up as the smoke of a furnace," but is at times pictured as an all-pervading distress, a weeping as though God had died, as though life had been laid to rest in the coffins of our hearts, as though there was an unfulfilled longing of which man had to die, for instance Else Lasker-Schüler's "End of the World" (1902). A poem with the same title by Jakob van Hoddis initiated, in January, 1911, the lyric poetry of the journal *Die Aktion*. Hoddis' world ended 14 years before Mr. Eliot's "not with a bang but a whimper." T. S. Eliot's irony is perhaps more sophisticated and devastating because of his turning liturgical forms into the ritual of children's games, but Hoddis achieves a similar effect by understatement and images reminding us of Humpty-Dumpty's fall. A prosy translation of Hoddis' rhymes gives at least the content, though not the flavor of his doomsday:

> From pointed heads of burghers fly their hats / The air is filled with shrieking everywhere / Roofers fall headlong and break in two / The flood is rising on the shore—the papers say. / The gale is here, the wild seas hop / on land to crush fat dikes / Most people have a cold / The railroad trains fall from the bridges.

The condensation and concentration of language and thought in lyric poetry makes it relatively easy to experiment in that medium. But it is a different matter with the prose of the storyteller and novelist. We want to read a well told story. We are looking for plot, action, character. We expect, in a novel, the long wind of an epic writer and, if the turns of the lan-

guage are interesting, accept even a certain pedantry, as in Thomas Mann's Joseph stories. Do we have a good expressionistic novel in Germany? The very tenets of expressionism, as stated in the fall of 1917 by Kasimir Edschmid's "On poetic expressionism," seem to deny everything that traditionally belonged to the epic genre. The love for detail, for the characteristic which belongs only to one individual, for local color—all this is, for Edschmid, part of bourgeois and capitalistic thinking. The artists of the new movement want to express their own feelings infinitely. They do not see, they have visions. They do not describe, they experience. They do not reproduce, they create. Their new picture of the world is like the great landscape of paradise which God originally created. It is more splendid, colorful, and infinite than that which our empirical blindness can see. Everything must show its bond with eternity and with the universe, the great existence of heaven and earth. A sick man must not be described as a suffering cripple, he must become sickness itself, the suffering of all creatures must shine forth from him and call down the pity from the creator. A house must not be an object with definite attributes and dimensions, it must rise above these particularities, it must be freed from the dull compulsion of a false reality and be resurrected as *the* house. Human beings in art are no longer individuals, bound by duty, morality, society, and family. Man in this art is nothing but the most sublime and the most miserable: *he becomes Man.* Neither inhuman, nor superhuman; but only Man, cowardly and strong, good and mean and splendid, as God released him from his creation. He is a cosmic man without need of psychology. Psychology and analysis are perverse ways of thinking; manmade and desecrated by man, guided by well-known causalities. But there can be no explanation for the inexplicable, for the world and for God. The new men do not reflect about the cosmos, they abandon themselves to the divine. They are direct. They are primitive. They are simple, because the simple is the most difficult and the most complicated, and leads to the greatest revelations.

Edschmid was aware of the dangers inherent in the new movement: for instance a cold abstraction, a mere theory, a conscious primitivism. Decisive for him is the *honesty* of the artist, his faith, the creative strength of his soul, the fervor of his spirit. But how does the reality and practice look, in Edschmid's own works for instance? There are many clever tricks, apparently *pour épater le bourgeois:* "By the way, the history of mankind is possible without Aischylos and Dante, but impossible without sailing. . . . The battle for Troy is a trifle, the fact that it was described is a joke. But that one was able to sail to Troy, that was the true achievement." A sample from his "Deadly May" of 1916 appears today funny and boring rather than exciting and novel:

> There was music. At times, the wind ran violently through the unhooked windows, and there was a wave of light which stormed over all. Then the violins from the music rose on high and trembled over space with nameless points. / There he was seized by the tumult of existence with a raving inebriation. He felt himself thrown from hottest excitement into rigid cold and then anew hurled against biting heat. An orchestra raged in his heart, organs burned upward, and the trumpets were lifted in long, cruel convolutions to a terrible blast.

Edschmid's own words at the end of his essay on poetic expressionism are prophetic in their warning against mistaking ambition and good will for achievement. "A good impressionist is a greater artist and has more chance to live in eternity than the mediocre creation of the expressionist looking for immortality. Zola's shameless, gigantic, stuttering, naked power will perhaps better stand the tribunal of the day of judgment than our great wrestling with God. But this, too, is fate." Yet are we confronted with the honesty of the artist or with an easy alibi when Edschmid closes with the words "Here, we do not know. This is in the hands of God who touched us that we should create. We have no judgment, only faith. We also serve in little things. This, too, is immortal."

There is much talk of God and of the New Man. The language of the Old and of the New Testament sounds through many expressionistic works. But is God more than a name to be invoked? Does he still exist as a reality of human experience, as the acknowledgment on man's part that there is something higher than man under whatever name it may appear? I do not think so. Man himself has taken over the creative functions of the deity. Expressionism is, in this respect, no more than the culmination of a development that began with the Renaissance. Much as the expressionists themselves may claim that this development came to an end with impressionism, they are in no way different from Rilke, for instance, who said that the artist does not stand opposite the gods, but looks with them in the same direction. This world is man-made, and only man can re-make it. It is a thoroughly secularized world; some would say a "humanized" world and be proud of it.

If we read Georg Kaiser's *The Citizens of Calais* (1914) as a literary drama and do not mistake it for "an argued condemnation of war" we have to admit that a historical incident, the surrender of Calais to the British in 1347, has been written up as a mystery play. Eustache de Saint-Pierre is the Christ who is willing to sacrifice himself so that the city and its harbor may live. He calls for the new deed and the new doers, changed men. The symbol presiding over the second act is a tapestry, presenting a capitalist history of salvation. The mighty tapestry shows, in its three fields ("with . . .) the strength of forms and colors of an early art, the building of the harbor of Calais." To the left is the steep coast, against which the sea beats violently. The center shows the finished harbor. The right panel represents lively activity during the building of the harbor. This is really the nineteenth century dream of the conquest of nature so that the citizen may live in the comfort of peaceful activity. Kaiser provides then the religion for this pursuit of wealth. He has to use religious forms of an early art: the last supper of the seven, the clamor of the populace similar to the cries of the Jews before Pilate, the mother of the third citizen like Mary, her heart pierced by swords, reminiscences of the garden of Gethsemane, countless echoes from Exodus, Judges, Jeremiah. In the third act, the blind father of Eustache can say of his dead son "I have seen the new man—in this night was he born." Self-sacrifice is the birth to a new life. The blind father is one of the blessed "that have not seen, and yet have believed." After the birth of the new man, it is almost too much when a British officer announces: "In this night a son was born to the King of England in his camp before Calais. On this morning the King of England will for the sake of the new life not destroy a life." Still the final stage directions once more underline the new gospel: "Light floods the tympanon over the door: in its lower part a burial is represented; the slender body of the judged man lies limp on shrouds—six stand bowed at the couch.—The upper part shows the apotheosis of the dead

man: he stands freely and weightless in the air—the heads of the six are turned toward him with astonishment."

The intellectual background of "The Citizens of Calais," as indicated in the title, was primarily the world of *Bürgertum*. In *Gas I* (1918), Kaiser grapples with the problem of an industrialized society in which human beings have become mere functions in a productive process. They are proud of their functional character, they are professionals and experts first and foremost; the Engineer is a specialist, the Secretary is a specialist, every worker is a specialist. Then the catastrophe occurs: the gas explodes. The formula is correct, the manufacturing process is without fault, no human error is involved, nor any mechanical failure. A limit has been reached, the calculations of man are correct in one way, they are incorrect in another way. What is to be done? "Forward, from explosion to explosion" is the general cry which the Billionaire's Son vainly opposes by a plea for a return to nature. His case would seem eminently sound as the only alternative to destruction, but no one wants to become a "peasant." When the Billionaire's Son argues for a true humanity, a new man who will function with the totality of his faculties and not just through the hypertrophy of one part, he is left alone with his widowed daughter—"alone like every one who wanted to become one with all." He asks: "Where is man? When will he appear—and call himself by his name: Man? When will he understand himself—and shake from the branches his knowledge? When will he pass the curse—and create the new creation which he spoiled:—Man ?!—. . . . Am I not a witness for him—and for his origin and arrival—is he not known to me through a strong vision? . . . Shall I still doubt?!!" "I shall bear him," says the kneeling daughter.

Gas II takes place some twenty years later. The Billionaire's grandson is now the Billionaire-Worker, one among many. The countries are at war. The Great-Engineer proposes a solution in the same spirit as his predecessor: gas should be turned into poison-gas, the workers shall become avengers—fighters—victors. The Billionaire's Grandson calls this seduction and pleads: "Formerly, you were great—become greater now—sufferers . . . be sufferers in your work—be released to yourselves!! . . . Build the kingdom!!—which you are in yourselves with a final confirmation! not of this world is the kingdom!!!!" The decision of the workers is unanimously against the millennium and for the Great-Engineer. Whereupon the Billionaire's Grandson sums up his own and his forebears' efforts with a partial quotation from the 29th Psalm. "Our voice could shake the wilderness—man grew deaf before it!! I am justified!! I can fulfill!!!" Seizing the sphere of poison-gas, he smashes it on the floor of the concrete hall. At the same moment the enemy barrage shatters the walls. After the smoke has cleared, an enemy soldier sees the grotesque shapes of the dead stripped of their flesh and scattered among concrete slabs. He telephones back to his own troops " . . .—turn the guns against yourselves and destroy yourselves—the dead throng from their graves—last judgment—dies irae—solvet—in favil—(With a shot, he smashes the rest of the word in his mouth)."

Quite possibly, this is the way our world will actually end. But Kaiser's romantic return to a rural mode of life is an escape, not a solution. Ernst Jünger, no expressionist, faced the same situation unblinkingly from which Kaiser tried to escape, either through the birth of a new Adam, or failing that, through an acceptance of the end, stated in terms of the Judaeo-Christian tradition.

In *The Worker* (1932), Ernst Jünger wanted to evoke the *Gestalt* of the new type of man. *Gestalt* is the indestructible totality of body and soul, not subject to the elements, but part of eternity. "Man's inborn, unchangeable, and imperishable merit, his highest existence and his deepest confirmation lies in his *Gestalt,* quite independent of every merely moral evaluation, every salvation and every "striving endeavor." Whatever this may mean, the *Gestalt* of Jünger's Man is not created in the image of God. Jünger draws the logical consequence from his image of man: "The result of this consciousness is a new relationship to Man, a more fervent love and a more terrible pitilessness. There results the possibility of serene anarchy which coincides with the strictest order—a spectacle already indicated in the great battles and the gigantic cities whose images stand at the beginning of our century. In this sense, the gasoline motor is not the ruler, but the symbol of our time, the emblem of a power for which explosion and precision are no longer opposites. It is the daring toy of a race of men who are capable of exploding themselves with a will and still see in this action a confirmation of order."

There are perhaps two reasons which may account for the absence of really great literary productions in the expressionist movement. One might be stated in T. S. Eliot's words in "Tradition and the Individual Talent": "Poetry is not a turning loose of emotion, but an escape from emotion; it is not the expression of personality, but an escape from personality. But, of course, only those who have personality and emotions know what it means to escape from these things." There were many personalities with strong emotions among German artists during the first quarter of this century. There are quite a few just as good as Eliot. But I should say that there are only three great poets who had "worked their emotions and personalities up into poetry," and they cannot be counted among the expressionists, even though they share with them common themes. I am thinking of George, Hofmannsthal, and Rilke.

The other reason may be elucidated by a quotation from Rudolf Blümner's *The Spirit of Cubism and the Arts.* Blümner found the justification for expressionism in the distinction which Thomas Aquinas made between *species impressa* and *species expressa.* Blümner wrote: "It is easy to understand my great delight when I read in him: the *species impressa* is a matter for sinful man, the *species expressa* is for the angels and for souls freed from the body."

Perhaps, that's just it. After all, we are sinful men, still a little lower than the angels, and it may not be good for our souls, at least as long as they are united with our bodies, to arrogate to us the work of angels. (pp. 8-24)

> *H. Stefan Schultz, "German Expressionism: 1905-1925," in* Chicago Review, *Vol. 13, No. 1, Winter-Spring, 1959, pp. 8-24.*

H. MACLEAN

[*In the following excerpt, Maclean discusses the principal themes and techniques of German Expressionist literature.*]

For a considerable time Expressionism has been seen as a part of a general literary revolution, which took place before and after the turn of the century. It was a revolt against traditional concepts, against values as typified in classical and romantic thinking, against the notion of man as central figure in a stable universe and against schematic and objective art forms.

The differences separating Expressionism from Naturalism on the one hand and from Neo-Romanticism on the other may be regarded as more a matter of variable emphasis than outright opposition. The Expressionist shared with the Naturalist his sympathy for misery and poverty, his indignation about social evils, but not his rôle of recorder and analyst of the human situation. Like the Naturalist, he noted the vulnerability and helplessness of man in his material environment, but felt more directly involved in the need to extricate him from his spiritual plight and give him new hope and new faith, or at least an awareness of his degraded condition. And he also made full use of the naturalist extension of theme and vocabulary to include the hitherto unacceptable in art, the technical, the ugly, the sordid and the diseased, but was not inclined to investigate causes and determining factors.

The Expressionist showed marked similarities with the Neo-Romantics, accepting "but in each case with a difference, the cult of the irrational, the representation of the dream-world, the application of the symbols, and the heightening of the emotional effect to the point of ecstasy." The difference consisted mainly in the rejection by Expressionism of the more passive and restrictive aspects of Neo-Romanticism, its aestheticism, its tendency to look backwards into the past, to use legend and fairy-tale, to create a hermetic world from which reality and vulgarity are excluded. Even the most withdrawn of the writers included under the Expressionist collective, poets such as Georg Trakl and Else Lasker-Schüler, cannot shield themselves from the intrusive reality of modern mass urban living.

All these points have been made many times and they remain, by and large, valid. But they do not stress the burning sense of difference, the violent reaction against the dominant and fashionable art forms of the day, which the young generation of writers and artists felt and expressed increasingly during the first decade of the twentieth century. Naturalism and Impressionism loomed in avant-garde circles as bigger bogeys than the comfortably bowdlerized ideas of romantic literature taught in school and home. What distinguishes the beginnings of Expressionism is the emergence of a more aggressive and emotional attitude towards art and life, or even more, the will to total dedication and absorption of the whole personality and mind into the work of art. It was in the visual arts that the new attitudes asserted themselves first, and most confidently and aggressively. Painters such as Kirchner, Pechstein, Schmitt-Rottluff and Nolde, who formed the *Brücke* group in 1905, turned away from the passivity and delicacy of Impressionism and took as their model, both technically and emotionally, artists such as van Gogh and Munch. For it is the most prominent of van Gogh's characteristics that his whole personality blazes out of the canvas and that he fascinates and repels at the same time. The Expressionist writer and painter was never so insulted as when his work was regarded coolly and indifferently, or worse, when it was simply "enjoyed" as entertainment.

It was from France that the main impetus came. The primitive themes of the south seas and negro art have as a corollary the suggestion of dynamism and surge of basic emotion which sweeps aside the sophistication of civilized controls and techniques. The *Fauves,* established also in 1905, made use of pure elementary colour, which, together with the disruption of realistic space concepts, are echoed and developed with greater emotional intensity in the works of *Die Brücke,* and in the *Blaue Reiter* school, which provided a highly articulate and theoretical backing to experimental work in art, and by a natural extension, to writing. The links between the visual arts and writing were particularly strong in the period before the First World War and parallels between painting and literature both in theme and technique, have been drawn. The closeness of the link is, however, most convincingly demonstrated by those, such as Ernst Barlach, Alfred Kubin and Oskar Kokoschka, who achieved considerable standing in both fields. All three are better known as artists than as writers, but Barlach and Kokoschka especially have enjoyed an increase in their literary reputations over recent years. It was from the visual arts too that the term "Expressionism" derived and it was to French artists that it was first applied. It appears not to have been used by the French themselves, but to describe a group of French artists, among them Braque, Dufy, Picasso, Vlaminck, who were represented in the exhibition of the Berlin Secession in the early summer of 1911. In the August number of *Der Sturm* in the same year Wilhelm Worringer used the term, and from that point it gradually gained currency. Yet it was at first assumed to apply exclusively to painting and was suspect in the literary world until after the beginning of the war. Indeed, despite its fashionable popularity from 1916 until the middle 'twenties, the term "Expressionism" has remained suspect to the present day.

It was in 1910 that the literary groups, no less aggressive or radical than the painters, began to form around clubs and journals. *Der Sturm* was founded in 1910 by Herwarth Walden who claimed more or less exclusive rights to the literary revolution and published in 1912 the German translation of the fierce Futurist manifestos written by Marinetti in 1909. Franz Pfemfert's *Die Aktion,* founded a year later as a rival to *Der Sturm,* was as provocative as the title indicates, and the founding of these two journals was followed by a whole host of new publications. Enthusiasm was colossal. In *Die Aktion* of 1913 a new age of poetry was announced, only half facetiously, which would change the tempo of the lives of bakers, tramwaymen and stock-brokers who, in capital letters, "hate everything which is not poetry." Some of the greatest talents remained isolated—Georg Trakl, Gottfried Benn, Franz Kafka, to name the most considerable—but most were unwilling to reserve their work for the select appreciative few. Literary clubs, *Der Neue Club* (1910), *Das Neopathetische Cabaret* (1910), *Gnu* (1911), sprang into being, and in numerous coffee-houses and halls up and down the length and breadth of the country writers and critics and a frequently bewildered, sometimes hostile, sometimes appreciative public met to hear and discuss the literary productions of an army of young writers whose numbers, fed by unrivalled opportunities for publishing, were increasing at a rate hitherto unknown in Germany.

The intrusion of the Futurist manifestos on the German scene in 1912 can be seen, superficially at any rate, as supporting the intentions of the German writers and giving them direction and cohesion. Marinetti claimed that speed, power, efficiency and aggressiveness were the prime needs of the future. He took up an extreme, unambiguous position by praising the city and the machine as the chief instruments in both the social and the aesthetic revolution, which would overthrow existing patterns and make a complete break with the past. But the Italian theorists not only noted the displacement of man from the centre of things, they drew the conclusion that, since he was dominated by museum, library and fixed thought patterns implanted in him by past ages, he must also be excluded as a subject for painting and literature. "The pain of a man

is just as interesting for us as the pain of an electric torch which suffers from a spasmodic twitching." The age of humanism was dead and man reduced to the level of material things.

Marinetti was fêted when he spoke in Berlin in 1912 and it would be false to underrate the stimulus which the Futurists gave to the more experimental groups, especially to the group centred around *Der Sturm.* But although they were presented with a novel clarity and precision which made its own impact, the content itself of the manifestos was not unfamiliar to the Germans, as Alfred Döblin pointed out at the time in an open letter to Marinetti: "Marinetti, you are not saying anything new to us; I may say: you embrace our cause." Moreover there were clearly differences. The Germans did not accept the Futurist doctrine in its entirety. Those of them who could lay claim to a defined political attitude were leftist and ignored the passages in the manifesto which glorified war and proclaimed the domination of the male sex. But there is another point of difference which is less obvious and which needs to be stressed considerably more. The German writers were generally conscious at the beginning that anarchy could so easily spill over into tyranny, that the means by which freedom could be achieved might be turned with bewildering suddenness against freedom. Again it was Döblin, who, despite his general approval of their radicalism, saw that the fanaticism of the Futurists could defeat itself, replace the dominance of the museum by the dominance of the machine, and subject them to a new kind of Naturalism:

> Surely you do not think that there could be only one reality, surely you do not identify the world of your automobiles, aeroplanes and machine-guns with the world? . . . Or do you ascribe to the world of angles, colours and sound an absolute reality, which we should approach as reverently as minute secretaries?

Döblin objected to specific aspects of Futurism. But his protests were also directed against a general tendency to bring everybody into their own fold. Although the Expressionists of the pre-war years had willingly entered into the communities of the clubs and the journals, they were chiefly distinguished by the individuality of their literary style and technique. It is true that the war and particularly the revolutionary period after the war produced a spate of political writing and an always increasing tendency to stereotyped techniques after the fashionable models of Werfel, Kaiser, Toller and others. This was accompanied by a mass of theoretical writing which followed the appearance of Hermann Bahr's *Expressionismus* in 1916 and reached its high point in Kasimir Edschmid's treatise [*Über den Expressionismus in der Literatur und die neve Dichtung*] in 1919 which is, despite the disservice done to it by too frequent quotation, still one of the essential documents of Expressionism. But the Expressionist before the war felt no temptation to ally himself to any literary mode and the few desultory attempts to formulate classifications point to the lack of any compelling binding relationship present at the time.

These writers did not want to be pinned down, to be labelled, to be forced into a new mould at a time when development seemed to be limitless. Their minds were reaching out constantly to grasp something which lay beyond the horizon of all those who had preceded them, they wanted simultaneously to form and yet not to be formed, to create and yet to remain forever in the enticing realm where everything is possible and not yet realized, for realization is a kind of death. "Christ became Church", said Kurt Heynicke, "and thereby failed." They wanted to lose themselves in a search for God and to be God themselves, to reform the structure of the world and to destroy that structure before it began to solidify around them. The only sphere in which the attempt to reconcile the irreconcilable is even remotely possible is in art, for art offers one of the few possibilities for man to assert his independence of environment.

This is a state in which only absolutes are acceptable, in which the compromises and modifications of ordinary life are rejected. A tension arises between permanence and change which is the basis of conflict in so many Expressionist works. Where permanence has established itself in its most rigid and monolithic forms the irresistible power of change is brought into play, pictorial and verbal images indicate the *action* of massive, often unseen and incomprehensible, forces in their disruption of the static and comfortably established. Thus Ludwig Meidner rejects nature in favour of city scenes in his pictures, and his apocalyptic visions show massive buildings collapsing in upon themselves, drunken structures in the first stages of rapid dissolution. Jakob van Hoddis, in his poem "Weltende," sees the end of the world as the formless strength of wind and sea sweeping aside the most rigid forms of civilization. The geometrical patterns of the bourgeois' pointed head fitting within his hat, roofs sealing off a fixed order of domestic living, the train neatly confirming the horizontal line of a bridge; all these are swept away, and in the middle of the catastrophe the cosmic ridicule of the little man who has caught cold. Even the vast serenity of sky and earth is resented by Alfred Lichtenstein, who longs for the storm to "tear the gentle world with iron claws . . . to rend the beautiful blue eternal sky into a thousand tatters" ("Sommerfrische").

The shattering of the cohesiveness of the universe by this juxtaposition position of extreme opposites, reflects a determined rejection of the more conventional aesthetic, the cult of beauty. The opposition had been expressed crudely but effectively by the Futurist slogan, "Death to moonlight". The old sensual moon, "with the beautiful warm thighs", is replaced by another ideal of beauty which is just as absolute, by the beauty of the electric moons which dim the radiance of ancient Luna. The glorification of the technical for its own sake, the speed and rhythm of the machine, the architectonic construction of steel and concrete, occurs among Expressionist writers, but it is not a dominant theme and in its extreme form barely represented among the better writers. What one does find is an exact inversion of the conventional idea of beauty contained in unusual combinations: in Georg Heym's poem, *Ophelia*, the dead girl with the nest of water rats in her hair and the long white eels slipping over her breast, or, in the short story, *Der Irre*, by the same author, the radiant universe of infinite peace and eternal rest which is the product of a bloodthirsty madman's imagination. Gottfried Benn's picture of the aster folded into the chest of a drunken beer-carter during a post-mortem is even more shocking in its conciseness, and the poem about the girl, in whose body a nest of rats is found, is entitled "Schöne Jugend". The dissonance between poem and title, and the obvious attack on cliché which is intended, represents Benn at his most sarcastic.

From the opposition to a cult of beauty it is logical transition to a cult of ugliness for its own sake, in which are contained in equal measure emotions of abhorrence and attraction, a salutary purging by the concrete expression of disgust. Very few regions which can supply loathsomely emotive details were left unexplored. The stench of pestilence and poverty, the prisons, the brothels and the thieves' dens, the insane, the crippled and the drunkards fill the landscape of the asphalt literature. This ugliness is all manmade and man is the sufferer. The factories and the hospitals are ugly enough, but they derive their horror from the wretched mass of human beings who inhabit them and who, whether seen in the mass or individually, are degraded to the point of being dehumanized. Men appear as "mucus spat on a rail" (Ehrenstein), dissected on a mortuary slab or washed by nurses "as one washes benches" (Benn), or an aimless, mindless whirling mass jerked hither and thither in a dance conducted by evil and cruel beings of whom they are totally unaware and whose gigantic stature dwarfs them to the size of ants (Heym). It is because he is not even aware of the fact that he stands on the lowest rung in the universal scale of things, because he does not know that above him and around him there is no firm protective fabric but a vast uncomprehended and uncomprehending hostility or indifference, that man excites the scorn or the pity of these writers.

This view of the predicament of man derives rarely from cynical indifference, but rather from a sense of universal agony and personal vulnerability, in which the poet himself is involved. Heym reserves the quality of love for those beings who are, like himself, tortured and torn by inner conflicts— for men such as Kleist, Grabbe, Büchner and Hölderlin, who despair in themselves, "as I daily despair in myself." It is the knowledge that these men had shared the despair of the human condition which draws Heym to them, whereas in his God this essential quality is lacking. God is without love and indifferent, he is "cold and dumb as the cloud formations which forever carry their heads turned away from earth, as though they knew some terrible secret and must bear it with them throughout all time to a dark, unknown and distant goal." And it is God's remoteness from human suffering to which Albert Ehrenstein points again and again in his poetry and in his prose fragments, *Briefe an Gott.* Ehrenstein can recognize God in nature, but "not, almost never in man, that illegible caricature of immortality, that transitory sketch of eternity."

The deepest religious feeling is to be found in those writers who acknowledge the immensity of distance, the impossibility of communication, between themselves and God. It is the combined hopefulness and hopelessness of the search for God which Franz Kafka has made the subject of one of his best-known parables, the story of the message from the dying emperor "to you, the humble subject, the insignificant shadow cowering in the remotest distance before the imperial sun." The messenger can never fight his way through the infinite multitude of obstacles, through "the centre of the world, crammed to bursting with its own refuse.—But you sit at your window when evening falls and dream it to yourself." In the plays of Ernst Barlach the need for God is urgent, for there is no alternative; when, in *Der Tote Tag,* the way to God is barred, the hope of man is turned in on itself and ends in self-destruction. But it is in the poetry of Georg Trakl that one can feel most keenly the crushing weight which lies on humanity in its vital need for a God, who is at every approach inaccessible and who is, one senses, in the last resort merely emptiness. But where Heym and Ehrenstein accuse God, Barlach and Trakl feel the deficiency in themselves; in Trakl's

"De Profundis," "God's silence" is within himself, plunging his whole being into darkness and sealing him off from any hope of contact. In Trakl's world, the moments of hope and ecstasy seldom maintain themselves and give way to melancholy and self-hatred; or they appear at several removes, as in the poem, "An die Verstummten," where he addresses, in the last lines, that section of humanity in whom the future hope of redemption rests, but which is now silent and in remote darkness.

The compelling sense of ineradicable evil and a threatening universe, the fear or conviction that human existence is ultimately meaningless, above all, the creation of an intensely personal literature, in which writers such as Heym, Trakl, Benn, Barlach, and Lasker-Schüler are more concerned in the struggle to come to terms with themselves than guiding the rest of humanity—this forms one end of the Expressionist spectrum. At the other end stand the so-called Activists whose chief characteristic is a fervid revolutionary optimism. They too were aware of the filth and wretchedness of a world which is hostile to mankind, but in more finite terms and not as an unalterable state of affairs. "Those who are aware should kill themselves—or acquire a will", said Kurt Hiller, one of the leading Activist theorists, in attacking the helplessness induced by resigned recognition. They believed, like so many of their contemporaries, that their own time had been given over to a deadening materialism, which had spread over the face of the earth like a disease and that a tabula rasa was necessary in all fields, whether cultural, political or religious. They shared the hatred for the Wilhelminian society which was dominated by a hierarchy of officialdom and militarism, by conventional and repressive morality in state, school and home, by a traditionalism in taste which had remained almost completely unaffected by new tendencies in the arts. They shared also the contempt for the philistinism of the middle classes—most of them were themselves of middle-class origin and the violence of their reaction was undoubtedly due in great measure to the degree of repression which they had experienced as children or were still experiencing as young men.

But the Activists also designated as philistines those who withdrew, in their estimation, into aesthetic strongholds and shut themselves off from the world. Evil was, for all practical purposes, palpable and readily comprehended, and could be overcome by perfectly rational means and by political action. Their programme was at least in part political—socialistic in the sense that it would lead to the annexation from the establishment of the outward forms of control. The greatest emphasis, however, was on the preparation for this utopia through the rehabilitation of the mind (*Geist*)—as opposed to "soul" which does not distinguish between right and wrong—which was capable of reaching out and transforming the minds of all men, changing the face of society from within. Thus the legions of depressed humanity were not condemned to the permanent status of marionettes. In the poems of Ernst Stadler, the drabness of factory workers, the anxieties of madmen are lit by the premonition of happiness. In Stadler's work is the crossing of the ways, the simultaneity of bitterness and hope; in the work of political writers such as Johannes Becher and Ludwig Rubiner, misery is used as a whip to scourge complacence and to stimulate revolt. They deliberately cut themselves off from organized society and identified themselves with its waste products, the "street filth" and the "human rubbish". "We are the scum, the offal," said Rubiner. "We are the holy mob." The acknowl-

edged subservience of art to politics, the obtrusive application of moral purpose promise banality. Add to this the habit of sustained ecstatic utterance—Becher's calls to unity, Franz Werfel's and Leonhard Frank's visions of the brotherhood and ultimate goodness of man—and the promise of banality was all too frequently fulfilled.

Yet it was rare for even Activist literature to ally itself with any specific political cause. It might be revolutionary, antimilitaristic, anti-capitalistic, but a vague socialism or uncommitted sympathy with Communism were the farthest point to which they were prepared to go. In the drama with a social mission especially, hopes were centred in an undefined leader figure, as unreally magnified as Heym's figures were reduced, who was to lead his generation out of the wilderness. Into such figures are compressed ideal attributes of humanity at large; they speak for and to all those who are awakened and ripe for awakening, are confronted not by antagonists but by antagonistic forces contained in just such representative figures as himself. The "poet," the "young man," the "son," all frequently encountered sobriquets, pass through stages or spheres, into which are concentrated vital facets of human experience; at the end comes the promise rather than the realization of the ideal, for which the hero prepares the way by what often amounts to self-inflicted martyrdom. These abstractions do not allow for normal dramatic interplay of characters or for the construction of a unified comprehensive plot (which are specifically rejected), but are contained in a series of largely independent scenes which are united by theme and metaphor, and supported by the symbolic effects of stage design and lighting. The weight of the play lies in the lyrical and rhetorical intensity of each scene, condensing the emotions and experiences of a lifetime into moments of utmost significance, which are heaped one upon the other with growing fervour until the climax is reached. In the nature of things, it can be an anti-climax, for there is a limit to the extent to which intensity can be "intensified," but there are superb examples of this genre, such as Georg Kaiser's *Gas I* (1918). In the fourth act of this play, the enlightened millionaire's son is arguing the case for humanity against the representative of the conventional materialistic world (Engineer) before a mass of assembled workers who punctuate the exactly constructed dialectic of the individual speeches with staccato cries. *Gas I* provides a genuine involvement, vastly different from Franz Werfel's *Die Versuchung* (1913), in which the poet resists Satan's offer of a noble martyrdom, decides to descend humbly into the world, expose himself to insult and misunderstanding, offer the whole world to men, who will "become rich from my poverty." This kind of arrogant humility is unfortunately not limited to Werfel. It can be found, understandably enough, in writers such as Hanns Johst and Kurt Heynicke, who later became Nazis, but it is also present to a quite unpleasant degree in Fritz von Unruh and not least in Georg Kaiser himself.

Such plays normally provide no concrete solution, but point forward to a coming era of light, so that in their end is a new beginning, occasionally symbolized by effects such as ascension (Kaiser: *Die Bürger von Calais*), resurrection (Johst: *Der junge Mensch*), actual rebirth after passing through the realms of the dead (Heynicke: *Der Kreis*). In place of a solution they present a constant searching, testing and questioning, demanding an answer, but seeing the ultimate answer receding interminably into the distance. In Reinhold Sorge's drama, *Der Bettler* (1911), the central figure appears successively as the poet, the son, the brother, the youth. In each of these functions an area of experience is explored, but the process cannot be finite and, at the end of the play, the poet stands on the edge of eternity: "I see many stages yet before me in the light / And many purities which I have not yet traversed. . . ." And the young man at the end of Ludwig Rubiner's *Die Gewaltlosen* (1919) says: "We must go on! Our way lies through many countries."

The two plays by Sorge and Rubiner illustrate one of the main differences between Expressionism and Activism as defined by Wolfgang Paulsen in his book on the subject. The Activist is, according to Paulsen, the theoretician for whom poetry is not an end in itself but an aid in forming the reality which he wishes to impose on society. He is less an artist than a politician, a politician of the "mind and idea." The Expressionist, who is first and foremost the poet, will make use of everyday reality, but ruthlessly subordinate it to his own vision and create his own world. Rubiner's play takes place in a revolutionary setting. The reactionaries who hold material power are overcome, their main representative is converted and, before his execution, voluntarily passes over his power to the suppressed, to the "powerless." Humanity (*will* and *mind*) has become visible in the political arena and will continue into the future. In *Der Bettler* the poet makes himself independent of a society which bars his way to self-fulfilment, he establishes sovereignty over his environment by drastic means and re-creates it in terms of his dream.

Whatever the difference in their final aims, both Activist and Expressionist were united in their realization of the need to throw off the controls which bind men to the increasingly circumscribed patterns of their existence. They objected particularly to the attempt to see people in terms of the psychological factors which create personality, for this seemed to proceed from the assumption that man was a prisoner of himself, that his behaviour resulted from an unalterable combination of physical and mental characteristics and that his whole development moved on rails. In order to impose his will on reality, in whatever form, man must be freed of all restraints, and above all he must be freed from himself.

An interesting pointer to the processes involved is contained in the prose piece by Alfred Wolfenstein, "Fragment eines Daseins" (1914). There is only one character, and there is no name or other identifying detail. The outer world, the world of normality is still there and he still makes physical contact with friends, relations and strangers, but none of these has any meaning for him or any power to affect the dominance of his own thoughts. The function of other people is purely negative and merely serves to underline his own liberty of action and invulnerability to outside stimulus—he seeks out acquaintances in the certainty that they will not be able to afford him company. He has cut himself off from his own past and his own future purpose, and his mind is free to examine, with a mixture of curiosity and fear, that unexplored universe, his own self. In Wolfenstein's story the procedure is described in extreme, mechanically contrived terms and its ultimate sterility is recognized, but it admirably maps out the territory into which so many writers ventured and points the dangers to which Expressionist characterization was exposed. The lack of any stable centre is made very clear in one sentence of the story: "Diese Nacht . . . wollte die Bodenlosigkeit vollenden, die er als Feind eines Müssens, als zerstörerischer Freund aller Möglichkeiten, als unaufhörlich *gegen sich Treuloser* lange vorbereitet hatte. . . ." One may of course insert into this paradoxical, self-cancelling, infinite-

ly elastic frame all the denials of organic development and causal relationships ("the enemy of compulsion"), the radical break with the past and the transformations of character ("constantly faithless to oneself") and the infinite possibility of new combinations and developments of personality which are opened up as soon as verisimilitude is thrown overboard ("the destructive friend of all possibilities").

In fact it is, one suspects, another case of the formula which, stretched to cover a large area of Expressionism, is so all-embracing as to be virtually meaningless. It is left to Bertolt Brecht, who so often in his early plays parodied and deflated Expressionism by the use of its own techniques, to put Wolfenstein's tour de force into perspective by somewhat drastic means. In his *Mann ist Mann,* written in 1925 eleven years after "Fragment eines Daseins," he creates an equally artificial situation by taking the simplest of harmless fellows, a piece of putty responsive to the slightest pressure, and re-moulding him by a series of farcical procedures into a bloodthirsty warrior. This is in one important respect an actual reversal of Wolfenstein's theme, since in Brecht a naturally insulated character is changed by pressure from without. Yet the basic assumption is the same. There is no such thing as psychological continuity or the permanent unity and consistency of character. Nor is Brecht's attitude only a negative one for the schematic formulation in *Mann ist Mann* points forward to his later realistic technique, in which opposite and apparently self-contradictory traits, courage and cowardice, nobility and meanness, are shown in the same character emerging under the stimulus of varying situations. Or one thinks of the close link between gluttony and intellectual curiosity in his *Galileo,* especially as interpreted with Brecht's approval by Charles Laughton.

"Fragment eines Daseins" appears in the anthology of Expressionist prose which the compiler, Karl Otten, has entitled *Ego und Eros,* and Otten is quoted as regarding "Fragment eines Daseins" and its companion piece, "Die künstliche Liebe," also by Wolfenstein, as central to the theme of the anthology. "Die künstliche Liebe" introduces one of the most typical manifestations of Expressionism, the combination of the spiritual and the material in the power of love and the erotic urge. Here there are just the two figures involved, man and wife. The woman's whole personality is absorbed in her one dynamic rôle which is expressed neither in her features nor her character, but in her body. This is a liberated personality in a much more positive sense than appears in "Fragment eines Daseins," for there is no alienation of the outside world; on the contrary, material things are subordinated to her existence and integrated into her activity. She is creative and acts from instinct, without any kind of self-awareness, whilst cerebration and too great a pre-occupation with self render her husband incapable of sharing genuine experience. "Ego" and "eros" are perfectly compatible, but not on any conscious or rational level.

The husband, a man with money and without occupation, has married his wife in the hope of discovering at least at second hand the enjoyment of experience. But he is unequal to the task of participating, his relegation to the rôle of observer soon palls and he realises that she too cannot maintain her powers with a passive partner. He decides to change himself or at least to make the appearance of a change, and to translate himself during love-making into a world of art, imagining that he is reading a book printed on fine paper, conjuring up in his mind a symphony or a painting. The pretence succeeds insofar as he is able to deceive her and give her happiness, he gains the cold satisfaction of achievement, of a certain selflessness even, but not of love; not even the sensation of her love is conveyed to him. What he has gained is "talent." He cannot bridge the gap and must bear the weight of loneliness.

The two factors in this story might be considered as dominant motifs of Expressionism. Firstly: eros as the liberating, creative force appears most frequently in the guise of prostitution. Prostitutes are idealized as representing the release of love from the restraints of marriage and thus in a general sense the release of creative strength itself. Even at the most sensual level there is idealization and even at the most idealized level, as in Werfel's poem "Veni Creator Spiritus," in which the divine spirit is called upon to break through man's imprisoning walls, there are clearly recognizable erotic overtones. However, the situation which Wolfenstein envisages in "Die künstliche Liebe" is more akin to the world of Frank Wedekind, whose formative work had begun some twenty years before—the woman in Wolfenstein's story is a rational abstraction of Wedekind's Lulu, as she appears in *Erdgeist* and *Die Büchse der Pandora* (1893-1902). In Lulu's vivid person is contained the elemental force which is in itself neither good nor bad and has creative potentialities, but will turn to destruction or even self-destruction, if contained or dominated. Her nature is as instinctive, innocent and direct as that of an animal and she lacks all trace of artifice or selfknowledge. All the men with whom she is associated attempt to possess her and to adapt her to their own stature. Only the intelligent egotist, Dr. Schön, recognizes the danger and tries to keep her at a distance, but he cannot save himself. The very strength of his intellect and will make him inferior to Lulu and Wedekind sums up their relationship as the destruction of the conscious intellect, which always overrates itself so extravagantly, by the unconscious element in man. Strikingly similar situations may be found in the drama of Georg Kaiser (e.g. *Die Jüdische Witwe*), and although handled in an immense variety of forms, the themes recur constantly in Expressionist literature: the primitive and the natural are at war with the conventional (hence the popularity of animal subjects in painting and literature), hope and creativity derive from irrational and dynamic forces, and the *dominance* of the cerebral and the artificial produces a frustration, which can be either tragic or comic in its effects. Isolated within themselves, the contrivers and the manipulators remain tragically aware, or ridiculously unaware, of the fact that the gulf between themselves and the outside world cannot be bridged.

Egotism, the other main motif of "Die künstliche Liebe," also appears in many guises. There is a clearly marked tragic frustration and isolation in the person of the husband in Wolfenstein's story. Especially in the beginning he is shown as the type of egotist who has no inner life of his own and tries to gain his sensations by living parasitically on the vitality of others. The clearest demonstration of such a relationship is contained in the drama, *König Hahnrei* (1913), in which Georg Kaiser makes use of the story of Tristan and Isolde. The absurd old king, Marke, literally warms himself at the fire of their youth, and eventually, by the burden which his weakness imposes upon them, destroys their love for each other. "In the realm of sensations I am the poorest beggar." This cry of Alwa Schön in *Die Büchse der Pandora* is the despairing acknowledgement of impotence, the tragedy of the author who has been unable to write since he has surrendered himself to a more vital personality. For a predicament of this kind Wedekind clearly felt a personal sympathy, but in his

play, *Die Junge Welt* (written in 1889), he bitterly attacked the literary vampirism of Naturalism. The playwright Meier, a gross caricature of Gerhart Hauptmann, obtains literary recognition by using the life story told to him in confidence by another person. Like Balzac, Meier carries a notebook in which he jots down every conversation he hears. He records the reactions of his fiancée at the moment when he is kissing her and complains bitterly of her unnaturalness and lack of spontaneity when she ceases to react at all.

Even more scathing in his treatment of characters with artistic and literary pretensions was Carl Sternheim. Both Scarron in *Die Hose* (1911) and Seidenschnur in *Die Kassette* (1912) are, like the weaklings in Wedekind's and Kaiser's plays, compulsive talkers. It is the poetry of cliché which Scarron adopts, compressed poetic cliché, in which the empty inflated phrases follow on one another with stunning rapidity, so that they are immensely funny when delivered with the staccato precision employed by actors in Sternheim plays. Seidenschnur's protestations of love, delivered with the same bombast, are deflated when they become entangled with the mechanics of the camera: "Your picture, Lydia, flows into the lens, into the chambers of my heart." Both Scarron and Seidenschnur are savage denunciations of the inadequacy of the romantic type, who claim to be preoccupied with their innermost selves, claim to be superior to bourgeois philistines, to which they, the artistic philistines, cling nevertheless like drowning men. They are in a way the false egotists, for they remain as empty at the end as they were at the start, they attach themselves to the body of the "shark," and seek not strength but only protection for themselves.

Sternheim's portrayal of the middle classes, annihilating as it is, is not intended, as Emrich forcefully reminds us, to be regarded as satire, it is not a "scourging" but a "recognition" of reality. His main characters, his Maskes, Krulls and Ständers, are not merely intended to show the emptiness of a life given over to materialism and middle class ambition. They are not there as warnings, but as signposts in a waste country. There is about them an aliveness, a vitality which is strangely attractive and survives dedication to a limited aim. Sternheim is therefore not sarcastic, but perfectly genuine when he describes them as heroes, for they have gained their freedom by overcoming the restraints which are imposed on them by society. This is very much the idea of freedom which activates the hero in Wedekind's *Der Marquis von Keith* (1900), who sets out to free himself from middle class society by dominating it. Keith fails, but Sternheim's characters have less inner life and more tenacity and grasp of reality than Wedekind's characters. Theobald Maske (in *Die Hose*) and in even more extreme fashion his son Christian Maske (in *Der Snob*) subordinate society to their own goals. Christian works quite cold-bloodedly and with exact machine-like calculation; he is the prince of the manipulators. In Christian and his other heroes, Sternheim has created characters who stand out as unique in Expressionism for two reasons: they are the only contrivers and manipulators to win their way to personal freedom and they are the only liberated personalities who do not represent some purpose greater than themselves. They are the pure egotists, egotists unsullied as it were by frustration on the one hand or by the intrusion of any moral, artistic or community ideal which transcends the individual and which Sternheim despised heartily. Yet these characters are not individuals in the orthodox sense. They achieve their power and urgency by the fact that the whole horrible world which Sternheim "recognizes," the wealth and status worshippers spread over all the rungs of the social ladder, is concentrated into them and shaped by them, or more accurately is shaped by the words that are spoken; for Sternheim's characters do not live by virtue of their individual fate or by their position in an unfolding story, but through their language.

Sternheim said of Gottfried Benn that he "destroys concepts from within, so that language totters and citizens lie flat on belly and nose"; like Benn, Sternheim was an uncompromising critic, not only of idealistic concepts, but also—and this is more characteristic of Expressionism in general—of the platitudes which are used to paper over unpalatable and unfamiliar realities. Conventional images are seen as masks concealing the essential attributes of a person or object, and the revolt against the lazy classification of people according to comfortable and familiar categories is a recurring theme from Wedekind's *König Nicolo* (1902) to Hans Henny Jahnn's *Die Krönung Richards III* (1920). Richard III is the perfect example of the popular image which has crystallized around a name through the main external features by which he is familiar to us: the murder of the princes and his physical ugliness. Jahnn makes his Richard bitterly conscious of the process: "Have you ever really known me? Was I not always an image to you, made up of shadows, ugliness and hellish instincts?" and adds in resigned recognition: "You have again not understood me . . . but this you should know, I am not quite identical with my counterfeit." Between these personal statements Richard speculates on the application of his case to life in general, on "the whole masquerade which is called life. It would be a joke to tear off their masks . . . people who are only stomachs, and women who are like cows—one covers them, they calve, give milk—and men who are only words, completely without meaning, and gifted with all the virtues of the word, with honour, wisdom, integrity! . . . And if one were to tear off the masks, some would appear who are shaped for eternity."

This one speech in Jahnn's play sums up large reaches of Expressionist literature, in which life is seen literally as a masquerade, men and women as puppets acting according to the dictates of an imposed or self-imposed image of themselves, and hidden amongst them the few (in the case of Jahnn mostly children) who contain the promise of regeneration. But words too contribute to concealment and constitute a barrier to real understanding. Language can also act as a mask unless it is rescued from its progression towards emptiness of meaning through the abrasion of common usage. In the passage about Benn quoted above, Sternheim writes of the "intoxication caused by separation from context" ("Rausch der Zusammenhangsentfernung"). If language is to regain its dynamic quality it must be delivered from its organization into familiar structures and associations, from the certainty that one word automatically follows another in speech and writing and—quite concretely—from the enslavement of syntax.

Language controlled by syntax was regarded as rational language and the "language of reason presupposes a world of repose and rigidity, an easily assimilable mosaic which can be mirrored in concepts and logical connections." This description appeared in Oswald Pander's essay, "Revolution der Sprache" in 1918 and is typical of many approaches which add nothing substantially new to the systematic and comprehensive statements on the language revolution contained in the Futurist "Technical Manifesto" by Marinetti which appeared in *Der Sturm* in 1912. Marinetti's opposition is directed basically against normal syntax as reflecting compartmentalized thinking. He advocates the removal of all defining and connecting elements. Conjunctions, adjectives and adverbs disappear, and together with them punctuation; the verb remains in the infinitive, so that it may adapt "elastically" to the noun. The "naked" nouns themselves thus retain and enhance their own essential character, and are linked directly by association and analogy, not by any logical train of thought.

In their most extreme form these requirements are scarcely practicable, but Marinetti's influence was clearly felt among members of the *Sturm* group of writers, led by August Stramm, and by certain Activists, such as Becher and Rubiner. In his poem, "Mensch stehe auf," Becher is concerned to make his voice heard in the most primitive fashion, by hammering repetition:

> Verfluchtes Jahrhundert! Chaotisch! Gesanglos!
> Ausgehängt du Mensch, magerster der Köder,
>   zwischen Qual
> Nebel-Wahn Blitz.
>
> (Cursed century! Chaotic! Songless!
> You man hung out, leanest of baits, amidst torment
>   fog-illusion
> flash.)

This is Marinetti's method adopted in almost literal fashion; there is the absence of any finite verb, the chain of single words and fragmented phrases, the row of four nouns—a single noun on either side of the double noun—juxtaposed and unpunctuated. Marinetti had wanted to avoid by his technique a too even tone, but Becher's words and images, though certainly forceful, are all on the same level of extreme emphasis and the emotions are shapeless and undirected. More truly dynamic is August Stramm's "Patrouille":

> Die Steine feinden / Fenster grinst Verrat / Äste
> würgen / Berge Sträucher blättern raschlig / Gellen / Tod.

The violence here, which is genuine and not a whipped-up emotion, is contained in each word, and each of the inanimate objects—stones, window, branches, hills, bushes—acquires a hostile attitude through the verbs with which they are associated. The tension mounts to the last word as the whole scene explodes in a final shriek of death.

The Stramm poem rests upon the suspension of time, the simultaneity of the various elements, each of which carries within itself the promise of the final word. In the following excerpt from Sternheim a similar effect is obtained where the passage of time is violently compressed as Christian Maske sums up his previous existence:

> Kämpfe ums Dasein. Die habe ich auch durchgemacht und dabei ganz anders als Myriaden Boden in mir aufgerissen; von Trieben geschnellt, flog ich durch den Brei der Bequemen, weil ich wusste, jenseits fängt erst das Leben an. Du sahst ja, wie ich ankam, Fetzen mir vom Leib riss und das flatternde Band am Hals zu fester Krawatte knüpfte. Mich allmählich zur Form erzog, der der höhere Mensch im Zusammenleben bedarf. (*Der Snob*).
>
> ["Struggles for existence. I've been through all that, too, and the turmoil taught me a lot. Impelled by an insatiable impulse, I waded through the mush of comfortable people because I had learned that life really only begins when you are through and out the other side. But you saw how I got there, how

I 'arrived', how I tore strips of living flesh from my own body and wore them, twisted into an elegant cravatte, round my own neck. Little by little I approached that form which the superior being must assume among his peers."]

The fragments of language illustrate the fragmentary nature of Christian's existence, the violence of the verbs his headlong destructive passage through life, and the whole is given a dynamic cohesion through the fusing of the fragments into a mass activated by the principle of flight, which forces him through the "mush of comfortable people" to the life which is always a stage beyond. In the second half of the passage the fragments take palpable form in the shreds of clothing which hang about him; the tatters and the fluttering ribbon are drawn together in the firmly knotted tie. It is Christian's mistress who literally knots his ties because he cannot manage them himself, who disciplines his formless existence and trains him to live the life of the "higher man."

In the Stramm poem the pressure expands outwards towards the explosion, in Sternheim's passage there is a forced contraction of exploded fragments into the confining image, providing a contrast of startling and absurd proportions. Furthermore, there is a levelling of the usual hierarchy of values; the trivial object, the tie, is given a life foreign to its own and is raised to a status far above its place in the normal scale of things, whilst the notion of the "higher man" is correspondingly deflated. It is the same process which Wolfenstein describes in "Die künstliche Liebe," where the inanimate objects which provide the environment of lovemaking—bed, lamp, room—are divested of their independence and their quality of "strangeness", and are drawn into the whole magical sphere of love. Here, objective reality is broken up or transformed, exterior objects are diverted from their normal functions and directed to the assumption of new roles which the hand and the eye of the artist have prepared for them.

These examples differ radically from the imaginative transformations of reality which one finds for instance in the description of a fever in Rilke's *Die Aufzeichnungen des Malte Laurids Brigge* (1910). Malte describes the way in which even the most trivial objects take a new form and life under the spur of fear: the fear that a thread of wool protruding from the edge of a blanket is as hard and sharp as a needle, that the button of his nightshirt is bigger than his head, that a bread crumb falling from his bed will break like a piece of glass and that everything will be broken for ever. With Rilke the fear is given an explanatory basis, for it derives from a fever which awakens childhood memories and terrors, the typical nightmares of childhood which are familiar to everybody. Moreover, no transformation has taken place and the whole passage in the original German is couched in the subjunctive, the hypothetical product of fear.

It is a characteristic of many Expressionist writers that the transformation is presented as complete, apparently without the involvement of the observer, and there is no insertion of the process of imaginative change or of the "as if" which prepares the way for a bold comparison. "Zerlumpte Bäume strolchen in die Ferne. / Betrunkene Wiesen drehen sich im Kreise." (Ragged trees stroll into the distance. / Drunken meadows turn in circles.) In these lines from Lichtenstein's poem, "In den Abend . . . ," the intermediate stage by which the everyday is changed into an intoxicated landscape is withdrawn and the inner vision of the poet has completely displaced objective reality. The point is made more sharply

in the familiar example of Kafka's *Die Verwandlung,* in English *The Metamorphosis.* As Sokel points out, there is no comparison between Gregor Samsa and an insect, no pointing to a relationship between one entity, Samsa, and the other entity, the insect. Samsa *becomes* the insect, a fact described in minute physical detail. In Barlach's *Der Tote Tag,* the instrument of observation itself becomes the metaphor; the vision of the artist is objectified and the eyes—the eyes of the blind seer Kule—are "two spiders crouching in the net of their sockets and catching the images of the world," but these images, at first full of sweetness and delight, multiply till they are "juicy with bitterness and greasy with horror; so that at last my eyes could no longer bear such bitterness and they spun a web over the entrance, crouched within, preferred to hunger and die."

The withering away of the physical sense of sight is, like the withering of the rational faculties of the madman, simply another pointer to the emancipation from the order and system of the representational world; but this emancipation is a constructive act which opens the way to an infinite range of possibilities, the new grouping of sensual images and the creation of new relationships which constitute the most fruitful aspect of Expressionist style. Entities which have previously had neutral contacts or no contact at all, like Samsa and the insect, lose their original identity when brought together in a meaningful relationship, and a third or transcendental identity is established.

In addition, the normal patterns of time and space, indeed the quality of both animate and inanimate objects may undergo a radical change. In Wolfenstein's sonnet, "Städter," the meaning may be summed up tritely enough—the loneliness of man in the crowd. But the violence of the compression created by the imagery produces a transformation of reality. The windows of houses are as close as holes in a sieve, the houses themselves are packed so tightly that the streets are as grey and swollen as strangled corpses. The townspeople suffer a double transformation of compression and petrification, they are locked together on the tram-seats like "two façades," and the reality of their new state is so completely established that the comparison, "Unsere Wände sind so dünn wie Haut" (Our walls are as thin as skin), has been exactly reversed and "skin" becomes the extended meaning of "walls." Or we are shown the relationship between man and nature, not personalization of nature in the simple sense, but a physical interpenetration, an actual linking of man and world in a composite picture of decay, such as one finds in Lichtenstein's poem, "Punkt," and in other poems contained in the anthology introduced by Benn, *Lyrik des expressionistischen Jahrzehnts.* In such relationships, the idea of the grotesque and the incongruous—grass growing from a skull, a man reduced to a hand operating a lever—no longer exists, any more than atonality exists in modern music. The shock which distortions of reality produce derives only from their unfamiliarity; the eye and the ear which has grown accustomed to these combinations will not be shocked, but stimulated.

Thus the process which is observable in the modern art forms is not merely a "destruction" of the familiar world or a "dislocation" of language; it is rather the process of using the flexibility thus made possible in an increasingly personal way—personal in the sense that images and symbols acquire an independence of external and generalized criteria and can properly be understood only in their own terms and by reference to each other. Nor is this process to be regarded as either subjective or arbitrary; Trakl, for instance, is one of the most personal writers in the above sense, but he was able to say in a letter about a poem which he had rewritten: "I am convinced that it (the poem) will say more and mean more to you in the universal form and manner than in the limited personal manner of the first draft." Moreover, the more accomplished writers were fully aware that discipline and form were necessary. It was not, however, the discipline of outward form which was the deciding factor—though in the lyric and the drama a formal framework was not infrequent—but the artist's need to construct in a way which corresponded with his own needs. Ehrenstein said of Napoleon that "he made laws but had no law in himself." The criterion of the Expressionist's work is therefore to be found, not in the application of an aesthetic or ethical system, but in terms of his own view of life, his own experience and his formulation of that experience. (pp. 257-77)

H. Maclean, "Expressionism," in Periods in German Literature: A Symposium, Vol. I, *edited by J. M. Ritchie, Wolff, 1966, pp. 257-80.*

EXPRESSIONIST DRAMA

ERNST TOLLER

[*A German dramatist and poet, Toller is often cited as the most talented and effective of the Expressionist writers. His dramas, which dominated the German stage during the early 1920s, reflect the primary concerns of Expressionism, including the regenerative power of love, the diabolical effects of industrialization, and the need for a peaceful overthrow of the existing social order. The last of these was of particular concern to Toller, who worked to effect social and political change throughout his lifetime. In the following excerpt, he explains the aesthetic and pragmatic goals of Expressionist drama.*]

I have been asked by the editor of the *Nation* to write a few words on post-war German drama. We are in the habit of using the term "post-war drama" without stopping to ask ourselves if there really is such a type, distinct in presentation, treatment, kind, and form from that of the pre-war period.

Did the war really cause this decisive change in German drama? Not at all. It is strikingly confirmed today, after ten years, that the present tendencies in the drama began their development years before the war, and that since then they have simply been in more rapid eruption.

The younger dramatists felt that an unbridgeable gulf divided them from the older generation. The struggle between the generations, the father-and-son problem, the fight between compromise and directness, between bourgeois and anti-bourgeois, had stirred young intellects before the war made a reality of what they had prophetically seen coming. To be sure, the war destroyed many moral and social, many spiritual and artistic values. But the foundations of these values had become rotten. In place of the idea, there had come to the fore a realpolitik which was leading to the abrogation of all reality. Freedom had become hypocrisy—freedom for the few, spiritual and economic bondage for the many. In the first dra-

mas of Sorge, Hasenclever, and Werfel this hatred toward our elders was already smoldering. And these were the same elders who did nothing to prevent the war but, tricking it out in romanticism, pitilessly and unfeelingly sent battalion after battalion of young German manhood out to die.

During the war very little got to the public through the strict censorship. But after the collapse, every day brought new works from the newly liberated minds. The form which this art took was called expressionism. It was just as much reaction as it was synthetic and creative action. It turned against that tendency in art which was satisfied merely to set down impressions, one after the other, without troubling to question their essential nature, justification, or the idea involved. The expressionists were not satisfied simply to photograph. They knew that environment permeates the artist and is reflected in his psychic mirror in such a way as utterly to transfigure this environment. Expressionism wanted to influence environment, to change it in giving it a brighter, more righteous appearance, to make it impossible, for example, for a catastrophe like the war ever to threaten mankind again. Reality was to be comprehended anew in the light of the ideal, was to be born again.

All activity resolves itself into outer and inner activity, both of equal importance and strength as motivating forces. In style expressionism was pregnant, almost telegraphic, always shunning the peripheral, and always probing to the center of things. In expressionistic drama man is no accidental private person. He is a type posited for many, and ignoring the limits of superficial characterization. Man was skinned in the expectation that somewhere under his skin was his soul. The dramatic exponents of expressionism were Sorge, Göring, Barlach, and Toller. Of their works may be mentioned Sorge's *Der Bettler,* Kaiser's *Von Morgen bis Mitternacht,* Hasenclever's *Der Sohn,* Unruh's *Ein Geschlecht, Der arme Vetter* by Barlach, and Toller's *Die Wandlung* and *Masse Mensch.*

During the epoch of expressionism a significant development took place. A new character appeared on the stage—proletarian man. Of course, there had already been plays whose action took place in a proletarian milieu. But something fundamental divided expressionistic proletarian drama from such a play as Hauptman's *Die Weber* or Bucher's *Wozzek.* In the old dramas the proletarian was a dull creature who rebelled against his fate with strong but rash impulse. The artist who picutred him wanted to awaken sympathy. In the new drama, the proletarian is active, conscious, rebelling against his fate, and struggling for a new reality. He is driven on by feeling, by knowledge, and by the idea of a brighter future.

It is useless to talk to the fiasco of expressionism, or to ask whether expressionism produced works which will still be remembered in fifty years. Expressionism wanted to be a product of the time and to react to it. And that much it certainly succeeded in doing. Never since Schiller's *Die Räuber,* since *Kabale und Liebe,* has the theater been so much a rostrum for current happenings or so much upset by the strife and counter-strife of public opinion; passionate partisanship on one side, and violent one-sided reproaches on the other.

Let us examine for a moment the reproach of "tendency" leveled against expressionism. When a piece of writing portrays spiritual behavior, feelings, reactions to the phenomena of life and knowledge it does not seem tendential to the bourgeois, because these things have become traditional and because they express his conception of the world, his philosophy, his naked economic interest. He overlooks the fact that such writing also has a tendency, namely his own.

But when new observations are made in a drama, in opposition to those ideas to which the bourgeois has been accustomed, he calls such a work tendential. The atmosphere in any work of art, in so far as it transects a given social milieu, always has a definite impress that one is safe in calling partisan. There is, however, one type of partisanship which the artist must avoid, namely that partisanship of the black and white kind which depicts all persons on one side as devils of the blackest sort, and all those on the other as angels.

But since the spirit, the idea did not succeed in changing the character of the times; since the old reality with the old abominations, with the old greed, the old rapacious striving, the old danger zones, simply reappeared; since the peace which all were yearning for turned out to be a grin behind which the next war is looming; since the spiritual had again become a veneer and a mockery, younger dramatists appeared who thought that as the ideal was lacking there was no reason for it, especially in art. They set out to portray life and nothing but life. But the decisive thing in life for them was the uninhibited accord or antagonism of the sexual impulse. The chaotic, the sexual, became the focus of the new drama which tended to the epic in form. Side by side with this the struggle between the generations played a definite role. Speech became naturalistic again, but it was distinguished from the old naturalism by a dynamic impetus that gave it a distinctive rhythm. As dramatists of this type one may mention Brecht, Bronnen, and Kuckmaier.

The later German dramatists were unquestionably influenced by America, but the German brand of Americanism did not represent the great minds of America. What was taken over was the tempo, the banal optimism, the superficiality, in short that new matter-of-factness which has very little meaning and no connection whatever with the major arts.

German drama exists, as does all German art, between two worlds. The bourgeois world is spiritually and ethically convulsed and the world of the workers is visible as yet only among small or petty groups. The generation now thirty years old, the war generation, appears to be living in an interval of rest—a creative interval, let us hope. Those who knew the war as children barely bestir themselves. What work of theirs we see is classic, amazingly senile, and very seldom original. The last few years have given us several important novels (the novel seems to be developing in Germany for the first time and German novelists are now worthy rivals of French and English masters of fiction) but few dramas that one can call important or significant documents of the time. (pp. 488-89)

Ernst Toller, "Post-War German Drama," in The Nation, New York, Vol. CXXVII, No. 3305, November 7, 1928, pp. 488-89.

JOHN GASSNER

[*Gassner, a Hungarian-born American scholar, was a great promoter of American theater, particularly the work of Tennessee Williams and Arthur Miller. He edited numerous collections of modern drama and wrote two highly regarded dramatic surveys,* Masters of the Drama (*1940*) *and* Theater in Our Times (*1954*). *In the following excerpt from the former, Gass-*

Walter Hasenclever (standing) and Ernst Toller in 1928.

ner discusses several of the most significant Expressionist dramas.]

[The] first step toward the nervous, half-realistic, half-fantastic drama that went under the name of "expressionism" during the first post-war decade was taken by an ultra-naturalist. Frank Wedekind, who was born in 1864, belonged to Hauptmann's generation and adopted its program with greater vehemence than Hauptmann himself. In order to describe the tabooed realities of sexuality and bring to this subject all the apparatus of medical and psychological science, Wedekind wrote a number of plays which even exceeded the candid camera shots of his contemporaries. After a negligible first comedy, he turned to his proper métier in 1890 with *Die junge Welt* or *The World of Youth,* which described conditions in a girls' boarding school. Although here he aimed a blow at naturalism in his ridicule of a character who resembles Hauptmann, Wedekind's picture revealed the girls as troubled by the libido and repressed by their instructors. A year later, moreover, came his *Frühlings Erwachen* or *The Awakening of Spring,* an unvarnished diagnosis of adolescence and a fierce attack on the educational system's obliviousness to the sexual problems that bedevil schoolchildren.

Like Ibsen, whom he long admired and recited professionally at public readings, Wedekind proved himself a bitter enemy of social hypocrisy, and he found the most injurious hypocrisies in the manner in which society denied or warped the sexual instinct. In this "children's tragedy," as he called his play, a group of adolescent boys and girls between the ages of fourteen and seventeen are variously preoccupied with the libido. But they receive no enlightenment or guidance from their parents and teachers. Fourteen-year-old Wendla, whose mother refuses to help her in the crisis that impends when she falls in love with the schoolboy Melchior, becomes pregnant. Her mother, who dreads scandal more than the loss of her child, engages a bungling midwife because one can count on her silence. Melchior, the culprit, is an earnest and brilliant student who would have behaved more discreetly if he had been better instructed. In his *gauche* manner he also figures in a second catastrophe when, imparting sexual information to his hypersensitive schoolmate Moritz, he drives him to suicide. Only Melchior refuses to be completely engulfed by the difficulties of adolescence. Expelled from school and sent to a reformatory, he is troubled by his conscience and entertains suicidal thoughts, only to reject them.

The Awakening of Spring exploded in the theatre like a bombshell. But what shall be said about Wedekind's reprise in *Erdgeist* or *Earth Spirit* and its sequel *The Box of Pandora!* In the former the woman Lulu, blithely unaware of her own evil, is a demoniac incarnation of the primal instinct and lover after lover is destroyed by this succubus. Her perfidy gives her first husband a stroke, and drives a second one to cut his throat; the third she kills herself after he has caught her intriguing with numerous men, including his own son, and boasting that she poisoned his first wife. In *The Box of Pandora* she reappears after escaping from prison. But she is no longer a triumphant demon and becomes the sordid victim of the same erotic force that led her to destroy her husbands. After murdering a blackmailer, she flees to London, starves in its streets, and is finally slashed to bits by one of her clients who proves to be a Jack the Ripper. The cycle of elemental lust thus comes to an end when the sadism of the female encounters the rawer sadism of the male. Here Zola's formula for naturalism—"to see the beast in man, and only the beast"—is carried to a more than logical conclusion. Ringing further changes on his primal theme, and writing penetratingly in *The Marquis of Keith, The Tenor,* and other works, Wedekind carved out the most pungent "slices of life" in the German theatre.

But Wedekind was an unstable personality who refused to be confined to any school even before he turned to manifestly romantic, symbolic material. He had begun his career by appearing in a cabaret where he recited grisly ballads, and his taste for the macabre remained with him even when he explored the same field as the naturalists. This taste, as well as his love of sensationalism and his impatience with organized artistry, led him to clap a fantastic ending to *The Awakening of Spring.* When Melchior, escaping from prison, visits the graves of his fellow-students, Moritz comes to life and insists that he join him in death. But a "Masked Man" appears and dissuades Melchior from suicide, whereupon Mortiz returns to his grave. The same tendencies led Wedekind in *Earth Spirit* and *The Box of Pandora* to create situations and characters that exist only partially in the real world. In the main, they are symbols of Eros, and Lulu is less of a real person than an allegorical representation of the sexual instinct. Thereafter Wedekind became increasingly inchoate and a late contribution by this anarchic genius like *Such Is Life* is a curious stew of philosophy and melodrama.

Wedekind, sex-obsessed and hopelessly neurotic, was shipwrecked by his morbid personality, and for all their dynamic quality his plays remain in the limbo of half-realized efforts. But his deficiencies and experiments were straws in the wind.

When the German nation began teetering on the edge of war, precipitated itself into the cataclysm, and emerged from it wrecked in body and soul, dramatic violence like his found strong incentives. The provocation to storm high heaven and thresh one's arms against a mad world with commensurate madness was too strong to be resisted. This began to be the case some years before he died in 1918.

Out of this turmoil came the work of Walter Hasenclever. His febrile talent, expressing itself in staccato dialogue and rapidly shifting extravagant situations, engaged such issues as the clash of generations, the evil of the war-making state, and the violence that arises in a maddened world. In *The Son,* completed in 1914, a young man resents his father's tyranny with such intensity that he would kill his parents. He is incited to the deed by a friend who declaims: "Destroy the tyranny of the family, the medieval blood-bath. . . . Do away with laws! Restore freedom. . . ." This adolescent fanfare was followed by two comparatively reasoned pieces: *The Savior,* in which a poet tries to stop the war at the risk of his life, and an adaptation of Sophocles' *Antigone* which Hasenclever turned into a pacifist drama. Since these plays were written in 1915 and 1917 respectively they were naturally suppressed. But when the lid was lifted from the insurgent drama, nothing short of exhaustion could stop the young writers.

Hasenclever's *Men,* in 1918, proved a veritable nightmare; the hero is a corpse who returns to life and sees the whole madness of the world unrolling before him until he finds peace in the grave. (Corpses or ghosts, not to speak of halfcorpses, were particularly favored by the post-war playwrights, and the habit is still with us in such recent products as Rice's *American Landscape* and Capek's *The Mother.*) A corpse was again the center of attention in *Jenseits* or *Beyond,* written in 1920. Here a husband who was killed in an explosion constantly interposes himself between his wife and her lover until in despair the latter stabs her and kills himself. The dead man's presence makes itself felt throughout when doors open and close by themselves, when the fire assumes the shape of his face, and when the house is at last demolished by invisible hands. Uprisings and chaos also reappeared in *Decision,* and this bitter satire on the failure of revolution was amply supported by the betrayal of the 1918 revolt by pussyfooting and smug Social Democrats like Scheidemann and Ebert.

Hasenclever continued to capitalize his fantastic and bitter vein to the end. In 1930, shortly before the collapse of the Weimar Republic, he brought Napoleon back to life in *Napoleon Enters the Scene.* Napoleon struts again, but it is not long before he is committed to an asylum because his dictatorial ambitions are too romantic for the modern practical world. As events were soon to show, Hasenclever proved himself more Shavian than prophetic. When a Napoleon reappeared in Germany in 1933 he succeeded so well that it was Hasenclever, a half-Jewish descendant of Goethe, who was forced into retirement.

Hasenclever's brothers-in-arms were numerous, and although it is difficult to find a definition which would cover all their work they discovered a slogan in the term "expressionism." All the arts shared the new viewpoint, and the very term first came to the fore when the new painters looked for an antonym that would express their divergence from the "impressionism" of Monet and Manet. Painting, sculpture and architecture were to turn from the duplication of nature to the "expression" of inner experience. It is not surprising to find in the ranks of the expressionist playwrights a painter like Kokoschka and a sculptor like Barlach.

Expressionism called for the presentation of inner states rather than outer reality, as well as for the distortion of the latter by the inner eye. This type of drama was in the first instance defiantly and flagrantly subjective, and it capitalized personal disillusionment and revolt. In more objective forms it could also be imaginative rather than completely distorted by the creator's ego, as in the case of *The Goat Song* and *R. U.R.* But even the more objective approach called for stylization of one kind or another and frequently strove to represent the anarchic state of the world by a corresponding anarchy of rapidly shifting elusive scenes, by an alteration of fantasy and reality, and by characters who are fantastic either in themselves or in their visions or moods. To use an elementary example, if a woman clapped into prison for revolutionary activity in *Masses and Man* mulls over the struggles in which she has just engaged, the playwright visualizes her thoughts in stylized, fantastic scenes. If the great world is essentially unreal to a character, as it is to the embezzling cashier of Kaiser's *From Morn to Midnight,* the play makes the world look commensurately unreal by means of extravagant and fugitive scenes. If a character himself is unreal or only half-alive the author may give him a mechanical appearance and supply him with a number instead of a name, as was the case in Elmer Rice's *Adding Machine.* As might be expected, work of this kind afforded a golden opportunity for modern theatrical art and designers, directors and actors met the requirements of the young playwrights with notable ingenuity. In fact, many directors like Leopold Jessner, and Jürgen Fehling, along with scenic designers and actors like the elastic Fritz Kortner, were frequently far more successful in justifying expressionism than were the playwrights.

No single formula can, however, cover the multifarious puerile aberrations and noble endeavors of this volcanic school. The plays ranged all the way from the most furious melodramas and fantasies to carefully conceived dramas of social protest written in a more or less expressionistic style. At the beginning especially one finds such exhibits as Reinhard Sorge's early *Mendicant* (*Der Bettler,* in 1912), Arnoldt Bronnen's *Parricide,* and Hanns Henny Jahn's sanguinary *Medea* and *The Coronation of Richard III.* The recently discovered Oedipus complex and a natural revolt against a war-mongering state were represented by plays in which a son is invariably flying at his father's throat in the name of freedom.

The horror of the World War could not lightly be forgotten, and the love of blood-letting appeared to have become a habit. Alfred Kerr, the eminent German critic who defended the new drama as long as it retained a grain of sanity, describing Jahn's *Richard III* in which "people were continuously being slaughtered, tortured and buried alive" ("on one occasion a gentleman's liver was cut out and eaten"), exclaimed sadly, "They actually produced that in the theatre. Oh, you know too little of this era of the German drama. . . ."

Paul Kornfeld, another disciple of the new "storm and stress" movement, honored his hero in *The Seduction* for strangling a bridegroom simply because he had found the latter's philistinism offensive. A girl admires him for the deed, her brother poisons him, and he in turn induces his murderer to commit suicide! A grocer's dozen of murders, all in the name of "love" is likewise glorified in Kornfeld's *Heaven and Hell.* Unquestionably taste had been debauched by four years of blood-lust and starvation.

However, this turbulent period was not entirely devoid of controlled direction. Expressionism had its moderates like Anton Wildgans whose *Poverty* is a powerful picture of a middle-class family embittered by destitution and whose *Love* mourns the attrition of happiness in marriage. Only by his combination of sordid reality with intense lyricism in these painful plays did Wildgans reflect the expressionist movement, although elsewhere (in *Dies Irae* and *Cain*) he shared the excesses of his compatriots.

The provocations of militarism, social injustice, and revolution, moreover, soon brought thoughtful and poignant works. Whatever sanity or nobility can be ascribed to the post-war German drama came largely from those writers who rejected adolescent posturings and addressed themselves to tangible realities in society or in the human spirit. No matter how febrile or mechanical their style, writers like Kaiser, Werfel, the Czech Capek brothers and Toller made some honorable contributions to the modern theatre because they navigated in the great stream of dramatic humanism.

Most open to suspicion was the talent of Georg Kaiser, who often proved himself an opportunist and a sensationalist. Kaiser, however, reached his maturity, not in his numerous easy concessions to the public among which the melodramatic *Fire in the Opera House* is one of the most pretentious, but in broadly relevant works. In his *Gas* trilogy, he created a symbolic history of modern civilization rushing headlong toward destruction by profit-motivated industrialism. In *From Morn to Midnight,* he satirized the cheapness and futility of this civilization, as well as the inability of its robots to recover their freedom and individuality. A robot-like cashier embezzles his bank's funds in order that he may court an exotic foreign lady, but she turns out to be a respectable woman. Since he has already crossed the Rubicon by stealing the money, he resolves to make the best of the situation and tries to capture the fullness of the great world beyond his cashier's cage. In successive nightmarish episodes, however, he finds this world deceitful and illusory. The pleasure-seeking crowds are automata and the girl who entertains him proves to be a pasteboard beauty with a wooden leg! Soon the jig is up and he can only kill himself to avoid capture when the Salvation Army lassie who pretended an interest in his soul informs the police. So ends the tragedy of a white-collar slave who tried to live like a man! So, too, ends the crucifixion of one who represents the masses, and Kaiser took pains to impress the symbolic nature of his hero's Passion with a variety of details. In one weird and lonely scene when the cashier spreads out his arms he looks as if he were nailed to a cross, and in this portentous moment he has premonitions of the end that bear a fugitive resemblance to the Agony in the Garden nineteen hundred years before. In this bitter summary of a soul's defeat and in the stenographic world-vision of the *Gas* trilogy, Kaiser wrote memorable, if by no means great, drama. His inability to create full-blooded characters and his chronic sensationalism would have relegated him to a speedy oblivion but for the fact that he put his shortcomings to effective use when he conveyed the hollowness and mechanization of the post-war era.

Franz Werfel, who also attained distinction as a poet and novelist, lost himself in confusion and metaphysics when he dramatized the conflict between the social and the anti-social self in his elaborate *Mirror Man* and in the psychiatric *Schweiger* which makes much of hypnotism and insanity. His non-expressionistic plays (*Juarez and Maximilian* and *Paul among the Jews*) have not been particularly effective; and his chronicle of the Jews *The Eternal Road,* although it was effectively staged by Max Reinhardt, was little more than a good pageant. But *The Goat Song* is, despite some tantalizing confusions, a memorable fantasy. Its story of an eighteenth-century insurrection on the part of the homeless drew a provocative parallel to the revolutions that followed the World War. Werfel, who has always distrusted the beast in man, symbolized the dangers inherent in such an upheaval when his revolutionists put an escaped monster at their head and make him the symbol of their revolt. They are crushed by the army, the monster is destroyed, and the old order is restored. But the masters, whose actions gave birth to both the revolt and the monsters, will not remain unchallenged. A woman is bearing the monster's seed in her womb. The cycle of oppression and revolution will not easily come to an end! Lacking the optimism of the true revolutionist who expects a triumphant new order, as well as the optimism of the reactionary who believes that he can stamp out the revolutionary spirit without readicating the provocations he himself is supplying, Werfel could not gratify either camp. But despite some confusion, *The Goat Song* is replete with dramatic excitement, and its overtones are stimulating. The embattled twentieth century has found few symbols in the theatre as comprehensive as this work. Werfel's pessimism was proved to have been prescient when the advent of a new monster—a monster of reaction—drove him into exile.

Prescience was also an attribute of his countrymen the Capek brothers who gave the Czechoslovak theatre its masterpieces. (Werfel who was born in Prague in 1891 was technically a Czechoslovak after the Treaty of Versailles, although he continued to write in German.) The liberal Czech republic established by the Treaty of Versailles counted among its many achievements a progressive stage distinguished by brilliant productions. The Czech drama was, however, too young to develop much individuality except for some patriotic plays. When Czech playwrights did not favor the light Austrian-Hungarian drama (sometimes with a Shavian touch) as in the work of Frantisek Langer, whose *Camel Through the Eye of the Needle* is known to the American public, they were attracted to expressionism.

Stirred by the German movement in 1921, Karel Capek wrote a memorable play in *R.U.R.* (Rossum's Universal Robots). Observing the growing mechanization of men by mass-production industry, Capek conceived a future in which all the workers would be automata or "robots." Their ultimate revolt when they acquire souls and the ensuing catastrophe comprise an exciting and vivid experience in the theatre. Here Capek succeeded in conveying a contemporary phenomenon in robustly melodramatic but imaginative and provocative terms. Although this fable suffers from Wellsian superficiality and didactic obviousness, it employed expressionism with more than ordinary force and intelligence.

Capek next addressed himself to the problem of longevity and spun out a thin fantasy in *The Macropoulos Affair* to prove the banal point that old age is not a blessing. Feeling the pressure of the horrible thirties, however, he retrieved his hold upon contemporary realities in two earnest and deeply troubled plays: *The White Plague* or *The Power and Glory,* a taut anti-fascist fantasy; and *The Mother,* a lament for the European mothers who lose their husbands and sons in its wars and discords, written shortly before the nearly simultaneous death of the author and his country. Although both plays

won esteem in England, Capek was unable to recapture the dramatic power of *R.U.R. The White Plague* was too obviously contrived, and *The Mother* proved static and repetitious. However, *The Insect Comedy* or *The World We Live In,* a collaboration with his brother Josef, must also be listed among the assets of Central European expressionism. This pessimistic allegory of man's rapaciousness and stupidity, as duplicated in the insect world, is as neatly contrived as it is uncomfortably true. Josef Capek's independently written *Adam the Creator,* was another but inferior pessimistic document, expressing the hopelessness of ever weaning mankind from its lust for property and power.

Pessimism was, in truth, the dominant note of those expressionists who revealed any maturity as artists. Kaiser, Werfel and the Capeks, all of them seated on the Central European volcano, looked out upon a crumbling world, and one can hardly be surprised if their writing hand shook with anxiety. To be a serene and rounded artist under the circumstances was impossible; to have tried to be one would have argued super-human power or a dubious talent for shutting both eyes. Only one writer, Ernst Toller, the noblest and most dramatic of all the expressionists, commandeered faith in a new world at least for a time. Like several other expressionists (among whom the Austrian Hans von Chlumberg contributed the occasionally effective, if operatic, *Miracle at Verdun*), Toller turned first to the tragedy of war. With Shelley-like confidence in man Toller celebrated a spirited conversion to pacifism in his immature *Transfiguration,* written in 1918 while he was in prison for supporting an anti-war demonstration. In both realistic and dream pictures a sculptor, who enlisted for foreign service, becomes a pacifist. Toller here envisaged a revolution without bloodletting—a conversion to reason and love that would make the soldiers beat their swords into plowshares.

Soon enough, however, Toller came up against the material reality of revolution and counter-revolution. After his release from prison for pacifist agitation, he was elected to the Bavarian National Congress and became a member of the Bavarian Soviet, although he deplored the untimeliness of the uprising. His five years' imprisonment in the fortress Niederschönenfeld after the collapse of the revolution could not crush his spirit. In prison he wrote the two noblest plays of the post-war German theatre *Masses and Man* (*Masse-Mensch*) and *The Machine-Wreckers,* as well as the beautiful and more consistently satisfactory poems of *The Swallow Book.* Neither play relinquished any faith in the ultimate triumph of humanity or countenanced violence. Both works expressed the idealism of communism without countenancing sanguinary methods. Both were consequently poems of suffering and aspiration rather than mere appraisals of reality.

In *Masses and Man* an upper-class woman deserts her husband and supports the common people in an anti-war strike. But when the masses get out of hand and commit violence she makes an impassioned effort to restrain them. She is mocked and overruled, and the resulting revolt is crushed. But it is she who is dragged to prison and forced to suffer for the people. Refusing to be saved by the nameless proponent of mob-violence and awaiting execution, she endures visions in her cell that fortify her instead of crushing her spirit. Memorable was Toller's fine presentation of the great dilemma of all idealists. "The Nameless," as the leader of the mob is called, insists that evil can be destroyed only by violence because the intractable masters cannot be overthrown by any other means. But Sonia cannot countenance murder from any source and in any cause: the masses, who have been poisoned by oppression and made murderous by their wrongs, must not build a new world of hatred. To the tactician of revolution poor Sonia (and, with her, Toller) is hopelessly "confused." But, like Toller, she is the incarnation of all the dreams of all the lovers of humanity. "You live too soon," says her antagonist.

Similarly in *The Machine-Wreckers,* a horrible picture of the first phase of English industrialism which led to the Luddite riots in 1815, it is an idealist who opposes violence. The enlightened worker Jim Cobbett calls upon the desperate weavers to desist from destroying the machines to which they attribute their plight. The machine can become the slave of humanity; and it can be turned into a blessing if the workers will only organize themselves into an effective body. The maddened and misled mob, braving the power of the English government, disregards his plea and kills him. But the ultimate effect of *The Machine-Wreckers* is far from dispiriting, for Cobbett—according to Toller—was only anticipating the day when the desperate mob would become an organized and intelligent working-class.

Even Toller's nerves, however, were affected by the war in which he had served as a student officer. In *Hinkemann* or *Broken-Brow,* the morbid domestic tragedy of a soldier who is unsexed in the war, bitterness overwhelmed the artist in Toller. Dismay also struck his heart as he watched the growing flabbiness of the opportunistic German Social-Democratic Party. The idealist in one of Toller's last plays *Hoppla* leaves an asylum only to discover that his erstwhile socialist comrades have become liberal time-servers and to be made responsible for the assassination of one of their number by a Nazi—a deed which he planned to commit himself for precisely opposite reasons. He is ultimately exonerated, but it is too late; he hangs himself in his cell.

Toller's later plays could not recapture the hopeful passion and superb lyricism of his youth, and his despair grew deeper until his sensitive soul could bear it no longer. After years of exile in England and America while his relatives suffered in German concentration camps, this Christlike poet, whose last act was a single-handed effort to bring relief to the starving children of Spain, hanged himself in his New York hotel. Perhaps his private demons were seconded by some vague belief that his death would shake the world and awaken its conscience. Perhaps he thought that his sacrifice would cleanse the world. Toller was one of those sons of man who cannot sacrifice others—they can only sacrifice themselves. Had he not written in *Masses and Man:* "Who acts may only sacrifice himself." (pp. 482-91)

John Gassner, "Hauptmann's Fellow-Travelers and the Expressionist Eruption," in his Masters of the Drama, *third revised edition, Dover Publications, Inc., 1954, pp. 467-94.*

WALTER H. SOKEL

[*In the following excerpt, Sokel examines the primary characteristics of German Expressionist drama.*]

What strikes one first about Expressionist plays is an extremism of theme, language, stagecraft, mixed with many features of realistic or classical drama. There are in these plays elements of distortion, exaggeration, grotesqueness, and implau-

sibility that clearly anticipate the alienating effects encountered in the avant-garde theater of our own time. We witness bizarre events. For example, we see a murdered man reappearing in the modern metropolis carrying his head in a sack, brought to court, and condemned as his own murderer. A woman floats out the window of her lover's apartment. A poodle changes into a psychologist. A cuckolded husband grows antlers on his head. A group of airplane pilots suddenly appears in a café, reciting verses in the style of Greek tragedy, and a group of prostitutes and their lovers engage in a stylized orgy while a literary conversation takes place in another section of the café. Plots are disjointed and confusing, or cease to be recognizable as such. Dialogue suddenly changes from prose to hymnic poetry and rhapsodic monologue, completely interrupting the action. Lyrical passages alternate with obscenities and curses. Characters speak past rather than to each other. Language tends to be reduced, in some plays, to two- or one-word sentences (the "telegraphic style"), to expletives, gestures, pantomime.

Some of these developments were simply an intensification of Naturalism. The Naturalists, in the wake of Ibsen, had brought to the stage subject matter which the "well-made play" of the Victorian era carefully avoided, and their language, especially in German Naturalism, increasingly flaunted an emotional directness that made the linguistic innovations of the Expressionists possible. Ibsen had made syphilis the theme of tragedy; Strindberg, in his Naturalistic phase, introduced the strait jacket on the stage; Schnitzler made sexual intercourse the structural center of each scene in his *La Ronde;* Hauptmann, in his *The Weavers,* made workers' dialect the language of tragedy. At first glance, an Expressionist play like Arnolt Bronnen's *Patricide,* in which a high-school boy has sexual intercourse with his mother on stage and mortally stabs his father, seems simply an extreme development of Naturalism, foreshadowing and even outdoing Tennessee Williams. But in spite of the play's many resemblances to extreme Naturalism, the spirit in which *Patricide* was written was diametrically opposed to Naturalism. In his autobiography, *Arnolt Bronnen Goes on Record (Arnolt Bronnen Gibt zu Protokoll,* 1954), Bronnen tells us that he wrote down not what he observed but what he felt and suffered; he not only dramatized the Freudian Oedipus complex in its primitive essence, he also exemplified the Freudian view of the artist—he had sublimated his misery into a dream and projected this dream on paper. With this, the keynote of Expressionism is struck: subjectivism. Dream became literature.

The extremism and distortion of Expressionist drama derive from its closeness to the dream. In its crude aspects, Expressionism is dramatized daydream and fantasy. In its subtler and more interesting examples, Expressionism parallels the concealing symbolism and subliminal suggestiveness of night dreams. Strindberg called the experimental plays he wrote when he passed beyond Naturalism "dream plays." In them projection and embodiment of psychic forces take the place of imitation of external facts; association of ideas supplants construction of plot based on logical connection of cause and effect. The old structural principle of causal interrelation between character, incident, and action gives way to a new structural pattern, closer to music than to drama—the presentation and variation of a theme.

Strindberg's "dream plays" became the inspiration of the Expressionists. Unlike the French Surrealists of the twenties and thirties, the Expressionists rarely reproduced actual dreams. Rather, the structure of many of their plays resembled, in some respects, the pattern of the human mind in dream and reverie. The influence of Strindberg coincided with that of psychoanalysis (Freud's *Interpretation of Dreams* appeared two years before *A Dream Play*). Both in its Freudian and in its Jungian form, psychoanalysis had decisive significance for Expressionism. But even before Freud and Jung, the intellectual atmosphere in the wake of Romanticism, and German philosophy from Schelling to Schopenhauer and Nietzsche, had given intimations of the concept of the subconscious. Even those Expressionists who were not conversant with the actual works of Freud and Jung could not help but be familiar with the climate of thought that had given rise to psychoanalysis in the first place.

Dream effects were achieved in a variety of ways. A comparison of two examples—the first act of Reinhard Sorge's *The Beggar* and Oskar Kokoschka's play *Job*—might illustrate the range. The choice of these two playwrights has special relevance, since they introduced full-fledged Expressionism to the German theater. Kokoschka, more famous as a painter, wrote the first Expressionist play, *Murderer the Women's Hope,* in 1907; Sorge composed *The Beggar* in 1911.

Sorge achieves dreamlike effects by scenic arrangements, light, the grouping of characters, and speech variations. Floodlight takes the place of stream of consciousness. The wandering of the floodlight over the stage, illuminating now one and now another section, symbolizes the process of the mind itself. When the latent substratum emerges, the center of the stage is obscured while a particular corner—significantly supplied with couches or benches—is highlighted. When the mind shifts back to the surface plot, the corner sinks into darkness, while the center is illuminated. The corner scenes, so puzzlingly unrelated to the main-action center stage, can now be seen as only apparently unrelated. These scenes function as symbolically disguised commentary and reflection on the themes discussed in the center, and in that lies their dreamlike quality.

This relationship between scenic interludes and main dialogue or plot was a radical extension of the multiple-plot structure of Shakespeare's plays, which had inspired not only Sorge but all those who, since the Storm and Stress of the eighteenth century, had rebelled against the neo-classicist unities and their modern successor, the "well-made play," with its neat logic and economy of plot. Those for whom theater meant more than drama and dramatic plot, for whom theater was play, show, and vision of the world, had to hark back to Shakespeare and beyond. The Expressionists benefited greatly from Max Reinhardt's imaginative stagings of Shakespeare and Strindberg, and from the general advances in stagecraft, especially lighting effects, associated with this master showman of the Berlin theater.

The historic importance of Sorge's play lies in its attempt to create on the stage something that happened to be akin to the interior monologue in the novel. This approach leads to musical, rather than dramatic, structure. Expressionist drama is theme-centered rather than plot- or conflict-centered. This factor constitutes the most marked break with the tradition of the "well-made play." The first impression given by Sorge's *The Beggar,* for instance, is one of bewildering formlessness. The play flies in the face of the plot-centered tradition of drama with which we are most familiar. Yet a closer examination of the play reveals the opposite of formlessness—careful craftsmanship and richly interwoven texture,

at least in the first three acts, the bulk of the play. The intricate arrangement of themes closely corresponds to the composition of a symphony rather than a drama in the traditional sense. The interludes of the first act echo the foreground theme in choral variations. The Prostitute interlude represents a counterpoint to the Girl theme. The Poet's visionary speech finds its exact counterpoint in the Father's enraptured vision in the second act. The insane Father's engineering "mission," which dominates Acts II and III, is the contrapuntal theme to the Son's poetic mission in Act I.

These few examples should help dispel the widespread notion that Expressionism was necessarily formless. The subtle musical structure of *The Beggar,* or the classically polished, lyrical grotesqueries of Kokoschka, show that the abandonment of a logical, unified plot does not mean the abandonment of theatrical form. Like abstract paintings or like *Finnegans Wake,* the experimental plays of Expressionism did not necessarily renounce aesthetic form and inner coherence merely because these offered greater obstacles to immediate appreciation.

In his play *Sphinx and Strawman (Sphinx und Strohmann),* performed by the Zurich Dadaists in 1917, the Austrian painter Oskar Kokoschka developed a kind of dream play which differed from Strindberg's and Sorge's type. He deepened, expanded, and changed this play from prose into poetry of classical smoothness and elegance, and so gave birth to his finest poetic achievement—*Job,* which created a theater scandal at its performance in 1919. Like Sorge, Kokoschka transforms aspects of the dream process into theater. His play revolves about the projection of psychic processes into visual terms. Unlike Sorge, Kokoschka relies less on light effects and stage division than on the transformation of metaphors, of figures of speech, into stage images. Job's tragedy consists in having his head turned by woman. The author shows this literally happening on the stage. In his helpless anxiety over his wife Anima, Job twists his head and cannot set it straight again. As his wife flagrantly deceives him, antlers grow on his head and become the clothes-tree for his wife's and her lover's undergarments. The metaphors contained in the figures of speech—"she turns his head," "she puts horns on him"—become dramatic image, visual fact. Intimately related to the dream and the workings of the human subconscious, as expounded by Freud in his *Interpretation of Dreams* and *Wit and Its Relation to the Unconscious,* Kokoschka's method constitutes the dramatic parallel to Kafka's art of projecting the repressed content of the mind into mysterious events. In Kokoschka's play, the projection of psychic situations into symbolic images, an essential function of the subconscious mind, becomes action on the stage. This principle offered Kokoschka, and Goll after him, a means of returning to the ancient nature of the theater as magic show, as visual and pantomimic liberation from the confining fetters of realism and propriety. As Esslin has pointed out, it is precisely this triumph of the image, this staging of the metaphor, which makes for the dramatic poetry in the works of Beckett, Ionesco, and Genet. The ash cans in which the senescent parents in Beckett's *Endgame* spend their lives, the audience of empty chairs in Ionesco's *The Chairs,* or the transformation of human beings into rhinoceros in his *The Rhinoceros*—such central stage images of the Theater of the Absurd are born of the same kind of inspiration as Job's twisted head or the Chagallian heroine floating out the window in Goll's *The Immortal One.* This particular form of Expressionist dream play not only points ahead to the avant-garde theater of our day, but also re-establishes connections with the ancient mainstream of European theater, which the "well-made" respectable play of the modern era had repudiated. Cabaret and circus, *commedia dell'arte,* Passion and miracle play, and, above all, the magic farce of the Vienna popular theater, which flowered in Mozart's and Schikaneder's *Magic Flute,* the whole baroque delight in the *spectaculum mundi,* contributed to that feast of theatricality and poetry—Kokoschka's *Job.*

In Georg Kaiser's play, *Alkibiades Saved,* a figure of speech becomes event and forms the brilliantly ironic plot. Kaiser's drama is a spectacle showing how "the thorn in the flesh" gives rise to Platonism, idealism, and spirituality. By preventing Sokrates from engaging in normal physical activity, the thorn lodged in his foot forces him to question and subvert the athletic-heroic values of his civilization and replace them with new values of intellect and spirit. The process of sublimation is acted out before our eyes. No one of the Athenians (except Sokrates himself and Xantippe, his wife) knows of the thorn, the invisible wound that makes Sokrates the subverter and scandalizer of the old and the prophet of a new civilization. But for us, the spectators, the invisible is visualized, the spiritual and psychological problem is projected into a vividly concrete, physical happening.

The projection of abstract ideas and psychic situations into symbolic images and happenings is one of the most basic features of Expressionist drama. Consequently, language loses the pre-eminent rank it held in traditional drama. Dynamic utilization of setting and stage (in *The Beggar,* for instance, the walls of the living room literally widen and part to let in the cosmos) expresses many things formerly expressed by language, or not expressed at all. Broad gestures, uninhibited overacting, as demanded by Kornfeld, the return to mask, buskin, and chanting—these are the demands made by Expressionist theory and frequently exhibited by Expressionist practice. An immediate appeal is made to the audience's visual sense rather than to its conceptual thought. The memory of empirical reality, with its demand for causal logic and plausibility, is suspended.

The single emotional word replaces the involved conceptual sentence as the basic unit of Expressionist language. Repetition, variation, modulating echo, and contrapuntal clash of single words are essential parts of Expressionist dialogue. The Expressionists utilize to their fullest extent the expressive possibilities of punctuation. Punctuation becomes one of the tools of visualization and attains a crucial role. The accumulation of exclamation points, or the linking of exclamation point and question mark, as in Kaiser and Sorge, and punctuation in general, are transformed on the stage into inflection and gesture and thereby augment and even create the emotional impact of their language. Punctuation becomes one of the primary tools of visualization and assumes a significance unknown in traditional drama. Concomitantly, the demands made upon the vocal apparatus and bodily effort of the actors greatly transcend those of traditional plays. As Kornfeld's essay shows, Expressionism stands at the opposite pole of Stanislawski. The Expressionist actor stands somewhere between actor, singer, and mime. Frequently his greatest impact must come from his stage presence rather than his speech. Sokrates, in Kaiser's play, dominates the scene in which he refuses the wreath simply by the visual contrast between his massive silence and static presence, and the frantic verbosity of the others. At the banquet, his presence falls like a shadow over the revellers. The chill that overtakes them is

conveyed by Sokrates' silences more than by his words. Bereft of the customary support of dialogue, the actor has to rely on the resources of his body to a much greater degree than in conventional plays, in which dialogue is the primary, and often exclusive, means by which meaning is conveyed.

Expressionist drama employs silence more frequently and more strategically than conventional drama, extending and further developing a tendency initiated by realism and Naturalism in their revolt against language-centered classical drama. Brecht in *Baal,* Kaiser, and Hasenclever use silence as a counterpoint to the meaning of the spoken dialogue. Words and pauses together form a kind of linguistic chiaroscuro, counterpart to the visible chiaroscuro of illumination and dimness or darkness on Sorge's stage. The deliberate use of the pause as a significant means of expression (indicated on the printed page by the abundance of dots and dashes in Expressionist plays) reveals most clearly the kinship between Expressionist drama and music. Dots and dashes are the equivalents of pauses in musical scores. The pause is an essential part of the Expressionist attempt to create or re-create a theater of depths inaccessible to conceptual speech, a "superdrama," as Yvan Goll calls it, conveying a "surreality" which is to empirical reality what depth is to surface. Such a theater would be a "total work of art," like the drama of the Greeks. It would restore the theater as cult. While the Expressionists sought to restore theater as cult, Brecht, going beyond Expressionism, sought to develop theater as seminar and laboratory. Both were equally opposed to the "culinary" theater of mere entertainment and commercial profit.

The displacement of conceptual language by exclamation and pantomime reached an extreme point in Walter Hasenclever's *Humanity (Die Menschen),* in 1918. The early silent films with their exaggerated gestures and miming influenced Hasenclever's modern Passion play. The mixture of sentimental pathos, social protest, and grotesqueness characteristic of the silent films is found here, too. Attracted by the new medium, Hasenclever, soon after *Humanity,* wrote the scenario of the film *Plague (Pest)* in 1920. The possibilities of the film intrigued other Expressionists as well. Yvan Goll celebrated Charlie Chaplin, along with Apollinaire one of his most decisive influences, in his scenario *Chaplinade.* The great film *The Cabinet of Dr. Caligari* (1919), which ushered in the classical period of the German film, was an excellent example of pure Expressionist theater on the screen. Fritz Lang's film *Metropolis* (1926) continued Expressionism in the German movies.

Because of its subjectivism, Expressionist drama does not allow genuine conflict to arise. With few exceptions, Expressionist drama conforms to an "epic" or narrative, rather than to a strictly dramatic pattern. It is not based upon the clash of independently motivated characters, but upon the showing and telling of themes. Ultimately its structure can be traced to the Christian miracle and Passion plays. The content of Expressionist drama is, of course, frequently the opposite of Christian: glorification of murder, blasphemy, pederasty, and vigorous anti-theism (a term more fitting than atheism in the context of Expressionism). Yet even though content may differ profoundly, structural pattern may be similar. The protagonist in Expressionist plays usually serves as an existential example, a paragon, very much like Christ in the Passion plays. The other "characters" are not so much characters as functions in his mission or martyrdom. They represent his opportunities, obstacles, parallels, variations, and counterpoints. Genuine antagonists do not exist. There are antagonistic characters, usually philistines, materialists, often scientists or engineers, moralists and sentimentalists. However, these antagonistic characters do not act as independent personalities motivated by aims of their own, but as foils to the protagonist. They do not carry the action forward. They are closer to the tempting devil in miracle plays or to Goethe's Mephistopheles than to Claudius in *Hamlet.*

The absence of conflict determines the pageant or pilgrimage-type structure of many full-length Expressionist plays, such as Hasenclever's *Humanity* and Brecht's *Baal.* A loosely connected "life story," a series of "stations," pictures, and situations takes the place of a well-knit plot. The major influences for this truly epic or narrative character of Expressionist drama are the Christian Passion play and Goethe's *Faust,* both of which deeply influenced Strindberg, and with him the Expressionists; Shakespeare; Storm and Stress playwrights like Lenz; Büchner (especially in his *Wozzeck*); and the modern cabaret, with its brief skits and numbers. From this type of Expressionist play, the left-wing director Erwin Piscator, Lion Feuchtwanger, and Bertolt Brecht developed in the twenties what is now known as the Epic Theater. Both Expressionism and Brecht's Epic Theater emphasized theater as "show" or demonstration rather than as drama with emphasis on action and suspense. The difference was that most Expressionists (although by no means all) sought to appeal to the emotions, while Brecht's Epic Theater tried to appeal to the critical intellect of its audience.

Kaiser's dramas offer by their taut construction a remarkable contrast to the "epic" looseness and disconnectedness of many Expressionist plays. "Writing a drama" meant for him "thinking a thought through to its conclusion." He compared dramas to "geometric problems" and considered Plato's dialogues perfect models for playwrights. However, subjectivism also formed the basis of Kaiser's work. It was a symptom of this subjectivism that Kaiser admired Plato as a "dramatist." For Plato's dialogues fail to present genuine conflict and dramatic encounter of ideas. They are not true dialogues, but thinly veiled monologues. Significantly, Kaiser noted and praised not the dramatic but the visionary quality of Plato's work. As Professor Wolfgang Paulsen pointed out in his recent work on Kaiser, Kaiser, unlike Shaw, was not a truly "dialectical" playwright. At best he dramatized antitheses, embodied in different characters, as he did in the Billionaire's Son and the Engineer of his famous *Gas I* (1918). Many of his plays even lack such an antithesis. Sokrates, in *Alkibiades Saved,* for example, has no real antagonists waging a real conflict against him. All action comes from Sokrates; the others merely react against him. They are blindly caught in a problem of which Sokrates alone is aware, and which is his own creation. Actually, it is not Sokrates, the character, but Sokrates' idea, to which the thorn in his foot gave rise, that moves the action, until nearly the end. The other characters, with the exception of the judges, are pawns in Sokrates' great enterprise of "saving Alkibiades," the tragic irony of which he alone can see. While more subtly expressed than in the works of other Expressionists, subjectivism informed Kaiser's dramas as much as it did theirs.

Subjectivism in Expressionist dramas entailed not only the absence of genuine conflict but of all real touch and communication between human beings. The most powerful example is Brecht's *In the Swamp* (*Im Dickicht der Städte,* 1922), which came at the end of the Expressionist period. With the

formulation, in theatrical terms, of the breakdown of human communication, Expressionist drama foreshadowed French Existentialism and almost all the serious literature of our time.

Expressionism had two faces: With one of these it looked back to Romanticism; with the other it looked forward to what is most significant and new in the theater of our own time. It was the positive content given to "mission" in Expressionist plays that harked back to Romanticism. It was the parody of "mission" that pointed to the future. What was the content of the Expressionists' "mission"? The Poet in Sorge's *The Beggar* proclaimed that his new theater would regenerate and redeem the world. Kaiser defined drama as "vision." The content of the vision was "the regeneration of man" (*"die Erneuerung des Menschen"*).

With their concept of the writer as visionary and savior, the Expressionists renewed the old dream of Romanticism. Shelley's definition of the poets as "unacknowledged legislators of the world" could have been their motto. The mission themes of Expressionist plays projected the authors' romantic self-pity and isolation in the modern world, as well as their equally romantic self-glorification, their dream of changing the world into a place in which they would feel at home.

There was another side to Expressionism, the counterpart of the idealism contained in its "mission" themes: the acid and macabre presentation of a meaningless, insanely materialistic world. It is in this respect that Expressionism shows an amazing relevance today. The insane Father in Sorge's *The Beggar,* the engineer who draws blueprints of fantastic machines he imagines having "seen" on Mars, strikes us as a truer, more convincing figure than the idealistic Son who hopes to save the world by poetry. The Father resembles the Engineer in Kaiser's *Gas I,* who, after a devastating explosion, calls upon the workers to push ahead from "explosion to explosion" to the conquest of the universe. In our age, shadowed by mushroom clouds and moon rockets, the technocratic nightmares of the Expressionists appear astonishingly prophetic, and much more realistic than at the time they were conceived. Distortion served the Expressionists as an X-ray eye for detecting the dynamic essence of their time, the direction in which history was moving. In caricature and nightmare they approached the truth. Their idealism, on the other hand, was a desparate attempt at self-deception, protecting them from the truth.

Kaiser's brilliant tour de force, *Alkibiades Saved,* amounts to a clear statement of the irony and paradox underlying the Expressionist position. Sokrates' mission is to endure suffering and court the death penalty in order to save Greece from absurdity. Only Sokrates, the intellectual, knows the trivial accident—the thorn in his foot—to which the hero, Alkibiades, owes his life, and the country its victory. If Sokrates discloses the absurd secret, the hero would become a laughingstock, and faith in history and human greatness would be shattered. Civilization could not withstand such a shock. Better to interpose new values, a new "message," between the traditional hero worship and the absurdity of truth than to allow truth to make all messages ridiculous. Subversive as these new values of intellect may be, they serve as a screen between man and the devastating insight into the absurdity of his existence.

This is the crux of the Expressionist sense of "mission": it is a last barrier, frantically held, against absurdity. Its ecstatic humanism is the surface froth. But beneath it lies a cynical, bitter, and sardonic spirit. This spirit informed some of the finest and most brilliant works of Expressionism, from Carl Sternheim to Bert Brecht. The parodying of the sense of mission, or, rather, the demonstration of its absurdity, lies at the heart of Sternheim's comedies and Brecht's early plays.

Carl Sternheim's comedies of "the heroic life of the bourgeoisie" lack the dreamlike distortions of much of Expressionist drama. Their hilarious caricatures and farcical situations remind one at first glance of conventional comedy. However, if we look a little closer, we discover qualities that profoundly distinguish Sternheim's comedies from the traditional type and make them the nearest counterpart to the grimly sardonic drawings of George Grosz.

There are not in Sternheim's comedies, as there are in Molière's, characters with moderate points of view, representing common sense—i.e., the common ground shared by author and audience. Sternheim fails to supply us with the convenient yardstick by which we can judge, while feeling comfortably above them, the comic characters as eccentrics. In Sternheim it is not the characters, but the world that has lost its center. His characters demonstrate a process that defines the whole of bourgeois society, and that might be called a quiet pandemonium of cold-blooded, insidious inhumanity. In *The Strongbox,* faith in securities, the new "soul of man," triumphs effortlessly over the older romantic, sensuous, and sentimental nature of man. But Sternheim does not weep for the lost glory of romantic man. He, too, is shown to be a self-drugging fraud. The aesthete and lover Silkenband is even phonier and more absurd than the tough-minded Professor Krull, with his monomaniac obsession with the securities contained in the strongbox. Sternheim's characters function grotesquely in a world become demonic through what is supposed to be most commonplace and sober in it—its monetary system. Instead of making love to his beautiful young wife, the materialistic professor locks himself in with the strongbox, counting the maiden aunt's securities, listing and relisting their numbers, and figuring their values. Yet neither does Sternheim hold any brief for the neglected young beauty, who turns out to be engaged in a ruthless struggle for power with her shrewd and terrifying spinster aunt. No single value is more rational than any other; beauty and art, romantic love, sensuality, legacy-hunting, and financial fever—all are absurd.

Sternheim's characters are "soulless" in the literal sense—they have no stable permanent core of personality. They are completely identified with their maneuvers and obsessions—their "masks." Many of Sternheim's comedies deal with a bourgeois family called Maske. The name symbolizes modern man's essence, which Sternheim "unmasks." The modern bourgeois's essence is his mask—his veneer, as in Dickens' Mr. and Mrs. Veneering, who foreshadow Sternheim's ruthless characters not only in their go-getting cold-bloodedness but even in their peculiarly staccato baldness of diction, which perfectly expresses their cold-blooded spirit. Yet the obsessions of these characters are not the idiosyncrasies of individual eccentrics nor the embodiments of timeless vices familiar to us from Molière. They embody the obsessions of society and the absurdity of the human condition itself. Lacking a stable center at his core, man in Sternheim is denatured.

Sternheim's "comedy" has a mission as its plot—the old aunt's strongbox pulls all men away from sexuality and passion to its own cold self. Not plot, but theme, is the center of interest. If the plot were the main interest—in other words,

if Sternheim had written a traditional comedy about greed—the question of whether or not Professor Krull would inherit the strongbox would be left in suspense until as near the end as possible. Instead, the disclosure of the aunt's will, which bequeaths the contents of the box to the Church, is put near the middle of the play. The play ends not with the ironic punishment and just comeuppance of a greedy and neglectful husband, but with a new convert to mammonism. Capitalism, as the modern truth, replaces the older "truths" of chivalrous mummery and romance, or bohemian idealism. However, the "mission" of capitalism is patently absurd, too, since we know that the securities in the strongbox will never belong to their worshipers. The strongbox becomes a symbol of absurdity, like the Mars machines "seen" by the Father in Sorge's play. An absurd mission, seriously and consistently engaged in, reveals the absurdity of the world.

Brecht wrote *Baal* (1918), perhaps the most poetic play Expressionism produced, as a parody and refutation of the romantic concept of the poet's martyrdom in the philistine world. Like the Dadaists of the same period, the twenty-year-old, guitar-strumming ex-medical orderly, whom war had shocked into "coolness" and nihilism, could not stomach the naïve dreams of grandeur and the lachrymose self-pity of many Expressionists. His intent was to show the truth of a contemporary poet's existence, stripped of sentimentality and pseudo-romantic claptrap. Hanns Johst's play *The Lonely One* (*Der Einsame,* 1917), which treated the life of Christian Dietrich Grabbe as a nineteenth-century, German-provincial version of a *poète maudit*'s fate, was the special target for Brecht's derision and became the cause for *Baal,* which Rimbaud's life also helped to inspire. However, Brecht took issue not only with Johst but with the entire stream of Expressionist "dramatic missions," which Sorge's *The Beggar* had initiated seven years earlier. It will therefore be helpful to compare these two poetic "missions," one at the beginning and one near the end of Expressionism, in order to assess its inner range and unity.

Both *The Beggar* and *Baal* deal with poets who are in radical opposition to past traditions and values. At the beginning of each play, the poet-protagonist is offered financial support by wealthy members of the bourgeoisie. Both rebuff this help and prefer isolation and a bleak, poverty-stricken existence to security. Both deliberately burn their bridges to society before our eyes. However, there is a profound difference. Out of loyalty to his ideal, his mission, the new theater he envisions, Sorge's Poet rejects the help of society. Needless to say, he is also frighteningly convinced of his own importance. His art, he feels, is so significant that he cannot tolerate even the slightest adulteration. His attitude is to the highest degree moral, duty-bound, and egocentric. The difference between him and an old-fashioned Prussian officer is that the Prussian officer's loyalty is to king and country, the Poet's to himself. However, since his self is of supreme importance only as the bearer of a sacred mission, the difference is considerably diminished. Obviously, Sorge was still deeply steeped in the traditions of German Idealism, which he received in a modernized, Nietzschean version. He substituted new and "higher" values of his own for the conventional values he rejected.

Although written only seven years after Sorge's play, Brecht's *Baal* strikes one as disturbingly up-to-date. Baal, a "beatnik" of genius, a link between Rimbaud and Genet, transforms twentieth-century despair into poetry. Baal rejects society not because he believes in a new ideal but because he is bored and revolted. In his boredom, which is his revolt, only one thing can inspire him—physical experience. While the rich publisher offers success and security, Baal only notices the fine body of the publisher's wife. He knows no inhibitions and propositions her in front of her husband, with the result that he will sleep with the wife and lose the husband's support forever. With his "cool," blunt proposition, Baal sweeps all values aside. He delivers a much more radical rebuff to society than Sorge's Poet. Sorge's Poet can still be understood by the bourgeois—although not approved. Brecht's Baal cannot be understood. His is a directness and immediacy which make civilization impossible.

We must not misinterpret Baal's motives as simply honesty or Rabelaisian *joie de vivre*. There is a cruel complexity, a tragic sadness about him, which makes his unending string of debaucheries not an expression of a thirst for life but a challenge to and a confirmation of the absurdity of life. Baal toasts in one everlasting carousal and orgy his knowledge that life lives by feeding on life, and God forgets his rotting creation. Sex is the means by which Baal expresses his revolt against and his enactment of the purposelessness of a universe in which nothing lasts. Not Rabelais's Pantagruel but Camus's "stranger" is his brother.

Baal is a return to nature, not as Rousseau and the Romantics had conceived it, but as Darwinism taught modern man to see it. Baal's sky is filled with vultures that wait to eat him, unless he manages to eat them first. And yet this sky is beautiful and loved by Baal. By stripping existence of meaning, *Baal* glorifies truth. In this lies its poetry. Several years after *Baal*, Brecht had his Sergeant Bloody Five, in *A Man's a Man*, emasculate himself to suppress his nature and fit more perfectly into the army code, which is only the most extreme form of organized society. Baal has no need for emasculation. He stays free of the compulsion to fit into any organized form of life. Civilization has been unable to conquer him; organization has been unable to touch him with its twisting grip. Seen by the social self in all men and women, Baal is a "degenerate beast" and deserves full contempt. Seen by their nostalgia for a pre-social state of freedom, Baal wears the halo of eternal childhood and arouses hopeless admiration. Men and women are erotically drawn to him because he awakens in them a buried memory of untrammeled vitality, the longing for an innocence that has nothing to do with moral codes. His life is entirely of the moment. It makes no claims to continuity, and is therefore able to burn in undivided intensity. For this same reason, Baal's fascination for the men and women who are involved with him must always end in their disaster because the undivided life can only be a life for moments and cannot recognize duration. Baal's only love that transcends the moment is homosexual. He loves a man whom he soon murders. Apart from the obvious Verlaine-Rimbaud model, there is this reason for the decisive role of homosexuality in *Baal*. It is the same reason that has made homosexuality a leading motif in mid-century Western life: No way of life is better fitted to express the refusal to fit into any accepted pattern of behavior.

Baal lives what Expressionists, like Ludwig Rubiner, envisioned and proclaimed. He is "man in the center," embodying "explosion," "intensity," "catastrophe," the rhythm and color of life uprooted from all traditions. However, in creating Baal, Brecht made Expressionism "realistic." He freed it from the remnants of Christian spirituality and the sweetish *l'art nouveau* or *Jugendstil* sentiment. He likewise stripped it

of the illusion that the explosive liberation of "essential man" could be compatible with humanism. Burning away all comforts, Brecht showed the Dionysiac essence of Expressionism. (pp. xii-xxix)

Walter H. Sokel, in an introduction to Anthology of German Expressionist Drama: A Prelude to the Absurd, *edited by Walter H. Sokel, Doubleday & Company, Inc., 1963, pp. ix-xxxii.*

MEL GORDON

[*In the following excerpt, Gordon discusses the performance style of German Expressionist theater.*]

Like other avant-garde movements, Expressionism developed both a dramatic literature and a theatrical style. Although they shared a similar philosophical underpinning, the Expressionist drama and theatre evolved separately, being created by different people, at different times. Occasionally, theatre scholars have analyzed one in terms of the other, producing a number of misconceptions. To be sure, the earlier Expressionist dramatic literature inspired the development of the Expressionist styles of performance. Yet, some of theatrical Expressionism's roots and influences came from sources that were antithetical to literary Expressionism. More often than not, however, theatrical Expressionism, particularly in the acting, advanced modes of performance that were uniquely its own.

Despite the fact that Expressionist plays were published and widely read beginning in 1912, only a few were physically enacted before 1917. In part this was due to the First World War, with many of the Expressionists and theatre practitioners at the fronts and a high degree of military censorship. Yet, one notices a kind of reluctance by the Expressionists to actually stage their works. Although they praised the theatre as their greatest potential medium, a utopic space where "Man explodes in front of Man," Expressionists like Walther von Hollander were clearly worried that the too quick realization of Expressionist productions, especially in the acting, could prove to be a very costly failing. And in a way, their fears of imperfection were not unjustified.

From its beginnings in 1910 to its demise as a movement in Germany some fifteen years later, literary Expressionism promulgated the existence of a higher order of humanity, of a certain kind of individual who was neither merchant nor "blond beast," of an intellectual who could act, of the New Man. Like the movement itself, the Expressionists' conception of this ideal type underwent numerous and extreme transformations. At first he was described as a Nietzchean Nay-Sayer, the slayer of fathers and teachers, the destroyer of all bourgeois traditions (i.e., the students in Gottfried Benn's *Ithaka* [1914]). Later, during the war, the New Man appeared as an apostle of peace; he became an activist Christian, one who was capable of great feats of leadership and self-sacrifice, a lover of Mankind (i.e., Antigone in Walter Hasenclever's *Antigone* [1917]). In the last phase of Expressionism, or its "Black Period," the New Man was revealed as an Übermensch/Gandhian *manqué*, the individual with all the conventional attributes of the enlightened hero except the powers of social or political potency (i.e., Jimmy Cobbett in Ernst Toller's *The Machine-Wreckers* [1922]).

Particularly in the second stage of Expressionism, the followers of Expressionism propagated the philosophy of the worth of Man—of *all* men. Essentially, they thought, Man was good, born good. Only a restrictive society and a denatured consciousness were preventing Man from searching and feeling the true, inner ecstatic reality of life. Instead, society's institutions—the family, the government, the military, the business and landowning classes—were pushing Mankind into cycles of materialism and misery. There was only one solution, the Expressionists felt: revolution—not necessarily the substitution of one government for another, but rather a revolution of the spirit. If Man could learn to trust his emotions, then he would love all men, would experience "new love," and therefore would be in touch with the laws of the universe.

What united all of these conceits was the New Man's unique awareness of Mankind's—as well as his own—place in the universe and his ability to act upon it. No books of philosophy or psychology could instruct the New Man in this cosmic understanding; instead, he would have to seek it directly. Sometimes this could be accomplished through the exploration of his unconscious in dream, hypnotic, trance, or drug-induced states. Occasionally in physical states of pure action where the brain's censor would not function adequately, the New Man could discover that ecstatic, ineffable condition of "absolute Rapture." Like the medieval mystics, the Expressionists believed that only the possessed individual was capable of transcending his daily existence to make contact with the *Seele,* or soul. (In such a primordial state, one's entire being is expressed outside space and time; the possessed's muscles and joints may be twisted and contorted, sounds akin to animal barks or single syllables may be produced in his throat. According to the Expressionists, a man in that condition was experiencing the Cosmos.)

For the Expressionists, the new, untested Expressionist actor was not just a symbol or the physical rendering of the New Man: His abilities to transform himself from one soul-state to another, to emote the broadest range of feelings, to express the ecstasy of the playwright, and to guide the audience made him the New Man incarnate. The failure of Expressionist performance, they thought, would doom Expressionism as an artistic movement and philosophy.

Most of the important Expressionist statements on acting were prescriptive, coming months and years before the heyday of the Expressionist theatre. To a large degree, these articles, often in a manifesto or declamatory style, were authored by Expressionist playwrights and theoreticians and not by the to-be Expressionist directors or theatre workers themselves.

First and best-known of these statements,"Epilog to the Actor," was written by the Expressionist playwright Paul Kornfeld in May 1916 as an afterword to his play, *The Seduction* (1913), a year and a half before it was produced at the *Schauspielhaus* in Frankfurt by Gustav Hartung on 8 December 1917. As did other playwrights, Kornfeld worried that the nascent Expressionist actors would misunderstand or prove inadequate to the task of presenting his play. In "Epilog to the Actor"—translated in full by Joseph M. Bernstein in Walter Sokel's *An Anthology of German Expressionist Drama: A Prelude to the Absurd*—Kornfeld exhorted the Expressionist actor not to behave

> as though the thoughts and words he has to express have only arisen in him at the very moment in which he recites them. If he has to die on the stage, let him not pay a visit to the hospital beforehand in order to learn how to die: . . . Let him dare to

> stretch his arms out wide and with a sense of soaring speak as he has never spoken in life; let him not be an imitator or seek his models alien to the actor. In short, let him not be ashamed of the fact that he is acting.

Only this sort of non-reality imitating actor could embody the single, pristine, emotional essence of the new drama, Kornfeld claimed. Through careful selection and avoidance of complex Naturalism, the new actor could be the necessary "representative of thought, feeling, or Fate." Despite the heavy Expressionist rhetoric, Kornfeld's model for the Expressionist actor was operatic—"The dying singer [who] still gives forth a high C"—and in some ways did not significantly differ from the conception of the Reinhardt or pantomimic actor.

Writing in the *Neue Rundschau,* Walther von Hollander defined the essence of the yet-unseen Expressionist acting as the search for the final removal of all corporal disguises—clothing, skin—in order to uncover the actor's own *Seele.* Unlike the performer from the Neo-Romantic theatre, who merely copied the established symbolic positions to signify his inner, soul-like feelings, the Expressionist actor would have to exhibit, through physical unmasking and submission, his own internal—cosmic—anxieties. Only then, after the actor had fully mined his deepest emotions, Hollander maintained, could his soul explode from the clutches of his body, gushing through his veins until his entire being became a physicalization of the *Seele,* Naturally, Hollander was not unaware of the difficulties in training for and in ultimately achieving such a state on the stage. But, he felt, the fate of Expressionism would rest upon its realization in the theatre: "If this form of acting does not develop of its own accord, then it will have to be consciously created."

There were also those who were more clearly optimistic, presuming that true Expressionism in acting was inevitable. Some believed that the correct recitation of Expressionist dialog and Expressionist acting would follow naturally from the production of intense emotions—and vice-versa. In the *Neue Schaubühne,* Friedrich Sebrecht affirmed that there was an intrinsic link between the actor's internal feelings and his physical actions, so that an actor could not feel—and therefore not express with his voice—a "concealed longing pain" without spasmatically convulsing his shoulders while speaking: he could not experience vocally and viscerally a deep melancholia without first forcing his vacuous, "chaotic and eternity-filled" eyes to bulge.

Some writers hoped that Expressionist acting, while expressing extreme emotions and demonstrating the inner, psychic transformations of the New Man, would also make concrete the entire human condition in a simplified fashion. Using Edschmid's dictum, "The sick man is not merely the cripple who suffers; he becomes sickness itself," they wanted the creation of absolute external states in the Expressionist acting and performance. But, for the most part, the Expressionist theoreticians were concocting theatrical manifestos in a vacuum.

Then in 1917 and in early 1918, a handful of Expressionist performances were mounted in Frankfurt, Dresden, Munich and Düsseldorf. Their reception was by no means a uniformly welcomed one. But, by the next year, as if they had come out of nowhere, Expressionist productions began to be viewed throughout Germany and to dominate the entire theatrical scene—particularly in Berlin.

Oskar Kokoschka. Kokoschka explained that he was angry at being characterized as a criminal in the press after the first performance of his play Murderer Hope of Womankind, *and he shaved his head "in order to look the part."*

Basically, the German Expressionist theatre can be divided into two distinct periods: 1) a stylistically pure early stage from 1917-1921 that culminated in the unusually vigorous 1919-1920 season in Berlin, and 2) a later period from 1921 to 1924, in which Expressionism having outlived its public novelty in the popular commercial theatre, combined with other avant-garde trends like Purism (Yvan Goll), the Bauhaus (Lothar Schreyer), Constructivism (Karl-Heinz Martin), and the New Objectivity (Leopold Jessner) along with various modern dance and operatic movements in Central Europe.

At the earliest stage, Expressionist directors and actors were most strongly affected by the proto-Expressionist (Strindberg, Wedekind, Kokoschka, Alfred Döblin, and Carl Sternheim) and Expressionist dramas themselves. The majority of these texts provided detailed, almost operatic instructions as to the performers' movement and voice: "inside, breathing heavily, laboriously raises his head, later moves a hand, then both hands, raising himself slowly, singing, withdrawing into a trance," "seeking each other's eyes—swing arms—gradually all rising—bursting out in a joint cry," "suddenly weak in one arm," etc. Even the speaking parts were relatively clear and simplistic; the telegraphic or lyric dialog frequently was keyed to unchanging stereotyped characters. Still, it was evident to the Expressionists that even the most descriptive stage directions and simple characterizations

could not furnish the essential creative basis for their performances. Other stimuli were needed.

Like the graphic Expressionists, the theatrical Expressionists were attracted to the crafts of the German Middle Ages and Renaissance. Both the German Passion Play's repeated use of exaggerated character-gestures and grotesque comic poses of the medieval traveling-troupes (i.e., the six conventional distorted hand-gestures of Hans Sachs) were known and discussed by the Expressionists. In his "Development of the Actor's Art" Hans Knudsen saw parallel uses of *mise en scène* in the Berlin premiere of Hasenclever's *Antigone* (1920) directed by Martin and the spectacle productions of the seventeenth-century Jesuit theatre with their mass scenes and "celebratory tensions." In both performances, huge and pathetic gestures of heroism were brought to the foreground as ceremonial choruses and oversized scenic effects moved across the backstage.

Despite their symbolic role of bourgeois fathers to the Expressionists' rebel/sons the Neo-Romantics greatly affected the modes of Expressionist acting. With the notable exception of Kokoschka and the *Sturmbühne,* most of the theatrical Expressionists were as likely to be active in the German theatre itself than with the Expressionist movement before 1915; many of them were schooled at Reinhardt's studios, the most prestigious in Germany. For example, Fritz Kortner, one of the two most celebrated Expressionist actors, trained as a choral leader in Reinhardt's production of *Oedipus Rex* (1912). There he was taught not only a particular choral voice and diction but also the appropriate statuesque gestures that were meant to project across gigantic staging areas. As Kortner was later to discover, the very same movements when applied to a much smaller stage and auditorium were to have a completely different effect on the spectator and the speaker.

However, in no other field of performance does one find a strong, if relatively unexplored, similarity with Expressionist acting than in the Middle-European dance and cabaret of the 1910's. Not only did the German and Swiss dancers and choreographers influence the early theatrical Expressionists in the areas of movement-philosophy and technique, they were also largely responsible for the evolution of a new critical understanding and journalistic analysis that explained the performer's craft in terms of self-motivation and private expression.

Before the outbreak of the First World War, two distinct dance styles evolved from the revolt against classicism in Central Europe. The first was an off-shoot of the imitative Greek, individually expressive, and earth-bound style of Isadora Duncan. "Skirt dancers," somewhat in the manner of Loie Fuller, like the three Wiesenthal sisters (Bertha, Elsa, and Grete), adapted Duncan's free-style technique to great success around 1910. Also, at this time, the Swiss composer, Émile Jacques-Dalcroze began to teach his concept of *eurhythmics* at Hellerau, outside Dresden. Essentially, *eurhythmics* was an intricate music-based system of precise movement training and practice that taught the performers to translate "into attitude and gestures all the esthetic emotions provoked by sound rhythms." Through the establishment of small studios elsewhere in Germany and through his own austerely rhythmic and classically styled opera productions beginning in 1913, Dalcroze and his methods became known throughout Europe. German theatre practitioners and directors, like the Goethean theosophist Rudolf Steiner—starting with his 1912 Mystery Plays in Munich—and Gottfried

Hass-Berkow in Dresden utilized their own theatrical versions of *eurhythmics.*

Later, the theatrical Expressionists would compress and join these two ways of moving and working—the lyrical, unrestrained, emotive flow of Duncanism with the musically symbolic, muscular posturings of Dalcroze—to form an abrupt series of gesture-combinations that were begun in one kind of tempo and intensity and completed in another. These movement-hybrids were executed from one style to the next without any transitional gestures. Frequently, the movements were initiated in a monumental, intense, laboriously slow, Dalcroze-like tempo and then suddenly exploded into a string of disjointed, separate, staccato emotional-gestures that resembled the projection of minute flashes of Duncan's counterparts.

A third modern force in the pre-war Central European dance was that of the Hungarian-born Rudolf von Laban. According to Laban, all human movement could be divided into centrifugal movements, radiating from the center (i.e., in the arms: "scattering") or peripheral movements, inward from the extremities (i.e., "scooping"). To distinguish it from the more static *eurhythmics,* Laban called his system *eukinetics.* Like Dalcroze, he developed movement-choirs to realize his theories, but Laban's dancers performed in a music-less, plastic environment. Using only the beat of a tambourine for punctuation, the Laban-Group shifted from one pure movement—sometimes expressing a single emotion like Joy, Wrath, Thoughtfulness, etc.—to another. The exercises were repeated until each dancer felt the "universal celebratory state" of motion. Laban was most interested in exploring the range and shape of human movement through his alteration of extremely emotional and expressive actions in the performer. Although his work was exhibited as early as 1910 in Munich, it was not until three or four years later that Laban's importance became recognized. By 1914, the year he moved to Switzerland—as did Dalcroze and Steiner—Laban had already pioneered the expressive study of the formal relationships between the performer's movements, his costume, and the shape and color of the stage and its decor.

Laban's most famous German pupil, Mary Wigman, developed an even more dynamic and personal style. Based in part on *eukinetics,* but with a greater emphasis on emotional intensity and freedom, Wigman's performance involved the spasmatic shift from complete tension to its complete retardation—of "thrust and pull-out." More concerned with primitive expressiveness and the grotesque (i.e., masking) than with pure scientific research of human motion, Wigman was closer to the central body of theatrical Expressionism. Still, her performances, although viewed quite early—1913 in Munich—probably had little effect on the Expressionists' work until late 1920 when she opened a dance school in Dresden. In fact, Wigman's influence on theatrical performance, still largely undocumented, was likely greater outside Germany than in it during the middle and late Twenties.

Another non-theatrical source of inspiration for the Expressionists were the German solo and cabaret dancers of the time. Some, like the hypnotic dream-dancer from Munich, Madeleine, performed pure *Seele*-states. Madeleine's hypnotic performances were confirmed by medical authorities and impressed theatre and dance critics alike. Writing in the early 1910's for *Der Tag,* Alfred Kerr described how Madeleine was transformed from a state of catalepsy to hysteria at the sound of a musical note. Kerr was especially excited by the changes in her tonal manner of speaking/singing and in her eye-focus. Valeska Gert, the young grotesque-dancer who performed in Kokoschka's *Job* (1917), was also a favorite of the Expressionists. In a certain way, she was considered more of a contortionist than a dancer. Later, her way of negating the normative beauty of dance and her uniquely demonic persona propelled her into the stardom of Berlin cabaret.

But among the cabaret performers, none excited the theatrical Expressionists more—nor served as a more common acting model—than Frank Wedekind (1964-1918), the author of the proto-Expressionist, sexually/emotionally sprung Lulu plays. His style of acting in Munich before the war was praised by the Expressionists, the Dadas, and even by the anti-Expressionist playwright Bertolt Brecht. Hugo Ball, later to found the Dada-movement in Zurich, described Wedekind's acting as "gruesome as *hara-kiri,*" "flagellant," and "hypnotic." According to Ball, Wedekind destroyed the societal structure between the inner and outside impulses. He ripped and mutilated himself while remaining as naive "as a pony." Reportedly, there were convulsions throughout his body, in his brain, his throat, his legs. Ball compared Wedekind's deformed physicality on stage to a grotesque woodcut. In Max Krell's anthology, *German Theatre of the Present,* Kasimir Edschmid recalled Wedekind's animal-like, tortured presence as the greatest acting experience that he ever witnessed. It is also noteworthy that the other most lauded Expressionist actor—along with Fritz Kortner—Werner Krauss, worked with Wedekind before entering the Expressionist stage.

Possibly the most coherent and detailed analysis of the philosophical / technical aspects of theatrical Expressionism was published in a book that appeared long after the Expressionists' apogee, Felix Emmel's *The Ecstatic Theatre.* In his chapter on Expressionist, or ecstatic, acting, Emmel differentiated and described two kinds of actors: 1) the actor of nerves—as exemplified by the Neo-Romantic actor, Albert Bassermann, and 2) the actor of blood—as exemplified by Friedrich Kayssler, also a Neo-Romantic actor. Although both performers essentially came out of the same Reinhardt tradition, they worked and acted from theoretically opposed points of view. Bassermann generally created his stage-characters from the study of other men. His final presentation would be based on a combination of many individual characteristics that he observed in scores of people. His character-performances revealed a finely-drawn, psychological mosaic of many types that were bound together after much practice until his nerves were automatically capable of reproducing the illusion of a new, single character. Kayssler, on the contrary, always played himself. He allowed his changing stage personas to grow from the character-emotions rooted in his "soul," or from the flood and unity of his "blood." His acting rhythms and character motivations always came directly from his own internal experiences and essence.

Emmel saw these two popular ways of establishing characters as modern theatrical developments of two basic ancient or medieval traditions of transcendence. The first, nerve-acting, had its roots in the primitive impulse toward imitation and masking; in the carnival, mummings, and fairground booth of the Middle Ages and Renaissance. Looking at the variegated, many-formed externals of life, the ancient nerve-actor, according to Emmel, sought to capture their ever-changing nature in acting-styles that demonstrated Man's constant physical transformations and in the wearing of the masks that signified new personages.On the other hand, always seeking transformation from within, the blood-actor and his roots were closely bound up with the ancient shamans and German mystics. Instead of linking his ecstatic feelings or "extraordinary states of being" with divine or religious communion, the blood-actor became entwined in the Expressionist playwright's text. Working from that in performance, he could allow "the tremendous ecstasies to soar from his soul," often—Emmel quoted from Kayssler's acting notes to make his point—in a conscious/subconscious/unconscious dreamstate. Not surprisingly, Emmel acknowledged enormous dangers in ecstatic acting. Besides risking possible psychological damage, the ecstatic actor could also appear comical at times or produce a pseudo-ecstasy reminiscent of nerve-acting.

Of course, it is unlikely that the majority of the theatrical Expressionists would have agreed to all of Emmel's tenets of Expressionist acting and his division into nerve and blood acting. (Certainly, most of the roots Emmel ascribed to the actor of nerves, like masking, were claimed by some Expressionists.) Yet, Emmel's further detailed and high praise of Kortner's dynamic-speech—"He compresses Fate into a single word or lets it zoom through his sentences. . . . His pauses reveal an overwhelming pressure of movement and inner tension. . . . His tonal strength is an echo of the soul's movement."—and Krauss' ecstatic-gestures—"Almost every one of his movements signifies an ecstatic bodily transformation."—were very much in line with other late analyses of Expressionist acting that frequently appeared in theatre reviews.

Although later critics and historians of the Expressionist theatre have long recognized its non-monolithic, changing nature and have been sensitive to the differences in Expressionist stage decor, many of these same critics have also treated Expressionist styles of production and acting as a single entity—and, not surprisingly, discovered ingenious contradictions: for instance, in the dramatic quest for pure human emotionalism and pure abstraction. Yet, to point up these discrepancies in the Expressionist theatre movement, as opposed to in individual artists, belies a misunderstanding of the philosophical and physical range of theatrical Expressionism.

At the center of the Expressionist universe was Man. All other objective or conceptual phenomena—every physical property, theory, idea, formal grammar, science, or methodology—that precluded Man was eliminated or diminished. This emphasis on Man, and Man alone, produced a variety of different performance and acting styles since the theatrical Expressionists themselves strongly disagreed as to the concept or mode of presentation of their Man-centered art; once the curtains were drawn and the stage-space revealed, the post-war German audiences could expect to viscerally experience one of several kinds of Expressionist utopias.

Borrowing some of the terminology from Bernhard Diebold's influential study, *Anarchy in the Drama* (1921), that was used to describe models of pre-Expressionist and Expressionist dramas, German Expressionist performances can be subdivided into three general styles based on their expressive relationship to the audience—the creation of ecstasy through induction, association, or identification—and their overall approach to acting. These three categories are 1) The *Geist* (purely spiritual or abstract) *performance*, which could be viewed as an ultimate vision of pure expression without the conventional intervention of dramatic characters or intricate plot—a sort of absolute communication between the playwright/director's *Seele*-mind and his audience; 2) the *Schrei*

(scream or ecstatic) *performance*, which could be likened to an actual, if hazy, intense dream-state where movement, exteriors, language, motivation, and inner logic were uniformly and bizarrely warped; and 3) the *Ich* (I or ego) *performance*, which resembled the second type in certain ways, but focused upon a central performer who acted less—*or more*—grotesquely than the other, often stereotypical, characters and who was the subject of the playwright's and audience's identification—a kind of dream told to another person or a dream remembered.

(As with Diebold's general divisions, there is a necessary, but dangerous, arbitrariness in differentiating all, particularly the late, Expressionistic performances according to this system. For instance, Martin's well-known production of Toller's *The Transfiguration* shared characteristics of both the second and third types, due to the nature of the play and the tiny staging-area. Other productions of the time, like the Deutsches Theater's *Lonely Lives* (1920), utilized the talents of actors from three theatrical generations—those of Otto Brahm, Reinhardt, and the Expressionists. However, the theatrical intent of most Expressionist directors was, by and large, clearly articulated in their contemporary writings and announcements.)

Historically, the *Geist* play precedes all other forms of Expressionist drama, with the possible exception of Kokoschka's *Murderer, the Women's Hope* (1909), which can be seen as the progenitor of all three types. As early as 1909, the Russian painter Vasily Kandinsky wrote the scenario *The Yellow Sound*, later published with an introduction in the *Blaue Reiter Almanac* (Munich, 1912). Kandinsky's theory of performance was based on the production of "delicate vibrations" that effect the "strings" of the audience's souls. In part, Kandinsky's program was a further development of Symbolist and neo-Symbolist theatrical tendencies in Germany, France, and Russia. But, unlike Wagner's idea of the *Gesamtkunstwerk*, which greatly influenced the French Symbolists, Kandinsky's theory called for a production style that abstracted and separated the various theatrical elements, rather than allowing them to overlap and re-enforce one another. Each expressive feature of the performance—like the music, "the physical–psychical sound and its movement," or colortone—while existing independently of the others, functioned only as a means to the artist's ultimate goal. In the text of the second picture of *The Yellow Sound*, for example, actors, dressed in assorted primary colors, were instructed to speak ecstatically in unison, then repeat themselves individually in various tones, keys, and tempos. Sometimes they were to shout as if possessed, then hoarsely, before their voices and costumes faded into the sounds of orchestra and stage-lights.

Although *The Yellow Sound* was not staged, Ball, a theatrical producer in Munich in 1914, asserted that Kandinsky's abstract performance theories would be the basis of "The Expressionist Theatre." Also about this time, August Stramm began to compose his telegraphically-worded and grotesquely violent plays that were soon printed in the periodical, *Der Sturm*, founded by the Expressionist Herwarth Walden. The technical influence of Italian Futurist poetry on Stramm has been noted, yet Stramm's dramatic tensions and abstract characterizations were unlike anything the literary Expressionists had read. Lothar Schreyer, who joined the *Sturm*-circle in 1916, arranged for dynamic recitals of Stramm's and Kokoschka's plays and poetry by Rudolf Blümner and Walter Mehring at the *Sturm*-evenings during the war.

A production of Stramm's *Sancta Susanna,* the first *Geist-performance,* was staged by members of the *Sturmbühne,* a section of Walden's *Sturm-*school, under the direction of Schreyer on 15 October 1918. Performances of *Sancta Susanna* continued through October of that year for audiences limited to subscribers of *Der Sturm* and were met with mixed reactions. Although Schreyer claimed otherwise, at least some Berlin theatre critics were sympathetic to and impressed by the production.

After the war, in 1919, Schreyer journied to his native Hamburg and established the *Kampfbühne,* a sister theatre to the *Sturmbühne.* With the help of two hundred supporters, Schreyer was able to mount premier performances of Walden's *Transgression,* Stramm's *Powers* and *The Bride of the Moor* as well as Expressionist adaptations of Hölderlin's *Death of Empedocles* and a German folk play. In 1920, Schreyer returned to Berlin to present his play *Man* with the *Sturmbühne* group at Reinhardt's Deutsches Theater. It was there, according to Huntley Carter, that the actors represented "Tones and Movement, Form and Color." However, Reinhardt felt that the production was too cultish and declined to promote other *Sturmbühne* projects. Schreyer's most abstract work *Crucifixion* was presented on 12 April 1920. Later that year in September, Walden directed *Geist-performances* of *Impulse* and his pantomime *The Four Deaths of Framettia* in Dresden. In 1921, Schreyer directed his best known play *Child-Deaths.*

Many of the *Sturmbühne's* scenic ideas were derived from the Zurich Dadas—the Berlin and Hanover Dadas, Mehring and Kurt Schwitters were frequent contributors to *Der Sturm*—and Futurism. Thus, we find in the *Sturmbühne* performances: brightly-colored backdrops of black, yellow, green, and red (*Sancta Susanna*); oversized cylindric costumes made from geometrically-painted cardboard and wire (*Child-Deaths*); gigantic—ten-foot high—masks (*Transgression*); bizarre instrumentation, like a West African xylophone (*The Bride of the Moore*), glass harmonica (*Child-Deaths*), or a violin-solo (*The Death of Empedocles*); all dramatic elements of other avant-garde theatres.

Like Kandinsky, whose search always lead to the "inner music" of a theatrical component, Schreyer was most concerned with the *sound* of a performance. The earlier work of modernist composers like Scriabin, Arnold Schönberg, and Paul Hindemith, and the unique word-formations of Stramm, were of the utmost importance to him. According to Schreyer, the actor was only the bearer of "form, color, movement, and sound"; and he trained his students at the *Sturm-*school to be "sound-speakers," who could reproduce any "vibration of the soul" with their mouths and throats. Hidden behind yards of thick paper and cardboard, however, the *Sturmbühne* actors were probably less successful in achieving this than in any other aspect of their acting.

Although Schreyer was appointed to direct the stage-workshop of the Weimar Bauhaus in 1921 and obviously influenced the more purely abstract director, Oskar Schlemmer, he always considered himself an Expressionist. In fact for this reason, besides being thought something of a mystic among functionalists, Schreyer resigned from his post in 1923. Like Walden, Schreyer maintained that only the *Sturmbühne* exemplified Expressionism in the theatre; everything else was pseudo-Expressionism. The *Geist-performance's* position is best summed up in Schreyer's statement in the final number of the *Sturmbühne* magazine.

Art is the artistically logical formulation of optical and acoustic relations. Art comes from the senses and appeals to the senses. It has nothing to do with understanding. The theatre is the formulation of focal color forms.

(October 1919)

Most critics associate the *Schrei-performance* with the bulk of Expressionist productions. Certainly, the premise of much of the Expressionist theories on acting was directed toward this style. As in the 1919 German film, *The Cabinet of Dr. Caligari,* the performer's acting constantly shifted from a kind of cataleptic stasis to a powerful, if epileptic, dynamism. The decor was marked by buildings and objects indicated with irregular, nonparallel lines and often shaded with impossible shadows. In terms of acting and scenography, the comparison of *Caligari* with the *Schrei-performance* is useful, despite the fact that there is some question whether *Caligari* should be thought of as an "Expressionist" film. Photographs of *Schrei-performances,* even posed ones, show the heightened states of the actors as they performed against a background of distorted stage properties and painted backdrops. Many early definitive descriptions of Expressionist acting were from *Schrei-performances* ("[in him] sounds became corporal and movements aural") yet the roots and development of the *Schrei-performance* differed from the *Geist* and *Ich* varieties.

The *Schrei-*directors and actors freely borrowed from the contemporary middle-European dancers and painters, just as the *Geist-*directors incorporated elements from the pre-Expressionist/Expressionist musicians and poets. Most of the *Schrei-*directors came from cities outside Berlin—cities such as Dresden, Frankfurt, Mannheim, and Munich—where the grip of the professional, commercial theatre was considerably looser, and where there was a greater access to German Expressionist and Swiss dance and art. Many of the *Schrei-*actors were university students selected or hired for the occasion. Consequently, there was often a free, spontaneous atmosphere in *Schrei-performances* that did not exist in the other types. (For example, in Heinrich George's Dresden production of three Kokoschka plays [3 June 1917], a cabaret-dancer, much to the audience's surprise and outrage, appeared naked in her role as Eve.)

Two of the best-known *Schrei-*directors were Gustav Hartung and Richard Weichert, both of whom staged their most important works at the Frankfurt *Schauspielhaus* between 1917-21 and then directed Expressionist productions in Berlin. One of Hartung's Frankfurt productions, Fritz Unruh's *A Generation* (16 June 1918) was particularly noted for its "total" intensity in the acting, the simple Expressionist settings, and its religious attitude—some of the performances were given on Sunday mornings, for instance. Weichert established himself as an Expressionist director with an early production of Hasenclever's *The Son* (18 January 1918) in Mannheim. In many of Weichert's later Frankfurt productions, such as *Penthesilea* (17 September 1921), there was a stylistic emphasis on a kind of emotive, primitive abstraction, more akin to Expressionist woodcuts than to the Futurist-inspired abstractions of the *Sturmbühne.*

But, if there was a less professionally rigid, programmed quality to these performances, the *Schrei-*directors were more doctrinaire—and more democratic—in their devotion to Expressionist philosophy; that is, in the molding of each ecstatic actor in the cloak of the New Man. Working with basically untrained performers, this creation of ecstatic-states in the actors had its dangers: speaking-lines were sometimes swallowed or lost; actors frequently had to be restrained in their relations with other actors and the audience. The actress Leontine Sagan later claimed in *Cinema Quarterly* (Summer 1933) that Expressionist acting began to have adverse psychological effects on the off-stage behavior of the performers.

Theatrical Expressionism came to Berlin in the Fall of 1919. Since the *Sturmbühne* performances of the previous year hardly met with the mass expectations that were fed by the Berlin reviews of the *Schrei*-performances from Dresden, Frankfurt, Munich, and Leipzig, the theatre-going public was most anxious to view theatrical Expressionism first-hand. At that time, the entire theatre structure in Berlin vastly differed from other German cities, being long dominated by Reinhardt and his co-directors. Indeed, when Expressionism became established in the Berlin theatre, it was in conjunction with Symbolist and Neo-Romantic esthetics.

The marriage of the *Schrei* acting style with Reinhardt's star-system and mass choruses formed the basis of the *Ich-performance*. Characteristically, an *Ich-performance* focused upon the single ecstatic-actor surrounded by or confronted with dozens of choral-performers who moved in unison, creating grotesque, but picturesque, poses. Frequently, the central actor, like Kortner or Alexander Granach, received his earliest training in both *Schrei* and Reinhardt productions. For the most part, *Ich*-directors absorbed much of Reinhardt's use of *mise en scène,* whether they worked in competition with him or under his auspices. The best known of these were Karl-Heinz Martin, Leopold Jessner, and Jürgen Fehling.

Beginning as a revolutionary director at the small leftist theatre, the *Tribüne,* Martin attempted to expressionistically bridge the gap between performer and audience. At the time of his first production, *The Transfiguration* (30 September 1919), Kortner's performance was thought to be the first standard by which all Expressionist acting could be judged. Martin soon became known as both an Expressionist and a "mass-director"—in the footsteps of Reinhardt. His Berlin productions of *Antigone, Europa* (5 November 1920), *Florian Geyer* (5 January 1921), *The Maid of Orleans* (22 February 1921), *The Robbers* (26 September 1921), and Toller's *The Machine-Wreckers* (30 June 1922) demonstrated a scenic trend away from Neo-Romanticism toward a Central-European abstraction. (This trend would culminate in an Expressionist/Constructivist collaboration with the Viennese architect Friedrick Kiesler in 1924.) However, Martin retained a purified *Ich*-style of acting in the later performances. Thus, we find in his stage-directions for *The Maid of Orleans,* instructions for the title character to rant, not only in changing tempos, but also to perform as if she were "speaking in tongues."

A few months after the opening of the *Tribüne,* Jessner mounted a version of Schiller's *William Tell* (12 December 1919) at the State Theatre with Kortner in the lead role. Kortner's ecstatic performance—his shrill manner of speaking and frenzied gesticulation—again, and Emil Pirchan's sparse *mise en scène* were both highly praised. In other productions, *Marquis of Keith* (12 March 1920), *Richard III* (5 November 1920), *Othello* (11 November 1921), and *Macbeth* (10 November 1922), Jessner retained this unique and celebrated combination of Kortner and Pirchan.

Heavily influenced by the scenic experiments of Appia and Dalcroze, Jessner reduced and abstracted all the dramatic elements that could be used to spotlight the essential poetic, human, Expressionistic vision, namely the soul-states of his central characters.

> The historical becomes the abstract, the human focuses itself into the symbolic, external fades into an adumbration, space and the scene are reduced to the simplest common denominator, costumes are resolved into masses of color. The poetry, the characters, and passions remain dominant, but with a treble, a tenfold force and meaning. It is indeed an expressionistic summary, but also a compressionistic one.
> Herman Scheffauer, *The New Vision in the German Arts*

In his desire to intensify the emotive aspects of classical and proto-Expressionist plays, Jessner was accused of abandoning every dramatic component except one and then "hammering that point to death." Jessner accomplished many of his mathematically-calculated effects through an unswerving reliance on heightened Symbolism: pure colored lights and carpeted platforms of red, gold, white, and black that signified the protagonist's mood and ultimate destiny; oversized, austere stage-properties; distorted shadows projected across vast spaces; and abstract, Appia-like levels called *Jessnertreppen*. It was this last Symbolist feature that caught the critics' attention. For instance, Lee Simonson enthusiastically described their use in *Richard III*.

> How immensely the movement of the second part was enhanced by the staircase when Richard appeared at the summit, when his men in red and Richmond's in white moved up and down it with all the symbolism of opposing forces, groups mounting toward its apex in imminent struggle. And what a contrast to all heightened movement as Richard descends slowly at the end in utter lassitude, to dream his last dream at its base.
> "Down to the Cellar," *Theatre Arts Monthly, VI* (April 1922)

The *Jessnertreppen* served many Expressionist purposes. It signified the relationships between characters and their individual psychic states; it increased the actor's plastic possibilities, allowing him to be more easily perceived in depth; it rhythmically heightened the impact of slow, fast, or disjointed movements; and it created a novel esthetic unity that was thought to be lacking in other Expressionist productions. Yet, an otherwise comic anecdote points up the peril of Jessner's multi-leveled scenery: at the premier of *Macbeth,* Kortner, in a "possessed" state of mind, lost his footing on the stairs and went sliding down the length of the platforms. While mass actors could be precisely choreographed in the negotiation of the complex staging, an ecstatic-actor could not.

Formerly an actor at the *Volksbühne,* Fehling achieved renown with his *Ich*-production of Toller's *Masse-Mensch* (29 September 1921). Both his work before and after that production reflected late theatrical Expressionism's growing interest in the conventional grotesque and comic irony—modeled after the fairground booth performance, circus, variety-stage, and the popular cinema—especially in *Marriage* (1 March 1920) and in *The Rats* (10 March 1922). Although it would be difficult to assess Fehling's major historic and scenic techniques, except for his central use of the *Ich-performance* style

Kokoschka's poster for a 1909 production of his Murderer Hope of Womankind.

of production and rhythmic choruses, in *Masse-Mensch,* which is finely documented in Kenneth Macgowan's and Robert Edmond Jones' *Continental Stagecraft* (New York, 1922), we find a number of innovations: characters are set off against a background of black curtains and intense beams of light. As in the Jessner productions, the abstract *mise en scène* and highly choreographed groups of actors allowed the audience to focus upon the expressions of a single performer (Mary Dietrich) or situation. Unlike Jessner, Fehling varied his formal sets for each scene and was not as insistent on the perfection of his actors' tonal qualities. Fehling's later successes with Expressionist plays from 1923 to 1930 marked the very last vestiges of pure Expressionism in the German theatre. (pp. 36-50)

Mel Gordon, "German Expressionist Acting," in The Drama Review, Vol. 19, No. 3, September, 1975, pp. 34-50.

EXPRESSIONIST POETRY

MICHAEL HAMBURGER AND CHRISTOPHER MIDDLETON

[*Hamburger is a German-born English poet, translator, and critic. An accomplished lyric poet in his own right, Hamburger has been widely praised for his translations of several German poets, including Friedrich Hoelderlin, Georg Trakl, and Hugo von Hofmannsthal. He has also written extensively on modern German literature. Middleton is an English poet and translator of German literature. His poetry is noted for its great technical skill and its assimilation of many of the experimental aspects of Modernism. Although some critics have called his poems unnecessarily obscure, others contend that his method of composition is intended to create a multiplicity of meanings and suggests an adherence to T. S. Eliot's Modernist ethic that "poetry can communicate before it is understood," which supports Middleton's own stated "predilection for stark-ambiguous style in any art." Middleton is also an accomplished and widely praised translator and anthologist of twentieth-century German literature. In the following excerpt, Hamburger and Middleton survey the work of major Expressionist poets and compare the early and later poetry of Expressionism.*]

The word *Expressionist* is sometimes loosely applied to style in painting and poetry other and older than that which began to take shape in Germany around 1910. This is in part due to the fact that Expressionism was one of the slogans popularized by the revolution which affected all the arts soon after the beginning of this century, and which made it possible and desirable to revaluate certain antecedents. With this revaluation it was found that some of the work of older poets and artists (not to mention "primitives") was not merely failed mimesis, art which failed to represent or to imitate observable realities, or art which was untrue to Classical principles. On the contrary, it was art which had distinct laws of its own, art which formed its image of reality by means never intended to be mimetic. Wilhelm Worringer, whose *Abstraktion and Einfühlung* (1909) was one of the pioneering works of revaluation, could thus in 1921 officially disparage mimesis to the extent of saying that imitation, though a basic impulse of the human mind, had nothing to do with art at all. The recognition of this other tradition in art, sometimes now called "Asiatic," as opposed to "Attic" or Classical art, was made largely possible after Expressionism in Germany and parallels in other European countries and in the United States had wrought radical changes in each of the arts in turn, not excluding music. The term *Expressionist,* first used in France to distinguish from the Impressionists certain new painters, was then applied to any art which was less mimetic than expressive, which did not present an image of an already realized or observable world, and which seemed to spring less out of eyesight than out of vision. The epoch of non-figurative art had begun. Benedetto Croce's esthetic, with its accent on intuition, helped to generalize the use of the term. But in German Expressionist poetry, it is less the intuition that matters than the modes in which such intuitive types as the early Expressionist poets reformed the idiom of German poetry, and made it into the proper creative speech of modern tensions and modern themes. Some of their formal innovations have parallels in other European literatures, including Russian literature. But though the modern movement was, from the start, an international one, German Expressionist poetry has certain unique features.

The modern movement as a whole began less with a formal

program than with a polemical acclamation of the modern for its own sake. Marinetti's *Futurist Manifesto,* published in Paris in 1909, proclaimed that "a roaring automobile is more beautiful than the Nike of Samothrace." In Germany, too, the desire for a new outlook, an outlook that would be up-to-date and would also axe the bourgeois idols of the Wilhelmine period, preceded the appearance of any definite programs or of any new styles. The periodicals *Die Aktion* and *Der Sturm* were, however, founded in 1910; and a year later a German translation of Marinetti's manifesto appeared in *Der Sturm.* In 1911, also, the German Expressionist movement in poetry began with the publication of two poems, both in *Die Aktion:* "Weltende" by Jakob van Hoddis, and "Die Dämmerung" by Alfred Lichtenstein. At about the same time, the French poet Guillaume Apollinaire, impressed by the *Futurist Manifesto,* started the literary movement which he called *Orphisme.* The first Futurist exhibition was held in Paris in 1912; in 1913 there was a similar exhibition in London, where Marinetti himself lectured. The year 1913 also saw the publication of the Imagist group's *A few Don'ts,* which was to determine many future developments in poetry in the English language.

The best early German Expressionist poetry satisfies three of the Imagist requirements: the creation of new rhythms, freedom in the choice of subject, and concentraton. But one must be cautious about attributing to the German poets the Imagist way of presenting an image. It is not that the German poets preferred generalities to the Imagist particulars, far from it: but what they wanted was less a clear rendering of a visual experience than a true rendering of visionary experience; and these two things are different. In Georg Heym or Georg Trakl, for instance, the image embodies tones of feeling to an extent which the Imagist, with his accent on the physical object of feeling, would not have admitted. Indeed, in early Expressionist poems the image can voice feelings precisely and be visually graphic, without using a realized or even realizable world as a source of objective correlatives. If it does not lean so heavily on the object as the image in Imagist poems, it does lean more heavily on tones of feeling as these crystallize in the configurations of images, of which the single image is an element. Accordingly, the early Expressionist image can seldom be isolated from context without losing some of its quality, whereas in Imagism it is precisely the isolated image of the particular realized object which exists to be appreciated. In Imagism the image's function is to isolate surface sharply; but the function of the early Expressionist image is to deepen the perspectives of the whole configuration of images within which it stands.

Yet Expressionism is more often distinguished from parallel movements in poetry less by contrasts like these, than by the tendencies which made it, after 1914, as much a sociological phenomenon as a literary movement. For, after 1914, its craft of imagery was vulgarized and, at the same time, its mental climate became predominantly political. We shall refer again to this development as "Phase II Expressionism," in order to distinguish it from the early Expressionist poetry of the years 1911-14.

The Imagist program led to a diversity of individual achievements. Expressionist poetry, too, is really a body of work by poets who had little in common except certain apprehensions in the face of a disintegrating culture, and a need to create individual styles which would present their peculiar tensions. The early Expressionist poets did not subscribe to a common

program. It has been suggested that the Imagist program was formulated in the face of crisis: in a world where all values were in doubt, sense-data were at least something to start from. But, as has been indicated, the German poets did not confine their attention to sense-data in this way. Neither were the best poets in a position to argue things out among themselves. Certainly, Berlin was the center. Here Jakob van Hoddis, Lichtenstein and Heym were working; here Herwarth Walden and Franz Pfemfert were editing their rival periodicals, *Der Sturm* and *Die Aktion.* Here, too, the literary club called the *Neuer Club* was active holding readings in its so-called "Neopathetic Cabaret," which in some ways foreshadowed the Dadaist Cabaret Voltaire in Zürich—both expressed disapproval of "literary" poetry and humbug. But Heym died early in 1912; and three other pioneers, Georg Trakl, Ernst Stadler and Franz Werfel, worked in places as remote from each other as from Berlin: Trakl in Salzburg and Innsbruck, Stadler in Strasbourg and Brussels, and Werfel in Prague and Vienna.

Jakob van Hoddis and Alfred Lichtenstein both lived in Berlin. The poem "Weltende" by van Hoddis appeared before Lichtenstein's "Die Dämmerung," and Lichtenstein admitted having used it as a model, though he rightly claimed to have improved on it. Both poems are rhymed and have regular stanzas. What was new about them was that they consisted of a deadpan concatenation of apparently dislocated images, derived from the contemporary scene, but not presenting a realistic picture. It was a new picture, because the viewpoint seemed to jump from line to line, and because the objects alluded to were not ones that can be ordinarily found in the same place at the same time. This was *collage,* a technique which was being tested at the same time in visual terms by Picasso (*Still Life with a Cane Chair,* 1911-12) and by Braque (*The Fruit Dish,* 1912), and which was to be developed drastically by the Zürich Dadaist poets five years later. Yet van Hoddis gave the game away in the title of his poem, "End of the World," the strident sarcasm of which does not allow the images to speak for themselves. In Lichtenstein's poem, the images do speak for themselves, and the title, "Twilight," is wryly ambiguous. The *collage* effect thus has much more force. (pp. xxi-xxv)

In Lichtenstein, as in a number of early Expressionist poems, the quality of the vision is not some previously fixed, definite idea which can be detached from the images. The quality of the vision is absorbed into the images without residue, and it is the hidden nerve which governs their association. Such poems do not present the sensibility wasting in reflection of much nineteenth century verse (e.g., Lenau), but a sensibility absorbed and active in construction, presenting simultaneously the *what* and the *how* of the perception. Lichtenstein's images are accordingly full of piths and gists. Though not free from the self-deprecation made familiar by Heine and Laforgue, Lichtenstein's irony does not thus merely unsay what he seems to be saying and so negate his negative image of the world; rather his irony, without ever making discursive statements, simultaneously bewails and derides the world whose collapse his images embody. With his irony and his sense of the absurd, Lichtenstein developed one of the first and most appealing forms of Expressionist imagery: near-caricature, at once clownish and terrified. The new freedom of association asserted in his work also contributed to one of the main trends of modern poetry: the liberation of the image from the tyranny of the object.

Lichtenstein died in battle at the age of twenty-five, soon after war broke out in 1914. Of the other early Expressionist poets, Heym had died two years before, at the age of twenty-four; Trakl also died in 1914, while on active service; Ernst Stadler was killed on the Western front in the same year; and August Stramm, whose innovations are among the most extreme, was killed in 1915 on the Eastern front. The premature deaths of these poets is the chief reason why later developments in Expressionist poetry did not fulfill its early promise. Another reason is the increasingly political strain of Phase II Expressionism. And a third reason is that, besides lacking a definite program comparable to the Imagist manifesto, the poets could depend on no poet-critic with the stringent authority of Pound or Eliot. The lack of all conviction which had brought some greatness into the poems of the pioneers, was superseded all to soon by a passionate intensity which first lowered and then lost the aims of the early poets.

Between 1909 and 1912, however, Georg Heym was writing his roughly 130 poems, which explore the new apocalyptic mood, the theme of doom and the milieu of the city, which in varying proportions constitute the world of early Expressionist poetry. "Umbra Vitae" is one of Heym's many poems in which the city is seen as a domain of demons. Heym's demons, as in his luridly macabre poem "Die Dämonen der Städte," pervade modern existence as irrational destructive forces. Yet these are not death-wish poems, even though Heym is a poet of bile and brainstorm. The suicides in "Umbra Vitae" are searching for their "lost selves." The German *verlorenes Wesen* also means "lost substance" or "lost being." And what Heym regards with horror is this loss of self and of substance (the medieval *inopia entis*) which hollows modern collective man. The only single individuals about whom he writes are outcasts and rebels (e.g., "Judas"). Even in his pastoral poems, and in such massive visionary poems as "Mond," the demons are near or present. Neither are the dead (as in the poem "Die Morgue") exempted from their grasp; for death merely accelerates the disintegration which the dead knew in life, who "without name, poor, unknown, / Died in empty cellars, and alone."

In his massive poems, like "Der Krieg," Heym frequently uses the device of personification to control perspective. But in "Der Krieg" his graphic and tumbled imagery of the city offsets any literary quality that might weaken the device. The horror of war is compressed into the image: war "crumples the moon in his black hand." Personification is fortified by the typical dynamic verb-metaphor; and it is with such verb-metaphors as this that he transmutes and transvalues the observable world. The Expressionist poet is not, like the Impressionist poet, a passive reflector of sense-data, or, in Hofmannsthal's words, "a soundless brother of all things." Moreover, Heym's metaphors move in clusters and by association. Attention is fastened not on any objects of reference, but on the images themselves as they crystallize and cluster around a central visionary focus. The poem "Und die Hörner des Sommers verstummten" exemplifies this procedure somewhat less forcefully than the massive poems like "Mond" or "Der Krieg." But this is not to say that Heym's metaphors are graphic phantasms. In fact, one of the more subtle qualities of his poetry is his faculty for absorbing a plain observation into a visionary context. He does this often imperceptibly, by manipulating small parts of speech, like verb-prefixes. If it were done otherwise, or not at all, a number of his poems would be crass.

Another feature in Heym is the suppression of the analogical *as if* element in the poetic metaphor. This element had persisted in most previous modes of metaphor in German poetry, even in Romantic metaphor, despite certain Romantic theories about poetry as a kind of absolute word-music. The Romantic poet still worked form observation to construction, or vice versa, keeping his analogies usually explicit. Metaphor therefore never lost its fictive quality. The Expressionist, on the other hand, aims to eliminate this fictive element. Either he submerges the analogy, or he suppresses it. The older parallelism of image and idea is superseded by a fusion of image and idea, in which "the expressive element swallows the representational element" [W. Sokel, *The Writer in Extremis*]. This meant that the image could cease to refer to an observable world; it could become an end in itself, that is, *autotelic*. If it consists exclusively of images on this pattern, the poem exists as a discrete and self-contained world. It exists as an autonomous configuration of images which have affinity to each other, as consorted voices of the complex of feelings crystallized in the whole configuration, but need have no direct affinity to actual objects of reference. The poem becomes a *heterocosm*. Many, if not most, of Trakl's later poems are heterocosms in this sense. To cite a familiar prose example: in Kafka's story *The Metamorphosis* (1914), Gregor Samsa, when he wakes up, is not in a state of mind which is insect-like; he wakes up to find that he has become an insect. In the image, object and idea are identical. Neither stands in an *as if* relation to the other; neither is a fiction based on the other; and the metaphor which results is free to conform to purely imaginative laws. Now the tendency of Expressionism after 1914 is to relax this principle, to write out in an often clumsy longhand what the pioneers had compressed into a vigorous and provocative stenography. In doing so, it ignored firstly the identification principle of early Expressionist metaphor; secondly, the Imagist (and not only Imagist) principle of concentration; and thirdly, T. E. Hulme's relevant precept about poetry being "a compromise for a language of intuition which would hand over sensations bodily," a precept which also rejects the fictive element and to which Heym's and Trakl's metaphors do often conform.

The poems of Ernst Stadler, a slightly older contemporary of Heym and Trakl, are not so image-packed as theirs. Another difference is that Stadler's poems about the squalor of city life, poems about the Jewish quarter in the East End of London, do not express the obsessive foreboding of a general doom which is common to nearly all the early Expressionists. For Stadler, the age was an end, but the end was a fresh start. And he interpreted it less as an age of anxiety and disintegration than as one of transformation and hope. He is about the most literal of the foremost early Expressionists; and in his poems one can detect his starting-point more easily than in those of Heym or Trakl. This starting-point may fire the inner vision; but the inner vision seldom detaches itself from the frame of externals to become autonomous. Yet Stadler's poems are dithyrambic. His line is long and athletic, at times Whitmanesque. And many of his poems show the true dynamic mentality of the Expressionist. Logical organization is, again, secondary; primary alone is the immediate presentation of a complex of feelings. The starting-point in experience may be a familiar one, a walk in early Spring, or waking as day breaks, or crossing a bridge in a train. In the poem "On Crossing the Rhine Bridge at Cologne by Night," a recognizable world of sense-data persists almost to the end: the chimneys, roofs, lights, the train's rumbling. Yet this observed world is in the grip of an inner vision advancing toward a point of ecstasy. Only when it has reached this point, at which perception is extinguished in the intensity of pure self-consciousness, does the vision break free from the frame of sense. In this poem, it is the syntax which presents, gestically rather than logically, the simultaneous associations provoked by the sense-data. The gestic syntax is more highly developed in Stadler than in Heym; Stadler, too, unlike Heym, coins new words by linking old ones, like *nachtumschient* and *nachtentrissene* [*Luft*] in the Rhine Bridge poem. Heym, on the other hand, creates more surprising verb-metaphors than Stadler. Both poets, in different ways, were cultivating the "associative style" perculiar to Expressionism. It is a style which, by telescoping normally consecutive impressions and making them simultaneous in the poetic image, aims to rescue essence from time's chaotic flux. This is a far cry from the Impressionist style at the turn of the century, as in Liliencron's or Dehmel's poems, in which not verbs but nouns, not gestic syntax but logical syntax, had been predominant.

Stadler worked in his native Alsace, at Oxford and in Brussels. Even though he knew and praised work by Heym, and by Gottfried Benn, he had no contact with any of the Berlin poets. Of all the early Expressionists, it is the poet who was most remote from Berlin, the Austrian Georg Trakl, whose work probably comes closest to the early Expressionist idea of the visionary poet. Trakl does not seem to have been influenced by any of his contemporaries, with the possible exception of Else Lasker-Schüler, an older experimental poet, whom he did once meet on a brief visit to Berlin. Karl Kraus, the Austrian critic of literature and *moeurs,* may also have had some influence on Trakl's outlook; and Trakl dedicated one of his richest small poems to him. But the actual formative influences on Trakl's poetry are chiefly Baudelaire, Rimbaud, and Hölderlin. Not least, Dostoevsky had a certain influence on Trakl's thinking—his novels were in general congenial to writers of the period. Trakl's long poem "Helian" (written during the winter 1912-13) also contains echoes from the Old and New Testaments; but here, as in other poems, Biblical motifs are wholly absorbed into Trakl's own image-world, even to the extent of being presented in the present tense.

One of the assumptions which Trakl shared with his contemporaries was that the materialistic bourgeois society of his time was doomed. But his attitude to this was as far from Stadler's vitalism as from Franz Werfel's utopian optimism. His apparent unconcern with political or other ideologies was shared by some of the best poets writing before 1914 (which is not to say that the age was not crazed by conflicting ideologies); but in Trakl, perhaps more than in any of his contemporaries, the vision of disintegration tells. He was certainly a poet of the generation which lay under Nietzsche's spell. Yet if we must look for beliefs in his work, we find that he believes in certain primitive Christian values: the reality of evil, and the expiation of guilt by suffering, values against which Nietzsche had levelled some of his harshest criticism. Trakl's beliefs, however, remain problematic—the decay of the faculty of belief does, after all, stigmatize the minds of many of the pioneers of modern poetry. Trakl's beliefs are implied in his poetry; but they are seldom stated, nor is it his intention to state beliefs. For he came closer than any of his contemporaries to creating a poetry of autotelic metaphor, in the sense outlined above. One approaches his meanings through the recurrent images and symbols which embody them; but even then it is hard to arrive at a generally acceptable interpretation, since much of his symbolism is ambiguous, and errors

of interpretation arise equally if one assumes that his symbolism is systematic (a typology), or that it varies from poem to poem. Trakl was reticent about his work. He left little or no indication of how it is to be interpreted. In an age of manifestos and polemics, he was intent only on writing poems.

His poems must not be read as egocentric confessions in metaphoric disguises. One of his ablest critics has suggested just the converse, in fact: that his work evolves toward a transparency of vision, in which things enact and interpret themselves through autonomous metaphoric forms. This would account for the luminosity of Trakl's inscapes. And his mature work at least (1912-14) fulfills the demands that Rilke made, but was himself able at best to postulate, of the true orphic poet. What Trakl himself called his "criminal melancholy" is a premise, but it is not the substance, of what he says. As Rilke first pointed out, Trakl's work is affirmative. But what it affirms is a spiritual order of being which may not be at once perceptible in his poems, because he inflects the imagery of this spiritual order so often with an imagery of disintegration. As the poem "Untergang" shows, Trakl does not exempt himself from this vision of disintegration. Of the poets so far discussed, Trakl had perhaps the most intimate intelligence of the moral and intellectual crisis through which his generation was passing. Thus he is concerned to evaluate freely the crisis of modern man in his relation to death and to evil, whereas Heym, for instance, often excludes crisis by projecting images of death and evil which make them all-pervasive and quite inexorable forces. The same difference exists between Heym's black image of nature and Trakl's variable image which enshrines, even if it does so tonally rather than visually, the changing shadows of a Paradise not irretrievably lost.

The poem "Klage" shows just this distinctive feature of Trakl's work. For here there is his lamentation, in the language of idyl, for the mortality of the idyl—as if the chant of this language could charm away the idyl's creeping death. This is one of Trakl's last poems, written just before his death in a military hospital in Poland, where he was under observation as a suspected case of schizophrenia. Although he suffered at this time under the delusion that he would be executed as a deserter, for breaking down after the Battle of Grodek, "Klage" is not Trakl's complaint for himself. It is a complaint for the "golden image of man," or man's true image, which he feared would be lost or obscured in "Eternity's icy wave." As often in Trakl, the image of the boat appears as a symbol of human existence. But that existence is now threatened with extinction. Here too, charactieristically, Trakl says "Eternity's icy wave / Would swallow . . .". He does not say "swallows." The German subjunctive permits a glance into the interior of Trakl's mind—how his vision embraces persistently, or hovers between, the extremes of idyl and anti-idyl. His double vision of a possible redemption of man and of the actual corruption of man, never spills over into a crass statement of either half-truth.

Trakl's rhythms and sound-patterns, too, are as expressive of meaning in his poems as are his recurrent symbols and images. In this respect he realized possibilities which were divined by the Romantic Novalis, sometimes realized by Brentano, and made programmatic by Mallarmé. But since these rhythms and sound-patterns sometimes seem to contradict, and not conventionally to match, the meanings embodied in his images, it might seem that Trakl is less a master than a slave of his ambiguities. Yet it must be realized that his ambiguities derive, firstly, from the tension in his thought between spiritual and temporal orders of being, and secondly, from the tension in his language between the autotelic image and the representational image. Here an analogy exists between Trakl's practice and modern musical harmony, as in Stravinsky's *Sacre du Printemps,* where we are asked to hear two contradictory harmonies at the same time. Also Arnold Schönberg was at this time (1912) developing his dodecaphonic system, which emancipates music from conventional harmony altogether. Kandinsky, the spokesman of abstract painting at the time, whose book *Über das Geistigge in der Kunst* also appeared in 1912, was describing the same phenomenon from a painter's standpoint, when he wrote: "The fact that the form may not match the color must not be regarded as something 'unharmonic' . . . but quite the reverse—it must be regarded as a new possibility, as another harmony [*auch eine Harmonie*]."

Sometimes the tension in Trakl's images prevents one from telling whether an image is to be understood descriptively or symbolically. It is true that each of his poems—of which there are about a hundred, excluding the juvenilia—offers a clue to the others. But the meaning of the same words varies according to the degree of literalness involved in each case. The same adjective may be primarily descriptive in one poem (or one line of a poem), synesthetic in another, and symbolic in a third. Yet the expectation of some "realistic" or "logical" connection between images presupposes the existence of a common and referable image of reality to which both the poet and his public implicitly assent. And it is precisely the absence of such an image of reality from Trakl's world that constitutes the ground of his poetry. Therefore it is wrong to conclude that he is enigmatic because he deploys images haphazardly, as euphonious formations made up of words that have been rooted away from normal usage, for use as integers in a private fantasy. Certainly, he is a poet of monologue. But not only are the individual words in his poems more often plain than precious (though his feats of association might suggest the opposite); also his laconic image-formations can, if it helps the reader at all, be traced back more frequently than one would expect to some objective source, if not in sense-experience, then in legends, or in the Bible (as in some of the darkest areas of the poem "Helian"). It is Trakl's genius for deep assimilation which brings a new kind of energy into the language of German poetry, and makes us newly sensitive to the enigma of the familiar world. His poetry is remote; but it is not rarefied. And the more one reads his poems, the more one finds them simultaneously enacting and interpreting sensuous and spiritual experience.

So far, only three years of early Expressionist poetry have been discussed. But it is not too much to say that these three years just before the First World War were some of the most productive in modern German literature. In 1912 also, Rilke began the *Duino Elegies,* and during the next two years wrote some of his best short poems (e.g., "Wendung" and "An Hölderlin"). Stefan George was writing *Der Stern des Bundes* (1914); Else Lasker-Schüler was writing her *Hebräische Balladen* (1913); Alfred Mombert published his mythic poem *Äon vor Syrakus* in 1911; and Theodor Däubler was writing his *Der sternhelle Weg* (1915).

The three last-named poets came close enough, in certain poems, to the Expressionist style to be included in most of the anthologies and miscellanies of the period. All three were accounted forerunners, and Däubler and Lasker-Schüler were

among the most enthusiastic apologists of the movement. Däubler's poem "Millionen Nachtigallen schlagen" ("Millions of nightingales are singing") merits special study for its functional sound-effects, its word-conjuring and its central cipher image (the latter kind of image was to be used systematically by Gottfried Benn).

But it is August Stramm, of the same generation as these older poets, who was the most radical experimentalist. His experiments in diction, meter and syntax were of a different order from those of the younger generation, who were concentrating chiefly on the essential image. Stramm's break with the logic of prose and with description—elements retained obdurately by Naturalists and Symbolists—had a strong influence on the development of poetry after Expressionism. Whereas Heym or Trakl composed mythic or symbolic landscapes, Stramm composed only abstract word-patterns. The poem "Schwermut," for instance, contains no images at all, no adjectives, and only one adverb. The poem voices a state of mind; but it refers to no recognizable objects or symbols. Stramm reverses the usual procedure for objectifying states of mind: he suppresses the world of the object altogether. The poem voices the gesture of the feeling itself which gives the focus. For this reason, verbs and neologisms abound in Stramm's poems. He often arrives at his neologisms by telescoping two or three normal synonyms. In the poem "Freudenhaus," for instance, the word *schamzerpört* telescopes *schamzerstört* and *empört,* to give a word with the sense, roughly, of "shamesexshattershocked." Gottfried Benn, too, in his poems published in 1917, was like Stramm far more a poet of the provocative single word, the *parole essentielle* of French Symbolism, than of the *image essentielle.* But the new words coined by Stramm were less cerebral than Benn's; at least, they were meant to be emotive. In other poems he invents onomatopoeic and pun-like sounds, to voice emotions which he believed could not be rendered by existing words. This was not in itself new: Paul Scheerbart had published the first German sound-poem, "Kikakoku," in 1897. But Stramm (and before long Hugo Ball in Zürich) used pure sound seriously for the voicing of mental states, just as he had abandoned, in other experiments, normal conjugations and declensions. Although it can be said of Stramm that his mental states, if different at all from those of any average sensual man, are bizarre rather than electric, it should be by now self-evident that the poet here assumes the role of absolute creator. To this role his function as communicator, using lexical and generally intelligible meanings, is strictly subordinated. One sees to what extremes poets at the time could be driven by the despairing scepticism with regard to normal language, of which Hofmannsthal wrote as early as 1902, in his *Brief des Lord Chandos.* It was only one step from Stramm's experiments to the abandonment of the mental state, as an expendable fiction, in certain Dadaist simultaneous poems and bruitist sound-poems which foreshadowed Kurt Schwitters' long long and elaborate *Sonata in Basic Sounds.* Hugo Ball, at the end of his Dadaist period in 1917, wrote in his journal: "The safety-valve of an abstract age has burst."

A certain abstractive strain is also found in Gottfried Benn's later poems. But Benn's first published poems, *Morgue* (1912), are realistic expressions of shock: mortuary poems about cancer-effects, about a nest of rats found in the corpse of a drowned girl, and so on. These poems are Expressionistic in their disillusion, aggression and disgust; but not in their form. It is only in such poems as "Caryatid," first published in 1916, that Benn emerges as the Expressionist poet of the subliminal. The image of Silenus at the end of stanza I in "Caryatid" shows what kind of distortion enters Benn's subliminal imagery at this stage of his work:

> from his loud blood forever drowned by roars
> shivered by alien music and unique,
> wine drips into his sex.

The distortion creates an image that is deliberately fused and turbid: the image of the essential Silenus at large in the living soul. This is not the involuntary distortion by bombast which is found in such Phase II Expressionist poems as those of Johannes R. Becher. "Caryatid" also has other important implications: the poem suggests that only the human imagination can emancipate man from the stony fixity of his actual state; but finally even this belief is put in doubt, for the moment of ecstasy is a *Glück-Lügenstunde* ("moment of joy and lie"). In this typical *parole essentielle,* the ecstasy and the doubt merge and are fixed. Nonetheless, the idea of transcendent imagination underlies the whole of Benn's subsequent work, with its irrationalism strangely consorting with a phrasing so urbane and a diction so near-scientific. It also underlies his attitude to distinctively modernist poetry: its ringdance of irrationality and intellect. In his later essays Benn often returns to "Nietzsche's assertion . . . that art is the only metaphysical activity to which life still obliges us."

Of the more important early Expressionists, only Gottfried Benn, Franz Werfel and Yvan Goll survived the 1914-18 war. Meanwhile the pioneers had been succeeded by poets whose first concern was not so much a new poetry as a new society. They were the poets whom Thomas Mann, with some justice, stigmatized at the time as "political literati" and against whom he wrote much of his book *Reflections of a Non-Political Man.* It was the literariness as well as the vaguely Utopian political ideas of the post-1914 poets which, in fact, contributed to the expiring, during the first years of the 1920's, of Expressionism as a coherent literary movement. Yet it is necessary to distinguish two phases of Expressionism within the decade 1910-20: the first from 1910 to 1914, and the second from 1914 to 1920. Phase I produced the best poems and the real revolution in poetic language, the impact of which continued during the 1920's, and can still be felt today. Phase II diluted the innovations of Phase I, to the extent of producing work in which mindless feeling and oratory combine to limit, if not to cancel, its value as poetry. Phase I ended early in the war, with the deaths of Lichtenstein, Stadler, Trakl and Stramm, and with the insanity of Jakob van Hoddis. The end of Phase II came during the two fatal years of counter-revolutionary gains which followed the 1920 splitting of the German Independent Socialist Party (USPD), whose policies for a bourgeois republic and for appeasing the masses had coincided broadly with the indecisive Marxism of most Phase II Expressionists. Of course, one can see continuity between the two phases. The earlier flight into the pure poetic image, or into the grotesque, oscillated between morbidity and regeneration no less than the succeeding flight into a political image. But the distinction of these two phases within the decade does at least aid understanding of the shift of accent and the change of style within Expressionism. It also allows for factors which are not discriminated in two other views of Expressionism: the Marxist view of Georg Lukács, and the *soi-disant* nihilist view of Gottfried Benn. Lukács confines Expressionism almost exclusively to the bourgeois left-wing writers of the 1914-20 period, e.g., Ludwig Rubiner, Karl Otten, Walter Hasenclever and Kurt Hiller; and he attacks these writers from a Leninist standpoint

(his views were written down in 1938). Benn, on the other hand, spreads his range of reference wider. He writes of a "Phase II of the Expressionistic style," which presupposes a *pre-Expressionist* Phase I, covering the period from the end of classical antiquity down to Nietzsche. This "Phase II" is not, therefore, a second Phase within Expressionism as a literary movement at all. It relates to Expressionism as a whole, as a manifestation of the intellect and art of modern Western man, as opposed to Western man before Nietzsche, in Benn's own cultural and anthropological perspective.

Much as some English poets used the innovations of the Imagists for quasi-doctrinaire ends in the 1930's, Expressionist poets after 1914 converted early Expressionist innovations and visions into ideological weapons. True, left-wing poets in Phase II believed that they were fighting to defend the status of poetry as a life-shaping force, and that poems could be used as invectives against reaction—the reactionary creeds which they believed to be responsible for the war. For the idealistic humbug of the materialistic society then involved in war they were, however, no less responsible themselves. Accordingly, they were rarely intellectually free or technically skillful enough to wield any weapon more subtle than a sandbag. The tocsin had first been sounded in Phase I by Franz Werfel. But Werfel also wrote some disturbing poems (e.g., "Der Ritt"); and his message was much less a political than an ethical one. He, no less than the Dadaists, who sat in the Café Odeon in Zürich at a table decisively apart from him and his confederates, was searching for what Hugo Ball called in his journal at this time, in 1916, "the specific rhythm, the buried face, of the epoch." But all too often, as Ball pointed out, Werfel's poems were a means to this end, not ends in themselves—a feature which relates them unfortunately to some of the more shapeless poems of the period. Werfel was for a time the accepted spokesman of Phase II. But after 1920 his poetry changed its manner, and his novels and plays took most of his attention. What was needed during Phase II was, in any case, less a spokesman than a critic. There was no critic who was sympathetic but ready to curb excesses. Neither was there a critic who had criteria by which to discern, cooly, the relations between the declamatory style and the politics of the Phase II Expressionists. Such a critic might, at least, have followed up the implications of Hugo Ball's penetrating remark: "The force of the modern esthetic consists in this: you can't be an artist and still believe in history."

Documents of the period relating to the aims of its poetry in Phase II have the same buskinading manner as many of the poems. Kurt Pinthus, advocate and anthologist of Expressionism, wrote from the trenches in 1915:

> The common will of the latest poetry is to free reality from the outline of its appeareances, to free ourselves from it [reality], to overcome it, not by its own means, not by evading it, but, embracing it all the more fervently, to conquer and master it by intellectual penetration [*des Geistes Bohrkraft*], by suppleness, by a longing for clarity, by intensity of feeling and by explosive force.

Pinthus then went on to say that Expressionist poets were wanting a total image of reality seen from the core, a poetry not of appearances and of ornament, but of "essence, heart and nerve." This theme is taken up by Kasimir Edschmid in his 1917 manifesto, "On Poetic Expressionism," in which he is groping, through the jargon of the period, toward an idea of poetry as stark inclusive vision, although, symptomatically, he deplores reality as fact. He dissociates Expressionism from the Naturalist and Impressionist trends which preceded it, and goes on:

> Above all, there was now, against the atomistic fragmentation [*das Atomische, Verstückte*] of the Impressionists, a great embracing cosmic feeling [*Weltgefühl*—a normal German locution] . . . A *new image of the world* had to be created, one that had no share in the Naturalist image—which could only be grasped in terms of experience, and no share in the fragmented space given by the impression; rather an image which had to be *simple,* literal [*eigentlich*] and therefore beautiful. . . . We had to create reality. The sense of the object had to be rooted out. No longer may one be satisfied with the believed, supposed, noted fact; the image of the world must be mirrored pure and unfalsified. But that image lies only within ourselves. Thus the Expressionist artist's whole dimension becomes vision. He does not look, he sees. He does not describe, he has the inner experience. He does not reproduce, he creates. The chain of facts no longer exists: factories, houses, sickness, whores, shrieks and hunger. What now exists is the vision of them.

This statement not only extends Pinthus' views; it is also a crude attempt to apply to writing the aims of those artists of the time, notably Hans Arp, who wanted to create an *ab initio* concrete art which was by definition non-figurative, and the aims of those artists who practised what Kandinsky had preached about abstract painting five years earlier. But Arp had rejected existing objects altogether, and Kandinsky had been defining truth to sensation and to feeling in an attempt to limit strictly the domain of objects within the free realm of imagination. What Edschmid does is to generalize both concretist and abstractist theories into bombast, and to add the postulate that poetic vision, which to him concerns not particulars but types, should define truth to objects. In the development of the modern esthetic, this is a decidedly retrograde step. As for its relevance to poetry, it divorces the typifying function of language from its truly creative particularizing function: the same process, in the name of "vision," is noticeable in the sprawling, jumbled poems of Johannes R. Becher. What the poets wanted, Robert Musil thought at the time, was some synthetic procedure. But, he wrote, "the Expressionist . . . is looking for the new feeling of life as a chemist looks for synthetic rubber. His limitation is this: there is no exclusively synthetic procedure."

In the 1920's, an Expressionist manner still prevails in many plays and novels, as well as in poems. Expressionist drama, which flourished between 1916 and 1922, now found a model producer in Erwin Piscator. Of the poets active in the 1920's, Yvan Goll, much of whose work is written in French, created an idiom which is both highly idiosyncratic and cosmopolitan enough to incorporate some features of French Surrealist poetry. Goll also avoided the provincialism which limited some other poets (not Rilke), and which marked a reaction against the "cosmic feeling" convention of Phase II. Erich Kästner, with his satiric "New Realist" poems, represented with Kurt Tucholsky a stronger reaction against the irrationalism and mind-exorcising oratory of Phase II. Goll, however, remained faithful to his early Expressionist beginnings. Though his first poems tend toward Whitmanesque oratory, the poems which he wrote during the long illness before his death in 1950, show a controlled freedom of imagery and

rhythm won only from years of careful experiment. These last poems of Goll's *Traumkraut,* mark one possible extreme of the liberation of the image initiated by the early Expressionists. But Goll's last poems are much more overtly personal in tone than any of the early Expressionist poems by poets discussed above. Much of his previous work had an intimacy of voice as well. But the new intimacy of *Traumkraut* is not merely that of a practised symbolist with a natural style, nor is it only consistent with Goll's knowledge that he was to die. It is consistent also with an awareness which has, directly or indirectly, informed much poetry during the last fifteen years, the awareness of the Bomb, about which Goll wrote (in English, while in the United States) one of the first Bomb poems, "Atom Elegy."

Oskar Loerke's work never lost density even in the oratorical climate of Phase II, and it retained it in the years which followed the collapse of Expressionism as a movement. Loerke was possibly the purest pastoral poet of the post-Expressionist period. It is noticeable that Lichtenstein's "Die Dämmerung" cadence returns again in Loerke's poem "Die Vogelstrassen." Into the pastoral he also brings the identification principle of early Expressionist metaphor. His observation, sharp as it is, is that of the disembodied eye detecting in the smallest natural phenomenon the mythology of the human soul. Wilhelm Lehmann, whose work was not widely known before 1945, is another poet of this quasi-mythopoeic vision into nature. Both Loerke and Lehmann exerted influence on poets after 1945, particularly since "nature" remained one of the few object-worlds which had not disintegrated when Germany fell. (pp. xxv-xli)

> *Michael Hamburger and Christopher Middleton, in an introduction to* Modern German Poetry, 1910-1960: An Anthology with Verse Translations, *edited by Michael Hamburger and Christopher Middleton, Grove Press, Inc., 1962, pp. xxi-xliv.*

MARK RITTER

[*In the following excerpt, Ritter assesses the early poetry of Georg Heym, Gottfried Benn, Jakob van Hoddis, and Alfred Lichtenstein.*]

"The heritage of Expressionism is not yet over, for it has not yet even been started." With these typically cryptic words, Ernst Bloch attempted to put an end to the famous "expressionism debate" in 1938. There is one group of Expressionists for whom the term "unfinished legacy" is especially apt: the lyric poets of early Expressionism. A number of these poets (Trakl, Benn, Heym and Stadler) are among the handful of Expressionists still known to other than specialist readers today. Benn was controversial his whole life, but the others tended to be eclipsed with the movement's demise around 1925 and were not rediscovered until the post-war period. In this sense their legacies were unfinished at the time of Bloch's essay.

It is also worth recalling that three of the four poets listed above (and at least half a dozen, less prominent, others) failed to survive the First World War. Had they been able to continue their creative activity, there is no doubt that literary Expressionism would have been considerably different, and probably better. In this sense, too, the legacy of Expressionism is unfinished.

But the most important aspect of the unfinished legacy of

Georg Trakl.

early Expressionism is its effects on later generations of writers. One would be hard pressed to find examples of actual copies by later poets, except for a spate of Benn imitations in the 1950s, but, consciously or not, later poets were working in territory staked out by the early Expressionists. This essay will seek to show that their primary contribution was a poetry of discontinuous and fragmented reality that reflected the fragmentations and upheavals of bourgeois society.

First, however, a caveat is in order. Many treatments of Expressionism, even a recent German survey for students, cultivate the assumption that Expressionism was a unified movement whose theoretical base is established in the manifestoes of Edschmid and others. In fact these documents stem from a later date and have precious little to do with early Expressionism.

One does much better to conceive of early Expressionism as a number of loosely connected circles, primarily in Berlin. The oldest of these is *Der neue Club,* founded in 1909 by a group of students led by Kurt Hiller. Members who became important poets of early Expressionism include Georg Heym, Jakob van Hoddis, Alfred Lichtenstein and Ernst Blass. From 1910 to 1912, the club presented a dozen or so "cabarets" in which members read from their works and those of poets they admired. These were held in various cafes, which

even more than for previous generations served as focal points of literary life. In particular, the *Cafe des Westens* on the *Kurfürstendamm* served as the clearinghouse and literary stock exchange of Expressionism. There new arrivals to Berlin checked in, and there too, Franz Pfemfert and Herwarth Walden, publishers of the two leading expressionist journals (*Die Aktion* and *Der Sturm,* respectively), held court. Other publishers and literary figures built up circles in the *Cafe des Westens* and elsewhere, which were intricately interlinked and constantly changing and feuding with each other. The atmosphere in those years on the eve of the World War, by all accounts, was electrified.

Beyond the feuding and the plethora of different styles, there are certain attitudes that all the early Expressionists share. All were opposed to contemporary Wilhelminian society in art as in life, but at this early date they were on the whole as apolitical as the middle class from which they came (Franz Pfemfert is a notable exception). Consequently one looks in vain in the works of these Berlin poets for utopian sentiments or appeals to brotherhood and love. Nor did the early Expressionists wholeheartedly condemn modern society's technology and cities. In a good many of their poems they betray a fascination with the urban landscape and modern means of transportation.

Perhaps the major tenet of this literary revolt was a conviction that the younger generation must restore honesty to a literature that had lost its way in sterile aestheticism or sentimental lyricism. Georg Heym's condemnation of Stefan George (whom he had imitated in his early years) and Kurt Hiller's polemic "Against 'Lyric Poetry' " illustrate different aspects of the same striving. The clearest formulation of the ideal of honesty occurs in Ernst Blass's preface to his collection of poetry, *Die Strassen komme ich entlang geweht* (1912), probably the closest approximation to a manifesto to be found in pre-war Expressionism. Blass justifies his selection of poems on the grounds that all reflect moods of his: "My feelings this evening are not in any poem in this book—nonetheless, the poems in this book are my feelings." These personal reflections soon give way to a discussion of the poetry of the future. Poetry must become intellectual: "One who understands while writing: that is what the poet of the coming decades will be." Such a poet will not be able to ignore the mundane aspects of day-to-day existence:

> This will be in his strains: knowledge of the flatness
> of life, its ordinariness, dullness, idiocy, shame and
> nastiness. The strains of the coming poet will not
> be "pure" and "from the depths." He will not be
> just a blissfully potent primitive, but a person who
> realizes and admits that one is sometimes stuck in
> quite ordinary situations.

Besides being honest in reflecting life as it is actually lived, the poet of the future must also be "someone who looks for the non-swampy ground for humanity's march forward, someone who struggles for progress (I know what I'm saying)."

These views are strongly influenced by Hiller and they also reflect Blass' personal style. Nonetheless, the preface expresses a general mood in literary circles of Berlin at the time. Not all poets adopted Blass's dry, urbane style, but most sympathized strongly with his call for poetry to deal with the real stuff of life rather than the artificial problems of aesthetes.

Nowhere was the trend to honesty more brutally apparent

than in *Morgue* (1912), Gottfried Benn's first collection of poems. Benn was attempting on one level to come to terms with the harsh realities of his practice as a young doctor in a Berlin hospital, but his subject matter was just as clearly intended to shock the bourgeoisie. Consider, for instance, the parodies of traditional sentiments in "Kleine Aster":

> A drowned beer trucker was lifted onto the table.
> Someone had stuck
> a dark bright mauve aster between his teeth.
> As I was cutting out
> his tongue and palate,
> starting from the chest and working
> under the skin with a long knife,
> I must have bumped it, because it slipped
> into the brain nearby.
> I packed it into his chest cavity for him
> in the excelsior
> while he was being sewed up.
> Drink your fill in your vase!
> Rest in peace,
> Little Aster!

The poem's style and form must have been nearly as shocking at the time as its subject matter and crass tone. The original German has only two pairs of rhymes, which may or may not be intentional, and the lines have no fixed meter. Their length is determined by considerations of effect; particularly important words are reserved for line endings and beginnings. It might seem far-fetched to consider this poem a forerunner of Brecht's "rhymeless poetry with irregular rhythms," but it must be conceded that Benn's type of free verse is closer to the latter than to the hymnic or dithyrambic modes that largely dominated German free verse from Klopstock and Novalis to Rilke. Besides directly assaulting bourgeois sensibilities with the poem's content, Benn clearly intended to parody the literature of preceding generations. The final lines are plainly enough a persiflage of sentimental nature lyrics for Philistines; less obviously, the rather precious adjective, "dark bright mauve" ("dunkelhellila"), and perhaps even the poems' clinically precise descriptions, mock the "impressionism" and "realism" of the culturally leading classes.

Benn's contempt for the bourgeoisie of Berlin is revealed much more directly in "Night Cafe" ("Nachtcafe"):

> 824: The Love and Life of Women.
> The 'cello has a quick drink. The flute
> belches throughout three beats: his tasty evening
>   snack.
> The drum reads on to the end of the thriller.
> Green teeth, pimples on his face,
> waves to conjunctivitis.
> Grease in his hair
> talks to open mouth with swollen tonsils,
> faith, hope and charity around his neck.
>
> Young goiter is sweet on saddle nose.
> He stands her three half pints.
> Sycosis buys carnations
> to mollify double chin.
> B flat minor. sonata op. 35.
> A pair of eyes roars out:
> Don't splash the blood of Chopin around the place
> for this lot to slouch about in.
> Hey, Gigi! Stop!
>
> The door dissolves: a woman.
> Desert dried out. Canaanite brown.
> Chaste. Full of caves. A scent comes with her.
>   Hardly scent.

It's only a sweet leaning forward of the air against my brain.
A paunched obesity waddles after her.

The dominant device of the first six strophes, metonymy, is known from classical rhetoric; Benn's innovation is to apply it more radically and consistently than had been done previously, and with medical terminology. The denizens of this cafe thus lose their individuality and their actions acquire a grotesque typicality. Only the exotic woman and the poetic subject are exempted from depersonalization. Their fleeting relationship, and the vision it engenders, are abruptly terminated by the entrance of an "obesity," presumably her husband.

A *curriculum vitae* that Benn wrote in 1921 for what he promised would be his final collected works provides insights into his state of mind in the expressionist period. He had experienced a crisis in his medical practice:

> I had originally been a psychiatrist, an assistant in an insane asylum, until at the age of 26 I began to notice an unusual phenomenon, which became more and more critical; in short, I was no longer able to muster any interest in an individual case.

Benn turned twenty-six in 1912, the year *Morgue* was written. Just as the persona of those poems displays no compassion for the individuals on his autopsy table, the poetic subject in "Night Cafe" has no interest in the individuals he sees there. Using his scientific training, Benn attempted to discover the source of his curious malady:

> I delved into descriptions of that condition known as alienation or depersonalization of the sphere of perception. I began to recognize that the ego was a structure that was striving with a force, next to which gravity is like the pull of a snowflake, for a condition in which nothing that modern culture calls an intellectual faculty is important, but where everything civilization, led by academic psychiatry, had made disrespectable and labelled neurasthenia . . . admitted the deep, limitless, mythically ancient alienation between the ego and the world.

Benn's realization of the disassociation of perception in bourgeois society is of central importance, both for his own poetry and for Expressionism in general.

Benn's concept of alienation is, of course, not that which is ordinarily used in sociology or political philosophy, but it is illuminated by the concept of "ego dissociation" used by Vietta and Kemper in their recent study of Expressionism. In their view, this psychological condition played as great a role in the development of Expressionism in general as it appears to have done in Benn's personal life. Doctor Benn's dilemma in fact expresses the crisis of subjectivity in bourgeois society.

At least as important for Benn as his alienation from the world is his belief that an overwhelmingly regressive force lurks within the modern civilized mind; the operative word in the passage quoted above is "mythically ancient." A large part of the woman's attraction in "Night Cafe" is her ability to call forth in the poet associations with Mediterranean antiquity ("desert," "Canaanite brown"). Benn depicted this "thalassic regression" in a number of his best known expressionist poems, such as "Karyatide" or "D-Zug," and in nearly all of his poetry from the 1920s and 1930s. He became progressively more obsessed with what he sometimes called "Ligurian complexes," that is, a series of visions of a blissful world of instinctual life and, often Dionysian ecstasy, in which the poetic subject can briefly overcome the fragmentation produced by modern intellectuality. "Songs" written in 1913, reaches what must be a peak in the glorification of the instincts (I quote only the first strophe):

> Oh, that we were our primal ancestors
> In a warm bog a little clump of slime
> That from our sap, mute plasm and blind spores
>   Cool deaths, calm lives to viewless growth might
>   climb.

It was this celebration of the instincts and the concomitant denigration of rationality which led Benn briefly into the arms of the Nazis, and which rouse the justifiable anger of Marxists. There was an irrational component in nearly all expressionist works, but nowhere was it comparable with Benn's position. Significantly, Bloch defended Expressionism against Ziegler's attacks, but not Benn himself.

Benn's formal development was as distinctive as his formal evolution. Both "Little Aster" and "Night Cafe" are in free verse, as is typical of Benn's early work, but the excerpt from "Songs" already displays rhyme and regular meter in the original. In a strict form Benn found the opportunity for "artistic transcendence," which seemed to offer the only defense against nihilism. Other Expressionists, to the extent that they underwent any formal development at all, tended to move away from traditional forms—either in the direction of experimentation (Stramm and other adherents of the *Wortkunst* propagated by Herwarth Walden) or of undisciplined rhetoric (Becher, Rubiner, and a host of others). None of them took up the dry, spare free verse of Benn's earliest work; that was left to the writers of the 1920's.

Georg Heym has become associated with the Expressionists because of the extraordinary power of his images, despite the fact that his poetry is formally very conventional. Born in 1887, a year after Benn, he died on January 12, 1912 when he fell through the ice while skating. Nonetheless, he left behind a large opus of poems which includes some of the most frequently anthologized expressionist poems that have inspired a great deal of critical literature. His earliest poetry (from 1903) follows the prevailing neo-romantic style, although even as a schoolboy Heym reveals an unusual fascination with death. His actual breakthrough to an expressionist style occurs around the beginning of 1910. Heym's opus includes some surprisingly tender love poems and striking nature poems, but he is most famous for his demonic visions of modern industrial civilization and the city, and it is these which had the greatest impact on other Expressionists.

Heym's diary, as might be expected, chronicles in great detail his puberty crises and his conflicts with his authoritarian Prussian father, but it also offers some historical insights. The salient feature of the bourgeois Wilhelminian world for which he was being prepared in school and university was monotony, a monotony so crushing that any change would be welcome: "If only something would happen . . . If they just start a war. Even if it's an unjust one." A contemporaneous text reveals a somewhat broader perspective: "Our disease is to be living in the twilight of history, in an evening that has become so stuffy one can hardly withstand the odor of its rottenness anymore."

In Heym's mature poetry one constantly encounters references to the end of history (a theme he and Van Hoddis inau-

gurated in Expressionism). "Umbra Vitae," for instance, begins:

> The people on the streets draw up and stare,
> While overhead huge portents cross the sky;
> Round fanglike towers threatening comets flare,
> Death-bearing, fiery-snouted where they fly.

The "fanglike towers" strike one as rather archaic, and illustrate how Heym transformed neo-romantic elements into modern poetry. The latent doom of "Umbra Vitae" becomes palpable in "War" ("Der Krieg"), of which I quote only the first strophe:

> He is risen who was long asleep.
> He is risen from beneath the vaulted keep.
> In the dark, unrecognized, huge, he stands
> And crushes the moon between his swarthy hands.

The "he" is of course a personification of war, who rises up from the midst of society, the city, where he has been kept prisoner. For Heym, the vision is utmost; hence he is not bothered by the incongruity in his description of a giant who is big enough to block out the moon, but can manage to go unnoticed.

Heym's aesthetically most felicitous poem with a demonic personification is "The God of the City" ("Der Gott der Stadt"), written in December, 1910. Since, unfortunately, no poetic translation is available, the following literal, prosaic rendering will have to suffice for present purposes:

> He sits sprawled atop a tract of houses.
> The winds lay black around his brow.
> He looks in anger out into the distance
> Where the last houses straggle into the country.
>
> The evening's red belly gleams at Baal,
> The great cities kneel around him.
> Enormous numbers of church bells rise up
> To him like waves from a sea of black towers.
>
> Wild as the dance of corybantes, the music
> Of the millions rumbles through the streets.
> The fumes of smokestacks, the clouds of factories
> Drift up to him like bluish incense smoke.
>
> The weather smoulders in his eyebrows.
> Dim evening is stupefied into night.
> Storms flapping around him like vultures
> Gaze out of his hair, which stands on end in rage.
>
> He sticks his butcher's fist into the darkness.
> He shakes it. A sea of fire races
> Through a street. And the glowing smoke roars
> And consumes it, until the day dawns, late.

The form of the original poem is quite conventional—iambic pentameter lines arranged into strophes with alternating rhyme—but its content was revolutionary in several respects. Heym's use of language is quite different from that of *fin-de-siecle* poets; throughout, he mixes words from the modern and the ancient, the sacred and the profane spheres, and his frequent use of active, even violent, verbs creates a dynamism that extends even to static objects. The purpose of this diction, like that of his descriptions generally, is visionary intensity rather than fidelity to nuances.

One is immediately struck with the matter-of-factness with which the poem announces the presence of the god; Heym is clearly operating on the visionary plane, where the logic of the dream or the hallucination is in force. This deity seems to be lord not only of the city (indeed, cities in general), but also of the weather. He has obviously antique and pagan features, but he is worshipped in a Christian manner by a modern city. The people in the city, or more precisely, their hectic activity as a crowd, are equally idolatrous, resembling the Dionysian dances of Greek Corybantes.

In view of past misinterpretations of this poem, it is important to note what it *does not* say. The god does not invade the city, indeed we have every reason to believe he is a normal part of it. Neither does he destroy the city; his random blow consumes only one street, and in the context, that destruction too should be viewed as a normal part of city life. Heym's poem thus provides no support for those critics who interpret it as a prophecy of the destruction later visited on German cities. Instead, Heym is personifying what he perceives to be the city's essence, what Schneider calls its "demonic excessiveness." He may be correct in asserting that for Heym the city was essentially a concentration of energy, life and sensations, but there are precious few signs of life in this particular poem. Much more prominent is the city's aggressiveness, not only in the form of self-destruction, but also in its anger at the remaining nature it has not yet incorporated (lines three and four of strophe one). In fact, the city has reached a stature equal to nature, or at least to the elements of the weather, which dwell on and around the god's head. Despite the images from antiquity, this is clearly an industrial city which shares many attributes with the "tentacular city" described by the Belgian poet Emile Verhaeren some fifteen years before Heym's poem was written. Heym's use of mythic imagery is not meant exclusively to glorify the subject, as was the case in some German naturalist urban poems. The god of the city is in fact a critique of the rapacity of modern industrialization and obliquely, of the mad and destructive pace of urban life.

Still, the god of the city possesses a certain grandeur—the poet does not find him totally negative. Nonetheless, Heym is among the least ambivalent of Expressionists with respect to what the Germans call *Zivilisation,* that is technology, communications, industry and politics. His demonic images, his obsession with death (as manifested, for instance, in his cycle *The Homeland of the Dead* and his fondness for images of decay (as in *Ophelia*) all indicate his revulsion at the modern world. Heym also wrote a number of poems about the French Revolution, but he exploited it largely for its seemingly pointless violence (as in "Robespierre") and not as an attempt at liberation. His poetic universe is oddly closed; it is full of movement, but movement in a circle. He likes to depict violence, but it too is usually inconclusive and not truly apocalyptic. In "Damnation of the Cities I" an entire city is inhabited by sadists, who parade around ceaselessly, mutilating and violating each other. A glowering red sky threatens, but does not deliver, an end to the misery.

Some would call Heym's static universe mythic, and certainly images from myths and antiquity are very common in his work, but his poems do not explain as a myth should. The stasis in Heym's poetry owes more to his basic disposition than to any beliefs he might have held. Heinz Rolleke has shown how intensely visual his imagination was; he even wrote in his diary that he would have preferred being a painter to being a poet. Heym's desire to fix in his poetry a number of images, some contradictory, some complementary, explains the stasis of his poems better than any philosophical conviction he might have held. Indeed, the very fact that he

held no creed, except hatred for his Wilhelminian surroundings, accounts for the pervasive mood of hopelessness and doom that haunts his work. His poems are an attempt to put the nightmare of his own life into words.

Heym was well respected in Berlin during his brief career and earnestly mourned when it came to an untimely end, but his rival in *Neuer Club*, Jakob van Hoddis (a pseudonym for Hans Davidsohn), could claim the honor of having written the most celebrated single poem of early Expressionism. The publication in 1911 of his "End of the World" ("Weltend") caused an immediate sensation and soon inspired imitations.

> The bourgeois' hat flies off his pointed head,
> the air re-echoes with a screaming sound.
> Tilers plunge from roofs and hit the ground,
> and seas are rising round the coasts (you read).
>
> The storm is here, crushed dams no longer hold,
> the savage seas come inland with a hop.
> The greater part of people have a cold.
> Off bridges everywhere the railroads drop.

"End of the World" strikes the modern reader as amusing, but hardly earth-shaking. . . . And yet, Johannes R. Becher recalls: "These two stanzas, these eight lines, seem to have transformed us into different beings, to have carried us up out of a world of an apathetic bourgeoisie which we despised and which we did not know how to leave behind." Such profound effects can hardly have been brought about by the poem's subject matter; only the first line makes any reference to the bourgeoisie, after all. What must have struck Becher and his colleagues in early 1911 was the poem's novel form. Its rhyme scheme is conventional and its rhythms almost monotonously regular; it is in fact consciously anti-poetic. Each line contains a distinct image, just as, with one exception, each line is a distinct syntactic unit.

Van Hoddis deliberately tries for disharmony within the poem, just as he consciously avoids the musical effects that, say, Rilke was able to achieve with flowing syntax. In this *Simultangedicht* ("simultaneous poem"), heterogeneity is raised to the organizing principle, and thus the individual elements are lowered to a common denominator. It was this to which Becher was referring when he said: "We seemed to be in the grip of a new universal awareness, namely the sense of the simultaneity of events." "The End of the World," Becher continues, shows that ultimately everything in the universe is related to everything else.

Becher's interpretation is written from his position as a comfortably situated Stalinist bureaucrat, and the ultimate connection he alludes to is doubtlessly his ideology. It seems more plausible that an unbiased reader would conclude that there was no connection behind events, or at least, that there is no correlation between what happens in the world and what the "bourgeois" or "most people" think and do. Trains may be falling off bridges, floods rising, storms blowing, but the bourgeois is affected only to the extent that he loses his hat or catches cold. Thus a recent critic has suggested that this is not the end of the world, but the end of the bourgeois world. Van Hoddis' affinities to Heym lie not in his vision of destruction, but in his conception of the world as something that was approaching a crisis people were powerless to avert.

Van Hoddis, oddly enough, wrote only a few more poems in the "associative style" (*Reihungstil*). His mind began to deteriorate soon afterwards, and he had ceased writing entirely by 1914. Alfred Lichtenstein, however, found the associative style exactly what he needed for his subject: life in Berlin. "Morning" ("Morgen"), written in 1913, provides an example of Lichtenstein's associative style:

> All the streets lie snug there, clean and regular.
> Only at times some brawny fellow hurries by.
> A very smart young girl fights fiercely with Papa.
> A baker, for a change, looks at the lovely sky.
>
> The dead sun hangs on houses, broad as it is thick.
> Four bulging women shrilly squeak outside a bar.
> The driver of a cab falls down and breaks his neck.
> And all is boringly bright, salubrious and clear.
>
> A wise-eyed gentleman floats madly, full of night,
> An ailing god . . . within this scene, which he forgot
> Or failed to notice—mutters something. Dies. And laughs.
> Dreams of a cerebral stroke, paralysis, bone-rot.

The final strophe, with its cosmic perspective, is atypical of Lichtenstein in any respect except its irony. His poems in associative style (as distinct from his grotesques in simple, almost free verse) generally leave the disparate images unresolved.

The first two strophes, however, illustrate the connection between the associative style and urban experience. Ten years before this poem was written, the philosopher-sociologist, Georg Simmel, had worked out a brilliant analysis of "The Metropolis and Mental Life." The fundamental fact of life in a great city is the chaotic flood of impressions to which the individual is subjected. The resulting psychic dislocations are responsible, in Simmel's view, for the excessive rationality, the blasé attitude and all the other traits generally considered typically urban. Benjamin applied Simmel's urban theories to the poetry of Baudelaire, and recently Vietta has extended them to the analysis of Lichtenstein's poems. He views the *Simultangedicht* (or associative style) as the formal analogue of urban dissociated perception.

These first eight lines of "Morning" also illustrate other typical aspects of Lichtenstein's work. Like most other Expressionists, he preferred to represent "little people" like the smart young girl, the brawny fellow, the four fat women and the two workers or even social outcasts. This affinity for the non-bourgeois types reflects the poet's own highly tenuous and marginal position in bourgeois Wilhelminian society, although it was, at least at first, purely emotional and not political. The lines that introduce each of the first two strophes are also typical of Lichtenstein's very sparse descriptions of the physical setting. His personifications, like the dead sun here, do not serve to invest something dead with dynamic vigor, as Heym's personifications do, but to denigrate the object being personified. Thus, in another poem, Lichtenstein compares streets to dog bones bleaching in the sun, or the moon to a "fat, foggy spider." The total effect is to provide a formal correlative for the grotesque contradictions of modern urban life.

Van Hoddis and Lichtenstein also deserve recognition for their conscious inclusion of the Bohemian subculture of Berlin in their poems. Each man produced poems that rank among the very first in Germany to deal with the new medium of film. Both authors were aware of and represented in their work the escapist functions of these media in modern society, but both were also too much a part of that society to deny the media's attractiveness (see Van Hoddis' "Variete").

The essential attitude in this case, as in so many others, is ambivalence, tempered in Lichtenstein's case by a healthy self-irony.

"The Patent Leather Shoe" (1913) expresses Lichtenstein's understated, sophisticated view of life in Bohemia:

> The poet thought:
> Enough. I'm sick of the whole lot!
> The whores, the theatre and the city moon.
> The streets, the laundered shirtfronts and the smells.
> The nights, the coachmen and the curtained windows,
> The laughter and the streetlamps and the murders—
> To hell with it!
> Happen what may . . . it's all the same to me:
> The black shoe pinches me. I'll take it off—
>
> Let people turn their heads for all I care.
> A pity though, about my new sock.

The poet is in fact tired of the entire Bohemian subculture of bourgeois society in which he moves. The individual elements he lists vary from being unavoidable to being truly obnoxious, and hence his curse is ineffectual, for all the passion with which it is uttered. It too is a pose, as artificial as the world he abjures. Lichtenstein surely meant to criticize the poet's superficiality, but he does so with affection and even sympathy.

Lichtenstein's poems seem at first glance light-hearted, but they are significant in German literature for two reasons. First, Lichtenstein and Van Hoddis, more than any other Expressionists (more even than Benn), subverted the traditional "seraphic" concept of poetry, which had only recently been strengthened by George and Rilke (as a poet, not as the author of *Malte Laurids Brigge*). These two Expressionists cleared the way for later poets to write as directly as they cared to do about nearly any subject. The associative style was used, for instance, by Paul Zech in the 1920s for socially critical poems about Berlin.

Secondly, they responded in an aesthetically significant way to fundamental changes in the structure of perception, as has been pointed out by Vietta and Kemper (following Benjamin's lead). In this respect, Van Hoddis, and especially Lichtenstein, are fulfillments of Blass's prophecy that the coming poet would write "from the depths," but about "quite ordinary situations." Their work also could have served as the model for Bloch's attack on Lukács' concept of objective reality:

> Perhaps Lukács' concept of reality itself still contains classical systematic traits; perhaps true reality is also interruption. Because Lukács has an objectivistic, closed concept of reality, he objects in the case of Expressionism to any artistic attempt to undercut and eventually bring down a world view (even if it is the world view of capitalism). For that reason, he sees subjectivistic destruction in an art which utilizes destructions of the superficial connection of reality and tries to find something new in the gaps; that is why he equates the act of subversion with the act of decadence.

No one seems yet to have found what lies in the gaps, but if present-day art is able to deal frankly and openly (and objectively) with modern phenomena, then it owes a debt to the unfinished legacy of such poets as Benn, Van Hoddis and

Lichtenstein, who subverted old artistic conventions and helped destroy old world views. Thus the unfinished legacy of early Expressionism remains open and challenging to poets today. (pp. 151-63)

Mark Ritter, "The Unfinished Legacy of Early Expressionist Poetry: Benn, Heym, Van Hoddis and Lichtenstein," in Passion and Rebellion: The Expressionist Heritage, *edited by Stephen Eric Bronner and Douglas Kellner, J. F. Bergin Publishers, 1983, pp. 151-65.*

EXPRESSIONIST FILM

LENNY RUBENSTEIN

[*In the following excerpt, Rubenstein discusses German Expressionist film.*]

From 1919 to 1925, expressionist techniques dominated the German silent film and through this national industry influenced the imagery and techniques of the world's infant cinema. Although Expressionism wasn't new in 1919, and several early silent films had been made of expressionist plays, Robert Wiene's *The Cabinet of Dr. Caligari* (*Das Kabinett des Dr. Caligari*) not only heralded the emergence of German film as an important new art form, but was also the harbinger of a theme and a number of cinematic devices that have left their marks on literally hundreds of films that came after it.

Seen today, *The Cabinet of Dr. Caligari* may appear almost primitive; the performers' exaggerated gestures, their peculiar eye-makeup, and the flatness of the painted set (although strikingly done) appear a bit comic and archaic. However, the stage set with its elongated streets radiating out in all directions, the trapezoidal houses with matching doorways and windowframes seem however a fitting environment for the major antagonists Dr. Caligari, (Werner Krauss), and his sleepwalker, Cesare, (Conrad Veidt) with their mad head movements and peculiar gaits. The film is much more the terrain of its villains, than of the erstwhile protagonist, Francis, (Friedrich Feher), who begins his story in the autumnal garden of a lunatic asylum. Krauss' Caligari and Veidt's Cesare are the more interesting characters to contemporary audiences which have not only accepted their performances in this film, but have continued to accept the latest permutation of the Caligari character whether as Dr. No in the James Bond film or as Dr. Strangelove in Stanley Kubrick's satire on nuclear war. All the mad scientists and obsessed tyrants of film are preceded by this 1919 production from Berlin's Decla Film studio which first introduced the character to movie-going audiences with an iris-in on the top-hatted individual with glasses and cloak who jerkily wanders through the carnival grounds at Holstenwall searching for a spot to display his creature.

The revolt in *Caligari,* however, was not only scenic, it was meant to be political, as well. In his classic study of German film, *From Caligari to Hitler,* Siegfried Kracauer has already detailed the story of how the original screenplay by Hans Janowitz and Carl Mayer was significantly altered to include a framing device, placing "reality" in Francis' lunatic asylum tale, thus undercutting to some extent the original attack on murderous authorities hidden within a rigidly hierarchical society. Both Janowitz and Mayer had learned to distrust governmental officials during the war, and their script could be seen as an open attack on a society that had countenanced murder by senseless people led by "respectable" leaders. Although the framing device reduced their attack to a madman's fable, the film still contains elements of social rebellion. The first example curiously enough is Caligari's confrontation with traditional, civil authority, the town clerk, in his effort to get a license to display his somnambulist. Seated on a tall stool decorated with legal and mystical symbols, the clerk disdains to recognize the hypnotist who cringes and schemes in his corner of the office; this is the visual realization of the famous quip by the Weimar Republic's prime satirist, Kurt Tucholsky, that it was the longing of every German to sit *behind* a desk, while it was their fate to stand *before* one. Hat in hand, bowing, Caligari endures the clerk's scorn, while already plotting his revenge. The clerk is the first victim in a series of murders engineered by Caligari with his nearly perfect weapon, Cesare who moves with the precision of a trained dancer, at once both graceful and ominous and emerges from his coffin-shaped box at the command of Caligari who brandishes his cane like a field marshal's baton—a gesture not lost upon a German audience in the years following the First World War, the *Nachkrieg*. Caligari's appearance is a study in contrasts; he wears the top hat and caped-cloak of a nineteenth century Biedermeier figure with the wire-rimmed glasses and wild white hair of an academic-gone-mad. Indeed the film takes many of the benevolent stereotypes of Germany and reverses them, just as the sets invert the normal geometry of house and street to create its disordered universe of bent streetlamps and truncated trees.

The protagonists, Francis and Alan, (Hans Heinz von Twardowski), a thinker and a poet, are also figures from a pre-Bismarckian Germany, who are seen amid their books and papers in garret apartments dressed in the appropriate nineteenth century styles for scholar and Bohemian. It is the poet, Alan, who rashly asks Cesare his future, only to learn that he will die before dawn, a prophecy Caligari has his somnambulist make good. Alan's murder, not only prompts Francis to investigate the mysterious hypnotist, but also adds a new device to film: the off-screen act shown only in a shadowed-silhouette, one of the great expressionist legacies to the cinematic form. Following this sequence, all the distortions and incongruities of the set designed by Hermann Warm, Walter Reimann and Walter Röhig become less comically intrusive and part of the world in which Caligari can stalk his victims. Part of the horror of these designs is not even linked directly to Caligari or Cesare, but to the local policemen whose flowing moustaches and pillbox caps make them appear as Central European Keystone Cops, until we see one of their prison cells. With its tapering walls, monstrously huge ball and chain, and cruel narrow window, the cell is not only an exemplary piece of expressionist design, but a hint of the tyranny beyond the confines of Caligari's show-place tent. Although many critics thought the stage-set an expression of Francis' lunacy—the visual representation of his subjective mood—Kracauer has noted that many of the design motifs remain even after the revelation of the narrator's madness.

That set was, of course, the lucky accident of its age—the Decla Film Studio had expended its rationed supply of electric power, so the trio of designers suggested painting in the perspectives and shadows to eliminate the need for expensive lighting and carpentry. The painted sets with knife-edged rooftops, chimney pots at oblique angles and houses drawn from a wild geometry text have an eerie beauty that impressed a small body of esthetes and film pioneers in both Europe and America, but the real terrain for expressionist successes were the Gothic and horror films that emerged from Germany in the first half of its Golden Age of film. *The Cabinet of Dr. Caligari* has become the acknowledged first film of this amazing output, and some of that productions' themes and formalist exercises appeared again and again in *Nosferatu, Waxworks, Vanina, The Golem, Raskolnikov* and *The Student of Prague.* Many of the performers and directors, as well as set designers and cameramen, who worked on these films found themselves the targets of lucrative offers from the American film industry, and Hollywood became one of the richest heirs of the Weimar Republic's cultural heritage.

Expressionist writers glorified the "demonic man" whose longings could never be assuaged, and German's silent films are replete with images of the demonic character—whether he is dressed in the heavy clothing of the nineteenth century bourgeois or the trappings of the fabled demon, the vampire. Directed by Friedrich W. Murnau in 1922, from a script by Henrik Galeen, *Nosferatu* used the shadow of the evil Count Orlok, (Max Schreck), to intimate his attack on the helpless insurance agent, Hutter (Gustav Von Wangenheim), and one sequence used *negative* exposure to convey the otherworldly evil of the Count's estate, (a device most recently employed in the televised PBS version of *Dracula*). In lieu of distorted painted sets, Murnau used abandoned mansions and a studio-built castle to create the backdrop for his story of evil and love. With his fanged teeth and claw-like hands, Orlok was the next stage in monstrousness after Caligari, whose gestures anticipated many of Orlok's, and his long fingers seemed only a more open threat after the white gloves ceremoniously worn by the mad hypnotist. Mad ghouls and tyrannical psychiatrists may have appeared as cinematic fictions far removed from the actual society a few miles outside the Neubabelsberg studios, and indeed the political implications of much of expressionist works were almost lost amid the finely crafted stage-sets and lighting patterns which earned universal acclaim, but there were occasional links to real authority and actual monarchs, if not to social types prevalent in Weimar Germany.

Nosferatu was followed, in 1922, by *Vanina* which supplanted the vampire with a sadistic royal governor who not only imprisons and tortures his daughter's lover, the leader of an abortive rebellion, but then allows her to believe he has relented and will permit their marriage to take place. Both rebel and daughter die, he at the gallows and she from a broken heart, a curiously apt allegory for the German Revolution of 1919. Directed by Arthur von Gerlach from a script by Carl Mayer, *Vanina* not only reversed the optimistic ending of *Nosferatu* where love destroys an evil creature, but appended the ruler's final cruel revenge. Besides the veteran script-writer, *Vanina's* other link to *Caligari* was the set designer Walter Reimann who here emphasized the lovers' fated doom by an emphasis on long, menacing corridors through which the pair attempt to flee. Malevolence and authority seem to co-exist ideally in these films, even when that authority is exercised for an ostensible noble cause.

Paul Wegener's *The Golem* (1920) retells the ancient Jewish legend of a man-made creature with super-human powers in a film that borrowed lightly from the expressionist armory of

devices, but which highlights the sense of powerlessness in the hands of fate. In an effort to dissuade the Hapsburg emperor from expelling the Jews from medieval Prague, the ghetto's wiseman, Rabbi Loew constructs out of clay an indestructible creature animated by mystic forces summoned by the Rabbi's alchemical and astrological skills. The free-floating mask of the demon and the walls of fire from which the Rabbi must protect himself and his assistant, as well as the smoking letters which serve as the titles for this sequence, are some of the expressionist features in this film. More intriguing perhaps are the twisted, onion shaped rooms and stairways designed by Hans Poelizig which lead the eye from the dark, cavernous laboratory to the huge blacksmith's fire which dominates many of the alchemical scenes. Lotte Eisner, in her recent study of German film, *The Haunted Screen,* has termed the major influence in *The Golem* impressionist rather than expressionist given its emphasis on texture and light, instead of abstracted, distorted designs. *The Golem,* however, still shares with *Vanina* and *Caligari,* an interest in the abuse of power and authority. Although the Golem does succeed in dissuading the emperor from expelling the Jews, Loew's creation, unleashed by his bungling assistant, turns on the ghetto and specifically on Loew's daugher. Having nearly destroyed the ghetto he was designed to save, the Golem is unstoppable, even by his creator, until he reaches the ghetto gates where amid the sunlight and flowers he is toppled by a group of garlanded blonde girls who toy with the magic amulet on the golem's chest. Authority, even the religious power wielded by Rabbi Loew, has its darker side, the film implies, and it is only childish faith that reduces the rampaging golem to a lifeless clay object once more.

A more pointed use of expressionist themes and formats can be seen in Paul Leni's 1924 film *Waxworks (Das Wachsfigurenkabinett)* which stars three of the German silent screen's biggest stars: Emil Jannings, Conrad Veidt and Werner Krauss. They play murderous historical figures whose images in a carnival wax museum conjure up three stories in the mind of an unemployed writer who was hired by the museum curator to compose a tale about each of them. The first story is about Haroun Al-Raschid, (Jannings), a grotesque onion-shaped despot whose very castle mirrors his own body with its sinuous towers and elastic looking walls and is peopled with cringing servants in over-sized turbans. A traditional parody of a moody and arbitrary tyrant, Al-Raschid condemns to death in one gesture and then tearfully regrets his decision the next. The second episode centers around the thin, stark Ivan the Terrible, (Veidt) who is not subject to such relief. The Czar, in Leni's film, is a murderous madman whose evil is highlighted by his regal stature. At one point, the Czar is seen flanked by the painted icons of a doorway, and the murderous ruler in his robe and crown seems to fit in with them. Besides watching the torture of his victims from a secret window, Ivan has his greatest pleasure in presenting his quarry with an hour-glass inscribed with his name so that he would know when the administered poison would take effect. The appropriately lighted hour-glass becomes the means by which Ivan is driven mad, since he finds one with his name on it and begins to insanely rotate the glass in an effort to stop time. A gift of religious art to the film-maker, the hour-glass has become a virtual symbol of ancient horror and it is certainly no accident that it is by a large, ornately-carved hour-glass that the Witch times Dorothy's life in the *Wizard of Oz.*

The final episode in *Waxworks,* however, is not removed in

time or space like the previous two, but brings a modern killer, Jack-the-Ripper, (Krauss), into the life of the writer and his lover. The third killer pursues the protagonist through the darkened, abandoned carnival grounds, with all the emphasis on shadows and distortions of space. This ending implies the reality of tyrannical murderers, since there is no resolution posed for the protagonist and his lover, the museum curator's daughter. The chase through the carnival grounds, the contemporary terrain for the film's story, as well as a symbol in German films for the chaos of modern life, brings the threat of lunatic murders into 1920's Germany. The image of the mass murderer, seen in the paintings by Georg Grosz and Max Beckmann years before the Nazis were actual political threats, or in films like *Waxworks* or Fritz Lang's *M,* had its basis in the actual reports of apprehended criminals who had lured any number of young men and women to their homes where they were cruelly killed.

Another Robert Wiene film, *Raskolnikov,* examines the protagonist of Dostoyevsky's *Crime and Punishment* to arrive at an understanding of the "demonic man" compelled to kill. Using sets designed by Andrei Andreiev, Wiene succeeded in overcoming the flat, one-dimensional look of the *Caligari* set, by constructing his shadows and oblique angles to match the disordered universe seen by the young student and to show the complementing effect of the protagonist's madness on the distorted environment. A later Henrik Galeen film, *The Student of Prague,* used a studio-fabricated forest to convey the sensation of impending evil and latent doom. In this familiar, old tale of the split-personality, a young student, (Conrad Veidt), is persuaded to sell his soul to another of those Biedermeier characters who seem to possess unnatural powers. Set amid the twisted trees of a wind-swept plain, the stranger (Werner Krauss), carries his umbrella like some sort of weapon or magic staff, and his silhouetted shadow haunts the student at critical points in the film's plot, until the tragic conclusion when the victim confronts his own image in a duel-to-the-death.

One of the problems in any discussion of the expressionist influence on German silent films is the conflict between the subjective experience of the character as caught by the camera and the objective view of the same sequence by the audience. In *Caligari* the set is seen as the world viewed by a madman rather than as an abstracted view of a society on the brink of lunacy. The use of wispy letters in place of printed inter-titles and the various tinted scenes, no longer seen in most prints of the film, reinforce the latter argument. In the expressionist canon, the actual world is seen as ajar, not the characters. This aspect was rapidly lost in film as many of the expressionist devices were used to convey purely subjective states, for example the collage of distorted, laughing faces in Murnau's *The Last Laugh,* or to serve decorative purposes as in Fritz Lang's *Nibelungen (Siegfried).*

Arthur Robison's 1923 film *Warning Shadows (Schatten),* however, is more purely expressionist. There is real confusion for both the audience and the main character concerning whether they are mad or whether it is their situation which is insane. Seen as ambiguous shadows, a series of infidelities, betrayals and murders cures a jealous Count of the suspicion that had been ruining his marriage. The film is basically a therapeutic role-playing in silhouette, so that the characters can have a peaceful resolution to a possibly murderous dilemma.

From 1925-1930 the expressionist devices entered the wider world of international film production. Paul Leni's *Cat and the Canary* (1927) is a Hollywood comic-thriller replete with all the trappings of a German horror classic: the long, dark corridors are haunted by peculiar breezes and mysterious creatures, while the film's mood of entrapment is constantly re-created by the cameras filming through stairway uprights and the slats of old-style chairs. Distortion for mere effect, not to underline the society's irrationality or to highlight a character's emotional instability, became an excuse for cameramen to film through refractive lenses, jars of water and clouded windows. Other film-makers with period plots could create countryside sets enshrouded in mist to provide their Wagnerian heroes with the appropriate backdrops. With improvements in camera equipment, film-makers were soon taking their performers and crews up mountain peaks for a popular kind of German film that helped launch Leni Riefenstahl's career (*The Blue Light*).

The decline of the expressionist film in the mid-twenties was mirrored by a period of relative stability in German society and government; the excesses of the inflation, as hinted at in Fritz Lang's *Dr. Mabuse,* or of the possibilities for dictatorship in Hitler's abortive putsch were old memories by 1925-6. The order beloved by a martinet was conveyed in cinematic terms by Lang's use of people as geometric formats in *Nibelungen* or *Metropolis* where individuals exist only as facets of a wonderously choreographed regimental whole. The expressionist theatrical chorus had been converted into a silent procession—while the only voice it was allowed, in *Triumph of Will,* was the Nazi Party's "German" greeting.

In one notable film, *The Revolt of the Fishermen,* directed by the famed veteran Erwin Piscator in a Soviet theatrical production, left-wing uses were made of expressionist devices, i.e. the geometric grouping of extras is used as a dramatic device to comment on the action, the strike by a number of impoverished fishermen. The film also has several remarkably staged sequences, such as a night-time brawl between strikers and strike-breakers, an appropriately murky scene illuminated faintly by moon-light in which class conscious workers fight it out with their less enlightened brothers. A later scene revolves around the denunciation of religious pacifism when troops attack the strikers at a funeral. Made in exile, *The Revolt of the Fishermen* was the last German film to merge distortion with a message of rebellion; the studies at Neubabelsberg were busy churning out the musical comedies and war films that were to become a staple of the Third Reich's film industry. Even before Hitler's appointment as *Reichskanzler,* however, the German film had turned almost wholly away from the traces of revolt that had once motivated its writers and directors.

The city, like the expressionist carnival, had become a symbol of conflict for directors; it was seen as a dangerous terrain dominated by criminals and corrupt geniuses, men like Lang's Mabuse and Haghi, the spy master. The number of urban tragedies that dot German cinematic history is indicative of the foreboding with which the modern industrial city was seen; *The Street, The Joyless Street, Asphalt, Tragedy of a Street* and *The Last Laugh* depict the doom that awaited the unwary, and of course Lang's futuristic morality story [*Metropolis*] took its title from a synonym for a large cosmopolitan city. Like the American gangster film or the contemporary "disaster" epic, the German silent "street" films catered to the audience's interest in, and obsession with, the worst aspects of urban life: crime, drug usage and sexual li-

Still from the Expressionist film Nosferatu *(1921).*

cense. Only a few consciously political films attempted to show urban life from the viewpoint of the average worker, *Mother Krausen's Journey to Happiness, Berlin Alexanderplatz* and *Kuhle Wampe* are probably the three most famous. However, except for an interesting sequence of multiple bicycle wheels shown racing against the symbols of continued joblessness—closed factory gates with signs that no-one need apply—the Brecht-Dudow film *Kuhle Wampe* is not very different from any number of street films about the plight of the impoverished bourgeois. The emphasis on the collective life of the political characters in the film seems a forced, optimistic after-thought. Both Kracauer and Eisner, who tend to differ sharply on their interpretation of the silent films, agree on the similarity between the leftist-youth in *Kuhle Wampe* and any similar Nazi group. Both Nazi and Communist films from the 1930's share a similar realism in style, and even end up with a similar image—the marching column. The Nazis made no distinction between the war they waged in the Berlin streets and the one that their spiritual antecedents had waged in the trenches in Flanders. This copy-book version of patriotism was voiced in one of the most successful early Nazi films, *Hitler Youth Quex, (Hitlerjunge Quex)*, which contrasted the regimented Nazis with the rowdier Communist youth group. Films like *Kuhle Wampe* and *Mother Krausen's Journey to Happiness* ended with the heroine alongside her Communist

lover in a protest demonstration march. The clash of rival marchers was to ruin Europe for more than a decade.

Like all legacies, the expressionist heritage in film has been shared and misspent by a veritable army of heirs. The Soviet film-makers borrowed heavily from the collection of madmen and killers in regal or bourgeois dress for their films, and it was certainly no whim that made Sergei Eisenstein arm his middle-class ladies with parasols in *October,* parasols with which they kill a young Bolshevik in the film's July Rising sequence. The early Soviet film-makers never hesitated to display their enemies as brutes with a thin veneer of middle-class culture, an image curiously enough well represented in the silent German cinema. Pabst's *Love of Jeanne Ney* featured Fritz Rasp as a particularly squalid example, while Kracauer cites the elegantly dressed Ivan the Terrible in *Waxworks* who gleefully watches his torturers at work. Besides the Russians, Hollywood was not only quick to borrow expressionist devices, but imported directors, performers, and cameramen as well. Even in the Germany that emerged from Hitler's "national revolution" there were strong hints of the silent film's contribution to Nazi stage-craft. Fritz Lang's heraldic display played its part in the filming of the Nazi Party's 1934 Party Day in Nuremberg, where all the devices of the entertainment film—cloud formations and an actual gothic city, the night sky punctuated by hand-held torches and anti-aircraft search lights, the imperious leader atop the reviewing block and the serried ranks of marching uniformed faithful— could be used in a documentary film extolling the German rebirth. Riefenstahl's *Triumph of the Will, (Sieg des Willens),* provided an ideal matrix for all the elements of the German film tradition, just as the political ideology it glamorized was the perfect combination of the need to rebel within a hierarchical framework with the desire for socialism without any consideration of economics or democracy.

While the Soviets adapted some of the expressionist film techniques and the Nazis adopted the decorative grouping and use of shadow (in many Nazi wartime newsreels the sense of victory was conveyed by the shadow of the advancing tanks cast on the roadway) the Americans utilized the atmosphere of the early silent films in horror films that have never been equalled: *Dracula, Frankenstein, The Invisible Man, The Mummy* and *The Bride of Frankenstein.* In each of these films the emphasis is always on the creature, never the protagonist, although both must operate and act in a universe shaped by the abandoned towers, gloomy mansions or deserted village streets designed by the film's artistic director. These sets owe as much to the German silent films from the early twenties as do the presentations by the performers. The look of half-mad cunning and menacing tyranny so frequently cast by the expressionist actor was developed, along with the proper vocal tone, by those Hollywood performers with whose names the early sound-horror films are inextricably linked: Boris Karloff, Bela Lugosi and Claude Rains, while a host of other performers personified the reluctantly obsessed scientist, the evil genius and the clumsy assistant: Colin Clive, Ernest Thesiger and Dwight Frye. Even today's films owe a serious debt to Decla's 1919 production, since the appropriate setting and garb for many a Hammer studio horror film is the nineteenth century with its heavy clothing and deceptively polite manner—just the atmosphere for Caligari. (pp. 363-73)

> *Lenny Rubenstein, " 'Caligari' and the Rise of Expressionist Film," in Passion and Rebellion: The Expressionist Heritage, edited by Stephen Eric Bronner and Douglas Kellner, J. F. Bergin Publishers, 1983, pp. 363-73.*

EXPRESSIONIST PAINTING

HORST UHR

[In the following excerpt, Uhr discusses the development and techniques of German Expressionist painting.]

Ranging from the representational to the nonobjective, the works that have come to be grouped under the label "German Expressionism" are as varied as the term itself is vague. For German Expressionism was less a unified style than an attitude, a state of mind that in the early years of the twentieth century existed among young artists in a number of different places—in Dresden, Berlin, and Munich, as well as in various cities in the Rhineland and northern Germany. Profoundly critical of the materialism of modern life, these artists probed man's spiritual condition in search of a new harmoni-

ous relationship between him and his environment. And though their methods differed, depending on the inclination of a given group or on individual temperament, all subordinated nature to a transcription of their subjective reactions to the world. Opting for the universal and prototypical rather than the specific and anecdotal, and for a deliberate antinaturalism manifested in intensified color and simplified form, they were less concerned with resemblance than with artistic vision, and sought to penetrate appearances in order to lay bare what they perceived to be the inner essence of things.

The term *expressionism* and the concept of self-expression in art, however, originated not in Germany but in France. More precisely, it originated in the atelier of Gustave Moreau. Moreau, one of the chief precursors of Symbolist painting, taught at the École des Beaux-Arts from 1892 to 1898, encouraging his students to express themselves according to their individual sensibilities. Moreau's advice was not lost on his most gifted pupil Henri Matisse, who studied with him between 1892 and 1897. In the first decade of the twentieth century, Matisse used the term *expression* repeatedly in conversations with his own students, stressing that pictorial results must always be based on the dictates of one's temperament and personal interpretation of nature.

The term *expressionist* is first documented as having been used in Germany in connection with the visual arts in April 1911. This occurred at the twenty-second exhibition of the Berlin Secession where, in a separate gallery specifically labeled "Expressionists," a group of French artists—associates of Matisse in Paris and members of the original Fauve group—showed some of their recent pictures; Pablo Picasso, represented by pre-Cubist works, exhibited with them. The term continued to be confined to contemporary French painting in both *Der Sturm,* an influential weekly founded in Berlin in 1910 by the enterprising Herwarth Walden, and in the first exhibition Walden organized at Der Sturm Gallery in 1912, even though this exhibition included German artists who have since been recognized as leaders of the German Expressionist movement. That year, at the famous Sonderbund exhibition in Cologne—the first truly international survey of contemporary European developments and the direct model for the 1913 Armory Show in New York—the term *expressionism* was applied to all Post-Impressionist work distinguished by the subjective use of color and form. This encompassed not only the work of pioneers like Paul Cézanne, Paul Gauguin, and Vincent van Gogh but also virtually every modern trend, including paintings and sculpture by the young Germans.

Only with Paul Fechter's book *Der Expressionismus (Expressionism),* published in Munich in 1914, was the term explicitly linked to the artists of Die Brücke (The Bridge), organized in Dresden in 1905, and of Der Blaue Reiter (The Blue Rider), founded in Munich in 1911. Identifying Dresden and Munich as the true birthplaces of Expressionism, Fechter not only discussed Die Brücke and Der Blaue Reiter as representative of two distinct German Expressionist directions, but also interpreted the movement as a typically Germanic phenomenon. Moreover, he saw the Expressionist not only as an artist who communicates his own feelings but also as one who gives expression to the conflicts and aspirations of his time.

Even today there is agreement neither on the chronological limits of Expressionism nor on its precise nature. Since the publication of Fechter's book, the term has been applied to the art of the early twentieth century as a whole, seen as an alternative to Cubist-derived abstraction, and equated with manifestations of German art from the Ottonian period in the tenth century to the present. Generally, however, Expressionism has come to be understood as designating a period in German culture spanning the years from 1905 to the rise of National Socialism in 1933, although as early as 1920 a reaction against Expressionism had begun to set in, and Max Beckmann, widely hailed as one of the chief exponents of the German Expressionist movement, continued to work in an Expressionist-derived idiom in America until the time of his death in 1950.

While all Expressionists were pursuing the same general goal, the development of each artist varied in accordance with local and personal conditions. Indeed, the context of the evolution of Expressionist conceptions of color and form differed considerably in northern, southern, and central Germany. Whereas in Dresden and Munich close-knit friendships and associations of artists encouraged the formation of a cohesive outlook and style, no such groups developed in northern Germany, where expressions of striking individuality tended to be the rule. On the other hand, it is impossible to view the art of Die Brücke and Der Blaue Reiter collectively. For while the Munich group in southern Germany was decisively influenced by Wassily Kandinsky's aesthetics and contemporary French developments, the work of both Edvard Munch and Van Gogh had a pervasive effect on the young artists of Dresden in central Germany.

The founding of Die Brücke in 1905 by Ernst Ludwig Kirchner, Fritz Bleyl, Erich Heckel, and Karl Schmidt-Rottluff, all of whom had originally gone to Dresden to study architecture, was as much an act of defiance of conventional bourgeois notions of success and respectability as it was the result of a burning desire for a type of creative and intellectual freedom that architecture did not allow. Indeed, the group's early years together were marked not only by the obsessive search for an intuitive form of pictorial expression, but also by a truly revolutionary belief in a new kind of man. In keeping with this spirit, the name of the group, "The Bridge," was intended as a metaphoric image signifying its members' pursuit of a new and inward-searching art, as well as their common quest for a new life. In 1906 Kirchner, who regarded himself as the spokesman of Die Brücke, made a woodcut of the group's emblem and reproduced in bold letters cut into wood the association's challenging manifesto:

> With faith in growth and in a new generation of creators and those who enjoy, we call all young people together, and as the youth that bears the future within it we shall create for ourselves elbow-room and freedom of life as opposed to the well-entrenched older forces. Everyone who renders directly and honestly whatever drives him to create is one of us.

The various studios of the Brücke artists, decorated with brightly colored wall hangings and hand-carved furniture, were the scenes of a truly bohemian life. Discussions about Friedrich Nietzsche, Feodor Dostoevsky, and Walt Whitman alternated with spurts of frenzied activity, as the young artists rushed from one pictorial idea to another, constantly urging each other on. Their group spirit resulted in marked resemblances among their works, especially in their graphic production which from the very beginning was especially lively.

In 1906 Emil Nolde and Max Pechstein joined Die Brücke.

Nolde was then well on his way to developing an independent style, and Pechstein, a graduate of the Academy of Fine Arts, Dresden, was more accomplished in terms of technical knowledge than the other members. Also new to the group that year were the Swiss Cuno Amiet and the Finn Axel Gallén-Kallela, although the two restricted themselves to occasional participation in the group's exhibitions. Nolde, always a loner at heart, withdrew after about a year and a half, while Bleyl resigned from the association in 1909 to return to the practice and teaching of architecture. The Dutchman Kees van Dongen, who had exhibited with the Fauves in the famous Salon d'Automne of 1905 in Paris, entered into an informal relationship with the German artists in 1908. The last important artist to join their circle was Otto Mueller, who became associated with the group in 1910.

The first artistically important period for the members of Die Brücke was the years between 1906 and 1911, when they exhibited extensively as a group. They made their debut in 1906 in the showroom of a suburban lamp manufacturer in Löbtau, a suburb of Dresden. Beginning in 1907, Die Brücke exhibitions were held in Dresden in Emil Richter's gallery and in the Ernst Arnold Gallery. By 1910 the list of exhibition sites included such major cities as Hamburg, Frankfurt, Leipzig, and Hannover, as well as Copenhagen and Prague. Nonetheless, the Brücke painters did not find themselves widely accepted. On the contrary, their work usually met with hostility and resistance. In 1910 several works by Pechstein were rejected by the Berlin Secession, which until then had been a fairly liberal forum for the European avant-garde. In response Pechstein founded the Neue Sezession (New Secession) and organized a counter-exhibition in one of the city's private galleries. Among the twenty-seven artists exhibiting with Pechstein were Kirchner, Heckel, and Schmidt-Rottluff. Seeking to preserve the unity of their artistic aims, however, the members of Die Brücke withdrew from the Neue Sezession the following year, pledging to exhibit their work in the future only as a group.

By 1911 all the Brücke artists had settled in Berlin, attracted by the cultural life of the metropolis and the prospect of finding acceptance among the city's potentially more broadminded critics and public. They contributed illustrations to *Der Sturm* and in the spring of 1912 had their first major exhibition in Berlin at the well-known gallery of Fritz Gurlitt, an event that finally brought them to the attention of several leading art journals. While Kirchner, Heckel, Schmidt-Rottluff, and Mueller received less than favorable comments, Pechstein was singled out as the leader of the group. All the Brücke painters also participated in the Sonderbund exhibition in Cologne that year.

Shortly after the Gurlitt show in Berlin, however, Pechstein was expelled from the association, apparently for having rejoined the Berlin Secession independently, thereby violating the group's pledge to exhibit only together. Die Brücke was officially dissolved in 1913, when Kirchner's subjective editing of a chronicle the artists had intended to publish that year was repudiated by the other members. Yet the controversy over the chronicle was probably hardly more than an excuse for the group's breakup. Not only had Pechstein's defection the previous year signaled recognition that the artists' youthful dreams of an artistic community could not be maintained forever, but also their work had long ceased to be characterized by a collective style, since in Berlin each artist had developed an increasingly personal form of expression. While henceforth they were to work and develop independently, the Brücke painters nonetheless remained friends, with the exception of Kirchner, who refused to exhibit with his former associates in later years and in 1919 even denied that Die Brücke had ever had anything to do with his own early progress. Yet in 1926, at his mountain retreat in Switzerland, he painted from memory a nostalgic group portrait. (pp. 10-13)

The aims and origins of Der Blaue Reiter, founded in 1911 in Munich by Kandinsky and Franz Marc, differed sharply from those of Die Brücke. While Kandinsky and Marc shared with their colleagues in Berlin a tendency toward inwardness, being similarly bent on a subjective interpretation of the visible world, the members of the Munich circle possessed a far greater intellectual openness. Not only did they readily accept and acknowledge international trends, but, unlike the close-knit Brücke, where communal activity in the early years had given rise to works of striking similarity, they never developed a unified style. Moreover, while Die Brücke was committed to social change, having been conceived as a revolutionary youth group, the basic ideology of Der Blaue Reiter was philosophical. At issue here was not the individual as a social being, but man's relationship to the innermost secrets of nature.

By the time Der Blaue Reiter was founded, Kandinsky, who had left Russia in 1896, had played an active role on the Munich art scene for some years, first through the pioneering exhibitions of Phalanx, an independent exhibition association he created in 1901, and subsequently through the Neue Künstlervereinigung (New Artists' Association), organized under his chairmanship in 1909 and intended, like Phalanx, as a forum for the European avant-garde. It was in response to ideological rifts developing within the Neue Künstlervereinigung in 1911 that Kandinsky, his friend Gabriele Münter, and Marc seceded from the group, and Marc immediately started to make preparations for the first Blaue Reiter exhibition, which opened at the Thannhauser Gallery in Munich on December 18 of that year. In addition to Kandinsky, Münter, and Marc, the major artists included in the show were Heinrich Campendonk, August Macke, the Russian brothers Vladimir and David Burliuk, and the French painter Henri Rousseau; the Austrian composer Arnold Schönberg was represented by a number of intriguing oil sketches.

Of major importance for the Munich artists were five works submitted by the Parisian Robert Delaunay, who as early as 1909 had developed an independent form of Cubism, combining expressive color with Cubist analysis of form. By 1911-12, fascinated by the rhythmic structure of medieval and contemporary architecture and the movement of the modern city, he was working on a series of window views in which he had virtually eliminated representational images in favor of interpenetrating, transparent planes of prismatic color and the predominant structural elements of the composition. Having separated color and form from description, Delaunay subsequently developed a conception of abstract painting in which he used pulsating color harmonies to reflect the intangible rhythms that pervade all of nature, a notion that not only had consequences for the development of the art of Macke and Marc but ultimately affected the pictorial thinking of Lyonel Feininger as well.

Exactly why the name "The Blue Rider" was chosen for the Munich group is not known. Kandinsky, when asked for an explanation many years later, jokingly replied that Marc liked horses and he himself riders, and that both of them had always been rather fond of the color blue. The horse and rider motif, first found in Kandinsky's work in a decorative painting of about 1901, represents, in fact, the most persistent theme in the Russian painter's oeuvre and one that he gradually transformed from a material representation to an abstract configuration. Based on such images as the medieval crusader-knight and the legendary warrior Saint George, both the theme and the name "The Blue Rider" were, like "The Bridge," doubtless intended metaphorically, signifying the conquest of the visible world in what was to become for Kandinsky, as well as for Marc, a dematerialized and thus spiritual art.

The first Blaue Reiter exhibition closed in Munich in January 1912, after which it toured several major cities. Inaugurating Walden's Der Sturm Gallery in Berlin in March, the exhibition was augmented by works by Alfred Kubin, Alexey Jawlensky, Marianne von Werefkin, and Paul Klee. The year 1912 also saw the publication of Kandinsky's trail-blazing book *Concerning the Spiritual in Art* (*Über das Geistige in der Kunst*) and of the anthology *Der Blaue Reiter,* a collection of essays edited by Kandinsky and Marc which, in addition to important contributions by the two editors, contained articles by Macke, David Burliuk, Schönberg, and others. Testifying to the group's enthusiasm for all artistic expressions untainted by convention, the anthology featured a remarkable series of illustrations, ranging from works by leading Post-Impressionists to peasant paintings, drawings by children, medieval illuminations, sculpture, prints, and various forms of non-European art.

Lyonel Feininger joined Der Blaue Reiter when the group participated in Walden's First German Autumn Salon in Berlin in 1913. The last exhibition of Der Blaue Reiter took place at Der Sturm Gallery the following year. Shortly afterward the association disbanded. The outbreak of World War I forced Kandinsky to return to Russia. Macke, one of the first to be called up for active military service, died on a French battlefield only weeks after the beginning of the war. Marc was killed in action near Verdun in France in 1916.

Although those Expressionists who have talked or written about their work have generally tended to guard the individuality of their achievements by denying any direct indebtedness to either tradition or contemporary models, it can be demonstrated that their art was not evolved without precedents. On the contrary, in their efforts to push aside the veil of visible reality they found helpful ideas in the immediate past.

As early as 1885 Gauguin had begun to turn inward from the exterior world. Convinced that pictorial harmonies can act upon the human soul the way music does, he believed in the psychological power of color and line, equating pictorial properties with emotional states. Indeed, he considered painting to be superior to music, since it can achieve a unity of expression that transmits itself to the senses in one instant, whereas music must be experienced over time. In his pictures, luminous colors unite with simplified and sweeping curves to form a decorative whole that defines the mood of a given composition. A similar awareness of the emotional power of color was to manifest itself in the art of Der Blaue Reiter, and a feeling for rhythmic compositions symbolically uniting man and nature became characteristic of many early works of Die Brücke.

Seeking a second, artistic reality beneath optical truth, Van

Gogh, too, had intensified color in order to convey what he felt, giving status to color as a purely expressive means. But it was not only the brilliance of his palette that appealed to the young Germans: his depth of feeling and empathy with his fellowman stirred them as profoundly. The austere yet poignant peasant pictures of Paula Modersohn-Becker are unthinkable without the context of both the mood and deliberately primitive form of *La Berceuse,* a painting Van Gogh did in Arles in 1889, showing Madame Roulin, the wife of the local postman, seated at her infant's cradle. Van Gogh painted five versions of this picture, intending it as a prototypical image of maternal consolation for all who are lonely and sad.

Although he provided an important impetus to the revival of the woodcut among the artists of Die Brücke, Munch influenced the German Expressionists even more as a kindred spirit. Having experienced a difficult youth, Munch felt keenly the emotional tensions that modern society inflicts upon the individual and for many years was unable to escape the torments of his own psychic maladjustment. What he wanted to paint were pictures expressive of states of mind, an idea he eventually developed in *Frieze of Life,* a series of canvases on the theme of human suffering. His subject matter—love, hate, life and death, illness, and the pain of loneliness—greatly appealed to the artists of Die Brücke. The brooding woman in *Melancholy,* for example, may be seen as the spiritual antecedent of the vulnerable and frail creatures of Heckel and Max Kaus.

By the time Munch painted *Melancholy* in 1899, German artists were also advocating an art of spiritual significance. Their ideas sprang from the fertile ground of the international arts and crafts movement as it developed in Munich. There it was dubbed "Jugendstil," following the founding in 1896 of *Jugend,* a Munich weekly that popularized the new style. One of the earliest supporters of the movement and its most vigorous spokesman was the designer Hermann Obrist. By the mid-1890s he had developed a vast vocabulary of decorative forms which, while based on nature, were transformed into evocative, semiabstract shapes. A wall hanging embroidered around 1895 with one of his designs, originally titled *Cyclamen,* became famous as *Whiplash,* since the configuration seemed less an image of a flower than a subjective expression of energy, an abstract representation of feeling. Obrist exercised a profound influence on August Endell, Munich's leading Jugendstil architect, who as early as 1897 had prophesied the development of abstract art in speaking of "forms that signify nothing, represent nothing, and recall nothing, but that will be able to excite our souls as deeply as only music has been able to do with tones." The expressive properties of Obrist's forms as well as his ideas directly touched the future Expressionists. From 1903 to 1904 Kirchner attended the Teaching and Experimental Studio for Applied and Fine Art that Obrist had founded with Wilhelm von Debschitz in 1901. Kandinsky became a close friend of Obrist in 1904. Indeed, nearly all the Expressionists went through a period of experimentation with the abstracted natural forms of Jugendstil, and Jugendstil's concepts of pure line, color, and form were fully developed by Kandinsky in *Concerning the Spiritual in Art.*

German Expressionism, in short, emerged from developments of the last quarter of the nineteenth century, a time in which the description of natural fact had increasingly come to be replaced by the artist's efforts to find a pictorial equivalent for personal experience. German Expressionism is also connected with the work of the Fauves, which not only matured contemporaneously with that of Die Brücke, but also was inspired by some of the same sources, such as the brilliant and emotional color of Van Gogh's work and Gauguin's evocatively "musical" art. Despite the striking stylistic similarities that can be observed in works of both groups prior to 1911, the expressive purposes of the French and German artists differed fundamentally. The French, under the leadership of Matisse, were primarily committed to problems of pictorial design, while the Germans expressed a far greater concern for the social and psychological situation of modern man. Of the French, only Georges Rouault revealed in his work a comparably serious, indeed tragic, view of life. (pp. 13-19)

While Matisse strove for an art of pictorial harmony, the German Expressionists sought to address themselves in their art to the spiritual needs of the time, needs rooted in their country's immediate past. Unlike England and France, which could look back on a well-established tradition of economic and political organization, Germany in the last quarter of the nineteenth century found itself faced with a belated industrial revolution, having been transformed in 1871 from a semifeudal collection of principalities into a nation state. Virtually overnight, commerce and industry began to grow at a dizzying rate, corporations and banks multiplied, and immense private fortunes were amassed. In 1872, just one year after the old Hohenzollern residence had officially been declared the capital of the newly founded empire, no fewer than forty new construction firms commenced operation in Berlin alone, gradually extending the city's perimeter farther westward. Before long, vast blocks of workers' tenements rose near Alexanderplatz in bleak contrast to the palatial villas of the Tiergarten quarter and the splendid façades of elegant shops and apartments on Kurfürstendamm.

Whatever the immediate material benefits, the accelerated changeover from an agrarian to an industrial society was bound to bring about a cultural shock. Young German intellectuals became increasingly distrustful of the crass materialism of the age and revolted against their own middle-class roots. Stage plays of family conflict, such as Walter Hasenclever's drama *The Son,* 1914, Frank Wedekind's tragic play about adolescent sexuality, *Spring's Awakening,* 1891, as well as Heinrich Mann's satires of bourgeois smugness and hypocrisy, all grew from a profound awareness of the dislocation of modern man.

Evident in the art of many Expressionists and their associates is a similar disenchantment with material values and sympathy for the alienated and downtrodden, often combined with an idealistic plea for the transformation of the existing social order. This informs the proletarian themes of Kollwitz, the joyless dancers of Heckel, and Kirchner's anxiety-ridden city views, inhabited by men and women whose stylish appearance is matched only by their soulless indifference to each other.

Accompanying the Expressionist criticism of modern industrialized society was a conscious effort to become uncivilized, a yearning for an unspoiled form of existence originating in Nietzsche's vision of a Dionysian return to the wellsprings of nature. At the turn of the century, national organizations like the Wandervögel (Birds of Passage) encouraged communal hikes into the countryside, while members of groups such as the Jugendbewegung (Youth Movement) or practitioners of *Freikörperkultur* (nudism) dedicated themselves to man's physical and spiritual renewal through contact with the out-of-doors. This new cult of primitive vitality was also part of the early communal lifestyle of the members of Die Brücke, who left their studios in the city during the summer months for the idyllic Moritzburg lake district near Dresden and the more distant beaches of the Baltic and the North Sea. There, accompanied by a number of women friends, they lived nude in tents and spent their days bathing, lolling about on the grass, and making love. They also painted and drew. Rejecting the pose of the professional model as artificial and sterile, they studied the nude human body moving freely in natural surroundings. While Pechstein's hedonistic bathers conjure up an image of primeval vigor, Mueller's wistful nudes recall the mythical world of the nineteenth-century German painter Hans von Marées, whose clearly structured compositions are pervaded by a similarly nostalgic air. Since 1908, when two large retrospective exhibitions of his work were held at the Munich and Berlin Secessions, Marées had become a major source of inspiration for the younger generation. They not only admired his ability to subordinate anecdotal detail to the rhythm of the composition, but also discovered a kindred spirit in the nostalgic mood of his art.

Indeed, as the open countryside became an antidote to urban life for the Expressionists, they increasingly invested nature with a transcendental significance reminiscent of the nineteenth-century German Romantic tradition. In the late 1790s the philosopher Friedrich von Schelling had postulated the existence of a world-soul stirring in all animate and inanimate things, though productively conscious only in the mind of the artist. Nowhere is this pantheistic notion more eloquently expressed than in the haunting landscapes of Caspar David Friedrich, who had been virtually rediscovered at the centennial exhibition of German painting in Berlin in 1906 after decades of neglect. For Friedrich nature was only the physical manifestation of his own inner vision. Though based on topographical fact, his landscapes are almost visionary in character. The quasi-religious, intensely spiritual communication of Friedrich's compositions, in which human figures, singly or in pairs, stand transfixed before nature, seemingly yearning to become one with the universe, is apparent in the work of the German Expressionists. Kirchner's coastal landscapes from Fehmarn and grandiose mountain views from Switzerland are similarly subjective projections of empathy with the mysterious forces of nature, as are Nolde's luminous seascapes and flower pictures from the north German plain. Marc and Klee also developed pictorial parallels to the rhythm they perceived flowing through all of nature. While the former found accord between living beings and their environment in his animal pictures, the latter combined color and form into poetic metaphors of the very processes of organic growth.

Their quest for a state of existence untouched by the strictures of modern life led many Expressionists to a new appreciation of primitive art. The tribal craftsman, they felt, not only lived in true harmony with nature, but also worked intuitively, guided solely by religious and spiritual goals. Kirchner played an important role in introducing the other members of Die Brücke to the rich collection of the Ethnological Museum in Dresden where, in 1904, he had encountered African sculptures and masks as well as painted carvings from the South Sea Islands. Most Brücke painters eventually not only owned primitive art themselves but also, as a substitute for Gauguin's life among the natives, adorned their studios with pseudo-primitive wall decorations and statues of their

own design. On the eve of World War I Nolde and Pechstein actually traveled to the South Pacific, and from the mid-1920s on Mueller carried on his search for the primitive among the Gypsy colonies of central Europe. Yet, while they deeply admired primitive art as a genuine form of expression, the artists of Die Brücke never slavishly copied their sources of inspiration. Primitive art served, rather, as an encouragement to explore the expressive possibilities of color and form, resulting, as in Nolde's *Two Peasants* or Schmidt-Rottluff's *Evening by the Sea,* in a generalized evocation of the elemental and archaic.

The painters of Der Blaue Reiter embraced a wider range of primitive art than did the artists of Die Brücke. Campendonk's development, for example, is unthinkable without his contact with the Bavarian peasant tradition of painting on glass, while Klee explored the linear drawing techniques of children. "I want to be as though newborn," Klee wrote in 1902, stating what was to become a fundamental Expressionist belief, "knowing absolutely nothing about Europe, ignoring poets and fashions, to be almost primitive."

Neither did the Expressionists ignore German art of the late Middle Ages. The angular forms, arbitrary proportions, and compressed space in late fifteenth- and early sixteenth-century paintings and prints appealed to them, since here, too, artists had obeyed their inner visions, using nature only as a point of departure. The willfully expressive style of Matthias Grünewald, in particular, became the touchstone of their own efforts to achieve a new synthesis of content and form. For them, Grünewald had used pictorial means entirely in the service of feeling, plumbing the very depths of human misery. An analogous attitude toward the art of the Middle Ages is found in Wilhelm Worringer's book *Problems of Form in Gothic,* 1912, in which the author made a distinction between classical and Gothic art, explaining the former as the result of a harmonious relationship between the artist and his environment and the latter as having sprung from conflict between man and his world. Interestingly, many Expressionists were drawn to religious subjects at various points in their careers, motivated not by any conventionally orthodox considerations, but by the sense of disaffection which, according to Worringer, had given rise to Gothic art. For Nolde, biblical themes offered a refuge from rational existence, and Ernst Barlach's religious imagery stemmed from an intense longing for a new relationship between man and God. Especially during the bitter years of World War I and the period following immediately thereafter, when questions of life and death touched millions and—if humanity were to survive—man's spiritual reorientation became more urgent than ever, themes of guilt and atonement through suffering took on a universal significance. In Christ's Passion, Beckmann found a surrogate for his own anguish. Schmidt-Rottluff, Pechstein, and Christian Rohlfs turned to the Old and New Testaments in search of symbols with which to express their sympathy for their fellowmen.

By the time war broke out in 1914, Expressionism had emerged as a major force in German art. Four cruel years later Marc and Macke were dead, and Kandinsky, Jawlensky, and Kirchner had left Germany. Some of the idealism, however, which had given direction to many works of both Der Blaue Reiter and Die Brücke prior to the war surfaced anew in the optimistic program of the Novembergruppe (November Group), founded in Berlin in the fall of 1918 under the leadership of Pechstein and the painter and stage designer

César Klein in order to help rebuild German society after the chaos of the war. During its brief span of existence in the very center of cultural life in Berlin, the Novembergruppe sought to explore possibilities of cooperation between artists and the socialist state of the nascent Weimar Republic. Through its Workers Council for Art, established in 1919, the group addressed itself to such issues as state support for the arts and the artist's responsibility toward society; through exhibitions, concerts, lectures, and evening classes for working people, it not only strengthened public acceptance of modern art, but also convinced many that social conditions could indeed be improved by an appropriate visual milieu.

The creation of an environment in which man's life achieves dignity and meaning was also the noble objective of the Bauhaus. Founded by the architect Walter Gropius in Weimar in 1919, this school was the only institution to come close to realizing the idealistic goal of placing the various arts collectively in the service of society. Named in analogy to the medieval *Bauhütte,* the cathedral workshop in which artists and artisans worked together to construct one mightly edifice, the Bauhaus was devoted to the investigation of principles of design and structure in the arts and crafts, especially with respect to objects intended to be mass-produced by modern industrial methods. In keeping with the school's lofty aims, Feininger, the first painter to join the Bauhaus staff, illustrated the cover of the initial announcement of the school's program with a woodcut depicting a soaring cathedral illuminated by radiant stars.

Not all artists, however, shared the idealistic aspirations of the Novembergruppe and the Bauhaus. Deeply scarred by the experience of war, men such as Otto Dix, Beckmann, and George Grosz met the physical and moral collapse of German society in the immediate postwar years with disillusionment and cynicism, taking refuge in a harsh and unsentimental form of expression.

At the same time, Expressionism was beginning to reach a wider public, and several of its leading exponents found themselves sought after as teachers. Kandinsky, having returned from Russia, joined Feininger and Klee on the staff of the state-supported Bauhaus. Several artists were appointed to positions at the academies in Dresden (Oskar Kokoschka), Breslau (Mueller), Düsseldorf (Campendonk), and Berlin (Carl Hofer, Pechstein, Schmidt-Rottluff).

But, as the demands for social renewal gradually diminished and youthful ardor was replaced by mature reflection, Expressionism inevitably lost its former urgency. Increasingly preoccupied with problems of pictorial structure from the early 1920s on, the pioneers of the movement began to subordinate the expressive features of their art to aesthetic considerations and eventually committed themselves to a more traditional interpretation of nature. Ironically, German Expressionism in its most authentic form was already a thing of the past when it was ruthlessly suppressed by the National Socialists. Nonetheless, having extolled subjectivity and freedom of expression, it did not fit Hitler's dream of a controlled society, and he had hardly acceded to power in January 1933 when he began his fanatic campaign of vilification against all forms of modern art. The doors of the Bauhaus were closed by the police in March, while Campendonk, Pechstein, Schmidt-Rottluff, and others were either summarily dismissed from their teaching positions or forced to resign before the year was up—a fate that subsequently befell many more. Henceforth, these artists were not only prevented from exhib-

iting their work, but some, like Schmidt-Rottluff and Nolde, were actually forbidden to paint. (pp. 19-26)

Horst Uhr, in an introduction to his Masterpieces of German Expressionism at the Detroit Institute of Arts, *Hudson Hills Press, 1982, pp. 10-28.*

EXPRESSIONIST MUSIC

HENRY A. LEA

[*In the following excerpt, Lea discusses German Expressionist music.*]

Musical Expressionism evolved in Vienna in the first decade of the twentieth century. Its chief composers, Arnold Schoenberg (1874-1951), Alban Berg (1885-1935) and Anton Webern (1883-1945), all began with highly romantic works but soon found this style exhausted and irrelevant. The chromatic and hyperemotional elements of the romantic style, found most notably in Wagner's *Tristan und Isolde,* led inevitably to the dissolution of tonality. It is this so-called atonality— the lack of a tonal or key center as an anchor for melody and form—that chiefly characterizes expressionist music, just as the lack of causality and logical sequence typifies expressionist art and literature.

The works that Schoenberg wrote between 1908 and 1913— following his late-romantic compositions, such as *Verklärte Nacht, Gurrelieder* and *Pelleas und Melisande,* before he reorganized music on the basis of the twelve-tone scale—are the primary examples of musical Expressionism. Its chief characteristics are the suspension of tonality, emotional extravagance, formal freedom, and an atmosphere of existential anxiety. Berg and Webern who shared Schoenberg's musical and spiritual outlook composed similar music, with Berg remaining predominantly expressionist while Webern moved quickly on to serialism. All three composers admired Gustav Mahler (1860-1911) as a visionary and musical nonconformist who anticipated certain stylistic and technical features of Expressionism.

Mahler's music is highly emotional and uses an extremely wide dynamic and instrumental spectrum. He likes to use instruments and voices at the outer limits of their range, which gives the music an irregular or distorted sound. It is a music of sudden contrasts in harmony and melody, pace and rhythm, tone and mood. Using a minimum of ornamentation and transition, it combines the earthy and the exalted, often simultaneously. Mahler writes intensely subjective music, expressing the full range of the composer's feelings in such a way that his music becomes a statement about the human condition.

Generally speaking, Mahler spiritualizes the external by transforming it into inner landscapes. Even when he uses the full orchestra the sound is not descriptive of outer reality, as in Strauss' tone poems, but other-worldly, as in Kokoschka's cityscapes in which the subject is projected into a cosmic perspective. A good example is Mahler's use of cowbells in the *Sixth* and *Seventh Symphonies.* A comparison with Strauss' cowbells in the *Alpine Symphony* shows that Strauss paints a realistic scene of cows grazing on a mountain meadow, whereas Mahler's cowbells, lacking such a context, are symbolic, transfigured sounds that are literally not of this world. Strauss' cowbells are specific and localized; Mahler's are disembodied and suspended in cosmic space. Strauss describes a day in the Alps; Mahler gives an expressionist synthesis of the Alpine spirit.

Closely related is the lack of a specifically national identity in expressionist works, since their setting is usually undefined in time and place. In Mahler, this tendency shows up in the increasingly free use of tonality and in the transformation of marches, dances and folksongs. One of his earliest works, *Waldmärchen* (Part I of *Das klagende Lied*) begins in harmonic ambiguity, with the orchestra playing in two keys simultaneously and thereby undercutting the firm harmonic foundation so characteristic of national music. In some of the later symphonies (Nos. 4, 5, 7 and 9) he abandons the idea of a basic key for an entire symphony altogether, and *Das Lied von der Erde* ends on an open chord, analogous to the open form of expressionist paintings and plays.

Mahler's treatment of marches, dances and folksongs shows a similar tendency to universalize what is inherently specific or regional. The grotesque funeral march in the First Symphony, based on the children's canon "Frere Jacques," monumentalizes this popular, cheerful little ditty by transforming it into a dirge. The piece exemplifies expressionist magnification and distortion: the orchestration is highly unorthodox, particularly in the use of high wood winds and percussion, while the sudden shifts in pace and rhythm and the use of syncopation make this composition a unique mixture of pathos and irony. By integrating the piece into a symphony, with the connotations of nobility and grandeur associated with that form, Mahler elevates this thrice-familiar tune into a "statement" and extends the emotional and stylistic range of the symphonic form.

A more extreme example of this mentality is Schoenberg's use of the well-known German song "Ännchen von Tharau" as the theme for a variation movement in his *Suite* (op. 29)— more extreme because the variations of this simple song, being atonal, remove the song even further from its origin by divesting it of its firm harmonic setting and stylizing it beyond recognition. What is expressionist about this piece is the anti-realist stance, the highly subjective point of view, the strong distortion and the estrangement of the simple-minded, comfortable, familiar and trivial.

Mahler and the Expressionists also radicalized dances, mainly the *ländler* and the waltz. Mahler's scherzos are to an increasing degree demonizations of these popular dances. Most of them begin diatonically, with a few instruments, but soon grow to enormous proportions and literally break open harmonically and rhythmically. An example is the Scherzo of the Fifth Symphony which Mahler makes the pivotal section of the entire work and in which the *ländler* becomes a metaphor for the human comedy; similarly Berg, in his opus 6, transforms the waltz into a dance to the abyss.

In the third movement of the *Third Symphony* an offstage posthorn transmutes a Spanish dance (*jota aragonesa*) into a haunting, lonely melody that suggests a lost paradise. Even in Mahler's wide-ranging work this episode is a remarkable evocation of cosmic musical dimensions. By transforming a popular national dance into an ethereal chant heard at a great distance and placing it at the center of a vast symphonic cosmos, Mahler anticipates certain expressionist tendencies: the

inclusion of widely disparate elements in a work of art, the denationalization of folk art, and the extreme disaffiliation of the artist from mimetic art.

Similar thoughts pertain to the march. Mahler's marches— insistent, vehement, distorted—are important not only as critiques of military music but as an integral structural device suggesting that man's course is a march to heaven or hell, or that life on earth is a martyrdom, in the manner of expressionist passion plays. These marches have stereophonic dimensions of time and space. Most of them are apocalyptic processions or at least suggest a fateful event; some of them, like the Frere Jacques march, are grotesque; all of them are extravagant; they predominate even in Mahler's songs. Marches pervade his music to an extent that exceeds all previous composers, with the possible exception of Tchaikovsky whose view of the march somewhat resembles Mahler's. Noteworthy is the occurrence of marches in opening movements, which is rare in earlier composers. Five of Mahler's symphonies open with marches (nos. 2, 3, 5, 6, 7), and the first movements of his other symphonies have a strongly processional character. His preoccupation with the threatening aspect of the march suggests a prophetic vision of war which also haunted many expressionist writers, especially Georg Heym, Georg Trakl and Albert Ehrenstein.

What sets Mahler's marches apart from those of earlier composers, even Tchaikovsky, is the built-in ironic note: they often sound like parodies of Central European band music. Being socially speaking an outsider, like many Expressionists, Mahler was skeptical about such music because he did not identify with the community which it served. An example is the gigantic march in the first movement of the *Third Symphony* which, as Mahler himself suggested, was influenced by Prussian and Austrian marching bands; but by comparison with their marches, Mahler's march abounds in irregularities: repeated shifts in tempo and harmony, off-beat accents marked "raw!", muted brass, satiric counter-melodies in the high woodwinds, a massive array of percussion instruments, and an ever-quickening pace that escalates the march to bedlam proportions before it collapses. Intentionally or not, it sounds like a band-music extravaganza gone wild, a march that has left military or patriotic or ceremonial considerations far behind; or in expressionist terms, a grotesquely heightened processional that raises the march to a metaphor of worldly tumult and simultaneously calls it into question. The closest expressionist example is the march in Berg's *Three Pieces for Orchestra* (op. 6), a truly Mahleresque work that sounds the death knell of the march.

Another link between Mahler and Expressionism is his conception of the symphony as the record of a spiritual quest. Like an expressionist artist, Mahler "invests forms with spiritual significance." With their ascending structure, from the worldly to the exalted, and their expressed or implied program, his symphonies, notably the metaphysically aspiring *Second, Third, Fourth* and *Eighth Symphonies,* resemble the expressionist *Stationendrama* or pilgrimage play which centers on the protagonist's search for salvation and identifies his soul struggle with the spiritual crisis of the age. As in Expressionism, the loneliness of the quest and the mood of upheaval in these symphonies make the negative examples of this form (the *Sixth* and *Ninth Symphonies* and *Das Lied von der Erde*) artistically more convincing. Mahler shares with the Expressionists an atmosphere of cataclysm, but while in literary Expressionism this is a necessary prelude to a New Man or a new world order, for Mahler it is the end of an era.

Mahler's symphonies and song cycles are the existential statement of a solitary man. As an idealist who fought against philistinism in art and life Mahler struggled largely alone, whereas the Expressionists formed communities, issued pronouncements and even took part in political action. This would have been foreign to Mahler, yet he was artistically speaking an activist. Violating accepted standards of beauty, harmony, balance and restraint, he wrote music of such naked emotional force and arrestingly vivid sound that its expressive weight overburdens the traditional form and harmony he used. One might say that it is unassimilated music, in the sense that it is not in the mainstream and lacks any trace of virtuosity or showmanship. It has something uncomfortable, exaggerated, larger-than-life, "traumatic," which constitutes Mahler's main affinity with Expressionism.

After he heard Mahler's *Third Symphony* under the composer's direction in 1904, Schoenberg wrote to Mahler: "I have seen your soul, naked, stark naked. . . . I saw a man in torment struggling for inner harmony; I sensed a man, a drama, truthfulness, the most relentless truthfulness!" Schoenberg revered Mahler's unsparing commitment as man and artist, his all-embracing music and his sense of mission, but there were also more specific relationships. Mahler had met Schoenberg early in 1904 at a rehearsal for the premiere of *Verkläte Nacht* which made a deep impression on Mahler. When shortly thereafter, in March 1904, Schoenberg and Alexander von Zemlinsky formed an "Association of Creative Musicians" in Vienna to promote the performance of contemporary music, they persuaded Mahler to serve as honorary president and guest conductor. During its first and only season (1904-05) Mahler introduced Strauss' *Sinfonia Domestica* and his own *Kindertotenlieder* and *Wunderhorn* songs, and Schoenberg conducted the first performance of his tone poem *Pelleas und Melisande.* His comprehensive study of harmony, *Harmonielehre* (1911), is dedicated to Mahler's memory.

A compositional link between Mahler and Schoenberg is their effort toward a more sparing, more individualized instrumentation to clarify textures and differentiate the various musical lines from each other. The lines themselves become increasingly angular and intense as they detach themselves from the underlying harmony. The goal is precision and sharpness of definition in opposition to lush writing, just as expressionist painters and writers are at pains to express themselves boldly by using strong, contrasting colors and exclamatory, unlyrical language. Expression of emotions and ideas preempts form and technique. This explains the avoidance of the usual generic forms (sonata, symphony, concerto) with their repetitions and sequential patterns—conventions that clash with the music in Mahler's symphonies. Expressionist music lacks for the most part the emotional and rhetorical argument so typical of romantic and late-romantic music. And it has no relation to nature, in contrast to Mahler's music, and completely lacks the expansive and pictorial quality of romantic music. Unlike Romantics and Impressionists, Expressionists do not depict; they create inner worlds.

The shift from Romanticism to Expressionism is palpable in Schoenberg's *First Chamber Symphony* (op. 9; 1906), a fascinating transitional work that Stuckenschmidt calls "the last tonal work of his early years." Though written in E major the

work is so chromatic that the few pure chords sound utterly incongruous. Apart from its unresolved dissonance, the expressionist aspects are the emotional intensity, the abrupt contrasts, the wide intervals in the musical line, the lightness and sharpness of its scoring, its uncompromising somberness, and the combination of high-voltage music and carefully wrought polyphony. Schoenberg writes music of intricate texture which brings together many disparate voices in an asymmetrical structure.

The *First Chamber Symphony* demanded much of performers and listeners. Many listeners hissed and left the hall during its first performance in Vienna on February 8, 1907. Its eerie blend of Romanticism and Expressionism shows Schoenberg on the way to a new style that is far more radical, at least for the listener, than any previous development in modern musical history.

The *Second String Quartet* (op. 10; 1907-08) is listed as being in F sharp minor. The first movement is written in this key and the quartet ends in an F sharp major chord, but the last movement does not have a key designation—the first piece by Schoenberg without an identified key. Schoenberg wrote that the quartet contained tonal chords at major structural points, but that "the overwhelming number of dissonant sounds can no longer be balanced by the occasional use of such tonal chords as are commonly employed to express a tonality." His reference to "the Procrustean bed of tonality" expresses his impatience with traditional composition and his compelling need to transcend it. The last two movements of the quartet are settings of two poems from Stefan George's *Der siebente Ring,* "Litanei" and "Entrückung." "Entrückung," describing the poet's withdrawal from familiar surroundings to uncharted regions, characterizes Schoenberg's search for new musical horizons.

Early in 1908 Schoenberg had begun the setting of a self-contained cycle of fifteen poems from Stefan George's *Buch der hängenden Gärten* and completed the work in the following year. The choice of George seems odd: his aristocracy of style and form seems antithetical to Schoenberg's vehement expressiveness. George's elitist aesthetic is the opposite of Schoenberg's volatile music which democratically gives equal value to all notes. The composer later said that these highly structured poems served to give structure to his music. Actually his music is more moderate in this work, in keeping with the dour tone of the poems which deal with the waxing and waning of a love. There are only a few expressionist outbursts, for example, toward the end of the fourth song when the glance of the beloved first reaches the lover. The very brief fourteenth song is one of those ghostly aphorisms which Adorno finds expressionistically bold, abstract and unstructured. Citing Schoenberg's essay "Das Verhältnis zum Text" with its emphasis on freely improvising on a poem rather than illustrating or depicting its content, Adorno concludes that Schoenberg composed against or away from a text.

In view of the repeated choice of *fin-de-siecle* texts by Schoenberg, Berg and Webern, the question arises whether they intended to set them off against the music or whether these poems simply appealed to them. Though the bleak atonal music does set off the rich imagery of the poems, the latter seems more likely, because this music possesses a similar *fin-de-siecle* quality, except that it is more searing and less resigned, which has to do with the difference in medium and the composers' less passive temperament. Moreover, expressionist poems began to appear somewhat later. Another difference is that the atonal music conveys none of the poems' nature symbolism. What it does convey is the interiority of George's lyrics and their declamatory style. Rosen notes that the Schoenberg-George cycle has an "implacably hostile view of the exterior world."

About the George songs, Schoenberg wrote that he was aware "of having broken all bonds of a bygone aesthetic" and that he was "following an inner compulsion which is stronger than upbringing." The year of their completion, 1909, was astonishingly productive for Schoenberg. He also composed the *Three Pieces for Piano* (op. 11), *the Five Pieces for Orchestra* (op. 16) and the opera *Erwartung* (op. 17).

The Five Pieces for Orchestra are Schoenberg's first nonprogrammatic work for full orchestra. The title suggests an "unsymphonic," more concise work that lacks the traditional sonata form because it lacks the tension between tonic and dominant which is the basis of sonata form. This tension is replaced by continual variation of motivic material and instrumental color. Pertinent to Expressionism is the brevity of motifs and their deployment. This resulted, as Rosen well explains, from the rejection of large, formula-type units— "blocks of prefabricated material"—such as ends of sections and accompaniment figures in classical and romantic music. These procedures, having lapsed into mechanical repetition, now sounded stale and superfluous, as in the last movements of Mahler's *Sixth* and *Seventh Symphonies.* This left the composer with only very brief units of music which had to carry the emotional and structural weight of much larger units. Perhaps this is the essence of expressionist music: brief motifs invested to the breaking point with musical intensity.

This intensity is evident in the first and fourth pieces, the shortest, fastest and wildest of the set. They abound in ominous brass snorts, sudden bursts of dissonance, heavy offbeat accents, piercing woodwinds, abrupt breaks, leaping intervals, extreme and sudden dynamic shifts. The other three pieces are quietly atmospheric: the extreme contrast among the five pieces is itself a mark of Expressionism. The most famous piece is the third with its brooding mood and subtly shifting tone color—so different from the impersonal tone painting of the Impressionists. The last piece has the rhythm of a *ländler,* but this is often obscured by the absence of a first beat, either because of a pause or a tie to the previous note. In general, expressionist music notably lacks rhythmic impulse.

The first publication of the *Five Pieces* (1912) had no titles. His publisher then asked Schoenberg to add a title to each piece, evidently to make them more acceptable to the public. The composer yielded reluctantly, making sure that the titles would be too general to give any clue to the music. Expressionist composers seek to avoid programmatic titles and descriptions, in the belief that the music should speak completely for itself. Also, by remaining unspecific, they can elevate the particular to the symbolic—a major tendency of Expressionism.

Schoenberg next composed two one-act stage works, *Erwartung* (op. 17) and *Die glückliche Hand* (op. 18). *Erwartung* was written in 17 days in 1909. A monodrama lasting about half an hour, it has only one character, an unnamed woman whose interior monologue is set to fragmented and overwrought music. Its Expressionism lies first of all in its undefined plot, place and character and its unreal atmosphere. The woman is searching for her lover and finds him mur-

dered, but few details are given. Schoenberg has suggested that it may be an anxiety dream.

The lack of realistic detail is matched by the lack of musical development which has traditionally determined structure and sequence in music. The music follows the broken phrases and jagged emotions of the woman with an even more unstructured score. All the traditional elements of musical form are missing. There are no recognizable themes, there is no tonality, no development, no continuity, no repetition, no variation, no rhythm, and above all, no "sense of cadence." It is an improvisatory work that communicates the woman's fear and memory with unprecedented immediacy, that is, without having undergone a shaping or sublimating process. Like most expressionist works, *Erwartung* is open-ended: after the last words "I was searching . . ." the music fades out in a chromatic scale, as if the woman's fantasy would continue.

In its theme, form and Freudian ambience, *Erwartung* invites a comparison with Strauss' *Salome* (1904-05), that helps define Expressionism. Oscar Wilde's libretto for *Salome* has a luxuriant eroticism that is lacking in Marie Pappenheim's text for *Erwartung*. Strauss writes appropriately lush, "culinary" (in Brecht's sense) music for characters that are bound by their particular identifiable circumstances. Marie Pappenheim's Woman is an existential figure, and the emphasis in her text is on dream versus reality, rather than on good versus evil, as in *Salome.* Schoenberg's music goes far beyond the non-expressionist text to create a work of extreme dissociation. In sum, *Salome* is a post-Wagnerian opera of rich, late-romantic, extroverted music for a well-defined theatrical plot with a beginning, climax and end that presents no musical problems for the listener; *Erwartung* is a Strindbergian outcry that makes severe demands on musicians and listeners and has not been assimilated even after seventy years.

Even more Strindbergian is *Die glückliche Hand* (op. 18), a "drama with music" written between 1910 and 1913. It is more concise than *Erwartung* and more fully formed and continuous. Though there are three characters and a chorus of six men and six women, the plot is again centered in one person, an unnamed Man, the only solo singing voice, who in this case is the Artist. Schoenberg himself wrote the libretto whose title refers to the good fortune of being artistically gifted. In true expressionist manner this work has a message, given by the chorus at the beginning and end: the artist must live for a higher truth rather than for earthly happiness, such as love of woman. Though a woman betrays him, he cannot overcome his desire for her, thereby ignoring his artistic mission. In expressionist terms he fails to achieve spiritual purification.

The staging and scenery for which the composer has given detailed instructions are expressionistically dreamlike and involve elaborate lighting symbolism. The music is highly dissonant and agitated, though somewhat less so than in *Erwartung*. Again it goes far beyond the banalities of the text and raises the question whether Schoenberg needed this kind of text to inflame his musical imagination. Since this is his own text, it is hard to argue, as Adorno does regarding the George cycle, that he is composing away from the text. What can be said is that Schoenberg's music radicalizes the text by abandoning the formal and syntactic conventions which the text still retains. He imposes expressionistic music upon a romantic text, in contrast to Berg whose chosen librettos for *Wozzeck* and *Lulu* already exhibit the dissociation so typical of Expressionism. In *Die glückliche Hand* the combination of literary cliche and searing music creates a work which is curiously out of joint.

The superiority and isolation of the artist in *Die glückliche Hand* is neo-romantic rather than expressionist, but this mixture is also found in contemporaneous expressionist plays by Sorge and Hasenclever, among others, where it develops into a savior complex. The vulgar off-stage music representing the crowd in opposition to the artist's dramatic onstage music—a device used by Mahler in *Das klagende Lied* and elaborated by Berg in *Wozzeck* but with different assumptions—creates a multi-level perspective characteristic of expressionist art. Undoubtedly *Die glückliche Hand* would make an impact on stage that it cannot have on a recording, but it is performed even more rarely than *Erwartung*. With these two stage works musical Expressionism reaches its farthest point.

The breaking open of a neo-romantic poem by expressionist music occurs in the song "Seraphita" (Stefan George's translation of a poem by Ernest Dowson), one of the most extreme of expressionist works. Set to a mystical, symbolist poem, this song, the first of the *Four Orchestral Songs* (op. 22), was written between 1913 and 1915 and is set for soprano and a huge orchestra which is, however, used in a way to set one group of instruments off against another. Since the opening melody contains every note in the chromatic scale, this work provides a bridge to Schoenberg's serial works which began to appear, after a silence of seven years, with the publication of the *Five Pieces for Piano* (op. 23) in 1923. With these pieces Schoenberg began to organize and systematize atonal music, making possible large-scale works but sacrificing much of the free-flowing, improvisatory, unfettered quality of the expressionist works.

Toward the end of his life the composer returned to the expressionist vein in a group of serial works of passionate intensity inspired by political events. The most dramatic of these works is *A Survivor from Warsaw* (op. 46; 1947), a short piece (less than ten minutes) for narrator, men's chorus and orchestra. It is an account of a group of Jewish prisoners about to be killed by the Nazis. As they are ordered by a sergeant to count off, they chant the Hebrew prayer Shema Yisroel. The highly concentrated, deeply moving work evokes the same macabre, nightmarish mood of the expressionist works, but in a topical context that is more characteristic of literary Expressionism. In subject matter it is closely related to Paul Celan's famous poem "Todesfuge," but in contrast to the poem's regular form which seeks to rationalize the irrational and at the same time to show the disparity between long-honored forms and their destruction, Schoenberg's work has the abrupt, jagged, eruptive quality of expressionist art that is appropriate to this eyewitness account. The clashing sounds, vivid orchestral effects and stark contrasts between the victims' screams, the sergeant's shouts and the religious chant make this work a striking example of Expressionism. It is a typically direct, unmediated expression of Schoenberg's feelings. As an outcry against inhumanity it recalls such anti-war poems as Trakl's "Grodek" and Werfel's "Der Krieg." In this work Schoenberg returned to the impassioned Expressionism of his earlier years.

Of the major expressionist composers, Alban Berg is the most accessible. Even his serial works are not strictly atonal, which explains why he has established greater rapport with the public. He met Schoenberg in 1904 and was his student from 1904 to 1910. By comparison with Schoenberg, Berg is musically more sensuous, more rhapsodic, less severe—in short,

more romantic. His style is less angular and less contrapuntal, his rhythm more traditional, his tone less forbidding than Schoenberg's or Webern's. Of these three composers who constitute the so-called Second Vienna Schoool, Berg is musically closest to Mahler and the *fin-de-siecle*. He stylizes marches and dances similarly, but compresses his material to a much greater degree. He uses similar tonal and rhythmic symbolism. And he shares Mahler's sense of personal and cultural catastrophe.

As his operas *Wozzeck* and *Lulu* show, Berg has a sense of theater. Unlike Schoenberg's operas which tend to be soliloquies or dialogues with an ideological program, Berg's are settings of highly dramatic plays of literary merit and human interest, with music that matches the text. In sum, Schoenberg is a more committed theoretician and advocate of the new music who had ties to the expressionist painters, while Berg, being temperamentally less austere, is the less doctrinaire composer of a more literary sensibility.

Of Berg's early work the *Three Pieces for Orchestra* (op. 6; completed in 1914 and dedicated to Schoenberg) is an outstanding example of musical Expressionism. It consists of "Prelude," "Rounds" and "March"—innocent-sounding titles for awesome pieces written for a very large orchestra. Since this work is not atonal—a strong C minor reference persists in "Prelude" and "March"—it is not difficult to listen to. Moreover, by comparison with Schoenberg's expressionist works it retains considerable impetus that recalls romantic music. It also has recurring themes and recognizable endings; quotations from Mahler and Debussy create another link with the past.

As usual in expressionist orchestral music, the instrumentation includes a large number of woodwinds and percussion instruments, including a hammer which is struck at the climax of the March and on its last note. Going beyond Mahler, Berg explodes and distintegrates the waltz and the march. *The March* which was completed on August 23, 1914, shortly after the outbreak of World War I, is a particularly dark work: recalling both symphonic and popular marches it destroys the march as a viable form of music. After the shattering climax (measure 126) only fragments remain.

Adorno, who was a student of Berg, reports that the composer distinguished sharply between symphonic works and character pieces. These are character pieces in the sense that they dispense with sonata form and offer perspectives on particular genres. Adorno interprets "Rounds" and "March" as grim commentaries on nineteenth century genre pieces that had degenerated into banality. He states further that Berg's "incorporation of the banal" into his music explains the "panic," "chaotic" tone of these pieces. This apt description takes account of the expressionist tendency to combine the elevated and the vulgar, yet Berg's pieces are so large in conception and somber in mood that he must have felt, like Mahler, a strong affinity for these forms. The sheer frequency and formal integration of dances and marches in these composers' music show a special kind of affection for these popular forms of music which are so much a part of everyday life in Central Europe—the affection of the sophisticated who are unable to identify with them and prophetically view them as symbols of a dying civilizaton.

The doom-laden mood and monumentalization of dances and marches recur in Berg's opera *Wozzeck* (op. 7; composed between 1917 and 1921 and dedicated to Alma Mahler). This work, a stark drama about a poor soldier who kills the woman he loves, is steeped in military, folkloristic and religious imagery which is distorted by Wozzeck's perspective. Büchner's play, written in 1836, is pre-expressionist in the sense that the realistic small-town background is preempted by the protagonist's visions and fantasies and by the caricatured portraits of his tormentors who are expressionist types without names. The resulting distortion is fully conveyed by the typically hypertrophied music, as for example in Wozzeck's end-of-the-world phantasms that recall the terror of the woman in *Erwartung*. Wozzeck's antagonists are overdrawn by wildly leaping vocal lines and falsetto notes. The march announcing the Drum Major's appearance recalls Mahler in its mixture of pathos and grotesque. But the most Mahleresque, multi-level music occurs in the tavern scene in Act II. There are two separate musics: one played by the main orchestra, the other by the dance orchestra on stage which plays *ländler* and waltzes for the carousing soldiers and apprentices. As Wozzeck watches Marie dance with the Drum Major to the tavern music, he neither speaks nor sings with the dance orchestra, signifying that he does not join the carousal. Between dances, a chorus of apprentices and soldiers bursts out with a romantic German hunting song ("Ein Jäger aus der Pfalz") which resembles the original setting in rhythm but is harmonically so distorted that one can almost speak of a Brechtian *Verfremdungseffekt* ["alienation effect"].

The Brechtian atmosphere is heightened by the instrumentation of the tawdry stage music which consists of two fiddles, a clarinet, an accordion, two to four guitars and a bombardon (bass tuba). The difference between Expressionism and the more realistic Brecht-Weill aesthetic lies in the function of the music and the attitude of the composer. Berg's opera is not didactic and follows no ideology; he does not distance himself from the music or from the text, as Brecht and Weill do. Furthermore, Berg's music is not a critical comment on the text and is not basically satiric. Berg shares Wozzeck's agony; when he introduces the hunting song he does not satirize it as such, but shows the gulf between the singing carousers and the suffering protagonist who is one of the world's hunted. The combination of the intensely dramatic main orchestral music, the cheap tavern music, the distorted folksong and the mostly spoken voice of Wozzeck is a classic example of the dissociative aspect of Expressionism and its tendency to bring together extreme disparities. And finally, Berg appeals to a much more limited audience than Brecht-Weill.

Much of the text of *Wozzeck* is declaimed in a *parlando* voice that makes the words more clearly audible, while retaining the emotional involvement that Brecht dismissed as "culinary." The score is extremely complex and uses traditional formal devices, such as passacaglia, fugue, sonata, rhondo, theme and variations, but as in other expressionist works these cannot be detected on hearing the music and are probably used to control the extreme expressivity of the music. Because it is a stage work of intense human emotions and because text and music are so well matched, *Wozzeck* is probably the most accessible work of musical Expressionism.

A more contained expressionist work is Berg's *Violin Concerto* (1935). As a piece of absolute music in a traditional form, it is a more composed work; as a personal memorial to a dear friend and as his last work, it has a transfigured quality unique among expressionist compositions. Its inner program deals with life, death and resurrection, a familiar pattern in

expressionist works. As in much expressionist music there are dissonant climaxes that mark a crisis, but in this work the first crisis leads to a chorale and the second to a serene close. The chorale is quoted from Bach's *Cantata No. 60,* with words written into the score by Berg that promise release in heaven from earthly woes. After the solo violin's intense variations on this theme, a reminiscence of a Carinthian *ländler* from the first movement is heard "at a great distance but much more slowly that the first time;" the chorale returns and leads to the work's conclusion on an open chord, like the chord at the close of *Das Lied von der Erde,* that suggests musical and spiritual infinities.

This work, too, though serial, is not fully atonal. Its instrumentation is more modest; exceptions are an alto saxophone (also used by Berg in the opera *Lulu* and the concert aria *Der Wein*) and the large number of percussion instruments that include a high and a low gong. The music ranges from jagged brass outcries to the peaceful opening and closing pages. In combining a Bach chorale with a Carinthian folksong, the composer encompasses the religious and the secular, the exalted and the popular in a remarkable and moving synthesis that marks the swan song of musical Expressionism. The circumstances of this rhapsodic work, its haunting music, the composer's imminent death and the engulfing political catastrophe in Expressionism's home base make the Berg *Violin Concerto* a retrospective and prophetic work in the history of modern music.

The link with Romanticism is very strong in musical Expressionism. The wide instrumental, dynamic and emotional range, the leaping phrases, the lack of rhythmic variety, the preference for vocal settings and the element of the fantastic show a close kinship with German romantic music. The big difference is the lack of tonality in expressionist music. It is the conflict between the recognizable provenance of this music and its extremely dissonant setting that makes it so strange to listen to.

Tonality in music may be likened to realism in literature and perspective in painting, but it is more deeply ingrained than either of them. Its abandonment is therefore a more radical development that the abandonment of realism. Giving up tonality makes music, the most abstract art, even more abstract. It is for this reason that expressionist music is harder to understand than expressionist literature and art. An important factor is the difference in medium. One can look at an expressionist painting or read an expressionist poem more easily because their representationalism does not depart from previous art or literature as greatly as works of musical Expressionism do from their predecessors. Furthermore, a painting or poem can be apprehended more directly—without the mediation of performers or previous technical knowledge—than a musical work.

Tonal music is in some way, no matter how distantly, derived from or related to folksong or dance. This is not the case with expressionist music which is both harmonically and rhythmically far removed from the pulse and spirit of folk music. Unlike the music of Bartok and Stravinsky, whose relation to folk music is more direct, expressionist music is highly stylized, lacking in rhythmic drive, and forbiddingly esoteric. It is extremely sophisticated music, being highly thought out and texturally complex. Having said this, one must also acknowledge its expressive power. At its best it reaches deep into the psyche; beginning with the piercing outburst in the first movement of Mahler's unfinished *Tenth Symphony,* this music is a cry from the depths. It expresses terror, agony, anguish, chaos, shock. More than expressionist art and literature which have an ecstatic dimension, expressionist music is somber and foreboding. It is music of unrelieved grimness.

For these reasons it remains a difficult stumbling block for listeners and even performers. Its importance lies in greatly extending the expressive and technical range of music, in its power to communicate spiritual torment. In contemporary music this influence can be heard in the compositions of Luciano Berio, Krzystof Penderecki and George Rochberg, to name only a few. While Expressionism has been most successful in the plastic arts, its impact on music has been the most radical. (pp. 315-29)

> Henry A. Lea, "Musical Expressionism in Vienna," in Passion and Rebellion: The Expressionist Heritage, edited by Stephen Eric Bronner and Douglas Kellner, J.F. Bergin Publishers, 1983, pp. 315-31.

EXPRESSIONISM AND POLITICS

HELMUT GRUBER

[*Gruber is a German-born historian and critic. In the following excerpt, he discusses the philosophical principles and political goals of the Expressionists.*]

Today, the public, following the lead of literary critics and historians, has consigned the writer to a stylistic and personal *Erewhon* from which he rarely ventures. In our age of experts, says Walter Sokel, we recognize the writer as an expert too, but only as an expert for the fabrication of linguistic patterns. "The present day writer must well look back with uncomprehending amazement to the arrogance which made the Expressionist hurl maledictions against his age and call, without the least self-irony, for the regeneration of mankind. How, our contemporary marvels, could the Expressionist have the stamina to step so far out of his expert's role which was, after all, nothing more than putting words together to desired effect? How could he dare to prescribe remedies and preach salvation which was not his business at all?" To be sure the aims of the Expressionists were often vague and their results confused. At times they appeared to be rebels without a clear cause, but they were among the first to feel the political awareness and responsibility that was to erupt among intellectuals everywhere in the years between the Great Depression and the Second World War. In the valiant attempt of Expressoinist writers to join art and politics lies one of the trends of modern literature that in the present thirst for revision is made to appear negligible.

It was the war that made Expressionism a fashionable intellectual movement even though its artistic novelty and contribution lay in the works of Reinhard Sorge, Carl Hauptmann, Carl Sternheim, Georg Trakl, Georg Heym, Ernst Stadler, Jocab van Hoddis and others, written between 1910 and 1914. Some Expressionists exhibited a political-ethical concern before World War I. This can be seen in the plays of Sternheim and Sorge and in the pages of *Die Aktion* which combined radicalism in politics and esthetics from its beginning in 1911. Heinrich Mann, who became the intellectual ancestor and advisor of later Expressionism, laid the political cornerstone of the movement in his essay of 1910 titled *Geist und Tat*. Here he directed German writers to become agitators and to ally themselves with the people against authority.

The Expressionists' conception of their work as a means in the awakening and instigation of the public made them ideologists as much as artists, but they were neither clear nor in complete agreement about the means of carrying out their mission. They were tormented by the incompatibility between their desire to be "acknowledged legislators" and the unprincipledness, temporizing, and violence of the world of practical politics. They appear to have been torn between their highly developed egos, which cast them as prophet-preachers into the midst of political currents, and their equally active superegos, which held them ethically aloof from the battle lines. Their sincere attempts, in their programs and manifestos, to resolve this conflict underlined their contradictions and self-doubts.

The Expressionists believed that there is an integral relationship between literature and politics. Their attempts to define it represented variations on a commonly accepted theme. Ernst Toller, Walter Hasenclever, and Johannes Becher were most representative of the belief that literature was capable of effecting profound changes in society. Their outlook was shared by Leonhard Frank, Kurt Hiller, Klabund, Ludwig Rubiner, George Kaiser, Rudolf Leonhard, and Reinhard Goering. "We often ask ourselves," said Toller, "can art influence reality? Can the writer at his desk influence the politics of his time? There are authors who answer this question in the negative; I in the affirmative." In commenting on an earlier introduction to his play *Der Sohn*, Hasenclever maintained that "this play was written in the Fall of 1913 and had the purpose of changing the world."

The widespread conviction among Expressionists that their literature could be an instrument of political action and social change often turned the writer into a militant agitator. Becher's directive to the writer was a call to arms.

> Der Dichter meidet strahlende Akkorde
> Er stößt durch Tuben, peitscht die Trommel schrill.
> Er reißt das Volk auf mit gehackten Sätzen.
>
> ["The writer shuns radiant harmony
> He blasts on tubas, flogs the drum piercingly.
> He tears open the nation with butchered sentences."]

More explicit was Toller's admission that in 1917 he regarded the drama as a means of propaganda in the service of revolution.

> In 1917 I considered the drama [*Die Wandlung*] as a broadsheet and handbill. I read scenes from it aloud to a group of young people in Heidelberg and wanted to uproot them (incite them against the war!). After my expulsion from Heidelberg I went to Berlin and again gave a reading of the play. It was always with the intention of arousing the apathetic, of inducing the reluctant to march, of pointing the way for the groping—and of winning them all for essential and detailed revolutionary labor.

Elsewhere Toller attempted to draw a distinction between political propaganda and political literature. Without deviating from his affirmation of the writer's political responsibility, he warned against turning literature into sheer propaganda and stressed the importance of "throwing light on human conduct" and awakening "the tragic sense of life." As we shall see Toller became increasingly disillusioned about the possibility of being an individual and mass-man at the same time. Only a few Expressionists took the path of subservience to political parties. Karl Otten, for example, declared himself to be a communist. He demanded that every revolutionary writer devote himself to furthering communism, correcting the errors of the German people, and subordinating literature to the exigencies of party politics.

A number of Expressionists, among them Kurt Pinthus, Ludwig Rubiner, Alfred Wolfenstein, René Schickele, and Fritz von Unruh, made the relationship between literature and society appear to be subtle and indefinable. The most general description of this relationship was that of Rubiner who argued that "every spoken word happens upon the world like a seed that produces facts. Every spoken word is a foreword to men's actions." Although Rubiner attempted to indicate the influence of literature on events, his vague formulation expressed little more than the axiom that the reader is affected by what he reads. More pointed perhaps—if one can understand the meaning of "the politics of mankind"—was Pinthus' appraisal of the connection between poetry and politics.

> The newest poetry [is] political poetry—political poetry of a higher order, for it does not strive for the overthrow or victory of political parties and politicians but for the politics of mankind and humanity from which alone, after the present chaos, the necessary construction can follow in art as well as in the formation of states [Staatengestaltung].

If the Expressionists were uncertain about the link between literature and politics, it was because of their desire to be both artists and ideologists and fear lest a preference for one weaken or annul the other. The proper balance between—or blending of—the commitment of the creative artist and the commitment of the tract writer was one of the Expressionists' most serious and presistent problems. They saw the strongest link between literature and politics in their own role as leaders. In the words of Klabund they were "God's silver sons," the "soldiers of the only salvation." They seemed to think that since the traditional leadership of society had not succeeded in keeping it from decaying, the responsibility for leading the reconstitution of society must fall on the writer. Rubiner, who believed that "the poet's effect is a thousand times stronger than that of the [practical] politician," attempted to show that the political poet's "goal is not to move his public but to lead it." Hasenclever directed the poet who would be a politician to leave his ivory tower and become a popular leader. (pp. 186-89)

At times this notion of leadership bordered on mania. Throughout his life Ernst Toller was driven by a sense of guilt about what he had not accomplished as a leader. He assumed personal responsibility for disasters which befell causes in which he had taken an active part. Somehow he held himself responsible for the failure of the Bavarian Soviet Republic, the collapse of the Weimar Republic, and the defeat of the Spanish Loyalists. Convinced that he had failed to forestall a number of catastrophies and filled with guilt about the suffering brought on innocent people by the causes he had supported, he committed suicide in a New York hotel room in 1939. Toller seemed to attribute powers to himself far greater than an individual, even a leader, could hope to command, and his guilt was out of proportion to his actual activities as

writer and crusader. The Zarathustrian powers and privileges claimed for the writer by Georg Kaiser illuminates the exaggeration of leadership by some Expressionists. Kaiser was convicted for selling furnishings and *objets d'art* from a house he had rented and sentenced to six months in prison. He defended himself by claiming to be beyond good and evil. He asserted that the artist, unfettered by the limitations of the philistine world, is entitled to steal in order to create.

Some Expressionists who regarded themselves as leaders thought of setting a model for others rather than of directing them. Although Paul Kornfeld called the artist the only savior, he insisted that salvation could not come about through social action. He refused to equate the artist's role with the improvement of man's physical condition and upbraided those writers who had catered or pandered to the masses. He insisted that the Expressionist must exercise his leadership by being above practical politics, by transforming himself into a worthy example for others. Arthur Holitscher carried this thought one step further by making the leader into a religious figure. He claimed that the function of these religious "magnetic personalities" is not to force formulas on others but to let the people sense (herausfühlen) a law from their profound and inexplicable natures. Having no clear conception of how they were to realize the idea of leadership, the Expressionists foundered on their own generalizations and consequently fell back on abstractions that were as unclear to them as to their audience.

Many Expressionists underwent a transformation in the front lines. They were so overwhelmed by events that their accepted beliefs were suddenly shaken, and they were gripped by the burning desire to discover the true purpose of life. They realized that war would have to be abolished for all time but believed that only the brotherhood of man would make such a plan feasible. Upon returning to their homes these men discovered that "soldiers of peace" were everywhere held in contempt. War had not been a catharsis for those who had not been at the front. The old chauvinism and warmongering continued as if no war had taken place. The Expressionists became convinced that the memory of war must be kept constantly before the eyes of the people. Armin Wegner maintained that war, as a weapon of peace, must continue to strike terror into the hearts of men. He prescribed one hundred years of nightmares "until the crimes of this century will be blotted out and men . . . recognize that no power but love may move their hearts."

Prompted by their revulsion against war the Expressionists became pacifists. Schickele went so far as to equate Expressionism with pacifism. Their mission was clearly to impress the absolute need for peace on the present and future generations. They all were in agreement with Klabund's essay "Bußpredigt" in which he asserted that the intellectuals were partly responsible for the war because they had failed to foresee it and, after its outbreak, to act against it. The writers can justify their existence, he concluded, only if they will launch a furious protest against the ideology of war.

A large number of Expressionists, including Hiller, Toller, Rubiner, Becher, Otten, Leonhard, Hasenclever, Wolfenstein, Klabund, L. Frank, Pinthus, Holitscher, Alfred Ehrenstein, Jomar Förste, and Armin Wegner considered the promotion of pacifism to be one of the most important political activities of the writer. They came to be known as "activists," a term coined in 1915 by Kurt Hiller, editor of *Das Ziel*, who with Heinrich Mann was the leader of the active pacifists in

Berlin. This group adopted the ideals of liberty, equality, and human brotherhood. The functions and goals of activism were laid down by Hiller in a manifesto in which the activist was described as a conscientious objector and leader in the struggle against conscription, a striker against armament production, and a wartime saboteur in word and deed. He was further characterized as the *true* patriot and champion of national defense, for he defended his countrymen from the danger that threatened them most—being killed. Hiller went on to say that he who died in the cause of pacifism died for life itself.

Although this program appeared to be practical politically, the activists were in conflict about the details of its realization. One question undermined the efficacy of their program: How can one actively combat war without the use of violence? This question proved unanswerable, for the activists' belief in participation was coupled with an even stronger affirmation of the sanctity of life—particularly the lives of others. Rudolf Leonhard gave voice to an idea that was to lead the activists into repeated contradictions.

> I am not completely against one's letting himself be killed for an idea but I am against one's killing for an idea. . . . Die for the idea—better yet, don't die—but die as you want and must without killing others.

Leonhard was anxious to provide pacifism with offensive weapons but could not find a way to overcome the activist's inconsistency. He did avow that force may be used, but added that it will be necessary only against force. The weapons of which he approved were the strike and boycott, but they were under the stricture of non-violence. Activists like Hiller, Toller, Rubiner, Leonhard, and Hasenclever believed that party politics should be subordinated to the pursuit of pacifism. Even socialism was awarded a secondary place, for the abolition of fratricide was deemed more important than the destruction of capitalism. Hiller distinguished between murder and killing for an ideal but condemned both.

> Certainly of two such mass-slaughterers as Trotsky and Horthy . . . Trotsky is the lesser evil. The murder which he commands is murder in the service of a progressive idea. But the spirit commands: don't murder even for the loftiest idea, for no idea is loftier than the living.

One group of Expressionists, including Kornfeld, Schickele, Unruh, S. Zweig, Däubler, and Werfel, was content to let their interpretation of pacifism rest on a general protest against war, for they were afraid that pacifism might be interpreted as a program for action. Schickele, one of the spokesmen of this group, attempted to make clear that pacifism was a spiritual frame of mind.

> Those people are mistaken who expect more from pacifism than the restoration and—if I may say so—consolidation of an atmosphere and [thereby] they wrong the representative leaders of pacifism. Pacifism is not a political movement but a spiritual state of mind in which individuals find and assert themselves and in which they act.

There can be no doubt that the Expressionists were tied to the war. Their work and lives attest the magnetic attraction of this event. In their struggles on behalf of peace they appear to have been unable to rise above the inconsistencies inherent in pacifism. Those who were passive were satisfied to relegate

peace to the realm of the spirit. For them, pacifism, like charity, began at home, and they hoped to make themselves a living model of non-violence before the world. They were unable to show how or why the regeneration of a single individual could affect mankind. The activists' position was even more ambivalent, for they desired to act on behalf of peace and, at the same time, abhorred force. Surely they knew those in Germany who supported ideas and conditions leading to war were prepared to act and did so. Yet, they were unable to reconcile the conflicting aspects of their idealism. The Expressionists never asked themselves whether peace could really be achieved by other than practical political means. They were so convinced that brute force could be replaced by the force of an ideal made imperative in poetry and drama that they refused to consider the possible ubiquity of human aggressiveness. They regarded the idea that man's aggressive tendencies might be diverted into channels other than warfare as a half-way measure of practical politics, and clung to the belief that "true" pacifism could eradicate aggressiveness altogether.

The theme of war and peace provided the steppingstone to the Expressionists' highest goal—the molding of the future. With a dogged persistence this generation of writers labored to bring the future into existence in the present, and to do so it acted as prognosticator and herald, as sibyl and the gods on Olympus.

Into whose hands shall the creation of the future world be entrusted? Kurt Pinthus, one of the important Expressionist literary critics, asserted that man, not the creature of flesh and blood but "infinite man," will perform this task. His conclusion summarized the movement's almost blind faith in the powers and abilities of the individual. Paul Kornfeld insisted that man's tremendous potentialities had to be studied and understood. He did not mean the superficial surface qualities of "psychological man" but the unique qualities of "souled man." Then everyone would be able to realize that an individual act of humanity could lift the world out of its axis. Most Expressionists rejected a psychological view of man because it made the individual appear to be inherently frail rather than omnipotent. Kasimir Edschmidt declared that the absence of traditional psychology was the essence of Expressionism. Kornfeld concluded that "psychology reveals as little about the nature of man as anatomy." This was an example of the Expressionists' unwillingness to define the nature of man in particular terms. They preferred to view him as an irreducible entity governed by his soul but willfully able to determine his future. In a world filled with dualities, reasoned Rubiner, man can and must decide between them.

> The world is good or evil. Just or unjust. Love or violence. Freedom or slavery. All above, beyond, or between that is deception. Deception in favor of evil, injustice, violence, slavery. Decision! And every man must decide anew each day and for all eternity for justice, devotion, and freedom.

Some of the more politically sophisticated Expressionists found it difficult to accept the idea that the individual is the only agent for reconstructing society. They were often swayed by philosophies emphasizing the importance of dialectics and the masses in the progressive march of mankind. While on trial as one of the leaders of the Bavarian Soviet Republic, Ernst Toller steadfastly maintained that the revolution of the masses could not be destroyed by the imprisonment and execution of its leaders. Behind this facade of political stalwartness were Toller's own doubts. By 1921 he had brought them into the open in his drama *Masse-Mensch*. More than a decade later he further exposed the workings of his hyper-sensitive conscience in his autobiography.

> Isn't man an individual and a mass-man at one and the same time? Isn't the struggle between the individual and the masses played out in man's mind as well as in society? As individual he acts in accordance with what he considers a moral idea. He is willing to serve it even if the world is destroyed in the process. As mass-man he is driven by social impulses and wants to reach his goal even if he has to sacrifice his moral idea.

In the midst of contemporary ideologies, movements, violence, revolution, political upheaval, and inflation, all of which made the life of the individual more and more uncertain and subject to the pressures of organizations, the Expressionists continued to believe in the power of the single human. From among the mass of individuals a new man was to arise not only with a Nietzschean will but also with the purity and selflessness of Saint Francis. The whole existence of these men was to be devoted to leading mankind into the future. Below the surface of this sublime vision there were serious discrepancies.

Many Expressionists agreed with Georg Kaiser that "man is perfect from the beginning." They believed that his limitations did not spring from his inner nature but were imposed on him from without, and that, endowed with the spark of inner purity, man showed promise of being renewed. Although they held society responsible for man's spiritual perversion, the Expressionists decided that it was more important to restore man from within than to alter society's effect on him, or at least they believed that the alteration of society depeded upon the transformation of man. The conviction became widespread that the discoveries, or laws, or inventions of the world could not save man; that only *he* could save himself. But how?

The Expressionists were unable to answer this question in anything but the most general and abstract terms. Although Unruh insisted that no outside miracle could accomplish it, he did no more than suggest the miraculous transformation of everyman. Rubiner also suggested that every man had the potential to become the leader of society. The new man was so pure and intellectual, so idealized and visionary, that he overstepped even the liberal bounds of literary verisimilitude. "It is not to important," wrote Kaiser, "that man should be able to do something as that he should be recognized. Man that is recognized becomes a reality. . . . I believe in this man to come, and belief is enough." The yearning for a new man meant also the yearning for a new world. For Becher this world represented a generation's desire to be different and the wish to make the twentieth century stand out against the century of its fathers. Wolfenstein considered it to be much more than merely a time of peace. Peace, after all, only followed war and alternated with it like day and night. The new world was to be beyond anything imagined so far; it was to be a creation of something that had never existed. Some Expressionists called it immediately into being. René Schickele hopefully dated its beginning from the outbreak of the November Revolution of 1918.

Virtually no one dared to say what the new world would really be like. Rubiner thought of it as the triumph of rationalism through which man would become the measure of all things.

He considered it to be the apogee of the three great periods of modern history.

> The geocentric consciousness: astrology, or: the cosmos exists for the sake of the individual. The heliocentric consciousness: natural science, or: the individual exists for the sake of the cosmos. The humanocentric consciousness: global orientation, or: man exists for the sake of man.
> Future of the next epoch: Man in the center!

Hiller was willing to be more specific. He called the new world a paradise that was utopian but not fantastic. It resembled a large city rather than the Garden of Eden, and all of its inhabitants were allowed to express their vitality. They lived in this paradise of man with the happiness of unconscious creatures but without the dullness of unconsciousness, for here there was not poverty only a variety of needs, no sickness only turgor. There was also "enmity but no malice, hatred for the sake of love but no lying, . . . activity but no work, enterprise but no service."

On occasion the Expressionists tried to examine and evaluate their utopian ideas, but in spite of the apparent unreality of their visions they refused to abandon them. Kornfeld, for instance, declared that to believe that everyone on earth will become good and pure was utopian, but to believe that man will be able to elevate himself through practical politics was nonsense. He concluded, therefore, that it would be better to strive for a utopia than to move along a hopeless path that would rob man of his utopian vision and the desire to realize it.

The belief in utopias was widespread during the height of the movement between 1917 and 1921. That the writers' conception of the future should have been utopian rather than practically political can be partially explained by the disrepute of traditional politics in intellectual circles. The feeling was current that politics, which had been largely responsible for tension and disorder within the nation, would sully any scheme for reconstruction. This attitude does not sufficiently explain why the Expressionists planned their regeneration of the world around the new man—an idealization of the individual. Surely, among them there must have been some who realized that ideologies, class interest, and power structures could not simply be wished or willed away. Not even the most politically committed writers, who proclaimed themselves propagandists, were able to propose anything but an imprecise and lukewarm humanitarianism. Perhaps the Expressionists chose the transforming power of the individual over the social and political action of the masses because they could not overcome their middle-class origins and ties; or their choice may have been determined by their overabundant ego, which projected the individual writer into the role of leader and savior.

There were few Expressionists who were not goaded into action by events in the postwar period. Most direct was their participation in the November Revolution of 1918 and the revolutions that continued throughout Germany until the summer of 1919. During the period they contributed idealistic and inflammatory speeches, read snatches of their latest works before mass audiences, and participated as rank and file and leaders of revolutionary organizations and governments. Pinthus acted as chairman of a Soldiers' Council during the November Revolution in Berlin, Leonhard was a functionary of the Spartacists during the January 1919 uprising in Berlin, and Ernst Toller and Klabund were officials of the Bavarian Soviet Republic in April 1919. Even Franz Werfel, who was basically apolitical, took to the barricades as a Red Guardist in a moment of revolutionary fervor.

A general sympathy with socialism led many Expressionists to become active in political parties of the left. Between 1917 and 1920 Becher, Brecht, Klabund, L. Frank, Hiller, Hasenclever, Leonhard, Rubiner, Pfemfert, Pinthus, Wolfenstein, Otten, Piscator, and Schickele were for some time affiliated with the Independent Socialist party (USPD). The large, well established Socialist party (SPD) received little if any support from the Expressionists, primarily because of its support of the war. In addition, its bureaucracy of union officals and party functionaries looked with suspicion on intellectuals who claimed to be leaders and who wanted to educate the party leadership rather than carry out the petty tasks of ordinary members. The USPD was created in opposition to the SPD support of the war. It abounded in theoreticians and intellectuals, and its lack of an established hierarchy made it possible for newcomers and new ideas to become prominent without having to work their way through a bureaucratic labyrinth.

A few Expressionists became well-known political figures. Ernst Toller's political career began in 1917 when he founded the pacifistic Cultural-Political Union of German Youth. To the strike in Munich that year he contributed broadsides with scenes from his drama *Die Wandlung* and also acted as a delegate for the stike committee. Following a short prison term, Toller became active among the young radicals surrounding the Bavarian Independent Socialist Kurt Eisner. After Eisner's assassination he became a leader in the Bavarian Soviet Republic, and after its collapse was tried for treason and sentenced to five years in prison.

One might expect that as active politician forced to make exigent decisions Toller should not have been plagued by the ambiguities and inconsistencies that troubled him as a writer, but this was not so. From the beginning of his Munich experience he was torn between his revolutionary zeal and his abhorrence of violence. Unable to accept the maxim about breaking eggs to make an omelette, he proposed to his fellow revolutionaries that they create a "dictatorship of love." In the midst of uncertain and fluid political conditions in Munich (the revolutionary government was never secure) he took a principled position that was ethically worthy but dangerously impractical. While in prison he remained politically active—he was elected to the Bavarian *Landtag* as an Independent Socialist and contributed articles to various publications—but was unable to resolve the conflict between his revolutionary and pacifistic self.

During the period of Toller's political notoriety Kurt Hiller, active as pacifist and essayist, was busy organizing intellectuals for politcal action. He refused to approve of any political party, for even the most pacifistic or radical party was based on government by the majority, which he considered government by mediocrity. As an alternative to democracy he suggested "Logokratic" or rule by an intellectual elite. To promote this idea he helped to organize the *Politischer Rat Geistiger Arbeiter*. Its program was a combination of activist pacifism, political action, economic reform, and utopianism. It proposed the formation of a league of nations and world parliament, the universal abolition of conscription and the prohibition of all military arrangements, the punishment by economic sanctions of all disturbers of peace, the just distribution of material possessions and the confiscation of "excess"

property, and the abolition of capital punishment. Members of this select organization were not to be elected; they appointed themselves by virtue of the "Kraft der Pflicht des Geistes zur Hilfe" ["power of the duty of the spirit to help"]. The most important provision of the program placed the government of Germany in the hands of representatives of the *Reichstag* and of the *Politischer Rat*.

With one stroke Hiller propelled the intellectual and artist into power, but his feat was accomplished only on paper. There were at the time numerous pressure groups in Germany that wished to assume political power, but they struggled toward their goal in accordance with a realizable plan. Hiller and most Expressionists failed to formulate schemes that might be translated from fancy into fact. Simply to propose a government dominated by highminded intellectuals and artists and to leave it at that was to invite ridicule and indifference. Yet more than fifty Expressionists approved Hiller's program. Among them were: Kasimir Edschmidt, Rudolf Kayser, Rudolf Leonhard, Kurt Pinthus, René Schickele, Fritz von Unruh, and Paul Zech. The Expressionists simply did not recognize the impracticality and hopelessness of their own and their fellow writers' formulations. When they did propose to become participants in politics, they often did so only on exaggerated idealistic terms that isolated them from the mainstream of political life.

The Expressionists' party affiliations were generally of short duration and involved frequent changes. During the height of revolutionary activity in 1918-1919 a number of writers, among them Becher, L. Frank, Leonhard, Rubiner, Pfemfert, and Otten, switched from the USPD to the more radical Spartacists, but few of them were to make the transition to the Communist Party (KPD). Only Johannes Becher and Karl Otten committed themselves to communism and only Becher remained a loyal spokesman for the party in later years. The extreme right with its symbols of folk, blood, and nation attracted Kurt Heynicke who became a Nazi sympathizer and Hans Johst who became the literary spokesman of the Third Reich. While the left in Germany was in flux and a political and social revolution still seemed possible most Expressionists identified with the left and were attracted to personalities such as the Independent Socialist Kurt Eisner and the dynamic Communist party leader Paul Levi. By the end of 1920, when the left had crystallized into the Social Democratic and Communist parties, most Expressionists had become convinced that their salvational program could not be achieved through party politics.

Participation in the world of affairs and the unlikelihood of drastic changes in German society helped to disillusion the Expressionists. By 1920 there were many whose belief in their mission had been shaken. Within the next few years they were overcome by a sense of failure. In their desire to retrench emotionally and intellectually they often turned their backs on the idealistic goals of their generation. In a letter written from prison in 1919, Toller poured out his heart to Unruh. "You are right," he wrote, "the ghosts of rottenness are more impudent than ever. Every day as I read the newspaper, I can smell the stench of decay." A year later, having become even more skeptical, he wrote: "I have believed in the redemptive power of Socialism; that, perhaps, was my 'life-lie'." Kornfeld had also had his fill of grandiose principles. "Enough of war and revolution and of the salvation of the world," he cried. "Let us be modest and devote ourselves to other, lesser things." Even Unruh, the staunch democrat, was discouraged by life in Weimer Germany. In an address during 1922 he told an audience of ten thousand that the fatherland of force had been recreated; that all those conditions that had led to war had been left unchanged or had been allowed to sprout again.

These testimonies of personal dejection were matched by the resignation of those Expressionists who summed up the failure of their generation. In the prologue to the last important Expressionist anthology published in 1921, Rudolf Kayser surrendered to a Spenglerian pessimism. He saw his time as one of decline; only the end of the era seemed clearly marked. Quietly he accepted the bitter fate of his generation. "Today, after years of youthful tumult, inflammatory exclamations and revolutions we must admit that for us there was no fulfillment. We are the pursued and the searching, waiting in the expanse of time between child-and-fatherhood." In an epilogue to the fourth printing of *Menschheitsdämmerung*, Kurt Pinthus admitted that his anthology did not mark the dawn of Expressionism as he had hoped when it was first published, but really signalled its twilight or end. Now he called it "a testament of the deepest suffering and happiness of a generation that believed fanatically, and wanted to make others believe, that through the will of all a paradise would immediately sprout from the ruins." Speaking for himself and for his generation, Hasenclever forswore all political views and artistic programs. He was tired of beautiful gestures and the kiss of brotherhood; he wanted simply to cultivate his garden.

The Expressionists' disillusionment about man's willingness to change himself, about the salvational powers of socialism, and about their generation's ability to lead mankind to the dawn of a universal utopia was the first sign of the disappointment Western writers and intellectuals were to experience in this century. During the nineteen thirties a disenchantment with Communism and political and social causes in general brought such writers as Panait Istrati, André Gide, André Malraux, Arthur Koestler, Ignazio Silone, John Steinbeck, Romain Rolland, and John Dos Passos to the same impasse the Expressionists had confronted nearly two decades before. The Expressionists' experiment with politics and their subsequent sense of failure was a prophetic preview of the crisis developing in Western literature.

The Expressionists retreated from the world of politics and shrank from the monumental themes that had previously fired their imagination. Programs and manifestos had not established them as leaders of a new humanity. Their mission had failed; they were spent and unable to make a new start although few of them realized it at the time.

The Expressionists were not content to be mirrors of and subtle influences on society but were intent on accomplishing a Herculean task. It is not surprising that they should have experienced a keen sense of failure in a Weimar Germany which was not altered radically by revolution or fundamental reforms. The Expressionists regarded this lack of change as a rejection of their programs and responded with apocalyptic maledictions against their society. As their disillusionment grew, the desire for destruction, the original purpose of which was to prepare the ground for the future, attained an independent value. It became the antidote for despair and ennui, the means of giving meaning to the meaningless, and the outlet for revenge against the world. Ultimately, the Expressionists ended in abdication and resignation and retreated to a triviality and banality that was an artistic and intellectual dead end. (pp. 189-201)

Helmut Gruber, "The Political-Ethical Mission of German Expressionism," in The German Quarterly, *Vol. XL, No. 2, March, 1967, pp. 186-203.*

FURTHER READING

I. Anthologies

Miesel, Victor H., ed. *Voices of German Expressionism.* Englewood Cliffs, N.J.: Prentice-Hall, 1970, 211 p.
   Credos and manifestos of German Expressionist artists.

Raabe, Paul, ed. *The Era of German Expressionism.* Translated by J. M. Ritchie. Woodstock, N.Y.: Overlook Press, 1974, 423 p.
   Reminiscences of the Expressionist era in Munich and Berlin by various participants.

Ritchie, J. M., ed. *Seven Expressionist Plays.* Translated by J. M. Ritchie and H. F. Garten. London: Calder and Boyars, 1968, 201 p.
   Oskar Kokoschka's *Murderer Hope of Womankind,* Franz Kafka's *Guardian of the Tomb,* Ernst Barlach's *Blue Boll,* Georg Kaiser's *Protagonist,* August Stramm's *Awakening,* Alfred Brust's *Wolves,* and Ivan Goll's *Methusalem.*

——, ed. *Vision and Aftermath: Four Expressionist War Plays.* Translated by J. M. Ritchie and J. D. Stowell. London: Calder and Boyars, 1969, 208 p.
   Carl Hauptmann's *War,* Reinhard Goering's *Naval Encounter,* Walter Hasenclever's *Antigone,* and Ernst Toller's *Hinkemann.*

Sokel, Walter H., ed. *Anthology of German Expressionist Drama: A Prelude to the Absurd.* Garden City, N.Y.: Anchor Books, 1963, 366 p.
   Collects numerous Expressionist dramas.

II. Secondary Sources

Allen, Roy F. *Literary Life in German Expressionism and the Berlin Circles.* Göppingen: Verlag Alfred Kümmerle, 1974, 722 p.
   Social history of the Expressionists focusing on the period known as the "Expressionist decade," from 1910 to 1920.

——. *German Expressionist Poetry.* Boston: Twayne, 1979, 158 p.
   Analysis of themes and techniques of Expressionist poetry.

Boyd, Ernest. "Expressionism without Tears." In his *Studies from Ten Literatures,* pp. 231-50. 1925. Reprint. Port Washington, N.Y.: Kennikat, 1968.
   Discusses theories and techniques of Expressionist literature.

Brinkmann, Richard. "Abstract Lyrics of Expressionism: End or Transformation of the Symbol?" In *Literary Symbolism: A Symposium,* edited by Helmut Rehder, pp. 107-36. Austin: University of Texas Press, 1965.
   Examines problems of communication and interpretation that result from the Expressionists' abstract use of language.

Chandler, Frank W. "Expressionists in Theory and Practice" and "Expressionism at Its Best." In his *Modern Continental Playwrights,* pp. 383-406, pp. 407-37. New York: Harper & Brothers, 1931.
   Discusses Expressionist dramatists. In the first chapter cited, Chandler examines the works of Kornfeld, Wildgans, Kokoschka, Goering, Von Unruh, Bronnen, and Brecht; in the second, he examines those of Kaiser, Toller, and Werfel.

Dierick, A[ugustinus] P. "Irony and Expressionism: An Examination of Some Short Narrative Prose." *New German Studies* 7, No. 2 (Summer 1979): 71-90.
   Examines the use of irony in Expressionist prose, arguing that

the failure to note this irony has led to widespread critical misinterpretation of the Expressionists' literary aims, most notably in Egbert Krispyn's emphasis upon pathos as the stylistic hallmark of their writing (see entry below).

————. *German Expressionist Prose: Theory and Practice.* Toronto: University of Toronto Press, 1987, 328 p.
   Analysis of themes and techniques in Expressionist prose.

Eisner, Lotte H. *The Haunted Screen: Expressionism in the German Cinema and the Influence of Max Reinhardt.* Translated by Roger Greaves. Berkeley and Los Angeles: University of California Press, 1969, 360 p.
   Analyses of early German films, many of which reflect the influence of Expressionism.

Furness, R. S. *Expressionism.* London: Methuen, 1973, 105 p.
   Study of German Expressionism, its aesthetic antecedents, and its influence in twentieth-century art and literature.

Goldberg, Isaac. "Germany." In his *The Drama of Transition,* pp. 269-325. Cincinnati: Stewart Kidd, 1922.
   Provides an assessment of German Expressionist drama and discusses plays by Hauptmann, Hasenclever, Kaiser, and Kokoschka.

Klarmann, Adolf D. "Expressionism in German Literature: A Retrospective of a Half Century." *Modern Language Quarterly* 26, No. 1 (March 1965): 62-92.
   Summarizes the aesthetic goals and achievements of the Expressionists and critical response to their works.

Krispyn, Egbert. *Style and Society in German Literary Expressionism.* Gainesville: University of Florida Press, 1964, 60 p.
   Study of German Expressionist writing. Krispyn argues that the Expressionists can correctly be classified as a literary movement, since their works consistently manifest a concern for "the human suffering caused by the discrepancy between reality and ideal."

Maclean, H. "Expressionism." In *Periods in German Literature,* edited by J. M. Ritchie, pp. 257-80. London: Oswald Wolff, 1966.
   Analysis of Expressionism in literature. Maclean concludes: "The criterion of the Expressionist's work is . . . to be found, not in the application of an aesthetic or ethical system, but in terms of his own view of life, his own experience and his formulation of that experience."

Middleton, J. C. "Dada Versus Expressionism; or, The Red King's Dream." *German Life and Letters* n.s. 15, No. 1 (October 1961): 37-52.
   Suggests that "diametrically opposed interpretations of . . . social revolution are at the root of the conflict between Dada and Expressionism."

Myers, Bernard S. *The German Expressionists: A Generation in Revolt.* New York: McGraw-Hill, 1957, 348 p.
   Study of Expressionist painting.

Newton, Robert P. *Form in the "Menschheitsdämmerung": A Study of Prosodic Elements and Style in German Expressionist Poetry.* The Hague: Mouton, 1971, 270 p.
   Comprehensive stylistic analysis of the poems collected in *Menschheitsdämmerung.*

Nicoll, Allardyce. "The Expressionistic Movement." In his *World Drama from Aeschylus to Anouilh,* pp. 764-810. New York: Harcourt, Brace and Co., 1950.
   Discusses the aims, techniques, and impact of Expressionism.

Perkins, Geoffrey. *Contemporary Theory of Expressionism.* Bern: Verlag Herbert Lang, 1974, 182 p.
   Seeks to clarify the "problematic nature" of any attempt to construct a single, coherent definition of German Expressionsim.

Pickar, Gertrud Bauer, and Webb, Karl Eugene, eds. *Expressionism Reconsidered: Relationships and Affinities.* Munich: Wilhelm Fink Verlag, 1974, 100 p.
   Collection of essays on various topics, including "Foreign Influences on German Expressionist Poetry," by Reinhold Grimm and Henry J. Schmidt; "'The City Is Dark': Conceptions of Urban Landscape and Life in Expressionist Painting and Architecture," by Reinhold Heller; and "The Expressionist Vision in Theater and Cinema," by Anton Kaes.

Raabe, Paul. "On the Rediscovery of Expressionism as a European Movement." *Michigan Germanic Studies* 2, No. 2 (Fall 1976): 196-210.
   Traces the evolution of critical studies of Expressionism from the 1920s to the 1970s.

Reinhardt, Kurt F. "The Expressionistic Movement in Recent German Literature." *Germanic Review* 6, No. 3 (July 1931): 256-65.
   Assesses the achievement of Expressionist writers, suggesting that while few of their works "reached the state of artistic perfection," their theories, techniques, and ideological convictions did exert a marked influence on subsequent generations of writers and artists.

Ritchie, J. M. *German Expressionist Drama.* Boston: Twayne, 1976, 198 p.
   Discusses theories, themes, and techniques of Expressionist drama.

Rose, William. "Expressionism in German Literature" and "The German Drama, 1914-1927." In his *Men, Myths, and Movements in German Literature,* pp. 201-24, pp. 225-44. London: George Allen and Unwin, 1931.
   Survey of Expressionist poetry and drama. Rose contends: "Expressionism has contributed much to literature which does not appear on the surface. It signified a new way of looking at and expressing things, and sprang from an intenser feeling and a profounder insight. Short-lived as the Expressionist movement was, it ensured that a superficial realism can never again be taken for literature."

Samuel, Richard, and Thomas, R. Hinton. *Expressionism in German Life, Literature and the Theatre, 1910-1924.* 1939. Reprint. Philadelphia: Albert Saifer, 1971, 204 p.
   Study of Expressionist themes and techniques.

Scheffauer, Herman George. "The Essence of Expressionism." In his *The New Vision in the German Arts,* pp. 1-41. New York: B. W. Huebsch, 1924.
   Discusses the theory of Expressionist art.

Schumann, Detlev W. "Expressionism and Post-Expressionism in German Lyrics." *Germanic Review* 9, No. 1 (January 1934): 54-66.
   Examines the trend toward objective use of language in the work of later Expressionist writers.

Selz, Peter. *German Expressionist Painting.* Berkeley and Los Angeles: University of California Press, 1957, 379 p.
   Comprehensive discussion of German Expressionist painters and their works.

Sokel, Walter H. "Expressionism from a Contemporary Perspective." In *Erkennen und Deuten: Essays zur Literatur und Literaturtheorie Edgar Lohner in memoriam,* edited by Martha Woodmansee and Walter F. W. Lohnes, pp. 228-42. Berlin: Erich Schmidt Verlag, 1983.
   Summarizes varying critical approaches to Expressionism from the 1960s to the present.

Styan, J. L. *Modern Drama in Theory and Practice, Volume 3: Expressionism and Epic Theater.* Cambridge: Cambridge University Press, 1981, 230 p.
   Discusses representative Expressionist dramatists.

Waller, Christopher. *Expressionist Poetry and Its Critics.* London: Institute of Germanic Studies, 1986, 190 p.

Applies the critical approaches of Rainer Maria Rilke, Thomas Mann, Georg Lukács, Stefan George, Friedrich Gundolf, and Robert Musil in analyzing the works of representative Expressionist poets.

Webb, Benjiman Daniel. *The Demise of the "New Man": An Analysis of Ten Plays from Late German Expressionism.* Göppingen: Verlag Alfred Kümmerle, 1973, 186 p.

Examines the portrayal of the "New Man" in late Expressionist dramas. Webb concludes: "The 'New Man' was an activist ideal which disillusioned its former advocates. Initially, he was considered to be the only hope for the war-torn world. . . . Ultimately, however, the ideal became a source of frustration; not only were people 'too immoral, too weak, too irresponsible' to accept the tremendous sacrifices demanded by the 'New Man,' but the former ideal himself was subjected to a re-evaluation. . . . Those who once called for his birth in drama reversed their position and began to depict his downfall."

Weisstein, Ulrich. "German Literary Expressionism: An Anatomy." *German Quarterly* 54, No. 3 (May 1981): 262-83.

Analysis of the unifying concerns of Expressionist art. Weisstein suggests: "In spite of the many difficulties presenting themselves to the scholar bent upon finding some degree of unity in the diversity of phenomena subsumed under the label 'German literary Expressionism,' there is no reason for despair. As long as one remembers that Expressionism is no organic whole but that, like moons or satellites circling around a planet, its varied, paradoxical and sometimes contradictory elements are ultimately centered in a common core of *Weltgefuhl* ["world-sense"], one is fairly safe in treating it as a cluster, provided that in the matter of ascription one casts aside all chronological and biographical misconceptions."

Werenskiold, Marit. *The Concept of Expressionism: Origin and Metamorphoses.* Translated by Ronald Walford. Oslo: Universitetsforlaget, 1984, 251 p.

Traces the development of Expressionist aesthetics and art.

Willett, John. *Expressionism.* London: Weidenfeld and Nicolson, 1970, 256 p.

Examines German Expressionism in the context of early twentieth-century social, political, and aesthetic developments.

The Muckraking Movement in American Journalism

INTRODUCTION

"Muckraking" was President Theodore Roosevelt's censorious term for a type of exposé journalism that flourished in the United States between 1901 and approximately 1912. During this period newspaper and magazine writers exhaustively documented unethical and dangerous practices in business, labor, politics, and industry. While exposure of wrongdoing has always been a part of journalistic endeavor, that practiced by the muckrakers was unprecedented in scope and thoroughness, presenting the facts about a corrupt system and those who profited from it. The attention focused upon such issues as dishonest officials, adulteration of food, dangerous or ineffective patent medicines, and hazardous working conditions aroused public indignation and supported the efforts of those working to effect positive change.

The first of the muckraking journals was *McClure's*. Editor S. S. McClure identified exposé journalism as a potentially popular trend and assigned his top reporters to investigate civic or corporate wrongdoing. Lincoln Steffens's series "The Shame of the Cities" exposed corruption in the city governments of St. Louis, Chicago, Minneapolis, Pittsburgh, Philadelphia, and New York. Ida Tarbell's history of the Standard Oil Company revealed that company's often unethical business practices. Other *McClure's* reporters produced similar studies of business, labor, and finance. In January 1903 an editorial by McClure called attention to the "arraignment of American character" in his magazine's examinations of "capitalists, workingmen, politicians, citizens—all breaking the law, or letting it be broken." The muckraking inquiries were approved by readers, in particular by the growing urban middle class which, commentators agree, was the primary audience of the muckrakers. Other popular magazines quickly embarked on investigative series of their own, and revelations about such diverse issues as patent medicines, slum holdings of rich corporations and churches, factory conditions, and child labor were taken up by writers for *Collier's*, *Everybody's*, *Harper's*, the *Cosmopolitan*, the *Outlook*, the *Forum*, and many other magazines and newspapers. Novels with muckraking themes appeared, such as Upton Sinclair's *The Jungle*, Frank Norris's *The Octopus*, and the works of Theodore Dreiser. As the movement gained in popularity and readers clamored for more exposures, the careful fact-checking, research, and substantiation that was the hallmark of *McClure's* was often subordinated to sensationalism by other magazines.

Historians of the period generally agree that the movement had begun to wane as early as 1906, before President Roosevelt branded the crusading journalists with the "muckraker" label. The president accused journalists of deliberately averting their attention from the wholesome aspects of American life to focus on a small deleterious element. Although he was primarily targeting the sensationalistic practitioners of "yellow journalism" who were producing wildly accusatory and damaging stories with insufficient factual bases, the president's condemnation helped to sway public opinion against the muckrakers. Many muckraking magazines went out of business at about this time, and numerous others abandoned muckraking for the more staid content of the literary or the family magazine. In 1906 Steffens, Tarbell, Ray Stannard Baker, and other investigative journalists left *McClure's* and jointly purchased the *American* magazine. After their departure, *McClure's* ceased to be a forum for crusading journalism, while the *American* lasted only a short time under the directorship of the muckrakers.

Although some chroniclers of the movement contend that the muckraking magazines were systematically driven out of business by advertisers, little evidence of this exists. Current scholarship suggests that the failure of some muckraking journals can reasonably be attributed to poor financial management, or seen as the inevitable result of an oversaturated market. Although muckraking articles on issues of topical interest continued to appear, they were no longer the primary focus of individual publications or of wide public interest. Historians concur that sometime between 1912 and 1914, muckraking was subsumed into the era's general climate of reform and political progressivism.

The muckrakers are often credited with instigating many of the reforms of the period. The Pure Food and Drug Act, for example, was enacted after Samuel Hopkins Adams's series "The Great American Fraud" explored patent medicines and Upton Sinclair's novel *The Jungle* exposed unsanitary and hazardous conditions in American meat-packing plants. Other historians more cautiously concur with Robert C. Bannister, Jr. that "even in the case of Sinclair's *The Jungle*, or Baker's series on the railroads—notable examples of muckrakers' influence in arousing public opinion—cause and alleged effect are imperfectly related." Whether the muckrakers instigated or simply reported on the massive social and political reforms that were taking place in early twentieth-century America, their accomplishment in chronicling some of the worst abuses of trust and power is undeniable, and in bringing public attention to rampant corruption the muckrakers helped to sustain the reform movements that characterized the period.

REPRESENTATIVE WORKS

Adams, Samuel Hopkins
  The Great American Fraud (journalism) 1906
Baker, Ray Stannard
  Following the Color Line: An Account of Negro Citizenship in the American Democracy (journalism) 1903
Lawson, Thomas W.
  Frenzied Finance: The Crime of Amalgamated (journalism) 1905
Myers, Gustavus
  History of the Great American Fortunes. 3 vols. (journalism) 1909-10
Norris, Frank
  The Octopus (novel) 1901
Phillips, David Graham

The Treason of the Senate   (journalism)   1906;
    published in *Cosmopolitan Magazine*
Riis, Jacob
    The Battle with the Slums   (journalism)   1902
Russell, Charles Edward
    The Greatest Trust in the World   (journalism)   1905
    *Lawless Wealth: The Origin of Some Great American
        Fortunes*   (journalism)   1908
Sinclair, Upton
    The Jungle   (novel)   1906
Steffens, Lincoln
    The Shame of the Cities   (journalism)   1904
    The Struggle for Self-Government   (journalism)   1906
Tarbell, Ida
    The History of the Standard Oil Company. 2 vols.
        (journalism)   1904

DEVELOPMENT, PRINCIPLES, AND MAJOR FIGURES

HARVEY SWADOS

[*Swados was an American novelist, short story writer, political
speechwriter, and critic whose works focus on the problems of
the industrial laborer. Charles Shapiro said of Swados's story
collection* On the Line (1952) *that "Not since Upton Sinclair's*
The Jungle *have we had such a direct, steady look at the worker's world, one of dullness, continual pressures, and very little
satisfaction." In the following excerpt from his introduction to*
Years of Conscience: The Muckrakers, *an anthology of excerpts from important muckraking articles, Swados discusses
the inception of muckraking journalism and assesses the success of the movement.*]

Something exhilarating happened to American journalism at
the beginning of the twentieth century. For a brief period, a
decade—roughly from 1902 to 1912—an extraordinarily
keen group of editors and publishers made common cause
with some of the nation's outstanding novelists, poets, historians, lawyers, economists, and researchers. The cause, which
changed the course of our history, was the exposure of the
underside of American capitalism.

Ever since the Civil War there had been plenty of editors and
writers willing and eager to inculcate a credulous public with
legends of wealth accumulated solely by thrift and canniness,
of progress achieved thanks to completely unregulated free
enterprise, and of the natural inferiority of the lower orders:
Ambrose Bierce argued against the socialists that slums and
child labor ought not to be combated because they were the
inevitable lot of those too stupid and shiftless to raise themselves and their offspring from the heap. But a new wind blew
in with the new century, reintroducing two qualities which
had for too long been relegated to the wings of the American
scene: honesty and compassion.

Honesty was now defined not merely as "discretion" or "balance" but as unflinching determination to bring to light the
reality behind the convenient myths about the rulers of
America, regardless of whether the rulers' power lay in the
political machine, in the corporate cannibalism tagged as the
trust, or even in the pulpit. Compassion was now defined not
merely as "charity" or "sympathy" but as outraged identifi-

cation with the friendless and the voiceless at the bottom of
society, regardless of whether they were illiterate croppers,
sweated newcomers, aggrieved laborers, or terrorized Negroes.

During this vigorous decade honesty in pushing the investigation of corporate and governmental corruption to its nether-
most reaches and in arriving at the ultimate logical conclusions was not mislabeled treason, subversion, *lèse majesté*, or
cynicism. Nor was compassion for the suffering of the exploited millions—as ruthlessly sacrificed in the rage to industrialize as the masses of any contemporary Communist ex-
colony—mistaken for sentimentality, or confounded with the
"square."

In fact, it was the Square Deal's father who also fathered the
name which has identified these journalists from that day to
this. On April 14, 1906, in the midst of the labors of this unusual band, Theodore Roosevelt unloosed an attack on them,
taking as his text a passage from *Pilgrim's Progress:* " . . . the
Man with the Muckrake, the man who could look no way but
downward with the muckrake in his hand, who was offered
a celestial crown for his muckrake, but would neither look
up nor regard the crown he was offered, but continued to rake
to himself the filth of the floor."

The presidential attack, sanctimonious and largely unjustified though it was, created a permanent label, one which has
entered the language as has the more recent "egghead"; but
it did not succeed in slowing the momentum of muckraking
journalism. That did not take place until the end of the Taft
administration, when B. H. Hampton, last of the great muckraking publishers, awoke one day in 1911 to find that financial control of *Hampton's,* a haven for writers displaced from
other journals, had been maneuvered out of his hands and
that the magazine was going to be scuttled—apparently by
underground agreement of some of the financial interests
which had been plagued by its revelations.

Historians differ as to whether muckraking was bought out
and killed off, or whether—regardless of what happened to
Hampton's—it would in any case have died with the ebbing
of the Roosevelt era. Certainly some of the muckrakers themselves, tired, disillusioned, or disoriented by American participation in World War I, directed their energies into other
channels: one became a corporation executive, another a
chronicler of romances, a third a biographer, a fourth a professional reactionary.

But just as certainly, during the first decade of this century,
these writers showed themselves at their best; and they, together with the editors and publishers who were bold and idealistic enough to commission and to print their exposés,
showed America at its periodic best. There is something to
be said for the notion that our country recuperates from its
greedy decades almost like a repentant drunkard recovering
from a debauch by trying to examine the causes of his drinking bout and by making earnest resolutions to sin no more.
The difference between the nation and the drunkard may lie
in the fact that in its moods of sober self-criticism the nation
really does redress many of the wrongs, really does help those
who cannot help themselves, and does thereby renew its
world image as a state concerned not solely, or even primarily, with self-aggrandizement, but much more importantly
with dignity, freedom, and decent self-respect.

This is not to say that the national mood during these intervals of thoughtful stock-taking is always one of unalloyed be-

The British humor magazine Puck *depicted the muckrakers as crusaders in a 1906 cartoon.*

nevolence, any more than were the pages of the muckraking magazines purely rationalistic or invariably redolent of Christian brotherhood. Just as the New Deal years were also the years of the Silver Shirts, the Liberty League, and the German-American Bund, so can one find in the pages of the muckraking magazines reams of nonsensical food-faddism and, worse, occasional articles about semibarbaric Negroes or aggressively acquisitive Hebrews which should have been beneath the contempt of any self-respecting editor; and it is perfectly true that a humane, passionately reform-minded editor like B. O. Flower could wax as eloquent in the pages of *The Arena* over the virtues of spiritualism or Christian Science as over those of civic reform or public ownership. But we speak here of an overall tone, a mood, and it is surely beyond dispute that in those years such periodicals as *Hampton's, Pearson's,* the *Cosmopolitan,* and *McClure's,* to say nothing of *Collier's* or *The Arena,* reflected in their major concerns everything that has been traditionally largest and noblest in the American spirit.

That may very well explain the twofold reaction to Theodore Roosevelt's epithet on the part of the journalists whom he attacked. If Gustavus Myers and Ida Tarbell were appalled at this parodying of their scholarly researches, others—Upton Sinclair and Charles Edward Russell among them—responded to the challenge by accepting the label and insisting on wearing it with pride, as a proof of the force with which their work was striking home.

"Now the Muckrake Men I know," insisted Upton Sinclair in the *Independent* in 1908,

are all men of personally clean lives and generous hearts; there is not one of them who would not have been something noble, if he had felt free to choose. Of those who come immediately to my mind, one would have been a metaphysician, another would have been a professor of ethics, three at least would have been poets, and one would have founded a new religion. Instead of that they are Muckrake Men . . . not because they love corruption, but simply because they hate it with an intensity which forbids them to think about anything else while corruption sits enthroned. . . .

As a rule, the Muckrake Man began his career with no theories, as a simple observer of facts known to every person at all "on the inside" of business and politics. But he followed the facts, and the facts always led him to one conclusion; until finally he discovered to his consternation that he was enlisted in a revolt against capitalism.

He is the forerunner of a revolution; and, like every revolutionist, he takes his chances of victory and defeat. If it is defeat that comes; if the iron heel wins out in the end—why, then, the Muckrake Man will remain for all time a scandal-monger and an assassin of character. If on the other hand, he succeeds in his efforts to make the people believe what "everybody knows"—then he will be recognized in future as a benefactor of his race.

History would seem to justify those who gloried in TR's diatribe; for, decades later, the surviving journalists of the era vied in asserting pride of rank in the muckraking elite and in reading others out of it. This was to be true even of those (a majority of the original group) whose political philosophy had shifted over the years: Mark Sullivan, become a spokesman for conservative Republicanism, was to insist in his later years that he and not Lincoln Steffens had fired the opening gun of the muckrakers' crusade. One hardly presses his claim to charter membership in a group which he cannot regard as representative of what is best in the national character.

It should not be thought that the muckrakers sprang full-blown from the brows of a handful of editors, any more than that their spirit was swept from the scene once and for all by the storm clouds of the First World War. Their fervor, their passionate denunciation of corporate aggrandizement at the expense of the individual American, their belief in the boundless possibilities of a better nation, instinct in every line they wrote—all these are to be found in Henry Demarest Lloyd's *Wealth against Commonwealth,* which was published in 1894.

"The men and women who do the work of the world," asserted Lloyd in his opening chapter,

> have the right to the floor. Everywhere they are rising to "a point of information." They want to know how our labor and the gifts of nature are being ordered by those whom our ideals and consent have made Captains of Industry over us; how it is that we, who profess the religion of the Golden Rule and the political economy of service for service, come to divide our partial existence for the many who are the fountains of these powers and pleasures. This book is an attempt to help the people answer these questions. It has been quarried out of official records, and it is a venture in realism in the world of realities. Decisions of courts and of special tribunals like the Interstate Commerce Commission, verdicts of juries in civil and criminal cases, reports of committees of the State Legislatures and of Congress, oath-sworn testimony given in legal proceedings and in official inquiries, corrected by rebutting testimony and by cross-examination—such are the sources of information.

Indeed the only thing wrong with this powerful book, from a journalistic standpoint at least, was that it was too far in advance of its time, for it anticipated in every area the main lines of attack of the muckrakers; to a modern reader its method and its commitment are all but indistinguishable from those of the muckrakers, and if it was less widely absorbed than their work this can only be attributed to the fact that the public was "not ready" for it—which may be another way of saying that it was not made readily available as an article of mass consumption.

A decade later, however, the public was ready. Or again we may put this another way by saying that the revelations of the muckrakers were made easily available to the public by a mass medium, the cheap popular magazine. If it is worth nothing that the traditional American periodicals—whether scholarly, historical, literary, or simply upper-class in general—played little part in the tumultuous activity of the decade, despite the fact that some of their most valued contributors blossomed as muckrakers in other journals, it is even more important to emphasize the mass circulation of those other journals. A low-price magazine which could vault to a circulation of nearly half a million in a country with, at the turn of the century, little better than a third its present population—and with a substantial proportion of newly arrived im-

migrants and native illiterates—was obviously saying something of value to millions of Americans. When we multiply this by the total number of magazines whose circulations were zooming upwards because they were encouraging and publishing the muckraking writers; when we remind ourselves that there were at the time no true picture magazines, no television, no radio, no movies, we begin to sense that we are here witnessing the birth of the modern mass media (the parallel—but distinct—development of yellow journalism is one which cannot be examined here). Isn't it worth pondering the fact that the mass magazine was born of this arousal of the American conscience by a band of bold editors making common cause with novelists, poets, and littérateurs?

In his brilliant early book *The Golden Day,* Lewis Mumford makes what seems to me a most telling argument against overvaluing the ultimate impact of the muckrakers. "In attack, in criticism," he says, "they did able work; but when it came to offering a genuine alternative, their picture became a negative one: industry without millionaires, cities without graft, art without luxury, love without sordid calculation. They were ready to upset every aspect of modern industrial society except the fragmentary culture which had brought it into existence" [see excerpt below].

Mr. Mumford goes on to point out a truth which the thirty-five years since he first committed it to paper have only strengthened—that capitalism itself *can* provide what it was attacked for not providing, and that the real indictment of it lies elsewhere: "the essential poverty of America was a qualitative poverty, one which cut through the divisions of rich and poor; and it has been this sort of poverty which has prevented us from projecting in the imagination a more excellent society. Life was more complicated in America but not more significant; life was richer in material goods but not in creative energies. These eager and relentless journalists were unaware of the necessity for establishing different kinds of goods than the existing ones; they had no notion of other values, other modes, other forms of activity than those practiced by the society around them."

Anyone who reads the literature, not the journalism, produced by the muckrakers, must be persuaded of the justness of Mr. Mumford's reproach. Those reformers who, like Brand Whitlock, invested all their indignation as well as all their creative energy not in journalism but in novel writing, produced books which, despite the polite references to them by American historians, are all but unreadable today. Those who divided their energies between poetry and muckraking—Edwin Markham, Ernest Crosby, Charles Edward Russell—produced poetry which is now hardly recalled even by specialists in the period. Those who were both storytellers and muckrakers, from novelists like Frank Norris and Owen Wister and David Graham Phillips (who did an occasional muckraking piece), to writers of the volcanic energy of Jack London or Upton Sinclair (who regarded both their fiction and their polemics as performing equivalent functions), produced rows of books which, even at their best, are simply not worthy of comparison with the great imaginative works of other epochs. (pp. 9-16)

Writing in the *Cosmopolitan* in 1906, Upton Sinclair, still flushed with the fantastic success of *The Jungle,* spelled out the reasons why the opening chapters of that bombshell of a book were (and still are) so explosively charged; at the same time he unconsciously exposed the roots of an aesthetic misconception that was to strangulate not only his own later fiction, but also much of the work of Sherwood Anderson and of the proletarian writers of the 1930's:

> In many respects I had *Uncle Tom's Cabin* in mind as a model of what I wished to do. . . . But now there is a stirring of life within the masses themselves. The proletarian writer is beginning to find a voice, and also an audience and a means of support. And he does not find the life of his fellows a fascinating opportunity for feats of artistry; he finds it a nightmare inferno, a thing whose one conceivable excellence is that it drives men to rebellion and to mutual aid in escaping. The proletarian writer is a writer with a purpose; he thinks no more of "art for art's sake" than a man on a sinking ship thinks of painting a beautiful picture in the cabin; he thinks of getting ashore, and of getting his brothers and comrades ashore—and then there will be time enough for art. . . . So far as I myself am concerned, the well-springs of joy and beauty have been dried up in me—the flowers no longer sing to me as they used to, nor the sunrise, nor the stars; I have become like a soldier upon a hard campaign—I am thinking only of the enemy. The experiences of my life have been such that I cannot think of them without turning sick; there is no way that I can face the thought of them at all, save as being practice for the writing of *The Jungle.* I see that it was necessary that some one should have had such experiences, in order that it might be impossible for any man to have them again.

Regardless of whether the novelist blocked his own development by imagining himself a soldier rather than an artist, or whether (as seems most likely in those whom we are considering) he simply lacked the necessary imaginative gifts from the very outset, the unhappy fact remains that the literary efforts of the muckrakers were not on a par with their journalistic labors.

But what of these labors? Can one go along with Lewis Mumford when he concludes: "For all the effect that these painstaking pictures had in lifting the worker onto a more active plane of manhood, one would willingly trade the whole literature for a handful of good songs. . . ."?

The best answer is to be found in the [work of the muckraking journalists], and in the course of America's social progress in the twentieth century, so profoundly influenced for the better by these pages themselves. Seldom if ever has the craft of journalism more responsibly served the individual conscience and the national interest. The ardent American notion of a free society, freely inclusive, freely elected, and freely helpful, had been cynically shoved aside in the closing decades of the nineteenth century. If it was revivified in the early years of the new century, to the benefit of every American who has come of age since then, that must be credited in substantial measure to the ringing voices of the muckrakers, recalling their fellow citizens to an honest understanding of their responsibilities and their potentialities in a democratic society. (pp. 16-17)

> *Harvey Swados, in an introduction to* Years of Conscience: The Muckrakers, *edited by Harvey Swados, The World Publishing Company, 1962, pp. 9-22.*

HARRY H. STEIN AND JOHN M. HARRISON

[*In the following excerpt from a collection of essays entitled* Muckraking: Past, Present, and Future *(1973), Harrison and*

Stein consider some principles and characteristics of muckraking journalism.]

Muckraking has been a phenomenon specific to the journalism of the United States. Its opportunities for practice and degree of popularity have always been related to conditions within the press and within the country. Muckraking has been a journalistic form continuously formed and reformed by its creators, by its channels of communication, and by those who receive its messages. From decade to decade in the twentieth century none of these elements has remained exactly the same. The first spirited generation of muckrakers fell away prior to World War I and, with few exceptions, were not replaced in number or influence until the late 1960s and 1970s. Today, a new generation of practitioners has different views of the issues and different means of analyzing and expressing them from those of Lincoln Steffens, Ida Tarbell, Ray Stannard Baker, and other muckrakers of the Progressive Era. Yet they often share the assumptions of their illustrious predecessors just as they sometimes dwell on similar problems. The country has changed and so too the media available for muckraking and the publics actually or potentially receptive to it. Nevertheless, continuity exists between the journalism of conscience of the Progressive Era and that of the present.

Muckraking is associated with four major press traditions in America. It bears closest resemblance to investigative journalism; less, to advocacy journalism. It has a distant relation to sensationalistic and to yellow journalism. (A crucial mistake of proponents and detractors alike has been to equate muckraking with one or another of these American press traditions.) The work of investigation, like muckraking, furnishes a careful, accurate, inevitably non-neutral account and analysis in words and images of a set of events, ideas, circumstances, or persons. Both usually expose or reveal fresh facts or patterns of meaning to their audiences and sometimes offer solutions to depicted problems. Investigative journalism encompasses the "watchdog" function of the American press: the surveillance of governmental and political institutions and personnel and their conformance to ordinances and regulations and to social values and norms resembling law. Muckrakers exercise a surveillance over a wider area than government and politics and so have probed the unique and the common in American society, the highest reaches of power and the everyday social patterns of the population. Also, muckrakers sometimes define as a removable evil a practice or view normally accepted as natural, inescapable, or beneficent. By helping to enlarge Americans' expectations of what is possible and desirable in their lifetimes, they illuminate fundamental intentions both to inform and to improve their fellows. Furthermore, the muckraking work, already selective in facts and emphasis to elicit indignation or anger, proceeds beyond the investigative form to indicate how extensive, not unique, are the practices and ideas exposed. It denounces or praises specific individuals, conditions, or values, and exhorts its audience, explicitly or by tone, to "take action" or to support specific remedies. In a sense, muckrakers have insisted directly and investigative journalists indirectly that Americans concern themselves with the norms of public and individual good, the nature of existing realities and social change, and the standards and needs of a representative democracy. In that manner, both forms have become segments of extended social action, more so as their representatives have often engaged in public speaking and testifying, pamphleteering, unofficial advising of leaders, and other nonjournalistic activities.

To become a propagandist or apologist for a particular viewpoint or organization has always been a seductive danger for journalists of conscience. Still, they have never *fully* entered the stream of the oldest press tradition in America, that of advocacy journalism. This tradition has been represented by the factional and party newspapers of colonial and nineteenth-century America, by the pamphlets and other writings of Thomas Paine, Theodore Parker, William Lloyd Garrison, and Henry George, and by such twentieth-century magazines as the *Commoner, Masses, Progressive, Nation,* and *New Republic.* Little or no pretense to detachment or neutrality exists in advocacy journalism. Advocacy has been characterized by deliberate silence on some topics, suppression of material uncomplimentary to its partisans, and intentional bias in selection of subjects, emphasis, and interpretations. Muckrakers have resembled advocacy journalists in making emotional appeals, in personalizing complex issues, and in thus placing a premium on public opinion to right wrongs, defeat conspiracies, or alter institutions, attitudes, or values. The line between the two forms can blur, as in the collection of *Ramparts* articles, *Divided We Stand,* which its editors described in 1971 as "positive muckraking." Indeed, partisan outlets have been normal refuges for muckrakers lacking access to general-circulation media.

Distinct from advocacy journalists, muckrakers have tried to preserve their autonomy, never irretrievably committing themselves to any single cause or person. They have checked their partisanship (but not their critical sensibilities) with a healthy skepticism, journalistic norms or instructions, and audience predilections. Supporting Theodore Roosevelt, they could, like Lincoln Steffens, praise Socialism and Robert M. La Follette and later shift support to Woodrow Wilson. Drew Pearson and Jack Anderson have spurred federal officials regardless of party. In the television documentaries, "Hunger in America" and "This Child Is Rated X," muckraking newsmen have not simply operated as spokesmen for liberal senators on charges that hunger and child abuse are routine in the United States. They verified, extended, and deepened the senators' charges and broadcast them to a national audience. But if they become too evenhanded or detached, muckrakers, as those connected with the magazine *KEN* learned by 1940, will never build a following.

Finally, sensationalistic journalism and its extension into a yellow journalism which manufactures news, banners misleading headlines, and luridly illustrates its stories have a few parallels with muckraking. Hearst, Pulitzer, and their many imitators treated subjects like scandal and corruption, sex, and violence in a provocative manner and in doing so touched the often inchoate needs and aspirations of millions of Americans. Sensationalism figured prominently in the muckraking of ex-New York *World* city editor Charles Edward Russell, less so in muckraking by his contemporaries before World War I. Like sensationalistic and yellow journalism, muckraking has supported political and social crusades, focused on nongenteel subjects, and adopted such techniques as human-interest stories to win attention and sympathy. The immense audience for the muckraking in the syndicated "Washington Merry-Go-Round" column since the 1930s might be due partly to the late Drew Pearson's and Jack Anderson's use of tantalizing gossip and slangy language. Nevertheless, while the sensationalistic and yellow journalist exposes in order to

entertain and titillate Americans, the muckraker labors to offer them a profound and specific education. Muckrakers distinguish, examine, and judge whatever has seemed to improve or lessen humankind and society. The thrust for moral social improvement is part of their design. (pp. 13-16)

Much has been said . . . regarding the public which muckraking has enjoyed or could potentially enjoy. In 1914 Walter Lippmann wrote in *Drift and Mastery* [see excerpt below] that "the mere fact that muckraking was what the people wanted to hear is in many ways the most important revelation of the whole campaign" the nation had just witnessed. Lippmann suggested that muckrakers had won quick approval because they both illuminated the real causes of public dissatisfaction and gave the appearance of doing something about them. Since the 1900s the muckrakers themselves have held a motivating premise that somewhere in the United States there existed a concerned, disquieted audience receptive to their messages. Any responsiveness by their *own* constituencies also has concerned individuals frequently touched by the work of muckrakers—the public officials, the corporation executives, the managers of competing communication media. They must ask if the number or influence of those actually or potentially roused by muckraking can safely be ignored or whether it is better to mount a prosecution, pass a law, launch an inquiry, initiate a publicity campaign, or change editorial direction. Like the muckraker, they too must be keenly interested in what public is being cultivated by muckraking. (pp. 18-19)

Most commentators and practitioners believe that the urban middle class has furnished the fundamental audience for muckraking in any decade of this century. A small following from the middle class persists whatever the national mood and whatever the inclinations of the bulk of middle-class Americans. The permanent following includes people who sympathized with Sinclair's muckraking in the 1920s and with I. F. Stone's in the 1950s, supporters of two small contemporary newspapers, the *Texas Observer* and the San Francisco *Bay Guardian,* and adherents to the muckraking appearing for many years in the small-circulation *New Republic* and *Nation.* Twice—from about 1902 to 1912 and again since the late 1960s (though support may now be dwindling)—muckraking has had an upsurge, thanks partly to the enthusiasm of a larger and more influential following from within the middle class. Finally, it is believed, a mass audience cutting across residence and class has been realized occasionally by muckrakers in this century when their efforts appeared in large-circulation newspapers or magazines or on television.

This overall conception may hide some important audiences of muckraking. Trade unionists belonging to the C.I.O. supported the muckraking newsletter *In Fact* in the 1940s. Working people admired Judge Ben Lindsey's muckraking of juvenile delinquency and crime before World War I. The Chicago *Daily News* and St. Louis *Post-Dispatch,* which printed muckraking for years, circulate in large metropolitan regions, reaching small and large communities, including the homes of readers who are distinctly not middle-class. The national interest tapped by exposures in the now-defunct *Saturday Evening Post* and *Life* magazines of criminal-political connections, by *Ramparts'* muckraking, and by particular television documentaries suggest a reservoir of responsiveness to muckraking not coterminous with the urban middle class. It is likely that muckraking addressed to *every* American has always been doomed not to be heard by these millions. It seems equally probable that muckrakers who only target their audience as the urban middle class or an elite segment within it have failed to realize the full potential of muckraking.

Muckraking has been associated with many traditions in twentieth-century America. Most commentators emphasize the intimate connection between muckraking journalism and American liberalism. Indeed, many, if not most, muckrakers have shared in the liberal tradition, found their best voice in liberal publications, identified theirs as liberal goals, and been treated as liberals by their audiences and students. But muckraking has not been exclusively connected to liberalism. Sinclair, Steffens, and some others, for example, identified themselves with ancient Judeo-Christian themes of prophecy and social justice. Others in the 1900s regarded themselves as heirs to such nineteenth-century reformers as the abolitionists. And a number of muckrakers today . . . prefer to think of themselves as reporters devoted to a general public interest but to no earlier tradition.

Despite its predominant connection to liberalism, muckraking journalism has also converged on occasion with the issues and usages of both American conservatives and American radicals. A number of important early muckrakers, including John Spargo, Charles Edward Russell, and Upton Sinclair, reflected their Socialism in their works. Others, including Steffens and Baker, flirted with and praised the Socialists. I. F. Stone and those connected with *Hard Times* and *Ramparts* in recent times have muckraked for their respective versions of radical change. Stone regards Sinclair's ideas as an important influence on his own journalism. The value of muckraking for conservatism has rarely been recognized because of conservatives' usual antagonism to muckraking. James B. Dill, a major promoter of trusts, quietly provided Steffens with material to attack certain monopoly arrangements for many years. Samuel Hopkins Adams' muckraking series on patent medicines was reprinted and given a half-million-copy distribution by the American Medical Association. The New York Stock Exchange, the Chicago Board of Trade, and individual financiers before 1907 endorsed and helped muckraking journalists so long as their attacks were being launched against "bucket shops" and a few other embarrassing Wall Street practices.

Muckraking has a ticklish association with the commercial needs of the media in which it normally appears. To profit from advertising dollars, to build and maintain audience acceptance, and simultaneously to advocate social change is a formula for conflict. The *American Magazine,* partly owned after 1906 by muckrakers who wrote for it, saved itself from economic foundering by casting overboard its muckraking. Some muckrakers turned to the partisan press, such as the privately subsidized *Nation* and *New Republic,* or like Sinclair published their own writings to bypass media barriers against controversial views. Interestingly, it was money making, some have charged, that caused the *Saturday Evening Post* and *Life* in their waning years and certain magazines copying *McClure's* early in this century to *add* muckraking to their usual pursuits. These media are alleged to have provided a kind of muckraking which entertained and reinforced audience attitudes—the usual service of popular journalism—in order to demonstrate to advertisers their appeal to a middle-class buying public suddenly "ready" for muckraking. Their subsequent investigations allegedly focused on "safe" topics, guaranteed to arouse indignation, such as trusts, organized crime, or pollution, without assigning spe-

cific responsibility or proposing harsh remedies. . . . [Such] muckraking journalism becomes a version of "inside dopesterism," loses its element of protest, and ends captive to mass entertainment and all the passing moods on which it seizes. Finally, after any noticeable shift in the winds of public attitudes, it is abandoned.

Not so, say proponents of muckraking who are alive to the dangers of advertiser pressure and audience fickleness. Advertisers and audiences are more quickly lost than gained by muckraking in the mass media. Muckraking by such licensed media as television raises additional threats of control by Congress, the White House, the F.C.C., and organized pressure groups. Just as small profits and small audiences do not attest to effective muckraking, they argue, neither does a mass audience for muckraking indicate a necessary dilution of investigation and exposure. Praise must be accorded the public which forces the big-audience media to direct their attention to real social needs. And who could be opposed to a responsive mass public for muckraking? (pp. 19-21)

Harry H. Stein and John M. Harrison, "Muckraking Journalism in Twentieth-Century America," in Muckraking: Past, Present and Future, *edited by John M. Harrison and Harry H. Stein, The Pennsylvania State University Press, 1973, pp. 11-22.*

LOUIS FILLER

[*Filler is a Russian-born American historian, biographer, and critic. His numerous studies of muckraking and the muckrakers include* The Muckrakers (*1976; revised and expanded from* Crusaders for American Liberalism, *1950*), Appointment at Armageddon (*1976*), Muckraking and Progressivism (*1976*), *and* Voice of the Democracy: A Study of David Graham Phillips (*1978*). *In the following excerpt from the first-named work, Filler considers what led some early muckrakers to the movement and briefly outlines their careers.*]

They came from everywhere, these journalists, sociologists, *littérateurs,* and it was often difficult to tell just what they were and whom they represented. Rheta Childe Dorr, a newspaper woman and feminist, was resentfully called a Socialist so often that she finally joined the Socialist Party. And Robert Hunter, who *was* a Socialist, could never understand why anyone should call him a muckraker. His book *Poverty* was the product of ten years of brilliant investigation and social work begun under the aegis of Jane Addams and her colleagues. It had been written in the spirit of the scientist and fact-finder. Why should it be dubbed "muckraking"?

Those who felt threatened or insulted by the investigations and exposés which appeared on every side had no time to choose words. So Hunter, William Hard, Florence Kelley, Dorr—they were all muckrakers, or no better than muckrakers; in a word, trouble-seekers. In these writers, muckrakers and near-muckrakers, worried men could find few easily distinguishing marks. Each writer borrowed from the other; yet a careful weighing of any one would have shown individual patterns of development that were not superficially apparent. Actually the rude attempts of disturbed critics of the time to pigeon-hole writers according to the "scientific," "literary," or "exposure" content of their work were uniformly inadequate and absurd. When journalists produced novels and novelists took to making investigations, when poets produced histories and politicians took to writing poetry, and when such things went on at an unheard-of tempo, the average critic was likely to lose his head and begin to strike out in all directions.

That was what happened. (p. 110)

[What] made the muckrakers what they were? It is safe to say that hardly one of those who made his name in that history-packed decade had any more intention than Steffens, Tarbell, or Baker of challenging the *status quo* in the way that he did. The muckrakers originally meant to be merely novelists, merely scholars, merely politicians, according to the tradition they had inherited. They wanted merely to make careers. And they became muckrakers, most of them, by popular demand.

This does not mean that muckraking was, as its enemies charged, a pandering to corrupt taste. The public's lust for information, for understanding, was enormous. It charged the air with vitality. It called into being a veritable army of writers to interpret and describe the accumulated history of thirty and more years. Naturally, mistakes happened. Cleveland Moffett was a mistake: his series, *The Shameful Misuse of Wealth,* was futility itself—a sermon in the key of moral indignation concerning the "excesses" of the rich. And there were such ridiculous articles as the one by Frederic Thompson, written in all seriousness, called *After the Salome Dance—What?* But there were surprisingly few such mistakes.

Most of the writers meant only to write, not to muckrake, as their biographies testify. Will Irwin, for example, who had been a classmate of Herbert Hoover at Stanford University, began his career on the San Francisco newspapers and then moved to New York to work with the *Sun* and then for McClure. He loved to write, and he wrote movingly of his own San Francisco. Otherwise he was as willing to report baseball as Chinatown. It was the drift of the times, as well as the palpable corruption of newspaper methods, that called forth the series which capped his work of the period. (pp. 111-12)

Among the fiction writers of the period, Samuel Merwin and Henry Kitchell Webster had together written the first of the "business novels": *The Short Line War,* published in 1899, described the struggle for control of a Midwestern railroad. *Calumet K,* also written in collaboration, told of the contest that marked the building of a grain elevator. Such subjects had been new; but the books lacked the disturbing quality which Frank Norris's detailed treatment and superior craftsmanship were soon to provide for the reader. For Merwin and Webster were primarily romancers, not social historians: as Arnold Bennett showed, they had simply applied the method of Dumas to American conditions. *The Road to Frontenac,* which Merwin wrote alone, was actually a romance, with all the trappings of swords and chivalry.

But again the times directed its writers. After the turn of the century Webster began writing such books as *The Banker and the Bear,* dealing with a corner in lard, and his friend wrote *The Whip Hand,* which dealt with a corner in lumber. Contemporary pressure forced Webster to adopt the shallow philosophy he finally evolved in *The Duke of Cameron Avenue,* a novelette of New York ward politics that touched on "practical" reform. But the times did better for Merwin. As contributing editor to *Success,* he made first-hand surveys of business and politics; as associate editor, he became a coworker with the most virile of the muckrakers; finally he became editor of *Success,* and it was while he held this position that the magazine became a powerful organ of exposure—

and was stamped out by interests which could no longer tolerate its existence. (pp. 112-13)

Charles Edward Russell, who began the century innocently enough, was one more of the group who had no intention of becoming muckrakers. He was an Iowan, born in 1860, the son of a newspaper editor who had been one of the founders of the Republican Party. The last fact alone practically committed him to early entry into the political differences of the Eighties. As early as 1881 he spoke out boldly in defense of free trade. That same year he founded with Henry J. Philpott a free trade journal and the first of the free trade leagues; and it was not long before the gospel was being preached vigorously throughout the West. Russell supported, in turn, Populism, Henry George, and miscellaneous reform movements. Early in his career, however, sturdy Republicanism practiced in the Lincoln tradition reduced the fortunes of the Russell family, and this youngest Russell was forced to earn his living. He went to New York, where he began with the *Commercial Advertiser* and then joined the staff of the *World* which sent him to Chicago in time to be present when the Haymarket riot occurred. With time Russell ran the gamut of newspaper experience, eventually becoming city editor of the *World* over an impressive corps of reporters and helping Hearst to found the Chicago *American.*

By 1902 Russell had saved enough money to ensure his freedom from want, and, after the hectic experiences of a score of years, issued his first book: *Such Stuff as Dreams.* Poems! It was amazing how such productions were passed over by those who pretended to interpret the age. Actually there was a poet burning in many a fierce muckraker—and Russell was one of the fiercest of them all: a proud, sensitive man who yearned romantically to accomplish worth-while things. The truth about Russell was that he had been hurt by the successive political and financial failures of old-time Republicanism, and he was anxious to keep away from it all; besides, he wanted more than a journalistic career. Yet he was no mere escapist; his purely literary ability and interest were genuine. Even at the height of muckraking, he was to issue studies and articles having nothing directly to do with exposure.

Russell, however, had not lost by any means his passionate belief in the necessity for democracy. His bitterness toward those who had stripped the Western middle-class of its former strength was soon to start him upon what was to be his real career. He became, in the following years, one of the most sincere, most partisan of the reform writers.

Russell's friend David Graham Phillips was less reluctant to do battle with his times. He had been anticipating a national upheaval for years. A Hoosier, bred somewhat like Russell, Phillips had been matured by Princeton and Park Row. An outstanding newspaperman, he might have gone on to high editorial honors. But he had cherished the determination since college days to paint America whole, to tell the truth and avoid the sentimentalities that had defined and limited the work of Howells and Twain and Bret Harte; so he had held on to the career of journalism deliberately, in order to learn his country thoroughly.

In 1901 Phillips broke away from the newspapers and set himself to writing with a resolution and regularity and capacity that, in the end, made him a legend. He wrote articles, stories, and novels, sounding his audience and experimenting with his material. Until about 1906 his articles were, in the main, more important than his fiction. He wrote on every subject: housing, charity (which he abhorred), the steel trust, travel; but he gravitated naturally toward pen portraits of outstanding men and events. These were the stuff of his fiction. And once muckraking was in full swing, Phillips's straightforward evaluations were being featured in *Cosmopolitan,* the *Arena, Everybody's,* and other magazines. Such an article as "The Real Boss of the United States" (dealing with Senator Aldrich) precipitated wide discussion and carried more than a suggestion of the great muckraking scoop that was brewing.

It cannot be too much emphasized that the reading public in those years was just beginning to understand that home things—ways of living, ideas, government—in a word, *Americana*—were as interesting, as worth knowing, as foreign things. "Confession" and other personal-experience stories, whatever their merit or lack of it, were being read eagerly and widely for their realistic accounts of everyday American life. They were a valuable supplement to muckraking because they created a background for the muckrakers' themes. Such work as Owen Kildare's, for instance, was extremely popular. Kildare had been a Bowery tough who, at the age of thirty, became respectable. By study and application he made himself an educated man, and he finally wrote the story of his life, the frontispiece of the book being a map of Manhattan with the Bowery indicated as though it were in a foreign country. Kildare became merely respectable, but his story was good, and it became a pattern for similar works.

Will Irwin reported *The Confessions of a Con Man,* Frederic Howe wrote *The Confessions of a Monopolist* (fiction, but based on fact), *World's Work* ran *The Confessions of a Commercial Senator.* Confessions were elicited from thieves and salesgirls and other men and women in every walk of life. Not all of these unburdenings of the soul were breath-taking. *Everybody's,* for example, printed among others the "confessions" of a life-insurance agent: this was standard writing and might just as well have come from the life-insurance companies themselves, for all the revelation it contained. It appeared before scandal in the life-insurance field broke loose. But even the most pedestrian "confession" was eagerly read for light on the country and the experiences of its people.

Among the writers who made a career of such work was Hutchins Hapgood, who never, in fact, considered himself a muckraker. Hapgood's newspaper training had given him a taste for loitering in the parks and among the colorful East Side people. Unlike his brother, Norman, who was pure intellectual, he looked for human interest and the East Side was particularly the place for it: the waves of immigration had crowded it with vivid and lively people, such as the Russian Jews who had fled from the Czar and his bureaucrats, bringing with them the finest of a gifted intelligentsia. Using this human material Hapgood wrote *The Spirit of the Ghetto* (1902). It was a remarkable production for a non-Jew, for it revealed an extraordinary effort to understand his subject and the people it involved. (pp. 114-17)

During the muckraking period Hapgood issued, in turn, *The Spirit of Labor, An Anarchist Woman,* and *Types from the City Streets*—all case studies and observations set down with extreme care. No one could complain that Hapgood was not eager to give the truth as he saw it among all kinds of people, from intellectual Socialist to street gamin.

If Hapgood was the sociologist of the muckraking movement, then Gustavus Myers, more than any other—certainly more than either Tarbell or Steffens or Baker—was its historian. He, too, never quite considered himself part of the movement; probably he resented the difficulties he encountered in the way to fame and influence, and coveted the prestige and national attention won by men like Steffens and Russell and Phillips. But he also harbored something of the scholar's feeling of superiority to the man of action. Writers like Russell and Phillips used their material to drive home points and call readers directly to reform; Myers was completely—too completely—the student.

As a young man Myers specialized in original historical research. In 1900 he wrote for the Reform Club Committee on City Affairs *A History of Public Franchises in New York City,* which was immediately recognized as required reading for any serious student of the franchise. Cold fact and history though it was, it constituted a sensational indictment of franchise practices. The next year Myers completed *The History of Tammany Hall,* which publishers refused to accept and which finally had to be issued on a subscription basis. Speaking of the book, Myers explained that he had begun his study in no partisan spirit; it was not he, but the evidence, that showed every prominent leader of Tammany to have been involved in some theft or swindle, public or private. But Myers's detachment—lack of guile—went unappreciated: seventeen years were to pass before a second edition of the book was published.

Myers's researches turned up staggering amounts of material on the great financiers of America—startling evidence which shook down all his preconceptions regarding them. While the other muckrakers captured popular attention with articles on trusts, insurance, labor trouble, impure food, and other national scandals, Myers patiently turned pages of old books, magazines, and newspapers to learn the true history of capitalism in America. Nine years passed before his book was ready for publication, and he was justified in considering it his masterpiece. But *The History of the Great American Fortunes* was not greater than all the other books produced by other investigators; it was merely different—it was history: tendentious, narrow-gauged, but history.

Alfred Henry Lewis was called a muckraker. It would have surprised the common critics to learn that he would be remembered—not if at all, but unquestionably—as a creator of substantial literature. They had already forgotten the excitement his first book, *Wolfville,* had caused in 1897, and the praise they themselves had accorded it. Criticism was, in fact, unequal to the task of weighing the numerous and varied books that Lewis had written by the middle years of the muckraking period. When Lewis died in 1914, he was buried as a muckraker, as a Hearst man, without honor.

Lewis was born in Cleveland in 1857. He became a lawyer, but when his health broke down he gave up law and went West, where he spent more than five years as a cattleman on the plains of Texas, New Mexico, and especially Arizona. There Lewis's rough, lawless kind of temperament—three-fifths of it pure individualism, the remainder a compound of learning and forensic aptitude—found itself. He was precisely the character who could understand the men who lived on the plains, played cards and drank and held life cheap, hated Indians and Mexicans, despised Negroes, had a placid irony and talked little. In this society Lewis's *Wolfville* was conceived, although it was not written until later. The central character of the book, which dated Bret Harte as no criticism could have done, was the Old Cattleman, now in the twilight of life, who sat by the hour telling tales of Wolfville, Arizona, where his best years had been spent. In Doc Peets, Texas Thompson, Dave Tutt, Cherokee Hall, and all the others of that permanent company, the Old Cattleman conjured up a pageant of the entire Far West.

After leaving Arizona Lewis spent a number of years practicing law in Kansas City, where he was subsequently attracted to newspaper work on the Kansas City *Star.* He began sending Western sketches to newspapers, including Hearst's *Examiner,* under the pseudonym "Dan Quin." These were gathered into *Wolfville,* dedicated to Hearst, and quickly found readers.

When Lewis returned East as Washington correspondent for the Chicago *Times* and other papers, he had the individualistic and comparatively lawless traits of a Westerner. Yet he was not naïve, for he had been born and raised in a large Midwestern city. Half-sophisticated, half-primitive, he took a peculiar role among the Eastern scribes. He had no faith in reform; he despised Socialism. Trying to reconcile the ethics of the West with those of the East, he wrote *Richard Croker,* a book that purported to be a history of the Tammany chieftain and his demesne. It was a fantastic production, a weird attempt to mix philosophy, history, and appraisal in the manner of Sterne—or, rather, in the manner of the Old Cattleman. Lewis was unable to make up his mind whether Croker was to be praised or condemned; he confused personality with principles; he alternately attacked and discussed his man without balance or sequence.

The Boss (And How He Came to Rule New York), which Lewis published in 1903, was supposedly a muckraking book but was actually a mere fictionalization of the Croker material. By this time Lewis had a grip on the Eastern method and was able to control his impulsive amorality. But the material wasn't his material; the story lacked life and depth. *The President* likewise was a failure, and so were the several other books and many articles which represented Lewis as a political thinker and observer.

Meanwhile Lewis produced a constant flow of stories about his beloved West. *Wolfville Days, Nights, Folks,* and others joined the original book as the garrulous Old Cattleman filled out the huge canvas of his memories. Lewis himself became large and imposing, the Dr. Johnson of a group of men who met in the back room of Considine's saloon on Broadway near Forty-Second Street. The group included, among others, Charley White, the prize fight referee; Bat Masterson, the famous Dodge City sheriff of the "bad man" period, whose life Lewis told fictionally in *The Sunset Trail;* Kid McCoy, the fighter; Eddie Foy, the actor; a famous crook; and Val O'Farrell, a detective sergeant, some of whose cases were told in Lewis's *Confessions of a Detective.* As they sat about the table with Charles Edward Russell, whom they accepted despite his radical point of view, they told marvelous stories of personal adventure. Here the real Lewis sat and warmed himself among his kind of men.

The other Lewis felt himself bound to attack despoilers of national wealth and honor. This was the "muckraking" Lewis who wrote voluminously on railroads, corrupt politicians, and trusts, and who, in the way of a Westerner, applied names prolifically. But muckraking was the least of Lewis. His unbridled violence little more than indicated how much the times could stand; it was nothing more than pyrotechnics, and only the historian or acolyte will ever interest himself in

it. It was his Wolfville stories that found their way into the American heritage. (pp. 118-21)

[Among] Socialists, Sinclair was throughout the decade most thoroughly the muckraker. The Socialism within which he worked was to the muckraking period almost what Populism had been to the period preceding. Socialist newspapers and magazines sold to wide strata of the middle-class and working-class. They were the last refuge for muckraking articles which could not find print elsewhere, but they worked on a premise different from that of the muckraking magazines proper. Having given up capitalism, intellectually at least, they felt more constrained to discuss fundamental social change than to make the wide-eyed and amazed announcements of the muckrakers. The muckrakers had not given up capitalism; it was still practicable to them, by no means damned.

The Socialist movement, however, in many of its phases only supplemented the muckraking movement. Some of the muckrakers, like Sinclair, were Socialists, and many of the muckrakers who did not become militant defenders of capitalism, and even capitalists, after the movement had been destroyed, became Socialists. "Can't you see it?" Sinclair urged Steffens, while *The Shame of the Cities* was devolving upon the public. "Can't you see it?" For Steffens was painting a picture such as no Socialist could have achieved. And it was precisely because Steffens could not "see it" that he was able to see so many things other than Socialism; and it was precisely because the public desired to "see" these many things that he was encouraged to do his work.

Sinclair was by no means certain that muckraking was by itself enough; others were certain. That was why David Graham Phillips pleaded with Russell not to join the Socialists when, in 1908, Russell so decided. It would destroy his influence, Phillips insisted. It did not, of course; but Phillips could no more foresee that than Sinclair could understand Steffens's position, than Sinclair could foresee thirty years ahead to his own principled break with the ideas which had guided him so far. Decisions regarding party support and alliances were made in the heat of daily work, and with the dogmatism of men who perforce must act with full conviction. It might be added that insincerity and intolerance of other men's decisions were not qualities which began or ended with the muckraking movement. (pp. 123-24)

Louis Filler, in his The Muckrakers, *revised edition, The Pennsylvania State University Press, 1976, 456 p.*

MUCKRAKING PUBLICATIONS

WILLIAM ARCHER

[A Scottish dramatist and critic, Archer is best known as one of the earliest and most important translators of Henrik Ibsen's plays and as a drama critic of the London stage during the late nineteenth and early twentieth centuries. In the following excerpt from an essay written in 1910, he considers some characteristics of American muckraking publications and assigns McClure's *precedence among the inexpensive American maga-*

zines that undertook investigative journalism. Unexcerpted portions of the article discuss the lack of such magazines in England.]

Of the many differences between America and England which do not altogether minister to our national self-complacency, none is more striking than the contrast between our sixpenny monthlies and the ten-cent or fifteen-cent magazines that crowd the American bookstalls. On the surface, the contrast is most humiliating; and though, when we look below the surface, we shall find reasons which diminish its significance, it remains, when all is said and done, a disquieting phenomenon.

In trying to work out the equation, I begin by cancelling the factor of fiction. To be candid, I seldom read magazine stories on either side of the water. So far as I know, there is not much to choose between the American and the English short story in its present development. It was the Americans, as a matter of history, who first cultivated the form in our language; but they have certainly no monopoly of it. The same stories will often appear in the magazines of both countries; and though America is probably more prolific of fairly readable matter in this kind, I fancy England holds her own in respect of quality. It is not on the score of fiction, at any rate, that I claim for the American cheap magazine an immeasurable advantage over our own.

Apart from fiction, what do we find in the English sixpenny magazines? May not the rest of their matter fairly be described as magnified, and scarcely glorified, tit-bits? There are articles of cheap personal gossip, addressed for the most part to popular snobbery; articles of pettifogging antiquarianism, on Old Inn Signs, or Peculiar Playing Cards; articles on homes and haunts of the poets, and on Royal Academicians, with reproductions of their masterpieces; articles on Indian snake-charmers and a woman's ascent of Fuji; articles on the Post Office and the Fire Brigade, the Bank of England and the Mint, all gossipy and anecdotic, with a careful avoidance of real information or criticism; articles on golf and billiards, "ski-ing," and salmon-fishing; articles on "A Day in the Life of a Call-Boy," or on "My First Speaking Part," by Miss Birdie Montmorency—articles, in short, on everything that can pass the time for an idle brain, and cannot possibly matter either to the individual or to the nation. The most serious papers ever admitted to these miscellanies are a few pages of illustrated statistics and an occasional peep into popular science. Nor, in the past ten years, does one notice any symptom of a drift towards better things.

Now, in America there are plenty of magazines of the same or even lower calibre—"all story" magazines, and repositories of mere intellectual slush. Also there are the old-established, finely illustrated, expensive, and—to put it frankly—somewhat conventional magazines, such as *Harper's, Scribner's,* the *Century.* But between these two classes—ranking in price with the lower class, in matter, to my thinking, at least on a level with the higher—stands a group of some half-dozen periodicals of extraordinarily vital and stimulating quality, which must be reckoned, I think, among the most valuable literary assets of the American people. There is nothing quite like them in the literature of the world—no periodicals which combine such width of popular appeal with such seriousness of aim and thoroughness of workmanship. None of them costs more than sevenpence-half-penny, yet their difference in intellectual value from our sixpenny magazines is not to be measured in money. In En-

gland it never occurs to me to buy a sixpenny magazine, unless it be to read a new Sherlock Holmes adventure or a sketch by Mr. Jacobs. In America there are at least four magazines which, if I lived there, I would buy every month, certain of finding in each of them some three or four articles of absorbing and illuminating interest. The range of their topics I shall indicate later; meanwhile I state for what it is worth this fact of personal experience.

It is difficult, and not very important, to settle points of precedence; but I believe that the bare idea of producing an illustrated magazine at sixpence or thereabouts originated in England. The *Strand Magazine* was probably the pioneer of the whole procession; and in America the *Cosmopolitan,* edited by John Brisbane Walker (now one of the Hearst group of publications), was early in the field. But the special character of the American cheap magazine as we now know it is mainly due to one man—Mr. S. S. McClure. He it was who invented and developed the particular type we are now studying. Mr. McClure is a very remarkable personality. He has been genially lampooned by Stevenson in *The Wreckers* and by Mr. Howells in *A Hazard of New Fortunes.* There is, indeed, something that lends itself to caricature in his feverish fertility of ideas, his irrepressible energy, his sanguine imagination. But besides being an editor of genius, he is a staunch and sincere idealist. When he determined to make his magazine a power in the land, he also determined that it should be a power for good; and he has nobly fulfilled that resolve. He has a keen instinct (though this he himself denies) for "what the public wants"—what is the opportune subject on which people are ready to accept information and guidance. He knows that it is neither good business nor good sense to try to force upon his readers topics which are either dead or not yet alive. Yet his view is far from being limited by the demands of the passing hour. He has his eye upon the topics of the future, no less than upon those of the present. He garners material for the men who are to work upon them; he leads up to them sedulously and adroitly. He does not edit his magazine from his desk, but will run all over America, to say nothing of crossing the Atlantic, in search of the matter he requires. While he is, as I have said, a staunch idealist, it is equally true that the new note he has introduced into periodical literature is the note of sedulous, unflinching realism. "Thorough" is his motto, and the motto he imposes on all his staff. It is in facts, as distinct from opinions, that he deals—not dead and desiccated facts of the Gradgrind order, but live, illuminating, significant facts. You need not go to his magazine for views, paradoxes, partisan arguments, guesses at truth. The style of article which has made its fame, and which may fairly be called the invention of Mr. McClure, is a richly-documented, soberly-worded study in contemporary history, concentrating into ten or twelve pages matter which could much more easily be expanded into a book ten or twelve times as long. If "Thorough" is the first of his maxims, "Under-statement rather than over-statement" is the second. He abhors exaggeration and sensationalism. His method is to present facts, skilfully marshalled, sternly compressed, and let them speak for themselves. And they *have* spoken for themselves, to the no small enlightenment, and to the lasting good, of the American people. The historian of the future may determine how much of the "uplift" that distinguished the Roosevelt administration was due to the influence of the McClure type of magazine. We cannot, at this distance of time, see things quite in proportion; but it seems to me certain that Mr. McClure both paved the way for President Roosevelt and potently furthered the movements with which his name will always be identified.

The "McClure type," as I have called it, did not spring into existence clear-cut and all of a sudden. It gradually differentiated itself from the English and lower American type. A series of articles on no more "actual" topic than Napoleon established the success of *McClure's Magazine;* and its popularity was confirmed and greatly extended by a series of articles on Lincoln. But the transition from history of the past to history of the present was soon made; and it was Miss Ida M. Tarbell, the writer of the Napoleon and Lincoln series, who was presently to give the world its first great object-lesson in "trust" methods, in her masterly and exhaustive history of the Standard Oil Corporation. Mr. Lincoln Steffens contributed to *McClure's* those brilliant investigations into municipal corruption, which he afterwards collected in a volume under the title of *The Shame of the Cities.* Articles on "The Needs of the Navy," and "Waste in the Navy-Yards," led to two Congressional investigations; and an article on "Government by Commission" in Galveston has had a far-reaching influence on American city politics. If, however, I were asked to point to a single article which exhibited the McClure method in its highest perfection, I think I should select Mr. George Kibbe Turner's study of Chicago, published some three years ago. It condensed into a few fascinating pages, without rhetoric or emphasis of any kind, the most amazing picture of organised, police-protected vice and crime—a picture every line of which was evidently the result of patient, penetrating investigation, and intimate personal knowledge. The same writer has since produced equally masterly studies of the history and methods of Tammany and of the "white slave" traffic in Europe and America—the elaborate machinery of force and fraud whereby the ranks of prostitution are recruited. It is one of the striking features of the American magazines that, though distinctly "family" productions so far as their fiction is concerned, they deal freely with social topics of the utmost delicacy, without either frightening their subscribers off, or achieving any "success of scandal." The reason is, I take it, that they treat their topics in a dispassionate, almost scientific spirit, as remote as possible from hysterical humanitarianism. I am no advocate, assuredly, for forcing knowledge of the horrors of civilisation upon the young and immature; but I have never seen an article in *McClure's* or any magazine of its class that was not perfectly fit to be read by anyone who could conceivably wish to read it. The sincerity and sobriety with which difficult topics are handled—the adherence to essential fact and avoidance of lurid and "picturesque" detail—are beyond praise.

It was not long before *McClure's Magazine* had several rivals in the field of social investigation; and there are now, as I have said, about half a dozen periodicals conducted more or less on the same lines, though most of them make concessions to the more trivial-minded public by devoting several pages each month to portraits of actresses and matter of that description. The *American Magazine* is a direct off-shoot of *McClure's,* founded by some seceding members of the staff, with Miss Tarbell at their head. Other noteworthy magazines of the same class are *Hampton's* (a newcomer in the field), the *Cosmopolitan,* the *Metropolitan, Munsey's,* and *Everybody's Magazine.* It may also be noted that there is an American *Pearson's Magazine,* partly reproducing the matter of the English magazine, but far more serious in tone.

I have before me some five-and-twenty numbers of these vari-

ous magazines, all published during the past ten or twelve months. Let me make a rapid survey of them, and note some of their contents. Space forbids me to attempt more than a mere enumeration of subjects. Some articles are, of course, much abler and more thorough than others; but I shall mention none that is not a product of more or less solid work and thought, honest investigation, and, in many cases, intimate personal experience.

I have attempted a rough classification under seven heads:

(1) Municipal Politics and Police.
(2) National Politics, including questions of Trusts and Finance.
(3) International Politics.
(4) Social Topics.
(5) Science, Medicine, &c.
(6) Sport.
(7) Miscellaneous.

Municipal Politics and Police.

In the particular bundle of magazines before me, municipal politics do not chance to take up very much space. If this be other than a pure chance, it must mean that the vein is for the present worked out; for, until quite recently, it was perhaps the most productive of all. I have already referred to Mr. Steffens' investigations of municipal corruption, to Mr. Kibbe Turner's studies of Chicago and of Tammany, and to the same writer's exposure of the "white slave traffic," which is a form of municipal corruption in every sense of the word. In the bundle before me, perhaps the most important articles are a series entitled, "The Beast and the Jungle," by Judge Lindsey, of the Juvenile Court of Denver (*Everybody's*). It tells an amazing and most dramatic story of the struggles of an honest and humane man to introduce something like honesty and humanity into the administration of the law in the capital of Colorado; and it ought to be read by everyone who is interested in the problem of reclaiming, instead of hardening, juvenile misdemeanants. Another striking article is "The Looting of New York," by Judge Gaynor, now Mayor of New York (*Pearson's*). It shows how, by a "monstrous traction conspiracy," "the poor city is being bled at every pore." Then we have "Policing our Lawless Cities" (*Hampton's*), "The Police Commissioner's Task" (*Metropolitan*), and "The Organised Criminals of New York" (*McClure's*), all by General Bingham, late head of the New York Police. An article in the *Cosmopolitan* deals with the history and exploits of the redoubtable "Black Hand" organisation; and in *McClure's* we have "The Story of a Reformer's Wife: an Account of the Kidnapping of Fremont Older, the Shooting of Francis J. Heney, and the San Francisco Dynamite Plots," by Mrs. Fremont Older. This is only the latest of several extraordinarily interesting articles dealing with the recent history of San Francisco.

National Politics and Finance.

Under this head the articles are so numerous that I can do little more than give a list of significant titles. "The Trust that will Control all Trusts," "Water-Power and the Price of Bread," "The Pinchot-Ballinger Controversy," "Mr. Ballinger and the National Grab-Bag," "The Story of Sugar," "Spreckels and the Philadelphia Sugar Trust"—all these appear in *Hampton's Magazine,* which is making a particularly spirited fight against the "grabbing" of national resources, such as water-power, forests, and Alaskan coal and copper, by the associated magnates of finance. Mr. Ballinger, Secretary of the Interior in Mr. Taft's administration, is roundly accused of favouring the Trusts in their evasions of the law; hence the recurrence of his name in these articles. Then we have: "The Heart of the Railroad Problem" (*Hampton's*) and "Hill against Harriman: the Story of the Ten-Years' Struggle for Railway Supremacy in the West" (*American*). On the question of tariffs, we have "Where the Shoe is Pinched," by Miss Tarbell (*American*); "A Tariff-made City: Pittsburg" (*American*); "The President Reports Progress" and "In the Supreme Court" (*Everybody's*); while an article closely relevant to the tariff question is "Aldrich, Boss of the Senate" (*Hampton's*). Miscellaneous articles under this head are: "The Financial Captains of To-morrow" (*Pearson's*), "The Cost of the Wall-Street Game" (*Everybody's*), "The Direct Primary" (*Munsey's*), "Postal Savings Banks" (*Pearson's*), "Oklahoma and the Indian: a Carnival of Graft" (*Hampton's*), "The Rebate Conspiracy" (*Cosmopolitan*), "The Yellow Pariahs" (*Cosmopolitan*), "The Negro in Politics" (*Hampton's*), "A Continent Despoiled" (*McClure's*). Almost all these articles are so clearly, vigorously written, and give such curious insight into significant phases of human nature, that even an outsider like myself, not directly concerned in the matters at issue, can read them with the keenest interest.

International Politics.

As the significance of the Atlantic Ocean diminishes, and America is being more and more swept into the general stream of world-affairs, it is natural that a new interest in the affairs of other nations should manifest itself. It has done so very strikingly of recent years. It was *McClure's,* for example, which published Kuropatkin's commentaries on the Russo-Japanese War; it is *McClure's* which has recently given us "The Ominous Hush in Europe," "The New Germany: an Object-Lesson," "Germany's Preparedness for War," and "The Secrets of the Schluesselberg." Among other articles on foreign affairs and personalities which I find in the pile before me, I may mention "The Terror on Europe's Threshold" (*Everybody's*)—a very remarkable paper; "England's Epoch-making Budget" (*Cosmopolitan*); "America and the Vatican" (*Metropolitan*); "The New Régime in China" (*Everybody's*); "Why Japan does not want to Fight," and "Will Japan become a Christian Nation?" two strikingly well-informed articles in *Hampton's;* "Barbarous Mexico," a series of papers in the *American;* "Spiking Down an Empire" (*Everybody's*)—an account of the new Canadian trans-Continental Railway; and in the *Metropolitan* articles on the Czar of Russia and the King of England, so much superior to the ordinary patchworks of gossip that they may fairly claim a place in this section.

Social Topics.

Under this somewhat vague heading a great number of articles may naturally be classed. I pick out only some of the more remarkable. In the *American* Mr. Ray Stannard Baker has written a series of articles under the general title of "The Spiritual Unrest." It includes such papers as "The Case against Trinity" (an exposure of scandals connected with the administration of property belonging to the richest church in New York), "The Godlessness of New York," "The Faith of the Unchurched," "Lift Men from Gutter, or Remove the Gutter—Which?" These articles are all founded on a genuine examination of conditions, and are full of actual first-hand knowledge. A somewhat analogous series has been running in the *Cosmopolitan* under the sensational titles of "Blasting the Rock of Ages," "Polyglots in Temples of Babel," "Chris-

tianity in the Crucible," and "Rallying Round the Cross." These papers deal with the very advanced views on religion, morals, and politics alleged to be disseminated in American universities, and with the counterblasts attempted by the churches. A series in *Hampton's* called "Beating Men to Make them Good" deals with the abuses and absurdities of the prison system; and in the same magazine a series entitled, "What Eight Million Women Want," describes the social and political activities of women's clubs throughout America, which have turned from the discussion of Browning and the musical glasses to questions of street cleaning, sanitation, housing, and progressive activities in general. A few more titles will show that topics of special interest to women predominate in this section: "Women and Occupations," "The Beauty Business," "Eugenics," and "A Servant on the Servant Question" (*American*); "The Bird Tribute to Vanity" (*Hampton's*); "The Story of a Spring Hat" (*Metropolitan*); "Divorce and Public Welfare" (*McClure's*). Miss Tarbell has recently begun in the *American* what promises to be a long series of articles on "The American Woman," beginning with studies of the women of the Revolutionary period.

Science, Medicine, &c.

Some of the ablest and most important work done for the American magazines falls under this heading. Here again it seems to me that *McClure's* takes a clear lead with such articles as "Conquering Spinal Meningitis," "What we know about Cancer," "The Vampire of the South" (the terrible hookworm), and "Pellagra, the Medical Mystery of To-day." All these articles are models of investigation and concentration, and I, for one, find them absorbingly interesting. In the same category come "The Red Cross and Tuberculosis," "War on the White Death," and Professor Münsterberg on "Nerves" (*Metropolitan*); "The Sacrifice of the Innocents" and "Exercise that Rests" (*Cosmopolitan*). Then we have "The Nature of Physical Life" and "Does the Weather Bureau Make Good?" (*Everybody's*); "In a Dynamite Factory" (*Metropolitan*); "The Coming Spectacle in the Skies" (*Hampton's*); "Psychology and the Market," by Münsterberg (*McClure's*). A considerable sub-section might be formed of articles on those "super-normal" topics which hover on the borderlands of science: such as "Telepathy" (*Pearson's*)—a destructive criticism; "Eusapia Palladino" (*McClure's*); "On the Trail of the Ghost," and Lombroso on "What I think of Psychical Research," in *Hampton's*. It is doubtful whether such articles as "Automobiles of the Air" (*Hampton's*) and "The Grand Week of Flying" (*Everybody's*) ought to take their place in this section or in the next.

Sport.

The comparative rarity of articles on sport in the magazines I am reviewing is worthy of notice. It cannot mean that the American public is uninterested in the topic, but rather, I suppose, that the field is occupied by the daily paper and by magazines of a lower class. It is no doubt to the interest aroused by Mr. Roosevelt's expedition that we owe "Trapping Big Game in the Heart of Africa" (*Hampton's*) and "Hunting in British East Africa" (*Metropolitan*). For the rest, there fall under this heading, "Sea Elephant Hunting in the Antarctic" (*Hampton's*), "Trapping Wild Horses in Nevada" (*McClure's*), "The Transformers of Baseball" (*Pearson's*), "The Fine Points of the Game" (*American*), "Golf in America" and "Behind the Scenes in Football" (*Metropolitan*). Here ends the list, so far as the magazines immediately before me are concerned.

Miscellaneous.

There are really few articles which might not at a pinch have been placed under one or other of the foregoing headings. Two papers in *Hampton's* on "Our Undermanned Navy" and "The Hitting Power of the American Navy," might have been assigned to the section of "National Politics"; and so might "The Lure of Gold" (*Hampton's*). "The Modern Church Building: What Should It Be?" (*Munsey's*) and "The Indecent Stage" (*American*) might have ranked under "Social Topics." But there is a small residue of articles which it is difficult to range under any general heading. Such are Ferrero's studies of "Nero" and "The Influence of the Vine," in *McClure's;* papers on "Cleveland's Opinions of Men" and "Cleveland as a Lawyer," in the same magazine; "Retrospections of an Active Life," by John Bigelow, in the *Metropolitan;* and papers on the Astors, the Goulds, and other great American families, in the *Cosmopolitan.* Under the "Miscellaneous" rubric, too, would come a good deal of cheap padding which most of the magazines admit: articles on plays and players, which are, as a rule, mere text for illustrations, and personal paragraphs accompanying portraits of notabilities of the moment.

One curious point to which I must call attention is the almost total absence from these magazines of the literary essay, the aesthetic appreciation, the article on painting, sculpture, or music. The traditional Bostonian spirit is wholly unrepresented in the modern cheap magazine. I find, indeed, articles on "Heroes and Heroines of the Violin" (*Everybody's*), and "Cosima Wagner, the Widow of Bayreuth" (*Munsey's*), but these consist of mere personal gossip, without any critical pretensions. The nearest approach to a purely literary article is one of a series in *Munsey's,* entitled "Famous Affinities of History: Thackeray and Mrs. Brookfield." For the rest, "Chatter about Harriet" is evidently not in demand. Literary and artistic topics are left almost entirely to the older and more expensive magazines. (pp. 921-30)

The United States present a phenomenon new to history—a land of vast natural resources in process of feverishly-rapid exploitation—a land of great cities expanding at an unprecedented rate. Under such conditions, immense prizes await the forceful, unscrupulous financier, and immense temptations beset both the municipal and the State politician. A "grab" of mineral lands or of water-power, or the filching from the community, on preposterous terms, of a rapid-transit "franchise," may mean the almost immediate acquisition of a gigantic fortune. What wonder that corruption is rampant, and that an infinitude of ingenuity, skill, and daring is devoted to evading inadequate and feebly-enforced laws, and securing the richest pickings from a treasure-cave, beside which Aladdin's was but a trumpery toy-shop! It is probable that England after the Norman Conquest may have presented in miniature a similar scene of rapine; but not since then has our slow-growing community offered anything like the same openings for unbridled acquisitiveness. The United States is like an enormously rich country overrun by a horde of robber barons, and very inadequately policed by the central government and by certain local vigilance societies. The cheap magazines find in this situation an unexampled opportunity. In writing historical and economic studies which have all the fascination of a detective story, they at the same time help to organise and reinforce the movement for what may be called, in the widest sense of the word, a more efficient national police. The opponents of this movement have nicknamed it

"muck-raking"; and it is probable enough that some of the clamour for reform has been either dishonest or insincerely sensational. But these accusations cannot lie for a moment against the best of the cheap magazines. Their work has been no less sincere than efficient, and they have been an incalculable force for good. The logical weakness of their position, it seems to me, lies in an insufficient thinking-out of the fundamental ideas on which their crusade is based. They do not see that most of the evils they attack are inevitable results of the national creed of individualism. They lack either the insight or the courage to admit that some form of collectivism is the only permanent check upon the enslavement of the people by the most amazing plutocracy the world has ever seen. (pp. 930-31)

William Archer, "The American Cheap Magazine," in The Fortnightly Review, *n. s. Vol. LXXXVI, No. DXXI, May, 1910, pp. 921-32.*

ROBERT CANTWELL

[*Cantwell was an American journalist, novelist, and short story writer. He served as literary editor and contributing editor of many popular periodicals from the 1930s through the 1950s, including* Time, Newsweek, *and the* New Republic. *Cantwell's two widely praised novels,* Laugh and Lie Down (*1931*) *and* The Land of Plenty (*1934*), *are often discussed with pro-Communist works of the thirties, although Cantwell himself stressed the distinction between the Proletarian and the Depression novel, considering his works representative of the latter. Cantwell worked with Lincoln Steffens in Boston in 1929, researching the life of merchant and social reformer E. A. Filene. In the following discussion of* McClure's, *he offers reasons for the muckrakers' widespread success and notes changes in American popular magazines after their decline.*]

Early in May, 1906, an extraordinary group of journalists walked out of the most sensationally successful magazine in American history. They left in a body. There were two men from the business department, an associate editor, the managing editor and his assistant, and three of the most celebrated magazine writers of the time—Ida Tarbell, Lincoln Steffens, and Ray Stannard Baker. Ida Tarbell was nearly fifty; she had written her lives of Lincoln and her famous *History of the Standard Oil Company.* Steffens was celebrating his fortieth birthday at the time of the walkout; he had published his *Shame of the Cities* and had been in Colorado, working on an article on Ben Lindsay, when the break came. Baker had not at that time written his best sellers under the name of David Grayson, but he was widely known, and he had been with the magazine through the six years of its greatest growth. These writers were joined by William Allen White and Finley Peter Dunne; they raised $200,000, bought the *American Magazine* and set out to rival the magazine they had left.

This was *McClure's.* Founded thirteen years before by the ambitious, volatile Samuel Sidney McClure, it had swept into an exhilarating financial, political, and literary success so rapidly that no other publication of its time could be compared to it. When it was founded, American periodical publishing was dominated by the four great, venerable, distinguished literary magazines—*Harpers, Scribners,* the *Atlantic* and *Century.* Modelled on the English magazines, printing genteel fiction by some highly skilled practitioners and a good deal of expertly composed but unexciting literary criticism, they had never been really popular. *Harpers* led them with

S.S. McClure, founder and editor of the muckraking journal McClure's.

a circulation of 130,000. This was, however, as great a circulation as any American magazine had up to that time, with the brief exception of *Godey's Lady's Book,* which had reached 150,000 in 1850. Indeed, it was commonly believed then that Americans were not magazine readers, just as it is generally believed now that they will not buy books: Poe had increased the circulation of *Gresham's* from 6000 to 30,000, but Henry Adams, despite some distinguished contributors and some timely articles, could not get *The North American Review* above 2000. That had been the tradition when McClure and Munsey launched their cheap magazines. By the time Steffens and Tarbell left in 1906, popular magazines were firmly established in American cultural life: *McClure's* alone had a circulation of 750,000. More importantly, a group of magazines with similar policies had swept up with it: *Hampton's* increased from 13,000 to 440,000; *Everybody's,* which had been the house organ for Wanamaker's department store, climbed to 735,000; *Collier's* had 500,000 by 1909 and one million by 1912; *Cosmopolitan* and the *American Magazine* grew in proportion. Consequently, when Steffens and Tarbell left *McClure's* it was no mere editorial squabble—American popular magazines, and not simply *McClure's* and the muckrakers, had come into existence during their careers. Largely, in fact, as a result of their bold and simultaneous editorial coups—*The History of the Standard Oil Company* and *The Shame of the Cities.* When they began

these works there were no popular American magazines; when they left *McClure's,* magazines had something of the popularity, and a good deal of the character, that they have now.

The term muckrakers applied to these people is as misleading now as it was when Ellery Sedgwick, then a young journalist, first tagged them with it—for it was Sedgwick and not Roosevelt who first applied Bunyan's phrase to describe them. Why had they been so sensationally successful? The commonly accepted answer has been that their exposures of the corruption of American political and social life coincided with a great stirring of popular revolt. Theirs was, [Vernon L.] Parrington says, "a dramatic discovery . . . when the corruption of American politics was laid on the threshold of business—like a bastard on the doorstep of the father—a tremendous disturbance resulted. There was a great fluttering and clamor amongst the bats and the owls. . . ." The political side of the muckrakers' contribution was unquestionably great, but it has been overvalued, and the simple journalistic boldness and effectiveness of their writing has been overlooked. After thirty years the simple bulk of their work is astonishing; in five years' time a handful of gifted writers conducted a searching exploration of American society—industrial, financial, political, and moral. Moreover, they did this with a wealth of local color, with wonderful savory names and places that had never been elevated into prose before. It was not because the muckrakers exposed the corruption of Minneapolis, for example, that they were widely read, but because they wrote about Minneapolis at a time when it had not been written about, without patronizing or boosting it, and with an attempt to explore its life realistically and intelligently.

They wrote, in short, an intimate, anecdotal, behind-the-scenes history of their own times—or, rather, they tried to write it, for they often fell down. They traced the intricate relationship of the police, the underworld, the local political bosses, the secret connections between the new corporations (then consolidating at an unprecedented rate) and the legislatures and the courts. In doing this they drew a new cast of characters for the drama of American society: bosses, professional politicians, reformers, racketeers, captains of industry. Everybody recognized these native types; everybody knew about them; but they had not been characterized before; their social functions had not been analyzed. At the same time, the muckrakers pictured stage settings that everybody recognized but that nobody had written about—oil refineries, slums, the red-light districts, the hotel rooms where political deals were made—the familiar, unadorned, homely stages where the teeming day-to-day dramas of American life were enacted. How could the aloof literary magazines of the East, with their essays and their contributions from distinguished English novelists, tap this rich material?

For literary, and not for political reasons, the muckrakers were successful. Their writing was jagged and hasty, and their moralizing now sounds not only dull but a little phony, yet they charged into situations that were deliberately obscured by the people involved in them; they sized up hundreds of complicated and intense struggles at their moment of greatest intensity; they dealt with material subject to great pressure and about which journalists could easily be misled. In a time of oppressive literary gentility they covered the histories of the great fortunes and the histories of corporations—something that had not been done before and that has scarcely been done well since—the real estate holdings of churches, the ownership of houses of prostitution, insurance scandals, railway scandals, the political set-ups of Ohio, Missouri, Wisconsin, Chicago, Cleveland, San Francisco, New York. The new huge cities of the West had not been explored after their growth through the 70's and 80's (just as, say, Tulsa, Oklahoma, has not been written about after its astonishing growth through the 1920's) and because they wrote of them, the writing of the muckrakers was packed with local color, the names and appearance of hotels and bars, crusading ministers and town bosses and bankers. They told people who owned the factories they worked in, who rigged the votes they cast, who profited from the new bond issue, the new street-railway franchise and the new city hall, who foreclosed the mortgage, tightened credit, and controlled the Irish vote on the other side of the river. Their exposures, as such, were not so sensational. People knew all the scandals, and worse ones. But they liked to read about towns they knew, characters they recognized, and a setting they understood. The old magazines had never given them that.

American popular magazines thus began by making an original contribution to American literature and to American social life. But from the start there had been a split between the people who wrote for the muckraking magazines and the people who owned them, and the break between owner and editors was symbolized by the walkout at *McClure's*. McClure had not wanted a crusading publication. He wanted a cheap one that would appeal to the masses, and he believed that the masses wanted sensational, if not lurid, general informative articles—short, easily digestible material like biographies of Lincoln and Napoleon. If he had to have muckraking, he wanted it to be non-political—an account of the increase in murders, for example. According to Steffens, McClure came to believe that democracy itself was responsible for the evils that the muckrakers exposed, and consequently tried to direct their exposures to attacks on democracy. Some stories had been killed, an attack on the insurance companies was shelved. Why the break came so dramatically was not made clear in either Steffens' or McClure's autobiography; writing to his father a few days after it occurred, Steffens said that McClure was planning to launch a giant stock promotion and organize a string of commercial companies. The significant point is that the direction of *McClure's* changed after the split—and the change was typical of that taking place in popular magazines in general. Willa Cather, who had not joined the insurgents, was made editor of *McClure's*. The type of writing that she did, finished and careful—far better in detail, in fact, than the hasty journalism of her predecessors—set the tone for American popular magazine writing. It bore only an indirect relation to current political and economic struggles; it cried no evils and proposed no remedies. After a brief flyer in what might be called right-wing muckraking (Ellery Sedgwick joined the staff after Steffens and Tarbell left) *McClure's* settled down to the printing of more fiction, the stories of the outstanding English romancers—and more advertising.

McClure's was only an episode in American periodical publishing history, but it throws a good deal of light on its entire thirty-year course. Popular magazines began by distributing a literature of information and inquiry—even of discontent—a kind of writing which, for all its unevenness, was calculated to inform readers of the life of communities like their own, and to stimulate skeptical discussion of their institutions. Having gained circulation in this way, they insensibly shifted and began to distribute a different kind of reading matter which has grown into the magazine literature we now

have. It would be wrong to imply that the owners and advertisers were solely responsible for this; the limitations of the muckrakers, their inability to set any new goal for themselves once their initial survey was completed, was as great a factor. In any event a literature that was, in a studied way, not political and not controversial came into being and became the chief product of the popular magazines. It still is. Their circulation did not fall, but it assumed a different character. The muckraking magazines grew almost without advertising and their income was based on their sales; in the later publications advertising income became at least as important as the income from newsstand sales. People continued to buy magazines, in other words, after magazines ceased to publish the type of material that had made them popular, but readers no longer carried the full cost of them. There are innumerable explanations of the economics of advertising, none of which carry much conviction, but in the history of popular magazines advertising has played a unique role: It has constituted, in effect, a gigantic subsidy placed behind a certain type of literature—a subsidy given by the biggest national corporations, making it possible for the magazines receiving it to be distributed for less than their cost of production. The literature that is thus supported is varied and sometimes it is so skillfully done as to seem brilliant—the magazines that carry it now are so competently edited that beside them the scratchy publications of the muckrakers seem as heavy as a Sears-Roebuck catalogue. But it is essentially a literature, not of inquiry, but of distraction, a literature least of all calculated to provoke questions or excite controversy, and with the strange characteristic of being unsuited for the communication of information or the analysis of ideas. (pp. 345-49)

    Robert Cantwell, "Journalism—Magazines," in America Now: An Inquiry into Civilization in the United States, *edited by Harold E. Stearns, Charles Scribner's Sons, 1938, pp. 345-55.*

PETER LYON

[*Lyon is an American biographer, travel writer, and critic. The following excerpt from his* Success Story: The Life and Times of S. S. McClure *outlines the role of editor S. S. McClure and of* McClure's *magazine in initiating the muckraking phase in American journalism.*]

[S. S. McClure was absent from the offices of *McClure's* magazine for much of 1901 and 1902 for health reasons. When he returned] he began to turn the office upside down, shaking the staff out of its shoes.

Bert Boyden, for one, was seriously annoyed at what seemed to him to be McClure's inexcusably meddlesome behavior. He sent off a letter of complaint to Miss Tarbell in Cleveland, where she was engaged in the exasperating work of tracing the devious development of the Standard Oil Company. Miss Tarbell sensed how angry Boyden was with McClure. Maternally she both soothed and scolded him:

> Dear Mr. Boyden:—
>
> . . . Things will come out all right. The General may stir up things and interfere with general comfort but he puts the health of life into the work at the same time. And there's nobody else who can to the same degree. When he's fussing & fretting & bothering you keep your eyes open, something is weak or wrong. He feels it and the rest of us are too much occupied with our little daily tasks to be con-

scious that there is a weakness. . . . Never forget that it was he & nobody else who has created that place. You must learn to believe in him & *use* him if you are going to be happy there. He is a very extraordinary creature, you can't put him into a machine and make him run smoothly with the other wheels and things. We don't need him there. Able methodical people grow on every bush but genius comes once in a generation and if you ever get in its vicinity thank the Lord & *stick.* You probably will be laid up now and then in a sanatarium recovering from the effort to follow him but that's a small matter if you really get into touch finally with that wonderful brain. . . .

Above all, don't worry. What you are going through now we've all been through steadily ever since I came into the office. If there was nothing in all this but the annoyance and uncertainty & confusion—that is if there were no results—then we might rebel, but there are always results—vital ones. The big things which the magazine has done have always come about through these upheavals. Try not to mind! . . . The great schemes, the daring moves in that business have always been Mr. McC's. They will continue to be. His one hundredth idea is a stroke of genius. Be on hand to grasp that one hundredth idea! . . .

Faithfully yours
Ida M. Tarbell

April 26

This upheaval was the genuine article, with department heads whirling apprehensively about as in a game of musical chairs. The head of the London office was summoned home to take charge of the book business; the editor of the syndicate's Woman's Page was dispatched to London in his place; nobody was safe. . . . [McClure] concluded that Baker should become editor-in-chief and urged him most earnestly to accept. "You can always call upon me for advice," he assured Baker, "and upon all of us, but mainly upon me, and in the conduct of the magazine you will be responsible to the American people first of all, and to me only." Baker reserved his decision.

What was so wrong, to have precipitated all this fussing and fretting? Quite simply, the magazine. In S. S.'s absence, it had not only lost its vitality, it had also lost some fifty thousand subscribers. He got all the editors together and launched into a long, rambling lecture, as mercurial as a passage of free association from a patient lying on a psychoanalyst's couch.

"The editors of *McClure's* magazine," he began, "should attempt to do something on every great event that happens that is great, such as McKinley's death, et cetera, that is of interest because it has happened. To produce a great deal each month of the proper material the men who do these great things must be met, seen, and talked with, no matter what they do, and these editors must learn by observation what is well done." At this point his editors could have been forgiven for thinking that perhaps McClure felt they should have published an article in praise of the anarchist Leon Csolgosz [President McKinley's assassin], but it developed that what McClure meant was that they were publishing nothing timely, nothing that reflected what people were concerned about.

"I am going to try the experiment of shifting this editorial work on the staff of *McClure's* magazine and see the result. It will be a different magazine, because every man makes a different magazine; it is simply judging men and women and seeing what should go in. I read the papers and when I find anything interesting cut it out." Now from one pocket after another he pulled forth enough clippings to cram a wastebasket. "For example I see this announcement in the newspapers of wonderful etchings . . . arrange to have them reproduced in the magazine . . . go and find out at the Grolier Club . . . perhaps nothing comes of it but perhaps something does. . . .

"Lord Kelvin in Rochester; he is one of the greatest scientists living . . . people have forgotten how much the present conditions in the world are due to his inventions. . . . Take Pupin who made the invention for telephoning to San Francisco. . . . This Harper advertisement is not very good, we can do better, but there are ideas there. . . . Here are a lot of men, the Columbia strong men, there are a lot of things to be had from those chaps, how they got strong. That is worth investigating. . . . Look it up sometime, every one of these ideas leads somewhere."

He brushed the clippings aside and said something startling: "The proper policy of doing business is never to originate if you can imitate. It is my policy. I let Munsey demonstrate the success of the ten-cent magazine in two ways, getting circulation and getting advertising, before putting the magazine down to ten cents. I am so conservative I am rarely willing to perform experiments myself. To Mr. Munsey's boldness is due the success of the ten-cent magazine largely.

"I mean to add to the size of the magazine," McClure said, a few minutes later. "I wish I were in form to talk about the beauty of the cover, human interest, inside grasp on vital movements of the times, but I cannot today. . . . This I have to let go, I cannot do it.

"There are two elements required in editing this magazine, one the proper brain and the other the proper environment. Get something out of everything, look everywhere for stuff, every man you meet is an original source of information. Now, the editor of this magazine has to read daily newspapers in different parts of the country. I read four hours a day during all those years of my editing. . . .

"Half of the stuff in *McClure's* is stuff that comes without work. There are three or four high-salaried members on the staff and we are short of articles. I don't understand it.

"My present plan is to found another magazine so as to have something for you all to do."

He nodded. The meeting broke up. Bert Boyden left with the others, no doubt wondering where was that one hundredth idea.

It came. There were, as McClure had said, three high-salaried staff writers, yet the magazine was short of articles. He considered, but only very briefly.

Miss Tarbell, as he knew, was hard at work on her history of the Standard Oil Company and had been ever since the previous October. (Indeed, McClure had been instrumental in supplying her with an unexpected and most authoritative source of information. Soon after the projected series was announced in the issue of November, 1901, McClure had run across Mark Twain, who asked him whether Miss Tarbell, in gathering her research, would care to talk to his good friend Henry H. Rogers. Since Rogers was one of the chief executives of Standard Oil, Miss Tarbell had of course grabbed at the chance.) McClure was eagerly looking forward to reading the first three of her articles, which were, she had told him, nearly finished.

Baker, as S. S. knew, had been industriously at work not only writing articles for *McClure's* under his own by-line but also doctoring the account of Miss Stone's adventures amongst the brigands.

But what in thunder had Lincoln Steffens been doing? (In fact, although McClure had no way of knowing it, Steffens had been seriously planning to chuck his job on *McClure's* either to buy and run a small Connecticut weekly newspaper or to have another stab at writing his novel.) It was clear that Steffens was not earning his salary at a desk in New York. Already McClure had once bid him get out, travel, look around, meet people, listen, learn. Now more firmly he issued the same orders, but this time he accompanied them with "that one hundredth idea." He instructed Steffens to scout the possibilities for a series of articles on state and municipal governments. It was in McClure's mind that William Allen White might write some of the articles; maybe Steffens might write some, too; but there was plenty of material for a series; McClure was sure of it; he had newspaper clippings in his pockets to prove it. Miss Tarbell agreed with him: she had learned enough about Cleveland, while researching her Standard Oil series, to be sure that there was an article in the reform mayor, Tom Johnson.

A reform mayor? Steffens sniffed. His heart wasn't in the assignment. But he permitted himself to be thrust out upon the road to fame.

At last McClure's two pet projects—the trusts and the iniquity of municipal government—were in capable, if reluctant, hands. As for the third of his high-salaried staff writers, McClure was still hopeful Baker would be editor-in-chief. Perversely, Baker would not. He went west in July and before long he was absorbed in another attempt at writing a novel.

Fortunately Baker was more journalist than novelist. He had the journalist's dream of The Great American Novel. It was to illumine all the murky forces in American life which he had himself witnessed in opposition: Debs and Pullman, Coxey's Army of the unemployed and the new prosperity of 1900, the invisible government of capital and the record floods of immigrants that were being channeled into reservoirs of exploited labor. When his work on the novel began to falter, when he found that even a close reading of Sidney Webb's *Industrial Democracy* gave him no hint as to how a man feels when he is out on strike, Baker showed that he was an instinctive journalist. He laid down his pencil and took a train to Wilkes-Barre, where the hard-coal miners had been on strike for nearly five months, so that he might gather material for his novel at first hand.

Here, forsaking his novel, Baker turned again to *McClure's* magazine like a filing to a magnet. For McClure was also in Wilkes-Barre.

Now S. S. had encouraged Baker to work on his novel—had insisted on paying him half his salary while he was doing so, had assured him that it would be a great success, and had even talked of selling a hundred thousand copies of it. But McClure was in Wilkes-Barre to chase down an idea that had interested him; in no time he had infected Baker with his enthusiasm.

The coal strike was about to be settled and even the manner of its settlement was a sign of the changing times. Earlier Presidents would have called out the army and driven the miners back into their pits at bayonet's point. But Roosevelt unprecedentedly stepped into the dispute and, bespeaking the rights and interests of the public, forced the owners and miners to submit their quarrel to arbitration. It was a long time since a President had not instinctively backed the business community.

Interesting; but something else had brought McClure here. There were seven thousand miners who had refused to go on strike and another ten thousand strikebreakers who had been brought into the area. Leaving aside the strikebreakers, what about the non-strikers? The press had been filled with lurid stories about their stormy life: their houses had allegedly been stoned and sometimes burned; allegedly many of them had been attacked, some seriously injured, and a few killed. The operators had naturally accused the union of these crimes; spokesmen for the union had hotly denied the charges and attributed all violence to "the coal and iron police . . . mostly city thugs with orders to shoot and kill." Where was the truth? And—no matter who was right—what had made seven thousand miners decide to stick to their jobs, no matter what the danger to themselves and their families? In 1902, these questions were still as sticky as fresh paint. In his room in the Hotel Sterling, McClure put the questions to Baker and, to his delight, Baker undertook to answer them.

In mid-November Baker's article reached the New York office. It was a dispassionate indictment of the lawlessness of a few members of the United Mine Workers. "This article," McClure wrote Baker, in congratulation, "will undoubtedly be the most important publication of this winter."

Meanwhile, Steffens's article on the corruption of municipal government in Minneapolis had likewise arrived in New York. "You have made a marvelous success," McClure wrote Steffens. "I think [your article] will probably arouse more attention than any article we have published for a long time, although we are going to get a hummer from Baker on the coal mines."

As for Miss Tarbell, her third article on the Standard Oil Company was already at hand. McClure scarcely needed to write her a letter of praise; he had already shown what he thought of her series by giving her a substantial block of S. S. McClure Company stock.

Here they were, then: three long, vivid, arresting, carefully documented articles, each probing deep into a sore in the American body social and politic. McClure could take deep satisfaction in them. They were the culmination of his editorial schemes; what he had been groping for in 1899 and 1900 was coming alive under his hand. He would publish all three articles in the issue of January, 1903. A lesser editor might have hesitated. Wasn't it poor policy to print three such contentious papers—arraignments of industry, labor, and government—all in one issue? McClure never hesitated. Each article interested him intensely: that was all that mattered.

But he was aware that he was making an extraordinary decision. He recognized that he had to show his readers he knew what he was doing. He wrote a special editorial, perhaps the most important ever to be published in an American magazine. "Concerning Three Articles in this Number of *McClure's*," he called it, "and a Coincidence that May Set Us Thinking":

How many of those who have read through this number of the magazine noticed that it contains three articles on one subject? We did not plan it so; it is a coincidence that the January *McClure's* is such an arraignment of American character as should make every one of us stop and think. How many noticed that?

The leading article, "The Shame of Minneapolis," might have been called "The American Contempt of Law." That title could well have served for the current chapter of Miss Tarbell's *History of Standard Oil.* And it would have fitted perfectly Mr. Baker's "The Right to Work." All together, these articles come pretty near showing how universal is this dangerous trait of ours. Miss Tarbell has our capitalists conspiring among themselves, deliberately, shrewdly, upon legal advice, to break the law so far as it restrained them and to misuse it to restrain others who were in their way. Mr. Baker shows labor, the ancient enemy of capital, and the chief complainant of the trusts' unlawful acts, itself committing and excusing crimes. And in "The Shame of Minneapolis" we see the administration of a city employing criminals to commit crimes for the profit of the elected officials, while the citizens—Americans of good stock and more than average culture, and honest, healthy Scandinavians—stood by complacent and not alarmed.

Capitalists, workingmen, politicians, citizens—all breaking the law, or letting it be broken. Who is left to uphold it? The lawyers? Some of the best lawyers in this country are hired, not to go into court to defend cases, but to advise corporations and business firms how they can get around the law without too great a risk of punishment. The judges? Too many of them so respect the laws that for some "error" or quibble they restore to office and liberty men convicted on evidence overwhelmingly convincing to common sense. The churches? We know of one, an ancient and wealthy establishment, which had to be compelled by a Tammany hold-over health officer to put its tenements in sanitary condition. The colleges? They do not understand.

There is no one left; none but all of us. Capital is learning (with indignation at labor's unlawful acts) that its rival's contempt for law is a menace to property. Labor has shrieked the belief that the illegal power of capital is a menace to the worker. These two are drawing together. Last November when a strike was threatened by the yardmen on all the railroads centering in Chicago, the men got together and settled by raising wages, and raising freight-rates too. They made the public pay. We all are doing our worst and making the public pay. The public is the people. We forget that we all are the people; that while each of us in his group can shove off on the rest the bill of to-day, the debt is only postponed; the rest are passing it on back to us. We have to pay in the end, every one of us. And in the end the sum total of the debt will be our liberty.

This editorial was a flaring balefire, rallying progressives and reformers all across the country. Its impact was felt first on the newsstands. The January number was sold out. At one stroke *McClure's* magazine had recouped all its lost circulation. "The greatest success we have ever had," McClure wrote exultantly to Baker. "Your articles have been more important than anything appearing in any other magazine," he

told Steffens. "Your articles are the great magazine feature of recent years," he wrote Miss Tarbell.

Other magazine editors, after their first shock of astonishment, hastily gobbled down the McClure formula. For some it meant an overhaul of format, even sometimes a change of title; but the direction in which they had to go was clear enough, and McClure had pointed the way. *Collier's, Leslie's, The Cosmopolitan, Success, Everybody's, Pearson's, Hampton's*—one after another they acquired new editors or owners, one after another they embraced the new journalism of exposure. Even *The Ladies' Home Journal* had a genteel fling at it.

The muckraking era had begun.

Was it, as McClure had insisted, just a coincidence? He wrote: "We did not plan it so"; and subsequent historians have agreed that the origins of the muckraking movement were largely accidental. Conceivably they might be considered accidental if Steffens, Baker, and Tarbell had all been freelance writers who, working independently of an editor and of each other, had simply happened to simultaneously submit their pieces to a receptive editor. But, as we have seen, they were staff writers directed and supervised at every step by an editor who knew precisely what he wanted, who regarded them, indeed, as extensions of his own intelligence. The only thing McClure didn't know about their work—for he generously afforded them every latitude to study their subjects thoroughly—was when they would have their articles ready. In that sense only was there any "accident" about the origins of muckraking in the issue of *McClure's* magazine for January, 1903. McClure himself, when he wrote, "We did not plan it so," was disingenuous. He had begun planning it two or three years before. (pp. 199-206)

Peter Lyon, "The Magazine—1893-1912," in his Success Story: The Life and Times of S. S. McClure, *1963. Reprint by Everett/Edwards, Inc., 1967, pp. 111-338.*

SOCIAL AND POLITICAL IDEAS

DAVID MARK CHALMERS

[*Chalmers is an American critic and historian who has written, edited, and contributed to several studies of the muckrakers and their era. He is also the author of* Hooded Americanism: The History of the Ku Klux Klan (1965) *and has edited an abridged edition of Ida Tarbell's* History of the Standard Oil Company (1966). *In the following excerpt, Chalmers discusses the social and political ideas of the muckrakers.*]

Lincoln Steffens told in his autobiography of accepting a challenge to prove that his home town of Greenwich, Connecticut, was typically corrupt. While he spoke, his assistant, Walter Lippmann, drew on a blackboard a diagram of the dishonest functioning of government in the average American city. Then with the help of the audience, Steffens filled in the names of the Greenwich exemplars. According to the traditional depiction of them, the muckrakers functioned like this, writing in the names of grafters on a ready-made chart. This interpretation, however, misses the real spirit and importance of the movement. The difficulty in understanding the muckrakers results from the nature of their crusade and the way it developed. The participants were journalists, not academicians or legislators. Their work was adapted to the medium of the popular magazines and tended to develop in installment fashion. Few of the writers initially began with a broad analysis of the national ills. They started with a particular city or industry and built up a picture of the nation as a whole, article by article, series by series. Each crystalized his philosophy before the end of the era of exposés. Nevertheless, the readers' initial impression of naivete and lack of direction was often the one that remained.

Theodore Roosevelt's label of "muck-rakers" entrenched this popular reaction by creating a simplified picture of aimless and often unjustified sensationalism. Though the people read and absorbed the message of these journalists, the stereotype stuck. But the effect of the President's phrase was not only upon the general public but also the writers themselves. Although Charles Edward Russell, Upton Sinclair, Thomas Lawson, and Alfred Henry Lewis gloried in the title, David Graham Phillips and Ida Tarbell were extremely upset, and Phillips soon gave up the magazines in order to concentrate on his novels. Some writers seem partially to have accepted T. R.'s criticism. The time came soon afterwards when Lincoln Steffens announced that he was done with exposés. "Now solutions," he proclaimed [in *Everybody's* magazine in 1908], although he had been so engaged all along.

The fact that the movement was educational, rather than legislative, adds an additional difficulty to understanding the era. The journalists, agreeing upon a common enemy, wished specific reforms and often whole programs of correction, but most of them did not feel that they were in a position to lead a political movement. Rather, they set themselves to creating an informed public opinion that would make progress possible.

The muckrakers were not intent on keeping aloof from political affairs. Charles Edward Russell and Upton Sinclair were hardy campaigners on the Socialist ticket. G. K. Turner testified in crime and vice investigations. Ray Stannard Baker soon gave up his anti-political ideas, took part in local politics in Michigan, and later became a campaign adviser to Robert M. La Follette. Lincoln Steffens was involved in practically every stirring of municipal and state reform.

There can be little doubt of the journalists' earnestness and sense of dedication. Russell's muckrake convictions led him to join the Socialist Party. The letters and diaries of Lincoln Steffens, Ida Tarbell, Ray Stannard Baker, and David Graham Phillips showed how their hopes for the good which they might do became the central force in their lives. Although this ego-involvement was responsible for Tom Lawson's flights of fancy, for the others it meant that their effectiveness depended on a high standard of honesty and integrity. This feeling was demonstrated when the top writers on *McClure's* resigned rather than be a party to S.S. McClure's speculative experiments.

But much more was involved in the movement than the seriousness of its participants. The muckrakers presented affirmative creeds, ranging from G. K. Turner's belief that big business should be released from the trammels of laws designed for a bygone competitive economy, to the socialism of Upton Sinclair and Charles Edward Russell. All of the writers realised that vast changes had taken place in the land.

More than any other group they made the people aware of what twentieth-century America was like. Quickly passing over the fields which had concerned previous generations of reformers, they evidenced little interest in currency or civil service improvements. Although they all attacked the tariff, only Ida Tarbell believed that it was a vital national problem. For the belated nineteenth-century answer to the growth of monopoly, the Sherman Anti-trust Act, there was only minority support.

Despite the diversity of their remedial views, all of the muckrakers laid the evils of society to the rise of new economic conditions. The journalists used a variety of terms: the "interests," "the System," high or frenzied finance, plutocracy, industrial aristocracy, the trusts and monopoly. In one way or another the writers were talking about the same thing. The specific agent in the national orgy of corruption was the corporations. Their highest utility, Ray Stannard Baker wrote [in an unpublished notebook entry], was that they enabled "reputable people to participate in the profits of disreputable business enterprises without disturbing their moral complacency." It was just this popular indifference and acquiescence that the muckrakers tried to upset. They attempted to educate the people to the realization, as Will Irwin stated it [in the *American* magazine in 1909], that "the crime of stealing the means of production through corrupt legislatures and corrupt market manipulations is as great and heinous, doubtless, as the crime of stealing silver spoons from the safe of a wealthy burgher." The fault was not in the corporate form itself but rather the use to which it was being put. The moral development of the nation failed to keep pace with an enormous material expansion. The profit motive, they pointed out, had been enthroned in America. They all believed that "Business" had become the ruling force in society and, with the exception of G. K. Turner, they did not like the results. Lincoln Steffens summed it up when he wrote [in *The Upbuilders* (1909)] that "Business, the mere machinery of living, has become in America the purpose of life, the end to which all other goods—honour, religion, politics, men, women and children, the very nation itself—are sacrificed."

Muckraking then, despite its gaudy show of accusations, was not directed toward seeking out individuals as scapegoats. The emphasis on prominent men as exemplification of evil was a matter of journalistic style rather than ideology. Although the muckrakers were concerned with the need for leadership, it rarely approached becoming a cult. Only Lincoln Steffens and Thomas Lawson seriously relied upon a theory of leadership. Lawson's messiah was himself, while Steffens looked to the outstanding men of business and politics to arouse a general sense of dedication to public service.

The disinclination of the journalists to tie their movement to the political chariot of any particular man in public life emerged clearly from the body of their writing. To most of them, Theodore Roosevelt initially promised the best chance for a great national readjustment. Alfred Henry Lewis and Will Irwin never faltered in their admiration, but the others became disillusioned with the President. His friends, Ray Stannard Baker and Lincoln Steffens, who held the highest hopes for him, were the most disappointed. He was, they came to believe, unconcerned about economic problems and hopelessly a trimmer. By the time most of the writers crystalized their ideas, they discovered that the Rough-rider from Oyster Bay had been left behind.

The muckrakers had no greater faith in the political parties than in outstanding individuals. Almost all of them rejected the standard national solutions of replacing the "ins" with the "outs," or "bad" with "good" government. Even the minority of Democrats among the journalists were not willing to claim that a shift in political power would in any way change conditions. Steffens, Lewis, Baker, Russell and Phillips repeatedly wrote that "Business" ruled in both parties. Nevertheless, few of the journalists became radicals. Only Charles Edward Russell was led to socialism during the muckrake era by the conviction that the traditional channels were hopeless. Upton Sinclair was already there before he turned to muckraking.

Corruption of politics was but one example of the failure of the traditional ways of doing things. Wherever the muckrakers looked they found that the national institutions no longer served the people. Politics, the law, education, the press, and religion had been diverted from their intended function and were, in varying degrees, the captive creatures of wealth. C. P. Connolly devoted his attention to the judiciary, but all the writers commented repeatedly on the failure of the courts to dispense justice. David Graham Phillips was the most concerned with the way the titans of industry corrupted the colleges with their gifts, but Ida Tarbell and the others also attacked what they considered to be false benevolence. Will Irwin made the fullest study of the press in an age of commercialism, but all were concerned with what seemed its vanishing freedom. Many of the muckrakers were particularly upset by the conservatism of organized religion. They felt that most of the churches had lost their social message and were seeking to make the people content with the world as it was, rather than inspiring them to create a better one.

Despite the growing aggregation of wealth and the inability of the country's institutions to protect the interests of the common man, the muckrakers were not prophets of gloom. All believed that the evils could be corrected and that the moment of crisis was at hand. Only Will Irwin and G. K. Turner felt that no action was necessary. To everyone, except Lawson and perhaps Turner, America meant the promise of a freer and more equalitarian land. They saw the story of the nation's march toward that goal as a dialectic process by which every struggle against a newly rising wave of reaction resulted in a new advance for the people. Both Baker and Phillips wrote of such waves, and Russell and Sinclair saw in their own times a repetition of the pre-Civil War unrest. As homemade evolutionists and environmentalists, even when they were not economic determinists, they accepted this as the path to progress.

With their firm belief that they were contributing to the progress of society, the muckrakers might have been justified in considering themselves a constructive force on the basis of their criticism alone. Sweep away the forces which hindered or corrupted public opinion, the muckrakers were convinced, and the battle was half won. Even so, each of the journalists developed his own reform theories. G. K. Turner believed that organized business would free the nation from the combination of vice and boodle. C. P. Connolly sought methods by which the machinery of the law might function effectively in the public interest. Will Irwin believed that with a certain amount of public awakening the competitive processes would be an effective barrier to business excess. Alfred Henry Lewis, Burton J. Hendrick, and Ida Tarbell relied on competition but felt that somewhat more drastic action was necessary to make it function. Lewis favored any legislation that would

end great fortunes, for he held that popular adulation of the rich had dulled the competitive individualism of the average citizen. Burton Hendrick felt that the states had the legal and legitimate right to regulate and require service from the corporations. Ida Tarbell believed that breaking the trust monopoly on transportation was essential, but that public scorn of unfair action was the best way to regain lost values.

Samuel Hopkins Adams and Thomas Lawson maintained that Wall Street lay at the heart of the trouble. They demanded that stock market gambling be prevented and that the government take steps to end the over-capitalization of industry which raised the cost of living. Ray Stannard Baker, David Graham Phillips, and Lincoln Steffens believed that certain key industries should be publicly owned and operated. Baker considered joining the Socialist Party but, while absorbing much of its ideology, he ended up by temporarily resting his faith in the pragmatism of La Folette's insurgent movement. Steffens and Phillips were also attracted by socialism but held back from Party membership. Charles Edward Russell came to believe that vast changes were needed in order to correct the evils of society. He and Upton Sinclair embraced socialism as the means by which society was to be rebuilt.

The writers of magazine exposés were basically moderates in most fields. They spoke as representatives of the middle classes of the nation's cities and towns. It would be difficult to apply Richard Hofstadter's thesis in the *Age of Reform* [see excerpt below] to the muckrakers and maintain that they were led to reform as members of the old middle class which was being shaded by the rise of the trusts and the great fortunes. The muckrakers, perhaps apart from their class confreres, were at the peak of their professional power and mobility. On the whole, they came to the Progressive movement through the discovery of national corruption, rather than by conscious or unconscious comparison of their class or status position. As a group, they looked neither backward to an intensely democratic small America nor forward to a highly centralized nationalistic state. With the exception of Charles Edward Russell, they did not understand or attach any great importance to the agrarian unrest of the previous decades. Nor did they preach a doctrine of class warfare. There were stirrings of the latter phenomenon in the writings of Baker, Phillips, Russell, and Sinclair, but even they saw class conflict as a peaceful force working within the democratic framework. The socialism of Upton Sinclair and Charles Edward Russell was not extreme and contained only a limited amount of the Marxian paraphernalia. It was primarily a sense of frustration that led Russell into increasing radicalism in the last days before the outbreak of the First World War. In the main, the muckrakers believed that they did not believe that virtue resided solely in any one group in the society. They were for "the public," whose interests, however, always seemed to be typically middle class.

This is clearly shown in the attitude toward organized labor. Although all of these journalists at one time or another wrote on the subject of unions and the plight of the wage earner, they were usually without conclusions. They merely cautioned against violence and lamented unfair union practices. None saw labor as a counter-balancing group to aggregate wealth in a compromise society. On the other hand, only Burton Hendrick was openly hostile. The sins of labor seemed less menacing than those of capital, and there was much talk of "the public" whose interests had to be protected against both the unions and the trusts.

One theme that was almost completely absent from the writings of the muckrakers was a consideration of "big government." Hendrick alone dealt with it explicitly. He opposed centralized national power, but he did not believe that it threatened to become a reality. When the magazine crusaders pondered the role of the national government, they were concerned only with the privileges which might be given to business. For the most part, the non-socialists believed that the existing type of government would endure if it could be made responsive to the will of an informed people. To this end, the muckrakers offered enlightenment in their columns and called for such reforms as initiative, referendum, recall, direct primaries, and the popular election of Senators. One might suppose from the Socialists' talk of public operation for the common good, that a super-bureaucracy was in the making. However, they did not discuss this possibility. Although control of the national administration was to affect the revolution, Sinclair talked of his cooperative commonwealth as though it were a series of individual utopian colonies. Russell never dealt with the problem at all.

Probably the outstanding weakness in the philosophy of the muckrakers was their lack of a broad knowledge of economics. Although highlighting many evils, most of them did not understand the workings of the industrial and financial mechanisms. As George Mowry, the leading authority on this era, has pointed out, the Progressives tended to talk in "moral rather than economic terms" [*The Era of Theodore Roosevelt: 1900-1912* (1958)]. This was surely true of the muckrakers. Whether or not it was a substitute for the middle class absence of a consciousness of class consciousness, they placed great emphasis upon the role of public-spirited altruism. However, if their outlook was moralistic because they believed that man could be made "good," the means was to pass laws to change the environment and conditions which made men "bad."

The strong point in the ideas of Samuel Hopkins Adams and Tom Lawson was their realization that there was much about the industrial machine which could not be controlled by public opinion and moral pressure. Having a better understanding of the financial organization of business, they explained why over-capitalization forced higher prices on the American consuming public. The muckrake-Socialists had the most detailed conception of how the economic mechanism worked. Charles Edward Russell cogently connected public buying power with industrial health, and he explained how over-capitalization and the drive for profits forced business to act in a way inimical to its own interests. The malignant force of "the surplus" held a central role in the analyses of Russell and Upton Sinclair. Their apocalyptic brand of economics, however, had the faults of its virtues. There is, perhaps something depressing and pessimistic about a social process—even when working toward the best of ends—which is not amenable to the control or direction of the men whom it is supposed to aid.

Most of the muckrakers were not looking backward. Perhaps, a few exponents of an anti-trust, competitive America, thought longingly of the days gone by. The vast majority of the others would have agreed with Lincoln Steffens when he attacked those who mistakenly believed that the nation could turn back the pages of history to the days of Thomas Jefferson or Andrew Jackson. Will Irwin, who felt that the existing institutions were satisfactory, maintained that competition would work because it would adjust the new industrialism to

the service of the common people. Steffens, Phillips, and Baker, as well as the muckrake-Socialists, were convinced that the forces of evolution were at work in human society. The Socialists saw a future of increasing progress and believed that trusts were an inevitable step in the movement toward a co-operative commonwealth. Others lauded the new industrialism and the good that might result from its enormous output. G. K. Turner, declining to blame big business for corruption, felt that it was bringing order to a chaotic competitive world. David Graham Phillips wrote the most enthusiastic message of praise in *The Reign of Gilt*. America, he explained proudly, was being emancipated by the machine. By raising the nation's standard of living, industry was working like science and education to break down prejudice and ignorance. By contributing to a new political fluidity, it would bring the end of the bosses and plutocracy.

Most of the journalists searched for hopeful signs of the growing productivity being applied to the service of the community. Burton Hendrick hailed the workers' villages of Gary, as well as the Carnegie and Rockefeller foundations, although the rest of the muckrakers strongly opposed anything that had the appearance of philanthropy or charity. Ida Tarbell was quick to seize upon the first encouraging instances of public-spiritedness on the part of the titans of industry. Steffens, with his interests in the techniques of leadership, relied upon the outstanding men of politics and business to bring the mass of citizens to a higher sense of community service. Many of the writers praised the scientific management theories of F. W. Taylor. Upton Sinclair alone raised a discordant note by demanding to know exactly how the greater profits were to be divided.

Although concentrating on the central problems of society, the crusading journalists sought a more complete democracy in all parts of American life. Together with Russell, Tarbell, Baker and Sinclair, Phillips examined the role of the woman in the partnerships of marriage and national affairs. Turner and Steffens found the city a unique opportunity for experimentation in progressive democracy. As a group, the muckrakers had no agrarian prejudice against city or immigrant, even though there were strong strains of love for the land and nostalgia for the small town in the writing of Baker and Phillips. Upton Sinclair alone displayed hatred for the life of the metropolis which he equated with plutocratic consumption and exploitation of the immigrant.

It would be difficult to maintain that the muckrakers followed at least some of their Progressive brethren along the paths of racism or Anglo-Saxon bias. Will Irwin was a little gullible on the subject of the Negro, but his failure to arrive at any solution to the West Coast prejudice was not based upon a belief in racial or cultural inferiority of the Oriental. Ray Stannard Baker's abandonment of his strident advocacy of Negro equalitarianism was in reality a retreat from socialism. Although he came to recommend a slower path, he did not give up his opposition to second-class citizenship for the Negro. Phillips and Russell were strongly critical of English society. Hendrick followed the liberal anthropology of Franz Boas in explaining varying ethnic stocks in terms of the plasticity of man responding to differences in environment. Lincoln Steffens, in writing of corruption in Philadelphia and Rhode Island, maintained that corrupt government was not ethnic, but American. Phillips hailed the immigrant as a strong force against aristocracy and tyranny. All of the muckrakers believed, with Charles Edward Russell [writing in *Cosmopolitan* in 1907], that any action which denied the "normal ties of sympathy and goodwill between men" exacted a cost too great for any nation to bear.

The wielders of the muckrake exposed corruption in order that it might be corrected. Their analysis of national life probed deeply into the vast changes that had taken place during the previous half-century. Collectively they presented one of the first comprehensive descriptions of the business civilization that had become the ideal and the motive force of the American nation. With their criticism the muckrakers helped lay the groundwork of public concern which resulted in many of the reforms of the next half-century. In addition, these journalists had positive reform views to express and were able to do so in the popular magazines for more than a decade. They explained that the corruption which had become general in American life resulted from the privileges sought and obtained by the giant business enterprises that had emerged in the United States after the Civil War. The muckrakers did not reject the new industrialism and the dominant corporate form, but rather insisted that both be used for the public good.

The best illustration of the nature of the muckrakers' message can be found in a letter which Lincoln Steffens wrote to Theodore Roosevelt in the spring of 1907:

> I am not seeking proof of crime and dishonesty. . . . What I am after is the cause and the purpose and the methods by which our government, city, state and federal is made to represent not the common, but the special interests; the reason why it is so hard to do right in the U.S.; the secret of the power which makes it necessary for you, Mr. President, to fight to give us a "square deal." In brief, I want to . . . explain why it is that you have to force the Senate to pass a pure food bill or one providing for the regulation of railroads. . . .
>
> And please don't misunderstand me. . . . This is a point on which you, Mr. President, and I have never agreed. . . . I am looking upward to—an American Democracy. You ask men in office to be honest, I ask them to serve the people. . . .

(pp. 104-16)

David Mark Chalmers, in his The Social and Political Ideas of the Muckrakers, *The Citadel Press, 1964, 127 p.*

RICHARD HOFSTADTER

[*Hofstadter was a distinguished American historian and social critic who challenged and reinterpreted the liberal reformist ideology of the Progressive historians, which he considered narrow-minded and undemocratic. In his studies, Hofstadter applied a pluralistic, inquisitive, and skeptical approach to historical investigation, never accepting plausible causal explanations of other historians. He received two Pulitzer Prizes: in 1956 for* The Age of Reform: From Bryan to F. D. R. *(1955), a dynamic work that chronicles the political and social climate from the 1890s through President Franklin D. Roosevelt's New Deal; and in 1964 for his* Anti-Intellectualism in American Life *(1963), which examines this phenomenon in American political, cultural, and educational systems through the 1950s. In the following excerpt from the first-named work, Hofstadter discusses the muckraking movement in relation to American political Progressivism.*]

The muckrakers had a more decisive impact on the thinking of the country than they did on its laws or morals. They confirmed, if they did not create, a fresh mode of criticism that grew out of journalistic observation. The dominant note in the best thought of the Progressive era is summed up in the term "realism." It was realism that the current literature and journalism fostered, just as it was realism that the most fertile thinkers of the age brought into philosophy, law, and economics. Although Western sectional consciousness, which was curiously united to a sort of folkish nationalism, made its own contribution to realistic writing, the chief source of realism lay in the city and city journalism. With few exceptions the makers of American realism, even from the days of Mark Twain and William Dean Howells, were men who had training in journalistic observation—Stephen Crane, Theodore Dreiser, Harold Frederic, David Graham Phillips—or men like Edward Kirkland, Edward Eggleston, Hamlin Garland, and Jack London who in some other capacity had also seen the rough side of life to which the reporters and human-interest writers were exposed. What they all had in common—the realistic novelists, the muckrakers, and the more critical social scientists of the period—was a passion for getting the "inside story."

Robert Cantwell once suggested that the primary reason for the success of the muckrakers was not political at all, but literary, and that their work was in a sense the journalistic equivalent of the literary realism that also flourished at the time [see excerpt above]. It had never been customary in America to write about America, but especially not about the life of industry and labor and business and poverty and vice. Now, while novelists were replacing a literature bred out of other literature with a genre drawn from street scenes and abattoirs or the fly-specked rural kitchens of Hamlin Garland's stories, the muckrakers were replacing the genteel travel stories and romances of the older magazines with a running account of how America worked. (pp. 198-99)

What the muckrakers and the realistic writers were doing in their fields the speculative thinkers and social scientists were also doing in theirs. As scholars reached out for their own "realistic" categories, the formalistic thought of an earlier and more conservative generation fell under close and often damaging scrutiny. Economists were pondering Veblen's effort to replace the economic man of the classical school with his wasteful consumer and his predatory captain of industry. Legal realists were supplanting the "pure" jurisprudential agent of earlier legal theorists with the flesh-and-blood image of the corporation lawyer dressed in judicial robes and stuffed with corporation prejudices. Political scientists were losing their old veneration for the state as an abstract repository of something called sovereignty and accepting the views of men like Charles A. Beard and Arthur F. Bentley, who conceived of the state as a concrete instrument that registered the social pressures brought to bear upon it by various interest groups. Historians were beginning to apply the economic interpretation of history. The new discipline of sociology, intimately linked with social-settlement work and Christian social reform, was criticizing the older notions of individuality and morality and developing a new, "realistic" social psychology. John Dewey was attacking formalistic categories in philosophy and trying to develop a more descriptive and operational account of the uses of ideas. (pp. 199-200)

The muckraking model of thought had brought with it a certain limiting and narrowing definition of reality and a flattening of the imagination. William Dean Howells, in one of his less fortunate remarks, had accepted the earlier tendency of American literature to deal with "the smiling aspects of life" that were more characteristically American. This complacency the realists reversed with a vengeance. Reality now was rough and sordid. It was hidden, neglected, and off-stage. It was conceived essentially as that stream of external and material events which was most likely to be unpleasant. Reality was the bribe, the rebate, the bought franchise, the sale of adulterated food. It was what one found in *The Jungle, The Octopus, Wealth against Commonwealth,* or *The Shame of the Cities.* It was just as completely and hopelessly dissociated from the world of morals and ideals as, say, a newspaper editorial on Motherhood might be from the facts about infant mortality in the slums.

To the average American of the Progressive era this ugly thing that presented itself as reality was not a final term. Reality was a series of unspeakable plots, personal iniquities, moral failures, which, in their totality, had come to govern American society only because the citizen had relaxed his moral vigilance. The failures of American society were thus no token of the ultimate nature of man, of the human condition, much less the American condition; they were not to be accepted or merely modified, but fought with the utmost strenuosity at every point. First reality must in its fullness be exposed, and then it must be made the subject of moral exhortation; and then, when individual citizens in sufficient numbers had stiffened in their determination to effect reform, something could be done. As Josiah Strong put it: "If public opinion is educated concerning a given reform—political, social, industrial, or moral—and if the popular conscience is sufficiently awake to enforce an enlightened public opinion, the reform is accomplished straightway. This then is the generic reform—the education of public opinion and of the popular conscience." First the citizen must reclaim the power that he himself had abdicated, refashioning where necessary the instruments of government. Then—since the Yankee found the solution to everything in laws—he must see that the proper remediable laws be passed and that existing laws be enforced. He must choose men of the highest moral qualities for his political leaders. It was assumed that such moral qualities were indestructible and that decent men, once found and installed in office, would remain decent. When they had regained control of affairs, moral rigor would not flag again.

An excellent illustration of the spirit of Progressivism as it manifested itself in the new popular literature is provided by a famous editorial by S. S. McClure in the January 1903 issue of *McClure's.* In this editorial McClure stood back and took a fresh look at his publication and suddenly realized what it was that he and his writers were doing. He observed that his current issue, which was running an article muckraking Minneapolis by Lincoln Steffens, another on Standard Oil by Ida Tarbell, and still another by Ray Stannard Baker on labor, showed a striking and completely unplanned convergence upon a central fact in American life: a general disrespect for law on the part of capitalists, workingmen, politicians, and citizens. Who, he asked, was left in the community to uphold the law? The lawyers? Some of the best of them made a living from advising business firms how to evade it. The judges? Among too many of them the respect for law took the form of respect for quibbles by which they restored to liberty men who on the evidence of common sense would be convicted of malfeasances. The churches? "We know of one, an ancient and wealthy establishment, which had to be compelled by a Tammany hold-over health officer to put its tenements in san-

itary condition." "The colleges? They do not understand." "There is no one left," concluded McClure, "none but all of us. . . . We all are doing our worst and making the public pay. The public is the people. We forget that we all are the people. . . . We have to pay in the end, every one of us."

The chief themes of the muckraking magazines are stated here. First is the progressive view of reality—evildoing among the most respectable people is seen as the "real" character of American life; corruption is found on every side. Second is the idea that the mischief can be interpreted simply as a widespread breaking of the law. I have remarked that Anglo-Saxon thinking emphasized governance by legal rules, as opposed to the widespread tendency among immigrants to interpret political reality in the light of personal relations. If the laws are the right laws, and if they can be enforced by the right men, the Progressive believed, everything would be better. He had a great and abiding faith in the appeal to such abstractions as the law and patriotism, and the efficacy of continued exhortation. Third, there was the appeal to universal personal responsibility and the imputation of personal guilt.

To understand the reform mentality, we must consider the vigor with which the Progressives attacked not only such social questions as the powers of trusts and bosses, but also such objects of reform as the liquor traffic and prostitution. The Progressive mind . . . was pre-eminently a Protestant mind; and even though much of its strength was in the cities, it inherited the moral traditions of rural evangelical Protestantism. The Progressives were still freshly horrified by phenomena that we now resignedly consider indigenous to urban existence. However prosperous they were, they lived in the midst of all the iniquities that the agrarian myth had taught them to expect of urban life, and they refused to accept them calmly. Here it was that a most important aspect of the Protestant personality came into play: its ethos of personal responsibility. American life and American mythology had been keyed to the conditions of rural simplicity and village neighborliness under which personal responsibility for the problems—and the morals—of others could in fact often be assumed. Moreover it was the whole effect of the Protestant ethic to heighten the sense of personal responsibility as much as possible. The more the muckrakers acquainted the Protestant Yankee with what was going on around him, the more guilty and troubled he felt. The religious institutions of Protestantism provided no mechanism to process, drain off, and externalize the sense of guilt. American political traditions provided no strong native tradition of conservatism to reconcile men to evils that could not easily be disposed of. The native ethos of mass participation in politics and citizenlike civic consciousness . . . confirmed the idea that everyone was in some very serious sense responsible for everything. (pp. 201-05)

One is impressed, in a review of the literature, with the enormous amount of self-accusation among Progressives. William Allen White saw it when he attributed much of the movement to the fact that "in the soul of the people there is a conviction of their past unrighteousness." The moral indignation of the age was by no means directed entirely against others; it was in a great and critical measure directed inward. Contemporaries who spoke of the movement as an affair of the conscience were not mistaken. Lincoln Steffens had the key to this sense of personal involvement when he entitled his famous muckraking volume *The Shame of the Cities.*

Nothing, indeed, illustrates better than the Introduction to

Steffens's volume the fashion in which the Yankee ethos of responsibility had become transmuted into a sense of guilt. Again and again Steffens laid the responsibility for the ugly state of affairs portrayed in his book at the doorsteps of his own readers. "The misgovernment of the American people," he declared,

> is misgovernment by the American people. . . . Are the people honest? Are the people better than Tammany? . . . Isn't our corrupt government, after all, representative? . . . There is no essential difference between the pull that gets your wife into society or for your book a favorable review, and that which gets a heeler into office, a thief out of jail, and a rich man's son on the board of directors of a corporation. . . . The boss is not a political, he is an American institution, the product of a freed people that have not the spirit to be free. . . . We are responsible, not our leaders, since we follow them. . . . The spirit of graft and of lawlessness is the American spirit. . . . The people are not innocent. That is the only 'news' in all the journalism of these articles. . . . My purpose was . . . to see if the shameful facts, spread out in all their shame, would not burn through our civic shamelessness and set fire to American pride.

Steffens closed his introduction by dedicating his book "to the accused—to all the citizens of all the cities in the United States."

Ida M. Tarbell, author of the muckraking History of the Standard Oil Company.

It may seem that there was remarkable boldness in this accusatory procedure, but such appearances are often deceptive. Steffens had good reason to know that the substantial American citizen accepted such accusation as valid. The people of Minneapolis and St. Louis had written not in resentment but in encouragement after his exposure of those cities had been published in *McClure's,* and—still more significant—hundreds of invitations poured in from citizens, as individuals or in organized groups, of many other cities inviting exposure on their own premises: "come and show us up; we're worse than they are."

Steffens's argument that it was the people, and particularly the "best" people, who were responsible for corruption cannot be taken, however, as an ultimate comment on human nature or the human condition. He was not preaching universal sinfulness as a token of the fact that most men would be damned, but because he hoped and expected that all could be saved—saved through this ardent appeal to their pride. This is the real function of the pervasively ugly character of reality that the Progressives so frequently harped on: pervasive as it was, it was neither impenetrable nor irremovable: it was an instrument of exhortation, not a clue to life but a fulcrum for reform. Steffens hoped, at bottom, "that our shamelessness is superficial, that beneath it lies a pride which, being real, may save us yet." For when the chips were down he could not but believe, as he said of the situation in St. Louis, that "the people are sound."

Among some reformers this ethos of responsibility to which Steffens appealed simply took the form of an effort to participate in what the rhetoric of the time called "the race life"—which meant, by and large, to get nearer to those who suffered in a more profound and poignant way from the burdens of "reality." As early as 1892 Jane Addams had delivered a fine, penetrating lecture on "The Subjective Necessity for Social Settlements," in which she explained how the sheltered and well-brought-up young Americans of her generation, reared on the ideal of social justice and on Protestant moral imperatives, had grown uncomfortable about their own sincerity, troubled about their uselessness, and restless about being "shut off from the common labor by which they live and which is a great source of moral and physical health." Similarly a character in [*Social Strugglers* (1893)], one of the social novels of H. H. Boyesen, the son of a rich contractor, professed "a sneaking sense of guilt when I am too comfortable," and left high society to plunge into what he called "the great discordant tumultuous life, with its passions and cries of distress." Characters with the same motivation were constantly to be found in the pages of *McClure's*—now, however, no longer only as the protagonists of fiction, but as the authors of articles. Where this impulse was translated into action it sent a host of earnest reformers into the field to engage themselves in various useful philanthropies. But on the purely verbal level, where of necessity it had to remain for most people, it resulted on occasion in a rather strenuous moral purgation, not unlike the pathetic proletarianism that swept over many American intellectuals in the 1930's. (pp. 207-11)

So the middle-class citizen received quite earnestly the exhortations that charged him with personal responsibility for all kinds of social ills. It was his business to do something about them. Indeed, he must do something if he was ever to feel better. But what should he do? He was too substantial a fellow to want to make any basic changes in a society in which he was so typically a prosperous and respectable figure. What he needed, therefore, was a *feeling* that action was taking place, a sense that the moral tone of things was being improved and that he had a part in this improvement. Corruption thus became a particularly fine issue for the moral energies of the Progressive. He was ready to be convinced that the country was thoroughly wicked, and the muckrakers supplied him with a wealth of plausible evidence.

In time the muckraking and reform writers seem to have become half conscious of the important psychic function their work was performing for themselves and their public, quite apart from any legislative consequences or material gains. They began to say, in effect, that even when they were unable to do very much to change the exercise of political power, they liked the sense of effort and the feeling that the moral tone of political life had changed. "It is not the material aspect of this," they began to say, "but the moral aspect that interests us." [In *The Old Order Changeth* (1910)] William Allen White dated the beginnings of this shift from "materialism" to "moral values" from the war with Spain when "the spirit of sacrifice overcame the spirit of commercialism," and the people saw "that if we could learn to sacrifice our own interest for those of a weaker people, we would learn the lesson needed to solve the great problem of democracy—to check our national greed and to make business honest." McClure himself gave characteristic expression to this high valuation of the intangibles when he praised Charles Evans Hughes's exposure of the New York life-insurance companies for the enormous "tonic effect of the inquiry," which, he felt, had very likely saved thousands of young men from making compromises with honor. They saw that "public disgrace" awaited evildoers, and "there is no punishment so terrible as public disclosure of evil doing" [*McClure's* (December 1905)]. Related to this emphasis on moral as opposed to material values was a fresh assertion of disdain for money and monetary success, very reminiscent of the disdain of the Mugwump type for the materialists. With this came a disparagement of material achievement. San Francisco, remarked George Kennan [in *McClure's* (November 1907)], was a successful and prosperous city, but it had put stress "upon material achievement and business prosperity rather than upon civic virtue and moral integrity. But what shall it profit a city if it gain the whole world and lose its own soul?" Probably no statesman of the time had a better intuitive understanding of the interest of the reform mind in moral intangibles than Theodore Roosevelt, whose preachments exploited it to the full. And no observer had a better insight into T. R.'s relation to his time than [William Allen White], who declared quite properly that "Roosevelt's power in this land is a spiritual power. His is not a kingdom of this earth. . . . It is immaterial whether or not the Supreme Court sustains him in his position on the rate bill, the income tax, the license for corporations, or the inheritance tax; not for the establishment of a system of statutes was he born into this world; but rather like all great teachers, that by his life and his works he should bear witness unto the truth" [*McClure's* (January 1907)]. This was a penetrating comment upon the meaning of the reform literature as a kind of symbolic action. For, besides such material accomplishment as they had to show for themselves, the Progressive writers could claim that they had provided a large part of the American people with a necessary and (as they would have said) wholesome catharsis. (pp. 211-14)

Richard Hofstadter, "The Progressive Impulse," in his The Age of Reform: From Bryan to F. D. R., *1955. Reprint by Vintage Books, 1961, pp. 174-214.*

TARGETS OF THE MUCKRAKERS

HAROLD S. WILSON

[*Wilson is an American educator and critic. In the following excerpt from his* McClure's Magazine and the Muckrakers, *he examines some of the chief muckraking series that appeared in* McClure's *magazine following the early sensational exposés by Ida Tarbell, Lincoln Steffens, and Ray Stannard Baker.*]

After January, 1903, *McClure's* perceptibly changed, although not as much as generally maintained. The magazine invented little; rather it accentuated principles which had characterized it since 1893. At *McClure's* it was difficult to maintain that there was a decisive split between the old mugwump generation and the new progressives. Rather *McClure's* was like a sprout worming its way about in the earth, finally breaking through to find the sun. By an alchemy as old as the Great Revival, *McClure's* had always closely identified the activities of the saloon and the dance hall with professional thievery and machine politics. But with Theodore Roosevelt's assumption of the Presidency, hailed nationwide by the reform press, the magazine's progressive principles became more obvious.

A careful reading of McClure's editorial in the January, 1903, issue gives the germ idea from which the magazine's contributions to muckraking ensued. The title, "The American Contempt of Law," wrote McClure, "could well have served for the current chapter of Miss Tarbell's *History of Standard Oil.* And it would have fitted perfectly Mr. Baker's 'The Right to Work.' All together, these articles come pretty near showing how universal is this dangerous trait of ours." The law, the law, all were "breaking the law, or letting it be broken." Who was to uphold it? Neither the lawyers, nor the judges, nor the churches, nor the colleges could do so. "There is no one left; none but all of us." Illegal rebates, he continued, traction franchises which sold for a bribe, as well as lawless and violent strikes were worse in America than elsewhere. Railroads in particular and corporations in general, the city machines and the unions, exhibited the fatal native flaw of lawlessness. A toleration of vice and a contempt for order meant that vice was on the throne and the disintegration of society had begun. Newton Bateman could not have spoken more apocalyptically.

A defense of order and propriety that would have been a credit to those more staid fixtures, *Century* and *Scribner's,* pervaded *McClure's* after 1903. Most of *McClure's* muckraking articles can be classified as dealing with the breakdown of order, the birth of lawlessness, and the end of propriety. As Henry Adams might have seen it, in 1903 McClure was trying to defend in the twentieth century a unity of values based on moral absolutes, a naive assumption that moral and political laws had a clear meaning, and that answers could quantitatively be proved black or white by counting strikes or murders or other such external results. Henry May, in his *The End of American Innocence,* finds this is a characteristic of most American literature at the turn of the century. The situation was to change remarkably within a season, but at any rate the McClure journalists dished up heavy heapings of moral law and by it challenged society as the abolitionists had the slavocracy.

To point ahead, it must be said that initially, except where traditional moral judgments were dealt with, any appeal to a higher law, natural and unwritten, such as suggested by the Brandeis brief and the rise of sociological jurisprudence, was rather limited. But a generation with its Adamses, Spenglers, Einsteins, Spencers, Stoddards, McKinters, and Turners showed an unusual tendency to wrestle with metaphysical speculations about the order of the world. It was slowly—and this is the subject of later chapters—that the muckrakers came to terms with natural law and the axiomatic superstructure upon which institutions were built.

But more important than moral law in the early *McClure's* muckraking were man's conscious rules for governing himself. These rules were deemed valid by assuming that democracy itself was a moral condition, a metaphysical value. Laws, constitutions, and charters were the cohesive forces of society whose inviolability *McClure's* insisted upon. This defense of law was made more frantic by the country's condition. The McClure writers, it seems, confused the natural fragmentation of society resulting from social and economic forces—such as immigration, concentration of wealth, specialization of labor, technological development, and the rise of the cities—with the deterioration of the old order familiar to them. The first principle of *McClure's* muckraking . . . was that the conscience of the nation must be aroused to enforce existing laws, not to draft new ones. Man's inability to live in conformity with these articulated rules was described *ad infinitum* by McClure as "lawlessness."

When the muckraking movement began, McClure proved more capable than ever of pressing his campaign against "lawlessness" through the magazine. None of the illnesses or absences of earlier years plagued him. After 1906 the magazine became a more accurate reflection of his mind and interests, for in that year many of the men who had acted as both a restraint and a catalyst for McClure's enthusiasm left the magazine. Probably the only person capable of awing McClure was President Roosevelt. Thus not infrequently Roosevelt's philosophy of government and society spilled into the magazine's pages under the name of one of the editors or staff journalists. Most of the staff knew the President well enough to write him informally for his views. McClure, at least partially in response to Roosevelt's attack on muckrakers in 1906, it would appear, made a substantial change in editorial policy. Not only did the magazine strive to portray more positive aspects of society, but it showed a limited evolution from its posture that reform consisted in getting various laws obeyed to the position that certain new laws and new organizational structures were necessary to preserve the old ideals. Indeed, this was the direction of the whole progressive movement. And so in time, for example, the magazine advocated the city manager and the city commission form of municipal government as a means of preserving the democracy inherited from the New England town meeting. And, still later, the very nature of social and economic laws had to be questioned.

Throughout the years of muckraking McClure held steadfastly to the axiom that a quantitative judgment could be made on the effectiveness of government. "Governments," McClure paraphrased Locke [in *McClure's* (December 1904)], "are established and maintained chiefly for the purpose of protecting life and property." The number of lives lost and the amount of property destroyed were unquestioned indexes to the ineffectiveness of government and the "lawlessness" of society. This theory, from the contract theorists of the seventeenth century, puts in perspective most of the muckraking publications of *McClure's* between 1903 and 1911, when McClure retired.

McClure's only important contribution to muckraking was "The Increase of Lawlessness in the United States," published in 1904. His article was filled with statistics gleaned from the *Chicago Tribune* which proved that crime had been significantly increasing since 1881 until the ratio of murders to the population in the United States was twenty times that of any European country. In a speech before the Twentieth Century Club during the spring of 1904, the doughty editor developed his theme. There were more lynchings than legal executions in the United States which resulted in "more murders in the United States during the time of the Boer War than the entire number lost by Great Britain in that war by bullets and disease." "You have," he pointed out to his sedate audience, "one man in the United States out of each two hundred and fifty who is a murderer." It was statistically safer to commit murder than to embezzle bank funds. Only in the medieval atmosphere of Imperial Russia was a man's life confronted with such dire probabilities as in the United States. McClure was quick to place responsibility on three classes who kept the government from functioning as it should: the saloon keeper, the franchise buyer, and the corrupt politician. "These men destroy the law." While McClure spent years intensely collecting and collating, at great expense, statistics on murder and criminality in nations, states, and cities, it was the broader question of lawlessness that was attacked by the magazine. This discussion has been developed at length because this is the matrix from which most of *McClure's* important articles sprang, including those of Tarbell, Baker, and Steffens.

The History of Standard Oil, wrote liberal New York lawyer George W. Alger in a review [*McClure's* (December 1904)], was "an obvious desire to be exact in statement and to give all the facts, so that the reader may judge for himself whether the conclusions are justified." Lawless rebates, coercion, bribery, and fraud were the gravamens of Miss Tarbell's detailed two-volume indictment, not size, efficiency, or even the demise of laissez-faire economics. "I was willing," she insisted [in her autobiography], "that they should combine and grow as big and rich as they could, but only by legitimate means."

When Miss Tarbell finished with Standard Oil, Burton J. Hendrick's history of "Great American Fortunes and Their Making" replaced it. In a much less critical vein than Tarbell or Gustavus Myers, Hendrick recounted the familiar successes of the Astors, Thomas Fortune Ryan, and Elkins, and then he turned his attention to other concentrations of wealth in "The Story of Life Insurance." In New York, Charles Evans Hughes had revealed shortcomings on the part of these supposedly conservative bulwarks of society who often behaved as "savings banks" or "lotteries." Hendrick followed the New York exposures of fraudulence in detail. He explained the Tontine system—a gambling system whereby the insured bought a policy with an indefinite face value, depending for that upon the number of policy holders who survived him. The system had little relation to actuary tables, and it burdened and penalized persons who lived long—because by then company funds would have been exhausted by extensive advertising, large commissions and executive costs, and matured policies. In 1910 *McClure's* last series on the malefactors of great wealth appeared as "The Masters of Capital," by George K. Turner and John Moody. John Moody, who authored *The Truth about Trusts* while editing *Moody's Magazine* and *Moody's Manual,* was a cousin of George Foster Peabody, who helped found the House of Morgan in America. A follower of John Stuart Mill's individualism and Henry George's humanism, Moody approached McClure about writing a series to counter-balance Tom Lawson's *Frenzied Finance* in *Everybody's.* Though Moody and Turner worked in a "scientific manner," they admitted the "inevitability" of the concentration of wealth which in the final analysis could be controlled only by the state.

Like Miss Tarbell, they criticized only the lawlessness of the economic system. The greed and lust of the great businessman was no more than that of lesser ones, they asserted in an article on Morgan [*McClure's* (November 1910)]. "What could be more vicious than the waste of the savings of the race in the duplication of machinery which it does not need to do its work?" *McClure's* had finally advanced to the New Nationalist position without ever forsaking the original principles by which it had criticized the trusts. They should grow only by "legitimate means." While Miss Tarbell was deriding corporate machiavellianism, Baker exposed that of labor.

The lawlessness of labor was the central theme of Baker's *The Industrial Unrest.* The important question, McClure explained [in *Philadelphia North American* (15 August 1905)], was why non-union men "stick to their jobs in spite of the most horrible forms of boycott, not simply social, but business boycott, even suffering abuse and sometimes death." Again McClure was particularly interested in the plight of the non-union miners of Colorado.

One of Baker's articles dealt with "The Reign of Lawlessness" in Colorado where a "State of insurrection and rebellion" followed the organization of the Western Federation of Miners in that state. After Baker left *McClure's* Christopher P. Connolly continued the theme of miner violence in the west with his "The Story of Montana" [August 1906]. A lawyer for twenty years and a county prosecuting attorney for one term, Connolly supplied the gruesome details of his state's "reign of lawlessness and its overthrow" by vigilantes who hanged from forty to fifty men. Before Connolly's revelations were finished in 1907, another shocking series was begun. Harry Orchard, who, as a paid assassin for the International Workers of the World, supposedly killed eighteen men, published his autobiography in *McClure's*—after he first turned state's witness against Moyer, Haywood, and Pettibone, charged with the assassination of ex-Governor Frank Steunenberg of Colorado.

When Baker finished *The Industrial Unrest,* McClure hoped to develop other studies of lawlessness. He particularly wanted a complete study of European crime. Finally he reneged, suggesting [in a letter to Baker of 27 May 1903] that "railroad accidents are also very interesting and something in the same proportion." Soon Baker was writing "The Railroads on Trial," showing that the disregard for the law and life caused the deaths of nearly 20,000 people yearly in railway accidents. Subsequently the magazine asked "Can American Railroads Afford Safety in Railroad Travel?" [August 1909] and demonstrated that Europe had seventy-five percent fewer accidents than the United States because of advanced safety equipment and strictly enforced governmental regulations. In 1909 the magazine attacked the steel trust for producing cheap rails in "The Problem of the Broken Rail." It was shown that low production costs resulted in increased accident hazards. A year later the magazine delivered its *coup de grace* against the negligence of railroads in "The Cruelties of Our Courts." After a half dozen years of muckraking and progressive legislation, the railroads still refused to provide workers' compensation coverage or assume liabilities for injured or dead workmen, and often the rail magnates perverted the judicial process to maintain these prerogatives. Bismarckian Germany was a generation in advance of the United States in its protection of life and limb.

While all of these articles fitted the *McClure's* pattern, still another subject, lynching, "was taken up by us simply as a study in lawlessness—the total overthrow of all restraints and forms of government . . . " [McClure, *Philadelphia North American* (15 August 1905)]. "What is Lynching?" was a short series by Baker on mob justice, North and South, that served to introduce him to the controversial race question. His conclusion was startling: A high incidence of homicides almost universally accompanied a high lynching rate. Roosevelt was immensely impressed with the series and sent Baker a list of the few crimes committed in the District of Columbia, designed to show that his administration did not abet lawlessness. But the President's article did not appear, probably because the staff agreed with Steffens that "there are no murders down in the District of Columbia, they are too busy stealing to stop for such a thing as murder."

McClure's abounded with articles on other aspects of crime: the justice of the courts, the psychology of crime, secret criminal societies, and famous trials of felons. In "Some Follies in Our Criminal Procedures," a lawyer analyzed the probability of a defendant's getting justice in an American court where juries were often swayed by considerations other than the evidence presented. Not surprisingly, the magazine held up as an example the efficiency of English courts, with fewer judges and less delay in litigation. Later *McClure's* pioneered the advocacy of probation as a part of the "New Gospel in Criminology," which would help eradicate crime and lessen prison costs at the same time. One of *McClure's* most knowledgeable writers in the field of criminology was Hugo Munsterberg, chairman of his department and head of the psychological laboratory at Harvard. Like Steffens and G. Stanley Hall, Munsterberg had studied under Wilhelm Wundt at Leipzig. As early as 1893 he had published his views on criminology in *McClure's,* but with the advent of muckraking he was called upon for more regular contributions. Munsterberg was responsible for several articles that viewed the criminal as a diseased person, sharing responsibility for his guilt with his environment. His behavioristic bent became obvious in his studies of the third degree, hypnotism and crime, and the prevention of crime. He voiced a plea for penal reform reminiscent of Charles Sumner and Horace Mann in Massachusetts before the Civil War.

A less sympathetic approach was that of George K. Turner, who wrote and collaborated on articles that exposed the organized criminality of the Black Hand in the politics of Tammany Hall [May and June 1908]. In turn Theodore A. Bingham, an ex-police commissioner from New York, explained how Tammany infiltrated and made use of the police services in "The Organized Criminals of New York" [November 1909]. Meanwhile the activities of Western crusaders against organized lawlessness—such as Ben B. Lindsey of the Denver juvenile court and William J. Burnes who investigated the timber frauds in Oregon—were chronicled by the magazine [October 1906 and November 1909]. But more sensational yet were the articles on famous trials: the I. W. W. leaders in Colorado; Ferrer, a revolutionary in Spain; and the Camorra trial of a Mafia chieftain in Italy, written up by Arthur Train [January 1910]. Baker's articles on labor and lynching naturally led the magazine to undertake investigations on the other aspects of criminality in a statistical way methodologically more convincing than that of Josiah Flynt. Steffens' *Shame of the Cities* served as the same sort of catalyst.

From St. Louis to New York Lincoln Steffens described the struggle between the law defenders and those men who McClure said "destroy the law." In *The Struggle for Self-Government,* his sequel which muckraked the states, Steffens continued to develop the theme of a lone fighter involved in a personalized fight against criminality. *The Upbuilders,* likewise, is filled with vivid portrayals of men attempting single-mindedly to defend the legal order against a host of villains. This technique was also fondly, but less speciously, cultivated by Samuel Hopkins Adams and William Allen White. Adams' work included an analysis of the breakdown of the legal process in the Appalachian region. "The State of Kentucky vs. Caleb Powers" [February 1904] dealt with the insurrection that developed over the murder of Senator William E. Goebel in a contested governorship, and "Dan Cunningham: A Huntsman of the Law" [June 1904] depicted a U.S. Marshal's fight against the mountain clan system with its moonshining ways. White, in turn, in his "Folk," wrote *McClure's* third article on the Missouri reformer in two years, and emphasized the fact that the young district attorney had won twenty of his forty cases against the St. Louis machine.

It can be seen that the writings of Steffens, Baker, and Miss Tarbell only stimulated further inquiries into the state of lawlessness current in the various fields of capital, labor, and politics, with the resulting loss of life and property through crime and accidents. But *McClure's* campaign against such destruction due to governmental inefficiency spread quickly into other areas such as public health and fire prevention.

McClure's was probably never as influential in the field of preventive medicine as *Collier's.* But Samuel Hopkins Adams, whose famous series on medical quackery appeared in *Collier's,* first wrote on the inadequacy of medical treatment for McClure. With articles on tuberculosis, typhoid, hookworm, and modern surgery, Adams blamed the unnecessary loss of human life on misgovernment. Tenements and slums rather than the lack of medical technology were responsible for the scourge of the contagious diseases. Unguarded sewers and polluted water supplies existed because of irresponsible local government. In typical *McClure's* fashion Adams' articles made much of the better examples afforded by Europe in disease control—where cities were cleaner, airier, and more sanitary. This son of a minister and a graduate of Hamilton College also wrote on the New Orleans conquest of yellow fever through a campaign against the mosquito, "Rochester's Pure Milk Campaign," and the activities of various public health boards. *McClure's* dealt with other facets of the health problem with articles on food faddism, pellagra in the South, and poisonous commodities. Undoubtedly, Upton Sinclair's *The Jungle* was more important than *McClure's* in securing the passage of pure food and drug legislation. But on occasion the magazine championed such projects vigorously. With editorial support Walter Fisher used the pages of *McClure's* to propagandize for a National Health Board in his "A Department of Dollars vs. a Department of Health" [July 1910].

Public and private agencies engaged in health campaigns

proved to be good copy. The Public Health Service had its successes publicized in "Our Duel with the Rats" in 1910. In much the same manner as Miss Tarbell had written of the Pasteur Institute earlier, Burton J. Hendrick explained the Rockefeller Institute's early researches into spinal meningitis [April 1909]. He also wrote other articles on municipal health problems, but this hardly exhausted *McClure's* concern with health.

To be expected, one of McClure's most aggressive programs was directed against the consumption of alcohol. George K. Turner wrote much on the evils of that drink. Other problems were studied by George Kennan, who usually wrote on Russian life but devoted some time to the question of suicides, and Georgine Milmine, who exposed the supposed cures of the Christian Scientists. All of this material, less graphic than Sinclair's *Jungle,* less masterful than Adams' series on patent medicines, *The Great American Fraud,* obviously was concerned with risks to life in an area far broader than that covered by the Pure Food and Drugs Act.

Much of McClure's concern for health grew out of his friendship with the vegetarian, James H. Kellogg, of Battle Creek, Michigan. Both John Phillips and McClure frequented Kellogg's "sanatorium" in Battle Creek and tried his "biologic living," as did many of the progressives, such as Irving Fisher and Ben B. Lindsey. Kellogg was the son of ardent abolitionists who grew out of the Millerite faith and who opposed the use of tobacco, alcohol, spices, tea, coffee, and meats. Reflections of this health magnate's theories often appeared in *McClure's.* McClure paid his bills at the resort by giving Kellogg advertising, and on several occasions attempted to get publishable articles written on the program of the food faddist. Surprisingly, it was the *American Magazine* which first openly endorsed "biologic living."

McClure's was no less concerned with the loss of property which resulted from misgovernment. McClure and his staff were particularly interested in the twin problems of conflagration and conservation. American municipalities, the magazine pointed out in "Fire—An American Extravagance" [November 1908], ignored the recommendations of such groups as the International Society of State and Building Commissioners in regard to fire prevention. Arthur F. McFarlane especially indicted New York City, which permitted the building of skyscrapers when its fire department was unequipped to fight fires in multi-storied buildings [September 1911]. Factory and tenement tinder boxes were also exposed. "The Newark Factory Fire," published in 1911, graphically pictured the unsafe laboring conditions of one hundred New Jersey factories. Frequently fires resulted in extensive loss of life because no provision was made for evacuating the workers and because, on one occasion, doors to the fire escape were kept locked by the management. The situation was worse in the slum dumb-bell tenements, crowded, with no fire escapes and little fire prevention care. Unsurprisingly, American losses from fire were from five to fifteen times as great *per capita* as those of Europe.

McClure's staff was also concerned with the conservation problem, although hardly as much as such magazines as *Collier's,* which first publicized the Ballinger-Pinchot controversy. McClure was content to follow in the wake, and never did he pursue this question systematically or aggressively. In "A Continent Despoiled," which appeared after Roosevelt left office, one writer lamented the national wealth lost through careless destruction of forests, mineral resources, and animal life [April 1909]. Later George K. Turner wrote what amounted to *McClure's* only indictment of Ballinger. In "Billions of Treasure" he accused Ballinger of acting contrary to the public interest in the disposal of Alaskan property to the Guggenheim trust [January 1910]. Articles on Gifford Pinchot and the "National Water Power Trust" [July 1908 and May 1909] completed *McClure's* concern with conservation.

This summation should show that on one level much of *McClure's* muckraking was remarkably simple, a plea for the enforcement of laws against lawlessness of corporations, labor unions, criminality, corrupt politicians, and especially municipalities which were derelict in their public duty to protect health and property. In every instance, like a Bryce or a de Tocqueville, McClure used the practices of Europe as a yardstick by which the effectiveness of American government might be judged. While not the whole reform message of *McClure's,* this defense of order ensured the magazine's appeal to the middle class, always concerned with the legal protection of life and property.

Before completing this analysis of the contents of *McClure's* in the muckraking era, it must be reasserted that muckraking did not change many aspects of the magazine. *McClure's* maintained its interest in popular science, exploration, and aerial navigation. The exploits of the Wright brothers, for example, were nationally publicized by George K. Turner's "The Men Who Learned to Fly" [February 1908].

Nor did *McClure's* with the advent of muckraking cease to publish considerable material on the Civil War, that great illustration of lawless rebellion. During its second decade many of *McClure's* manuscripts came through the offices of Frederick Bancroft, and Miss Tarbell, working on Standard Oil, willingly surrendered much of her responsibility in this area to him. Perhaps their most significant collaborative venture was the securing of Carl Schurz's memoirs. Since Bancroft had worked with the old independent reformer in the campaign of 1884, the two had developed a close friendship. It took twenty-seven installments for Schurz to get from the insurrection in Germany, where he drew a lasting portrait of Karl Marx, to his election as Senator from Missouri. While the series was in progress, Schurz died in 1906.

In addition to his memoirs, Schurz published a review of the race problem for *McClure's* which no one else could have written and no other magazine would have published. This article, which preceded four attempted rebuttals by Thomas Nelson Page and Baker's progressive analysis of lynching and *Following the Color Line,* was a discussion of the aims of Reconstruction in the light of contemporary Negro disfranchisement and demogogic appeals by Vardaman and Tillman. Joshing the South for its fluttered feelings over Booker T. Washington's invitation to dine at the White House, Schurz strenuously argued that modern attempts to reassert peonage over the Negro were doomed [January 1904]. Booker T. Washington immediately responded to this brilliant article: "I spent a portion of Christmas Day in reading your article in *McClure's Magazine,* and must say to you what I have just said to Mr. Baldwin in a letter, that it is the strongest and most statesmanlike word that has been said on the subject of the South and the Negro for a long number of years, and I want to thank you most earnestly for the article. I earnestly hope that it will have a large circulation in the South. *McClure's Magazine* is read a good deal by Southern white people, and I hope the results will be far-reaching."

Undoubtedly Schurz's great reform mind influenced Baker's approach to the race problem.

In its earlier years, the magazine continued to cultivate even minor aspects of the Civil War. Together Bancroft and Miss Tarbell served as a sort of Civil War brain trust for the magazine, ready to help any of their colleagues.

On the other hand, with the genesis of muckraking, *McClure's* fiction underwent as much change as the politically oriented articles. One would like to say that the muckraking movement spelled an end to Victorian modesty, opened new areas for factual commentary, and ended the guise of fiction which factual articles had to carry. But such was not totally the case. Even *The Thirteenth District* and *The Jungle* paraded as fiction. Perhaps Henry May's setting of the pivotal year for the end of American innocence at a later date is justified.

But . . . *McClure's* fiction did change. In a sense it resumed its burden to entertain. The political fiction became a less serious way of commentary. For example, James M. Palmer published numerous stories on "Colonel Lumpkin." Lumpkin often gave long monologues on how to take over a city or a business, or he instructed a Mr. Boodle on the art of using the "pigeonhole vote," the party vote. Or else he revealed delightful accounts of rapid transit scandals of "Finances of the Shark System." Undoubtedly Colonel Lumpkin was based to a great extent on Washington G. Plunkitt, the Tammany chieftain who held sway at a shoeshine stand in Greenwich Village, educating listeners on the distinction between honest and dishonest graft. With only slightly more pathos Harvey O'Higgins, who served an apprenticeship with Steffens on the *Commercial Advertiser,* wrote in dialect of Irish ward politics. His "Tammany's Tithes" appeared in 1906 and was about the police-machine combine. The suffragettes were the subjects of other humorous accounts.

Although earlier writers such as O. Henry, Rex Beach, and Jack London continued to appear occasionally, slowly the field of short story writing was taken over by such writers as Theodore Dreiser, James Hopper, Mrs. Woodrow Wilson, Kathleen Norris, and Willa Cather. Octavia Roberts, a confidante of Brand Whitlock, was occasionally published, as was Alfred Damon Runyon, who wrote "The Defense of Strikesville" in 1907, a character sketch of a professional soldier who helped to put down strikes. After 1905 an increasing amount of *McClure's* fiction came from the pens of its own staff. Miss Roseboro', Miss Cather, Steffens under the pseudonym of Adrian Kirk, James Hopper, and George K. Turner all supplied material. The poetry of Miss Roseboro' along with that of Witter Bynner often appeared, as did that of *McClure's* protégée, Miss Florence Wilkinson. (pp. 148-65)

In conclusion, muckraking brought to *McClure's* a deepening concern for law, a concern that relegated literature to a secondary status but permitted Civil War themes to be continually developed. The magazine's reform program was built upon the design of the old Galesburg reformers who wanted the heavenly city, with temperance, racial justice, feminine rights, and Sabbath observance. Lawlessness had no place in such a universe. But these noble aims were threatened by numerous ills when progressive journalism had scarcely come into its own.

In the first place, several members of the staff felt an indictment of lawlessness might appeal to the middle class but the magazine needed to balance its rather negative attitude with something more positive. Baker was one of the first members of the staff to show such a concern. Although writing of the industrial unrest, lynching, and the railroads with great skill, he saw both sides of these great questions. He admitted his doubts to McClure, who responded in 1903: "I think you are right, that we should in some way offset the critical campaign of the magazine by some articles that would show the real and conquering American in his true character and aspect. It is, of course, a little difficult to formulate such articles. . . ." The President's growing impatience with muckraking only further encouraged McClure to emphasize what he called the upbuilding nature of the American people. Hendrick's series on "Great American Fortunes" and Steffens' on "The Upbuilders" seem efforts in this direction. By 1910, in what could be considered either as a joke or an attempt at objectivity, the magazine published the memoirs of Senator Thomas Platt. This was the same Platt who threatened to sue the magazine over William Allen White's portrait of him a half decade before. And so the second decade at *McClure's* witnessed an increasing dialectical strain between concern for "upbuilding" and for "lawlessness." It was becoming necessary for the staff to make crystal clear what its metaphysical notions were.

But there were many other problems that came with muckraking. Financial difficulties with mounting costs and competition were a major concern, and personality differences were no less significant. When the *McClure's* staff split up in 1906, the most articulate of the middle class monthlies suffered an irreparable blow to its prestige and well-being. This contributed in no small degree to the final disaster that befell McClure in 1911 when he lost control of his magazine. (pp. 166-67)

> *Harold S. Wilson, in his "McClure's Magazine" and the Muckrakers, Princeton University Press, 1970, 347 p.*

ARTHUR WEINBERG AND LILA WEINBERG

[*Arthur Weinberg and Lila Weinberg are American biographers, editors, and critics. Their collection* The Muckrakers: The Era in Journalism that Moved America to Reform *reprints representative muckraking articles written between 1902 and 1912, arranged by topic, with introductory essays prefacing each section. In the following excerpt from that work, the Weinbergs discuss some of the principal issues addressed by reform journalists as well as some of the reforms attributed to muckraking.*]

An earthquake in 1906 practically wiped out half the city of San Francisco.

The journalistic earthquake of the year was the series of articles by David Graham Phillips in *Cosmopolitan* magazine, "The Treason of the Senate." It was this series which prompted President Roosevelt to give to Phillips and other writers the name which has tagged them ever since: muckrakers.

Inspiration for the articles had come from Charles Edward Russell, also a journalist. While sitting in the press gallery of the U.S. Senate one day, he became aware of "well-fed and portly gentlemen," and was struck with the idea that "almost nobody in that chamber had any other reason to be there than his skill in valeting for some powerful Interest." Russell then conceived the idea that a series of articles "might well be written on the fact that strictly speaking we had no Senate; we had only a chamber of butlers for industrialists and financiers" [*Bare Hands and Stone Walls* (1933)].

He suggested the idea to William Randolph Hearst, who had just purchased *Cosmopolitan*. Hearst liked it, and Russell started to gather facts. But he dropped the project when he was given an assignment by *Everybody's* magazine, and *Cosmopolitan* looked for someone else to do the series.

Hearst picked the handsome, meticulously dressed Phillips, who at the age of thirty-nine was already a novelist of some repute. He was also a political journalist whose writing had appeared in the Cincinnati *Star* and the New York *Sun* and *World*.

In spite of his attention to fiction, Phillips was first and foremost a reporter. His name was familiar to readers of *Everybody's*, *McClure's*, *Collier's* and *Harper's*. A series of articles in *Everybody's* touched such subjects as "How Roosevelt Became President," "The Man Who Made the Money Trust," and "The Madness of Much Power."

Though Phillips wrote the series, the research for "The Treason of the Senate" was done by Gustavus Myers, who had already written *The History of the Great American Fortunes*. Myers specialized in historical research.

In announcing the series [February 1906], *Cosmopolitan* proclaimed: "This convincing story of revelation, to be told in several chapters, and to run well through the magazine year, has been called 'The Treason of the Senate' for the reason that that is a fit and logical title for this terrible arraignment of those who, sitting in the seats of the mighty at Washington, have betrayed the public to that cruel and vicious Spirit of Mammon which has come to dominate the nation."

The series began in March 1906. Its theme, taken from the Constitution of the United States, Article III, Section 3: "Treason against the United States shall consist only in levying war against them, or in adhering to their enemies, giving them aid and comfort."

Its opening article charged: "The treason of the Senate! Treason is a strong word, but not too strong, rather too weak, to characterize the situation in which the Senate is eager, resourceful, indefatigable agent of interests as hostile to the American people as any invading army could be, and vastly more dangerous: interests that manipulate the prosperity produced by all, so that it heaps up riches for the few; interests whose growth and power can only mean the degradation of the people, of the educated into sycophants, of the masses toward serfdom. . . . The Senators are not elected by the people; they are elected by the 'interests.' "

[New York senators] Chauncey M. Depew and Thomas Collier Platt were the first to be put on the carpet. Phillips pointed out that Senator Depew was a member of the boards of directors of seventy corporations. He received more than $50,000 as fees for his services from these firms, which Phillips claimed was part payment from "the interests." He described Platt as having a "long . . . unbroken record of treachery to the people in legislation of privilege and plunder promoted and in decent legislation prevented."

After Depew and Platt, Phillips singled out Nelson W. Aldrich, the senator from Rhode Island, a Republican, and called him the right arm of "the interests." Senator Arthur Pue Gorman of Maryland, a Democrat, was called the left arm.

The series also included articles on John C. Spooner of Wisconsin, Joseph Weldon Bailey of Texas, Stephen B. Elkins of West Virginia, Philander C. Knox of Pennsylvania.

Phillips referred to Henry Cabot Lodge as "the familiar coarse type of machine politician disguised by the robe of the 'Gentleman Scholar.' " He called William B. Allison of Iowa the Interests' "craftiest agent," and Joseph Benson Foraker of Ohio the "best stump speaker" for "the interests."

The records of William J. Stone of Missouri, Shelby M. Cullom of Illinois and Winthrop Murray Crane of Massachusetts were reviewed, as well as a number of other senators, both the leaders and those who were led.

The series concluded: "Such is the stealthy and treacherous Senate as at present constituted. And such it will continue to be until people think instead of shout about politics; until they judge public men by what they do and are, not by what they say and pretend. However, the fact that the people are themselves responsible for their own betrayal does not mitigate contempt for their hypocritical and cowardly betrayers. A corrupt system explains a corrupt man; it does not *excuse* a corrupt man; it does not *excuse* him. The stupidity or negligence of the householder in leaving the door unlocked does not lessen the crime of the thief."

Upon the conclusion of the series [17 November 1906], *Collier's,* which had been doing its own share of muckraking, commented: " 'The Treason of the Senate' has come to a close. These articles made reform odious. They represented sensational and money-making preying on the vogue of the 'literature of exposure,' which had been built up by truthful and conscientious work of writers like Miss Tarbell, Lincoln Steffens and Ray Stannard Baker. . . . Mr. Phillips' articles were one shriek of accusations based on the distortion of such facts as were printed, and on the suppression of facts which were essential."

President Roosevelt, writing to the editor-in-chief of the *Saturday Evening Post,* George Horace Lorimer, said: "I do not believe that the articles that Mr. Phillips has written, and notably these articles on the Senate, do anything but harm. They contain so much more falsehood than truth that they give no accurate guide for those who are really anxious to war against corruption, and they do excite a hysterical and ignorant feeling against everything existing, good or bad. . . ."

Professor Louis Filler contends [in *Crusaders for American Liberalism* (1939)] that the political consequences of the series of articles "had at least broken down those adamant walls of the Senate. Freer discussion of Senatorial personages and powers followed. A number of Senators were unseated in the next election, and others were dropped from the rolls in succeeding years until, by 1912, the composition of the Chamber had changed completely. . . . An amendment to the Constitution was drafted and triumphantly adopted, and the power of direct election of Senators was at last given to the people."

Phillips himself was disturbed about the outburst which followed the publication of the articles. He considered the series the one failure in his life.

He did not live long enough to derive the satisfaction of knowing what he had accomplished. An assassin's bullet killed him at the age of forty-three. But his series on the treason of the Senate was a major influence in the passage of the Seventeenth Amendment, which gave to the people the direct election of senators. (pp. 68-70)

The idea of publishing articles on trusts in *McClure's* magazine was that of its publisher, S. S. McClure. It was his intention to present a series on "the greatest American business achievements."

Trusts and monopolies had been a topic of discussion in the United States since the end of the Spanish American War and the coming of prosperity. "The feeling of the common people," recalled McClure in his autobiography [*My Autobiography* (1913)], "had a sort of menace in it; they took a threatening attitude toward the Trusts, and without much knowledge."

At an editorial conference at *McClure's,* it was decided not to discuss trusts in the abstract but to take one trust, give its history, its effects, its method of operation.

As the Standard Oil Company was the most important trust at that time, the company was earmarked for study. It was the creation of one man—John D. Rockefeller—of whom McClure said: "There is no question that he is the Napoleon among business men." To McClure and his editors, Standard Oil represented the "Mother of Trusts," and it acted as a model or an inspiration for others.

Ida Tarbell was already on the staff of *McClure's Magazine* when she was assigned to write the articles. She had lived for years in the heart of the Pennsylvania oil country. She was born not more than thirty miles from the first oil well, and its discovery shaped her father's life. She had grown up "with oil derricks, oil tanks, pipe lines, refineries, oil exchanges."

Tragedy had hit her own household during the ten years that Standard Oil completed its monopoly. Her father's partner, "ruined by the complex situation shot himself, leaving [her] father with notes" to pay. In order for her father to pay these notes, he had to mortgage their home, which to him "in his modest economy was unsound and humiliating" [Tarbell, *All in the Day's Work* (1939)].

In her research for the Standard Oil series, Miss Tarbell turned to records of Congressional investigations, state investigations, testimony of Mr. Rockefeller and other Standard Oil officials in suits brought against Standard Oil, and also information from those who had fought the "Mother of Trusts."

Through Mark Twain, Miss Tarbell met Henry Rogers, a top executive in Standard Oil, and a man whom she saw regularly for two years in her preparation of the series. Through Rogers she was able to meet and talk with other officials of the company.

[As she recounted in her autobiography] Rogers and Miss Tarbell made a "bargain." She was to take up with him each case in the company's history as she came to it, and he in turn would give her documents, figures, explanations, and justifications—"anything and everything which would enlarge my understanding and judgment."

In case of a disagreement, Miss Tarbell's judgment about these cases would prevail.

Her visits to Rogers ended when one of her articles disclosed that the shipments of independent oil companies "were interfered with, their cars side-tracked en route while pressure was brought on buyers to cancel orders. There were frequent charges that freight clerks were reporting independent shipments."

Before the article appeared, Miss Tarbell told Rogers that she had come upon repeated charges that Standard Oil got reports of independent shipments from the railroad and that they stopped them.

"Do you have the help of railroad shipping clerks in the operation?" Miss Tarbell asked.

Rogers responded: "Of course we do everything we legally and fairly can to find out what our competitors are doing, just as you do in *McClure's Magazine.* But as for any such system of tracking and stopping, as you suggest, that is nonsense."

"Well," said Miss Tarbell, "give me everything you have on this point."

Rogers said he had nothing more than what he had already given her.

After the article in which she mentioned these charges was written, Rogers asked Miss Tarbell: "Where did you get that stuff?"

"Mr. Rogers," responded the reporter from *McClure's,* "you can't for a moment think that I would tell you where I got it. You will recall my efforts to get from you anything more than a general denial that these practices of espionage so long complained of were untrue, could be explained by legitimate competition. You know this bookkeeping record is true."

There were no more interviews between the reporter and her company source.

Originally, "The History of the Standard Oil Company" was to be a three-article series, but before publication it was changed to six, and before the series was completed it ran to nineteen articles. It was published in book form in the fall of 1904. Though Ida Tarbell was already famous as a biographer before the appearance of *Standard Oil,* the series catapulted her into national fame and her name became a byword in many homes throughout the country. The author, however, was particularly interested to learn what kind of reception the book would get from the Standard Oil people.

A friend of hers reported to her that Rockefeller at one time thought of answering the McClure articles, but "it has always been the policy of the Standard to keep silent under attack and let their acts speak for themselves."

Nevertheless, answers did come. For example, Elbert Hubbard of the Roycroft Shop of East Aurora, New York, wrote an essay on the virtues of the centralization of the oil industry by Standard. Miss Tarbell says in her autobiography that she had it "from various interested sources that five million copies were ordered printed in pamphlet form [as *The Standard Oil Co.*] by the Standard Oil Company and were distributed by Mr. Hubbard."

Hubbard wrote: "Up to this time, or until very recently, the Standard Oil company has declined to answer its assailants. . . . The Standard Oil company should have nailed a few of the Ida Tarbell fairy tales, ten years ago."

He went on to say:

> Ida Tarbell . . . is an honest, bitter, talented, prejudiced and disappointed woman who wrote from her own point of view. And that view is from the ditch, where her father's wheelbarrow was landed by a Standard Oil tank-wagon. . . . She shot from cover, and she shot to kill. Such literary bush-

whackers should be answered shot for shot. Sniping the commercial caravan may be legitimate, but to my mind the Tarbell-Steffens-Russell-Roosevelt-Sinclair method of inky warfare is quite as unethical as the alleged tentacled-octopi policy which they attack.

When the book itself was published, most reviews were laudatory. The only voice of dissent came from a reviewer in the [5 January 1905] *Nation,* who wrote: "This book seems to have been written for the purpose of intensifying the popular hatred. The writer has either a vague conception of the nature of proof, or she is willing to blacken the character of Mr. John D. Rockefeller by insinuation and detraction. . . ."

On the other hand, the magazine *Public Opinion* said [5 January 1905]: "The author never gets excited, however exciting her story may become; she sets forth the facts, and to a considerable extent leaves inference and conclusions to her readers. . . . It is, in effect, a liberal education in the fundamentals of the trust problem; it is the Blackstone of the literature that is growing up around this problem, in its entirety the most important of all in commercialized America."

Will Irwin in his articles on the American newspapers in *Collier's* in 1911, more than half a decade later, wrote of the series: "Never was a contemporaneous history so temperately and accurately written."

From a vantage point of more than twenty-five years after its appearance, Professor Allan Nevins in his two-volume biography of John D. Rockefeller, published in 1940, refers to *The History of the Standard Oil Company* as "the greatest book produced by the muckraking movement . . . its most enduring achievement."

"Readers today," wrote Dr. Nevins, "are likely to find . . . its sober, factual method difficult to read; and nine people out of ten who talk of the book actually know it only at second hand. But in 1902-4 the public had a background of knowledge which lent the articles a stirring interest." (pp. 242-44)

A franchise was granted to Trinity in 1697 by the English kingdom for a parish church to be located at the head of Wall Street for "the use and in behalf of the inhabitants from time to time inhabiting and to inhabit within our said city of New York, in communion of our said Protestant Church of England, as now establisht by our laws." The franchise specified that this should be the "sole and only parish church in the city of New York." Eight years after this, the church was given a grant of land which later became the great bulk of its holdings. In 1788, after the separation of the United States from England, the corporation name changed from "Protestant Church of England" to "Protestant Episcopal Church in the State of New York."

By 1788, the corporation had three churches: Trinity, which was the church proper, and two chapels: St. George's on Beekman Street and St. Paul's on Vesey Street. The city and the number of people grew. By 1793 Christ Church, a separate and rival congregation, was created. It was refused admission to the Convention because Trinity was by franchise the "sole and only parish" in the city. Later, however, St. Mark's, first a Trinity chapel, was set apart as a separate church and Trinity gave some land, and then followed other separate churches, to which Trinity gave both her blessings and some land.

The land originally given Trinity developed as the city grew, and by the early twentieth century was rich with all types of property. That part used for church and educational purposes was not taxed. Along much of their other property, particularly that surrounding the church proper at the head of Wall Street, a horde of tenements had sprung up, and Trinity was reaping huge financial benefits.

The downtown neighborhood started to change and the wealthy moved uptown. In 1852 Trinity Corporation appropriated $230,000 to build Trinity chapel on West Twenty-fifth Street. In 1890 St. Agnes on West Ninety-second Street was built for $500,000. At the same time, the corporation discontinued its missionary work downtown. In 1909 Trinity summarily tried to close St. John's, one of its oldest chapels in downtown New York, with close to 500 members, on the theory that it didn't pay and they could use the money elsewhere to better advantage.

This brought forth a comment from Dr. John P. Peters, rector of St. Michael's Protestant Episcopal Church, New York: "The appropriation granted for the maintenance of St. John's was counted as a benevolent dole given to the poor; the similar appropriations to the well-to-do congregations of Trinity and St. Agnes were regarded as their right. The well-to-do congregations had representatives in the Corporation, the poor congregations had none. In principle, the methods of the insurance scandal were repeated here."

The Trinity tenement properties were notorious for their squalor and filth; they were breeding places for disease, particularly tuberculosis. Hundreds of rickety firetraps; sanitation limited to backyard sheds. Trinity fought each new improvement law—one case even going to court, where they lost and eventually had to comply by installing tap water on each floor of a tenement building.

Originally, the muckrakers had focused their attention on national and business affairs. Eventually, however, they began to study local conditions and it was not long before Trinity with its tenement housing came under the muckrake.

Ray Stannard Baker's "The Case Against Trinity" in the *American Magazine,* July 1909, indicted Trinity Church for the way it ran its holdings, and its autocracy over its chapels. He criticized the church in that it failed to live up to its duty, but made it clear that it was the institution he was criticizing, and not religion. This particular article was part of a series Baker did for the magazine on "The Spiritual Unrest" which was published in 1908 and 1909.

In April-May 1908, Charles Edward Russell told the story of "Trinity: Church of Mystery," in *Broadway* (later *Hampton's*) *Magazine.*

Russell in his autobiography [*Bare Hands and Stone Walls* (1933)] says: "The series, with its photographs of conditions and its array of indubitable facts, started a cyclone of resentment, particularly in our highest social circles.

"The Reverend Morgan Dix, chief pastor of Trinity, died in the midst of the engagement and it was poignantly suggested that grief and chagrin over the attacks upon his corporation had caused his death."

Everybody's in July 1908 published Russell's "The Tenements of Trinity Church." In introducing the article, *Everybody's* editors wrote that it "aims to describe the actual condition of some of these Trinity tenements and to give an idea of their relation to the health and security of the city. It also

raises a very great and interesting question: whether the good wrought by the charitable and philanthropic enterprises of Trinity equals the evil wrought by the tenements that finance the charities."

In answer to letters of criticism which appeared in *Everybody's* after Russell's article, Russell wrote an article titled "Trinity's Tenements—The Public's Business," in which he stated that the public was minding its own business, as it was told to do by a reader, whom Russell took to be a Trinity trustee. It is up to the public, wrote Russell, to take care of the public health. In this respect, the fact that the tenements are laden with germs makes it its business. On a business basis, since the tenement properties are depressed, taxes are low, and the rest of New York's citizens must make up the difference.

In his book *The Battle with the Slum,* Jacob Riis said, "Trinity, the wealthiest church corporation in the land, was in constant opposition as a tenement house landlord, and finally, to save a few hundred dollars, came near upsetting the whole structure of tenement law that had been built up in the interest of the toilers and of the city's safety with such infinite pains."

Twenty-five years after his articles on Trinity appeared, Russell wrote in his autobiography: "The smoke of battle finally cleared away. Trinity had the usual vindication, the wickedness of the muckraker was satisfactorily demonstrated and all was once more peace. Then Trinity began quietly to pull down its objectionable tenements." It is estimated that in the next three years after the articles some scores of these "filthy old barracks disappeared from the face of the earth."

In April 1910, *Hampton's* editorialized: "We are as ready to praise as to attack. Therefore, we are glad to announce, upon reliable authority, that Trinity Corporation has torn down, since the publication of these articles [about two years previously] about four blocks of its miserable tenements in New York City, and is showing a disposition to clean up at least a part of its property." (pp. 309-10)

Exposure of prison conditions during the era of the muckrakers was in most instances accomplished by specialists in the field. The one exception was Charles Edward Russell, who as a muckraker contributed to the literature of exposure in varied fields, including that of prison conditions.

The muckraking magazines carried a number of articles which decried the inhuman conditions found in prisons. For example, *The Arena* in 1904 published an article by Dr. G. W. Galvin of the Emergency Hospital in Boston on "Inhuman Treatment of Prisoners in Massachusetts." The article excited protest and produced some amelioration of the conditions in the Massachusetts penitentiaries.

A letter to *Everybody's Magazine* from an ex-prisoner, telling about his experience in the Georgia prison system, initiated Russell into the field of prison muckraking. *Everybody's* sent him to investigate the man's accusations. "A Burglar in the Making" resulted.

In announcing "A Burglar in the Making" [June 1908] *Everybody's* editor noted: "For apparent reasons, the man's identity must be carefully guarded here; but all the essentials of the narrative are exactly as recited. Many of them Mr. Russell has been able to verify from his own observations; the others can be accepted upon faith. They reveal clearly the shameful system by which the State of Georgia surrenders for profits the solemn duty of correcting her wrongdoers. . . ."

Prior to the Civil War, convicts in Georgia were kept in a prison, but after the war, with an upsurge of crime, penitentiary facilities were inadequate to house all the convicts, so the state adopted the policy of leasing prisoners to contractors. At first it was on public works projects; later this was changed so that the state could lease them to private individuals for a period of five years. In 1879, the state started to lease the convicts to three companies under an agreement to run for a period of twenty years. These companies were to pay the state $500,000 in twenty annual installments for the use of the convicts.

Eighteen years later a law was passed to the effect that when the companies' contracts expired (in two years), the convict leasing system would be amended.

Under the law, a prison commission was appointed to obtain a prison farm where the old, the young and the sick would be housed apart from the hardened criminals. Convicts with sentences of five years and under were to be sent to a chain gang; those with sentences of more than five years were to be leased to contractors. The contractor paid $100 a year for the more "desirable" convicts, the others went to the highest bidders.

Russell made this system the target for his articles.

In the November 1908 issue of *Everybody's,* its publishers commented: "Georgia didn't waste any time finding fault with us for calling attention to the spot on her pretty gown. Georgia cleaned the spot off quicker'n scat—that's Georgia—and, looking up smiling, said, 'What was that last remark of yours?' We didn't really kill the bear—Georgia did it. . . . All we did was to criticize. . . . We are proud to have had a little share in the good work."

That same issue quoted a Georgia citizen as saying that Russell's article was "the spark that set off the powder that is now exploding in the legislative halls of the state of Georgia."

And there was an explosion in the Georgia legislature. The hearings made page-one news. (pp. 322-23)

But the lower and upper houses of the legislature could not reach agreement on how to handle the leasing situation. The upper house wanted complete repeal of the leasing system. The lower house desired amendments. . . .

The regular session of the legislature adjourned with no action on the problem. But it did call for a special session to discuss the convict bill. At this session, several weeks later, once again there was "floundering," but eventually a bill was passed which satisfied both houses and was signed by the governor.

The new law provided that the governor and the prison commission might lease for one year any "overs" after cities, municipalities and state institutions had been accommodated with their needs for convict labor.

"The law does not 'unconditionally' terminate the lease system upon March 3, 1909 as repeatedly demanded by the upper house. However, it takes a long step toward that much needed result," reported the Atlanta *Constitution* [20 September 1908]. (p. 324)

The editor of *Everybody's Magazine* in a note preceding William Hard's [November 1907] article "Making Steel and Killing Men" asks three questions. But these questions are asked after presenting certain comments by the superintendent of a steel mill and reports from the records of the Chicago coroner's office. The comments:

"The English idea with regards to blast furnaces is to run moderately and save the lining," Charles S. Price, superintendent of the Cambria Steel Works at Johnstown, Pennsylvania, is quoted as saying. "What do we care for the lining? We think that a lining is good for so much iron, and the sooner it makes it the better."

From the records of the Chicago coroner's office, the editor cites the statistic: "Forty-six men were killed in accidents last year [1906] in the South Chicago plant of the United States Steel Corporation. There was no great casualty. The largest number killed at any one time was four. Two other accidents accounted for two men apiece. All the rest were killed singly. During the course of the year, therefore, there were 41 separate accidents that resulted in the destruction of the one valuable thing in the world, human life."

The editor now asked his three questions: "Have we in America the same attitude toward human beings that we have toward the linings of blast furnaces? Do we think that a man is good for so much iron and steel, and the quicker he makes it the better? Must he then go to the graveyard just as the lining of the blast furnace goes to the junk heap?"

Several years after the publication of "Making Steel and Killing Men," and another article by Mr. Hard, "The Law of the Killed and Wounded," *Everybody's Magazine,* in an editorial roundup on what the magazine had accomplished [June 1912], cited these articles as "unquestionably influencing much of the humanitarian legislation of the past few years." The editor asked his readers to "wade through" the list of articles which the editor considered "our apology for being alive."

Several months after six girls were burned to death and nineteen others died as a result of jumping from fourth-floor windows in a Newark factory fire, Mary Alden Hopkins in *McClure's Magazine* showed that the loss of life was mainly due to defective doors and fire escapes.

She concludes that article with: "If an employer has provided broad, easily accessible fire escapes, and enough of them, if he has provided interior staircases constructed in a flameproof manner; if he has provided interior fire-alarms, and has taken enough interest in the safety of his people to establish a fire drill, then he has at least given his employees a chance for their lives."

Soon thereafter, safety committees were named in factories, safety rules formulated and continuous inspection decreed. Here again the muckrakers detailed the problems and their exposures sparked the movement for safety, which resulted in legislative action in the various states.

By 1912, thirteen states had passed Workmen's Compensation laws. By 1917, about forty states had enacted such regulations. (pp. 340-41)

The country had been reading about the alliance between business and politicians and the corruption of both. This was the theme of Lincoln Steffens. Now the public began to read the muckrakers' stories about the connection between liquor, gambling, crime, political corruption and prostitution.

The nation was shocked with the sensational charges in *Mc-Clure's Magazine* about the highly organized, efficient, and wide extent of traffic in women and its association with political corruption.

S. S. McClure had given George Kibbe Turner the assignment of exposing vice. Turner had been associated with the Springfield *Republican.* He joined the staff of *McClure's* soon after Ray Stannard Baker, Lincoln Steffens, Ida M. Tarbell, Finley Peter Dunne and others left the magazine to publish and edit their own *American Magazine.*

S. S. McClure had had an idea for a story on Chicago. He had been clipping news stories from Chicago newspapers for some time as a basis for this. However, before he published his article, he sent Turner to Chicago to study the situation. What resulted was Turner's "City of Chicago," which appeared in April 1907. The article pointed to the "business of dissipation" that came from the liquor trade, prostitution and gambling.

"The effect of this single article was indescribable. Coming as it did four years after Steffens began his investigations into municipal crime, it found a national audience ready and able to appreciate it and apply its lessons at home. Prostitution had hitherto been mentioned in generalities; it was significant that the public now seized upon it rather than upon municipal corruption as a whole. Prostitution was the subject the people wanted elaborated" [Louis Filler, *Crusaders for American Liberalism* (1939)].

The article acted like a clarion call to Chicago reformers and a vice commission was named by the Mayor in 1910 which resulted in its report "The Social Evil in Chicago."

A month later, McClure's article, "Chicago As Seen by Herself; Epidemic of Crime," appeared.

U.S. Congressman Barratt O'Hara, who at the time of the Chicago Vice Commission was lieutenant-governor of Illinois and who later was to be chairman of the Vice Commission of the Illinois State Senate, which investigated vice and low wages, writes [in a letter to Arthur and Lila Weinberg, 23 February 1960]: "I am not in a position to say that the Turner article in *McClure's Magazine* in April 1907 was responsible for the creation of the vice commission . . . but I have no doubt it was a large contributing factor. . . . This committee did a really good work. . . . But because of some of the personnel of the commission the large emphasis in the placing of blame was put on dance halls, manner of conduct of houses of prostitution and similar phases. The fact that at that time it had been established that no girl could live on less than $8.00 a week, and that at least 50% of the girls in such respectable establishments as Marshall Fields and Sears Roebuck were getting considerably less than that amount in wages was not given what I thought the proper emphasis . . . .

"While I cannot say that in any direct sense did the writings of the McClure 'muckrakers' influence the creation or the investigation of the Senate Vice Committee, it is undoubtedly true that these writings had a large indirect influence. That is, the 'muckrakers' had prepared the climate for the public reception of the exposures, and inasmuch as the wide public indignation over the fact brought out by the Senate Vice Committee that women workers were being paid less than they could live on, resulted in the enactment of the first State Minimum Wage laws.

George Kibbe Turner, whose muckraking articles about prostitution helped bring about passage of the Mann Act.

"I think that in this area you must give the 'muckrakers' plenty of credit."

Turner followed his Chicago article two years later with an exposé of the social evil in New York City. "Tammany's Control of New York by Professional Politicians" charged that prostitution had been practically legalized in that city. Five months later, Turner wrote "Daughters of the Poor," which was a tale of immigrant girls caught in the white slave trade of New York.

In announcing "Daughters of the Poor," *McClure's Magazine,* using an advertisement in *Collier's* [23 October 1909], called it "the most startling and important article published in years—a plain story . . . of how the White Slave Trade in American girls developed in New York under Tammany Hall and has spread to every large city of the United States."

Two months after "Daughters of the Poor" appeared, a grand jury was impaneled in New York to investigate white slave trade in that city. It was headed by John D. Rockefeller, Jr.

The *New York Times* of January 4, 1910 announced:

ROCKEFELLER HEADS
VICE GRAND JURY

———

Son of the Standard Oil Man
Demurs Because of Youth and
Business, but Is Overruled.

———

TO TAKE UP WHITE SLAVERY

———

Judge O'Sullivan, in Strong Charges,
Says Organized Traffic Should Be
Thoroughly Investigated

(pp. 386-88)

[In October 1910, a] year after the publication of "Daughters of the Poor," *McClure's* referred to the article "as one of the most notable things that the magazine ever published . . . largely instrumental, together with reports to the national Government of the Immigration Commission, in causing legislation dealing with the 'white slave' traffic to be passed in many States. So influential, indeed, was this article that in the public mind it has gained a large share of the credit which is due to the two years' investigation of the national Government. . . ."

The impetus to investigation, as a result of these three Turner articles, also led to such vice commission reports as that in Minneapolis, 1911; Portland, 1913; and Hartford, 1913.

A strong case can also be made out that these writings had their effect in helping to pass the Mann Act. Designed to deal with the traffic of women through the Federal power over interstate commerce, the Mann Act was first introduced in December 1909 by Representative James R. Mann of Chicago, and passed by Congress on June 25, 1910. (p. 388)

The muckrakers believed in fair play and in democracy; they believed that if man knew of the wrongs, he would rise to his stature and do something about them. They muckraked because they loved the world. Though they were angry at the injustices, there was no bitterness, no hatred.

They were writers and reporters interested in human nature. Sometimes they worked together; mostly they worked alone. Though they were not organized as a group, they had a common cause: to expose. Generally they offered no cures.

Some of their paths crossed again after the era of the muckraker was over; others found themselves in different arenas. Some turned conservative; a few—like Sinclair, Steffens and Russell—veered to the left. With the mass-circulation magazines no longer interested in publishing muckraking articles, these writers whose words had blazoned across the American scene to awaken an apathetic public now began to look toward other areas of activity.

Upton Sinclair, in reminiscing, calls his muckraking colleagues simply "men of courage." He explains: "The times required a great deal of it, for the things they were after were certainly serious defects in our political, social and economic life."

Ida M. Tarbell, on the other hand, wrote that she often heard the comment that it required courage on the part of *McClure's* to undertake her series on Standard Oil. "But courage implies a suspicion of danger. Nobody thought of such a thing in our office. . . . We were neither apologists nor critics, only journalists intent on discovering what had gone into the making of this most perfect of all monopolies. What had we to be afraid of?" [*All in the Day's Work* (1939)].

Sinclair recalls some of his fellow writers of the muckraking era: "Ida Tarbell was largely a conventional-minded lady, sweet and gracious. David Graham Phillips never classified himself, but he expressed an old-fashioned American radicalism not identified with any economic theory. He associated with Socialists.

"Lincoln Steffens was very enthusiastic in the early days about Communists, but later he became disillusioned and disappointed with them.

"Ray Stannard Baker was very mild, sweet, kind, a New England conscience, cultured. He muckraked conscientiously; he was shocked by the wrong. I tried to make a fighting radical out of him, but Baker was too gentle; he had no economics, or very little.

"Finley Peter Dunne made fun with Mr. Dooley and he laughed freely; he had a wonderful sense of humor," recalls Sinclair.

William Hard, who during the muckraking era wrote about child labor, politics and industrial accidents, is today proud of his muckraking, and asserts [in a letter to Arthur and Lila Weinberg] that "in my opinion, the best of us muckrakers was Lincoln Steffens. He dealt principally, of course, with politics and government. He was a charming character as well as a great magazine writer." (pp. 431-32)

Arthur Weinberg and Lila Weinberg, in The Muckrakers: The Era in Journalism That Moved America to Reform—The Most Significant Magazine Articles of 1902-1912, *edited by Arthur Weinberg and Lila Weinberg, Simon and Schuster, 1961, 449 p.*

JAMES HARVEY YOUNG

[*Young, an American educator and historian, has written and contributed to several studies of medicine and the medical profession, including* Drugs in Our Society, *edited by Paul Talalay (1964),* The Medical Messiahs *(1967), and* American Self-Dosage Medicines *(1974). In the following excerpt from his* Toadstool Millionaires: A Social History of Patent Medicines in America before Federal Regulation, *he discusses muckraking of patent medicines. An unexcerpted portion of the chapter from which this excerpt is taken discusses mid- to late-nineteenth-century exposés of dangerous patent medicines and early efforts toward their regulation.*]

The most famous series of articles in American patent medicine history began on October 7, 1905, in the pages of *Collier's, The National Weekly.* They were written by a free-lance journalist named Samuel Hopkins Adams, and his conclusions were succinctly rendered in the title he gave to the series, "The Great American Fraud." Adams did not say much that had not been said before in the long decades during which patent medicines had been criticized. But in the *Collier's* series he made a major campaign out of what had been an occasional skirmish, and he reached an audience not only vastly larger than had ever before heard nostrums castigated, but one enthusiastic about supporting reform.

Adams' "muckraking" journalism came during the Progressive period. The first major attack on patent medicines had been part of that earlier upsurge of reform sentiment associated with Jacksonian democracy. It had been led by perceptive physicians and pharmacists, who belabored Swaim's Panacea and saw hazards to American health in other packaged pills and potions. Denunciation of nostrums continued in the years that followed, as in the case of R. G. Eccles, that relentless foe of Radam's Microbe Killer, who was both doctor and druggist. He and his fellows in both professions could aim anti-nostrum weapons of improving accuracy, as medical science and pharmaceutical chemistry advanced. The target also kept expanding, as the volume of patent medicine production boomed and the blatancy of advertising increased during the last quarter of the 19th century. (pp. 205-06)

[In the late nineteenth century several magazines] had spoken out in opposition to medical quackery. Orange Judd's *American Agriculturist,* begun in 1859, had excluded objectionable nostrum advertising and had set aside a special page on which to expose frauds. Wilmer Atkinson's *Farm Journal,* started in 1877, had adhered to the policy described in the circular announcing the first issue, that it would accept no "quack medical advertisement at any price." *Popular Science Monthly* took a perennial interest in quackery and through the years printed a series of able attacks. Even the staid *Atlantic Monthly* in 1867 published Dr. S. Weir Mitchell's *The Autobiography of a Quack,* a novel which revealed the shabbiness of the fake remedy game so vividly that it was reprinted in the *Century* when the anti-nostrum movement had heated up.

It was during the 1890's that the *Ladies' Home Journal* first got interested in patent medicines. Cyrus H. K. Curtis, the publisher, came to the decision that proprietary ads must go, and, when the treasurer protested, the taciturn New Englander withered him with a look. In full agreement with his publisher and father-in-law was editor Edward Bok. He kept the *Journal* columns clean and occasionally wrote a harsh word about nostrums, particularly the bitters of high alcoholic content. Many of Bok's feminine readers were ardent members of the revived temperance crusade, and WCTU leaders, more sophisticated than they once had been, were now well aware that Hostetter's Bitters and Peruna might provide an unwitting or a secret tipple. Through pamphlets, speeches, and propaganda in the schools, they battled the demon rum disguised as medicine. Bok gave them a helping hand.

The *Journal's* random attacks on nostrums turned into a vigorous campaign in 1904. The change of tempo owed much to a chance error. In an editorial condemning "The 'Patent-Medicine' Curse," Bok listed the ingredients of various nostrums, citing a document issued by the Massachusetts State Board of Health. One of the remedies was Doctor Pierce's Favorite Prescription, and it contained, said Bok, relying on his source, alcohol, opium, and digitalis. The company promptly launched a $200,000 libel suit, asserting that the medicine contained none of these. The editor found he had made a careless and costly mistake. The Massachusetts analysis he had depended upon was a quarter of a century out of date; new analyses run by chemists hired for the purpose confirmed the Pierce contention. So did a visit to the manufacturing plant. Bok printed a retraction, prepared for the trial, and stepped up his denunciation of the patent medicine business.

The *Journal* editor hoped that he might be able to find an old bottle of Pierce's remedy, perhaps in some isolated rural store, which would contain alcohol, opium, and digitalis. To make this hunt he needed an able and trustworthy man, and Bok hired a young Harvard-trained journalist and lawyer named Mark Sullivan. Despite a diligent search, the *Journal's* sleuth could find no such bottle as his employer needed for the trial. The woman's magazine lost its suit, and the jury awarded Pierce $16,000. In the meantime Bok had given Sullivan other undercover tasks to do, and, shadowed by detectives, he probed into the workings of the patent medicine business. Using assumed names, Sullivan advertised in the papers of various cities as if seeking to hire men skilled in different branches of the industry. Then he interviewed those who struck at his bait, the chemists, the experts in direct mail selling, the advertising specialists. Eager for better jobs, these men bragged about their own ability, revealing to Sullivan the tricks of the trade, confiding the formulas. He learned that letters written by ailing men and women in response to adver-

tisements were sold, after the company had fully exploited them, to other proprietors. These pathetic and confidential missives ended up in huge bundles, packaged according to disease, and brokers sold or rented the letters for several dollars a thousand. Sullivan bought some packages and had them photographed. Another photograph became more celebrated. Sullivan soon learned that, although advertising showing Lydia Pinkham's maternal face might be read as suggesting that she would answer letters of inquiry from suffering women, the venerable lady had long been dead. Accompanied by a friend who owned a camera, he set out on a tour of the Pine Grove Cemetery near Lynn, Massachusetts, and found the imposing tombstone inscribed with the date of Mrs. Pinkham's passing, May 17, 1883. The picture soon appeared in the pages of the *Journal.*

It was Sullivan who found out about the "red clause" in advertising contracts. As a result of some delicate maneuvering, he secured a copy of the minutes of the Proprietary Association meeting at which Cheney had made his boastful speech. With this clue, Sullivan tracked down and photographed similar "muzzle-clauses" in the contracts of several major medicine advertisers. He also obtained pictures of letters written by proprietors to newspapers when danger loomed, and he secured direct quotations from Dr. Pierce's son praising the newspaper publishers' association for help in defeating inimical bills.

All of this sensational information Sullivan drafted into an article which he called "The Patent Medicine Conspiracy Against the Freedom of the Press." Bok liked it but felt it too "legalistic" and long for the *Ladies' Home Journal* and offered it to Norman Hapgood, the sober, scholarly editor of *Collier's.* Hapgood took it and Sullivan's article appeared in the magazine during November 1905. At the time that it was printed *Collier's* was in the midst of the most earnest campaign ever waged against patent medicines by an American magazine.

The crusade had started with a jest. William Jennings Bryan had been belaboring corporations in the pages of his personal organ, the *Commoner,* a paper which contained full-page advertisements for Liquozone, a nostrum promising to cure everything from dandruff to dysentery. Hapgood chided Bryan editorially, asking if it were not inconsistent for him to attack the immorality of corporations and at the same time countenance such an absolute therapeutic monopoly. Bryan did not appreciate the joke and wrote a letter of injured innocence. Liquozone's proprietor did not appreciate the joke and sent his lawyer to talk with Hapgood. "In a short time," the editor later wrote, "we were launched into a field we occupied for years."

The more Hapgood looked into the matter, the more he was affronted by the fraud and effrontery of the patent medicine business. *Collier's* own hands were not clean, as Bryan had pointed out. The magazine was running advertising for such remedies as Vapo-Cresolene, which promised to cure whooping cough and diphtheria, and Buffalo Lithia Water, which possessed a "Marvelous Efficiency in Gout, Rheumatism, [and] Gastrointestinal Dyspepsia" lauded by no less a figure than the Physician in Ordinary to the Pope. Such ads Hapgood ordered expunged from his magazine, and he set out to find a reporter capable of digging out the facts and writing a hard-hitting full-scale exposure of medical quackery. The man he found was Samuel Hopkins Adams. The choice was one of the shrewdest in the annals of journalism.

Adams was no doctor, although he was not unfamiliar with matters medical. As an undergraduate at Hamilton College, he had pursued for a time a course in pre-medical studies. Journalism won him away from science, but Adams did not abandon his interest in disease and health. After graduating, he became a reporter, spending nine years perfecting his craft on the staff of one of the nation's distinguished newspapers, the *New York Sun*. He became adept at crime reporting and covered the major sensational cases of robbery and murder. Sleuthing techniques here developed were later to stand Adams in good stead. In 1900 he left the *Sun* to enter the employ of that driving temperamental genius of the journalistic world, S. S. McClure. Adams first edited the syndicate that distributed stories and articles to newspapers, and later served as advertising manager for the McClure publishing house.

While Adams was associated with these enterprises, *McClure's Magazine* suddenly became the most exciting periodical in America. On its staff were topflight reporters like Lincoln Steffens, Ida Tarbell, and Ray Stannard Baker. They began to write articles asserting that the American dream had been blighted. Big business had grown so huge, these journalists stated, that it had crushed American freedom, ruining small business, thwarting freedom of speech, and subverting all branches of government. Charges like these had been made before, but seldom so explicitly and never with such a wealth of circumstantial detail. *McClure's* authors were not content with generalities. They named names, mentioned places, and cited dates. There was already a reform spirit astir in America, here and there, when *McClure's* writers began to write. With their exposure articles they fanned local fires into a searing national flame. They were joined in this task by other writers on other magazines, for the booming circulation figures of *McClure's* led to widespread imitation. Never before had so many Americans, especially the great middle class, bought so many magazines. Never had the magazines treated the evils of society with such a combination of exact description and moral passion. Never—unless the abolition crusade is excepted—had exposure literature played such a compelling role. The leadership of American thought, said the philosopher William James, was leaving the universities and entering the ten-cent magazines.

In 1904, a year after the McClure authors had brought "muckraking" journalism to fever heat, Samuel Hopkins Adams resigned his post as advertising manager in order to write. No longer on the regular payroll, he continued to receive *McClure's* checks, since his important early articles appeared in the magazine shoulder to shoulder with pieces by Steffens, Baker, and Miss Tarbell. With them Adams shared a dedication to factual accuracy and a zeal for improving the lot of mankind, both of which marked his discussions of certain aspects of the public health. For Adams had turned to his continuing interest in medical science for themes, writing on tuberculosis, yellow fever, typhoid fever, and surgical techniques. These subjects, good as they were, lacked one essential ingredient of the full-blown "muckraking" essay: the human evil-doer. Such a sinister figure was by no means absent from the medical scene. So Adams turned to patent medicines.

Ray Stannard Baker, as Adams recalled it, first suggested to him that he prepare a series on American nostrums. The idea struck him most favorably. He had done some thinking but no research when he was approached by Norman Hapgood.

Adams owed first loyalty to McClure, who could have published the series, but for some unaccountable reason—his staff could never predict his reactions—McClure was lukewarm to the idea. Hapgood, however, was in earnest. Adams signed a contract and set to work.

The build-up for the Adams series lasted from April to October. Week after week, in editorial, jingle, and picture, *Collier's* whacked away at the nostrum menace. E. W. Kemble drew a "DEATH'S LABORATORY" cartoon, depicting a skull with patent medicine bottles for teeth. Hapgood wrote an article bemoaning the fact that America's most reputable newspapers opened their pages to disreputable ads, and he surrounded his words with a pictorial border linking patent medicine appeals with the mastheads of papers from which they had been clipped. The rhymster, Wallace Irwin, like countless other Americans, perused an advertisement and discovered to his horror

> That mushrooms were growing all over my liver,
> That something was loose in my heart,
> That due to my spleen all my nerves had turned
>   green
> And my lungs were not doing their part.
> I wrote Dr. Sharko and got as an answer,
> "The wart on your thumb is incipient cancer."

Adams, in the meantime, was hard at work. He was gathering and studying examples of nostrum advertising. He was buying the medicines advertised, transporting the bottles to his Hamilton chemistry professor or experts at a pharmaceutical laboratory, and requesting them to find out what was inside. He was getting counsel from state agricultural chemists and consulting editors of pharmaceutical journals. With a list of curative claims and a list of ingredients, he was asking experts in medical research if the former could possibly derive from a dose of the latter. Adams was doing lots of leg work. He was selecting choice testimonials and then seeking to find the testators and get their stories at first hand. Nor was the busy journalist diffident about approaching nostrum princes themselves. One of the leading proprietaries of the day, a remedy so influential that babies were named for it, was Peruna. The maker of this much-vaunted tonic was a genial old German named Samuel D. Hartman, a trained physician. Adams journeyed to Columbus, Ohio, to talk with Hartman and was accorded a friendly reception. The medicine man told the reporter everything, even after being warned that the planned article was bound to be critical.

Not all remedy proprietors took such a charitable view of Adams' researches, and he found that his goings and comings were being followed by a private detective. Suddenly events took a nasty turn. One weekend Adams was invited to a house party in Connecticut. In the station in New York, he met the wife of a close friend, also on the guest list, and they rode together on the train. Soon thereafter it was brought to his attention that this episode had been observed and that the story of his train trip with another man's wife might be made public in an unfavorable way if he was so injudicious as to continue his investigations.

The suggestion of blackmail made Adams' blood boil, yet he was worried, for he shrank from any course that might bring embarrassment to the lady. As luck would have it, Adams was well acquainted with the mayor of the city where the nostrum proprietor lived whom Adams believed to be chiefly responsible for the threat. Hastening west, Adams told the mayor his plight. The city official knew just the facts which the journalist required. Not long before, the mayor reported, the nostrum maker had been surprised in a roadhouse room with another man's wife. When detectives had knocked on the door, the startled medicine proprietor had jumped from a window and broken his leg.

Adams cautiously let it be known that he was privy to this tale. Not only did he hear no more of the threat, but the detectives were immediately withdrawn.

Safely past this contretemps, Adams returned to his researches with a new zest. "A character inherited from a line of insurgent theologians," noted a *Collier's* colleague, "gave him firm conviction in his beliefs." And Adams "gloried in combat." In this respect appearances were perhaps deceptive, for the reporter looked younger than his thirty-four years and his face, rather than being pugnacious, was relaxed and pleasant, with soft contours and rounded features. His hair was cut long and parted just to the right, and he wore a high stiff collar and flowing cravat. Adams' amiable, indeed aesthetic, appearance may have fooled the patent medicine tribe into thinking him a less than worthy foe. No such miscalculations were made after October 7, 1905.

On that date *Collier's* carried the first chapter of "The Great American Fraud." Adams' vigorous words appeared under a page-wide illustration showing a hooded skull in front of patent medicine bottles exuding noxious vapors. Sinewy serpents, so often the nostrum maker's symbol of evil, had now turned coat and slithered among the vials.

"Gullible America," Adams began, "will spend this year some seventy-five millions of dollars in the purchase of patent medicines. In consideration of this sum it will swallow huge quantities of alcohol, an appalling amount of opiates and narcotics, a wide assortment of varied drugs ranging from powerful and dangerous heart depressants to insidious liver stimulants; and, far in excess of all other ingredients, undiluted fraud. For fraud, exploited by the skilfulest of advertising bunco men, is the basis of the trade. Should the newspapers, the magazines, and the medical journals refuse their pages to this class of advertisements, the patent medicine business in five years would be as scandalously historic as the South Sea Bubble, and the nation would be the richer not only in lives and money, but in drunkards and drug-fiends saved."

After this sweeping introduction, Adams got down to cases. He rebuked Pond's Extract for "trading on the public alarm" by running an advertisement boldly headed "MENINGITIS" while New York was suffering an epidemic. Next to his criticism was a reproduction of the offending ad. Adams described how proprietary manufacturers inserted into their advertising contracts with newspapers the restraining clause printed in red ink. Beside Adams' words was a picture of a contract which had been offered by the Cheney Medicine Company to the *Emporia Gazette*. Adams explained that patent medicine testimonials were gathered from gullible ignoramuses or secured through various pressures from people in public life. He told the tale of the visit to the advertising manager of a Chicago newspaper by an agent for Paine's Celery Compound. The agent showed the manager a full-page advertisement with blank spaces in the center.

"We want some good, strong testimonials to fill out with," he said.

"You can get all of those you want, can't you?" asked the newspaper manager.

"Can *you*?" returned the agent. "Show me four or five strong ones from local politicians and you can get the ad."

"The Nostrum Evil," as Adams entitled his initial article, contained other generalizations buttressed by specific instances. It was, indeed, a sort of broad preview of what he intended to treat in more detail in the articles to follow.

Adams followed his first general attack on nostrums with the exposure of Peruna, about which he had warned its friendly proprietor at the beginning of their conversation. The article opened with a quotation from a public health official.

"Let us," the man had suggested to Adams, "buy in large quantities the cheapest Italian vermouth, poor gin, and bitters. We will mix them in the proportion of three of vermouth to two of gin with a dash of bitters, dilute and bottle them by the short quart, label them '*Smith's Revivifier and Blood-Purifier; dose, one wineglassful before each meal*'; advertise them to cure erysipelas, bunions, dyspepsia, heat rash, fever and ague, and consumption; and to prevent loss of hair, small-pox, old age, sunstroke, and near-sightedness, and make our everlasting fortunes selling them to the temperance trade."

"That sounds to me," Adams had replied, "very much like a cocktail."

"So it is," the health official noted. "But it's just as much a medicine as Peruna and not as bad a drink."

Peruna's alcoholic content, Adams discovered, ran about 28 per cent, and a dollar bottle of the remedy cost its manufacturer—including the bottle—between fifteen and eighteen cents. As a medicine Peruna was promoted to cure nothing but catarrh, but catarrh in Dr. Hartman's pathology was a term encompassing appendicitis, consumption, mumps, and female complaints. Adams reported on Peruna "alcoholics" he had met, at least one of them a member in good standing in the WCTU, and he reproduced an Office of Indian Affairs order to Indian agents prohibiting the sale of Dr. Hartman's product as an intoxicant "too tempting and effective." Among the many Peruna testimonials written by men in high places, Adams was particularly fond of the assertion by a North Carolina Congressman: "My secretary has as bad a case of catarrh as I ever saw, and since he has taken one bottle of Peruna he seems like a different man."

Next in the series came Liquozone, the nostrum which had started *Collier's* on the muckraking trail. Like numerous other remedies, it trafficked on the public's wariness of bacilli, and paraded as a universal antiseptic. Like Radam's Microbe Killer, Liquozone was 99 per cent water, though devoid of red wine. The one per cent was made up of sulphuric and sulphurous acids, with occasionally a trace of hydrochloric or hydrobromic acid. The risks a sick man ran in relying on Liquozone were those of neglect; proper medical treatment was not initiated. This was a serious charge to bring against the fake antiseptics, but it was still not so brutally fiendish a crime as that of which "The Subtle Poisons" were guilty.

These were, Adams believed, "the most dangerous of all quack medicines." They were less transparent in their quackery than Peruna and Liquozone, so even highly intelligent people fell prey. Not only did they pose an immediate danger; they also created "enslaving appetites." What were these insidious poisons? They fell mainly into two classes, Adams said. One was made up of catarrh powders that contained cocaine and soothing syrups that contained opium. Medicines of this sort might threaten sudden death, but, almost worse, they led innocent victims into narcotic addiction. It was a "shameful trade," Adams asserted, "that stupefies helpless babies, and makes criminals of our young men and harlots of our young women." The second class—nostrums loaded with acetanilide—were nearly as dangerous. These too were habit forming and sometimes, because of a personal susceptibility or through an overdose, led to death. The names and addresses of twenty-two such victims Adams listed in a box accompanying his article. The symptoms of still-living victims of acetanilide were also grim. Adams quoted a medical report: "Stomach increasingly irritable; skin a grayish or light purplish hue; palpitation and slight enlargement of the heart; great prostration, with pains in the region of the heart; blood discolored to a chocolate hue." And yet Orangeine, one of the acetanilide mixtures in widest use, claimed that it would strengthen the heart and improve the blood. "Thus far in the patent medicine field," wrote Adams, "I have not encountered so direct and specific an inversion of the true facts."

The same statement, however, he might have applied to much of the advertising written by proprietors who were "Preying on the Incurables." "There are being exploited in this country to-day," Adams stated, "more than one hundred cures for diseases that are absolutely beyond the reach of drugs. They are owned by men who know them to be swindles, and who in private conversation will almost always evade the direct statement that their nostrums will 'cure' consumption, epilepsy, heart disease, and ailments of that nature." From two New York Sunday papers of the same date Adams clipped nearly a score of ads categorically promising to cure cancer, consumption, and fits, and reproduced these false promises in "A Fraud's Gallery." He reported the ingredients which some of these purported remedies contained, drugs like chloroform, opium, alcohol, and hashish, which could well hasten the course of the diseases they promised to eradicate. Adams concluded his discussion in somber mood: "Every man who trades in this market, whether he pockets the profits of the maker, the purveyor, or the advertiser, takes toll of blood. He may not deceive himself here, for here the patent medicine business is nakedest, most cold-hearted. Relentless greed sets the trap, and death is partner in the enterprise."

In February 1906 Samuel Hopkins Adams concluded his series on "The Great American Fraud." He set to work immediately on another series, directing his detailed facts, his wit, and his scorn against the advertising doctors with their fake clinics and institutes. Editor Hapgood, in the meantime, kept up the pressure in his editorial columns, through his own barbed words, letters from grateful readers, and promises from newspapers which, with blinders removed, were joining the anti-nostrum crusade. Opposition evoked by the *Collier's* campaign also was quoted. The magazine was "A Yellow Weekly," said a Philadelphia editor, and its survey of the medical scene "a hideous and ghastly caricature." Medicine makers themselves felt aggrieved. One company threatened to sue *Collier's* for $50,000. The magazine did not court the suit, Hapgood replied, although it did not fear it. "The mere threat . . . will furnish the Proprietary Association of America with material for press notices: 'Another worthy medical firm grossly libeled!' "

Adams, indeed, avoided the embarrassment and *Collier's* the expense which had afflicted Bok and the *Ladies' Home Journal* as a result of carelessness. No statement was printed about a nostrum in Adams' articles, unless the ingredients were listed on the label, without a chemical analysis being made. Some 264 medicines, doctors, and firms were mentioned in the ten articles which Adams wrote. Four months after the last one had appeared, Hapgood asserted, the only damage suffered had been two personal protests "filed" with the magazine and two libel suits still on the docket.

By no means all the medicine men who smarted under the *Collier's* lash protested to the magazine. They had other channels through which to express their anger: the receptive pages of friendly papers, certain drug and medical journals, anonymous pamphlets. One of the latter [entitled *Memoranda Concerning Recent Sensational Attacks upon Proprietary Medicines* (1905)] termed Bok guilty of "gross misrepresentation" and called Hapgood "ignorant or . . . malicious." These men, the pamphleteer charged, "*want a sensation. . . .* They could not make a sensation if they merely told 'the truth and nothing but the truth.' So they simply prevaricate—affirmatively and negatively—directly and indirectly—by implication and by suppression and in every other way which serves their purpose; and they have the presumption to ask reputable publishers of this country to follow their lead!"

This pamphlet and others like it also included harsh words aimed at physicians who condemned proprietary medicines. *Collier's* had been pleased to cite praise received from doctors for the Adams series, although Hapgood believed, just as Bok did, that the medical profession had been tardy in assuming its full measure of responsibility in the fight against medical quackery. "So far," Hapgood editorialized, ". . . the Medical Societies have done little but pass resolutions." It was a sentiment with which even the *Journal of the American Medical Association* reluctantly agreed. Nonetheless, the remedy proprietors were not wrong in fearing both doctors and journalists and in seeing a connection between the two. During the same months that the muckraking of nostrums was at high tide, the medical profession was assuming a much more aggressive role. The American Medical Association began a campaign that would at long last eliminate suspect advertising from its *Journal*. To provide a clear basis for separating proprietaries of value from those of disreputable stamp, a Council on Pharmacy and Chemistry was created. Its members, skilled physicians, pharmacists, and chemists, set about analyzing the ingredients in proprietary products and studying their techniques of promotion. The results, good or bad, not only determined the *Journal's* advertising policy but also appeared in the news pages for all who wished to read.

Nor did the Association limit its scrutiny to nostrums advertised directly to doctors. As proof of their wider concern with quackery, the American Medical Association reprinted Adams' vigorous articles in a booklet which was sold for a nominal price. In time nearly 500,000 copies of *The Great American Fraud* were bought by disturbed Americans. Doctors were also engaging in deliberate and effective pressure to achieve the goal which *Collier's* and the *Ladies' Home Journal* most desired, the action which the nostrum makers most opposed: national legislation regulating the patent medicine trade.

The manufacturers of proprietary remedies were right. There was a plot against them. It included not only muckraking writers and doctors, not only pharmacists and chemists.

There was also a governmental contingent. State legislators were seeing the light and feeling the pressure. Members of the national House and Senate were growing increasingly concerned. In the executive branch, President Theodore Roosevelt had said a few words, and down the chain of command, in the Department of Agriculture, was a man who had said a great many more: Harvey Washington Wiley, chief of the Bureau of Chemistry. Wiley had long been pleading for a national law. While gathering material for "The Great American Fraud," Samuel Hopkins Adams had sought help from many sources, one of them Wiley's laboratory. To the red-brick building in Washington also had gone many other men and women desiring to tell the American people why laws were necessary if nostrum abuses were to be restrained.

The manufacturers of proprietary remedies were right. There was a conspiracy against them. And so many American citizens were becoming party to it that the outlook at long last was favorable that a protective measure might be passed. (pp. 212-25)

> *James Harvey Young, "'The Great American Fraud'," in his* The Toadstool Millionaires: A Social History of Patent Medicines in America Before Federal Regulation, *Princeton University Press, 1961, pp. 205-25.*

ROBERT C. BANNISTER, JR.

[*Bannister is an American educator and critic and the biographer of Ray Stannard Baker. In the following essay from the collection* Muckraking: Past, Present, and Future *(1973), he examines the muckrakers' treatment of racial issues.*]

During the Progressive era, many black Americans felt that the national press seriously ignored their grievances. "The magazines," charged the editor of the *Voice of the Negro,* "want to hold their southern subscribers and so they have thrown open their columns to the Vardamans and Dixons. When reply to such vile rot is submitted, the manuscript is returned with the statement that 'we do not care to open our columns to controversy'." When Theodore Roosevelt attacked the muckrakers, this same editor wished only that T. R. had scored the magazines for "muckmaking" on the race issue. The *Crisis,* the journal of the NAACP, charged that *McClure's* had required Jane Addams to delete a paragraph criticizing the "lily-whitism" of the Bull Moosers. Another popular magazine allegedly commissioned an Englishman to study the race issue but, having paid him, suppressed the results when they proved too favorable to the Negro. Even the *Survey,* spokesman for more enlightened opinion among charity and settlement workers, required an author to omit a plea for equal social rights. By the end of the period it seemed that, as one black reader wrote to the muckraker Ray Stannard Baker, "the press has entered into a 'conspiracy of silence' on the wrong the nation is heaping upon the colored population."

Several historians, questioning this indictment, have noted that whatever the policy of the press in general, the muckrakers made a considerable contribution to the cause of Negro rights. *McClure's, Cosmopolitan,* and the *American Magazine,* joining older journals like the *Independent, Nation,* and *Outlook,* denounced a rising tide of discrimination and violence. Ray Stannard Baker's *Following the Color Line* (1908) was an especially outstanding contribution. Thanks to their efforts, wrote one observer, "the Negro problem was taken out of the hands of reactionaries and scattered forces of well-wishing individuals and societies, and . . . raised to its rightful place among the most important social issues."

Others have been more skeptical. "The Negroes," John Hope Franklin concluded, "could look neither to the White House nor to the muckrakers for substantial assistance." Not only were the contributions of the muckrakers few in number, but their efforts resounded with racial stereotypes now offensive to many whites. Even Baker's *Following the Color Line* has drawn criticism. Although generally praising the work, Gunnar Myrdal termed it a monument to the "static assumption" that benign neglect would best solve the race problem, an assumption Myrdal's *American Dilemma* (1944) explicitly challenged. The author of a study of the Atlanta riot of 1906, the event which triggered Baker's serious interest in the race problem, censured the reporter for failing to "transcend the racist assumptions of his era." Similarly, the author of a recent survey of "The Muckrakers and Negroes," while admitting that these journalists took "some serious interest" in the Negro, concluded that to have enlarged their "restricted" achievement would have required changes in attitude impossible for the pre-War generation [see Herbert Shapiro (1970), Further Reading].

More generally, the question of the muckrakers and the race issue goes to the heart of recent charges that twentieth-century liberalism—the tradition of progressivism—has consistently ignored the interests of the urban and rural poor, especially the blacks, and is thus unable to provide solutions in the present crisis. That many pre-1914 liberals condoned new forms of discrimination seems abundantly clear. Yet the question remains whether some groups with some success opposed the emerging consensus, thus tempering the reaction. The several dozen writers and editors who spearheaded muckraking, because of their general contribution to progressivism, are especially significant in this connection. Sensitized by profession to public opinion, they provided one channel through which enlightened sentiment on the race issue might awaken an apathetic public. Their success, and the personal and institutional pressures that limited their efforts and their sympathies, provide valuable insight into the nature and promise of muckraking in the liberal reform tradition.

Concerning the muckrakers and race, three sorts of questions have been central. First, what precisely was their response, and how did it compare to discussions of race in the older journals? Second, in what ways did personal bias and/or editorial policy influence this response? Finally, insofar as one may speak of influence, what impact did the muckrakers have?

Although much of the interest and excitement of muckraking derives from alleged contrasts between a "new" and older journalism, it is easy to exaggerate the extent of this departure, especially on the race issue. A number of journals, although limited in circulation in comparison with *McClure's* and the others, led in reporting racial injustice during the Progressive era. The religious press, in sheer quantity, was foremost. The *Independent,* edited by William Hayes Ward and Hamilton Holt, was the Negro's steadiest champion among national journals. Not coincidentally, this journal published William English Walling's significant article on the Springfield riot of 1908, an account directly responsible for the formation of the NAACP. The *Outlook,* edited by Lyman Abbott, also gave the race issue considerable space, but emerged finally as a spokesman for a brand of Rooseveltian equivocation which the NAACP branded "Bourbonism."

The *Nation,* the *Arena,* and *Charities,* more exclusively concerned with politics and society, also focused the attention of their readers on the race issue. Although the *Nation,* since its founding in 1865, had diluted its initial devotion to absolute equality, it never entirely abandoned its early idealism. During the Progressive years it emerged as an outspoken critic of Jim Crow and disfranchisement. The *Arena,* a radical journal edited by Benjamin Orange Flower, regularly included three or four articles a year (of sixty to seventy) on the race issue, some also critical of the emerging consensus. *Charities,* which devoted an entire number to the race issue in 1905, thus provided a group discussion of the issue that was perhaps the most significant to appear in America to that date.

Although the respectable monthlies often disseminated highbrow racism, some gave the Negro sympathetic attention on occasion. The *Atlantic Monthly* and the *North American Review* in particular printed a number of articles that one black observer termed articles of "the greatest permanent value," a judgment reflecting their relatively balanced consideration of the Negro cause. The *Atlantic,* concerned by the spread of disfranchisement laws, openly wondered what position should be adopted by "those who believe, as the *Atlantic* does, in the old-fashioned American doctrine of political equality, irrespective of race or color or station." To help its readers decide it ran during 1902 a series of thoughtful articles, one of which led to the forced resignation of its author, an Emory University professor, for its forthrightness. The *Century* and *Harper's,* in contrast, gave the issue less space and generally deserve the criticism they have received. In 1903 Richard Watson Gilder of the *Century* refused the article by Carl Schurz which would subsequently launch *McClure's* into this area. In turning it down, Gilder revealed a policy of caution. "Your essay would probably be read more calmly in cooler weather," he urged, suggesting a delay. Finally he refused it outright, citing its excessive length. Although the usual *Century* article was shorter, the magazine's receptiveness to articles highly critical of the Negro indicates that more than length was involved.

In sum, the muckrakers did not operate in a vacuum. When in 1903 Sam McClure launched the "literature of exposure" the race problem, like trusts and corruption, was not unknown. There had been and would continue to be sympathetic discussion of the issue, especially in smaller magazines which may be termed "muckrakers" only at the peril of considerable confusion. A nucleus of enlightened opinion existed. What was needed was a stark recitation of the mounting tide of discrimination in the style in which the new journalism excelled, and publicity that would carry the issue to a broader audience than the older periodicals served, awakening "Middle America." The muckrakers, dramatizing injustice, might thus mobilize the public on an issue that white Americans rather preferred to forget.

A superficial look at the response suggests they met the challenge with characteristic boldness. *McClure's,* again the pioneer, led in January 1904 with a widely heralded discussion "Can the South Solve the Negro Problem" by Carl Schurz. Drawing on his experience in the post-Civil War period, Schurz condemned the reactionism that threatened the South with a new "peculiar institution" of semislavery. Attacking the new state constitutions, he insisted that disfranchisement by "direct or indirect" means was clearly in opposition to the

Fifteenth Amendment. Although not muckraking in a strict sense, his article suited the mood of *McClure's.* What he offered, he admitted, was a "diagnosis" rather than a "definite remedy." What was needed was not more law or legal action (he purposely omitted reference to a popular proposal to punish the South by reducing representation) but a change in "public sentiment."

Although many white southerners were outraged, black leaders were pleased beyond measure. Booker Washington joined with DuBois and others to distribute reprints to the legislators and governors of all southern states, representatives of every branch of the federal government, and officials of all southern colleges. Reprints also appeared in *Liberia* and the African Methodist Episcopal *Church Review.* One Negro leader suggested that if the northern press generally were as brave as *McClure's,* "many of the abuses which bring such disgrace upon the Nation would be wiped out."

During 1905, other contributions more clearly in the new genre appeared in both *McClure's* and *Cosmopolitan,* the latter purchased in 1905 by William Randolph Hearst. In *McClure's* Ray Stannard Baker, already acclaimed for his studies of the labor situation, initiated a two-part discussion of lynching. In *Cosmopolitan,* Herbert D. Ward, a popular novelist, attacked the peonage system. Neither writer presented solutions but rather documented the evils in crisp detail. The problem, Baker stressed, was lawlessness: the "only remedy," "a strict enforcement of the law, all along the line, all the time." Ward agreed. "We have laws enough," he wrote, "we need only an aroused public opinion and fearless officers to enforce these laws."

The riot in Atlanta in the fall of 1906, like Watts and Detroit six decades later, triggered new interest. For the next two years the popular magazines looked more deeply than ever into the race question. The *American Magazine,* which Baker, Ida Tarbell, and others from the *McClure's* staff purchased in mid-1906, took the lead. An analysis of "The Negro Crisis" by the Social Gospeller Washington Gladden in January 1907 prefaced the appearance of Baker's *Following the Color Line.* The *American* also published a steady stream of poems and stories which, however condescending in tone they may appear today, were designed to soften the hearts of middle-class whites. In March 1907 *Cosmopolitan* renewed its attack on peonage in an article by a young California journalist, Richard Barry. *Collier's,* which dabbled in muckraking, tried unsuccessfully to get Baker to do a series, and eventually published several sympathetic pieces which stood in marked contrast to the magazine's defense of Thomas Dixon and *The Clansman* in 1905. *McClure's,* again judged only on the number of articles, continued to focus attention on the race question.

By 1908 the muckraking crusade was changing character, and with it came a new phase in the discussion of race. Not content merely to arouse public opinion, individual muckrakers attempted to translate indignation into positive programs for change. Charles Edward Russell followed Upton Sinclair to socialism; and Lincoln Steffens had well begun the pilgrimage to radicalism he later described in his *Autobiography.* Baker, after also toying with radicalism, began to fashion a philosophy designed to resolve to his own satisfaction the growing tensions he perceived in American life, an enterprise he undertook simultaneously in his journalism and in the "Adventures in Contentment" he wrote under the pseudonym David Grayson. These muckrakers also essayed solutions to the race problem. Baker, reversing his original intention to report only the facts, ended his *Following the Color Line* series with a statement of "Personal Conclusions." Russell, for some time sympathetic to black aspirations, joined Lincoln Steffens in signing the "Call" that led to the formation of the NAACP.

Meanwhile several new arrivals kept the muckraking spirit alive. Harris Dickson, a native southerner, contributed a series on the race issue to *Hampton's Magazine* in 1909. *Pearson's,* like *Hampton's* an heir of the original crusade, added several further discussions in 1910 and 1911. The *Twentieth Century,* successor to the *Arena,* published a sympathetic history of black writers. In another issue editor B. O. Flower wondered if the "caucasian cowardice" underlying lynching was "congenital."

Indeed, from this superficial review, one might with some justice conclude that muckrakers gave the race issue national exposure, and to some degree opposed discrimination. Their response in fact followed the general pattern of the muckrake crusade: *McClure's* pioneered during the Roosevelt years; indignation yielded to more constructive analysis toward the end of the decade; and there occurred a brief revival between 1909 and 1912 in such magazines as *Hampton's* and *Pearson's.*

A closer look, however, raises problems requiring further analysis. Although the newer journals proved occasionally receptive to attacks on discrimination, the leading muckrakers, with a few exceptions, were remarkably silent. Steffens and Russell, whatever their personal views, barely mentioned Negroes in their published work. Most others ignored the issue entirely, publicly and privately, during the Progressive era and in their autobiographies. Like other social issues race relations were primarily the province of what may be termed "special interest" contributors, many of whom differed in age or background from the typical muckraker. When Schurz's article appeared in *McClure's,* one reader noted that it was "refreshing to hear the fearless tones of the anti-slavery 'old guard'," a characterization that equally fits others who preserved, in however fractured a form, something of the Civil War idealism: Oswald G. Villard of the *Nation;* William Hayes Ward and Hamilton Holt of the *Independent;* Lyman Abbott of the *Outlook.*

Moreover, despite the articles cited above, *McClure's* and the others failed to make even the departures that distinguished their contributions from those of the older magazines on other issues. In range they were narrower, and in tone as unfavorable to the black cause as many articles in other periodicals. In the pure muckraking phase (as opposed to the extended analysis of *Following the Color Line*) the newer journals had essentially two concerns, lawlessness and corruption, primarily as evidenced in lynching and peonage, practices already widely condemned in both North and South. Idealistic impulses of idealism, while occasionally producing attacks on other forms of discrimination, characteristically yielded to support for a minimal reading of the Booker Washington program, or even to the sanction of segregation, colonization, or disfranchisement. To understand the forces that set these limits, it is necessary to weigh the impact of two crucial factors: the racial attitudes of the individuals involved, and the editorial policies of their magazines.

Although a great deal has been written concerning the racism of the Progressives, the subject must be approached with cau-

tion. Few muckrakers underwrote the extreme pseudoscientific racism that I. A. Newby and others have described. If in some cases, outright or subterranean bias explained hostility or straddling, certain muckrakers partially transcended racial bias.

For some, perhaps many, a lack of contact with blacks bred simple indifference. As youths the muckrakers grew up in communities in which the black population was considerably less than 2%. In only one was it higher than 7%. As adults, to judge from their published work, many remained ignorant of and indifferent to black America.

Innocence in other cases sustained a color blindness that combined idealism with naivete. William Allen White, the Kansas editor, sometime muckraker, and associate of Baker and Tarbell on the *American,* was truly repulsed by racial bias. Responding to a report that the University of Kansas was discriminating in its athletic facilities, he described prejudice as a "curious psychological mania" which, although personally unknown to him, was responsible, he had been told, for a "great deal of sorrow and injustice." During the 1920s, White battled the Ku Klux Klan in his native state. Ida Tarbell, although less explicit in denouncing prejudice, also apparently assumed that simple justice required equal treatment for blacks. Jacob Riis, who generally ignored the race issue, asserted that in twenty-five years of reporting in New York's "Old Africa" and other black districts he had seen no crime or other activity sufficiently peculiar to blacks to warrant mention by color.

At the other extreme lay a racism of varying degrees. Both *Pearson's* and *Hampton's,* two magazines that rekindled muckraking after 1909, demonstrated how well racism fit the tested formulae of the new journalism. Side by side with revelations concerning corporate and political malfeasance, these journals "exposed" the dangers of racial amalgamation, black criminality, black political rule, and the "fallacies of the hysterical philanthropists and negrophiles." The results were articles which, better even than those in *McClure's* or the *Cosmopolitan,* may be genuinely termed muckraking applied to the race issue. Their tone and rhetoric was early *McClure's.* "Facts" would allay a "fog of misunderstanding" bred by "sentimentalism and idealism," *Hampton's* proclaimed, introducing a series by the southerner, Harris Dickson. Replying to readers who condemned Dickson's overt racism, the editors noted they were "simply printing the plain, unvarnished truth that every American should know." *Pearson's,* summoning white Americans to their "responsibilities" in preserving "race purity," pronounced miscegenation "the real 'nigger' problem." The story of race mixture, "plainly told," was a "shocking revelation of the depravity of man."

Although the earlier and more important muckraking magazines avoided such explicit appeals to racial fears, such were not entirely absent. Will Irwin, describing the "saloon evil" in *Collier's,* played on similar apprehensions in a controversial piece titled "Nigger Gin." Certain brands of cheap gin, picturing on their labels lewd pictures of white women, were directly responsible for race conflict and worse, he alleged. Imagining the gin an aphrodisiac, the ignorant southern black as Irwin described him, "sits in the road or in the alley at the height of his debauch, looking at that obscene picture of a white woman on the label, drinking in the invitation which it carries. And then comes—opportunity. There follows the hideous episode of the rape and the stake." When readers subsequently charged Irwin with "apologizing for the Negro brute," he firmly denied that such was his intention.

Even in the offices of the *American,* the most sympathetic of the newer journals, crude prejudice provided a counterpoint to the sympathy Baker and other writers revealed in their work. "Darkey," originally a sentimental description of the allegedly carefree rural black, was there applied indiscriminately to all members of the race. "Sounds just like a darkey," an anonymous hand scrawled across the bottom of a letter from Booker Washington's secretary, Emmett Scott. "An Oberlin darkey," another editor commented at the bottom of a request from Ida Hunt Gibbs that "Afro-American" be substituted for "Negro." "Don't mention me to her or she'll blow in for lunch some day." Baker, before he learned better, adopted the jargon naturally. "You would be amused by the darkies here," he wrote his wife when his investigations were underway. "Darkies," and other descriptions of the "savagery" of blacks figured prominently in his earliest installments.

Yet these varying degrees of bias must be set in perspective. If *Pearson's* and *Hampton's,* in a frenetic attempt to revive a wilting genre, exploited racial fears, the ambivalent attitudes in the editorial room of the *American* were probably more typical. Moreover, as important as such bias may have been in muting sympathy or destroying interest, equally significant is the manner in which several muckrakers made their way around it to support the Negro cause. For Sinclair, socialism apparently provided one answer by allowing the translation of "blacks" to "exploited workers." In *The Jungle,* blacks appeared in crude stereotype, a testament to Sinclair's instinctive bias. Yet in the *Appeal to Reason,* the radical weekly to which Sinclair was a frequent contributor, the black worker received a modicum of sympathy because, as was explained, "Socialism regards race problems as secondary to economic problems." Steffens, although his reasoning was less explicit, also supported the Negro cause despite occasional willingness to indulge popular conceptions concerning the hierarchy of "races." In this hierarchy the "nigger," as he referred to the race in his private letters, clearly ranked lowest. Thus, as Steffens explained to the readers of *Collier's,* the American Negro was inferior to the Japanese on every count, especially when measured by standards of efficiency and organization. Yet such views did not bar Steffens from signing the "Call" for the NAACP, making him one of the two muckrakers to do so.

Charles Edward Russell, like Steffens a signer of the "Call," also believed that race was at root an economic matter. The "Philosophy of Pigment," as he branded racism in his autobiography, was to him reprehensible because it masked class distinction, and denied proper recognition to a fellow professional like W. E. B. DuBois. Baker, sharing many of the biases of his time, and like Russell keenly sensitive to the "tragedy of the mulatto," also transcended instinctive prejudice to allow a measure of growth. During his early years an idealism inherited from Abolitionist ancestors mingled with the crude bias that infected his home and professional environment. Yet, tutored by Washington, DuBois, and others, he steadily revised both his rhetoric and his outlook between 1905, when his first article on lynching appeared, and 1908 when *Following the Color Line* was complete. Concerned initially with lawlessness more than with the Negro, he provided finally an optimistic vision of racial harmony to be attained through a process of evolution whereby blacks absorbed the values of the white (progressive) middle class.

Editorial policy, a second factor setting limits, made growth difficult, however, and personal prejudice almost irrelevant. "To interest our magazines," wrote William Walling [in an unpublished letter], "a given piece of work must either have very exceptional literary merits, or else must be 'cooked up' in exactly the manner to which the American public is accustomed." Racial bias was no doubt a factor, he conceded, but any subject could be made tempting enough to make editors "overlook their prejudice."

Behind this observation lay an important truth. Progressive reform, insofar as it was spearheaded by various professionals working within the confines of organizations, owed much to the dynamics of these professions. For journalists and editors, certain facts concerning publishing for a mass national audience were crucial. As television and the fate of certain metropolitan dailies illustrate, an audience of millions is no assurance of success if a comparable vehicle for advertising offers relatively greater exposure. With the cost of printing and paper virtually equal to the selling price, as was the case with *McClure's* and the others, advertising was the key to survival. Concern over circulation, dressed up in a seemingly equalitarian devotion to "reader interest," shaped presentation of the Negro issue from first to last.

The appearance of the Schurz article in the January 1904 *McClure's,* often cited as a breakthrough, in fact owed as much to coincidence, even commercial calculation, as to idealism. Contrary to the claim of *McClure's* biographer [Peter Lyon] and others, there is no evidence that the editor solicited the piece, or "contrived a national debate" between the liberal Schurz and Thomas Nelson Page, whose conservative defense of a southern solution followed in successive issues. Rather, both contributions were apparently unsolicited. The Page articles, which McClure judged "a very temperate and interesting expression of the best informed southern opinion," arrived first and might well have appeared alone, thus adding *McClure's* voice to a growing demand to let the south solve the problem. The arrival of the Schurz article coincided with negotiation over the highly prized rights to Schurz's memoirs. If there was an element of concern for the Negro it might have come from Ida Tarbell, who later perfunctorily thanked Schurz for saying "a number of things which need to be said just now."

Whatever the motive, the departure proved temporary. Although the Schurz article, breaking the silence that *McClure's* had maintained on this issue since its founding, boosted circulation to a near-record high, the risks on balance apparently seemed not worth the benefit. The magazine refused a request to open its column to discussion of the Page piece, rejected a second contribution on the subject from Schurz, and in subsequent years turned down material from H. G. Wells, DuBois, and Mary White Ovington. Commenting on the Wells proposal, an editorial assistant voiced the policy of caution. "I felt sure," she wrote to McClure, "you would not for a moment consider this proposition. You know well Mr. Wells' general views and how much antagonism was excited by the work he did for *Harper's* touching upon this difficult problem." After 1905, the Negro appeared in *McClure's* infrequently, most notably in sentimental and patronizing fiction, in another plea from Page to let the South alone, and in a proposal by an English observer that a black state be created, travel rights curtailed, and the Fifteenth Amendment repealed. The Baker articles on lynching, an apparent exception, were as Sam McClure saw it, a case study of the lawlessness of American life, a concern that was an obsession with him at the time of the assignment.

At the *American Magazine* principle was more obviously a factor than at *McClure's.* Baker himself was enthusiastic, quickly shedding the cruder biases that surfaced in his lynching articles. William Allen White, commenting on the proposed series, termed it vital in view of agitation for repeal of the Fifteenth Amendment and several undisclosed "stories Steffens has heard about the Booker Washington school." Editors Bert Boyden, John Siddall, and John Phillips, seeing the favorable publicity the project was engendering, dropped their initial reserve and even appeared on occasion genuinely moved by Baker's findings.

But profit could not be ignored. "Everything depends on the method of treatment," Phillips cautioned the reporter at the outset; "so long as your articles are good journalistically and you can hold the public interest, we can go on with them." At first there seemed to be no problem. "You have been getting us some fine publicity down there in the south," Boyden wrote as Baker launched his study. "It all helps." When Baker strayed, Phillips gently reminded him of "the importance of working as long as possible with the Southerner of the best type and to the limit." At the same time he urged Baker to revise his second installment. "After all," he lectured, "they are the people whom we wish to reach and enlighten." Baker, to his roots a journalist, and as a partner in the *American* keenly aware that his series could make or break the new venture, never questioned this wisdom. Years later, in his lengthy autobiography [*American Chronicle* (1945)], he devoted one paragraph to this work, now widely hailed as his best effort. It was, he remembered, "a 'real success' from the editorial point of view."

Baker's revisions of his articles, revealing the way in which such pressures moderated his instinctive outrage, showed what his concern for "reader interest" meant in practice. Disturbed by evidences of struggle and conflict in American life he tried to reconcile divergent positions, making room for the Washingtons and the DuBoises. On balance, however, the Washington-southern-white-educator group was the greater influence. In his "personal conclusions," for example, Baker accommodated Mary White Ovington, later an organizer of the NAACP, by changing a critical reference to "foolish agitation" to a grudging acknowledgment that "there must always be men like Dr. DuBois." But he also removed, at the request of James Dillard of the Rural Education Board, a lengthy discussion of "social contact." In its place he put a statement that the less said about the issue the better, a direct paraphrase of Dillard's letter on the point. Interestingly it was precisely this sentence that Gunnar Myrdal later cited to illustrate the "static assumption" that governed American thought on the race issue after 1908. In response to Baker, Dillard wrote that he was happy to hear that "the *American* circulation has not lessened in the south," and predicted Baker's book would have a "wide reading." In many respects Baker's accomplishment, the outstanding one of the muckrakers on this issue, testified to the possibilities of personal development. Yet in other ways it was, as Mary White Ovington wrote [in an unpublished letter] when his series was complete, "just as much radicalism as . . . a popular magazine will stand."

Financial considerations, indirectly a factor in the general decline of muckraking after 1908, probably also produced reluctance to pursue the race issue further. At any rate, most magazines dropped the issue, making Baker's work the high point of the muckrakers' interest. *Cosmopolitan* and *Collier's* returned to silence on the issue. Although the *American* supported the insurgents in Congress, it too lost interest in the cause of Negro rights long before it became the purveyor of sweet sentimentality for which it was soon noted. *McClure's,* if the NAACP charge concerning the Jane Addams article may be believed, was unwilling to inform its readers of Progressive Party lily-whitism. The discovery by *Hampton's* and *Pearson's* that muckraking could consider the race issue best by pandering to racist sentiment was a frank acknowledgement of the growing mood of reaction, and a significant admission, as Ray Stannard Baker had earlier found out, that the *McClure's* canons had definite limits where race was concerned. Since these same years witnessed a renewed attack on Negro rights, the NAACP, formed in 1909, rightly saw the silence of the press as a major problem and established a press bureau to overcome it. Newspapers, the organization reported on one occasion, could sometimes be pressured. But the magazines remained another matter.

If muted racism and editorial policy limited the interest and tempered the response of the muckrakers, was their influence not salutary nonetheless? The question is a difficult one. Even in the case of Sinclair's *The Jungle,* or Baker's series on the railroads—notable examples of muckrakers' influence in arousing public opinion—cause and alleged effect are imperfectly related. On the race issue such connections are even more tenuous, the evidence more fragmentary. Scattered data suggest that while the muckrakers had little effect on national policy, they stimulated some action on the local level. Moreover, in throwing their weight to the Washington camp in a time of crisis the magazines may well have affected the developing struggle over Negro rights. How one judges this overall impact will clearly depend on an assessment of the local action and the struggle between Washington and his opponents.

National policy remained immune. President Roosevelt's reactions to the *McClure's* articles of Schurz and Baker illustrate the degree to which early muckraking, with no solutions of its own, depended on the energy of public officials in translating indignation into concrete programs. Where irrigation or the railroads were concerned, T. R. was willing. In the case of suffrage restriction and lynching, he was not. Writing Schurz about his "noteworthy article" [in a letter of 24 December 1903] the President first rehearsed the bold actions he had taken in *other* areas of public concern. "But," he continued, "as regards the race problem in the South I have been greatly puzzled. . . . I feel just as you do about the nullification of the 14th, 15th, and even 13th Amendments in the South; but as it has not as yet seemed absolutely necessary that I should notice this, I have refrained from doing so."

With Baker his dealings were similar. The article on lynching, T. R. wrote Baker [on 2 January 1905], was the best the President had seen anywhere. In private conversation with the reporter he said that the Southerners, in their racial attitudes, were "only overgrown children!" But the public Roosevelt, as recent studies have demonstrated, was rapidly abandoning the Negro. By the time *Following the Color Line* appeared he was openly critical, chastising the reporter for placing too much emphasis on the economic aspects of the race struggle.

Locally the muckrakers' articles had greater impact, although not always that which the modern reader might expect. The movement against peonage (the convict-lease system) which swept the South during the Progressive era may have profited by the exposures in *Cosmopolitan.* Mississippi defeated the system in 1906, and Oklahoma progressives forbade the selling of convict labor the following year, as did Georgia under the administration of Hoke Smith.

Action against lynching and rioting, however, took a less direct form. Praising Baker's study of lynching, a public official in Springfield, Ohio, the scene of one of the ghastlier outrages he described, credited his account with leading to passage of an ordinance prohibiting the use of screens or other obstructions to the view of the interior of saloons after closing hours. This ordinance, Baker wrote in the revision of the article for his book, "has proved of great assistance to the police department in controlling the low saloons where the riot spirit is bred." In Atlanta, as Charles Crowe has shown in tracing the effect of the riots of 1906, reports such as Baker's precipitated a rash of prohibitionist legislation, much of it prejudicial to the interests of lower-class whites and blacks alike. Baker, also reporting this outcome for the book version, again celebrated such reform. In this way Baker's articles, despite his relative sympathy toward the Negro, served an end not unlike the one Will Irwin directly espoused in his article on "Nigger Gin."

More significantly, reports of riots and racial tension stimulated the movement to formalize Jim Crow laws. Again Baker's role is especially revealing. In his reports instinctive outrage over discrimination battled with a desire to dampen struggle by further separating the races. Although he had been told that Jim Crow exacerbated tensions, he finally convinced himself that the uncertainties of the older, informal system were most at fault. Since a formalization of Jim Crow would avoid the "dangers of clashes between the ignorant of both races," such regulations might be allowed as "the inevitable scaffolding of progress." Although he suspected that economic discrimination bred misery, he decided finally that such segregation was producing a vital black business community. Thus, as Allen Spear has remarked [in *Black Chicago* (1967)], Baker exemplified those of his generation who mistook a forced accommodation to unpleasant realities for something more than it was.

Baker's support of the Washington approach, evidenced in his description of successful black businessmen, was only one instance of the general influence of the press on the developing struggle between Washington and his opponents. The organizers of the NAACP, aware that Baker in particular would be a useful ally, early attempted to interest him in their plan. Although the reporter attended a preliminary organizational meeting, he refused finally to sign the "Call" issued in the late spring of 1909. Subsequently, Baker became increasingly a direct spokesman for the Washington position, in various articles and even in a speech he delivered before the second annual convention of the NAACP. Although the segregation policies of the Wilson administration gave Baker pause, he supported the President in a number of articles, in none of which did he mention the race issue. Although aware of "Gathering Clouds along the Color Line," as he titled an article in 1915, Baker insisted that the race issue demanded "statesmen" not "agitators." In this way, his vision of a harmonious social order, to be achieved if necessary by a "scaffolding" of Jim Crow, reinforced racial attitudes and editorial pressures.

Baker's silence concerning the NAACP, and his continued optimism in the face of racial turmoil, mirrored the position

Editorial cartoon of 1910 by Frederick Opper, depicting the "trusts" abusing the "common people."

of the popular press in general in the period after 1909. When on one occasion the *Independent* published a piece dealing with the new organization, the enthusiastic reaction of one leader revealed the novelty of the occasion. Although the *Survey* reported annual meetings of the NAACP, and the *Independent* and the *Nation* continued to oppose a deepening pattern of discrimination, the popular magazines were unwilling or unable to mount even the modest indignation of a decade earlier.

For present-day liberal reformers the muckrakers provide both inspiration and a warning. Despite a poisoned ideological atmosphere, professional and institutional restraints, and a deep-seated fear of social disorder, some of these journalists found courage to expose the worst, if not all, of the racial evils of their day. Despite the limitations described here, they broke important ground: in stressing that race was a national issue; in opposing extreme racism of the Thomas Dixon variety; in condemning lynching and extremist demands for further discrimination; perhaps even in furthering a rhetorical revolution whereby readers of the popular magazines learned that the "darkies" of their generation preferred to be called "Negroes," and this name capitalized.

But their shortcomings on the race issue warn how uncertain a vehicle is muckraking in dealing with an issue on which there is little basis in popular feeling for indignation or outraged innocence, no consensus to structure "facts" however scientifically reported. If the Negro had champions during the Progressive era they were most likely to be found in journals with more limited, one might even say highbrow, circulation, journals similar to those which in our own day continue to alert readers to various abuses glossed over by allegedly "liberal" organs of mass opinion. Muckraking, a perennial force in American life, will no doubt continue to inspire reform where there exists a basis for popular indignation. It will be less effective, this survey suggests, where the most powerful forces against change reside not merely in the "interests" but in the "people" themselves. (pp. 45-60)

Robert C. Bannister, Jr., "Race Relations and the Muckrakers," in Muckraking: Past, Present and Future, edited by John M. Harrison and Harry H. Stein, The Pennsylvania State University Press, 1973, pp. 45-64.

MUCKRAKING FICTION

LEWIS MUMFORD

[*Mumford is an American sociologist, historian, philosopher, and critic who has written extensively about city and regional planning. His studies* The Culture of Cities *(1938),* City Development *(1945), and* The City in History *(1961), examine the interrelationship between cities and civilization and display Mumford's conviction that firm moral values are necessary to the growth of civilization. In the following excerpt, Mumford questions the value of the work produced by turn-of-the-century muckraking novelists.*]

The shadow of the muck-rake fell over [the late 1800s and early 1900s]. That was to its credit. But business went on as usual and the muck remained. Those who defended the sweating of labor, the building of slums, the bribery of legislatures, the piratical conduct of finance, the disorderly and short-sighted heaping up of very evanescent material goods were inclined to blame the muck-rake for the existence of the muck, just as they would blame the existence of labor agitators for the troubles they attempt to combat—which is very much like blaming the physician for the plague. As a result of the muck-rake, whitewash cans and deodorizing solutions came into general use: philanthropic bequests became more numerous and more socialized; social work expanded from the soup kitchens and down-and-out shelters to social settlements; and the more progressive factories even began to equip themselves with gymnasiums, lunchrooms, orchestras, and permanent nurses. If modern industrial society had in fact been in the blissful state its proponents always claimed, it would be hard indeed to account for all these remedial organizations; but in the widening of the concept of "charity" the claims of the critics, from Owen to Marx, were steadily being recognized.

Frank Norris, in *The Octopus* and *The Pit*, Upton Sinclair in *The Jungle*, and Jack London in the numerous biographic projections he called novels, faced the brutal industrialism of the period: they documented its workings in the wheatfield, the prison, the stockyard, the stock exchange, and the vast purlieus of *la ville tentaculaire* ["the tentacular city"]; Mr. Robert Herrick, a little more restrained but just as keenly awakened, added to the picture. The work that these men accomplished could scarcely be called a spiritual catharsis; for it left the reader the same man that it found him; it was rather a regurgitation. To their credit, they confronted the life about them: they neither fled to Europe nor fancied that all American aspects were smiling ones. But these vast cities and va-

cant countrysides were not something that they took in and assimilated and worked over into a new pattern: it did not, in fact, occur to these writers that the imagination had an important part to play in the process. They were reporters, or, if they thought of themselves more pretentiously, social scientists; their novels were photographs, or at any rate campaign documents.

With unflinching honesty, these novelists dug into the more putrid parts of modern American society and brought to light corruption, debasement, bribery, greed, and foul aims. Fight corruption! Combat greed! Reform the system! Their conclusions, implicit or expressed, could all be put in some terse admonition. They took these symptoms of a deep social maladjustment to be the disease itself; they sought to reach them by prayer and exhortation, carried on by street corner evangelists, by legislative action—or, if necessary, by a revolutionary uprising in the fashion of 1789.

Perhaps the most typical writers of this period were implicated in political programs for reform and revolution. In their reaction against the vast welter of undirected forces about them, they sought to pave the way for political changes which would alter the balance of political power, drive out the "predatory interests," and extend to industry itself the republican system of government in which the nation had been conceived. Upton Sinclair's *The Industrial Republic*, which followed close on his great journalistic beat, *The Jungle*—the smell of tainted meat, which accompanied the United States Army to Cuba, still hung in the air—was typical of what was good and what was inadequate in these programs. To Mr. Sinclair, as to Edward Bellamy some twenty years earlier, the Social Commonwealth, full-panoplied, was just behind the horizon. He was hazardous enough to predict its arrival within a decade. With Mr. Sinclair's aim to establish a more rational industrial order, in which function would supplant privilege, in which trained intelligence would take the place of inheritance, in which the welfare of the whole community would be the prime end of every economic activity, I am in hearty sympathy. What was weak in Mr. Sinclair's program was the assumption that modern industrial society possessed all the materials essential to a good social order. On this assumption, all that was necessary was a change in power and control: the Social Commonwealth would simply diffuse and extend all the existing values. These writers accepted the trust, and wanted the principle of monopoly extended: they accepted the bloated city, and wanted its subways and tenements socialized, as well as its waterworks; there were even authoritarian socialists, like Daniel De Leon, who believed that the corporate organization of workers, instead of being given added responsibility as guilds, would disappear entirely from the scene with the Socialist State. Concealed under revolutionary phrases, these critics could envisage only a bourgeois order of society, in which every one would have the comforts and conveniences of the middle classes, without the suffering, toil, anxiety, and frustration known to the unskilled worker.

What was lacking in such views was a concrete image of perfection: the "scientific" socialists distrusted utopias, and so made a utopia of the existing order. In attack, in criticism, they did able work; but when it came to offering a genuine alternative, their picture became a negative one: industry without millionaires, cities without graft, art without luxury, love without sordid calculation. They were ready to upset every aspect of modern industrial society except the fragmentary culture which had brought it into existence.

Now, were the diffusion of existing values all that was required of a better social order, the answer of capitalism was canny and logical: the existing regime could diffuse values, too. Did not bank accounts spread—and Ford cars—and movies—and higher wages in the skilled trades? What more could one want? Why risk one's neck for a Social Commonwealth when, as long as privilege was given a free hand, it would eventually provide the same things? Thus the socialist acceptance of the current order as a "necessary stage," and the socialist criticism, "Capitalism does not go far enough" have been answered by the proposition that it actually does go farther: the poor do not on the whole get poorer, but slowly march upward in the social scale.

The evils of privilege and irresponsible power in America were of course real; but the essential poverty of America was a qualitative poverty, one which cut through the divisions of rich and poor; and it has been this sort of poverty which has prevented us from projecting in the imagination a more excellent society. Life was more complicated in America but not more significant; life was richer in material goods but not in creative energies. These eager and relentless journalists were unaware of the necessity for establishing different kinds of goods than the existing ones; they had no notion of other values, other modes, other forms of activity than those practiced by the society around them. The result is that their works did not tend to lead out of the muddle. Their novels were interesting as social history; but they did not have any formative effect: for they sentimentalized the worker to the extent of always treating him as a victim, and never making out of him a hero. The only attempt to create a heroic portrait of the worker came towards the end of the muck-raking period; it was that of Beaut McGregor in Sherwood Anderson's *Marching Men,* a half-wrought figure in an imperfect book.

What the American worker needed in literature was discipline, confidence, heroic pictures, and large aims: what he got even from the writers who preached his emancipation was the notion that his distressing state was only the result of the capitalist's villainy and his own virtues, that the mysterious external forces of social evolution were bound eventually to lift him out of his mean and subservient condition and therefore he need not specially prepare himself to bring about this outcome—and that anyway the odds were always against him! It is doubtful whether this analysis could be called accurate science; it certainly was not high literature. For all the effect that these painstaking pictures had in lifting the worker onto a more active plane of manhood, one would willingly trade the whole literature for a handful of good songs. I am not sure but that the rowdy, impoverished lyrics of the wobblies were not more stirring and formative—and that they may last longer, too. (pp. 239-46)

> *Lewis Mumford, "The Shadow of the Muck-rake,"
> in his* The Golden Day: A Study in American Experience and Culture, *Boni & Liveright Publishers,
> 1926, pp. 233-69.*

ALFRED KAZIN

[A highly respected American literary critic, Kazin is best known for his essay collections The Inmost Leaf *(1955) and* Contemporaries *(1962), and particularly for* On Native Grounds *(1942), a study of American prose writing since the era of William Dean Howells. Having studied the works of "the critics who were the best writers—from Sainte-Beuve and Matthew Arnold to Edmund Wilson and Van Wyck Brooks" as an aid to his own critical understanding, Kazin has found that "criticism focussed many—if by no means all—of my own urges as a writer: to show literature as a deed in human history, and to find in each writer the uniqueness of the gift, of the essential vision, through which I hoped to penetrate into the mystery and sacredness of the individual soul." In the following excerpt, Kazin discusses the development of muckraking fiction during the era of muckraking journalism and American political Progressivism.]*

From the time Howells took up the cudgels for realism to the time Dreiser published *Sister Carrie* in 1900 only to see it withdrawn, the story of the modern spirit in American literature is a chronicle of lonely and defeated individual ventures, of courageous struggles by a few isolated spirits. With the turn of the century and the coming of a national interest in reform under the Progressive period, however, all the forces that had been pressing on the new literature from the late eighties on were suddenly released in a flood, and a mood of active insurgence seized American writing. The long-awaited reckoning with the realities of the new industrial and scientific epoch was at hand, and a spirit of active critical realism, so widespread in popularity that it seemed to come directly from Theodore Roosevelt in the White House, now swept through politics and journalism, gave a new impetus to young realistic novelists, and stimulated American liberal thought in every sphere.

The significance of the Progressive period to literature is not that it marked a revolution in itself; it simply set in motion the forces that had been crying for release into the twentieth century. It was a catalyst, as Theodore Roosevelt, who seems in retrospect to have given the period so much of his own moral character, was one of its agents. The new spirit of insurgence had been bound to come, as the whole trend of American thought for twenty years and more had been heading in its direction. Yet when it did come, it became less a central movement of insurgence in itself than a medium through which flowed all the borrowed and conflicting European ideas, all the amorphous tendencies toward political reform, all the hopes for a different social order, all the questioning and nostalgia, aspiration and impatience, that had been dammed up so long at the back of the American mind. (pp. 91-2)

The new spirit was abroad; there was change in the air. And everywhere one saw sudden stirrings in the literature that had been waiting for its charter of freedom—in the profound hunger for fresh leadership that fastened on Roosevelt; in the revulsion against ostentatious wealth that united the novelists of the early nineteen-hundreds; in the endless, excited journalism that now flooded the scene and became the tracts of a new time. The technique of the new social novels was not always subtle and the tone was often shrill; but though many of these writers limited themselves to political ends and were deceived by political appearances, they helped to introduce what was virtually a resurgence in all the avenues of American life. The uneasiness, the hesitant half-hopes, remained; but one thing was now clear: The energies of the new century were no longer arrested; American writing had entered upon the Years of Hope.

If we think of all the repressed influences that were set loose by the insurgency of the Progressive period, all the exuberant romanticism out of the West that was to find its expression in the adventurousness of the new decade, it is easy enough to see why Frank Norris, who died on the eve of the Progressive period in 1902, must yet seem always so representative of it. For Norris, with his boundless energy and worship of force, his delight in life and willingness to learn from every source, was the perfect child of the Roosevelt era. In fact, if Theodore Roosevelt had had a taste for novels and an admiration for Zola, he might have produced huge transcripts of contemporary life not much different from Norris's. Where Stephen Crane seems so significantly a symbol of the fin de siècle, the last glowing ember of a dying century, Norris, who was his almost exact contemporary, was the counterpart in literature of the tough and muscular new men of the new century—Roosevelt and Big Bill Haywood, Borah and Darrow.

At *McClure's Magazine*, where the first muckrakers were provided with shovels, Frank Norris worked along with Ida Tarbell, Lincoln Steffens, and Ray Stannard Baker. He had been hired on the strength of his early romantic stories, and a romanticist he significantly remained to the end. (pp. 96-7)

Norris became a naturalist by that hatred of "pure literature" which developed in Europe after Flaubert into the social studies of Zola. "Who cares for fine style!" he wrote in 1899. "Tell your yarn and let your style go to the devil. We don't want literature, we want life." With a certain boyish opportunism that was characteristic of him, he selected from the naturalist creed chiefly its delight in violence, and accepted its determinism only as it satisfied his dramatic sense. The philosophy behind naturalism in Europe, with its attempt to imitate the studious objectivity of science, its profound tragic sense, he ignored. Studying Zola as the high priest of naturalism, he may, however, have shown a shrewder understanding of Zola, as Franklin Walker has suggested, than of the naturalist creed itself. While still at college Norris wrote:

> Naturalism, as understood by Zola, is but a form of romanticism after all. . . . The naturalist takes no note of common people, common in so far as their interests, their lives, and the things that occur in them are common, are ordinary. Terrible things must happen to the characters of the naturalistic tale. They must be twisted from the ordinary, wrenched from the quiet, uneventful round of everyday life and flung into the throes of a vast and terrible drama that works itself out in unleashed passions, in blood and in sudden death. The world of M. Zola is a world of big things. The enormous, the formidable, the terrible, is what counts; no teacup tragedies here.

This was hardly what the naturalists had sought in their hope of observing human life under conditions of "clinical objectivity," but it was characteristic of Norris's spirit. He was obsessed by size and violence, and his delight in bigness was a curious blend of his love for the California frontier and an invincible youthfulness that was not exhausted in the thumping romances he wrote as a boy—the autobiographical *Blix* and the red-blooded *Moran of the Lady Letty* so plainly derived from Kipling. Like Roosevelt and Jack London, he had more than his share of the facile Nordicism of his day; yet he believed so passionately in a literature close to the masses that he once wrote that "a literature that cannot be vulgarized is no literature at all." His love of quantity came out most strikingly in the technique of his sprawling novels and particularly in the rhetorical perorations that spoil so many of his books, a trick of piling detail on detail in one grand symphonic swell to suggest the hugeness of Nature. To that overflowing vitali-

ty, however, he owed the extraordinary feeling for the common brutality of life that makes his best novel, *McTeague*, one of the great works of the modern American imagination.

For the key to Norris's mind is to be found in a naïve, open-hearted, and essentially unquenchable joy as radiant as the lyricism of Elizabethan poetry, a joy that is like the first discovery of the world, exhilarating in its directness, and eager to absorb every flicker of life. Norris wrote as if men had never seen California before him, or known the joy of growing wheat in those huge fields that could take half a day to cross, or of piling enough flour on trains to feed a European nation. It is out of the surge and greed of that joy that his huge, restless characters grow, men so abundantly alive that the narrow life of cities and the constraints of the factory system can barely touch them. He was the poet of the bonanza, teeming with confidence, reckless in the face of that almost cosmological security that was California to him. Every object in his books was huge, brought up to scale—the wheat fields in *The Octopus* that are like Napoleonic duchies, the eating and drinking in *McTeague*, the fantastic debaucheries in *Vandover and the Brute* (like a Boy Scout's daydreams of ancient Egypt), the Renaissance prodigality in *The Pit*, and even the back-alley slugging and thievery in an adventure yarn like *Moran of the Lady Letty*, whose heroine, characteristically, is a Viking princess in blue jeans.

When Norris planned his trilogy of wheat, inevitably it became "an idea big as all outdoors." It was to span two continents and, as he boasted to Bruce Porter, deal with the primitive, record man's struggle with nature, depict the conquering of the frontier, the growth of business enterprise, and at the last take in Europe. It was to be the last affirmation of nature's promise in an America rapidly veering away from even industrial promise. The conflict between the railroads and the farmers, as he revealed it in *The Octopus*, was unconsciously conceived in terms of the Biblical legend of evil. It is this fact that explains the book's sentimental mysticism and the shambles he made out of its sequel, *The Pit*. The San Joaquin Valley (rather like Steinbeck's Salinas) is Eden; Magnus and Derrick and his fellows Nature's children; and the Southern Pacific the serpent in the garden. *The Octopus* was, in a sense, the first muckraking novel, and it remains the most confused. Norris was still torn between Zola and Kipling, and though he was already a considerable artist, he was still a boy. He knew that in the society of which he wrote, an agricultural community geared to industry, a railroad could do nothing else; but his appreciation of economic necessity yielded to his desire to pay a last—and majestic—tribute to the frontier. Powerful as the book is, its fervor remains sentimental, its heroes and villains stock figures in a conflict Norris could project passionately but did not comprehensively understand. In the end the rascally railroad agent, S. Behrman, falls to his death amid circumstances reminiscent of the cheapest Victorian melodrama, the railroad takes all the land, and Norris is left to the celebration of the wheat that brings the book noisily to a close.

In *The Pit* Norris intended to tell the second phase of the wheat story, its fortunes on the Chicago market; but he succeeded only in completing a mediocre counterpiece to the stock novel of finance that became popular six years later. Like so many of these novels, it inevitably became a sentimental study in marriage, and proved no more than that the hold of the pit over Curtis Jadwin was exactly like the hold of drink over the good but erring father in a temperance novel. Exciting in its detail, *The Pit* was astonishingly uncritical of the very financial framework Norris had sought to expose in *The Octopus*. Norris's characteristic esteem for pure achievement led him to inflate the commonplace figure of Jadwin into an almost romantic type of adventurer, kindly at times and even magnificently generous, but one hardly typical of his world and certainly never a clue to its morality. As the story of Jadwin and his wife occupied Norris's mind, the place of the market in the blueprint of his epic obviously lost all significance for him. No one turning to *The Pit* first would guess its purpose in the projected trilogy. There is not even an echo of the struggles of *The Octopus,* for the novel rapidly dwindles to a romantic story rooted in one place and centered in one theme. Narrow and compact, it does, however, illustrate that mastery of episode which Norris attained beyond most novelists of his day.

Norris's ambition, it is clear, was to make America equal to the cosmic, to find a literary equivalent for his nation's bigness. Yet it is in *McTeague,* that history of degeneration, that he lives. In his wheat novels he tried to expand local scenes, and that local patriotism which has no parallel in the literature of the frontier, into the cosmic view that fascinated him; it was in this early book, much of which was written before he left college, that he exposed the crude foundations of a whole civilization in his bitterly remorseless drama of one soul's failure. There was a certain coarseness in Norris which was the obverse side of his boyish sentimentality, and if it was sadistic and painfully "literary" in *Vandover,* it lifted Norris's passion for reality to new heights in *McTeague.* "The Dentist," as he referred to the book in letters to his friends, became at once the portrait of a city and the matchless reproduction of its culture. Norris crammed into it the darkness of that world of the poor which always beckoned to him like Nemesis, a world frozen in necessity, merciless to those who lost their foothold, savagely inexorable even in death. It was a melodrama, as all Norris's books were melodramas; but the violence was something more than his usual exhalation of boyish energy; it supported a conception of life. The tragedy of McTeague and Trina was arranged, for once, on a scale of genuine determinism; blindness became the arena and accident the avenging angel; the universe was a wasteland in which men grappled for bread, and life was emptied into the sewers of the city.

Yet perfect an object lesson in naturalism as the book is, despite all its extravagance and crudity, the novel glows in a light that makes it the first great tragic portrait in America of an acquisitive society. McTeague's San Francisco is the underworld of that society, and the darkness of its tragedy, its pitilessness, its grotesque humor, is like the rumbling of hell. Nothing is more remarkable in the book than the detachment with which Norris saw it—a tragedy almost literally classic in the Greek sense of the debasement of a powerful man—and nothing gives it so much power. For McTeague himself, it is safe to say, Norris cared very little; but out of his own instinct for brute force he invested McTeague's own brutality with an imperishable significance. The red-blooded, aggressively tough novelist to the end, he had almost casually improvised a livid modern tragedy out of his own sensitiveness to McTeague's failure; and the tragedy was perhaps more real than he knew. For Norris's gift, to the very end, was a peculiarly indiscriminate one; he was still trying his hand, still the inveterately curious, overgrown boy alternating between Kipling and Zola; still a precocious master of violence whose greatest pride was that he was tough as any in his imperialist genera-

tion. "I never truckled," Norris boasted before his death. "I never took off the hat to Fashion and held it out for pennies. I told them the truth. They liked it or they didn't like it. What had that to do with me? I told them the truth."

Shaped to the size of the smaller men who followed Norris, this boast might have been the epigraph of the muckraking novelists who now came on the scene. So far as they could see it clearly before them, they certainly did try to tell the truth; and it was not their fault if they saw a new St. George in Theodore Roosevelt. "Theodore Roosevelt is the ablest living interpreter," Robert M. La Follette wrote in his autobiography, "of what I would call the superficial public sentiment of a given time, and he is spontaneous in his response to it." To Roosevelt, so perfect a child of his time, was it given by Boss Platt, fate, and Czolgosz to enjoy the leadership that stamped his influence on the literature of the Progressive period. As a literary influence he has no parallel in the Presidency. He inspired dozens of political novels that seemed to have been written out of his speeches, invented the militant slogans gratefully received by a generation eager to be militant, gave public opinion something of his own Rough Rider vigor, and set a nation to flexing its muscles, if he did not always set it to thinking. (pp. 98-103)

Roosevelt talking, Roosevelt grinning, Roosevelt hunting beasts in the jungle and writing about beasts with the same studied bravado, Roosevelt grimacing and thundering at Armageddon, gave the democracy of his day a token of its real or imagined potency. He was a force in a day that yearned after force; he enlivened the air. What did it matter that his antitrust suits had almost no effect upon the earning power of guilty corporations, or that the conservative, slow-moving Taft proved himself a more conscientious, if less spectacular, opponent of the great trusts? What did it matter that Teddy had summoned the Japanese and the Russians after their 1904 war to a peace conference of whose issues he was sublimely ignorant? What did it matter that he excoriated the muckrakers themselves in public and in private admitted the prevalence of corruption more fetid than any they had reported? Genuinely anxious to heal the surface wounds of the American organism, Roosevelt radiated indignation against "wrong" and cheerful encouragement of "right" in terms of such stentorian vagueness that he encouraged and made respectable the whole reform movement. He was blindly ambitious, he did not always have a proper respect for truth, and he worshiped pure energy. Yet because he believed with fierce emotional patriotism, as he proclaimed in *The New Nationalism,* that the history of America was the central event in the history of the world, he made a whole generation believe it. Driving America before him like an errant child, he made people conscious of the great tasks that lay ahead for America; and no one knew it better than the journalists and novelists who were now coming up to the front.

Muckraking, which was to lead from "exposé" journalism to "exposé" fiction, was christened by Roosevelt, though he publicly denounced it. (pp. 103-04)

Muckraking, Roosevelt complained to Taft while still in the White House, was ineffective; at the same time he sensed in alarm that it could go too far. Thus he sneered that most of the muckrakers lacked intelligence; some were Socialists, he felt, and some "merely lurid sensationalists; but they are all building up a revolutionary feeling." In this respect he secretly agreed with Lincoln Steffens, who was trying to prove to him, as the more conservative, that muckraking could never remain on the level of journalistic exposure. "You, who have the democratic sense," he wrote to T. R. in 1907, "know that most of the good done in the last few years has been done by the exposure, not by the conviction of the rascals. . . . You seem to me always to have been looking down for the muck, I am looking upward to—an American Democracy. You ask men in office to be honest, I ask them to serve the public." Ever since he had returned from his graduate studies in Germany to be a reporter in Wall Street, Steffens had seen that "the struggle for existence is very animal-like. The abler the man, the farther he goes over the lines they agree to as the unsafe ones to cross." Now, after two decades of industrious research into the life of the big cities in America, he had a clear insight into the general social pattern. "My gropings into the misgovernment of cities," he wrote in *McClure's* in 1904, "have drawn me everywhere, but always, always out of politics into business, and out of the cities into the state."

The evangelist of the reformer-muckrakers, Steffens had already proved himself a social philosopher—gay, cynical, casually wise, yet growingly impatient with the slowness of reform. The other muckrakers generally had no social philosophy. They had been assigned and encouraged to expose, and they exposed—and how much there was to expose! For the rest, they had little historical curiosity, and the nature of the capitalist state remained as mysterious and inscrutable to them as Melville's white whale. Yet it is too easy to indict them for not transcending the normal boundaries of journalism in their day or in our own. The chief grievance of some contemporary critics against them is that they were "naïve"; that is, that they were not Marxists. Yet if they were "naïve," who was not in their time? Lincoln Steffens, whose growing contempt for democracy led him after the war to become an unashamed admirer of dictatorship, was certainly not less naïve when he found the true religion in Soviet Russia. If any of the muckrakers now deserve censure, it is those who tried to become novelists on the strength of a few facts and a little indignation (rather like some proletarian novelists in the nineteen-thirties); or romantic novelists like Winston Churchill, who set out in "reform" novels like *Coniston* to write truthfully about politics and ended up by sentimentalizing the very political bosses whom they seemed to attack. In the same way some of the early "political" novels, like Alfred Henry Lewis's *The Boss,* Brand Whitlock's *The Thirteenth District,* and Elliott Flower's *The Spoilsman,* were ingenuous transcriptions of newspaper stories—novels exactly as profound, John Chamberlain wrote in his study of the Progressive mind, *Farewell to Reform,* "as the mind of Theodore Roosevelt, no more and no less." It was when muckraking now began to drain into fiction, carrying the romantic subsoil of the period with it, that the essential quality of this second generation of pioneer realists stood clearly revealed. Social realists, they were not yet novelists or even ambitious for the novel; it was enough for them that they had learned some first facts about society in America. With all the essential optimism and energy of their times, they moved exuberantly from journalism into fiction, ready to attack.

The muckraking novel was essentially a reporter's novel; at first it was called the "political" novel and later the "economic" novel, as insurance companies turned out to be as corrupt as Tammany elections, and the trusts as coolly wicked as a Philadelphia district leader. Of all the reporters who turned to fiction, David Graham Phillips soon emerged as the shining example. He was a kind of superior archetype of all the people who went into "reform fiction"—bred and trained in the Middle West, a great reporter, stubbornly honest, prudent, handsome, the dashing ideal journalist in a day when all the great reporters were as romantic as foreign correspondents. He had been born a reporter, as it seemed; enormously prolific, a legend on Park Row before he became the perfect reporter-novelist, his importance to realism lay in his exceptional news sense. One of the most famous of all the muckrakers, his most distinctive contribution was his "Treason of the Senate," but it is in his collection of articles, *The Reign of Gilt,* that the design of his social novels is most clearly seen. Phillips, in whom the nostalgic Jeffersonianism of the Progressive period became a passion, had no higher aspiration than to lay bare the debasement of the old middle-class spirit in the new plutocracy. As it happens, he succeeded only in documenting, out of the overflowing knowledge he had gained as a reporter, the surface corruption in contemporary politics and business. Yet in reading *The Reign of Gilt* one glimpses the hidden intensity of Phillips's essential purpose in the bitterness with which he there described the manners of the new rich and their cheapening of tradition, their comic efforts to found a social caste of their own, their grappling for favors, their monumental bad taste, and their essential cruelty. The rising tide of wealth, most conspicuously displayed in the great trading capitals of New York and Chicago, disgusted him. It was with inexpressible indignation that the small-town Indiana banker's son now recorded it as his authenticated observation that it took no less than three-quarters of a million dollars a year to live at the peak of fashion on Fifth Avenue at the turn of the century.

Like so many in his generation, of course, Phillips knew that to attack the new plutocracy in this spirit was not enough. He was a reformer passionately eager to inculcate a new respect for democracy in America, and it was with this aim in mind that he wrote until 1908 that group of novels by which he is best remembered. Yet perhaps it is because he tried to do too much that his failure as a social novelist is now so marked. He wanted, as it were, to write the great symbolic epic of what had happened to his country and to his generation; but he wanted to write it from the city room, and he remained so much the reporter in his novels that he succeeded only in dramatizing the headlines of the Progressive era and in packing into his books an unparalleled density of newspaper data. For Phillips was above all a great reporter, and like the great reporters he covered everything: politics in *The Plum Tree,* finance in *The Deluge* and *The Cost,* the "penalties of wealth" in *The Master Rogue,* the insurance scandals uncovered by Charles Evans Hughes in *The Light-Fingered Gentry,* national corruption in *The Fashionable Adventures of Joshua Craig,* municipal corruption in *The Conflict,* state corruption in *George Helm*—twenty-three novels in all. He even wrote an editorial in novel form, *The Second Generation,* that was a general criticism of contemporary industrial ethics.

Yet though Phillips was able to establish precise case histories of stock-juggling and political "fixing," monopoly practice and industrial politics, it was as a novelist of marriage that he tried to give artistic significance to his books. Away from his muckrake, Phillips was a frank romanticist; and like his greater contemporary, Robert Herrick, he seems to have based his criticism of a competitive society on the dangers it presented to the marriage equipoise. He always wrote of Wall Street with loathing, but the great danger of a life on Wall Street for him was that it kept husbands away from home. Though toward the end of his life he began to write eagerly about "the new woman" and published a gusty American

Moll Flanders in *Susan Lenox,* the women in his "reform" novels were pastel heroines out of Tennyson. What he saw in them, it is clear, was the unburnished old-fashioned idealism that their lovers and husbands had lost on 'change, and by their sweet-smiling patience and fastidiousness they were presented as good examples to their men, enslaved to the industrial or political machine. When a husband and wife are reconciled on the last page of a Phillips novel—and they usually are—you may be sure that the stock market will never see him again. The pattern rarely changed, and was so much like that of the old-fashioned temperance novels that it remains an interesting commentary on Phillips's resources as a novelist. If the hero is essentially a good man, as most Phillips heroes are essentially good, but caught in the toils of the netherworld of corruption, like Matthew Blacklock in *The Deluge* and Horace Armstrong in *The Light-Fingered Gentry,* they must wait until they have broken with corruption to be forgiven by their wives. If the man is good enough to begin with, but hopelessly gone in his greed, an incorrigible rascal like James Galloway in *The Master Rogue,* John Dumont in *The Cost,* or Harvey Saylor in *The Plum Tree,* he dies unshriven and unloved.

Phillips's greatest asset as a novelist of society was his appreciation of the extent to which economic necessity governs middle-class lives, but he was often faithless to his own recognition of that necessity. There is a kind of determinism that reaps its victims in his books as inexorably as in any naturalistic novel, but he always weakened and brought in some deus ex machina at the end to send his characters off in a shower of bliss. Whatever intensity he had sprang out of his deep-felt hatred for ostentation. "Conventionally, it is man's chief business to get rich," he wrote in *The Light-Fingered Gentry,* "woman's chief business to keep young looking." He wrote of "that hungry look, sometimes frankly there, again disguised by a slimy overlayer of piety, again by whiskers or fat, but always there," which he detected on the faces of the new rich. Respectability, as he saw it work out in hundreds of careers that wasted a man's best talents and frustrated his good instincts, often seemed to him a pitiful ambition. It was to the greed for wealth that he laid the corruption of American life, and with equal simplicity, it is by sentimental renunciation in his most positive novel, *The Second Generation,* that men leave the beast world of the big city to build Jerusalem again in Indiana's green and pleasant land. The muckraker's apotheosis was always the same—a vision of small, quiet lives humbly and usefully led; a transcription of Jeffersonian small-village ideals for a generation bound to megalopolis, yet persistently nostalgic for the old-fashioned peace and the old-fashioned ideal.

In the eyes of the young Socialist intellectuals who were now beginning to come up, the muckrakers were bourgeois reformers who lacked a comprehensive grasp of the social problem; but they did not always claim that leading Socialist novelists like Jack London and Upton Sinclair were doing a better job. The Socialist intellectuals did not, in fact, seem to have too much respect for the novel, or for their own artistic achievements generally. It was a young Socialist critic named Van Wyck Brooks who commented at about this time on the social conscience in writers like Upton Sinclair which enables them "to do so much good that they often come to think of artistic truth itself as an enemy of progress." The scholars in the movement, such as Brooks and Walter Lippmann, were always a little appalled by the boisterous and raucous and inordinately prolific comrade-novelists like London and Sin-

clair. Socialists generally were proud that they had novelists of their own, but they must have wondered just how authentically their message was getting across. For the curious thing about these leading Socialist "fictioneers" is that they were the most romantic novelists of their time. London's greatest desire was to slip backwards, away from capitalism, into the lustier and easier world of the primitive frontier; Sinclair, as Robert Cantwell has pointed out, went back to the amiable faddism of a nineteenth-century visionary like Bronson Alcott, and was then, as he remains, the most enthusiastic and angelic of Utopians, a Brook Farmer who gave as much passion to vegetarianism as he did to Socialism and fiction. Indeed, both of these pioneer Socialist writers were amazingly like the romantic archetypes which benighted bourgeois opinion then made Socialist rebels out to be. To the America of Roosevelt and Taft, Socialism was still an exotic mushroom growth, though progressing rapidly—a movement too easily confused with surface phenomena like Sinclair's attempts to set up a Utopian community at Helicon Hall in New Jersey, or Maxim Gorki's expulsion from a New York hotel for living with a lady not his wife. Against this background, London and Sinclair, who lived and wrote in the feverish grand style of romantic revolt, seemed to suggest that Socialism was only a new and wilder romanticism.

Naïve the muckrakers were, but was there ever such a Dick Dare in modern American writing, so incarnate a confusion of all the innocence and lust for power in his day, as Jack London? Grandiloquent without being a fraud, he was the period's greatest crusader and the period's most unashamed hack. A visionary and an adventurer, like no other in his time he now seems cut off from the brave new world of Socialist comradeship to which he called all his life. In a period of "strong men" and worshipers of strong men, London the Socialist was the leading purveyor of primitive adventure tales. His Socialism was his greatest adventure, yet in nothing was he so tragic—and so impatient—as in his Socialism. A leading hero of the movement, he signed his letters with a dashing "yours for the revolution," but he was a prototype of the violence-worshiping Fascist intellectual if ever there was one in America; the most aggressive of contemporary insurgents, he was at bottom the most cynical. Yet like Norris he was pre-eminently a child of the Roosevelt-Kipling age, and his paradoxes were only its own. If he seems to be slipping away even as a boy's hero, he remains significant because his work, with its terror and bombast, is like a feverish concentration of all the adventurous insurgence and obsession with power that came to the fore in the Progressive period. (pp. 105-11)

There is a note at the end of the first volume of Lincoln Steffens's correspondence that illuminates the bouncing optimism of the Progressive period as nothing else could. When the war broke out in 1914, Steffens had been preparing to muckrake Europe! Today, when Upton Sinclair actually has been muckraking the Europe of Munich and Hitler in his recent novels with the same combative innocence that he once muckraked the Chicago stockyards, the mining and oil industries, the ways of Hollywood finance, and his own unsuccessful campaign for Governor of California in 1936, it is not difficult to see where he learned the reformer's and historian's passion that has carried him irrepressibly through four decades of American literature and conflict. If Sinclair lives to survive all the bright young novelists of today and to publish a thousand books (and he may yet), he will remain a touching and curious symbol of a certain old-fashioned idealism and quaint personal romanticism that have vanished from American writing forever. Something more than a "mere" writer and something less than a serious novelist, he must always seem one of the original missionaries of the modern spirit in America, one of the last ties we have with that halcyon day when Marxists still sounded like Methodists and a leading Socialist like Eugene V. Debs believed in "the spirit of love."

Sinclair burst into fame with the most powerful of all the muckraking novels, *The Jungle,* and he has been an irritant to American complacency ever since. His life, with its scandals and its headline excitements, its political excursions and alarums, its extraordinary purity and melodrama, is the story of a religious mission written, often in tabloid screamers, across the pages of contemporary history. As a novelist, he has suffered for his adventures, but it is doubtful if he would have been a novelist without them. The spirit of crusading idealism that gave Sinclair his chance inevitably made him a perennial crusader as well, and if his books and career have become hopelessly entangled in most people's minds, they have been entangled in his own from the day he leaped to invest his royalties from *The Jungle* in the single-tax colony of Helicon Hall. That confusion has always given his critics the opportunity to analyze his works by reciting the adventures of his life, and it is inevitable that they should. For what Sinclair had to give to modern American literature was not any leading ideas as such, but an energy of personal and intellectual revolt that broke barriers down wherever he passed. At a time when all the pioneer realists seemed to be aiming at their own liberation, Sinclair actually helped toward a liberation greater than his own by making a romantic epic out of the spirit of revolt. From the first he was less a writer than an example, a fresh current of air pouring through the stale rooms of the past. Impulsive and erratic as he may have been, often startlingly crude for all his intransigence, he yet represented in modern American literature what William Jennings Bryan represented in modern American politics—a provincialism that leaped ahead to militancy and came into leadership over all those who were too confused or too proud or too afraid to seize leadership and fight for it. (pp. 116-17)

Sinclair was full of grandiose projects, and when his early romantic novels failed he planned an ambitious epic trilogy of the Civil War that would record his family's failure and make him rich and famous. He took his family to a tent outside of Princeton, where he did the research for the first volume, *Manassas,* and supported himself by more hack work. But when even his historical novel, a work which he had written with all the furious energy that was to distinguish him afterwards, fell on a dead market, he found himself in the very situation that he had portrayed with such anguish in the story of Arthur Stirling, the epic of the romantic genius who had stormed the heights and failed.

The Jungle saved him. Tiring of romantic novels which no one would read, he had turned to the investigation of social conditions, and in his article on "Our Bourgeois Literature," in *Collier's,* 1904, he exclaimed significantly: "So long as we are without heart, so long as we are without conscience, so long as we are without even a mind—pray, in the name of heaven, why should anyone think it worthwhile to be troubled because we are without a literature?" Although he still thought of himself as a romantic rebel against "convention," he had come to identify his own painful gropings with the revolutionary forces in society, and when he received a chance to study conditions in the stockyards at Chicago, he found himself like St. Paul on the road to Damascus. Yet into

the story of the immigrant couple, Jurgis and Ona, he poured all the disappointment of his own apprenticeship to life, all his humiliation and profound ambition. *The Jungle* attracted attention because it was obviously the most authentic and most powerful of the muckraking novels, but Sinclair wrote it as the great romantic document of struggle and hardship he had wanted to write all his life. In his own mind it was above all the story of the betrayal of youth by the America it had greeted so eagerly, and Sinclair recited with joyous savagery every last detail of its tribulations. The romantic indignation of the book gave it its fierce honesty, but the facts in it gave Sinclair his reputation, for he had suddenly given an unprecedented social importance to muckraking. The sales of meat dropped, the Germans cited the book as an argument for higher import duties on American meat, Sinclair became a leading exponent of the muckraking spirit to thousands in America and Europe, and met with the President. No one could doubt it, the evidence was overwhelming: Here in *The Jungle* was the great news story of a decade written out in letters of fire. Unwittingly or not, Sinclair had proved himself one of the great reporters of the Progressive era, and the world now began to look up to him as such. (pp. 118-19)

In his own mind Upton Sinclair had become something more than a reporter; he was a crusader, and after joining with Jack London to found the Intercollegiate Socialist Society, a leading Socialist. "Really, Mr. Sinclair, you *must* keep your head," Theodore Roosevelt wrote to him when he insisted after the publication of *The Jungle* on immediate legislative action. But Sinclair would not wait. If society would not come to him, he would come to society and teach it by his books. With the same impulsive directness that he had converted Jurgis into a Socialist in the last awkward chapter of *The Jungle,* he jumped ahead to make himself a "social detective," a pamphleteer-novelist whose books would be a call to action. In *The Metropolis,* an attack on "the reign of gilt" which Phillips and Robert Herrick had already made familiar, Sinclair took the son of his Civil War hero in *Manassas,* Allan Montague, and made him a spectator of the glittering world of Wall Street finance. In *The Moneychangers* he depicted the panic of 1907; in *King Coal,* the Colorado strike; in *100%,* the activities of a labor spy. Yet he remained at the same time a busy exponent of the "new freedom" in morals, wrote the candid story of his own marriage in *Love's Pilgrimage,* "novelized" Brieux's famous shocker of the early nineteen-hundreds, *Damaged Goods,* and between pamphlets, fantasy plays, and famous anthologies like *The Cry for Justice* ("an anthology of the literature of social protest . . . selected from twenty-five languages covering a period of five thousand years") wrote stories of "the new woman" in *Sylvia* and *Sylvia's Marriage.*

Wherever it was that Sinclair had learned to write millions of words with the greatest of ease—probably in the days when he produced hundreds of potboilers—he now wrote them in an unceasing torrent on every subject that interested him. Like Bronson Alcott and William Jennings Bryan, he had an extraordinary garrulity, and his tireless and ubiquitous intelligence led him to expose the outrages of existence everywhere. He used his books for "social purposes" not because he had a self-conscious esthetic about "art and social purpose," but because his purposes actually were social. Few writers seemed to write less for the sake of literature, and no writer ever seemed to humiliate the vanity of literature so deeply by his many excursions around it. First things came first; the follies of capitalism, the dangers of drinking, the iniquities of wealthy newspapers and universities came first. "Why should anyone think it worthwhile to be troubled because we are without a literature?" His great talent, as everyone was quick to point out, was a talent for facts, a really prodigious capacity for social research; and as he continued to give America after the war the facts about labor in *Jimmie Higgins,* the petroleum industry in *Oil!,* the Sacco-Vanzetti case in *Boston,* Prohibition in *The Wet Parade,* it mattered less and less that he repeated himself endlessly, or that he could write on one page with great power, on another with astonishing self-indulgence and sentimental melodrama. He had become one of the great social historians of the modern era. Van Wyck Brooks might complain that "the only writers who can possibly aid in the liberation of humanity are those whose sole responsibility is to themselves as artists," but in a sense it was pointless to damn Sinclair as a "mere" propagandist. What would he have been without the motor power of his propaganda, his driving passion to convert the world to an understanding of the problems of labor, the virtues of the single tax, the promise of Socialism, the need of Prohibition, a credence in "mental radio," an appreciation of the sufferings of William Fox, the necessity of the "Epic" movement, and so much else? In a day when the insurgent spirit had become obsessed with the facts of contemporary society, and newspapermen could write their social novels in the city room, Sinclair proved himself one of the great contemporary reporters, a profound educative force. He was a hero in Europe, and one of the forces leading to the modern spirit in America; it seemed almost glory enough. (pp. 120-21)

> *Alfred Kazin, "Progressivism: The Superman and the Muckrake," in his* On Native Grounds: An Interpretation of Modern American Prose Literature, *1942. Reprint by Harcourt Brace Jovanovich, Inc., 1963, pp. 91-126.*

WILLIAM PARMENTER

[*Parmenter is an American educator and critic. In the following excerpt, he examines the revelations of Upton Sinclair's novel* The Jungle *that led to passage of the Pure Food and Drug Act.*]

The struggle to insure the food and drugs that Americans consume are pure and properly inspected dates at least to the 1880s. A number of people over two decades contributed to that cause by performing experiments, giving lectures, introducing legislation and writing articles and books. Of those contributors, Upton Sinclair's muckraking novel, *The Jungle,* had one of the greatest public impacts. This was ironic, as a major purpose of Sinclair's book was to plead for the substitution of a socialist state for what he considered the flawed capitalistic society of his day. Instead, the official public reaction to Sinclair's novel was to pressure for legislation insuring proper inspection and purity of food and drugs, and to overlook his socialist ideas. (p. 14)

A number of persons and events were involved in the attempt to properly label, inspect and purify America's food and drugs either before or at the same time as Sinclair. These included Dr. Harvey W. Wiley, of the U.S. Department of Agriculture, the furor created by American soldiers in the Spanish-American War being fed putrid meat and scholarly articles written for a British medical journal by Adolphe Smith. Muckraking journalists writing for large-circulation, popular magazines in the early 1900s included Charles Ed-

ward Russell, Ray Stannard Baker and Edward Bok. Russell focused on the meat-packing industry, Baker on the connection between the railways and meatpacking, and Bok on fraudulently labeled patent medicines.

An outstanding figure in the crusade for pure food was Dr. Wiley, chief chemist for the Department of Agriculture. He came to the department in 1883 with a medical degree from Indiana Medical College, and fought for pure food for 29 years. Although Dr. Wiley's scientific work was a valuable public service, he did not have the lobbying power to get a pure food and drug law passed without the publicity generated by the muckraking journalists.

In 1899 William Randolph Hearst exposed the "embalmed beef" scandals that brought on a U.S. Senate investigation of the canned meat shipped to American soldiers in Cuba during the Spanish-American War. Theodore Roosevelt testified he would just as soon eat his old hat as that tinned beef. General Nelson Miles, who investigated the scandal for the Army, claimed, "3,000 American soldiers lost their lives because of adulterated, impure and poisonous meat."

Later, Adolphe Smith did much to document the unsanitary conditions of the Chicago stockyards in a four-article series appearing in the January, 1905 *Lancet,* a British medical journal. Smith spent 14 years researching the conditions of slaughterhouses in various countries for *Lancet.* Smith found that the Chicago slaughterhouses were unsanitary and dirty factories, lacking proper working conditions, lunch rooms and lavatories. Due to unhealthy conditions, he wrote, several thousand workers died of tuberculosis and blood poisoning each year.

Muckraking journalists, who mainly wrote for popular magazines, exposed conditions in the food processing field to a wider popular audience than Smith. Socialist muckraker Charles Edward Russell depicted the rise, machinations and economic depredations of the beef trust in a seven-article series titled "The Greatest Trust in the World." Russell's series started in *Everybody's* in February, 1905, the same month the socialist weekly newspaper, *The Appeal to Reason,* started serializing Sinclair's *The Jungle.*

In his densely factual articles Russell charged that the beef trust, run by J. Ogden Armour, was more powerful than state governments and intimidated railroads. The beef trust fixed the low prices ranchers received for their cattle and the high prices Eastern butchers charged for their meat, according to Russell. Political action against the trust was made unlikely, said Russell, by the trust's publicity bureaus' effective newspaper advertising and publicity campaigns.

Meanwhile, another muckraker, Ray Stannard Baker, wrote a six-article series on railroad monopolies, "Railroads on Trial," for *McClure's* magazine in 1905-6. One article, "The Private Car and the Beef Trust," described how the beef trust augmented its profits via railway charge rebates and high charges on refrigerator cars it rented to railroads. Baker sarcastically concluded that the public was an "unconscious philanthropist" which ended up paying railway freight overcharges and excess retail beef prices to trust magnate Armour.

Prominent in the fight against patent medicines was Edward W. Bok, editor of the *Ladies' Home Journal.* Bok disclosed that by trying to save money on doctor's fees, people consuming patent medicines ingested alarming amounts of alcohol, opium and cocaine. Samuel Hopkins Adams also attacked the false claims of patent medicines in a series called "The Great American Fraud," published in 1905 and 1906 in *Colliers.* Mark Sullivan, likewise contributed to the exposure of the false labeling and sometimes poisonous contents of "cure-alls" in articles in *Colliers* and *Ladies' Home Journal* in 1905 and 1906.

This was the scene in regard to exposures of impure food and drugs when *The Jungle* was published in book form in February, 1906. (pp. 14-15)

On Sept. 20, 1904, Sinclair's 26th birthday and three days after his challenge to the meatpackers had appeared in the *Appeal to Reason,* he checked into the Stockyards Hotel in Packingtown, the Chicago meatpacking district. He presented a letter of introduction to Mary MacDowell, who presided over the University Settlement in the stockyards district. For the next seven weeks he roamed the packing plants and housing areas of the meatpacking workers collecting facts, impressions and stories for the novel he intended to write.

To do his research, Sinclair wore old clothes and carried a workman's lunch pail. He claimed he gained access to all parts of the immense packing plants. He said he made mental notes, wrote them down later, checking his findings against the knowledge of the University Settlement social workers. In the evenings Sinclair went to the homes of the mostly immigrant workers and made notes of their stories and experiences. He visited lawyers, doctors, dentists, politicians, policemen, nurses and real-estate agents, so he could record details on all aspects of the meatpackers' lives.

After a month of gathering a mass of detailed facts, which give *The Jungle* its air of verisimilitude, Sinclair still did not have a story line or any characters. One Sunday afternoon he followed a Lithuanian wedding party into the rear room of a beer saloon. While he watched in fascination, he conceived of making his novel the story of a band of Lithuanian immigrants and their misadventures with the meatpacking industry. And the colorful wedding scene would start the novel. That is the way he wrote it, and the wedding scene was one of his best sketches ever.

After the general election of December, 1904, in which the Socialist Party presidential candidate garnered some 500,000 votes, Sinclair wrote another article for *Appeal to Reason.* In it he announced his intention to write a socialist novel, which was to be *The Jungle,* and stated he had made arrangements with the newspaper to run it as a serial. His intention was "to open the eyes of the American people to the conditions under which the toilers get their bread." The book was dedicated to "the workingmen of America," showing that Sinclair's major interest was in exposing industrial working conditions in hopes of seeing dramatic social improvement.

On February 25, 1905, the *Appeal to Reason* started running *The Jungle* as a serial, titled "The Jungle, A Story of Chicago," indicating that it was meant to represent industrial conditions in Chicago's largest industry. In a larger sense, Sinclair meant the novel to be an allegory of how American capitalism butchered its workers like so many hogs. The serial ran each week in the weekly paper, with rare exceptions, until Nov. 4, 1905.

Sinclair kept working on *The Jungle* until summer, 1905, when he stopped, because he was stuck for an ending. Sin-

clair's problem was he was not prepared to accept the hopeless situation he had created for the novel's characters, and he did not know what to do about it. While he was groping for an ending, Sinclair turned his attention to the organization of the Intercollegiate Socialist Society. He invited all the socialists he knew to an organizing meeting at Peck's Restaurant in New York in September, 1905. The successful organization of the society gave Sinclair the heart to finish his novel. The society's formation induced Sinclair to think that the real life counterparts of his novel's characters could expect eventual salvation through the educative power of organized socialism. And, so, when *The Jungle* was published in book form it contained an ending composed of a 48-page tract on socialism. Unfortunately the tract was intellectual and didactic and did not fit in with the character and mood of the rest of the book, which was a fast-paced action melodrama. (pp. 15-16)

The Jungle paints in bold colors the social impact of industrial capitalism in the early 1900s. The chief characters are a family group of Lithuanian peasants, who came to work in the Chicago slaughterhouses, having been lured by tales of freedom and affluence in America. Their American dream quickly turns to a nightmare, as industrial and social conditions they are powerless to surmount subject them to a series of unspeakable sufferings and degradations. The protagonist's wife is seduced by a scheming boss, forced into prostitution and dies in childbirth. A female cousin likewise ends up in prostitution and addicted to drugs. The protagonist's father contracted probably tuberculosis at the packing plant and dies. A young child of the family dies from eating what is most likely tuberculer pork. A teenage member of the family is attacked by rats when he falls asleep at his post at an oil factory and dies.

The book is flawed with events that strain credulity, with hyperemotional melodramatics and poorly developed characters. Yet it is a book of emotional power, which relates the suffering of the protagonist's family with verve. The immediate appeal of *The Jungle* throughout the Western world indicated the novel's capacity to touch upon and illuminate the theme of the moral logic of early 1900s capitalism. *The Jungle* ruthlessly exposes the social consequences of capitalism's widely accepted business ethics. *The Jungle*'s capacity to shock moral sensibilities echoed the achievement of Harriet Beecher Stowe's *Uncle Tom's Cabin* (1852). Both novels produced stormy public reactions.

Analysis of *The Jungle* reveals that Sinclair dissected two levels of noxious social conditions, and that he articulated a social critique of contemporary society. The first level of baneful social conditions dealt with his exposé of specific abuses to workers and the public in the meatpacking industry. Sinclair spent the most time working on this level, documenting and researching the specific abuses he exposed. It was to this level that the official public response and much public outcry directed itself.

Sinclair gave graphic accounts of such abuses as spoiled meat, meat covered with rat dung and poisoned bread being ground up for sausage; sausage workers being dyed the color of sausages; sausages being adulterated with potato flour; workers cowering in fear as a boss blazed away with a rifle at a steer loose on the killing beds; acid eating away the flesh of pickle-room workers and of wool pluckers; condemned meat diseased with tuberculosis, and poisoned with ptomaines, sold in Chicago though it was banned from export trade.

Among Sinclair's other meatpacking industry revelations: children labored on machines; the slaughterhouses butchered pregnant cattle and steers that died in transit; old pickleroom scraps were periodically cleaned from traps and then processed with the rest of the meat; people were summarily dismissed from their jobs after long service, and there was no job security or pension plans; and only evil schemers were able to rise above entry-level jobs due to predatory working conditions. Sinclair claimed documentation could be secured for all his charges except one, namely that men who fell into hot lard vats were rendered into pure leaf lard. Documentation was unavailable, he said, because in each case the beef trust had paid off the family and shipped it far away.

The second level of social conditions dissected by *The Jungle* places the novel in the era's muckraking literature. On this level Sinclair mirrored many of the charges made in magazine muckraking articles, thereby reciprocally corroborating Sinclair's and the other muckrakers' charges. The book's charges in aggregate constitute a kind of muckrakers' view of the ugly side of America, as many of society's worst conditions were woven into a frightening unified vision.

Sinclair claimed that the public's food was adulterated, preserved and dyed, as did Samuel H. Adams in an October, 1905, *Colliers* article. *The Jungle*'s protagonist witnessed industrial accidents in a Chicago steel mill, a subject treated by William Hard in a November, 1907 article in *Everybody's.* The novel touched upon the white slaving practice of kidnapping servant girls into brothels, which George Kibbe Turner discussed in a November, 1909 article in *McClure's.* A child in *The Jungle* toiled as a newsboy, and child labor was William Hard's topic in a January, 1908 *Everybody's* article. Sinclair described Chicago's press as giving slanted coverage of the meatpacking employees strike, a complaint voiced in Will Irwin's series on the press in *Collier's* in 1911.

The ultra rich's conspicious consumption lifestyle in their palatial mansions was discussed in *The Jungle,* a subject treated by Cleveland Moffett in his "Luxurious Newport" article in the August, 1908, *Cosmopolitan. The Jungle* depicted political bosses corrupting the political process by paying blocs of illiterate immigrants to vote. Both Lincoln Steffens with his "Shame of the Cities" series in *McClure's* and David Graham Phillips with his "Treason of the Senate" series in *Cosmopolitan* won reputations for exposing political corruption. Sinclair charged police with protecting vice rings, such as gambling syndicates, a topic dealt with by George Kibbe Turner, in his exposure of Chicago's police protected vice, in an April, 1907, *McClure's* article.

Although the general public did not accept Sinclair's radical remedy for the social ills he depicted, Sinclair, in his turn, rejected the gradualist solution favored by the majority of the public. In *The Jungle* he disdainfully characterized the efforts of a Packingtown settlement worker as, "standing upon the brink of the pit of hell and throwing in snowballs to lower the temperature." The filthy conditions of Chicago's slaughterhouses was a secondary concern with Sinclair, who was mostly a vegetarian. When the public ignored Sinclair's socialist message in *The Jungle* and focused its attention on filthy meatpacking conditions instead, Sinclair wryly observed, "I aimed at the public's heart, and by accident I hit it in the stomach."

To Sinclair only a leap to the solution of Christian socialism would suffice. Jesus Christ was to Sinclair a socialist who ex-

coriated lawyers, the rich and the respectable, and who was a symbol of the emotionally solacing and loving place that would be created. Under Sinclair's socialism there would be scientific farming, automatic dishwashing, healthful eating and scientific political administration. These notions were described in detail in the last 48 pages of *The Jungle,* a sort of idealistic but unpersuasive socialist tract. The key to attaining Sinclair's socialist state was for Americans to vacate self-interest and vote in love and brotherhood. (pp. 16-17)

[The] novel's impact was enormous. The book became a best seller in America and Great Britain for six months. Within a short time editions appeared in 17 translations, and *The Jungle* became a world sensation. The New York *Evening World* wrote: "Not since Byron awoke one morning to find himself famous has there been such an example of worldwide celebrity won in a day by a book as has come to Upton Sinclair." Winston Churchill, later England's war-time prime minister, added to the chorus the comment, that Sinclair made "the beef trust stink in the nostrils of the world." Reporters and photographers from the leading papers flocked to Sinclair's New Jersey farm for interviews.

The reaction to the meatpacking industry and of public officials was at the lowest level, focusing on the immediate facts of Sinclair's charges regarding meat purity. The din of the furor centering on this narrow issue obscured the fact that public officials ignored many other valid complaints aired in *The Jungle.* The issues of job security for workers, industrial safety, child labor and a slanted press, which all affected the meatpacking workers, were not addressed. Neither were the larger issues, which echoed the magazine muckraking articles, such as white slavery, narcotics addiction, conspicuous consumption by the rich, corrupt political bosses and police protecting vice rings. In time, however, legislation was passed or more vigorously enforced that dealt with some of these areas. Finally, Sinclair's generalized indictment of the business ethics of capitalism, and the social wastes consequent of practicing those ethics, was officially ignored.

In assessing public reaction to *The Jungle,* it appears that the issues ignored far outweigh the issue addressed in public importance. In mitigation of official reaction, however, it may be pointed out that remedial steps were taken in the area where Sinclair was most painstaking in his documentation. The perception that public officials chose to overlook the bulk of important issues stands as a comment on officialdom's capacity and willingness to deal with the issues Sinclair raised. It suggests that despite the technological advancement of the period, America was still a morally primitive society.

Although public attention riveted itself on the question of pure meat, quite a battle had to be fought before progress in that area was achieved. The packers attempted to cover up. The month after publication of *The Jungle,* the [10 March 1906] *Saturday Evening Post* hit the newstands with a vigorous defense of the meatpacking industry signed by J. Ogden Armour, head of the beef trust. Armour insisted the meatpackers' impact upon America was beneficial. He categorically defended Armour's meat. Armour insisted that at his plant, "not one atom of any condemned animal or carcass finds its way directly or indirectly from any source, into any food product or food ingredient."

Sinclair and Doubleday, Page and Company rushed into the fray to defend and uphold their charges. Sinclair solicited the support of President Theodore Roosevelt and challenged Ar-

Upton Sinclair in 1906, the year The Jungle *was published.*

mour's statements in articles in the New York *Times,* and the May issues of *Everybody's* and *Independent* magazines.

Sinclair wrote to President Roosevelt on March 13, 1906, to enlist his support. Roosevelt responded two days later by mail, saying he had already read "a good deal" of *The Jungle.* He invited Sinclair to lunch at the White House during the first week in April, closing his letter with the postscript that ". . . the specific evils you point out shall, if their existence be proved, and if I have power, be eradicated." At the White House lunch, Sinclair met members of the Cabinet, and heard Roosevelt voice his negative attitude toward the meatpackers. Roosevelt personally disliked the packers as he had eaten the meat they shipped to the soldiers in Cuba during the Spanish-American War. To obtain authoritative evidence, Roosevelt ordered two men, Labor Commissioner Charles P. Neill, and a settlement worker, James B. Reynolds, to personally investigate conditions in the meatpacking industry and to prepare a report. (p. 17)

Sinclair wrote a series of charges against Armour, which appeared in the May 4, 1906, New York *Times,* challenging a libel suit, so he could prove his claims in court. His article, "The Condemned-Meat Industry," in the May *Everybody's* bluntly called Armour a liar. It also reproduced an affidavit attesting that Armour's had sold meat to the public from diseased and recently expired cattle. The article also reproduced court records of two cases where Armour was convicted of selling impure meat. In a May 17, 1906, article, "Is *The Jungle* True," in the *Independent,* Sinclair identified *The Jungle*'s sources of information and said he had witnessed the prepa-

ration of impure meat for sale and seen rats running about the sausage storage room in the meatpacking plant.

To keep public pressure on the meat packers, Sinclair started up a publicity bureau in a New York hotel, writing statements and giving interviews to the press. He arranged to send Mrs. Ella Reeve Bloor, a socialist who played a role in a 1901 meatpacking exposé, to Chicago to put Roosevelt's inspection team of Reynolds and Neill in touch with stockyard workers. In addition, leading newspapers in New York, Chicago, Kansas City, Philadelphia and Boston issued a stream of articles, editorials, and cartoons on the pure meat subject. Underscoring that pure meat was the major issue of the day, the New York *Times* had a front page story on the subject nearly every day in June 1906. Current events magazines such as *Arena, Literary Digest, Review of Reviews* and *World Today* printed surveys, reviews and summaries of the controversy.

This clamor contributed to the passage of two federal laws tightening up meat purity and inspection. The first was a tighter meat inspection bill, initially called the Beveridge Amendment for Sen. Albert J. Beveridge of Indiana, who introduced the bill to the U.S. Senate on May 21, 1906. The bill was unanimously passed by the Senate on May 25, in the form in which it had been drafted by the Department of Agriculture, as an amendment to the agricultural appropriation bill. It was a tough bill requiring post-mortem examination of cattle, inspection of meat products, sanitation control, and exclusion of harmful chemicals and preservatives. The bill required meatpackers to pay costs, inspection dates to be placed on labels, and gave final decision over condemned meat to Department of Agriculture meat inspectors.

The bill ran into trouble in the House. Influenced by the meatpacking lobby, Rep. James W. Wadsworth's Agriculture Committee diluted the bill.

Enraged at the meatpacking lobby and its House allies for watering down the Beveridge Amendment, Roosevelt decided to pressure them publicly by releasing the findings of the Neill-Reynolds investigation. Roosevelt sent the first part of the report to the House on June 4, 1906, strongly urging passage of the stronger Beveridge Amendment. The President informed the solons that the report showed stockyard conditions to be "revolting."

The report's release created a profound stir. The meatpackers engaged in "frenzied attempts" to clean up every department of the stockyards. Carpenters, plumbers and cleaners whitewashed, cleaned, scraped walls and put in washrooms. The New York *Times* reported that cleanliness at the stockyards improved 50 per cent in one day. The meatpackers were additionally alarmed by the President's threat to deny them the government meat inspection label if the Beveridge Amendment was not passed. That would severely damage their export trade with Europe.

Public pressure contributed to the House Agriculture Committee strengthening its version of the bill by specifying that meat inspectors had to be civil servants and not allowing court review of condemned meat orders. This was the bill the House passed on June 19, 1906. A House-Senate conference committee met June 28 to negotiate differences between the House and Senate versions. Senators Beveridge, Henry Cabot Lodge and others were not satisfied with the House Bill. But they did not have the political leverage to add two clauses they thought important—dating of meat inspection labels and making the meatpackers bear the expense of government inspection. Thus it was the House version of the Meat Inspection Bill that was passed and signed by the President on June 30, 1906, the last day of the Congressional session.

The second federal law passed was the Pure Food and Drug Act. It had been languishing in a House committee since Feb. 21, 1906, the day it had been passed by the Senate. The bill specified purity and labeling standards for food, patent medicines, whisky and drugs. Publication of *The Jungle* was credited by Dr. Harvey W. Wiley, of the Department of Agriculture, as being "largely" responsible for firing public indignation to where it demanded legislation. President Roosevelt, roused by the public uproar, and reaction to release of the Neill-Reynolds report, rescued the Pure Food and Drug Bill from threatened oblivion. Timely magazine muckraking exposes of patent medicines contributed to the aggregate of pressures influencing the House to pass the bill on June 23 by a 240 to 17 margin. After a House-Senate conference committee ironed out differences between the House and Senate versions of the bill, it was passed again by both houses and signed into law by the President on June 30.

Thus Upton Sinclair's *Jungle* contributed large measure to the passage of the Meat Inspection Act and the Pure Food and Drug Act of 1906. His achievement, measured narrowly on the issue of pure meat, was considerable indeed. No other muckraker of the period created such a public stir or contributed so immediately to the passage of two acts of remedial legislation. For this contribution Sinclair's name is secure in the annals of American public benefactors.

Measured against Sinclair's larger purpose of contributing to the creation of a socialist state in America, *The Jungle* did not succeed. Of this purpose Sinclair wrote a fellow muckraker, Ray Stannard Baker, on June 19, 1906: "The meaning of all this to me is simply that it has added a degree to the intensity with which the American people hate the system. If it were not for that I assure you I should not be wasting my precious time in the fight." Later, in his *Autobiography,* Sinclair commented during this period it seemed to him ". . . that the walls of the mighty fortress of greed were on the point of cracking." To other observers the walls of the social system seemed to be trembling too, as 1906 was one of the peak years of social ferment of the Progressive Era. But the social system's walls did not fall, as the American public was not ready for radical change. Instead, American society gradually evolved during the Progressive Era and in subsequent years.

That leaves as *The Jungle*'s chief legacy its contribution to social justice literature. People of the period sensitive to social conditions shuddered when they saw the portrait of American society Sinclair had outlined, and they reacted to it. As a result, today *The Jungle* has an honored place among other beacons of American social justice writing, in the vein of Harriet Beecher Stowe's *Uncle Tom's Cabin* and John Steinbeck's *Grapes of Wrath.* (pp. 17, 33)

William Parmenter, " 'The Jungle' and Its Effects," in *Journalism History, Vol. 10, Nos. 1 & 2, Spring & Summer, 1983, pp. 14-17, 33-4.*

DECLINE OF THE MOVEMENT

THEODORE ROOSEVELT

[*Roosevelt, the twenty-sixth President of the United States, befriended many journalists and editors, maintaining regular correspondence and meeting frequently with some of the most influential. The following is the text of his "muckrake" speech of April 1906, which condemned the flourishing exposé and reform movement and, some commentators believe, initiated its downfall. See the excerpt by John E. Semonche below for an assessment of the impact of this speech.*]

Over a century ago Washington laid the corner-stone of the Capitol in what was then little more than a tract of wooded wilderness here beside the Potomac. We now find it necessary to provide by great additional buildings for the business of the government. This growth in the need for the housing of the government is but a proof and example of the way in which the nation has grown and the sphere of action of the National Government has grown. We now administer the affairs of a nation in which the extraordinary growth of population has been outstripped by the growth of wealth and the growth in complex interests. The material problems that face us to-day are not such as they were in Washington's time, but the underlying facts of human nature are the same now as they were then. Under altered external form we war with the same tendencies toward evil that were evident in Washington's time, and are helped by the same tendencies for good. It is about some of these that I wish to say a word to-day.

In Bunyan's "Pilgrim's Progress" you may recall the description of the Man with the Muck-rake, the man who could look no way but downward, with the muck-rake in his hand; who was offered a celestial crown for his muck-rake, but who would neither look up nor regard the crown he was offered, but continued to rake to himself the filth of the floor.

In "Pilgrim's Progress" the Man with the Muck-rake is set forth as the example of him whose vision is fixed on carnal instead of on spiritual things. Yet he also typifies the man who in this life consistently refuses to see aught that is lofty, and fixes his eyes with solemn intentness only on that which is vile and debasing. Now, it is very necessary that we should not flinch from seeing what is vile and debasing. There is filth on the floor, and it must be scraped up with the muck-rake; and there are times and places where this service is the most needed of all the services that can be performed. But the man who never does anything else, who never thinks or speaks or writes, save of his feats with the muck-rake, speedily becomes, not a help to society, not an incitement to good, but one of the most potent forces for evil.

There are, in the body politic, economic and social, many and grave evils, and there is urgent necessity for the sternest war upon them. There should be relentless exposure of and attack upon every evil man whether politician or business man, every evil practice, whether in politics, in business, or in social life. I hail as a benefactor every writer or speaker, every man who, on the platform, or in book, magazine, or newspaper, with merciless severity makes such attack, provided always that he in his turn remembers that the attack is of use only if it is absolutely truthful. The liar is no whit better than the thief, and if his mendacity takes the form of slander, he may be worse than most thieves. It puts a premium upon knavery untruthfully to attack an honest man, or even with hysterical exaggeration to assail a bad man with untruth. An epidemic of indiscriminate assault upon character does not good, but very great harm. The soul of every scoundrel is gladdened whenever an honest man is assailed, or even when a scoundrel is untruthfully assailed.

Now, it is easy to twist out of shape what I have just said, easy to affect to misunderstand it, and, if it is slurred over in repetition, not difficult really to misunderstand it. Some persons are sincerely incapable of understanding that to denounce mud-slinging does not mean the indorsement of whitewashing; and both the interested individuals who need whitewashing, and those others who practise mud-slinging, like to encourage such confusion of ideas. One of the chief counts against those who make indiscriminate assault upon men in business or men in public life, is that they invite a reaction which is sure to tell powerfully in favor of the unscrupulous scoundrel who really ought to be attacked, who ought to be exposed, who ought, if possible, to be put in the penitentiary. If Aristides is praised overmuch as just, people get tired of hearing it; and overcensure of the unjust finally and from similar reasons results in their favor.

Any excess is almost sure to invite a reaction; and, unfortunately, the reaction, instead of taking the form of punishment of those guilty of the excess, is very apt to take the form either of punishment of the unoffending or of giving immunity, and even strength, to offenders. The effort to make financial or political profit out of the destruction of character can only result in public calamity. Gross and reckless assaults on character, whether on the stump or in newspaper, magazine, or book, create a morbid and vicious public sentiment, and at the same time act as a profound deterrent to able men of normal sensitiveness and tend to prevent them from entering the public service at any price. As an instance in point, I may mention that one serious difficulty encountered in getting the right type of men to dig the Panama Canal is the certainty that they will be exposed, both without, and, I am sorry to say, sometimes within, Congress, to utterly reckless assaults on their character and capacity.

At the risk of repetition let me say again that my plea is, not for immunity to but for the most unsparing exposure of the politician who betrays his trust, of the big business man who makes or spends his fortune in illegitimate or corrupt ways. There should be a resolute effort to hunt every such man out of the position he has disgraced. Expose the crime, and hunt down the criminal; but remember that even in the case of crime, if it is attacked in sensational, lurid, and untruthful fashion, the attack may do more damage to the public mind than the crime itself. It is because I feel that there should be no rest in the endless war against the forces of evil that I ask that the war be conducted with sanity as well as with resolution. The men with the muck-rakes are often indispensable to the well-being of society; but only if they know when to stop raking the muck, and to look upward to the celestial crown above them, to the crown of worthy endeavor. There are beautiful things above and roundabout them; and if they gradually grow to feel that the whole world is nothing but muck, their power of usefulness is gone. If the whole picture is painted black there remains no hue whereby to single out the rascals for distinction from their fellows. Such painting finally induces a kind of moral color-blindness; and people affected by it come to the conclusion that no man is really black, and no man really white, but they are all gray. In other words, they neither believe in the truth of the attack, nor in the honesty of the man who is attacked; they grow as suspi-

cious of the accusation as of the offense; it becomes well-nigh hopeless to stir them either to wrath against wrong-doing or to enthusiasm for what is right; and such a mental attitude in the public gives hope to every knave, and is the despair of honest men.

To assail the great and admitted evils of our political and industrial life with such crude and sweeping generalizations as to include decent men in the general condemnation means the searing of the public conscience. There results a general attitude either of cynical belief in and indifference to public corruption or else of a distrustful inability to discriminate between the good and the bad. Either attitude is fraught with untold damage to the country as a whole. The fool who has not sense to discriminate between what is good and what is bad is well-nigh as dangerous as the man who does discriminate and yet chooses the bad. There is nothing more distressing to every good patriot, to every good American, than the hard, scoffing spirit which treats the allegation of dishonesty in a public man as a cause for laughter. Such laughter is worse than the crackling of thorns under a pot, for it denotes not merely the vacant mind, but the heart in which high emotions have been choked before they could grow to fruition.

There is any amount of good in the world, and there never was a time when loftier and more disinterested work for the betterment of mankind was being done than now. The forces that tend for evil are great and terrible, but the forces of truth and love and courage and honesty and generosity and sympathy are also stronger than ever before. It is a foolish and timid, no less than a wicked, thing to blink the fact that the forces of evil are strong, but it is even worse to fail to take into account the strength of the forces that tell for good. Hysterical sensationalism is the very poorest weapon wherewith to fight for lasting righteousness. The men who with stern sobriety and truth assail the many evils of our time, whether in the public press, or in magazines, or in books, are the leaders and allies of all engaged in the work for social and political betterment. But if they give good reason for distrust of what they say, if they chill the ardor of those who demand truth as a primary virtue, they thereby betray the good cause, and play into the hands of the very men against whom they are nominally at war.

In his "Ecclesiastical Polity" that fine old Elizabethan divine, Bishop Hooker, wrote:

> He that goeth about to persuade a multitude that they are not so well governed as they ought to be, shall never want attentive and favorable hearers; because they know the manifold defects whereunto every kind of regimen is subject, but the secret lets and difficulties, which in public proceedings are innumerable and inevitable, they have not ordinarily the judgment to consider.

This truth should be kept constantly in mind by every free people desiring to preserve the sanity and poise indispensable to the permanent success of self-government. Yet, on the other hand, it is vital not to permit this spirit of sanity and self-command to degenerate into mere mental stagnation. Bad though a state of hysterical excitement is, and evil though the results are which come from the violent oscillations such excitement invariably produces, yet a sodden acquiescence in evil is even worse. At this moment we are passing through a period of great unrest—social, political, and industrial unrest. It is of the utmost importance for our future that this should prove to be not the unrest of mere rebelliousness against life, of mere dissatisfaction with the inevitable inequality of conditions, but the unrest of a resolute and eager ambition to secure the betterment of the individual and the nation. So far as this movement of agitation throughout the country takes the form of a fierce discontent with evil, of a determination to punish the authors of evil, whether in industry or politics, the feeling is to be heartily welcomed as a sign of healthy life.

If, on the other hand, it turns into a mere crusade of appetite against appetite, of a contest between the brutal greed of the "have-nots" and the brutal greed of the "haves," then it has no significance for good, but only for evil. If it seeks to establish a line of cleavage, not along the line which divides good men from bad, but along that other line, running at right angles thereto, which divides those who are well off from those who are less well off, then it will be fraught with immeasurable harm to the body politic.

We can no more and no less afford to condone evil in the man of capital than evil in the man of no capital. The wealthy man who exults because there is a failure of justice in the effort to bring some trust magnate to an account for his misdeeds is as bad as, and no worse than, the so-called labor leader who clamorously strives to excite a foul class feeling on behalf of some other labor leader who is implicated in murder. One attitude is as bad as the other, and no worse; in each case the accused is entitled to exact justice; and in neither case is there need of action by others which can be construed into an expression of sympathy for crime.

It is a prime necessity that if the present unrest is to result in permanent good the emotion shall be translated into action, and that the action shall be marked by honesty, sanity, and self-restraint. There is mighty little good in a mere spasm of reform. The reform that counts is that which comes through steady, continuous growth; violent emotionalism leads to exhaustion.

It is important to this people to grapple with the problems connected with the amassing of enormous fortunes, and the use of those fortunes, both corporate and individual, in business. We should discriminate in the sharpest way between fortunes well-won and fortunes ill-won; between those gained as an incident to performing great services to the community as a whole, and those gained in evil fashion by keeping just within the limits of mere law-honesty. Of course no amount of charity in spending such fortunes in any way compensates for misconduct in making them. As a matter of personal conviction, and without pretending to discuss the details or formulate the system, I feel that we shall ultimately have to consider the adoption of some such scheme as that of a progressive tax on all fortunes, beyond a certain amount either given in life or devised or bequeathed upon death to any individual—a tax so framed as to put it out of the power of the owner of one of these enormous fortunes to hand on more than a certain amount to any one individual; the tax, of course, to be imposed by the National and not the State Government. Such taxation should, of course, be aimed merely at the inheritance or transmission in their entirety of those fortunes swollen beyond all healthy limits.

Again, the National Government must in some form exercise supervision over corporations engaged in interstate business—and all large corporations are engaged in interstate business—whether by license or otherwise, so as to permit us to deal with the far-reaching evils of overcapitalization. This

year we are making a beginning in the direction of serious effort to settle some of these economic problems by the railway-rate legislation. Such legislation, if so framed, as I am sure it will be, as to secure definite and tangible results, will amount to something of itself; and it will amount to a great deal more in so far as it is taken as a first step in the direction of a policy of superintendence and control over corporate wealth engaged in interstate commerce, this superintendence and control not to be exercised in a spirit of malevolence toward the men who have created the wealth, but with the firm purpose both to do justice to them and to see that they in their turn do justice to the public at large.

The first requisite in the public servants who are to deal in this shape with corporations, whether as legislators or as executives, is honesty. This honesty can be no respecter of persons. There can be no such thing as unilateral honesty. The danger is not really from corrupt corporations; it springs from the corruption itself, whether exercised for or against corporations.

The eighth commandment reads: "Thou shalt not steal." It does not read: "Thou shalt not steal from the rich man." It does not read: "Thou shalt not steal from the poor man." It reads simply and plainly: "Thou shalt not steal." No good whatever will come from that warped and mock morality which denounces the misdeeds of men of wealth and forgets the misdeeds practised at their expense; which denounces bribery, but blinds itself to blackmail; which foams with rage if a corporation secures favors by improper methods, and merely leers with hideous mirth if the corporation is itself wronged. The only public servant who can be trusted honestly to protect the rights of the public against the misdeed of a corporation is that public man who will just as surely protect the corporation itself from wrongful aggression. If a public man is willing to yield to popular clamor and do wrong to the men of wealth or to rich corporations, it may be set down as certain that if the opportunity comes he will secretly and furtively do wrong to the public in the interest of a corporation.

But, in addition to honesty, we need sanity. No honesty will make a public man useful if that man is timid or foolish, if he is a hot-headed zealot or an impracticable visionary. As we strive for reform we find that it is not at all merely the case of a long up-hill pull. On the contrary, there is almost as much of breeching work as of collar work; to depend only on traces means that there will soon be a runaway and an upset. The men of wealth who to-day are trying to prevent the regulation and control of their business in the interest of the public by the proper government authorities will not succeed, in my judgment, in checking the progress of the movement. But if they did succeed they would find that they had sown the wind and would surely reap the whirlwind, for they would ultimately provoke the violent excesses which accompany a reform coming by convulsion instead of by steady and natural growth.

On the other hand, the wild preachers of unrest and discontent, the wild agitators against the entire existing order, the men who act crookedly, whether because of sinister design or from mere puzzle-headedness, the men who preach destruction without proposing any substitute for what they intend to destroy, or who propose a substitute which would be far worse than the existing evils—all these men are the most dangerous opponents of real reform. If they get their way they will lead the people into a deeper pit than any into which they could fall under the present system. If they fail to get their way they will still do incalculable harm by provoking the kind of reaction which, in its revolt against the senseless evil of their teaching, would enthrone more securely than ever the very evils which their misguided followers believe they are attacking.

More important than aught else is the development of the broadest sympathy of man for man. The welfare of the wage-worker, the welfare of the tiller of the soil, upon these depend the welfare of the entire country; their good is not to be sought in pulling down others; but their good must be the prime object of all our statesmanship.

Materially we must strive to secure a broader economic opportunity for all men, so that each shall have a better chance to show the stuff of which he is made. Spiritually and ethically we must strive to bring about clean living and right thinking. We appreciate that the things of the body are important; but we appreciate also that the things of the soul are immeasurably more important. The foundation-stone of national life is, and ever must be, the high individual character of the average citizen. (pp. 415-24)

> *Theodore Roosevelt, "The Man with the Muck-Rake," in his* American Problems, *Charles Scribner's Sons, 1926, pp. 415-24.*

JOHN E. SEMONCHE

[*Semonche is an American historian, lawyer, critic, and biographer of Ray Stannard Baker. In the following excerpt, he assesses the circumstances, intention, and impact of Theodore Roosevelt's "muckrake" speech (see above)*].

On a sunny day in April, 1906, President Theodore Roosevelt delivered a much anticipated public address that has been less a subject for study than for clichés. Generally it has been assumed that the "Man with the Muck-rake" speech was more spontaneous than planned, that Roosevelt suddenly "lost all restraint" with the sensationalism of the magazine campaign of exposure [Louis Filler, *Crusades for American Liberalism.* Rev. ed., 1950]. Some writers have contended that the President's aim was to "appease the right wing" [Henry F. Pringle, *Theodore Roosevelt: A Biography* (1931)], while others have felt that Roosevelt took the occasion to divorce himself from what was commonly referred to as "the militant left" [Mark Sullivan, *Our Times: The United States 1900-1925* (1928-35)]. Still others have sought to deemphasize the attack on the muckrakers and stress Roosevelt's constructive proposals. Actually much of this comment, when not incorrect, is misleading. The address is of historical import not only for its effect upon the muckraking movement, but also for the light it sheds upon its author. Given both Roosevelt and the movement, a clash was inevitable.

The President's basic attitude toward men of the muckraking stamp was thoroughly consistent and apparent as early as July, 1901. Commenting to Owen Wister on Frank Norris's new novel, *The Octopus,* Roosevelt said that the author's picture of California in the grips of control by the Pacific and Southwestern Railroad was an "overstatement . . . so utterly preposterous as to deprive his work of all value. A good part of it reads like the ravings which Altgeld and Bryan regard as denunciation of wrong." Ever unwilling to accept fiction on its own terms, Roosevelt continually demanded literal truth and balanced impressions. He concluded his letter to

Wister: "More and more I have grown to have a horror of the reformer who is half charlatan and half . . . fanatic, and ruins his own cause by overstatement."

When the assassin made what was to be the successful attempt on President William McKinley's life, the then Vice-President labeled the crime "a fearful comment . . . on the teachings of yellow journalism and of the Altgeld type of politician." In a letter to his friend Senator Henry Cabot Lodge, Roosevelt said that "every scoundrel like Hearst and his satellites who for whatever purposes appeals to and inflames evil human passion, has made himself accessory before the fact to every crime of this nature, and every soft fool who extends a maudlin sympathy to criminals has done likewise."

Roosevelt's intense feelings were not lessened by his assumption of the Presidency, though he became more cautious in their expression. In the fall of 1904, almost two years after the coordinated campaign of magazine exposure had begun, the President considered an "infamously false attack" by the prominent journalist Lincoln Steffens the cause of the fatal illness of the Wisconsin senator, Henry C. Payne. Though Steffens was on friendly terms with the President, his articles frequently annoyed Roosevelt.

Early in the summer of 1905 the President expressed some of this feeling to Steffens personally. The occasion was an article the journalist had written on corruption in the state of Ohio. Roosevelt objected to the "unfounded gossip of a malicious or semi-malicious character" which he found in the article. He then went on to comment on an earlier article on Rhode Island in which the journalist had called Senator Nelson Aldrich of that state "the boss of the United States." The President lectured the writer [in a letter of 24 June 1905]:

> . . . such an absurdity has a sinister significance, for in my judgment, we suffer quite as much from exaggerated, hysterical, and untruthful or slanderous statements in the press as from any wrongdoing by businessmen or politicians. . . . When I come upon statements that I do know about and find them without foundation, it shakes my faith in the rest.

Later that same summer Roosevelt wrote to one of Steffens' colleagues on the *McClure's Magazine* staff, Ray Stannard Baker, a reporter who had already garnered many notes of commendation from the man in the White House. Returning proofs of a Baker article calling for governmental regulation of the railroads, the President said that he wanted to free the drive for regulation "from all rancor and hatred." With growing alarm Roosevelt had been watching the growth of the Socialist party; its class conscious appeal, he contended, would only encourage rancor and hatred.

Probably with some thought about the coming battle for effective railroad regulation, Roosevelt became even more intent in trying to ward off this class feeling that he felt the many magazine exposures were unconsciously, if not consciously, promoting. In a revealing letter to the owner and editor of *McClure's,* Samuel S. McClure [4 October 1905], the President amplified upon an earlier conversation. He asked the magazine's staff to

> Put sky in the landscape, and show, not incidentally but of set purpose, that you stand as much against anarchic violence and crimes of brutality as against corruption and crimes of greed, as much

against demogogic assaults on the well-off, as against crimes by the well-off.

Great good could be accomplished by *McClure's,* the President continued, but only if hostility were not confined to the wealthy and indignation not confined to corruption. He conjured up the French Revolution and the Terror, which, he said, had resulted from just such class agitation. In a postscript Roosevelt added that the sentiments expressed pertained to the writing of Ray Stannard Baker as well as to the others. Baker had most carefully been stressing "evolution rather than revolution" and was somewhat surprised and hurt by Roosevelt's admonition. When the journalist responded that "strong language" was necessary in defense of the public's interest, the President paid no heed.

At the year's end Roosevelt confided to the creator of the comic Mr. Dooley, Finley Peter Dunne [in a letter of 15 December 1905], that he was "sick of the people who are always insisting upon nothing but the dark side of life." Here the President was expressing a sentiment definitely on the rise throughout the country—a certain fatigue with exposure writing.

Into this atmosphere burst one of the most sensational of the muckraking exposés, "The Treason of the Senate," written by the prolific and reform-minded novelist, David Graham Phillips [the series began in *Cosmopolitan* in March 1906]. William Randolph Hearst, a man whose publishing policies Roosevelt especially detested, had recently purchased the *Cosmopolitan Magazine* and was now seeking to boost its circulation with the widely publicized series which placed the public spotlight on individual Senators. At least since the time of Mark Twain's *The Gilded Age,* the Senate had been a choice subject for attack; its undemocratic composition seemed anachronistic in this age of reform. The appearance of the first article in the March 1906 issue of *Cosmopolitan* created a furor. As Chief Executive, Roosevelt had always felt a certain respect for the representatives of the people; in part they held the key to his success. Now the enraged President did not hide his feelings in private correspondence.

In a letter to Alfred Henry Lewis [on 17 February 1906], a contributor to the offending magazine, Roosevelt said that the liar was more harmful to society than the thief. Then he continued:

> Now some of the articles in the *Cosmopolitan* consist of nothing but a mixture of hysteria and mendacity; and in others, in which there is a great deal of truth, there is so much suppression of the truth, or assertion or implication of the false, and so much sensationalism, that I do not think very much good will follow.

Writing to Lyman Abbott of the congenial *Outlook* [on 16 March 1906], Roosevelt became more emotional:

> I am not at all sure that the sensation-mongers, the demagogues, the hysterical panderers to the spirit of unrest, the preachers of wild and foolish creeds of social discontent, are not quite as damaging as the corruptionists. . . . These make-believe reformers, these preachers of rabid hatred, these ranters against corruption and in favor of social reform, these socialists who preach the creed of envy—in short, the people like those who write in the pages of the *Cosmopolitan,* are the real enemies of every effort to secure genuine reform, to secure social, civic and political betterment.

Obviously Roosevelt was disturbed, but the disturbance was more deep seated than a single series in the Hearst periodical could provoke. This whole campaign seemed to be getting out of hand.

The President amplified upon this concern in a significant letter to William Howard Taft [on 15 March 1906]. In it he referred to "the dull, purblind folly of the very rich men . . . ," saying that their reactionary opposition to reform has "tended to produce a very unhealthy condition of excitement and irritation in the popular mind, which shows itself in part in the enormous increase in the socialistic propaganda." But then he continued:

> Nothing effective, because nothing at once honest and intelligent, is being done to combat the great amount of evil which, mixed with a little good, a little truth, is contained in the outpourings of the *Cosmopolitan,* of *McClure's,* of *Collier's,* of Tom Lawson, of David Graham Phillips, of Upton Sinclair. Some of these are socialists; some of them merely lurid sensationalists; but they are all building up a revolutionary feeling which will most probably take the form of a political campaign.

This need for some effective, honest and intelligent countermove Roosevelt set himself to fill. On March 17, 1906, two days after his letter to Taft, the President seized the opportunity of a Gridiron Club dinner to set loose a trial balloon. At this special dinner, given by Speaker of the House Joseph G. Cannon for the Washington correspondents assembled in the Gridiron Club, the President took nearly three-quarters of an hour to deliver the longest speech of the evening. It was [assessed by the Washington *Star,* 18 March 1906, 95] "an earnest, at times passionate, exhortation against the tendency in certain quarters, notably among the magazines, to decry public institutions and public men."

Since remarks at the dinner were governed by the traditional "no reporters present" standard, Roosevelt's speech was not specifically reported, but rumors as to its content spread widely. The President quickly sensed that he had struck a popular chord. In his responses to the many supportive letters and editorials, he condemned both reactionary and radical and urged the enlightened course of Rooseveltian moderation.

Immediately after the Saturday evening speech Roosevelt said that he had been motivated by his indignation at "magazines like the *Cosmopolitan"* and at the way the leaders of the Western Federation of Miners had been garnering class sympathy in their trial for complicity in the murder of the former governor of Idaho, Frank Steunenberg. Roosevelt said that he wanted "to stamp on the liars, and yet cordially to join with honest men in eradicating the mistakes which are sure from time to time to occur. . . ." Ida Tarbell's remark that the President was disturbed because the muckrakers were stealing his thunder contains at least a kernel of truth, for Roosevelt wanted to define the "mistakes."

Encouraged by the enthusiastic response which greeted his private remarks, the President decided to make his sentiments public. Some of the journalists with whom Roosevelt had willingly cooperated were worried about the constant rumors of a broad-gauged attack on the campaign of exposure. Would not such a public denunciation by the President himself be harmful? In asking this question Ray Stannard Baker admitted that some of the articles had been extreme, but, he concluded, the movement had generally "been honest and useful. . . ." Baker warned the President [in a letter of 7 April 1906] that the most reputable writers would be the first to withdraw from the field, thereby leaving the work to the "outright ranters and inciters." "Already," Baker continued, "there exists an indiscriminating attack upon the so-called exposures which may prevent the careful study of modern conditions and the presentation of the facts in a popular form." The journalist's letter had made clear the potential results of such a Presidential attack, but then Roosevelt was already well aware of these results.

In replying to Baker the President singled out Hearst's newspapers and magazines along with the New York *Herald* as the subjects of his attack. He also added that he would be sure in his address to discourage the opinion that he was advocating or supporting the whitewash brush. Roosevelt also took time to answer the worried editor of *McClure's Magazine,* who also feared the consequences of an indiscriminate attack. Far from reassuring, the President replied that his speech would have universal applicability. (pp. 114-20)

Roosevelt [soon] found an opportunity to make his sentiments public. The occasion was the laying of the cornerstone of the House of Representatives Office Building. Both Houses of Congress along with a large crowd were present when the President began his speech in a pleasant and jovial mood. As he spoke of "tendencies toward evil," he waved his hand over the assembled Senators and provoked their laughter. Shortly thereafter, however, the President settled down to deliver the remainder of the speech in what he called his "best Methodist-lay-preacher style." (p. 121)

[The famous muck-rake speech] was loosely constructed, repetitive and far too imprecise. Its moral strictures, though well within the consensus of the times, strike a later generation as especially naive. Though all this can be granted, the speech still remains one of Roosevelt's most significant political addresses. With it he sought to accomplish a number of important aims, all of which hinged upon checking this movement of journalistic exposure. Muckraking not only offended the President's taste, but also, according to Roosevelt, it was having a deleterious effect upon the country as a whole. The articles were aiding and abetting the radicals, the socialists, whom Roosevelt viewed as subverters of the American way of life. Though the vast majority of muckraking articles were far from socialistic in their viewpoint or implication, they did attack the status quo. With the socialists preaching a fundamental and grand alternative, it was inevitable that their cause would receive considerable, albeit indirect, support.

The President was also worried about the possible political implications of the campaign of exposure. After decades of apathy, the American people were developing a sense of political awareness. With Roosevelt's own party threatened by internal divisions, the fear that muckraking might groove new political channels was all the more intense. The Chief Executive continued to feel that the future of the country and the unity of the Republican party were inextricably woven together. He tried to use the muck-rake speech to establish his position as a new Republican consensus, a position right of the left and left of the right.

Lastly, though Roosevelt had not hesitated in the past to utilize the moral energy generated by muckraking, by 1906 he was worried that the movement was escaping his control. To assert again his leadership, he proposed both the inheritance tax and a federal licensing system to provide for governmental control of large corporations. The true guardians of the public welfare, the President assumed, were men of wealth with a sense of responsibility to the nation. Not only were they fair and just, but even more important, they were free from the class prejudice that characterized both left and right.

The success of the President's speech would depend in part upon the public's response. That response demonstrated once again that the Chief Executive had felt the public's pulse. The "attack" (and this is Roosevelt's own assessment) on the muckrakers was headlined across the country and even received considerable space in European dailies. As Brander Matthews predicted [in a letter to Roosevelt of 22 April 1906], the words of condemnation came at a time when they would stick. The terms "muckraker" and "muckraking" were derived by members of the daily press, who were generally unconcerned about discriminating among the various writers in the field. The terms of opprobrium took hold and disturbed many of the more sensitive writers, but this seemed only to add to the President's enjoyment of his triumph. With pride he referred to his "muck-rake speech," saying [in a letter to Jacob A. Riis, 18 April 1906] that it had expressed his "deepest and most earnest convictions."

Roosevelt's failure to distinguish between writers bewildered some of them, but this failure was quite conscious, for he realized that specific distinctions would only blunt the attack. In his attempt to check muckraking, Roosevelt could not afford to spare anyone. Besides all were equally guilty in adding to the momentum of the movement. Even to this generation which saw truth as something attainable, Roosevelt's standard of absolute truth was one that no reporter could meet. The initial, indiscriminate image of the man with the muck-rake caught the public's attention and held it.

Though historians of muckraking have noted the continuation of exposure after the speech, much of the unity, purpose and mission went out of the magazine crusade in 1906. The laudable *McClure's* staff agreed almost to a man that the speech had marked the beginning of the end of muckraking. Abuse mixed with the ridicule that followed the speech permanently affected many of the more honest writers. Even Louis Filler, who charted another high point in the history of exposure in 1910-1911, admits that after 1906 there was a shift away from exposure toward the support of specific reform proposals. As such it was a retreat, for the essence of muckraking was exposure. And certainly the muck-rake speech deserves an expanded role in the story of the decline of muckraking.

With a single blow, then, Roosevelt did much to check the effects of exposure writing. Still the hoped-for consequences did not materialize: the appeal of the socialists was not weakened; Roosevelt's leadership was not appreciably strengthened; and the unity of the Grand Old Party was not assured. These failures, however, cannot be attributed to the speech; instead they belong to the grandeur of the President's hopes. (pp. 123-25)

John E. Semonche, "Theodore Roosevelt's 'Muckrake Speech': A Reassessment," in Mid-America: An Historical Review, *Vol. 46, No. 2, April, 1964, pp. 114-25.*

MICHAEL D. MARCACCIO

[In the following excerpt, Marcaccio examines and largely discounts the theory that financial interests conspired to drive muckraking magazines out of business.]

In 1914, in a passage that would be often quoted, Walter Lippmann wrote that "not once but twenty times have I been told confidentially of a nation-wide scheme by financiers to suppress every radical and progressive periodical" [*Drift and Mastery: An Attempt to Diagnose the Current Unrest* (1914)]. Although Lippmann did not believe these stories, by 1914 a substantial body of literature charged that a plot existed by financial interests to crush muckraking. Fears that the muckrakers would be forced out of business by hostile interests, evident for some time, had reached a new intensity in 1911 and 1912 when several reform magazines either folded or changed ownership. Early in 1911, after Standard Oil had filed $350,000 in libel suits against *Hampton's* because of an article written by Cleveland Moffett, the harrassed author warned "we are up against the powers of darkness. The right of free speech in America is in jeopardy. They are trying to muzzle the magazines." Less than two weeks after Moffett's charges, the *New York Press* published a much talked-about article "J. P. Morgan Takes a Strangle Hold on Big Magazines." In January 1912, *Collier's Weekly,* one of the most eminent of the reform magazines, lamented that "the forces of special privilege are making a determined effort to control directly and indirectly as many magazines and newspapers as possible." Shortly thereafter the *Independent* noted the fear of a conspiracy.

Charles Edward Russell, a well-known muckraker, presented the conspiracy theory in a more organized fashion [in "The Magazine Soft Pedal," *Pearson's* (February 1914) and in his *Bare Hands and Stone Walls* (1933)], but Upton Sinclair's *The Brass Check,* published in 1919, a book primarily about newspaper journalism, marshalled the available evidence in a compelling fashion. Finally, in 1939, Louis Filler, in his classic study of muckraking, *Crusaders for American Liberalism,* gave the suppression thesis its strongest scholarly support [The critic cites the 1939 edition of Filler's book and comments that "subsequent reissues of *Crusaders for American Liberalism* have simply repeated the chapter on the demise of muckraking"].

The debate over the end of muckraking has not been one-sided. There have always been individuals like Lippmann who have doubted that various business interests, unable to tolerate muckraking any longer, crippled it. C. C. Regier, the first historian of the subject, conceded that a conspiracy smashed a few magazines, but concluded that a lack of interest was chiefly responsible for muckraking's demise [*The Era of the Muckrakers* (1932)]. Richard Hofstadter and John Semonche have argued that although there are possibly a few instances of suppression, most magazines collapsed for other reasons. Frank Luther Mott, David M. Chalmers, and Harold S. Wilson were even more inclined to blame business problems. Although there is now perhaps more skepticism than ever about a conspiracy to destroy muckraking magazines, recent scholarship has focused on only a magazine or two; overall treatments of the periodicals have been cursory. (pp. 58-9)

Trying to establish the financial condition of magazines in the early twentieth century presents a formidable challenge. Magazines were business enterprises that had to sell both to

Widely reprinted editorial cartoon, based upon a quote by John D. Rockefeller, Jr.: "The American Beauty rose can be produced in all its splendor only by sacrificing the early buds that grow up around it."

the public and advertisers as well as appeal to creditors or potential creditors such as paper manufacturers, printers, bankers, and even to investors or potential investors. Like most American businesses of the early twentieth century, magazines were secretive about their financial standing. But some public data remains. *N. W. Ayer and Son's American Newspaper Annual* and Rowell's *American Newspaper Directory* published circulation figures, although before the creation of the Audit Bureau of Circulation in 1914, these figures were often unauthenticated and unreliable. *Printers' Ink,* a trade journal, published all the major magazines' advertising linage figures monthly. While these figures are precise, they do not include the rate charged for advertising or indicate whether the magazines paid the established rate. One of the most valuable sources, balance sheets, are rare. Letters by insiders often prove indispensable to gaining a picture of financial performance.

Upton Sinclair was in some respects an odd person to bemoan the demise of muckraking. Although one of the most famous and talented of the breed, he often berated a number of the magazines for their shabby treatment of him. Furthermore, as a committed socialist, he concluded that the capitalist press was a means of class domination, and the most that could be expected from it were occasional glimmerings of truth. Despite pique and ideology, he treated some of the magazines he earlier had lambasted as martyrs when they collapsed or became dominated by new groups. With his warnings of the dangers of too rapid an expansion of circulation, the hostility of business and the success of trashy magazines, Sinclair unintentionally presented a strong case against ever taking up muckraking.

Louis Filler's work, in contrast, was much more scholarly. He had no personal ax to grind and, unlike Sinclair, he regarded the muckrakers, not the socialists, as the more serious threat to the established order. Despite these differences, Sinclair and Filler reached similar conclusions. Sinclair found:

> For, of course, the industrial autocracy very quickly awakened to the peril of these "muck-raking" magazines, and set to work to put out the fire. Some magazines were offered millions and sold out. Those that refused to sell out had their advertising trimmed down, their bank-loans called, their stockholders intimidated—until finally, in one way or another, they consented to "be good".
>
> [*The Brass Check* (1919)]

After blaming the war as well as the desertion of muckraking by its practitioners on a conspiracy, Filler concluded:

> The movement to put a stop to exposure was systematically begun by those who felt they could no longer tolerate interference in their affairs. If no executive council met solemnly to discuss ways and means to corrupt or liquidate the muckraking magazines, it was only because enough minor disagreements existed among the interested parties to make such cooperation impossible. It is no less true that the destruction of the magazines was deliberately planned and accomplished in short order—in the case of individual organs, within a few months.
>
> [*Crusaders for American Liberalism*]

Specifically, both charge that *Hampton's, Success, Twentieth Century,* and *Harper's Weekly* were crushed in the years between 1911 and 1916. Moreover, the muckraking owners of *McClure's* and the *American Magazine* were forced out in 1911, and in 1912 conservative interests gained control of *Collier's Weekly* albeit not actual ownership. All were conscious efforts to silence muckraking. These seven instances constitute the heart of the thesis. *Human Life, Pearson's,* and *Everybody's* are less clearly mentioned, but Filler also alleged that *Arena* was destroyed by the American News Company and an advertising boycott in 1909.

The demise of *Hampton's* has often been regarded as the best documented case of the suppression of a muckraking magazine. Known as *Broadway Magazine* when Benjamin B. Hampton purchased it in 1906, *Hampton's* led in numerous exposures and played a particularly conspicuous role in the Ballinger-Pinchot Affair. The chief pieces of evidence in the *Hampton's* episode are contained in an article by Charles Edward Russell in 1914, and, most importantly, in Hampton's letter to Upton Sinclair reprinted in *The Brass Check.*

Hampton contended that after his refusal to withhold from publication an unflattering article about the New Haven Railroad, a stranger appeared in his office and warned him that he would lose his magazine in retribution. The magazine was also, Hampton believed, the victim of sabotage—one of its accountants was working for its enemies and copied a list of stockholders, who then were sent malicious rumors. Hampton asserted that his credit was cut off, and could not obtain a $30,000 loan. The paper manufacturer, with whom he had a $300,000 line of credit, pressured him to pay his accounts. In June of 1911, Hampton was forced to sell out to the Columbian-Sterling Company.

Hampton complained to Sinclair [in a letter quoted in *The Brass Check*]:

> Never in the history of magazine-publishing was there such a great success in such a short time as that of *Hampton's.* That is not my conversation. It is simply the records of the American News Com-

pany. We had, I think, 425,000 circulation, and we broke all records for the same length of time. No other magazine ever succeeded with an investment as small as ours. When they took the magazine away from me I think we had nearly thirty thousand dollars a month advertising.

Although this is clearly one of the more powerful charges of suppression, Hampton's story is inconclusive and sometimes false. Advertising may have been at $30,000 but advertising linage, which had grown spectacularly during most of 1910, had dropped precipitously during the first four months of 1911—down 36.7 percent. Although circulation and advertising figures are important, they do not necessarily portray a magazine's true financial condition. The example of *McClure's* readily comes to mind. From 1908 to 1911 circulation and advertising had risen, but a heavy debt was undercutting the magazine. Profit and debt were the more valid measures of a magazine's financial standing than circulation or advertising. It must be emphasized that when Hampton talked of "success" he was speaking of popularity, not profit. Hampton stated that the magazine's profit had been certified at between $3000 and $7000 a month during the first four months of 1911. Hampton's assertion, in a confidential letter to S. S. McClure, that a certified public accountant's report declared that *Hampton's* had "turned the corner" in early 1911, suggests that there had not been any profits in 1910 or that they had been very small. Hampton's remark that "no other magazine ever succeeded with an investment as small as ours" might indicate capital problems. Although "the indebtedness was not large," actually about $200,000, the figure is somewhat misleading because much money, about $700,000, had been raised through public stock sales. Hampton had also invested another $200,000 of his own money. In other words, the magazine had been largely financed through stock sales rather than through borrowing. Despite this advantage, profits were very low and represented an extremely low rate of return on capital.

Hampton wrote that when he was on the verge of losing the magazine, "Mrs. Hampton and I were having a time to buy clothing for the children, . . . and we had put all our money in the undertaking. In fact, we were near the line of desperation, we were so hard up." In the next sentence of his letter to Sinclair he recounted how he had tried to buy quantities of *Hampton's* stock to stabilize its price on Wall Street! Hampton also alleged that one banker, Edward Earl of the Nassau National Bank, who was willing to defy the Morgan interests by helping him, "was put out of business himself within a few months. . . . The way the Morgan crowd drove him out of the banking business was one of the coldest-blooded things I ever heard of. They punished him for trying to accept perfectly good banking-paper to help me out of my crisis." Earl was not forced out within a few months, but in 1914, and, according to his own account, was let go because of rumors of mismanagement circulated by a few disgruntled stockholders.

In June 1911 Hampton sold out to the Columbian-Sterling Publishing Company, received a little cash and unsecured, non-interest-bearing, long-term notes. Within a few months the new owners were in deep financial trouble and several officers of the concern were indicted for using the mails to defraud, though they gained acquittals due to insufficient evidence.

The *Hampton's* debacle makes for a difficult assessment. Several critical pieces of evidence are suggestive rather than decisive. Did increased advertising rates or continued stock sales account for the modest profits of early 1911? What about the supposed threat? It was made in September 1910. The article about the New Haven Railroad was published in the December issue, and the advertising drop took place when the January 1911 issue appeared. Advertising linage, however, which had soared through most of 1910 had stabilized by the December 1910 issue. The problem in dealing with the possibility of the suppression of *Hampton's* is that by the time of the alleged implementation of the conspiracy, there were persuasive reasons for denying *Hampton's* credit.

It is important to note that the credit crunch began at least by early 1911 and probably in late 1910 before the profits. An audit was made in response to difficulty in paying bills. By early 1911 increased skepticism about magazines that relied heavily on stock sales to the public became evident. It is conceivable that a poor reputation as a business might have brought on many of these difficulties. There were legitimate grounds for denying Hampton credit, including the magazine's nearly chronic inability to make money, although the business did rest on a more solid base than *Success*, for example. Although bizarre things happened to *Hampton's* after Columbian-Sterling acquired it, no one has produced evidence that the new owners were in any way linked to interests hostile to *Hampton's*. In conclusion, while the *Hampton's* incident is too confused to evaluate definitively, it is at least as plausible that financial troubles rather than a conspiracy caused the magazine's failure.

The demise of *Hampton's* was a profoundly important event for the magazine business. In the end, the Columbian-Sterling debacle would drag through the press for quite some time. When it was over some 124,000 investors had lost almost $2.7 million. This ugly and well-publicized incident made creditors even more suspicious of the magazine business, especially of those that sold stock to the public. For example, *Pearson's*, which sold stock, was hurt by an unfair article on the subject in the *New York Sun*. Not only were the magazines under increasing scrutiny, but the efforts of the Taft administration to raise second class postage rates—an important expense for magazines—created a vitriolic fight that lasted from 1909 to 1912.

Hampton's is the only magazine for which even a modest, if inconclusive, case can be made. *Success*, which had been founded by Orison Swett Marden, a noted proponent of self-help, and which came to muckraking late—its chief contribution being an attack on Speaker Joseph Cannon—went out of business in late 1911. The demise of *Success* is sometimes regarded next to the *Hampton's* episode as one of the more persuasive examples of a muckraker being crushed by the denial of credit. Failure to get additional credit destroyed the magazine but it does not therefore follow that credit was withheld to destroy a muckraker. In fact, ample evidence exists to suggest that *Success* was a concern whose critical and persistent financial troubles brought it down. (pp. 59-64)

According to some accounts, five less important magazines were destroyed in retaliation for muckraking: B. O. Flower's *Arena* (1909) and *Twentieth Century* (1913), *Human Life* (1911), *Harper's Weekly* (1916), and *Pearson's* (1916). Although Sinclair did not mention the *Arena*, and some consider it a reformist but not a muckraking magazine, Filler concluded that the American News Company forced Flower out. Strangely, Filler then said that the *Arena* fell to "the advertis-

ing boycott." Actually the *Arena* had been in poor financial condition when a new publisher took it over in 1904, had suffered from chronically low circulation, and was terminated in 1909 when the publisher, Albert Brandt, was on the verge of bankruptcy. Flower's *Twentieth Century* was also a magazine of low circulation—apparently peaking at just over 13,000 but declining to about 12,000 by 1913. Peter N. Barry has demonstrated [in an unpublished doctoral dissertation] that it collapsed because of unsuccessful business practices. *Harper's Weekly,* which did some muckraking under the editorship of Norman Hapgood, from 1913 to 1916, allegedly fell to "the advertising boycott." Yet there is no reason to believe that outside forces were trying to crush it. *Harper's Weekly* inherited a very poor reputation as an advertising medium from its previous management, and suffered from low circulation, poor management, weak intellectual content, and a consistent failure to make money. *Pearson's* continued to muckrake with much ballyhoo until about 1916. The conscious change of 1916, while accompanied by some feeling of business pressure, was due basically to publisher Arthur W. Little's desire to pursue a more popular style of journalism, which he hoped would be more profitable.

If the serious financial problems of the muckraking magazines seem to explain their demise, a perceptive question asked by E. A. Van Valkenburg, publisher of the *Philadelphia North American* [in a letter to Ray Stannard Baker of 13 February 1911], arises: "Is it not remarkable that millions of money await, eagerly, investments in independent publications which are now not on a dividend paying basis?" In other words, why buy a financially troubled magazine? The most important muckraking magazines that experienced a change in ownership (except for *Hampton's* which was a peculiar case) or serious efforts to take them over along with charges that such efforts were attempts to silence their muckraking, were *Everybody's, McClure's, American Magazine,* and *Collier's Weekly*. These four were among the most popular and respected magazines that did muckraking. Each had a particular appeal to potential acquisitors. S. S. McClure lost control of his magazine in 1911 to a group of financiers headed by his son-in-law. Although both Sinclair and Filler concluded that McClure was forced out because of his reform zeal, Peter Lyon and Harold Wilson, who have written excellent studies of *McClure's,* have reached a different conclusion. Lyon found that McClure "had only himself to blame" for the loss of the magazine. McClure was saddled with a large debt and was paying, by 1911, sixteen percent interest on borrowed capital. Further, one could ask whether by 1911 McClure posed any serious threat to corporate interests. Pinned by its debt to such firms as the West Virginia Pulp and Paper Company, which often figured prominently in the conspiracy demonology theory, *McClure's* had printed far fewer socially concerned articles since 1909.

The case of *Everybody's* can be quickly summarized. A leader in circulation and advertising and generally profitable, it was one of the most attractive muckraking properties. The Butterick Publishing Company acquired it in early 1910 from E. J. Ridgway. No evidence exists that Ridgway was forced to sell, nor can Butterick be linked to any overwhelming drive to stifle muckraking. Since the purchase price of *Everybody's* amounted to one-quarter of the Butterick Company's capitalization, profit, not suppression, constituted the chief motive. In truth, the new owners in time rejected muckraking, but *Everybody's* had often been regarded as less than loyal to that style of journalism.

A familiar story occurred with *The American Magazine.* Established out of *Frank Leslie's Popular Monthly* by such *McClure's* stars as John S. Phillips, Ida M. Tarbell, Ray Stannard Baker, and Lincoln Steffens, among others, and acquired by the Thomas Y. Crowell Company in 1911, the magazine has been subjected to careful study by John Semonche. Plagued by constant shortage of capital, *American Magazine* managed to turn a profit—in 1910—but was still hard pressed. The editor, John S. Phillips, had to ask for $20,000 from the wealthy reformer William Kent, who found someone else to contribute the money. Phillips, hurt by the situation and sorely tried by the incessant financial problems, sold out to the Crowell Company. The new owners apparently were able to work with the old staff for about a year until things became difficult, then terminated the older employees.

Collier's Weekly, the famous muckraking magazine that had played a conspicuous role in the patent medicine crusade, the Ballinger-Pinchot controversy and the fight against Speaker Joseph Cannon, was a fourth example of a change in control. Sinclair charged that the National Association of Manufacturers pressured *Collier's* with an advertising boycott and a threat from bankers. Filler contended that the *Weekly,* because of Robert Collier's mismanagement, fell on hard times and ran up a large debt that permitted bankers to step in and order a halt to muckraking. But like a song's refrain, there is no evidence that the National Association of Manufacturers instituted an advertising boycott of *Collier's.* In both 1911 and 1912 the *Collier's* advertising linage increased over the previous year's and increased at a rate comparable to that of the overall weekly market. *Collier's* definitely fell on hard times, but whether bankers ordered a halt to muckraking is debatable. *Collier's Weekly* had never been very profitable and the much discussed resignation of editor Norman Hapgood in October 1912, a resignation that raised issues of business domination of the *Weekly,* clouded issues as much as it clarified them.

A convincing interpretation is needed of the role of Thomas W. Lamont, who had been associated with several New York banks and had been an important figure in the Crowell Company since 1908 and a partner in J. P. Morgan and Company since 1911. Both Lamont and Crowell appear frequently in talk about magazine takeovers during these years. For example, in 1911 Lamont made a proposal—rejected by McClure—to help *McClure's* with its debt in return for bonuses of preferred and common stock. When Crowell purchased the *American Magazine* in 1911, Lamont's prominence at Crowell "excited most attention about the transaction." In 1912, Lamont tried without luck to gain control of *Collier's Weekly.*

These have sometimes been seen as attempts by J. P. Morgan and Company to smash muckraking, but a careful reading of the evidence reveals otherwise. For one thing J. P. Morgan and Company did not own any Crowell stock, although Lamont did. The extent of Lamont's investment is hard to determine. In a letter written in 1934, Lamont termed his investment "small," but his close associate in the enterprise, Joseph Palmer Knapp, stated that both had invested heavily. More importantly, the activities of Lamont and Crowell can best be explained by immediate business considerations rather than primarily as an effort to thwart the muckrakers. Crowell was looking for magazines, in part, according to William Chenery, later a famous editor at *Collier's,* to make maximum use of the need of its chief stockholder, Joseph Palmer

Knapp, for printing orders. The idea of increasing efficiency by printing several magazines—Crowell already owned *Fireside* and *Woman's Home Companion*—was very popular at that time.

McClure's obviously had a respected name. The crux of its problems rested with its debt, which Crowell would have refinanced, thus reducing the burden drastically. Under Lamont's proposal, McClure would have had to accumulate a surplus of one-half to one million dollars before any dividends could be paid on common stock—a shrewd strategy to curb *McClure's* well-known tendency to squander money. Crowell's interest in *McClure's* was not new and in fact antedated Lamont's association with J. P. Morgan and Company. Crowell had attempted to purchase *McClure's* in 1908, before extensive talk of financial interests buying out magazines took place. Further, one might note that if Crowell's prime interest was to stop *McClure's* muckraking, it would have been easier to destroy the magazine than to make the acquisition. When Crowell purchased the *American Magazine,* it had clear plans for making changes. One might also note Knapp's anxiety when the magazine was losing money. This acquisition was no lark to stifle exposure but a calculated move to add to Crowell's profits. In the case of *Collier's Weekly,* it must be remembered that the most profitable part of P. F. Collier and Son had always been the book business. Widely circulated rumors stated that Robert Collier's extravagance had hurt the business. The Collier empire appealed to Crowell, whose practice was to purchase established magazines, not launch new ones. The Collier book business would nicely complement Crowell's and was the most attractive part of the property. It is worth mentioning that although unsuccessful in 1912, Lamont and Crowell would stalk Peter F. Collier and Son for several years and eventually purchase the business in 1919, long after *Collier's Weekly* had given up muckraking.

A number of muckraking magazines clearly had financial difficulties. It is conceivable, however, to argue that the weaknesses might have been caused by the efforts to suppress the magazines or simply might have made it easier to destroy them or seize control over them. But neither position holds up under analysis. Most of these magazines were floundering before serious talk arose of anyone having a vendetta against them. Furthermore, there is no convincing documentation of a concerted effort to smash these magazines. Not only does evidence in individual cases prove to be slight, but on a number of other tests the thesis fails. It would appear logical that a so-called advertising boycott would not only punish its enemies but reward its friends. This was not the case. As the *New York Press* noted in early 1911 just after Crowell acquired the *American Magazine,* it was widely believed that advertising largesse would be bestowed on this magazine. Advertising linage actually dropped precipitously, at first out of fear that the takeover indicated weakness in the property and then later over the loss of the famous staff. One might also expect that a muckraker might find it very difficult to acquire another magazine. Norman Hapgood, while shopping for a new periodical after leaving *Collier's Weekly,* had access to *Leslie's Weekly* and *McClure's,* each of which had close ties to a corporation sometimes associated with hostility to muckraking—Standard Oil and the West Virginia Pulp and Paper Company, respectively. He did not find closed doors.

The conspiracy theory of the end of muckraking overestimates the financial performance of the muckraking magazines, and tends to see muckraking as the decisive characteristic of a magazine. The sole motive of various business interests in the thesis was the desire to quell muckraking. But in nine cases out of ten the conspiracy theory overdramatizes the hostility between muckraking and business. It should be rejected by historians. Instead, a more plausible explanation would emphasize the business problems of the magazines, and the reasonable and defensible concerns of creditors and potential creditors. Finally, a new thesis would relate the acquisition of magazine properties to the overall situation of the purchaser. It's time to cast out the business conspiracy thesis and substitute a more believable model. (pp. 66-71)

> *Michael D. Marcaccio, "Did a Business Conspiracy End Muckraking? A Reexamination," in* The Historian, *Vol. XLVII, No. 1, November, 1984, pp. 58-71.*

IMPACT AND ACCOMPLISHMENTS

WALTER LIPPMANN

[*Lippmann was one of the twentieth century's most influential political journalists. He began his career as a research assistant and investigative reporter for Lincoln Steffens, and later helped found the leftist* New Republic *in 1914, serving for several years as associate editor and literary critic of that publication. During the 1920s, his interest shifted from literature to politics, and he worked as editor and political writer for various American periodicals for the rest of his life. In the following excerpt from his* Drift and Mastery *(1914), Lippmann speculates upon reasons for the widespread popularity of the muckraking movement.*]

There is in America to-day a distinct prejudice in favor of those who make the accusations. Thus if you announced that John D. Rockefeller was going to vote the Republican ticket it would be regarded at once as a triumph for the Democrats. Something has happened to our notions of success: no political party these days enjoys publishing the names of its campaign contributors, if those names belong to the pillars of society. (p. 23)

You have only to write an article about some piece of corruption in order to find yourself the target of innumerable correspondents, urging you to publish their wrongs. The sense of conspiracy and secret scheming which transpire is almost uncanny. "Big Business," and its ruthless tentacles, have become the material for the feverish fantasy of illiterate thousands thrown out of kilter by the rack and strain of modern life. It is possible to work yourself into a state where the world seems a conspiracy and your daily going is beset with an alert and tingling sense of labyrinthine evil. Everything askew—all the frictions of life are readily ascribed to a deliberate evil intelligence, and men like Morgan and Rockefeller take on attributes of omnipotence, that ten minutes of cold sanity would reduce to a barbarous myth. I know a socialist who seriously believes that the study of eugenics is a Wall Street scheme for sterilizing working-class leaders. And the cartoons which pictured Morgan sitting arrogantly in a chariot drawn by the American people in a harness of ticker tape,—these are not so much caricatures as pictures of what

no end of fairly sane people believe. Not once but twenty times have I been told confidentially of a nation-wide scheme by financiers to suppress every radical and progressive periodical. But even though the most intelligent muckrakers have always insisted that the picture was absurd, it remains to this day a very widespread belief. I remember how often Lincoln Steffens used to deplore the frightened literalness with which some of his articles were taken. One day in the country he and I were walking the railroad track. The ties, of course, are not well spaced for an ordinary stride, and I complained about it. "You see," said Mr. Steffens with mock obviousness, "Morgan controls the New Haven and he prefers to make the people ride."

Now it is not very illuminating to say that this smear of suspicion has been worked up by the muckrakers. If business and politics really served American need, you could never induce people to believe so many accusations against them. It is said, also, that the muckrakers played for circulation, as if that proved their insincerity. But the mere fact that muckraking was what people wanted to hear is in many ways the most important revelation of the whole campaign.

There is no other way of explaining the quick approval which the muckrakers won. They weren't voices crying in a wilderness, or lonely prophets who were stoned. They demanded a hearing; it was granted. They asked for belief; they were believed. They cried that something should be done and there was every appearance of action. There must have been real causes for dissatisfaction, or the land notorious for its worship of success would not have turned so savagely upon those who had achieved it. A happy husband will endure almost anything, but an unhappy one is capable of flying into a rage if his carpet-slippers are not in the right place. For America, the willingness to believe the worst was a strange development in the face of its traditional optimism, a sign perhaps that the honeymoon was over. For muckraking flared up at about the time when land was no longer freely available and large scale industry had begun to throw vast questions across the horizon. It came when success had ceased to be easily possible for everyone.

The muckrakers spoke to a public willing to recognize as corrupt an incredibly varied assortment of conventional acts. That is why there is nothing mysterious or romantic about the business of exposure,—no putting on of false hair, breaking into letter-files at midnight, hypnotizing financiers, or listening at keyholes. The stories of graft, written and unwritten, are literally innumerable. Often muckraking consists merely in dressing up a public document with rhetoric and pictures, translating a court record into journalese, or writing the complaints of a minority stockholder, a dislodged politician, or a boss gone "soft." No journalist need suffer from a want of material. (pp. 23-5)

> *Walter Lippmann, "The Themes of Muckraking," in his* Drift and Mastery: An Attempt to Diagnose the Current Unrest, *edited by William E. Leuchtenburg, Prentice-Hall, Inc., 1961, pp. 23-34.*

DAVID MARK CHALMERS

[*In the following excerpt, Chalmers assesses the impact of the muckraking movement.*]

What is the significance of the muckrakers? What did they do and how much did it matter? The historian Alexander B.

Callow, Jr., in writing about New York City's Tweed Ring (1859-1871) scandals, stated that the essential elements for a crusade against civic corruption are "moral indignation and facts." The muckrakers supplied both and projected them on a national level. The muckrake trademark was the detailed factual story, complete with names, dates, documents, and mind-staggering tally sheets about the extent and cost of the corruption. The journalists shuttled in and out of New York City to write on municipal elections in St. Louis, land frauds in the Pacific Northwest, bosses in Cincinnati, capital-labor strife in Pennsylvania and Idaho, vice and corruption in Chicago (their favorite municipal target), rebates in the oil fields, and manipulation on Wall Street.

Ward bosses protected crime and prostitution. Aldermen and mayors sold franchises and stole from city treasuries. Legislatures did the same things on the state level, and sent businessmen to the United States Senate to do the same thing nationally. Land frauds, mineral frauds, timber frauds, water frauds, tariff frauds, and stock frauds abounded. Not only were favors bought and the government corrupted at all levels, but the public was cheated and squeezed, labor was exploited, consumers poisoned, investors swindled, companies looted, and poverty perpetuated. This was the muckrake picture of a twentieth-century urban and capitalist America.

The muckraking journalists performed an important role. First, they made the American middle class conscious of corruption. Second, they linked together all of the different kinds of wrong-doing into a broad picture of the malfunction of American society. Third, they offered an explanation for it all. The effective cause of the national corruption was the concentration of vast economic power. They had many

names for it: the Corporations, High Finance, Frenzied Finance, the Trusts, the System, the Interests, Plutocracy, and Monopoly. Although the new economic giants were the instruments of national wrong-doing, the basic fault lay in the values and institutions of society. The laws and moral codes of a more placid agrarian system did not hold for a major urban and industrial society.

Before the end of the second decade of the twentieth century, a majority of Americans would live in towns and cities, an increasing number in the great exploding metropolises. Urban America needed more than the profit motive, the trolley car, and the ward boss to guide it. The prime collective achievement of the muckrakers was to point out the conflict between the growth of large scale private economic power and the needs of the new national American society.

The term the muckrakers used for this conflict was "lawlessness," but they used it in such a way as to cause confusion. Sometimes it meant felonious assault and crime in the streets, sometimes industrial warfare, sometimes institutional malfunction, sometimes the behind-the-scenes "invisible government" of the political and economic bosses, and sometimes the aggressions of capital. The muckrakers were no more successful than anyone else in working out the degree to which the criminal codes governing the behavior of individuals could be made to apply to the behavior of large economic organizations.

Otis Graham, Jr., who has studied the biographies of several hundred progressives, sums up the muckrakers [in his *An Encore for Reform* (1967)] by saying that most of them merely tried to warn the middle class that "its food was adulterated, its insurance funds misused, its stocks watered, and its government full of graft." If this were all they did, then the muckrakers would rank as important forerunners of the still infant field of consumer protection. Consumerism, however, was only a part of their concern.

The muckrakers represented a principle much discounted today by political realists, radicals, and conservatives alike. Like most progressives, the journalists did not see society as divided and subdivided into a multitude of interest groups, primarily economically based. Many subsequent commentators have pointed out that this was their weakness, but perhaps it was also their strength. Basically optimistic, they believed that democracy and progress went hand-in-hand. The people were good. With information and guidance, the people would be capable of selecting proper principles and leaders. Accumulating wealth and the materialistic standards which Ida Tarbell summed up with the phrase "commercial machiavellianism" could be overcome through public opinion, altruism, a return to moral standards, and the regeneration of political and economic leadership. Society could escape from its lawlessness, or anarchic, materialistic disorganization, and regain proper moral solidarity.

Lincoln Steffens sought to convince tycoons and bosses that running a city for the benefit of its people was more exciting than running a railroad for profit. He called it "practical Christianity," and probably most of the muckrakers would have accepted such a term to describe their goal. Excepting only Tom Lawson ("Frenzied Finance"), they were serious about their efforts to do good for America. When the press referred to them as crusaders, it fitted their own self-image.

Caricature of Lincoln Steffens and Ray Stannard Baker from 1905.

The most frequent criticism of the journalists is that they saw the world as divided between good and bad men, and that they offered little more than the old political cry of "throw the rascals out." This is the common textbook image. The fact that the journalists focused their stories on the industrialist, the railroad magnate, the banker, the senator, and the political boss was misleading. Most of the muckrakers didn't much care whether the Democrats or the Republicans were in office. Both parties were much alike, and party was a device to mislead the public, not inform or represent it.

Nor was the "business government" a solution for any of the muckrakers, except G. K. Turner. Businessmen in government constituted much of the problem. The lure of special privilege was too strong for them. As Lincoln Steffens recalled explaining it to the elite Jonathan Club in San Francisco, special privilege was the prize which society gave for evildoing. "Let's take down the offer of a reward," he had said. "Let's abolish—privileges." In reply to an Episcopal Bishop who asked where it all began, Steffens went on, "You want to fix the fault at the start of things. Maybe we can. Most people, you know, say it was Adam. But Adam, you remember, he said it was Eve, the woman; she did it. And Eve said no, no, it wasn't she; it was the serpent. And that's where you clergy have stuck ever since. You blame the serpent, Satan. Now I come and I am trying to show you that it was, it is, the apple."

The muckrake ethic developed into a demand for a new political morality in an age of organization. The men in power acted "treasonably," to use David Graham Phillips' and Lincoln Steffens' term, when they squeezed their great fortunes out of the tenement dwellers, subway riders, farmers, shippers, small businessmen, investors, oil producers, workers, and consumers.

The muckrake instrument for the creation of the national morality was education. "Facts, facts, and more facts," were the way to reform. That path did not lead back to American individualism, which a majority of the muckrakers soon left behind, but to an awakened leadership and public. As "reform" Darwinists, they believed that public concern and enlightened public interest leadership could produce the proper environment for a better society. The great William James, at Harvard, perceived the role which the journalists had taken as social educators. The leadership of American thought, he commented, was shifting from the universities to the ten-cent magazines.

The muckrakers agreed that the problem was one of monopoly, greed, and institutional failure. They differed on how to solve it. At one end of the spectrum, there were those who believed that individualism, competition, or business government was the answer. For the majority of the journalists, whether they believed in competition or bigness, the proper instrument for change was the regulatory state. During the progressive period, that state began to emerge. Today, the United States is a system of regulatory capitalism, mixed with some natural resource socialism, Keynesian or indirect business cycle controls, occasional crisis-time direct controls on wages and prices, and corporate, state, and national welfarism. Still the nation has remained an enterpriser society, with the key production decisions in the hands of the businessmen, somewhat circumscribed and prodded by government. Although they did not foresee the other developments, the muckrakers saw the necessity of basic components of regulation and private enterprise. Only a few, G. K. Turner and A. H. Lewis on the Right, and Upton Sinclair, Gustavus Myers, Charles Edward Russell—and perhaps Lincoln Stef-

fens—on the Left, believed that the economy could do without either the government or the enterpriser-businessman.

In a very real way, the journalists shared an uneasy partnership with Theodore Roosevelt. Most of them were originally enthusiastic about the President, but came to cringe under his attack and to doubt his sincerity. He, in turn, refused to share the middle of the road with anyone else. He feared that the muckrakers were not politically "realistic" and were stirring up a popular discontent that might take a dangerously socialistic direction. Actually, the muckrakers helped prepare public support for the President's regulatory solutions and softened up the political opposition. They collaborated on the major progressive era achievements: the Pure Food and Drug Act (1906), the Meat Inspection Act (1906), the Hepburn Act (1906) strengthening the Interstate Commerce Commission, and conservation. They helped bring about New York State's regulation of the insurance industry, and the Seventeenth Amendment to the national Constitution for the direct election of senators.

In an electoral republic, the attack which the popular journals waged against "corrupt" public officials whom the muckrakers identified as "friends of the interests" was an important political factor. On the plus side, Tom Johnson was reelected Mayor of Cleveland; Joseph Folk went to the state house in Missouri; Robert M. La Follette became a United States Senator, and Nelson W. Aldrich, "the representative of all the interests," retired from the Senate. Joseph T. Hadley in Kansas and Theodore Roosevelt would probably have filed anti-trust suits against Standard Oil without Ida Tarbell's articles. The muckrakers did not dream up the income tax amendment, tariff reform, or Woodrow Wilson's Clayton and Federal Trade Commission Acts. Probably as many of Lincoln Steffens' municipal reformers were defeated as got elected, and despite G. K. Turner's grand jury testimony, prostitutes still walked the streets of American cities. On the whole, the muckrakers were more the supporters of reform laws and publicizers of the results of grand jury investigations than the originators.

For a decade, the magazine journalists were dramatic spokesmen on popular issues and probably second only to President Theodore Roosevelt in reaching a national audience. Democratic governments are dependent on two-way communication between the people and their government. Periodic elections need continual supplementation. In most cases there is no way to measure the impact of public opinion on the governmental process. Presidents, legislators, and bureaucrats follow it when they find it convenient, ignore it when they feel they can or must, and usually rationalize their actions, even to themselves. At the same time, particularly in the public life of a democratic society, the values of men in power and the tasks they set for themselves and their societies are often touched by popular attitudes and demands. Between 1902 and 1912, the muckrakers had a prominent role in such a shaping.

Historians give the muckrakers credit for helping father the modern, middle-class, regulatory state, but there is growing question over whether they should be praised for it. Modern critics tend toward two critical conclusions. They assert that regulatory capitalism is run by and for the capitalists. "Public morality" and "the public interest" are decried as meaningless guidelines which conceal the nature of interest and power in society. The middle classes pass off their own comfortable place within society as universal morality. "Public morality" is their morality, and "the public interest" is their interest. Political realists such as George Mowry and Richard Hofstadter have described the muckrakers and their fellow progressives as members of the old, Protestant, middle-class leadership, which reacted to the loss of status, prestige, and power to the big corporations and an organizational society.

Neither the muckraker-socialists nor the muckraker-enterprisers understood the nature of bureaucracy and modern government. It is questionable whether they did much better with the nature of groups and interests. Interests and groups conflict; the muckrakers thought in terms of order. They were rationalists. Their middle-class backgrounds and "practical idealism" dulled their awareness of the nature of power. Seeing the havoc which unrestrained economic power was creating in society, their solution was an ethical one. They assumed that there was basically one public rather than many, and therefore they believed that everyone could be educated to the acceptance of a single "public interest" as a guide. This would do away with private or group use of power. They did not recognize the pluralistic or interest-group society which A. F. Bentley wrote about in his pioneering *The Process of Government* (1908) or that Charles Beard was describing to his government classes at Columbia University. Basically the appeal of both liberals and socialists was that men should rise above group, faction, and greed. While the conservative muckrakers saw interest and greed as healthy individualistic forces, the muckraker-progressives believed that national regulation and the public interest would lift society above corporate and group selfishness. The muckraker-socialists looked to collective ownership to perform the same feat. None recognized the highly heterogeneous nature of American society.

More than half of the magazine journalists had been recruited from the big city newspapers. They often wrote about the problems of labor, the immigrant, the black, the Oriental, the women who worked in the sweatshops and the children who tended the looms, and the tenements and the poor. They called for social and welfare reforms, as well as regulation of the railroads and an end to municipal corruption. Social reform had to come from the public-spirited citizenry. By progressive standards this meant their own, old stock, white, middle-class America. Somewhat fearful of the masses, the muckrakers did not consider sharing power with labor and the other underclasses or groups in society.

Though less followers of John Locke's absolute defense of property and less committed to individual economic enterprise than they have been accused of being, most of the muckrakers were liberals. On the crucial "liberal" values, they believed in the people and in change, were not distrustful of government, and were reservedly critical of private property. The people were good and would be trustworthy when informed. Great changes had already taken place, and more were necessary. There was a tendency to believe that reform and major changes came periodically, rather than continuously. Abolitionism and the Civil War were one such wave. Another, they believed, was cresting. As the other Roosevelt, FDR, would phrase it a quarter of a century later, they believed that their own generation had that "rendezvous with destiny." They tended to see the conflict of property vs. individual rights in consumer, wage, and small property terms. The governmental role was primarily that of a regulatory agent in the economy.

The muckrakers did not like concentrated wealth or misbe-having trusts, but they rejected a return to a Jeffersonian world of small-scale individual enterprises. Most wanted a regulatory capitalism, but even the muckraker-socialists did not glimpse either the possibilities or the dangers of big government.

Upton Sinclair used the royalties from *The Jungle* to build a communitarian colony on the palisades of the Hudson River, which he called Helicon Home Colony. In *The Industrial Republic* (1907) he described this experiment in group living. Drawing together the various socialist doctrines of alienation, corporate concentration, the surplus, and the capitalist breakdown, Sinclair hoped for a world based on the community of interest of the workers, not on increasing production. Once the output was no longer set by profit-dictated maldistribution, there would be enough for everyone. While his path toward this cooperative society was no more clear than today's communitarianism, Sinclair alone among the muckrakers sought this form of radical transformation of the capitalist society. It was because he believed in such a goal that he had become a muckraker in the first place.

Only Charles Edward Russell and Gustavus Myers found that their muckraking carried them all the way into the socialist camp. Lincoln Steffens hovered vaguely around socialism, more interested in the public-spirited use of power, than doing away with power. Charles Edward Russell had been an Iowa Greenbacker, a single-taxer, and an early foe of the railroads. His experience with a capitalist society that produced the slums, prisons, and poverty, led him to working-class sympathies and an analysis based upon surplus production. Much more than Upton Sinclair's brand, Charles Edward Russell's radicalism was typical of the American brand of eclectic socialism.

The basic problems of regulatory capitalism are how to regulate and toward what ends. The attention of muckrakers, historians, and the general public has usually focused on the battle to get legislatures and congresses to pass laws. The anti-trust suit against Standard Oil, the struggles for the Pure Food and Drug law, the Hepburn Act, and the Federal Trade Commission were dramatic. The press and history books concentrate on the passing of such bills but do not usually examine what happens afterwards. Neither the Sherman and Clayton Anti-trust laws nor the regulatory system have prevented the growth or misbehavior of concentrated economic and political power.

Although United States Senators seldom go to jail, judges, congressmen, legislators, and former governors are from time to time likely to. Processors adulterate and corporations pollute. Standard Oil was dissolved by the Supreme Court in 1911 and is today the largest industrial corporation in the world, and five oil companies, not one, head the list of American giant corporations. Prisons deprave rather than correct, and the inmates of the Arkansas penitentiary probably would not have been much worse off if the state had started to lease them out again. Safety laws are not enforced in the mines. Undereducated and undernourished children may be out of the factories, but they still work in the migratory stream or languish in the ghettos of the inner cities. Once the principle of regulation is accepted and an agency created and empowered to regulate, the problems have really just begun. The question has always been more complicated than simply a choice between private profit and public interest. The public interest is complex, multiple, and contradictory.

The corporate firm and industry employ and produce. Their financial health is a vital part of "the public interest." Historians who decry the failure of the muckrakers to offer objective or working standards for regulatory capitalism have been just as unable to provide them. However, the critic does not have to accept the radical view that business created the regulatory state as its own instrument, to agree that business and inertia have captured and held most state and national regulatory agencies.

The regulatory state is staffed by individuals from those industries that it is supposed to supervise. Governors and presidents have failed to appoint effective public interest representatives. The political system, the voters, and the media have failed to demand legislators and regulators who will combine a concern for the public interest with the long range, healthy development of industry. The impartial expert, anchored within the protected civil service strata of the regulatory agency and government, has often turned out to be a timid and routineering bureaucrat. Legislative failure to fund properly has often been as deadly as economic interest and political pressure. Judicial paths have often been as slow as bureaucratic ones, and the complexities of the American legal system have often made the political problems seem simple by comparison. The regulatory system has never shown any signs of being an automatic mechanism. It needs a great deal of pressure from outside to get and keep it going, and it usually has received the wrong kind. The consumer's champion of the 1960s and 1970s, Ralph Nader, has pointed out that he is unlike the earlier muckrakers because they had no follow up. He intends to be different.

Probably what regulatory capitalism needs most is to develop and institutionalize public-interest pressure and follow-through. The error of the muckrakers was the belief that government—the regulator—itself could produce this follow-through. The regulatory experience clearly indicates that sufficiently financed and mandated structures, such as consumer counsels and representatives, are needed. So is continuous pressure from outside, representing the public or general interest, as well as more narrowly directed labor and farmer interest groups. Such pressures must be focused on the political parties as well as on the regulatory agencies. Consumer leagues and cooperatives, lobbies and public interest law firms, unions, study groups, and "raiders" need the spur, support, and platform that the muckrakers and the media of their day, the popular magazines, provided in initiating the system of regulatory capitalism in the first place.

The great contribution of the muckrakers was that they developed a new form of detailed, factual, investigatory journalism which exposed the problems and confusion of the American social system at the beginning of the twentieth century. The existence of the need was indicated, as young Walter Lippmann pointed out, by the remarkable interest with which the American middle-class public read the muckrake writing. The journalists and Theodore Roosevelt helped lead the silent middle classes into progressivism. The main resources of the journalists were honest indignation, the facts, and the belief that there was some sort of essential value in society which could be called "the public interest." If they were naïve to believe that a public interest existed, more sophisticated modern critics are also naïve if they believe that either communitarian withdrawal or the power competitions of different "interest" groups alone can handle society's problems and directions.

The muckrakers focused their attack on giant capitalism without, for the most part, being willing to seek an alternative to the capitalist system. They looked to regulation without an understanding of the nature and difficulties of big government, or regulation itself. They sought to help the underclasses without a sufficient awareness that they were themselves a class. They did not realize that an important part of the solution to the problems of the underclasses lay in sharing the possession of power, not just in the conscience of governments and the overclasses.

The problems, limitations, and failures in defining what the public interest is stands at the core of their failure to remake society. But without a continuous reawakened and fueled concern for some value called "the public interest"—however it is defined, and however much it changes—any modern society is in peril.

The Pulitzer prize-winning historian, Richard Hofstadter, wrote in his book on *The Progressive Historians* (1968), that what the muckraking journalists and the popular novelists were getting at was a picture of what their society was actually like. "Reality" was "the inside story." It was "the bribe, the rebate, the bought franchise, the sale of adulterated food, the desperate pursuit of life in the slums." Such "reality" was not to be found "in the standard textbooks on constitutional law, political science, ethics, economics, or history." It was to be found, Hofstadter wrote, in the writing of Henry Demarest Lloyd, the novelists Frank Norris and Theodore Dreiser, and in Upton Sinclair's *The Jungle,* David Graham Phillips' *Susan Lennox,* Ida Tarbell's *The History of Standard Oil,* and Lincoln Steffens' *The Shame of the Cities.* (pp. 64-74)

David Mark Chalmers, in his The Muckrake Years, *D. Van Nostrand Company, 1974, 161 p.*

C. C. REGIER

[In the following excerpt, Regier reassesses the muckraking era.]

It is clear that muckraking is not something that was discovered by a group of men in the first decade of the twentieth century. What does distinguish that decade is the fact that there then existed a muckraking movement, a concerted effort on the part of a large number of writers, using as their medium books and pamphlets but more especially the popular magazines which had sprung up in the late eighties and early nineties and had, by the turn of the century, achieved large circulations. Muckraking, as a movement, began late in 1902, became militant in 1903, in 1904 and 1905, and by 1906 was a force that was felt throughout the nation. By 1908 it was dying down, but the Taft administration revived the interest in the literature of exposure and gave a new incentive to the cause of liberalism in politics. The activities of the insurgents in Congress in 1909 and 1910 provided a center for agitation, and the tariff legislation enacted at that time proved a source of dissatisfaction and a subject for criticism. In 1911 muckraking was again at a high point, and many of the muckrakers participated in the campaign of 1912. But even before that three-cornered struggle, muckraking was again on the decrease, and soon nothing was left that could be described as a movement. Some writers and some magazines continued to expose corruption and vice, but whatever fragments of the movement remained were crushed by the entrance of this country into the war. Since the World War, attempts to revive muckraking have largely proved abortive, and "debunking" was for a time the only popular form of the literature of exposure.

Looking back on the muckraking movement, we can readily see that it was part of a larger social, intellectual, and political development. In the nineties . . . the average man acquiesced in the methods of industry and commerce. Industrial expansion seemed as much a matter of "manifest destiny" as geographical expansion had seemed in the days before the Civil War, and no more thought was given to those who were ruined by the ruthless methods of the business men than had been wasted on the Indians and Mexicans whose land was taken from them. For the poor there was sympathy and even charity, but few people stopped to consider the conditions which made poverty inevitable. The majority threw themselves into the struggle for wealth with as little consideration for abstract theories of right and wrong as the pioneers had shown in the struggle for land. Even those who were beaten in the struggle were inclined to look upon their defeat as produced by the very laws of nature, and not through the operation of controllable social forces.

Of course there were movements of protest in the nineties, but it was not until the next decade that there came a definite revolt against Big Business. Gradually, but on the whole with surprising rapidity, people, partly because of the facts which the muckrakers revealed, partly because of the visions of better things which the reformers held before them, partly because of chastening personal experiences, began to regard the corporations as enemies rather than as friends. In particular, the comfortable middle classes, who had viewed the earlier stages of the growth of monopoly with considerable complacency, now began to fear the power of the trusts. And they turned to the government as their bulwark in the struggle against the great interests. Formerly, they had accepted the view that the function of government was to protect and encourage the growth of business enterprise; now they demanded that the state and federal legislatures enact laws which would defend the rights of the common people by restraining the activities of the large corporations.

It is significant that there came to be much talk about the "social conscience." Forward-looking men in the churches and in public life began to say that too much attention had been paid to the sins of the individual. They pointed out that men who were kindly, thoughtful, and high-principled in their private lives condoned and even practised business methods which brought poverty, misery, and disease to millions. Washington Gladden noted our discovery that no society could march hellward faster than a democracy under the banner of unbridled individualism. A "Golden Rule" movement was started in 1901, and it was the intention of the founders that the Golden Rule should be practised in business and political relations. Dr. Max Farrand holds that every twenty or thirty years a wave of "moral hysteria" passes over the country, and practices that were once regarded as proper and honorable come to be condemned and scorned. "Hysteria" may or may not be the right word, but it is true that, with almost the suddenness of conversion, the attitude of the American people toward industry and toward government underwent a complete reversal.

The expression of the attitude was twofold: exposure and reform. It is important to note that, taking the most conservative figures available, those given in Ayer's *American Newspaper Annual and Directory,* we find the total circulation of the

ten magazines which engaged in muckraking to run over three million. These periodicals devoted a considerable proportion of their space, sometimes as much as 20 per cent, to articles of exposure. And in addition to the magazines we have books and the newspapers. Several of Russell's books sold more than thirty thousand copies, and both *The Brass Check* and *The Jungle* went over the hundred thousand mark. A few newspapers, particularly the New York *World* and the Kansas City *Star,* aided materially in the campaign. We have every reason, then, to suppose that the muckrakers touched in one way or another the great majority of American citizens.

Parallel with the muckraking movement went a political movement which took shape in a variety of ways. Some of the muckrakers were Socialists, but others, probably the majority, believed that the capitalistic system could be so altered as to meet the needs of the nation. During the Roosevelt administration the hopes of the liberals were pinned on the President, and much of the legislation for which he was responsible met with their approval. With the Taft administration reaction set in, and the liberals linked themselves with the insurgents in Congress. In 1912 the liberal movement was divided. Many of the men who had worked for reform supported Roosevelt and the Progressive party, but others gave their allegiance to Wilson and "The New Freedom" of which he eloquently spoke and wrote. But at no time from 1902 to 1912 were the muckrakers and the reformers without some political figure who seemed to embody more or less adequately the ideals which they held.

Since Roosevelt was the outstanding statesman of the muckraking era, and since he was intimately associated with many of the measures which were intended to remedy the evil situations which the muckrakers exposed, it is interesting to note the judgments expressed in 1922 by some of the leaders. Mr. S. S. McClure, in a letter to the present writer, stated:

> President Roosevelt was the most influential force in getting good things done that the country ever possessed. He assisted all good causes and hindered all bad causes.

William Allen White expressed a similar opinion:

> Roosevelt was the leader of the liberal movement. At the famous Gridiron Dinner in which Roosevelt spoke about the muckrakers, Uncle Joe Cannon spoke up, and said, "Yes, you're the chief muckraker," which was literally true.

More critical was the verdict of Ray Stannard Baker:

> In the beginning I thought, and still think, he did great good in giving support and encouragement to this movement. But I did not believe then, and have never believed since, that these ills can be settled by partisan political methods. They are moral and economic questions. Latterly I believe Roosevelt did a disservice to the country in seizing upon a movement that ought to have been built up slowly and solidly from the bottom with much solid thought and experimentation, and hitching it to the cart of his own political ambitions. He thus short-circuited a fine and vigorous current of aroused public opinion into a futile partisan movement.

John S. Phillips and Charles Edward Russell went even further. The former wrote:

> The greatest single definite force against muckrak-

ing was President Roosevelt, who called these writers muckrakers. A tag like that running through the papers was an easy phrase of repeated attack upon what was in general a good journalistic movement.

And Russell, when asked what place Roosevelt had in the muckraking movement, replied:

> None of any honor. He did much to hamper and discourage it, but never a thing to help it. His speech in which he first misapplied . . . a passage of Bunyan to this work of righteousness, frightened some timid editors and greatly emboldened those malefactors of great wealth to whom he was afterward supposed to be hostile.

But the fact remains, whatever individual muckrakers may think of Roosevelt, that muckraking was closely bound up with the progressive movement for reform, and that both movements were expressions of the attitude of the decade. It was a period not merely of bitter criticism but also of high hopes. The liberals of the period felt that they were getting results, and that they would go on getting results. It seemed as if a new Golden Age were at hand, not only for American business and government, but also for American letters and art. Much of the writing of the nineties . . . was infinitely removed from the realities of life, but the authors of the early nineteen-hundreds were eager to grapple with American problems and to find their subjects on American soil. Robert Herrick, in a series of novels on the American scene, criticized the shallowness and crassness of his contemporaries, especially the women. Theodore Dreiser was beginning his distinguished career. William Allen White's immensely popular *A Certain Rich Man* (1909), portrayed the growth of the Middle West since the Civil War, ending on a note of high optimism and ardent faith. Brand Whitlock was writing about politics; Winston Churchill shifted from historical romances to critical studies of politics, business, and the church; Edith Wharton was achieving realistic works of distinction. In American literature, especially in the novel, a new spirit was evident: a determination to utilize typically American material; a willingness to criticize unflinchingly what was unseemly in American life; a note of confidence in America's future.

Frederic C. Howe, in his *Confessions of a Reformer* (1925), describes the attitude of the liberals in the years just before the outbreak of the war in Europe, and much of what he says is equally applicable to the decade before 1912. He writes:

> The years from 1911 to 1914 were a happy interim for me. Working with college men and women who were convinced that the old order was breaking up, living in a world that had confidence in literature and in the power of ideas, it seemed to me that a new dispensation was about to be ushered in. A half-dozen magazines had built up their circulation on disclosures of corruption and economic wrong; Lincoln Steffens, Ida M. Tarbell, Ray Stannard Baker, Charles Edward Russell had the attention of America; forums were being opened in the churches, city reformers were springing up all over the country. A dozen insurgents had been elected to Congress; direct primaries, the direct election of United States senators, the initiative and referendum were being adopted, while municipal ownership, labor legislation, woman suffrage, and the single tax seemed but a short way off. It was good form to be a liberal. Conservative lawyers, bankers, and men of affairs stepped out from their offices and

lent their names to radical movements. They presided at meetings and contributed to causes. Branches of the Intercollegiate Socialist League were being organized in the colleges, woman suffrage was enlisting the most prominent women of the country, President Roosevelt was providing catchwords for radicals to conjure with, while Woodrow Wilson was taken from the cloisters of Princeton to be made governor of New Jersey, to be later elected to the presidency.

> "The new freedom" was to replace the old serfdom of bosses, the younger generation was to achieve the things that had been denied my own—a generation ignorant of the old Egypt of small capitalism, aware of the crude feudalism of the new. The political renaissance was now surely coming. It would not stop with economic reform; it would bring in a rebirth of literature, art, music, and spirit, not that which came to Italy in the thirteenth century after the *popolo grasso* had made their pile and then turned to finer things. The colleges were to lead it; it was to have the support of the more enlightened business men; it would call forth the impoverished talents of the immigrants and the poor. The spirit of this young America was generous, hospitable, brilliant; it was care-free and full of variety. The young people in whom it leaped to expression hated injustice. They had no questions about the soundness of American democracy. They had supreme confidence in the mind. They believed, not less than I had always believed, that the truth would make us free.

Such was the spirit of the age, and such was the optimism of the muckrakers, the reformers, the leaders of liberal opinion. And now we naturally ask ourselves what was accomplished by these workers, more especially, of course, by the muckrakers. We wish to know not merely what laws were passed as a result of their agitation but also what effect their exposures had on business. For it was business, as we have said many times, that bore the brunt of the muckraking attack. The muckrakers discovered that the great corporations were behind the corruption in municipal, state, and national politics, behind the suppression of liberal magazines, and the perversion of news, behind the pollution of foods and the misrepresentation of medicines. It was the opinion of most of the muckrakers that almost all the evils of American life were directly traceable to the aims and methods of industrialists and financiers, and it was in the hope of arousing public opinion and thus changing these aims and methods that they did their work.

It is impossible to prove that business methods were bettered in such and such a way by such and such an attack, but it is quite possible to argue that the whole tone of business in the United States was raised because of the persistent exposures of corruption and injustice. As early as 1909 John Forbes stated that in his early business career "things were done without a thought of their being wrong that the public would not for an instant stand for to-day." The Rev. Hugh Black declared in 1922, "during the sixteen years that I have been in America the whole basis of commercial morality has changed." In 1921, Dr. Frank C. Doan, comparing the public attitude a quarter-century ago with that of his own time, said that whereas old men had once advised him to rid himself of his dreams of social justice, he found intelligent men everywhere willing to listen to talk of the Sermon on the Mount and the Golden Rule. Even Charles Edward Russell, who has remained militant in his attitude, believes that business methods have been remade, that the old tactics of monopoly have been abandoned, that business has been humanized and made decent so far as that is possible under our competitive system, that there is a general interest in the conditions of labor, and that competitors are no longer put out of business without regard to law. President Wilson, in his message to Congress in January, 1914, summarized an opinion that was widely held when he said, "At last the masters of business on the great scale have begun to yield their preference and their purpose, and perhaps their judgment also, in honorable surrender." One of the most impressive statements on the subject is to be found in an article entitled "Higher Standards Developing in American Business," written by Judge Elbert H. Gary, and published in *Current History* for March, 1926. Judge Gary, after contrasting the business ethics of to-day with the practices current twenty-five years ago, writes:

> To my personal knowledge many men of big affairs have completely changed their opinions and methods concerning ethical questions in business. The majority of business men conduct operations on the basis that right is superior to might; that morality is on a par with legality and the observance of both is essential to worthy achievement. They regard employees as associates and partners instead of servants. Executives have come to understand that stockholders are entitled to any reasonable information, so that under no circumstances can there be preferential rights and opportunities. At last it has been perceived—and this belief is spreading everywhere—that destructive competition must give way to humane competition; that the Golden Rule is not an empty phrase, but a golden principle. Finally, business as a whole sees that full and prompt publicity of all facts involving the public weal, not only must be made possible, but must be insisted upon as a primary tenet of good faith.

It is something to have great industrialists and financiers rendering even lip-service to ethical principles and humane considerations.

The achievements of muckraking and the liberal movement in the field of legislative accomplishments can be more easily tabulated. The list of reforms accomplished between 1900 and 1915 is an impressive one. The convict and peonage systems were destroyed in some states; prison reforms were undertaken; a federal pure food act was passed in 1906; child labor laws were adopted by many states; a federal employers' liability act was passed in 1906, and a second one in 1908, which was amended in 1910; forest reserves were set aside; the Newlands Act of 1902 made reclamation of millions of acres of land possible; a policy of the conservation of natural resources was followed; eight-hour laws for women were passed in some states; race-track gambling was prohibited; twenty states passed mothers' pension acts between 1908 and 1913; twenty-five states had workmen's compensation laws in 1915; a tariff commission was established in 1909, abolished in 1912, and revived in 1914; an income tax amendment was added to the Constitution; the Standard Oil and the Tobacco companies were dissolved; Niagara Falls was saved from the greed of corporations; Alaska was saved from the Guggenheims and other capitalists; and better insurance laws and packing-house laws were placed on the statute books. Some changes can be traced directly to specific muckraking articles. *Hampton's* maintained that Charles Edward Russell's articles on the Southern Pacific Railroad were instru-

mental in breaking the power of that corporation in California politics. Mr. Russell himself states that the articles of John L. Mathews were responsible for defeating the plans of the Water Power Trust. And it is fairly clear that it was because of Russell's articles that Trinity Church destroyed the vile and unsanitary tenements from which it had long been drawing income.

The period also witnessed a number of important changes in the machinery of government: the popular election of United States senators, direct legislation through the initiative, referendum, and recall, direct primaries, corrupt practices acts, campaign expense laws, commission form of government for cities, and women suffrage—reforms all of which were intended to remedy the abuses pointed out by the muckrakers. William Allen White, in 1909, stated that the shackles of democracy—direct bribery, party bribery, machine rule, and unresponsive legislative control of the states—had been thrown off. The muckrakers probably deserve credit also for the introduction of congressional investigations, for the development of sociological surveys, for the devising of methods of popular exposition which the later essayists and the conservative magazines adopted, and for the destruction of the awe and reverence in which wealth had been held. *Everybody's,* in 1909, offered a somewhat exuberant summary of what had been accomplished:

> Wall Street cannot gull the public as it once did. Insurance is on a sounder basis. Banking is adding new safeguards. Advertising is nearly honest. Rebating is unsafe. Food and drug adulteration are dangerous. Human life is more respected by common carriers. The hour of the old-time political boss is struck. States and municipalities are insisting upon clean administrators. The people are naming their own candidates. Independent voters, and that means thinking men, are legion. The children are having their day in court. Protection is offered to the weak against the gambling shark and saloon. Our public resources are being conserved. The public health is being considered. New standards of life have been raised up. The money god totters. Patriotism, manhood, brotherhood are exhalted. It is a new era. A new world. Good signs, don't you think? And what has brought it about? Muckraking. Bless your heart, just plain muckraking. By magazine writers and newspapers and preachers and public men and Roosevelt.

We may discount as much as we like the enthusiasm of the editor of *Everybody's* and of other commentators on the achievements of the era, but it still remains obvious, even from so cursory a survey as we have offered, that a great many important and valuable reforms were adopted, as the result, in part at least, of muckraking. What the muckrakers tried to do was necessary; the evils were there, and there was no hope of removing them until the public was aroused to a recognition of their existence. What they accomplished was significant; the public was aroused and conditions were improved. Why, then, did muckraking cease?

The first, and most obvious answer, in view of what has just been said, is that muckraking was no longer needed because the conditions against which it was directed had been abolished. This seems plausible enough, and there is indeed some truth in it. The more flagrant evils, both in politics and in industry, had been eliminated. Moreover, the public had been aroused, and Congress, together with the state legislatures, was carrying on investigations of its own and was apparently

S.S. McClure with former McClure's *staff members Willa Cather, Ida Tarbell, and Will Irwin.*

committed to a policy of reform. On the other hand, in 1911, when muckraking ceased, many important reforms, some of which were adopted during the first Wilson administration, were still unrealized, and, furthermore, it was already apparent that many of the old evils were appearing in new guises. Monopoly had been abolished in theory, but it still existed in fact. Despite the amendment providing for direct election, senators were frequently chosen by the same old bosses. The direct primary, for which so much had been hoped, was proving a disappointment in many states. Business might be less open in its defiance of law, but there were many subtle ways of evading legislation that clamored for exposure. Finally, it is to be noted that many of the muckrakers were themselves dissatisfied with what had been achieved, while the liberals in politics put forth their greatest efforts in 1912, a year in which there was almost no muckraking. Quite probably belief that muckraking was no longer needed had something to do with the decline of public interest in exposure, a point which will be discussed shortly, but it is wrong to suggest that the muckrakers ceased their efforts of their own accord because they believed that their work was finished.

We must go on, then, to discuss other factors in the cessation of muckraking, and immediately there comes to mind another possibility: perhaps muckraking did not stop; perhaps it was stopped. . . . [It is difficult to analyze the facts, but]

there is considerable evidence to show that financial interests did manage to suppress more than one magazine that had been antagonistic to Big Business.

William Allen White, however, believes it was a "natural phenomenon" that the liberal magazines should fall into the hands of their creditors, mostly financiers, when liberalism declined and with it the popularity of these periodicals. He writes, "There is absolutely no truth in the story that there was a deliberate plot on the part of the great financial interests to grab the magazines." And we have, in support of his position, the fact that the costs of publishing had greatly increased, making advertising necessary if magazines were to survive.

To the present writer it seems possible to find much truth in both these statements. To him the evidence seems overwhelming that some muckraking magazines, which might otherwise have survived for some time longer, were deliberately and ruthlessly put out of business by the interests which they had antagonized. On the other hand, it is reasonable to suppose that these magazines could have continued, in defiance of the financiers, if the public interest in muckraking had been maintained and circulation had remained large. And it is quite clear that other magazines gave up muckraking, not because their existence was threatened by the financiers and industrialists, but because articles devoted to exposure did not serve to sell copies. Financial pressure may have hastened the demise of muckraking, but there is no conclusive evidence that it was a case of murder in the first degree.

We come inevitably, then, to the conclusion that muckraking ceased, primarily, because the American people were tired of it. John S. Phillips, in a letter to the author, states:

> This phase of journalism died down because of the unwarranted and exaggerated imitations done without study and containing much that was untrue. The result of these things was a revulsion and a loss of public interest. Journalistically, the scheme was given up because readers didn't want to read that sort of thing any more. The same thing happened in the political field. Victor Murdock and Senator Beveridge both told me they couldn't get any response to the former kind of speech. The people at large, as readers and auditors, are changeable and when they get tired of a certain kind of thing they stop reading and stop attending lectures and speeches.

John O'Hara Cosgrave, editor of *Everybody's* during the muckraking period, says much the same thing: "The subject was not exhausted but the public interest therein seemed to be at an end, and inevitably the editors turned to other sources for copy to fill their pages."

But why the change in public interest? Why, indeed? Why does public interest permit one play to run on Broadway for five years, while another, and a much better, according to the critics, dies in its first week? Why does public interest send this book, rather than that, to the head of the list of best-sellers? Why did the public interest in muckraking ever develop? These questions cannot be conclusively answered, for public taste is largely incalculable. "The wind bloweth where it listeth." But, even as we tried to show some of the reasons for the beginning of public interest, so we can now seek a partial explanation for its decline.

In the first place, as already suggested, it is possible that many people believed so many important reforms had taken place that there was no need for muckraking. In the second place, it may be that the excitement wore off in time, with the result that the magazine readers found more of a thrill in stories about cowboys and bandits than they did in articles about senators and industrialists. In the third place, as Mr. Phillips says, the increased sensationalism of the latter years of the era may have sickened people with the whole business. In the fourth place, intelligent citizens may have become impatient with exposure and may have begun to demand what they should do to remedy conditions. And, in the fifth place, the mere fact that muckraking had gone on for ten years may be enough to explain why the reading public was weary of it.

We come, in short, to the conclusion that to a considerable extent muckraking was little more than a fad. Many writers took up muckraking because, for the time being, it was more profitable than other forms of writing. They gave up writing pretty romances, western thrillers, or ingenious yarns about detectives, in order to "expose" real or imagined abuses. Naturally they turned to other fields the moment it seemed likely that greater profit lay therein. Some of the editors were much the same. They had little of the social vision which brought the *Arena, McClure's, Collier's,* and *Hampton's,* to mention without invidious intent only a few names, into the muckraking campaign. They sought only to capitalize a tendency of the times. Such writers and such editors, of course, did not hesitate over sensationalism, and accuracy was of only minor concern. By their attitude and their conduct they did much to bring muckraking into discredit, and when the public would have no more of it, they blithely turned to other things.

We have said enough, perhaps, to explain why muckraking ended, but it is important to devote a little more attention to those writers who were both purposeful and competent, to those periodicals whose editors were sincerely devoted to the general good, to that section of the public which examined with seriousness and intelligence the literature of exposure. Probably the decline of muckraking was hastened by the insincerity of certain writers and editors, the cheapness of what they wrote and published, and the superficiality of the interest they aroused. But we should study the movement at its best, noting the criticisms which have been directed against it, and endeavoring to discover if there were inherent weaknesses that may have contributed to its cessation.

It has been frequently charged that the muckrakers were not fundamental enough in their diagnoses and in their prescriptions. Walter Lippmann, for example, in *Drift and Mastery* (1914), charges the muckrakers with failing to understand the great changes in American life. They did not realize how the nature of industry had been altered, and they were content to denounce this abuse and remedy that evil without ever touching the bases of the whole problem. William Archer reached a similar conclusion, declaring in his article on "The American Cheap Magazine" that the muckrakers were never willing to admit that collectivism was the only permanent check upon the enslavement of the people by the most amazing plutocracy the world had ever seen. Frederic C. Howe, in his *Confessions of a Reformer* (1925), argues that the whole liberal movement was on the wrong basis. The liberals thought that it was enough to make people see what was wrong; they did not realize that the mind "refused to work against economic interest."

In all these criticisms there is more than a grain of truth. Of course it cannot be said that all the muckrakers were afraid of collectivism, for Sinclair and Russell, and at one time Lincoln Steffens, were Socialists. But most of the muckrakers described themselves as "liberals," meaning by that term much or little, as the case might be, and even the Socialists did not seem fully to understand how their dogmas were to be applied to American life. As Lippmann has said, the muckrakers were not leaders, showing men and women how to rise above the chaos of individualistic industrialism; they were, rather, symptoms and expressions of that chaos. Their exposures were unquestionably fruitful, but more than muckraking was necessary for healing the sores of American civilization. Of far-reaching and fundamental philosophy the muckrakers had little; as a result their movement could be only a passing phase in the long struggle for justice and liberty.

Other criticisms have been leveled against these men. It has been charged that the muckrakers were not sufficiently accurate and painstaking in their studies, and that their articles consisted of rhetoric instead of facts. This was true of the more sensational muckrakers, but it was not true of the revolutionary exposures made by such investigators as Steffens, Tarbell, Baker, Connolly, and their confreres. John S. Phillips, who served on both *McClure's* and the *American,* says: "So thorough was the work then, that, although we dealt with libelous materials all the time, there was only one suit for libel sustained against the magazine [*McClure's*]." And this suit was successful simply because a document on which an article was based turned out to be inaccurate.

It is amazing, when one considers the kind of material these men were using, how few successful libel suits were brought against them. A single article might blast a political reputation or ruin a business. Naturally, the people who were attacked sued for damages if they dared. Samuel Hopkins Adams says that he was threatened with suit after suit but usually all he needed to do was to point out that he had far more information than he had thus far used, and the threat was forgotten. Of all the threats produced by his patent medicine articles, comparatively few materialized into cases, and of these cases he lost but one. Will Irwin had six suits filed against him, but only one was brought to trial. . . . Steffens, despite the fact that he was constantly destroying the prestige of eminent politicians, never had to pay a cent in damages. The victims of muckraking were on the lookout for the slightest inaccuracy and yet the muckrakers lost very few cases.

This is some indication of the reliability of the better type of muckraking, but there are other proofs. . . . [It should] be noted that articles were subjected to the most rigorous editorial scrutiny, and that the advice of experts was occasionally obtained. In the better type of muckraking, matters of hearsay were entirely eliminated, and merely personal charges were never included. Of course there were muckrakers who were reckless, and there were muckrakers who could not distinguish between evidence and rumor, but the general level of accuracy in the leading magazines was astoundingly high.

If we wish to find other criticisms of the movement, criticisms many of which were voiced by men who took part in it, we need only turn to the *Survey Graphic* for February, 1926, in which are printed twenty-three answers to the question, "Where are the pre-war radicals?", raised by Mr. Howe in his *Confessions of a Reformer.* The criticisms contained in these statements are directed against the liberal movement, but some of them apply to muckraking. Stuart Chase pleads for a more careful study of facts, declaring that "the Uplift . . . is comatose if not completely ossified—strangled both by the war and its own ineptitude. It was inept because its moral judgments took the place of sound analysis." Ray Stannard Baker says that he and his fellows were on the wrong track because they believed that what they wanted could be had by "adopting certain easy devices or social inventions," and he insists that more understanding is necessary. "Think of us," he writes, "as having gone back to get acquainted with life; of liking better for a while to ask questions than to answer them; of *trying to understand.*" (pp. 194-212)

These criticisms all point to the conclusion stated a moment ago: muckraking, however necessary and however valuable it might have been for the time being, was essentially a superficial attack upon a problem which demanded—and demands—fundamental analysis and treatment. If we paraphrase Mr. Howe's provocative question and ask ourselves "Where are the pre-war muckrakers?" we are likely to find some indication of what happened to the movement.

We see, in the first place, that the spirit of many of these men remains unchanged. Upton Sinclair is still a muckraker, but, until very recently, he has found it necessary to publish his own books in order to get them before the public. Charles Edward Russell also remains critical, but, unable or unwilling to follow Sinclair's example, he has failed to secure a medium through which his political and social ideas could reach the reading public. Thus these two writers illustrate the influence which economic pressure has had in checking the movement.

Others of the old muckrakers are engaged in what is a modern approximation of muckraking. Will Irwin has done important service in his exposures of the horrors and the futility of war and in his articles on the scandal in the Veterans' Bureau. Samuel Hopkins Adams, devoting himself chiefly to fiction and writing under a pseudonym as well as under his own name, has used one of his novels, *Revelry,* in order to make a startling exposure of the Harding regime. (pp. 212-13)

In one way or another, the muckrakers have adapted themselves to the changes that have taken place in the life of the nation. The transformation which brought us David Grayson in place of Ray Stannard Baker [Grayson is the pseudonym under which Baker published pastoral novels] is significant because it reveals Baker's belief that we must have understanding, and Baker's present devotion to the history of the Wilson administration still further illuminates his decision that quiet study rather than noisy assertion is the present need. Mark Sullivan, though writing on politics, seems to have tempered his views, and he, too, is devoting himself to history. Ida M. Tarbell, apparently, has made an even more drastic change; at least her life of Judge Gary shocked those readers who remembered with approval her history of the Standard Oil Company. (pp. 213-14)

Because muckraking was to some extent merely a fad—of which the public grew tired, because of the pressure of financial interests, because some of the evils exposed had been remedied, and because of inherent weakness in the movement itself, muckraking came to an end. Even liberalism, of which muckraking was but a part, received a stunning blow when the United States entered the World War.

After this colossal "atrocity" the public mind was in no mood to become excited over mere political and business exposures at home. The absolute apathy in the face of the Teapot Dome scandals is sufficient indication of the way "times have changed." The genteel sort of exposure which such periodicals as the *Nation,* the *New Republic,* and the *World Tomorrow* carried on could hardly be dignified with the term muckraking. The editorials and books of Mr. Mencken, the novels of Mr. Lewis, the many critical biographies of Washington and the "eminent Victorians"—these represent a social philosophy quite unlike that of the muckrakers.

Is muckraking likely to return? A few years ago the historian would probably have answered that the era of the muckrakers was a unique phenomenon in American history, and that the chapter was definitely closed. Today he is not so sure. Liberalism seems to be coming back. The fanaticism and provincialism and conservatism of the post-war period are passing away; and Progressives can carry elections, as was demonstrated in 1930.

Is there need for further muckraking? What brought about muckraking in 1902? S. S. McClure's desire to satisfy the people—for journalistic reasons—on such vexing subjects as the trusts, labor unions, municipal corruption. Are there any public problems that puzzle the American people today? Certainly. There is the problem of the gangsters. Everybody is interested in it and very few understand it. There is the whole problem of the relation of the underworld to the so-called respectable classes. There is the problem of the relation of the police to communists and other "undesirables," there is the problem of prohibition, and there is the old alliance of business and politics, in state and nation. These are a few of the things that need to be exposed.

At present (1932) we find ourselves in a world-wide depression. Millions of working men and women are out of employment because, so they are told, they have "produced" too much. The Kansas farmer sells his wheat for twenty-five cents a bushel—the lowest figure in forty years. The Texas farmer dumps many tons of fruit and vegetables to rot in the sun while the West Virginia or Pennsylvania coal miner starves for want of food. People are beginning to ask fundamental questions. Has capitalism failed? Or has it not been allowed to go far enough? Perhaps political power should be delegated to the managers of capital as well as economic power. In that case we should approach the contemporary Russian ideal of unified control, only we should reach it from the opposite direction. Or should our government definitely and finally give up the old theory of laissez faire and actually plan and enforce a unified and harmonious scheme of economic, cultural, and political life for all of its citizens? We want to know; and before we can know much we must have the facts; and how can we get the facts except by further honest and scientific exposures? It would almost seem that before we can have another intelligent progressive movement we will have to have some more muckraking. How this can be brought about it is not easy to see. What magazine would undertake such a task? What magazine has a staff of trained social scientists who can write interestingly and significantly, and is willing to pay them for their investigations? Or is there any other plan of bringing such information before all the citizens who would care to read it?

In conclusion we shall quote two prominent muckrakers on the value of muckraking magazines and on the need for further exposures. Charles Edward Russell wrote thus to the present writer: "Looking back, it seems to me clear that the muckraking magazine was the greatest single power that ever appeared in this country. The mere mention in one of these magazines of something that was wrong was usually sufficient to bring about at least an ostensible reformation." And Ray Stannard Baker wrote a few years ago that "there is a greater opportunity now than ever before for clear-headed criticism by writers, and a greater need than ever for an illuminating presentation of conditions." (pp. 214-16)

C. C. Regier, in his The Era of the Muckrakers, *1932. Reprint by Peter Smith, 1957, 254 p.*

FURTHER READING

I. Anthologies

Swados, Harvey, ed. *Years of Conscience: The Muckrakers.* Cleveland: World Publishing Co., 1962, 409 p.
   Representative anthology of reform journalism arranged under the headings "Corruption in City, State, and Nation," "The Robber Baron and the Trust," "Brave Women and Working Children," "The Worker and the Negro," "Land and Power," "Food, Drugs, and the Nation's Health," "Religion and Hy-

pocrisy," "Crime and Punishment," and "The Press." Swados's introduction to this collection is excerpted above.

Weinberg, Arthur, and Weinberg, Lila. *The Muckrakers: The Era in Journalism that Moved America to Reform.* New York: Simon and Schuster, 1961, 449 p.
   Thematically arranged collection including entire muckraking articles as well as excerpts from long series. Portions of the editors' critical commentary are excerpted above.

II. Secondary Sources

Beasley, Maurine. "The Muckrakers and Lynching: A Case Study in Racism." *Journalism History* 9, Nos. 3 & 4 (Autumn-Winter 1982): 86-91.
   Considers Ray Stannard Baker's sometimes noncondemnatory investigations of violence against blacks representative of the failure of the muckrakers to satisfactorily address this issue.

Bloomfield, Maxwell. "Muckraking and the American Stage: The Emergence of Realism, 1905-1917." *South Atlantic Quarterly* 66, No. 2 (Spring 1967): 165-78.
   Maintains that the popularity of muckraking journalism influenced the first Realist writers for the American stage.

Bradshaw, James Stanford. "The Journalist as Pariah: Three Muckraking Newspaper Novels by Samuel Hopkins Adams." *Journalism History* 10, Nos. 1 & 2 (Spring-Summer 1983): 10-13.
   Discusses *The Clarion* (1914), *Common Cause* (1918), and *Success* (1920)—novels "with a newspaper background and with a strong muckraking flavor," that "explored, in a fictionalized form, the state of American journalism, what it was, and what, as a liberal, [Adams] felt it should be."

Bridges, Lamar W. "George Kibbe Turner of *McClure's* Magazine." *Journalism Quarterly* 61, No. 1 (Spring 1984): 178-82.
   Considers Turner's series of muckraking articles on prostitution and crime for *McClure's* instrumental in spurring the formation of the Chicago Vice Commission and eventual passage of the federal Mann Act, designed to curtail prostitution.

Cassady, Edward E. "Muckraking in the Gilded Age." *American Literature* 13, No. 2 (May 1941): 134-41.
   Contests the claim that "the muckraking era followed a long period of public and literary complacency toward social evils," maintaining that many writers of the 1860s through the 1890s produced journalism and fiction of the muckraking type. This essay is refuted by L. A. Rose (below).

Cassady, James H. "Muckraking and Medicine: Samuel Hopkins Adams." *American Quarterly* 16, No. 1 (Spring 1964): 85-99.
   Examines Adams's muckraking exposés of patent medicines and his later career of investigative medical journalism.

Chalmers, David M. "The Muckrakers and the Growth of Corporate Power: A Study in Constructive Journalism." *The American Journal of Economics and Sociology* 18, No. 3 (April 1959): 295-311.
   Contends that the muckrakers, while exposing corrupt practices common to the huge business concerns that arose in the United States after the Civil War, "did not reject the new industrialism and the dominant corporate form but rather insisted that both be consciously directed toward the public good."

Chamberlain, John. "The Muck-Rake Pack." In his *Farewell to Reform: The Rise, Life, and Decay of the Progressive Mind in America,* pp. 119-43, rev. ed. New York: John Day Co., 1932.
   Outlines the social and political conditions that fostered the "literature of protest" of which muckraking was a part.

Cook, Fred J. *The Muckrakers: Crusading Journalists Who Changed America.* New York: Doubleday & Co., 1972, 182 p.
   Introduction to the muckraking era and some of the principal practitioners of muckraking journalism.

Filler, Louis. "The Muckrakers: In Flower and in Failure." In *Essays in American Historiography: Papers Presented in Honor of Allan Nevins*, edited by Donald Sheehan and Harold C. Syrett, pp. 251-70. New York: Columbia University Press, 1960.

Calls for a renewal of scholarly interest in the muckraking journalists of the early twentieth century and disparages much of the extant critical material on this topic.

————. *Appointment at Armageddon: Muckraking and Progressivism in the American Tradition.* Westport, Conn.: Greenwood Press, 1976, 476 p.

History linking exposé journalism to American political Progressivism. The chapter "Writer-Reformers" focuses specifically upon the muckraking era of the early twentieth century.

Forcey, Charles. "Walter Lippmann: Voluntarist Liberal, 1909-1913." In his *The Crossroads of Liberalism: Croly, Weyl, Lippmann, and the Progressive Era, 1900-1925*, pp. 88-120. New York: Oxford University Press, 1961.

Includes an account of Lippmann's work as a research assistant for Lincoln Steffens, who "had bet the editor of *Everybody's* . . . that he could create within six months an accomplished magazine writer from some intelligent college graduate."

Fuller, H. de Wolf. "The Realism of the American Stage: The Drama of Exposure and the Reforming Spirit." *The Nation* 102, No. 2646 (16 March 1916): 307-10.

Theater review article in which Fuller pronounces Ida Tarbell "the mother of dramatic realism in this country," stating: "It was she who gave rise to the flood of muckraking which swept over us during the first decade of the century, and it was undoubtedly the muckraking spirit which begot the first serious attempts to bring the American stage into close contact with life."

Geiger, Louis G. "Muckrakers—Then and Now." *Journalism Quarterly* 43, No. 3 (Autumn 1966): 469-76.

Contends that the muckrakers failed to establish a widespread national "climate of reform" because the principal muckraking periodicals reached a primarily urban and middle-class audience and failed to engage the large agrarian portion of the population.

Graham, Otis L., Jr. "Appendix I: The Derivation of the Sample." In his *An Encore for Reform: The Old Progressives and the New Deal*, pp. 187-204. New York: Oxford University Press, 1967.

Notes that the muckraking movement supplied publicity and impetus for the Progressive movement.

Grenier, Judson A. "Muckraking the Muckrakers: Upton Sinclair and His Peers." In *Reform and Reformers in the Progressive Era*, edited by David R. Colburn and George E. Pozzetta, pp. 71-92. Westport, Conn.: Greenwood Press, 1983.

Surveys Sinclair's muckraking career and discusses many of his contemporaries.

Hapgood, Norman. *The Changing Years: Reminiscences.* New York: Farrar & Rinehart, 1930, 321 p.

Autobiography that includes discussion of Hapgood's editorial work at *Collier's* during the muckraking period. Hapgood offers his explanation of why *Collier's* refused the opportunity to serially publish Upton Sinclair's *The Jungle*.

Holbrook, Stewart H. *The Golden Age of Quackery.* New York: Macmillan, 1959, 302 p.

Entertaining and informative history of patent medicines, including extensive discussion of Samuel Hopkins Adams's muckraking series "The Great American Fraud" for *Collier's*, which Holbrook credits with aiding the passage of the Pure Food and Drug Act.

Hornung, Alfred. "The Political Uses of Popular Fiction in the Muckraking Movement." *Revue française d'études américaines*, No. 17 (May 1983): 333-48.

Examines popular novels with muckraking themes by Upton Sinclair and Winston Churchill.

Kielbowicz, Richard B. "The Limits of the Press as an Agent of Reform: Minneapolis, 1900-1905." *Journalism Quarterly* 59, No. 1 (Spring 1982): 21-7, 170.

Examines the relationship between political muckraking and specific reforms effected in early twentieth-century Minneapolis.

Kittle, William. "The Making of Public Opinion." *The Arena* 41, No. 232 (July 1909): 433-50.

Surveys the popular muckraking magazines that were instrumental in forming public opinion.

Kolko, Gabriel. "Roosevelt as Reformer, 1904-1906." In his *The Triumph of Conservatism: A Reinterpretation of American History, 1900-1916*, pp. 79-112. Chicago: Quadrangle, 1963.

Discusses Roosevelt's involvement with various reform movements instigated by the muckrakers, concluding that "he worked with reformers if it suited his purposes, but he virtually regarded them as the cause of evils by their consciousness of them."

Link, Arthur S. "The Progressive Movement." In his *American Epoch: A History of the United States Since the 1890s*, pp. 68-91. New York: Alfred A. Knopf, 1955.

Discusses the role of the muckrakers in social justice and political reform movements of the early twentieth century.

"The Man with the Muck-Rake." *Literary Digest* 32, No. 16 (21 April 1906): 605.

Reports on press reaction to President Roosevelt's "muckrake" speech.

"More Remarks on the 'Muck-Rakers'." *Literary Digest* 32, No. 17 (28 April 1906): 639-40.

Presents aspects of the ongoing controversy regarding President Roosevelt's comments about muckraking journalism.

Martin, Jay. "The Visible and Invisible Cities." In his *Harvests of Change: American Literature, 1865-1914*, pp. 240-48. Englewood Cliffs, N. J.: Prentice-Hall, 1967.

Considers muckraking journalism primarily an expression of middle-class concerns about urban conditions, providing a focus for "vague feelings of hostility and frustration."

McClure, S. S. "Concerning Three Articles in this Number of *McClure's*, and a Coincidence that May Set Us Thinking." *McClure's* 20, No. 3 (January 1903): 336.

Editorial calling attention to three investigative series in *McClure's* and exhorting readers to be aware of and to combat corruption.

————. *My Autobiography.* New York: Frederick A. Stokes, 1914, 266 p.

Includes McClure's account of the founding of *McClure's* magazine and the inception of the muckraking movement, as well as anecdotes about many of the principal muckrakers.

Mott, Frank Luther. "Great Journals and Journalists of the West." In his *American Journalism: A History, 1690-1960*, pp. 561-77. New York: Macmillan, 1962.

Briefly assesses the muckraking movement.

Mowry, George E. "Genesis." In his *Theodore Roosevelt and the Progressive Movement*, pp. 3-35. Madison: University of Wisconsin Press, 1947.

Includes discussion of reform and muckraking movements during Roosevelt's presidency.

Pattee, Fred Lewis. "The Muck-Rake School." In his *The New*

American Literature: 1890-1930, pp. 144-59. New York: Cooper Square, 1968.

   Traces the rise of muckraking, calling S. S. McClure the "prime mover" of the campaign and mentioning the chief practioners of muckraking journalism and fiction.

Piott, Steven L. "The Lesson of the Immigrant: Views of Immigrants in Muckraking Magazines, 1900-1909." *American Studies* 19, No. 1 (Spring 1978): 21-33.

   Discusses short stories published in muckraking journals in the early 1900s that deal with the immigrant experience.

Reaves, Shiela. "How Radical Were the Muckrakers? Socialist Press Views, 1902-1906." *Journalism Quarterly* 61, No. 4 (Winter 1984): 763-70.

   Examines ways that Socialist publications responded to the muckraking movement.

Reynolds, Robert D., Jr. "The 1906 Campaign to Sway Muckraking Periodicals." *Journalism Quarterly* 56, No. 3 (Autumn 1979): 513-20, 589.

   Recounts the efforts of United States Senator John F. Dryden—who was president of the Prudential Life Insurance Company—to suppress publication of a negative article about his business practices in the October 1906 *Cosmopolitan.*

Rose, L. A. "Shortcomings of 'Muckraking in the Gilded Age'." *American Literature* 14, No. 2 (May 1942): 161-64.

   Refutes Edward Cassady's "Muckraking in the Gilded Age" (above), maintaining that it is inadequately supported by insufficient research.

Russell, Charles Edward. "Muck-Raking and Muck-Rakers." In his *Bare Hands and Stone Walls: Some Recollections of a Side-Line Reformer,* pp. 131-47. New York: Charles Scribner's Sons, 1933.

   Discusses some of the chief muckraking series by Russell and others in *Everybody's,* the *American,* and several other muckraking journals.

Schultz, Stanley K. "The Morality of Politics: The Muckrakers' Vision of Democracy." *The Journal of American History* 52, No. 3 (December 1965): 527-47.

   Attempts to abstract a consensual view of political ethics from the writings of the muckrakers.

Semonche, John E. "The *American* Magazine of 1906-15: Principle vs. Profit." *Journalism Quarterly* 40, No. 1 (Winter 1963): 36-44, 86.

   Finds that the *American* magazine did not become a significant moneymaking concern until most of the muckrakers left the staff and "the journal made an unabashed, sentimental appeal to the family audience."

Shapiro, Herbert. "The Muckrakers and Negroes." *Phylon* 31, No. 1 (1970): 76-88.

   Assesses the coverage of racial issues by early twentieth-century exposé journalists, commenting that "it is remarkable how little imprint the race question made upon some of the outstanding muckrakers."

———. "Steffens, Lippmann, and Reed: The Muckraker and His Protégés." *Pacific Northwest Quarterly* 62, No. 4 (October 1971): 142-50.

   Discusses the personal and professional relationships that developed among Lincoln Steffens, Walter Lippmann, and John Reed.

———. "Lincoln Steffens: The Muckraker Reconsidered." *The American Journal of Economics and Sociology* 31, No. 4 (October 1972): 427-38.

   Considers Steffens's impact on his times and his continued relevance as a thinker.

Sinclair, Upton. "Revolt." In his *The Autobiography of Upton Sinclair,* pp. 99-126. New York: Harcourt, Brace & World, 1962.

   Includes an account of the circumstances under which Sinclair researched and wrote *The Jungle* and the difficulties he encountered in finding a publisher.

Steffens, Lincoln. *The Autobiography of Lincoln Steffens.* 2 vols. New York: Literary Guild, 1931.

   Anecdotal autobiography that includes lively accounts of Steffens's early days as a newspaper reporter and his work as a muckraker.

Stein, Harry H. "Theodore Roosevelt and the Press: Lincoln Steffens." *Mid-America* 54, No. 2 (April 1972): 94-107.

   Explores President Roosevelt's relationship with Steffens and his dealings with the American press.

———. "The Muckraking Book in America, 1946-1973." *Journalism Quarterly* 52, No. 2 (Summer 1975): 297-303.

   Considers the practice of muckraking American business and politics to be flourishing well into the twentieth century.

———. "American Muckrakers and Muckraking: The 50-Year Scholarship." *Journalism Quarterly* 56, No. 1 (Spring 1979): 9-17.

   Surveys fifty years of scholarship devoted to American muckraking journalism.

Tarbell, Ida M. *All in the Days Work: An Autobiography.* New York: Macmillan, 1939, 412 p.

   Includes reminiscences about muckraking for *McClure's,* research, writing, and publication of *The History of the Standard Oil Company,* and an account of the staff exodus from *McClure's* in 1906.

Ziff, Larzer. "The School in the Cemetery: Newspapers." In his *The American 1890s: Life and Times of a Lost Generation,* pp. 146-65. New York: Viking, 1966.

   Examines muckraking efforts of early twentieth-century newspaper reporters.

New Criticism

INTRODUCTION

The New Criticism comprises various theories and practices advanced by a loosely affiliated group of American critics who reacted against prevailing methods of literary criticism in the 1930s. Turning away from critical methods that employed a psychological or sociological approach, the New Critics examined a work of literature as an object in itself through close analysis of such literary elements as symbol, image, and metaphor. For the New Critics, a literary work was not a manifestation of ethics, sociology, or psychology, and could not be evaluated in the general terms of any nonliterary discipline. They considered the old notion of personal taste unimportant, championing instead a methodology that could be "learned and imitated." Drawing on critical theories advanced by T. S. Eliot, I. A. Richards, and others, the New Critics—so labeled after the publication of John Crowe Ransom's *The New Criticism,* which identified the criticism of Ransom, Cleanth Brooks, and Allen Tate with the views of Eliot, Richards, William Empson, Yvor Winters, and R. P. Blackmur—are considered revolutionary for their attempt to establish definitive standards of literary excellence.

With the publication in 1938 of *Understanding Poetry: An Anthology for College Students,* a textbook containing poetry with accompanying analyses by Brooks and Robert Penn Warren, New Criticism entered the university classroom and during the 1940s and 1950s enjoyed a period of wide acceptance. Opponents of the movement viewed the New Critics as advocating a program of art-for-art's-sake and denigrated their neglect of the biographical and historical context of works. Eventually, other critical doctrines emerged and drew attention away from New Criticism, and its influence largely faded in the 1960s. The revolutionizing legacy of the New Criticism may be seen in the modern nature and perception of criticism, which in the twentieth century has developed from a combination of subjective impressions and extraliterary scholarship into a professional academic discipline.

REPRESENTATIVE WORKS

Blackmur, R. P.
The Double Agent: Essays in Craft and Elucidation (criticism) 1935
Language as Gesture: Essays in Poetry (criticism) 1935
The Expense of Greatness (criticism) 1940
The Lion and the Honeycomb: Essays in Solicitude and Critique (criticism) 1955
New Criticism in the United States (criticism) 1959
Brooks, Cleanth
Modern Poetry and the Tradition (criticism) 1939
The Well Wrought Urn: Studies in the Structure of Poetry (criticism) 1947
The Hidden God: Studies in Hemingway, Faulkner, Yeats, Eliot, and Warren (criticism) 1963

A Shaping Joy: Studies in the Writer's Craft (criticism) 1971
Brooks, Cleanth, and Heilman, Robert B., eds.
Understanding Drama (textbook) 1945
Brooks, Cleanth, and Warren, Robert Penn, eds.
Understanding Poetry: An Anthology for College Students (textbook) 1938
Understanding Fiction (textbook) 1943
Brooks, Cleanth; Purser, John Thibaut; and Warren, Robert Penn, eds.
An Approach to Literature: A Collection of Prose and Verse with Analyses and Discussions (textbook) 1941
Eliot, T. S.
The Sacred Wood: Essays on Poetry and Criticism (criticism) 1920
The Use of Poetry and the Use of Criticism: Studies in the Relation of Criticism to Poetry in England (criticism) 1933
After Strange Gods: A Primer of Modern Heresy (criticism) 1934
Empson, William
Seven Types of Ambiguity (criticism) 1930
Heilman, Robert B.
This Great Stage: Image and Structure in "King Lear" (criticism) 1948
Leavis, F. R.
Revaluation: Tradition and Development in English Poetry (criticism) 1936
Ransom, John Crowe
God without Thunder: An Unorthodox Defense of Orthodoxy (criticism) 1930
The World's Body (criticism) 1938
The New Criticism (criticism) 1941
Poetics (criticism) 1942
Selected Essays of John Crowe Ransom (criticism) 1984
Richards, I. A.
Principles of Literary Criticism (criticism) 1924
Science and Poetry (criticism) 1926
Practical Criticism (criticism) 1929
Coleridge on Imagination (criticism) 1934
Tate, Allen
Reactionary Essays on Poetry and Ideas (criticism) 1936
Reason in Madness: Critical Essays (criticism) 1941
On the Limits of Poetry: Selected Essays, 1928-1948 (criticism) 1948
The Hovering Fly, and Other Essays (criticism) 1949
The Forlorn Demon: Didactic and Critical Essays (criticism) 1953
The Man of Letters in the Modern World: Selected Essays. 1928-1955 (criticism) 1955
The Poetry Reviews of Allen Tate (criticism) 1983
Warren, Robert Penn
Selected Essays (criticism) 1958
Wellek, René, and Warren, Austin
Theory of Literature (criticism) 1949

Wimsatt, W. K., Jr.
   The Verbal Icon: Studies in the Meaning of Poetry
      (criticism) 1954
Wimsatt, W. K., Jr., and Brooks, Cleanth
   Literary Criticism: A Short History (history) 1957
Winters, Yvor
   *Primitivism and Decadence: A Study of American
      Experimental Poetry* (criticism) 1937
   *Maule's Curse: Seven Studies in the History of American
      Obscurantism* (criticism) 1938
   Anatomy of Nonsense (criticism) 1943
   In Defense of Reason (criticism) 1947
   The Function of Criticism (criticism) 1957

DEVELOPMENT AND IDEAS

ARNOLD L. GOLDSMITH

[*Goldsmith is an American critic and educator. In the following excerpt, he examines the critical principles of the major figures associated with the New Criticism.*]

The most important critical movement of the first half of the
twentieth century is the one often called the Analytical or
Formal or, adopting the title of John Crowe Ransom's study
of four contemporary critics in 1941, the New Criticism. To
a considerable extent it developed as a reaction against [ethi-
cal, sociological, psychological, and impressionistic schools
of criticism]. Despite its excesses and internal controversies,
its approach to literature has probably been more influential
in this country in the last thirty years than all the other
schools combined. Its practitioners have repeatedly insisted
that to understand and appreciate a literary work, particularly a poem, you have to read it closely. In the hyperbole of the
English critic David Daiches, "The New Criticism has taught
a whole generation to read."

From the beginning—and this has been one of its limitations—the New Criticism has been interested primarily in poetry. Its main objective has been to discover the unique qualities of a poem, the craftsmanship and poetic use of language
which distinguish it from all other uses. Whether the critic's
favorite terms are *intension* or *extension, paradox* or *irony,
texture* or *form, ontological* or *dramatic,* all are bent on seeing
the poem as a whole after divorcing it as completely as possible from its historical and social context. In a sense, the New
Criticism is an attack on the value of the old survey courses
with their treatment of literature as documents in the history
of ideas. It is a rejection of Carlylean hero worship and the
biographical approach. This extrinsic approach is replaced
with an intrinsic analysis of a work's structure and texture
in order to get at its totality of meaning.

The ambivalences of the New Criticism reveal its complexity.
[In his *An Age of Criticism: 1900-1950*] William Van
O'Connor sees the movement as actually "a continuation of
nineteenth-century criticism" stemming from Coleridge. It is
new only in the sense that it "borrows from contemporary anthropology, philosophy, and psychology. . . ." The New
Critics shared with Coleridge an interest in the psychology
of poetic creativity and the organic unity of the created work.

On the other hand, they reacted against an impressionistic,
romantic criticism with its emphasis on the personality of the
author and the emotional reaction of the critic. From the
nineteenth century the New Critics inherited a distrust of science and technological domination, but in their distrust of
anarchic individualism and their quest for tradition and
order, they sometimes seemed as neoclassical as the New Humanists. One further paradox is seen in their rejection of the
eighteenth-century neoclassical view that literature should be
both decorative and didactic. At the same time, as Murray
Krieger has observed in *The New Apologists for Poetry* (1956),
they "had equally to eschew an 'art for art's sake' position
which would trivialize literature. They had somehow to assert at once the autonomy of art and its unique power to give
meaning to our experience, a power allowed only by its autonomy."

Of the many influences on the New Criticism, three are especially significant: T. E. Hulme, I. A. Richards, and Ezra
Pound. Hulme, the bright young English philosopher who
was killed in World War I, led the attack on the subjectivity
and vagueness of Wordsworth and Coleridge, calling instead
for objectivity, discipline, and hard dry images in poetry.
These challenging new concepts soon became the foundation
of the Imagist movement, but actually Hulme was a conservative influence on twentieth-century British and American
criticism (e.g., Eliot, Pound, Richards, and Tate) with his
philosophical belief in man's tragic limitations and his classical concept of art and criticism as the handmaiden of political
conservatism and religious orthodoxy.

Pound's influence can be seen in his catholic taste in literature, his dislike of the nineteenth century, his comparative
method, his theory of the impersonality of the artist, and his
practice as a poet-scholar. Both Pound and Eliot introduced
French Symbolist poetry to English literature, and the new
techniques they employed soon found a receptive audience.
The French Symbolists placed their hard, clear images so
skillfully into the poem's total pattern of meaning that the
consequent overtones gave the verse a subtlety and texture
which could not be found in ordinary prose. Equally important to the development of the New Criticism was Pound's
early interest in psychoanalysis, which gave him insights into
the function of imagery.

The English critic I. A. Richards, credited by Ransom with
being the founder of the New Criticism, was another pioneer
in the use of the psychological approach to literature, particularly interested in the reaction of the feeling and motor impulses in the poetic reading experience. In *Principles of Literary Criticism* (1924) and *Science and Poetry* (1926), he explored the "referential meaning" of science and informative
writing as against the emotive meaning of verse, a difference
which has obsessed so many of the New Critics. Richards's
close reading of poems, with his concentration on semantics,
imagery, irony, and metaphor, became an important part of
the method of the New Critics, even though they fought over
the views he expressed in *Coleridge on Imagination* (1935).
Unlike Pound and Eliot, Richards favored the Romantics,
and combined their theories with the new psychology.
"Thus," as Walter Sutton has observed, "although ostensibly
developing a critical theory 'scientific' in its language and
methods, Richards [was] actually using the resources of science to refurbish and translate into twentieth century terms
nineteenth century romantic ideas."

No one label can adequately describe the wide range of the

contribution of T. S. Eliot (1888-1965) to modern criticism. . . . Eliot's close reading of the works of his predecessors also places him in the tradition of such famous poet-critics as Jonson, Dryden, and Coleridge. At the same time he has been one of the guiding lights of the New Criticism.

To the disapproval of Ransom, Wilson once described Eliot's kind of comparative criticism as "non-historical." By this Wilson meant that Eliot saw spread out behind him all of past literature in one continuum, "as if the whole of literature existed simultaneously in a vacuum. . . ." By comparing works of different times and places, but unconcerned with the influence of time and place, Eliot was able to arrive at generalizations about what a literary work should be. Each new work added to the mainstream changes in some way our understanding and appreciation of both the past works and the total accretion. In this way, Wilson explained, ". . . Sophocles is no longer precisely what he was for Aristotle, or Shakespeare what he was for Ben Jonson or for Dryden or for Dr. Johnson, on account of all the later literature that has intervened between them and us." The critic thus views literature "as God might; he calls the books to a Day of Judgment. And, looking at things in this way, he may arrive at interesting and valuable conclusions which could hardly be reached by approaching them any other way." Eliot was thus the first to see "that the French Symbolist poetry of the nineteenth century had certain fundamental resemblances to the English poetry of the age of Donne." (pp. 102-05)

Though it has become traditional for histories of modern criticism to discuss Eliot's aesthetic theories as influential on the development of the New Criticism, some scholars, like Murray Krieger, have argued that the New Critics should not even be considered as a school or group with "a single and defined entity." As he and others have pointed out, even though Ransom gave the movement its name with his book, several earlier critics, namely Brunetière, Lewisohn, and Spingarn, not considered New Critics today, once labeled their work as "new criticism." Furthermore, objected Krieger, the movement lacked a "foundation of aesthetic theory." The three main concerns of the New Critics, as he saw them, were 1) "the psychology of poetic creativity," 2) "the structure of the poem as aesthetic object, viewed in terms of a definition of the aesthetic experience," and 3) "the unique function of poetry." The leading figures who shared these interests are John Crowe Ransom, Cleanth Brooks, Allen Tate, R. P. Blackmur, Yvor Winters, René Wellek, and Robert Penn Warren. (Kenneth Burke could also be added to this list. . . .)

The chairman of the board of the New Critics was John Crowe Ransom (1888-1974). "Perhaps I use a distasteful figure," he wrote in 1938 in *The World's Body,* "but I have the idea that what we need is Criticism, Inc., or Criticism, Ltd." Reacting against the didacticism of the Victorians, Humanists, and Marxists, and finding the current state of criticism deplorable, he urged all university teachers of English to join the movement and raise the level of professional criticism to new heights. Despite his own looseness of terms, his restricted range and oversimplifications, as teacher, editor (*The Kenyon Review*), critic, and theoretician, he won the respect of and had great influence on many of his colleagues.

Like some of the other conservative Southern Agrarians, Ransom began his career with a defense of orthodox religion and an attack on science in *God without Thunder* (1930). In 1934 he turned to literary criticism in "Poetry: A Note on Ontology," pointing out the limited achievement of the Imagists, attacking the didactic and moralistic verse which he called "Platonic" or "bogus" poetry, and lavishing praise on the metaphysicals' startling use of figurative language.

In "Criticism as Pure Speculation," a paper Ransom delivered as part of a symposium in 1941 with Norman Foerster (representing the New Humanism) and Edmund Wilson (Marxism), Ransom continued his attack on the moralistic and sociological approaches to literary criticism with "their equal inadequacy to the reading of the poet's intention. The moralistic critics wish to isolate and discuss the 'ideology' or theme or paraphrase of the poem and not the poem itself," he complained. To Ransom, "the business of the literary critic is exclusively with an esthetic criticism." For one thing, "ethical character is not universal" in poetry and even though the poet might consider an ethical situation, his view is not the same as the moralist's, which would be defined in prose. Ransom considered himself in partial agreement with Schopenhauer, who described poetic creation as an objectification of an act of will—in other words, a contemplative act, not an actual deed, "and therefore qualitatively a very different experience, knowledge without desire." But Schopenhauer's theory was too negative. Ransom preferred to express the difference this way: "Art is more cool than hot, and moral fervor is as disastrous to it as a burst of passion itself."

In this same essay Ransom elaborated on two of his favorite terms, while giving his personal definition of poetry: "A poem is *a logical structure* having *a local texture.*" To Ransom, the prime interest of the critic is his examination of the poetic "increment," that is, the texture enveloping the substance which, incidently, might be an ethical situation. To clarify this distinction, he drew an analogy from architecture. Beams, boards, and plaster all have a functional purpose and can be considered structure, whereas painting, wall paper, and tapestry are all part of texture. "The values of the poem would be intrinsic, or immediate, and they would include not only the value of the structure but also the incidental values to be found in the texture. . . . In saying intrinsic or immediate, I mean that the poet is fond of the precise objects denoted by the words, and writes the poem for the reason that he likes to dwell upon them." Drawing on music for another analogy, Ransom referred to the affective nature of tones which combine to make brilliant harmony.

One of Ransom's favorite words was *ontological,* which he used in conjunction with his structure-texture duality to get at the essence, the very being and reality of poetry. This essence is ultimately metaphysical. It goes beyond the paraphrasable structure of the poem (i.e. its logic, its rational guidelines) and incorporates all the inexhaustible enrichments of texture which give the sophisticated reader such intense pleasure.

Though a leading spokesman for the New Criticism, Ransom showed no reluctance to find fault with others associated with the movement. His traditional concept of a poem's logical structure, with its beginning, middle, and end, and all the necessary transitions as well as conventional meter and rhymes, led to his dislike of modern verse experimentation, in particular his early attack on Eliot's *The Waste Land.* Though he praised Eliot highly as a scholarly critic, he questioned Eliot's evaluative ability and his fixation on the past. Yvor Winters, whose concept of structure was closer to Ransom's own than that of any other New Critic, he ironically criticized for ignoring texture, and because of Winters's insistence on morality, he considered him primarily a critic of prose. And though Ransom continued to argue that moral criteria have no place in literary criticism and that the critic's undivided attention must be given to technical matters, he censured Cleanth Brooks's exclusive treatment of such matters in *The Well Wrought Urn.* The reason for this apparent contradiction was his fear that Brooks's obsession with paradox and the interrelationship of words was too fragmentary an approach and needed the counterbalance of an attempt at synthesis. Too exclusive a study of texture in this case resulted in the neglect of structure and the poem as a whole.

Reading the criticism of Burke, Blackmur, and Wimsatt in the 1940s and 1950s reinforced Ransom's fear that the New Criticism was losing sight of the human meanings, the ideology, supporting the texture of poetry. Aristotle he saw as the successful critic synthesizing both the lower level of "academic scholarship" (i.e. study of language, period, and biography) and the higher, which is the more speculative and ontological. From the New Critics' fascination with the abstractions of Coleridge, Ransom turned to Wordsworth, who realized that human "affections focus upon concretions." Even his Southern Agrarian antipathy to science softened. However, underlying both his poetry (for which he won the National Book Award in 1964) and almost forty years of criticism was his fundamental concept of life as a constant tension between irreconcilable opposites.

In 1938, the same year that Ransom challenged America's English professors to elevate the level of criticism, Cleanth Brooks (1906–), one of his students at Vanderbilt, and Robert Penn Warren (1905–) published their revolutionary new textbook, *Understanding Poetry: An Anthology for College Students* (rev. 1950, 1960). Introducing the New Criticism with commendable clarity to an undergraduate audience, the authors taught new generations of students how to read poems of all periods. Minimizing the traditional biographical, sociological, and moral approach to poetry, Brooks and Warren analyzed the effect of words, rhythms, structures, and poetic techniques on the total meaning of those poems selected for analysis. The underlying premise of all three editions of the book was underscored in 1960, when Brooks and Warren wrote: "The knowledge that poetry yields is available to us only if we submit ourselves to the massive, and subtle, impact of the poem as a whole. We have access to this special kind of knowledge only by participating in the drama of the poem, apprehending the form of the poem."

The problems of unity and form became the obsessions of the New Critics. Brooks laid down their basic beliefs in 1951 in *The Kenyon Review,* when he wrote that "the primary concern of criticism is with the problem of unity—the kind of whole which the literary work forms or fails to form, and the relation of the various parts to each other in building up this whole." Above all, "in a successful work, form and content cannot be separated" because "form is meaning" and "literature is ultimately metaphorical and symbolic." The formalistic critic is interested not in the author or the audience but the work itself. Speculation on the author's mental or psychological state "describe[s] the process of composition, not the structure of the thing composed, and [it] may be performed quite as validly for the poor work as for the good one. [It] may be validly performed for any kind of expression—nonliterary as well as literary." Concentrating on the work itself, the formalist critic makes two assumptions: first, "that the

author's intention *as realized* is the 'intention' that counts, not necessarily what he was conscious of trying to do, or what he now remembers he was then trying to do." And second, that he is dealing with "an ideal reader: that is, instead of focusing on the varying spectrum of possible readings, he attempts to find a central point of reference from which he can focus upon the structure of the poem or novel." Reducing a poem or story "to its causes does not constitute literary criticism; nor does an estimate of its effects." Furthermore, what the formalist critic insists upon "is that literature does not simply 'exemplify' ideas or 'produce' ideas," but, at the same time, neither does he claim "that the writer is an inspired idiot. . . . Literature is not inimical to ideas. It thrives upon ideas, but it does not present life patly and neatly. It involves them with the 'recalcitrant stuff of life.' The literary critic's job is to deal with that involvement."

Another important statement of Brooks's critical theory can be found in "Irony as a Principle of Structure" (1949), a discussion of the interaction of metaphor, image, symbol, and irony. It is the poet's "commitment to metaphor" that he considered the essential technique of modern poetry. In rejecting the static concept of a poem as a bouquet of beautiful images, he argued for "a principle of organic relationship," and like Kenneth Burke, conceived of each poem as "a little drama." It is the context of the poem which "endows the particular word or image or statement with significance. Images so charged become symbols." In this way "The part is modified by the pressure of the context," and "the *obvious* warping of a statement by the context we characterize as 'ironical'." Following the lead of Eliot and Richards, he saw poetry as arriving at some kind of synthesis of opposite forces involving "thrust and counterthrust." The result is an organic relationship between the parts, "which means each part modifies and is modified by the whole."

In *The Well Wrought Urn* (1947), in which he analyzed ten poems in the main stream of English poetry from Donne to Yeats, Brooks developed more fully his theory of organic structure. To Brooks the "essential structure" of a poem "resembles that of architecture or painting: it is a pattern of resolved stresses." Ballet and music furnished him with further analogies, but ultimately he came back to the Burkean idea of drama and conflict. "The dynamic nature of drama, in short, allows us to regard it as *an action* rather than as a formula for action or as a statement about action." The end of the poem "is the working out of the various tensions—set up by whatever means—by propositions, metaphors, symbols," and the unity of a poem is achieved "by its ability to resolve the conflicts which have been accepted as the *données* of the drama." In this way metrical pattern and metaphor are not mere embellishment but function relevantly in that they "modify, qualify, and develop the total attitude which we are to take in coming to terms with the total situation."

Brooks objected to any school of criticism which considered poetry a "formula" or "logical process." To him it was a "dramatization, . . . a controlled experience which has to be *experienced*" by the reader. The great danger in reading a poem for its theme only is reductivism. The reader ends up with a substitution for the "complex of attitudes" which is the poem. "To do this, is to take the root or the blossoms of the tree for the tree itself." Extending this organic image further, Brooks complained that "Our staple study of literature consists in investigations of the root system (the study of literary sources) or in sniffing the blossoms (impressionism), or—

not to neglect Yeats's alternative symbol—in questioning the quondam dancer, no longer a dancer, about her life history (the study of the poet's biography)."

In the final chapter of *The Well Wrought Urn* Brooks returned once again to the idea of structure, which he considered much more important than subject matter. Struggling with the inadequacy of terminology, he redefined the key word. *Structure* does not mean " 'form' in the conventional sense in which we think of form as a kind of envelope which 'contains' the 'content'." By *structure* Brooks meant "a structure of meanings, evaluations, and interpretations; and the principle of unity which informs it seems to be one of balance and harmonizing connotations, attitudes, and meanings." By *balance* and *harmony* Brooks did not mean "homogeneous grouping pairing like with like. It unites the like with the unlike. It does not unite them, however, by the simple process of allowing one connotation to cancel out another nor does it reduce the contradictory attitudes to harmony by a process of subtraction. The unity is not a unity of the sort to be achieved by the reduction and simplification appropriate to an algebraic formula. It is a positive unity, not a negative; it represents not a residue but an achieved harmony."

Brooks's critique of Eliot's "The Waste Land" in *Modern Poetry and the Tradition* (1939) is an excellent example of the New Criticism at its best. Rejecting Wilson's interpretation of the poem as essentially pessimistic and full of despair, Brooks concentrated on Eliot's techniques of contrast and complexity: "The poet works in terms of surface parallelisms which in reality make ironical contrasts, and in terms of surface contrasts which in reality constitute parallelisms." The result is "a sense of revelation out of material apparently accidentally thrown together. I have called the effect the obverse of irony, for the method, like that of irony, is indirect, though the effect is positive rather than negative." In other words, underneath the poem's intentional ambiguity and surface negativism is the core of Christian material which is always dealt with indirectly. "Eliot's theme," then, which Wilson failed to see, "is the rehabilitation of a system of beliefs, known but now discredited":

> To put the matter in still other terms: the Christian terminology is for the poet here a mass of clichés. However 'true' he may feel the terms to be, he is still sensitive to the fact that they operate superficially as clichés, and his method of necessity must be a process of bringing them to life again. The method adopted in *The Waste Land* is thus violent and radical but thoroughly necessary. For the renewing and vitalizing of symbols which have been crusted over with a distorting familiarity demands the type of organization which we have already commented on in discussing particular passages: the statement of surface similarities which are ironically revealed to be dissimilarities, and the association of apparently obvious dissimilarities which culminates in a later realization that the dissimilarities are only superficial—that the chains of likeness are in reality fundamental. In this way the statement of beliefs emerges through confusion and cynicism—not in spite of them.

Throughout *The Well Wrought Urn* Brooks ignored the historical backgrounds of the poems he analyzed and sought instead their universal qualities. He pointed out the richness of connotative language and many paradoxes, both conscious and unconscious, in Wordsworth's sonnet "Composed upon Westminster Bridge" and his famous "Ode." He showed how

Milton's symbolic use of light in "L'Allegro" and "Il Penseroso" helped "bring the patterns of opposites together—to build up an effect of unity in variety." He delved into the ambiguities of Keats's "Ode on a Grecian Urn," avoiding the intentional heresy by asking "not what did Keats the man perhaps want to assert here about the relation of beauty and truth," but rather, "was Keats the poet able to exemplify that relation in this particular poem?" By carefully analyzing the poem's metaphors and paradoxes and its reiteration of certain motifs, he demonstrated the way the closing lines have been "dramatically prepared for."

The difficulty so many readers have with modern poetry, Brooks explained, is caused by its indirection. "The reader must be on the alert for shifts of tone, for ironic statement, for suggestion rather than direct statement." Readers used to poetry as history are unable to read *"poetry as poetry."* They are conditioned by the "heresy of paraphrase." Once "we allow ourselves to be misled by the heresy of paraphrase, we run the risk of doing even more violence to the internal order of the poem itself. By taking the paraphrase as our point of stance, we misconceive the function of metaphor and meter. We demand logical coherences where they are sometimes irrelevant, and we fail frequently to see imaginative coherences on levels where they are highly relevant."

The weaknesses of Brooks's criticism have not gone unnoticed by his detractors. Herbert Muller argued that Brooks "considers only technique, mechanism, outward show. He overlooks the underlying attitude, the world view, the quality of mind, the informing spirit—all that makes Donne's poetry much greater than Herbert's, and very different from Mr. Ransom's, and that enables a Shakespeare or a Goethe to be as simple, forthright, eloquent as he pleases." In his defense Brooks simply pointed out that he was less interested in the poet's mind than the work itself. Critical relativism, he argued, will only result in the eventual death of criticism. Once the methods of the formalist critics are accepted, "We will then judge Wordsworth, not by the standards of the Age of Pope nor by those of the Age of Donne. Each period will be considered *sui generis;* we will have criticisms, not *Criticism.*" Brooks was "convinced that, once we are committed to critical relativism, there can be no stopping short of a *complete* relativism in which critical judgments will disappear altogether."

Another incisive complaint brought against Brooks was that of Murray Krieger, who felt that Brooks placed too great a premium on complexity as though "the more complexity a poem has, the better it is. Indeed to make such a demand, as Brooks seems to, is to set up complexity as a mechanical demand, one that would violate the integrity of the poem as much as would other mechanical demands which Brooks would abhor." As Krieger wisely observed, complexity is only a subordinate, relative attribute of poetry, "limited by the formed and orderly entity which is the total poem."

Despite the valid criticisms of Muller and Krieger, Brooks's contributions to the New Criticism remain impressive. As persuasive a theoretician as Ransom, he has gone beyond his teacher with the close application of his theories to the poetry of Donne, Wordsworth, Yeats, and others. His sensitive analyses of metaphor, paradox, and irony have pointed up the aesthetic blindness of sociological criticism to the organic nature of poetry, and his reminder that "the poet is most truthfully described as a *poietes* or maker, not as an expositor or

Allen Tate, Richard Chase, William Empson, Cleanth Brooks, John Crowe Ransom, and F.O. Matthiessen at Kenyon College, 1948.

communicator," is one of the great lessons of the New Criticism.

Another prominent member of the Southern School who disapproved of the sociological approach to literary criticism is Allen Tate (1899-1979). Reacting sharply against the Marxist criticism of such men as Rahv, Gold, Calverton, and Hicks, he wrote in the preface to his appropriately named *Reactionary Essays* (1936) that "a political poetry, or a poetical politics, of whatever denomination is a society of two members living on each other's washing. They devour each other in the end. It is the heresy of spiritual cannibalism." To Tate, who also rejected the other extreme (i.e. Richards's arguing that ultimately poetry "has no meaning at all"), poetry "is the art of apprehending and concentrating our experience in the mysterious limitations of form."

According to one of his detractors, Alfred Kazin, Tate's criticism is "a fantastic inversion of the Marxist system; and in him the extremities met as in no other critic of the time. The Marxist critic could study a work of art only in terms of its social relations; Tate would study literature—that is, only poetry of a certain intensity and difficulty—precisely because it had no social relations at all." To Kazin, "The Marxists made life and literature indistinguishable; Tate made life indistinguishable in literature." In other words, in rescuing lit-

erature from the scientists, and criticism from the impressionists and historians, Tate got rid of positivism, history, and "all extraneous vulgarities of circumstance. . . . Only the poem remained, and before it the critic worshiped as at a shrine, since in it was all human knowledge and all spiritual insight."

Kazin, of course, has overextended himself in the passion of his dislike for Tate. The latter, as John Pritchard and others have pointed out, has never been impervious to ideas. On the contrary, Tate has shown that the major philosophical poets like Donne and Milton have dealt with traditions and ideas so imbedded in their readers' minds that their poems do not have to be didactic. "Poetry does not dispense with tradition," Tate wrote in his essay on Emily Dickinson; "it probes the deficiencies of a tradition. But it must have a tradition to probe." Like Eliot, Tate has argued that literature must have "a social, or moral, or religious purpose," but these ideas should be so blended with the author's sensibility as to produce a work of art, not a sociological or religious tract.

One of Tate's pet dislikes was what he called the "heresy of the will." Poetry is not "a document to be used by the social will"; on the contrary, it "finds its usefulness in its perfect inutility." Thus the allegorical and moral poetry of the seventeenth century represents "the spirit of the practical will," which is inferior to the "poetry of genuine imagination." To Tate, even the works of I. A. Richards are just "the latest version of the allegorical, puritan and utilitarian theory of the arts—a theory that is rendered, by Mr. Richards, the more plausible because it seems to give to the arts a very serious attention." Tate saw Richards as ultimately doing a disservice to poetry: "his desperate efforts to make poetry, after all, useful, consist in justly reducing its 'explanation' to nonsense, and salvaging from the wreck a mysterious agency for 'ordering our minds'."

Tate's critical theory is most famous for his concept of tension. In "Tension in Poetry" (1938), Tate explained that he derived this term "from lopping the prefixes off the logical terms *ex*tension and *in*tension. What I am saying, of course, is that the meaning of poetry is its 'tension', the full organized body of all the extension and intension that we can find in it." Where Tate used the word "extension," another New Critic might have preferred "abstractness" or "denotation"; "intension" he identified with concreteness and connotation. According to Tate, the rationalistic metaphysical poets began on the extensive or denotative side, while the romantic symbolists began on the intensive, and each tried "by a straining feat of the imagination . . . to push his meanings as far as he [could] towards the opposite end, so as to occupy the entire scale." In short, what Tate is saying is that more significant than both the development of the paraphrasable point of a poem (its *ex*tension) and the original emotion and its metaphorical presentation (its *in*tension) is its *tension,* the complex patterning of the whole meaning.

An American poet who succeeded in bringing about this equilibrium, who perfectly fused sensibility and thought in the tradition of the great metaphysical poets, is Emily Dickinson. Tate scoffed at popular biographical approaches to Miss Dickinson's poetry: "All pity for Miss Dickinson's 'starved life' is misdirected. Her life was one of the richest and deepest ever lived on this continent." In her mastery of the world by rejecting it, Tate placed her in the tradition of Cotton Mather, Edwards, Hawthorne, and James. Because she faced life squarely, there is in her poetry "a clash of powerful opposites, and . . . it issues in a tension between abstraction and sensation in which the two elements may be, of course, distinguished logically, but not really." In the manner of Donne, "she *perceives abstraction* and *thinks sensation.*" Emily Dickinson "cannot reason at all. She can only *see.*" Another important source of tension in Miss Dickinson's poems is "the verbal conflict" which results from her unconscious mixture of words of Anglo-Saxon origin with those deriving from Greek and Latin.

Like the other New Critics, Tate has done his best work with poetry. In a statement reminiscent of Poe, Tate made clear in "Techniques of Fiction" (1948) the major problem of the formalist critic when confronted with a novel like *War and Peace* or *The Wings of the Dove.* Because of their length he "could not pretend to know them as wholes, and without that knowledge I lack the materials of criticism." A compromise could be reached, however, in analyzing the poetry of individual scenes, and that is just what Tate did with a brilliant analysis of a long scene from *Madame Bovary.* Acknowledging his debt to Henry James, with the novelist's interest in "all the major problems of 'picture and drama,' symmetry, foreshortening, narrative pattern, pace and language," Tate analyzed Flaubert's imaginative handling of "the complex texture of scene, character and action." Flaubert's success in rendering the action "in terms of situation and scene," without authorial intrusion, concluded Tate, is truly the "art of fiction."

The influence of Henry James can also be seen on the style, aesthetic sensibility, and dedication to a life of art of one of the most exacting of the New Critics, R. P. Blackmur (1904-1965). Like Richards, Blackmur showed great interest in linguistic analysis, but in "A Critic's Job of Work" he criticized Richards for trying to "transform literary criticism into the science of linguistics." The scientific approach, he argued, cannot be used as "an implement for the judgment of poetry. Actually, it can handle only the language and its words and cannot touch—except by assertion—the imaginative product of the words which is poetry: which is the object revealed or elucidated by criticism. Criticism must be concerned, first and last—whatever comes between—with the poem as it is and as what it represents is felt."

With his focus then on the poet's craftsmanship in unifying idea and imagination, Blackmur, in *The Double Agent,* evaluated the poetry of Marianne Moore, Hart Crane, E. E. Cummings, Wallace Stevens, T. S. Eliot, and others. In Cummings, whom Blackmur did not like, he found "the extreme form, in poetry, of romantic egoism: whatever I experience is real and final, and whatever I say represents what I experience." Examining closely some of the types of distortion Cummings used, Blackmur criticized his "vagueness of image and a constant recurrence of words." For example, Cummings added so many personal connotations to his favorite word *flower* that he divorced it from all historical meanings. "But when a word is used in a poem it should be the sum of all its appropriate history made concrete and particular in the individual context . . . ." Cummings heaped so many words together that "he destroy[ed] their individuality" and failed to communicate.

The vocabulary of Wallace Stevens is a different matter. Blackmur defended the poet's diction against the charges of "preciousness": not a word from the poems under discussion was "used preciously; not one was chosen as an elegant substitute for a plain term; each, in its context, was a word definitely meant. . . . It is the way that Mr. Stevens combines kinds of words, unusual in a single context, to reveal the substance he had in mind, which is of real interest to the reader." Both Cummings and Stevens are ambiguous poets, "but the ambiguity of Cummings is that of the absence of known content, the ambiguity of a phantom which no words could give being; while Mr. Stevens' ambiguity is that of a substance so dense with being, that it resists paraphrase and can be truly perceived only in the form of words in which it was given." Blackmur's conclusion is a perfect example of the New Criticism's attack on what Eliot called "the dissociation of sensibility," that separation of thought and feeling which had once been so perfectly fused in the best poetry of the metaphysicals:

> Mr. Stevens is a genuine poet in that he attempts constantly to transform what is felt with the senses and what is thought in the mind—if we can still distinguish the two—into that realm of being, which we call poetry, where what is thought is felt and what is felt has the strict point of thought. And I call his mode of achieving that transformation rhetorical because it is not lyric or dramatic or epic, because it does not transcend its substance, but is a reflection upon a hard surface, a shining mirror of rhetoric.

In *The Lion and the Honeycomb, Essays in Solitude and Critique* (1950), Blackmur turned his attention to prose, with studies of Henry Adams, Melville, Babbitt, and Henry James, along with general essays on critical theory and technique. His inability to appreciate the genius of Melville ("He added nothing to the novel as a form, and his work nowhere showed conspicuous mastery of the formal devices of fiction which he used") and his implied preference for the earlier, more dramatic novels of James are less satisfactory than his incisive comments on the success in failure of Adams in his search for the heresy of unity. In "Notes on Four Categories in Criticism," Blackmur formulated a hierarchy of critical levels, starting with the category of "superficial techniques," involving analyses of such primary devices as meter and plot, progressing to linguistic techniques (images and figures of speech) and then to "the ulterior technique of the imagination" (how the creative mind tries to recapture the richness of the original experience). The highest level is the investigation of "the symbolic imagination."

One of the most important essays in *The Lion and the Honeycomb* is "A Burden for Critics" (1948), in which Blackmur complained that the New Criticism, with all of its brilliance, has been too "facile." To him it had "dealt almost exclusively either with the executive technique of poetry (and only with a part of that) or with the general verbal techniques of language." Such criticism worked well at first with poets like Donne, Eliot, and Yeats, but "For most older poetry it is not suited for anything but sidelights, and has therefore made misjudgments when applied. It is useless for Dante, Chaucer, Goethe, or Racine. Applied to drama it is disfiguring, as it is to the late seventeenth- and all the eighteenth-century poetry." Above all, what criticism must do, said Blackmur, is develop "aesthetic judgment," and this is where the New Criticism often fails. Eliot's comparative, analytical approach is not enough.

Blackmur saw the critic as a double intermediary—between the reader and the work of art and between the artist and the art object. Blackmur wanted modern criticism to turn its attention to "symbolic techniques" so that it could explain "what happens in the arts—*what gets into the arts*—that makes them relatively inexhaustible so long as they are understood. I mean what happens in the arts by means of fresh annunciations of residual or traditional forces, whether in the language, culture, or institutions of the artist's society." What the critic must make clear is the rational way the executive, conceptual, and symbolic techniques ("the logic, the rhetoric, and the poetic") work together to make "the rationale of that enterprise in the discovery of life which is art."

Disapproving of the excessive obscurity of some potentially good modern poetry (which could benefit from a knowledge of meter) and the unfashionableness of "the full narrative mode" among writers of fiction and drama, Blackmur claimed that the effective critic can influence writers "to develop a skill in making positive statements, whether generalized or particular, whether in verse or in prose." What he sought "in the arts is rational intent, rational statement, and rational technique; and I want to do it through technical judgment, clarifying judgment, and the judgment of discovery, which together I call rational judgment." Despite all of his emphasis on the rational, Blackmur's ultimate ideal of literary criticism was almost mystical: a poem is to be judged "as a soul is judged finally, quite apart from its history, for what it really is at the moment of judgment."

In the essay "The Lion and the Honeycomb" (1950), deploring the excesses of both methodological scholarship and criticism, Blackmur called for a combination scholar-critic who would model himself after Aristotle and Coleridge, freely borrowing from these men certain key terms, such as *esemplastic, synergical,* and *praxis.* Fortunately, however, Blackmur, in his own writing, thought better of adding further confusion to the already esoteric terminology of the New Critics. In this same essay, after pointing out certain limitations in the criticism of Ransom, Brooks, Empson, and Burke, Blackmur feared that such specialization might result in an "omnicompetent methodology," a risk which "is underlined by the rhetorical nature of the skills. To put it another way, it is a natural sequence to move from art for art's sake to criticism for criticism's sake." Looking to the future, Blackmur concluded the essay with a call for the New Criticism to be applied to fiction—the direction in which he himself was moving with his essays on the European novel.

Probably the most balanced evaluation of Blackmur's contribution to literary criticism is Hyman's. After calling Blackmur's "lofty evaluation of art and the symbolic imagination" an "almost mystic religion," he observed how close it comes to being "precious, snobbish, out-of-the-world; in general, dilettantish." But "To balance the snobbishness there is his eloquent insistence on the social responsibility of the artist" and his refreshing humility. Above all, "Outweighing all the tentativeness and finickiness is the one certainty: of the high and absolute value of art and the human imagination." Although at times he skirts dangerously close to the very overspecialization he feared, he is, "with Empson, . . . the sharpest and closest reader of poetry we have. . . ."

It is impossible to categorize the exact affiliations of Yvor Winters (1900-1968), whose critical principles and practices allied him at one and the same time with the Neo-Humanists, the Impressionists, and the New Critics. Various commentators have placed him in direct line of descent from such earlier dogmatic evaluators of literature as Rymer, Dennis, Johnson, and Landor, with their classical and conservative biases. Hyman saw him also in the tradition of Sidney, Arnold, and Newman, his concept of art as "the permeation of human experience by a consistent moral understanding" an echo of Arnold's moralistic view of art as "the criticism of life."

In 1947, in his foreword to *In Defense of Reason,* Winters himself chose "moralistic" (for "lack of a better term") to distinguish his critical position from the "didactic, the hedonistic, and the romantic" critics who have been theorizing about literature for twenty-five hundred years. "The theory of literature which I defend in these essays," he went on to explain, "is absolutist. I believe that the work of literature, in so far as it is valuable, approximates a real apprehension and communication of a particular kind of objective truth." Admitting the theistic implications of his absolutism, he insisted that his "critical and moral notions are derived from the observations of literature and life," and that his theism stems from his "critical and moral notions. I did not proceed from the opposite direction."

Winters's unique theoretical synthesis of the moralism of the Neo-Humanists and the close analysis of the New Critics was clearly outlined in *The Anatomy of Nonsense,* where he listed the five key steps in the critical process. He began with the acceptance of "such historical or biographical knowledge as may be necessary in order to understand the mind and method of the writer," and supplemented this with an "analysis of his literary theories as we may need to understand and evaluate what he is doing." His third step was "a rational critique of the paraphrasable content (roughly the motive) of the poem," but his fourth separated him from the Neo-Humanists and allied him with the New Critics: "a rational critique of the feeling motivated—that is, of the details of style, as seen in language and technique . . . ." And it is in his metrical analyses of specific poems, his at times brilliant analyses of poetic structure, and his attempt in *Maule's Curse* to relate the history of ideas with a study of literary forms that Winters has tried to practice this fourth step in the critical process.

Winters's fifth point, however, revealed his singular contribution—his willingness to go beyond analysis and interpretation to evaluation of the literature he was studying. Thus the fifth step in the critical process is "the final act of judgment, a unique act, the general nature of which can be indicated, but which cannot be communicated precisely, since it consists in receiving from the poet his own final and unique judgment of his matter and in judging that judgment. It should be noted that the purpose of the first four processes is to limit as narrowly as possible the region in which the final unique act is to occur."

In all of his criticism, the one principle Winters consistently adhered to was his insistence on what he called the "moralistic" quality of literature. Poetry, he argued, should "increase the intelligence and strengthen the moral temper." Certainly Babbitt, whose influence he acknowledged, would have approved Winters's belief that "Poetic morality and poetic feeling are inseparable," and Winters's attack on Frost as "a spiritual drifter" who mistakes "whimsical impulse for moral choice" could have come from the pen of one of the New Humanists (whom Winters attacked for their "bastard impressionism," "moral Mechanism," and "spiritual bankruptcy").

In *Maule's Curse: Seven Studies in the History of American Obscurantism* (1938), Winters applied these same moral standards to the evaluation of the minds and works of seven major nineteenth-century American writers from Cooper to James, all of whom were "abnormally sensitive to the influence of European romanticism" and thus cursed, despite their varying degrees of talent. All seven, to some extent, contributed to that subjective disease of romanticism known as obscurantism, that is, "the development of the feeling in excess of the motive." Poe, whose reputation was at a peak before Winters's attack, was annihilated as being "exceptionally bad" in both theory and practice, his deficiency traced to his "failure to understand the moral basis of art, to his view of art as a kind of stimulant, ingeniously concocted, which may, if one is lucky, raise one to a moment of divine delusion." Cooper, whom Winters favored, "displays a great traditional moral sense corroded by the formulary romantic sentiment of his own period, and apparently with no realization that the two are incompatible." Emily Dickinson was "one of the greatest lyric poets of all time," but "of all the great poets, she is the most lacking in taste; there are innumerable beautiful lines and passages wasted in the desert of her crudities . . . ." Henry James, "one of the five or six greatest writers of any variety to be produced in North America . . . ," suffered from having tried to accomplish the impossible: "he was so obsessed with the problem of moral judgment in its relation to character, that he not only constructed his plots so that they turned almost wholly on problems of ethical choice, but he sought to isolate the ethical

problems as far as possible from all determining or qualifying elements, an effort which in any period would have led to difficulty, and which in his period would have been sufficient to dissolve in complete obscurity any talent save one of the greatest."

In *Primitivism and Decadence*, published a year before *Maule's Curse*, Winters analyzed some of those techniques in modern poetry which have also resulted in obscurantism. The first of these was what he called "pseudo-reference," such as Eliot's reference to a nonexistent plot involving Mr. Silvero, Hakagawa, and Madame de Tornquist in "Gerontion." Here the poet keeps his syntactic forms and "coherence of feeling," but without rational meaning. Similar techniques are the poet's referring explicitly or implicitly to "a non-existent symbolic value" or a purely private one—again the kind of subjective romanticism which Winters detested. Another kind of "pseudo-reference" Winters objected to was that found in the *Cantos* of Ezra Pound where there is "no attempt whatever at a rational progression," the poet proceeding "from image to image wholly through the coherence of feeling." Although he found unity of mood, variety, and aesthetic control, Winters rejected the poems as irreparably flawed because of their lack of rational content.

Winters's traditionalism is sometimes disappointingly superficial or scientifically inaccurate. In "Problems for the Modern Critic of Literature" (1956), he claimed that the difference between poetry and prose is simply "verse," verse being "metric or measured language. The measure controls the rhythm, and provides precision of rhythm. The resulting rhythm is more expressive of emotion than is the relatively loose rhythm of prose." In *Primitivism and Decadence* he claimed that free verse is actually scannable with an indefinite number of unaccented syllables or light accents within a long foot with one heavy accent. Another of Winters's questionable metrical theories is what Hyman has called "the fallacy of imitative rhythm, the idea that meters and metrical variations alone serve to suggest (rather than to reinforce) meaning or mood."

In attacking Milton's *Paradise Lost* and Spenser's *Fairie Queen* in *The Function of Criticism* (1957), Winters revealed his preference for the short poem which is essentially "expository." In the twentieth century he saw two different directions in poetry: "the decay of form has progressed rapidly in men such as Pound and Eliot; on the other hand there is a recovery of form in the best work of others, for example, Robinson, Stevens, Tate, Louise Bogan, Cunningham, Kunitz, and Bowers."

It is relatively easy to find fault with Winters's "reactionary" views (the adjective is his own), some of his erratic judgments, his cantankerous impoliteness in assaulting those who disagreed with him, and his incomprehensible ignorance of essential source materials (e.g., Hawthorne's *Journals*) which were available to him, but he nevertheless succeeded in helping to instigate—as he claimed in *The Function of Criticism* that he always tried to do—"a revolution . . . in critical thinking." He should be remembered for his critical dicta that poetic "feeling and technique, or structure, are inseparable," that it is an error to assume that "one can determine the ideas governing a work of art without making any attempt to understand the art as art," that good poetry is written for intelligent readers, that the best critical and historical analyses "are mere aspects of a single process," and that the logical structure of a poem is as important as its texture. One can easily ignore his somber insistence that the modern novel is almost dead, but his parting advice is well worth pondering:

> Unless there is a serious reconsideration of materials and methods, not merely in the interests of what may seem to the uninstructed to be novelty, but in the interests of intelligent achievement, the next generation will see the novel as dead as the drama is now. The most damnable fact about most novelists, I suppose, is their simple lack of intelligence. . . . They do not find it necessary so far as one can judge, to study the other forms of literature, or even forms of the novel other than those they practice; they do not find it necessary to think like mature men and women or to study the history of thought; they do not find it necessary to master the art of prose.

In 1949, the same year as Winters's *In Defense of Reason,* René Wellek (1903-) and Austin Warren (1899-) collaborated on *Theory of Literature,* unlike any other book previously published in the United States. Not a textbook or anthology like the influential volumes of Brooks and Robert Penn Warren, *Theory of Literature* was a novel attempt, its authors explained in their preface, "to unite 'poetics' (or literary theory) and 'criticism' (evaluation of literature) with 'scholarship' ('research') and 'literary history' (the 'dynamics' of literature, in contrast to the 'statics' of theory and criticism)." Here, then, is their acceptance of the challenge laid down by Ransom in 1941 in the final chapter of *The World's Body:* "Criticism must become more scientific, or precise and systematic, and this means that it must be developed by the collective and sustained effort of learned persons—which means that its proper seat is in the universities." Wellek and Warren realized that since each work of literature is both individual and general, "Literary theory, an *organon* of methods, is the great need of literary scholarship today." Arguing for the compatibility of scholarship and criticism, they nevertheless insisted on focusing literary study on the work itself, not its historical, sociological or psychological background.

Laying the groundwork for later chapters, they began with the preliminary observation that a literary work is "a highly complex organization of a stratified character with multiple meanings and relationships." The old separation of form and content is superficial and misleading. To analyze a work of art today the critic "has to begin with more complex questions: its mode of existence, its system of strata." As for the function of poetry, though its contributions of pleasure and usefulness cannot be overlooked, "Its prime and chief function is fidelity to its own nature."

In the chapter on "Literary Theory, Criticism, and History," Wellek added his voice to the attack on what Wimsatt and Beardsley have called "the intentional fallacy." "The meaning of a work of art is not exhausted by or even equivalent to, its intention. . . . The total meaning of a work of art cannot be defined merely in terms of its meaning for the author and his contemporaries. It is rather the result of a process of accretion, i.e. the history of its criticism by its many readers in many ages." What Wellek wanted was to understand a work of art in terms of both "the values of its own time and of all the periods subsequent to its own." He called this view "Perspectivism," which he defined as the recognition "that there is one poetry, one literature, comparable in all ages, developing, changing, full of possibilities. Literature is neither a series of unique works with nothing in common nor a series of works enclosed in time-cycles of Romanticism or Classi-

cism, the age of Pope and the age of Wordsworth." Aware of the charge of absolutism that can be brought against this theory, Wellek, like Cleanth Brooks, expressed a greater fear of relativism, with its "anarchy of values." Carrying his theory one step further in the next chapter, he called for a "universal literary history" that will "trace the growth and development of literature without regard to linguistic distinctions."

The next section of *Theory of Literature* turned to "The Extrinsic Approach." Here the intentional fallacy gave way to the "fallacy of origins." What starts out as the extrinsic study of literature in terms of its social context and antecedents often turns out to be "a 'causal' explanation, professing to account for literature to explain it, and finally to reduce it to its origins . . . ." To Wellek and Warren, a causal study of art, whether it investigates biography and psychology; economics, sociology and politics; intellectual history, theology, and the other arts; or "the Zeitgeist, some quintessential spirit of the time, some intellectual atmosphere or 'climate' of opinion," can never take the place of a descriptive analysis and evaluation of a literary work.

In the chapter on "Literature and Biography" Wellek continued the attack on the extrinsic approach with the statement that "The whole view that art is self-expression pure and simple, the transcript of personal feelings and experiences, is demonstrably false." The biographical approach is filled with too many traps. Writers "cannot be assigned the ideas, feelings, views, virtues, and vices of their heroes" because "Even when a work of art contains elements which can be surely identified as biographical, these elements will be so rearranged and transformed in a work that they lose all their specifically personal meaning and become simply concrete human material, integral elements of a work." Furthermore, the duplicitous nature of literature is such that "A work of art may rather embody the 'dream' of an author than his actual life, or it may be the 'mask,' the 'anti-self' behind which his real person is hiding, or it may be a picture of the life from which the author wants to escape." To end this chapter, Wellek listed some of the ways that the biographical approach can help scholarship if used intelligently (e.g., explaining allusions; showing an author's growth, maturation, and decline; his readings, friends, and travels). However, Wellek warned, "No biographical evidence can change or influence critical evaluation."

Although psychology can illuminate the creative process, Warren argued, it can never evaluate the work of art. In literature, "psychological truth is an artistic value only if it enhances coherence and complexity—if, in short, it is art." To Wellek, "Marxist criticism is at its best when it exposes the implied, or latent, social implications of a writer's work," but the critic must never forget (and this is the war cry of the New Critics) that "literature is no substitute for sociology or politics. It has its own justification and aim." Wellek offered similar arguments against the "History of Ideas" approach despite all of its illuminating insights. The real job of the critic is to study the way "ideas actually enter into literature."

The next section of the book was concerned with "The Intrinsic Study of Literature" which Wellek and Warren so obviously favored. To them the literary work should be "considered as a whole system of signs, or structure of signs, serving a specific aesthetic purpose." After rejecting the popular theory that all the arts have much in common, Wellek raised the ontological problem: "What is the 'real' poem; where should we look for it; how does it exist?" Four popular answers to this question struck him as inadequate. A poem is considerably more than the printed version, more than a sequence of sounds, more than "the mental experience of the reader," and more than the experience of the author (the intentional fallacy again). In his attempt to get at the structure, sign, and value of a work of art, Wellek suggested several strata which can be investigated, such as the sound stratum (which includes meter and rhythm), "the units of meaning which determine the formal linguistic structure of a work of literature," and image and metaphor, which in turn become symbol and myth. Also on his list were problems of literary genres, the special modes and techniques of narrative fiction, "the nature of literary history," and "the central problem of all criticism . . . evaluation." Subsequent chapters discussed these strata in turn.

One conclusion that Wellek arrived at was that sound and meter cannot be separated from meaning and should be studied as part of the totality of a poem. Another was that "stylistic analysis seems most profitable to literary study when it can establish some unifying principle, some general aesthetic aim pervasive of a whole work." Warren, in turn, carefully defined different types of metaphoric imagery, the pathetic fallacy, "the anthropomorphic imagination," and myth, rejecting biographical and psychological analyses of a poet's choice of images and concluding that the pattern of imagery "is part of the syntactical, or stylistic, stratum" and must be seen as part of the total picture. When Warren turned to the narrative mode of fiction and discussed such things as plot, characterization, setting, and point of view, he claimed that criticism of the novel has been far inferior to that of poetry, an opinion apparently shared by other New Critics as Tate, Blackmur, and Brooks began to turn their attention to fiction. And finally, Warren called for a return to the genre approach in criticism—without, of course, the rigidity of the classical view or that of the seventeenth and eighteenth centuries. To Wellek and Warren, a genre is "a grouping of literary works based, theoretically, upon both outer form (specific meter or structure) and upon inner form (attitude, tone, purpose—more crudely, subject and audience)." Their preference, however, was for genre criticism to "lean to the formalistic side," in other words, limited to " 'literary' kinds, not subject-matter classifications as might equally be made for nonfiction."

In the penultimate chapter Warren came to grips with the main problem of literary criticism—how to evaluate a work of art. He suggested that criticism start with problems of "organization and function. It is not what elements but how they are put together, and with what function, which determine whether a given work is or is not literature." Warren then summed up the formalistic approach: "The valuing of the poem is the experiencing, the realization, of aesthetically valuable qualities and relationships structurally present in the poem for any competent reader."

In the final chapter, Wellek, reminiscent of Eliot, conceived "of literature as a whole system of works which is, with the accretion of new ones, constantly changing its relationships, growing as a changing whole." Criticizing the traditional literary histories which usually divide periods according to political, social, or intellectual developments, he urged that "the literary period should be established by purely literary criteria." Critics should realize "that a period is not an ideal type or an abstract pattern or a series of class concepts, but

a time section, dominated by a whole system of norms, which no work of art will ever realize in its entirety."

Though *Theory of Literature* will surely be recognized as one of the monumental works of the New Criticism, its most conspicuous limitation is its slighting of the various extrinsic approaches and the importance of ideas in literature. Trilling, writing in *The Liberal Imagination,* justifiably complained that Wellek and Warren "presume ideas to be only the product of formal systems of philosophy, not remembering, at least on the occasion of their argument, that poets do have their effect in the world of thought." More recently, Walter Sutton, who found much in the book to praise, challenged such sweeping pronouncements as Wellek's "There is great literature which has little or no social relevance," and, "No biographical evidence can change or influence critical evaluation," and complained that they "have the effect of excommunicating from the body of true literary scholars . . ." all those critics who have successfully made use of the extrinsic method. To Sutton, Wellek's assertions cannot "withstand close scrutiny." (pp. 107-29)

Arnold L. Goldsmith, "The Intrinsic Approach: The New Criticism," in his American Literary Criticism: 1905-1965, Vol. III, *Twayne Publishers, 1979, pp. 102-31.*

GEORGE CORE

[*In the following excerpt, Core discusses the development of New Criticism, focusing on the influence of Southern culture on the New Critics and their progress through the Fugitive and Agrarian movements.*]

The New Criticism as we know it today is the issue of a complicated lineage. The modern progenitors are T. S. Eliot, I. A. Richards, and T. E. Hulme; their chief descendants on the English side are William Empson and the *Scrutiny* group, notably F. R. Leavis; on the American side, John Crowe Ransom, Allen Tate, Cleanth Brooks, Robert Penn Warren, R. P. Blackmur, Francis Fergusson, and Yvor Winters. (The list is not intended to be exhaustive; I am speaking of the progeny of principal houses—not of distant cousins and bastard offspring.) The grandfather of this line is of course Coleridge.

A good many common assumptions about literature are shared by these men whom I have so indiscriminately lumped together. They believe that literature embodies the highest values of the culture from which it springs and that it conserves those values through the order of art, an order which is fundamentally moral but not didactic. They are formalists in a technical sense, but none of them finally believes that art is a simple matter of technique which can be fully explained or exhausted by formal considerations. What they have most in common is a willingness, almost obsessive, to assay a literary work in the closest way possible—to bring it under the most searching scrutiny. They are also intensely interested in the relation of culture and art but seldom confuse either dimension with the other. They tend to be religious men, though not necessarily in a church-going sense. Many of them have been involved in great controversies about the ground and nature of art, especially as art is affected by, and reflects, politics. In short, they all believe that the importance of art is revealed in the universals it incorporates and reveals, not in the order of its tactics or the relevance of its contemporary design. Art for them is experience refracted by form, but quickened and elevated by value. Criticism is an act which involves a restless seeking after the essence of art, and to be good it must illumine the necessary relation between art and life, individual life and the life of society.

I turn now to the Southern branch of the American house, my essential subject. Many of the Southern new critics were first Fugitives and later Agrarians. They were fugitives from the moonlight and magnolia South of Thomas Nelson Page and John Pendleton Kennedy and from the New South of Henry W. Grady and Walter Hines Page. They then ventured, on the eve of the depression, into the field of political philosophy and proposed an old deal for the South which was based upon agrarian economics. Later they gave themselves wholly to the profession of letters, which included teaching and editing. Always they were poets, novelists, critics. In the beginning of their careers most of them were students of history; towards the end many have turned to autobiography and memoir.

The guiding voices—Donald Davidson, Ransom, and Tate—began as stern and enthusiastic followers of the Muse, as Davidson has put it; and probably no other group in recent literary history has devoted itself to the discipline of art, specifically to poetry, with better purpose than did the Fugitives. Yet in the late twenties and early thirties they saw fit to enter into the political arena and to launch a frontal assault upon the industrial state—Leviathan. The most famous document was the first, if we discount Ransom's *God without Thunder:* it was *I'll Take My Stand.* The continuing importance and vitality of this symposium derive from the fact that it goes beyond polemics and presents an image of what the good life can be. It is also far less utopian than its New England counterparts—including Thoreau's *Walden.* Of course they were interpreted in the most literal way by their detractors who liked to say that the Agrarians were advocating that everyone get out and plow, as Frank Owsley said at the Fugitive reunion in 1954. In 1936 *I'll Take My Stand* was followed by another symposium—*Who Owns America?,* and in 1939 Donald Davidson's *Attack on Leviathan* was published.

In the same year John Crowe Ransom founded the *Kenyon Review. The World's Body* was issued by Scribners the year preceding, and in 1941 another book by Ransom appeared. It was entitled *The New Criticism.* These books and Cleanth Brooks's *Modern Poetry and the Tradition* (1939) announced that the Agrarians were no longer chiefly interested in a reformation of society in the South—and that they had returned to their proper sphere—the world of letters. This is not to say that they forgot political issues or withdrew entirely from them; but it is significant that Ransom has never written another essay on Agrarianism nor has Tate or Warren. At this point Agrarianism and its advocates went into deliberate exile in the Middle West and the Northeast, as Richard Weaver has shrewdly observed; this was especially true when Brooks and Warren left Louisiana State University in 1942 after the *Southern Review* was curtailed for lack of funds. Ransom had already left Vanderbilt for similar reasons. By this time, it should be added, the revolution that the New Criticism was beginning to effect was already reaching into classrooms throughout the land: *Understanding Poetry,* perhaps the most famous textbook of this century, was first published in 1938.

So by the eve of the United States' entry into the Second World War these men were wholly engaged in the business of literature. It is interesting that no new critic suffered the pangs of disillusionment which overwhelmed socialist and communist critics of the thirties when Hitler entered into the cynical non-aggression pact with Stalin. Granville Hicks's nervous collapse and his retreat to the country is symptomatic of this breakdown, which is fictively rendered in Trilling's *The Middle of the Journey.*

The high-water mark of the New Criticism probably occurred during the late 1950's. At that time the *Kenyon Review* and the *Sewanee Review* were at the height of their influence, having continued the near hegemony of the *Southern Review.* Murray Krieger's book-length anatomy of the New Criticism [*The New Apologists for Poetry*] had appeared in 1956. Since 1960 the New Criticism has come under increasingly more intense (and sophisticated) attack, and its opponents are more articulate and better equipped than in the past. Today Cleanth Brooks is the only new critic of the original group who is still really active, although Ransom, Tate, Warren, and Lytle occasionally publish fine essays.

The New Criticism has lived through various critical fads. In the beginning it reacted principally against the humanism of Irving Babbitt and Paul Elmer More—and the old Germanic historical scholarship of George Lyman Kittredge and John Livington Lowes. Later critical movements included Freudianism and Marxism. At the moment the wave of the future appears to be with "myth criticism"; and its great panjandrum, Northrop Frye, is a brilliant critic. One should not neglect the men who have popularized American studies (Roy Harvey Pearce and Leo Marx for instance) as scholars with broad appeal; nor should he overlook the wizards of linguistics who are headed by Our Man in Vietnam—Noam Chomsky. I do not mean to ignore any thriving branch of criticism, and certainly I must mention two other "schools" which are not that at all. The first is Edmund Wilson, who has used everything from Freudian psychology and Marxism to historical scholarship to become the finest critic of this century: Wilson is a whole school by himself. Philip Rahv, Lionel Trilling, and George Steiner all have something of his range, sophistication, and authority, especially Rahv. The other involves the very capable men who have written the best literary biographies of the past decade or so—notably Richard Ellmann.

Yet, for all those who will see, it is obvious the best criticism of our time is still the New Criticism. To support my contention I call the names of B. L. Reid, R. W. B. Lewis, James M. Cox, and many of those associated with the *Hollins Critic,* particularly Daniel Hoffman, George Garrett, Walter Sullivan, and Louis D. Rubin, Jr. These men have made more use of the tactics and strategies of the New Criticism than they have of any other critical procedure, and their work is demonstrably rooted in that criticism. This fact should be perfectly clear but it is not: it is as obscure today as the real contributions of Ransom, Tate, Brooks, Warren, Davidson, and Lytle—and their closest associates, Blackmur and Fergusson. Why this is true and how it has come to be are the subjects to which I now address myself.

The many commentators who have considered the work of the Southern new critics—both the criticism itself and the art which accompanied it—have never really provided a satisfactory equation which shows the relation of the one to the other. Herein lies the mystery. All other matters, if not peripheral, are of lesser importance.

The misconceptions about the New Criticism spring from the fact that its detractors handle evidence the way Clarence Darrow did at the Scopes trial: they use simple and unrepresentative texts on which to base their arguments: *Under-standing Poetry* (and occasionally the related books by Brooks and Warren or Brooks and Heilman), *The Well Wrought Urn,* and an amorphous body of second-rate criticism which has been written according to what are often accepted as canonical new critical principles. The list of books here is almost endless: two which are representative of one method—the symbolic—and which have produced a good deal of transcendental voyaging are *The Literary Symbol* by William York Tindall and *Symbolism and American Literature* by Charles Feidelson.

In *Understanding Poetry* and its companion volumes Brooks and Warren were striking a pose in an attempt to sweep away much of the post-Romantic and post-Victorian miasma which lingered on in the classroom in the late 1930's; they were also dealing with the thick gas of Marxism. They wanted to bring the work of art itself to the attention of the student, to encourage close thinking about the text at hand, and to put biography and literary history in their proper places. In a freshman text one can, after all, accomplish only so much. That the accomplishment of Brooks and Warren in this respect is real cannot be argued; that its effects in the long run were salutary is equally unarguable; that this is not the only way to teach or to read poetry these men would be first to say. (Both have said repeatedly, as Warren did some fifteen years ago: "There is no *one, single, correct* kind of criticism, no *complete* criticism.") But in the circumstances a certain amount of overstatement and oversimplification were required: as Flannery O'Connor has said, "To the hard of hearing you shout, and for the almost-blind you draw large and startling figures." The success of the book is a commonplace: look at the popular freshman English texts today which are poor men's versions of *Understanding Poetry*. Laurence Perrine's *Sound and Sense,* now in its third or fourth edition, is as unthinkable without Brooks and Warren as the New Deal is without Roosevelt—or the Nixon administration without Mr. Agnew and Mrs. Mitchell. I do not have to add that it is far inferior to its prototype.

The case about *The Well Wrought Urn* is a far more complicated matter. This book, like *Modern Poetry and the Tradition,* is in part a specific response to the dominant critical trends of its time. But it is principally an elaboration of the idea that poetry is something more than cultural anthropology with a specific political or religious or moral purpose which can be translated by a literary historian as easily as Egyptian hieroglyphics would yield to the Rosetta stone. Brooks is arguing that a poem entails something more mysterious and universal than the expression of particular values which were present at its creation. One can disagree with Brooks at many points and can argue persuasively against the touchstones he uses—ambiguity, irony, paradox, and metaphor (as Ransom often has); but when all is said and done, it is plain that Cleanth Brooks has acutely interpreted more major poems than any other critic in the business, now or in the past; and this is in itself a considerable achievement. Many of Brooks's readings have not been surpassed or even equalled. "*The Waste Land:* Critique of the Myth," an essay now thirty-odd years old, is only one instance. Nobody but Brooks could have written "Poetry Since *The Waste Land*," a comprehensive treatment of contemporary poetry which was published in 1965; nobody but Brooks could have written *The Yoknapatawpha Country.* I will rest my case by noting that the radical change in taste about classic English litera-

ture was predicted by Brooks in 1939 in his "Notes for a Revised History of English Poetry."

Pointing to scholarly and critical studies which lean heavily on the New Criticism is far more difficult than noticing textbooks which are blurred copies of *Understanding Poetry*. Neither Tindall's book nor Feidelson's is really poor, but both are characteristic of the craze for symbolism which was in vogue before academic critics put their money solidly on Frazer and Jung and invested heavily in myth. The reader of these works may be led to think that the symbol is everything and that once it is identified, the entire meaning of the fiction which embodies it will be revealed in a blaze of light. The presumption is that the presence of symbol and its elaboration—symbolism—are the absolute indices of a fiction's greatness. Moreover, everything in the hands of a skilled sleight-of-hand artist like Mr. Feidelson becomes a symbol, even the printed word: "To consider the literary work as a piece of language is to regard it as a symbol . . . ," he blandly informs us. The conclusion is that literature is symbolic or it is nothing, just as to later critics it is either mythic or unworthy of the most serious attention. The symbolic critic would have us take leave of the literal world; the myth critic attempts a similar escape from history into the fixed and often stagnant world of a timeless past. Needless to say, symbolism appears in tenth-rate art, as does myth.

The search for symbolism came about in consequence of the renewed interest in the text itself—and because it is a method easily learned and practiced. Myth criticism is only a slightly more difficult trade. That symbolic interpretation and myth criticism eventuated in part from the New Criticism is obvious, but this is mainly an accident or a sequence of accidents. To hold the new critics responsible for these methodologies is like finding Hegel and Nietzsche culpable for the appearance of Herr Schicklgruber.

All criticism is of course open to the objection that it somehow distorts art's true meaning and makes art less, rather than more, accessible. The informed general reader (who is as frequently seen as the dodo) presumably likes his art neat, uncontaminated by soda water or even branch water. And there is something to be said for this. But the rise of modernism has made criticism all the more necessary; and when the writer cries out against criticism, we can usually be sure he is speaking with tongue in cheek or writing with the left hand. Randall Jarrell, for instance, often complained about criticism, saying that "Art is long, and critics are the insects of a day." Moreover, according to Mr. Jarrell, the critic is likely to be querulous about the very eccentricities which make a poet distinctive and significantly inform his work. Yet, when Jarrell died at fifty-one, he left behind three volumes of criticism, much of it excellent.

It is instructive to remark that the rise of criticism began at almost precisely the same time that the artist became alienated from society and from the general audience—in the Romantic period. (Lewis Simpson has felicitously called this movement the Great Literary Secession.) Prior to the Romantic period the artist had frequently been so much a part of his society as to be virtually indistinguishable from it; and there were relatively few professional writers or men of letters. Most writers were amateurs in the old and honored sense, or they had patrons. Many were clergyman.

The Romantic poets were alienated from the church and from society by virtue of choice for the most part. This is especially true of Byron and Shelley; the American writer Poe generally conforms to the pattern. The Romantic poet therefore began the process which taken to its limits would result in aestheticism—"art for art's sake." Art of this kind is addressed to a small select audience, and it exists in a rarified atmosphere far from the world's body, in a hothouse inhabited by those who think that life imitates art and that art is far more important than life. Criticism written for these devotees is a form of narcissistic worship before the altar of Art.

That the reading public should take a dim view of this behavior is understandable; that the view should persist when that reader is confronted by modernist literature is equally understandable; and we would be silly to think this attitude will change in the immediate future. The artist grows more eccentric as time goes on: for every Wallace Stevens, quietly working as an insurance executive, there are now a double handful of Ezra Pounds, with one great exception—the genius is missing. The general reading public today probably has no greater distrust of the New Criticism than of Freudian criticism or historical scholarship.

Despite all this, the present day is still a pre-eminently critical age: criticism in the academy and among the truly informed public is a more powerful force than ever before. It is also still being practiced occasionally in a few large-circulation periodicals as well as quarterlies. In the pages of the *New York Review of Books* one can find perceptive and thorough reviews, if he looks hard enough and is not put off by diatribes against the war in Southeast Asia. On the whole, criticism today is manifestly superior to fiction and poetry; we are in what Arnold calls an age of expansion when criticism rules. We are confronted by a pre-eminent criticism, pre-eminent over the literature it purports to criticize; yet paradoxically that criticism has few distinctive and important voices. The most compelling of these voices belong to the old hands—the new critics and the others who won attention in the 1930's, 40's, and 50's. My point is that the very proliferation of criticism may be a cause of a new mediocrity, a general levelling down. The new mediocrity I speak of involves a high level of competence but offers little or nothing which partakes of the classic qualities of criticism, the qualities one associates with Coleridge, Arnold, the early Eliot, and Wilson: the ability, in short, as Arnold put it, to make the best ideas prevail. We might ask who in this country will "replace" Wilson, Rahv, Ransom, Tate, or Malcolm Cowley. Most of the leading candidates have been largely educated by the New Criticism.

Today good criticism must be what it has always been—an act of the highest intelligence and the most demanding judgment; but there is a new urgency which the critic must feel. The signs of the time are generally bad: the artist in and out of the South is bereft, probably for the first time in history, of almost every vestige of shared belief. Ours is very nearly a post-Christian age: chaos looms at every hand; anarchy is celebrated throughout the land; order in society and in art have never had a lower valuation; the forces of darkness seem to be getting the upper hand. Everywhere one is confronted by the demonic, and the various bizarre figures who are parading across the stage today are strikingly reminiscent in many respects of the specters who appeared at the end of the Czarist regime and of the monsters who gradually took over in the dying throes of the Third Reich.

The progressive decay of modern culture has by now overtaken the country as a whole, and, with it, finally, the South. In the 1920's, when the Southern literary renascence began,

the reawakening was made possible, at least in no small part, by a painful historical consciousness which invested the writer. He could see that the culture of the Old South, as much of it as had remained during the long Indian summer in the late 1800's and early 1900's—and that was a good deal—was fast disappearing. That the South had rejoined the American Union after the first world war and that this signalled the triumph of the New South which was the wave of the future. Decay in the fabric of society drove the Southern writer at last to make his stand in both literature and in politics. But since the end of World War II that rottenness seems to have become so general that it has overwhelmed the Southern writer who was not given that special consciousness through the accident of birth and the shaping force of his society. Without it he cannot bring past and present into a significant relation and truly render the configurations of human experience. (The illness described may be terminal, and we should stop to ask ourselves whether literature is possible for modern man.) The decay in the bone and marrow of society is no longer paradoxically bringing forth fine fruit; the literary harvest in the South as elsewhere is now sporadic, lean, and worm-infested; the moment of fruition has passed. I do not see a renascence taking place elsewhere in the nation. The decadence in our society is truly reflected today by the decadence of our art. The Southern writer is presently planting crops in fields which have been exhausted and which are insufficiently tilled and fertilized. There has been inbreeding as well as exhaustion.

In such a time literature tends to become mere propaganda: revolution is its sermon, disorder its means. The artist is often accepted as prophet, priest, hero, and saint, whether he wants to be or not. The critic therefore has a great obligation, a heavier burden, than ever before. In order to fulfill the critical office he must know more than at any time in the past, and he must find a secure vantage point to view the chaos unfolding about him. He must be free of the commercial pressures which are the very pulse of our economy and often our lives. In short, the critic, looking about him today, has little cause for rejoicing. As he sits fishing upon the shore (itself threatened by the high tides of change), with the arid plain behind him and the murky waters stretching out before, he can do worse than speculate upon the situation which faced the Nashville poets at the time of Mencken's devastating and accurate indictment of Southern literature in 1917—"The Sahara of the Bozart." Some few years later Tate succinctly described the bleak situation: "We lack a tradition in the arts; more to the point, we lack a literary tradition. We lack even a literature."

The Fugitives first withdrew from society, specifically the South; and then they returned to it. Their commitment to the South was all the more significant and informed in consequence. After their literary secession, their worship of the muse of poetry, they set about earning their Southern inheritance, and as Mr. Simpson has pointed out, nobody has ever worked harder at recovering his past and earning his birthright.

On March 1st, 1927, Tate wrote to Ransom that he had "attacked the South for the last time, except in so far as it may be necessary to point out that the chief defect of the Old South was that in it which produced, through whatever cause, the New South." Ransom wrote at the same time: "Our fight is for survival; and it's got to be waged not so much against the Yankees as against the exponents of the

New South. We must . . . take some very long calculations ahead. . . ." The battle was joined. The Fugitives subsequently used every literary means at their disposal: history, political and economic theory, criticism, fiction, and poetry; but they never confused polemics with art. This is one great difference between their work and the socialist and proletarian literature of the thirties.

The Fugitive-Agrarians went about recovering their usable past through the means of history: from that discipline and its enactment came biography grounded in a thorough understanding of the past: John Donald Wade's *Augustus Baldwin Longstreet* (1924), Tate's *Stonewall Jackson* (1928) and his *Jefferson Davis* (1929), Warren's *John Brown* (1929), and, a little later, Lytle's *Bedford Forrest and His Critter Company* (1932). From the interest in politics and economics, the driving forces in contemporary society, came the books I have mentioned, especially *I'll Take My Stand;* from the fictive impulse came Lytle's *The Long Night* (1936), Tate's *The Fathers* (1939), and Warren's *Night Rider* (1939). The New Criticism was born between the writing of polemics and fiction, but it should be remembered that all the while Ransom, Davidson, Tate, and Warren were writing some of their finest poetry. The New Criticism had a long period of gestation: it was not created overnight.

In examining this curious phenomenon one is struck immediately by the conjunction of the creative impulse and actuality with the critical attitude and practice. Nothing precisely like this has occurred before or since in American literary history insofar as a group is concerned. Literary coteries generally tend to produce an unfortunate interaction and reaction among the people who make them up: the "lost generation," for example, is mainly remembered as a loose collection of uprooted souls who fought vigorously and pointlessly among themselves. (There is even some reason to wonder how much Hemingway learned from Gertrude Stein.) The same is by no means true of the Bloomsbury group or the Eliot-Pound association (including the Vorticists) or the members of the Cheddar Cheese; yet probably no group relation since the English renaissance has been so fruitful as the Fugitive-Agrarian connection. Generally the author must work by himself, without the benefit of criticism from close friends whom he can depend upon; or occasionally he can work closely with another man as Pound and Eliot did in the early days, or as Conrad and Ford did about the same time. The greatest genius, needless to say, almost invariably pursues a solitary course: James, Joyce, and Faulkner are good examples. This kind of writer writes criticism incidentally or not at all.

What brought the Fugitives and Agrarians together were a common background and hence common values, the coincidence of a shared place, and the sense of cultural shock and recoil from the prevailing tendencies which followed in the train of that series of shocks—World War I, the Dayton trial, the great depression. What began as regular and serious conversation on Saturday nights in Nashville ended in a large proportion of a new and significant Southern literature and in a criticism which provided a philosophical and aesthetic complement to that literature. The literature was tempered by the criticism; the criticism was proved by its relevance and exactitude for the art of its makers.

It should be remembered that these men in particular and the new critics in general have always been critically tough on one another—and have not expended as much effort in pursuing arguments outside their own ranks. The correspondence

of Tate and Davidson about the finest early poetry of each is a case in point as is Ransom's argument with Brooks over the nature of poetry. (The battle which went on between Yvor Winters on the one hand and Tate and Ransom on the other was one of the fiercest critical engagements of the century.) This kind of fruitful disagreement occurred repeatedly at the Fugitive reunion in 1954 and at the Agrarian reunion in 1968; it continues today.

This wrangling was part of the process of recovering the past through working individually for a common inheritance. That it involved a high seriousness and an unflinching pursuit of excellence is beyond doubt, although there were admittedly creative and critical failures along the way—and more of the former than the latter. The enactment of this purpose shows that Tate knew what he was talking about in 1930 when he said that the Southerner could take hold of his tradition by one means only—violence. By that he meant that the Southerner of his generation had to ignore or to cut through the old atavism and sentimentality—the flag-waving and hollow ritual of the grave celebrants who were Professional Southerners—in order to earn the enduring truth of Southern history. In so doing the Fugitive-Agrarians and their closest associates achieved a developed sense of allegiance, a conviction which informs their work. As one of them, R. P. Blackmur puts it, conviction is that quality which gives the writer "objective authority in his work." Or, put differently, it is the "inward mastery of the outward materials of experience."

I do not mean to imply that writers and critics must periodically huddle together at a convenient university and create a group aesthetic and a group literature. On the contrary, nothing could be further from what the facts of this particular case entail. As Warren has said, there was "no systematic program behind the Fugitive group." Nor was there a systematic program behind what has come to be known as the New Criticism: only its critics have been systematic in imposing a dogmatics. Tate has said the critic's position is untenable; Ransom has looked in vain for a satisfactory critic and a satisfactory criticism; Lytle has said that criticism is the last stand of the creative mind; Blackmur has written that criticism must be "consciously provisional, speculative, and dramatic"; and so on.

What finally characterizes the New Criticism, aside from the common background and the friendships of many new critics, is the insistence upon looking steadily at the literary work itself and determining its form and value from within—not without. The principle is more flexible and fertile and accurate than any other single approach, many of which tend to be mechanical, indeed allegorical. So long as the critic constantly seeks "to see the object as in itself it really is," then he should not go far wrong in attending to its virtues and defects—its uniqueness and its representative quality. "To see the object as in itself it really is"—the words are Matthew Arnold's—not Eliot's or Brooks's.

The principal accomplishment of the Southern new critics, I take it, was to restore the profession of letters to the South. They did this in an astonishingly short time, but only after intense labor. When one thinks of the profession of letters in the true and highest sense—and thinks of its practice in this country—there are very few names he can enter into evidence. The obvious Anglo-American examples are Pound, Eliot, and Auden. In England there are a good many—E. M. Forster, Robert Graves, Edwin Muir, Herbert Read, and Ford Madox Ford. Of the Southern new critics Ransom,

Tate, and Warren are all men of letters in the exact sense; this is true, with qualifications, of Davidson, Lytle, Blackmur, and Fergusson.

The man of letters is not simply a fiction writer or a poet or a dramatist or a critic: he has many parts, one of which is an intense commitment to the profession of letters: he is committed to it and by his commitment, his behavior as a writer, he helps make letters an honorable and important profession. By so doing he increases the importance of literature for society and culture. The South desperately needed this professionalism in the twenties; the entire country sorely needed it at the same time; the entire country desperately needs it today.

Traditionally the man of letters has been a critic-poet or a poet-critic, and I do not play with words here. Sidney, Ben Jonson, and Keats are critic-poets, whereas the new critics are poet-critics in general: this is certainly true of Fergusson, Blackmur, and Winters, who have all written fine poetry; it is essentially true of Tate; it is true of Ransom when one merely weighs his work quantitatively. When he looks at it qualitatively, even if he doesn't agree with Tate that Ransom is one of the great elegiac poets in the language, it is still clear that Ransom's greatest and most enduring contribution to letters is his poetry. Warren is of course the most various of the men I am looking at, but Tate has nearly as much technical expertise in various literary modes. Again we are brought to an awareness of the subtle relation between the criticism of a practicing writer and his creative work, and we may remember that Eliot said on more than one occasion that the best critics are more often than not creative artists. The literary achievement of the Southern new critics ensues naturally from the enkindling reaction of criticism and literature which are written by the same hand—or, if written by more than one hand, which finds a sympathetic and informed audience within close proximity, a proximity of the heart and head, of sensibility and intellect.

The Fugitive-Agrarians brought respectability to the poet-critic's relation to the university, a quality it has sorely lacked. There are exceptions in the history of American letters—Longfellow and Lowell might be mentioned; but when one considers the early twentieth century things were entirely different, and the man of letters had all but disappeared from the American academic scene. Think of Robinson and Frost; of Hemingway, Fitzgerald, Dos Passos, and others of the lost generation; of Ellen Glasgow and James Branch Cabell; of Dreiser and Sinclair Lewis; of Van Wyck Brooks and Edmund Wilson; and so on. As Blackmur has said: "What we want . . . is not to save a few individuals, but to secure and elevate the profession. . . . This is where the university comes in, at least indirectly, to help re-establish the writer, in his *profession,* as an effective force in the great world. . . ." It seems clear enough now that John Crowe Ransom, more than any other man, made this relation possible through his behavior as teacher and man of letters.

The greatness of Ransom, Davidson, Tate, Warren, and Brooks as teachers is too large a subject for me to embark upon at length; but it should be observed that all have been long established as brilliant teachers, though each in his differing way. As Tate said of Ransom, "He was not so much teaching us literature as teaching us how it is possible to think about literature." Here we confront, second- or third-hand, the athletic vigor and the elastic grace of the New Criticism in the classroom. Again (as in the New Criticism proper) there is really no communicable body of received dogma

which can be passed on, no pedagogical method other critics and teachers can learn by rote and successfully apply. The list of critics, poets, and novelists that studied under these men would be far more impressive than that which has come out of, say, Harvard or the University of North Carolina in a comparable period of time. In one generation we could mention Peter Taylor, Randall Jarrell, and Robert Lowell; in the next, James Dickey and Madison Jones; and so on. A kind of tradition has been established which is likely to be vital for years to come, and it has been made possible by smaller schools like Vanderbilt, Kenyon, and Greensboro.

We may conclude that the community of letters has been immeasurably strengthened by the New Criticism because these men have not only contributed to it as scholars and critics and teachers but as artists, and because they have always respected both the integrity of society and the integrity of art. They have always understood that art is life at the remove of form, that art contributes to the vital quality of the life of society, that the health of art depends upon the health of the society from which it springs and vice versa, and that criticism is a force which provides a current between art and society but which can reform neither.

This is not to say that the new critics did not make mistakes, even serious ones. I do not think that Agrarianism was a mistake in the long run: the strategy proved sound even if individual tactics were faulty. Only Davidson clung to Agrarianism too fiercely. But the new critics' running battle with the scholarly community as such has often been unfortunate—mainly because it has given their students a trifling bias towards historical scholarship. (Allen Tate could call Douglas Bush's bluff about metaphysical poetry, but Tate's students lack a classical education, not to mention his wit and intelligence.) It is also regrettable that the Nashville group has had a strong continuing aversion to certain men, or kinds of men, who take a different view of the South than they. I speak of Thomas Wolfe—and of H. L. Mencken, W. J. Cash, and James Agee. Their informed prejudice, like their bias towards historical criticism, has often degenerated into a reflexive attitude on the part of followers. (This blind defensiveness has led to much nonsense and wasted motion). Furthermore, there has been a hardening in recent years in the attitude towards religion and western man. The argument here is that since the late Middle Ages western civilization has undergone a steady decline in religious belief—hence in sensibility. This frame of mind may be described as post-Eliot Old High Church Toryism: sometimes it genuinely works as a historical perspective for a critical essay (as in any number of pieces by Tate); more often it does not.

The achievement of the Southern new critics has not been earned without great expense, an expense which almost necessarily excludes greatness for its makers. One could argue that were not these men forced to create a community of letters in the South—and hence a literary tradition—through teaching, editing, and writing criticism, they might have been more important as creative writers. Davidson spent an enormous amount of time and energy on his *Nashville Tennessean* book page and, later, in continuing the Agrarian campaign after the mid-thirties; Brooks and Warren gave much of themselves to the first series of the *Southern Review* and to their textbooks; Tate is forever helping a writer like Hart Crane or Robert Lowell, and he has spent some time making the *Sewanee Review* an important journal; Lytle has given many years to the same periodical; Ransom has not published a really new book since he started the *Kenyon Review;* and so it goes. In consequence only Warren has written enough fiction or poetry to be considered a major writer; the others have not. But insofar as their creative accomplishments are concerned I do not think that things would have turned out very differently had all of them more fully pursued fiction and poetry. I believe the Fugitive-Agrarians were individually too various and learned and self-conscious to become great writers; they were also not ruthless enough, not devoted enough to art in the pure form (as opposed to letters), to produce a more comprehensive and universal literature, even though their common subject—what Tate has called "the opposition of an heroic myth to the secularization of man in our age"—is sufficient to bear greater force than they levied upon it. Had these men been more concerned about themselves and less concerned about the profession of letters, their art would not have been appreciably affected for the good; but their contributions to the world of letters would have been considerably diminished, if not lost altogether. Had they behaved thus, the South would still be lacking a true profession of letters and a vital literary tradition, although it would admittedly have a great deal of literary talent. And the nation as a whole might have only impressionistic and pseudo-scientific criticism.

The present time is a dry season for art. The death of modernism is at hand, and clearly no literature as great will displace it in the foreseeable future. The New Criticism was born in part because modernism made it necessary: other criticisms could not cope with Yeats, Pound, Eliot, Joyce, and the others in the nineteen twenties and thirties. Now that the end of modernism looms before us . . . , one might ask if the death of the New Criticism is not also within sight—if, having performed its function, it will not also disappear. I think not—since the example of the new critics, which extends far beyond mere analysis of a given body of work—should remain permanently valuable to anyone who is interested in seeing literature steadily and seeing its whole. Each age has to write its own criticism, yet no critic can afford to ignore Ransom, Tate, Brooks, Blackmur, and Fergusson.

The new critics more than any others in this century have known the expense of criticism, the difficulties of going haunted in a society indifferent to art and the supreme agony of momentarily bringing together that society and the world of letters. It is equally apparent that few other critics in the United States have seen so clearly and so well and have so convincingly transformed insight into abiding judgment. Theirs has been the common pursuit of true judgment—the standard which Eliot proposed nearly fifty years ago.

The spreading field is experience; the circumference drawn against the recalcitrant landscape, the reach of the imagination; the area within, the work of art which ensues from the conjunction of vision and technique. The Southern new critics have fired consistently and accurately on many significant targets, whether they or (far more often) another artist fashioned the work. The range and sight conditions have often radically changed: it is a great distance from Shakespeare to Wordsworth; from Donne to Frost; from Milton to Hart Crane; from Keats to Eliot; from Gray to Hardy; from Aristotle to Johnson: but these men have always seen the stillness at the center of the target and have acted without regard to fashion. By so doing they have established a vital connection between art and society. The New Criticism thus joins the profession of letters and the profession of life, and that is the highest office any criticism can perform. (pp. 413-31)

George Core, "Southern Letters and the New Criticism," in The Georgia Review, *Vol. XXIV, No. 1, Spring, 1970, pp. 413-31.*

ROBERT WOOSTER STALLMAN

[*Stallman is a leading scholar on the life and works of Stephen Crane and has written extensively on American fiction and criticism. In the following excerpt from an essay originally published in 1946, he discusses New Criticism in the context of twentieth-century critical trends, traces the central themes upon which it is based, and defines the principal attitudes of its most prominent theorists.*]

There is one basic theme in modern criticism; it is the dissociation of modern sensibility. The loss of a spiritual order and of integrity in the modern consciousness is T. S. Eliot's major premise. The issue of our glorification of the scientific vision at the expense of the aesthetic vision is the central theme in both the poetry and the criticism of the Southern poet-critics. It is this theme of spiritual disorder which the late Paul Valéry exploited; it shows through the current of the critical writings of I. A. Richards, F. R. Leavis, Yvor Winters, R. P. Blackmur, and the Southern critics. The New Critics, while differing among one another in theory or in practice, are as one through the unifying relation of this obsessive burden.

To what use does the critic put it? My purpose in this essay is to order into a synthesis the critical ideas and methods of the New Critics, and for my starting point I shall trace the ways in which this theme operates at the critical level.

One variation upon the theme is *the loss of tradition.* We lack a religious and a social tradition which would extend moral and intellectual authority to the poet. Dante and the poets of other great ages of poetry had at hand a body of ideas and a faith in them. There is no such agreement today. Never were poets more profoundly divided from the life of society than in our time. The effect upon our Experimental Generation of the loss of an antecedent discipline such as tradition provides forms the subject of Yvor Winters' *Primitivism and Decadence.* The loss has resulted in a poetry of structural confusion. The theme of Eliot's *After Strange Gods* is the limiting or crippling effect upon our literature of our dislocation from a living tradition. The effect is twofold: (1) confusion as to the boundaries of criticism, and (2) extreme individualism in viewpoints—the expression of a personal view of life, the exploitation of personality. Allen Tate, following Eliot, defines tradition as "a quality of judgment and of conduct, rooted in a concrete way of life" that we inherit from our immediate past, or, if we are makers of tradition (and it demands our constant rediscovery), the quality of life that we create and pass on to the next generation. Tradition, no less than religion itself, is formed of a structure of absolutes—points of moral and intellectual reference "implicit and emergent in experience at all times, and under certain conditions, explicit and realized." This conception of tradition is the foundation for the critical outlook of both Eliot and Tate. Eliot's conception of an immutable order is ultimately religious; like Valéry's, Tate's is ultimately aesthetic.

The theme is repeated in other terms—from Hulme to Blackmur—as *the loss of a fixed convention* providing the poet a unifying relation to his society. The modern poet, deprived of some rational structure from which he might derive discipline and authority, is under the constant necessity of either resurrecting a dead convention (Millay) or erecting a new one of his own (Yeats). A tradition or a culture manifests itself in the language, in the medium of the poet's words. It is only in terms of language, which may be defined as the embodiment of our experience in words, that a convention exists or survives. The work of a great poet is the creation of a new convention, a new order of language. A convention is simply the way in which language has been used by the poets of a preceding generation, used so powerfully that we can but carry on its major significance. The operation of this principle in Tate's criticism is best illustrated by his judgment on Millay. By using the language of the preceding generation to convey an emotion peculiar to her own, and by making that language personal, Millay restored life to a dead convention. This is her distinction, but it is also her limitation. She preserved, in the traditional style of the preceding decadent age, the personality of her own age—without altering either. The criticism of Tate, Brooks, and Blackmur is built upon this principle of the language: does the poet make "a genuine attempt to use in his poems the maximum resource of poetic language consonant with his particular talent"?

A third thematic variation is the loss of an objective system of truths imbedded in a homogeneous society—*the loss of belief* in religion and in myth. Eliot claims that what Blake's genius required and lacked "was a framework of accepted and traditional ideas which would have prevented him from indulging in a philosophy of his own, and concentrated his attention on the problems of the poet. . . . The concentration resulting from a framework of mythology and theology and philosophy is one of the reasons why Dante is a classic, and Blake only a poet of genius." Eliot's theme informs Tate's standard for judging such poets as Robinson, MacLeish, and Cummings. Because they had no systematic philosophy or external framework of ideas to sustain them, they substituted their own personality as the core of experience and meaning. MacLeish lacked what Milton had, namely "an objective convention that absorbed every implication of his personal feeling." Lacking an epos or myth, E. A. Robinson had to repeat his ground again and again, writing a poem that would not be written. On Cummings the criticisms of Tate and of John Peale Bishop come to the same point: Cummings' poetry is an image of his unique personality. In ages which suffer the loss of religion there is chaos and violence expressed, and that is what Eliot's *The Waste Land* means. It means "that men who have lost both the higher myth of religion and the lower myth of historical dramatization have lost the forms of human action; it means that they are no longer capable . . . of forming a dramatic conception of human nature. . . ." In place of the dramatization of the soul, as we find it in Emily Dickinson's poetry, we get from a contemporary poet like MacLeish the dramatization (in "Conquistador") of personality against an historical setting.

Another form the theme takes is *the loss of a world order,* a world order which can be assimilated to the poetic vision. Shakespeare had such a world order in his medieval pattern of life, and Emily Dickinson had one in her New England and Puritan Christianity. Without moral and intellectual standards the poet has no means for measuring and testing his personal experience. Our age lacks what Shelley called the "fixed point of reference" for the poet's sensibility. The assumption—a fallacy common to contemporary poets—that order or adequate form can be created simply by the poet's

act of self-expression, by his imitation of the world disorder in what Winters has labeled as Expressive or Imitative Form—fails the poet as a solution for the problem of poetic structure. For Winters, Tate, F. R. Leavis, John Crowe Ransom, or R. P. Blackmur—a poem for these critics must have a rational structure, a core of meaning, a scheme of objective reference which orders and gives meaning to the poet's emotions. "Shelley, at his best and worst, offers the emotion in itself, unattached, in the void" (Leavis in *Revaluation*). In MacLeish's "Conquistador" a mechanism of personal sensation is substituted for theme or meaning; the personality attached to Cummings's "Viva" is the only meaning in Cummings's poems; the coherence of "The Bridge" is merely the coherence of the tone or poet's attitude. Tate sets down Crane's career as "a vindication of Eliot's major premise—that the integrity of the individual consciousness has broken down." The failure of "The Bridge," by virtue of its structural disorder, is symptomatic of the failure of modern poetry generally. Tate's analysis of Crane's poetry extends beyond the poems to the outer area of disorder and cross-purposes in the contemporary milieu. Tate relates the world disorder to the poetic one. Likewise, in examining other poets (Eliot, Pound, Dickinson, Bishop), his criticism scrutinizes both the conscious intention of the poet, the intention which is framed within the poem, and the unconscious intention—the cultural mind of the poet's world order as it is expressed in the poetry.

Intellectual chaos has been the background of American poetry and criticism during this period. The problem confronting a poet is to transfer to the poetic process a unified point of view synthesized out of the social and intellectual climate; but in our world today the complexity of these relations is not readily resolvable into a unity. "The modern can never avoid the suspicion," Samuel Hoare observes, "that whatever attitude he takes up is only a partial expression of himself and a partial activity. And he has no scale of values which would justify him in concluding that this part is the most important, that this activity is the fundamental activity. Without this great poetry is impossible." It is a commonplace of criticism, I repeat, that our present-day world is in radical disintegration and that the artist is severed from a living relation to society. Both W. H. Auden and Stephen Spender have explored this theme in their critical writings, Auden pointing out that when there is no organized dogma within society the artist becomes self-consciously didactic. As D. S. Savage says (in *The Personal Principle*), "The modern artist cannot take his values from contemporary society, because that society lacks all coherent standards and values. This it is which explains the artist's isolation from society. In his isolation he is forced to depend upon what values he can find within himself, and this makes a 'classical' art impossible."

The critics tell us that ours is an age of intellectual chaos and spiritual disunity, and yet, despite the prevailing disjuncture between artist and society, it is an age of great poetry. The dilemma of the modern poet, according to Tate, has its counterpart in the disfranchised intellect of the critic. (Blackmur singles out Yvor Winters as a conspicuous example.) It is claimed that the dissociation of sensibility—a theory which has echoed throughout criticism since it first appeared in Eliot's definition of the Metaphysical poets—transposes into the split mind of the critic. And yet it is an age of great criticism. Order, system, and (notwithstanding all the cross-currents of disagreement) unity toolmark the total achievement of the critics of our time.

Criticism is the positing and criticizing of dogmas, and its quest is standards of judgment and value. Though Tate disclaims the act of the systematic literary critic, Tate's criticism nevertheless is systematic as an aesthetic theory and as a synthesis of dogmas. The critical ideas do not conflict with each other, as they do in Herbert Read's criticism, but form a coherent system of principles. The system is unified by a single point of view. The point of view, which is that of T. E. Hulme, derives from Bergson. There is a radical division between the realm of faith and the realm of reason; between, on the one hand, the intuitive and qualitative, and, on the other hand, the intellectual and quantitative. It was Hulme's thesis that our spiritual disunity is the result of our failure to recognize the division which exists between the Religious Attitude, which postulates absolute values by which man is judged as limited and imperfect, and the Humanist Attitude, which regards man as fundamentally good and life as the source and measure of all values. Hulme designated the confusion of these two orders as the essence of Romanticism. "The view which regards man as a well, a reservoir, full of possibilities, I call the romantic; the one which regards him as a very finite and fixed creature, I call the classical." Hulme's identification of humanism with romanticism and of the religious attitude with classicism is followed by Eliot, and likewise by Tate.

Classicism means the discrimination between reason and faith; and romanticism, the confusion of reason and faith. This confusion, Eliot complains, has been the background of the modern consciousness since the Renaissance. But as Read remarks, our age "is not clearly either a romantic or a classical age, nor are the categories of a romantic or a classical tradition applicable to it." More significant and fundamental is the dichotomy between art and science. This post-Renaissance dichotomy, which replaces the Renaissance antinomy between faith and reason, represents an opposition between qualitative knowledge (art) and quantitative knowledge (science). The modern problem, as John Middleton Murry sees it, is to reach a synthesis between these two orders of knowledge. He maintains that not until a new synthesis is posed will any work of art of the first magnitude be possible again. In advocating the medieval synthesis as projected into the Thomist system, Murry suggests that "the Classicism of the Middle Ages can serve us only as a symbol, not as a pattern, of a new synthesis" ("Towards a Synthesis," *Criterion:* May, 1927). Tate sums up our modern dilemma through the same perspective and in similar terms. In the decay of Protestantism is to be found the chief clue to our understanding of English literature. Tate's opposition to the modern positivist procedure, the reduction of all knowledge to the quantitative kind, has the same foundation as Murry's opposition to the scientific materialism of our time.

Both Eliot and Tate have thoroughly orientated themselves in Hulme's *Speculations.* As his critics have observed, Hulme's dicta, in the same or in different settings, appear throughout Eliot's writings. They show up also in Tate's. In Hulme is grounded, for instance, Tate's objection to Emerson's conception of man. (It was Emerson's conception which dissipated all tragic possibilities in that culture for dramatizing the human soul, as Robert Penn Warren points out.) Hulme might have phrased this accounting for the great wastes in Emily Dickinson and Walt Whitman:

> The great bulk of the verse of each appears to have been written on the sustaining pretense that everything was always possible. To see boundless good

> on the horizon, to see it without the limiting discipline of the conviction of evil, is in poetry as in politics the great stultifier of action. . . . With no criterion of achievement without there could be no criterion of completion within.
>
> (R. P. Blackmur in *The Expense of Greatness*)

Hulme defined the mood and perspective of our age; and this is his importance, almost exclusively. He is important not because he was an original thinker, but because of his influence upon those who have dominated and largely directed the course of contemporary criticism. Tate is a disciple of Hulme in his campaign against scientism, romanticism, and humanism ("the belief that the only values that matter are human values"). Tate accepts as necessary a system of religion because it provides standards by which man can measure his own imperfections. ("The religious unity of intellect and emotion, of reason and instinct, is the sole technique for the realization of values.")

The affinity between the Southern critics and Hulme lies in their common claim that our present disunity has been created by the confusion of two categories: the aesthetic vision, which is concerned with quality, and the scientific vision, which is concerned with quantity. The disunity of the modern mind is the single theme of Tate's *Reason in Madness.* It is the scientism of our age that has forced out the religious attitude and reduced the spiritual realm to irrelevant emotion, under the illusion that all experience can be ordered scientifically. It is the decline of organized religion that has given rise to utilitarian theories of art. Dewey's theory of the integrating power of art attributes to art all the psychological virtues of a religion. Under the formula that all art is action, he identifies art and religion and science as "satisfying the same fundamental needs." Tate, of course, rejects this equation. In "The Aesthetic Emotion as Useful" (in *This Quarter:* Dec., 1932), he exposes the fallacy of the pragmatic aesthetic. Both Tate, in *Reason in Madness,* and Ransom, in *The New Criticism,* attack victoriously the positivists' position and thereby perform for modern criticism, as one of their critics acknowledges, an invaluable service. In line with an aesthetician like Eliseo Vivas, the Southern critics regard the aesthetic and the practical as opposites. Contrary to Dewey's pragmatic aesthetic, art is neither another kind of religion nor another kind of science. Poetry is poetry and not science or religion.

The canon of the Southern critics is based upon a division of art and science into two independent, objective and equally valid categories of experience. Science and poetry are the opposite poles of truth; art and religion, though both are the vehicles of qualitative experience, are not identical. It was Arnold's faith that poetry, since religion had yielded to science, could take over the work of religion. (Though the facts of science had undermined religion, they could still support poetry!) Arnold's viewpoint has its contemporary version in I. A. Richards's *Science and Poetry.* Richards here endorsed Arnold's dictum that what is valuable in religion is its aesthetic aspects. Tate's analysis of Arnold shows his position as giving the case for poetry away to the scientist. Arnold's poetics turns poetry into a "descriptive science or experience at that level, touched with emotion." Tate and Ransom attempt to solve anew Arnold's problem. They attempt to place poetry on an equal footing with science. They do so by claiming that poetry is primarily of the intellect and that poetry is "an independent form of knowledge, a kind of cognition equal to the knowledge of the sciences at least, perhaps superior." They

Allen Tate and T.S. Eliot in Washington, D.C., 1948.

claim for art those cognitive ingredients which the early Richards, by his former positivist position, discredited. The knowledge which poetry gives us is a special kind of knowledge and not, as Richards once persuaded us to think, merely an inferior kind of science. Richards misunderstood the aesthetic emotion and equated poetry with life, so Montgomery Belgion declared in his critique, "What Is Criticism?" (*Criterion:* Oct., 1930). The later Richards of *Coleridge on Imagination* (1934), however, has repudiated his former utilitarian theory of art, and with his present definition of poetry—"Poetry is the completest mode of utterance"—Tate acknowledged an essential agreement. (Paul Valéry and T. Sturge Moore have expressed similar insights.) As Tate frames it, "the high forms of literature offer us the only complete, and thus the most responsible, versions of our experience." The arts "give us a sort of cognition at least equally valid with that of the scientific method."

Ransom's theory of poetry as knowledge is fundamentally the same as Tate's. Science and poetry present two different descriptions of the world. Science presents an abstract description, poetry attempts a total description of the object. Poetry's representation of the world is an alternative to that pictured by science. The abstract structures of science sacrifice "the body and substance of the world." Poetry, by virtue of its concrete particulars, restores "The World's Body." (The difference between art and science is marked out in similar

terms by Ramon Fernandez: art qualifies, individualizes; whereas science schematizes, collects relations.) "The local, the immediate, and the concrete are the take-off of poetry," Tate remarks (in *Poetry:* May, 1932). The problem of the poet is essentially a problem of aesthetics: what shall the poet "imitate" and to what end? "Art arises in particulars, and it arrives at order at the point of impact between the new particulars and whatever recognized experience the poet has been able to acquire" (*New Republic:* August 2, 1933). Ransom, practising his imitation theory of knowledge upon a poem by Hardy, observes that Hardy's language "is not content with the concepts, but is constantly stopping to insert or to attach the particularity which is involved in images; a procedure which might be called the imaginative realization of the concepts. A genuine poetic energy will work with both these dimensions at once." (*Southern Review:* Summer, 1940). Translated into Tate's terms, the two dimensions embodied in a poem are "extension" and "intension," and the meaning of a poem is its "tension" of these two extremes of language. A good poem achieves a unity or fusion between abstraction and concretion. Idea and image are in tension. On the term *tension* Tate has built his entire aesthetic. (This key word is to Tate's criticism what the term *paradox* is to Brooks's critical theory.)

For Tate, as for Schopenhauer, art aims at nothing outside itself. This formalist creed has brought against the Southern critics the charge of art for art's sake, but their principle of art for art's sake must be interpreted very differently from the aestheticism of the Nineties. Rightly understood, the principle has tremendous implications. Tate's position again squares with John Middleton Murry's: "Art is autonomous, and to be pursued for its own sake, precisely because it comprehends the whole of human life; because it has reference to a more perfect human morality than any other activity of man." Tate's stand puts him at odds with any critical program which inflicts upon art the values of science, or of metaphysics, or of social philosophy. He repudiates, for instance, the program of Edmund Wilson for an art-science. Wilson's view is that art and science, as they come to apply themselves more directly to life, may yet arrive "at a way of thinking, a technique of dealing with our perceptions, which will make art and science one." Wilson's optimism is based on Whitehead's idea that the poetic and the scientific impulses, being radically different, must unite harmoniously in a compromise. This proposal of a compromise is at the heart of Wilson's rejection of the Symbolists (in his *Axel's Castle*). His optimism has kinship with Wordsworth's faith, as Edwin Muir interprets it, that as soon as the world of science becomes somehow as "familiar" as the primitive world of religious myth, our cultural integrity and our literature will be restored. "This belief ignores the hopeless breach between the abstractionism of science and the object itself, for which the abstraction stands and to which it is the business of the poet to return" (Tate in *The Nation:* November 17, 1926). (pp. 488-95)

The most important American critics who have organized our critical attitudes are Eliot, Tate and Ransom, Winters, and Kenneth Burke. Burke is the Aristotle of our criticism, the Aristotle who constructs vast systems. Of all our critics no one has done more towards revolutionizing our reading of a poem than Cleanth Brooks, and no critic has been of greater practical influence. While Brooks and Warren have brought the New Criticism into the universities, it is Tate and Ransom who have furnished it with systematic aesthetic studies. Their critical ideas constitute a single doctrine, their critical positions being basically identical. True, Ransom is the *point de repère* of American letters, as Donald A. Stauffer says; but Tate stakes out the issues more resolutely, and without Ransom's ironic detachment. As the spokesman for the Southern school of poet-critics, he has the greatest eye for the facts of the times and he is downright and persuasive in declaring them. It is this which accounts for my placing of Tate at the center of this present perspective. In these critical cross-currents there are violent disagreements, but, as Ransom remarks, any one of the New Critics shows the influence of the others, and the total effort amounts to a sort of collaboration.

Tate's critical writings constitute a campaign against all schools of critics who judge art for its pragmatic values. Art proves nothing; "it creates the totality of experience in its quality; and it has no useful relation to the ordinary forms of action" (*Reactionary Essays*). According to Tate's theory of art, art springs from the irresistible need of the mind for an absolute experience, one which cannot be adequately satisfied in ordinary experience. The only coherent reality that we can experience is in art, for it is here alone that the disparate elements of our experience attain coherence and form. Art apprehends and concentrates our experience within the limitations of form. The poet as maker strives toward a signification of an experience, emotion or idea, until it becomes, with-

in the dimensions of the poem, "absolute." Poetry is the fusion of "an intensely felt ordinary experience, an intense moral situation, into an intensely realized art." The great poems are absolute: there is nothing beyond the poem. Tate offers the critic no formula for recognizing this quality of absolutism. Ransom follows Tate's doctrine here in his insistence that "Good critical writing is always more or less empirical in method, which means that the critic looks first and last at the poem, while he tries to determine what poetic theory will be the one to accomplish its analysis. Each poem is a new poem, and each analysis is probably the occasion of a new extension of theory in order to cope with it" ("Ubiquitous Moralists," *Kenyon Review:* Winter, 1941). In "Poetry and the Absolute," which contains the core of Tate's poetics, Tate made the same point, namely that the test of a poem must be applied *a posteriori.*

> One may say that Yeats's poems, *Upon a Dying Lady,* survive the test, in any formulation. . . . He has presented a newly-created *emotion* never before felt by anyone and never to be felt creatively by anyone else; has contributed an absolute signification to an old and relative fact. It is absolute because it is unique and contains no point of relation to any other signification of that fact.

In the perfectly realized poem there is no overflow of unrealized emotion, no emotion or action in excess of the object or situation which should be the objective equivalent for that emotion. Poets must be selected by some absolute, even if it is only a provisional one. If there is any originally ulterior motive, such as Dante's moral contempt for his enemies in Hell, the ulterior motive "is absorbed and becomes implicit in form, rather than explicit and didactic." Paul Valéry has described the perfect poem by way of a simile, comparing it to "a distant sailing-vessel—inanimate but articulate, seemingly with an absolute life of its own."

Eliot's Impersonal Theory of Art, which he announced in *Tradition and the Individual Talent* and elaborated in *The Sacred Wood* (1920), is repeated in scattered instances of Tate's critical dicta. A poem is not the secretion of personal emotions. The emotion or idea embodied in a work of art is impersonal. "The more perfect the artist," Eliot declares, "the more completely separate in him will be the man who suffers and the mind which creates." Contrary to Coleridgean theory, which has led criticism out of the poem and into the mind, Tate's poetics asserts that the specific poetic element is an objective feature of the poem, rather than a subjective effect. We can never determine whether a work is a work of art by establishing its subjective, or purely personal, correlatives. The critic who asserts that he is investigating poetry from the psychological approach is actually leading us away from the fact of the art-work, Tate observes. His stand is poles apart from Herbert Read's "ontogenetic" criticism, as practiced on Shelley in his *In Defense of Shelley,* "which traces the origins of the work of art in the psychology of the individual and in the economic structure of society." But literary criticism (the definition is Desmond MacCarthy's) is concerned with values, not with the psychological origin of such values. The traditional critic like Tate, as distinguished from the experimental critic like Read, investigates the nature of the poem *as* poem; not the origin of the poem (Read), nor its effect upon the reader (Richards), nor its value for civilization (Dewey).

For Ransom, likewise, the business of the literary critic is exclusively with an aesthetic criticism. Aesthetic values are anchored within the poem; it is solely the aesthetic structure, the internal organization of the poem, that gives any poem its value. Its value as a poem does not lie in its relation to the mind of the author. In "The Objective Basis of Criticism" (*Western Review:* Summer, 1948), Eliseo Vivas defines an aesthetic structure to be one "which successfully excludes the irrelevant values and controls vigorously the values and meanings it communicates." A work of art, I contend, contains but a single intention, and all the seemingly disparate and conflicting elements which are enclosed within the dimensions of the work accrete around and function towards that one intended end. As for Tate and Eliot, a work of art has a life of its own. True, the ultimate question concerning a work is out of how deep a life does it spring? But the critical question which determines whether it is a work of art is: has it a life of its own? "The life of art is in its form" (Bishop). The difference between art and its germinal event is absolute. The expression of those elements which give art its aesthetic identity and its absolute quality, Roger Fry states in his *Vision and Design,* is never identical with the expression of these elements in actual life. Though Fry limits his discussion to the field of the plastic arts, the concept is open to more general application. Consideration of poetry bears this out. In poetry, life and art can in no way be made equivalent because the emotions or experience which poetry offers are not the actual emotions or experience which everyday life presents, they are specifically aesthetic emotions. (Fry defines the aesthetic experience to be the apprehension of the purely formal relations of a work of art.) This distinction between life and art is also made by Belgion in criticizing Richards' supposition, in *Practical Criticism,* that there is no gap between the two realms. Not only is the aesthetic emotion different from the emotion we should have if we experienced the poem's subject in actual life, but it can be produced without having originated in life at all. And Tate attests to this fact in his Preface to his *Selected Poems:* " . . . that, as a poet, I have never had any [original] experience, and that, as a poet, my concern is the experience that I hope the reader will have in reading the poem." We as readers, T. Sturge Moore comments in his study of Valéry, come to poetry not to know what poets feel; "we read poems because they are wholes, composed of harmonized words and meanings which inter-echo symphonically."

To analyze and elucidate the formed meaning of a poem or novel is the prime job of the critic; but criticism must also make judgments as well as analyses, and therefore criticism cannot stand apart from theory. For technical criticism we look to Brooks, Blackmur, or Empson; for theoretical formulations of the nature of poetry, to Burke, Ransom, Tate, Winters, or Richards. Ransom, like Burke, is a philosophical critic. As critic his prime interest is in the metaphysics of aesthetics; it is only incidentally that he is committed to the technical criticism of poetry. As in *The World's Body,* he begins with aesthetics as the starting point for a philosophical defense of poetry. He gives us a poetics, and the core of it lies in his principle that the differentium of poetry is a metaphysical or ontological one. Poetry is ontology. Poetry, Charles Maurras similarly points out in his Preface to *Musique Intérieure,* is ontology, "for poetry strives . . . towards the roots of the knowledge of Being." Ransom transposes the problem of being, which is for him the basic problem in aesthetics, to the plane of the imaginative content of literature and art. He examines the "ontology" of a work and makes a metaphysical or aesthetic judgment upon it. In the principle that the intellect is the foundation of poetry and that the criterion of judg-

ment is a qualitative one, Ransom and Tate are Aristotelian. To quote Tate, Ransom "has explored possibilities of an Aristotelian criticism of the poetic disorder of our time." He has attempted to establish poetic truth as objective. A poem is a self-enclosed world which "recovers for us the world of solid substance." Its status is "objective," even as the criticism which is a criticism of that poetic structure is objective. Poetry is one way of knowing the world. The knowledge obtainable from poetry is unique. It is radically or ontologically distinct from the prose or scientific formulation. In any scientific formulation objects exist not as solid objects but as points in a structural pattern which controls them. The thought pattern controls and subordinates them to the realization of a thesis. Now in a poem what is analogous to the prose or scientific formulation is its logical structure-meaning. The structure of a poem is its prose argument (the universal); but a poem has not only this determinate meaning, which attaches to the structure, but it has a texture-meaning as well. The texture is the context of indeterminate and heterogeneous details (the concrete). These many-valued texture-meanings are significant since they function in the total meaning of the poem, but they are logically irrelevant to the structure-meaning alone. (This tissue of concrete irrelevance is more valuable for its own sake than for its contribution to the prose argument of the poem.) "A poetic discourse embodies within itself . . . a prose discourse. I think this is a law of poetry. . . . No prose argument, no poem. The prose argument is the poem's 'structure'; and then 'texture' suggests itself for the name of the ubiquitous and unstructural detail" (*The Inorganic Muses*).

The flaw in much of modern poetry, and for Ransom this is the flaw in *The Waste Land,* is that it is all texture and no structure. "Poetic texture without logical structure is not the right strategy." The differentium of poetry is this texture-structure order of objectivity. And the critic's job is to examine and define this texture-structure formulation in individual poems under his scrutiny. To do this, Ransom insists, requires an aesthetician's understanding of what a poem generically "is." "The thing that makes a lyrical poem supreme over other literary forms, and indeed the epitome and standard of literary forms, is its range of content; or, what is the same thing, its density" ["Mr. Empson's Muddles," *Southern Review* 4 (Autumn 1938)]. It is by the content or subject matter that Ransom differentiates a poetry from a poetry—on the basis of the ontology of the poem, "the reality of its being." In *God without Thunder,* he poses the view that though poetry and religion are agents of the irrational, they nevertheless yield a greater reality than science does. "Art is radically not science." What distinguishes a poetic discourse from a scientific one is the degree of irrelevant and indeterminate concreteness, the texture.

Permanent poetry, Eliot holds, is a fusion of these two poles of the mind: emotion and thought. For Tate it is a fusion of concretion and abstraction, image and idea, or (to substitute Ransom's dichotomy) texture and structure. Tate reframes Eliot's view: poetry does not give us "an emotional experience," nor "an intellectual experience"; it gives us a poetic experience. In commenting on Wallace Stevens' *Ideas of Order,* Blackmur defines the poetic experience from a parallel viewpoint. Ideas are abstractions, but they are also things seen. "It is the function of poetry . . . to experience ideas of the first kind with the eyes of the second kind, and to make of the experience of both a harmony and an order: a harmonium" (In *The Expense of Greatness*). In all great poetry there is a clash of opposite elements issuing in a tension between abstraction and sensation. In Donne and in Emily Dickinson, "There is no thought as such at all; nor is there feeling; there is that unique focus of experience which is at once neither and both." Dickinson's abstractions are not separately visible from her sensuous illuminations of them; idea and image are in tension. Like Donne, "she *perceives abstraction and thinks sensation*" (Tate in *Reactionary Essays*). The genuine poem embodies both the emotion (or thought) *and* the situation which provokes it. Tate regards Hardy's abstractions as beyond the range of his feelings, since Hardy "rarely shows us the experience that ought to justify them, that would give them substance, visibility, meaning" (*Hardy's Philosophic Metaphors*). He judges Crane and Cummings by the same criterion. (It is the criterion of the Objective Correlative.) Winters' formula that poetry is technique for dealing with irreducible emotion, which Tate attacks in *Confusion and Poetry* (*Sewanee Review:* April, 1930), conceals a contemporary version of the romantic dogma that poetry is emotion. Emotion is not the exclusive subject matter of poetry. As Auden says, "abstractions are empty and their expression devoid of a poetic value." And the poet's emotions, these too have no value in themselves. In his Preface to Valéry's *le serpent,* Eliot states the point: "Not our feelings, but the pattern which we make of our feelings is the centre of value."

The New Critics have found their standards for great poetry in the seventeenth century Metaphysicals. Using Richards' viewpoint, Brooks defines metaphysical poetry as a poetry of synthesis and claims for it the highest order. It is a poetry which joins widely divergent and conflicting elements in imagery that is functional rather than decorative, and it achieves thus the desired union of emotion and thought. In Donne's poems the comparisons are not illustrations attached to a statement, as they are in Arnold's. In Donne "The comparison *is* the poem in a structural sense." The poetry of synthesis as defined by Richards is synonymous with the poetry of the imagination as defined by Tate (in contradistinction to the poetry of the will—allegory or propaganda art). A poetry of the will, as distinct from a poetry of the imagination, ignores the whole vision of an experience for some special moral, or political, or social interest; the meaning is forced and the total context of the human predicament oversimplified or unexplored. Such didactic poetry is "one-sided"; it is therefore inferior both as a poetic discourse and as a prose or scientific one (*Three Types of Poetry*). "Platonic poetry" is Tate's and Ransom's descriptive term for this didactic poetry which brings poetry into competition with science, falsifying their relationship. Unlike the Metaphysical poet, the Platonic poet discourses in terms of things, "but on the understanding that they are translatable at every point into ideas"; or he elaborates ideas as such, "but in proceeding introduces for ornament some physical properties." Platonic poetry deals with ideas, Physical poetry deals with concrete things. For Ransom, all genuine poetry is a phase of Physical poetry (*A Note on Ontology*).

Brooks's *Modern Poetry and the Tradition* (1939) is a critical synthesis of this modern revolution in our conception of poetry. The revolution, in sum, has consisted chiefly in a return to the Metaphysicals and hence in a repudiation of their heretical deviators: the Augustan Neo-Classicists, who regarded metaphor as a decoration of poetic thought-content; and the nineteenth century Romantics, who discredited irony or wit (the essential ingredient of metaphysical poetry) and regarded poetry as an elevated way of expressing elevated be-liefs. Milton and Shelley have been the two main points of attack in this revised perspective of the poetic tradition. We have witnessed the thorough repudiation of Shelley (by Leavis, Tate, and Eliot), and the dislodgment of Milton—for which Eliot was wholly responsible. We have paid homage to Dryden, especially to Dryden the critic, with Eliot and Mark Van Doren as the chief instigators of his ascendant reputation. Pope, placed by Leavis and Brooks in the Metaphysical line (in *Revaluation* and in *The Well Wrought Urn*), has finally come into his own again. But it is Donne who has dominated our poetic and critical climate. While the New Criticism begins with Eliot's *Sacred Wood,* it had its taking-off in Hulme's pronouncement that the Romantic convention had reached a point of exhaustion and that, of immediate necessity, it was now the moment for a new convention or technique to replace the dead one. For the new convention, modern poetry drew upon the school of Donne and, sharing with it, the school of the French Symbolists—both schools representing radical departures from the common poetic tradition. The New Criticism was created out of this new convention—to explain it and to make it accessible. (pp. 496-502)

The sole purpose of criticism is to enlighten the reader, to instruct the reader, to create the *proper* reader. The critic prepares the reader to appreciate the ascendant artists of his time by defining for him standards of taste and examples of taste in operation. The chief end of criticism is to elucidate the relation of the poet, or the reader, to the poem. All critical writings can be classified under one or more parts of this three-part poet-to-poem-to-reader relationship. Everything of Richards' criticism, for instance, fits into this framework. This schematic idea is epitomized in his theory of poetry as communication: a poem is an organization of experience, a resolution and "balancing of impulses," and the reader gets the same harmony or "ordering of the mind" as the poet originally experienced. Though neither Brooks nor Tate fully assents to Richards' theory of poetry as communication, Brooks holds similarly that we, as the poet's readers, in a process akin to the poet's exploration of his material, "refabricate from his symbols . . . a total experience somewhat similar, if we possess imagination, to the total experience of the poet himself." Eliot's idea of the Objective Correlative suggests a parallel correlation: the objects or chain of images in a poem, if it is the objective correlative of the poet's original emotion about it, immediately evokes in the spectator the same emotion.

The poet-poem-reader relationship is again illustrated by the Problem of Belief: the question whether it is necessary for the reader to share the poet's beliefs in order to enjoy fully his poetry. The problem of the poem as related to the poet's, or the reader's, beliefs is resolved by Eliot thus: "When the doctrine, theory, belief, or 'view of life' presented in a poem is one which the mind of the reader can accept as coherent, mature, and founded on the facts of experience, it interposes no obstacle to the reader's enjoyment. . . ." With this interpretation, which Eliot makes in *The Use of Poetry* (1933), all later critics concur. The question of the specific merit of a poetic statement as truth or falsehood does not arise when the beliefs of the poet are ordered into an intrinsic whole. It is on this ground that Tate rejects Shelley's poetry, not because Shelley's ideas are immature but because his statements are not an integral part of a genuine poem. As Eliot notes: "Both in creation and enjoyment much always enters which is, from the point of view of 'art,' irrelevant." One irrelevance is the truth or falsity of the belief expressed in the poem *as* poem.

It was a mistake of the early Richards to think that what, in the way of acceptance, is demanded of a poem is the poet's own beliefs. All of Spender's best poems convey single emotions, but, as Tate says (in *New Verse:* May, 1933), "these *single emotions* are created, in the sense that a table or chair is created; they are not believed."

Belief, as applied to the arts, is a sociological category. To assign objective status to the content of a poem apart from its form is to reduce the poem's meaning to its original state, and this is to locate it in the historical process. Within terms of this affirmation the critic is testing poetic subject matter by its correlation with the world it represents—the correlations being either historical, psychological, ethical, or economic. This doctrine of relevance is false. The only relevance the New Critics subscribe to is the relevance which subject ideas have to each other within the formed meaning of the work itself. Poetry, as Blackmur affirms (in *The Double Agent*), "is life at the remove of form and meaning"; criticism has to do with "the terms and modes" by which this remove was made, that is, with the relation between content and form. A work of art is autonomous. It is a construct having a life of its own, and it is limited by its own technique and intention. The New Critics isolate the meaning of a poem only in terms of form.

Their critical practice is consistent with their critical theory. Contrary to Jacques Barzun, Tate does not repudiate the validity of textual exegesis (his own explication of his "Ode to the Confederate Dead" is proof enough). A paraphrase is not the work itself; a paraphrase defines only the poem's structural plan. It is the inferior poem alone that can be replaced by a statement; to paraphrase such a poem is to reduce it to something like its originally unrealized condition. The aesthetic whole, however, resists practical formulation. Tate's whole point is that there is no substitute for the poem itself. The poem "is its own knower, neither poet nor reader knowing anything that the poem says apart from the words of the poem." Brooks and Ransom take of course the same stand.

In the manner of Empson, Blackmur, or Brooks, who are our most expert technical critics, the critic lets the reader in on the poem's intention. He digs out the facts (and not alone the subsurface ones) and the principle governing the facts; he elucidates the poem's intention (the meaning objectified within the work, which is its form); he analyzes the texture-structure strategy of the poem, and he makes comparative judgments about its technical practice. Such judgments are not abstractions. These critics make analyses and judgments that are informed by a body of principles, but their approach is empirical. The Southern critics and the critics of the *Scrutiny* school are Aristotelian in their method: they analyze the aesthetic object in and for itself. H. A. Mason, in his defense of "F. R. Leavis and 'Scrutiny' " (in *The Critic:* Autumn, 1947), points out that the reader of Leavis' criticism "tends to forget the critic entirely and fails to note that in the process he has appropriated a good number of Mr. Leavis's judgments as his own." The point holds similarly for Empson and for Blackmur. "As there is no Leavisian doctrine or philosophy, there is nothing to seize on in his criticism but the example of first-hand valuation and there is no interference in the triangular interplay between reader, author and critic." The standards of these critics are aesthetic ones, and this sets them apart from other critics whose standards are sociological (Auden), historical (Wilson), psychological (Burke), or ethical (Winters).

The critical writings of Tate and Leavis show a close kinship in their sources, their aims and critical attitudes, and particularly in their conception of the critic's function. Leavis is at one with Tate's rejection of critical relativity, with his dogma of authority in absolute standards which allow the reader no choice in point of view or taste, and with his contention for the values of a tradition as imperative. The critic, directly or by implication, deals with a tradition. He deals with tradition in terms of representative poets (and with individual poets in terms of representative samples of their work). The poet's objective is the same as the critic's. The poet probes the deficiencies of a tradition. As Tate explains, the poet, in the true sense of Arnold's dictum that poetry is a "criticism of life," criticizes his tradition "either as such, or indirectly by comparing it with something that is about to replace it . . . he *discerns* its real elements and thus establishes its value, by putting it to the test of experience" (*Reactionary Essays*). Always the business of criticism, Leavis states in his Introduction to *Towards Standards,* is "to define, help form, and organize the contemporary sensibility [the traditional mind which lives in the present or not at all], and to make conscious the 'standards' in it."

Both Tate and Leavis derive their critical position from Eliot. They have crystalized and expanded germinal ideas planted in *The Sacred Wood.* As Leavis makes clear in *Education and the University* (1943), he opposes, however, Eliot's doctrinal approach. Both critics reject Richards' theory of art and, for the past two decades, they have vigorously assaulted his pseudo-scientific, pseudo-psychological, and semasiological approach. It was only in the early Richards that Leavis felt points of agreement, his *Practical Criticism* providing incitement towards Leavis' program for instructing public taste and reforming literary education, for which he pioneered in *Mass Civilization and Minority Culture* (1930) and in *How to Teach Reading* (1933). Like Brooks, Leavis insists upon the importance of critical study in the university education of general intelligence, and, like Ransom, he sets strict boundaries to the conception and practice of literary criticism, contending that it "should be controlled by a strict conception of its special nature and methods." Literary criticism "should be the best possible training for intelligence—for free, unspecialized, general intelligence, which there has never at any time been enough of, and which we are peculiarly in need of to-day."

In comparison with Tate, Leavis has more scholarship to buttress his criticism, and, in comparison with Brooks, he has a somewhat wider range. It is Johnson whom Tate and Leavis resemble, for their criticism is a dogmatic and rational criticism. Tate's prose is savage in tone. Where Leavis defends the fort, Tate pursues the enemy. Brooks's debt is chiefly to Empson and Richards, but a striking parallelism is provided by Leavis' work, namely between his *Revaluation* and Brooks's *The Well Wrought Urn,* and again between his *New Bearings in English Poetry* and Brooks's *Modern Poetry and the Tradition.* In the first instance their criticism is technical criticism, in the second instance it is historical rather than critical in approach. The work of Martin Turnell, the leading associate of Leavis' *Scrutiny* school, is likewise both technical and historical criticism. I mention Turnell because I think that he and Leavis represent the two most important critics in England today.

Our age is indeed an age of criticism. The structure of critical ideas and the practical criticism that British critics—Leavis, Turnell, Empson, Read—and American critics—Ransom,

Tate, Brooks, Warren, Blackmur, Winters—have contrived upon the foundations of Eliot and Richards constitute an achievement in criticism the like of which has not been equaled in any previous period of our literary history. (pp. 502-06)

Robert Wooster Stallman, "The New Critics," in his Critiques and Essays in Criticism: 1920-1948, Representing the Achievement of Modern British and American Critics, *The Ronald Press Company, 1949, pp. 488-506.*

RICHARD STRIER

[*In the following excerpt, Strier discusses New Critical poetics and the insights it affords into the nature of literary language.*]

In an essay written in 1940, Cleanth Brooks attempted to formulate the poetics and the general attitude toward language of the New Criticism (indeed, for this criticism, as we shall see, "poetics" *means* "attitude toward language"). The title of Brooks' essay, "The Poem as Organism," is an acknowledgment of the historical origins of New Criticism in Coleridge's critical and philosophical vocabulary; the central claim of the essay is that "what has to be considered the recalcitrancy of language (when viewed as the material which resists the single-minded expositor) may be viewed on the other hand as an amazing fertility and richness, a vitality with which combinations of words seem sometimes of themselves to urge upon us new meanings." "All that is necessary" to effect this change of attitude, Brooks claims, is that we do not conceive of words in sentences as "sharply isolated entities, like beads on a string, each opaque and impervious to the others except for the thread of logic which links them together." Rather, he continues, "we have to think of them not as beads, but as burrs—predisposed to hang together in any fashion whatever."

Brooks is making two separate but closely related assertions in this passage, and each of these assertions is crucial to the poetics he is seeking to enunciate. The first is of the relative autonomy of verbal configurations from conscious intentions in a thinker, speaker, or writer. The key term in Brooks' simultaneous description and positive evaluation of this phenomenon is "vitality," while most of the strictly descriptive work in his characterization is done by the almost parenthetical phrase, "of themselves"—"combinations of words seem sometimes *of themselves* to urge upon us new meanings." In this phenomenological account, the non–"single-minded" thinker or "expositor" is presented as passive, while certain "combinations of words" are seen as actively "urging" new meanings upon him (Brooks' plural indicates that he takes this experience to be familiar to all non–"single-minded" users of language). Brooks' argument is that a proper appreciation of the significance of this experience is essential to the understanding and production of poetry and that this appreciation also necessarily leads to a rejection of what might be called the algebraic model of language—words as "sharply isolated entities" related to one another solely by the "thread" of syntactical and logical operators.

Brooks' second proposition about language is never actually very carefully or successfully articulated by him. It is implied in his description of the results of "autonomous" combinations of words as "new meanings" but is obscured by his exhortation that we think of words "not as beads but as burrs." An implicit contradiction in Brooks' description of these

"word-burrs" points to the fact that Brooks is not quite saying what he means here. To describe something as "predisposed" to act in a *random* manner borders on the contradictory. "Predisposition" implies a determinism, a tendency (based upon prior history or development) to act in certain specific ways—the range of possibilities can be enormously large, but it must be, at least in principle, delimitable. The assertion that I take it Brooks wants to make is that the combinations of words which seem to emerge into the thinking consciousness "of themselves" are, if not predictable, ultimately intelligible—they are, that is, new *meanings,* not simply random phonetic patterns.

This belief in the ultimate intelligibility and potential cognitive content of (what seem to be) nonlogical connections between words is perhaps the fundamental premise of the New Criticism. It might be said that in the theory of language behind New Critical poetic theory the very notion of a "purely verbal" association between words in the mind of a speaker or writer is being seriously questioned; the sharp Cartesian or Platonic distinction between ideas and matter, thought and words, meanings and the vehicles of meaning, is being denied. W. K. Wimsatt has suggested [in his study *The Verbal Icon,* 1954] that even the pun—that most despised form of "purely verbal" connection between words—is not always wholly adventitious: "I wonder," he muses, "if it may not even be possible to say that the long survival of such basic and homely homonymies as *son-sun, rest-rest* testifies to the fact that there is nothing repugnant in the ideas thus linked (though clearly distinguishable), or even that there is some harmony in the linkage." The New Criticism conceives of concepts as dissolved or "submerged" in the "matter" of words and holds that the "autonomous" movements of words are ultimately intelligible because they are based on and include (coherent) relations between the meanings of the words involved. Language, on this view, is thought of as concrete and material rather than as abstract (recall "the *material* which resists the single-minded expositor"). The claim is that words have "lives of their own" independent to a certain extent of logical and syntactical relations because they have had a history and development of their own.

William Empson [in his *Seven Types of Ambiguity,* 1961] remarked that the position of the critic wishing to apply Empson's type of verbal analysis to poetry is analogous to that of a scientist "wishing to apply determinism to the world"—that is, like the scientist, the critic of this kind must assume that the context in which a given (verbal) event takes place has made it necessary for that event to take place in precisely the way it did and that past relations between the components of the (verbal) situation under consideration have conditioned the "present" ones. Words are considered to include at least potentially, within their appearance in a given setting, (all) the meanings they have had (that is, the ways in which they have been used) in previous contexts. An "autonomous" movement of words is considered to be potentially intelligible in terms of meanings potential (through usage and prior contexts) in each of the individual words. The system of meanings can relate at any point, but the relation constituted by the point at which they do meet will be discursively assertible.

Like the determinist, the New Critic must proceed by assuming what he hopes to prove; he assumes the existence of "objective" relations between the words of the poem he is studying and then attempts to perceive such relations. The distinction between "objective"—that is, in some sense verifiable—

and purely subjective or personal meaning must necessarily be a central one for this type of poetics. New Critics are constantly protesting that they are not "reading into" works, that the meanings they ascribe to the words or images of a literary text are objectively there rather than subjectively imposed. Empson declares, speaking of a recurrent image in Donne's poetry [in "Donne and the Rhetorical Tradition," *Kenyon Review 11* (Autumn, 1949)], "the point is not so much what 'connotations' this 'image-term' might have to a self-indulgent reader as what connotations it actually does have in its repeated uses by Donne"—there is clearly a semantic distinction to be made here, for Empson is using the same term, "connotation," to describe both what he does and what he does not mean.

In *Poetic Discourse,* Joan Hungerland suggests that there is a sharp distinction to be made between "personal association," which "may or may not be idiosyncratic," and "word association," which "must be based on shared experience." She notes that the associations which give *connotation* to a word are "communal" and that connotation is a matter of "the associations of words with other words" in which contexts of employment are a major factor. Ms. Hungerland points out, as does Max Black in a well-known article on metaphor [*Proceedings of the Aristotelian Society* (1954-55), No. 54 (London, 1955)], that the commonly accepted attributes of the *referent* of a word tend to become part of the word's connotation. *Connotation,* then, is objective, empirically verifiable by appeal to history and/or any competent speaker of the relevant language who has the relevant range of experience. This seems to me both a helpful and true distinction. Empson's comment on Donne, moreover, suggests another way, more purely literary, in which the associations of a writer's words can attain something like the status of objective connotations: this will happen when a reader or critic recognizes that, in a number of unrelated employments by a writer, a given word consistently tends to have certain fixed or specific associations which are roughly predictable. To a careful reader, then, these associations will be *connotations* within the context of this writer's *oeuvre.*

In dealing with texts, particularly poems, in which the relations among the words or images involved are not immediately intelligible, the New Critic seeks for connecting connotations. He will, therefore, attempt to screen out as far as possible his own personal associations (this is what Empson's "self-indulgent reader" does not do) and to respond to what might be termed the "connotative flow" of the language of the text he is reading. The New Criticism might be said to demand of the critic something very similar to what Keats meant by "negative capability" and "the poetical character"—a capacity to suspend the judging and "irritable" ego and "enter into" the "life" of other entities. In the "Preface" to *Understanding Poetry,* Brooks and Warren assert that "the knowledge poetry yields is available only if we submit ourselves to the massive, and subtle, impact of the poem as a whole," and they insist that the reader "must surrender as fully as possible to the impact of the whole." Since, as we shall see shortly, the connotative flows between words and, especially, images in poems constitute a great deal of what the New Critics consider to be the "massive and subtle impact" of poems "as wholes," "surrender" to the connotative flow of a poem becomes a—indeed, *the*—crucial means of access to the special "knowledge poetry yields." This brings us back, of course, to what I earlier termed "perhaps the fundamental premise" of the New Criticism—a faith in the ultimate intelli-

gibility and potential cognitive content of (what seem to be) non-logical connections between words.

The attitude toward associations between words which I have been attempting to sketch is obviously related to the problem of the peculiar unity or "logic" of poetry. Poetry is considered by the New Critics to be characterized by language peculiarly rich in connotation and peculiarly conscious of its own connotative content. The language of poetry is seen as distinctively "vital" in the number and significance of the links between its words and images. If a critic can point to the "sub-surface" connotative flow of the language of a poem and show it to have cognitive content relevant to the apparent or literal content of the poem as a whole, he has found a way to establish the unity of a work which may appear to have no unifying principle at all, and to account for the experience of unity which he has, presumably, already had in reading the work.

In poetry which is highly metaphorical and does not provide explicit transitions between its metaphors, the problems of unity and "logic" (in the sense of discursive coherence) are particularly urgent, and the possibility of revealing a coherence in, and thereby establishing a unity upon, the connotative flow of the poem's language is particularly attractive. It is in these cases that the New Critic's faith and "application of determinism" are most immediately called for, and it is in these cases, as in that of puns, that the "autonomy" of language can most clearly be seen in operation. The New Critics have been only too eager to test their faith in relation to sequences of metaphors or poems which proceed almost wholly through metaphors. Metaphor, for Cleanth Brooks, is "the essence of poetry"; the first case of "ambiguity" in poetry that Empson considers is "the comparison of two things which does not say in virtue of what they are to be compared." The whole process of explication is often a process of "explicitating" the implied cognitive content of metaphors or other figures in a poem. Metaphors necessarily generate specific connotations, a set of possible relations between the things compared. Metaphor is the preeminent instance in language of what Walter Ong (in a somewhat Hegelian or Whiteheadian phrase) has termed "meaning in the concrete."

When Coleridge wrote [in *Biographia Literaria*] that "poetry, even that of the loftiest and, seemingly, that of the wildest odes, has a logic of its own, as severe as that of science; and more difficult, because more subtle, more complex, and dependent on more, and more fugitive, causes," he was referring primarily to highly metaphorical poetry, poetry like that of Shakespeare or Pindar. It is this kind of poetry, as Coleridge was keenly aware, that lies most open to the charge of incoherence. When Eliot asserted that "there is a logic of the imagination as well as a logic of concepts," he was defending St.-John Perse's *Anabase* specifically against those who "find it difficult to distinguish between order and chaos in the arrangement of images."

It is worth noting that the problem of the "logic of imagery" that Eliot speaks of in his "Preface" to *Anabase* and that Coleridge refers to as the fugitive and subtle "logic of poetry" is not the logical problem which Aristotle saw metaphor as raising. Like the New Critics, Aristotle emphasized the cognitive content of metaphor: he saw the chief pleasures metaphor provides as vividness and *"making us learn something"* (italics mine). But Aristotle was interested in the internal logic of single metaphors, the logic of the relationship between the object, event, or situation to which the metaphorical word or words in a statement literally refer and the object, event, or situation to which the statement as a whole actually refers. The "logic" Eliot and Coleridge are speaking of is the relation between the cognitive content of a metaphor and the rest of the *total context* of which it is a part (which may, of course, contain many other metaphors). The "logic of imagery" of which Eliot speaks is a question of justifying a *sequence* of metaphors—as in *Anabase* or much of Shakespeare's poetry. It is a question of relating in a coherent discursive manner the cognitive content of a number of metaphors.

As the quotations from Eliot and Coleridge suggest, in attempting to establish the "logic" of a sequence of metaphors, a critic has to demonstrate order in verbal situations which appear to be random—in poems, that is, in which metaphors are "mixed" or apparently unrelated. In an essay entitled "The Hinterland of Thought," [in *Metaphor and Symbol*, edited by L. C. Knights, 1960] D. W. Harding concludes an analysis of *Adonais* with some remarks which are clearly relevant to the "surrender" which Brooks and Warren urge upon the reader of poetry. Not surprisingly, however, the subject of Harding's remarks is the poet rather than the reader:

> The contrasting and sometimes barely consistent ideas in these stanzas [48-52] seem to have reached expression partly *through verbal associations that might be called accidental,* were it not that they evidently gave openings for important variants of idea and attitude to emerge. "Time's decay" which the kings of thought defy [st. 48] leads to a contemplation of material decay in the Roman ruins [st. 49]; the monument of Caius Cestius, called a "refuge" for his memory [st. 50], later [st. 51] produces "the shelter of the tomb"; the tears and gall that await us in life suggests the world's "bitter" wind that immediately follows [1.457]. In this way the *partial surrender to the seeming accidents of language* has become a means of releasing partly-formed ideas and attitudes. . . . And if we feel that in the earlier fluctuations of his attitude toward death Shelley gives evidence of confusion, there is a good case for arguing that in the last of these stanzas [st. 52] he achieves a very real complexity, and especially through the uses he makes of the word "stains" in [1.463]. [Italics mine]

This analysis points to a problem in poetics which is particularly pressing for the New Criticism—the problem of distinguishing "complexity" from "confusion" on rational grounds (recall Eliot's scorn for people who "find it difficult to distinguish between order and chaos in the arrangement of images"). "Complexity" is clearly an honorific term in Harding's vocabulary, and "confusion" clearly a negative one. The distinction between them, therefore, is crucial. In following the connotative flow implicit in some apparently purely verbal links among Shelley's words and images, Harding perceived a thoroughgoing ambivalence in Shelley's attitude toward his subject. He holds this ambivalence not to be damaging to the coherence of the poem because the poem comes to focus directly upon it. He shows apparent "accidents of language" to have cognitive content, and he shows the movement of the poem from one image to another to be expressive of or related to the thematic development of the poem as a whole. The images are revealed to be the theme in embryo.

Harding's procedure excellently demonstrates the strategy which the New Critics regularly employ in defending the "logic" of a poem's apparently illogical metaphors: the

"logic" of these metaphors is their relevance to thematic content. The criterion which Empson suggests in *Seven Types* for distinguishing between "good" and "bad" ambiguities in poetry corresponds exactly to the criterion Harding employs for distinguishing between complexity and confusion in highly imagistic poems: an ambiguity is bad, Empson asserts, "when the interest of the passage is not focussed upon it." In the chapter on "Figurative Language" in *Practical Criticism*, Richards comments negatively upon a poem ("Poem 9," the original version of Noyes' "For the Eightieth Birthday of George Meredith") not because its metaphors are inconsistent with one another—"to say this settles nothing about the value of the passage"—but because these inconsistencies *are unconnected*; they do not, says Richards, derive "from some one central liberty taken by the poet," but rather each is "a separate crack in the fabric of the sense." The essential difference, on this scheme, between complexity and confusion, good and bad ambiguity, emerges: complexity is systematic and thematically central. A highly metaphorical poem is said to be complex rather than confused if the possibilities or problems implicit in its imagery are realized in its theme, if the "autonomous movements" of the poem's language are identical with or parallel to developments of thought or attitude amenable to coherent thematic explication.

For critics mainly concerned with poetry in English, the question of the cognitive content and discursive coherence of highly metaphorical poetry based on apparently "purely verbal" links inevitably comes to a head in relation to Shakespeare. John Crowe Ransom, who insisted upon a sharp distinction between the material and the conceptual aspects of language—its "texture" as opposed to its "logical structure"—attacked Shakespeare's poetry for apparently progressing through accidental associations rather than through a structure worked out in advance. He calls for a poetic language completely controlled by the intellect; he condemns the poet who "partially surrenders" to "seeming accidents of language." Ransom calls for images which exemplify thoughts rather than for thinking in or through images, for the foreground of thought rather than that "hinterland" in which associational flows release "partly-formed" ideas and attitudes. "Much of the effect of Shakespeare's poetry," says Ransom [in "Shakespeare at Sonnets," in *The World's Body*, 1938], is "accidental or mechanical, because it is oral or verbal; it is word-play" and word-play, according to Ransom, belongs to the "loose" poetry of "association"—a kind of poetry of which the cognitive content must necessarily be "of low grade." Against this kind of poetry, Ransom opposes the "tight," "coherently" organized poetry of Donne.

The New Critics have denied both halves of Ransom's claim, that about Shakespeare and that about Donne. The second essay in *The Well Wrought Urn*, is an elaborate "explicitation" of the cognitive content of two passages in *Macbeth* which seem, even for Shakespeare, extraordinarily incoherent and arbitrary in their metaphorical structure. Brooks demonstrates the "logic" of Shakespeare's metaphors in these passages by showing that the relations between the metaphors therein correspond to and express central thematic concerns of *Macbeth* as a whole. Brooks demonstrates in Shakespeare's "mixed" metaphors what Harding discovers in Shelley's accidental linkages: a coherent structure of attitudes. Empson and others have done the same for other sequences of mixed metaphors in Shakespeare. Moreover, in a later essay in *The Well Wrought Urn*, Brooks attempts to demonstrate, in direct response to Ransom, that in spite of its facade of logical argument, Donne's poetry as much as Shakespeare's takes its essential movement from the connotative flows among its images.

Ransom's method involves concentrating on individual images in poems and counting connections between images as logical only if they are explicit; for Ransom, images are (as Brooks said words are not) "isolated entities like beads on a string." Brooks argues that in Donne's "A Valediction: Forbidding Mourning"—a poem that is famous for the supposed logical rigor of its figures—the connections between the figures are associational in just the same way the connections between Shakespeare's less fully elaborated figures are. And Empson, arguing against Tuve's contention that the "stiff twin compasses" image in this poem is properly responded to only in terms of the explicit point of connection between the separateness of the legs of the compasses and the separateness of the lovers, suggests that in its total context even this celebrated explicit comparison has an important and relevant "associational" dimension: "surely," says Empson, "the reality, the solidity, the usefulness and the intellectual uses of the compasses, their reliability in situations where native intuition cannot give the answer unaided, are all relevant to the comparison [in its context]." John Middleton Murry enunciates the New Critical attitude toward metaphor and the "logic of metaphor" in a passage [in *Countries of the Mind*, 1931] that amounts to a New Critical *credo* and includes within it the content of almost all the statements from Coleridge, Empson, Eliot, Harding, and Brooks that I have quoted in this section: "The greatest mastery of imagery does not lie in the use, however beautiful and revealing, of isolated images, but in the harmonious total impression produced by *a succession of subtly related images.* In such cases, the images appear to grow out of one another and to be fulfilling *an independent life of their own.* . . . Yet this apparent autonomy is *as strictly subordinated to a final impression* as the steps of a logical argument are to their conclusion." (pp. 171-80)

> *Richard Strier, "The Poetics of Surrender: An Exposition and Critique of New Critical Poetics," in* Critical Inquiry, *Vol. 2, No. 1, Autumn, 1975, pp. 171-89.*

DEBATE AND DEFENSE

WILLIAM VAN O'CONNOR

[O'Connor was among the many American exponents of the New Criticism. In the following excerpt from an essay that first appeared in the journal College English *in 1950, he discusses New Critical theory and defends its basic premises. For a response to O'Connor's comments by David Daiches, see the excerpt below.]*

William Morton Payne . . . believing that the concept of evolution would make for a new critical method, had spoken about a new criticism around the turn of the century; Joel Spingarn, finding Croce's doctrine of expressive form equally promising, had written "The New Criticism" in 1910. But the term "new criticism" as used more recently derives from John Crowe Ransom's *The New Criticism* (1941), a volume in which he discusses I. A. Richards, William Empson, T. S.

Eliot, Yvor Winters, and a few other critics. The characteristic common to all these latter critics is intensive analysis of the literary work. A designation more useful than "new criticism" would be "analytical criticism."

In William Elton's *A Glossary of the New Criticism* (1948) there is a lineal table of contemporary criticism listing Pound, Eliot, and the Southern Regionalists in direct descent from Coleridge; and Richards, Burke, and Empson in direct descent from Jeremy Bentham. There are also collateral influences, with the British critics Richards (who is also indebted to Coleridge) and Empson influencing Brooks and Warren, and Yvor Winters being at once in the debt of Burke and Eliot. But if one remembers that John Stuart Mill called Coleridge and Bentham the two seminal minds of the nineteenth century, the table, although interesting, merely implies that contemporary criticism is involved in the philosophical, sociological, psychological, and aesthetic currents of its time.

The interests of T. E. Hulme, who is commonly held to have influenced Pound, Eliot, and others in the years immediately prior to World War I, may be taken as representative. In his *Speculations,* published posthumously [in 1924], there are dicta, sometimes worked out, sometimes not, about scientism, romanticism, the structure of poetry, and the need for a system of religious values. Hulme discussed the breakup of religious belief and the awful burden thereby thrown on the individual poet to establish not only his own scale of values but the vehicles for giving them literary expression. He attempted to define the contemporary sensibility and to help "make conscious the 'standards' " in it. Like many another critic, Hulme was concerned with the way cultural developments are manifest in language and literary forms.

I. A. Richards, whose *Principles of Literary Criticism* (1924) was equally influential with Eliot's *The Sacred Wood* (1920), has been greatly concerned with the role of literature in a scientific-minded world. In *Science and Poetry* (1926) he discussed as pseudostatements those statements which are not verifiable in scientific terms but which satisfy our emotional needs. Poetic statements were useful but not true. The later Richards of *Coleridge on the Imagination* (1935) and *Philosophy of Rhetoric* (1936) got away from the notion that poetry although valuable in ordering our minds is irrelevant to the real world. In the volume on Coleridge he says, *"Poetry is the completest mode of utterance."* He places poetic language in the realm of myth, with no such pejorative connotations as those clinging to the term "pseudo." Myths, he adds, "are those hard realities in projection, their symbolic recognition, coordination and acceptance. . . . Without his mythologies man is only a cruel animal without a soul . . . a congeries of possibilities without order or aim."

Eliot too, of course, has been preoccupied with literature in relation to its own generation and the generations preceding it. His first book, *The Sacred Wood,* ended for many, particularly for younger readers, the era of Victorian literary standards. He became a symbol of an intellectual criticism that drew on the scholarship of various fields as well as a knowledge of Sanskrit, Greek, Latin, Italian, and French. For many years he was the leader of the younger generation, ignored by those whose tastes had been formed before World War I and occasionally attacked by those who misunderstood the pessimism of *The Waste Land,* as well as by those who disapproved of his growing religious interests, his politics, or his unsettling of Victorian literary standards. Recently the

I.A. Richards, circa 1928.

controversies have been less heated, but his work continues to be studied and to be influential.

Writing the Preface in 1928 for a new edition of *The Sacred Wood,* Eliot stated that the volume had as its center "the integrity of poetry" and that he was much indebted to Rémy de Gourmont. In the volume appear "Tradition and the Individual Talent" (which epitomizes many of the themes that run through his work), pieces on the art of criticism, as well as brief studies of Dante, Marlowe, Shakespeare, Jonson, Massinger, Blake, Swinburne, and others. Many of the subjects which recur in his later work are here: the objective correlative, the impersonal nature of art, the need for a sense of history, a pointing to the most usable parts of the literature of the past, and the meaning of tradition.

Homage to John Dryden (1924), which included essays on Marvell, the metaphysical poets, and Dryden, established even more clearly Eliot's belief that the most usable part of the English literary tradition was the literature of the sixteenth and seventeenth centuries. Subsequently it has become evident that Eliot's criticism was not entirely, in Arnold's sense, *disinterested.* His discovery of certain poets and his comments about them were grist for himself as a working poet. There are immediately evident connections between statements in "The Metaphysical Poets" and his own practice in *The Waste Land.* There are connections between "Song for Simeon," "Journey of the Magi," as well as "Gerontion" and

the title essay in *For Lancelot Andrewes* (1928). And there are connections between *Dante* (1929) and *Ash Wednesday.* In his Milton lecture, delivered several times in the United States in 1947 and published in *Sewanee Review,* Eliot explained his earlier playing-up of the metaphysicals and playing-down of Milton. In the 1920's one of the principles stressed by Pound and Eliot was that poetry should have the virtues of prose, that "the subject-matter and the imagery of poetry should be extended to objects related to the life of a modern man or woman." In neither respect would the study of Milton have helped their contemporaries. Eliot concluded the lecture by saying, "it now seems to me that poets are sufficiently removed from Milton, and sufficiently liberated from his reputation, to approach the study of his work without danger, and with profit to their poetry and to the English language." In "The Function of Criticism" in *The Sacred Wood,* Eliot stated that "the poetic critic is criticizing poetry in order to create poetry." In other words, Eliot's earlier criticism records the growth of his own mind and the development of his sensibility at the same time that it records the direction of one of the most significant lines of development in modern poetry and criticism.

The method of his criticism is less easy to characterize. First and foremost, he requires the co-operation of his reader. He analyzes and compares. Quite often Eliot's own comments, in a restricted and transparent style, simply prepare the reader for a long quotation. The reader is obliged to engage himself with the passage in order to relate it to what Eliot has said. That this is his intention seems to be indicated in another sentence from "The Function of Criticism": "In matters of great importance the critic must not coerce and he must not make judgements of worse and of better. He must simply elucidate: the reader will form the correct judgement for himself." The occasionally cryptic expressions, according to his own statement in *Homage to John Dryden,* are intentional. Certain notions presented as cryptograms would, if expressed directly, "be destined to immediate obloquy, followed by perpetual oblivion." He generally uses a historical method, not in the sense of establishing the milieu of a given work but by drawing upon poems of various periods in order to distinguish the character as well as the level of excellence of the given work. In his later criticism, as in *The Use of Poetry and the Use of Criticism* (1933) and *After Strange Gods* (1934), he is likely to be closer to the method of Arnold than to an aesthetic emphasis or an analytical method.

Arnold, of course, was preoccupied with the culture of Victorian England and tended to see literary works as they related to it. He was able to perceive many of the qualities that differentiated one writer from another, but he rarely discussed these differences in other than moral, social, or cultural terms. Samuel Johnson, on the other hand, was much more likely to focus attention not only on moral earnestness but also on metaphor, diction, metrics, and so forth—in other words, on form. But it is probably Samuel Taylor Coleridge who furnishes the most characteristic example of the method and considerations which recur in the new criticism, especially in the study of "Venus and Adonis" in *Biographia Literaria.* He treats of imagination as it relates to versification and the ability to reduce a multitude of feelings to their proper proportion in relation to the total unity of the work; dissociation of the literary work from its origins in the writer's own life, so that the work, as Eliot has demanded, lives impersonally and with its own kind of wholeness; dramatization, or as James would say, rendering not reporting; union of "creative power and intellectual energy," or as we say more commonly now, the union of thought and feeling; complexity in the sense that one perceives "the flux and reflux of the mind in all its subtlest thoughts" and in the sense that imagery, versification, tone, and other things contribute in the most minute ways to the dominant feeling and thematic lines unifying the work.

Richards and Hulme are both indebted to Coleridge. So too are later critics like Herbert Read and Kenneth Burke. In fact, Coleridge is so much a part of the preconceptions in contemporary criticism that there is probably no critic who is not greatly in his debt. In this sense, then, the new criticism is not *new*—it is a continuation of nineteenth-century English criticism. It is undoubtedly more intensive than Coleridge's. And it is undoubtedly new in that it borrows from contemporary anthropology, philosophy, and psychology—just as Coleridge borrowed from German philosophy. However, it is hardly just to consider contemporary critics members of a literary guild. One might think of T. S. Eliot (at least in his earlier work), William Empson, R. P. Blackmur, Robert Penn Warren, Cleanth Brooks, and John Crowe Ransom as being in agreement about most of their critical standards. Undoubtedly there is a considerable body of agreement among them, but anyone reading through Ransom's *The New Criticism* will also be struck by the extent of their disagreements. Ransom's theory, most neatly expressed in "Criticism as Pure Speculation," that much of the concrete detail of the poem is to be looked upon as interesting and pleasant in its own right but irrelevant to the logical or prose meaning of the poem, is not evident in the work of these other critics; some of them are explicitly in disagreement with it. *The Anatomy of Nonsense* (1943) offers abundant evidence that Yvor Winters is in very considerable disagreement not merely with Ransom's theory but with that of most of their contemporaries.

A simple way of demonstrating the diversity in method among contemporary critics is to compare the work of R. P. Blackmur and Kenneth Burke. Blackmur's criticism is eclectic, indebted to Eliot, Richards, Empson, Burke, and others and is perhaps impossible to label easily. Like James, whose prefaces he has edited, he has insisted on the high value of art. And, as witness his work in *The Double Agent* (1935) and *The Expense of Greatness* (1940), he has insisted on arduous labor in criticism. He wants the critic "constantly to be confronted with examples of poetry" for the practical purpose of helping readers to understand its meaning and value. In explicating a poem by Wallace Stevens or Hart Crane he explores all possible meanings in a word in terms of its context. Ransom opens his account of *The New Criticism* by presenting Blackmur's analysis of a poem by Emily Dickinson as a distinguished example of the illumination possible as the result of close and imaginative reading. Blackmur's readings are usually detailed and subtle, but too often his prose is unnecessarily contorted and difficult. In staying close to the specific work of literature or to the work of a specific writer, Blackmur typifies the practice of many contemporary critics. Burke, on the other hand, is more characteristic of the movement in its liking for critical terminology.

In his later books like *A Grammar of Motives* (1945) and *A Rhetoric of Motives* (1950), Burke is a theoretician of a kind almost unique among literary critics. Aside from whatever values Burke's "dramatism," as he calls his generating principle, may have in settling or precluding the quarrels between the positivist-minded and their critics over the claims of poetry or the other arts to be called "knowledge," his critical observations are usually shrewd and sometimes transferable to other contexts. In "Musicality in Verse" from *Philosophy of Literary Form* (1941), for instance, he says there is a "concealed alliteration" in Coleridge's "bathed by the mist" because *b* and *b* are "close phonetic relatives" of *m.* " 'B-b-the-b-' would be blunt. But in deflecting the third member from a *b* to an *m,* the poet retains the same phonetic theme, while giving us a variation upon the theme." In "Caldwell: Maker of Grotesques," from the same volume, Burke furnishes clues that plausibly explain some of the effects Caldwell frequently manages. Caldwell's characters, Burke says, are to real people as deracinated frogs are to whole frogs. What they lack in humanity the reader supplies. "When the starved grandmother in *Tobacco Road* lies dying, with her face on the ground into the soil, and no one shows even an onlooker's interest in her wretchedness, we are prodded to anguish. When these automata show some bare inkling of sociality, it may seem like a flash of ultimate wisdom." With this as a beginning, one could read much of Caldwell with an increased critical awareness. Burke is hard reading for the most part, however, because he is working out, as he says, a "theory of the criticism of books (a theory that should be applicable, *mutatis mutandis,* to any specific cases)." When he has completed his work, much that now appears scattered and piecemeal will probably be more coherent and readily useful.

Such differences in belief and method could be documented at length. On the other hand, it should be noted that most contemporary critics do attempt to analyze the literary work carefully and in detail. Despite the varying approaches implied by a critic's emphasis on texture, tension, ambiguity, expressive form, pseudoreference, paradox, irony, or other such terms, each critic is attempting to establish a body of definable criteria. Each is concerned with developing useful terms and techniques so that the reader may be able to explore the complex parts of the literary work and to make some attempt to evaluate its worth.

There has been a good deal of attention paid in recent years to what W. K. Wimsatt and M. C. Beardsley [in *The Verbal Icon: Studies in the Meaning of Poetry*] called "the intentional fallacy." The general point is that critical inquiries about the meaning of a poem are not to be settled by consulting the intention of the author. (The British critic C. S. Lewis in *The Personal Heresy* disagreed with E. M. W. Tillyard's contention in *Milton* that *Paradise Lost* is about the state of Milton's mind when the poem was written. Lewis says it is about Satan, the angels, and so forth. And he adds: "Every work of art that lasts long in the world is continually taking on . . . colors which the artist neither foresaw nor intended.") In the final section of his essay on *The Ancient Mariner,* "A Poem of Pure Imagination: An Experiment in Reading" (1946), Robert Penn Warren has made a neat summary of most of the issues relevant to the problem of intention. The primary consideration, he concludes, is the criterion of "internal consistency."

Because of the concern of critics with literature as literature, it was inevitable that there would be protests against centering the critical process in the antecedents or origins (the intentional fallacy) of the work as well as against centering it in the psychological reactions or responses to it (the affective fallacy). Wimsatt and Beardsley define the affective fallacy as "a confusion between the poem and its results (what it *is* and what it *does*). . . . It begins by trying to derive the standard of criticism from the psychological effects of the poem and ends in impressionism and relativism." As a result, "the poem itself, as an object of specifically critical judgement, tends to disappear." Examples of affective criticism are Emily Dickinson's remark that in reading genuine poetry she had the sensation that the top of her head was taken off and A. E. Housman's comment about feeling a shiver run down his spine when he recalled a good line of poetry. References to one's feelings in the presence of a literary work will indicate approval or disapproval of some kind, but they are likely to be vague and untranslatable into cognitive terms.

Many contemporary critics also object to the old dichotomy of content and form. Like the earlier proponents of organic form and expressive form they believe that if the writer alters his expression he has probably affected not merely the appropriateness of his manner or style but the actual meaning of what he has said.

The dichotomy of content and form is seen as a Cartesian and Kantian inheritance. Meaning was commonly held to have a mind-body relationship; rhetorical figures were a dress put upon meaning, like the glove put on the hand. (The attempted divorce of meaning from matter, which was a part of the effort to achieve mathematical unfeeling or objectivity, is discussed in the new criticism usually as a part of the phenomenon labeled by T. S. Eliot the "dissociation of sensibility.") The concern with structure in the new criticism implies some degree of recognition that abstraction emerges from matter. Walter J. Ong in "The Meaning of the 'New Criticism'" (1943) writes: "The understanding is defective if it does not observe that, however they may be handled in mathematics and minor logic, the most abstract abstractions always come to us in ways which reflect their origins out of material existents. . . . Abstractions cannot be preserved and packaged, but are known and used only as they are being drawn in some way or another out of matter." Form or structure is understood not as an envelope or even as a vehicle of the total meaning or total abstraction the writer has made available. As Yeats wrote in "Among School Children":

> O body swayed to music, O brightening glance
> How can we know the dancer from the dance?

I. A. Richards was the first of the contemporary critics to address himself to the problem of "total meaning."

In *Practical Criticism* (1929), Richards considers meter, diction, metaphor, and methods of organizing the poem not as ornaments but as parts of the total meaning. The poet's attitude toward his subject matter is, or should be, implicit in his meter (the use of the spondee, for example, to slow the metrical movement) and in his diction (the "Mister Death" phrase in Cummings's poem on Buffalo Bill, for example, suggests the poet's attitude toward death in this particular context). The meter and the diction are among the factors that produce the tone. The method of organizing the elements in the poem—the incidental ironies, the juxtaposing of unlike elements, the bringing together of homogeneous elements, the use of alliteration, of internal rhyme, and so forth—also contribute to its meaning. The employment of assonance, for example, can enable a poet to echo and stress a word he does not want to repeat explicitly. The interest in total meaning is related to the belief that, ideally, in literature there can be no true separation of form and content.

Empson in *Seven Types of Ambiguity* (1930) extended Richards's work by demonstrating that language tends to be highly connotative, or, in Wheelwright's term, "plurisignificant." The older preconception was that cognitive language implies simple denotation. But Empson took words like "rooky" from *Macbeth* and demonstrated that *all* of the meanings listed by the Arden editors were plausible. If they seemed plausible to the various editors they would have seemed plausible to the first-night audience and would have "seemed plausible to Shakespeare himself, since he was no less sensitive to words than they." (Ong quotes Hugh Blair, a late neoclassic rhetorician whose *Lectures on Rhetoric* was widely studied in the nineteenth century: "Simple expression just makes our ideas known to others; but figurative language, over and above, bestows a particular dress upon that idea; a dress, which both makes it to be remarked and adorns it.") Empson, by showing that the new meaning (tenor) and metaphor (vehicle) interact, thereby suggesting a considerable number of meanings (abstractions), is showing that meanings have their origins in matter, in the concrete. Meaning is involved with structure or form down to the slightest connotation or suggestion.

After Richards and Empson, criticism became much more conscious of the details which carry the meaning of a poem. In "Hardy's Philosophic Metaphors" (*Reason in Madness,* 1941), for example, Tate criticizes "Nature's Questioning" on the ground that its structure, the metaphors, contradicts the working content—Hardy's belief in a deistic unknowable

God. Hardy conceives a God who in one place is an automaton, in another an imbecile, but in still another a schoolmaster. "Even in the magnificent image of the 'God-head dying downwards' we get a certain degree of contradiction between tenor and vehicle: in order to say that God has left the universe to chance after setting it in motion, Hardy can merely present us with the theistic God as blind and imbecile." To this Tate adds: "So generally of Hardy it may perhaps be said that his 'philosophy' tends to be a little beyond the range of his feeling: his abstractions are thus somewhat irresponsible, since he rarely shows us the experience that ought to justify them, that would give them substance, visibility, meaning." Similarly, Tate's analyses of verses by Edna St. Vincent Millay, James Thomson, and John Donne in "Tension in Poetry" are examinations into patterns of coherent relationships between denotative and connotative meanings in poetry.

The reader of *The Well Wrought Urn* (1947) will be able to observe that Cleanth Brooks also thinks of the poem as a structure or form in the sense indicated above. He justifies his use of "paradox" and "irony" as the most available terms to suggest the kinds of indirection and the kinds of qualification he has observed to be characteristic of the total statement (or structure) that composes the poem. To substitute a paraphrase, a simplified meaning, is to destroy a part of the structure and therefore a part of the meaning.

Structure or form is also a key concept in the criticism of the novel. A novelist succeeds or fails in terms of his structure. Mark Schorer in "Technique as Discovery" [in *Forms of Modern Fiction,* edited by William Van O'Connor (1948)] says: "What we need in fiction is a devoted fidelity to every technique which will help us discover and evaluate our subject matter, and more than that, to discover the amplifications of meaning of which our subject matter is capable." To take a specific instance, Robert Penn Warren's Introduction to Hemingway's *A Farewell to Arms* has as its center the concept of an appropriate structure. He explains first what he calls the "characteristic Hemingway 'point' ": this includes comments on the initiates in Hemingway's God-abandoned world, the hard-bitten, disciplined men and women who savor not only drinking and sex but who have a sharp awareness of the physical world and of light and darkness. Drinking and sex are dramatized as forces that dull the sense of *nada* (death and the meaninglessness of the physical world), except that with love a margin of human significance or meaning is achieved, and so forth. The successful Hemingway stories occur, Warren says, when "the essential limitations of his premises" have been accepted. The "failures occur when we feel that Hemingway has not respected the limitations of his premises." In the failures not merely the moral significance or judgment, which we expect to be implied in the action, becomes blurred, but the characteristic irony and the simplified style sound empty and pretentious. Warren's focus, in other words, is on the structure of the stories. Joseph Warren Beach, R. P. Blackmur, M. D. Zabel, and comparable critics, we may assume, look to James and to Conrad, because in them they find artists who have learned how to inform a given subject matter with maximum resonance, meaning, and significance.

An argument sometimes directed against such criticism is that by emphasizing form it fails to emphasize moral values and other extra-aesthetic values (content). This argument, again, is dependent upon the old assumption that form and content are readily separable. The analytical critics might, in reply, point to their concern with synthesis, tension, irony, complexity, and inclusiveness, as opposed to the sentimental, the arbitrary, the merely asserted, and so forth. The maturity, as Henry James insisted, with which a moral or political view emerges from the aesthetic form is dependent in part on how well, how impressively, and how vividly the view has been investigated and refracted through the aesthetic medium. The nature of literary form, demanding as it does stylization, that is, selection of detail, understatement, parody, or the manipulation of characters within a given concrete situation, precludes the possibility of its offering easy rules of thumb for moral, political, or social action. (It may develop that critical studies in the immediate future will furnish further studies of literary conventions and, more particularly, what is implied by the term "stylization.") In the final analysis, statements about the moral or philosophical elements in a literary work are made inside an aesthetic framework, in terms of the structure that makes these elements available for discussion.

Another argument directed against this criticism is that it is antihistorical and antibiographical. The argument probably oversimplifies the attitudes of most of the analytical critics since they, as well as other students of literature, understand with Mme de Staël that there are reciprocal relationships between literature and a society's laws, manners, and religion, just as they understand the general significance of Taine's oversimplified statements about a work of art being the product of "race, milieu, and moment," or just as they understand, with Arnold and Sainte-Beuve, that a writer's work can often be better interpreted in the light of his personal life. Yet most of them would insist that historical studies can be, and frequently have been, carried on in such a fashion that they become almost divorced from any significant concern with the values of literature as literature. They would also insist that scholarship divorced from an aesthetic criticism will fall into the genetic fallacy, will attempt to explain a piece of literature not in terms of what it is but in terms of its social or biographical origins.

In their *Theory of Literature* (1949), René Wellek and Austin Warren have mediated these arguments by treating the poem, or literary work, as a thing in itself, as unique but also with characteristics common to its genre, and as having persistent as well as shifting meanings depending upon the audience and historical context in which it is read. "A poem, we have to conclude, is not an individual experience or a sum of experiences. . . . Thus the real poem must be conceived as a structure of norms, realized only partially in the actual experience of its many readers." They discuss the division of the literary work into such factors as sound, meaning, character, setting, and point of view, each factor having its subordinate considerations and each interrelated with the other factors. It is true, they admit, that each work of art has unique aspects, but to overstress uniqueness invites complete critical relativism and an indifference to the similarities and common elements that would make it possible to discuss not merely genre but literature in general. "The work of art, then, appears as an object of knowledge *sui generis.* . . ." Wellek and Warren admit that the *Iliad* as understood by the Greeks is not identical with the *Iliad* we are capable of understanding. Nonetheless, there must be a "substantial identity of 'structure' which has remained the same throughout the ages." Again, not all the viewpoints in terms of which the "structure" is seen will be equally capable of grasping it most meaningfully. Therefore, some "hierarchy of viewpoints," a criticism of the grasp of norms, is implied in the concept of the "adequacy of interpretation." This dependence on a "system of norms" more or less completely realized by various generations of readers (as well as by individuals) would avoid the extremes of absolutism and relativism. It would seem to follow also that one might, after all, by knowing a good deal about the potentialities of literary form or structure be able to say that particular generations of poets or novelists or dramatists held viewpoints that enabled them to make excellent or relatively poor use of their medium.

The job of the critic is to help us perceive the nature and worth of the literary work. It is not his function to offer us coherent systems of philosophy, coherent theories of the nature of language, or even ideological systems that include accounts of poetry as a substitute for religion and the relation of the poet to the economic order. He can use all the information he can get, but he can employ his knowledge, as a critic, only insofar as it is relevant to the particular work or works he is discussing and attempting to make more available to the reader. Occasionally someone offers to subsume the study of literature under sociology—which would mean the end of the study of literature as an art. It would be ironic if a few zealots in criticism managed to raise a complex edifice composed of interrelated lines of knowledge of philosophy, anthropology, and linguistics that was so massive that the literary work beneath it became merely an excuse for the superstructure. Almost everyone in the twentieth century is looking for a kind of knowledge that will be as a Second Coming. It is too much to hope that such knowledge will arise from critical analyses, that it is resting like a genie in the bottle labeled the "new criticism." In "The Function of Criticism," Eliot refers to a criticism that is self-serving as autotelic. Tate, in a more homely phrase, has compared such criticism to the picture apologizing to the frame.

Probably it is true, as some of its practitioners claim, that no body of criticism in the history of English and American literature is comparable in bulk, variety, or intensity to the criticism produced in our half century. Since this accomplishment is likely to invite a considerable degree of smugness among those who sympathize with the movement, it may be well to close this survey with a little fable devised by Robert Penn Warren:

> Critics are rarely faithful to their labels and their special strategies. Usually the critic will confess that no one strategy—the psychological, the moralistic, the formalistic, the historical—or combination of strategies, will quite work the defeat of the poem. For the poem is like the monstrous Orillo in Boiardo's *Orlando Innamorato.* When the sword lops off any member of the monster, that member is immediately rejoined to the body, and the monster is as formidable as ever. But the poem is even more formidable than the monster, for Orillo's adversary finally gained a victory by an astonishing feat of dexterity: he slashed off both the monster's arms and quick as a wink seized them and flung them into the river. The critic who vaingloriously trusts his method to account for the poem, to exhaust the poem, is trying to emulate this dexterity; he thinks that he, too, can win by throwing the lopped off arms into the river. But he is doomed to failure. Neither fire nor water will suffice to prevent the rejoining of the mutilated members to the monstrous torso. There is only one way to conquer the monster: you must eat it, bones, blood, skin, pelt, and gristle. And even then the monster is not dead,

for it lives in you, is assimilated into you, and you are different, and somewhat monstrous yourself, for having eaten it.

So the monster will always win, and the critic knows this. He does not want to win. He knows that he must always play stooge to the monster. All he wants to do is to give the monster a chance to exhibit again his miraculous powers.

(pp. 156-75)

William Van O'Connor, "Analytical Criticism," in his An Age of Criticism: 1900-1950, *Henry Regnery Company, 1952, pp. 156-75.*

DAVID DAICHES

[*Daiches is a prominent English scholar and critic who has written extensively on English and American literature. He is especially renowned for his in-depth studies of such writers as Robert Burns, Robert Louis Stevenson, and Virginia Woolf. His criticism in general is best characterized as appreciative in content and attached to no single methodology. In the following excerpt, Daiches responds to William Van O'Connor's defense of New Critical theory, taking exception in particular to the concept of "affective fallacy." For O'Connor's comments, see the excerpt above.*]

Mr. William O'Connor's article on the "new criticism" provides an interesting conspectus of some of the main trends in modern critical thought, written by one who is in substantial agreement with the whole modern movement. It seems to me, however, that it shows an insufficient awareness of possible alternatives to that "new" approach which regards the primary problem in the critical examination of a work as the demonstration of its "internal consistency." The only alternatives he actually mentions are "scholarship" (he points out early in his essay "the chief differences between the new criticism and scholarship") and the method which employs "the old dichotomy of content and form." Now, in the first place, "the chief difference between the new criticism and scholarship" as explained by Mr. O'Connor is the difference between *any* criticism and scholarship. Scholarship throws light on the social and biographical origins of a work, on the cultural environment out of which it sprang, and on the transmission of the text, and thus often enables the critic to understand in some degree how the work came to be written and to see more clearly the meanings of certain parts of the text; but his job as a critic, whether his brand of criticism be old or new, remains the assessment of the literary worth of the work in question. The new criticism has no monopoly in this perception. As for the escape from the dichotomy of content and form, this has been sought by generations of critics and has been achieved in one fashion or another by many who take wholly different positions from those taken by any representative of the new movement—by R. L. Stevenson and John Middleton Murry, to mention only two, who are as different from each other as from any of those mentioned by Mr. O'Connor. I think it is not unfair to say that many who appreciate and have profited from the achievements of the new critics (and I consider myself one of those) nevertheless resent the assumption of some of their spokesmen that they alone are really critics, all others being mere scholars, historians, *Einfluss*-hunters, "positivists," or unprincipled impressionists.

One can see, of course, what it is that leads them to such a view. The new critics have taken criticism more seriously—

grimly, even—than representatives of other schools of thought, and, at least from Dr. Leavis on, have seen the function of the critic as central to a civilization. Not only have they taken every opportunity to differentiate between criticism and other kinds of literary investigation, but they have also, unlike the more traditional critic, refused to start by a consideration of the impact of the work on the ordinary cultivated reader and then proceed to explain that impact in terms of the work's qualities. Instead, they have made critical analysis a tool for the total reassessment of the impact. They have striven by every possible means to widen the breach between amateur and professional criticism: even their vocabulary helps to serve this purpose, so that when Mr. John Crowe Ransom writes an essay on the nature of poetry, he does not call it, as critics of other schools would, "The Nature of Poetry," but "Poetry: A Note in Ontology."

There is both good and bad in this, just as there is both good and bad in the criticism of criticism which the new critics encourage (and of which the present discussion is an example). Criticism of criticism is, after all, an intellectual luxury and may lead to an inability to enjoy more nourishing fare. "It is the chief penalty of becoming a professional literary man," Mr. T. S. Eliot once remarked to Mr. William Empson, "that one can no longer read anything with pleasure." The phrase "curl up with a good book" has been cheerfully abandoned to the Philistines, and people who take literature seriously are supposed to have more rigorous methods of dealing with the work of poets and novelists.

Of course, there is much gain in this rigour. The scrutinizing of literary theories is not only a valuable philosophical activity calculated to throw light on the differentiating characteristics of the literary work of art but it also sometimes helps us to approach individual works with a clearer understanding of what they are and so of how to read them with greater understanding and satisfaction. These are two separate, though related, functions of criticism—one might call them roughly the "philosophical" and the "appreciative"—and when their separate nature is not realized much confusion may result. It would be absurd to maintain that no Greek appreciated Sophocles until Aristotle had written the *Poetics,* or that English playgoers had to wait for A. C. Bradley or Professor Heilman before they could understand and enjoy *King Lear.* Appreciation can be independent of critical theory—a proposition which the new critics do not explicitly deny but a denial of which seems to be implicit in much of their writing. But if we do not concede that it is possible to enjoy art without formal training in criticism and without possessing general ideas about aesthetics, we are flying in the face of experience, setting up a priestly critical profession to mediate between artists and their public, and encouraging the growth of the most barren kind of academicism in matters artistic and literary.

We all agree that criticism is valuable, but we must be clear about its kind of value. Eliot has defined criticism in the sense in which we are using the term as "the commentation and exposition of works of art by means of written words"—a reasonable, if inelegant, definition; but it should be noted that the definition itself says nothing of what this "commentation and exposition" is supposed to achieve. In the same essay, as Mr. O'Connor has reminded us, Eliot denies that criticism is "autotelic" (it should be said that this essay was written in 1923, before Eliot had rid himself of that pontifical pretentiousness in manner and vocabulary which mars some of his

early prose) and specifically asserts that it must always profess an end in view, which he roughly defines as "the elucidation of works of art and the correction of taste." But we must go further than this. "Elucidation" is an ambiguous word, and "the correction of taste" an even more ambiguous phrase. Elucidation itself will vary according to the purpose of the elucidator. Miss Lily Campbell's elucidation of Shakespeare's historical plays is very different in nature and purpose from the elucidation supplied by, say, John Palmer in his *Political Characters of Shakespeare,* a fact which Mr. O'Connor sees but which he might have explored further. A poem or a play or a novel can be very many things at the same time—a reflection of the cultural climate of its age, a document in the mental history of its author, a carefully patterned arrangement of words, ideas, images and situations, a fable, a piece of rhetoric, and the communication of a unique insight into an aspect of human experience through one or several of these means. We may choose to elucidate the work as any one of these things, or as any two, or as so many as we think we can handle.

But our new critic, with his awareness of the difference between criticism and scholarship, has his answer at once: "There is no real difficulty here," he will reply. "What the literary critic should concern himself with is the work qua work of art. He should ignore it as a document in the history of ideas, as an expression of the writer's personality, or as anything but a poem or a play or a novel, and the problem is to find out what a poem or a play or a novel really is, what it is *uniquely,* what it is that no other form of written expression is. Having done this, he can proceed to demonstrate its special formal qualities and exhibit it as a literary work of art." He then proceeds to find a formula which will define the *quiddity* of a literary form and goes on to the analysis of individual texts which demonstrates that any given example conforms to this definition.

This is all very appealing. The human mind has a fondness for definitions and categories, for contrasts and exclusions, for analytic demonstrations. Nevertheless, a sense that the true quality of a poem somehow escapes this sort of defining and categorizing and demonstrating has persisted throughout the history of criticism and has given rise to every kind of evasive impressionism in order to avoid coming to grips with the basic question of whether and why a given poem is good. "It were as wise to cast a violet into a crucible that you might discover the formal principle of its colour and odour, as seek to transfuse from one language into another the creations of a poet," wrote Shelley; but the modern critic, in spite of his awareness of the uniqueness of a given work of art, is made uncomfortable by such statements because they open the door to autobiographical chatter masquerading as criticism. And there again we can understand and sympathize with this insistence that without a stern formal discipline real criticism is impossible.

But in a sense "real criticism" *is* impossible. This is not by any means to say that there are no standards of value, that we must fall back on personal taste, or vague impressionism, or on mere gush. We do, however, mean that no critical statement about a work of literary art—least of all, about a poem—can be a complete statement of what it is and why it is good. On the level of aesthetic theory, it may be possible to construct a set of valid general principles, but practical criticism, criticism designed to demonstrate the nature and quality of a work and so to increase understanding and appreciation, must always be fragmentary, indirect, approximate, and can never be a complete and wholly satisfactory description of what in fact takes place in the work of art.

It is not difficult to see why this should be so. A poem is an immense complex of meaning which is nevertheless simple and immediate in its impact, and it is impossible to describe that complex and simultaneously to account for its impact. To resolve the poem into mere complexity by analytic discussion is often useful and helpful, but it hardly begins to explain the reasons for its total impact on the experienced and sensitive reader, nor does it necessarily increase appreciation for the inexperienced. The richness and uniqueness of poetic statement, so rightly insisted on by the new critics, is far too often underestimated in their practice, for in their desire to concern themselves only with literary criteria they are liable to narrow their analysis so as to exclude all elements that are not exclusively related to those criteria. But the fact is that there is no such thing as a purely literary work of literature. A work of literary art is necessarily a mixed form. It produces its effect by being several things at once—not by mere complexity but by operating simultaneously on several different levels not only of meaning but of existence.

Our search for "criteria that make possible judgments about literary worth," in Mr. O'Connor's phrase, if pursued with a disinterested desire to find out what a work of literary art really is rather than with a desire to find merely a consistent method, will eventually turn up the fact that literary discourse is by its very nature several kinds of discourse at once. A poem is a structure with "internal consistency," but it is also often a fascinating record of the poet's mind, a period-piece reflecting with moving brilliance the climate of an age, and a story. We may differentiate uses of language in a poem which are not to be found in other ways of writing, but this does not mean that the full impact of a poem can be determined by examining only its differentiating qualities. Who can hear Mozart played on the harpsichord without enjoying, as part of his reaction to the actual music, the poignant feeling of listening to the gaiety of a lost civilization? Is this reaction "impure," sentimental, irrelevant? If, in seeing *Hamlet,* we appreciate its dramatic structure and its poetic magnificence while, at the same time, seeing it as the work of Shakespeare the Elizabethan, are we being aesthetically wicked? A work of literary art, which, because of its richness, its use of so many elements of expression, can be so many things at once, is often, also, a work of history and of autobiography and of moral philosophy; and its impact on us is the more profound because it is all these things. In appreciating a work of art, we have only one ear cocked for "internal consistency," for the purely "formal" aspect. And often when such consistency has been demonstrated we do not read the work with any richer enjoyment.

The new critics, of course, have their answer here. Messrs. Wimsatt and Beardsley, in a widely discussed article ["The Affective Fallacy" in *The Verbal Icon: Studies in the Meaning of Poetry* (1954)] (duly cited by Mr. O'Connor), have in their very title boldly stigmatized as a "fallacy" the consideration by the critic of the impact of a work on the reader. Their concern with what a literary work *is,* uniquely and formally, rather than with the reasons for which it is enjoyed, logically leads them to dismiss the testimony of those who enjoy literature as irrelevant. The new criticism tends, in fact, to be impatient with the testimony of readers. A poem, the argument seems to run, *should* be enjoyed for those of its aspects which

differentiate it from other forms of discourse; whether it is ever so enjoyed is considered an irrelevant question. This is a seductively tidy way of looking at things—as though we were to enjoy people only for such of their attributes as distinguished them from all other kinds of living creatures and not for their total selves—but it leads, in criticism as in morality, to a puritanism which does violence to the values found in experience.

Why, it might be asked, is the "affective fallacy" in any sense a fallacy? The value of literature surely lies in its actual or potential effect on readers—admittedly, on experienced and sensitive readers, on readers who have had sufficient exposure to this kind of thing to have developed a proper responsiveness and discrimination. To deny this is to fall into the "ontological fallacy" of believing that a work of art fulfils its purpose and achieves its value simply by *being,* so that the critic becomes concerned only to demonstrate the mode of its being by descriptive analysis. This is comparable to saying that a body of moral laws exists in order to have an internal logical structure and that to consider the effect of obeying any given law would be to move from questions of moral philosophy to questions of social or individual behaviour. Literature is a phenomenon produced by men in order to communicate in a certain way with their fellows. In the last analysis, the test of its value can be judged only by the receiver, and judged by him on some kind of "affective" theory. Of course the critic must consider the means by which this special kind of communication—in virtue of which literary discourse differs from other kinds of discourse—is achieved, and this in turn leads him to an examination of internal consistency as one among many characteristics of a work of art. (The new critics generally talk as though it were the only essential characteristic.) But we must distinguish between means and ends. Poetry, in the largest sense of the word, is a unique method of making a unique kind of communication, and it is the real or potential effectiveness of the communication which justifies the method, not vice versa.

There is, of course, the question of communication *to whom.* Who is the ideal reader whose reactions are to be taken as the norm? We must not take a purely pragmatic view and send out pollsters to find out who are most affected by which works—to that extent Messrs. Wimsatt and Beardsley are right. The ability to discriminate between more and less effective uses of the medium of poetry is achieved by deep and wide experience in reading. The most brilliant literary mind, if faced only by the poems of Eddie Guest, might believe that they represented the height of poetic expression; but, given the opportunity to read widely and richly, he will change his views. Deep and wide reading provides a better training in critical appreciation than a thousand ingenious analyses of poems. If critical analysis be provided as well, the process can be speeded up, and the reader may be made aware of how the effects which he appreciates are achieved—and that in itself increases appreciation.

The best "appreciative" criticism is that which enables the reader to get a glimpse of the real life in a work: having glimpsed it, he can proceed to enter into all its rich vitality. No critical method is absolute, foolproof, or "true." I have known students who have been more effectively brought to see the essential life in a poem by hearing it read aloud slowly than by the most careful analysis of its structure. Art is meant to be experienced, and the function of criticism is to assist that experience. After reading some of the new criticism, one might imagine that an effective stage performance would achieve less towards an understanding of *Hamlet* than an analysis of its internal consistency made in the study. Criticism of any work of art is a kind of performance, a sort of substitute for performance. Part of the true glory of a scene in *Hamlet* may be brought out for students by having them act it out. There are, of course, other ways, and the careful discussion of structure, imagery and similar points can be of immense help. But to say that what matters about a work of art is not its communicative potential but its internal consistency is to put the cart before the horse completely.

One must not forget the pedagogical aspect of criticism. As far as its classroom use is concerned, the function of criticism is to increase awareness of what a work of literary art really is and by so doing to increase appreciation of it. To teach a student that criticism always and necessarily involves demonstration of internal consistency, or of paradox, or of ambivalent meanings, or what have you, *may* be useful but is often fatal. If the student does not learn that such devices are means to achieve a communicative effect and that the reader remains dead to the work so long as that communicative effect remains unachieved, then he has learned only to be a pedant. How often have I seen a student who has got it into his head that ingenuity of analysis is the mark of the good critic proceed to make a pretentious fool of himself by demonstrating with misguided ingenuity the existence of manifestly absurd meanings in some poem or story. There is such a thing as a "feeling" for a work and its period which can save one from such barren stupidities. Our new critics generally have this feeling, because they are men of wide reading and historical knowledge. They have assimilated a whole historical tradition, and they know, before they approach *Hamlet* as professional critics, to what area of human sensibility and significance it belongs. In their demand that all works should be treated as though they were contemporary and anonymous they are in effect requiring the student of today to do without tools which they themselves are continually using, though often not consciously. There is, in fact, no limit to what ingenious analysis can achieve by way of demonstrating complexity and consistency of structure in any work at all, good or bad: how far you can go is taught you by your "taste"—and taste is the sum of what you have learned about art by willing and interested exposure to it. It necessarily includes an element of historical discrimination, since wide reading experience is bound to produce in a reader of any native sensitivity at all some awareness of the difference between the cultural points of reference of, say, Milton and Matthew Prior. This does not mean that there may not be even greater differences between two contemporary writers.

It is not wise to give the student the impression that the end-product of literary activity is the critical analysis of the work and not the work itself. I do not suggest for a moment that the new criticism would maintain such a preposterous position, but its practitioners often implicitly suggest this attitude. Literature exists to be read and enjoyed, and criticism, at least in its pedagogical aspect, exists in order to increase awareness and so increase enjoyment. The purely philosophical critic may entertain himself by trying to isolate the quiddity of poetry (but I should maintain that the quiddity of poetry is that, unlike all other forms of communication, it has no single quiddity), but the "appreciative" critic will use any means at his disposal—analytic, descriptive, histrionic, yes, even historical—to arouse alert interest, to produce that communicative impact without which all further critical discussion is useless.

Another objection might be brought against much (but not all) of the new criticism. Even if we agree that it is possible to isolate and define the differentiating qualities of a work of literary art, we may not agree that those qualities are to be discussed in terms of structure. To many of the new critics all criticism is analysis of structure, and demonstration of value is demonstration of structural complexity and coherence. There are, however, many valuable kinds of literature whose value does not reside in their structural effectiveness. There is not even a single poetic use of language. Good verse can consist of propositional statements neatly phrased, with an agreeable rhythm and pleasantly chiming rhymes serving more or less as pleasing decoration (as in John Pomfret's "The Choice," for example), or, at the other end of the scale of poetic expression, it may be like a poem of Donne's or of the later Yeats, a flaming organic unity in which every element in the expression contributes equally to the total communication. To place a poem in this scale is not necessarily to pass any value-judgment on it, for there can be good poems at any place in the scale. We may with some justice hold, however, that the potentialities for really impressive poetic expression are less likely to exist at the lower end of the scale and that the most effective poems are those which come in the middle or higher parts of the range. Such questions can only be resolved by reading poems and considering what each achieves. One might say that at the lower end of the scale of poetic expression the handling of language is nearer to that of prose or perhaps to that of non-artistic literary expression and that it makes less use of the characteristically poetic ways of handling language. But is this necessarily a value-judgment? Is the best poetry the most poetical poetry, poetry which uses most of those aspects of language which differentiate the poet's use of it from other kinds of use? And, anyway, is this difference to be explained in terms of structure? The point is, to say the least, arguable.

By concentrating on what they deem to be the differentiating qualities of poetic expression (in the widest sense of "poetic") and by seeing these qualities in terms of complexity and coherence of structure, many of the new critics often find themselves unable to cope with such simpler forms of literature as the verse-essay or the song-lyric. The new criticism is incapable, for example, of demonstrating the magnificence of Burns's songs (which I have recently seen dismissed with something very like contempt by a young critic). The devices by which Burns, in "Auld Lang Syne," sublimates nostalgia for the past in present good fellowship to close with a formal social gesture which holds past and present together for one tenuous moment by ritual, man's way of marking permanently the fleeting meanings of things—this sort of thing cannot be handled or even discussed by the new criticism without embarrassment. And what of the devices by which lyrics are fitted to music? These are some of the areas in which modern criticism, largely because of its persistence in considering every "affective" theory as a "fallacy" and thus clinging to what I have called the "ontological fallacy," is seriously inadequate.

This has an effect on the vocabulary of the new criticism and, indeed, on its prose style, which as a rule is ugly and clotted. There seems to be a tendency to equate grace and clarity with superficiality and a preference for a technical jargon which is not, in fact, necessary in order to communicate adequately.

Some of the results of this—for example, the comical "Glossary of the New Criticism" which appeared in *Poetry* some time ago—are likely to encourage the worst kind of verbal exhibitionism and, among the hangers-on of the movement, have often done so.

But it would be unjust to judge the new criticism by its more ragged camp followers. All I am concerned to do here is to point to some limitations and inadequacies of its characteristic method. I certainly recognize its great achievement in helping to abolish from our colleges the mumbling survey course consisting of biographical facts combined with lists of adjectives appropriate to each writer and in insisting on the close reading of individual texts. But the alternative is not necessarily to throw out all that Mr. Ransom, for example, or Mr. Wimsatt would like to throw out, to remove from our critical vocabulary all adjectives designed to point to the nature of the work's impact on the qualified reader, to manipulate a few pretentious technical terms. We can learn from the new critics without using their jargon, adopting their puritanism, or employing their Procrustean method of forcing every literary work into a pattern of complex coherence or ambivalence or paradox or some such criterion. We can learn to read carefully, sensitively, critically, without losing sight of the richness and essential "impurity" of all effective literary art and without forgetting that, as the rejected Saintsbury once remarked, "in the house of poetry are many mansions." What we want is a richer, not a narrower, aesthetic than the traditional combination of autobiographical impressionism and description. Catholicity of taste does not mean the abandonment of standards, nor does the recognition that different kinds of value may legitimately be called "literary" imply the loss of critical principles. In the last analysis, the characteristic method of the new criticism—immensely helpful though it has been, and brilliantly as it is often employed—is inadequate because it is too easy. Its tendency towards what Professor [R. S.] Crane has called "critical monism" leads to a drastic oversimplification of what in fact a work of literary art is, what kind of pleasure it gives, and why it is valuable. It is the invention of ardent but simple minds and, too often, of minds that are really happier talking about literature than reading and enjoying it. (pp. 167-79)

David Daiches, "The 'New Criticism': Some Qualifications," in his Literary Essays, *Philosophical Library Publishers, 1957, pp. 167-79.*

HUGH KENNER

[*A Canadian-born American critic, Kenner is the foremost chronicler and commentator on literary Modernism. He is best known for* The Pound Era *(1971), a massive study of the Modernist movement, and for his influential works on Samuel Beckett, T. S. Eliot, James Joyce, and Wyndham Lewis. In addition to his reputation as an important scholar, Kenner is also noted for his often eccentric judgments and a critical style that relies on surprising juxtapositions and wit. In the following excerpt, Kenner discusses the academic climate of the early twentieth century and how it shaped New Critical theory.*]

There seem to be no New Critics in business today, and if they are judged as extinct as the wild pigeon or the dodo, that may be because surly folk clubbed them all to death, or because they go disguised as old critics now. More likely they are extinct for the same reason that the unicorn is extinct. Expeditions find no unicorns because none have existed. It is arguable that the New Critic in the same way was always a gen-

teel fiction. His art had little to do with literary criticism but much to do with the teaching of literature, and teaching is the most evanescent of performances, unless we count skydiving, than which however teaching makes more difference to the nonpractitioners.

The importance of the teacher—particularly the college teacher—in the American scheme of things cannot be overestimated. If we want some quantitative measure we may reflect that some 40 percent of the young Americans of an age to attend some institution of "higher learning" do in fact attend one. No effort has been made anywhere in history to detain so many people in classrooms for so many years, and if it is proposed that not a great deal of learning goes on, it may be countered that the tacit point is not really the learning of skills and subjects, in which it is true that the average grade is C. What gets learned is a common language, at a level of abstraction that grades cannot touch. At that level we may describe a language as a body of inarticulate shared assumptions; no one makes grammatical errors, and eloquence of performance, in fact performance itself, is not at issue. This does not sound much like language as most of us understand language, and yet it is the most powerful set of vectors in the language field: the invisible tensile network that holds the words together, as gravitation, invisible likewise, holds the mere objects in the solar system together, setting limits within which they move with seeming freedom.

To call this nonverbal cohesiveness an aspect of language is especially appropriate in America, so much importance have Americans from the outset accorded to sequences of words and to the very act of uttering and naming. William Carlos Williams more than once reflected on the fatefulness of the decision, centuries ago, to name a certain orange-feathered bird a robin, after a different bird remembered from England. Like the cities the colonists called New Amsterdam and New London, the birds they chose to call robins could be stripped of alien identity and transformed into tokens of a continuity for which men hungered. Symptoms of the alien, by nothing more than a name, had been conjured out of existence: for better or worse. (Williams thought it a fateful act of self-deception.)

Then the nation declared its novel identity by means of a declaration and a written constitution: two historical documents, but also two pieces of canonical prose, to be examined and memorized. To their number President Lincoln was to add the Gettysburg Address. American schoolchildren read the address intact, and study it sentence by sentence. We should reflect on the oddity of this fact. England's history has occasioned no such canonical writing, with the complex exception of the King James Bible. It abounds in consecrated gestures: Cromwell saying, "Take away that bauble"; Victoria affirming her nonamusement. What this connoisseurship of theatrical moments may have to do with the fact that England's principal author was a man of the theater would be a theme for a different inquiry. Suffice it to say that it is America, where the national prose is allegedly barbarous, that makes a cult of connected pieces of prose writing; and it is England, where men of no other discernible credentials can generate fluent five-thousand-word book reviews, that can hardly scrape up three consecutive sentences anyone can remember.

It was into this highly language-conscious milieu that pedagogy in the nineteenth century introduced the classroom study of English literature. Acquaintance with a range of vernacular literature had become a synonym for being cultivated. But fiction and poetry written in another country could scarcely be expected to have other than a classroom existence, and that is the kind of existence literature in America has tended to have. Even among nonprofessional people with leisure, which in America until recently meant chiefly ladies with servants, it has tended to be something to *study.* But the American classroom is like no other: not only the place where rudiments are inculcated, "for the instruction" (as Jefferson put it) "of those who will come after us," but the place where that which is taught chiefly exists: where a considerable part of the nation's mental life is actually conducted.

Imagine, then, the translation into an American classroom of a poem by John Keats:

> Season of mists and mellow fruitfulness,
> Close bosom-friend of the maturing sun;
> Conspiring with him how to load and bless
> With fruit the vines that round the thatch-eaves
>   run;

Move that into Idaho and mark how it is orphaned. It enters the New World naked, cold, uncertain of all save that it enters. How bound up it is, first of all, with an alien weather. American autumns are not misty but crisp. California students stare numbly at that word *mists* and puzzle over the import of *mellow.* Neither word accords with any experience that they have had of the month of October (when it does not rain in Southern California) or November (when it may, and between rains the skies are fiercely clear). And "thatch-eaves": A Disneyland décor. And those home-grown vines in the eaves; and that biblical locution *bless with fruit*—these touch on areas of vague feeling where Bible Christianity interacts with a lifelong experience of not trusting the weather, so that weeks of beneficent weather are remarkable and call for an ode. Keats goes on: "To bend with apples the moss'd cottage-trees. . . ." Mossed because old, because weathered by centuries of damp; cherished by cottagers; and a cottage something other than a vacation retreat, rather a humble, substantial shelter for generations of immovable folk. It is like deciphering the Greek of Sappho, and wondering what flowers exactly were before her mind, in those unforgettable catalogues of flowers.

It is worth a real effort to conceive how desperately philological is the effort to Americanize something like that, because if we can begin to glimpse the difficulties we can see how inevitable were the strategies that got employed. One was a natural one for young readers: the biographical. Its gambit, since the poem would not attach itself readily to the students' experience of autumn, was to attach it to their experience of being alive and young and having feelings. Keats was an impassioned young man whose time was short. "To Autumn" was one precipitate of his soul's obscure but vigorous chemistry. He *felt* like that. (You can't argue with a feeling.) Professionalize this tactic, and when you are in graduate school you will be giving your attention to Keats's letters, among which his poems will take their place as documents, on the whole less penetrable than the letters are.

Another strategy, suitable for more mature students whose attention spans may be judged rather long, is to place the poem in some historical process which it will serve to illustrate. An ideal history for this purpose is that of romanticism, which one can decorate, if it seems unsuitably abstract, with remarks about "nature-feeling." Apples on mossed cottage-trees are assuredly part of Nature, and for Nature it is good to have feelings.

Then there is the Moral Strategy, apt to dwell upon final words: "And gathering swallows twitter in the skies." They gather to depart, and twitter in calling attention to this fact. Here is the teacher's cue to devise a peroration about the worth of feelings of composure. The poet composes the transience of autumn fruition into his celebration of its fructiveness: seeing steadily and whole. This strategy works better with "Ode on a Grecian Urn," which makes some kind of philosophical statement just as it is ending, and so fits the paradigms we learned from McGuffey's reader, which McGuffey himself would have learned in classrooms where Horace was the approved schoolmaster-poet, assuring unruly boys that the prudent course is after all the middle course.

To assimilate an English poem—it is the story of the robin over again. As men newly arrived from England drew security from misnaming an unfamiliar bird, so later people long resident in the new world did violence—could not but do violence—to English writing (so much of which is, after all, indifferently written—can anyone feel sure he remembers exactly the words in which Oliver Twist asks for more? The Theatrical Moment again, masquerading as literature). And those modes of violence were institutionalized; that is a short history of the North American English department, up to about 1945: "the old brass-bound English department," Cleanth Brooks used to say, referring to an impressive mindless curiosity like a Victorian railway train. What had begun as a set of strategic necessities had turned into a profession, a way of life, and a stultifying of literary sensibility. The methods of the Germanic seminar made matters worse by equipping mindlessness with the pretensions of method. (pp. 36-40)

What the New Criticism did was return the study of literature—of poetry, primarily—to the central American intellectual concern, which is Language.

It looked, in those days, like a New Scholasticism for Poloniuses to shake their heads over after the prince had averred that what he read was words, words, words. We began to hear of wit and irony, of paradox and tension. Whole chains of imagery interacted, in likeness and in difference. Fanny Brawne's name went unmentioned, and Shakespeare's deer-stealing. Dates were omitted. Spellings were modernized, and one was encouraged to read seventeenth-century words as though they had been written yesterday—

> I wonder, by my troth, what thou and I
> Did, till we lov'd?

and words written nearly yesterday as though all the time since Shakespeare had hallowed them—

> Here I am, an old man in a dry month,
> Being read to by a boy, waiting for rain.

The Poem Itself—that was what the New Criticism purported to be about.

About the New Criticism Itself, now that we have worked our way up to it, I want to make several interrelated observations. The first is that in treating the poem as a verbal artifact the New Criticism reached deep into the American linguistic sensibility. William Carlos Williams in 1945 had called the poem "a small—or large—machine made out of words," and that was how the New Critics also thought of the poem, though as good agrarians they avoided the word *machine.* Such a sense of things is intimate with the American Grain. It was an American, Edgar Allan Poe, who spun out an outrageous theory postulating that the last thing for a poet to bring to mind, after he has his form and his rhymes and some of his words, may be his subject. He is making a verbal clockwork which appropriates some subject. It was an American linguist, Benjamin Lee Whorf, who elaborated a theory that our language does not report but creates our simplest perceptions, as though we all lived inside a collective poem. Again it is the words that come first. More recently it was an American engineer, Claude E. Shannon, who devised information theory, which has us attend not to the speaker but to the system of encoding. (Ransom's comments on how his own poems were changed by his revisions direct our attention in a similar way.)

Neither for Poe nor for Whorf nor for Shannon does language proceed from a human interior, though we can reconstruct a human intention from it if we are skilled. The New Critic in the same way warned us not to mistake the poem for an utterance of the poet, and an intricate terminology of "speaker" and "persona"—not Keats or Donne but "Keats" and "Donne," each in the role that he plays on this occasion—admonished readers that biography was irrelevant and that all there was to know of the poet in connection with this poem was what this poem could be persuaded to yield. This entailed the formulation whereby all poetry is dramatic, with the incidental advantages both of incorporating Shakespeare's prestige and of coping with the fact that the life of so great a poet has so little to offer us.

My second and third observations are interrelated: that the New Critical thrust was toward facilitating classroom discussion, and that its procedures tended to move into prominence chiefly those poets whom they rendered lengthily discussable. Hence the odd paradox that Williams, despite his dictum about the word-machine, was almost totally neglected. This neglect proceeded from no bias against modernity, since part of the benefit of these novel preoccupations was supposed to be the quantity of contemporary work that they made accessible. Moreover by concentrating on the chemistries of language you could draw comparable satisfactions from poets who made "statements" and from poets who didn't, unembarrassed by the absence of summarizing sentences. *The Waste Land*—not a favorite of Ransom's by the way—became a young critic's obstacle course, through which he was expected to scramble beneath a hail of live ammunition from the battlements of brassboundery, before being adjudged fit for intelligence work. No, the difficulty was that when disassembled by the approved methods, the Williams machine was insufficiently complicated. Not even "The Crimson Cyclamen"—as close a thing, I would argue, to a metaphysical poem as we have in modern English—lends itself to the isolation of "tensions" and "paradoxes" that are effective in the classroom and lend themselves well to the blackboard. And as for "The Red Wheelbarrow," what do you put on the board after you have put the sixteen words of the poem on the board?

Which permits me to elide into my fourth observation, that in subjecting the words on the page to their famous scrutiny, the New Critics tended to scrutinize rather than to listen. A typical blackboard at the end of the hour would display words encircled, with little colliding arrows; would show lines broken into phrases, with perhaps some stresses marked; and would generally be faithful to the discussion of which it carried the traces, since a blackboard permits no interest in what lines sound like, and generally the classes

didn't either. It was perhaps as part of the ritual exorcism of Tennyson, "mouthing out his hollow oes and aes," that this order of omission was tolerated; partly too it stemmed from a certain fear of vulgarity—sound can *impose*—and partly from the persistent though usually unspecified metaphor of the artifact: the precision machine, the well-wrought urn. The persistent neglect of Pound throughout the new critical years was sometimes excused by the allegation—I once heard Cleanth Brooks make it—that Pound never made a poem that was a finished whole. But Pound's poems are apt to be completed—not merely enhanced—by their metrical and vocalic components, so we have here an instance of the field of interest being diminished by critical preoccupations. (And it was Donne, who Ben Jonson thought "for not keeping of accent deserved hanging," who was apt to be deemed the poet par excellence.)

The cult of the blackboard sponsored other distortions: early Yeats underrated, late Yeats sometimes overrated; Wallace Stevens's work unsorted into the categories it demands, the live parts distinguished from the parts that are rhythmically dead. An indifference persisted, for that matter, to rhythmic deadness in modern after modern, just so sufficient surface complication was discoverable.

My purpose behind this catalogue of omissions and distortions is not to denigrate the critic-pedagogue, but to define his characteristic limits of activity, by way of defining what he can do superlatively well, and why, in the 1940s and 1950s, it mattered so much.

What he does is trace the play of mind through a poem, in a way that depends as little as possible on knowledge the students won't have and shouldn't be distracted by. All that is in front of the naive student is the poem, and every minute that is spent on the biography of Yeats or the topography of Sligo is a minute during which his capacity for getting interested in the poem will dissipate by several quanta. A half-hour spent on the doctrines of romanticism insures that meanwhile a dozen odes will die in their entirety. Any strategy for entering directly into the text, and encountering the strange capacity of its words for engaging one another and absorbing attention, is clearly preferable to a pedagogic habit that lingers amid peripheral data, because in no other way can the life of the poem be saved, the life that alone confers interest on other orders of lore. (What interest whatever can romanticism possibly have, unless we first find some romantic poems interesting? Unless they interest the mind to the point where the mind possesses them, they simply are not "there," and without the poems the movement isn't "there" either, and time spent on its study is spent on precisely nothing.)

The curious thing is how a classroom strategy could come to mistake itself for a critical discipline. Not to distract students with peripheral information, that is one thing; to pretend to oneself, as some New Critics did, that the information has no status whatever, is something else. It is possible at all because poems are very tough, viable in strange environments, even in the zero environment of absolute ahistoricity, with only the circulatory system of Language itself to nourish them. How they can protect their existence by mutation is a theme that deserves more attention than it has received. Shakespeare's "golden lads," for instance, has exerted power over countless imaginations despite the virtual loss of the information that what he wrote down was a Warwickshire idiom for dandelions. And Ransom's influential discussion of "Lycidas" ("A Poem Nearly Anonymous") illuminates the poem despite the demonstrable inaccuracy of its postulate—that Milton "roughened" a poem he had first written "smooth." Despite missing information, misinformation, even downright wrong information, it is possible for discussion to proceed a long way without losing itself in nonsense. We may hope to see the way of this elucidated, as information (we may also hope) works itself (duly subordinated) back into our classrooms.

There is no way of not emphasizing classrooms. Criticism is nothing but explicit reading, reading articulating its themes and processes in the presence of more minds than one. It is natural for more minds than one to be concerned, because it is natural to want to talk about what interests one, and also because language itself can only exist at the focus of many minds. And it is in the classroom that, for better or worse, this process of shared and explicit reading is destined to localize itself. (The Browning study groups are, thank heaven, dead.)

What is important is that the very terms on which poems exist shall not surrender once more to the exactions of the beginning student. More than twenty years ago Walter J. Ong described a whole department of human thought, the "arts-course scholasticism" of the late Middle Ages, as having been shaped almost wholly by the need to devise a "philosophy" that could be taught to bright adolescents. It existed only in classrooms, and prepared the minds that, both by penetration and by reaction, prepared the renaissance. By analogy we may call the New Criticism the scholastic phase of an American poetic, rescuing poetics in the New World both from naiveté and from disappearance by absorption into other subjects such as psychology and history.

That, we may say, is accomplished; at least that. In the decades ahead we shall see what we shall see. (pp. 41-6)

Hugh Kenner, "The Pedagogue as Critic," in The New Criticism and After, *edited by Thomas Daniel Young, University Press of Virginia, 1976, pp. 36-46.*

RENE WELLEK

[*Wellek's* A History of Modern Criticism *(1955-1986) is a comprehensive study of the literary critics of the last three centuries. Wellek's critical method, as demonstrated in* A History *and outlined in his* Theory of Literature *(1949), is one of describing, analyzing, and evaluating a work solely in terms of the problems it poses for itself and how the writer solves them. For Wellek, biographical, historical, and psychological information is incidental. Although many of Wellek's critical methods are reflected in the work of the New Critics, he was not a member of that group, and rejected their more formalistic tendencies. In the following excerpt, Wellek defends New Criticism against charges of reviving aestheticism, denying historical context to literary works, employing an overly scientific outlook, and engaging in pedagogical practices of limited usefulness outside the classroom. For an opposing view, see the excerpt by Gerald Graff below.*]

Today the New Criticism is considered not only superseded, obsolete, and dead but somehow mistaken and wrong. Four accusations are made most frequently. First, the New Criticism is an "esoteric aestheticism," a revival of art for art's sake, uninterested in the human meaning, the social function and effect of literature. The New Critics are called "formalists," an opprobrious term used first by Marxists against a group of Russian scholars in the twenties. Second, the New Criticism, we are told, is unhistorical. It isolates the work of

art from its past and its context. Third, the New Criticism is supposed to aim at making criticism scientific, or at least "bringing literary study to a condition rivaling that of science." Finally the New Criticism is being dismissed as a mere pedagogical device, a version of the French *explication de texte,* useful at most for American college students who must learn to read and to read poetry in particular.

I want to show that all these accusations are baseless. They can be so convincingly refuted by an appeal to the texts that I wonder whether current commentators have ever actually read the writings of the New Critics. Inevitably one must ask what the reasons are for this ignorance and these distortions, and one will have to come up with answers that allow a statement of the limitations and shortcomings of the New Criticism. Still, I think that much of what the New Criticism taught is valid and will be valid as long as people think about the nature and function of literature and poetry.

Before we enter into the merits of the case we must come to an agreement as to whom we should consider New Critics. The term itself is old. The Schleger brothers, early in the nineteenth century, called themselves "neue Kritiker," and Benedetto Croce, when he did not want to use the pronoun "I," referred to his own views as "la nuova critica." Joel E. Spingarn, the historian of Renaissance criticism, took the term from Croce when he expounded Croce's theories in a little book, *The New Criticism,* in 1911. E. E. Burgum edited an anthology with this title in 1930, and finally John Crowe Ransom, the founder of the *Kenyon Review,* wrote a book, *The New Criticism,* in 1941 which seems to have established the term in common usage, even though the book was far from being a celebration of the New Criticism. Ransom discusses there not contemporary American criticism in general but only three critics: I. A. Richards, whom he criticizes sharply; T. S. Eliot, against whose views on tradition he makes many objections; and Yvor Winters, whom he rejects in the strongest terms. It earned him a virulent reply in Winters' *Anatomy of Nonsense.*

In 1941 when Ransom's book was published the views and methods of the New Criticism were long established. One can best observe their gradual emergence by thinking of them as reaction against the then prevalent trends in American criticism. Without too much simplification we can distinguish four main trends in American criticism before the advent of the New Critics. There was, first, a type of aesthetic impressionistic criticism, a type of "appreciation," ultimately derived from Pater and Remy de Gourmont, prevalent in the first decade of this century. James G. Huneker may stand here as the representative figure. Then there was, second, the Humanist movement, of which Irving Babbitt and Paul Elmer More were the acknowledged leaders. In 1930 there was a great public commotion around them, but this date is misleading. The main writings of both Babbitt and More appeared in the first decade of the century: the first seven volumes of More's *Shelburne Essays* between 1904 and 1910, Babbitt's *Literature and the American College* in 1908, *Masters of Modern French Criticism* in 1912. Then there was, third, the group of critics who attacked the "genteel" tradition, the American business civilization, the "bouboisie," and propagated the naturalistic novel, Dreiser's in particular. H. L. Mencken and the early Van Wyck Brooks were in the limelight in the twenties. Finally there were the Marxists or near Marxists who flourished during the Great Depression in the early thirties. Granville Hicks is their best-known spokesman, but the much more versatile critic Edmund Wilson was also deeply affected by Marxism, though his actual methods were rather revivals of appreciation or of historicism in the wake of Taine. None of these critics can be mistaken for New Critics.

The new methods, the tone, and new taste are clearly discernible first in the early articles and books of John Crowe Ransom, Allen Tate, R. P. Blackmur, Kenneth Burke, and Yvor Winters, and somewhat later in Cleanth Brooks, Robert Penn Warren, and William K. Wimsatt. A date such as 1923 when Allen Tate spoke of a "new school of so-called philosophic criticism" [in Thomas Daniel Young, *Gentleman in a Dustcoat,* 1976] cannot be far off the mark for the earliest stirrings in the United States. The influence of T. S. Eliot was obviously decisive, to which later that of I. A. Richards should be added. Eliot's *Sacred Wood* dates from 1920, Richards' *Principles of Literary Criticism* from 1924.

If we look at this list of names we soon discover that the group was far from unified. Ransom, Tate, Cleanth Brooks, and R. P. Warren may be grouped together as Southern Critics. Burke and Blackmur stand apart, and Yvor Winters was a complete maverick. I could collect and quote a large number of their pronouncements violently disagreeing with their supposed allies and show that they hold often quite divergent and even contradictory theories. Even Ransom, the teacher in different years of Allen Tate, Cleanth Brooks, and R. P. Warren, holds views very different from those of his pupils. Burke and Blackmur later rejected the New Criticism in strong terms, and Winters never was happy with the association. The view that the New Criticism represents a coterie or even a school is mistaken. With the evidence of disagreements among these critics—which it would take too much time to develop in detail—it may seem wise to conclude that the concept and term should be abandoned and these critics discussed each on his own merits. I have done so in the . . . fifth volume of my *History of Modern Criticism,* where I give individual chapters to each of these men. (pp. 611-13)

Still, something tells us that there is some sense in grouping these critics together. Most obviously they are held together by their reaction against the preceding or contemporary critical schools and views mentioned before. They all reject the kind of metaphorical, evocative criticism practiced by the impressionists. Tate, Blackmur, Burke, and Winters contributed to a symposium highly critical of the neo-Humanists, and others voiced their rejection elsewhere. They all had no use for Mencken and Van Wyck Brooks, particularly after Brooks became a violent enemy of all modernism. Furthermore, they were almost unanimous in their rejection of Marxism, with the single exception of Kenneth Burke, who in the thirties passed through a Marxist phase and, anyhow, after his first book moved away from his neo-critical beginnings. What, however, in the American situation mattered most was that they were united in their opposition to the prevailing methods, doctrines, and views of academic English literary scholarship. There, in a way the younger generation may find it difficult to realize, a purely philological and historical scholarship dominated all instruction, publication, and promotion. I remember that when I first came to study English literature in the Princeton graduate school in 1927, fifty years ago, no course in American literature, none in modern literature, and none in criticism was offered. Of all my learned teachers only Morris W. Croll had any interest in aesthetics or even ideas. Most of the New Critics were college teachers

and had to make their way in an environment hostile to any and all criticism. Only Kenneth Burke was and remained a freelance man of letters, though he taught in later years occasionally at Bennington College and briefly at the University of Chicago. But he very early deserted the New Criticism. It took Blackmur, Tate, and Winters years to get academic recognition, often against stiff opposition, and even Ransom, R. P. Warren, and Cleanth Brooks, established in quieter places, had their troubles. Ransom's paper "Criticism, Inc." (1937) pleaded for the academic establishment of criticism, and thanks to him and others criticism is now taught in most American colleges and universities. But it was an uphill fight. I still remember vividly the acrimony of the conflict between criticism and literary history at the University of Iowa, where I was a member of the English Department from 1939 to 1946.

The New Critics with one voice questioned the assumptions and preoccupations of academic scholarship with different degrees of sharpness. The wittiest and most pungent was Allen Tate. In a lecture, "Miss Emily and the Bibliographer" (1940), Tate exposed the vain attempts to emulate the methods of science by tracing influence conceived in terms of forces, causes and effects, or biological analogies of growth and development, or by applying psychology, economics, and sociology to literature. They all shirk, Tate argues, the essential of criticism, "the moral obligation to judge," for "if we wait for history to judge," as they plead, "there will be no judgment." We must also judge the literature of our own time. "The scholar who tells us that he understands Dryden but makes nothing of Hopkins or Yeats is telling us that he does not understand Dryden" [*Essays of Four Decades,* 1968]. As early as 1927 Tate said that "the historical method has disqualified our best minds for the traditional functions of criticism. It ignores the meaning of the destination in favor of the way one gets there" [*New Republic* 41]. Winters argues similarly. The superstition of a value-free literary history ignores the fact that "every writer that the scholar studies comes to him as the result of a critical judgment" [*The Function of Criticism,* 1957]. The professors who engage in "serious" literary study—bibliography, philology, textual criticism, and related disciplines—not only hold criticism in contempt and do their best to suppress it in the universities, but also, Winters tells us bluntly, "were fools and where they still flourish they are still fools." Blackmur also rejected the methods of what I shall call "extrinsic" criticism. Scholarship, he grants, is useful in supplying us with facts but becomes obnoxious when it "believes it has made an interpretation by surrounding the work with facts" [*The Lion and the Honeycomb,* 1955]. The mild-mannered Ransom could become caustic at the expense of "the indefensible extravagance in the gigantic collective establishment of the English faculties" that fail to teach criticism [*Kenyon Review* 2 (1940)]. Many more voices could be added to a revolt against the positivism of nineteenth-century scholarship, which in the United States was vigorously stated as early as 1908 by Irving Babbitt in *Literature and the American College* and was widespread and effective on the continent of Europe, especially in the twenties.

Still, one should understand that this rejection of academic historical scholarship must not be interpreted as a rejection of the historicity of poetry. Cleanth Brooks has, in many contexts, mostly in interpreting seventeenth-century poems, shown that the critic "needs the help of the historian—all the help he can get" [*English Literature Annual,* 1946]. "The critic," he argues, "obviously must know what the words of the poem mean, something which immediately puts him in debt to the linguist (or rather lexicographer, the OED, I might add); and since many of the words are proper nouns, in debt to the historian as well." In order to interpret the "Horatian Ode" of Andrew Marvell correctly we must obviously know something of Cromwell and Charles I and the particular historical situation in the summer of 1650 to which the poem refers. But historical evidence is not welcomed only as a strictly subordinate contribution to the elucidation of a poem.

Brooks and all the other New Critics reinterpret and revalue the whole history of English poetry. It was an act of the historical imagination (however prepared before) to revise the history of English poetry: to exalt Donne and the Metaphysicals, to reinstate Dryden and Pope, to sift and discriminate among the English Romantic poets, preferring Wordsworth and Keats to Shelley and Byron; to discover Hopkins, to exalt Yeats, and to defend the break with Victorian and Edwardian conventions as it was initiated by Pound and Eliot. Brooks' "Notes for a Revised History of English Poetry" (1939) sketches the new scheme clearly. Winters' books, particularly his last, *Forms of Discovery* (1967), do the same, with a different emphasis, more dogmatically. But it is not enough to refute the allegation of lack of historical sense by pointing to the interest in historical elucidation and even in literary history properly conceived. Rather I would argue that the New Criticism embraces a total historical scheme, believes in a philosophy of history, and uses it as a standard of judgment.

History is seen substantially in the terms of T. S. Eliot. There used to be once a perfectly ordered world, which is, for instance, behind Dante's poetry. This world disintegrated under the impact of science and scepticism. The "dissociation of sensibility" took place at some time in the seventeenth century. Man became increasingly divided, alienated, specialized as industrialization and secularism progressed. The Western world is in decay, but some hope seems to be held out for a reconstitution of the original wholeness. The total man, the undivided "unified sensibility" which combines intellect and feeling, is the ideal that requires a rejection of technological civilization, a return to religion or, at least, to a modern myth and, in the Southern critics, allowed a defense of the agrarian society surviving in the South. The basic scheme has a venerable ancestry: Schiller's *Letters on Aesthetic Education* (1795) was the main source for Hegel and Marx. In the American critics, particularly in Tate and Brooks, the scheme is drawn from Eliot's view of tradition. In Eliot the "unified sensibility" comes from F. H. Bradley, who knew his Hegel. Brooks is confident in focusing on Hobbes as the villain; Tate singles out Bacon, Gibbon, and La Mettrie as the destroyers of the old world view. Ransom puts out a different version blaming "Platonism," which means presumably any generalizing abstracting view of the world. Tate praised Spengler's *Decline of the West* [in an essay in the *Nation* 122, (1926)] and gave the scheme a peculiar twist in his practical criticism. He was most interested in poets who come at the point of dissolution of the original unity, who dramatize the alienation of man: Emily Dickinson and Hart Crane in particular. Tate sees poems always within history and echoes Eliot saying, in 1927, "My attempt is to see the present from the past, yet remain immersed in the present and committed to it" [*The Literary Correspondence of Donald Davidson and Allen Tate,* edited by John Tyree Fain and Thomas Daniel Young, Athens, Ga.: 1974].

The role of criticism is great for the health of poetry, of the language, and ultimately of society. The charge of rejecting history, of having no "sense of the past" (voiced even by Lionel Trilling, in *The Liberal Imagination*) is easily refuted. Its refutation has already answered the other main accusation, that of aestheticism, of an art-for-art's-sake view of literature. It is based on the insistence of the New Critics that the aesthetic experience is set off from immediate practical concerns: from rhetorical persuasion, bare doctrinal statement, or mere emotional effusion. The aesthetic state of mind can be induced only by the coherence and unity of a work of art. These views have an ancient lineage long preceding the art-for-art's-sake movement. The distinctions among aesthetic contemplation, scientific truth, morality, and practical usefulness were most elaborately drawn in Kant's *Critique of Judgment* (1790), and the idea of the coherence, unity, and even organicity of a work of art is as old as Aristotle. It was modified and amplified by the German critics around 1800, from whom Coleridge drew his formulas, and Coleridge is the most immediate source for English and American critics. One may raise doubts (as Wimsatt has) about the metaphor of organism if it is pushed too far in application to a work of art, but there seems to me a simple truth in the old view that a successful work of art is a whole in which the parts collaborate and modify one another. Much of the "close reading" practiced by Cleanth Brooks and followers demonstrates this truth even on recalcitrant material. But this insight is grossly distorted if it is supposed to lead to the conclusion that poetry is cut off from reality, is merely self-reflexive, and that it is thus only an inconsequential play of words. When Brooks combats the "heresy of paraphrase" he objects to reducing a work of art to a statement of abstract propositions, or to a moral message, or to any literal verifiable truth. But this emphasis on the specific "fictionality" of all art, its world of illusion or semblance, cannot mean a lack of relation to reality or a simple entrapment in language. Tate, for instance, emphatically condemned "that idolatrous dissolution of language from the grammar of a possible world, which results from the belief that language itself can be reality, or by incantation can create reality: a superstition that comes down in French from Lautréamont, Rimbaud and Mallarmé to the Surrealists, and in English to Hart Crane, Wallace Stevens, and Dylan Thomas" (*Essays*). Poetry is turned to the world, aims at a picture of reality. It cannot be absolute or pure. It remains impure, like anything human, a theme eloquently developed in R. P. Warren's essay "Pure and Impure Poetry" (1942).

Both Brooks and Ransom uphold a version of imitation, of *mimesis*. Brooks asserts that the poem, if it is a true poem, is a "simulacrum of reality" [*Well Wrought Urn,* 1947] or "a portion of reality as viewed and valued by a human being. It is rendered coherent through a perspective of valuing" [*Literary Criticism,* 1957]. In Ransom poetry is a display, a knowledge and restoration of the real world: a celebration of the beauty of nature, even a "representation of natural beauty" [*Poems and Essays,* 1955]. None of the New Critics could have believed in the prison-house of language. This supposed consequence of any view of the unity, self-reflexiveness, and integration of a work of art has been debated thoroughly, for example, by Murray Krieger in *The New Apologists for Poetry* (1956) and by Gerald Graff in *Poetic Statement and Critical Dogma* (1970), but it poses a false dilemma. A poem may have coherence and integrity without losing its meaning or truth. The very nature of words points to the outside world. In *A Window to Criticism* (1964) Murray Krieger speaks of a "miracle," but such a gesture toward the irrational seems unnecessary unless we consider the reference of almost every word a "miracle." It points to or may point to an object in the outside world and at the same time is part of a sentence, of a phonemic and syntactical system, of a language code. The parallel to painting is obvious: a painting is enclosed in a frame, is organized by a relation of colors and lines, but simultaneously may represent a landscape, a scene, or the portrait of a real man or woman.

In the writings of the New Critics the coherence of a poem is not studied in terms of form, as the label "formalism" suggests. Actually the New Critics pay little attention to what is traditionally called the form of a poem. Brooks and Warren in their textbook, *Understanding Poetry* (1938), inevitably pay some attention to the role of meter and stanzaic forms, and Winters expounded his view on "The Audible Reading of Poetry" (*Function of Criticism*). But the New Critics reject the distinction of form and content: they believe in the organicity of poetry and, in practice, constantly examine attitudes, tones, tensions, irony, and paradox, all psychological concepts partly derived from Richards. The concept of irony and paradox is used by Brooks very broadly. It is not the opposite of an overt statement "but a general term for the kind of qualification which the various elements in a context receive from the context" (*Well Wrought Urn*). It indicates the recognition of incongruities, the union of opposites that Brooks finds in all good, that is, complex, "inclusive" poetry. Brooks has most consistently held a strictly organic point of view. Other critics desert it. Thus Ransom draws a distinction between structure and texture which reverts to the old dichotomy of content and form. A poem, he says strikingly, is "much more like a Christmas tree than an organism" [*Kenyon Review* 7 (1945)], with the metaphors thought of as ornaments. Winters comes to a similar conclusion with a different emphasis. A poem is for him "a statement in words about a human experience" [*In Defense of Reason,* 1947]. The charge of formalism in any sense that is valid for the Russian school is completely off the mark. The New Critics are overwhelmingly concerned with the meaning of a work of art, with the attitude, the tone, the feelings, and even with the ultimate implied world view conveyed. They are formalists only in the sense that they insist on the organization of a work of art which prevents its becoming a simple communication.

The allegation that the New Critics want to make criticism a science seems to me even more preposterous. It might have emanated from those who felt hurt by their attack on "appreciation," on loose impressionism and mere self-indulgence in "adventures among masterpieces." More recently it often comes from defenders of a hermeneutics that assumes a mysterious identification with the author's *cogito* or rejects interpretation in favor of an "erotics of art," as Susan Sontag does in *Against Interpretation* (1964). Actually the New Critics are enemies of science. Science for Tate is the villain of history which has destroyed the community of man, broken up the old organic way of life, paved the way to industrialism, and made man the alienated, rootless, godless creature he has become in this century. Science encourages Utopian thinking, the false idea of the perfectability of man, the whole illusion of endless progress. Tate says bluntly: "Poetry is not only quite different from science but in its essence is opposed to science" [*This Quarter* 5 (1932)]. In Ransom, in particular, poetry is conceived as the supreme antidote against science. He makes the conflict of art and science the leading theme of history. "In all human history the dualism between science

and art widens continually by reason of the aggressions of science. As science more and more reduces the world to its types and forms, art, replying, must invest it again with body" [*The World's Body,* 1938]. The investment with body, the reassertion of the particularity of the world against the abstractions of science, is Ransom's leading theme: the restoration of what he calls the "thingness" (*Dinglichkeit*) of the world is the aim and justification of poetry. None of the New Critics has any sympathy for the mechanistic technological views of the Russian formalists. The New Critics have completely shunned modern linguistics: the use of phonemics or of quantitative methods. If they sometimes spoke of criticism as a systematic, rational discipline they could not mean a modern value-free social science, for they always stressed the necessity of judgment, the qualitative experience poetry gives us. In the attempt to defend poetry against the accusation of irrelevancy, they put forward claims for the truth of poetry, for the knowledge conveyed which is conceived as superior to that of science. Over and over again Tate says that literature provides "the special, unique and complete knowledge" (*Essays*), "knowledge of a whole object, its complete knowledge, the full body of experience." This is not a claim like that of the Romantics for some visionary power, some special insight into a world beyond, which might lead to an obscurantist theory of double truth. It is rather a view of knowledge as "realization," as full awareness in the sense in which we can say, "You don't really know what it is like until you have lived through it." It is ultimately a version of the unified sensibility of T. S. Eliot, the union of feeling and intellect achieved in poetry. Criticism cannot be neutral scientism: it must respond to the work with the same totality of mind with which the work is created. But criticism is always subordinated to creation. Its humility contrasts precisely with the aggressions, the impositions of science.

None of the New Critics would have thought that their methods of close reading were "scientific" nor would they have identified criticism with close reading. Ransom, Tate, Blackmur, Winters, and Burke had developed their theories of poetry and their general point of view long before they engaged in anything like close reading. Tate's first excursion into close reading is the essay "Narcissus as Narcissus" (1938), a commentary on his own "Ode to the Confederate Dead." The examination of a poem apart from biography and conventional literary history became, no doubt, an important innovation in the teaching of literature in American colleges and universities. The turn to the text was mainly accomplished by the success of *Understanding Poetry* by Cleanth Brooks and Robert Penn Warren, which invaded the strongholds of philological scholarship in the early forties. The method of close reading became the pedagogical weapon of the New Criticism. One should grant that the proliferation of "explications" became later a dreary industry, but it is a mistake to consider close reading a new version of *explication de texte.* Close reading as practiced by Cleanth Brooks differs from *explication de texte* by offering critical standards, leading to discrimination between good and bad poems, resolutely pursued in the textbook and in many other articles since. The aim is understanding, "interpretation," which is the other name for the now fashionable term "hermeneutics." The method of the New Critics may differ from the intuitive identification proposed by the phenomenologists in the wake of Poulet or from the fusion of horizons in the mode of Gadamer, but the aim is the same. It is hard to see how a study of literature can get along without interpretation of individual works and how one can be "against interpretation," as Susan Sontag entitled her book, or declare "interpretation" to be "the real enemy" [Jonathan Culler, in *Comparative Literature* 28 (1976)]. The view voiced by Richard E. Palmer in his book on *Hermeneutics* (1969) that the New Criticism has "a technological concept of interpretation" mistakes its aim of suppressing irrelevant subjective preconceptions or biographical explanations for an indifferent scientism. It seems to me far-fetched to bring in T. S. Eliot's belief in original sin as Gerald Graff does [in "What Was New Criticism? Literary Interpretation and Scientific Objectivity," *Salmagundi,* No. 27 (1974)] to explain the New Critics' emphasis on impersonality. It comes rather from Flaubert's and Joyce's desire for an objective art, "impersonality" meaning a rejection of overt didacticism and confessional display. The New Criticism surely argues from a sound premise, that no coherent body of knowledge can be established unless it defines its object, which to the New Critic will be the individual work of art clearly set off from its antecedents in the mind of the author or in the social situation, as well as from its effect in society. The object of literary study is conceived of not as an arbitrary construct but as a structure of norms which prescribes a right response. This structure need not be conceived of as static or spatial in any literal sense, though terms such as the well-wrought urn, or Joseph Frank's spatial form, or Wimsatt's verbal icon suggest such a misinterpretation. All these metaphors aim at a genuine insight: although the process of reading is inevitably temporal in criticism, we must try to see a work as a totality, a configuration, a gestalt, a whole.

I hope I have succeeded in refuting the common misconceptions about the New Criticism, but I have studied the history of criticism long enough to know that there must be reasons for the fact that the New Criticism is currently so in disfavor that, for instance, Geoffrey Hartman could not only entitle a book and an essay *Beyond Formalism* (1970; the essay dates from 1966) but quote there Trotsky, of all people, attacking the very different Russian formalists from his Marxist point of view and then conclude that "there is good reason why many in this country, as well as in Europe, have voiced a suspicion of Anglo-Saxon formalism. The dominion of Exegesis is great: she is our Whore of Babylon, sitting robed in Academic black on the great dragon of Criticism and displaying a repetitive and soporific balm from her pedantic cup" and say that "Explication is the end of criticism only if we succumb to what Trotsky called the formalist's 'superstition of the word'." Hartman and others have tried to overcome this superstition either by appealing to a purely intuitive identification with the author behind the work or by advocating a complete liberty of interpretation in an attempt to exalt criticism to the status of art, to obliterate the distinction between criticism and creation for which Roland Barthes has invented the convenient common term "*écriture.*"

But the objections to the New Criticism do not come only from this new apocalyptic irrationalism. They are much older and more serious. The New Critics were immediately attacked from two sides long before the new movements imported from France. The Chicago Aristotelians, who exalt plot, character, and genre, strongly disapproved of the New Critics' concern for language and poetic diction. Language according to the Chicago School is merely inert matter, a material cause of poetry, a view which seems to go back rather to the Renaissance scholar Scaliger than to Aristotle himself. The New Critics fared badly in their hands. R. S. Crane attacked Cleanth Brooks' "critical monism," deploring his preoccupation with paradox and his conclusion that the structure of poetry is the structure common to all literary works (*Critics and Criticism*). Crane also criticizes the New Critics for their "morbid obsession with the problem of justifying and preserving poetry in an age of science," as this was no problem for Crane and his group. Crane accepts pleasure as the aim of art and imitation as its procedure in which we find pleasure and instruction. One must admit that the Chicago critics scored many points against the overreadings in R. P. Warren's study of "The Ancient Mariner" and the attempts of Robert Heilman to read *King Lear* as an almost spatial pattern of images. Still the Chicago Aristotelians were on some points the allies of the New Criticism. Crane was one of the first to defend and to recommend the study of criticism in the university ["History versus Criticism in the Study of Literature," in *The Idea of the Humanities,* 2 vols., 1967]. The whole group advocates a rational systematic study of poetics even though their insistence on strict genre conventions and neutral analysis was unacceptable to the New Critics concerned with the nature of poetry in general and with criticism as evaluation.

The next, much more effective rejection of the New Criticism came from the so-called myth-critics. Myth as a system of metaphors or symbols is a central device in much of the New Criticism, but in the myth-critics it becomes the one overriding concern. Poetry is simply (and I think wrongly) identified with myth, and myth is used so broadly that it includes any theme, any story you can think of: Huck Finn floating down the Mississippi with Jim is a myth. Myth-criticism allows a discussion of content apart from the poem: it often became mere allegorizing. Every work of literature is a quest, or a version of the death of God and His rebirth. Still, one should recognize that Northrop Frye in his *Anatomy of Criticism* (1957) has not entirely discarded the achievements of the New Criticism, though he rejects criticism as judgment in theory (though hardly in practice).

The New Criticism was then totally rejected by the Critics of Consciousness, the so-called Geneva School and its followers in this country. Georges Poulet, their most articulate spokesman, does not want to analyze a single work of art, is uninterested in its form or specificity, for he is searching for the author's *cogito* behind his total *oeuvre.* The other French group which must not be confused with the Geneva School, the Structuralists, who come from Saussure's linguistics and from Lévi-Strauss' anthropology, have some affinities with the New Criticism in their concern for a microscopic analysis of texts and a general poetics. Roman Jakobson was the link between the Russian Formalists and the Paris Structuralists, and all his recent work, hailed by I. A. Richards as the fulfillment of his own ambitions, demonstrates his concern and skill in interpreting individual poems. But Jakobson's methods are linguistic, attentive to the grammar of poetry, and pointedly ignore criticism as judgment or ranking. Still, there is one trend in Parisian Structuralism, particularly the acute analyses of fiction or symbol practiced by the Bulgarian Tzvetan Todorov and by Gérard Genette, which is not incompatible with the ambitions of the New Criticism. Many others in France and here in the United States aim at an all-embracing structure of universal poetics and finally at a science of semiotics: an ambition beyond the ken of the New Critics. Their *ethos,* unlike the often religious motivation of the Geneva School, is scientific; the philosophy, implied positivistic or materialistic: some of the French group have embraced Marxism and even Maoism. The distance from the New Criticism is obvious.

Surely one of the reasons for the demise of the New Criticism is the distrust many feel toward the political and religious views of the main New Critics: toward T. S. Eliot's Anglicanism, which is shared for instance by Cleanth Brooks, or toward the Roman Catholicism of Allen Tate (a convert) or William K. Wimsatt, as well as toward the participation of three of the Southern Critics (Ransom, Tate, R. P. Warren) in the so-called Agrarian movement, formulated in the symposium *I'll Take My Stand* (1930). But the New Critics—unlike the later Eliot and the early Richards—never tired of rejecting the amalgamation of poetry and religion. Tate says expressly that "literature is neither religion nor social engineering" (*Essays*), and Brooks and Wimsatt always kept the two realms rigorously apart in their critical practice. But one cannot deny that ultimately poetry with several of the New Critics turns out to be, if not religion, then a preparation for religion: it is assigned a role comparable to the imagination in Wordsworth and Coleridge. The poet and his reader are each brought back to the totality of his being, are restored to their original humanity.

If one rejects this version of history, one can see the justification of a new turn in poetic taste. The revival of the English Romantics as the Visionary Company centered in Blake and the current attempts to dismiss T. S. Eliot both as poet and critic and to reduce the role of all Modernism imply a rejection of the New Criticism also in the everyday matters of selection and ranking of poets and poems.

Still even more profoundly the New Criticism is affected by the general revolt against aesthetics per se, by the whole rejection of any distinction between the aesthetic state of mind and any other activity. It goes back to the German theory of empathy, even to Benedetto Croce, wrongly suspected of aestheticism, though he abolished the distinction between art and any act of intuition; and to John Dewey's *Art as Experience* (1934), which denies all distinction between aesthetic and other experiences of heightened vitality; and paradoxically to the literary criticism of I. A. Richards, who had such an influence on the American New Critics with his book on *Practical Criticism* (1929) but propounded a behavioristic theory which ignores the difference between aesthetic and other emotions completely. Thus the very basis of any concern with poetry or literature as an art is undermined. The New Criticism has become a victim of the general attack on literature and art, of the "deconstruction" of literary texts, of the new anarchy which allows a complete liberty of interpretation, and even of a self-confessed "nihilism."

One limitation of the New Critics seems to me serious, possibly because of my commitment to comparative literature. They are extremely anglocentric, even provincial. They have rarely attempted to discuss foreign literature or, if they have done so, their choice has been confined to a very few obvious texts. Dante is discussed by Allen Tate; he also comments on passages in *The Idiot* and *Madame Bovary*. Winters admires the poems of Paul Valéry. Blackmur, late in his life, did write, often vaguely and obscurely, on Dostoevsky, Tolstoy, and Flaubert. A recent excursion of Kenneth Burke into Goethe seems most unfortunate. That is about all. The justification of this preoccupation with texts in English is presumably the conviction of the critics that poetry is implicated closely in the language, and lyrical poetry, the nature of poetry in general, was their first concern. Still it *is* a limitation, considering the inexhaustible wealth of the world's literature speaking to us in many tongues, crying to be interpreted and judged.

I will not conceal my own conviction that the New Criticism has stated or reaffirmed many basic truths to which future ages will have to return: the specific nature of the aesthetic transaction, the normative presence of a work of art which forms a structure, a unity, coherence, a whole, which cannot be simply battered about and is comparatively independent of its origins and effects. The New Critics have also persuasively described the function of literature in not yielding abstract knowledge or information, message or stated ideology, and they have devised a technique of interpretation which often succeeded in illuminating not so much the form of a poem as the implied attitudes of the author, the resolved or unresolved tensions and contradictions: a technique that yields a standard of judgment that cannot be easily dismissed in favor of the currently popular, sentimental, and simple. The charge of "elitism" cannot get around the New Critics' assertion of quality and value. A decision between good and bad art remains the unavoidable duty of criticism. The humanities would abdicate their function in society if they surrendered to a neutral scientism and indifferent relativism or if they succumbed to the imposition of alien norms required by political indoctrination. Particularly on these two fronts the New Critics have waged a valiant fight which, I am afraid, must be fought over again in the future. (pp. 613-24)

> René Wellek, "The New Criticism: Pro and Contra," in Critical Inquiry, Vol. 4, No. 4, Summer, 1978, pp. 611-24.

GERALD GRAFF

[*Graff is an American educator and critic whose works often discuss modern critical theory. In the following excerpt, he challenges René Wellek's defense of New Criticism (see excerpt above).*]

Yes, the New Critics have taken a lot of abuse for things they did not really do—or for things they did do that were sensible. I myself have objected, in the publications René Wellek mentions, to oversimplified characterizations of New Criticism as "formalism" and "scientism" and to the irrationalist politics that often goes along with such caricatures. But I think Wellek himself oversimplifies the issues and lets the New Critics off too easily on several of the charges he takes up. Wellek promises us a "statement of the limitations and shortcomings of the New Criticism," but since I could not find any reference to limitations and shortcomings except a minor one (the New Critics were "anglocentric," I have dealt with his essay as an unqualified apology.

1. History.—Wellek regards as baseless the common charge that the New Critics ignored "the historicity of poetry." To prove his point, he cites some statements by Cleanth Brooks conceding that the critic "needs the help of the historian—all the help he can get"—for information about the meanings of words, references lost to the modern reader, and so forth. It is true that Brooks and other New Critics often acknowledge the need for this rather pedestrian kind of history as a supplement to the work of the critical analyst. From my viewpoint, the problem is not that the New Critics rejected history but that they held a somewhat trivial conception of it. When William K. Wimsatt and Monroe C. Beardsley talk about history in their influential "Intentional Fallacy" essay, what they have in mind is either a rather mechanical sort of history of ideas (Charles M. Coffin's *John Donne and the New Philosophy*, 1937, is one of their prime exhibits) or else isolated documents and facts. Wimsatt, for instance, speaks of "revelations (in journals, for example, or letters or reported conversations) about how or why the poet wrote the poem—to what lady, while sitting on what lawn, or at the death of what friend or brother" [*The Verbal Icon,* 1954]. Wellek quotes a remark by R. P. Blackmur about the limitations of "surrounding the work with facts" that could illustrate this atomized view of history.

It was, of course, the positivistic historians against whom the New Critics were reacting who first reduced history to a congeries of disconnected ideas and facts, as opposed to a continuous, coherent process. But instead of seeking to rehabilitate and redefine the concept of history from the diminished article it had become when they arrived on the critical scene, the New Critics incorporated this positivistic view of history into their own outlook. (I am surprised Wellek is not more alive to this trivialization of history, since his own essay "The Concept of Evolution in Literary History" in his *Concepts of Criticism* [1963] is an important analysis of how it got started.) However many concessions the New Critics may have made to the historians, they never came close to the insight that neo-Marxists and others have been trying to reformulate, that literature is in some important degree not simply extrinsically conditioned but intrinsically constituted by an historical process.

But Wellek is ready with an answer to this kind of charge. He argues that "the New Criticism embraces a total historical scheme" and "believes in a philosophy of history." This philosophy, which he traces in its derivation from Eliot by way of Bradley out of Hegel and Schiller, conceives history as a fall into "dissociation of sensibility" resulting chiefly from the industrial and democratic revolutions, a fall that has been followed by a struggle for recovery of unity. Wellek's description is right, but it confirms rather than refutes the accusation. Scholars who have found New Critical interpretations of sixteenth- and seventeenth-century works anachronistic—for example, Rosemond Tuve (*Elizabethan and Metaphysical Imagery* [1947] and *A Reading of George Herbert* [1952]), Dame Helen Gardner (*The Business of Criticism* [1959]), and J. V. Cunningham (*Tradition and Poetic Structure* [1960])—have understood perfectly well that the New Critics embraced "a total historical scheme." That was just the problem. The New Critics were so deeply concerned with the post-industrial crisis of dissociation that they read this issue into every work they encountered, including those which happened to have been written before intellectuals had become preoccupied with it. If being historically conscious means trying to understand the past on its own terms, then the New Critical revision of the history of English poetry which Wellek cites was not very historically conscious, for it reinterpreted the past in terms of modernist interests and biases. The whole problem is complicated, but if the New Critics are to be cleared of charges of ahistoricism, the many telling critiques by qualified historical scholars will have to be disposed of.

2. Formalism.—Wellek takes up the charge that New Critical theory led "to the conclusion that poetry is cut off from reality, is merely self-reflexive, and that it is thus only an inconsequential play of words." This he counters by quoting a number of statements by New Critics defending literature as a form of mimetic knowledge or condemning aestheticism, art-for-art's-sake, and formalism. Wellek observes, correctly, I think, that "actually the New Critics pay little attention to

what is traditionally called the form of the poem," and that concepts such as irony, paradox, and tension are after all not formal but psychological. The New Critics "are formalists," he says, "only in the sense that they insist on the organization of a work of art which prevents its becoming a simple communication." Critics like Murray Krieger and me (from different viewpoints) have posed a "false dilemma" in thinking there is a contradiction between the New Critics' insistence on the internal self-sufficiency of literature and their attempts to reconcile literature to knowledge and reality. What Krieger and I mistake for a contradiction was actually a healthy comprehensiveness: "A poem may have coherence and integrity without losing its meaning or truth." This, according to Wellek, is all the New Critics were getting at in attacking various extrinsic critical approaches—"the insistence . . . that the aesthetic experience is set off from immediate practical concerns: from rhetorical persuasion, bare doctrinal statement, or mere emotional effusion."

Wellek makes the New Critics sound so mild and reasonable that I began to wonder if I had imagined those extreme and programmatic assertions of the "autonomy" of literature which I thought I remembered in New Critical writing. The New Critics turn out to have been defending doctrines that "have an ancient lineage"; their concept of coherence is "as old as Aristotle," though, Wellek concedes, not quite the same. But Wellek's portrait is incomplete. He mentions little of the terminology used by the New Critics in order to neutralize or eliminate the propositional and referential aspects of literature—terms like "autonomy," "self-sufficiency," "intransitivity," "autotelism." He does not mention New Critical strategies, such as the "principle of dramatic propriety," which assume that because literature is dramatic "action" or "embodiment" it therefore makes no reference to external states of affairs. He says nothing about the questionable distinction between literary and nonliterary language, except to imply that anybody who objects to it is participating not only in the "rejection of any distinction between the aesthetic state of mind and any other activity" but "the general attack upon literature and art."

Wellek writes of Brooks as a theorist in the mimetic tradition and quotes Brooks describing poetry as "a simulacrum of reality." The full statement in which this phrase appears is slightly more equivocal: "The poem, if it be a true poem, is a simulacrum of reality—in this sense, at least, it is an 'imitation'—by *being* an experience rather than any mere statement about experience or any mere abstraction from experience" [*Well Wrought Urn,* 1947]. The antithesis here between experience and statements about experience—as if a poem could not be both at once—is just the sort of formulation that got the New Critics into logical muddy waters and made it easy to read them as formalists even if they did not mean to be.

Wellek turns to Allen Tate, pointing out that "over and over again Tate says that literature provides 'the special, unique and complete knowledge . . . knowledge of a whole object, its complete knowledge, the full body of experience'." Yes, Tate did say this sort of thing over and over, but he said other things too, things that sometimes seemed to take back what such statements had given. For instance, Tate says "if the poem is a real creation, it is a kind of knowledge that we did not possess before. It is not knowledge 'about' something else; the poem is the fullness of that knowledge" [*Essays of Four Decades,* 1968]. Perhaps Wellek will not accuse me of creating a "false dilemma" if I suggest that Tate's appeal to a knowledge that is not "about something else" raises some questions about how Tate is using the word "knowledge." Either Tate's formulation is incompatible with a mimetic view of literature or else Tate did not say what he meant and should have worded it some other way.

The question, it seems to me, comes down to this: Is literature answerable to some standard of truth or adequacy to life, a standard beyond purely internal coherence, or is it not? Wellek wants us to believe that the New Critical answer was "yes," coherence and correspondence are *both* admissible demands. My impression, on the contrary, is that the New Critics frequently answered "no" to this question and then began hedging. One type of hedging was to declare that literature should not be held liable to any external standard of correspondence, and then to warn the reader that this declaration should not be taken to *mean* that literature is not ultimately about life—as if such a rhetorical disclaimer could blunt the logical force of the categorical overstatement. Another type of equivocation was to smuggle terms like "complexity" into the discussion while pretending that one is not, in doing so, appealing to any standard external to the literary work. For example, in the chapter on "Evaluation" in Wellek and Warren's *Theory of Literature,* the authors object to Eliot's call for "maturity" and "truth to experience" in poetry because it "goes beyond any formalism" (!) and is "an appeal to worlds outside the work of art, a call for the comparison of art and reality." They go on to reply to Eliot that "the maturity of a work of art is in its inclusiveness, its awareness of complexity . . . ," as if such a strategy did not itself patently involve us in drawing comparisons between art and reality.

Perhaps such contradictions can be explained by the fact that critics like Brooks, Tate, and Wellek and Warren are groping to express that peculiarly experiential quality of literature that we obviously do not find, say, in laboratory reports or railway timetables, but I think we do not help matters by making this experiential quality the antithesis of general ideas and references to the world. It is possible to defend these New Critical moves as tactical correctives to various didactic heresies and propagandistic reductions, but as soon as one takes them seriously as statements within a universe of logical consequences, they pose problems that should not be brushed aside as imaginary.

Wellek is surely right in arguing that the New Critics did not intend to behave as formalists, but I think he needs to explain why they came so close to doing so in spite of themselves. One explanation may lie in a sphere Wellek mentions but might have probed even more fully, the long-standing Romantic and modernist revolt against the culture of science, positivism, and utilitarianism. In *Culture and Society, 1780-1950* (1958), Raymond Williams argues that the Romantic reaction against industrial-utilitarian society led to a specialization of literature that attenuated literature's claims in a self-defeating way. Instead of contesting the realm of objective knowledge, the defenders of literature conceded this territory to science and commerce, either celebrating literature for its very freedom from such knowledge or claiming for it some alternate form of knowledge (not "about" anything) that could not be made rationally respectable. One could argue that the same pattern of misplaced reaction is seen in the New Criticism, that its revolt against the utilitarian, "Platonic" drives of science and positivism took the form of an attempt to divest literature of objective "truth of correspondence." Having equated this kind of truth with the most reductive

forms of scientism, moralism, and propagandizing, the New Critics made it difficult to justify their own ambitious claims for the humanistic knowledge embodied in literature. Their way of reacting against the depravities of technological culture continues to be a common one today and can even be found in such adversaries of the New Critics as the cultural revolutionaries, the phenomenologists, and the deconstructionists—all of whom express the paradigms of our modern "adversary culture." It is an understandable and even perhaps an admirable reaction, but it has led to distortions in our conception of the humanities—one of which is the aggravation of that very dissociation of sensibility into scientific and poetic components that we all say we want to have done with.

3. The High Priori Road.—Wellek refers to R. S. Crane's attacks on the New Criticism but does not mention their most telling point. This is Crane's charge that the New Critics, like some of their adversaries the historians, took "the high priori road" in their theories of literature and their applications of these theories to specific works. By starting out with the assumption that *all* poetry must be the "language of paradox," or some comparable thing, the New Critics, in effect, knew the meanings of poems before they had read them. The current critical fashion of reading all works as self-consuming artifacts, as commentaries on their own problematics, or as language that "knows and names itself as fiction" illustrates a similar a priorism. In this respect I do not think it farfetched to see this new mode of interpretation as New Critical "ironic" reading raised to a sublime degree.

Crane asked a simple question of the New Critics: How did they *know* that poetry—or specific poems—consisted of the language of paradox? The answer, he saw, was that they had derived this thesis not from empirical study of particular poems, submitting the thesis to a rigorous and skeptical test, but rather from that philosophy of culture and history that Wellek describes. Starting with a view of culture as a warfare between the forces of positivism and the forces of humanity, the New Critics polarized language accordingly. In Crane's own words, they begin "by dividing all language into two opposing and incommensurable kinds—the language of 'logic' and the language of 'symbolism' " and then proceed to deduce "from this initial assumption that the 'symbolic' language of poetry must necessarily possess the contraries of all qualities commonly asserted of 'logical discourse' " ["Criticism as Inquiry; or, The Perils of the 'High Priori Road'," *The Idea of the Humanities and Other Essays Critical and Historical,* 2 vols., 1967]. It was not, according to Crane, that the New Critics were necessarily *wrong* in what they said about literature but that, right or wrong, the method by which they arrived at their generalizations and interpretations derived not from a genuine inquiry into the subject but from a deductive scheme formulated in advance.

Wellek thus seems to have missed the point of Crane's reference to the New Critics' "morbid obsession with the problem of justifying and preserving poetry in an age of science" when he retorts sardonically, "this was no problem for Crane and his group." Crane's phrasing may have been needlessly caustic, but his point was not that the problem of justifying poetry in a scientific age is not a real problem but that this problem should not be permitted to dictate our understanding of what literature is or what a particular work means. But this brings me back to my earlier point: that many of the confusions and extravagances of the New Criticism—and of much that has come after—are symptomatic of a distorted, if understandable, reaction against technological society.

I suspect some readers may be wondering why any of this is important. I think it is important because the way we talk about literature, the terms we decide to use to define it, the things we contrast it to and align it with—all this has consequences in our behavior, both inside and outside the literary sphere. Whether we accept or reject the term "autonomy" as a description of literature's formal integrity, whether we choose to contrast literature with "representation" or "statement" or put these things on the same side, may seem to be merely verbal questions, of concern only to those with rarified theoretical interests. But these and other terms in the vocabulary of criticism are implicated in the moral and political warfare of modern culture—so deeply, in fact, that it is often difficult to keep the literary and the cultural issues distinct. And though literary theory has lately become an esoteric subject (as it was not for the New Critics, to their credit), its controversies mirror the cultural politics played out in society at large. In this sense, the question of whether a particular way of talking about literature is useful or self-defeating is of great importance. On this point, if not on others, perhaps Wellek and I can agree. (pp. 569-75)

Gerald Graff, "Critical Response: New Criticism Once More," in Critical Inquiry, *Vol. 5, No. 3, Spring, 1979, pp. 569-75.*

CLEANTH BROOKS

[*Brooks is the most prominent of the New Critics. His most characteristic essays are detailed studies of metaphoric structure, particularly in poetry. According to René Wellek, "Brooks analyzes poems as structures of opposites, tensions, paradoxes, and ironies with unparalleled skill." For Brooks, irony is the most important of these elements and, as Wellek notes, "indicates the recognition of incongruities, the ambiguity, the reconciliation of opposites which Brooks finds in all good, that is, complex poetry." In the following excerpt from an essay Brooks wrote for the* Sewanee Review *in 1979, he recalls the aims of the New Critics and defends the movement against some common charges.*]

I have been asked by the editor [of the *Sewanee Review*] to write on the New Critics, but to engage to do such an essay is very much like embarking on the hunting of the Snark. The New Critic, like the Snark, is a very elusive beast. Everybody talks about him: there is now rather general agreement as to his bestial character; but few could give an accurate anatomical description of him. Even when one believes that the Snark has actually been netted, he usually turns out to be not a Snark at all but a Boojum.

Who, after all, are the New Critics? John Crowe Ransom, who almost accidentally supplied them with a name? R. P. Blackmur? I. A. Richards? T. S. Eliot? People like these do not fit the stereotype neatly. Richards, for example, contradicts the current stereotype by his heavy stress on the reader, not the work. Allen Tate breaks out of the stereotype by showing from the beginning a keen interest in history. Two of his earliest books are biographies and many of his later essays are concerned with cultural history.

One could name other critics who fail to fit the pattern. In fact, after some preliminary sorting and sifting, I am usually the person chosen to flesh out the agreed-upon stereotypical diagram. In short, if a genuine Snark can't be found, then a

Boojum will have to do. I'm not, of course, very happy with this state of affairs. I am well aware that no compliment is intended when I am so often pointed out as "the typical New Critic" or when a fashionable young critic sneers at what he calls "Well-Wrought-Urn-ism."

In view of this situation, I think it just as well to make this essay on the New Criticism a personal one. I shall prefer to talk about my own position rather than defend the occasional lapses, deficiencies, or biases of the so-called New Criticism. So much for the negative side. On the positive side, if I am to be forced to accept the term after all, then I want to define it so that it will actually reflect my own values and beliefs, not those of others, least of all those of a strawman.

Let me begin with a bit of ancient history. When in the early 1930s Robert Penn Warren and I found ourselves teaching "literary types and genres" at a large state university, we discovered that our students, many of whom had good minds, some imagination, and a good deal of lived experience, had very little knowledge of how to read a story or a play, and even less knowledge of how to read a poem. Some had not been taught how to do so at all; many had been thoroughly mistaught. Some actually approached Keats's "Ode to a Nightingale" in the same spirit and with the same expectations with which they approached an editorial in the local

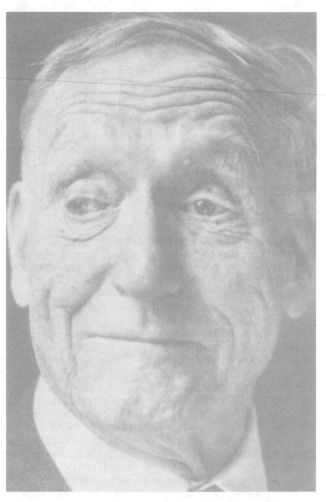

Robert Penn Warren.

county newspaper or an advertisement in the current Sears, Roebuck catalogue.

In this matter the textbooks that had been put in their hands were almost useless. The authors had something to say about the poet's life and the circumstances of his composition of the poem under study. Mention was made of Keats's having listened to the song of a nightingale one evening as he sat in the garden of his residence in Hampstead. But the typical commentary did not provide an induction to this poem—or into poetry generally. The dollop of impressionistic criticism with which the commentary usually concluded certainly did not supply the need. The editor's final remarks on the poem were vague, flowery, and emotive. The only person who could make sense of these remarks had to be a person who was already able to read the poem and who had become reasonably well acquainted with it.

Faced with this practical problem, we set about to produce a textbook of our own—two, in fact: *An Approach to Literature* and *Understanding Poetry*. Neither book was long on biographical and historical background—nor on the editors' warm pulsing feelings about the poem or story. These calculated omissions were noted almost at once and put down as proof of the fact that we had no use for biography and history, and that we were cold-blooded analysts who found no pleasure—certainly no joy—in literature.

Yet in a small cheaply manufactured book—*Understanding Poetry* in 1938 sold for $1.40 a copy—how much commentary do you have space for? We were trying to apply the grease to the wheel that squeaked the loudest. Besides, the typical instructor, product as he was of the graduate schools of that day, had been thoroughly trained in literary history, or so we assumed. (Clearly he had not been taught much else.) We believed that he could be counted on to supply historical and biographical material. We were concerned to provide help of another sort.

Warren and I were not out to corrupt innocent youth with heretical views. Our aims were limited, practical, and even grubby. We had nothing highfalutin or esoteric in mind. We were not a pair of young art-for-art's-sake aesthetes, just back from Oxford and out of touch with American reality.

Our personal interest in biography and history was never taken into account. Warren's first published book was a biography and his first volume of fiction, a historical novel. As for myself, my thesis at Oxford had been an edition of an eighteenth-century correspondence—brassbound research indeed, with many pages showing a fairly thin layer of text resting solidly on two columns of footnotes in finer print. My first published book concerned the derivation of pronunciation in the southern states from English county dialects such as those of Devonshire, Dorset, and Sussex. No precious aestheticism here either.

Yet the notion that we dismissed the importance of history clung to us. My publication of *The Well Wrought Urn* (1947) probably served to confirm the indictment. The experimental character of that book was, I assumed, quite plain. It was devised frankly to test an idea—namely that authentic poems from various centuries possessed certain common elements. In stressing the common elements in all literature, I was consciously cutting across the grain of English studies as then established. Yet the very plan of the book should have made the experimental character unmistakable. In any case I had not left it to mere inference: it was spelled out on several

pages. In the preface, for example, the charge that I had neglected history or discounted its importance was predicted and dealt with: "I have been anxious to see what residuum, if any, is left when we have finished subtracting from [a poem] its references and relations to the culture out of which it came."

In my chapter on Wordsworth's Intimations Ode I observed that it might "be interesting to see what happens when one considers the 'Ode' [not primarily as a document in Wordsworth's spiritual autobiography, but] as an independent poetic structure, even to the point of forfeiting the light which his letters, his notes, and [his] other poems throw on difficult points." I went on to add, however, that this "forfeiture . . . need not, of course, be permanent." Looking back at this passage some thirty-odd years later, I still do not think the proposal I made there unreasonable or excessively doctrinaire. The cautious reader is given sufficient notice of what kind of commentary to expect on Wordsworth's ode, and, by implication, on the other nine poems discussed in the book.

But the title! An urn is something static, shaped, rigid. Surely a poem is fluid, dynamic, a transaction between poet and reader. Yet what has happened to the reader's metaphoric sense if an obviously figurative title, borrowed from one of the poems discussed in the book, has to be frozen into a literal application? I thought that, for a book which sought to find a structure common to all genuine poetry, Donne's praise of a well-made object, however small, was apt. After all, what he sets up as its opposite is the vulgarly ostentatious "half-acre tomb." Donne was not the only poet who compares a poem to a static object. A very different kind of poet, Wordsworth, compares the body of his poetry to a gothic cathedral, with its "ante-chapel," and "the little cells, oratories, and sepulchral recesses, ordinarily included in these edifices." Readers have allowed Wordsworth his analogy without imputing to him the notion that poems are "static."

When Hugh Kenner came to write his essay "The Pedagogue as Critic" [see excerpt above], he obviously had very much on his mind the detailed treatment of individual poems such as one finds in *The Well Wrought Urn* and in *Understanding Poetry*. In fact he reduces the New Criticism to a classroom strategy. The aims, limitations, and possible achievements of *Understanding Poetry* constitute, as he sees it, the boundaries of the New Criticism. This maneuver provides him with a handy means for dismissing the New Criticism—at least under that name—as having any real substance. Thus he is able to ignore such questions as whether T. S. Eliot or Yvor Winters or Allen Tate is, or is not, a New Critic. This, as I have already suggested, may be to the good. But his essay amounts to a clever caricature, with the bold exaggerations and oversimplifications that an effective caricature demands. He depicts the pedagogue chalking up his key words and his diagrams on the blackboard for the enlightenment of his students. For Kenner's pedagogue conceives of a poem as a verbal machine. Thus he devotes himself to explaining the workings of its gears, pistons, and ignition system. He remains oblivious to the fact that the poems are meant to be intoned rather than merely perceived as characters on a printed page.

Kenner does point out extenuating circumstances. He concedes that the American cultural scene in the 1940s and 1950s needed something of the kind. In fact Kenner remarks that in making up his "catalogue of omissions and distortions" of which he asserts the critic/pedagogue was guilty, his purpose is "not to denigrate the critic-pedagogue, but to define his characteristic limits of activity, by way of defining what he can do superlatively well, and why, in the 1940s and 1950s, it mattered so much." (Question 1: Have the students of the 1960s and 1970s become so adept at reading that they no longer need what the New Critic could do so "superlatively well"? The literacy rate continues to fall nationwide. Question 2: How can Kenner believe that his New Critics ever did this job superlatively well when he accuses them of regarding a poem as merely a verbal machine, a kind of mechanism?)

Kenner's bill of particulars against the New Critic/pedagogue is powerfully urged, and the implication clearly is that we need now something different and something that goes beyond the New Critic's "characteristic limits of activity." Presumably critics like Kenner will provide it. To this point I shall return, but for now I quote Kenner's summation: "The curious thing is how a classroom strategy could come to mistake itself for a critical discipline."

Is this sentence a politely figurative way of avoiding saying that the New Critic/pedagogues, including the authors of *Understanding Poetry,* mistook their proffered teaching methods for a true critical discipline? Or does Mr. Kenner mean that the college teachers who bought the book—or books like it (Kenner got into the game by once writing such a book himself)—mistook a teaching method for a critical discipline? Perhaps it doesn't matter. In any case there is a more important question to be asked. Doesn't any teaching strategy have some relation to a critical discipline? I think it does. Though none of the so-called New Critics—least of all I—ever set up as a system-builder, a definition of literature and a conception of its function are clearly implicit even in my own critical writings.

It would seem that Kenner's principal objection to the New Critic's classroom strategy (critical discipline?) consists in what Kenner takes to be the New Critic's misguided dismissal of the cultural background of a work. With this we return, not surprisingly, to an old and still prevalent indictment that I shall presently consider. But first I must point out that Hugh Kenner offers a strong hint that he himself can show the proper way to manage literary criticism.

Kenner tells us: "Not to distract students with peripheral information, that is one thing; to pretend to oneself, as some New Critics did, that the information has no status whatever, is something else." But what is peripheral information and what is central? Kenner does not say directly, but he remarks that "Shakespeare's 'golden lads' . . . has exerted power over countless imaginations despite the virtual loss of the information that what he wrote down was a Warwickshire idiom for dandelions."

A footnote directs us to his *The Pound Era* (a truly rich and interesting work), in which Kenner discusses this bit of information more fully. After quoting the first stanza of the song at Fidele's grave (*Cymbeline* 4.3), which concludes "Golden lads and girls all must / As chimney-sweepers, come to dust," Kenner runs the changes on the meaning of "golden": " 'golden,' because once precious when they lived; 'golden,' touched with the nobility and permanence of gold . . . ; 'golden,' in contrast to 'dust': a contrast of color, a contrast of substantiality, a contrast of two immemorial symbols, at once Christian and pagan: the dust to which all sons of Adam return, the gold by which human vitality braves time; dust, moreover, the environment of chimney-sweepers, against whose lot is set the promise of shining youth, *la jeunesse dorée,* who may expect to make more of life than a chimney-

sweeper does, but whom death at last claims equally. 'Golden,' magical word, irradiates the stanza so that we barely think to ask how Shakespeare may have found it."

Kenner's account of "golden," I should say, is standard stuff, the sort of thing that an old-fashioned New Critic might have written; though Kenner speaks in a more exalted strain than mere pedagogues are wont to reach. The phrase *golden lads* has indeed "exerted power over countless imaginations," whether or not we ask how Shakespeare came by the words. This is why some of us think that this kind of information (i.e., the meaning and associations of the words as used in the poem) is *central* information, not peripheral.

Nevertheless it would be highly interesting to learn how Shakespeare came by the words—if we can indeed ever gain such information. Kenner tells us how he did, and in doing so, he presumably advances beyond what he takes to be the narrow frontiers of the New Criticism. A "visitor to Shakespeare's Warwickshire"—Kenner does not name him but I too have met him—told Kenner that he once "met a countryman [in Warwickshire] blowing the grey head off a dandelion" and remarking, "We call these golden boys chimney-sweepers when they go to seed." This circumstance allows Kenner to imagine that "perhaps on the afternoon of the first performance [of *Cymbeline*] if there were no Warwickshire ears in the Globe to hear that Warwickshire idiom, the dandelions and their structure of meaning simply dropped out. Yet for 350 years no one has reported a chasm." True enough, but perhaps they have failed to do so because there was no chasm to report.

Let us see how Kenner explains the dandelion simile for us. Speaking like a good pedagogue himself, he asks his reader: "And all is clear?" But he takes nothing for granted. The dandelions that have gone to seed "are shaped like a chimney-sweeper's broom." But are the terms of Shakespeare's comparison the golden lads (and let us not forget that he mentions golden girls too) and the blackened little urchins who cleaned the chimneys, or is the second term of his comparison the special brush used to clean the chimneys? It is the long-handled brush with bristles at the end of it that resembles the gone-to-seed dandelion with its long stem and fuzzy top.

The *OED* indicates that *chimney-sweeper* can refer to either the boy or the brush. The *OED*'s first meaning refers to the boy who climbed the chimney; the second reads: "A stiff radiating brush fixed on a long jointed rod, used for cleaning chimneys." But if the *OED* is correct, to the ears of Shakespeare's Warwickshire neighbors watching a performance of *Cymbeline* in the Globe the word *chimney-sweeper* could not have meant anything other than the boy who cleaned the chimney, for the special brush that resembles the gone-to-seed dandelion was not introduced until 1805. Dandelions may have been referred to as golden boys in Elizabethan Warwickshire. Who knows? But the second meaning simply wasn't available in the early 1600s. Mr. Kenner seems here to have supplied us with information that is not even peripheral information; but instead with some highly ingenious speculation, charming enough in its way, yet without factual support, biographical or historical.

I do not mean to imply—let me repeat—that the study of how particular literary works came about, detailed accounts of authors' lives, the history of taste, and the development of literary conventions and ideas are not obviously worthy of pursuit. That is not the issue here, though it is true that a number of the so-called New Critics have preferred to address themselves primarily to the writing rather than to the writer; and a few of us to regard as the specific task of literary criticism the interpretation and evaluation of the literary text. To borrow a term from Austin Warren and René Wellek's *Theory of Literature,* such an *intrinsic* criticism is to be distinguished from *extrinsic* criticism and general literary scholarship.

If some of the New Critics have preferred to stress the writing rather than the writer, so have they given less stress to the reader—to the reader's response to the work. Yet no one in his right mind could forget the reader. He is essential for "realizing" any poem or novel. Moreover readers obviously vary extremely in their sensitivity, intelligence, and experience. They vary also from one cultural period to another: the eighteenth century apparently tended to find in Shakespeare something rather different from what the nineteenth century found or the twentieth century now finds. Reader response is certainly worth studying. This direction is being taken by many of our more advanced critics today. Yet to put the meaning and valuation of a literary work at the mercy of any and every individual would reduce the study of literature to reader psychology and to the history of taste. On the other hand to argue that there is no convincing proof that one reader's reaction is any more correct than another's is indeed a counsel of despair.

Let me summarize by using the most homely analogy that I can think of. The real proof of the literary pudding is in the eating thereof. It is perfectly proper to look at the recipe the cook says she followed, to take into account the ingredients she used, to examine her intentions to make a certain kind of pudding, and her care in preparing it—or her carelessness. But the prime fact for judging will still be the pudding itself. The tasting, the eating, the experience is what finally counts.

It is time to drop such analogies and to turn to more detailed and systematic discussions. "The Intentional Fallacy," when W. K. Wimsatt and Monroe Beardsley published it in 1945, was thoroughly misunderstood. Most readers have concluded that the authors dismissed the poet's intentions as unimportant, or that they believed that the poet had no intentions and that his work issued from a kind of mindless "trance" as described in Plato's *Ion,* or that they forgot that literary works were produced by warm-blooded human beings whose heads were filled with ideas, beliefs, prejudices, and who were themselves the products of a particular cultural environment.

"The Intentional Fallacy" as an essay has its difficulties, but a careful reading of it today would rectify the worst of those misconceptions. In any case the discussion of intentionalism in Beardsley's *Aesthetics* (1958) or the whole subject as reviewed and reassessed in Wimsatt's "Genesis: An Argument Resumed" (1968) would do so. In his 1968 essay Wimsatt considers and appraises a host of objections and rejoinders, and disposes of them in masterly fashion.

One or two brief examples will have to suffice. For example, Wimsatt affirms that it is perfectly reasonable to use a literary work to throw light on its author.

> From the work to the author (when one wishes to be biographical) is not the same as from the author (outside the work) to the work. These directions remain opposites no matter how numerous and complicated a set of deflectors and baffles we set up between the two termini.

The fact is that we can, if we wish, learn with relative certainty from biographical evidence that some personae are close to or identical with the author and some are much different from him. . . . Almost everybody rushes to confuse the persona of Gray's "Elegy Written in a Country Churchyard" with Gray himself. In fact it can be shown on quite convincing biographical evidence that the melancholy poet who is the anonymous speaker of that poem is very close to the melancholy poet Thomas Gray. . . . Nevertheless, the "Elegy" is not *about* the historic person Gray. The self-contemplative speaker remains anonymous. The poem itself, if it were anonymous, would be intact.

Surely this passage cannot be quoted to the disparagement of literary biography or literary history; nor does it make any unreasonable separation of the author and his work. For example, if we want to read Byron's *Childe Harold* primarily for the light it throws on Byron, why not? *Childe Harold,* particularly cantos 1 and 2, is not very impressive as poetry; perhaps it is most useful as a kind of register of the moods of that world-weary young man. Human nature being what it is, a good many people, if the truth were known, would much rather read a life of Byron than *any* of his poetry. Gossip is more interesting than fiction—even to many of the literati.

Another passage from "Genesis" constitutes as good a brief summary of the issue as I can find.

> The closest one [can] ever get to the artist's intending or meaning mind, outside his work, would still be short of his *effective* intention or *operative* mind as it appears in the work itself and can be read from the work. Such is the concrete and fully answerable character of words as aesthetic medium. The intention outside the poem is always subject to the corroboration of the poem itself. No better evidence in the nature of things can be adduced than the poem itself.

To use a metaphor drawn from the law courts, "evidence outside the poem" is always secondhand (or even hearsay) evidence as compared with the evidence presented by the text itself. Such a position seems to me not in the least unreasonable. It does not deny the suggestive value of evidence from outside the poem; moreover it leaves literary biography and literary history intact, for it does nothing to inhibit our human interest in or systematic study of writers and the whole process of literary creation. Nor does it forbid the study of reader response. Finally it does not conveniently overlook the fact that every critic is himself a reader who needs to be continually conscious of his own prejudices, possible blind sides, and imperfect responses to the work he is reading. Clearly he must try to become the ideal reader.

In her interesting *On the Margins of Discourse* Barbara Herrnstein Smith heaps a bit of polite scorn on the concept of the ideal reader as providing a way out of our problems in the interpretation of literary texts. But no one claims that the ideal reader actually exists in flesh and blood. The ideal reader is a platonic idea, an ideal terminus never actually attainable. Nevertheless common sense and an appeal to the dictionary and to the text in question would indicate that some of us read more sensitively and intelligently than others. If "better" is a demonstrable fact, then "best" is at least a useful ideal, something we must try to approximate as nearly as possible, even if it is never fully attainable. To say that there is no way to prove that one reader's interpretation is better than another's means the end of any responsible study of literature.

Besides a preference for emphasizing the text rather than the writer's motives and the reader's reaction, does there exist any other possible common ground occupied by the so-called New Critics? If so, it is probably "close reading." But it might be more accurate to substitute "adequate reading." "Adequate" is, to be sure, a relative term; but so is "close." (How close is close enough?) The substitution of "adequate" might help relieve the New Critic of the jeweler's eyepiece with which he is equipped as he is commonly pictured when engaged in a microscopic study of a text. Some documents do require a more careful reading than others; that again seems a reasonable surmise. "Twinkle, twinkle, little star" requires less careful reading than Wordsworth's "The Solitary Reaper." (I'm not forgetting, of course, that some modern theorists could turn even "Twinkle, twinkle" or "Mary had a little lamb" into a verbal labyrinth, "and [find] no end, in wandering mazes lost." Consider, for example, the number of meanings of "lamb" and the number of analogues for "Mary." To a richly stored literary mind these two words offer almost infinite possibilities. In fact only weariness of the flesh or the adoption of an arbitrary terminus need bring such a free-ranging process to an end.)

In January 1979 Hillis Miller published (in the *Bulletin of the American Academy of Arts and Sciences*) an account of Wordsworth's "A Slumber Did My Spirit Seal." It is a truly remarkable example of how much one can read out of a poem (if he first allows himself to read almost anything he likes into it). Miller begins with an account of the poem that, in spite of some elaboration, resembles very closely that of the so-called New Criticism. (I published, for example, such an account in 1948.) But Miller's first several paragraphs serve only as a runway for the takeoff into what amounts to an intercontinental—possibly interplanetary—flight.

One of the several contrasts in the poem has to do with the terms in which the girl is described in the first stanza and in the second. In the first she is called a "thing" that "could not feel / The touch of earthly years." In the second she becomes a "thing" like a rock or stone. Miller properly points out that as described in the first stanza Lucy had "seemed an invulnerable young 'thing': now she is truly a *thing,* closed in on herself like a stone." His next several paragraphs elaborate this point. We are told that Wordsworth's play on the word *thing* exists also in German. Miller then quotes two passages from Martin Heidegger. In the second of these passages Heidegger refers to the story in Plato's *Theaetetus* about the "whimsical maid from Thrace" who laughs at the philosopher Thales because he, failing to see "the things in front of his very nose," fell down a well. Heidegger observes that the philosophical question "What is a thing?" will always cause housemaids to laugh. Such a question, Miller opines, would also provoke laughter in Wordsworth's Lucy.

As items in a process of almost free association, all of this is interesting—the more so perhaps because one is allowed to nod to Heidegger and to Plato. But Miller has taken us all around Robin Hood's barn—even though a pleasant excursion—in order to make a rather obvious contrast between two senses of "thing." The old folk-song about Billy Boy's prospective bride, a song that Wordsworth may well have known, as he could not have known the writings of the yet unborn Heidegger, would have provided him with the mean-

ing of "thing" that Miller would like to invoke for the term as used in the first stanza.

> "Can she bake a cherry pie, Billy Boy, Billy Boy?
> Can she bake a cherry pie, charming Billy?"
> "She can bake a cherry pie quick as a cat can blink
> its eye,
> But she's a young thing, and cannot leave her
> mother."

Though poets do not necessarily go by the dictionary, consider the *OED.* Meaning 10: "Applied to a person, now only in contempt, reproach, pity or affection (especially to a woman or child)." But if one reads still further, he notices that all the *OED* examples of *thing* as expressing pity or affection have a qualifying adjective such as "sweet thing," "noble thing," "poor thing." As used without a qualifier (10b) *thing* seems always contemptuous or reproachful—senses that would be inapplicable to Lucy. If one takes this circumstance seriously, noting that "thing" in the first stanza of the Wordsworth poem has no qualifying adjective, one might feel constrained to look further to find just what Wordsworth meant by "thing" in his first stanza.

OED's meaning 7 ("An entity of any kind") can be applied to human beings, and this meaning would sufficiently justify "thing" as Wordsworth uses it in the first stanza. The girl once seemed an immortal being, an entity impervious to time. Keats uses "thing" in this sense in his "Eve of St. Agnes." In stanza 25, to Porphyro, Madeline seems more than mortal: she wears "a glory, like a saint"; she seems "a splendid angel" as she kneels, "so pure a thing, so free from mortal taint." "Thing" as applied to a young woman is used here not in affection or pity but rather in awed wonder—as I suggest it is in the first stanza of "A Slumber." Later, in stanza 37, Madeline uses "thing" when she refers to herself as "a deceived thing;— / A dove forlorn and lost." But here we have the qualifying adjective.

In Wordsworth's second stanza Lucy has clearly become a "thing" in a sharply contrasted sense, that designated by *OED* meaning 8b: "A being without life or consciousness; an inanimate object, as distinguished from a person or living creature." This contrast between meaning 7 (an entity, a being, which may be a human being) and meaning 8 (an inanimate object) is surely the basic contrast in Wordsworth's poem. That contrast is actually indicated in one of the *OED*'s illustrative quotations: "He that getteth a wife getteth a good thing; that is, if his wife be more than a *thing.*"

Yet any forced implication made in Miller's interpretation of "thing" seems negligible in the light of some of his further extrapolations. Thus Miller tells us that among the oppositions to be found in this eight-line poem are: "mother as against daughter or sister, or perhaps any female family member as against some woman from outside the family; that is, mother, sister, or daughter as against mistress or wife, in short incestuous desires against legitimate sexual feelings." (Shades of the late F. W. Bateson!) Miller later says that it perhaps does not matter "whether the reader thinks of Lucy as a daughter or as a mistress or as an embodiment of his feelings for his sister Dorothy. What matters is the way in which her imagined death is a re-enactment of the death of [Wordsworth's] mother as described in *The Prelude.*"

Though I of all people have to feel abashed at quibbling over other people's discovery of paradoxes, I confess that I find absurd some that tumble forth in Miller's exegesis. For example: "To be touched by earthly years is a way to be sexually penetrated while still remaining virgin"; or "the poet has himself somehow caused Lucy's death by thinking about it."

Miller remarks that this poem "in the context of the other Lucy poems and of all Wordsworth's work enacts one version of a constantly repeated Occidental drama of the lost sun. Lucy's name of course means light. To possess her would be a means of rejoining the lost source of light, the father-sun as *logos*." The woman in this poem, of course, is not actually named. Miller calls her "Lucy" because "A Slumber" belongs to a grouping of poems which Wordsworth's editors have themselves made and decided to call the "Lucy poems." Yet if we are to be free-ranging, what about Wordsworth's poem "Lucy Gray"? Here the girl is specifically named Lucy, and the poem is again about the death of a girl. Would "Gray" hinder our considering this Lucy as also a daughter of the sun? (Should Wordsworth have named her Lucy Bright or Lucy Ray instead of Lucy Gray?) Or is the contradiction between "light" and "grayness" intended and somehow meaningful? Wordsworth's editors have not assigned "Lucy Gray" to the Lucy group. If they had, I have no doubt that some ingenious explanation, paradoxical or otherwise, would be discovered to clear up the difficulty. But enough of excerpts. The reader will need to peruse the whole of Mr. Miller's essay to be able to do justice to his argument and to my reactions to it.

I have to confess that there is a certain mad plausibility in this and such other ventures in interpretation. Granted an agile mind and a rich stock of examples from the world's literature, granted modern theories about the doubleness of the human mind and the ways in which secret meanings can underlie surface meanings (and one can sometimes "mean" one thing by uttering its opposite), it is possible to construct readings that make a kind of glittering sense. The real trouble is that the game is almost too easy to play. With so lax a set of rules to govern the play, one might be able to do something with even "Humpty Dumpty sat on a wall" or "Hey diddle diddle, the cat and the fiddle."

In ambitious interpretations of this sort it helps, of course, to deal with an author about whose life we have a great deal of information. A writer such as Shakespeare would be more difficult, but even here the game is not impossible. By reading back from the work into a hypothetical life, one could doubtless construct a base from which to find further meanings in the texts themselves.

How typical of the new movements in criticism is this essay of Hillis Miller's? It would be hard to say, and I shall simply note that Miller's subtitle reads: "The Crossways of Contemporary Criticism," and that he prefaces his account of "A Slumber" with a general review of the recent history of critical theory and practice. Apparently he means for his reader to assume that in this essay he is exploring some of these newest paths.

In a recent article René Wellek writes that "surely one of the most urgent problems of literary study today" is that of putting some kind of "theoretical limits on [literary] interpretation," now that "total willfulness has been running riot." Wellek's essay was written well before Miller's essay appeared, and I do not suggest that Wellek had this essay or any other by Miller in mind. Yet Miller's extraordinary construction does illustrate what can happen when there is a lack of theoretical restraints. Literary interpretation becomes a game

of tennis played without a net and on a court with no backlines.

In *Literature against Itself* Gerald Graff vehemently denounces all such license, but he does not stop at that. Almost everything that has happened in literary criticism since the heyday of Henry Seidel Canby and George Lyman Kittredge gets roundly swinged—the Structuralists, the Deconstructionists, the proponents of an affective criticism, the Northrop Fryes and the Hillis Millers, the Jacques Derridas and the Frank Kermodes, and many another. They make up a strange assortment of bedfellows. A more apposite figure here might be a motley group of wrongdoers hustled before the bar.

In his attack Graff lays about him so indiscriminately that he sometimes slashes innocent bystanders and even potential allies. I, for example, agree with, and even applaud, some of his indictments. But I cannot accept his contention that the New Critics are themselves responsible for all or most that has gone awry since the 1950s. Specifically I beg to be excused from being cast as the Pandora who, though not meaning any harm, nevertheless foolishly opened the fateful box and loosed all the present evils upon the literary world. Graff's scolding of the New Critics signally fails to take into account recent powerful movements in philosophy and in western society generally. The kind of debacle that Graff describes would have occurred had not a single New Critic ever been born. More unjust still is the fact that Graff's censure derives from a misunderstanding and an essentially false assessment of what most of these critics were saying. Let me say that my reference to Graff here is not gratuitous. One of his eight chapters is entitled "What Was New Criticism?", and he rings the changes on the New Criticism throughout the whole book.

Graff believes that the basic sin of the New Critics was their repudiation of the referentiality of literary language. True, their purpose was merely "to expunge from the mind of the educated middle class . . . the genteel schoolmarm theory of literature, which had defined literature as a kind of prettified didacticism." Though Graff says he finds it difficult to mourn the disappearance of the schoolmarm theory of literature, what the New Critics succeeded in doing, he insists, was to cut literature loose from any connection with reality.

I dispute his conclusion. Allen Tate, for instance, asserts that a true poem provides "knowledge of a whole object, its complete knowledge, the full body of experience [the object] offers us"; and in an early work I wrote that a genuine poem offers us "a simulacrum of experience." It may be said to imitate experience by "*being* an experience rather than any mere statement about experience." But I want to raise a prior question that Graff never answers: What kind of didacticism would be substituted for the schoolmarm didacticism? A PhD's didacticism? Would that necessarily be any better? What didacticism would be a proper and wholesome kind of didacticism? And if all literature is didactic, how would Graff distinguish between a poem and a sermon or a poem and an essay? I think that sermons and moral essays are valuable and have an important place in the human economy, but I don't want to confuse them with poetry or fiction. Poems and novels have their own character and function and their own characteristic relation to reality. On this whole matter Graff remains distressingly vague.

He does relieve his general censure of the New Critics by

making a few concessions. He admits that "to repudiate art's representational function is not necessarily to leave no link between art and reality." I'm not sure that the New Critics repudiated anything more than literal copying and the necessity for a one-to-one correspondence with reality. Yet, though this qualification makes his concession seem generous, Graff insists that such a repudiation "is to reduce reality to a trivial role in the partnership." It doubtless could, but I see no signs of that in, say, Eliot or Auden or Tate, or in many others that Graff would call New Critics. They all are very much in earnest about the importance of reality—if *that* is the issue.

The strength of *Literature against Itself* is almost wholly negative: Graff's sharp condemnation of certain excesses in critical theory and practice. But he is very vague in setting forth positive solutions. He seems reluctant to face crucial problems. He sometimes writes as if some of the problems have not been with us from almost the beginning. For example, he deplores "an implicitly defeatist acceptance of art's disinheritance from its philosophical and social authority." But how far back in history do we have to go to find art in undisputed possession of philosophical authority? At least back to pre-Socratic times; for Plato explicitly denied it such authority. The issue here is not whether Plato was correct, but the age-old character of the issue.

In general Graff lays too heavy a burden on literature. He implies that unless one can find philosophical authority in it, we have nowhere else to find such authority. Unless we can claim an easy and obvious referentiality in a poem, then we have lost our hold on reality itself. It is as if philosophy, religion, and even common sense were not available to us. These may not be available to some of the people that Graff is attacking. But if I must be birched, I want my punishment to have some relation to my own sins of omission and commission.

Years ago T. S. Eliot remarked that we were still living in the age of Matthew Arnold, who believed that literature could and should take over the burdens once performed by a now-exploded religion. I believe with Eliot that it cannot, for literature has its own and indispensable function, which does not duplicate that of religion or of philosophy, or certainly that of science. In a special sense, then, Graff's enemy's are Arnoldians; but Graff may be the noblest Arnoldian of them all in that he too would apparently lay upon literature the whole burden of acquainting us with reality. Certainly he wants a stable and responsible philosophy. So do I. But I do not ask that literature provide the ultimate truth about reality. Graff sometimes writes as if he thinks it does.

For a more detailed and carefully objective answer to Graff (and others) I refer the interested reader to René Wellek's two recent articles in *Critical Inquiry:* "The New Criticism: Pro and Contra" (summer 1978) [see excerpt above] and his rejoinder to Graff's "New Criticism Once More" (spring 1979). [For Graff's comments, see the excerpt above.] In his 1978 essay Wellek agrees with my view that those persons commonly designated as the New Critics were "far from unified." He even considers the wisdom of abandoning the "concept [of a New Criticism] and [the] term." But he decides that, after all, there is "some sense in grouping these critics together" and proceeds to make what I consider the best case that can be made for seeing them as a group.

His description and assessment of the New Critics is summed up in the final paragraph:

> I will not conceal my own conviction that the New

Criticism has stated or reaffirmed many basic truths to which future ages will have to return: the specific nature of the aesthetic transaction, the normative presence of a work of art which forms a structure, a unity, coherence, a whole, which cannot be simply battered about and is comparatively independent of its origins and effects. The New Critics have also persuasively described the function of literature in not yielding abstract knowledge or information, message or stated ideology, and they have devised a technique of interpretation which often succeeded in illuminating not so much the form of a poem as the implied attitudes of the author, the resolved or unresolved tensions and contradictions; a technique that yields a standard of judgment that cannot be easily dismissed in favor of the currently popular, sentimental, and simple. The charge of "elitism" cannot get around the New Critics' assertion of quality and value. A decision between good and bad art remains the unavoidable duty of criticism. The humanities would abdicate their function in society if they surrendered to a neutral scientism and indifferent relativism or if they succumbed to the imposition of alien norms required by political indoctrination. Particularly on these two fronts the New Critics have waged a valiant fight which, I am afraid, must be fought over again in the future.

Speaking for myself, at least, the preceding paragraph is the best concise summary that I know of what some of us thought we were doing. As for our accomplishments, I am happy that Wellek believes that we waged "a valiant fight" for those ideals. In any case, as I contemplate the present literary scene, I agree with him that the war is not over. The same issues will have to be fought over again and again in the years ahead. (pp. 592-607)

Cleanth Brooks, "The State of Letters: The New Criticism," in The Sewanee Review, *Vol. LXXXVII, No. 4, Fall, 1979, pp. 592-607.*

WILLIAM J. HANDY

[*Handy is an American formalist critic. In the following excerpt from his study* Kant and the Southern New Critics *(1963), he reevaluates the formalist approach to literature.*]

If one principle could be singled out as basic to the theory and practice of John Crowe Ransom and his students, [Allen] Tate and [Cleanth] Brooks, that principle necessarily would be concerned with the nature of the language of literary art. Perhaps it might be stated like this: *The very core of the artistic intention is concretion, which is a "growing together" intention, not an intention to abstract.* Every aspect of their poetic theory and critical practice derives, directly or indirectly, from this source principle. It explains why they believe poetry to be a separate and distinct form of knowledge; it determines the role they assign to the moral and practical content of the poem; it relates directly to their belief that the poem must be considered as an objective cognition; it provides a basis for their theory of the structure of the poem; and it conditions the manner in which they approach the poem in their critical practice.

In the view of the Southern New Critics, the difference between the language of science and the language of literary art is directly related to the difference between the language of abstraction and the language of concretion. Yet this is not merely a preoccupation with form and technique. Underlying their concern with poetic language is a deep conviction regarding the vital nature and function of poetry. They take the meaning of *abstract* in its original sense of "taken away." Thus they see the practice of science as the process of "reducing" whatever aspect of experience it formulates, of thereby altering its real existence. Ransom considers poetry's chief reason for being is to act as the necessary restorative for the emasculations of scientific formulations. In *The New Criticism,* he declares: "We live in a world which must be distinguished from the world or the worlds, for there are many of them, which we treat in our scientific discourse. They are its reduced, emasculated, and docile versions."

The language of poetry on the other hand is the language of concretion. Here again the original meaning of *concrete* as "grown together" is central to Ransom's theory of poetry. As is evident in the statement quoted above, Ransom's concern is not simply with form and technique but with the deeper function poetry has in offering a more complete formulation of human experience. Ransom concludes: "Poetry intends to recover the denser and more refractory original world which we know loosely through our perceptions and memories. By this supposition it is a kind of knowledge which is radically or ontologically distinct." Or, as he had put it in *The World's Body:* "What we cannot know constitutionally as scientists is the world which is made up of whole and indefeasible objects, and this is the world which poetry recovers for us."

The scientist wishes to indicate one meaning, not a plurality of meaning; he avoids distracting elements such as the communication of personal attitudes, imagistic associations, and words to which emotional overtones have become attached. In short, he consciously conditions himself against any usage which would fall outside the normal patterns of logical formulation. His vision is directed at the principles which determine the object, and which relate it to other objects. His method is abstraction. On the other hand, when language is used to communicate the object itself rather than information about it, the intention is to seek presentational effects. The literary artist strives for a fullness or plurality of meaning which he knows the object exhibits before it has been reduced to a general concept. He is fully aware of the reader's propensity to grasp eagerly at the structure of logical ideas implicit in any language formulation, and he means to distract his readers from the practice by offering presentations of qualitative meaning rather than patterns of ideational meaning. Thus, the writer must use language in a way which resists the logical pattern. His method is concretion.

Exactly here the principle of poetic particularity becomes apparent. The very fact of logical discourse—the fact that our communication of any judgment, from the simplest sentence to the most complex dissertation, operates to impose a habit pattern on the way we ordinarily use language—gives rise to the possibility of poetic particularity. The reason is obvious: *Every poetic device constructed to function as a literary presentation must, in some way, interrupt or violate the established norm of the logical language pattern.* Without deviation from the normal language pattern, only logical meaning is possible. The poet strives for relevant departures from the logical. Ransom offers a general statement of the principle: "A feature that obeys the canon of logic is only the mere instance of an universal convention, while the one that violates that canon is an indestructibly private thing."

Ransom's point is simply that poetic structures characteristi-

cally violate the conventional pattern of logical discourse. To give an example: In Wordsworth's lines: "The World is too much with us; late and soon, / Getting and spending, we lay waste our powers," there are several such departures from the logical or expected thought pattern. The logical statement of the first poetic phrase would be formulated in some such terms as these: "Worldliness is too much a part of our interests." The second phrase, "late and soon," to follow the expected thought pattern should read, "late and early," or more precisely, "early and late." The metaphor "Getting and spending, we lay waste our powers" is based on the analogy between the materialistic urge destroying the other faculties of the mind and, for example, the activity of a mercenary horde destroying a city. The poetic phrase has other ramifications of meaning which function by indirection, in contrast to the direct, unambiguous meanings of logical discourse. "Getting and spending" suggests the cheapness, the crassness, which the poet associates with materialistic cravings. The same attitude is expressed in man's thoughtless destruction of his valuable powers, which is like the soldier's wanton destruction of the city's precious cultural objects.

But to lay waste is also to let lie and rot, and the analogy in this sense is to the farmer's neglect of his harvest. The farmer's failure to tend his fields is a failure of stewardship just as we fail in stewardship of ourselves by neglecting our intellectual and aesthetic capacities, i.e., "we lay waste our powers." It is obvious that science must carefully avoid structures like these. The scientist must seek one-to-one correspondences between his symbol and its referent and between his predicate and its intended meaning. But the poet's most effective structure is the metaphorical analogy, which in every instance represents some variation from the logical form.

None of the critics in the formalist tradition has emphasized the importance of irony as a device for achieving the full particularity of poetic meaning as often as has Cleanth Brooks. Here the literal or strictly logical meaning is purposely not intended. It is the violation of the expected straightforward use of language that results in a literary presentation. In *The Well-Wrought Urn,* Brooks explains irony as a strictly literary device:

> Irony . . . is to be found in Tennyson's "Tears, Idle Tears" as well as in Donne's "Canonization." We have, of course, been taught to expect to find irony in Pope's "Rape of the Lock," but there is a profound irony in Keat's "Ode on a Grecian Urn"; and there is irony of a very powerful sort in Wordsworth's "intimations" ode. For the thrusts and pressures exerted by the various symbols . . . are not avoided by the poet: they are taken into account and played, one against the other. Indeed, the symbols—from a scientific point of view—are used perversely: it is the child who is the best philosopher; it is from a kind of darkness—from something that is "shadowy"—that the light proceeds; growth into manhood is viewed, not as an extrication from, but as an incarceration within, a prison.

> There should be no mystery as to why this must be so. The terms of science are abstract symbols which do not change under the pressure of of the context. They are pure (or aspire to be pure) denotations; they are defined in advance. They are not to be warped into new meanings. But where is the dictionary which contains the terms of a poem? It is a truism that the poet is continually forced to remake language. As Eliot has put it, his task is to "dislo-

cate language into meaning." And, from the standpoint of a scientific vocabulary, this is precisely what he performs: for, rationally considered, the ideal language would contain one term for each meaning, and the relation between term and meaning would be constant. But the word, as the poet uses it, has to be conceived of, not as a discrete particle of meaning, but as a potential of meaning, a nexus or cluster of meanings.

Thus, the poetic use of language is one in which "the symbols—from a scientific point of view—are used perversely," and "the poet is continually forced to remake language," to "dislocate language into meaning."

The device of paradox functions to achieve poetic particularity by the quite obvious violation of the expected ideational pattern. Brooks contrasts the use of paradox as a method for communicating "the important things which a poet has to say" with the "more direct methods" which "enfeeble and distort what is to be said":

> And how necessary are the paradoxes? Donne might have said directly, "Love in a cottage is enough." "The Canonization" contains this admirable thesis, but it contains a great deal more. He might have been as forthright as a later lyricist who wrote, "We'll build a sweet little nest, / Somewhere out in the West, / And let the rest of the world go by." He might even have imitated that more metaphysical lyric, which maintains, "You're the cream in my coffee." "The Canonization" touches on all these observations, but it goes beyond them, not merely in dignity, but in precision.

> I submit that the only way by which the poet could say what "The Canonization" says is by paradox. More direct methods may be tempting, but all of them enfeeble and distort what is to be said. This statement may seem the less surprising when we reflect on how many of the important things which the poet has to say have to be said by means of paradox: most of the language of lovers is such— "The Canonization" is a good example; so is most of the language of religion—"He who would save his life, must lose it"; "The last shall be first." Indeed, almost any insight important enough to warrant a great poem apparently has to be stated in such terms.

Later in the same passage Brooks shows what would happen to the poet's pronouncements if they were reduced from their function as literary symbols to the pure symbols of abstract science:

> Deprived of the character of paradox with its twin concomitants of irony and wonder, the matter of Donne's poem unravels into "facts," biological, sociological, and economic. What happens to Donne's lovers if we consider them "scientifically," without benefit of the supernaturalism which the poet confers upon them? Well, what happens to Shakespeare's lovers, for Shakespeare uses the basic metaphor of "The Canonization" in his *Romeo and Juliet*? In their first conversation, the lovers play with the analogy between the lover and the pilgrim to the Holy Land. Juliet says:

> For saints have hands that pilgrims' hands do touch
> And palm to palm is holy palmer's kiss

> Considered scientifically, the lovers become Mr. Aldous Huxley's animals, "quietly sweating, palm to palm."

The passage indicates not only the profound difference in meaning of poetic symbols considered first as literary language and then literally, but it also indicates the significant contribution to a whole formulation of human experience made possible by the literary meanings furnished by the poet.

Tate distinguishes the "poetic experience" in terms of the fuller meanings which the poem offers in contrast to the reduced version offered by the logical statement: "If you find that exhaustive analysis applied to the texture of image and metaphor fails to turn up any inconsistency, and at the same time fails to get all the meaning of the poem into a logical statement, you are participating in a poetic experience." Thus the poetic device, itself determined by the principle of logical violation, contains a fullness of meaning that cannot be encompassed by the logical statement.

The formalist critics use such terms as "embodiment of meaning," "the literary presentation," and the "concrete image" or "icon." Each of these is a way of saying that something has been done to the language which is different from the straightforward logical use of it. Even the concept of "poetic quality" denotes that what is communicated is a kind of meaning generically different in intention and essence from what is communicated by any use whatsoever of a logical formulation. Tone, attitude, and atmosphere may be qualities which are distinct and significant in their meanings in the poem. They are not so clearly recognized as the sharp-edged concrete image, but they possess the same quality of being particular, and they are the direct result of an intended nonlogical use of language. In a strictly logical assertion, such qualities are intentionally neutralized because they offer meanings which distract. The scientist, recognizing the fact, strives for qualitative neutrality in his formulations.

The poet, on the other hand, continually works to achieve a poetically meaningful distraction from the logical pattern. Ransom calls the formation of these literary distractions, "irrelevances." In the sense in which he uses the term, an irrelevance is any poetic phrase, which, as has been shown, derives from some meaningful variation from, or violation of, the logical norm. It is *logically* irrelevant, which is the necessary condition for poetic relevance:

> An "irrelevance" may feel forced at first, and its overplus of meaning unwanted, because it means the importation of a little foreign or extraneous content into what should be determinate, and limited; but soon the poet comes upon a kind of irrelevance that seems desirable, and he begins to indulge it voluntarily, as a new and positive asset to the meaning. And this is the principle: the importations, which the imagination introduces into discourse, have the value of developing the "particularity" which lurks in the "body," and under the surface, of apparently determinate situations. When Marvell is persuaded by the rhyme-consideration to invest the Humber with a tide, or to furnish his abstract calendar with specifications about the Foood, and the conversion of the Jews, he does not make these additions reluctantly. On the contrary, he knows that the brilliance of the poetry depends on the shock, accompanied at once by the realism or the naturalness of its powerful particularity.

Literary meanings cannot be the outcome of logical thinking;

they are more accurately described as discoveries, or the result of artistic experimentation. But in any case they represent presentational meanings which are logically irrelevant but which successfully embody the particularity of experience in its unabstracted state.

The historical critics have charged the formalists, especially Ransom, Tate, and Brooks, with seeking nothing but aesthetic meanings, without a full acknowledgement of what the formalists intend by their emphasis on aesthetic meanings. On the other hand, the Southern New Critics have attacked the historical scholar for reducing the poem to historical, biographical, and philosophical meanings, and have not sufficiently recognized that the poem does contain, however poetically transcribed, such meanings. Yet it is now evident that a meeting ground is possible for these opposing schools of critics. The recent critical study of Blake and Yeats by Hazard Adams and the new analysis of Milton by Kester Svendsen . . . are sufficient testimony that a critical evolution is underway. In the criticism of fiction, Edwin Bowden's *The Themes of Henry James* and A. J. Guerard's *Conrad the Novelist* follow a similar critical approach. Most important is that all of these writers seem to reflect an insight that colors their critical practice—a recognition that literature must be regarded as a distinctive language, as a special symbolic form into which meaning is uniquely embodied. Not only are these works characterized by sound literary scholarship, but all are excellent examples of formalist criticism, of close analysis based upon sensitive interpretation.

To say that meanings are embodied in literature is to suggest that they are not directly offered as they are in logical discourse, that they are vital presences invested with body. But a body is a concrete thing, a particular. Its individual particularity we apprehend with an immediacy; it is a sense presentation, rich in qualitative meanings. As such, the poetic body resembles the objects which we encounter all about us as part of our conscious experience, not in being a pictorial duplication of them, but in being a special symbol which adequately represents their full unabstracted particularity. Ransom sees the embodiment of meaning in the poem as its "texture," that part of the poem which fulfills its function by symbolizing the fullness of bodiness of experience. He says that "we attend also to the texture as the body behind the abstract. Otherwise I cannot see that what we call a poem is specifically anything at all; or for that matter, what we call the fullness of experience." Thus, in Ransom's view, the meanings which are invested with body in the poem formulate, through a special employment of language, the "world's body." The critical belief which holds consciously to this principle must necessarily be concerned with the technique and devices through which literary art is able to construct its unique achievement. Such a view is hardly art for art's sake; it is more nearly art for the sake of capturing man's real experience—which, the Southern formalist critics insist, is a full-bodied, not an abstracted, experience.

Although the techniques for achieving concretion in fiction are often markedly different from those of poetry, the basic principle is the same. The novelist does not write about a world; he presents one. He seldom gives information about a character; he offers his developing image directly. Even in those instances when the author seems to obtrude his own presence into the action, the intention, if the work is successful, is to present qualitative rather than ideational meanings. Whether the writer's task is the development of a scene

through dialogue, description, or narration, his employment of language is always in the direction of concretion. How a writer develops concrete presentations defines his particular style, which is simply to provide a designation for the deviations from the logical norm of language that a writer discovers when he constructs a literary work.

The task of the critic of fiction is to discover and disclose the particular language forms which are operating to embody meaning. His approach cannot be so much a method of analysis as it is an attitude toward analysis. Paradoxically he must at once strive toward a developing sophistication, an ever-increasing sensitivity toward the complexities of fictional forms, while at the same time he must practice a humility which will permit the inherent forms within a work to disclose themselves—a process too often blocked when the critic is not on guard against imposing critical criteria and preconceived categories upon the work. (pp. 33-44)

> *William J. Handy, in his* Kant and the Southern
> New Critics, *University of Texas Press, 1963, 112 p.*

INFLUENCE AND LEGACY

RICHARD FOSTER

[*In the following excerpt from the conclusion to his* The New Romantics: A Reappraisal of the New Criticism *(1962), Foster praises the development by New Critics of "criticism-as-poetry" in literary essays that reveal their essentially romantic approach to literature.*]

"One looks in vain through the writings of subtle and 'philosophical' minds like I. A. Richards, William Empson, Kenneth Burke, and the younger men who have adopted their terminology," Henri Peyre complained several years ago, "for *one* excellent article of criticism." Of course, anyone even a little conversant with the writings of these men (who, by the way, are the "younger men" that have been searched through "in vain"?) would feel unhappy at Professor Peyre's having allowed his irritability to make him appear ignorant. But for the critic himself, or the student of criticism, the professor's statement would have other echoes of interest. It would recall, first of all, the whole ethos of the contemporary critics' assault upon the institutionalized inertia of mind and imagination characteristic, until recent years, of the study of literature in the universities. But more important, it introduces two words, "excellent" and "criticism," which symbolize perhaps the most vitally strategic ideas in the former war between the Professors and the Critics, and which, even now, any critic or critic-of-critics has to be responsible for making clear to himself.

But whatever "good" or "excellent" criticism may finally be, I think it is striking how frequently and consistently the New Critics and their associates have been blamed or praised for doing things essentially unrelated to criticism, things *noncritical* or *other than* critical—at least if we hang on to a fairly common-sense idea of what literary criticism is. Isn't this at the heart of Professor Peyre's complaint when he puts "philosophical" into a little scoff of quotation marks? Stanley Edgar Hyman once charged [in his *Armed Vision*], a charge variously echoed by other commentators, that Ransom, Tate, and others who produced "manifestoes" in behalf of "close technical reading of texts" failed, on the whole, to practice their own preachments. This was the point of Harry Levin's objection many years ago [in the *New Republic* 103 (23 December 1940)] to Blackmur's proliferating mannerisms ("a fondness for onomatopoetic suggestion, a deliberate cultivation of the malapropism, a tendency to fall victim to his own metaphors; epigrams that fizzle, paradoxes that turn out to be mere contradictions, desperate efforts to achieve a platitude"), all of which were signs of a flourishing self-consciousness that was essentially irrelevant to the business-like pursuit of criticism. But Robert W. Stallman, in contrast, certainly implied no disapproval in describing Ransom as "primarily a philosopher . . . only incidentally committed to the technical criticism of poetry" [see excerpt above]. And more recently Professor Hugh Holman [in "The Defense of Art: Criticism since 1930," in *The Development of American Literary Criticism,* edited by Floyd Stovall] implied praise when he described Ransom as having "fostered and practiced a criticism that is philosophically oriented," and Tate as having a "sharply logical and profoundly philosophical mind."

So it appears that at least in some eyes the critics are up to something that is much of the time other than criticism, if criticism, reduced to the lowest common denominator of probable agreement on its meaning, denotes the analysis and evaluation of literary works. This other than critical something—an irrelevancy or an enrichment, depending on your viewpoint—would seem to range somewhere between general philosophy (Hyman, for example, praises Empson and the early Blackmur for examining texts while the other critics are preoccupied with "general critical problems, some of them remote from literature") and self-realization (John Edward Hardy [in "The Achievement of Cleanth Brooks" in *The Hopkins Review* 6 (1953)] praises the "plain, steady, utilitarian" manner of Cleanth Brooks as an antidote to the dangers of "inspired" criticism). The intent realized in Brooks' critical style as described by Hardy would be a rather far cry from Ransom's notion that the critic ought to write literarily. The "plain, steady, utilitarian" style would be close, I would judge, to the "schoolmaster's" style. Certainly it would not easily if Leslie Fiedler's conception [in "Toward an Amateur Criticism," *Kenyon Review* 12 (1950)] of the "true" language of criticism as "the language of conversation—the voice of the dilettante at home." Among the major New Critics, only Cleanth Brooks comes to mind—and perhaps also Empson— as engaging mainly in the detailed and selfless analysis of particular works of literature, even though these analyses may also serve as examples in support of theory. With the exception of a few brief analytical "notes" from Tate, of Blackmur's earlier textual studies of certain poets, of an occasional illustrative passage from Richards and a few special items like Ransom's study of Shakespeare's language and Tate's detailed discussion of his own "Ode," we have mostly general or "speculative" essays from the critics. In the manner of the essayist, the critics, even when they begin with a text or a corpus of texts, will tend to move away toward general considerations of the imagination, the modern world, the nature of poetry, even the nature of reality. As a consequence of such subjects and intentions, "style," as the expression of the necessarily personal mood of reflection or speculation, assumes the importance of individuality. Thus the effect of "personality" being realized in or obtruded into so much of the work of the New Critics.

There is a certain paradox—which makes a fine point of attack for the opposition—in this fact of the New Critics, who, after all, hounded the age back to the text and the conscious analytical reading of it, giving so much of their energies to writing "literary essays," essays on the whole *un*analytical and often not unlike, perhaps, the literary "impressionism" they once resisted. But of course not all literary impressionism is of the same value. Assuming the practical worth of impersonal textual and technical analysis, the sort of thing done so well by Brooks and by the many inheritors of his skills who write for the literary magazines and the best academic journals, I should like to explore possibilities for the defense of the other voice of the New Criticism. Call it the "personal," the "impressionistic," the "speculative" voice, as distinguished from the "impersonal" or "analytical" voice. It is the voice that . . . [betrays] the critics' shared sensibility as a romantic one, the voice of "criticism-as-poetry." Because the inadequacies of the critical positions represented by the old-fashioned academician and the journalist-reviewers make one wary of seeming to abet their causes in any way, it seems both fitting and necessary to consider fully the available virtues of this "criticism-as-poetry"—or, to neutralize the term, the "literary essay" as it has been variously practiced by the New Critics.

An obvious defense might be derived from the New Critics' doctrines against "scientism" and the anti-humane worship of method. The literary essay, by its very looseness and tentativeness, tends, perhaps, to keep the mind liberal, free, responsive, and thus preserves it from the habits of what Eliseo Vivas calls "methodolatry." But there are other possible important defenses, based on what such essays have actually accomplished. I. A. Richards, who has really done so little as a practical critic (and very little more, though he has *written* a lot, as a "theorist"), has almost singlehandedly motivated the modern critical revolution by haranguing against modern man's educated inabilities to read and understand. And, again almost singlehandedly, he has institutionalized the key concepts of the revolution—"Imagination," the complexity of language's "meaning" as experience, and the bogey of "stock response," which fathered psychologistically the New Critics' descriptions of good poetry in terms of "irony," "paradox," "tension," "impurity"—largely through the pure fervor of his wonder at the ways of words. Because he was perhaps the first to see both what was wrong and what was needed, he deserves the recognition he now has—along with Eliot, the great rediscoverer of the literature of the past in terms of contemporary sensibility—as an established classic of modern criticism.

There have been a great many gestures toward theory among critics following Richards, some pretty systematic, like those of Wimsatt, Wellek and Warren, and the allied aestheticians, but most of them more casual and essayistic—by Tate, Penn Warren, Brooks, Blackmur, and Ransom, to name only the major people. These excursions into theory have been made usually for the purpose of coming back with some definition of the nature of poetry, or of good poetry, and of its importance to us. And most of them have yielded what Richards likes to call "speculative instruments"—that is, metaphors or catchwords by which to conceive or "see," or to inquire further into, the nature of poetry. Of all the New and related critics who have gone in pursuit of theory, it seems to me that John Crowe Ransom has had the largest and best success. In his whole critical life work he has devoted himself to only two or three major ideas, running them through and through his essays, refining them and perfecting them into, as I believe, the truest speculative instruments of this kind that we have had from any of the critics, including Richards, or Coleridge via Richards. The key virtue of Ransom's achievement is that he has taken the pains to give us not a mere clever tag, but an *idea*. For in the trope of the texture-structure dichotomy and its refinement into the idea of the Concrete Universal, Ransom, by identifying the special nature of poetry with the experienced concretions' relation of abundant excess to the rational meaning, has made a definition both of poetry and its psychological reception by a proper reader. The poem has more detail than the meaning requires. And *because* of this we *care* for the poem beyond its use as "meaning." This is what all the critics have always been saying, of course, even those who have protested Ransom's "inorganic" theory. But none has said it so clearly or so well. And in these days when the reigning ambition is to huddle all the arts indiscriminately together under one great universal formula, Ransom's theory has the additional value—his own belief to the contrary—of being formulated so as to fit verbal art best if not exclusively. Taking for granted the indisputable grace and wit of his essays as essays, I think a sound defense of Ransom as a literary essayist could be made, then, on the grounds of his having constructed with such care and sensitivity a particularly effective theoretical idea or metaphor, a useful speculative—or persuasive or pedagogical—instrument for the examination and defense of poetry in a world where such instruments and defenses are peculiarly necessary.

Tate has been spoken of almost as often as Ransom as a "philosopher" among New Critics. But I think that his essays, seen as a whole, are closer to Eliot than to the theoretical pursuits of Richards and Ransom. One always feels the personality in Eliot's essays. It has its formal public face on, but behind that face is a living sensibility, a cultivated intelligence that eschews "method" and records its awarenesses and judgments pretty immediately. In Tate's essays the personality is more vivid, less formal—at least it seems so much less formal that the essays as a body take on the immediacy and drama almost of the confessional. As Tate himself very well realizes and, if we may believe his prefaces, intends, the essays are the record of the progress of a mind. The overpowering sincerity of Tate's essays, even the ingenuousness of their occasional vanities and posturings, make something very special of them. Most of them cannot quite be called criticism. But they are something rarer, richer in substance finally than "pure" criticism—like Ransom's essays, they are literature themselves: they are the biography of the conscience and sensibility of a deeply responsive and complicated man of letters in a peculiarly troubled time. And as that they create part of the myth of our time. Sometimes, in addition, they discover special and unforeseen responses to certain familiar writers—to Poe particularly, but also to Dante, Emily Dickinson, Dostoievski, and of course to Tate himself—that change one's own perception of them for good. They are always handsomely written, too. All this, it seems to me, makes them not only defensible, but indispensable.

Blackmur's criticism is also remarkable for the power, found occasionally in Tate, of creating or recreating one's mode of perception of some work or works. It is in fact *the* characteristic, understood as more vivid and radical in Blackmur's work than in Tate's, and as increased to many more instances, that I shall make the principal basis for arguing that Blackmur is the most important of the New Critics under discussion. Blackmur's peculiar talent has been not merely for

analysis or exegesis of texts, but for actually readying in the reader special variations of sensibility necessary for special understanding. . . . Blackmur's earlier style, while never so direct and utilitarian as Brooks', was simpler than the later style about in proportion to his then stricter attention to specific texts. But even his earlier criticism in its final intentions, was quite a different thing from "analysis." Though the earlier essays are full of the analytical work of explaining meanings and scrutinizing the effects of certain technical features of the poem, Blackmur always made these procedures subordinate steps toward the end of creating a mode of perceiving the special quality and receiving the special experience provided in the work of a particular writer. The 1931 essay on Wallace Stevens is a good example. It contrasts Stevens' surface "nonsense" with the meaning*less*ness of Cummings' language and the special compressive techniques of meaning in Pound and Eliot. It then inculcates, by close attention to some "examples" of Wallace Stevens, an understanding of Stevens' particular technique as one of seeing and accumulating ambiguities and pressing them to the point of virtual meaning. This characteristic technique having been isolated, elucidated, and variously exemplified, is thus made available to the reader as a technique of understanding or sensibility, paralleling Stevens' own, with which to surround and possess a poetry whose generalized difficulty is assumed by the critic on behalf of the reader. As in Blackmur's studies of Cummings' diction of sentimental unmeaning, of Marianne Moore's technique of reducing experience by idiosyncrasy and formalism, of Pound's technique of masks and voices, of Yeats' technique of conception and perception by "magic," this same, more than analytical intention informs most of the earlier essays.

It informs the later essays, too, but its objective there is more complex. In the later essays sensibility is prepared and provided not merely for the appropriate reception of a given, but also for a felt understanding of the disordered time in which we live, of the problems both of artists generally and of particular artists in our time, of what it is that the arts peculiarly "do" with reality, and finally of what essential reality itself is like as immediate unspeakable experience. All these themes may be distinguished, for example, in the long and exotically written essay on Eliot called "Unappeasable and Peregrine." It evokes a sense of our time as deprived of live and valid formative institutions like the Church. It presents the predicament of the artist in such a time in his necessarily makeshift and perhaps chaotic search for the forms and substance in which to create the formal sense of his experience, and delineates Eliot's special act, as a Christian convert, of *realizing* and *recreating* in poetry the substantial experience of the disused form to which he has personally reverted. It demonstrates that art in all times, but particularly in our time of severance from the coherences of the past, is a way of compassing the disorder and flux of experience, of giving it form, of giving us location in it, perhaps even of discovering it for us. And it convinces, finally—accomplishing, like successful art, a suspension of disbelief—that there are depths and mysteries in experience, in "reality," beyond prose and common sense, and graspable only by poetry and imagination. All these subjects are to a degree "talked about" in the Eliot essay; but principally they are evoked, incanted into existence, made intuitively sensible to the reader if he reads successfully. A smaller and more accessible example of Blackmur's performance is this evocation of understanding [in his *Language as Gesture*] for Yeats' "The Apparitions":

> One tends to let poems stay too much as they are. Do they not actually change as they are read? Do they not, as we feel them intensely, fairly press for change on their own account? Not all poems, of course, but poems of this character, which engage possibility as *primum mobile* and last locomotive? Is not the precision of the poem for the most part a long way under the precision of the words? Do not the words involve their own opposites, . . . not for contradiction but for development?

These rhetorical questions are not "analysis." But they are part of the almost poetic means by which Blackmur takes the reader into the poem. He also assists the reader to "ad-lib" the poem as Yeats ad-libbed it from the original given iota of insight, and one has the direct experience of how the poem might have gone differently at several junctures. The total effect of all this is to provide an approximate experience of the processes of sensibility with which Yeats himself must have written the poem.

This provision of multiple understandings "from within," so to speak, is the substance not only of the later essays on Yeats and Eliot, but of most of Blackmur's other essays of the forties and fifties. These later essays have a greater sameness about them than the earlier essays, for they all concern themselves with the more general themes of the modern world and the modern artist. But they are also crucially distinct, for each treatment of an individual writer—Mann, James, Dostoievsky, Tolstoy, Flaubert—recreates something of the necessarily individual quality of sensibility needed to grasp the special and different ways each artist had of compassing reality. Mann's "diabolism" is a different thing from Flaubert's exorcising by objective fiction his subjective romantic

R.P. Blackmur.

"demon." Such individuations are certainly an important part of the burden of Blackmur's later efforts as a poet of criticism. For that is what, on the whole, he is—a poet *creating* consciousness, *creating* in his readers a preparatory semblance of the essential experience to come in the poem proper, the experience that, without this readying, might have been missed or violated. Like a poet he *renders* his subjects. Or, as he once said about himself [in a contribution to "The Situation of American Writing" in *The Partisan Reader*] at the same time denying that his essays "expressed" either himself or a group or institution larger than himself, "I try to express what I am writing about."

We can say very frankly of Blackmur that though his later criticism contains analytical textual examinations, it is in bulk an evocative, insight-giving, impressionistic semi-poetry. Though he can be ludicrous or embarrassing or plain boring, when the frenzy fizzles or when he goes burning on and on without giving light, I believe there is no critic within the New Criticism as it has here been limited that can match him in sensitivity and catholicity and weight of accomplishment. Outside the New Criticism there is only Kenneth Burke, so like him in vitality and reach of imagination and intelligence, so opposite in principle and practice. (pp. 193-206)

All "good" criticism, certainly, must nourish upon "sensibility"—the cultivated but free vision to see according to your living and natural lights what is before you, and from what is given to imagine what is not. This may almost be a description of the poet. And it smacks of the romanticism, the interestingly ironic, the occasionally irritating romanticism of the New Critics.

But what have we as we look toward Chicago and the surviving memorials there of the only other important critical movement of the past twenty years? We have this from Elder Olson [in "An Outline of Poetic Criticism" in *Critics and Criticism,* edited by R. S. Crane]: "By 'beauty' I mean the excellence of perceptible form in a composite continuum which is a whole; and by 'excellence of perceptible form' I mean the possession of perceptible magnitude in accordance with a mean determined by the whole as a whole of such-and-such quality, composed of such-and-such parts." And this from Norman Maclean [in "Episode, Scene, Speech, and Word: The Madness of Lear" in *Critics and Criticism*]: "The tragedy with depth is compounded out of a profound conception of what is tragic and out of action tragically bent, with characters commensurate to the concept and the act—and, finally, it is composed out of writing." As so often with the Chicagoans, we have the pseudo-philosophic style of the supposed classic color—an imitation of the manner of a bad translation of Aristotle. We have intellectual bathos and circular exterminations of meaning achieved only after the most elephantine laborings of diction and syntax. And these are high points—moments of definition and principle. We have, finally, in the place where sensibility ought to be, huge abstract machineries for the processing, packaging, and labeling of literary produce. But after all the noise and exertion of its construction, the Neo-Aristotelian factory produced hardly anything very memorable—a lively essay or two, at its best, against New Critics—and it now seems to have shut down altogether, though presumably it still stands firm.

It is no doubt significant that most of the major New Critics have been artists as well as critics (Ransom, Tate, Blackmur, Penn Warren, Empson, recently I. A. Richards, and even a poem or two of Brooks' have seen print), and around them have gathered many of the finest younger writers of the time. Sensibility, that agile awareness that for better or for worse dominates the literary essay at the expense of "method," and that in a different dilution is the artist's special medium, is perhaps the chief thing lacking in the work of the Aristotelians and other mechanical critics, including that large majority of academics for whom the chief and lasting legacy of the New Criticism is what they call "explication," or "formalistic analysis." A viableness of sensibility, a readiness for "speculative fury," a susceptibility, at bottom, even to moments of romantic frenzy, these are qualities that gave the New Critics their original impetus to move against the sterility of literary study in their time and to challenge the dehumanizing conditions of the world that bred it. Now that the skills of literary study have been refurbished and revitalized, it may be worth turning back once again to the New Criticism, the chief movement for literary humanism of this century, this time to discover its vision of a humane commitment and belief that can provide for the user of those skills a deepening and liberating idea of their place in the human enterprise at large. We are all necessarily, in this place and time, if we are serious and humane, "romantics" in reaction. The New Critics have created, willy-nilly, by the hard personal labor of their extemporizing a structure of value in the midst of chaos, a major testament of that modern necessity. And perhaps accusations of romantic heresy are a tolerable enough scourge to bear for the privilege of such felicity. (pp. 207-10)

> *Richard Foster, in his* The New Romantics: A Reappraisal of the New Criticism, *Indiana University Press, 1962, 238 p.*

WILLIAM E. CAIN

[*In the following excerpt, Cain examines the influence of New Criticism on modern trends in critical theory, especially as New Critical assumptions have become institutionalized through university teaching.*]

In this essay I shall argue that the New Criticism is alive and well. To say this may seem perverse, since there is such general agreement that the New Criticism has lost its prestige and authority. All of us are keenly aware of its failings: it ignores the reader's role, denies the importance of authorial intention, cuts off literature from history, and favors some groups of texts (metaphysical poetry, for example) at the expense of others (Romantic and Victorian poetry in particular). Attacks on the New Criticism have in fact been so sustained and, apparently, successful that it is common today to discover references to the "decline" or "death" of the movement— as though the New Criticism were already in the grave or rapidly on its way there. Sometimes the references are slightly more charitable, as when Morris Dickstein remarks [in "The State of Criticism," *Partisan Review* 48 (1981)] that individual New Critics exist but as a species of "toothless lion." This implies that they possess a certain nobility, if not the power to do us harm.

But we have been hearing reports of the death, decline, or harmlessness of the New Criticism for decades, and they have always been greatly exaggerated. . . . Murray Krieger noted [in *Approaches to the Study of Twentieth-Century Literature* (1961)] that "we are told on all sides that the New Criticism is dead, that a reaction has set in against it." Many others said the same or similar things, and as the eighties begin, the dirge

still sounds. Everyone agrees that the New Criticism is dead or declining, and is obviously no longer an influential force. But at the same time, everyone feels obliged to keep dismissing the New Criticism yet once more. Its power is said to be negligible or nonexistent, yet it still compels interest and renewed attention, and arguments for its overthrow or displacement continue to be made. Critiques of the New Criticism, even in its so-called decline or death, crop up frequently in books and journals. And it is standard practice for literary theorists to begin their discussions of "new" approaches by first assailing the New Criticism, as though its errors still needed to be exposed.

For several decades, then, critics and theorists have been saying that the New Criticism is neither vital nor influential. Even the New Critics themselves—and at a relatively early stage—expressed doubts about the movement. John Crowe Ransom, for example, observed [in the *Kenyon Review*] in 1948 that New Critical "stock" was low, having taken a "dip in the market," and he suggested that a revaluation was in order. A year later [in a forward to *Critiques and Essays in Criticism, 1920-1948,* edited by Robert Wooster Stallman], Cleanth Brooks also called for a "general stock-taking," adding that the New Critical era "has come to fruition, or has arrived at a turning point, or, as some writers hint, has now exhausted its energies." So widespread was this sense of closure that by 1951 Austin Warren could state [in "The Achievement of Some Recent Critics," *Poetry* 77] as a "commonplace" the fact that the New Critical movement "had come to an end."

What we have is a curious phenomenon. From one point of view, the New Criticism appears powerless, lacking in supporters, declining, dead or on the verge of being so. No one speaks on behalf of the New Criticism as such today, and it mostly figures in critical discourse as the embodiment of foolish ideas and misconceived techniques. But the truth, I believe, is that the New Criticism survives and is prospering, and it seems to be powerless only because its power is so pervasive that we are ordinarily not even aware of it. So embedded in our work are New Critical attitudes, values, and emphases that we do not even perceive them as the legacy of a particular movement. On the contrary: we feel them as the natural and definitive conditions for criticism in general. It is not simply that the New Criticism has become institutionalized, but that it has gained acceptance as the institution itself. It has, in a word, been transformed into "criticism," the essence of what we do as teachers and critics, the ground or given upon which everything else is based.

The New Criticism leads two lives. Or rather, it is dead in one sense and very much alive in another. It is dead as a movement, as the many critiques and attacks demonstrate. But its lessons about literary study lead a vigorous life, setting the norms for effective teaching and marking the boundaries within which nearly all criticism seeks to validate itself. It is the New Criticism that defines and gives support to the central job of work that we perform—"practical criticism," the "close reading" of literary texts. "Close reading" forms the substance of most critical essays and books, and it is reinforced in our classrooms where we teach verbal analysis to our students. It is also an evaluative principle, the norm by which we assess new theories of literature. If a new theory cannot generate close readings, if it fails the test of practical criticism, if it seems unable to make us understand the classic texts in new ways and appears unlikely to work well in the classroom, then it is usually judged to be irrelevant. A new theory must have consequences for the analysis and explication of texts; it can only make modest claims for itself and should serve, above all, to direct us back to the text and thus enrich our "close readings." It is the single text that stands, in Malcolm Bradbury's words, [in "The State of Criticism Today," in *Contemporary Criticism,* edited by Malcolm Bradbury and David Palmer, 1970] as the "irreducible literary minimum," and our essential duty is to read it with as much sensitivity to tone and nuance as we can manage and to teach others to do the same.

In his essay "Beyond Interpretation," published [in *Contemporary Literature* 28] in 1976, Jonathan Culler argued against this over-riding emphasis on the "close reading" of texts. The chief and most "insidious" legacy of the New Criticism, he stated, is the "unquestioning acceptance of the notion that the critic's job is to interpret literary works." Culler's argument upset many people, who, on the one hand, claimed not to be New Critics at all, yet who nevertheless insisted that the critic's function is obviously to explicate literary texts. To insist on the "obviousness" of interpretation, however, is not to refute Culler's argument but to confirm it. We are so accustomed to seeing ourselves as "close readers," and we are so committed to producing more interpretations of texts, that when we practice close reading we believe that we are engaged in the inevitable work of criticism. No one, of course, is opposed to the detailed, attentive reading of texts, and I am not making a case for its elimination. But I think it is important to recognize that what was once the aim of a particular critical movement now defines the general aims of criticism. Close reading of literary texts is the ground that nearly all theories and methods build upon or seek to occupy. And this holds true even for those that are explicitly set up in opposition to the New Criticism. To put this point another way: the New Criticism is not so much declining or dead as it has won eternal life as the core or essence of criticism.

In . . . ["Tory Formalists, New York Intellectuals, and the New Historical Science of Criticism," *Sewanee Review* 88 (Fall 1980)] Louis D. Rubin, Jr. affirms this identity between the New Criticism and "criticism" in general, and thereby brings into the open what most critics take for granted and leave unsaid. "If the New Criticism as a movement is concluded," he explains,

> it is because its job has been done: it has made us read poems closely and in their own right, so that we could gain access to the poetry written in English during the first half of the twentieth century. But I remain unconvinced that it is kaput, because I don't see its job as having been done. Certainly its faddishness is over; it is no longer a novelty. But in ceasing to be New it has not thereby become Old Criticism. Instead it has become simply criticism.

New Critical techniques, Rubin points out, are especially suited to the analysis of difficult modern texts, the poetry, for instance, of Yeats and Eliot. But instead of highlighting the historical conjunction of modern poetry and criticism, and instead of commenting on the kinds of poetry the New Criticism cannot help us to read well, Rubin endows the New Criticism with a permanent validity. "The best criticism of literature," he concludes,

> as long as it is criticism *of* literature, will have to be that which starts with the text and, no matter how far it may stray, or whatever it brings to the

text, will find its validity in the text. . . . Somebody is always going to say, eventually, after the New Historical Scientist or the structuralist or the Marxist or the reader-psychologist or whatever has erected his glittering paradigm or simulacrum or manifesto or document or who knows what: "Yes, but how do you *know* it's so?" And the only convincing response will have to be "Let's look at the text."

The text, in Rubin's view, is our point of departure and the instrument by which we measure the accuracy of an interpretation. The meanings situated in the text will prove or disprove what we say about it, however caught up we may be in our newfangled theories. When all the preliminaries and distractions are out of the way, we will be obliged, Rubin asserts, to return to the text, reading it scrupulously and hence seeing (and abiding by) its meaningful signals.

Such a "New Critical" understanding of the text is debatable at best, and it has been challenged by Gerald Graff, Richard Strier, and others. But Rubin's definition of the text concerns me less than his belief, uttered in that weary voice we reserve for basic truths in danger of being forgotten, that the basic fact of "criticism" is the close reading of texts. When we undertake the task of interpretation, keeping our sight focused on the words on the page, we are not, Rubin suggests, merely fulfilling the job of work prescribed by the New Critics. Rather, we are living up to the responsibility that every rightminded critic must acknowledge. We are not practicing the New Criticism, but "simply criticism."

Rubin's argument is not unique, and it is in fact surprising to realize, in this era of proliferating methods, theories, and approaches, how widely it is shared. Even for those who scorn the New Criticism and declare that something else replace it, the close reading of texts remains the normative procedure, the way of showing that the proposed replacement for the New Criticism is useful and worthwhile. Whenever a critic wishes to state the essential truth of criticism, or intends to demonstrate what a new theory has to offer, he or she returns to the literary text for an exercise in practical criticism. At this point the theoretical debates and conflicts are set aside, factional strife ceases, and teachers and critics urge one another to accept the facts of interpretive life—that we remain faithful to the discipline of "close reading" and to the class of specifically *literary* texts for which this skill was devised.

In his recent call for the "oral interpretation" of literature [in "How to Rescue Literature," *New York Review of Books* (17 April 1980)], Roger Shattuck does not present himself as a New Critic, but his argument is informed by the terms that the New Criticism canonized. He advises us to

> keep our heads, eschew intellectual fashions, avoid cleaving to one method as suitable to all circumstances, and attempt to approach a work of literature without rigid preconceptions, without a grid of theory. No, there is no "innocent reading" any more than there is an "innocent eye." But it is possible to temper experience and mastery with a kind of induced innocence—negative capability or *lacher prise*—which discourages the kind of usurpation I have been deploring. And in the domain of teaching . . . I would also favor certain kinds of exercises—busy-work even—that have fallen totally out of favor: word for word copying dictation, reading aloud, summarizing (precis writing), mem-

orizing, and translation. All of these activities enforce close attention to what a piece of writing is actually doing without requiring an elaborate theory
of literature to begin with.

This argument presents itself as straightforward and commonsensical even as it bypasses the contestability of its assumptions. It is a paradoxical kind of argument, since Shattuck wants something and concedes that it cannot be attained, but then tries to have it anyway. He admits that there
cannot be an "innocent" reading, yet he then asserts, without
any explanation, that we can "induce" this innocence or
something like it in ourselves and thereby guard against the
perils of "experience" and our arrogant desire to "master"
the text. Shattuck's words sound persuasive to many people,
but his argument is not very rigorous. It is in fact loose and
rather sloppy, but Shattuck succeeds in reaching his audience
because his argument is based on what many teachers and
critics assume as a matter of course—that we should always
attend to the text and remember that *any* "theory of literature" will necessarily be "elaborate," interfering with the text
rather than helping us to understand it in more complex
ways. Like Louis Rubin, Shattuck believes that he is reiterat-
ing commonplaces which, in our waywardness, we occasionally lose sight of but basically agree with. He knows, on the
one hand, that many of his proposals appear dated and old-
fashioned, yet he also senses how appealing these will be for
readers—and they constitute the majority of the profession—
who are tired of all the talk about theory and are anxious to
get back to the practical criticism of literature. To be a teacher and critic is to "enforce"—the word is somewhat disconcerting—the "close attention to what a piece of writing is actually doing." And this means that we should not sully our
discipline with theory, non-literary topics and approaches, or
even preconceptions. Just read the text closely and the disciplined nature of "Criticism, Inc." (Ransom's term) will be
ensured.

"Literature," Shattuck admits,

> is not autonomous and unrelated to our daily lives;
> on the contrary, we all to some degree live by and
> through it. But it does not belong to any domain
> outside the domain of art, and we are shirking our
> responsibilities if we look the other way while self-
> styled "literary" critics deliver literature into the
> hands of one or another of the social sciences.

Shattuck states that literature is not "autonomous" and
therefore *is* connected, in some way that he does not specify,
to our daily lives. Yet no sooner does he make this point then
he appears to take it back or at least diminish its force. Literature belongs to "the domain of art," and it is our obligation
to prevent traitors within the "literary" ranks from handing
over "literature" to the social sciences. Once again, Shattuck's words strike a high-minded tone, but this should not
disguise the fact that he is concerned about the territorial
privileges of English and other departments of literature.
Like Ransom and the other New Critics, he seeks to keep the
discipline "autonomous." A responsible critic, Shattuck insists, must affirm the autonomy of his or her discipline and
must examine *literature as literature,* not as some other
thing—and certainly not something as abstract and fussy as
one of the social sciences, which traffic in the world outside
the "domain of art."

What is especially revealing about Shattuck's argument is his
lack of confidence in the "literature" whose merits he claims

to be supporting. Shattuck believes that other disciplines are
making "raids" on literature, and his assumption is that these
raids are dangerous, that they threaten a literature unable to
defend itself. Any exchange between literature and other disciplines must, Shattuck implies, occur at literature's expense.
He could have maintained that literature naturally tends towards being enriched and supplemented by other disciplines;
from this point of view, he could have argued that precisely
because "the domain of art" is itself powerful, it enables and
encourages us to move beyond its secure boundaries. But
rather than emphasizing the range and resilience of literature,
Shattuck worries about its weakness. Literature, to quote the
title of his essay, needs to be "rescued." And this rescue-
mission is undertaken, as one might have predicted, by a return to the text, to "close attention" to the words on the page.
This will enable us to safeguard literature or "at least delay
the abduction of the text by method, theory or system." As
this last phrase suggests, perhaps the most curious paradox
of all is that Shattuck's modest claims for the role of the critic
barely conceal what is certainly a major claim: literature is
best served not by method or theory but by the virtues of its
protectors. Those who truly serve and strive to "rescue" literature do not require critical terms, theoretical models, or interpretive machines, but just themselves.

A similar, though more eloquent, proposal is at the heart of
Helen Vendler's [1980] presidential address to the Modern
Language Association. In her capacity as our spokesperson,
Vendler articulates the mission that we perform as critics and
teachers of literature. And she does so by repeatedly drawing
upon New Critical language about the close reading of texts.
"We are all, by now, scholars," she observes.

> But I would wish for us all a steady memory of the
> time when we were not yet scholars—before we
> knew what research libraries or variorum editions
> were, before we heard any critical terms, before we
> had seen a text with footnotes. It was in those inno-
> cent days that our attachment to literature arose—
> from reading a novel or seeing a play. In every true
> reading of literature in adult life we revert to that
> early attitude of entire receptivity and plasticity
> and innocence before the text.

Like Shattuck, Vendler feels that there is something impure
about our scholarly pursuits, and she recommends that we
try to recover our lost "innocence," that time before we knew
"critical" terms. This is, at first sight, a peculiar argument,
primarily because it seems to be directed *against* the various
practices in which the literary institution deals and which,
one assumes, Vendler ought to be defending: it is as if the
products of our research and scholarship were, for her, consequences devoutly to be wished away. But while this appears
to be an anti-institutional argument, it is actually one of the
oldest, most institutionalized arguments of all. The New Critics first made this point in the 1930's when they stated that
literary history, source-study, and the like were overwhelming the literary texts themselves; for the New Critics, the essential truth about literary experience is that it puts the reader into intimate contact with a particular text. And this is a
belief that Vendler, Shattuck, and Rubin share: we cherish
the literary text, seek always to return to it for close reading
and practical criticism, and view this task as the ground upon
which our discipline is constructed. It enables us to reaffirm
our sense of mission and justify our work to the world.

"No matter how elementary or specialized the written inquiry," Vendler adds, "it originated in problems raised by

human submission to, and interrogation of, a text." Nothing, perhaps, seems more understandable, in the face of our institutional chores and routines, than the desire to escape our consciousness of them and "revert" to purity and innocence—Vendler even characterizes the reading of texts as, at its best, a "state of intense engagement and self-forgetfulness." But this desire signifies a form of nostalgia that was itself institutionalized a long time ago, so much that it has become the basis for our conception of ourselves as teachers and critics. We read texts, poems in particular, because we believe that they are far better, richer, more deeply textured and organically unified than any world that we know from our daily experiences. Returning to the text means, in this sense, turning away from the world and dwelling within the verbal structures that literature provides.

I do not want in this essay to seem unfair or ungrateful to Ransom and his colleagues. As Richard Poirier has rightly emphasized [in his *The Performing Self: Compositions and Decompositions in the Languages of Contemporary Life,* 1971], the New Criticism made a necessary case against the bad effects of a certain kind of excessively "historical" approach, and in this sense it was truly liberating. But the spirit of reversion, withdrawal, and isolation remains deep-rooted in literary studies, and the New Critics are in large measure responsible for it. Once the Agrarian movement failed, Ransom and the others focused their attention on the reform of criticism and teaching. These reforms required, first, that "English Studies" be separated from other disciplines, and second, that literature not be made impure by contact with the world—the world that the New Critics, in their Agrarian phase, had sought to reform but now thought beyond repair. When Ransom was asked to organize and edit a new journal at Kenyon College, he insisted that such a journal should deal exclusively with literature and the other arts; and he did so despite the fact that the President of Kenyon College had originally proposed and hoped for a journal that would examine philosophy and public affairs as well as the arts. As this symbolically charged decision implies, the injunction to return to the text and the privileging of literary experience are not, contrary to Vendler and others, *anti*-institutional. These do not allow us to escape from the burdens of the literary institution but rather establish what the literary institution *is,* assumes as its central job of work, and regards as its justification.

"We love in *King Lear,*" Vendler affirms,

> precisely what distinguishes it from *Hamlet* or *Doctor Faustus,* the quality that makes it not simply a Renaissance tragedy, not simply a Shakespearean play, but the single and unrepeatable combination of elements we call *King Lear.* It is from the experience of one or two such works that we are all led to the place where we are now, and it is from that original vision—of the simple, unduplicatable, compelling literary object—that we must always take our final strength in university life and public life alike, whatever combinatorial tactics prudence may occasionally recommend.

Vendler inherits her conception of our submissiveness before the literary text from the New Critics, and the zeal that is evident throughout her essay suggests her feeling for its importance. It is not really the case, however, that she is addressing an audience that needs to be won over to her point of view. Most teachers and critics already share it, for their attitudes, too, have been formed by the New Criticism. Vendler is thus speaking to an audience that was converted long ago. New Critical beliefs and practices, though no longer in fashion, are also no longer in dispute, because they have been widely accepted as the foundation for criticism. Vendler does not name herself as a New Critic, but that is part of my point about her, and about Rubin and Shattuck as well. The New Criticism is so woven into the fabric of critical discourse that its assumptions are not recognized as assumptions at all.

This emerges with unusual clarity in John M. Ellis's . . . ["The Logic of the Question 'What is Criticism?'," in *What Is Criticism?,* edited by Paul Hernardi, 1981]. Ellis contends that most of the criticism being written today is wrongheaded and contemptible. As he surveys the critical landscape, he sees battles and disagreements that are fought without real point or purpose. The main problem, Ellis says, is that many critics now view their enterprise as a "creative" one, in competition with the literature that criticism ought in fact to be serving. "Modern critics," he states,

> seem less and less inclined to let the text speak for itself, through close attention to its emphases; they seem far more concerned to impress than to allow the text to do so, readily substituting their own ideologies and conceptual systems for those of the literary work. They seem often to be trying to rival the uniqueness of literary language by their own dazzling conceptual pyrotechnics, and to display their own erudition and intellectual feats instead of the literary text's subtle individuality. Never have we been so faced with criticism which so obviously strains for originality at all costs. Critical essays by well-known and well-regarded critics seem often to ramble from one ill-defined but grandiose concept to another, attempting to enrich a vacuous argument with fashionable jargon and names, as well as bons mots and aphorisms of questionable relevance. The result is a veritable caricature of discussion, a reduction of criticism to an entertainment for scholars, a narrowly clubby kind of discourse.

The issues, Ellis believes, are clear. Critics should not impose their systems (or their personalities) on the literary text, but should "let the text speak for itself." If criticism is to lay claim to being a discipline, then its practitioners need to recall that it is the literary text, not the critic, which is our foremost concern. The goal of "actual criticism," Ellis maintains, is to "discern the unique emphasis of a given text." Some people, he adds, will judge such an emphasis to be "old-fashioned," a throwback to the "New Criticism." Yet "nothing will be as enduring as the plain confrontation of reader and text, the fundamental literary experience which will still be going on long after our current critical fads are forgotten." Like Rubin, Ellis advocates a return to the text itself; like Shattuck, he hopes to rescue the literary work from the theorists and self-serving critical performers; and like Vendler, he regards the "plain," direct encounter between the reader and the literary text as the essential truth to which the critic must remain loyal. These four critics doubtless disagree about many things, but all of them are in agreement about the necessity of "close criticism" and its central place in the study of literature.

Rubin, Shattuck, Vendler, and Ellis are to be commended for their efforts to reorient and justify the "discipline" of criticism. But it is their arguments on behalf of criticism that suggest, I think, why criticism is in trouble and receives so little respect. As we are all keenly aware, literature departments suffer from the pressures of our faltering economy: the stock of "Criticism, Inc." appears even lower today than when Ransom and Brooks worried about it in the late 1940's. Obviously we need to renew our discipline and vitalize the work that we perform, making clear the value of our labor and the importance of its survival. Yet even as literary study seems to be collapsing and in dire need of basic repairs, many of our most prestigious critics devise sophisticated theories, draw upon philosophy and the social sciences to buttress their interpretations of literary texts, and pay scant attention to the texts themselves. Must criticism, Rubin and the others ask, be so rarified and detached from literature? Isn't it time to get back to the fundamentals and re-acquaint ourselves with specific texts? Criticism should, it is argued, return to the text, concern itself with close reading, and resist the temptations of theory, ideology, politics, social and cultural commentary. It is the encounter with the literary text—and not anything else—that establishes the discipline of criticism and gives direction to our common pursuit.

But to see the dispute as one that sets practical critics against vanguard theorists, close readers against deconstructionists, advocates of a return to the text against proponents of French and other continental methods, is misleading. Whatever their differences of opinion on other matters, both sides share a commitment to "close reading" and the production of more analyses of texts. Most of the major theorists, including Paul de Man, Geoffrey Hartman, and J. Hillis Miller, seek to demonstrate the usefulness of their speculations in the "reading" of texts. As the spate of recent books and articles testify, these theorists and their clientele have created a booming industry in new kinds of textual explication. The results are not "New Critical" in any obvious sense; the form of the analysis differs; the terms vary; and the philosophical rationale is not the same. But the aim is identical—to generate more close readings, and to describe this activity as the inevitable job of the critic. Hillis Miller's defense of deconstruction [in his *Deconstruction and Criticism,* 1979] makes this abundantly clear: "The ultimate justification for this mode of criticism, as of any conceivable mode, is that it works. It reveals hitherto unidentified meanings and ways of having meaning in major literary texts." Deconstruction, in a word, feeds the growth-rate of literary studies, assuring us that still more readings can be gotten out of the classic texts that critical exegesis might seem to have exhausted.

Thus it is no accident that deconstruction, of all the new theories, has gained the largest group of supporters. It can be readily acquired by anyone versed in the techniques of the New Criticism, and so it holds out the promise of something radical and innovative even as it fits comfortably into the standard ways of doing business. At the same time, it is also no accident that of all of the theories being advanced today, deconstruction is the one against which the so-called practical critics fight most strenuously. They recognize, I believe, a certain—perhaps one should say a sneaking—kinship between the usual forms of "close reading" and deconstruction; but they cannot understand why the explication of texts needs to be theorized about—why invoke the terms of a theory to justify the basic procedure of criticism? And this in turn helps to explain why de Man, Miller, and the others are praised for the rigor and intensity of their analyses *and* chastized for their pretensions and overblown rhetoric; their readings are often stimulating, but their theories, it is charged, are foolish and extravagant. The deconstructive critics are, I think, pretentious in many ways, but not for their philosophical grandeur as much as for their insistence that they are

breaking free from the New Criticism and, at last, moving beyond formalism. As Edward Said has noted [in "Interview," *Diacrits* 6 (Fall 1976)], these "new New Critics, like their predecessors, confine literature to language and the problems raised by language." Deconstruction has not made a decisive change in our understanding of our discipline, but has merely enabled critics to refine familiar techniques, generate more close readings, and indulge in controversy without consequences.

My argument tends toward an obvious and double-edged conclusion—first, that the New Critics' placement of close reading at the center of literary studies was mistaken, however necessary it might have seemed at the time; and second, that we are wrong to assume that this New Critical practice defines the essential task of criticism, however inevitable it may strike us. But "close reading" is clearly here to stay, and I cannot pretend that I wish it could be dislodged. This essay is not, as I have already indicated, a plea for the end of careful, detailed study of specific texts. But I do believe that we need to acknowledge the costs of our too often single-minded emphasis on textual interpretation of the masterpieces: the rejection of other methods and other kinds of texts; the misguided attempt to define (and thus defend) the *teaching* of literature as, above all, "close reading"; the skepticism shown towards literary theory; and the refusal to see other disciplines as having relevance for "*literary* criticism." It is not that "close reading" is itself misconceived but rather that the case for it has always been made at the expense of other important things. In making arguments for our discipline, we invariably exclude too much. We seek to defend criticism, but in fact restrict and delimit it. Literary studies are at once exalted—they alone can teach us to read closely and perceive the powers of language—and diminished—they become tainted when they are involved with theory, other analytical techniques, other disciplines, and the burdens of worldliness.

During the 1930's and 40's, when Ransom and the New Critics were clashing with literary historians in America, F. R. Leavis was conducting a similar campaign in England. He, too, felt that useless data about sources, backgrounds, and influences were overwhelming literary texts themselves; and he also argued that it was time to focus on the "words on the page" and acquire practical skills in analysis and judgment. In terms that remind us of Ransom and his fellow New Critics, Leavis contends that we must examine "poetry as poetry," and he envisions a program for criticism that wrests control from the enemies of literature—both the pedants inside the institution and the journalists outside it. Criticism, both Leavis and the American New Critics stress, must be firmly grounded in the close reading of literary texts.

But Leavis differs significantly from the New Critics, in that he sees the "close criticism" of literature as leading to serious work in other disciplines, to the study of literature written in other languages, and most important of all, to the criticism of culture, society, and contemporary civilization. Leavis states these proposals in a number of books and articles, of which *Education and the University: A Sketch for an "English School,"* published in 1943, is the most concrete and compelling example. And this book is all the more illuminating when it is read in conjunction with Ransom's and the New Critics's writings during this period. Leavis's proposals indicate a significant road not taken in the charting of our American "New Critical" institution.

Like the New Critics, Leavis emphasizes the necessity of defining "English" and distinguishing it from other disciplines. But he then stresses that the study of English demands that we engage in historical research, cultural analysis, and social commentary. We take our bearings, he contends, in literary criticism, in the interpretation of particular texts; and then we proceed, inevitably, to other, more general studies. We are critics of both literature and more than literature, and viewing ourselves as concerned with the first job should not prevent us from doing the second one as well. To affirm that literature must be studied in its historical richness, its relevance to the present, and its relation to modern society is not, Leavis maintains, to weaken or disfigure the integrity of criticism. It is, rather, a sign of our confidence in the power of literature and criticism that we feel able to teach and write "critically" in other ways and through other disciplines. This confidence will seem misplaced only to someone who is so defensive about his or her discipline—to say nothing of being defensive about literature itself—that he or she judges the best argument for criticism to be the one that describes it in the most exclusive terms.

There were, of course, a number of important American critics in the 1940's and 50's who, like Leavis in England, sought to progress beyond the close reading of texts. Here are several representative statements:

> Like every other agent in this life, the critic has to be understood from what he does, what changes he effects or seeks to effect in the world. . . . The critic cultivating too zealously his critical autonomy may be consuming a great deal of energy defending himself against a threatening situation of which he does not want to be too conscious. We know that in life a man is sometimes most victimized by his fellows when he seeks to remove himself from them.
>
> [William Barrett, "A Present Tendency in American Criticism," *Kenyon Review,* 11 (Winter, 1949).]

> The New Critic's attention to the text is valuable insofar as he does not resemble the ostrich, with his head in the sand while round his oblivious baser parts sweep the contentious gales of personality and culture. . . . A viable critical movement needs its own idea of the artist as a type of moral man living in or out of a type of culture; and the New Criticism should have developed such an idea.
>
> [Richard Chase, "New vs. Ordealist," *Kenyon Review,* 11 (Winter, 1949).]

> In becoming a general critic, the literary critic does not betray his vocation but fulfills it. The "pure" literary critic, who pretends, in the cant phrase, to stay "inside" a work all of whose metaphors and meanings are pressing outward, is only half-aware. And half-aware, he deceives; for he cannot help smuggling unexamined moral and metaphysical judgments into his "close analyses," any more than the "pure" literary historian can help bootlegging unconfessed aesthetic estimates into his chronicles. Literary criticism is always becoming "something else," for the simple reason that literature is always "something else."
>
> [Leslie Fiedler, "Toward an Amateur Criticism," *Kenyon Review,* 12 (Autumn, 1950).]

But while these and similar statements by Philip Rahv, Lionel Trilling, Alfred Kazin, and others should not be discounted, they finally represent no more than a minority report. It was the New Criticism, and not a social or cultural or histori-

cal criticism, that became, in Richard Foster's words, "the dominant Anglo-American" literary movement of the twentieth century. It not only survived but "absorbed" its adversaries, Foster explains [in his *The New Romantics: A Reappraisal of the New Criticism,* 1962], making it "now almost impossible to identify the individual species *New Critic* as something distinct from the general run of competent literary academics." This was written in 1962, just when Krieger and others were observing that the New Criticism had died.

"One of the virtues of literary studies," Leavis argues, "is that they lead constantly outside themselves," and we should remember this point whenever we are inclined to defend the "autonomy" of our discipline. "While it is necessary," Leavis adds, that literary studies "should be controlled by a concern for the essential discipline, such a concern, if it is adequate, counts on associated work in other fields." Close reading is obviously important, "but a serious concern for education in reading cannot stop at reading":

> Practical criticism of literature must be associated with training in awareness of the environment—advertising, the cinema, the press, architecture, and so on, for, clearly, to the pervasive influence of this environment the literary training of sensibility in school is an inadequate reply.

This marks a commitment that the American New Critics and their successors generally do not share. For Ransom and those who have followed him, the critic's task is to mark the boundaries of the discipline and to work within them, whereas for Leavis, "literary" criticism is simply what we begin with. Indeed, it is precisely because we know the strengths of the literature that we study, and also have faith in our own discipline, that we are not threatened by other disciplines and procedures. We can relate our critical skills to other studies and allow our interpretive work to be informed by them. The "literary training of sensibility," in and of itself, is not adequate to the goals of criticism.

Leavis's words appear to make very good sense. Criticism ought to mean more than simply *literary* criticism, for surely the explication of classic texts needs to be supplemented by other modes and methods of analysis. Yet the situation today, as Rubin's, Shattuck's, Vendler's, and Ellis's essays attest, still reflects an extreme anxiety about any kind of criticism that seems non-literary, interdisciplinary, abstract, theoretical, or not primarily devoted to "close reading" of particular texts. On the one hand, most people acknowledge that the New Critical movement erred in limiting itself to the words on the page; but at the same time, this New Critical practice retains its potent influence, because it is so firmly in place as the natural form for "criticism" to take. It is true that many departments of literature include in their course offerings the study of topics and issues similar to those to which Leavis refers. But many do *not,* and most of us, I believe, condescend towards such courses: they are not "literary," and are therefore unserious and tolerated only for the sake of departmental enrollments. The "close criticism" of literature is our means of explaining and justifying our discipline to ourselves—this New Critical habit dies hard. It disturbs us to feel that the survival of "literature" departments depends on courses in media, popular culture, contemporary critical theory, interdisciplinary studies, and the like. And this has the effect of making our public calls for a return to the close reading of literature all the more fervent—as if by promoting "practical criticism" passionately enough, we could recast criticism and make it once again a discipline nearly autonomous.

But invoking this New Critical tenet is the wrong way to defend our discipline. For it is, in fact, the New Critical determination to identify our discipline as one that emphasizes "close reading," to the exclusion of all else, that has led to that crisis in literary studies which many feel so acutely. To put the matter as directly as possible: "close reading" is the problem, not the solution. It is unquestionably basic to the discipline, but is not the discipline itself and does not specify the only or the essential task that the teacher-critic undertakes. "Literature" forms one group or body of texts that we study; there are other kinds of texts, and we turn to them because we realize, as Leavis points out, that the practical criticism of literature is not enough to fulfill the demands of a responsible, truly critical mind. Literature, however much we cherish it, is not what Ransom suggests that it is—"the best of all possible worlds." And criticism cannot be purely "literary"; other studies should enrich our interpretive work, and we involve ourselves in them in order to extend our critical practice, turning it, finally, into more than just the close reading of classic texts. Instead of perceiving interdisciplinary, theoretical, and cultural studies as interfering with the real business of criticism, we should see them as further evidence of how capacious and wide-ranging criticism can be.

In his account of a revised plan for the English Tripos, Leavis notes some of the areas and issues that criticism ought to embrace. His list concentrates on the seventeenth century and is too lengthy to quote in its entirety, but it consists of more than twenty topics—for example, "the rise of capitalism," "economic individualism," "the changing relations between sophisticated and popular culture," "the rise of the Press," "general comparison with French development." Undertaking this work, as a natural outgrowth of training in literary criticism, prepares and shapes the mind as a "co-ordinating consciousness." Such a critical enterprise attempts to integrate various kinds of analysis and research, and it strives to demonstrate the relationships among the materials that are now divided up according to the discipline that claims the sole right to study them.

Identifying criticism with the close reading of classic texts has not served us well, and we ought to be aware of the cost that it exacts when we seek to ground our discipline upon it. Many of our students—to say nothing of their teachers—are skilled at textual interpretation but are at a total loss when asked to speak in a critically informed manner about their politics, attitudes towards history, and "awareness of the environment" in which they live. And they are at a loss, at least in part, because we confine criticism to literature, devaluing other techniques and other kinds of texts and materials. No wonder it sometimes seems both to us and to our students that their critical thinking ends when there are no more literature courses to be taken in school: it is as though the close reading of the classics is the only way in which criticism may be exercised, as though the only "criticism" is the New Criticism.

The essays by Rubin, Shattuck, Vendler and Ellis might appear to indicate otherwise, but there have been signs in recent years that the New Critical reign is at last coming to a close. Much contemporary theory can be dismissed as a set of passing fads and fancies, but the revival of "history" as an instrument for criticism is a truly important development. This has come about through the labors of a number of theorists and critics, including Michel Foucault, Edward Said, Fredric Jameson, and others. What they have shown, in their different ways, is that "history" does not have to imply—as it did for the scholars the New Critics attacked in the 1930's—a narrow and naive review of sources, backgrounds, and influences. For Foucault and those influenced by him, "history" means the formation of an archive, the building up of a rich, detailed, and complex discursive field. The ground for criticism, from this point of view, is not the classic literary text, but inter-textual configurations and arrangements; "criticism" thus entails the study of power, political uses of language, and orders of discourse. This seems to me immensely productive, and the research that has already begun to emerge strikes me as extremely promising. There is reason to hope that the kinds of suggestions made by Leavis in the 1940's can finally be realized, and in ways far more sophisticated than anything he could imagine or doubtless would wish to sponsor.

But it is precisely because certain signs are hopeful that I see all the more reason to be wary and suspicious, and all the more need to recognize that the lines of resistance to significant change are still strong. In the years ahead, as our profession is faced with declining enrollments, budget cutbacks, and the other hard realities that accompany living in a diminished world, we will be urged by people, both inside and outside the institution, to get back to basics—a core curriculum, expository writing, and "close reading" of the masterpieces. This will tighten the hold of the New Criticism upon us, and it will become increasingly difficult to give more than momentary attention to other programs and proposals. As in the past, other forms of criticism may appear for a time to displace the New Critical hegemony. But the New Criticism always seems able to outlast its competitors and to draw upon their methods to reinforce the techniques of "practical criticism." The New Criticism has been extraordinarily resilient and has survived many challenges. Even as it is declared dead or on the decline, it remains powerfully present—alive and well, "simply criticism." (pp. 1100-17)

William E. Cain, "The Institutionalization of the New Criticism," in MLN, *Vol. 97, No. 5, December, 1982, pp. 1100-20.*

SANFORD SCHWARTZ

[*In the following excerpt, Schwartz emphasizes the importance of New Criticism in the formation of contemporary approaches to literature.*]

New Criticism was inspired by Modernism, and it turns on the same crucial distinction between instrumental abstraction and immediate experience. It should not surprise us, then, to find the New Critics employing the same set of argumentative strategies as Hulme, Pound, and Eliot. Like their predecessors, the New Critics emphasize both the recovery of immediate experience and the construction of forms that reorder experience. They, too, argue that poetry should maintain a tensional relationship between form and flux. The ideal New Critical poem, like Pound's ideogram and Eliot's "new wholes," holds together rational coherence and experiential complexity, the unity of conceptual form and the diversity of sensory particulars.

The appeal to immediate experience is especially crucial to the Southern New Critics. Ransom and his colleagues opposed the mentality produced by scientific (i.e., Northern) technology, and expressed the abstraction/experience dichotomy in terms of a distinction between scientific discourse, which is abstract and reductive, and poetic discourse, which is concrete and inclusive. Ransom, for instance, asserts [in *The New Criticism*] that poetry must penetrate beneath instrumental abstractions to the reality of immediate experience "dense with its cross-relations and its interpenetrations of content":

> I suggest that the differentia of poetry as discourse is an ontological one. It treats an order of existence, a grade of objectivity, which cannot be treated in scientific discourse. . . . We live in a world which must be distinguished from the world, or the worlds, for there are many of them, which we treat in our scientific discourses. They are its reduced, emasculated, and docile versions. Poetry intends to recover the denser and more refractory original world which we know loosely through our perceptions and memories. By this supposition it is a kind of knowledge which is radically or ontologically distinct.

Ransom in effect reiterates Bergson's distinction between the abstract, quantitative knowledge of science and the concrete, qualitative knowledge of poetry, which brings us back to immediate experience.

However, the New Critics readily shift from this Bergsonian stance to its opposite, identifying poetry not with the experiential flux but with the intelligible forms that order it. Indeed, their emphasis on rational control over the sensory stream seems even more insistent than that of Pound and Eliot. Surveying more than two decades of literary innovation, some of the New Critics were appalled by the excesses of Modernist experimentation, which seemed to sacrifice logical clarity for experiential immediacy. Winters and Blackmur were especially concerned with this indifference to principles of order. In *Primitivism and Decadence* (1937), Winters condemns the fallacy of "expressive" form—the attempt to present the sensory stream directly by abandoning the mediation of the rational intellect. It is characteristic of modern poets, Winters asserts, "to express a state of uncertainty by uncertainty of expression; whereas the sound procedure would be to make a lucid and controlled statement regarding the condition of uncertainty, a procedure, however, which would require that the poet understand the nature of uncertainty, not that he be uncertain." Similarly, in *The Double Agent* (1935) and *The Expense of Greatness* (1940), Blackmur argues that the modern artist should order his immediate impressions into intelligible form:

> Form, we might say, is the only sanity—the only principle of balanced response—possible to art: as lyric form will make the right nonsense into poetry; and to force your material—which is to say to condense, to elaborate, to foreshorten and give perspective and direction—into your chosen form so as to express it primarily by actualizing it—that is the minimum of your rational responsibility.

For Blackmur as for Winters, form is closely allied to reason: it is the poet's "rational responsibility" to impose coherent principles of order on the otherwise chaotic flux of sensations.

This insistence on rational control notwithstanding, New Critics such as Blackmur position themselves between the extremes of form and flux. Blackmur urges the poet to resist not only the lapse into sensory chaos but also the lure of reductive

ideologies. Other New Critics adopt the same position. Ransom wants to combine the logical "structure" of rational argument with the felt "texture" of concrete experience. Tate wishes to balance the "extensive" comprehension of the intellect and the "intensive" power of direct intuition. Winters, in a similar manner, seeks to unify thought and feeling, rational "denotation" and emotional "connotation." The ideal for all these critics is poetry that establishes order without violating our sense of experiential complexity. The New Critics, like Pound and Eliot before them, envision a tensional relationship between identity and difference, the stability of conceptual form and the free play of the sensory flux.

It has been years since anyone regarded Modernism as truly modern or New Criticism as really new. "The Waste Land" has receded into the postwar gloom of the Twenties, and John Donne has returned to the company of mere mortals. Signs of change began to appear in the late Fifties. Robert Lowell published his *Life Studies* in 1959, and his turn from the style of Ransom and Tate to a poetry of direct self-disclosure was a portent of things to come. A similar change was taking place in the academy, where interest in Romanticism started to revive and scholars began to challenge the Classicism of Eliot and the New Critics. At the same time critics grew tired of paradox and ambiguity, and began to look for new sources of inspiration, first from critics such as Northrop Frye and then from a succession of Continental sources, which provided new strategies for reading and awakened interest in disciplines once considered marginal to literary study. After several decades of dramatic change, New Criticism now seems as quaint as the tradition it replaced. In books with titles such as *After the New Criticism* it has become a point zero from which to measure the gains of the last twenty-five years. Many now look back upon their New Critical heritage as a kind of provincial embarrassment, a reminder of the humble origins they have left behind.

Nevertheless, there is a widespread suspicion, common to advocates and adversaries alike, that the new modes of criticism bear an unmistakable resemblance to the old. This suspicion is well-founded, and at least one reason for the continuity between past and present is that Modernist/New Critical poetics is related more closely than is ordinarily assumed to Nietzsche, Saussure, and other sources of contemporary theory. As we have seen, Modernist views of abstraction and experience proceed from the same inversion of Platonism that engaged Bergson and Nietzsche in the late nineteenth century and attracts post-structuralist critics today. Modernist poetics also anticipates the contemporary "decentering of the subject," which derives from the common turn-of-the-century assumption that ordinary consciousness is structured by forces of which it is unaware. In addition, we have seen that the Modernist emphasis on the "swift perception of relations" is tied to Nietzsche's approach to literal and figurative language, which plays an important role in post-structuralist criticism. In this respect as well as others, Modernist and New Critical poetics prepared the way for more recent developments in literary theory.

To be sure, the continuities between old and new should not be overstressed. While they address similar problems, Modernism and post-structuralism respond with different answers. The differences, however, are not as great as they may seem, and they are akin to those that distinguish James and Nietzsche. The Modernists, like James, are less extreme in their challenge to the traditional hierarchy that privileges rational form over sensory flux. Their strategy is to employ constructs that hold together identity and difference, conceptual unity and sensory multiplicity. Like James, they hold that invention is tied to discovery: a new form projects a coherent system of relations that may disclose new aspects of reality itself. In response to the same issue, post-structuralism assumes the more radical posture of Nietzsche. It does not merely challenge but deliberately subverts the hierarchy that grants priority to form over flux. Instead of maintaining tensional relationships between opposing terms—abstraction/sensation, unity/multiplicity, identity/difference—it resolves the traditionally privileged term into a special case of the subordinate term. In other words, Modernist identity-in-difference yields to the free play of difference. The text that embodies a unified system of relations gives way to the "absolutely plural text," which is irreducible to a determinate network of relations and suggests ever new ways of ordering its various elements. Interpretation no longer involves the unification of discordant or opposing elements but rather the "teasing out of warring forces of signification within the text itself." Here again we find the long shadow of Nietzsche, whose vision of the cosmic flux as a ceaseless play of differences set the stage for contemporary criticism.

These differences between old and new are not to be minimized, and their implications for critical practice are significant. But the very terms that distinguish these two traditions suggest the affiliations between them. These terms are often identified with post-structuralism but rarely with Modernism and New Criticism; that is to say, we have failed to appreciate the conceptual foundations of the Anglo-American tradition, which is deeply involved with philosophical issues that are generally considered the exclusive province of the Continental tradition. Paradoxically, the failure to grasp this dimension of the Anglo-American heritage can be attributed in part to New Criticism itself, which aggravated the development of highly specialized and relatively isolated disciplines in English-speaking universities. The New Critics maintained that a poem is irreducible to the viewpoint of history, philosophy, or any other extrinsic discipline, and in their effort to preserve the integrity of the text, they encouraged the study of literary texts in isolation from their surrounding contexts. While students learned how to cope with ambiguity, paradox, and other complex features of Modernist verse, they were not encouraged to investigate the intellectual milieu in which these features rose to the fore. (pp. 210-15)

> Sanford Schwartz, *"The New Criticism and Beyond," in his* The Matrix of Modernism: Pound, Eliot, and Early Twentieth-Century Thought, *Princeton University Press, 1985, pp. 209-15.*

CLEANTH BROOKS [INTERVIEW WITH AYYAPPA PANIKER]

[*In the following excerpt from an interview conducted in 1982, Brooks responds to recent developments in literary criticism, contrasting them with the New Criticism.*]

Paniker: I should like our discussion to lead on to some comments on the current developments in American literary criticism, especially those emanating from Yale. I have in mind such things as the theory of de-construction, the theory of the anxiety of poetic influence, and the theory of subjective criticism based on reader-response. Would you like to say anything about them as a kind of corrective to New Criticism?

Cleanth Brooks in the 1940s.

Brooks: Yes. I don't know the various criticisms very well. I am doing a lot of reading on them just now. I would say—I would use this term first—the best definition of a heresy, a religious heresy, say, is to regard it as a partial truth which is masquerading as primary truth or as the whole truth. It seems to me that all of these people maintain some partial truths. Thus I think I would agree with Harold Bloom that some poets are very conscious of earlier poets, master poets, that they feel they are competing with. But I don't think, all poets do. I know many poets who tend to feel that they are competing with themselves rather than with some poetic ancestor. An anxiety of influence may occur. On the other hand, I don't see it as typical and certainly not as necessarily present. I think it can be pushed to absurdity. As far as writers like Stanley Fish are concerned well, yes, he also has a partial truth. We do need readers, and, there are linguistic communities with their own conventions. Richards showed the importance of the reader, how various his reactions to the same work may be long ago in his *Practical Criticism*. I don't think Fish has added much new. I think that his claims for reader-response are extravagant. As far as the de-constructionists are concerned, it seems to me that there is an instance of where logic has got itself out of hand. It reminds one of the centipede which has got so self-conscious about which foot to move first that he could not walk at all.

I would insist that we do communicate with each other, we do give signals and are understood. I would also say that on any pragmatic basis poems do mean something about the world, about reality. Some of us here at Yale and at other places think that de-constructionism is born out of the despair of Western Europe after the second World War, where some intellectuals feel that here is man alone in an empty and meaningless universe and that human beings cannot know anything about reality at all. Thus, we can say nothing about it. I disagree. I admit that this logic, this philosophy, is intriguing. I admit that I am not up to dealing with it, such as having a refutation to Derrida, though I think there are philosophers who can, do so. But I am inclined to think that commonsense finally has to assert itself here. If I really thought that literature has no reference at all to reality, I would stop bothering with literature.

Paniker: Professor Brooks, you have, I believe, all along been a champion of synthesis, which really is an enlargement of sympathies; and what I find in the practice of deconstructionists is that they are also giving close readings, they are also going behind the appearances, and the techniques are at times similar to what you have done to the poems of Donne or even of Milton. You didn't fall into the group of those who started an unjustifiable attack on Milton. You have always kept out of that. So it seems that as long as they resort to close reading and are able to derive some kind of an interpretation from reading the text closely, whether between the lines or even behind the lines, there should be some way of connecting the earlier Yale school and the present one.

Brooks: I think there are two theories with reference to this matter, and I don't know which one I believe in. I am not really much concerned with them. But here they are. The first is that the newest critics are the offspring of the so-called New Critics. The second is that they have no relation to them whatsoever. I am in no position to give an answer, but I would suppose the latter view was the correct one.

Paniker: The newest critics must have their agony with their father figures: the one that you wrestle with is your father, but then only the strong ones, whether poets or critics, have to wrestle at all.

Brooks: I have heard this view, but again I am not in a position to comment. I can't presume that I am the father of anyone.

Paniker: Struggle is perhaps their way of absorbing the father. It is not rejection or indifference; it is one way of taking the best out of their father into their own self.

Brooks: Perhaps so. As for Derrida, I can mention two people who are friends of mine. One of them has a book, the manuscript of which I have been reading, which argues that Derrida, properly understood, has done something very interesting and very valuable. But he goes on then to develop it in terms of Buddhism and Eastern religions, and then in the last section uses it as a brilliant way for coming to understand the Christian doctrine of Trinity. Well, this is very interesting. This would be, I suppose, turning Derrida on his head, or at least the current interpretation of Derrida upside down. I can't pass judgement, for I don't know enough about Derrida. There is another friend who again is fascinated by Derrida, and thinks that what Derrida has really done is not to dethrone the so-called New Criticism, but only to open up some further avenues for criticism, critical ideas that are in fact compatible with it. I am eager to see his book. But again, I don't know whether its argument is convincing.

Paniker: The critic also, you will grant, has to be a creator, like the poet who is a maker. And there is some destruction involved in any act of creation.

Brooks: I think that is true, although I want to be very careful here. I think, the critic ought to be very humble. If he claims to be a creator, and a case can be made for him as a creator, well and good. But I think the current tendency to turn the critic into a man of poetic powers calls for scepticism. I prefer for the critic to be content with his secondary role.

Paniker: Well, when you interpret a poem like Wordsworth's "A slumber did my spirit seal," can it not be considered a kind of creative "misreading"? And to the extent you have done that, you may be said to anticipate the revisionists and the de-constructionists.

Brooks: It may be true. But, again, I want to look very warily at that. Such a creative role is quite limited. It is true occasionally a critic has found something in a poem, of which the poet was hardly conscious, or perhaps quite unconscious. If the critic's discovery is compatible with other aspects of the poem and actually makes it richer, more interesting, and finally more coherent, again well and good. He has indeed participated in the creative process. But if he is a true poet, why bother to de-construct someone else's poem? Let him scribble something of his own and then de-construct it into poetry— or, better still, start from scratch and write his own poem.

Paniker: Isn't it the same kind of "misunderstanding" or "misinterpretation" that the New Critics too had been blamed for in their time?

Brooks: We were accused of taking the poem away from the poet. Oh, yes.

Paniker: Isn't this something similar to that?

Brooks: It is certainly; it begets the same charge. But the real question is how far is the charge true with the New Critics, and how far is the charge true with the newest.

Paniker: Perhaps when the first flush of enthusiasm is over, some synthesis will be achieved.

Brooks: I wrote something very brashly in my early days, and perhaps have made further brash statements since. On the other hand, I cannot ever remember ever pretending that I was doing anything more than helping the reader read the poem. I never claimed that I could push the poet aside.

Paniker: Maybe, when you discover the hidden God in Hemingway you too are engaged in creative "misreading," ignoring the claims or protests of the author.

Brooks: Maybe so. But you see I would deny that this is Bloom's kind of misreading. What was it that Hemingway was trying to say? It is at least possible that Hemingway, if he were alive, might say that I had interpreted him properly, though I think it unlikely that he would admit that any interpretation of any sort was necessary. In any case, my view was not that I had a licence to misread him. I was simply attempting clarification.

Paniker: Of course, "misreading" is always within quotes.

Brooks: But Bloom's view seems to be that nobody can read a poem correctly. Well, I will go along with him this far: if he means that every reader does his own reading, which is probably tinged with his own personality, his own myopia. I would agree with that. We don't have in the flesh a truly ideal reader. But that is very different from saying: since we all misread, long live misreading!

Paniker: I would say that Bloom too is equally free from historicism and sociological obsessions, and in that sense close to the Formalists and the New Critics.

Brooks: In a way he is. On the other hand, it is very interesting that the people he prefers to deal with have come from certain historical periods. He doesn't deal with Shakespeare. He doesn't deal with Chaucer.

Paniker: That is because they came before the Flood.

Brooks: But then I would question, you see, who sanctioned his driving a flood right through our cultural history. To posit a "flood" calls for sociological and historical reasons.

Paniker: That is perhaps purely incidental. Just as you had to focus attention on Donne and the Metaphysical Poets for proving the efficacy of irony and the relevance of wit.

Brooks: My memory—though it may be an error—is that I came to a realization of the power of irony more from reading modern poets like Eliot and Ransom than through Donne. But I would appeal to the text to evidence that it can occur also in a Wordsworth or a Keats. In any case, what would seem to count is to establish fully that it occurs in poetry of every period. I will be more easily persuaded of the importance of the anxiety of influence if it could be shown to be universal with examples from Chaucer and Shakespeare as well as from Wordsworth and Wallace Stevens. (pp. 142-46)

> Cleanth Brooks and Ayyappa Paniker, in an interview in The Literary Criterion, *Vol. XVII, No. 2, 1982, pp. 127-46.*

MURRAY KRIEGER

[*In the following essay, Krieger compares the New Criticism with the later critical schools of Structuralism and Post-Structuralism.*]

It was when I read J. Hillis Miller's survey of last year's books in literary criticism (in the November 29, 1975 issue of *The New Republic*) that I realized it was time to consider again, in such new light as he throws, the contributions of the New Criticism—as represented, say, by John Crowe Ransom in *The World's Body* (1938) and *The New Criticism* (1941), by Allen Tate in *On the Limits of Poetry* (1948) and *The Forlorn Demon* (1953), and by Cleanth Brooks in *The Well Wrought Urn* (1947). I have been told that my book, *The New Apologists for Poetry* (1956), helped bury the New Critics 20 years ago; if so, Miller's essay prompts me to try to exhume them. For I had hoped that post-New-Critical movements, while sophisticating their epistemology and resisting their mystifications, would build upon their insights. But Miller's essay reminds us how thoroughly all vestiges of that old New Criticism have been swept away by the new wave of our newer criticism, dominated by recent continental influences. As he shows us, recent critical fashions in the academy have sprung forth from assumptions that altogether preclude those of the New Criticism, thereby denying us their methods of literary analysis and the considerable fruits which such methods could bear. If our newer new criticisms go as Miller sees them going, then all continuity with earlier criticism in our century is severed, and we must unsay some rich decades of critical sayings. So I thought it worth looking again at what was being recanted and measuring the cost of that recantation.

What seems, from Miller's alien perspective, most central and unifying in the varied writers we (sometimes unfairly) have lumped together as New Critics is their insistence on the linguistic presence of (and *in*) the poem. Because they attribute to each poem the power to generate its verbal form, they see poems as entities uniquely privileged to struggle with and overcome the (otherwise) universal character of language, which, for them as for the Structuralists, tends to degenerate into empty signs. This claim to the victory of verbal presence in poems—and, through it, the refounding of meaning in words—is the common conclusion of Ransom's licensing of a self-generating ontology (in "Poetry: A Note in Ontology," the key essay in *The World's Body,* and "Wanted: An Ontological Critic," the all-resolving final chapter of *The New Criticism*), of Tate's notions—at once hybrid and synthetic—of "tension" and "proximate incarnations" (in "Tension in Poetry" from *On the Limits of Poetry* and "The Symbolic Imagination" from *The Forlorn Demon*), and of Brooks' paradoxical justification of poetic irony (throughout *The Well Wrought Urn*).

I have suggested what may sound surprising: that these New Critics hold certain notions about the workings of language in common with the Structuralists, who represent a dominating force in that continentally influenced criticism championed by Miller. But I also suggested, as a qualification to this agreement, that critics like Ransom, Tate and Brooks argue for the emptiness of verbal signifiers only while insisting upon exempting poetry from such general linguistic incapacities, building the very function of poetry upon this exemption. That is to say, they see the poem as generating a verbal form which reveals itself in its power to fill its signifiers with meanings—those very signifiers which, in their habitual use, have previously lost all meaning. Despite this crucial qualification, it remains important for us to see the similarities between the New Critical and the Structuralist conception of normal language behavior.

One may see I. A. Richards functioning for these New-Critical claims much as Ferdinand de Saussure functioned from Structuralism, with each providing a rudimentary linguistic analysis which becomes the basis for the criticism that followed. The New Critics derive from Richards' dualistic opposition between sign and thing in his argument for the referentiality of science and the nonreferentiality of poetry, much as the Structuralist needs Saussure's opposition between signifier and signified to define discourse as the manifold dispositions of empty signifiers. The difference, of course, is that New Critics, anti-positivists all, tended to be less faithful to Richards' dichotomy than Structuralists have proved to be to Saussure's. The New-Critical contribution consists in their struggle to convert Richards' linguistic reductionism into a theory that can account for the newly embodied world they find in poems, even if it is but a world of words. For *these* words are full, and their fullness is one with their meaning, though a meaning founded (and found) only in their form. Ransom, for example, freely grants the arbitrariness of language in its sensory dimension as sound—grants it as freely as any Structuralist would—but he sees the poem as parading that arbitrariness with a self-consciousness that makes it the necessary precondition for the poem's presence—as well as for the presence and fullness of its meaning.

Here, then, is the parting of the ways between the New Criticism and the Structuralism with which it seems to share a common view about the general workings of language.

Though both may agree that there is an absence of proper signifieds in language generally, the New Critic insists on allowing for the presence in poems of a discourse that generates and fills itself with its own signifieds. As esthetic elitists, they see the debased democracy of *écriture* being forced to yield the privilege that each true poem earns for itself as a closed verbal system. If humanists these days view the world of words as one emptied of meaning just as the world itself has been emptied of God, these humanists see that world as being forced to sustain—though it is belied by—a word now made flesh by man as poet, who creates a verbal identity within a linguistic system of ineluctable differences. It is their holding open this opportunity to create a verbal presence that has left them vulnerable to the monolithic positivism of spirit that has succeeded them.

I press this comparison between the New Criticism and Structuralism because of the extent to which—as Miller reminds us in his survey—all academic criticism that "counts" today (which is to say, all criticism that is currently fashionable in the academy) is continentally derived, the dominant continental modes being assumed to be Structuralist and Post-Structuralist. Indeed, in the Miller essay itself it seems enough to dismiss the sensitive study of George Herbert by Helen Vendler (the first book Miller mentions) by praising her as "the most distinguished contemporary practitioner of the New Critical tradition of 'close reading.'" Since such an attachment means that she is likely to be "implicitly hostile to continental criticism or indifferent to it" (and is "mostly innocent, whether innocently, or not, of any continental tinge"), it is clearly time, after the single sentence mentioning the book, for Miller to move past it toward what he sees as theoretically more consequential (which is to say, theoretically more fashionable) works, which he can treat at his leisure. About the Herbert volume we are left with the implication, splendid work, though quaint.

What accounts for the current domination of the critical scene by the continental ideas we associate with the terms "Structuralism" and "Post-Structuralism" is their antagonism to verbal and poetic presence, which is the very heart of New-Critical doctrine. Wary of presence as mythical delusion, they succumb to metaphysical emptiness and would have it sanction a verbal emptiness that not even poetic powers can replenish. Seeing all our books authorized by the original Book authored by God, the Structuralist finds the belief in the word to die with the death of our belief in the Creator whose Word gave all words meaning: when God evacuates our world, meaning evacuates our language. All wordly signifieds follow the Transcendental Signified out of our realm, the empty shell of Word and words. Such are the existentialist assumptions behind the Structuralist negations, the latter being the linguistic consequences of "the disappearance of God" (to borrow the title of one of Miller's books).

The work of Paul de Man, to whose importance Miller testifies in his essay, continually emphasizes the desperate inability of our language, since the early Romantics, to bridge the gap that separates the word from its would-be references in the world. This hopeless distance between signifier and signified is a reflection of the chasm between the interiority of the human subject and the deadly indifference of the object out there on its own. But, de Man to the contrary notwithstanding, the New Critic can claim that a dualistic thematic like his, for all it denies to language and for all the existential failures it visits upon the poet as human subject, need not preclude the poem from creating a monistic verbal structure that contains such denials within its expressive unity. On the one hand for de Man, and for the Structuralist and Phenomenological view he in part inherits, man's existential failure to remake a now alien nature must be echoed by the failure of the poem to remake its language—again a linguistic analysis that masks the theorist's existential anguish. So for him the possibility of poetic union in the created symbol dissolves into the dualism of a hopeless allegory. Poetic absence, with God's, overwhelms us.

Like the New Critic, de Man has inherited the shambles left by the collapse of faith of which Matthew Arnold despaired as he vainly sought to relate poetry to religion. Coming from Arnold, we can go either of two ways: we can view poetry as a human triumph, the creation of verbal meaning in a blank universe to serve as a visionary substitute for a defunct religion, or we can—in our negation—extend our faithlessness, the blankness of our universe, to poetry as well as to our religion. In the latter case, we tend, like de Man, to reject the alternative, affirmative claim as a mystification arising from nostalgia and from metaphysical deprivation. But, retrograde as I am, I am concerned about the loss of the filled and centered word, so that I must recall again the virtues that have now been demythologized, to lament the small gains given us in return for all we have given up.

It must be conceded that the New Critics habitually reified their poetic experiences into an absolute, if mythic, object. What we may see today as a fictional claim about the poem's integral self they uncritically asserted with epistemological naïveté. But their lesson for us today is their unquestioning willingness, consistent with their (and our) critical tradition, to treat the poem as a creative centering of words. It is true also that, in echoing the humanist's insistence on man's obligation to re-fill word and world with meaning—*his* meaning as a lower-case, still creative, creature—the New Critic may be seen, especially from the Structuralist perspective, as falling victim to his own mythologizing powers, which will not face up to the emptiness of his universe. Of course, a critic's defense of the power of the poet, as fiction-maker, to fill his world of words can be made without his turning it into a metaphysical defense of the world's fullness. Must such a critic be charged with invoking the myth of metaphysical presence if he claims no more than a constructed verbal presence?

If belief in the poet's power to find embodiment in the world is a myth, it has been, for the critical tradition in the West from its beginnings, the necessary fiction that has permitted more than two millennia of our greatest poems to speak to us. Few critical schools in our history have done more than the New Critics did to give them voice. Thanks in large part to these critics—but before them as well—the poems have been *there,* speaking as they do, as if there is a presence in them. They make their own case for presence, and it is out of no mere nostalgia that we continue to value it in them. For presence is present tense, and while we live we must not allow ourselves to be reasoned out of it.

It may well be that the Post-Structuralist mood is the most appropriate one to account for the revolutionary art produced in our culture these last decades: an anti-esthetic for an anti-art. The philosophical assault on man's symbols may both mirror and justify what man has been of late doing with them—or refusing to do with them. It would hardly be a flattering comment to suggest that, if Post-Structuralism turns out to be a theoretical partner of recent activities in the arts, they deserve one another. And I trust it is more than just a reactionary comment to suggest that the recent wars on metaphysics and art alike hardly produce worthy successors to the tradition they would destroy. In reconsidering the New Criticism here, I mean to stimulate us to reconsider at the same time the brilliant and extensive artistic repertoire which it was created to serve. These works in our tradition still stand, demanding the traditional esthetic to account for them. It was this esthetic of which the New Criticism represented a climactically productive moment.

I have made more of a school than is perhaps warranted by the several writers whom Miller treats jointly and favorably. Miller admits considerable differences among them, although he goes on to claim their common importance in light of the attention they pay to directions in continental theory, whether sympathetically or not. Certainly the exclusively extended treatment he accords Jacques Derrida, Paul de Man, Geoffrey Hartman and Harold Bloom suggests the embarrassing fact that the only school represented by these critics is Yale University. Yet there is what I have called a Post-Structuralist mood, if not a unified doctrine, in the work of these critics, and it is a mood that is now attracting academic critics throughout the country. That we should find a tentative alliance built on a mood, a temperamental rather than an ideological affinity, attests to the existential rather than the linguistic or methodological motive behind their varied writings.

Even Bloom's recent books can be viewed as making common cause with the others, unlikely as that may at first seem. Bloom licenses the critic to use the present critical occasion to undo and replace the primacy of the historically prior piece of writing (as its author had sought to use his poetic occasion to displace *his* precursor). Any potential presence of the poem that confronts the critic is thus dispersed into what Derrida would term "traces" of the burdensome past, now exploded by the present critic's self-gratifying ego. So the critic, indulging his narcissistic moment as the latest in a sequence of such moments indulged by the poets whom he deceives us into believing to be his subjects, tries to win his competition with his predecessor-poet, substituting his presence for that of the poem which, thus transformed, recedes as an unrecognizable point of origin. The critic supplants his precursor-father, remaking his work into his own. This self-conscious usurpation by the critic of the primary role of the literary work is another version of the Post-Structuralist's reduction of that work to the common domain of *écriture*, which equalizes all discourse and de-privileges the poem, denying its pretense to presence.

It would seem to be this radical reorientation of the role of the critic and the role of the poem as it spins out of our general discursive habits that characterizes the continental mood which Miller, probably accurately, sees as currently most influential. And it is in light of this tendency that the New Critics seem obsolete with their traditional sense of the poem as the critic's object. As we are reminded by Miller of the place of Yale in history's vengeful conspiracy to "de-center" the poem, we may muse ironically about the fact that Yale was not too long ago the equally well-armed bastion of another all-dominating movement—the New Criticism now so severely declared outmoded, one fashion undone by another. Let me compound the irony: if Bloom's theory, so different from and yet finally in tune with some continental theorizing, legitimizes and indeed issues a summons to literary patricide,

it is appropriate, after all, that his generation of Yale critics make this place for themselves by annihilating the preceding generation of Yale critics—and with an intensity and exclusiveness equal to theirs. In its consequences for our culture, however, the act is a negative one, an enactment of the murder of the past which modern society through its art has generally been practicing. The New Criticism reminds us that we can de-center past objects and can undo their presence only by obliterating all entities, ours among them. The murder of our fathers leads not to the assertion, but to the denial, of ourselves. (pp. 32-4)

> *Murray Krieger, "Reconsideration," in* The New Republic, *Vol. 175, No. 14, October 2, 1976, pp. 32-4.*

FURTHER READING

Arac, Jonathan. "Coleridge and New Criticism Reconsidered." In his *Critical Genealogies: Historical Situations for Postmodern Literary Studies,* pp. 81-95. New York: Columbia University Press, 1987.
    Revision of his "Repetition and Exclusion: Coleridge and New Criticism Reconsidered," which appeared in *Boundary 2* 8, No. 1 (Fall 1979). Arac examines Robert Penn Warren's "A Poem of Pure Imagination" (1916), which he considers "a crucial document in the struggle that allowed criticism to supplant scholarship as the major activity by which even academic teachers and students of literature defined their relations to the texts they read."

Barrett, William, et al. "The New Criticism." *The American Scholar* 20, Nos. 1, 2 (Winter 1950-51; Spring 1951): 86-104, 218-31.
    Transcript of a discussion involving Barrett, Kenneth Burke, Malcolm Cowley, Robert Gorham Davis, Hiram Haydn, and Allen Tate.

Bové, Paul A. "R. P. Blackmur and the Job of the Critic: Turning from the New Criticism." *Criticism* 25, No. 4 (Fall 1983): 359-80.
    Considers Blackmur's relationship to New Criticism, his rejection of the Humanism of Irving Babbitt and the Rhetoric of Kenneth Burke, and his response to Modernist literature.

Bradbury, John M. *The Fugitives: A Critical Account.* Chapel Hill: University of North Carolina Press, 1958, 300 p.
    Includes chapters on the critical theories of Cleanth Brooks and Robert Penn Warren, Allen Tate, and John Crowe Ransom.

Bradbury, Malcolm. "Introduction: The State of Criticism Today." In *Contemporary Criticism,* edited by Malcolm Bradbury and David Palmer, pp. 11-38. London: Edward Arnold, 1970.
    Defines and assesses New Criticism's place in the history of twentieth-century criticism. According to Bradbury, "In trying to define the appropriate aspects of its activity, [New Criticism] increasingly pointed to one primary object of critical attention—not the critic's own appreciative sensibility; not the writer's biography or psychological background; not his intellectual, social or historical context; not the creative process or the readerly response; but the one central, ascertainable object that critics could discuss in common and constantly refer to: the text, the 'words on the page'."

Bredin, Hugh. "I. A. Richards and the Philosophy of Practical Criticism." *Philosophy and Literature* 10, No. 1 (April 1986): 26-37.
    Close examination of Richards's assertions about literature, language, and reading as set forth in his *Principles of Literary Criticism.* Bredin concludes that "Richards has been extraordi-

narily influential both on literary theory and on critical practice. In his separation of poem and context we find the seeds of the intentional fallacy; and in his separation of readers from one another we find the seeds of the affective fallacy. His identification of a poem with the experience of it, and the distinction of poem from text, are ideas often discussed nowadays as if they had been newly minted."

Bromwich, David. "Revisiting the New Critics." *Commentary* 54, No. 5 (November 1972): 79-82.

Retrospective essay occasioned by the publication of *Beating the Bushes: Selected Essays 1941-1970* by John Crowe Ransom and *A Shaping Joy: Studies in the Writer's Craft* by Cleanth Brooks. Bromwich discusses similarities and differences in the critical approaches of the New Critics.

Brooks, Cleanth. "The Critics Who Made Us: I. A. Richards and Practical Criticism." *The Sewanee Review* 89, No. 4 (Fall 1981): 586-95.

Appreciative overview emphasizing Brooks's debt to and departure from Richards's critical theories as expounded in *Practical Criticism* and *Principles of Literary Criticism.*

Bush, Douglas. "The New Criticism: Some Old-Fashioned Queries." *PMLA* 64, Part 2 (March 1949): 13-21.

Disparages the general disregard for scholarship he finds in the works of several New Critics.

Core, George. "New Critic, Antique Poet." *The Sewanee Review* 77, No. 1 (Winter 1969): 508-16.

Assesses Ransom's place in literary history as a critic and poet. According to Core, "Ransom is the most philosophical of the group he labelled 'New Critics,' yet he denounces the abstraction that is frequently associated with philosophical thinking and demands concreteness and specificity in poetry. For him the true richness of a poem is found in its local texture of language and metaphor—not in the intended fable and theme, the logical structure or argument."

Crane, R. S. "I. A. Richards on the Art of Interpretation." In *Critics and Criticism: Ancient and Modern,* edited by R. S. Crane, pp. 27-44. Chicago: University of Chicago Press, 1952.

Aristotelian reassessment of Richards's general concepts and particular practices in the study of language, literature, and interpretation. Crane's essay was written in 1939 and originally appeared in *Ethics* (January 1949).

Day, Douglas. "The Background of the New Criticism." *Journal of Aesthetics and Art Criticism* 24, No. 3 (Spring 1966): 429-40.

Sketches currents in early twentieth-century literary criticism and how they influenced the leading figures of New Criticism.

Elton, William. *A Glossary of the New Criticism.* Chicago: Modern Poetry Association, 1949, 48 p.

Catalogs and defines many of the technical terms used by New Critics.

Graff, Gerald. "Cleanth Brooks: New Critical Organicism." In his *Poetic Statement and Critical Dogma,* pp. 87-111. Evanston: Northwestern University Press, 1970.

Examines Brooks's critical theory as a New Critical model, focusing on the validity of its definition of poetry as organic and essentially dramatic rather than assertive or propositional.

————."What Was New Criticism? Literary Interpretation and Scientific Objectivity." *Salmagundi,* No. 27 (Summer-Fall 1974): 72-93.

Contends that New Criticism did not represent a literary form of scientism as numerous detractors of the movement have maintained. According to Graff, "To view New Critical interpretation as analogous to empirical-scientific method is a misrepresentation, based on stereotyped prejudices about the nature of objectivity and a failure to examine what the New Critics actually said and why they said it."

Hardy, John Edward. "The Achievement of Cleanth Brooks." *The Hopkins Review* 6, Nos. 3-4 (Spring-Summer 1953): 148-61.

Appreciative overview of Brooks's contributions to literary criticism and education.

Harth, Phillip. "The New Criticism and Eighteenth-Century Poetry." *Critical Inquiry* 7, No. 3 (Spring 1981): 521-37.

Seeks the polemical origins of New Criticism through an examination of its practitioners' esteem for the poetry of John Dryden, Alexander Pope, and others.

Holman, C. Hugh. "The Defense of Art: Criticism since 1930." In *The Development of American Literary Criticism,* edited by Floyd Stovall, pp. 199-245. 1955. Reprint. Westport, Conn.: Greenwood Press, 1980.

Outlines the development of New Criticism and discusses the major tenets advanced by its most prominent advocates. Holman also surveys Marxist criticism, psychological criticism, and other recent theories.

Jayne, Edward. "The Rise and Fall of New Criticism: Its Brief Dialectic History from I. A. Richards to Northrop Frye." *Amerikastudien/American Studies* 22, No. 1 (1977): 107-22.

Traces the development and codification of Anglo-American New Criticism as it was shaped by Richards, Frye, Cleanth Brooks, John Crowe Ransom, René Wellek, W. K. Wimsatt, and Yvor Winters.

Knickerbocker, William S., ed. *Twentieth Century English.* New York: Philosophical Library, 1946, 460 p.

Includes "The Meaning of the 'New Criticism' " by Walter J. Ong and "The New Criticism and Scholarship" by Cleanth Brooks.

Krieger, Murray. *The New Apologists for Poetry.* Minneapolis: University of Minnesota Press, 1956, 225 p.

Analyzes and compares the critical theories of T. S. Eliot, T. E. Hulme, I. A. Richards, and the American New Critics, in a study focusing on the psychology of poetic creativity, the structure of the poem as an aesthetic object, and the function of poetry.

Lee, Brian. "The New Criticism and the Language of Poetry." In *Essays on Style and Language: Linguistic and Critical Approaches to Literary Style,* edited by Roger Fowler, pp. 29-52. London: Routledge and Kegan Paul, 1966.

Discusses attempts to define the nature of poetic discourse, including theories advanced by R. P. Blackmur, Cleanth Brooks, Isabel Hungerland, John Crowe Ransom, and I. A. Richards, examining the growing preoccupation of modern critics with literary language.

Leggett, B. J. "Notes for a Revised History of the New Criticism: An Interview with Cleanth Brooks." *Tennessee Studies in Literature* 24 (1979): 1-35.

Reflections on Brooks's participation in the New Critical movement, including discussion of its major figures and responses to opponents.

MacCabe, Colin. "The Cambridge Heritage: Richards, Empson, and Leavis." *Southern Review* (Adelaide) 19, No. 3 (November 1986): 242-49.

Discusses strengths and weaknesses of I. A. Richards's theory of language, William Empson's studies in literary language, which build on Richards's work, and F. R. Leavis's contribution to the subject in emphasizing the social nature of language.

Marcotte, Paul J. "What the 'Ontological Critic' in the Authors of *Understanding Poetry* Adds to the 'New Criticism' of Brooks and Warren." In *The Modernists: Studies in a Literary Phenomenon: Essays in Honor of Harry T. Moore,* edited by Lawrence B. Gamache and Ian S. MacNiven, pp. 46-60. Rutherford, N.J.: Farleigh Dickinson University Press, 1987.

Appreciative examination of the New Critical conception of poetry as it was outlined and revised in successive editions of Cleanth Brooks and Robert Penn Warren's *Understanding Poetry.*

Mastrangelo, Aida. "Benedetto Croce and the New Critics." *Studi Americani* 9 (1963): 455-65.

Examines similarities and differences between the aesthetic theories of Benedetto Croce and the New Critics.

Misra, Sadananda. "New Criticism vs. Structuralism." *Indian Journal of American Studies* 10, No. 2 (July 1980): 40-9.

Critiques structuralism and discusses the widespread adoption of its tenets, comparing its usefulness and validity for literature with that of New Criticism. According to Misra, "New Criticism's contribution has a permanent value in that it has brought about a harmony between the poetic consciousness and the formal elements in literary art. Structuralism, on the other hand, is formalism run amuck."

Muller, H. J. "The New Criticism in Poetry." *The Southern Review* (Baton Rouge) 6, No. 4 (Spring 1941): 811-39.

Discusses *The Expense of Greatness* by R. P. Blackmur and *Modern Poetry and the Tradition* by Cleanth Brooks in a review of several contemporary critical works. Muller praises New Criticism's "fine apprehension of the imaginative object, fine appreciation of the concrete poetic experience, [and] fine criticism of purely aesthetic values" but warns that New Critics "are beginning to suffer from inbreeding and to become victims of their half-truth. They are tending toward a narrow aestheticism in which they not only distinguish but disparage the 'ulterior' bearings of literature."

Narasimhaiah, C. D. "New Criticism: An Assessment." In *Indian Essays in American Literature: Papers in Honour of Robert E. Spiller,* edited by Sujit Mukherjee and D. V. K. Raghavacharyulu, pp. 267-84. Bombay: Popular Prakashan, 1968.

Considers the backgrounds, methods, assessments of major authors of English literary tradition, and impact of New Criticism on the future of literary criticism. According to Narasimhaiah: "(1) [New Criticism] taught us how to read poetry, that is, to realize that literature has a validity which is expressed in language and that poetry must be read as poetry and not something else. . . . (2) It made revaluations of the poetry of the past. (3) It focussed attention on contemporary achievement as reflecting contemporary consciousness. (4) It enlarged the frontiers of criticism by showing the necessity for a knowledge of other disciplines than literature proper."

Nath, Raj, and Elliot, William I., eds. *Essays in Modern Criticism.* Allahabad, India: Kitab Mahal, 1976, 176 p.

Includes "T. S. Eliot and New Criticism" by Ram Sewak Singh, "A Critique of New Criticism" by Naresh Chandra, and "New Criticism and the Aesthetic Experience" by Y. Sahai.

Ninkovich, Frank A. "The New Criticism and Cold War America." *The Southern Quarterly* 20, No. 1 (Fall 1981): 1-24.

Looks at the role of New Critics and New Criticism in the controversy surrounding the awarding of the Library of Congress's Bollingen Prize in Poetry for 1949 to Ezra Pound, a dispute in which the prevailing aesthetic preoccupations of the era were manifested.

Patnaik, J. N. *The Aesthetics of New Criticism.* Atlantic Highlands, N.J.: Humanities Press, 1983, 96 p.

Emphasizes and analyzes the New Critical concern with form. According to Patnaik, "The New Critics illuminate life by concentrating on form which reflects a sense of integration against the menace of fragmentation and by asserting human values against the pragmatic forces of materialism."

Phillips, William, and Graver, Lawrence. "The State of Criticism: New Criticism to Structuralism." *Partisan Review* 47, No. 3 (1980): 372-96.

Papers outlining the history of modern criticism delivered at Boston University's September 1979 conference on the state of criticism. Phillips focuses on New Criticism, Marxist literary theory, and structuralism; Graver's response and a transcript of ensuing discussion follow.

Plottel, Jeanine Parisier. "New Criticism and Current French Criticism: 'New Criticism' and 'Nouvelle Critique'." *The Hebrew University Studies in Literature* 3, No. 1 (Spring 1975): 93-9.

Defines the relationship between Anglo-American New Criticism, which was largely unknown in France until the late 1960s, and French nouvelle critique. According to Plottel, "To be sure, both *new criticism* and *nouvelle critique* focus on rhetoric and language. But the *new critic* studies the literary object, the poem, the novel itself, while *la nouvelle critique* . . . deals with literary discourse, and uses poetry to illustrate 'la langue poétique'."

Pole, David. "Cleanth Brooks and the New Criticism." *British Journal of Aesthetics* 9 (1969): 285-97.

Close study of Brooks's critical theory. According to Pole, Brooks's "work incorporates and sums up a large tradition, indeed, sums it up and sets it forth systematically; he also quotes and carefully answers his several critics. Brooks, in other words, consciously theorizes—among writers in the field a relatively rare and welcome merit."

Richmond, H. M. "The Dead Albatross: 'New Criticism' as a Humanist Fallacy." *College English* 33, No. 5 (February 1972): 515-31.

Asserts that New Critical concern with style, texture, and manner has altered society's perception of poetry, diminishing, for the most part, the value of poetry for modern individuals except as a recreation for critics.

Robey, David. "Anglo-American New Criticism." In *Modern Literary Theory: A Comparative Introduction,* edited by Ann Jefferson and David Robey, pp. 65-83. Totowa, N.J.: Barnes & Noble, 1982.

Defines the major concepts of New Criticism and compares the movement with Russian Formalism.

Roellinger, Francis X. "Two Theories of Poetry as Knowledge." *The Southern Review* (Baton Rouge) 7, No. 4 (Spring 1942): 690-705.

Focuses on the centuries-long debate about the nature and value of poetry, citing the New Critical ideas of Allen Tate in *Reason in Madness* and John Crowe Ransom in *The New Criticism* as two modern theories defending poetry against positivist assertions that reduce it "to the realm of irresponsible emotion and irrelevant feeling."

Rubin, Louis D., Jr. "Tory Formalists, New York Intellectuals, and the New Historical Science of Criticism." *The Sewanee Review* 88, No. 4 (Fall 1980): 674-83.

Review of Grant Webster's *The Republic of Letters: A History of Postwar American Literary Opinion* (1979; cited below) disparaging his assertion that New Criticism is obsolete. According to Rubin, "If the New Criticism as a movement is concluded, it is because its job has been done: it has made us read poems closely and in their own right, so that we could gain access to the poetry written in English during the first half of the twentieth century."

————."Robert Penn Warren: Critic." In *Renascence Man: Views of Robert Penn Warren,* edited by Walter B. Edgar, pp. 19-37. Baton Rouge: Louisiana State University Press, 1984.

Counters charges that Warren's criticism promotes a bourgeois "conspiracy to propagate the notion of a fixed, unchanging reality" and defines the importance of his criticism in respect to modern criticism in general and to his own creative works. According to Rubin, "To the extent that Mr. Warren is a critic, he is a New Critic. The importance that he places on rendering the complexity of human experience, his belief that there is little in this world that is easy or certain, his assertion of the constant need for exercising discrimination, and his unwillingness to jump at conclusions about one part of a poem without first testing them against other parts of the poem, make the identification inescapable."

Ruoff, Gene W. "The New Criticism: One Child of the 30s that Grew Up." In *The Thirties: Fiction, Poetry, Drama,* edited by Warren French, pp. 169-74. Deland, Fla.: Everett Edwards, 1967.

Recalls the cultural and academic climate of the 1930s against which New Criticism reacted, eventually flourishing as it gained a foothold in university classrooms.

Russo, John Paul. "I. A. Richards in Retrospect." *Critical Inquiry* 8, No. 4 (Summer 1982): 743-60.

Chronological survey of Richards's works and career. According to Russo, "The great strength of Richards' criticism is that it forces attention back toward the work of art. He makes the interaction between the mind and the work of art the center where the process of intelligence takes place, the center from which criticism departs on its theoretical exploration and to which it returns to gain its bearing. For this reason, his aesthetic and semantic methods are humanistic, a celebration of what the mind's reasoning powers can accomplish, down to assessing the ultimate premises of formalism and humanism."

Simpson, Lewis P., ed. *The Possibilities of Order: Cleanth Brooks and His Work.* Baton Rouge: Louisiana State University Press, 1976, 254 p.

Collection of essays by Robert B. Heilman, Walter J. Ong, Monroe K. Spears, Allen Tate, Robert Penn Warren, René Wellek, and Thomas Daniel Young, devoted to Brooks's critical theory and its influence.

Spears, Monroe K. "The Criticism of Allen Tate." *The Sewanee Review* 57, No. 2 (April-June 1949): 317-34.

Review of *On the Limits of Poetry: Selected Essays, 1928-1948* and general discussion of the major tenets of Tate's literary criticism. According to Spears, Tate's criticism is valuable as an aid in understanding his poetry, exemplifies prose of imaginative power and accomplishment equal to his poetry, and offers insightful critical conclusions and masterful analyses of individual works.

Steiner, Wendy. "The Case for Unclear Thinking: The New Critics versus Charles Morris." *Critical Inquiry* 6, No. 2 (Winter 1979): 257-69.

Traces the opposition of New Critics, who held that poetic knowledge is different from scientific or any other type of knowledge, to Morris's semiotics, which is based on the unified science assumption that all reality is one and all disciplines therefore united.

Subbarao, C. "Intrinsic Criticism: Claims and Counter-Claims of the New Critics and the Chicago Critics." In *Asian Responses to American Literature,* edited by C. D. Narasimhaiah, pp. 353-57. Delhi: Vikas Publications, 1972.

Discusses the "distinction between interpretation and criticism, description and evaluation" in the methods of approach of the New Critics and the Chicago Critics.

Swardson, H. R. "The Heritage of the New Criticism." *College English* 41, No. 4 (December 1979): 412-22.

Discusses the development of academic attitudes toward New Criticism and the implementation of New Critical practices in university classrooms.

Szili, József. "The New Criticism." In *Literature and Its Interpretation,* edited by Lajos Nyírő, pp. 115-61. The Hague: Mouton Publishers, 1979.

Focuses on the poetics of Cleanth Brooks, John Crowe Ransom, and Allen Tate, and discusses their development through Fugitivism and Agrarianism.

Thompson, Ewa M. *Russian Formalism and Anglo-American New*

Criticism: A Comparative Study. The Hague: Mouton Publishers, 1971, 160 p.

Outlines the histories, philosophical backgrounds, main concepts, and applications of both movements.

Trowbridge, Hoyt. "Aristotle and the 'New Criticism'." *The Sewanee Review* 52, No. 4 (October-December 1944): 537-55.

Compares the critical principles held by New Critics, particularly Cleanth Brooks and Allen Tate, which draw on Platonic concepts, with the Aristotelian theories advanced by critics of the Chicago school, including R. S. Crane, Richard McKeon, and Elder Olson.

Valentine, K. B. " 'New Criticism' and the Emphasis on Literature in Interpretation." In *Performance of Literature in Historical Perspectives,* edited by David W. Thompson, pp. 549-65. Lanham, Md.: University Press of America, 1983.

Outlines the development of New Criticism and discusses its influence on oral interpretation. Valentine concludes that "After absorbing the basic ideas of New Criticism, interpreters have been stimulated to develop analogous strategies for a new aesthetic of performance. In a sense, Ransom's dictum that human experience can be fully realized only through art has been taken further by interpretation teachers' conviction that literary art can be fully realized only through performance."

Van Deusen, Marshall. "Criticism in the Thirties: The Marxists and the New Critics." *Western Humanities Review* 17 (1963): 75-85.

Considers Marxists and New Critics the two most interesting literary groups of the 1930s and asserts that—though distant on many issues—they shared interests in literature as knowledge and in "the scholarly history of literature as a study of value rather than as a study of fact."

Warren, Austin. "The Achievement of Some Recent Critics." *Poetry* 77, No. 4 (January 1951): 239-43, 245.

Favorable review of *The Importance of Scrutiny: Selections from "Scrutiny: A Quarterly Review," 1932-1948* edited by Eric Bentley and *Critiques and Essays in Criticism, 1920-1948: Representing the Achievement of Modern British and American Critics* edited by R. W. Stallman. According to Warren, "These books illustrate the 'new criticism' at its best, with its virtues of straightforwardness, courage, will to interpret the masters of the past in terms of their relevance to us, not as the vested interests of accredited specialists."

Webster, Grant. "Part II: The New Critics as Tory Formalists." In his *The Republic of Letters: A History of Postwar American Literary Opinion,* pp. 63-206. Baltimore: Johns Hopkins University Press, 1979.

Renames New Criticism "Tory Formalism," a term which, in Webster's opinion, better characterizes the social and intellectual beliefs of the group; defines its basic critical practice as "a method of explication, chiefly of poetry, that is marked by a sense of discipline, a concern with the past as found in the allusions and form of the poem, and an intensive study of the text itself as the embodiment of a paradoxical but ultimately meaningful truth"; and outlines three stages of development of the group: the making of the Tory charter in the 1920s, the Age of Explication (1938-1948), and the Age of Theory (1949-1978). For a review, see Rubin (1980) cited above.

Young, Thomas Daniel. "Editors and Critics." In *The History of Southern Literature,* edited by Louis D. Rubin, Jr., et al., pp. 407-14. Baton Rouge: Louisiana State University Press, 1985.

General survey of the major critical works and concepts of Cleanth Brooks, John Crowe Ransom, Allen Tate, and Robert Penn Warren.

World War I Literature

INTRODUCTION

World War I was the first great international conflict of the twentieth century and is remembered as the first war in which modern technological weapons were used extensively, resulting in massive human casualties and conclusively changing the nature of combat. For many intellectuals, the utter devastation of the Western Front shattered the optimistic belief that a new era of human achievement and cooperation would emerge through continued scientific and social progress. Machine technology, which had previously been regarded as a source of prosperity and comfort, now aided in widespread slaughter, and the brutal nature of combat reminded observers that moral enlightenment could not erase humanity's essential animal nature. Even as it was unfolding, the war presented a vast human drama and an absorbing literary subject, and, viewed historically, the World War I period remains among the most fascinating eras of the twentieth century.

Many European writers and intellectuals actually welcomed the outbreak of war in the summer of 1914; among them were young German and English poets inspired by romantic patriotism who volunteered for service, and, like English poet Rupert Brooke, wrote passionately of their willingness to die for their respective countries. For the most part they offered a poetic summons to battle, espousing such traditionally valorous ideals as honor, duty to the fatherland, and courage in the face of the enemy. As the dehumanizing nature of machine-age warfare became apparent, old values were reassessed by combatants writing from the trenches, and the great battles of the Western Front became the settings of new, realistic portrayals of combat, often containing bitterly satiric portraits of commanding officers, whom many writers blamed for the sweeping casualties in the front lines. Under the uncertain conditions of trench life complicated by disease, inexperienced leadership, and the constant threat of death, the early enthusiasm and optimism of volunteers yielded to a pervasive disillusionment that haunted many writers of the World War I generation for the rest of their lives. Eventually, a compassionate tone—unknown in previous war literature—emerged in the works of several trench poets, who sympathetically portrayed enemy soldiers suffering the same dehumanizing experiences at the front. Although a number of battle chronicles and memoirs found publication in the postwar period, interest in war literature generally declined as society returned to peacetime concerns.

The late 1920s brought a profusion of realistic war literature, prompted by the huge commercial success of Erich Maria Remarque's novel *Im Westen nichts Neues* (*All Quiet on the Western Front*). Controversy arose over the merit of many war books as critics debated the criteria by which they were to be judged. The term "soldier-poet," for instance, had not existed before World War I, and many critics began to consider war poetry as somehow separate from poetry in general due to the pressured, tragic circumstances under which it was written. These commentators considered the candid, explicit presentation of the brutality of modern combat more important than such purely artistic concerns as narrative technique and literary style, while others maintained that war works deserved no allowances for the special nature of their subjects or the author's intention in writing.

Once the "war books" period of the late 1920s and early 1930s subsided, interest in war literature waned. As the renewed threat of war became apparent in the late 1930s, many critics, among them survivors of the World War I generation, mourned the failure of the war testimonies to have any effect in preventing succeeding generations from reenacting the outrages of war. The devastation and horror of combat on the Western Front receded into memory as the destructiveness of technological combat advanced further during World War II, and a new generation of war writers superseded the old.

REPRESENTATIVE WORKS

Aldington, Richard
  Death of a Hero (novel) 1929
Anderson, Maxwell, and Stallings, Laurence
  What Price Glory? (drama) 1924
Barbusse, Henri
  Le feu (novel) 1916
  [*Under Fire,* 1917]
Blunden, Edmund
  Undertones of War (autobiography) 1928; revised edition, 1930
Boyd, Thomas
  Through the Wheat (novel) 1923
Brittain, Vera
  Testament of Youth (autobiography) 1933
Brooke, Rupert
  1914, and Other Poems (poetry) 1915
Cummings, E. E.
  The Enormous Room (novel) 1922
Dorgelès, Roland [pseudonym of Roland Lécavelé]
  Les croix de bois (novel) 1919
  [*Wooden Crosses,* 1920]
Dos Passos, John
  One Man's Initiation: 1917 (novel) 1920; also published as *First Encounter,* 1945
  Three Soldiers (novel) 1921
Duhamel, Georges
  Vie des martyrs: 1914-1916 (short stories) 1917
  [*The New Book of Martyrs,* 1918]
Faulkner, William
  Soldier's Pay (novel) 1926
Ford, Ford Madox
  On Heaven, and Poems Written on Active Service (poetry) 1918
  *Some Do Not . . . (novel) 1924
  *No More Parades (novel) 1925
  *A Man Could Stand Up (novel) 1926
  *The Last Post (novel) 1928
  (*These works were published together as *Parade's End,* 1950.)
Graves, Robert
  Fairies and Fusiliers (poetry) 1917

Goodbye to All That (autobiography) 1929; revised edition, 1957
Grenfell, Julian
  Battle: Flanders (poetry) 1915
Gurney, Ivor
  Severn and Somme (poetry) 1917
Hašek, Jaroslav
  Osudy dobrého vojáka Švejka za světoné války (novel) 1920-1923
  [*The Good Soldier Schweik and His Fortunes in the World War,* 1973]
Hay, Ian [pseudonym of John Hay Beith]
  The First Hundred Thousand (chronicle) 1915
Hemingway, Ernest
  A Farewell to Arms (novel) 1929
Jones, David
  In Parenthesis (poetry and prose) 1937
Latzko, Andreas
  Menschen im Krieg (short stories) 1917
  [*Men in Battle,* 1918; also published as *Men in War,* 1918]
Mackenzie, Compton
  Gallipoli Memories (autobiography) 1929
Manning, Frederic [as Private 19022]
  The Middle Parts of Fortune (novel) 1929; also published as *Her Privates We* [abridged edition], 1930
Maurois, André [pseudonym of Emile Salomon Wilhelm Herzog]
  Les silences du Colonel Bramble (novel) 1918
  [*The Silence of Colonel Bramble,* 1919; rev. ed.; 1943]
Montague, C. E.
  Disenchantment (essay) 1922
Mottram, R. H.
  The Spanish Farm Trilogy: 1914-1918. 3 vols. (novels) 1927
  (This work includes: *The Spanish Farm,* 1924; *Sixty-Four, Ninety-Four,* 1925; and *The Crime at Vanderlynden's,* 1926.)
Nichols, Robert
  Ardours and Endurances (poetry) 1918
Owen, Wilfred
  Poems (poetry) 1920
Read, Herbert
  Songs of Chaos (poetry) 1915
Remarque, Erich Maria [pseudonym of Erich Paul Remark]
  Im Westen nichts Neues (novel) 1928
  [*All Quiet on the Western Front,* 1929]
Renn, Ludwig [pseudonym of Arnold Friedrich Vieth von Golssenau]
  Krieg (novel) 1928
  [*War,* 1929]
Rolland, Romain
  Au-dessus de la mêleé (essay) 1915
  [*Above the Battle,* 1916]
Rosenberg, Isaac
  Poems by Isaac Rosenberg (poetry) 1922
Sassoon, Siegfried
  The Old Huntsman, and Other Poems (poetry) 1917
  Counter-Attack, and Other Poems (poetry) 1918
  Memoirs of an Infantry Officer (fictionalized autobiography) 1930
Sorley, Charles Hamilton
  Marlborough, and Other Poems (poetry) 1916

Stramm, August
  Twenty Two Poems (poetry) 1969
Thomas, Edward
  Collected Poems (poetry) 1920
Tomlinson, H. M.
  All Our Yesterdays (novel) 1930
Trakl, Georg
  Poems (poetry) 1973
Trumbo, Dalton
  Johnny Got His Gun (novel) 1939
Unruh, Fritz von
  Der Opfergang (novel) 1919
  [*The Way of Sacrifice,* 1928]
Walpole, Hugh
  The Dark Forest (novel) 1916
Wells, H. G.
  Mr. Britling Sees It Through (novel) 1916
Williamson, Henry
  The Wet Flanders Plain (novel) 1923
  A Chronicle of Ancient Sunlight. 15 vols. (novels) 1951-69
Zweig, Arnold
  Der Streit um den Sergeanten Grischa (novel) 1928
  [*The Case of Sergeant Grischa,* 1928]

WORLD WAR I LITERATURE—AN OVERVIEW

EUGENE LÖHRKE

[*Löhrke is the author of* Armageddon: The World War in Literature *(1930). In the following excerpt from that study, he introduces the major works of World War I literature and discusses the resurgence of interest in the war as a literary subject in the late 1920s.*]

Although little more than a decade has elapsed since the armistice, it is becoming apparent that no event in world history has ever called forth a richer or more varied body of literature than the World War.

That this should be so is logical. It is not enough to say that since the beginning of time war and love have furnished inevitable themes for the creative writer. Whatever its final form literature has for its inspiration the impulses and emotions of men under stress and strain. And from 1914 to 1918 the minds, imaginations and feelings of a good half of the civilized world were torn as never before in history. (p. 1)

That the greater part of the civilized world should have been drawn into the war is, probably, merely a logical development of the intricate physical organization of the age. The shot at Sarajevo ignited a powder train that spread into a ring of fire and destruction, across Europe and a good part of Asia, penetrating remote desert places and jungle swamps in Africa. For the first time in history it became apparent that material civilization was its own greatest enemy; that Science could draw the death mask over its Godhead; that Progress wore the two faces of Janus, fronting backward along the slippery, dark trail of human improvement as well as ahead toward what men call the light. And if to the artist mind of the world, the war furnished a picture, ranging in colour from the blazing sunrise of glory to the vision of humanity crucified, to the thinker it furnished a particularly desperate enigma.

War had reached a stage in development where the individual no longer counted, and in any state of affairs where the individual no longer counts the artist revolts. Whatever the objectives that set the flame of 1914 smouldering, the general outline of them was lost under the ruin. Where antagonisms were merely civilian hysterics, where one had to scrutinize the purpose of the whole thing with even more care than one watched for the head of an enemy through a trench periscope, the vast balloons of war idealism collapsed slowly; and naked and desperate, an aspect of human nature fought its way to the front that men had thought to forget.

Logic and reason had fled; madness alone could avail. The nations of the earth clutched and tore at each other with one final object looming across the red-grey horizon. Exhaustion or extinction—in the last analysis these were the goals.

Yet the nations of the world moved to the war as to some glorious pageant of re-creation which all had long awaited. However bitter the later protest, however staring and horrifying the final negation, such the fact was and remains. However meagre the political pretexts that launched the avalanche of destruction, however the masses were blinded or fooled by their leaders, the first cry that went up was one of mighty surrender to the event. "Now thank we our God. . . ." The few scattered voices of protest were lost in the mighty hymnal that welled out from millions of throats, from Austria, from Russia, from France, from Germany and England as well. The assassination of Jean Leon Jaurés by a son of a clerk of the civil court of Rheims on August 1 was an example of the pitch to which the war fury had mounted. The crowd that gathered in front of Buckingham Palace and shouted for war on that fateful day of August 4 found its echoes tossed up and rolled back in waves of sound and fury from the throat of all Europe. *Men wanted this,* this terrible release from the penalties of safety and monotony. The day had come when the petty exactions of living could be swamped in the mighty ocean of self-surrender. The armed God would lead his friends to victory no matter what language they spoke or what creed they professed. The spirit that seized the nations was profoundly and deeply religious, as religious as the emotion of a crowd that sings its men to victory at a great football game. Even the inarticulate could weep and wave their flags. . . . Three years later when America joined in, when European eyes were drained of their tears, when life there was too hopeless even to be mourned over, when the dead in their shallow graves ringed in the living, we of America could still weep and cheer and wave our heroes to conquest in a storm of mob emotion.

Rupert Brooke, Alan Seeger, John Masefield, Ernst Lissauer, Gerhart Hauptmann were only a few of many poets and artists who, in the beginning, saw the dawn of a great new hope flame-coloured on the horizon of man's pettiness. Germany's poet-prophets had long anticipated the event, and those of France were not slow in joining in on the chorus. We may look back on all this, through the mist of blood and tears, with the eyes of disillusionment now. But that very remote literature of war idealism was often very pure. Its appeal, thin and fine as a bugle note, is not to be resisted. The literature of protest followed and grew to mammoth proportions. But the literature of idealism comes first in any consideration of the authentic imaginative writing that the Great War produced. (pp. 1-3)

One would not, of course, be drawn to lost causes unless there were the bright possibility of exaggerating their hope. [One] can look back on those days now and say what fools we were. "If each recruit in 1914 had been an à Kempis or a Rochefoucauld, he would have known that if you are to love mankind you must not expect too much from it," C. E. Montague notes in *Disenchantment.* But the world is not philosophic, other than by occasional mood or whim, and stupidity is as much our portion as wisdom.

Besides, no play, however exaggerated, is ever funny to the actors in it, if only because they have rehearsed it too long; and the great drama of 1914-1918 left much to be desired even from the viewpoint of the spectator. Whatever its folly or lack of humour, the disenchantment was normal to the original illusion. What was strictly abnormal was the spectacle of nations slaughtering each other on a large scale with the most improved scientific devices. And the first protest was as genuine as any simple cry of horror.

On the intellectual side of it, Romain Rolland, surveying the scene from the safe austerity of his Swiss mountainside, scattered the kernels of his prophetic sentimentality to the doves of all nations. Here, as elsewhere, one might question M. Rolland's common sense, but never his sincerity. His *Au-dessus de la mêleé* is, to-day, one of the most curious of the anti-patriotic documents, a mixture of Rousseauistic loose thinking with jingoistic chatter relieved by an occasional ray of disinterested and objective thinking. But M. Rolland was too self-conscious about it all to be very useful. He might furnish pacifists and conscientious objectors of all nations with an occasional rallying cry, but between the lines of his writings one perceives that he was quite as much alarmed at his own predicament as at the downfall of the nations. In England, Mr. Wells remained Mr. Britling throughout; safely and sanely Mr. Britling. Pessimism, remorse, Great Hope, foreboding, prophesy flowed indifferently from his pen. In Germany, Leonhard Frank had gloomily foreboded catastrophe and gloomily fled. And by 1916, Henri Barbusse had completed *Under Fire* out of his reaction to the scenes of Verdun.

It was the first important book of any literature to show the lengths to which a man of imaginative nature might recoil from the actual scene of the war nightmare, and it had its German counterpart in Fritz von Unruh's unbalanced *Way of Sacrifice,* suppressed by no less an authority than the General staff itself. In the meantime, Andreas Latzko, lying sick at Davos in Switzerland had told what an Austrian officer might think of it in two books *Men at War* and *Women in the War.* These are all works of direct observation with the war as the protagonist. And this very definite phase of war writing had its culmination in 1929 with the publication of Erich Maria Remarque's *All Quiet on the Western Front,* the most ultimately disquieting of all war books yet written.

They were, one and all—these early books—anti-militarist documents; the point being not one of intention but, overpoweringly, one of unconscious reaction. No "sensitive soul" could possibly stand the full vision of war, at the front, in the trenches and dug-outs, without revolting from it. Even if the spirit were strong enough, the flesh was bound, sooner or later, to rebel or break down. Discounting actual or imaginary cases of shell-shock, the state of usefulness of a soldier, unwounded, exposed to the ordinary bombardments, that is, to the ordinary routine of life in the trenches and rest billets, might range from six to eight months. He might be able to stand the turmoil, the constant imminence of danger, the continued and prolonged spells of sleeplessness and exhaustion a few weeks longer without permanently damaging himself, if his nervous system in the first place were of the best. After that neurosis of some kind or other developed until he had recuperated; in other words, he ceased to think and function as a normal human being. The time limit, of course, varied with the quality of hardship he was exposed to—some sectors were quieter than others—but the results of any prolonged "exposure" to front line conditions even in the cases of hardy and healthy men were often disastrous.

We should not lose sight of this when reading the blood-red horrors of Latzko's *Men at War*. The mind sensitive enough to render such impressions in detail could not, by the mere force of its nature, escape from rendering them as nightmares. What we read in Von Unruh's unstrung and ghastly pages is as much the record of a shattered nervous system trying to balance its own sense of horror as it is a picture of the horror itself.

It is always the vision of the thing that one reads from the pages of a worthwhile book, never the thing itself; and one has only to read more deeply in war literature to see how, as the years slipped by and the actual scene grew remote, that vision altered and shifted. But the immediate emotional duress during the war years was terrific. Never before had so many minds and imaginations been simultaneously wrenched and torn, the dream of a new world to rise phoenix-like from the ashes of the old settled into the despondencies of an intermittent nightmare; and the bitter war aftermath increased the sense of shock. It may have been the protective wisdom of the world that chose to forget the war so quickly—that labelled it as madness and nightmare and tried to turn its eyes away to the future once more. But no one who was at the front when the news of the armistice was brought will remember the scenes there as anything else but a strange tragi-comedy. The widest conceivable chasm of unbelief and disillusion divided those who had fought at the front and those who had warred at home. While the cities were blowing off the last remnants of their pent-up hysteria, the armies sat silently through the night on the frozen November earth; a silence not of calm but of utter unbelief and apathy. Bonfires were lit; rockets went up; the assurance of waking up in the morning, alive, was felt as a relief. No one really believed that the war was over, and only a very few seemed to care. War had called up into the grey, mud-covered hosts huddled under the lowering autumn skies a state of mind at the farthest remove from civilian passions and enthusiasms. The precious, formative years of character had been spent in turning millions of men into that highly specialized and anti-civilian being—the fighting man. If these men were to receive their due, they would have to be retrained and adjusted to peace again as they had been disciplined and adjusted to war. They had been gathered in by an immense drag-net, from schools and colleges, from soft homes, from prairie hamlets, from the city streets and slums. They had trained their bodies to endure the fatigue of long marches, of winters in frozen holes in the ground, of living and killing under conditions as primitive as their ancestors of thousands of years ago. They had been forced to forget their old values and standards to make the new ones endurable. They would now be asked to forget this in turn, to return to their little box-holes and offices, their streets that were no longer the same, their friends who had not changed with them. That is the theme of Remarque's book, and that, it seems to the editor, is the war's least understood tragedy. . . . And now, gradually, these pent-up emo-

tions, these adjustments and maladjustments, this enormous consciousness of nightmare and futility, these springs bent back and strained, began to function. The great nervous release of creative writing began to loosen the strain, all over the world.

It was like the ticking of many clocks in a room that had hitherto been filled with a heavy silence. One clock set off another. In ten years that room was full.

The war was over; but its consequences on the state of mind and on the literature which was its reflection had really barely begun. The intellectual revolt, excitedly stifled during the war years when propaganda was felt to be essential to every "cause," was now more or less the order of the day. In France, Romain Rolland might return from his Swiss retreat as unremarked by the general public as his writings addressed to the thinkers of the world had been when they appeared in Switzerland in 1915. He was forty-six years old when the war broke out, hence liable for duty; but the French public, as distinct from the French literary world, is not, as a rule, vindictive. To a weary nation, savagely chauvinistic and utterly exhausted by turn, he might even appear in the guise of a prudent man where Pierre Loti, who had written such unctuously patriotic letters to the admiralty at the outset of the conflict offering an old man's courage, etc., might seem rather monotonous. Professor Loisy's "War and the Pope" and "War" written in 1916 were too scholarly to reach the general public. Many of the professional men of letters in Paris, like their compatriots in Germany, had, from the first set their independence of thought at the service of the government, either as a result of intimidation or through a feeling of genuine patriotism or both. The battle that ensued between the intellectuals on both sides would make, today, one of the most amusing chapters of war history, if there were not something a little painful in the spectacle of professional wisemen turning somersaults at the behest of politicians. The Academy of Moral Sciences, through its President, Henri Bergson, was the first, apparently, to announce that "struggle of civilization against the barbarians" which was to give the sound thinkers of both sides a chance to exploit their ingenuity. Germany was first at the guns to accuse France of the rape and violation of Belgium and Professor Karl Lamprecht seems to have been the first to call attention to the resemblance between the French armies and the Huns of Attila, which was later to be caught up by the whole allied side and flung back at the Germans. In the propaganda field, Germany was outdone from the start simply because the British controlled the cable lines and coloured the news to suit themselves, and the industry and perseverance of the French savants in opening perspectives on German terrorism could, therefore, find a world audience. The peak of professorial ingenuity was, perhaps, achieved by E. Perrier of the French Academy of Sciences who discovered a certain unmistakable resemblance between the skull of Bismarck and the skulls of a hitherto unknown race of Stone Men called the Allophyles, but German men of letters were racing their French brethren to a tie at the time, and no absurdity was too pronounced to be debarred from the Press.

Anatole France, who had offered his services from the first, wisely forebore from making any too overt comment. André Gide, considering discretion the better part of valour for a man of military age, devoted himself to refugee work in Paris. Yet much had been written and published in France during the war years of a nature no whit less rebellious than Bar-

Georges Duhamel in Verdun in 1916, where he was serving as a doctor in a mobile surgical unit.

busse's *Under Fire*. P. C. J. Bourget's *The Night Cometh* was contemporary with Jean des Vignes Rouge's *Bourru*, and if in both the patriotic note is present, the voice of horror drowns it out. A host of inconspicuous and industrious scribblers could still fan the patriotic flame with the wind of the Great Illusion, but war diaries and letters from men at the front were leaving little doubt as to what soldiers were actually seeing and suffering. France, unlike America, and to a far greater degree than England, was too close to the theatre of conflict to permit any long standing disguise of its real nature. When the enemy is thundering at your gates and has tramped through your fields on and off for four years, it does not take a telescope or the glass eye of an editorial writer to see what is actually going on. Conscientious objectors and the inconspicuous lesser fry were hounded and bounced and tortured by the police to the edification of the mob which always needs its whipping boys, but the long hand of French justice wore the velvet glove where matters deeply controversial were concerned. Justice, when it can be satisfied by crucifying a carpenter's son between two thieves, seldom needs to go further afield, and for the rest the French jails were kept quite full enough to satisfy people that "steps were being taken." In the field of fiction, again, no new note was struck in Georges Duhamel's *Vie des Martyrs*, and Roland Dorgeles' *Wooden Crosses*, when they appeared toward the closing years, and if

they did push back the goal for other French writers on war themes, still the pace had long since been set. It has not been greatly varied or accelerated since, which may account for the astonishing monotony of two score French war books, very few of which, with the exception of *Under Fire*, have ever reached an international audience.

In Germany, the war had from the beginning created two parties among the thinkers and writers. Gerhart Hauptmann had written his "Vaterlandslied," Dehmel sang "Heilige Flamme Glüh," as a call of the nation to arms and Ernst Lissauer is still remembered for his "Hymn of Hate against England." The "Address to the Civilized Nations," found its subscribers among such distinguished thinkers, artists and scientists as Eucken, Haeckel, Wundt, Südermann, Humperdinck, Roentgen, Ostwald and Liebermann. Bruno Frank and the Austrian author, Wildgans, took on the appropriate patriotic coloration early in the war as writers in France and England had done, but the young poet, Gerrit Engelke broke into revolutionary strains in his "Rhythmus des Neuen Europas." He fell in the great retreat during October, 1918, and died in an English field hospital. Rene Schickele, editor of *Weisse Blätter*, had long since gathered around him an important group of anti-war writers, and Hermann Hesse's *Demian*, was published under a pseudonym. Across the border, Karl Spitteler, the Swiss poet, was inveighing against the conflict, and Franz Masereel, the Belgian artist, was beginning his career with woodcuts for a Geneva newspaper. Leonhard Frank, who had been prosecuted following the publication of *Der Mensch ist Gut*, in 1916 and who had made good his escape to Switzerland, returned, after the Armistice, something of a hero. The book had been brought out in Zurich in 1917. It was published by Kiepenheuer in Berlin during the Winter of 1919 and became a "best-seller" overnight. In the meantime, the old order had passed out of the picture; November, which began the troubled peace of the world, brought fresh conflict to Germany. Revolution marched the streets with red flags and machine-guns; the spectre of starvation haunted the houses of wealthy and poor alike; only the profiteers could drink to the new era with a confidence born of a full stomach and pocketbook. And the picture of a world in ruins was to permeate literature for some time to come.

In the theatre, Reinard Goering's *Seeschlacht* and *Scapa Flow* were anticipating the more vivid revolutionary effects of Bert Brecht's *Trommeln in der Nacht*. On the part of Germany's greatest writers there was a silence—a silence not unlike that which reigned in France and England for a while. Südermann had yet to be heard from. Heinrich and Thomas Mann had drawn close to the fringe of the Socialist-Democratic Party in essays looking to a future of reconstruction. Frank Thiess and Joseph Roth were beginning to make the weight of the younger writers felt in the vexed question of readjustment. But the first post-war outpourings were followed by a strange hiatus, until in 1927 Arnold Zweig broke the silence with *The Case of Sergeant Grischa*, one of the solidest literary achievements that the World War has produced.

In England, where the return to peace conditions was effected without the chattering of revolutionary machine-guns and the echoing crash of bombs in the city streets, the forward-lookers had picked up the first steps of a new *danse macabre*. Mr. Wells was relishing his vision of the world in ruins as he had never, properly, been able to enjoy the war itself. In a few years the rats and wolves would be gnawing at us all, unless the school teachers and intellectuals came to the rescue. J. M. Keynes, more straightforwardly, set the key for the politico-economic rebellion in his *Economic Consequences of the Peace.* His analysis of the personalities of the council of four was a master-piece of literary irony. Arnold Bennett, W. L. George, John Galsworthy, had all caught at varying refractions of the conflagration and had given the realities of war life at home a certain dignity and value. William McFee sensibly contributed to the cause of peace—or of bigger and brighter wars—in a very early book *Six Hour Shift.* Francis Brett Young had taken the promise of his early literary abilities along with his doctor's degree to East Africa with him, and had painted vividly the war in the bush. In poetry, the thin, silver call to higher hope had died with Rupert Brooke, although the mild verses of Thomas Hardy reiterated the patriotic wistfulness of the stay-at-homes. As in Germany, the young war poets were pressing to the fore to fix the scene in the glamour of their stark disillusion. The nightmare lines run riotous across the page. One could not speak one's mind, perhaps, but one could think one's thoughts and brood over the terrible dream—take notes on the margin, as it were, of the thing itself. The sedate levels of the wistful Masefield were deluged slowly in the oncoming waves of sound and fury. Siegfried Sassoon's coloured and fevered outcries were echoed, more soberly, by the heavy refrains of Robert Graves, Edmund Blunden and Richard Aldington, and Wilfred Owen died, leaving one of the few poetic legacies of any importance to the world, with the Great War as its theme. In fiction, again England had produced at least one good war book during the early years of conflict. It was Hugh Walpole's *Dark Forest,* published in 1916. Russia was busily quarrelling with herself in the name of revolution and progress while Italy, too conscious of coming storm clouds to watch the literary horizon, observed a certain reticence on matters pertaining to the war. But Prezzolini's anthology of Soldier's Letters, *Tutta La Guerra,* had been published to point out in some detail what the common people thought of it all. Soffici's *Kobilek* and Monelli's *Scarpe al Sole* are both additions of importance to the world's war works. And Borgese's *Rube,* dealing with the unhappy aftermath, was soon to unwind laborious coils in English translation.

Such was the scene abroad, while at home we were returning to normalcy and enjoying such revelations of Hun horrors and Allied manliness as were still being dispensed in the prescriptions of Mary Roberts Rinehart and Vicente Blasco Ibañez. It was an attitude, which, since it had become a matter of pride and presidential elections, was more than resistant to such foreign importations as pretended to show the war in its true colours. The desire to forget the war was tantamount to admitting that the American coals had been carried to Newcastle; and all that remained for us to do was to congratulate ourselves on possessing a race of heroes which we already suspected we possessed anyway and insist on the prompt payment of war loans. Latzko's *Men at War* when it was published here in 1919 was regarded as something between a freak and an intrusion. Barbusse had made an impression, but merely because *Under Fire* with all its obvious defects, its blundering crudities, was as inescapable as the tread of a heavy-shod infantry regiment. It was not, one submits, an impression comparable to the appearance of Rudolph Valentino in *The Four Horsemen of the Apocalypse.* And the reception accorded John Dos Passos' *Three Soldiers,* when it appeared in 1921 left a good deal to the imagination.

It was at once the finest American war book since Stephen Crane's *Red Badge of Courage,* and in its field—that of peculiarly sensitive realistic etching—a work of absolute sincerity,

of singular appeal and depth. It was not until 1929 when Mary Lee disburdened herself of a woman's wartime impressions in *"It's a Great War!"* that it was to find a rival in its own proper field. On its keystone of impassioned revolt was laid the structure of a solid, thoughtful novel that compares with the best "realistic" works of any literature. It came from the pen of a very young man who had never been heard from before and has had little enough of importance to say since. It was as rich and deep in human observation and sympathy as Ernest Hemingway's enormously popular, *A Farewell to Arms,* written ten years later is thin, pointless and weak. It was a success, but after all a minor one. The public was not "war-minded" yet.

So, at least, the publishers felt or seemed to feel—and continued to feel as late as 1928 when several of them turned down Remarque's *All Quiet on the Western Front* as being unsuited to the popular taste. For in America, as in Germany and England, in the years between 1920 and 1927, war literature continued at a discount. The formula, "the public won't stand a war book," was honestly believed and rigidly adhered to—possibly because it was true. In the meantime *What Price Glory* had opened in New York, and the public became aware that the best efforts of the Y.M.C.A. had not succeeded in preserving the virginity of the A.E.F.; that our boys, in short, were human beings; that they were engaged in a war and not in elevating Continental manners and morals. The police censorship suggested that the God be left out of the Goddams, and the scandal helped the box office enormously. Laurence Stalling's *Plumes* was followed by *The Big Parade.* The movies were in it now, but William Faulkner's bitter *Soldiers' Pay,* was quite forgotten in the shuffle. Even granting that our boys would swear and fornicate on the slightest provocation, still the "devil dogs" had beaten the Huns. Such was the progress of popular psychology. Willa Cather, however, chose to believe otherwise, and another case for the American hero, *One of Ours,* was crowned in 1922 with the Pulitzer Prize for "wholesome" literature. Abroad, and exiled from the scene of his Cossack charges, Krassnoff was heavily at work on his ponderous *From Double Eagle to Red Flag.* Russia was coming into her own again and Orenburgksy's *Land of the Children* followed hard on Babel's *Red Cavalry.* In England Ford Madox Ford was publishing his tetralogy of wartime stresses behind the lines and at home. It was the first definite sign that careful and skilful literary workmen might find in the war something more than fresh tar from the barrel of horrors. From *Three Soldiers* to *No More Parades* was, after all, a far cry forward in the analysis of war for its literary shades and values, but between the two was all the difference between a young poet with a song of revolt to sing and a mature artist more conscious of his materials than of his own heart. Later on we were to have more impassioned outcries, and still more sober analyses of the scene, the causes, the situation. But the dam was still holding back the water. The popular prejudice against war literature still existed or seemed to exist. . . . In 1928, ten years after the signing of the armistice, the dam was broken, and war literature flooded over, reaching its crest of popularity in Erich Maria Remarque's *All Quiet on the Western Front.*

The new impetus to war interest that marked the opening of the second decade since the armistice seems to have come in large measure from Germany. Whatever the politicians and peace-adjusters had done in ten years to sow the seeds for further wars in Europe, the inflated balloons of popular antagonism had long since gone flat. The American public had graduated from Ibáñez, gradually. The Hun was no longer the Scourge of God but an intensely Progressive industrialist—a coming trade rival. Dr. Henry Van Dyke's "Weir Wolf of Potsdam," was a harmless old man with a beard and whiskers like Bernard Shaw playing tag with matrimonial possibilities around the parks at Doorn. The economic atrocities of the French in the Ruhr were vastly more to the point than the rapings and shootings in Belgium vouched for by the Bryce Committee. Returning soldiers had already pointed something of a moral in their pointed refusal to hate anyone bitterly but their Allies and superior officers.

Obviously there were several factors at work here. In the first place it had taken the public ten years to forget, sufficiently, what the war actually was to afford a glimpse in retrospect. The war had become a memory, and memories are proverbially more grateful than actualities. And in the second place Germany was "having her say." She had not been heard from so far—except in Germany. The book reading world was quite ready to listen.

A good deal of this amazing popularity of war literature in the last year or so springs, undoubtedly, from romantic sources. As Señor Madariaga has been at some pains to point out, we accept the horrors of war in literature now because, shocking as it seems, they entertain us. We may be appalled by *All Quiet on the Western Front,* but so are we horrified by Poe's murder tales—and we continue to read both. The crowds, which, month after month, thronged to see *What Price Glory,* and, later, *Journey's End,* whatever the more obscure factors of terror, pity or wonder involved, came and left in the name of entertainment. Between these two plays are all the gradations of emotional experience that exist between an impressive elaboration of the blood-and-thunder formula and the pathos and beauty of a human experience simply and poetically rendered—a gradation in the finer interpretation of war emotions that seems to have reached its peak, now, in Paul Alverdes' *The Whistlers' Room,*—but still the fact remains that people do not see plays or read books unless they enjoy them. Another generation with its eyes dimmed by the enchantment that distance lends, may well look back on the Great War as the stupendous expression of some more vigorous race that has since vanished from the densely tragic peace-ways of men—or it may engage in another war to prove to itself how very limited the possibilities of human experience—and even of tragedy—are. We may scuttle our battleships and dismiss our armies. In that event the days when armies marched and ships sailed the seas will be revealed to backward-looking eyes in an aura of power and of beauty, and the World War veterans, as their ranks are thinned by time, may yet come into their own. "Old soldiers never die . . ." runs the cockney song. They live, instead, to become garrulous. Well, they are beginning to become garrulous now.

Yet *The Case of Sergeant Grischa,* the first break in the long literary hiatus in Germany as far as the war was concerned, was not a garrulous book. It was an intensely effective literary document—no outshoot of the war and revolutionary years but a work of solid merit grafted on the old, humanistic tradition of German letters; the spirit of kinship with all and partisanship with none that has found its most complete efflorescence in the work of Thomas Mann. We have already seen much the same method, if less of the spirit, at work in the conscientiously constructed war façades and interiors of Ford Madox Ford. Another year or two in England and it had rip-

ened into the thoughtful undertones of R. H. Mottram's *Spanish Farm Trilogy.* Whatever the war had been to the young generation who were trained or broken by it, whose vivid outcries form the greater part of the literature of protest, to more mature minds, or more stubborn nervous systems—no spectacle that was, after all, human, could escape a humane rendering. . . .

It would be purposeless here to enumerate and discuss all the books, important and trivial, that the breaking of the dam in early 1928 threw into the flood of war writing that is still under way. The pendulum, once set in motion, was bound to swing in wider arcs. It swung far to the realistic side again in other German war books, Ludwig Renn's *Krieg* and the anonymous *Schlump.* The final strength of the protest was measured to the whole world in the curious fixed intensity—almost as of a madman's stare—in Remarque's *All Quiet on the Western Front.* It touched a new height of irony in E. E. Cummings' *The Enormous Room,* at once the most remarkable and most neglected of all American war books. It drew out the hot sparks of Mary Lee's protest in *"It's a Great War!"* the single war book of any importance written by an American woman. It came to rest on the older levels again in James B. Wharton's *Squad,* in Thomas Boyd's vivid, *Through the Wheat,* in William Scanlon's stark recitative *God Have Mercy on Us!* It brought to light the acid and shallow comedy of Ernest Hemingway's *A Farewell to Arms.* In England it touched its drabber levels once more in Edmund Blunden's *Undertones of War,* and in the uninspired war chapters of Richard Aldington's otherwise brilliantly written book. It touched the humanistic level again in C. R. Benstead's *Retreat* and soared up to the clear-eyed perspectives of Robert Graves in *Good-bye to All That,* and H. M. Tomlinson's *All Our Yesterdays.* It struck a quiet note of retrospect in Henry Williamson's *The Wet Flanders Plain.* It brought out the staccato echo and low rumbling of the great guns of the war fleets in *Des Kaiser's Kulis,* the only war book of permanent literary value dealing with the war on the seas. The old year died, and the new year brought in Ben Ray Redman's *Down in Flames,* as an addition of literary distinction to the casual array of aviators' diaries and reminiscences. The ways and minds of hospital units and their workers were exposed in Frederick Pottle's *Stretchers* and in Morris Werner's *Orderly.* The door that had been set ajar in *Journey's End* was opened wider in Paul Alverdes' gently tragic *The Whistlers' Room.* And still the pendulum keeps on swinging and the waters flooding the dam.

And for the future—what? The publishers' lists for 1930 show that the authors continue to be "war-minded" whether the public is lapsing behind them or not. A new perspective has been opened through the hazes to the realities of the past. The war has ceased to be a theme for semi-realistic nightmares. We may look on the scene now through new eyes with greater poise and detachment. Even the caricaturists are coming into their own; and those, better equipped, who understand the nature of tomorrow as the nature of today and war, in some part at least, as the nature of man.

"The old soldier . . ." Henry Williamson notes in *The Wet Flanders Plain,* "sees many things by which he may recall with a sort of quiet glamorous melancholy, those days of the war that are almost romantic because of their comradeships, activities, immense fears, turmoils, miseries, light-thrilling barrages—dwelt on in the dimness of memory, now that he is safe, free and happy. Romantic! Yes, sometimes late at night the War is recalled with an indescribable feeling of immense, haunting regret. The human spirit haunts its old actions in time and space, and, it may be, having sloughed an essence of itself upon the vacant air, would stray its old way again. . . ."

Romantic? But unless there were a glamour to our yesterdays we would forget them all. The world has changed in the ten crowded years of peace—changed more than we are willing to admit even to ourselves, perhaps. A wide gap stretches between the ever-dawning future and the greatest tragedy ever known to or recorded by mankind. A new generation grows which carries the war as the dimmest of childhood memories, untouched by its healed wounds and scars. Already people begin to speak of the Great War as they used to speak of the earthquake at Messina. Soon they will speak of it as they speak of the war at Troy. And then it will be put on the Curriculum of Required Courses, and they will speak of it no more.

And as it fades out on the horizon, consciousness of it will also fade; and, more specifically, that artist consciousness that saw it in terms of an appalling drama; that saw the veil of the Temple rent and the voice of the terrible God crying out in the midst of thunder and of flame. And the retrospect, we may suppose, will show more of the frame and background, and less of the picture itself, as a memory here and there searches back through those years for a something . . . a something that seemed at times to crown the terror in an aura of new hope, a something irretrievably lost, a flame, seared against the darkness of calamity; the terrible searching of minds, wills and hearts in the face of disaster, the terrible and bitter surrender, the disillusionment, the loss, the nightmare that broke from the eternal dream of life and death. (pp. 5-21)

> *Eugene Löhrke, "Introduction: The World War in Literature," in* Armageddon: The World War in Literature, *edited by Eugene Löhrke, Jonathan Cape and Harrison Smith, 1930, pp. 1-27.*

FRANCES WINWAR

[*Winwar is an Italian-born American biographer, novelist, critic, and translator, who is best known for her entertaining studies of the lives of a diverse group of literary and historical figures, including Joan of Arc, Napoleon Bonaparte, William Wordsworth, and Oscar Wilde. In the following excerpt, she focuses on antimilitarism and protest in the literary responses of American, English, French, and German writers to the war.*]

Culturally the war bore fruit long before its close as a result of the effective propaganda of hate and misrepresentation on which the people of all countries were fed. Atrocity stories shrieked in headlines from the press and found credence with hitherto sane people who, forgetting the purported noble motives for which the war was being fought, shouted for the extermination of the enemy. In Germany, in England, in France, in America, it was unpatriotic—and unsafe—not to agree with the majority. A prominent political figure of proved integrity, the father of Charles A. Lindbergh, Lone Eagle of 1927, was ostracized for opposing America's war mania and died a broken man in consequence of his courage. People dared not speak their minds even before friends and found it the better part of valor not only to be discreet, but to echo the accepted lie. "Taisez-vous! Méfiez-vous! Les oreilles ennemies vous écoutent!" ["Shut your mouth! Be-

ware! Enemy ears are listening!"] exhorted the warning tacked on the doors of trains, hotels, and public buildings in France. Faithfully people kept their mouths shut and mistrusted everyone for fear of the listening ears of the enemy.

With few exceptions, writers and artists either howled with the crowd, submerging their individuality in the multitude, or sought safe havens of escape in the past, in fantasy, in the future—anywhere, anywhere out of reality. In Italy D'Annunzio, once the archangel of revolt, not only glorified war but took part in it. Others, more or less great, followed his example, pouring out rabid novels and verses that heightened the war fever till intellect became delirium. With Coningsby Dawson scores of otherwise pacific writers produced volumes of inciting fiction, or like Robert W. Service, beat the war drums in rhythms that even the illiterate could understand. Painters who had hitherto found their greatest joy in pure art forsook it for propaganda, doing their bit by daubing patriotic posters appealing to the emotions of the mob. Everything was sacrificed to feed the war god whose first victim was the white-clad figure of truth.

Nevertheless an infinitesimal minority in each country carried on the battle of the one against the many. "The children of a new generation," said Stefan Zweig many years after the armistice, "will scarcely find it possible to realize what those who belonged to this minority had to suffer." Because he had felt the need of expressing himself and others like him—the unheard, the outcast, the despised—he chose as his symbol the Biblical Jeremiah, through whose mouth, in his play of that name, he said the things he could not otherwise have uttered. Thus his allegorical protest against war reached an audience in spite of the stringency of the censorship.

In France Romain Rolland, while also adopting symbolism in his drama *Liluli* to show the futility and the folly of war, nevertheless voiced his condemnation of its barbarity in terms so unmistakable that he fell foul of the authorities. His prosecution became a *cause célèbre,* but few gave him moral support in his unpopular and risky crusade. Self-righteous patriots accused him of defeatism; *embusqué* heroes, well ambushed in safe posts, taunted him with cowardice. Out of his experience came one of the noblest works indirectly produced by the war, *Clerambault,* the bitter Odyssey of an independent spirit in a time of herd hysteria. The book is not a novel, though it has some elements of fiction; neither is it autobiography, in spite of Clerambault's resemblances to Rolland himself; the study is too objective, too universal for that. It might be taken rather as the searching soul-portrait of an individualist in the cataclysm, as he gropes toward the light of truth when all about him are denying its existence. In his strength as in his weakness, Rolland portrays him to that final moment when at the cry of his murderer, "I have killed the enemy," the words flash through his darkening brain: "My poor friend, it is within you yourself that the enemy lies."

Rolland wrote an explanatory note to an instalment of *Clerambault* that appeared in the Swiss press in 1917. Better than anything one can say, he delivers his message, a daring one even for less fanatical days: "He who makes himself the servant of a blind or blinded nation . . . does not truly serve it but lowers both it and himself. . . . Sincere thought, even if it does run counter to that of others, is still a service to mankind."

The experiences of Zweig and Rolland were common to independent spirits everywhere. The moment a country plunged into the war, the whole process of repression and censorship began. Newspapers either conformed or were ruthlessly suppressed. Periodicals remained organs of opinion only so long as that opinion followed the policies of the government. As a result many of them went out of existence or became vapid, pseudo-literary magazines whose closest contact with life took place in some safe Cloudcuckooland.

The working of the repressive method in America was perhaps best shown in the case of the *Masses.* For some time, since the veering of public opinion toward the side of the Allies, the Department of Justice had been watching each issue of the magazine as it came off the press. There was plenty of matter both in the drawings and in the editorial comment to worry the censor who, however, found nothing on which to build a case until, several months after President Wilson's war-entry speech, the troublesome little magazine boldly published a number of anti-militarist cartoons. Immediately the *Masses* was forbidden the mails. Notwithstanding, the magazine continued to appear, more openly anti-war than ever, even though the editors were aware of a very slaughter of the innocents among radical publications throughout the country. Defiantly they declared in the issue of August, 1917: "The *Masses* is the only one which has challenged the censorship in the courts and put the Government on the defensive. Each month we have something vitally important to say on the war. We are going to say it and continue to say it. We are going to fight any attempt to prevent us from saying it."

The government, however, had other views on the subject, which it conclusively demonstrated by suppressing the *Masses.* By the close of the year, with the December issue, the *Masses* ceased to exist. Worse, its editors, Max Eastman, Floyd Dell, Art Young, Merrill Rogers, the business manager, and later John Reed, who was given time to return from Russia, were brought to trial for sedition and for interfering with enlistment. At first the outcome seemed none too bright, for it was no trifling offense during the war to challenge the government's policies. Finally, after a lengthy procedure, the jury disagreed and the stage was set for a second trial in September. For weeks the process went on, the oratory of the defense and prosecution proving so soporific on one occasion that Art Young, forgetting the nightmare of Atlanta Prison hanging over him, fell asleep. Again the jury disagreed, but as the war was by then almost over the matter was dropped on what amounted to a verdict of acquittal. (pp. 200-03)

Whatever the preoccupations of the government with seditious writing might be, the people had to have something to read, and the soldiers in the trenches must be supplied with books—books that should at once sustain their morale and hold the door open to human hope. David Garnett, looking back upon the war years, recalled in a recent article that of all literature the soldiers at the front liked nothing better than sentimental stories. The trenches in France, he says, were littered with copies of Gene Stratton Porter's *Freckles* which sold in the tens of thousands. What was its attraction? Simply its memories of home and peace and innocence, and those simple values which the war had suddenly overturned. The soldiers wanted life as they remembered it before they entered No Man's Land. "I was kept warm by the ardor of life within me," wrote Wilfred Owen. "I forgot hunger in the hunger for life." The actualities of the front, death, the barbarity, the suffering, the needless human waste were the last things the men wished to be reminded of. If the war had to be written about,

they preferred it in such versions as Smith's *Dere Mabel* and Empey's *Over the Top.*

Next to sentimental fiction the soldiers liked poetry which could compress a wealth of emotional content in a brief space. Anthologies, therefore, were favorites with the men. Hence recently, to meet the present need, the English house of Routledge brought out two such collections designed for the soldiers at the front, *The Knapsack* and *The English Vision,* the one to remind them of the blessings of home, the other to keep before them the heritage of England.

From 1914 to 1918 books of war verse, the inspirational variety written comfortably from the depths of an armchair, and the vivid, poignant poems of the trenches flooded the market. In their patriotism the reviewers hailed a new genius with every edition of the literary supplements, sentimentalized over each week's crop of fighting Byrons, and praised the war that had produced them.

From a distance of twenty-five years, however, the poetry of the war seems hardly to have justified the critical acclaim. There were individual poems that achieved a certain fame for meeting the emotional need of the time: some of Rupert Brooke's stirring *1914* sonnets, for instance; Alan Seeger's "Rendezvous with Death" and a half-dozen others. But the only poets of any stature produced by the war were the two Englishmen, Wilfred Owen and Siegfried Sassoon.

Owen enlisted in the beginning of the war and saw two years of service. Then for more than a year he was invalided. In October, 1918, he returned to the front, only to be killed, shortly before the armistice, while leading his men, the Artists' Rifles, across the Sambre Canal. He was twenty-five when he died. A dreamy, imaginative youth of wonderful sensibility, he had hated war as much as he had loved humanity in those grim, brave semblances of men who were his companions. It was at the hospital that he produced the greater part of his poetry under the guidance and encouragement of Sassoon, whom he met there. He wrote of the things he himself had known, but although he drew from the horror and gruesomeness of war, he endeavored to raise the mind to the ultimate values that could survive such a test.

> I, too, saw God through mud—

he wrote in "Apologia pro Poemate Meo,"

> The mud that cracked on cheeks when wretches
>   smiled.
> War brought more glory to their eyes than blood,
> And gave their laughs more glee than shakes a
>   child.
>
> Merry it was to laugh there—
>   Where death becomes absurd and life absurder.
>   For power was on us as we slashed bones bare
>   Not to feel sickness or remorse of murder. . . .

Raids, bombings, the torturing asphyxiation of gas shells, all found their place in poetry that had gone far in its passionate indictment since those early days when everyone was drunkenly proclaiming the sweetness of sacrifice. He had seen how sweet such sacrifice could be, and from the agony of his anger he wrote it in letters of blood before he died:

> If in some smothering dreams, you too could pace
> Behind the wagon that we flung him in,
> And watch the white eyes writhing in his face,
> His hanging face, like a devil's sick of sin,

If you could hear, at every jolt, the blood
Come gurgling from the froth-corrupted lungs . . .
My friend, you would not tell with such high zest
To children ardent for some desperate glory,
The old Lie: *Dulce et decorum est*
Pro patria mori.

Siegfried Sassoon, slightly older than Owen whose poems he edited in 1920, was in active service through the duration of the war except for several months on two occasions when he was severely wounded. He came out of it a violent pacifist. Indeed, before the war ended, and after he had been awarded a Military Cross for bravery, he enacted a rebellion of his own, threw down his arms, and refused to go on fighting. His was such unheard-of behavior, especially when he emphasized his resolution by flinging his Cross into the sea, that he was pronounced insane and sent away for a change of air. On his return he suffered his second wound. But the war was soon over and he no longer had need for personal protest. In the books of prose and verse which he began publishing after the war, he continued, however, to carry on his fight against the ordeal that had shattered him and the best youth of his generation. His message is clear and forceful though with less of the emotional intensity of Owen's. Today he is the gadfly of English society whose snobbery and chauvinism he mercilessly punctures.

War's disillusionment, however, had made itself felt among the actual participants at the front long before the orators at home had exhausted their vocabulary on the grandeur and glory of death on the field of battle. On both sides feeling men were revolted by the cruel illogicality of it all. They had entered the war, most of them, inspired by the highest motives, on the Allied side sustained by the conviction that they were battling the Antichrist in the hated Kaiser; on the German, that they were carrying on God's fight. *"Gott mit uns,"* the slogan rang; and because God was with them, they were against the forces of evil, the loathed imperialists who were encircling Germany and preventing her from achieving the expansion that divine right had decreed. Church and state combined on both sides to keep the myths alive, but they reckoned without a force more potent than propaganda: common humanity which succeeded at last in piercing through the smoke screen of lies and prejudice. There is an eloquent bit of dialogue in R. C. Sherriff's *Journey's End,* laid at the time of the German offensive in 1918, which has its counterpart in almost every work that deals directly with the war.

It occurs during the scene wherein Osborne, representative of the best in the British army, tries to make young Raleigh understand what war is. "The Germans are really quite decent, aren't they?" the boy remarks, catching himself quickly. "I mean, outside the newspapers?" "Yes," Osborne answers, continuing after a pause:

> I remember up at Wipers we had a man shot when he was out on patrol. Just at dawn. We couldn't get him in that night. He lay out there groaning all day. Next night three of our men crawled out to get him in. It was so near the German trenches that they could have shot our fellows one by one. But, when our men began dragging the wounded man back over the rough ground, a big German officer stood up in the trenches and called out: "Carry him!"— and our fellows stood up and carried the man back, and the German fired some lights for them to see by. . . . Next day we blew each other's trenches to blazes.

Sherriff, it is true, was writing in 1928, from the perspective of distance that had helped to give facts their just proportion; but as early as 1917, Bernard Shaw, assuming an allegorical style, had striven to waken the conscience of thinking men in his so-called fantasia in the Russian manner, *Heartbreak House,* a play which unmasked the Europe which made the World War possible. In a preface which later accompanied the published work he tells some wholesome truths, not the less important for coming after the evil they sought to correct: "Not only were Shakespeares and Platos being killed outright, but many of the best harvests of the survivors had to be sown in the barren soil of the trenches. And this was no mere British consideration. To a truly civilized man, to the good European, the slaughter of the German youth was as disastrous as the English. Fools exulted in 'German losses.' They were our losses as well. Imagine exulting in the death of Beethoven because Bill Sykes dealt him his death blow!"

Almost continuously for the next ten years and more, other writers were dramatizing the gigantic catastrophe. Somerset Maugham in 1920 wrote *The Unknown;* Ernst Toller, imprisoned as a dangerous revolutionist, produced in 1919 *Die Wandlung* in the white heat of his fury against the war machine, following it four years later with his expressionist drama, *Hinkemann,* which traces so harrowing a picture of one man's calvary in the aftermath that only the chaotic unreality of the dramatic form makes it possible to bear.

In France H. R. Lenormand, a master of the new psychology, explored in his play of the coward, *Le lâche,* the mind and emotions of an artist who, physically weak, abhorred every form of violence and went through agonies of spiritual torture to avoid being sent to the front. It is the inner tragedy of the contemned, those who "die many times before their death" for a fault chargeable to nature and a necessity imposed by man. The subject, antipathetic to most writers, found an able exponent in Lenormand who in his almost medieval belief in the active power of evil, revealed its influence, through the medium of war, upon one of the darker aspects of the human psyche.

These, with Zweig's and Rolland's allegorical dramas, are but a few chosen from the hundreds, to indicate the various directions taken by the creative mind. In the United States the first and at the same time the best war play exploded with the shock of a powerful shell at the Plymouth Theatre, New York, during the season of 1924. Laurence Stallings, co-author of *What Price Glory?* had fought in the war. He had been in it at the worst period, and had returned maimed and, like the rest, emotionally shattered. He had seen men brutalized by trench life; he had watched, day by day, the disintegration, physical and moral, of pitiful wretches who could no longer be recognized as human beings. His resentment cried for expression, but it was only after his experiences had crystallized into the material for art that, with Maxwell Anderson as collaborator, he wrote his tremendous indictment.

"*What Price Glory?* is a play of war as it is," the program warned the audience, "not as it has been presented theatrically for hundreds of years. The soldiers talk and act much as soldiers the world over. The speech of men under arms is universally and constantly interlarded with profanity. . . ."

Wilfred Owen had commented upon the fact in one of his poems:

> I have perceived much beauty

In the hoarse oaths that kept our courage
straight.

Barbusse in *Le feu* had made it the subject of a pathetically
amusing scene when, while he is writing in the trenches, one
of his men expresses the suspicion that he will make them talk
like proper folk—the way the people back there, at home,
would have them talk, all the *gros mots* chastely indicated by
asterisks.

What Price Glory? shook New York out of all complacence.
Here the evils of war were no longer wrapped in sentimental
glamor, but shown naked for what they were, in the convincing art of the theatre. For two breathless hours the audience
lived with the men in the French farmhouse behind the lines,
followed them in their wine-cellar dug-out, and groaned with
desperation when, returning spent and wounded from their
terrific battle, the soldiers were ordered back to fight. People
sat tense through revolting scenes, not knowing whether to
admire or shudder at those creatures, impervious now to everything but death. Pious souls, missing the burning message
of the play, tried to have it closed on moral grounds. But the
public now wanted the truth and *What Price Glory?* remained
for the rest of a successful run.

In the novel the protest against war was heard even earlier,
coming, as was to be expected, from men who had been
thrown into the fray in its initial stages. *Men in War* by Andreas Latzko, an Austrian army officer, was perhaps the first
of the hundreds of war books to receive universal attention.
Its vivid sketches, compacted in their fidelity of the mud and
blood of the trenches, appeared in America in 1918, just in
time to make the nation reflect whether it had done wisely
to send the flower of her youth to so futile a carnage. Two
years later Latzko published a novel, *The Judgment of Peace.*
A powerful arraignment, it was still too close to the facts for
the author to write without bias. Full of hate though it was
for war, the makers of war and the cruelties of a vindictive
peace, it showed little of that brotherhood of man which it
advocated, and differed only in its honest attempt at fairness
from such partisan accounts as *My Memoirs* by Grand Admiral von Tirpitz, and *Ludendorff's Own Story,* both published
the same year.

But by that time Henri Barbusse had written *Le feu,* his searing document of the war, which, as if the picture he painted
were too black for mortal eyes, he alleviated with the light
of hope in *Clarté.* Both novels were the outcome of the early
years of the war. In *Le feu* he used the simple device of a journal recording the vicissitudes of his squad. With uncanny visual lucidity he sought out the least detail, omitting nothing,
however degrading, to reveal the unmitigated horror of the
thing he condemned. Never, before or since, has such a picture been drawn of war, from the physical misery of trench
life, to the soul-killing effect of the profession of murder.
There are scenes which even in the distance of years lose none
of their power: the shooting of the young soldier for running
back from the line of fire; the finding of Eudoxie's rotting
body by the man who had loved her, hopelessly. But it is in
the scenes of actual battle, toward the end of *Le feu,* that the
author dares to look into the very depths of the abyss.

Perhaps because of his despair at the futility of it all Barbusse
sought to persuade himself that it had not been in vain, and
that out of the fearful devastation some great truth might
arise for humanity. With renewed faith in society, he announced his message of hope in *Clarté,* out of which grew the

international group of that name, preaching peace, the solidarity of nations, and the social equality of all citizens—to
which high aims time has made sardonic commentary in the
wars which have since spilled blood in Ethiopia, in Asia
Minor, in China, in Africa, in Spain—in Europe!

More realistic because earlier disenchanted in their life,
American writers saw no ray in the blackness. "War is hell,"
they agreed, and as hell they wrote of it, some well, some not
so well, a few superbly. The first two notable war books, *One
Man's Initiation* and *Three Soldiers* brought John Dos Passos
to the fore as a realist of the first importance though as yet
he had not discovered the swift, cinema technique of his social novels. Both books stripped war of all romance, and certainly *Three Soldiers* will hold its place as a valuable human
record. It is in the later novels of Dos Passos, however, most
particularly in his trilogy published as *U.S.A.,* that he has
made the most effective use of his assimilation of world
events. In the largeness of its scope *U.S.A.* is in itself a history
of the war and its effects on America.

For the present generation, and probably for generations to
come, it is *A Farewell to Arms* that will remain the book of
the war for its tragic love story and the still starker tragedy
of Caporetto. When Ernest Hemingway wrote his novel he
was some ten years removed from the events he described. He
had come back from his self-imposed exile in France and
from his tutelage to Gertrude Stein; and he had a considerable amount of work behind him in published novels and
short stories. In *A Farewell to Arms,* however, he realized to
the full the strength of which he had so far given only intimations. In the rushing narrative it is not so much Lieutenant
Frederick Henry who is the protagonist as the army of which
he is a part, not alone the army, but the whole, unholy complex of war, which one entered for the fun of the thing but
which in the end when love, friendship, body, and spirit had
been crushed by it, wrung out the wormwood wisdom: "I was
always embarrassed by the words sacred, glorious, and sacrifice and the expression in vain. . . . I had seen nothing sacred, and the things that were glorious had no glory and the
sacrifices were like the stockyards at Chicago if nothing was
done with the meat except to bury it."

Hemingway has been called the American Byron; but Byron
had had no such real causes to be obsessed by violence and
death. If Hemingway is Byronic it is because he has wished
to be an active participant in life, seeking out by preference
its stronger passions whether of love or of war. Again, Hemingway has been accused of having no political or social convictions, of being attracted, for example, by the spectacle of
war instead of searching into the causes that make it. But
then, is there not conviction enough in the manner of a novelist's treatment of his subject? Hemingway could have glorified Caporetto—as no doubt it has been done—into a lofty
sacrifice, appropriately epitaphed with *Dulce et decorum. . . .* Instead he has us see it as a huge Golgotha, one
of the many sky-reaching mounds which mankind has been
fond of raising only to find at their summit a grinning skull.
It was Hemingway whom Gertrude Stein had in mind when
for a moment uncryptic she evolved the meaningful phrase
of the "lost generation"; and him it best suited perhaps, until
recently, when from his barren research of death in the bull-
ring and in the green hills of Africa, he saw it for the first time
ennobled among the fighters for freedom in Spain.

Edward Estling Cummings it was, however, who, before he
became the poet e. e. cummings, produced the most unique,

and some would have it, the best, book of the war when his connection with a letter-writing friend brought him to a concentration camp on suspicion of espionage. There was no evidence against him except that he knew Mr. B. It was enough, nevertheless, for the French government to take him from the Norton Harjes Division for which he had been driving an ambulance, and send him off under guard to Macé, a virtual prisoner "for the duration of the war." *The Enormous Room* was the outcome. Though only indirectly an arraignment of the war, its implications reaching as deep and as far as the perceptions of an extraordinarily keen artist, it conveys a more annihilating sense of the debasement of the individual under the conditions produced by war than any description of the shambles of the battlefield. For here it is human dignity that is every day degraded, and the human spirit that is done to death.

It remained for an Englishwoman to write the heart-wrung testament of war's youth. Vera Brittain's personal record of the war did not appear until 1933; even after such lapse of time it must still have taken great courage to recall and set down scenes so harrowing, and to reckon again losses so cruel. *Testament of Youth* is a narrative of the war as deceived young idealists saw it at the front, and as their sisters and sweethearts lived it in the war hospitals and at home during the anguished years of the actual fighting and the disheartening period of reconstruction when post-war Europe was struggling to rise out of the wreckage of civilization. More than all that, it is the story of another lost generation, one that never found its way back to the world of the living. (pp. 204-12)

Frances Winwar, "The World War and the Arts,"
in War in the Twentieth Century, *edited by Willard*
Waller, The Dryden Press, 1940, pp. 192-232.

ENGLISH LITERATURE OF WORLD WAR I

ARTHUR WAUGH

[*In the following excerpt from an essay published during the final month of the war, Waugh discusses the nature and value of English war poetry.*]

The experience of the present war ought surely to have taught believers in prophecy a trenchant lesson. Never in the history of the world can there have been a time when the prophets have proved more consistently wrong; and nowhere have they wandered further astray than in those doleful predictions which foretold the temporary overthrow of literature and literary interests. In the first months of the war it seemed generally agreed by critics and creative artists alike that the genius of expression itself was doomed to disappear in the immediate future. Works of imagination, we were assured, must cease to trouble the mind of man; no poetry worthy of the name was likely to be written during the next twenty years. It was a depressing prospect; but fortunately the prophecy was no sooner uttered than the event asserted its fallacy. A torrent of poetry began at once to pour from the press; and the voice of criticism found itself obliged to swing round to the opposite pole. The war, we were then told, had become

a very forcing-ground of poetry; it was recreating the poet's heart out of its own fires; we were face to face with an almost miraculous renaissance of the poetic spirit. This access of enthusiasm has also faded in its turn; and its wild confidence is shown to have been no less deceptive than the vain depression which preceded it. We are beginning, in short, to arrive at a more equable condition of judgment, and to see things in more accurate perspective.

The time therefore appears propitious for taking stock of the influence which the war has exercised upon contemporary poetry, and, conversely, for considering the contribution which this poetry has of its own initiative made towards an understanding of the true meaning and significance of War. Of the two considerations, the second is likely to prove the more fruitful. For it would seem to be not so much a fact that the war has made poetry, as that poetry has, now for the first time, made War—made it in its own image, with all the tinsel and gaud of tradition stripped away from it; and so made it perhaps that no sincere artist will ever venture again to represent War in those delusive colours with which Art has been too often content to disguise it in the past. From that dual point of view, at any rate, it is proposed in the following pages to consider the best of the war poetry of the last four years, and to attempt to estimate its spiritual effect upon the character of the nation.

It has been widely argued that the war must have been an inspirer of poetry because so many volumes of verse have been published during the last three years, written by young officers who have fallen in active service. It is the war alone, we are asked to assume, that has of its own creative power forced these otherwise "mute, inglorious Miltons" into song. But every one who has owned friends among public-school and University men must know that the impulse to record emotion in verse is one of the commonest attributes of educated adolescence. As a rule these youthful exercises languish in the privacy of the author's bureau; and it is only the perfectly worthy ambition of bereaved parents, to raise some personal memorial to a dead son, that has recently haled so many of these manly tributes into the light of publicity. Many of them bear witness to very creditable metrical proficiency; most of them are distinguished by highly meritorious sentiment. But it would be the falsest of compliments to pretend that they make any real addition to the poetry of War. For the most part they record pleasant memories of school and college, breathe a boyish loyalty to grey cloisters and green glades, but touch the essence of life no deeper than is possible to the soldier's honest determination to go out and do his best. Their mental and spiritual attitude to war, in short, is radically conventional; and they are thus entirely separated from the really significant poetry of the present war, of which the outstanding characteristic is its absolute freedom from convention, demonstrated in an eager, almost passionate determination to picture War as it reveals itself, not to the outsider, but to the enlightened combatant himself.

And here, at the outset, we find ourselves face to face with the differentiating quality of the best new poetry of War. It is written, not by lookers-on, but by the soldiers themselves. The relation between war and poetry, of course, is as old as either war or poetry itself; and we stand in no need of the picturesque *pastiches* of Sir Walter Scott to remind us of those wandering minstrels who strayed from castle to castle, singing by the fireside of the doughty deeds of dead heroes, to the end that the young men might be stirred to go out and fight, and the maidens' hearts preserved from breaking while their lovers were away. Most of the war poetry of the past has been the legitimate descendant of these glib eulogists, of whom the first thing to remember is that their whole business is to encourage and to praise, to set romance twittering among the leaves—in short, to tell noble lies about War, that the purpose of the country may be served. Poetry, in fact, has to plead guilty to misrepresenting War, in the cause either of politics or of art—of misrepresenting it as something intrinsically splendid, beautiful, and inspiring. It has persistently confused the issue with the process. Splendid things are done in war, of course; but they are the issue of war, not its process.

For the mere process of warfare is indisputably a vile, inhuman, devilish abomination, plunged in squalor and filth. It is approached through seas of mud, and pursued amid vermin and all uncleanness. It degrades the body of man; more than that, it would destroy his very soul itself, were it not for the divine fire that burns at the heart of humanity, and consumes even the weapons of war in the white heat of its truth. And in the present war, when, for the first time since the nation became articulate, fighting has ceased to be the business of a professional class, and has become perforce the bitter duty of the whole manhood of the race, we have had something approaching its true meaning revealed to us in poetry; not because war had any virtue in it that would "make a poet out of a man," but simply because the poet has himself turned soldier, and concentrated upon the ugly and monotonous business of war the keen searchlight of interpretation. The professional soldier is inevitably an unimaginative product; of all classes of the community, he is, perhaps, most completely the victim of tradition. His "not to reason why"; his, in the very nature of things, to do what he is told, and to do it as quickly and as effectually as possible. But, now that war has ceased to be the concern of a professional class, its secrets have been revealed to the world at large. And so, for the first time, we have had the clear lights of intellect and interpretation playing upon the battlefield; and, whatever may be thought of the gain or loss to poetry, there can at least be no question about the extraordinary actuality of this new presentment, about its sincerity, or about the arresting revelation which it affords of the evil and the horror of modern warfare between civilised communities.

The contrast is the more vivid because of the high ideals and the exalted purpose with which the yoke of battle was at first accepted by the nation at large. It has been repeated so often as to have grown tedious that no nation ever entered upon war with a cleaner conscience than Britain in the summer of 1914. And repetition does not dull the edge of that truth; it is indisputably true. No one could accuse Mr. Thomas Hardy, for example, of sentimentalising a situation of this kind. If there had been an atom of false pretence about it, his searching gaze would have tracked it down in its secret corner. But for once, as the drums are heard in the village street, the old poet is stirred out of his cynicism, and stands, as it were, to attention at the window in the dim light of the early dawn, proud of his fellow-countrymen, and confident in their cause.

> What of the faith and fire within us
>   Men who march away
>   Ere the barn-cocks say
>   Night is growing gray,
> To hazards whence no tears can win us?
> What of the faith and fire within us
>   Men who march away? . . .

> In our heart of hearts believing
>   Victory crowns the just,
>   And that braggarts must
>   Surely bite the dust,
> March we to the field ungrieving,
> In our heart of hearts believing
>   Victory crowns the just.

This sense of a just cause, almost of a sacred crusade, may be said to have inspired all the war poetry written during the closing months of 1914. In Mr. Laurence Binyon's rich and high-hearted "For the Fallen" it is presented as the one sure amulet of consolation.

> With proud thanksgiving, a mother for her children,
> England mourns for her dead across the sea.
> Flesh of her flesh they were, spirit of her spirit,
> Fallen in the cause of the free. . . .

Something of the same sentiment, too, broods over the harvest-fields in Mr. John Masefield's "August, 1914," linking to the present sacrifice all those sons of the soil who in the past have left home and loved ones and hope, for the sake of an immortal dream of freedom:

> And died (uncouthly, most) in foreign lands
> For some idea but dimly understood
> Of an English city never built by hands,
> Which love of England prompted and made good.

This was the universal sentiment of our poetry at the outset of the war; but it was a sentiment which, in the nature of things, would scarcely survive the insistent claim of personality. In particular, it could not be expected to survive the ordeal of individual experience. It was detached, remote—the sentiment, in a word, of the onlooker. It was once more the true descendant of the old ballad poetry, made by men who stood outside the fiery trial of battle. It philosophised the situation, but it did not embody it realistically.

Now, as it happened, the chief tendency in English verse for several years before the outbreak of the war had been a tendency towards crude realism, finding its inspiration in themes which had hitherto, perhaps, been considered impossible to the idealising spirit of poetry. The younger generation, perceiving that the idyllic school of verse had inevitably exhausted its capacities, appeared to have set its heart upon proving that no subject lies intrinsically outside the limits of poetic treatment, and that poetry can draw to its service, and ennoble by its interpretation, even the most uncouth and hideous circumstance. The war, therefore, may be said to have afforded our young realists the richest possible opportunity for concentrating their art upon the vital moments of life and death. It was an opportunity at once pictorial and psychological. Its appeal was equally to the eye and to the heart; and it was immediately accepted with the eager frankness characteristic of our younger writers, and with the prevalent determination to speak the truth about the ugly things of life, and to strip suffering bare of all concealing veils of sentimentality and pretence. The work of revelation has been undertaken with untrammelled honesty; and its completion raises a very important problem. How far, we must ask, can poetry proceed in the vivid portrayal of death and destruction, and yet remain what poetry must always be, if it is to be worthy of its traditions—a spiritual interpretation of the soul of man in conflict with his environment?

The first stage, at any rate, of the poet's initiation in the

Manuscript of Rupert Brooke's patriotic sonnet "The Soldier."

school of war brings with it no difficulty at all; it is purely and intimately introspective. It follows tradition with unfaltering step; and the first change to be observed is a rather startling retrogression from the universal to the purely personal point of view. It is comparatively easy for the onlooker to be eloquent in behalf of a cause; but the man who is swept into the field of action becomes, at the first onset, disconcertingly conscious of his own individuality and of his immediate personal risk. The young man trained to an intellectual life, with the plans for his future career plain before him, can scarcely break with so many associations unmoved by a sense of sacrifice; and the first poems to be written by soldier-poets were almost inevitably touched by a certain irresistible sense of self-pity. Rupert Brooke's sonnet "The Soldier" is the natural utterance of a young man who is leaving behind him everything that made life worth living, and who, faced by the prospect of an untimely death, seeks his consolation in bringing the future into some sort of permanent relation with the past. Wherever he falls, he will carry with him some spirit of his home, some tribute to his training, some memorial of his love. And other poems, like Mr. Robert Nichols's "Farewell," and the "Into Battle" of Julian Grenfell, are inspired by the same vague uncertainty, the same tremulous trust that a man may be remembered as having shown the courage which all the education of his youth was designed to breed.

They shall not say I went with heavy heart:
Heavy I am, but soon I shall be free,
I love them all, but oh, I now depart
A little sadly, strangely, fearfully,
As one who goes to try a mystery.

And again:

The kestrel hovering by day,
    And the little owls that call by night,
Bid him be swift and keen as they,
    As keen of ear, as swift of sight.

The blackbird sings to him, "Brother, brother,
    If this be the last song you shall sing,
Sing well, for you may not sing another;
    Brother, sing."

In these first moments of solitude it is perhaps inevitable that a man should be thinking of himself, but the mood passes with extraordinary rapidity; and the next change in the poet's attitude to War can be traced in almost every one of the young writers who have actually been into the front lines. The sense of a cause vanishes; the sense of self vanishes; and over all spreads an impenetrable, absorbing prepossession that War is after all merely another form of toiling, moiling business, beset with detail, loaded with obligation, in which the individual soldier is of no more significance than the proverbial cog in a vast mass of labouring machinery.

Men, as Mr. Gilbert Frankau sees them clearly, have become the slaves of the guns.

> These are our masters, the slim
>   Grim muzzles that irk in the pit;
> That chafe for the rushing of wheels,
>   For the teams plunging madly to bit
> As the gunners swing down to unkey,
>   For the trails sweeping half-circle-right,
> For the six breech-blocks clashing as one
>   To a target viewed clear on the sight—
> Dun masses, the shells search and tear
>   Into fragments that bunch as they run—
> For the hour of the red battle-harvest,
>   The dream of the slaves of the gun.

In these Kiplingesque lines the creak of the machine has practically drowned the voice of poetry altogether; but the authentic note sounds less uncertainly in Mr. Robert Nichols's "On the Way Up."

> The battery grides and jingles,
>   Mile succeeds to mile;
> Shaking the noonday sunshine,
>   The guns lunge out awhile
> And then are still awhile.
>
> We amble along the highway;
>   The reeking, powdery dust
> Ascends and cakes our faces,
>   With a striped, sweaty crust.
>
> Under the still sky's violet
>   The heat throbs in the air . . .
> The white road's dusty radiance
>   Assumes a dark glare.
>
> With a head hot and heavy,
>   And eyes that cannot rest,
> And a black heart burning
>   In a stifled breast,
>
> I sit in the saddle,
>   I feel the road unroll,
> And keep my senses straightened
>   Towards to-morrow's goal.

These pieces, which are grouped together in Mr. Osborn's suggestive anthology [*The Muse in Arms*, 1917], under the general title of "The Approach," may be said to bridge the gulfs that separate the three stages in the poet's initiation. In the first, where the battery has halted by the wayside, a sudden paroxysm of fear attacks the soldier. For a moment he is absorbed once more in himself. In the next, he has become a part of the machinery of war; the battery itself is the unit, and community of task the whole duty of life. In the third, community of task has opened out into human sympathy. "Men I love about me!" The machinery of war has revealed itself as composed of an infinity of human atoms, every one with a history, and a significance of its own. The man has passed out of himself into the heart of others; and, while life is seen to be made up of an endless sequence of little things, nothing in life, now so perpetually at odds with death, appears to be unworthy of care and consideration. This is, perhaps, the one and only helpful lesson that war brings home to the common soldier's heart, and it is instilled in a variety of different guises.

The life of the soldier lumbers along, revealing itself in broken glimpses through a mist of grey monotony. One thing which home-keeping age finds it difficult to realise is the interminable dulness which slowly settles down upon what once promised to be an heroic campaign. There are stretches of irksome inaction, during which the mind labours to reconcile itself with its uncongenial occupation. Weary detail, uninspired vigil, perpetual repetition of duties only half understood, throw the mind back upon itself and feed it with memory. In such lonely hours the impressions of the past become importunate, and flashes of the old life penetrate through the most unlikely environment. Wyndham Tennant describes this poignantly in "Home Thoughts in Laventie."

> Hungry for spring, I bent my head,
>   The perfume fanned my face,
> And all my soul was dancing
>   In that little lovely place,
> Dancing with a measured step from wrecked and
>   shattered towns
>   Away—upon the Downs.
>
> I saw green banks of daffodils,
>   Slim poplars in the breeze,
> Great tan-brown hares in gusty March
>   A-courting on the leas;
> And meadows with their glittering streams, and silver scurrying dace,
>   Home—what a perfect place!

And gradually the very contrast between the broad calm of the past and the infinite restlessness of the present draws the man out of himself into some sort of philosophic resignation.

> Here there are the great things, life and death, and
>   danger,
> All I ever dreamed of in the days that used to be,
> Comrades and good-fellowship, the soul of an
>   army,
> But oh, it is the little things that take the heart of
>   me.
>
> For all we knew of old, for little things and lovely,
> We bow us to a greater life beyond our hope or fear.
> To bear its heavy burdens, endure its toils unheeding,
> Because of all the little things so distant and so
>   dear.
>   ["A Highland Regiment," by E. A. Mackintosh]

Many of the soldier-poets recur naturally to their schooldays, fighting old battles over again on field and in classroom. In this context in particular there emerges the new type of student-in-arms, the bookman, the classical scholar, the meditative yet virile public-school product, bred on good literature and good sport, who carries Homer in his haversack, and dreams of Achilles in the trenches. Of this type a brave and stimulating example is afforded by Charles Hamilton Sorley, whose imagination seems to flood the squalid present with the picturesque heroism of the past. He carries the sunlight of ancient Sparta into the drab, drenched flats of Flanders, and sees the end of conflict in an ideal city of dreams, built "half in heaven" and half upon the windy Marlborough downs.

> Soon, O soon, I do not doubt it,
> With the body or without it,
> We shall all come tumbling down
> To our old wrinkled red-capped town.
> Perhaps the road up Ilsley way,
> The old ridge-track, will be my way.
> High up among the sheep and sky,

Look down on Wantage, passing by,
And see the smoke from Swindon town;
And then full left at Liddington,
Where the four winds of heaven meet
The earth-blest traveller to greet.
And then my face is toward the south,
There is a singing on my mouth:
Away to rightward I descry
My Barbury ensconced in sky,
Far underneath the Ogbourne twins,
And at my feet the thyme and whins,
The grasses with their little crowns
Of gold, the lovely Aldbourne downs,
And that old signpost (well I knew
That crazy signpost, arms askew,
Old mother of the four grass ways).
And then my mouth is dumb with praise,
For, past the wood and chalkpit tiny,
A glimpse of Marlborough ερατεινη!
So I descend beneath the rail
To warmth and welcome and wassail.

So Rupert Brooke, in a well-known poem, dwells with love and longing on the calm beauty of Grantchester, familiar to generations of Cambridge men.

Dreams like these mingle inextricably with the rough-and-ready consolations of companionship. Life has run to waste in a tangle of things imagined and things seen; in the confusion of values the mind grasps at any kind of respite or relief, and, when the pressure is relaxed, and the company is back in billets, as in Captain Charles Scott-Moncreiff's cheery ballad, the simplest, silliest jests have a savour, merely because they help the soldier to forget the perpetually-brooding cloud that lies ahead. Here is no longer, it must be recognised, any dream of heroism, of a cause or a crusade, of broidered banners or a watchword. As dreams merge into reality, men, and men alone, become the material of life; and through the machinery of war the young officer is drawn into sympathy with all who are part and parcel of the same machine. There is no sentimentality about it. The communion of endurance makes them all kin.

Mr. Siegfried Sassoon, perhaps, has expressed better than any one else this emancipation of the soldier's heart from the taint of selfishness. It is the animating spirit of his vivid little piece of realism, "In the Pink." The young subaltern, who records the impression, has entered into the very soul of the private, as he scrawls a letter home to his rustic sweetheart, comforting her with consolations which his own environment belies.

So Davies wrote: "This leaves me in the pink."
Then scrawled his name: "Your loving sweetheart,
   Willie,"
With crosses for a hug. He'd had a drink
Of rum and tea; and, though the barn was chilly,
For once his blood ran warm; he'd pay to spend.
Winter was passing; soon the year would mend.

He couldn't sleep that night. Stiff in the dark
He groaned and thought of Sundays at the farm,
When he'd go out as cheerful as a lark
In his best suit to wander arm-in-arm
With brown-eyed Gwen, and whisper in her ear
The simple, silly things she liked to hear.

And then he thought: to-morrow night we trudge
Up to the trenches, and my boots are rotten.
Five miles of stodgy clay and freezing sludge,
And everything but wretchedness forgotten.
To-night he's in the pink; but soon he'll die.

And still the war goes on; *he* don't know why.

The war goes on, moreover, through a panorama of cruel inequalities, which serve to strip militarism of its last vestiges of glamour. David, as Captain Graves reminds us, no longer triumphs picturesquely over his towering giant. Brute force is stronger than the human heart.

The inevitable response to such experiences is, on the one hand, an honest, deep, and undemonstrative sympathy with the men who suffer; and, on the other, an intolerant contempt for the false sentiment with which ignorant people at home so fatuously invest the horrors of war. Sometimes, as in the late Lieut. Mackintosh's touching "In Memoriam," the sentiment wavers towards an almost feminine air of protectiveness. The young officer pictures himself as filling a parental relation to his men, losing something of his own life with every man who falls.

Oh, never will I forget you,
   My men that trusted me,
More my sons than your fathers',
   For they would only see
The little helpless babies
   And the young men in their pride.
They could not see you dying,
   And hold you while you died.

The same feeling, revealed in a scene of the finest dramatic quality, animates Mr. Robert Nichols's "Comrades," where the dying subaltern, Gates, struggles back to the trenches, mortally wounded, every movement an accentuation of his suffering, out of sheer determination to die among the men for whom he is responsible.

Inch by inch he fought, breathless and mute,
Dragging his carcase like a famished brute. . . .
His head was hammering and his eyes were dim,
A bloody sweat seemed to ooze out of him
And freeze along his spine . . . then he'd lie still
Before another effort of his will
Took him one nearer yard.
                              • • • • •
                    The parapet was reached.
He could not rise to it. A look-out screeched,
"Mr. Gates!"
             Three figures in one breath
Leaped up. Two figures fell in toppling death;
And Gates was lifted in. "Who's hit?" said he.
"Timmins and Jones." "Why did they that for me?
I'm gone already!" Gently they laid him prone
And silently watched.
                    He twitched. They heard him moan,
"Why for me?" His eyes roamed round and none
   replied.
"I see it was alone I should have died."
They shook their heads. Then, "Is the doctor
   here?"
"He's comin', sir, he's hurryin', no fear."
"No good . . . Lift me." They lifted him.
He smiled and held his arms out to the dim,
And in a moment passed beyond their ken,
Hearing him whisper, "O my men, my men!"

So powerful indeed does the immediate influence of a common life become that by degrees all other associations fade before its white-hot vehemence. The present detaches the soldier altogether from the past. Home, love, even the one loved above all, are forgotten. Tenderness seems like a far-away memory; the soldier's concern is with the soldier's life alone.

Faces cheerful, full of whimsical mirth,
Lined by the wind, burned by the sun;
Bodies enraptured by the abounding earth,
As whose children, brothers we are and one.

And any moment may descend hot death
To shatter limbs! pulp, tear and blast
Belovèd soldiers who love rough life and breath
Not less for dying faithful to the last.

O the fading eyes, the grimed face turned bony,
Oped, black, gushing mouth, fallen head,
Failing pressure of a held hand, shrunk and stony!
O sudden spasm, release of the dead!

Was there love once? I have forgotten her.
Was there grief once? grief still is mine.
O loved, living, dying, heroic soldier,
All, all my joy, my grief, my love, are thine!

To those whose life has for months been riddled with visions such as these it is no wonder that a return to home, and the sudden recognition of its false sentiment and falser humour should assault the mind with the sting of intolerable resentment. The old, familiar glosses upon war are indeed effectually held up to scorn by our young realists. Mr. Siegfried Sassoon's "They," with its bitter arraignment of episcopal platitude, is well-balanced by the same poet's almost vindictive cameo of a London music-hall in war-time.

The House is crammed; tier beyond tier they grin
And cackle at the Show, while prancing ranks
Of harlots shrill the chorus, drunk with din;
"We're sure the Kaiser loves the dear old Tanks!
I'd like to see a tank come down the stalls,
Lurching to rag-time tunes, or "Home, sweet
    Home,"—
And there'd be no more jokes in Music-halls
To mock the riddled corpses round Bapaume.

The reflective attitude of modern poetry to war can hardly go further. Sympathy has merged itself in a furious detestation of all those false pretences which in the past have presented the military spirit as a sort of enclosed garden of the poets' fantasy. The men who have seen the thing as it is have left the rest of us in no sort of doubt upon one indisputable fact. The poetry of the future will hardly venture to sentimentalise an experience which can prompt so sincere and so overwhelming an indignation. And indeed it is already to be noted that among those poets also who have not themselves made personal trial of war a new and restrained spirit may be recognised.

The truth has come home to the civilian no less than to the soldier. Mr. Harold Monro's picture of the family gathering the night before the soldier returns to the front labours under no vain illusion with regard to the compensating glory of loss. Every moment, viewed from the stay-at-home's standpoint, is heavy with apprehension; every tick of the clock is like the warning of a death-watch. Suffering has become personal, intimate, homely, as all deep suffering always is. And when the news of loss comes home, as in Mr. J. C. Squire's exquisitely poignant poem "To a Bull-Dog," it is no longer decorated with conventional comfort, but accepted, simply and honestly, for the devastating thing it is. The dog and one of his masters are left alone; the other master has fallen at the front. The poet addresses his dumb companion.

When summer comes again,
    And the long sunsets fade,

We shall have to go on playing the feeble game for
    two
    That since the war we've played.

And though you run expectant as you always do
    To the uniforms we meet,
You'll never find Willy among all the soldiers
    In even the longest street,

Nor in any crowd; yet, strange and bitter thought,
    Even now were the old words said,
If I tried the old trick and said "Where's Willy?"
    You would quiver and lift your head,

And your brown eyes would look to ask if I was se-
    rious,
    And wait for the word to spring
Sleep undisturbed: I shan't say *that* again,
    You innocent old thing.

Simple, direct pathos could scarcely be expressed in simpler, more direct phrase; and yet the metrical scheme of the poem is full of subtlety, rising on the wave of the long line just as the thought rises in intensity, and sinking back into repose in the short. Expression seems to be matched quite perfectly with thought; and the sentiment, purged of all self-pity and protestation, becomes almost intolerably sincere.

Sincerity, indeed, is the essence of the light with which the poetry of the last four years has slowly and increasingly flooded the crowded theatre of war. The quotations which we have given may surely speak for themselves. They must be acknowledged as presenting a broad panorama of the soldier's life from the day he leaves England until the hour of his death upon the field of honour; and their outstanding virtue is the penetration with which they probe to the essential spirit of warfare. Springing from various and diverse temperaments, they illustrate in turn the honest soldier's fear of fear, his pilgrimage from self-consciousness to altruism, his absorption into the machinery of war, and his gradual appreciation of that complex machine as a collection of human characters, each individual and all interacting, combining at last into a unity in which self is merged absolutely in a sense of common purpose and general obligation. The comparison of this poetry with the poetry of any other war in the history of the world can hardly fail to reassure the critic that, so far as the spiritual interpretation of war is concerned, the poets have risen manfully to their opportunity, and have abundantly justified the claim to sincerity and directness which appears to be the staple ambition of modern poetry, whatever its theme and occupation.

So far, it will be noted, we have been considering the function of Poetry in offering a representation of War, psychologically and through its influence upon the soldier's mind; there remains to be considered the value of the material which War in its turn has offered to poetry, from the actual or realistic standpoint. And here, we believe, there has been a general tendency to overrate the value of the contribution. It has been claimed, for instance, that in the sister-art of painting the war has furnished artists with inspiration of the liveliest possibility. Can this be said with equal truth of Poetry? It seems very doubtful; and in any case the ground was ready-made for Poetry long before War had been dreamt of outside the impenetrable councils of Berlin. In the years immediately preceding the war there had been, as we have already noted, a growing fashion in English verse to seek crude and violent subjects for poetry; and this fashion was perilously fostered by the popular success of such realistic exercises as Mr. John Masefield's

"The Everlasting Mercy" and "The Widow in the Bye-Street," which may perhaps be said to display the method to its most effectual advantage.

The fashion was already exhausting itself before the autumn of 1914, but it has been adopted by a few experimentalists in an attempt to represent the outward aspects of War, condensed and vitalised to a single vivid and entirely external impression. It is noticeable, however, that the attempt has not been so much encouraged by those who had already affected this particular kind of realism, as accepted by others in a sort of faint discipleship. Such poems as Mr. Masefield himself has devoted to the war have been almost entirely psychological and interpretative; and of the older of the Georgian poets it has been left to Mr. Gibson to whittle poetry down to its barest core, in the effort to present a keen and undecorated outline of fact. It cannot be said that the experiment is altogether fortunate.

> This bloody steel
>   Has killed a man.
> I heard him squeal
>   As on I ran.
>
> He watched me come
>   With wagging head.
> I pressed it home,
>   And he was dead.
>
> Though clean and clear
>   I've wiped the steel,
> I still can hear
>   That dying squeal.

Or again:

> I watched it oozing quietly
>   Out of the gaping gash.
> The lads thrust on to victory
>   With lunge and curse and crash. . . .
>
> The lads thrust on to victory,
>   With lunge and crash and shout.
> I lay and watched, as quietly
>   His life was running out.

The consensus of critical judgment would almost certainly decide that such experiments as these are failures. They fail, because they are concerned exclusively with external facts; imagination has not got to work upon them; the poet's art has not even made the effort of fusing the fact with the idea. And the same is true of Mr. Robert Nichols's "Assault," an elaborate attempt to give instant and compelling expression to the sights and sounds of onslaught, which nevertheless falls completely short of the true, interpretative service of poetry to life.

> I hear my whistle shriek
> Between teeth set;
> I fling an arm up,
> Scramble up the grime
> Over the parapet!
>
> I'm up. Go on.
> Something meets us.
> Head down into the storm that greets us.
>
> A wail!
> Lights. Blurr.
> Gone.
> On, on. Lead. Lead. Hail.
> Spatter. Whirr. Whirr.

The true test of poetry must always be the test of reading aloud. Unless a poem can bear recitation, its workmanship is condemned. And to read Mr. Nichols's "Assault" aloud is to be persuaded of a creaking chain of artistic improprieties, which strain vehemently towards effect, only to end in incoherence.

> Ha! Ha! Bunched figures waiting.
> Revolver levelled: quick!
> Flick! Flick!
> Red as blood.
> Germans. Germans.
> Good! Oh, good!
>
> Cool madness.

This is neither metre nor *vers libre.* It has no form or true proportion; the fever of war has infected it, and left it void.

The fact is, of course, that Poetry can only be produced when imagination has fused fact; and that this fusion is possible, even to emphatically realistic verse, is proved by the impressive success of Captain Robert Graves's "It's a Queer Time," where the poet reproduces, with provocative fidelity, that familiar state of mind under which a man is conscious of acting with his bodily functions in one world while he is living with his brain in another. Past and present are commingled in a riot of confusion.

> You're charging madly at them yelling "Fag!"
> When somehow something gives and your feet
>   drag.
> You fall and strike your head; yet feel no pain
> And find . . . you're digging tunnels through the
>   hay
> In the Big Barn, 'cause it's a rainy day.
> O springy hay, and lovely beams to climb!
> You're back in the old sailor-suit again.
>   It's a queer time.
>
> Or you'll be dozing safe in your dug-out—
> A great roar—the trench shakes and falls about—
> You're struggling, gasping, struggling, then . . .
>   hullo!
> Elsie comes tripping gaily down the trench,
> Hanky to nose—that lyddite makes a stench—
> Getting her pinafore all over grime.
> Funny! because she died ten years ago!
>   It's a queer time.

This realism of the intellectual aspect of War, as contrasted with the merely material realism of lamp-black and lightning, has indeed afforded poetry a new scope for the imagination; and particularly in the work of Captain Graves, Mr. Siegfried Sassoon, and some of that of Mr. Robert Nichols, it has produced verse of a quality which could not, perhaps, have found inspiration at all in times of peace and contentment. But it will be noted at once that it is a realism which depends, for its very essence, upon a transcendental interpretation. The war, in other words, has only furnished poetry with material, when Poetry has brought to its aid a secret interpretation which is, in effect, the very antithesis of War itself. The concomitants of War are noise, squalor, filth—the worst antagonists of the poet's art. So long as the poet is content with merely superficial pictures of noise, squalor, and filth, War affords him no adequate opportunity. Its entire world is too barren, too hard, too hideous to issue in poetry. Even Captain Graves goes artistically wrong with his bloated portrait of the dead Boche. The image is starkly repellent; imagination has failed to light it up. But directly imagination gets to work, it finds the soul beneath the surface, and then at last Poetry issues from the union.

A comparison of the spirit of this new poetry with that of the generation which preceded it would seem to suggest that War has most certainly not been without its purging influence upon the artistic soul of youth. For the new poetry is honest; it is strong; and it is often very beautiful. Decadence, at any rate, has vanished; triviality is no more; eccentricity has almost disappeared. And with these inadequate tricks of manner there has also disappeared a certain narrowness or selfishness of outlook upon the world around. The old formula of youth in the Ibsen period, the formula that clamoured for every man to live out his own life after his own fashion, has yielded before a realisation that no man's life can belong to himself, even for a moment; and that, when all is said and done, the individual life is of very little concern to the world at large. Sentimentality has been most healthily lived down; there is an almost universal distrust of conventional consolation. Religion, perhaps, has lost the vigour of its hold upon the imagination, and one can trace very little faith in any survival of personality after death. But a larger and an austerer hope still finds the dead inseparable from every haunt of old association.

> Walking through trees to cool my heat and pain,
> I know that David's with me here again.
> All that is simple, happy, strong he is.
> Caressingly I stroke
> Rough bark of the friendly oak.
> A brook goes bubbling by: the voice is his.
> Turf burns with pleasant smoke:
> I laugh at chaffinch and at primroses.
> All that is simple, happy, strong, he is.
> Over the whole wood in a little while
> Breaks his slow smile.
>   ["Fairies and Fusiliers," by Robert Graves]

We end, then, with the conclusion that Poetry, in spite of many tribulations, is well justified of its supreme ordeal. It has gone down into the darkness, and has carried light in its hand. Our young men, indeed, have grown old, as befits those who have been face to face with death. It may be true that the war has made Stoics of our Hedonists, but in the process it has also made men. And, being men, they have not feared to speak the truth about the bitter discipline under which they have emerged into manhood. It is a terrible truth, wounding the speaker and the hearer alike; but it is a truth that may yet help to set free the soul of humanity for nobler victories in the years of peace. (pp. 380-400)

Arthur Waugh, "War-Poetry (1914-1918)," in Quarterly Review of Literature, *Vol. 230, No. 457, October, 1918, pp. 380-400.*

JOHN H. JOHNSTON

[*An American educator and critic, Johnston is the author of* English Poetry of the First World War: A Study in the Evolution of Lyric and Narrative Form *(1964). In the following excerpt from that work, he discusses the creation by English soldier-poets of a poetic system that enabled them to fully render their experiences in verse.*]

According to the well-known judgment of Dryden, the heroic poem is "undoubtedly the greatest work which the soul of man is capable to perform." Although we no longer subscribe to rigid literary hierarchies, we still admire—perhaps the

more profoundly because we find them so difficult to attain—the classic qualities of epic narrative, whether Greek or Germanic in origin: comprehensiveness, objectivity, and a sense of proportion and restraint, together with a positive, assertive attitude with respect to the values upon which motivation and action are based. In reading the poetry of World War I we are inevitably impressed by the absence of these qualities. We see a body of verse limited to a rather narrow range of personal experience, subjective and impressionistic in mode, marked by emotional excess, and motivated by disillusionment, anger, or pity. A tenuous but generic relationship exists among all types of literature devoted to the subject of war, and some of the deficiencies of modern war poetry may be assigned both to the lapse of the epic tradition and to the conditions of modern warfare which made that tradition seem impracticable and irrelevant. Other deficiencies may be traced to the immediate lyric tradition as practiced by the Georgians, for most of the young war poets shared the Georgian outlook and modeled their early verse upon established Georgian techniques. The evolution of World War I poetry is characterized by a spontaneous effort on the part of these young men to improvise some means of contact with a particularly ugly and violent revelation of the contemporary reality, and by a corresponding intensification of the lyric response. Later in the war, as the result of a deepening sense of tragic involvement, most of the soldier-poets began to understand the inadequacies of mere emotional or realistic intensification; they sought, or thought of seeking, a larger and more comprehensive mode for the interpretation of wartime experience. They tried the lyric sequence; they tried the verse narrative; and they tried to enlarge and unify the vision behind the lyric by means of the theme of pity. Significantly, the purpose of these varied experiments was realized, long after the war, in a remarkable narrative poem of heroic temper and scope—proving that the epic spirit was not defunct, and that a critical invocation of epic standards with regard to World War I poetry is not altogether beside the point.

The rapid transition from the "deep meadows" of Georgian peace and security to the shocking conditions of trench warfare in France was accompanied by a powerfully negative psychological reaction. If the epic glorified primitive combat as a heroic occupation and a test of individual worth, the main tendency of contemporary war poetry has been to deglorify modern warfare, to strip it of its falsely romantic and adventurous aspects, to emphasize its futility, and to portray it as shameful and degrading. The poets of World War I made it clear that man could no longer depend on his personal courage or strength for victory or even survival; mechanization, the increased size of armies, the intensification of operations, and the scientific efficiency of long-distance weapons destroyed the very elements of human individuality: courage, hope, enterprise, and a sense of the heroic possibilities in moral and physical conflict. Needless to say, the old epic standards of heroic achievement have disappeared entirely or are invoked only as implicit points of bitterly ironic contrasts. The modern soldier is portrayed as a passive and often degraded victim of circumstances. Siegfried Sassoon's infantrymen, for example, succumb to hysteria ("Lamentations"), take their own lives ("Suicide in the Trenches"), or perish in an ill-conceived attack ("The General"). In "Third Ypres" Edmund Blunden's soldiers die ignominiously or, stunned and helpless, crouch amid the ruins of a shell-blasted pillbox. The weapons of modern warfare add new terrors to death: mutilation, dismemberment, the agony of poison gas (Wilfred Owen's "Dulce et Decorum Est"). In terms that reverse all idealistic conceptions of death in warfare, Isaac Rosenberg's "Dead Man's Dump" depicts the pitiable degradation of the slain. After the war a succession of novels confirmed or enlarged these earlier impressions of violence, horror, and brutality; personal narratives and autobiographical accounts, such as Edmund Blunden's *Undertones of War* (1928) and Robert Graves's *Good-bye to All That* (1929), corroborated the imaginative projections of the novel. Although all of these writers differ in their degrees of specification and emphasis, not even the most meditative can deal with his material without some reference to the demoralizing conditions of modern warfare. Amid such conditions a mood of bitter disillusionment was inevitable; this attitude, of course, provided the poetry of World War I with its major themes and materials. The generally negative character of modern war poetry thus contrasts directly with the positive, affirmative character of epic battle literature, with its proud sense of past glories and its total commitment to the imperatives of heroic action.

A further point of contrast bears more directly upon the development of certain less obvious attitudes and their effects on poetic technique. Unlike the epic poet, who usually wrote of the distant past and was thus able to enlarge and transform his subject imaginatively, the harassed soldier-poet was in the very midst of the events which he attempted to depict. He was confined to a historical reality well known—at least in its superficial aspects—to those who might read his verse; he could take no large imaginative liberties with the facts and phenomena of the struggle. The soldier-poet, indeed, was seldom inclined to take such liberties; he felt it his special role—even his obligation—to see and portray the war as a starkly contemporaneous event. His material was the reality of the war as personal experience revealed it to him, and the unadorned expression or communication of that reality was his urgent concern. If the function of the epic poet was to entertain his audience with tales of heroic adventure set in the distant past, the modern war poet presents his impressions of suffering and tragedy not as a matter for simple entertainment but as an implicit or explicit protest against the very aims and methods of that conflict in which he is engaged.

Doubtless the fact that the epic poets dealt with the distant past has some relation to the qualities of objectivity, proportion, and restraint that are characteristic of epic and heroic narrative. Well removed in time from the men and events of his tale, the epic poet could hardly be emotionally subject to the issues of a legendary past; divested of its urgency and immediacy, purified of all extraneous feeling, the drama of the epic narrative exists in a separate, self-sustaining dimension of its own. Modern war poetry, on the other hand, is deprived of the aesthetic advantages of temporal remoteness; it is inextricably involved in the whole physical and psychological complex of warfare and takes its particular spirit from a dedicated and often desperate representation of that complex. This situation is further intensified by the mood of disillusion and rejection, which lends particular animus to the presentation of the disagreeable aspects of modern warfare and raises special problems of selection and control.

In World War I the great mission of the poet who had some prospect of publishing his verse was to communicate his sense of the reality of war to the millions at home who would not or could not appreciate the magnitude of the experiences and sacrifices of the common soldier. Even the poet who had no ready public outlet for his verse seems to be aware of his mission as spokesman and his voice has nearly the same degree

of urgency. Granting the imperative nature of that mission, the artistic virtues of objectivity, proportion, and restraint hardly seemed useful or even desirable. During the second winter of the war, when the true nature of the struggle was becoming apparent, poets began to react to the horrors around them with a directness almost unprecedented in verse. This literature of angry protest employed the weapons of satire, irony, and a savage realism, since realism seemed the only effective mode for depicting the disaster being enacted in France. As might have been expected, there were attacks upon civilian profiteering and indifference; upon official optimism; upon military incompetence and favoritism; and of course upon the continued prosecution of a war that had become particularly senseless to those who were fighting it. But most frequently of all, and most significantly from a literary point of view, we have accounts of the experiences of the common soldier amidst a new kind of warfare—a warfare that utilized to the maximum every species of concentrated scientific violence. As a partial and natural consequence, we have a tentative, episodic, disconnected, emotional kind of writing, a desperate insistence on the shocking facts of life and death, a compulsive focus on the obscene details of crude animal needs and reactions, on wounds, death, and decomposition. Never before in literature had war been described with this painful compression of action and incident, with this narrowing of focus, this fragmentation of reality, this obsessive emphasis on isolated and irrelevant sensory details. It is not really necessary to point out the almost incredible contrast between these tortured effects and the graceful, weightless songs of the Georgians. The "static lyric" had suddenly been forced to accommodate a flood of experience too vast for it to assess, too various for it to order, and too powerful for it to control.

If objectivity and restraint, selection and control are rare in modern war poetry, so also is that perspective which both orders and stabilizes the events of the present and unites them with a significant historical continuity. In the epic the distant past impinges upon and sometimes actually pervades the present narrative reality; depicted in the light of a compelling historical analogy or continuity, present events assume a special meaning and a particular force and depth. Most contemporary war poetry, on the other hand, is characterized by a sense of abrupt discontinuity with the past. The violence and intensity of mechanized warfare, the unprecedented scale of death and destruction, and the total national involvement all contributed to this feeling of complete historical severance. The war was seen, with some justice, as an absolutely unique event; it was hopeless to seek parallels in the past or to unite the shattering experiences of the present so that they would have some kind of relation to eras of past aspiration and endeavor. . . . [This] lack of historical perspective in World War I poetry resulted in a lack of both temporal and moral depth, since any event ceases to have real significance unless it is in some way related to other events. Further, if an event seems to have no real significance, the physical phenomena of which it is composed are likely to be presented as erratic, disordered, and void of meaning. Giving both an impression of temporal depth and a thorough notation of particularized reality, the great epics never sacrifice moral or physical proportion to the demands of crude realism; the epic poet's sense of proportion always preserves the elementary distinctions between large and small, relevant and irrelevant, trivial and momentous, real and unreal. The war poets, however, obviously felt (in the words of one of their sympathetic successors) that they must "let the wrong cry out as raw as wounds," that the voice of the poet should be as direct and as spontaneous as the voice of anger or pain.

In addition to reducing the historical perspective and the sense of moral and physical proportion, the conditions of World War I tended to obscure the very aims and ideals for which the struggle was being waged. In his brief critique of the war novel [in *The Lie about the War*, 1930], Douglas Jerrold thus describes the factors which limited the soldier's conception of his role in the conflict:

> To the individual personally, all operations of war are meaningless and futile. He has no sense of personal contention with his enemies, not because they are not his enemies, not because the issue of the struggle is immaterial, but simply because the smallest fighting unit is, in modern national warfare, not the individual, the section or the company, not even the battalion, the regiment or the brigade, but the division. And that on rare occasions only. The movements which made history, which broke in succession the power of the Czar, the Turkish Empire, the Austro-Hungarian Empire and the German military bureaucracy, were the movements, the hammer blows, of Armies and Army groups. In relation to these movements, the agonies, the ardours, and the endurances of individuals assume a tragic and heroic dignity. Divorced from them, related not to the will of their Commanders, the moral, physical and economic resources of their nationals and the aims of their statesmen, but to the limited horizon of the individual soldier, the wanderings and sufferings of the squad, the platoon, or the company, not only appear to be, but are, utterly futile and without meaning.

Though it is made with reference to the novel, Jerrold's analysis applies with equal accuracy to certain effects observable in modern war poetry. The epic, of course, dealt with a much smaller scale of conflict; during the heroic ages military organization had not yet developed to the stage of mass attack and maneuver, and the purposes of any military action were comparatively simple and direct. Furthermore, the epic was concerned only with aristocratic personages, the "leaders and lords" whose exercise of the heroic virtues constituted the major interest of the story. Unlike the epic, modern war poetry is almost exclusively concerned with the experiences of the ordinary soldier; this figure, elevated by his obscurity, his sufferings, his patience and endurance, is the anonymous "hero" of contemporary poetry. He is, however, a passive rather than an active figure; as a mere unit in a vast military machine, he is controlled by directive intelligences remote from the field of battle. As the poet depicts him, he is a victim rather than a hero; what he does is not so important as what is done to him. Since the individual soldier can know little of the war outside his limited and generally passive experience of it, this fact—as the passage from Jerrold implies—contributes even further to the reduction of perspective and the consequent loss of temporal, moral, and physical proportion. If we had to depend upon World War I poetry for our knowledge of the causes and aims of the struggle, the ideals involved, and the military purposes which governed the fates of so many millions of men, our understanding of these matters would not only be meager but in some cases rather seriously distorted. Here, as with Georgian poetry, we have something of an index to the nature of the contemporary lyric as it sought to adjust itself to the demands of a reality that seemed almost retributive in its manifestations of savagery and chaotic violence. The "lies, and truths, and pain" vaguely sensed but ignored by Rupert Brooke and his contemporaries became the substance of daily existence for those who fought in the trenches. Having become brutal in its exposure of the lies and its revelation of the truths, poetry became all too human in its function as the voice of pain.

If it is obvious that the novel conditions of modern warfare strongly influenced the attitudes and techniques of World War I poetry, the effects of Georgian lyric practice are not so obvious—or at least these effects have not been very clearly designated or described. The literary discontinuity, like the historical, is so abrupt that we fail to notice the few important continuing strands that tend to support and confirm the patterns of the wartime lyric response.

William Butler Yeats, as editor of *The Oxford Book of Modern Verse* (1936), confessed "a distaste for certain poems written in the midst of the great war." He excluded all such poems from his anthology, remarking in his Introduction that "passive suffering is not a theme for poetry. . . . When man has withdrawn into the quicksilver at the back of the mirror no great event becomes luminous in his mind; it is no longer possible to write *The Persians, Agincourt, Chevy Chase:* some blunderer has driven his car on to the wrong side of the road—that is all." Yeats's judgment, though it refers in passing to a certain physical or historical effect—the theme of passive suffering—is really an aesthetic judgment; it may be applied, as Yeats's actual selections seem to indicate, to nearly the whole range of poetry directly inspired by the war. The intrusion of strong subjective elements into any work of poetic art, to the detriment of its necessary objective relationships, brings loss of perspective and ultimately loss of proportion and value; the real world exists only as it is partially and inaccurately reflected in the beholder's mind and is thus subject to his personal emotional reactions. The trivial or irrelevant detail thus becomes more important, through its emotional effect, than the general situation of which it is a part. The poet, "withdrawn into the quicksilver at the back of the mirror," becomes a mere sensorium and a transmitter of sensations which the reader must sort and assess for himself.

Functioning largely as the exercise of personal sensibility, Georgian poetry failed to go beyond the limits of carefully chosen "poetic" situations—situations that evoked a predictable, somewhat self-conscious personal response to rural beauty. Whatever they lacked in vision or genius, the Georgians made up for by their comforting sense of numbers and by their illusory impression of a poetic "renaissance." With the war, therefore, came a vaguely idealistic reaction developed in highly personal, self-dramatizing terms—an emotionalized response which interpreted the conflict as an opportunity for the poet's own moral regeneration. Just as the Georgians had refused to venture outside their accustomed modes of thought and expression, so the early poets refused to go beyond the personal implications of their involvement in the war. Apparently oblivious of causes, issues, and practical effects, they exploited the "poetic" aspects of the situation and indulged themselves in romantic fantasies of honor, sacrifice, self-redemption, and immortality. These were safe, traditional themes which could provide numerous elegant variations; but they had nothing whatever to do with the objective historical reality, even when patriotism was the source of inspiration. No previous body of poetry in English literature, inspired by momentous national events, has been marked by such limited knowledge and by such an excess of self-contemplation.

"Above all I am not concerned with Poetry," wrote Wilfred Owen late in the war, signifying his dissociation from the earlier response. Knowledge had replaced ignorance, but even in the shift to more realistic attitudes we find evidence that the Georgian sensibility had not been totally transformed. The deliberately shocking techniques of the new realism may be seen, in part, as a frequently exaggerated reaction to Georgian blandness and decorum. Brought to life by its contact with living materials, the "static lyric" suddenly became dynamic, deriving its motive and effect not only from the physical conditions of the war but also from a consciously exercised contrast to the Georgian mode. However, the personal response, though intensified and liberated from self-consciousness, was no less personal in its depiction of experience; instead of a formal artistic principle of selection and control, we have an emotionalized sensibility offering glimpses, impressions, fragments. The external reality had changed, but there had been no fundamental enlargement of the lyric vision. Still "withdrawn into the quicksilver at the back of the mirror," the poet could not present his experiences objectively, nor could he discriminate clearly with respect to experiential values. Even the emotions of anger and pity remain, in the end, personal reactions that fall far short of encompassing the reality of modern warfare. Though the vision of pity comprehends most of what the later soldier-poets were struggling to say, it interprets only one aspect of war—that of passive suffering—rather than embodying the broader reality of which that suffering is a part. Certain poets, as we shall see, rejected the Georgian inheritance and successfully drew upon other resources, personal and traditional; these exceptions, together with the general effort to break away from the limitations of the personal response, simply accentuate the major tendencies we have been tracing.

Yeats's dictum concerning objectivity and proportion has an even more important corollary with respect to that tragic tone to which all serious art aspires. A tragic event which is understood only in terms of personal misadventure ceases to be tragic. Tragedy implies a relationship between the part and the whole, between man and the mysteries of the moral universe. Since the modern war poet can discern no significant relationships among the phenomena that confront him, he cannot positively relate his experiences to the moral whole of which they are necessarily a part. Of pity, grief, and fear there is much in World War I poetry, but these emotions rarely attain the nobility proper to genuinely tragic emotions. Although the war poet was frequently a witness to tragic situations, he never seems quite sure what these situations are worth; he deplores, pities, attacks, and rejects, but aside from the compassionate vision (as set forth in Wilfred Owen's "Strange Meeting"), he has no values to apply or standards to affirm. He functions as conscience, as sensibility, and as the voice of anger or pain; but he seldom rises above these functions and the aspects of ugliness or suffering upon which they are based. Enveloped in the tragedy of war, he sees only magnified particulars and details—no event becomes "luminous" in his mind. If it is a function of poetry, as Wordsworth claimed, to follow the effects of science on man's life, it may be that poetry deals with the phenomena of technological warfare at the sacrifice of values which alone can make events luminous—the values of the tragic or heroic vision. Yet it is impossible to believe, as we follow the developments of World War I verse to their culmination in the late 1930's, that either poetry or the particular vision that happens to animate it can succumb to forces which invariably provoke

man's instinctive rebellion and encourage his reassertion of the values by which he lives. (pp. 9-20)

> *John H. Johnston, "Foreground and Background," in his* English Poetry of the First World War: A Study in the Evolution of Lyric and Narrative Form, *Princeton University Press, 1964, pp. 3-20.*

JON SILKIN

[*Silkin, an English poet and critic, edits the poetry review* Stand, *which he founded in the 1950s. In the following excerpt from the preface to the 1987 edition of his* Out of Battle: The Poetry of the Great War, *Silkin reassesses the poetic validity of wartime subjects, themes, and sentiments in the works of several English poets of the war.*]

Some subjects are swallowed whole by literature, others, a very few, may engorge not only literature but writing itself. For some, war elicits responses that no other activity can. It is, we are told, the ultimate test. In Wilfred Owen's view, for instance, war sometimes elicited *caritas,* or greater love. "The Poetry [was] in the pity." Certainly war, in this formulation, appears to swallow up poetry: "But they are troops who fade, not flowers / For poets' tearful fooling."

We cannot, he seems to be saying, manipulate the experience of war or combat and hope for that experience to remain meaningful; it is the unshapeable, to which we must all adapt. "The true Poets must be truthful." And yet there is only a seeming antinomy between experience (war) and art. It is not that art fails in its attempt to *distil* the horror and pity of war, but that it must grow in its attempt to recreate it. Yet here we come upon a distinction that Desmond Graham makes in his *The Truth of War* (1984) which consists in his ensuring that the reader distinguishes between his being moved by the horror contained in a poem, and of thinking that he or she has endured or been witness to that horror. Coleridge makes a parallel but different point in his "Fears in Solitude" (1798): "All read of war, / "The best amusement for our morning-meal!" We are spectators and not combatants.

War and combat. Like a million other children, my childhood and early adolescence took place during the Second World War. Others—Keith Douglas for instance—fought in it, and died. For him, as for Owen and Isaac Rosenberg, war was combat. For the Hebrew kingdoms defeated by the armies of the Assyrians and Babylonians, war was exile.

With all this in mind, I want to re-consider briefly the poetry of the First World War, in the context of the late 1980s.

In a recent conversation with my fellow-poet and colleague Jon Glover I learned that—as one of his younger students expressed it—suffering and compassionate indignation were not thought by some to be germane to considerations of the style of a poem, and that such responses were of little value since poetry involved, by definition, an almost total preoccupation with style and language. Suffering as a preoccupation of a poem (shades of Yeats) was not only an irrelevancy but an impediment. The poetry is in the poetry. We pride ourselves on an uncaring survival, it seems.

But who, the reader may ask, are "we"? For those brought up in the Second World War, war is a reality. For those who were not—for some of those—war is other people's history, Northern Ireland notwithstanding.

Blake makes an angel sing:

> Mercy, Pity, Peace
> is the world's release.

But he also tells us:

> I heard a Devil curse
> Over the heath & the furze,
>
> "Mercy could be no more,
> If there was nobody poor,
>
> And pity no more could be,
> If all were as happy as we."
> At his curse the sun went down,
> And the heavens gave a frown.

War then is not the only activity that provides a medium for pity. It is merely the "most universal" opportunity to hand where, since the ending of the Second World War, there has been no lasting peace, or amity. That is surely the context for the "war poets" rather than an historical or even a literary one. In such a context in which there is so much suffering, responsiveness is a crucial factor; that is the principal meaning of Owen's "Strange Meeting" and "Insensibility."

Thus the usefulness of the "war poets," always supposing they need to be justified, could be seen to be in reciprocal proportion to the attitude that sees suffering and horror in a poem as disrupting a concern for style—"if a poem is not a literary artefact, what is it?" The implicit question turns upon itself, and we must, if we can, disengage the dog from its snarl—like a set of *false* teeth. Because, to make a poem a literary consideration exclusive of its theme and its responsiveness to the world outside that helped cause its existence is to dichotomize the reciprocal activities of writing and reading a poem. Is it true, and if true, is it right that considerations of style—stylistics—have not so much obscured as effectively disjoined style and sympathetic concern? If we no longer find the "war poets" relevant it is perhaps we, not the poets, who are deficient. Such is the pain of teeth gnashing at the indifferent reader who turns, in disdain, from these poets except in as much as they provide kinds of moral adventure stories.

The "war poets" coped with dire experience in language, it is as simple and miraculous as that. It is not so much, or only, that their writing mediated between such experience and a desire to create literature, but that they made their writing in response to that experience. Literature and writing may be two different if overlapping creations. At any rate, writing does not for some time become literature. We may consider this question differently by being advised by Karl Shapiro who, in *In Defense of Ignorance,* states that today poetry does not have readers, but critics. And by taking this sad fierce leaf from his book we may add that poetry does not have readers so much as students of it. Is it possible for these students to become readers?

For most of the poets of the First War period, combatant or noncombatant, war was a new experience—the "strange and extraordinary new conditions of this life"—as Rosenberg expressed it to Laurence Binyon in Autumn 1916, from the trenches. For us, war is familiar in the way that pictures without *our* experience being enshrined in them can become familiar. We can handle the images that hold the context of so many lives, or pay to see them on a screen. These images are repeatable in a way particular experience is not. And because they are repeatable, we, the recipients of them, may become bored. Or they may prove lethal to us as we become accom-

plices in an internalized adventure, connoisseurs or scholars of suffering.

These are some of the possibilities that await a concern with others' suffering, and Owen is right to warn us civilians against identifying with war's victims:

> You shall not hear their mirth:
>   You shall not come to think them well content
>   By any jest of mine. These men are worth
>   Your tears. You are not worth their merriment.
>   ("Apologia pro Poemate Meo")

Empathy not sympathy is what is required. But, as Owen less frequently observed, it is necessary to recognize that the soldier-victim is also a killer. That is surely part of the value of his "Mental Cases" (and his "Spring Offensive"). The mad are so not on account of what they have suffered but because of what they have inflicted or witnessed:

> —These are men whose minds the Dead have rav-
>   ished.
> Memory fingers in their hair of murders,
> Multitudinous murders they once witnessed.

The width of the "war poets'" responses is diminished if we consider only their suffering and dissolve our guilt in that anodyne of pity.

The other part of the rubric is, however, to do with the form and character of the poem itself that recreates the experience. Herbert Read, in *The Contrary Experience,* records how he came to feel that the literary apparatus of the Imagists could not adequately express the direful experience of war. Yet he deployed the strategies of Imagism, and even when most successful, as in his long, sustained "The End of a War," he merely modified his practice. Even so, his deployment of a set of rigorous if limiting principles has the cutting-edge of the newly-honed. These are principles operating in all their freshness, sharp partly because they are new. I-Thou has not yet become I-it.

One of Owen's most perceptive critics, D. S. R. Welland, asserts that Owen is a link-figure between nineteenth- and twentieth-century poetries, and this view is, I think, correct. Yet to see him thus may be to blur at once his more traditional role (his capacity to adapt not only the styles but the purposes of those earlier poets whom he admired) and his shrewd, knowing, contemporary-seeming self-awareness. To use Lionel Trilling's tools, Owen travelled between sincerity and authenticity. So that even the didactic, occasionally hectoring energies do not dissolve the self-awareness. Owen is himself his own link-figure. He himself joins up and endures the contradictions between recreation and experience, theme and response, literature and writing—that which is written to make sense of experience rather than to make, or only make, a poem. Sometimes literature dodges experience—as, in precisely the opposite way, writing suffers and responds to it.

We may see this self-transforming process in the work of Ivor Gurney, as he moves unevenly from being a traditional poet into becoming a raw writer, one whose experiences force him to be at the nub of himself. It is the story of a man who moves, not all of a piece, from producing aureate literature, a kind of psychic gold, to squeezing forth a rawness of expression:

> Save when the Gloucesters turning sudden to tell
>   to one
> Some joke, would remember and say—"That joke
>   is done,"

Since he who would understand was so cold he
    could not feel,
And clay binds hard, and sandbags get rotten and
    crumble.
                            ("Butchers and Tombs")

The purring melancholy of literature has ceased.

Sassoon and Rosenberg, their social backgrounds notwithstanding, are very different poets concerned with realizing,
despite their common subject of war, different apprehensions
of experience. Where, for instance, Rosenberg uses detail as
the microcosmic representation of a total experience, Sassoon
blesses the detail because it assists in his enterprise of an overall realism. This is the experience, he tells the reader; the very
thing. Isn't it horrible? You need search no further for meaning.

In his lecture "On Poetry" (1939), Sassoon said of himself:
"Thinking in pictures is my natural method of self-
expression. I have always been a submissively visual writer."
This statement is a pointer to Sassoon's "war poetry." Once
it has purged itself of its subjection to patriotic idealism, it
is poetry almost entirely uniform in attitude; that is, it wholeheartedly impugns war; and it deploys experience realistically
in order to make this clear. Even the more reflective poems
stem more or less directly from experience. With Rosenberg's
so-called "Trench Poems," although they more intimately
and sometimes more immediately respond to the experience
of war than Owen's, unlike Sassoon's poems, they nearly always fuse experience, evaluation and sensuous understanding. Where Sassoon's poetry "is" experience, Rosenberg's is
mostly a consciously representative instance of it. Thus there
is nearly always more beneath the surface of Rosenberg's
poems than there is beneath Sassoon's. Rosenberg loathed the
War (and the Army's endemic bullying militarism) but he is
more willing to digest the experience and then come to some
evaluative conclusions than Sassoon. Sassoon comes to judgment, and sticks to that judgment. His poems are judged
splinters of a core of belief, and they proceed upon the assumption that the poet must communicate his insight. Thus
in 1916 Rosenberg wrote, with almost speculative wonder, to
Binyon:

> I am determined that this war, with all its powers
> for devastation, shall not master my poeting; that
> is, if I am lucky enough to come through all right.
> I will not leave a corner of my consciousness cov-
> ered up, but saturate my self with the strange and
> extraordinary new conditions of this life; and it will
> all refine itself into poetry later on.

In his by now famous protest of July 1917 Sassoon wrote:

> On behalf of those who are suffering now I make
> this protest against the deception which is being
> practised on them; also I believe that I may help to
> destroy the callous complacency with which the
> majority of those at home regard the continuance
> of agonies which they do not share, and which they
> have not sufficient imagination to realize.

To say it once more, the difference is not merely one of class
although, notwithstanding that both men had Jewish ancestry, that is a factor. It is that where Sassoon's poetry is in
some sort a translation of a programme for action, Rosenberg's is more considering, more sensuous, where the poet
comes at length to make the poem out of re-creative distillation of experience, quite often in a version of synecdoche. The

leaf may be different from its plant but it is a representative
part of it.

Gurney's background was not one of literacy in depth. Unlike Wilfred Owen's mother who had, judging from Owen's
letters, middle-class literacy, Gurney's mother was not much
more than literate. But her letters have a vivid, queer directness:

> Mother could sing very nicely she was always sing-
> ing Scotch songs and English Irish and Welsh Fa-
> ther was alto in the Bisley Choir but he didn't sing
> at home like Mother did my dear old Grandfather
> and his brother uncle Robert he was a Batchelor
> and Mother said he nursed his Mother till she died
> and wouldn't let anybody else do a thing for her
> arm chair was covered with white dimity and he
> used to wash everything himself and after he had
> dug the garden the spade and the fork and all the
> diggers were shone like silver and put down in the
> cellar and the white stones which showed up
> through the dirt was scrubbed white and he would
> give us some flowers if we wouldn't put them on the
> graves that was popery well I wish I knew where
> they came from they were not the regular sort of
> Bisley people they had too much in them. . . .
>
> Grandfather was a good man the Luggs round
> Stroud are the most respected of anybody and you
> can say what you like a good ancestor is something
> to be proud of but Ivor hasn't seen a lot of the
> Luggs he knew the Gurneys better and they hadn't
> a note of music in them.
>   (Florence Gurney, undated letter to Marion
>   Scott; [quoted by Michael Hurd in his
>   biography *The Ordeal of Ivor Gurney,* 1978])

Vivid, snobbish, unstable yet direct—here are some of the
characteristics that Gurney uses, and partly overcomes, in his
poetry.

Within the 1919-22 period (see *Collected Poems*), Gurney
found a way of being contemporary without, it would seem,
his even trying to be so. It meant for Gurney his setting aside
the educated aureate diction of the poetic, and of finding in
himself direct utterance, the odd, the quirky, even the peculiar—anything that would match his apprehension of what
Rosenberg in that letter to Binyon (1916) described as "the
strange and extraordinary new conditions of this life." Rosenberg had been describing the "hell" of the trenches;
Gurney was now writing of that as well as of the "strange
hell" of existing within his own life:

> The wind frightens my dog, but I bathe in it,
> Sound, rush, scent of the spring fields.
>
> My dog's hairs are blown like feathers askew,
> My coat's a demon, torturing like life.
>   ("April Gale")

Gurney's directness there is close to speech, and he obtains
this effect by having short completed units of syntax which,
however, coincide with line-endings. The result is that he
makes the hurled, almost gasping, speech appear both exclamatory and contained. The speech-units resemble speech.
But at the same time they are tied down in such a way as to
indicate that the line-unit, a basic component of poetry, is a
controlling factor.

In the fine "Mist on Meadows," Gurney re-enacts his memo-

ry of the War, interleaving it in a comparison with his sense
of his own damaged, even wrecked, life:

> Mist lies heavy on English meadows
> As ever on Ypres, but the friendliness
> Here is greater in full field and hedge shadows,
> And there is less menace and no dreadfulness
> As when the Verey lights went up to show the land
>   stark.
> Dreadful green light baring the ruined trees,
> Stakes, pools, lostness, better hidden dreadful in
>   dark
> And not ever reminding of these other fields
> Where tall dock and clover is, and this sweet grass
>   yields
> For that poisoned. . . .
>
> But they honour not—and salute not those boys
>   who saw a terror
> Of waste, endured horror. . . .

I quote at length to suggest the hurtful effect of the War upon
Gurney; for although the clamping effect of the Army may
have temporarily given his life the support it needed, the experience of the battlefield did nothing for him. How should
it? One is especially struck by the disarming, appealing combination of directness and vulnerability (not self-pity)—in for
instance

> And there is less menace and no dreadfulness.

The abstract noun "dreadfulness" is deprived of its vagueness
by a tone of voice that conveys a man in much pain, and
much in need of succour, without, that is, his seeming to ask
for it. "Friendliness" uses the token word in a similar way.
More striking still is "lostness," where a greater sense of desolation is obtained through the abstract noun than through
the use of the word "lost," either as adjective or noun. By
means of this coinage, the hellish experience of the trenches,
and the hellishness of self-fear and the self's contingent madness, are each interleaved:

> Stakes, pools, lostness, better hidden dreadful in
>   dark
> And not ever reminding of these other fields . . .
>   and this sweet grass yields
> For that poisoned.

"Stakes, pools, lostness" are features of the Front; "these
other fields" are those of pre-war and, arguably, post-war experience which are in danger of "contamination" from the
memories of war. Refracted through recent memory, these
give way to the grass "poisoned" in war. The current life is
like a series of infinitely reflecting mirrors, in which these
meadows are not only haunted by the "War," but by the present "dark" fear of mental collapse. The poem conveys acute
unease and distress, at the point at which it makes the disclaimer—

> And there is less menace and no dreadfulness.

What Gurney does in "Mist on Meadows," finely, and with
directness, is to interleave, interfuse, his horror of war with
horror at incipient madness; and by bringing the two together, he faces, with delicate control, this double hauntedness.
He is not trying to demonstrate, by means of mutually reflecting metaphors, the horror of war and madness; on the contrary he offers these experiences which together, perhaps *only*
together, can begin to convey the full measure of each other.
And here we see the nature of Gurney's directness. It is not
that one experience is used as a metaphor for the other, in

order to make a literary apprehension, but that both these
materials of experience exact from him a candour and directness which only the most truthfully engaged psyches can
maintain.

When Gurney is writing at his best, it does not seem to matter
to him if what he is writing is poetry. In turn, this disregard
or rather this undivided consciousness permits him a deep
connection with his concerns and with his molten language.
Thus his poetry is the natural product of such connectedness,
and the urgency of the creation bestows upon the work its
own set of controls.

With Herbert Read it is almost entirely the other way about.
Like Owen and Sassoon, Read seems to have entered upon
the War with a poetic—a group of ideas or assumptions as
to what constituted a poem. Read's poetics derive, however,
not from the Romantic tradition nor the practice of the Georgians, but from the newer and on the whole more stringent
demands of Imagism. Thus unlike Gurney who, under pressure, wrote out of no set of poetics expressed in a critical
credo, Read's poems derive from his appreciation of Imagism. When Read modifies this practice, as he does in "The
End of a War," the modifications are made with respect to
style rather than with reference to or in connection with those
responses engendered by the turmoil of dire experience. I am
not, at this point, making value judgments on Read or
Gurney but noting the different kinds of poetic practice. It
is nevertheless ironic that despite the injunctions of "make it
new" it is Gurney, at his best, rather than Read whose work
feels not only fresher, but newer. This is not a depreciation
of Read's achievement; it is a way of marking a difference between them.

In an unpublished essay on Rosenberg's plays, Charles Tomlinson wrote of beauty, harmony, and music—that is, he examined the ideas of *The Amulet/Unicorn* dramatic fragments. As often as they refer to Rosenberg, which is not
often, critics have noted Rosenberg's dramatic energy. In *English Poetry 1900-1950*, C. H. Sisson says:

> It is a mark of Rosenberg's potential as a poet that
> the experience he sought to present was not merely
> a reportage of his personal life but an apprehension
> of the complexity of a wide universe. For this he
> found drama a natural medium.

And a few pages later: "In *The Unicorn* . . . he took to a dramatic form to give objectivity to his expression." That last
sentence is of course a confirmation of the ideas Eliot had put
about in "Tradition and the Individual Talent" (1919) concerning the desirability of impersonality. Many critics have
continued to echo this assertion, but the valuable point Sisson
makes is that Rosenberg "found drama a natural medium"
for expressing his apprehension of a complex universe. Yes,
and yet the obvious additional point is that Rosenberg had
in him that capacity to uncover his natural technically adventurous medium. In fact, we find in his dramatic writing some
of his strongest verse. Rosenberg admired Bottomley's
plays—"as a poetic drama [*King Lear's Wife*, 1915], it is of
the very highest kind"—but where Bottomley plays with sensationalism, Rosenberg's drama emerges from the pain of
having to perceive, and experience, the conflict of huge forces
struggling to destroy each other on the one hand, and on the
other, of attempting to survive. The energy in Rosenberg's
work derives from these necessities, and it produces a verse
that is original and yet, without its sacrificing movement and
energy, formal. Apart from Bottomley, there is no one with

whom to compare Rosenberg's verse drama—no other "war poet," that is. Where Rosenberg is impelled into drama, Owen narrates. And the stichomythia in Read's second section of "The End of a War" is argument not drama, a device that serves to heighten the intellectual debate. This is far from being dramatic verse.

On the other hand one would not suppose that the sophisticated pastoral distress in Edmund Blunden's war verse could be made into drama. Yet as Rosenberg's conflicts are impelled into the form of drama, so elements of conflict in Blunden are potentially (though never actually) drama. In *Pastoral Poetry and Pastoral Drama* (1906), Walter W. Greg wrote:

> What does appear to be a constant element in the pastoral as known to literature is the recognition of a contrast, implicit or expressed, between pastoral life and some more complex type of civilization.

War is that type of more complex civilization. In the instance of Blunden the situation is both more complex and more ironic in that not only is he the sophisticated living being almost within whose grasp is the pastoral life; he is also the link between that life and the War, both as soldier and poet. He records the pastoral life that he intensely values, but he is also the soldier who unwillingly contributes to its destruction. His "Report on Experience" voices an awareness of some of this.

Blunden's "drama" derives from the settled contrast between a peaceful rurality echoing in ironic recall either through scenes of carnage, or false deceitful lulls in fighting—and the degradation of the trenches which is redeemed, if that is the word, only by the comradeship with one's fellow-sufferer and victim. As Paul Fussell observes of Blunden's *Undertones of War* and of his pastoralism in general:

> every rhythm, allusion, and droll personification, can be recognized as an assault on the war and on the world which chose to conduct and continue it.

And:

> With language as with landscape, his attention is constantly on pre-industrial England, the only repository of criteria for measuring fully the otherwise unspeakable grossness of the war.

All of which is honed by the "Et in arcadia ego" formulation which may be translated as "I too once lived in Arcadia" or "I (death) am present even in Arcadia." Blunden's drama, whose conflicting constituents are often prevented from breaking out into open conflict by (among other things) the device of a reconciling irony, would have sprung up from deep (and wounded) sources—had it come into actual as opposed to potential existence.

These brief characterizations and comparisons are intended to bring back into the context of the late 1980s minds that are not ours yet whose relevance to us is, or should be, plain. The material and the literary modes feel as new now as when, one guesses, first produced. What keeps the work new is (to adapt an idea of Rosenberg's) the poetry's resistance to paraphrase. The poems also resist being split into their supposed components, such is the pressure of experience upon their genesis and composition, and therefore the strength needed for their creation. Work written out of such shared distress is likely to be of use to us. (pp. vii-xviii)

Jon Silkin, in a preface to his Out of Battle: The Po- etry of the Great War, *1972. Reprint by Ark Paperbacks, 1987, pp. vii-xviii.*

M. S. GREICUS

[*In the following excerpt, Greicus surveys the most important English prose works written about the Western Front.*]

In Britain it was the soldier poets who first took the measure of the war and reflected its changing mood. (p. 7)

Yet, the four years of war were not barren of significant prose treatment by major novelists. Arnold Bennett and H. G. Wells both examined the period from the point of view of civilians, and their novels during the period reveal an acuteness of vision' which makes them interesting reading today. Bennett's *The Pretty Lady* (1918) and Wells's *Mr. Britling Sees It Through* (1916) survive as remarkable studies of the disillusionment at home with the final stages of the war.

The earliest outstanding war novel was by a French author, Henri Barbusse's *Le Feu: Journal d'une escouade,* published in 1916. It was also the first anti-war novel of real merit, and its English translation, *Under Fire* (1917), prepared the way for the developing mood of disenchantment that was so well captured by the soldier poets writing in 1917-18. Written in the impressionist tradition, *Under Fire* focused on the true character of war for its participants. The long hours of waiting, the filth, the lice, the dead, the cold and the mud. English equivalents were not, however, to appear until some time after the war.

Three British novels of the war published between 1914 and 1919 by combatants do offer substantially more than the common patriotic and sentimental prose of the time. John Hay Beith, Hugh Walpole and A. P. Herbert each wrote remarkable studies that have escaped the bane of topicality. Beith's novel was the story of Kitchener's New Army, or "The First Hundred Thousand" as the first volunteers came to be known. More like the regular army than any later units, its officers and men were trained together, went to France in the same drafts, and were deployed in their original units—until the remnants were so few as to be of more use as replacements than as regiments. The first civilian volunteers had a sort of individuality which does not really belong to the armies of mass warfare.

In January 1915 Beith published the first instalments of "The Diary of a Subaltern" in *Blackwood's Magazine.* In December the series was published in book form as *The First Hundred Thousand* under the pseudonym Ian Hay. Written in diary form for monthly publication, the completed work is unlike its many predecessors in print. The episodes in the narrative are not loosely strung together on the cord of wartime adventure. Beith, by tracing his unit's progress through training into its initiation into battle at Loos, managed to capture for posterity the birth, short life and death of a pioneer effort in a new military epoch.

The finest achievement of the book is the honest picture it gives of life in the first volunteer army. Although military humour has become an overworked subject, the treatment of the intricacies of training by Beith remains as fresh as the experience itself was in 1915. Take for example, his commentary on bombs and hand grenades:

> So the bomb has come to its own, and has brought with it certain changes—tactical, organic, and do-

mestic. To take the last first, the bomb-office, hith-erto a despised underling, popularly (but malicious-ly) reputed to have been appointed to his present post through inability to handle a platoon, has sud-denly attained a position of dazzling eminence. From being a mere super, he has become a star. In fact, he threatens to dispute the pre-eminence of that other regimental parvenu, the Machine-Gun Officer. He is now the confidant of Colonels, and consorts upon terms of easy familiarity with Bri-gade Majors. He holds himself coldly aloof from the rest of us, brooding over the greatness of his re-sponsibilities; and when he speaks, it is to refer darkly to "detonators," and "primers" and "time-fuses." And we, who once addressed him derisively as "Anarchist," crowd round him and hang upon his lips.

(*The First Hundred Thousand*, 1915)

The last chapters on the Battle of Loos, while somewhat sen-timental in tone, effectively record the first major British of-fensive in France. It is a fitting climax for the book. Loos marked the beginning of Britain's awareness of the cost of modern war, and the end as a fighting unit of Kitchener's Army. The battle offered the irony for Beith's story; The First Hundred Thousand's eagerness to see action ended in reality, as in the novel, with their annihilation. The same Scotsmen, who are the representative battalion of the New Army de-scribed by Beith, did break through to the right of Loos, but a poorly co-ordinated covering movement exposed their flank and forced what was left of them into a withdrawal from the gap they had forged.

Hugh Walpole began his career as a novelist before the war. In 1914, Henry James in an essay for *The Times Literary Sup-plement* had recognized him, along with Compton Macken-zie, D. H. Lawrence and Gilbert Cannan, as the most promis-ing of a new generation of novelists. Of the four, Lawrence and Cannan, though profoundly affected by the war, re-mained civilians. Lawrence's experiences were to be fictional-ized in *Kangaroo* (1923). Cannan suffered a series of break-downs and was never to treat the war years in fiction. Mac-kenzie was to become a romantic figure in the Dardanelles, where he was attached to Ian Hamilton's staff; his memoir of the period, *Gallipoli Memories*, appeared in 1929.

Hugh Walpole alone responded immediately to the war with a novel. Bad vision kept him from enlisting, but he had taken an assignment as war correspondent in Russia. In March 1915 he managed to join a Red Cross unit and go on active duty at the front. Immediately he began to exploit the experi-ence in a novel he initially called *Death and the Hunters*. His diary of the period describes the events on which the plot of the novel was based. In its final form the novel was entitled *The Dark Forest* (1916). Walpole thus used a journalistic ap-proach for his frame, but where Beith had found a plot in the progress of the war itself, the close friend of Henry James and Arnold Bennett saw instead a setting for a psychological study.

Arnold Bennett measured the difficulty and the achievement of the novel in a letter to Walpole at the time:

> In my view you may make your mind easy about this book. You attempted an exceedingly danger-ous feat—making fiction out of a mass of violent new impressions that could not possibly have set-tled down into any sort of right perspective in your

mind . . . you have brought the affair very success-fully off, with the help of an A.I. central idea. . . .
(Quoted in Rupert Hart-Davis, *Hugh Walpole*, 1952.)

In the heat of the Russian campaign Walpole found very little that resembled ordinary experience. What he did see con-vinced him of the necessity of new values with which to weigh experience. But he did not accept those that arose out of a new system of order and personal discomfort. Walpole's three months of active service were not enough to make the necessity of survival outweigh all else. Rather, he looked to the problem of death for a key to the experience of war. "What I wanted to do," he said in his introduction, "was to create some sense of the dark and divine mysteriousness of war." Further on in the same passage he defines this quality:

> By divine I do not mean transcendent or noble or inspired or any grand thing at all. I mean that as you move inside the heart of war, you are in a world other than the material one, or, at least, your truest and most penetrating moments in it are not materi-al. And by this I do not mean any absurd romanti-cism. The truth about war is that the imminence, the commonness, of death alters all your customary values of life.

(*The Dark Forest*)

The result was gothic in its intensity and suggestive of the su-pernatural. The influence of Dostoevsky was unmistakable, yet the world Walpole described with such accuracy was not the distorted vision of a paranoiac, but real battle scenes. In fact almost every serious novel of the First World War sug-gests the parallel between the reality of trench warfare and the torments men undergo in the psychological studies of Poe, Dostoevsky and Andreyev. The confusion of time and sequentiality, the incapacity of the harried mind to connect the aspects of its immediate surroundings into a comprehen-sible picture: these were the result of being thrown into a war of attrition, as well as the symptoms of paranoia. Walpole captured them in *The Dark Forest,* but he went even further by working out a pattern of relationships that were created in the stress of the unnatural world of war.

The novel did not pass judgement on the war. The time was to come when such a work would have been nearly impossi-ble, but in 1916 a book that on one level supplied a day-to-day description of life on the Russian Front and at the same time used that description only as the background for a complex psychological tapestry was a creditable thing. War was horri-ble. It was a nightmare. But it offered an awakening to the young British protagonist which was itself a justification for the experience.

The forest of the novel's title is an unnatural, broken, blasted place hung with the drapes of war. There is a vivid descrip-tion of a food transport into a village stricken with cholera, and of a confused trip through the forest in search of a front-line battalion. Walpole had found an appropriate setting for a mature—if somewhat romantic—novel, a work whose in-herent mysticism would have been a farce without the mat-ter-of-fact experience of the war to justify its psychological analysis of love and death.

That the individual in battle could accept new ways of evalu-ating experience was brought home by descriptions of front-line action which come from life rather than the imagination. Instead of trying to express an emotional state with poetic, metaphysical passages, he depended on flat description of a character's view of his surroundings to convey his state of mind.

The novel was well received in 1916. For Frank Swinnerton it was the book that placed Walpole as a leader of the younger generation.

> I should say that for the first time he was considered to be the best of the lot. His work was still in a literary sense derivative, but he had seen and felt strange, thrilling things, and a literary tea-party was no longer his ideal form of entertainment. His ambitions had expanded.
>
> (*The Georgian Literary Scene,* 1935)

It was not a reputation he retained for any length of time. The scenes he had worked with so well in Russia were being repeated *ad infinitum* in France, and that truth inevitably was to reach the public. For the remainder of the war and for fifteen years afterwards it was impossible to view frontline action as dispassionately as Walpole had. Today the work seems Walpole's best. Certainly it is a good treatment of the subject of war.

A. P. Herbert's *The Secret Battle* appeared in May 1919, less than seven months after the Armistice. The quickness with which Herbert came to terms with his own wartime experience in this first novel was a personal attribute that characterized his long political and literary life. And his response was right in that *The Secret Battle* showed the way for the hundreds of anti-war novels which were to follow in the next fifteen years. The frequency of its reprinting during the 1920s is a testament to its staying power. Sir Winston Churchill, in his introduction to the 1928 edition, called it "one of those cries of pain wrung from fighting troops by the prolonged and measureless torment through which they passed; and like the poems of Siegfried Sassoon should be read in each generation, so that men and women may rest under no illusion about what war meant."

Herbert himself served in Gallipoli and in France, and his novel involves both fronts over the four years. The narrator, in an easy conversational manner, describes the progress of an idealistic young officer in his regiment through the campaigns in Gallipoli and later on the Western Front, closing with his execution for cowardice.

No finer account of the warfare in Gallipoli has been written. Simple, straightforward descriptions are the characteristic of a good writer, and the novel abounds in passages like the following:

> Mid-June came with all its plagues and fevers and irritable distresses. Life in the rest-camp became daily more intolerable. There set in a steady wind from the north-east which blew all day down the flayed rest-areas of the Peninsula, raising great columns of blinding, maddening dust. It was a hot, parching wind, which in no way mitigated the scorch of the sun, and the dust it brought became a definite enemy to human peace. It pervaded everything. It poured into every hole and dug-out, and filtered into every man's belongings; it formed a gritty sediment in water and tea, it passed into a man with every morsel of food he ate, and scraped and tore at his inside. It covered his pipe so that he could not even smoke with pleasure; it lay in a thick coating on his face so that he looked like a wan ghost, paler than disease had made him. It made the cleaning of his rifle a too, too frequent farce; it

> worked under his breeches, and gathered at the back of his knees, chafing and torturing him; and if he lay down to sleep in his hole it swept in billows over his face, or men passing clumsily above kicked great showers upon him.
>
> (*The Secret Battle*)

But Herbert was not writing simply a good novel. *The Secret Battle* is a polemic on the evils of the First War. While it was to share that characteristic with most serious British war fiction written from first-hand experience, the book has been unfairly ignored since the years of the "war books controversy," in large part because of the sheer number of well written books with a similar theme.

The greater part of British commentary on the First War—novels, reminiscences, autobiography and histories—appeared in publishers' book lists between 1928 and 1932. At the height of the war-books fad, in late 1929 and 1930, heated exchanges took place in the letters columns of *The Times,* and a spate of articles on "war books" appeared in literary and mass circulation journals. In dispute were the politics and the integrity of the writers of war books in their representation of the war.

C. E. Montague prophesied the anti-war boom in 1922. *Disenchantment* contains the finest writing of Montague as well as the most direct summation of the war's cost in terms of public spirit:

> The limp apathy that we see at elections, the curious indifference in presence of public wrongs and horrors, the epidemic of sneaking pilferage, the slackening of sexual self-control—all these are symptomatic like the furred tongue, subnormal heat, and muddy eye.
>
> (*Disenchantment,* 1922)

The journalist, who at forty-six had dyed his hair in order to enlist as a private, spoke for himself as well when he argued: "Now that most of our men in the prime of life have been in the army we seem to be in for a literature of disappointment."

Fiery Particles (1923), *Rough Justice* (1926) and *Right Off the Map* (1927) were his contribution in fiction to the memory and cost of the war, but they did not match the quality of his long essay. It remains today the best analysis of the First War's immediate effects on British society, and perhaps the best tracing of the changing mood of the war in England and at the fronts between 1914 and 1918.

By March 1929, when Erich Remarque's *Im Westen nichts Neues* appeared in translation as *All Quiet on the Western Front,* the resurgence of interest in the First War was at its height. The posture of Remarque was romantic in the extreme, and appropriate for the time. His doomed soldiers went about their lives—and their deaths—frankly, coarsely, and in the company of their comrades. His book personified "the horror school" of war fiction. The arguments which followed established the opposing principle involved in response to war books. Pacifist was set against militarist; the proponent of the survival of the individual will found himself in opposition to the defender of collective spirit. In a matter of months the argument completely diverted attention from the quality of war books as literature.

When Richard Aldington's *Death of a Hero* appeared in the same year, a literary evaluation was already impossible. In every way it was the most imposing novel of "the horror school." While he could compare his novel with the rants of Shakespeare's Timon, he felt the book belonged to a humanist tradition. He cited in the preface his belief "in a certain fundamental integrity and comradeship, without which society could not endure" (*Death of a Hero,* 1929). *Death of a Hero* must be seen in the tradition of rebellion that had begun with Samuel Butler's *The Way of All Flesh* (1903). Aldington equated the war with the stupidities of antiquated Victorian values. His story involves the discovery that the intelligentsia, who were behind the movement against those values, were themselves as corrupt as the morality they opposed. He saw his generation caught in the middle at a time when public attitudes were shifting toward the new values. His hero is broken in the war by the pressures of a wife and a mistress belonging to the circle of London's literary dilettantes. The narrator, a *persona* of the author who intrudes throughout the narrative, offers the bitter evaluations:

> The death of a hero! What mockery, what bloody cant! What sickening putrid cant! George's death is a symbol to me of the whole sickening bloody waste of it, the damnable stupid waste and torture of it.
>
> (*Death of a Hero*)

Such hysterical evocations are at once a virtue and a major flaw in the novel. The work captures the mood of his generation, its sentimentality, its *naïveté,* its disarming expectation of justice. It is also guilty of every charge levelled against the "war books." Its subject-matter combines the sensationalism of "modern sex" with the "horrors" of war, through a narrator who holds all of modern civilization in contempt. The pose has considerable interest for the contemporary reader, as has the careful delineation of trench warfare. Aldington, like the man he greatly admired, D. H. Lawrence, used his descriptive passages to reflect the mental state of his character. The Western Front lent itself to that treatment:

> The days passed into weeks, the weeks into months. He moved through impressions like a man hallucinated. And every incident seemed to beat on his brain Death, Death, Death. All the decay and death of battlefields entered his blood and seemed to poison him. He lived among smashed bodies and human remains in an infernal cemetery. If he scratched his stick idly and nervously in the side of a trench, he pulled out human ribs. He ordered a new latrine to be dug out from the trench, and thrice the digging had to be abandoned because they came upon terrible black masses of decomposing bodies. At dawn one morning when it was misty he walked over the top of Hill 91, where probably nobody had been by day since its capture. The heavy mist brooded about him in a strange stillness. Scarcely a sound on their immediate front, though from north and south came the vibration of furious drum-fire. The ground was a desert of shell-holes and torn rusty wire, and everywhere lay skeletons in steel helmets, still clothed in the rags of sodden khaki or field grey. Here a fleshless hand still clutched a broken rusty rifle; there a gaping, decaying boot showed the thin, knotty foot-bones. He came on a skeleton violently dismembered by a shell explosion; the skull was split open and the teeth lay scattered on the bare chalk; the force of the explosion had driven coins and a metal pencil right into the hip-bones and femurs. In a concrete pill-box three German skeletons lay across their machine gun with its silent nozzle still pointing at the loop-hole. They had been attacked from the

rear with phosphorus grenades, which burn their way into the flesh, and for which there is no possible remedy. A shrunken leather strap still held a battered wristwatch on a fleshless wrist-bone. Alone in the white curling mist, drifting slowly past like wraiths of the slain, with the far-off thunder of drum-fire beating the air, Winterbourne stood in frozen silence and contemplated the last achievements of civilised men.

> (*Death of a Hero*)

Death of a Hero underscores the relationship which the disillusioned ex-soldier-turned-writer contracted between himself and his audience. Although alienated, he was anxious to communicate with as large a reading public as possible, even at the expense of being labelled a political writer. His wartime experience required it of him; and rather than lessening the interest of such novels today, that commitment makes them the more challenging.

H. M. Tomlinson offered the civilian equivalent of Aldington's novel. Too old for the army, he had been war correspondent for *The Daily News,* and like the ex-soldiers he had needed a decade to gain the proper perspective of the war. *All Our Yesterdays* (1930), like Montague's *Disenchantment,* was the work of a writer already established by 1914. Thus, he was capable of working from a larger view—that is, he tried to suggest the presence of forces and symbols which represented Europe's history in the twentieth century. His novel escaped the charges of *naïveté* and subjectivism levelled against younger writers like Aldington.

All Our Yesterdays begins with the Boer War and ends just after the Armistice in 1918. Tomlinson combines history, prophecy and satire as vehicles for his testimony. The result is a rather loose collection of separate pieces which have a much tighter interior unity than has the novel itself. His commitment reinforces the sense of fragmentation, for Tomlinson indicted his society for each of its sins.

The novel contains a memorable dream sequence in which the Europe of 1900 is described metaphorically as a cardboard ship that crumbles even as it is launched. The senseless squabble between nations over remote, valueless colonies takes place in a setting reminiscent of Joseph Conrad's *Heart of Darkness.* The sections covering the war in France are the best done by a non-combatant. Even the pontificating of the intruding narrator has a charm characteristic of Tomlinson's best travel books:

> The urgent battle plans of the Somme turned blind; they went astray and were lost in autumn's unfathomed mud. The soldiers settled into the mud, and occasionally sank out of sight in it, helmets and all, wherever they were benighted at the time when their generals decided that no more progress could be made towards whatever prize they wished the troops to win, an object which had been as vague as the desire which is behind the sacred mask of stone of a heathen god.

> (*All Our Yesterdays*)

Three of the major war poets, Siegfried Sassoon, Edmund Blunden and Robert Graves, contributed to the "war-books controversy" with autobiographical or semi-fictional accounts of this war. Blunden and Graves, like Tomlinson, used writing as a means of coming to terms with their own experiences to discover some pattern or meaning in what had happened to their generation. Blunden best phrased the need to write the experience out of his system in *Undertones of War* (1928):

> I tried once before. True, when the events were not yet ended, and I was drifted into a backwater. But what I then wrote, and little enough I completed, although in its details not much affected by the perplexities of distancing memory, was noisy with a depressing forced gaiety then very much the rage. . . . And I have been attempting "the image and horror of it" . . . in poetry. Even so, when the main sheaves appeared fine enough to my flattering eye, it was impossible not to look again, and to descry the ground, how thickly and how innumerably yet it was strewn with the facts or notions of war experience.
>
> I must go over the ground again.
>
> (*Undertones of War*)

The book was the calmest, most detached treatment of the war that a poet has written. Unlike Aldington, Sassoon and Graves, Blunden quietly accepts even the most painful and violent of experiences, which he faithfully records. *Undertones of War,* along with Graves's memoir, is one of the few autobiographical masterpieces produced by 1914-18.

Good-bye To All That (1929) concerns Graves's childhood, his active service and his post-war years up until the mid-twenties. Yet the war is a dominating motif in the autobiography. The comic as well as the horrifying aspects of war are realistically described, and the book itself is a careful measure of the war, not only for a sensitive poet, but for the generation he was part of. The absurdities of the military became Graves's frequent butt, yet his commentary is quite without bitterness. In one passage which describes a lull in the action at a rest camp there is an ironic picture of battle-hardened veterans being treated literally as schoolboys and such passages offer a necessary relief from the realistic descriptions of trench warfare:

> We went along to the school room and squeezed into one of the desk-benches.
>
> When Scatter entered, the room was called to attention by the senior major; David and I hurt ourselves attempting to stand up, bench and all. Scatter told us to be seated. The officers were in one class, the warrant-officers and N.C.O.s in another. Scatter glared at us from the teacher's desk. He began his lecture with general accusations, saying that he had lately noticed many signs of slovenliness in the battalion—men with their pocket-flaps undone, and actually walking along the village street with hands in trouser-pockets and boots unpolished; sentries strolling about on their beats at company billets, instead of marching up and down in a soldier-like way—rowdiness at the *estaminets*—slackness in saluting—and many other grave indications of lowered discipline. He threatened to stop all leave to the United Kingdom unless matters improved, and promised us a saluting parade every morning before breakfast which he would attend in person.
>
> All this was general axe-ing; we knew that he had not yet reached the particular axe. It was this: "I have here principally to tell you of a very disagreeable occurrence. As I left my orderly-room this morning, I came upon a group of soldiers; I will not particularize their company. One of these soldiers was in conversation with a lance-corporal. You

may not believe me, but it is a fact that he addressed the corporal by his Christian name: *he called him Jack!* And the corporal made no protest! To think that the First Battalion has sunk to a level where it is possible for such familiarity to exist between N.C.O.s and the men under their command! Naturally, I put the corporal under arrest, and he appeared before me at once on the charge of 'conduct unbecoming to an N.C.O.' I reduced him to the ranks, and awarded the man Field Punishment for using insubordinate language to an N.C.O. But I warn you, if any further case of this sort comes to my notice—and I expect you officers to report the slightest instance to me at once—instead of dealing with it as a company matter. . . ."

> (*Goodbye To All That*)

Siegfried Sassoon's response was the most elaborate of the war poets, requiring three volumes of an autobiographical novel, *The Complete Memoirs of George Sherston,* and an official autobiography, *Siegfried's Journey,* published in 1945. *Memoirs of a Fox-Hunting Man* (1928) began the trilogy with the by then common contrast between the idyllic countryside of pre-war England and the shattered landscapes of the Western Front.

The second volume, *Memoirs of an Infantry Officer* (1930), carefully traces the changing mood of the war after the battle of the Somme, and of Sassoon's *persona,* George Sherston. His anger expresses itself in terms of Sherston's behaviour

Siegfried Sassoon.

rather than through the subjective commentary of an omniscient narrator. His experiences explain his progressively anti-war sentiments. Viewing unseasoned troops relieving his battalion in the trenches at the Somme, he records a developing awareness of his contempt for war:

> Visualizing that forlorn crowd of khaki figures under the twilight of the trees, I can believe that I saw then, for the first time, how blindly War destroys its victims. The sun had gone down on my own reckless brandishings, and I understood the doomed conditions of these half trained civilians who had been sent up to attack the Wood. . . . Two days later the Welsh Division, of which they were a unit, was involved in massacre and confusion.
>
> (*Memoirs of an Infantry Officer*)

For the curious pursuer of literary history there is a delightful fictional account of Sassoon's famous protest against the war, his subsequent court martial, where he was represented by his fellow officer, Robert Graves, and his subsequent confinement at Craiglockhart Hospital. Sassoon's narrator has the ability to laugh at himself throughout the trilogy, which alone makes it one of the more memorable of the anti-war books.

The most vehement of the novelists involved in the "war-books controversy" was Henry Williamson. *The Wet Flanders Plain* (1929) and *The Patriot's Progress* (1930) both attacked in fictional form the absurdities of British politicians, generals and war profiteers. As little more than political tirades they are of historical interest only; but Williamson had by the 1950s found a more tempered and dispassionate view of the events of his time, and one which patiently delineated the reactions of an over-sensitive young man like Williamson himself. *A Chronicle of Ancient Sunlight,* his *roman fleuve,* devotes five novels in the series to his central character's wartime experience: *How Dear Is Life* (1954), *A Fox under My Cloak* (1955), *The Golden Virgin* (1957), *Love and the Loveless* (1958), and *A Test to Destruction* (1960). Moving from his service in 1914 as a private in the Territorials to the rank of acting Lieutenant-Colonel in the last year of the war, the books carefully, almost journalistically, reconstruct Phillip Maddison's every reaction to the ordinary affairs of the four years. *A Chronicle of Ancient Sunlight* is also an in-depth psychological study which frequently subordinates Maddison's fortunes in war to the overriding problem of his relationship with his unsympathetic father. The mass of details from France and the home front has no equal in war prose. Considerable research on the official and unofficial histories of the war has resulted in frequent asides and commentaries from the major military figures, quoted from dispatches and memoirs, and intended to give an overview of the action. Surprisingly, the British High Command is treated with considerable respect—a reversal of Williamson's earlier stands.

In descriptions of critical battles such as the German breakthrough in the spring of 1918, Williamson shifts his narrative between Phillip Maddison's immediate involvement at the front, staff reactions and scenes in Britain:

> While Phillip wrote a report small fires were being started to boil canteens. Smoke was hanging in the mist when the hare rushed back again. Shots were heard and the thuds of stick-bombs to the left. The flanking Lewis gun opened up. The sergeant with the waxed points on his moustache ran up, red-faced. "They're coming, sir! They're in the wood on the left!"

Later that morning, south-west of where Phillip and his men were retreating, the Commander-in-Chief motored in his black Rolls-Royce flying Union Jack pennant on bonnet to see Sir Hubert Gough, over whose *château* at Villers Bretonneux hung the banner of the Red Fox. There he learned to his surprise that the troops of the Fifth Army were already *behind* the line of the Somme river.

That night the Field-Marshall wrote in his diary,

> "Men very tired after two days' fighting and the long march back. On the first day they had to wear gas-masks which is very fatiguing, but I cannot make out why the Fifth Army has gone so far back without making some kind of a stand."

". . . Listen to this!" said Richard [Maddison] sitting in his armchair of green Russian leather. It was a bitterly cold night; his coke fire, halved by extra fire-bricks, burned dully. It was his last free evening before resuming duty with the Special Constabulary. "Can Prussian effrontery go further? Here in the evening paper is a copy of the Kaiser's telegram to the Kaiserin, Hetty!

> 'Pleased to be able to tell you that by the Grace of God the battles of Mouilly, Cambrai, St. Quentin, and La Fere have been won. The Lord had gloriously aided. May he further help.
> Wilhelm'." (*A Test to Destruction*)

The attention to such detail sometimes grates, but it frequently enlivens and gives depth to the narrative. The work comes as close to a complete perspective of war on the Western Front as will ever be written. The atmosphere created carries the reader through even the most prosaic passages. More than most novels, it makes the reactions of the writers of "war books" seem logical, even reasoned. Though Williamson does not state it as such, the sense of violation which his generation suffered is thoroughly chronicled in the five novels covering Phillip Maddison's war years.

After the war an increasing number of writers and critics began to identify themselves as, and to write for, the "cultural minority." For the war novelist the techniques adopted by James Joyce, Virginia Woolf and D. H. Lawrence, with their implied commitment to a limited reading public, seriously constricted fiction's potential national impact. He had no mandate for an exercise in minority culture. His subject-matter and his experience during the war required a commitment to the general reading public, and if he was at all serious that audience was the one he wanted to reach. Further, the idea that good literature could come out of rage at an existing order, out of writing associated with leftist and anti-war pieces, has not been well received in the twentieth century. As a result few war novels have survived harsh literary judgements in the last fifty years. Yet, three works rise above the rest as major achievements in British fiction.

Ford Madox Ford, R. H. Mottram and Frederick Manning each avoided more than superficial ties with the partisanship and commitment of "war books." Ford and Mottram finished their war novels before the debate had assumed major proportions, and Manning prefaced his 1929 edition of *Her Privates We* with a statement of intended objectivity. Though they avoided the uncontrolled rage and the common sentimentality of most war fiction, they each represented that sense of individual isolation which has typified post-First World War fiction.

Ford was too old for active service. He managed a commission in the Welch Regiment in August 1915, and by the following July was in France with a line regiment. He had already written what a contemporary of Ford's, John Rodker, had termed "the finest French novel in the English language" before the war. In the months prior to his commission he had completed two propagandist exercises for the allied cause, *When Blood Is Their Argument* (1915) and *Between St. Dennis and St. George* (1915). In 1918 he published a collection of war poetry, *On Heaven, and Poems Written on Active Service,* and by 1923 he had embarked on the "Tietjens" novels, his interpretation of the years between Edwardian England and the end of the war. Ford did not distinguish between the pressures of Edwardian and wartime life. For him they had been the same:

> My own observation of active warfare had led me to a singular conclusion. . . . What preyed most on the mind of the majority of not professionally military men who went through it was what was happening at home. Wounds, rain, fear, and other horrors are terrible but relatively simple matters; you either endure them or you do not. But you have no way by which, by taking thought, you may avoid them. . . . But what is happening at home, within the four walls, and the immediate little circle of the individual—that is the unceasing strain!
> *(It Was the Nightingale,* 1934)

In capturing the period, Ford was guided by his own experience and that of many major novelists. What they seemed to have in common—Wells, Aldington and Lawrence, among others—were marital difficulties which hampered their work. The war, causing among other things a limited emancipation of women, also acted to ease sexual relationships that would have been agonizing in 1914.

Ford's early collaboration with Joseph Conrad and his subsequent comments on the importance of techniques for an impressionist writer are well known. In the "Tietjens" novels, published in a single volume, *Parades' End,* in the United States, Ford applied the theory he and Conrad had worked out, and the result is one of the most remarkably structured fictions in this century.

The central involvement of the series is relatively simple and quite "real," in that it seems to have paralleled the fate of many intellectuals whose wartime intimacies were revealed long after the Armistice. A biography of a well-known poet of the time, *Edward Thomas: The Last Four Years* by Eleanor Farjeon, describes a relationship between Thomas, his wife and a "good friend" which bears a striking resemblance to the plight of Ford's hero. Aldington employed a similar embroilment in *Death of a Hero,* and of course Ford himself was writing from experience when he described Tietjens's problems with an antagonistic Catholic wife who refused to divorce her husband.

Some Do Not . . . (1924) offers, in terms of setting and character, a social panorama of pre-war England. Suffragettes and marital difficulties seem the key to a society on the verge of cataclysm. Shifting to 1917 in the second half of the novel, Ford reveals in the action of an afternoon and evening the impact of the war on his hero, Tietjens, or "the last Tory" as Ford calls him.

No More Parades (1925), the middle novel of the original trilogy, concerns military life at a base camp in France. It captures the endless muddle and mud of war operations, and the way they affect the mind far more than the body. The novelist's sensitivity to his characters and their suffering evokes a sense of the sublime. The novel, by itself, is a remarkable achievement.

A Man Could Stand Up (1926) continues the description of the Western Front and rounds out Ford's view of the war by having as settings a quiet morning's action in the trenches, and the celebration of Armistice Day in England. The tone of the concluding scene is triumphant, and a validating demonstration of Ford's ability to consider his characters dispassionately, a feat which few other writers attempted:

> This then was the day!
>
> The war had made a man of him! It had coarsened him and hardened him. There was no other way to look at it. It had made him reach a point at which he would no longer stand unbearable things . . . what he wanted he was prepared to take. . . . What he had been before, God alone knew. A Younger Son? A Perpetual Second-in-Command? Who knew. But today the world changed. Feudalism was finished; its last vestiges were gone. It held no place for him. He was going—he was damn well going—to make a place in it for. . . .
> *(A Man Could Stand Up)*
> (pp. 7-25)

Ford succeeded better than any other writer in describing the war period. He had proposed to show "what the late war was like," and he managed it without overstating its horrors or heroisms.

R. H. Mottram had also seen in the war an entity to be described. He, too, depended on his immediate experience for a vision of that entity, but where Ford had meticulously sifted his fiction through history and thus revealed his vision of its meanings, Mottram went to the events themselves and used them in a chronicle-like manner. His actual war experience followed rather closely that of the two main English figures in *The Spanish Farm Trilogy.* The second novel of the work he admitted having taken from his war diary. When he was discharged he returned to his bank job, only to discover "how completely the pre-war world had been blown away, and how specious was the pretence that we had come back to anything recognizable." During the long delays between campaigns he had begun to write and had found it amazingly easy.

> The War moved me very little to poetry, and it was in the hospital at Hazebrouck in 1916 that I turned to prose. I felt already then that the romance and heroics usually woven around war were as futile as the hysterics and black despair about it which, even then audible, became vociferous thirteen years later. Experience of the actual front line trenches, and an extraordinary run of luck in being called out to administrative jobs convinced me then of its portentous silliness and ineffectiveness and subversion.
> (R. H. Mottram, "How *The Spanish Farm* Came to be Written," in Gilbert H. Fabes, *The First Editions of Ralph Hale Mottram,* 1934)

In 1919 he had rewritten his "diary" into a sort of "chronicle" and tried unsuccessfully to publish it. Even the backing of John Galsworthy was not enough to get the work accepted. In October 1922, Mottram began his "last" novel before he gave up writing for insurance. Curiously enough, his basis for the work was similar to that Ford had employed in *No More Parades.* The result could not have been more different from Ford's, yet it arose from the same intentions and involved as unique a method. For as Galsworthy was to note, *The Spanish Farm* seemed neither novel nor chronicle, but an odd combination of the two. Mood and subject had guided Mottram in a new direction, toward what John Galsworthy, echoing Joseph Conrad's comments on the novel, could describe only as "highly humanized history."

The Spanish Farm developed naturally out of Mottram's preoccupation with his war experience. The Ferme l'Espagnole itself was typical, and the characters who gradually came to move around it were equally familiar.

The novel begins somewhat obscurely because of Mottram's efforts to establish this universality of experience. The central figure of the narrative is used as the consciousness witnessing the action, but the novel opens with a depiction of the Spanish Farm as a common experience of the British Expeditionary Force:

> English officers and men who billeted in the Spanish Farm (and practically the whole English army must have passed through or near it one time or another) to this day speak of it as one of the few places they can still distinguish in the blur of receding memories, one of the few spots of which they have nothing but good to tell.
>
> (*The Spanish Farm*, 1924)

By focusing on the land, and the people whose land had become the Front in France, Mottram manages a depth in this first novel of the trilogy which might have been missed had he concentrated on a single British officer.

Sixty-Four, Ninety-Four (1925) had not begun as an integral part of *The Spanish Farm.* It was the hitherto unpublished "chronicle" reworked and judiciously edited with the help of Galsworthy. Yet it meshed with the other novel, complemented it. This second book considered the same period of time, and occasionally the same events related in *The Spanish Farm,* but it told the story from Lieutenant Skene's, the British officer's, point of view. In a sense Mottram had employed Arnold Bennett's earlier method in the *Clayhanger* trilogy. And to this he was later to add Galsworthy's contribution to the form of the trilogy: a series of short portraits, poetic in mood, to link the three novels.

The novel takes its name from the doggerel soldiers adapted to fit the notes of "Sick Call":

> Sixty-four, ninety-four—
> He'll never go sick no more,
> The poor beggar's dead.

These three lines contain everything the novel expresses. There is a feeling of irretrievable loss, a quiet bitterness, that every trench soldier has experienced. The plot involves an officer's experience first as an infantry subaltern and later as a staff officer. Enlisted men hardly figure in the story. Lieutenant Skene is isolated by his responsibilities, and as the war progresses his isolation increases. From being an intense young subaltern anxious to get into the fighting before it ends, he becomes a sly old soldier who, by 1918, can identify himself with nothing but army life in France. After the first few weeks of the Somme campaign his original regiment disappears. In England the death of his uncle leaves him without

family; the society of wartime London is completely alien to him. His one tie is with the France that is represented by the mistress of the Spanish Farm whom he imagines is still interested in him. For Skene, their affair is a melancholy interlude between periods in the trenches. When they form a liaison they consciously fall into a make-believe world which ignores the abnormalities of the war:

> For in their secret hearts both of them were domesticated, conventional to the core. Both of them loathed the War and all it had brought. It was the queerest of contradictions that forced them to comfort their ultra-respectable aspirations in such a place and such a manner, both spoken of even in wartime, by many people, as "irregular."
>
> (*The Spanish Farm*)

The War hardens Skene and his fellow officers. These men take it for granted that the England they know is gone. The good times they remember of the army seem to be lost in the remembrance of men who died with the war. But Mottram is too clear-sighted to sentimentalize emptiness, and he closes *Sixty-Four, Ninety-Four* with the note too many war writers have refused to recognize:

> He had gone into the thing neither because he was paid, nor because he was forced—and that was something. Processions and speeches were empty show—even the eventual effect on Europe was irrelevant—but deep within himself he had fulfilled a need, worked out a destiny. In what an abyss of self-contempt would he now be sunk had he not gone to that War—he, fit and of age?
>
> That was it—the call had come, and he had answered; surely he had his reward in: "I was there!"
>
> (*Sixty-four, Ninety-four*)

The Crime at Vanderlynden's (1926) is serious farce, the comic relief of the trilogy. It is an analysis of war built around a very minor incident at the Spanish Farm that symbolizes the whole paradox of the war. The crime is against all those on whose land the war was fought, and the criminal is every soldier. What Mottram attempts is to capture in a minor altercation over a French civilian claim for damages all the nuances of the *entente cordiale* and of the war behind the lines.

Mottram traced in the novel the gradual progression of the mood of the soldiers across the war years. In a very moving end to the trilogy his staff officer crystallizes the emotions of the returning British soldier. They are, as well, a final comment on the chronicle of four years.

> The Crime at Vanderlynden's showed the whole thing in miniature. The English had been welcomed as Allies, resented as intruders, but never had they become homogeneous with the soil and its natives, nor could they ever leave any lasting mark on the body or spirit of the place. They were still incomprehensible to Vanderlynden's, and Vanderlynden's to them. . . . To him [the staff officer], at that moment, it seemed that the English Effort was fading out, leaving nothing but graveyards. . . . [But] the Crime at Vanderlynden's was behind him. He had got away from it at last.
>
> (*The Crime at Vanderlynden's*)

What distinguishes *The Spanish Farm Trilogy* from its counterparts is Mottram's vision of the war. His technique, focus and organization are closely related to those of his friend, John Galsworthy. There is no real examination in depth of an individual's psychological responses to war, no elaborate weighing of value on the part of the individual characters; rather, the trilogy reflects, in much the same way as *The Forsyte Saga* before it, the surface convolutions of a society in the process of change. Mottram achieved precisely what he intended to in *The Spanish Farm Trilogy*. It is at once a monument to the war and its dead, and a fair record of its cost.

Neither Ford nor Mottram had attempted to write in tragic terms about the war. They had described the tragedy that war is, but they had not tried to use the conflict as a subject for a tragic novel. That remained for others and though attempts to deal with the war as a subject for tragedy were made, the usual result was hysterical, often offensively sentimental fiction. Only one writer has succeeded in mining the tragic themes of the war for the novel. In 1929 "Private 19022" published *Her Privates We*. Immediately Arnold Bennett, E. M. Forster, St. John Irvine and T. E. Lawrence all acclaimed it. The last named also recognized in it the hand of the author of *Scenes and Portraits*. But Frederick Manning was little known as a writer, and it was only after his death in 1935 that his authorship of *Her Privates We* was revealed. He had preferred anonymity to emphasize his concern with the anonymous ranks of the British Army. (pp. 26-30)

Her Privates We is tragedy in the classical sense of the word. At the same time, however, it fairly represents the private soldier's life "in the round." The irony of the novel is not in the reader's general foreknowledge of trench life, but in his realization of the fate it holds for the private soldier. In filling out its action the novel uses all those characteristics of men in war that had first been introduced by Barbusse. Comradeship and courage take their place beside the individual's ultimate isolation and his fear. Boredom and terrible stress, cynicism and hope, petty ambition and complete unselfishness—all the paradoxes of trench warfare are depicted. But over and above these things is the insistent echo of fate. Throughout the novel the expectation of Bourne—death in action—is sounded in the deaths of those around him. The irony is like that of Sophocles, for Bourne cannot admit to himself that the war will kill him too. When he sees a man blown up beside him, he forces himself to avoid the inevitable conclusion.

> One forgets quickly. The mind is averted as well as the eyes. It reassures itself after that first despairing cry: "It is I!"
>
> "No, it is not I. I shall not be like that."
>
> And one moves on, leaving the mauled and bloody thing behind: gambling, in fact, on that implicit assurance each one of us has of his own immortality.
>
> *(Her Privates We)*

The novel is filled with unfounded optimisms and their immediate contradiction by fate. Bourne is inextricably caught up in "the sausage machine," as the Western Front came to be known to infantry men after the Somme campaign. The means of escape open to him—Officer's School—he rejects, partly out of pride and partly because of a sense of comradeship with the men he would have to leave. When he does finally agree to become an officer and so gain a brief respite from the front, it is already too late. His orders come through as he is returned to the line again, and the last revolution of the wheel has begun.

Manning develops and then explores the strange mysticism that arises from so constant an association with death. *Her*

Privates We is not unlike Walpole's *The Dark Forest* in that respect. As Manning described it:

> Life was a hazard enveloped in mystery, and war quickened the sense of both in men: the soldier also, as well as the saint, might write his tractate *de contemptu mundi,* and differ from him only in the angle and spirit from which he surveyed the same bleak reality.
>
> *(Her Privates We)*

Manning gives Bourne heroic stature by setting him apart from the other soldiers. He is a gentleman ranker of sorts—that is, he has money and intelligence. Yet he at first refuses a commission and prefers to serve with the common soldier. His past is a mystery to his comrades and remains so to the reader, but he becomes a legendary figure for the ranks because of his extraordinary talent at "scrounging" a comfortable existence out of the lot of the private soldier.

The novel has been criticized as being an inaccurate portrayal of the ranker's experience. The argument has been made [by A. C. Ward in *The Nineteen Twenties,* 1930] that "a man of letters does not become a private soldier by the simple step of enlisting, nor can he do it in any other way." He must remain throughout an educated and imaginative man experiencing his own sensations and not those of the uneducated and unimaginative. What must be added, however, is that while a man of letters sharing experience may not see things from the common man's point of view, he can describe the men he has known and seen. And Manning succeeds in bringing the anonymous ranks to life better than any other British novelist dealing with the First World War.

The novel ends with a picture of the lifeless body of Bourne and of the men waiting silently near it. The sergeant-major's thoughts capture the very essence of the thing the war had done to its survivors.

> He was sorry about Bourne, he thought, more sorry than he could say. He was a queer chap. . . . There was a bit of a mystery about him; but then, when you come to think of it, there's a bit of a mystery about all of us. He pushed aside the blanket screening the entrance, and in the murky light he saw all the men lift their faces, and look at him with patient, almost animal eyes.
>
> Then they all bowed over their own thoughts again. . . . They sat there silently: each man keeping his own secret.
>
> *(Her Privates We)*

That same vision can be found in the "Tietjens" saga and in *The Spanish Farm Trilogy*. The war had left all its heroes in isolation, groping into themselves, forever looking for the small group of intimates or the way to love that would ease the pain of their aloneness. Ford's Tietjens had escaped a bleak, lonely existence after the war through his love for Valentine. Mottram's Lieutenant Skene had been left isolated in a friendless world. Bourne and his comrades had been left with a "faith in nothing but themselves and in each other." Such was the heritage of war experience.

The prose of The First World War is remarkable for the variety of settings, activities and subjects covered. The majority belonged to the period of the "war books controversy," and they reflect the trauma of the war before all else. Yet their merit reaches beyond the limits of political and social commentary, and the best of them have been forgotten or ignored

Frontispiece by David Jones for his In Parenthesis.

in the past thirty years more because of the flooding of the booklists with "war books" between 1928-32 and because of the movement of Europe into a Second World War, than because of any lack of quality in the works themselves. (pp. 31-4)

David Jones's *In Parenthesis* is the one serious artistic effort in the direction of an epic on the war but it can be defined neither as fiction nor poetry. As in Djuna Barnes's experimental work of the same period, *Nightwood* (1936), and in E. E. Cummings, *Eimi* (1933), poetic imagery and verse fragments are intertwined with prose narrative until they are inseparable. Like most innovations of this sort in literature the merits of the work are often obscured by an unfamiliar method. Because the novel has always been the most plastic of forms, quick to espouse the cause of numerous hybrids and bastard children, *In Parenthesis* may be considered a relative at least, and as such, no study of First War fiction would be complete without mention of it.

The work is of epic form partly because Jones worked his tale of trench warfare into a parallel with the Welsh national poem, *The Gododin of Aneurin.* He felt there was in the first two years of the conflict (up to the Battle of the Somme) the existence of a landscape and a code of behaviour that was embedded deep in the traditions of English literature, especially in the work of Shakespeare, Malory, Spenser, and the epic poets of the Middle Ages.

My companions in the war were mostly Londoners with an admixture of Welshmen, so that the mind and folk-life of those two differing racial groups are an essential ingredient to my theme. Nothing could be more representative. . . . Together they bore in their bodies the genuine tradition of the Island of Britain, from Bendigeid Vran to Jingle and Marie Lloyd. These were the children of Doll Tearsheet. Those are before Caractacus was.

(*In Parenthesis,* 1937)

The epic stature of the work is further strengthened by Jones's avowal that he did not intend *In Parenthesis* as a "war book." He wrote, "it happens to be concerned with war. I should prefer it to be about a good kind of peace—but as Mandeville says, 'of Pardys ne can I not speken propurly I was not there; it is fer beyonde and that for thinketh me. And also I was not worthi'." The work could not have caught the magical and the humorous elements of war if it had been an anti-war tract. As it is, *In Parenthesis* has been able to "see formal goodness in a life singularly inimical, hateful to us." Not, however, at the cost of an underlying reality.

In order better to present "the complex of sights, sounds, fears, hopes, apprehensions, smells, things exterior and interior," Jones intended *In Parenthesis,* like epic poetry, to be read aloud. The presentation of his complexity, however, is hampered by the many annotations he felt obliged to supply. Not only has he explained his war terminology and slang usages, he has cited the sources of half-lines of older verse, and he has footnoted contexts intentionally paralleled with traditional poetry. All of these were a part of the soldiers' conscious and unconscious perceptions, but the effect of footnoting every point does tend to draw the reader outside experiences he ought to share with the writer. As an epic should, *In Parenthesis* reflects a sort of racial consciousness in action during the war. Yet, having once cited direct sources and having annotated his verse, Jones removes his reader from poetic experience of the unconscious heritage of his race and offers him intricate scholarship instead.

To write of the 1914-18 War on an epic scale required a subject complete in itself. For the struggle in modern Europe did not cease with the Armistice but was simply delayed and so created a lull between eruptions. Jones seems to have been aware of this in 1937:

This writing is called *In Parenthesis* because I have written it in a kind of space between—I don't know between quite what—but as you turn aside to do something; and because for us amateur soldiers . . . the war itself was a parenthesis—how glad we thought we were to step outside its brackets at the end of '18—and also because our curious type of existence here is altogether in parenthesis.

(*In Parenthesis*)

He made his epic narrative a dramatic whole by forging it within the confines of a short period before and during the Battle of the Somme. In this brief interval he managed to formulate a total experience from The Great War. His careful presentation of the war as a poetic adventure, as a complex of sensual experiences in a "place of enchantment" which seemed, for all the new weapons, to be a reconstruction of an older heritage—it is this which makes *In Parenthesis* an artistic success. Ironically, it is also this hyperconcentration of reality and fancy, requiring so many annotations, which has left the work, after thirty years, an experimental oddity rather than a memorable piece of literature.

In Parenthesis offers an interesting vantage point for an examination of the extent of war literature. It is, in a sense, an exploration of the myth of battle. In developing the underlying sameness of experience that is visible in the war literature of the past, Jones hit upon the major feature of First War novels and uttered a last word on them. Their authors had shared an adventure that was as old as time. When they came to write about the war, it involved not only their own personal background but their cultural heritage as well. For no matter what far-flung field of action they described, there was for these writers "a culture already developed there, already venerable and rooted." Their work is good evidence of it, and of the commitment that culture had come to require. (pp. 40-2)

> M. S. Greicus, in his Prose Writers of World War
> I, edited by Ian Scott-Kilvert, Longman Group Ltd.,
> 1973, 49 p.

GERMAN LITERATURE OF WORLD WAR I

PATRICK BRIDGWATER

[*Bridgwater is an English educator and critic who specializes in German language and literature. In the following excerpt, he surveys German poetry of the First World War.*]

When 1914-18 war poetry is mentioned in histories of German literature, it is almost invariably the manufacturers of patriotic outbreak-of-war verse who are named as the war poets. This is nonsense. In Germany, as in England, "war poetry" is a term which covers many different kinds of poetry. Beside the monumental impersonality of Georg Heym's prophetic "Der Krieg" (1911), one of the truly great poems about war, there are the impersonal oracular poses of Rilke and George. Beside the unquestioning patriotism of 1914 there is the anti-war and pacifist poetry of 1914 onwards. There is the English-type irony of Alfred Lichtenstein, the "expressionism" of Stramm and Trakl, the compassionate realism of Anton Schnack, Wilhelm Klemm, Heinrich Lersch, Karl von Eisenstein and others. And so on. The real German poetry of the war is the work of a hundred-odd poets, many of whom only produced one or two outstanding poems and are now completely forgotten (e.g., Peter Baum, Richard Fischer, Gerhard Moerner, Siegfried Schlösser, Hugo Zuckermann).

Georg Heym, one of the major poets of his generation, was obsessed by a foreboding of war. His poem "Der Krieg" is a visionary and prophetic picture of war, written in 1911. It is written in a heavy six-beat trochaic line so that the accent stalks through the poem like the incarnate demon of war through his apocalyptic landscape. The rhythm and imagery of the poem underline the violence of its subject matter. Occasional deviations from the metrical pattern give the impression both of the poet's vision dominating and threatening to violate his formal resources, and of violence continually erupting through the surface of life; the old world represented by the trochaic metre is continually burst open by the violence of the subject matter. The use of rhymed couplets throughout, with all the rhymes masculine ones, is highly appropriate since the rhyme scheme thus reflects and expresses the primitive, elemental quality of Heym's subject. The poem is "lyrical" above all in its concentration. What strikes the reader at once is the monumental impersonality and barbaric grandeur of the poem. Indeed, "Der Krieg" differs from most 1914-18 war poems (*cf.* Owen, Schnack) in being not at all subjective; what Heym gives is an objective picture of war as such, war as an elemental feature of life. There is terror in this objectivity, as there is later in Ludwig Renn's novel *Krieg*. In poems actually written during the war such objectivity is found only in poets who are, for one reason or another, far from their subject (*cf.* Rilke's "Fünf Gesänge," George's *Der Krieg,* Max Dauthendey's *Des grossen Krieges Not*). Heym's poem aims to shock; it consists of juxtaposed explosive images which burst like shells in the reader's mind (*cf.* Stramm). Since the poet sees war as an elemental feature of life, "Der Krieg" ultimately conveys a visionary and prophetic picture of reality itself. Georg Heym, like T. S. Eliot's Tiresias, "perceived the scene, and foretold the rest."

The opening of "Der Krieg" is majestic in its barbaric grandeur:

> He is risen now that was so long asleep,
> Risen out of vaulted places dark and deep.
> In the growing dusk the faceless demon stands,
> And the moon he crushes in his strong black hands.

War is immediately personified into an infernal demon who rises from below, from the collective unconscious, from the most primitive depths of life, and at the end stands in all his grim majesty over the apocalyptic landscape that is both his own true element and the scene of mankind's Fall and Passion. The demon War rises before our eyes on the repeated word "aufgestanden." One changed syllable—"auf*er*standen"—and the word would refer to a god rising from the dead. But "auf*ge*standen" is appropriate here, for War is a chthonic god or demon, a great and unknown power, a figure of utter profanity. Just how terrible this power is, is suggested in the last line of the first stanza, where War is shown crushing the moon in his black hand; his colour is the colour of evil and death, for war is the product of evil, and the product of war, the whole point and purpose of war, is death. Heym's demon War reappeared in August, 1914, in Rilke's "Fünf Gesänge":

> For the first time I see you rising,
> Hearsaid, remote, incredible War-God
> . . . now he uprose; stands: higher
> Than standing towers.

These and other lines show that Rilke, like Petzold and others, is deliberately echoing Heym. But Rilke's "War-God" is a far more ambiguous and less terrifying figure than Heym's demon; he is a mythical god—"At last a god," Rilke wrote—and as such at most a source of awe rather than terror. Rilke's "War-God" is a sacred figure, while the whole point of Heym's demon is his profanity. Rilke's god comes ultimately from Olympos; Heym's demon comes straight from Hell.

In the course of the poem we see this demon moving out into the landscape of war, a landscape that becomes increasingly a prophetic picture of what has been called "the lunar waste of the Somme," until it finally assumes the proportions of myth: the demon War assumes the proportions of something wholly uncontrollable. Again and again personification is used to control the perspective and gain depth. Thus in the sixth stanza night, the abode of demons, is touched into independent existence by Heym's use of the plural "nights" which implies a black world full of night demons. Similarly fire is animated into "a red hound with the screaming of wild mouths": the mythical hell-hound itself carrying off the broken animal bodies of the dead to eternal damnation.

All through the poem War is presented as the sign of evil, and at the end we see the original monster city destroyed by War, destroyed, that is, by the awakened evil within itself. Its fall is made to echo the Fall of Babylon the Great. The earth is reduced to a wasteland dominated by the gigantic figure of Death Triumphant. Within five years this wasteland was to assume concrete form on the Somme.

"Der Krieg" is a magnificent poem about war, even if it is not a "war poem" as such. It is the best of several poems in which War is personified; others include Stefen Zweig's "Polyphem," and Albert Ehrenstein's "Der Kriegsgott," in which war appears as Ares (Mars), the bloody war-god abominated by all other gods. It is also the best of a number of poems by Expressionist poets prophesying war. Since Heym was well known in *avant-garde* literary circles, "Der Krieg" became a potent influence on the poetry of the First World War. The reason for this is evident: Heym was the first German poet to give adequate expression to the modern, tragic conception of war.

With the prophetic grandeur of Heym's poem, it is interesting to compare the prophetic poses of Rilke and George. Rilke's "Fünf Gesänge, August 1914" ("Five Hymns, August 1914") were written in the first days of the war amid the intense patriotism unleashed by the Declaration and subsequent mobilization. That Rilke starts by echoing the nationalistic and militaristic sentiments of the day is hardly surprising. While avoiding the jingoism of so many lesser poets, in the first and second of these hymns Rilke welcomes war in a way which not only points straight back to Heym, but which is also highly reminiscent of Hölderlin in terms of diction, syntax and attitude. The rhetorical first and second hymns are based on Hölderlin's view of the poet as the prophetic voice of his people, and on his cyclic view of history, which enables Rilke to view the war as something necessary. The borrowed prophetic mien is remarkable and basically spurious.

Three days later, however, in the third hymn, the poet's attitude has changed. The god of war is still seen as a primitive, demonic force, and as such is described in language reminiscent of Heym's "Der Krieg"; but now Rilke begins to have doubts about the way in which he had welcomed the advent of this legendary war-god. He begins to realize that he has allowed himself to be carried away by his amoral (aesthetic) enthusiasm for this radical phenomenon, an enthusiasm shared by his fellow-countrymen. This very reminder that he is speaking for so many others brings the realization that war, however "great" in a purely aesthetic sense, is a blind and destructive power. So far, so good. If the hymns had ended here, it would have been better. Rilke after all has realized the true nature of war long before most of his contemporaries. The trouble is that the hymns continue and, in so doing, become increasingly irrelevant. Rilke now sees it as his task to praise not the feeling of being "in gloriously experienced danger, holy to all," but rather the pain and grief which underlie this feeling and which are the real product of war. In the final hymn this "endless lament" leads to a mystique of *Schmerz*, so that war is virtually idealized for the depth of the grief that it causes.

In the course of the cycle Rilke's language becomes more and more clearly the rhetorical, emotionally charged and yet abstract language of the *Duino Elegies*. The real events of August, 1914, are absorbed into Rilke's esoteric view of life; war is turned into so much poetry. The real insight of the third hymn deserves all praise, but the cycle as a whole begins and ends with an aestheticism which is arguably amoral. These hymns are certainly the work of the most considerable German poet of the time, and they contain some of the best poetry written during the war; but it could be argued that they are too poetic, too literary and rhetorical to rank highly as war poetry. The decisive criticism was made in August, 1914, by the worker-poet Gerrit Engelke: "There's too much 'Hölderlin' here." Rilke's reactions may be sensitive, but he is in some ways too far from his subject. The great war poetry of 1914-18 was written by the front-line poets for whom the "horrible beastliness of war" (Wilfred Owen) was a matter not of sensitivity, but of grim personal experience and terror. Whereas Wilfred Owen rightly said "Above all, I am not concerned with Poetry. My subject is War . . . ," Rilke by contrast appears to be too much concerned with "Poetry." While Owen's poetry, for instance, is deeply personal, Rilke's hymns are personal only in the sense of being esoteric. Otherwise they are, like George's *Der Krieg,* impersonal in their lack of deep and genuine emotion, a masterful mistake. It would have been better if Rilke had refused, like Oskar Loerke, to leave his real, inner world.

Stefan George's *Der Krieg* (1917) shows an objectivity altogether different in kind from that of any other war poetry except Rilke's hymns. Singularly little emotion is present in George's poem, which appears to have been written solely because he felt that an utterance was expected of him. His impassive, prophetic stance conveys nothing so much as a monumental indifference to the war. George had, of course, looked forward to a holy war which would renew the spiritually moribund society of his time; but the particular war that came must have struck him as merely vulgar and brutal. In *Der Krieg* the opening quotation from Dante's *Divina Commedia* and the Biblical allusion in the first line serve to underline the impassive dignity of George's prophet-persona, the "hermit on the mountain." Asked "Are you silent still at this time of prodigious destiny," he replies: "I take no part in the struggle as you experience it." Except where the death of his own friends is concerned—and George's best "war poems" are those written in their memory—the war leaves him completely cold. His attitude is altogether too exalted: "Thanks never fall to the prophet's share. . . . To HIM what is the slaughter of hundreds of thousands / compared with the slaughter of life itself." Though the poet's proper concern may be the "slaughter of life itself," George shows a brutal indifference to the actual deaths that constitute this slaughter. Of the old prophet—himself—he says: "HIS office is praise and blame, prayer and atonement / . . . HE is gripped by a deeper dread," but this again surely underlines his almost total lack of commitment to real suffering and therefore to real life. His objectivity is at times little short of inhuman. He realizes that "The old god of battle is no more," realizes that modern war is bestial rather than heroic: "Diseased worlds are raging to their end in that frenzy" (his contempt for his time is matched only by Ezra Pound in "Hugh Selwyn Mauberley"). He is right, and his prophetic stance is momentarily justified, when he writes that "There is no call for rejoicing: there will be no triumph, / only many deaths without dignity . . . ." It was precisely "many deaths without dignity" that this war produced. George was right, too, in saying that "A nation is dead when its gods are dead."

In the penultimate section of the poem George's attitude changes and he expresses his love of Germany in a noble and moving way: "O land / too beautiful for foreign feet to ravage / . . . Land in which much promise still resides— / which therefore shall not perish!" But after this flash of real and deep feeling, the oracular pose returns in the final, wholly Hölderlinian section, where the mythical allusions are unnecessary adjuncts to his pose (contrast the ritual and mythical allusions in David Jones' *In Parenthesis*).

The conclusion is therefore inescapable that for all its linguistic brilliance and moments of real insight, George's *Der Krieg* as a whole is uninspired, unconvincing, unnecessary. The poem is essentially a belated reaction to the events of August, 1914, to which we should now turn our attention.

The fantastic flood of war verse produced in Germany in August, 1914, is a reflection of the immense national enthusiasm (most memorably summarized in Rilke's phrase "hearts full of homeland") that followed the Declaration. On both sides there had been those who had wanted war even before it arrived; "Oh, if only there were war! If only war would come!" Gustav Sack had written in 1912, and on the Allied side Rupert Brooke was not alone in greeting the advent of war with relief. Poetic reactions to the Declaration were almost without exception intensely enthusiastic, idealistic, blindly patriotic. It must, of course, be remembered that the German people regarded themselves as innocent of starting the war. For most Germans the issue was simple: the Fatherland had been attacked, the Fatherland must be defended. The Declaration was therefore inevitably an event about which countless poets and poetasters felt obliged to record their—mostly unthinking—reactions. This is true, especially, of the older, established poets, all of whom adopted a pro-war attitude.

In August, 1914, Richard Dehmel, for instance, wrote his famous lines "A flame was blown into the house, / A holy flame," and volunteered for military service at the age of 51. He retained his irrational patriotism to the bitter end; this is shown by his war diary *Zwischen Volk und Menschheit* (1919), a bombastic, self-important document which justifies Kurt Tucholsky's comment that even in 1919 Dehmel was "still bursting with enthusiasm for a Teutonism which no longer exists"; of Dehmel's war poems it is the "Hymnus barbarikus" (1917) that remains most valid. In August, 1914, too, Gerhart Hauptmann (whose attitude was to be so disappointing to Ernst Toller and others of the younger generation) wrote his once-famous patriotic song "O mein Heimatland," based on Gottfried Keller's poem "An mein Vaterland," and addressed an open letter to Romain Rolland in which his patriotism is no less clearly expressed. It was to this letter that Rolland replied with the famous question: "Êtes-vous les fils de Goethe ou les fils d'Attila?" ["Are you the sons of Goethe or the sons of Attila?"]. The controversy between Rolland and Hauptmann was highly characteristic of the time. Hauptmann was also one of the signatories of the German manifesto "To the Civilized World" of 2 October, 1914, which proclaimed the civilizing effects of German culture and went on to state: "It is not true that we have criminally violated the neutrality of Belgium. . . . It is not true that our troops have brutally destroyed Louvain." This statement was itself quite untrue; the ashes of Louvain spoke for themselves, while Chancellor Bethmann-Hollweg had admitted in the *Reichstag* on 4 August that "Our invasion of Belgium is contrary to international law. . . ." It must be said that the 93 intellectuals who signed the manifesto acted as irresponsibly

as did the 1314 intellectuals who submitted a memorandum supporting the most extreme Pan-German war aims in July, 1916. But then intellectual irresponsibility was the order of the day on both sides.

The civilizing effects of German culture bring us to Thomas Mann. The hitherto "unpolitical" Thomas Mann reacted strongly to the outbreak of war, and until 1916 his attitude was outspokenly nationalistic; this is shown by the essays "Gedanken im Kriege" (November, 1914), "Friedrich und die grosse Koalition" (December, 1914), "An die Redaktion des 'Svenska Dagbladet,' Stockholm" (April, 1915), and "Gedanken zum Kriege" (August, 1915), three of which he later refused to have reprinted. These mainly topical essays were followed in 1917 by the highly personal *Betrachtungen eines Unpolitischen,* which Hans Kohn has aptly described as "the most brilliant and penetrating summation of anti-Western and anti-liberal German nationalist sentiment." Briefly, Thomas Mann was enraged by Bernard Shaw and other British and French writers who spoke of the need to democratize and civilize Germany; he for his part welcomed the war as "a purification, a liberation, an enormous hope." "The victory of Germany," he wrote, "will be a victory of soul over numbers. The German soul is opposed to the pacifist ideal of civilization, for is not peace an element of civil corruption?" For the nationalist Thomas Mann this was indeed a "holy war," a "German war," a war between strong, pagan, militaristic German "culture," and effete, Christian, pacifistic Western "civilization." His nationalism, like that of Walter Flex, had a strong religious element; and this religious enthusiasm was only partly derived from Christianity in the form of Prussian Protestantism, for, as Hermann Löns wrote, "We Germans pretend that we are Christians, but we are nothing of the sort and never can be." A Christian, after all, could hardly have approved the German atrocities, the violation of Belgium and the sinking of the *Lusitania,* as Thomas Mann did. At this period of his life Thomas Mann was not only not a democrat; he was completely opposed to the very idea of democracy, which he regarded as "bourgeois" and "un-German." And of course it must be remembered that in August, 1914, Germany itself was emphatically not a democracy, for 69 per cent of the seats in the *Reichstag* were held by the opposition parties; throughout the war the real political power, including the power of censorship, lay with the Army High Command.

The crux of the matter is that Thomas Mann, having been turned down for the *Landsturm,* regarded it as his job "to devote at least [his] head to the German cause" (letter to Richard Dehmel of 14 December, 1914). That this view caused him to be violently attacked by Romain Rolland, who described Thomas Mann's "Gedanken im Kriege" as "le plus terrible [article] que j'aie encore lu d'un intellectuel allemand," is not surprising, for Rolland believed that the intellectual should think and act as a European and a human being rather than as a German or French or English nationalist. Thomas Mann was also bitterly attacked by his brother Heinrich; in his famous essay on Zola (first published in the anti-war periodical *Das Forum* in November, 1915) Heinrich Mann saw his country as dominated by the "tyranny of Fatherland-happy incompetents," by those who "eloquently oppose truth and justice." Heinrich Mann was himself a member of the anti-war group *Bund Neues Vaterland.*

To do Thomas Mann justice, it must be stressed that by February, 1916, his views on the war had changed considerably.

On 25 February, 1916, he wrote to the pacifist Paul Amman that he was sick of all the hatred, sick of the war itself. By this time he had realized that the "solemn national war" of August, 1914, had turned into a European revolution; this realization was shared by Hugo von Hofmannsthal who in 1916 wrote that the war was "the open outbreak of a revolution which in the course of the century will deny everything we are and everything we ever possessed."

Thomas Mann's reactions to the outbreak of war were typical of the reactions of the majority of German writers and intellectuals. Intense patriotism and national enthusiasm were the order of the day and are seen in all the once famous poems of August, 1914: R. A. Schröder's "Deutscher Schwur," Richard Dehmel's "Deutschlands Fahnènlied," Gerhart Hauptmann's "O mein Heimatland," Rudolf Herzog's "Das eiserne Gebet," Isolde Kurz's "Schwert aus der Scheide," etc. Throughout the war there is the closest connection between poetry and political propaganda; the majority of poets not only write about political events, they accept and propagate the official interpretation of these events. The very titles of series such as the *Tat-Bücher* (pro-war) and *Aktions-Bibliothek* (anti-war) indicate the active political rôle which poets of the time assigned to themselves. (pp. 150-58)

The two most famous outbreak-of-war poems, Karl Bröger's "Bekenntnis" and Heinrich Lersch's "Soldatenabschied," are also among the best. This is especially true of Bröger's "Bekenntnis" which illustrates, as no other poem did, the simple, almost inarticulate patriotism of the man in the street:

> All along we were aware of our love for you,
> Only we never put a name to it.
> When we were called, we set off in silence,
> Not on our lips, but in our hearts the word
> Germany.

Bröger's lack of subtlety is compensated by his transparent honesty and lack of rhetoric. His poem is an elaboration of the words of the Social Democratic Party leadership in the *Reichstag* on 4 August, 1914: "In its hour of peril we shall not leave the Fatherland in the lurch." It was with these words that the Socialists, hitherto regarded as "enemies of the *Reich*," announced their decision to vote for the war credits, a decision which was immensely popular. On 27 February, 1917, Chanceller Bethmann-Hollweg alluded to Bröger's "Bekenntnis" in the *Reichstag;* an obvious parallel here is with Rupert Brooke's "The Soldier" being quoted from the pulpit of St. Paul's by Dean Inge on Easter Sunday, 1915. Bröger's poem was also quoted with approval by a later German Chancellor, Adolf Hitler, in a speech given on 10 May, 1933; this is mentioned because it is a fact that National Socialist "literature" largely derived from the patriotic and nationalistic literature of the First World War, notably the outbreak-of-war poetry and the nationalistic war novels which began to appear in about 1930. In justice to Bröger it must be stressed that he, unlike some other "worker-poets," resisted Hitler's blandishments; but it must also be pointed out that his collected poems were published by Eugen Diederichs in 1943 under the title *Sturz und Erhebung.*

Another once famous poem which voiced similar simple patriotic sentiments was Heinrich Lersch's "Soldatenabschied," written on 4 August, 1914, which ends: "A free German knows no cold compulsion: / Germany must live even if we have to die." The poem as a whole, however, is spoilt by its rather whimsical diction. At this stage Lersch lacked the language to match his idealism, which is itself as yet un-

original. When his idealism developed in a personal direction, and he found the visionary language to match it, Lersch went on to produce one of the most remarkable poems of the war, "Massengräber"; he also produced the best genuinely religious poetry of this war in which Christianity was all too often a bloodthirsty parody of itself.

In the case of most outbreak-of-war poems the poetic expression was as commonplace as the sentiment itself. Among the German responses to the Declaration there is nothing that matches the poetic quality of Isaac Rosenberg's "On Receiving News of the War" or the understanding of Charles Sorley's "To Germany." But on the German side too the best of such poems were those in which deep personal feeling was involved, such as Paul Zech's "An meinen Sohn."

The patriotic blustering of August, 1914, reached its nadir in the virulence of Ernst Lissauer's notorious "Hassgesang gegen England" and Kipling's scarcely less deplorable "The Beginnings." Lissauer is said to have bitterly regretted writing a song of hate for England rather than a song of love for Germany. But in retrospect it might be argued that his poem was hardly more negative, only slightly more deplorable than the average pro-war patriotic poem. All he did was to take his patriotism to its logical conclusion. As a poem, the "Hassgesang gegen England" is worthless; but it was, and is, an important document. In 1914 German hatred was soon directed at England alone because the British declaration of war, which was unexpected in Germany, was regarded as *Rassenverrat,* treachery motivated by envy, and because "Great Britain seemed to be wantonly interfering in Europe, in order to prevent unification under German leadership instead of being content with the Empire." "Gott strafe England" became the most popular German slogan (it is the punch line in a number of poems and the title of at least one book of verse), and writers such as Max Scheler and Werner Sombart contrasted the German nation of heroes with the British "nation of shopkeepers" (the phrase was, of course, originally Disraeli's). Certainly Lissauer's "Hassgesang" was not unique; indeed, it triggered off many other hymns of hate, including one extreme example ("Deutschland, hasse!") by Heinrich Vierordt which was even banned by the German General Staff. Dozens of minor German poets, chiefly those who later became supporters of Nazism, wrote similar verses, and an anthology of more than 100 songs of hate was published under the title *Weh dir, England.* (pp. 159-60)

In 1914 patriotism was so widespread and so intense that it might be thought invidious to criticize the average poet of the time for his attitude, though the fact remains that this attitude alone made the war possible. There are in any case as many sorts of patriotism as of pacifism, and what we see in 1914 is the most savage and prejudiced variety. Besides, it is a fact that some poets, and most of the countless amateur war poets, remained fixed in a chauvinistic, pro-war posture even when the tragic realities of the war had exposed the folly of such an attitude.

The war poetry of Walter Flex is a case in point. Flex's *Das Volk in Eisen* (1914), *Sonne und Schild* (1915), and *Im Felde zwischen Nacht und Tag* (1917), which were among the most popular of all the German books of war verse are naïvely idealistic and sometimes in deplorable taste. It is one thing to write "We fell for the glory of Germany," but quite another to write of "the bayonet which mother kissed." The grotesque mixture of sentimentality and barbarism here springs from an excessive idealism, from an "ethical fanaticism" which has gone so far as to become its own opposite. The most popular of all Flex's war poems was the "Preussischer Fahneneid" of 1914 which idealizes the man who overcomes all selfishness and devotes his whole life and soul to Prussia: "He who takes his oath on the Prussian flag / No longer has anything which belongs to him alone." However vulnerable to rational argument lines such as these undoubtedly proved a genuine inspiration to many young Germans of the war generation. The poem may have been weak, but it worked. Yet this national devotion elevated to a quasi-religious or mystical level is surely much less impressive when repeated in the poem "Deutsche Schicksalsstunde" in 1917. The trouble with Walter Flex's poetry is that it does not develop. If the public on both sides wanted patriotic verse—and they certainly did—only an extremely naïve or irrational poet could go on giving it to them in 1916-18. A patriotic poem written after the Battle of the Somme is surely a very different proposition from one written in 1914.

In any discussion of the metapolitical aspect of the German linguistic crisis in the twentieth century, the poetry of August, 1914, is a landmark, for it is here that we first see the barbarization of the German language that was to reach its climax in the National-Socialist jargon of euphemism and hyperbole. The idea of mass violence held a fatal aesthetic attraction for the "intellectuals" of 1914, and the hysterical campaigns of hatred led by the intellectuals and writers of the time prepared the way for the deliberate genocide which was to become a feature of the war (*cf.* General Falkenhayn's decision to "bleed France white of able-bodied men" at Verdun). Until August, 1914, the German language (among others) had never been so barbarically and irresponsibly abused; in 1916 we find members of the French Academy in all seriousness discussing whether it should not be outlawed. It is no chance that the political "verse" of the Nazi period was so heavily indebted to the worst types of 1914-18 war verse, no chance that the Nazis took over the meaningless jargon of 1914 conservatism in referring to Hitler's war as a "heiliger Krieg" ("holy war"), a phrase which effectively robs the word "heilig" of any real meaning and thus makes it impossible to speak of the sanctity of human life. The "over-kill," "mega-death" mentality first became vocal in August, 1914.

As the war began to go its own senseless way, the pathological patriotism of Lissauer, Flex and others gave way to the compassion of the Expressionist anti-war poets and of some of the "worker-poets" (notably Heinrich Lersch and Gerrit Engelke), to say nothing of individual poets such as Karl von Eisenstein and Siegfried Sassoon:

> O German mother dreaming by the fire
> While you are knitting socks to send your son,
> His face is trodden deeper in the mud.

In both England and Germany the transition from an heroic to a tragic conception began as soon as the poets reached the trenches, although it was not until about 1916 that the transition was virtually complete. With some exceptions the romantic idealism of both sides was short-lived. Most important of the various forms of realism to which the initial euphoric idealism gave way was the "compassionate realism" of Owen and Rosenberg, Lersch, Klemm and Anton Schnack. (pp. 161-63)

Recent writers on the English poetry of the First World War are generally agreed that patriotism, idealism, and savage realism are alike inadequate as poetic attitudes to war, and that it is the "modern attitude" of "compassionate realism" which originates with Walt Whitman and is seen in the best work of Owen and Rosenberg, that comes closest to conveying a true and truly tragic conception of war. The truth of this is confirmed by the German poetry of the war. Mere patriotism, however noble (and frequently it is but a mask for prejudice), does not and cannot take account of the gruesome realities of modern war. Idealism alone is similarly inadequate and in this context is often merely prejudice in the most literal sense. Simple and savage realism too are not enough, simple realism because it lacks the compassion necessary to convey the tragic aspect of war, savage realism because it lacks humanity. Realism must in fact be combined with a compassionate objectivity. This combination one sees in all the best poetry of the war. On the German side it appears in the work of Wilhelm Klemm and Anton Schnack, and, in a somewhat different form, of the worker-poets Heinrich Lersch and Gerrit Engelke, both of whom were influenced by Walt Whitman. Gerrit Engelke wrote in a letter dated 15 July, 1918, of "my dear father Walt Whitman. He is always in the breast-pocket of my tunic. This man and poet is inexhaustible," and the last book that Engelke read, shortly before his death on 13 October, 1918, was a monograph on Walt Whitman. Remembering Sassoon's and Rosenberg's acknowledgement of their indebtedness to Whitman, the tragedy of this war in which poet fought—and probably killed—poet is again brought home. Of all the worker-poets Engelke was quite the least enthusiastic about the war, which he hated.

Compassion is the key feature of the work of Heinrich Lersch, as, for example, in his famous poem "Brüder" ("Brothers") addressed to a dead French soldier. Lersch is at his best when his realism gains visionary depth, as in poems such as "Massengräber" or "Vor der schmerzhaften Mutter Maria." But this visionary quality is more common in the war poetry of the Expressionists than of the worker-poets. The Expressionists were visionary idealists concerned with their vision of an ideal humanity, whereas the worker-poets were patriotic Christian idealists concerned with their country, their class, and Christianity (something very different from the Pan-German nature mysticism of a Walter Flex; Lersch and Engelke were Catholics). The worker-poets were social democrats, and as such were concerned with the brotherhood of man in a rather more empirical and political sense than the earlier Expressionists; it was only after the Russian Revolution that both groups of poets tended to identify their idealism with Marxian Socialism.

Foremost among the compassionate realists on the German side was Wilhelm Klemm, who served as an army surgeon on the Western Front throughout the war. A little-known poet of the "expressionist" movement and one of the anti-war poets of *Die Aktion,* Klemm is seen at his best in his war poetry. One of the outstanding front-line poets on either side, he was opposed to the war from the beginning. His first collection, *Gloria,* is said to have been published by Albert Langen after he had read in the foreign press the opinion that Klemm's war poems were the "only humane utterances" on the German side. His attitude is invariably humanitarian and compassionate. It is as a realistic war poet that he is outstanding; his realism is always exact and usually heightened, and is frequently combined with an ironical vision (*cf.* Alfred Lichtenstein) that allows him to show the grotesqueness of what he is describing. Many of his poems are antithetical in structure; war is presented as the antithesis of life. Like Robert Graves, and like Anton Schnack, Klemm defines war by making contrasted definitions of peace; his anti-war attitude is usually expressed this way. Among the best of his war poems are "An der Front" and "Lazarett." "An der Front" is a clear example of his realism combined with irony, for in it he gives both a true picture of the front-line scene and a clear impression of the absurdity of it all; "Lazarett" is starkly realistic—except for the final simile (in which the thunder of battle is likened to "the words of God"), which makes all the difference. Although there is little stylistic variation in his work, Klemm was certainly one of the best German poets of the war. Among the realists his only equal is Anton Schnack, whose range—both thematic and stylistic—is, however, more limited than Klemm's. Both Klemm and Schnack are normally accounted Expressionists in this period of their work and certainly both were connected with Expressionist groups. But in their war poetry they both use a basically impressionist technique: the images they juxtapose are mostly realistic, and it is only because the reality of the war itself is so grotesque, that their war poetry looks expressionistic.

Perhaps the most impressive single poem produced by a front-line poet in German is Anton Schnack's "Nächtliche Landschaft" which must be quoted in full:

> A constellation like a day; and behind it a horizon
>   by light and flare fingered and shrouded,
> Which went or came, fell or stood, restless, spectral; and if it went, there was deep night;
> And if it came, a forest was made, somewhere a village lay looking furtive and white,
> And a valley full of sleep, with torrents, tangled things, with graves and towers of churches, in ruins, with rising mists, moist and big-clouded,
> With huts where sleeping men lay, where a dream walked, full of fever, full of strangeness, full of animal splendour, where there suddenly burst
> Open a curtain of clouds; behind it rose a sea of stars or a realm of rockets, a light sprang up out of the ravine,
> Terrible, roaring, wheel-clatter rattled on roads, a man stepped darkly into the dark, his face dazed with the dread of what he had seen,
> Saw the flight of questing fires, heard butchery down below, saw behind the darkness the city by fire forever accurst.
> Heard a rumbling in the belly of the earth, ponderous, powerful, primal, heard traffic on roads, heading into the void, into the extended night, into a storm, dreadful in the West. Unquiet the ear
> With the thousand hammers of the front, with the riders who came, stamping, headlong, with the riders who rode away to turn into shadows, engulfed by the night, to decompose,
> Death slaughters them, leaving them lying among weeds, weighty, fossilized hands full of spiders, mouths crusted brown,
> Eyes full of bottomless sleep, on their brows the bloom of obfuscation, blue, waxen, decaying in the smoke of night,
> Which sank down, which shed its shadows far, which stretched vaulting from hill to hill, over woods and decay, over brains full of dreams, over the hundred dead, without repose,
> Over the uncounted fires, over laughter and madness, over crosses in fields, over pain and despair, over rubble and ash, over river and ruined town. . . .

This is the best of the sixty-odd poems in Schnack's *Tier rang gewaltig mit Tier* (1920), a collection which has rightly been said to contain "the most inclusive extant image of front-line war as seen by a young man." Anton Schnack, who served on the Western Front throughout the war, is virtually unknown as a poet; he is hardly ever mentioned in literary histories or surveys of German war poetry. Yet *Tier rang gewaltig mit Tier* is without question one of the best books of war poetry produced on the German side in 1914-18; it is a book of very considerable poetic and documentary value. As Anton Schnack has said, "the book contains no jingoistic poems, but is rather a book of sorrow and mourning."

The poems in Schnack's collection are dominated by night and death. He writes more vividly about war than any of his contemporaries. Though he too is normally accounted an Expressionist, his method in this war poetry is, like Klemm's, essentially impressionistic; it is again the grotesqueness of his subject matter which makes his work look expressionistic. Schnack writes in the long rhymed line in free rhythms developed in Germany by Ernst Stadler, whose early death robbed Germany of a potentially great war poet; but his technique is also highly reminiscent of Wilfred Owen, whose work he could not have known. His treatment of war has much in common with the heightened compassionate realism of his British contemporary, and, like Owen, Schnack also frequently uses internal rhyme, alliteration, assonance and reduplication to give his raw material poetic form; there is a tendency to mannerism in his threefold epithets. Several German war poets have been compared with Wilfred Owen. In the case of a poet like Alfred Vagts such a comparison has little substance, whereas in the case of Anton Schnack both attitude and technique are demonstrably close to Owen. (pp. 164-68)

The only group of poets to be opposed to the war right from the outbreak were the Expressionists, and more especially the poets of *Die Aktion* (Lichtenstein, Klemm, Werfel, Ehrenstein), who were moved by an ideal sense of brotherhood and compassion. Franz Werfel's rather bombastic poem "Der Krieg," for instance, is outspokenly opposed to the war, and this on 4 August, 1914. The Expressionists alone did not fall victim to chauvinism. Some of them acted patriotically by volunteering for military service, but one looks in vain in their poetry for the loaded patriotic words of the time. There is no Expressionist "song of hate," for the typical Expressionist philosophy is based on internationalism. The aesthetic *raison d'être* of the movement is a belief in art as self-expression, while the chauvinistic variety of war poetry is a denial of the individual and therefore of art.

In terms of war poetry *Die Aktion* is the most important Expressionist group. Though there were many war poets among the contributors to *Der Sturm,* there were few among the members of the *Sturm* circle in the narrower sense. Indeed, the only outstanding war poet associated with *Der Sturm* was August Stramm, though Kurt Heynicke (*Das namenlose Angesicht,* 1919) and Peter Baum (*Schützengrabenverse,* 1916) must also be mentioned. In the nature of things the more politically aware and active *Die Aktion* was far more important in this context.

Die Aktion, which published its anti-war anthology *1914-1916: Eine Anthologie* in 1916, had been opposed to the war even before it broke out. Franz Pfemfert's editorial of 4 July, 1914, was a cogent and outspoken attack on the whole idea of patriotism:

> So long as people remain patriotic, so long as they

retain their sentimental devotion to the country in which they happen to be born, they will also believe that their country is more valuable than the neighbouring one, [and] that it is honourable to die for it—as long as this attitude persists, it will be impossible to end international war. . . . If we are serious in striving towards the "united states of Europe", i.e., if we want lasting peace between the nations, then we must feel ourselves to be Europeans, or, better, compatriots and partners of the whole world.

No less blunt was the editorial of 1 August, 1914: "Chauvinism is a perpetual threat to mankind. It, and it alone, can turn millions of rational beings into madmen overnight." This latter editorial caused the journal to be banned from public sale, though it continued to be distributed to subscribers both at home and at the front. Later in the war the sub-title of the journal made it clear that *Die Aktion* stood for radical pacifism, while the anthology *1914-1916* carried the following note for new readers: "This book—poems from the field of slaughter—refuge of a currently homeless idea, I throw in the face of the age . . . F.P." War poems appearing in *Die Aktion* were entitled "Gedichte vom Schlacht-Felde," which made it clear that they were not mere "war poems" (*Kriegslyrik*), or even "poems from the battlefield," but "poems from the field of slaughter." They were excluded from all contemporary patriotic anthologies. In terms of political and artistic integrity, *Die Aktion* was the most important journal in wartime Germany.

When war came, the Expressionist poets had been concerned for some four years with the collapse of the old order and the impending irruption of the new. Expressionist *Aufbruchsdichtung* is therefore not "outbreak-of-war poetry" in the usual patriotic sense, but poetry concerned with the dawn of a new era. Because the Expressionists saw the outbreak of war as the beginning of this social and intellectual revolution, the practical issues of patriotism, victory or defeat, etc., no more arose for them in August, 1914, than they did for the Russian Bolsheviks; yet by its very nature Expressionism was far more intimately involved in the war than any other artistic movement of the time.

So far as Expressionist war poetry is concerned, two serious misconceptions need to be corrected. These are, first, the view that the Expressionist poets failed to respond to the war until pacifism became widespread after 1916 and, second, the view that Expressionist war poetry as such was insignificant. Both views are completely unfounded. The truth of the matter is that "Expressionist" war poetry (the work of Klemm, Schnack, Stramm, Lichtenstein and others) is on the whole the best written in German and is equalled only by the work of one or two individual poets such as Karl von Eisenstein and Heinrich Lersch. And Klemm, Lichtenstein and Stramm all began to produce their work shortly after the outbreak of war; by 1915 two of them had already been killed. Generally speaking, Expressionist war poetry started by being anti-war in the sense of being opposed to the war but having no other practical political aim, and ended by becoming radically pacifistic. Essentially the Expressionists are concerned with the brotherhood of the combatants, with humanity rather than Germany, with compassion rather than hatred. It is only later in the war, after the Russian Revolution, that some of the surviving Expressionist poets, and particularly those in Switzerland (including Ludwig Rubiner and Albert Ehrenstein), become pacifists and Socialist radicals. Because com-

passion is central to the typical Expressionist view of life, Expressionist war poetry overlaps with compassionate realism. Klemm and Schnack are normally accounted Expressionists at this time; but here it seemed more appropriate to consider their work in the context of compassionate realism, and to take Stramm and Trakl as exemplifying Expressionist war poetry, not because their attitude is any less compassionate, but because their work is not realistic in the same sense. Lichtenstein is also included, because his work belongs to the "absurd" category of early Expressionism.

August Stramm served as an Infantry Captain on the Eastern Front, where he fell on 1 September, 1915, having refused an offer to be released from the army. Most characteristic and in my view the best of Stramm's work are the war poems (*Tropfblut,* 1919), in which he seeks to "communicate the sights, sounds and horror of war more directly than would be possible in a reasoned and punctuated statement." This intention is both simple and admirable. He seeks to make war, and one man's reaction to war, speak for itself. In order to do so, he "chooses his words to act as missiles that will explode in the reader's mind, with the impact of a shell. With Stramm's work there is no longer any question of "emotion recollected in tranquillity," quite the opposite: he seeks "with raw immediacy to convey not a picture or a recollection but the actual sensations of the moment itself." Thus in perhaps the best of all his war poems, "Patrouille," he simply tries to convey what it feels like to be out on patrol in 1914/15:

> The stones malice
> window grins treachery
> branches strangle
> loomy bushes leafrattling feign
> shrieking
> death

The first line is immediately effective: the very stones are hostile (in German the neologism *feinden* is used for *anfeinden*). So it must seem to the soldier on patrol in no man's land who faces so many real and imagined dangers. The first line points to one of these dangers: mines. Another obvious danger was from snipers, hence the equally concentrated second line "window grins treachery." What Stramm is saying here is that to the soldier out on patrol it seems as though the very stones he treads are hostile, it seems as though a sniper is lurking behind every window, it seems (third line) as though every branch which brushes against him is someone trying to strangle him. It is all a question of his own nervous reactions. Each of the first three lines could have a full-stop at the end, and the third would normally require it, for after it the second half of the poem begins. The rhythm in the first three lines has been stealthy, suggesting soldiers creeping along with their nerves on edge, waiting for the sudden danger and death by which their minds and bodies are obsessed. The fourth line is longer and quicker—one imagines the men running for cover as they come under fire—and also even more concentrated. Mountainous bushes (*berge* suggests *bergige*)—that is, bushes which seem mountainous or loom overlarge to them in their overwrought condition—shed their leaves and disintegrate with a whistling sound; but *berge* also suggests *bergende* and therefore alludes to the shelter which these bushes fail to give, and to the danger which they hide. After the frantic fourth line, the poem tails off into the silence of death: two syllables, followed by one, followed—there is no full-stop—by silence. . . .

This is surely an excellent example of the Expressionist war poem. Highly condensed and highly expressive, it conveys in an absolute minimum of words, and with total precision, the state of mind in question. Because the war which provokes this state of mind is unparalleled, Stramm's neologisms are fully justified.

Now let us consider briefly two more of Stramm's raids on the inarticulate. First, "Schlachtfeld" ("Battlefield"):

> Clod softness lulls iron off to sleep
> bloods clot manoozed patches
> rusts crumble
> fleshes slime
> sucking ruts around decay
> child eyes
> blink
> murder upon murder

"Clod softness" (*Mürbe* stands for *Mürbigkeit*) "lulls iron off to sleep": this radically condensed opening line suggests the omnipresent mud of the battlefield, the continual need for vigilance, and the continual threat of exhaustion, the threat of metal and the threat of earth, to which man and his works will return. The use of the plural instead of the singular in the next three lines is most effective. "Bloods" and "fleshes" in particular are more suggestive than the singular forms would be, for they remind us that it is the blood of many men that clots the patches where they oozed to death, that it is the flesh of many men that is turning to stinking slime around which "sucking ruts [or: lusts]." The verb *brunsten* (*brünsten*) is most appropriate for conveying the beastliness of war which is caused by man's greed but satisfies only the worm's greed. And this scene is endless; murder upon murder is still to come, murder that "blinks" in "child eyes" because most of the contestants were only children when they arrived at the front, child murderers and child victims.

Another highly evocative miniature is "Krieggrab" ("War-Grave"):

> Stakes implore crossed arms
> writing falters the pale unknown
> flowers impertinence dusts intimidate
> faint light
> runs with tears
> glazes
> forgetfulness

There is nothing here of the eloquence of Owen's "Anthem for Doomed Youth." But without any pathos whatsoever Stramm too conveys the absolute futility of war: the fate of those who "die as cattle" (Owen) is to be forgotten, for peace has different heroes.

Stramm's *Tropfblut* (1919) is one of the really outstanding volumes of German war poetry. From the point of view of literary history too it is important because it shows that an imagistic technique could be used to excellent effect in war poetry (contrast the dearth of successful imagistic war poems in English).

Georg Trakl served as a lieutenant in the Austrian army medical corps on the Eastern Front, where he died on 3 November, 1914. The earliest of his few war poems is "Im Osten" ("On the Eastern Front"):

> The wrath of nations aroused is dark
> As the wild organ notes of a winter storm,
> The crimson wave of battle,
> Defoliated stars.

> With shattered brows, with silver arms
> Night softly beckons to dying soldiers.
> In the shadow of the autumn ash
> The spirits of the slain are sighing.

> A thorny wasteland encircles the town.
> From doorsteps sticky with blood the moon
> Chases terrified women.
> Wild wolves came pouring through the gates.

War is seen in Hölderlinian terms—and it is Hölderlin who is revealed as the German national poet at this time—as the embodiment of "the wrath of nations," the epithet "dark" implying that this anger is damnable. By saying that the nations' wrath, war, is like the wild organ notes of a winter storm, Trakl seems to imply that war is as necessary as winter; such a cyclic view of history, possibly deriving from Hölderlin, is found elsewhere in his work. The third and fourth lines of the first stanza incorporate Trakl's characteristic symbolism: the epithet "crimson" in "the crimson wave of battle" refers not only to violence, but to man's guilt, to the "crimson body" of man as opposed to "the golden image of man" (see "Klage," below). That the stars, signs of the spiritual, are defoliated, suggests that man is bereft of all spirituality. War is accordingly seen as a sign of man's literal beastliness or animality. The second stanza is by comparison straightforward (silver is here one of the colours of death). It is characteristic of Trakl to switch constantly from one type of meaning (literal, symbolical, etc.) to another within the poem. What should be noted here is the sequence: sinfulness, of which the war is the sign, leads to death. The last stanza opens with an allusion to the Passion: "Thorny wasteland" refers to Golgotha, the place of the skull (*cf.* the Eastern Front), thus implying that what is being enacted in Galicia in 1914 is the passion of mankind. The poem ends with a reference to the unrestrained animal ("wild wolves") in man. "Im Osten" is basically a Christian poem of despair. The cyclic view of life implied, and the reference to the Passion, are the only notes of hope. There is no sign of salvation because the animal in man has the upper hand. Man is not only doomed, but damned by his own actions. Although "Im Osten," like most of Trakl's poetry, is rooted in reality, his images constantly point beyond themselves to a greater reality. The result is that his poem has an objectivity and a depth unusual in front-line poetry.

Both Trakl's other war poems, "Klage" and "Grodek," were written when he was in the garrison hospital in Cracow as a mental patient, having been driven out of his mind by the terrible plight of the wounded under his care and his own despair at being unable to do more to help them. This despair is expressed in "Klage": the poet's greatest fear is that the war may mark the end of man as a spiritual being; he sees mankind in danger of sinking into permanent brutishness. In "Grodek," his last poem, Trakl implies that Western civilization has reached a turning-point: there is a contrast between autumn, 1914, and a previous age of golden plains and blue lakes, over which the sun now rolls more darkly. Night embraces dying warriors, the wild laments of their broken mouths, *cf.* Charles Sorley's famous lines:

> When you see millions of the mouthless dead
> Across your dreams in pale battalions go,
> Say not soft things as other men have said. . . .

No one could accuse Trakl of saying "soft things," for the key line in "Grodek," the one certainty among so many ambiguities, is the line "all roads lead to black decay." The phrase "black decay" refers not only to physical decay, but also to spiritual corruption; black is more than one of the colours in the spectrum of putrefaction, it is the colour of damnation. The poem ends with a somewhat ambiguous image ("the unborn grandsons," "unborn" having both its literal meaning and the figurative meaning of innocent) which implies that Trakl sees the Fall of Man being re-enacted on the battlefields of 1914; future generations of innocents will not now be born because man has finally lost his innocence.

Alfred Lichtenstein fell on 25 September, 1914, at Vermandovillers, near Reims. One of the main innovators of his generation, Lichtenstein might well have developed into a major poet. As it is, he was one of the most original of the German war poets. He was a great ironist, even his war poems being "self-deprecating, bitter, and funny," which makes him unique on the German side. His particular form of irony is in fact essentially English, and if one thinks of Siegfried Sassoon and the other satirical poets on the English side, it is clear that Lichtenstein's work falls into one of the main categories of war poetry, that of satire (*cf.* also Karl Kraus), in which "human beings seek relief from insupportably nerve-racking experiences . . . by satirizing them." The best, and funniest, of his war poems is "Gebet vor der Schlacht" ("Prayer before Going into Action"), which is totally, and uproariously, anti-heroic ("Don't let me snuff it like a dog / For my dear Fatherland"), and this on (?) 13 August, 1914, the eve of the first great infantry battle of the war. It is a remarkable poem, both true to life and funny, and with a highly personal attitude towards its subject. Although Lichtenstein is normally accounted one of the most important early Expressionists, his war poetry reflects above all his own highly individual and ironical vision; it has at least as much in common with the work of the pacifist satirists (Hugo Ball, Kurt Tucholsky and others) as with that of the Expressionist war poets. He shares with Wilhelm Klemm a sense of the grotesqueness of war. He had no illusions at all. In "Abschied" ("Leaving for the Front") he wrote: "Once more the good old sunset's glowing red. / In thirteen days I'll probably be dead." Seven weeks later he *was* dead.

It is time that we considered the question of pacifism. But perhaps enough has been said to make it clear that there is more poetry, more originality and more clear-headedness in the work of the Expressionists than among any other group of war poets. (pp. 169-76)

In Germany patriotism and pacifism proper were for the most part mutually exclusive. German patriotism was mostly chauvinistic. True, there were poets such as Hugo Ball, Max Barthel, and Heinrich Lersch, who combined the two attitudes; but on the whole this combination was commoner in Austria than in Germany. We have seen that in the early months of the war the vast majority of German poets were patriotic idealists, blind to the real significance of the events in which they were involved, like so many of their British counterparts. This idealism was eroded by a series of events, notably the growing doubts about Germany's real war aims (from the spring of 1915 onwards), the Battle of the Somme (1916), and the Russian Revolution (1917). We have seen too that all the major poets became opposed to the war once they had personal experience of it. The number of poets who started out as patriotic idealists and soon became anti-war idealists is legion. But if most of the real war poets, and especially the Expressionists and compassionate realists among them, are in effect anti-war poets, there is nonetheless an obvious

difference between the war-sickened front-line poet and the pacifist intellectual writing his anti-war satires from the safe distance of, say, Zürich. It is in fact necessary to distinguish between anti-war and pacifist writers. Anti-war literature as such is the work of individualists and has no necessary political aim beyond the ending of the war, whereas pacifist literature as such is mostly the work of left-wing radicals with a definite long-term political aim. In general it is true to say that anti-war literature dates from August, 1914, and is the work of combatants, whereas pacifist literature dates from 1916 onwards and is chiefly the work of noncombatants. But there are many exceptions to this rule of thumb, so that it will be most helpful to end by discussing briefly the work of the most prominent pacifist poets: Hugo Ball, Ivan Goll, Kurt Tucholsky and Bertolt Brecht.

No survey of German war poetry would be complete if it omitted Hugo Ball's "Totentanz 1916" ("Dance of Death, 1916"). This poem, in some ways uncharacteristic of the (Dadaist) poet Ball—it is a parody of a popular cabaret song of the time—was not only written two years before Brecht's "Legende vom toten Soldaten"; it also anticipated the anti-war satires of the neo-realist writers (such as Erich Kästner) by a whole decade. Like most of his contemporaries, Hugo Ball was carried away by the mass hysteria of August, 1914, and volunteered for military service. But in his case disillusionment came within a matter of weeks (the German atrocities in Belgium played a large part), and he got himself released from the army. His disillusionment came to a head in the spring of 1915, when we find him writing of the "idiocy" and "brutality" of the war (letter of 10 March, 1915). In May, 1915, he left Germany for Switzerland because the war and its "patriotism" was completely contrary to everything in which he believed. In 1917 he became assistant to Hermann Roesemeier, editor of the anti-German nationalist weekly *Freie Zeitung* (Berne). But although he became an opponent of the war, he himself said: "I am no pacifist *à tout prix*" (1918). His real position has been best expressed by Emmy Ball-Hennings [in her introduction to Ball's *Die Flucht aus der Zeit*, 1946]: "He was like a desperate patriot who slowly frees himself from nationalism and works devotedly and incessantly to open the eyes of his people, with whom he identifies himself." The crux of the matter is that Ball retained his love of Germany although it drove him to despair. He had no time at all for the bombastic, Pan-German variety of war poetry; his hatred of "Kriegslyrik" was shared by most front-line poets. In 1917 he wrote: "When things get serious, these tub-thumpers will crawl back into their literary dog-kennels." He himself believed in simplicity and moral commitment, and this is what we see in his own war poetry.

"Totentanz 1916" would have been treasonable if Ball had been living in Germany, the more so as it was one of a number of poems and other literary works dropped over the German lines by the Allies in August, 1918. Also used as anti-German propaganda were Schiller's "Die unüberwindliche Flotte," Erich Mühsam's "Die lustige Witwe," Prince Lichnowsky's *Meine Mission in London,* Siegfried Balder's (= Wilhelm Eckstein's) *Das Sturmläuten* and *Zwei Fragen,* as well as writings by Hermann Fernau and others. That this direct use of German war literature as anti-German propaganda worried the Supreme Command is shown by the fact that they offered a reward of about 3s. for each such leaflet handed in, and that Hindenburg himself warned the German people in September, 1918, against these leaflets "which are supposed to break our morale." Ernst Jünger for one found it appropriate that the armies of this "country of poets" should be bombarded with poems. . . .

Ivan Goll, another outstanding pacifist poet who spent the war years in Switzerland, was the most genuinely cosmopolitan of all the poets who wrote about the war: "Ivan Goll has no home: by fate a Jew, by chance born in France, designated a German by a piece of paper with an official stamp on it." Bilingual and bicultured, Goll wrote his first war poems in French (*Élegies Internationales. Pamphlets contre la guerre,* 1915). His *Requiem pour les morts de l'Europe* (1916) he republished in German (*Requiem. Für die Gefallenen von Europa,* 1917). This *Requiem* is one of the major poetic works of 1914-18, an admirably humane and poetic memorial to all those who died in the war. Like Hans Arp, Goll was "revolted by the butchery of the world war"; he fled to Switzerland on the outbreak and was subsequently associated with both German and French anti-war groups; he edited one of the main anti-war anthologies: *Le coeur de l'ennemi. Anthologie de poèmes contre la guerre* (1919). Other prominent pacifists from a similar Franco-German background were Annette Kolb and René Schickele.

Kurt Tucholsky served in the German army from 1915 to 1918, on the Eastern Front, and must have been among the least military figures ever to wear the German uniform. Though he did not react strongly to the outbreak of war, his anti-war poems dating from 1916 onwards range from "Zum ersten August" (1918)—a parody of the 90th Psalm ("Lord War, thou hast been our dwelling place in all generations . . ."), prompted, no doubt, by the chauvinism of the churches in 1914-18—to some of the most bitter anti-German satires ever written in German. These satires reach their climax in "Krieg dem Kriege" (1919) and "Nach fünf Jahren" (1919); the latter both makes Tucholsky's pacifist position quite clear, and also forms a grimly ironic and poetically just contrast to the nationalistic hymns of hate of 1914:

> And so we stand there in our shabby old uniforms
> And think of the old days.
> And hate,
> And hate that Prussian spirit
> Which brought us down and deceived us.

Paul Zech too, who started out in August, 1914, as a patriotic idealist, ended by writing a "Hassgesang gegen die Alldeutschen" (1918), as did several other poets. One of the most brilliant and bitter attacks on the Pan-Germans is Karl Kraus's savagely satirical "Lied des Alldeutschen," subtitled "Barbarische Melodie." In 1914-18 Karl Kraus kept his head when others all around were losing theirs. His gigantic visionary-documentary tragedy of mankind at war, *Die letzten Tage der Menschheit* (1919), is the supreme monument to those "unreal, unthinkable years." Both there and in the essays of *Weltgericht* (1919) and the poetry of *Worte in Versen* (1916-22) Kraus mercilessly attacks the barbarism of the war and the meaningless vulgarity of the advocates of this tragedy of mankind. The Expressionist poet Albert Ehrenstein was an equally, if less eloquently, bitter opponent of the war and of the barbarism of contemporary Europe ("Barbaropa," as he called it); his *Der Mensch schreit* (1916) and *Die rote Zeit* (1917) are among the most important collections of radically pacifist poetry.

And so we come, finally, to Bertolt Brecht who was studying medicine at Munich University in the spring of 1918 when the 17-year-olds and the over-age were called up. He was called up himself and placed in a hospital in Augsburg as a medical orderly; he later commented that "I saw how they patched people up in order to ship them back to the Front as soon as possible." Brecht, having recovered from his own initial patriotism (*cf.* his poem on Hans Lody), had made clear his attitude to the war in 1915 in a school essay on the subject "Dulce et decorum est pro patria mori." His view is similar to Wilfred Owen's ("that old lie" was how Owen described the patriotic tag): he contemptuously dismissed the saying as so much propaganda, thereby causing a scandal at his school. Though he was only called up in 1918, Brecht wrote perhaps the most bitterly anti-war poem of the whole war, the now-famous "Legende vom toten Soldaten" (1918). When the schoolboys and old men were called up in March, 1918, it was popularly said that "Man gräbt die Toten aus" ("They're digging up the dead," *scil:* to make them serve again). It was this popular saying which provided the starting point for Brecht's poem, which takes the form of a popular ballad. The poem tells of a dead body which is dug up, pronounced "ka-fau" ("fit for general service"), cleaned up ("to stop it stinking"), painted in the national colours and marched through the streets. The patriotic excitement is such that in the end nobody even notices the dead soldier: "But the soldier, as he's been taught, / Goes off to die a [second] hero's death." As Sir Maurice Bowra has said [in his *Poetry and the First World War,* 1961]:

> Brecht's gruesome and yet heart-felt myth exposes, among other pretences, the popular notion of glory. The parade of a corpse as a living hero marks the absolute discord between what is said at home and what is known at the front, between sentimental make-believe and the ruthless finality of death.

For all the formal differences, Brecht's bitter hatred not only of war, but of the patriotic lie which made this war possible, brings the "Legende vom toten Soldaten" close to Wilfred Owen's "Dulce et Decorum Est" and Ezra Pound's "Hugh Selwyn Mauberley" (1920):

> Died some, pro patria,
>   non "dulce" non "et decor" . . .
> walked eye-deep in hell
> believing in old men's lies, then unbelieving,
> came home, home to a lie,
> home to many deceits,
> home to old lies and new infamy;
> usury age-old and age-thick
> and liars in public places.
>
>   • • • • •
>
> There died a myriad,
> And of the best, among them,
> For an old bitch gone in the teeth,
> For a botched civilization.

We have come full circle from the unquestioning patriotism of August, 1914. In the last two years of the war the patriotic, nationalistic and militaristic concepts which had been accepted without question in 1914 ("Fatherland," "the altar of the Fatherland," "holy cause," "hero's death," "field of honour," "roll of honour," "duty," etc.) were debunked one after another until all that was left was tragic disillusionment:

> Until the end of 1914 we were carried away by the immense enthusiasm of the time in Germany. By the beginning of 1915 we realized that this enthusiasm had vanished into thin air and that its place had to be taken by the idea of duty. And then— after the Battle of the Somme—we became har-

dened front-line soldiers. . . . *The war was not at all as we had imagined it would be.*

That this disillusionment and resentment finally gave way to revolution is hardly surprising, for 21 million human beings had died unnecessary and indeed completely futile deaths. (pp. 181-86)

Patrick Bridgwater, "German Poetry and the First World War," in European Studies Review, Vol. I, No. 2, April, 1971, pp. 147-86.

WM. K. PFEILER

[*In the following excerpt from his* War and the German Mind: The Testimony of Men of Fiction Who Fought at the Front *(1941), Pfeiler surveys German novels about the First World War.*]

The first important—and lasting—literary efforts based on the life at the front were made in 1915 and 1916: Walter Flex's *Wanderer zwischen beiden Welten* [*Wanderer between Two Worlds*] and the *Der Opfergang* [*The Way of Sacrifice*] of Fritz von Unruh. They created no new forms, they were expressed with no original style, but both are of great importance in the development of the war novel. For they represent two idealistic and highly influential attitudes towards the war which find expression in the later novels. What is of the first significance is that these two attitudes show the fundamental cleavage . . . in the German intellectual and emotional reaction to the World War: Flex is ethnocentric, but Unruh is an individualist. Beyond this basic difference we do not find too pat a parallelism with later development, for the rationalism . . . associated characteristically—but certainly not universally—with the egocentric writers is not a quality of Unruh. Both Flex and Unruh tend toward the irrational in approach and solution.

Flex is a romantic idealist. In the hero of his story he gives a glowing example of the high idealism of the *Wandervögel*, the group of young men who originated the German youth movement. This movement had begun after the turn of the century and was the impetuous reaction against an unjust, inefficient, and hypocritical social order and an unnatural form of living. Against the degrading forces of a machine civilization, the age of Moloch, against the dead formalism and rigidity in the educational system of an ossified class-torn state, youth evoked the genius of Goethe and the classic-romantic idealism; it conjured in the spirit of Rousseau the healing powers of nature; it strove for the dionysian joy of living as preached so forcefully by Nietzsche, and found direction and consolation in the ideal of Christian faith and charity as expounded by the New Testament. A strange combination of ideals, indeed! And if the young men of the movement stressed the different elements differently, they sought the best from all these spiritual forces in the synthesis of the living individual. While each insisted on the right of self-determination, he recognized his ordained place as a member of a higher whole.

Flex's story depicts this higher type of man, the ideal *Wandervögel*. There is no development of character; the hero's personality is mature and his education finished. The discussion is about rivers, mountains, forests, sun, and clouds. There is the ever-readiness of the soul to receive from God and to fight against weak human nature. Man must live in both worlds, the eternal and the temporal, or he will be at home in neither; and nothing more can be demanded from life than to learn its true meaning. Therefore the war, with its revelation of vileness, cowardice, weakness, egotism, and vanity, affords a chance to see the true values of man through all the embellishments of pretense. The hero of the story, Lieutenant Wurche, hates the concept of mass heroism. Duty, obedience, loyalty may be discussed, but heroes are exceptions. There is no need to talk about them. His greatest concern is the German soul and humanity, as these were to be rejuvenated through the spirit of the *Wandervögel*. From his mature viewpoint he can consider calmly even the death of his own nation, for *all* is transitory. When the task of a nation is done, a few days of existence more or less do not matter. Yet with all the fibers of his being he is a part of his people. For six months he serves as a common soldier, and when called upon to serve as a leader he did not cast off his past like a wornout coat, but carried it with him like a secret treasure. For the people open their store room as well as their treasury only to him who has lived and suffered with them. He who with keen and kind eyes has gone through all experiences as one of the people, may well be chosen to be one of the leaders.

The story begins in the early spring of 1915 when the wandering geese pass north at night. From the front in Lorraine the young volunteers are called to an officers' training camp. After receiving their commissions they are sent to Russia. After a time of quiet trench warfare the offensive begins; in it Wurche finds his death. It is fall again, and the geese fly south.

The war as action never moves into the center of the story. The great tragedy is seen through the eyes of a finished character whose soul and mind are firmly anchored. In community with the eternal and with his people, he never loses his head, but remains calm and self-possessed; the physical dirt and mental defilement about him can not dim his clear eyes. Yet he is aware of the tragic dualism in life—it is also manifest in him: from an ecstatic oneness with God to a passionate desire for revenge and the intoxicating glory of an attack on the enemy is but a brief step, as he tragically realizes. (pp. 82-5)

For this type of man death has no sting. Against the charge that the destruction of life is meaningless after the long and careful training given to the individual, just for taking this one step into death, Wurche counters that all labor was not for the execution of this one step but rather in order that it might be taken with light and steady eyes, with human eyes. As Wurche had been an example in life, so he is in death. Shot in the abdomen, he remains calm and serene until he dies. He is laid to rest in the grave, holding in his right hand a sun flower, and in his left his beloved sword.

The critic [Albert] Soergel has said that here the story should have ended. The substance of the story, meager as the plot is throughout, is finished, yet continuing it does not extend it into a vacuum but rather into the final contemplative discussion of the apparent meaninglessness of death when such a valuable life is ended. The friend who is left behind has to settle for himself this age-old problem. His heart is like a barn full of wild horses, a barn set afire, but ultimately the dead comrade brings solace to his troubled soul. The dead should not be specters. They should be given a place in the heart; and it can be done without destroying happiness. Aging life must be rejuvenated through the eternal youth of death. This is the will of God. The German soldier finds himself in a house afire. He is to save the common possessions of his people. A burning oath for Germany makes him disregard any privation, suffering, or danger. What does it matter if laughter has died in him while he served in the war? He is to be the father of happy and laughing grandsons. And the little watch of the dead friend ticks: You live *his* time, do *his* work.

"Stay pure in heart and ripen" is the motto of the story, which was to have been followed by a large novel dealing in detail with Flex's own personal development. But since Flex died in action in 1917, only two chapters of the sequel, *Wolf Eschenlohr,* were finished; they were published in 1919. A non-compromising idealism was to solve the social question on a wide national basis. The cleavage between the classes of the people was to be done away with through genuine brotherhood. The war and the experience of the front had paved the way to this comradeship of the nation. (pp. 85-7)

Flex made a general human appeal, it is true, but he believed that the perfect form of the moral progress of man is in a nation [*Volk*]. This he always maintained clearly, and this he held for the sake of the individual, since to Flex's mind, "love for all mankind" [*Menschheits-patriotismus*] means the ethical disintegration of the individual. Natural human selfishness will be restrained by love for one's folk, but it is set free by the abstract "love for all" and will thus be egotism in its crudest form. But Flex is not always consistent. While he says that all men are children of God, he states also that the word *Bruderliebe* "brotherly love," had "too deep a ring" to be wasted on a southern Frenchman, or on a Cossack.

Flex's nationalism is of an ethical type. In 1917 he was in his heart as much a volunteer as in 1914, not so much because he was a national, as an "ethical fanatic." His is a moral faith which can also accept defeat, or as his hero Wurche had said, it can be realized even in the heroic death of a nation.

Even if Flex were not known to have had influence on others, his work would seem to have been a pattern for numerous war novels written later, not so much throughout in technique and style, as in its basic ideology. Therefore it must be placed at the beginning of all German ethnocentric, idealistic World War literature. Although its scene is laid predominantly in the first half of the war, before the war reached its insane climax of wholesale massacre, there is no doubt that even through the hell of later war years, this type of man would have kept his idealistic faith. (pp. 88-9)

For Flex the war served only as an intensifier of a philosophy of life of which the basic features were well established before the great conflict started. He was firmly rooted in his social group, and while his view of life took cognizance of the urgent necessity for national improvements, the determining forces in him were essentially traditional and conservative. There was nothing radically wrong with the economic and political structure of the fatherland. History would go its fate-ordained course, and before the concepts of fatherland, duty, and God all rebellious questions were stopped.

But where Flex and his kind halted, others were just beginning their demand—often ecstatic—for clarity, meaning, and justice. The youngsters who had not yet found social and philosophical security, and the sensitive ones, had more difficulty in adjusting themselves to the maelstrom of war than did Wurche with his happy and somewhat naïve outlook on life. They were torn between the rational condemnation of war as utter nonsense—in expressions that range from sardonic cynicism to torpid resignation—and the idealistic view

of war as a "bath of steel" for the rejuvenation of the nation. They tried to reconcile themselves with the real world of the front by interpreting it in terms of their own personality, projecting themselves by sheer will power into unity with events greater than themselves.

This method of approach to the world had already been developed before the war in expressionism. It manifested itself chiefly in the graphic and plastic arts, in painting, and in poetry, and there were some remarkable achievements in the drama. The epic art with its broad inclusiveness and character delineation was not a natural medium for expressionism, and Unruh does not exactly belong to the expressionist group. Still, in attitude and form *Der Opfergang*—it first appeared in 1919—shows clearly expressionist idealism. He was an officer in the Prussian army when his dramas had made him a reputation before the war. During the first months of his war experience a remarkable development took place in this traditional officer. He changed from a soldier who drew his inspiration from duty and honor and looked for death in battle as the fulfillment and meaning of life into a man who struggled for a real meaning behind all the inhuman horrors of war. As early as October 1914, he wrote the mystical play *Vor der Entscheidung* [*Before the Decision*] in which can be seen the great, initial effect of the war on Unruh. But it was not until 1916 in the *Opfergang* that he gives best expression to his experience.

The story depicts a company of soldiers from the first stages of their transport to the Verdun front to the climax of the attack and the subsequent decrescendo. Realistic description blends with visionary ecstasy to create a remarkable specimen of expressionistic technique in the field of the war novel. The characters of the story are real enough, rather as symbolic types of a complex humanity projected into artistic reality, than as individuals exactly observed. Captain Werner is the traditionalistic, conscientious leader of his men, who before the loyalty he sees in the eyes of the men he has to lead to death, longs for the bullet that would end the nightmare of his thoughts. . . . Deeply pessimistic, he despairs of lasting peace as long as human beings are as they are, and resignedly considers the path of duty as ordained by God.

Werner is nobody but Unruh himself, or rather one of the aspects of the author's protean soul, which, as a light broken up by a prism, appears in the various figures of the book. Unruh speaks also through the platoon leader Clemens, who, contemplating the insanity and nonsense of it all, sees the soul of the world bandied away and wonders whether true brotherhood of men can be enforced only in death. But in the clairvoyance of overstrained nerves, he sees also the spirit win in the end. He knows the soldiers bring about the decision in the world catastrophe, and it will therefore be theirs to determine the future. After the war nobody will ever seduce their hearts again and reach out with greedy fingers for the sacred lives of men. When Captain Werner suggests that after all some power might do this very thing, Clemens violently contradicts him. Power is ephemeral, and the soldiers will henceforth look only to what offers permanence and will endure, even if they themselves are torn to pieces by the next shell.

Unruh's nature also appears in the firm, controlled attitude of Sergeant Hillebrandt, who is sure to fight the good fight for the fatherland, and feels in the world about him for the first time in his life a mighty fate approaching; this he welcomes, for it will perfect him. It is a blessing to be rescued from one's own ego. The word *Tod* "death" is like tender music of warmth, sleep, and peace. In a spell of weakness longing for home makes him cry out desperately, but he collects himself resolutely by forcing into his thoughts over everything else the fatherland and its security. He wants not to be disturbed by Clemens' doubts, for his strength is drawn from the deepest wells of the national community and therefore he knows that man does not meet God on the path of his own desires. He advises Clemens: If you want to be a man, crush everything within you that destroys your faith. How can we win over this hell unless we are masters over our own thoughts? Our friendship must be action, our oath must be action. Man, we are to be examples!

Then there is the drummer, representing the sensuous side of human nature. His sensuality changes into a concentrated ambition to rise high, but transitory as his values are, his mind is destroyed by the scorching flame of the inhuman sufferings about him, and in company with the volunteer he buries the crucifix and his own Iron Cross. At home he tells of the hell of Verdun, only to find his voice drowned in unbelief, scorn, and laughter. The volunteer with his love of nature, his high idealism, is crushed by his own bloody deeds; he stands for a *Weltanschauung* like that glorified by Flex. The lieutenant, a minister by profession, deplores the lack of understanding among men—a confusion due to carnal life, according to him. That is why there is now a French, an English, and a German God. Kox, the sapper, is a sober, unimaginative, matter-of-fact type. He hates enthusiasm and big words. A firm jaw bone is more than a handful of glory. Victory is just a business like any other craft. If you want to continue to exist, get hand grenades and secure sufficient powder. Following the company in action is the cook Fips, formerly in the service of Greek royalty. His commentaries on his poor contemporaries are of a very simple, common-sense kind, often delivered in burlesqued exalted language, affording a touch of grim irony in an otherwise humorless world. All these men, personified aspects of a highly differentiated humanity rather than idealists, move with retarding, halting steps toward their doom.

Although it is broken up into many scenes, the story presents a complete rounded picture. There is sustained, gradually increasing tension to the very point of attack. Then in an unsuspected pause Captain Werner hesitates for several minutes in giving the signal to advance because the explosion of a mine fails to take place. But finally the attack commences, and all the tension is released. The behavior of the soldiers in action is fully consistent with their characters as they were unfolded before the climax. In the bedlam of chaotic and ecstatic action the innermost nature of men is revealed in a flash. (pp. 89-94)

Where Flex humbly subordinates himself to the destiny of his folk, even when he realizes that his nation is in dire need of reform, Unruh feels differently. No organized group, no state has a right to take precedence over the individual when the dignity of man is involved. He dares to rebel against the powers of the state which demand absolute and unquestioned coördination and submission. His soul rejects this imposition as presupposing the monstrous claim of an infallible human authority, which not even the state can have. The result, reminiscent of Hebbel, is the tragic destruction of men as physical beings, but the ultimate triumph of the spirit over matter.

The individualistic character of the book can be seen from other angles also. When all are exalted over the success of the attack, Werner's spirits sink low. He reflects on the attack and analyzes the victory, and nothing worth-while remains. For who can hold the enthusiasm and make it stay? Who can truly appreciate the achievement of this victory? Tomorrow strangers will again make their quarters here in the conquered village, and life will go on as if it had never been different, and in a few days all will be forgotten. The trite everyday world will keep on grinning. Werner's only true confidant is his diary. When it is temporarily lost, he is frantic. Conscious of the dualism in his life, he wonders: Did I step out of the framework of permitted thoughts? Can I not express doubts? "Doubts grow in me, loathsome as toadstools. I root them out ten times a day. They come back a hundredfold." Can I not ask questions? Are we a flock of sheep driven here and there? Assault troop? For whom? For what?

These and similar thoughts and incidents reveal the introvert who shares in the general suffering but is unable to become truly one with his fellow men. He will always stay apart from group experience.

At the end there are left Clemens, the man of the spirit, who ecstatically but somewhat nebulously sees the morning of a new humanity dawning, and Kox, the sober utilitarian. Uniting in action they both go ahead, together. The book closes with superb and tragic irony. The full morning light shines on Clemens' determined brow as he hurls his company forward out of the trenches—for more than three meters.

Unruh sees war as a catastrophe which, despite everything, suggests a deeper meaning than mere wholesale slaughter. It gives a man a chance to assert himself in chaos. Significantly, the book is named after its last chapter, *Opfergang* "the way of sacrifice"; here there is a metaphysical implication which is well justified, in view of the irrational tenor of the work. Whether it suggests the way of sacrifice of his own people, as [Hermann] Pongs sees it, or whether it refers to the experience of the individual on his way to a higher knowledge and a more genuine humanity, which seems to be more likely, Unruh does emphasize values which are of little import to the egotist, whose type is represented in the *Opfergang* by the actor Cäsar Schmidt. To him all is just a show. He is the self-styled rational individualist who does not "give a damn about the whole world."

In the works of Flex and Unruh man advances toward a positive solution of the problems of war. Flex sees in war an experience for a greater and more genuine ethnic community, his German people; Unruh, though he lacks national emphasis, snatches from war—and in the face of his very destruction—a more profound conception of man as an individual. Both writers are idealists and have in common an irrational appreciation of transcendental values in view of which the individual physical life has only secondary importance. Their beliefs are rooted in the emotional and spiritual world and have little in common with a matter-of-fact realism. In their family backgrounds both writers were conscious of and accustomed to think in terms of social ties, and as such they are prototypes of many later war authors.

During the war itself a great antiwar literature developed in Switzerland. Lyrics and stories poured forth, witnessing to the feverish activity of the pacifists of every nation. There was no lack of Germans among the writers of this material—which appeared preferably in magazines or pamphlets—and by the nature of the situation, most of them were noncombatants.

One of the antiwar writers, however, was not a civilian. Andreas Latzko, a disabled officer from the Austro-Hungarian army, wrote German war stories which quickly made a sensational appearance in all countries. Latzko had actually undergone the experience of the front. He shows the most uncompromising spirit of hatred for war, so characteristic of books of a later period. There are no considerations of ideal aspects. War is a bitter and horrible curse in which not a shred of anything is found that could be called good. The books of Latzko were *Menschen im Krieg* [*Men in War*] (1918), and *Friedensgericht* [*Judgment of Peace*] (1918), veritable compendia of antiwar sentiment.

Menschen im Krieg is a collection of short stories and sketches, showing "man" rather than "men" in war. The single individual is outraged by a group of which he feels himself no part. He is to pull the chestnuts from the fire for the mighty ones; he is to die for ideals that are not his. Brutal force reigns. The masses of people are inert. The sensitive individual, as, for instance, the artist, suffers inhuman agony. The central figures are mostly high-strung, nervous people. The approach to a judgment on war and its condemnation is most varied. There are women who let their men go to war because it flatters their vanity and because it is not fashionable to be without a hero. Here is the youth burning with ambition, for which he prodigally sacrifices the lives of other human beings. Then a commanding general struts by, safely behind the front but directing the fate of thousands, who from a dull peacetime existence has now come to such financial independence and munificence of living that war is to him a Santa Claus with a bag full of wonderful gifts and prospects. What good has *he* to expect from peace? Thank God, there is still war!

There is the insane officer who can not erase from his mind the picture of a horribly mutilated soldier whom he must regard as his second self. He feels himself sane and those diseased in mind who stretch a wall of flags between themselves and their humanity. Is he sick because he can not utter the word "front" without intense hatred? Are not the others mad, who look with combined religious devotion, romantic longing, and shy sympathy upon this wholesale "cripple-and-corpse factory?" Is he sick because he sees millions of human beings on either side slaughtered into a bloody hash? Is the dish of peace to be cooked from this? And for whom? Is it not for the lucky ones at home who sell the meat of their calves and oxen for a hundred-percent profit to their respective fatherlands instead of carrying their own flesh to market for the pennies of a soldier's pay? No, he is too honest and too sane for such an insane world. He will not swallow the cowardly stuff written by the war bards who try to make the "World War" brand famous, even if he has to stay behind iron bars as a seer over the blind.

In another story a young, strapping peasant boy returns home with his face terribly mutilated. Now he is abhorred by his girl, who in the time of his absence has become the mistress of his profiteering master. Fatherland? Would she go to the altar with the fatherland? What had happened to another fellow who had been crippled in the service of the fatherland? Never had the fatherland been mentioned when Peter the cripple went by. They called him contemptuously the village pauper, and that was all there was to it. (pp. 95-100)

The two books of Latzko [*Menschen im Krieg* and *Friedensgericht*] are interesting to us not because of literary merit, but because they contain virtually all of the arguments that later found such wide expression in the antiwar literature. That is

why he commands attention. He claims that the "higher" individual is and must remain free. He aims to prove the injustice and outrage done to this higher type. Suggestions of a personal responsibility and an obligation to higher values do occasionally emerge, but vanish soon before the all-important concern for the ego. No German war novel presents more definitely the attitude and the fate of the exclusively egocentric individual. Even the redeeming feature of comradeship is lacking in the books of Latzko. Appeals to a higher humanity, occasionally made, compare poorly with the dynamic and persuasive force of passages that express the hatred for the masses. . . . Utter pessimism with suicide as the logical end seems a natural consequence of such an attitude. Therefore the view of war presented by Latzko is extreme in its exclusive stress upon the individual. In the presentation of the realities of the front the books evince enough factual substance to be called realistic. There are indeed impossibilities and contradictions in the story, but they are not so numerous as to make it possible to brand Latzko's books as inventions or fabrications. Many accounts and incidents are authentic enough and could easily be corroborated by men of the front.

In evaluating Latzko's work we notice first that he presents the experience of the front realistically enough, but he lacks the power to create men and situations convincingly. Occasional scenes have real force, but sustaining and creative strength is lacking. Everything ends up in individual ranting and palaver. Latzko's sincerity is beyond question. The rights of man, his outraged individuality are matters of true concern, and not objects of mere sentimentalism, as we find them in many a writer of a later period. But by confining himself to the interests of his own person and by refusing to identify himself even partially with his fellow men—not even with men destined like him, far less with an ethnic community— Latzko's art was bound to be barren in a field where the social factor is of supreme importance. The world of his heroes is filled with their own egos so exclusively that outside themselves there is only nonsense or vacuum.

It is probably because they lacked creative power that Latzko's books fell into the background in Germany in favor of Henri Barbusse's famous French war novel, *Le Feu* [*Under Fire*]. Although it was written before Latzko's books appeared, it naturally did not become known in Germany until after the war. As the strongest artistic antiwar novel written during the war, it made a deep impression on a people utterly weary and disillusioned by the great world calamity. In its wake, during the first years of the Weimar Republic, there followed a flood of pacifist publications. Yet they vanished as they had come, despite the lofty sentiments and glowing hopes expressed, according to which a new era was shortly to arrive for mankind. The brotherhood of man was imminent, and no opinion not in conformity with this faith was tolerated. The pacifist sentiment, with its radical hatred of war, its belief in the primacy of the individual, held the public stage, and it was only natural that the work of Barbusse led in the field of the war novel. But the World War as theme and substance of literature lost ground rapidly. In politics and economics, the Versailles treaty replaced the war as the focus of interest for almost a decade, and literature and art turned their attention to anything that might help men to forget the bloody conflict.

During the dominance of pacifism in the Weimar Republic and the growing indifference of the public toward everything connected with the war, it was difficult for an author to find acclaim for a work that would try to depict the war experience as something more than senseless butchery. So it is understandable that Ernst Jünger had to wait many years until his reports of the thoughts and actions of a shock-troop leader received due recognition. *In Stahlgewittern* [*Storm of Steel*] (1919) is a book of achievement and import; it is, so to speak, the last word spoken for some time in favor of a positive view of war. It appeared at a time when objective evaluation of books on the war was still very difficult, and cheap glorifications of war could hardly have been produced successfully. It was a time, indeed, when, under the impact of the actual war experience, all the emotional and intellectual forces of the human defense mechanism against war were still actively at work. Since it is a book which reveals the nearness of the events in its realism and yet shows marks of detachment toward them, *In Stahlgewittern* is a fitting close for a period comparatively poor in artistic creation in the field of narrative war prose.

We have seen that Flex's idealism was the logical outgrowth of a firm *Weltanschauung,* that Unruh's expressionistic visions served him as an inner stronghold, and that Latzko's extreme egocentric thought led logically to suicide. We now find in Jünger an author whose "realistic idealism" arose from a sheer act of the will. This, it seems, is the explanation of Jünger's synthesis of the two opposing pictures, romanticism and realism, which resulted from the impact of the experience of war on a man who was at once a born romantic and a keen observer. If Jünger accepts without question duty, honor, and sacrificial death for the fatherland, we are sure that the acceptance must proceed from a positive refusal to question them, for how else can we reconcile his idealism with the pessimistic realism that often prevails in his work?

Jünger was a soldier—he had enlisted briefly in the French Foreign Legion before the war—and an artist of decidedly impressionistic talent. His iron control enabled him to fuse the rapturous vision of an ecstatic and the sober calculations of a war technician. He keeps his vision free of disturbing elements and holds speculation well in check. Factual, detailed descriptions are followed by breath-taking scenes full of the intoxication of battle. He says himself "in the cold light of reasoning everything becomes utilitarian, contemptible, and pale." He seeks to relegate reflections to the background, and the purpose of the book was to describe "factually" what he had experienced as soldier and leader, and "what he thought about it as it happened." Yet here and there are passages of deeper reflection which give us insight into the author's essence, many important features of the philosophy of his later works.

Upon his irrational nature he imposes a rationalistic method. And this highly individualistic man establishes for his *Weltanschauung* a hierarchy of values in which group interests take precedence over the ego. These center, characteristically, in his own social group, the officer class, and it is through this group that he arrives at the higher value of a folk, of Germany.

The picture of war is drawn soberly. The battlefield was a desert of insanity. Life was carried on wretchedly under ground. Ruins and crosses lined the path of the soldiers. A shell hole strewn with duds, tin cans, and shreds of uniforms, with a corpse or two lying on the edge: this the unvarying world of every one of the millions of soldiers. The character and tempo of the fighting had changed after the Somme offensive in 1916. War was not now a sparkling experience,

transient and bloody, but something which carved itself, over weeks and months, into the minds of men. What was a human life worth in a desolation where the stench of thousands and thousands of rotting corpses fouled the air? Gallantry was gone forever, and in its stead there was only an intensified tempo of mutual destruction. All noble and personal feelings stopped, as is true wherever the machine gains control over humanity. For here for the first time the machine civilization of the new Europe showed its face in battle. Man had to become hardened and ruthless, and his outward appearance showed this change. The German soldier began to wear the steel helmet. Into his features was hewn the stereotyped and overstrained energy that is drawing upon its last resources, reproducing so strikingly the enigmatic and grandiose facial expressions found on the faces of men in monuments of classical antiquity or of the Renaissance. The soldier was the patient day laborer of death burdened with iron. Ruthlessness became his mode of living, for he was constantly under the shadow of death. And since the human sense of self-preservation remained ever the same, adaptation was impossible. He did not become more courageous, and he did not care to parade his courage, but in night, desolation, and under fire he did his duty. He did it at the expense of his nervous energy, and he was able to carry on only through a strong sense of the inner values of honor and duty. The fighters became the conquerors of fear, towering in their brutal grandeur. They turned into the supple tigers of the trenches; they learned to become past masters in the handling of explosives and all the complicated means of destruction. Yet while the German soldier made his iron fist felt by the whole world, he was poorly clothed and fed in comparison with the splendid equipment and more adequate food of his adversaries. Could there, in view of this, be a greater proof for the impelling force of the idea? To die in moments of great enthusiasm is much, but to go on fighting for your cause in hunger and privation against overwhelming odds is more. (pp. 106-12)

Jünger's account finds its climax in a description of the great German offensive of March 1918. The moment for the last great effort has arrived. The fate of nations is to be settled by blood and iron. The stake is "the possession of the world." Jünger is conscious of the historic meaning of the hour. He is sure that every man feels his individuality dissolve under the impact of historical responsibility now descending on him. Moments like these leave no doubt for him that in the last analysis the history of the nations rises and falls with the turn of battles.

The atmosphere is charged with highest tension. The officers stand around exchanging nervous jokes. Nobody can keep his mind clear in the terrible pandemonium of artillery fire, mines, etc. The nerves no longer register fear. Everybody is raging and unpredictable in his actions. Death has absolutely lost its meaning, for the "will to live" has "passed over collectively into the nation." It makes everyone blind and indifferent to his own personal fate. In a mixture of emotions aroused by bloodthirstiness, rage, and alcohol the advance toward the enemy begins, inextricably commingling in man the beastly and the divine. The army is urged on by the overpowering desire to kill. Bitter tears of rage trickle down cheeks. . . .

In 1914 Jünger had thought of going to a brisk and joyful war. Little had he bothered about the idea and meaning of the fighting. Now, as he looks back over four years passed among a generation destined to die, he sees the idea of the fatherland emerge. It is the one lasting profit in a game which had been played with everything at stake. The nation was no longer an empty concept shrouded in symbols. It was a reality; otherwise how could so many have laid down their lives in its defense? Out of the four years of schooling in brutal materialistic warfare, Jünger arrives at the conclusion that life achieves deeper meaning only through the sacrifice of the self for an idea, that there are ideals in the face of which the life of the individual and even that of a people do not count. And even if the high goal he fought for has not been attained, if the "machine," the forces of materialism, have won out after all—well, he had learned how to stand up for a cause and, if need be, die for it, as befits a man. Hardened in all fires, the soldiers of the front can step into life and face what fate has in store for them, whether friendship, love, politics, or professional life. Not every generation has such a privilege. They have stood in blood and mud, but their thoughts have turned to great, exalted values. And if ever the time shall come—and Jünger is sure it will—when it is no longer understood why a man would give his life for his country, when the idea of the fatherland has died out among men, then, perhaps, the war generations will be envied for the irresistibility of their inner strength, just as the medieval saints and martyrs are envied today for the fervor of their faith. For all great and solemn ideas grow from a feeling deeply rooted in the blood. Fortunate and blessed are they who live in the aura of great emotions! To have realized this in war will always be an inestimable gain. The book closes: "Germany lives, and Germany shall not perish." (pp. 114-16)

In 1927 appeared [*Der Streit um den Sergeanten Grischa*] the novel of Arnold Zweig about the Russian sergeant, Grischa, who fell victim to a power-intoxicated Prussian war machine. It was the first published part of a tetralogy intended to give a broad picture and criticism of the World War as it resulted from and reacted upon a class-torn, capitalistic society. The titles of the tetralogy are, briefly: *Junge Frau von 1914, Erziehung vor Verdun, Grischa,* and *Einsetzung eines Königs.*

The individual is always in the center of interest; all approaches to the problems raised by the war proceed from him. Community values are recognized in terms of social class and a future socialistic society, though references to racial affinities are also not infrequent. A transcendental law is conceived within the teachings of the Torah.

The Grischa book was Zweig's best. Here he presents a sequence of events in a well-knit plot. At the same time he depicts a social organism, the German army of the World War. All the various classes and types appear side by side, from the common labor-service man to the commander-in-chief. The flight of a Russian prisoner, his adventures, recapture, trial, and death sentence as a result of mistaken identity, the establishment of his innocence, and his final judicial murder make up the thread of the plot. The story leads with inevitable logic through the various military strata, which thereby become the colorful milieu of a strong narrative.

The artist's mastery of his form controls his creative imagination, and freedom of poetic disposition is tempered by Zweig's knowledge of persons and situations. A genuine sympathy for suffering humanity is coupled with objective realism. The presentation in Zweig's books has that degree of inner probability which reports, describes, and entertains, and at the same time creates in the reader a true basis for a vicarious experience.

Right versus might is the central theme. Its supreme repre-

sentatives are the generals Schieffenzahn (i.e., Ludendorff) and Lychow, who in a terse dialogue bring out the basic principles of their respective positions. Schieffenzahn intends to put God in his proper place, and climaxes his views with the statement: "After all, to make war seems to have practically the purpose of putting your dear Lord in his proper place. The State creates justice; the individual is a louse" [*"der Staat schafft das Recht, der Einzelne ist eine Laus"*]. But such a view, if true, would make Lychow feel no better than a dog. He had learned as a boy that justice preserves a state and gives meaning to life. Might must not be divorced from right. All human institutions are imperfect, but nothing can justify a state in using the machinery of the law against the innocent, and thus destroying the nation's sense of justice, which must be a symbol of divine justice.

Lychow loses and Schieffenzahn wins, but only outwardly. Though he motivates his act by casual reasoning and deludes himself about the impression Lychow has made on him, Schieffenzahn tries to rescind the death order. But a snow storm has interrupted the system of communications, and Grischa must die—in the last analysis a victim, not of the Schieffenzahns, but of a fate that through many incidents had brought his small life to the attention of the mighty one. Fate carries the day, and Grischa realizes it in his primitive way.

Taught by the Talmudic wisdom of the carpenter Täwje, Grischa found his case in order. He had blindly accepted as right the tradition of killing the enemy, and he had killed many; now he knows the law: Whoso sheddeth man's blood, by man shall his blood be shed. It had nothing to do with "good" or "bad." His case seemed to him no longer a miscarriage of justice. It was quite in order.

Though Zweig here projects his plot into a metaphysical and cosmic sphere, he does so convincingly and with restraint. The robust life of man on earth, intensified and distorted by war, is really the substance he deals with. Historical, economic, and psychological realities lend depth to the picture he draws, as they also help to distribute justly the lights and shadows of a humanity basically tragic. Schieffenzahn, for example, is not only indicted and exposed as the imperialistic and materialistic protagonist of the ruling classes, but is also shown by psychoanalytical method to be the product of his environment and class. (pp. 131-34)

The story ends as it begins with a cosmic note of poetic impact. At the moment of Grischa's death, the mighty source of life casts into his brain a faint but definite certainty that parts of his being will live on. It makes him feel that there is a continuation of the ego, the immortality of his individual entity which at that very moment has been extinguished. And with clear symbolic significance, his daughter is born at the very time of his death.

The book ends with a significant episode in the sphere of economic, political reality. A long train is stopped by the engineer to permit one single lance-corporal to board it, who would otherwise have lost valuable time from his meager furlough. An unbelievable incident in the realm of Prussian order! Yet it happens, and it indicates the coming social revolution. In disgust the officers comment on how the workers are beginning to be aware of themselves. Theirs is the power. They do not know it yet, but when they do know it. . . .

The next two books of Zweig, the plots of which precede the Grischa story in time, followed at four-year intervals. *Junge Frau* gives the story of the relationship between the writer

Bertin and his wife in the fateful year 1914. It is of interest to us only as it reveals the character and background of Bertin, whose person gives a sort of unity to the four novels and who is the main figure in *Erziehung vor Verdun*. At first he is shown as a loyal Prussian patriot willing to follow the state wherever it leads; but at the same time he is a typical individualistic intellectual who, as a Jew and as a child of the lower middle class, is predisposed toward social resentment. There are some inconsistencies in Bertin's character in *Junge Frau*. He seems a rather unconvincing patriot of the common run. In fact, he is that only in conversations; in character and in action he is the individualistic aesthete who recognizes as his needs not so much a weaning from conformity as an education for a true knowledge of human nature, including his own. Verdun provides it. As the motto of *Erziehung vor Verdun* states, he learns about his position, his enemies, and himself. (pp. 134-35)

In form and style Zweig is a master; his novels, as creations of artistic merit and as documents of an era, are among the best the war has produced. Their length and scope are directly proportional to the importance of their sociological and critical theme. (p. 139)

Neither in length, scope, nor importance can the work of Erich Maria Remarque, whose novel, *Im Westen nichts Neues* [*All Quiet on the Western Front*] (1928), became a world sensation, be compared to the epic achievement of Zweig. Its success will perhaps never be satisfactorily explained, but one fact seems certain: it cannot be due exclusively to extraordinary merit.

Remarque is an artist. By his impressionistic talent he knows how to draw characters and situations that engage attention and arouse deepest sympathy. His language is versatile and concise; his narrative is rich in contrast of situations and reflections, and his composition is done with a brilliant stage technique. Lyric and idyllic scenes alternate with the most lurid and coarsest sort of realism. The intricate problems of life and of the War are cleverly reduced to such plain propositions that even the poorest in spirit can grasp them. Just at the most favorable psychological moment, when Zweig had broken the ice and the universal antiwar sentiment had reached its very climax, Remarque's story gave expression to the cry "No More War!"

But what are the facts and ideas of this book which claimed to tell of the fate of a whole generation?

A number of adolescents, college students, have been induced by their teacher to volunteer for war service. They and a few older men form a group somewhere at the Western Front. Their fate is the subject of the story, which was to be "neither an accusation nor a confession" but an attempt to give a report of "a generation that was destroyed by war, even though it might have escaped its shells." These pretensions of the author must be refuted. Ample evidence shows that the heroes of Remarque are not representative of a whole generation, but only of a certain type. This is not to criticize Remarque for military and other inconsistencies, but it is significant that in a book which claims to be a report of the front by a front soldier, of 288 pages of text only about 80 pages deal with situations at or right behind the front, and even they are heavily interspersed with reflections. Furthermore, it may be characteristic that the actual life at the front is described in general terms without ever a definite location given, while scenes behind the front, at hospitals, at home, in the barracks, etc., are

Front wrapper for Erich Maria Remarque's Im Westen nichts Neues (All Quiet on the Western Front).

given in a more clearly outlined realism. The implication is obvious; it leaves little doubt that many of his situations are fictitious.

What is more, the ethical character of the book provokes critical reflection. Through sordid detail and the description of gruesome and inhuman happenings, through reflection and innuendo, the condemnation of war amounts in the last analysis to a sweeping indictment of the older generation. It is as simple as that, and it would not evoke any criticism on our part, the guilt of the elders being a genuine problem, were it not for the superficial way in which Remarque goes about his task. Their teachers get the blame for the boys' being in a war which is of use "only to the Kaiser and the generals." With adolescent swagger, they call all culture "nonsense" [*Quatsch*] because they have to be out at the front, and when they have a chance they will pay their torturers back. For example, we find the hero on leave at home and looking at his books, among them all of the classical writers. He says: "I have read them with honest zeal, but most of them did not quite appeal to me; so much the more did I appreciate the other books, the more modern ones." This statement provides a good insight into the mind of the hero and his lack of appreciation for the values of the classical tradition. Again Lieutenant Mittelstedt "gets even" with his former teacher, now a drafted private. This particular scene, told with the malicious glee of an adolescent, is typical of the immature and sophomoric attitude of the heroes. So is the ever-recurring swagger and boastfulness of the young men who pose as old warriors well versed in all the tricks of warfare, though there is not one description of a feat actually executed, such as we find so abundantly and realistically in many other war books.

Individual incidents are given typical significance, less by an abstract process than by the exclusiveness with which they are presented. Thus the reader gets the impression that all officers are brutes; all teachers are cowardly shirkers who let others do the bloody and dangerous job of fighting for Germany's glory while they stay safely at home; and all doctors are inhuman monsters. Against this world of brutality are set off in shining lights the simple but genuine virtues of the common soldiers. They are all good fellows, and it arouses our sympathy to see them fall prey to power-drunk, sadistic superiors.

Immaturity and partiality by omission detract from the ethical import of this work which must be admitted to have force and human appeal. That the writer projects his 1927 mentality into the life of young World War soldiers is perhaps not so great a defect as is his wilfully narrowed outlook. *Im Westen nichts Neues* is scarcely a serious ethical document. Rather it is symptomatic of an age that saw the final revelation of the war in the adolescent self-pity, resentment, and sentimentality the novel embodies. Really it is the story of an egocentric, immature youngster of whom one may well wonder how he would have developed without the war. There is, indeed, plenty of authority for holding that the war helped many to find themselves and prove their mettle, and that it also exposed the brittle human substance that might have been broken by life anyway, without ever having been exposed to the destructive shells of war. It goes without saying that this observation—contradicting point-blank Remarque's claim to speak for a whole generation—implies neither that the war did not destroy the best of human values, nor that war was justifiable because it developed character.

Artistic powers of creation of Zweig's caliber are very rare. And they have even proved unnecessary in many a forceful war book. The reality of the war was so overpowering that a faithful account of it often found its own adequate form; that is to say, the subject matter made the writer. This can be seen in the failures of many sequels to war novels. Few of the war writers produced more than one successful novel. One of these rare exceptions is George von der Vring, whose book *Soldat Suhren* [*Private Suhren*] (1927) is a novel of finest artistic and human quality. Here again is the story of a group of men who are trained for and put into the mill of the war; here, too, we see the common scenes and incidents of the soldier's life. If we consider artistic composition, however, and seriousness of judgment, *Suhren* justifies a position of its own.

The title reflects the individualism and the humility of heart prevailing in this story. The experience of a young artist, a painter, and his closer comrades, their progress from their first uncertain steps as recruits to their first battle, is told with directness and restraint but intense sympathy. The reality of external details is well balanced by revelations of the inner life; and these are reserved and given with pathos, humor, and lyric quality. Von der Vring is a master in creating atmosphere, in conjuring moods and aesthetic effects, but he is also

an honest reporter of the ugly aspects of war which he sees always with the trained eyes of the artist.

Private Suhren is an individualist and remains one, for the meaning of his being herded off to war does not become very clear to him, and he does not see himself fully as a part of a common destiny. But if in his heart he stays aloof from his fellow men, this attitude has nothing defined about it. His reserve is the natural result of uncompromising intellectual honesty and a deep feeling of responsibility toward his destiny as a human being and an artist. He has no delusions about himself; he is not an eagle, as he would like to be, but neither is he a domestic chicken. Rather he compares himself with a partridge, that likes to live its life in freedom. Although he could well have escaped service through malingery skillfully executed, he continues in a service of self-effacement. It makes him happy, after all, since he feels it the honorable thing to do, even though the meaning of his duty remains obscure. He loves the fatherland and his home town, in memory of which he writes a most charming lyrical poem, but he also realizes that God created all nations. The nations are like the petals of a flower painted by an artist; they gleam around God in a single beautiful color. Similarity and an equal claim to life and light is the essence of the petals; and so it is also of the peoples. There are slight variations, certainly, yet it is the equality which makes the wonderful flower we call mankind. It is clear to Suhren that the front against the enemies of Germany is confusing. Good fights against good, evil against evil, good against evil, and evil against good. It is a front deranged and perverted a thousand ways that the men are fighting on, and nobody can make out its final form. But one front does exist, which is clear, simple, and straight, hidden deep in a secret place, in the conscience itself. It is the front of kind thoughts and deeds of human worth, of clasped hands and loyal faith.

In the crushing experiences of his environment he finds refuge in his dreams, dreams of human and artistic substance, of love, childhood memories, and art, dreams which do not enervate but strengthen. The superiority—under the stress of the reality of war—of these elements of Suhren's strong and simple faith over philosophies and conventional religion is well pointed out.

Suhren's individualism is not determined by an inflated ego, but by a sense of responsibility vis-à-vis a system which denied in its representatives the principles of a true community. Later works of von der Vring show a consistently developed approach toward a true spirit of community. They reveal much more of an ethnocentric character, and need not be regarded as contradictions to Suhren; rather they indicate Suhren's natural evolution.

Von der Vring presented the war through the eyes of an artist whose outstanding qualities were honest simplicity, lyrical charm, and unpretentious human sympathy. Suhren moves in a class of people among whom the leading elements are teachers in grade schools. The circle of the artist hero of Ernst Wiechert's *Jedermann* [*Everyman*] (1931) is of quite a different sort.

Johannes is a law student, but he can live only the creative life of a poet. The nailed boots of soldiers seem to him to trample into the dirt the individual qualities of life and of the spirit, so much that not even the name of a man remains. The soul becomes a figure, an entity for which only the indefinite personal pronoun "one" is justified. His whole life has prepared him to keep from giving himself over to collective concerns that demand subordination and devotion to a passion that has its origin in the mass of men and its character determined thereby. He can only mistrust everything in the line of tradition, school, teachers, authorities, and he hates to be *eingesetzt* "inserted," like a letter of type which attains meaning and significance only through combination with others. All purpose in the life of an individual is extinguished by war because one fate awaits everyone: exhaustion and senseless, lawless dying, that begins long before actual death terminates a wretched existence.

Despite his utter unfitness for war, Johannes stands up to the duty he assumed when he volunteered. But unlike von der Vring's Suhren, who generated out of his own individual resources the decision for a responsible active participation in war, Johannes needs and receives powerful aid from the outside to see him through.

There are first the friends in his group who help him. Count Percy's unfailing and self-assured conduct, bred in him in a fixed, aristocratic world, challenges Johannes to match these qualities with the forces provided by the aristocracy of the spirit. His dejected and weak friend Klaus, like Percy a former schoolmate, arouses in him deep and genuine sympathy, which, leading to a true helpfulness in spirit and deed, also benefits the helper. And then there is Comrade Oberüber, the homeless vagabond, whose common sense and earthiness serve as a wholesome corrective for the dangerous oversensibility of the poet.

But the real strength comes from the Eternal Feminine. To his mother and his love he owes endurance, sanity, honor, and a faith in the ultimate meaning of life. He learns that it is for his mother when he fights in the war, and if he dies in action, it will be for her. The mother becomes to him a symbol into which merge all the forces of life eternal; indeed, elements of the "Oedipus complex" are also in evidence, and play a part throughout the story.

With these supports Johannes finds he is able to save the remnants of his real self from the war, which otherwise means emptiness of heart and abandonment of all thinking, a war that is an endless road in storm and rain, an eternal waiting, a wasting of all values, and above all, the loss of the self.

Wiechert is bitterly abusive towards war, for example, "Whenever death feels hungry, then we are sold to him like bread, which he digests to dung." But he recognizes other than egocentric values as parts of the defensive mechanism of the individual; thus, it is the feeling of being one with his column that shelters the lost soul.

The justification for Wiechert's attitude of positive individualism is that the artist or poet as an individual creating for all humanity should have nothing to do with war, any more than mothers, the eternal bearers of life.

A definite weakness of the book is the number of unexplained allusions to experiences in the pre-war lives of the characters. It is chiefly on account of these that Wiechert fails to make the story a more satisfactory literary achievement. Indeed, the advantages of outlining in more detail the pre-war lives of the men depicted at the front are so apparent that it is surprising that this has been done in the German war novel so seldom. It certainly would have lent depth of focus to many stories. Among the few books that lead a character from a typical pre-war setting into and through the war is the novel

of Friedrich Eisenlohr, *Das gläserne Netz* [*The Net of Glass*] (1927). Here the egocentric attitude shows no responsibility toward a creative task or mission; rather it is a crude and unscrupulous egotism, made unpalatable by the camouflage of a high-sounding "new" morality. The book depicts a certain pre-war type of impressionistic man and his conduct in war, seven hundred pages of reflections and deeds of a rather unimportant, if representative, ego.

Arthur, the son of a high German official, is still a student. After having often changed his mind about his future profession, he breaks with his father and goes to the free atmosphere of Paris to develop his talents in his own fashion. On a trip to Germany he is caught by the outbreak of the war and must serve in the army, where he soon becomes a lieutenant, due to previous training and social position. Slightly wounded in the beginning, he hastens away from the front. Through clever and consistent malingering he removes himself from the combat zone for the rest of the war. He occupies comfortable and remunerative posts in the rear, where he can in safety "develop his higher personality." Numerous erotic adventures help in his education. He averts the occasional danger of being called back to the front by ruthless blackmailing methods. Thus, to the influential father of his former fiancée he reveals and threatens to publicize the intimacies he has had with her. Again he subtly hints about his knowledge of his superior's addiction to morphine. Having large war pay, he lives in luxury with his mistress, rejecting bribes of harassed Belgians only because they would put him under obligation to the despised plebs. Meanwhile his mother is growing weaker and weaker from lack of food. She dies. And in the end, after all these years of self-indulgence, he faces the future with pompous words of maturity and resolution.

This gentleman, who has brought misery and grief to many people, regards himself and his welfare as important out of all proportion to the rights of his fellow men. Consequently much of his argumentation about ethical and social problems sounds hollow. He will not give up the claim to individuality for the sake of the "superstition of ideals of community" and authority, which have their roots in romantic subordination. Only supreme, courageous loyalty to oneself gives back to life its true color and fertility; hence no heed should be paid to the civilization of modern society, that patina of cowardice, stupor, poverty, and brutality.

Through a world catastrophe, a proletarian revolution, salvation will come for sexual, public, and private ills. One may seem to drift aimlessly from adventure to adventure, but the only meaningful existence is to wait for this catastrophe. When it comes, a newer and truer life will be built on the foundation of unbiased personal freedom and individual responsibility. The state, whose very basis he rejects, has no right to throw men into the witches' cauldron of war without first giving aims, ideas, and faith that stand up against individual skepticism. Nothing and nobody can do good to the mass as a collective being. Only the individual can help himself by shaking off each and every authority, for authority exists only by falsifying human reality in terms of romantic idealism. Moral scruples must be resolutely left behind as bourgeois atavism, and the result will be a sublimated individuality on the basis of natural and eternal laws. Only the anarchists can be truly international, because they occupy themselves exclusively with themselves.

The ethics of this individual and his conduct in war are perfectly congruent. The egocentric attitude per se has found an extreme and presumptuous formulation. The hero is an isolated, atomistic individual and remains one, and many of his theories are more the outgrowth of his selfish character than the results of insight and logical conclusions.

Self-preservation is natural, and no moral stigma is attached to it. Man recoils from the horror of war and tries desperately to save himself. The varied ways he follows for this purpose can be readily appreciated, yet the cloaking of crass egotism with a mantle of a higher ethics is painful and embarrassing. Eisenlohr has succeeded well in presenting the development before and during the war of an intellectual and moral snob who does this. Fortunately, this sort of inflated moralizing is not very frequent. (pp. 141-52)

> *Wm. K. Pfeiler, "Two Idealists," in his* War and the German Mind: The Testimony of Men of Fiction Who Fought at the Front, *Columbia University Press, 1941, pp. 82-97.*

HELMUT GRUBER

[*Gruber is an Austrian-born American educator and critic whose works reflect his interests in history and the social sciences. In the following excerpt, Gruber examines German objectivist novels of the late 1920s and early 1930s that took the First World War as their subject.*]

The term *neue Sachlichkeit* lacks an appropriate English equivalent. At various times it has been referred to as critical realism, reportage, new realism, and matter-of-fact style. None of these translations really captures the essence of a term that became the unifying rubric for much of German literature during the twenties and early thirties. The term "objectivism," suggested by Rudolf Kayser in 1930, is the most appropriate characterization for the writers of this period. They sought to attain an objectivity in bringing life in all its complexity before their public through an unadorned and undramatized collection of facts. To do this they were willing to debase the traditional loftiness of language by introducing slang and dialect and the shopworn phraseology of the journalist into their works. Objectivity was not an end in itself; it was a means of educating the masses about the "true" circumstances under which they lived and about their power to alter the institutions of society. The quest for objectivity led these writers to believe that they were the only source of uncompromising truth in a society that had learned to live on illusions.

Objectivist literature arose during a period of stability, between 1924 and 1927, when the threat of revolution had passed and economic recovery was in progress; gained momentum during the years of the depression; and was of continuing importance until the end of the Weimar Republic. As the twenties drew to a close Germany entered a serious crisis; the depression led to widespread discontent and disillusionment, and public confidence in traditional politics largely disappeared. This crisis, threatening to undermine international stability and casting up the spectre of another war, seemed to be world-wide. At this juncture Objectivism was at its height, and against the background of uncertainty there appeared a spate of books dealing with the World War.

The new literature about the World War began to appear ten years after the event. Its aims and techniques were markedly different from those of works appearing immediately after the war. The Expressionists had regarded the war as a symbolic

point of departure leading to the creation of a "new man" and "new world." The Objectivists sought minutely to describe and analyze the war, and by an exposition of details to make the public discover its full meaning, which had been obliterated by the passing of years.

The Objectivists' treatment of the war had certain common features. Their interest in the immediate and tangible in human experience led them to undertake an uncompromising representation of naked reality. Everywhere the horrors of war were emphasized and heightened through detail and repetition. Man at war was made to appear as a puny creature at the mercy of an inhuman technology. This group of writers searched diaries, notebooks, archives, and memories to document a testament that the men of the trenches would have wanted everyone to share. Although the writers went to great lengths to make their work objective it was also autobiographical, for they appeared as narrators and leading characters of their work.

The Objectivists' motives in writing about the war were political, for they hoped to elicit from it a moral and message for present and future conduct of public affairs. Three divergent paths were taken to reach this didactic end. The first was descriptive and aimed at promoting pacifism. The second was analytic and attempted to illuminate the relationship between war and society. The third was mythological and, unlike the other two, approved of the war and sought to highlight its positive features. Although the representation of reality was a common feature of Objectivist war literature the purpose to which it was put—the moral to be drawn from it—differed for each of the three approaches to the public's enlightenment and conversion.

Many Objectivists were intent on promoting pacifism by portraying the effect of war's destruction on individuals and groups of men. War was made to appear as an impersonal force that degraded and dehumanized man; all that happened during its course seemed to defy rational explanation and lack justification. War was not simply hell; the writers pictured it as a monstrous process in which there were no victors and only man was the loser. He stood to lose not only his life but his identity and his humanity. In describing the process by which man was reduced to insignificance these Objectivists hoped to demonstrate that death was not the greatest evil that befell man in wartime and to explode the myth that war is an expression of heroism and national vitality.

In *Im Westen nichts Neues,* the most celebrated book of its time, Erich Remarque attempted to convince the reader that a whole generation was consumed by the war which gave it an identity that made it unfit for society. He introduced us to a group of eight young men who were the victims of the dangerous monotony of trench warfare interrupted by sorties into no-man's-land and rest periods behind the lines. They have been degraded from men into numb and unfeeling brutes lacking all the earmarks of civilization even in the act of dying. War has turned them into brutish instruments of battle and into nihilists who want to escape from life. "We are no longer the youth. We no longer want to take the world by storm. We are escapists. We're escaping from ourselves and from our lives. We were eighteen and had begun to love the world and life; on them we had to shoot. The first grenade that exploded hit our heart. We don't believe in them any more. We believe in the war." Peace and its uncertainty has become alien to these men whose minds appear to have been reduced to *tabulae rasae* on which only the know how of soldiers has been recorded. They performed their duty under fire or behind the lines like automatons. Their past as young men and as students meant nothing. All those venerable classics that had formerly inspired them were only fleeting shadows and memories.

Remarque permitted one spark of life and hope to appear among his dehumanized generation. Paul Bäumer, the narrator, was shaken out of his somnambulistic trance when he killed a French soldier in hand-to-hand combat. The dying man's agony made Paul realize for the first time the enormity of what he had been doing for years and awakened his hatred of war. "Comrade, I say to the dead man across from me, but I say it calmly: today it's you, tomorrow it's me. But if I survive, comrade, I will fight against that which destroyed both of us: your life and—my life too. I promise you comrade, it must never happen again." But war rained down on the awakened and the numb with equal disregard and in the last October days of 1918, when the shooting had all but stopped, Paul Bäumer became one of the war's last victims. The insignificance of his lot was recorded by the communique for the day of his death: "All quiet on the western front."

Arnold Zweig illustrated the horrible impersonality of war which played havoc with the life of man by reducing him to an indistinguishable number. In *Der Streit um den Sergeanten Grischa* the war was made to appear as an all-encompassing system the total effect of which was far greater than the sum of its specific horrors. Grischa, an escaped Russian prisoner of war, made his way through the forests of the enemy to reach his native village and his mother. He obtained the papers of a dead Russian to gain safe conduct through the enemy lines which lay before his destination. His new identity proved to be his undoing, for he was caught, his papers were checked, and he was imprisoned for the crimes committed by his double. Grischa was sentenced to death and in desperation blurted out the truth. But once set in motion the wheels of the system could not be reversed and efforts to save him failed. The high command had checked the records and a punishment was required to cancel out the crime and close the case. Grischa faced the firing squad.

Grischa suffered from injustice in two distinct but related ways. He was the victim of a war that violated his basic goodness and set him adrift in situations he could not understand. He also became an object in the hands of the bureaucracy that accompanies war. Here he was condemned to die by a system that did not care about guilt or innocence, but had to satisfy its mania for statistical accuracy and bureaucratic neatness.

Remarque and Zweig depicted the loss of identity and dehumanization of specific individuals. Other Objectivists described the meaninglessness of war in cold factual detail, and their narrations resembled chronicles in which the destiny of the individual was not permitted to stand out among the myriad misfortunes of everyman. In his novel *Vier von der Infantrie* Ernst Johannsen presented a factual account of the Somme battles at the end of the war. Four men were welded into a fraternity by the need for survival but the flying steel, the impersonal tools of war, recognized no immunity. Each one died in turn and shared the meaningless end of the hundreds who succumbed with each recoil of the big guns and foray into no-man's-land. "They died without hope or consolation, indifferent and resigned to their fate." Johannsen held out no hope that the tremendous sacrifice of life would be remembered in twenty years. "No monument recounts their suffering and words float away like leaves in the wind. On top

of ten million dead, life goes on as usual." Private Renn, who represented all soldiers in Ludwig Renn's *Krieg*, also seemed to be a typical victim of an unfathomable fate. He marched through four years of war, took part in numerous battles, and witnessed every possible human degradation. He was neither immature nor naive; yet was driven along unquestioning, was unaware of the forces directing him, and was unable to grasp the meaning of the spectacle of which he was a part.

The Objectivists who hoped to promote pacifism with their work concentrated on describing the horror of war without examining its causes or deeper meaning. Their characters, whether callous trench-fighters or mere objects of fate, were apolitical. Renn's typical soldier, for instance, remarked that he had never thought about politics and that he considered it something abhorrent and dirty. Pacifism in these works seemed to rest on the belief that a full revelation of the horrors of war would turn the public against it.

There were some authors who went beyond descriptions of violence to analyse the causes of the war. They looked upon war as the expression of underlying contradictions in society and sought an explanation for its origin in economic, political, and social relationships and institutions. With this analytic approach they attempted to probe below the common suffering of a population at war in order to demonstrate how war heightens the injustices suffered by man at all times.

An attempt at analysis was made by Theodor Plivier in *Des Kaisers Kulis*. This was the record of the German navy during the war years: the meaningless manoeuvres and mock actions of the fleet, the undermining of morale by inactivity, drill, and "spit and polish," and the naval rebellion of 1917 and other acts of desperation against injustice. Plivier showed how the sailors lived and what they thought. He pictured them as human beings driven to desperate measures by the officers and the endless war. Class antagonism was aggravated by the sailor's sympathy for the economically exploited civilian population and by their resentment of the luxurious life of their officers. The inactivity of the fleet allowed the crews to spend much time ashore mingling with local workers in waterfront bars, exchanging news about conditions on the ships, and reading the social democratic newspapers and illegal handbills. These contacts and activities increased the sailors' desire to understand why they were at war. Most of them had only a vague notion about the causes and were consumed by petty grievances. There were a few, whom Plivier designated as unsung heroes, who rose above the mass and blamed the outbreak of war and its continuation on a variety of oppressors. Köbis, one of these men, told his comrades that the war was only a continuation of the exploitation which the masses suffered from in peacetime.

> There are the war contractors, industry: steel, iron, leather! Makes no difference, all of them are making money, and all raised their dividends.
>   We're slaving for them!
>   We're starving for them!
>   We're being ruined for them!

In his treatment of war on the high seas Friedrich Wolf insisted that an understanding of causes was not enough. He revealed how the action of ordinary men faltered for lack of political experience. A mutiny of the Austrian fleet stationed at Cattaro in the Adriatic was initially successful, only to be defeated by the leaders themselves. They spent precious hours in negotiations and the drafting of demands. Their indecision permitted the Austrian Admiralty to send a task force, surround the mutinous fleet, and imprison the leaders. Wolf indicated that at the crucial moment of a revolutionary situation one man or a handful of men must act resolutely to prevent catastrophe. In his essay "Warum schrieb ich *Matrosen*?" he had stated that this play was intended to reveal the means of carrying out a successful revolution. This was precisely what the sailors of Cattaro were unable to do, and the thought "Kameraden, das nächste Mal besser" seemed to be an insufficient solace. Will it be better next time? Can a revolution led by ordinary men go further than this one? By insisting that the next time the revolution will be successful without giving the slightest indication of why this should be so Wolf asked the reader to accept an empty promise. The reader could just as easily have drawn the conclusion that rebellions are hopeless. Perhaps the most politically militant war book to be written in this period was Peter Riss's novel *Stahlbad Anno 17*. In the words of the author it was an "accusation, outcry, curse, reminder, and warning against the war criminals of all nations who are again arming for mass-annihilation." In this chronicle the soldier Riss was educated by a few enlightened comrades about why he was fighting and learned to look upon his surroundings with new insight. He marched with an army of the people—"factory workers, day-labourers, clerks, bakers, tailors, mechanics, masons, journeymen; the mysterious unknown mass." He discovered that this was not their war but that of the owners, rulers, oppressors, profiteers and their henchmen. The soldiers were reduced to sheep who knew only "obey and die" and were sacrificed to a fatherland that was nothing but the selfish interests of industrialists, Junkers, and the clergymen and professors who are their spokesman.

Everything and everyone seemed to be driven by an inexorable fate, but private Riss was not deceived by appearances. He knew that powerful human forces directed the destiny of the millions in the trenches. The enemy was not the man on the other side of the barbed wire. "Oh you poor comrades on the other side of the border who among you knows us, who among you hates us? You drivers, bakers, miners, mechanics, and journeymen from over there. You are poor devils like us; how could you hate us? After all, we are all victims of a common enemy!" Nor was the enemy the older generation, the foreigner, the civilian, or even the staff officer behind the lines. It was the exploiter and oppressor in war and peace. As the group of the enlightened of Riss's company experienced the endless months of slaughter they began to dream of vengeance and retribution against those who had unleashed the war. They looked forward to the time when their arms would be used to liberate man; when an army of the dead would arise to lead the revolution.

> A violent era will come and for it we are serving, suffering, and being murdered. Then we, the poor of the earth, will rise up as a large army, a different army, and will march again and will again shoulder rifles. We will march for our liberation; then our death will have meaning. We are the furthest outposts; we stand alone. Our murderers want to destroy us but we will remain alive even if we are long since decayed. We are the first; we are the first.

Riss did not regard war as cataclysmic and inexplicable or as the hellish experience of soldiers. He viewed war as an extension of peacetime society and therefore subject to its structure and functions. To understand the causes of war was held to be impossible without knowledge about the foundation of German society, just as it was impossible to understand German society without knowledge of the whole world. Riss conceived of the arena of war as being much larger than the thousands of acres of battlefield. It extended to the roots of society where power was located and decisions were made and included the working population of the belligerent nations. *Stahlbad Anno 17* more than any other war book went beyond the obvious suffering of the soldier to expose what its author believed to be the constant suffering of man at the hands of an unjust society.

Some Objectivists glorified the war and interpreted it in mythological terms. They recorded the violence of the battlefield but saw in it something quite different from hell, oppression, or an expression of the contradictions of society. From the actions of Germany's manhood in the war they deduced a myth that could serve to resurrect the vitality of the nation. Their narrations of war experience were secondary to the symbols that could be conveyed by them—symbols that bore a striking resemblance to those used by the ideologists of the "conservative revolution."

This group of Objectivists viewed war as the "existential moment" when man grows conscious of his capabilities and exults in being. There was little sympathy for the suffering, starving, and wounded soldiers or concern with the brutality of commanders and the irrationality of death. Man was taking part in a vast adventure and was wrestling with fate in a game in which the most daring were rewarded. Joseph Wehner illustrated this moment as follows: "To Bernhard Buchholz it seemed as if he were flying between heaven and earth. He took part in an attack for the first time and did not yet know that exultation of the male which is stronger than any pleasure. But now he sang in the midst of the assault. He hardly heard the muted rumble of the German shells above him. . . . His chest burned and his eyes shone."

The hero of this, man's greatest drama, was the warrior. He was a model of discipline and adaptability, was accustomed to obey and command, was mindful of his duty, and was able to surround himself with the charisma of the leader or to blend unobtrusively with the community. These paragons of German manhood and virtue instilled the whole army with the spirit of self-sacrifice. The soldiers seemed never to tire of fighting and after forty-four months of war threw themselves against the enemy with the same enthusiasm as in August 1914. Wehner went so far as to maintain that if the spirit of the warrior had been allowed to prevail, instead of the short-sightedness of the old staff officers, the battle of Verdun would have been won.

The writers who gave currency to the symbols of war signifying a new mythology saw in war a purpose and goal. They pictured the German soldier as driven by an idea with a dedication akin to that of the Christian martyr. All his daring and sacrifice, his will and individuality became instruments in the historical life and death struggle of peoples and nations. In the midst of the existential moment the fatherland stood out like the holy grail growing ever stronger in the soldier, forcing its way from his blood to his mind. For these writers it was only a short step from the metaphysical fatherland to the physical empire. The fatherland was the mystique; the *Grossdeutsche* state based on heritage of blood was its concrete counterpart. Wehner spoke of it in terms reminiscent of the programmes of the Pan German League and the shibboleths of nationalist propaganda.

> The empire, the empire and the Middle Ages once

again! Verdun, two hundred years ago it was still a free imperial city. Now we bleed where our ancestors have plowed. The empire, that is the German Empire and it exists wherever we once were. . . . We don't have space, we don't have room. We must go forth knowing and united. Not a drop of our blood must be dissipated among foreign peoples as it has been for hundreds of years. The migration begins anew; we are the outermost wave. And where we stand, there is the German Empire. For me that is the meaning of war.

With such emphasis placed on the worthiness of German national aspirations, it is not surprising to find the enemy depicted as degenerate and inferior. The French were even considered unworthy enemies because their military power rested on black colonial troops who, savages that they were, neither practised nor respected the warrior's code of honour.

These writers attempted to show how German manhood could be cleansed of the heritage of liberalism by a physical and primordial act through which virtues dating from a more glorious period of German history could be recaptured. The picture of war as a heroic and ennobling experience was the end product of skilful and often absorbing narratives that gave the appearance of being factual and impartial. These were not crude works of nationalistic propaganda but subtle confessionals seeking to make the reader believe that he too was part of the purifying events. The war was a prelude leading to Germany's true destiny, and the participants awaited the nation's call. Jünger predicted an era of brutality in which the tiresome debates of shopkeepers, writers, and weaklings would be swept away by a blood-crested tidal wave, in which deeds and swords would carry the day.

Although the interpretation of the war differed among the Objectivists whose approach was descriptive, analytical, or mythological, these differences were blurred in some important respects. A striking quality of the war literature was a similarity of tone asserting itself in spite of the writer's intentions. This gave the impression that all war books were essentially similar; the repetition of subject and setting in the large number of books published reinforced this impression.

The Objectivists seemed to agree that war engendered a marvellous feeling of comradeship among soldiers, and by making it absolute and without limits they elevated it to the status of a myth. Jünger, Stellrecht, Carossa, Remarque, Johannsen, and Renn all pictured camaraderie arising because or in spite of the horrible suffering the men were forced to endure. Even those writers who depicted war mainly as a holocaust implied that things were not so bad. They showed the development of a spirit of equality and fraternity that would have been unthinkable in peacetime. Remarque went so far as to characterize front-line comradeship as a relationship that obliterates all differences of class and education. The writers of a nationalistic bent extended the fraternity of men to include the officers who usually assumed the role of the fatherly figure within the group.

If the image of the good comrade suggested that the war had had its positive side, the portrayal of escapades appealing to the juvenile made war into a first class adventure. As the sale of *Im Westen nichts Neues* began to reach astronomic figures an astute critic pointed out that Remarque's book was filled with incidents representing the wish dreams of the immature. For evidence he pointed to the twenty year olds' Pantagruelian feasting, weeks of personal uncleanliness, beating of their

former sergeant and task-master, moonlight conquest of French women with loaves of bread, and the mishap of a haughty staff officer in the trenches. Such or similar events may actually have taken place, but Remarque endowed his generation of young men with a playfulness and conspiratorial delight certain to make their escapades exciting. Their antics are particularly incongruous considering Remarque's attempt to picture his young men as dehumanized victims of war. Even more remarkable was Jünger's presentation of the German soldier as both warrior and carefree youth. Interspersed throughout his book there were episodes that make one forget there was a war. Jünger recounted that behind the lines there was time for him to read, write, ride horseback, take walks, and start a beetle collection. In his billet in town there was nightly singing and romantic adventure reminiscent of student quarters. At the front there also seemed to have been plenty of time for diversion and entertainment: afternoon coffee hours, wine with supper, reading, chocolates and story telling, and, for exercise and sport, patrols behind the enemy lines.

The purpose of Objectivist war literature was didactic, but the lessons that could be drawn by the reader were often contrary to the intentions of the writers. Most of the Objectivists considered their work to be in the service of pacifism and viewed the war from a historical perspective as an event that must not be allowed to take place again. They hoped that realistic descriptions of violence and human sacrifice would convince the public of the need for universal and perpetual peace. Yet they managed to depict war as an inexorable fate that governs the lives of men. Zweig's Grischa as well as Johannsen's four comrades, Remarque's young men, and private Renn were its victims. It appeared as though destruction rained down on man like an act of providence the cause of which was unknown and the repetition of which rational means would be powerless to prevent. The reader could easily be led to conclude that since war was an emanation of an unknowable fate, conscious struggles for peace would be in vain.

Even those Objectivists who went beyond description to analyse the conditions underlying the war implied that man was powerless. The forces of exploitation and oppression identified by Plivier's and Wolf's sailors and by Riss's soldiers seemed to constitute a system the power of which was unshakable. In showing the causes of war to lie within society these writers seemed to substitute omnipotent economic, political, and social forces for blind fate. Man still remained an object and instrument in the hands of a system he identified and understood without knowing how to control or alter it. Despite Wolfe's aim to reveal the means of carrying out a successful revolution and Riss's desire to incite the youth against war, their work fell short of their propagandistic intentions. Their analysis of the foundations of war abounded in ambiguities so that rather than the need for social revolution it was the failure of the sailors of Cattaro and the soldiers of Stahlbad that left the most lasting impression. It seems that it was easier for these writers to formulate a radical political literary-programme than to carry it out. In their work singlemindedness gave way to dualities and nuances that strengthened artistic and dramatic values and at the same time weakened or counteracted the intended message.

The objective neutrality of many writers was coupled with a tendency indirectly to glorify the war. Descriptions of comradeship, exhilarating adventure, and selflessness in the trenches could easily seem attractive when compared to the boredom and egotism of daily life in peacetime. Writers in the service of nationalistic and conservative ideologies greatly elaborated on the glory of battle. They strove to make the war a rallying point for the revival of German greatness and sought to convince their readers that the heroism of the warrior could serve as a model to guide the nation out of the morass of parliamentary confusion and economic chaos.

In the seething political situation at the time, which momentarily threatened to erupt into open violence and in which clear-cut and simple solutions were demanded by the German public, nationalistic pro-war propaganda had an overwhelming advantage over neutralistic pacifism. (pp. 138-47)

Helmut Gruber, " 'Neue Sachlichkeit' and the World War," in German Life & Letters, Vol. XX, 1966-67, pp. 138-49.

AMERICAN LITERATURE OF WORLD WAR I

WAYNE CHARLES MILLER

[*Miller is an American educator and critic whose works reflect his interests in the military history and ethnic minorities of the United States. In the following excerpt he discusses cultural protest implicit in American war fiction by Thomas Boyd, John Dos Passos, William Faulkner, Ernest Hemingway, Laurence Stallings, Dalton Trumbo, and others.*]

Masses of Americans became directly involved [in World War I] and more than in any previous war they wrote about it. As a group, their novels emerge as a protest against the culture which had led them, so innocent, to the slaughter. Few were politically sophisticated enough to offer alternatives to the economic-political structure they criticized, but an untested Communism often looms as a possible panacea. In any case, for the first time since Melville, American novelists dealt critically with an entire social structure through a consideration of a military situation, and, by and large, they wrote in the mood of the young Melville of *White Jacket.* Only William Faulkner, in *A Fable,* approximates the elegiac tone of *Billy Budd.*

After establishing the idea that most of the World War I novelists are at least somewhat political, it may seem peculiar to begin discussion of them with a consideration of the early work of Ernest Hemingway. On the surface, at least, he seems the least political of any of them, but his subject matter is representative, his style best captures the tone of war-weary disillusionment, and, beneath the surface, political and cultural criticism exists in the work. In a purely literary context, Carlos Baker [in his *Hemingway: The Writer as Artist*] emphasizes the novelist's admitted debt to [Stephen] Crane, and [in his *Ernest Hemingway*] Earl Rovit discovers parallels between him and [Ambrose] Bierce. Compared to the direct impact of the war, however, literary influences seem less significant. In the most perceptive treatment of Hemingway's attitude toward war in general, John Atkins, in *Ernest Hemingway: His Work and Personality,* argues convincingly that for Hemingway war was somehow the most truthful condition of man's existence—a condition that best exemplified the general post-war disenchantment with western world culture.

"War, or more exactly battle, gave Hemingway his real chance to exhibit a world which consisted entirely of things. Millions of things, most of them broken, most of them useless, and filling the spectator with a sense of despair and desolation. . . ." While Atkins admits that Hemingway, as a novelist, may have regarded the war as just another useful landscape or milieu, it seems clear that this particular landscape, with its death, mutilation, destruction, and despair, was the particular one which summed up the author's sense of postwar western world culture. Most things are shattered, broken, and the totality of the conflict had reduced man to minuscule dimensions, dwarfed by the mechanism of his own creation.

Although Hemingway resembles Crane in his description of the war, his intention in the creation of Frederick Henry and Nick Adams is radically different from Crane's intention for Henry Fleming. Crane never permits his protagonist to become fully self-reflective concerning his insignificance within the total structure of the war and the universe, and he never serves as a reliable spokesman for the author's attitudes toward the conflict and the culture that produced it. He is, in the last analysis, a little man in search of social adjustment. In contrast, the Hemingway hero, like his creator, becomes aware of the cultural significance of the war and seeks escape from the absurd conflict in order to attempt a formulation of a meaningful rationale for his existence. In this pattern of involvement, revelation, and escape, he sets a pattern that a number of protagonists of World War I novels follow. Atkins suggests that "Hemingway did more to set the tone for writing about war than any other modern writer," and if one wishes to understand the American novelist's reaction to this first global conflict, one should first consider the tone and the subject matter of *In Our Time, A Farewell to Arms,* and *The Sun Also Rises.*

In the interchapter pieces and in several of the stories of *In Our Time,* Hemingway imagistically presents a number of broken lives and broken things—natural objects sufficient in their totality to suggest a shattered culture: a world, in [J. F. C.] Fuller's words, gone mad. It is an environment in which a column of drunken soldiers, the officer and authority figure drunkest of all and placed anachronistically on horseback, march toward engagement; a world in which a procession of displaced persons, seemingly without end and without beginning, move through rain and mud to nowhere, reminiscent of Bierce's products of war: widows and childless mothers and husbandless wives; a world in which men take pride in building perfect barricades of destruction and in properly killing the men who happen to be the enemy; a world of brutal and apparently pointless executions both in Europe and in the United States; a world in which, back in the heartland of America, two cops, Drevitts and Boyle, kill two Hungarians Boyle mistakes for "wops" in a personal expression of the grander scale nationalistic and bigoted behavior of the European countries. It is a world in which traditional political and social values have lost meaning and so one seeks one's separate peace.

Although Hemingway is normally considered to be decidedly apolitical and his one "political" novel, *To Have and Have Not,* an artistic failure, there are subtle political implications in *In Our Time.* For instance, the sympathetically drawn communist in "The Revolutionist" is in marked contrast to Drevitts and Boyle whose interchapter piece precedes the story. But although he may offer a social theory in opposition to the capitalist world of the munitions manufacturers, Hemingway holds no hope for his success, having his narrator report that "the last I heard of him the Swiss had him in jail near Sion."

Also, in the closing piece of the original *in our time*, "L'Envoi," Hemingway drops a hint that all revolutionaries eventually sell out and that belief in political amelioration is illusion. In that brief story, the revolutionary committee is keeping the king in good whiskey and the queen in roses, and one gets the feeling that these nobles will keep themselves alive and that, finally, there must be change in order that things remain the same. It is true that Hemingway does not make a political "statement," if by that one means propagandistic oversimplification in the name of a cause, but, like Melville's concern for the defeat of the forces of innovation, so Hemingway implies similar concern for his revolutionist and the ideals he embodies. Hemingway, then, is concerned with politics primarily because man is, at least partially, a political animal. (pp. 99-103)

In short stories specifically concerned with the war, such as "In Another Country," "Now I Lay Me," and "A Way You'll Never Be," Hemingway deals with disheartening physical and psychological maiming in which the wounded are trying to learn to live with what has happened to them; and, in "A Natural History of the Dead," he is self-consciously hard-boiled in detailing the various horrors of death—as if he too must write it out of his system in order to get used to it. In any case, a statement in *Green Hills of Africa* reveals how much he valued the war experience: "It was one of the major subjects and certainly one of the hardest to write truly of and those writers who had not seen it were always very jealous and tried to make it seem unimportant, or a disease as a subject, while, really, it was just something quite irreplaceable that they had missed."

In his single major novel directly concerned with the war experience, Hemingway traces Frederick Henry's awakening to this sense of "nothingness," and the World War I world of broken things is the environment in which he makes his discoveries. John W. Aldridge, in *After the Lost Generation: A Critical Study of the Writers of Two Wars,* sees Henry's withdrawal from the retreat after Caporetto as a withdrawal from an absurd political and social structure—from a system no longer defensible. Philip Young [in his *Ernest Hemingway*] identifies Henry as an American culture-hero whose pattern of "complicity, bitterness, escape" approximates the nation's involvement in the European war. Both seem correct, and, as the reevaluation of Hemingway's work continues, it is interesting to note that the validity of the novel is increasingly identified with its depiction of war and not with the love relationship between Catherine Barkley and Henry. George Snell [in his *The Shapers of American Fiction: 1798-1947*] depicts that relationship as outrageously sentimental but respects the treatment of the war. Two critics most favorably inclined toward *A Farewell to Arms,* Malcolm Cowley and Carlos Baker, also seem to judge Hemingway's handling of the war more favorably than his handling of the love relationship. Cowley concludes [in his *Exile's Return: A Literary Odyssey of the 1920's*] that "only *The Red Badge of Courage* and a few short pieces by Ambrose Bierce can be compared with it," and Baker, after somewhat overextendedly describing Frederick as Romeo and Catherine as Juliet, makes good sense in viewing Miss Barkley's death in a larger social context, "associated and interwoven with the whole tragic pattern of fatigue

and suffering, loneliness, defeat and doom, of which the war is itself the broad social manifestation." Leslie Fiedler, while the most critical of the novel's sentimental element, also has respect for the war material: "Hemingway's *A Farewell to Arms* in its earlier chapters captures the sense of disorganization and loss of identity typical of modern war, particularly at a moment of retreat, but quite soon becomes a love story, which is to say, an erotic dream of escape and pure sensuality, so haunted by unconfused guilts that it can only end in death and eternal separation" [*Love and Death in the American Novel*].

So, in the last analysis, it would seem that *A Farewell to Arms* is of particular value insofar as it portrays the war, the individual American's reaction to it, and, by implication, his reaction to the culture that produced the war. In a single pronouncement, Frederick Henry sums up the essential tone of many of the novelists' reactions.

> I was always embarrassed by the words sacred, glorious, and sacrifice and the expression in vain. We had heard them, sometimes standing in the rain almost out of earshot, so that only the shouted words came through, and had read them, on proclamations that were slapped up by billposters over other proclamations, now for a long time, and I had seen nothing sacred, and the things that were glorious had no glory and the sacrifices were like the stockyards at Chicago if nothing was done with the meat except to bury it. There were many words that you could not stand to hear and finally only the names of places had dignity. Certain numbers were the same way and certain dates and these with the names of places were all you could say and have them mean anything. Abstract words such as glory, honor, courage, or hallow were obscene beside the concrete names of villages, the numbers of roads, the names of rivers, the numbers of regiments and the dates.

Implied is the individual's disgust with absurd patriotism, chauvinistic politicians, and a culture that could permit the massive killing in the name of national interest that Henry must become toughened to: "At the start of the winter came the permanent rain and with the rain came the cholera. But it was checked and in the end only seven thousand died of it in the army." Frederick and Catherine may be, in Mr. Fraser's words, "some of the best of the people" insofar as they pursue sexual love as their escape, but, like their prototypes in the earlier "A Very Short Story," they are doomed to be additions to the landscape of broken things and shattered illusions. In Pound's words, the best among them died for "battered books" and "broken statues." They died for that "old bitch gone in the teeth"—yes, that "botched civilization."

Frederick Henry, like most Hemingway heroes, begins a retreat from traditional Christianity and other western world values toward a tough-skinned individuality which protects him from the illusions of that shameful world. When the heroes emerge from this cocoon of personal protection, as Robert Jordan does in *For Whom the Bell Tolls* and Harry Morgan somewhat belatedly does in *To Have and Have Not*, they are, like the revolutionist, inevitably aligned with the forces of innovation and change and in opposition to totalitarianism and capitalism. Just as inevitably, they are destroyed. In *A Farewell to Arms* Henry discovers the troublesome sense of "nothingness" at the center of western world values; Jake

Barnes, crippled by the war, lives with it in *The Sun Also Rises.*

Barnes lives his life according to the forms, however, and is hard working, technically religious, and genuinely romantic. As a traditional figure, he provides the moral focus of the novel, but in a meaningful ironic ploy, Hemingway presents him as emasculated—one might suspect as emasculated as the values he represents. Like them, he has been ruined by the war that ravaged the continent, and Hemingway hints that the real representative of the culture is not Jake Barnes but the composite of homosexuality, nymphomania, and drunkenness that surrounds him and that he abhors. He is a kind of caretaker for Lady Brett Ashley, who, while not gone in the teeth, does suggest a botched civilization. Frederick Hoffman views *The Sun Also Rises* as Hemingway's best war novel, and his insight helps clarify the novelist's intention in creating Adams, Henry, and Barnes. Unlike Crane, whose interest lay in depicting the plight of an average boy under the stresses of war, Hemingway attempts in all three characters the creation of culture-heroes who embody both the sense of western world disenchantment and the emptiness of western world values during and after World War I. However subtly, he criticizes those forces he thinks particularly responsible for that slaughterhouse in Europe: totalitarianism, absurd patriotism, and technically ritualistic but morally ineffectual Christianity. In the military structure of *A Farewell to Arms,* Henry comes in contact with representatives of those forces. The Carabinieri, who would kill him, are the blind and unthinking agents of a blind and unthinking totalitarianism, patriotically doing their duty, and the simple priest, who, like Frederick and Catherine, belongs in an Eden-like simplicity of the Abruzzi, is almost totally ineffectual in the real Europe at war.

Although perhaps the best, Hemingway is not the first American novelist to write of World War I. In fact, John Dos Passos, Thomas Boyd, Willa Cather, E. E. Cummings, Elliot Paul, William Faulkner, Leonard H. Nason, and Laurence Stallings all have works preceding the 1929 publication of *A Farewell to Arms.* Almost all write in the same mood of disenchantment, but most are more overt in their cultural and political criticism. Although Cummings' *The Enormous Room* is one of the most forceful antiwar novels ever written and an indictment of tyranny in any form, it does not deal directly with an American military unit or with the war itself. Alfred Kazin defines Cummings' attitude toward war as "compounded equally of resignation, hatred for all authority, and an almost abstract cynicism," and Norman Friedman correctly describes the thematic center of the work [in his *E. E. Cummings: The Growth of a Writer*]: "What Cummings is really after is implied by the emotional tone of the book, the joy he feels when the individual triumphs over the system which has done its best to destroy him." Much of the poetry suggests a similar theme; inevitably, "I Sing of Olaf Glad and Big" comes to mind.

Although Cummings captures the essential thematic thread that binds most of the World War I novels together and although Hemingway's style best encompasses the tone of disenchantment that results from the war, John Dos Passos, in *Three Soldiers* and *First Encounter,* breaks new ground, and, in effect, establishes the form that most of the novels occasioned by World War II and the Korean War would take. In fact, his concentration on an American unit, representative of various ethnic groups and social strata within United States culture at large, becomes standard for an avalanche of novels out of the two wars.

Joseph Warren Beach may exaggerate its value when he suggests [in his *American Fiction, 1920-1940*]: "*Three Soldiers* was the first important American novel, and one of the first in any language, to treat the War in the tone of realism and disillusion. It made a deep impression, and may be counted the beginning of strictly contemporary fiction in the United States." Certainly the novel had terrific impact and presented the American war effort in a way that shocked the folks back home. While Crane, in the last analysis, may be more ironic than any of the World War I writers, he presents, on the surface, a traditional tale of a young man's initiation and his acceptance of the rite; Dos Passos, and many who follow him, present protagonists who reject the usual initiation in war, and, in so doing, voice protests about the culture as a whole. John H. Wrenn, while pointing out Dos Passos' great debt to Crane, suggests [in his *John Dos Passos*] an important difference in regard to their attitudes toward maturation: "Like Crane, he [Dos Passos] considers the problem of courage of central importance in war as in life. But to Dos Passos the courage that each man must attain is a courage to face life, not death; for life is the ultimate reality." For Dos Passos in *Three Soldiers,* the commitment to life means commitment to personal freedom in the face of the monstrous machine of law and tradition that encloses the individual in the military structure. His protagonist, John Andrews, unlike Henry Fleming, runs from the machine, acts defiantly, and is destroyed. If [U.S. Secretary of War] Elihu Root, as early as 1899, had envisioned the American soldier as a cog in a vast machine, Dos Passos, in 1921, began a campaign in fiction to combat such dehumanization and denial of personal liberty.

Three Soldiers, among other things, is a novel of social statement, and Dos Passos, encompassing little of the complexity of Melville's world, is occasionally guilty of painful oversimplification. He strikes out at the vast machine by detailing the fates of three individuals caught in it: Fuselli, Chrisfield, and John Andrews. Dos Passos emphasizes the thrust of his criticism by meaningfully entitling sections of the book: "Making the Mould," "The Metal Cools," "Machines," and "Rust." All three characters, products of the army, are destroyed by it. The Italian-American, Fuselli, sees the service as providing him with social mobility: "'. . . this war's a lucky thing for me. I might have been in the R. C. Vicker Company's store for five years an' never got a raise. An' here in the army I got a chance to do almost anything'." He hungers for promotion, hoping for a sick corporal's death in order that he may attain his position. In order not to "get in wrong," he accepts what he regards as slavery and avoids those enlisted men of whom the officers are suspicious. Fuselli, like the soldier in Hemingway's "A Very Short Story," ends up with venereal disease and, in addition, the rewards of constant kitchen duty in a labor battalion. He never makes corporal. Thus, the ignorant immigrant is defeated in his efforts to enter the social structure and reap its rewards of status and personal advancement.

Chrisfield, a somewhat dim-witted boy from Indiana, kills an officer who had earlier arranged for his court-martial. After feeling a "warm joy" upon hurling the grenade that kills the man, he discovers the remedy for guilt. "He did not feel lonely any more now that he was marching in ranks again. His feet beat the ground in time with the other feet. He would not have to think whether to go to the right or to the left. He

I

1

We had spent almost three four of our six months at the section
sanitaire, my friend and I, and at the Moment which subsequent
experience served to capitalize had just finished the job of
cleaning and greasing--nettoyer is the convenient French verb--
the chef's own Flivver. Neither of us, as I recollect, were intensely thrilled by this form of service to France, which had constituted
owing to Jupiter pluvius and the tranquility of that section of
the French line wherewith our section was affiliated our donation
and almost unique form of heroism in the service of France.
Of course if I wanted to I could write a thrilling enough dairy
of things that almost didn't fail to occur, inserting voluminous accounts of hair-raising gas scares, trips by night with
wounded poilus along roads infested with thundering ravitaille
ment trains coming in the opposite direction--guns and groceries
are generally brought up by night to the trenches--occassional
ponderings on the ultimate location of certain merrily whistling
obus, etc.etc. But America is crammed at the present moment with
many conducteurs volontaires of the ambulance service whose
experiences (according to themselves, who should certainly
somebody said, know best) far surpass my own
comparatively measly thrills, that I will not presume upon the
thrill-saturated readers in that particular. My tale is of othe
matters, and begins, as I started to explain with the cleaning
of the chief's peculiar Fliv., said Fliv. being dirtier than
herein like ourselves might have expected an cold as we viewed
the spectacle before we got through.

I had washed up--do not forget this, reader, when you hear of
subsequent proceedings--and was strolling carelessly from the
cook wagon toward the tent which housed our huddling forms by
night, munching a historic morseau de chocolat, when a spick not
to say span gentleman in a suspiciously quiet uniform allowed
himself to be driven up to the bureau in a Renault whose pain-
ful cleanliness shamed my recent efforts. Two French soldiers(as I assumed) in tin derbies formed the
stranger's retinue. This must be a general at least, I thought,
regretting the extremely undress character of my uniform at the
moment, which consisted of overalls and a cigarette.
The gentleman allighted, received a conventional welcome from
the chef and the French officer who accompainied our section for
translatory reasons, and betook myself with all haste to the

Typescript of E.E. Cummings's The Enormous Room.

would do as the others did." This loss of individuality and morality, for Dos Passos, seems the system's ultimate achievement: the reduction of the human being to the role of automaton in a machine of death. Chrisfield is perhaps the most brutalized. Mechanically, he seeks sexual release and the enjoyment of killing; through most of his appearances later in the novel he seems hardly conscious. Fuselli remains self-reflective enough to occasionally feel lost in the machine, but the artist, John Andrews, is most aware of the debilitating effects of army life and so becomes the moral center of the novel, the focus of Dos Passos' antiwar and antimilitary statements.

"Andrews thought suddenly of all the tingling bodies constrained into the rigid attitudes of automatons in uniforms like this one: of all the hideous force of making men into machines." He sees himself as a slave in a brutal system and would risk death to escape that degradation. Throughout, he pictures the men as automatons and sums up his feelings by suggesting that the Army made "the warm sentient bodies into coarse automatons who must be kept busy, lest they grow restive, till killing time began again." As a composer, he wishes to present in music the "thwarted lives" and "the miserable dullness of industrialized slaughter," and there can be little doubt that Dos Passos dedicated his novel to the same task. Like Hemingway, however, he maintains little aesthetic distance between himself and his hero, and Andrews often seems altogether too romantically conceived and unduly naïve. Wilbur Frohock [in his *The Novel of Violence in America*] sees him as paranoid in his attitude toward the Army, insofar as Andrews views it as "one vast conspiracy to take away his liberty." At times, his naïveté seems unbelievable, and he becomes somewhat histrionic in his refusal to contact the authorities after his encounter with the brutal military police, and his escape in the river to an idyllic respite with Genevieve Rod. This pattern of action directly parallels Frederick Henry's escape to Catherine, and, like Hemingway, Dos Passos seems more interested in his hero as a symbolic culture-hero than as an individual character. Just as Thoreau bathed in Walden Pond as a religious exercise, both Andrews and Henry undergo baptisms into new identities through their plunges into rivers. They emerge confirmed in their individualism and in their opposition to the culture.

Frederick Hoffman points out [in his *The Twenties*] that the army in *Three Soldiers* is "a machine for which traditional values no longer had a meaning." Andrews, in fleeing the microcosm of the military unit, like Frederick Henry, flees western world values in general. Early in the novel, Dos Passos indicates that Andrews, in entering the army, wished to submerge his personality in the mass, and is racing from an American society for which he has great distaste and in which he is unable to find happiness. Of course, he finds in the army a reflection of the culture he flees, and Dos Passos characterizes that culture as brutal, prejudiced, and hypocritically Christian. Violence and anti-Italian and anti-Jewish feelings are frequent, but Dos Passos concentrates most on what he and his protagonist regard as the moral bankruptcy of Christianity. The representatives of the religion, the YMCA men, are, without exception, stupid, absurd, or downright malevolent. One of them remarks that he has discovered the essence of America in the army and reminds Andrews that the war is a Christian undertaking. In a hospital talk, the Reverend Mr. Skinner announces that the allies should have crushed Germany completely without the least thought that Germany is also a "Christian" country. An-

drews asks a "Y" man why he so totally hates the Huns: " 'Because they are barbarians, enemies of civilization. You must have enough education to know that,' said the 'Y' man, raising his voice angrily. 'What Church do you belong to?' " After this particular revelation, Andrews thinks: "So was civilization nothing but a vast edifice of sham, and the war, instead of its crumbling, was its fullest and most ultimate expression." Christianity, thus, becomes a part of a decadent tradition, devoid of meaning, and servant to nationalistic unleashings of power. In a conversation with Genevieve Rod, Andrews dismisses the whole tradition in a manner similar to Frederick Henry's: " 'Oh, those long Roman words, what millstones they are about men's necks!' " Thus, he implies, it is in the wartime army that one discovers the truth about the culture, and what he discovers is organized brutality, sanctioned by Christianity, within a system of autocratic control, supported by arbitrary laws and brutal police. Andrews foresees the crumbling of the system, and his heroics at the end are symbolic of the honest individual's desire to avoid complicity in a culture he sees as morally corrupt.

Just as *Three Soldiers* resembles *A Farewell to Arms*, Dos Passos' earlier novel, *First Encounter*, resembles the war stories of *In Our Time*, containing vignettes of war and men at war and concentrating upon the cruelty and absurdity of the conflict itself. The hero, Martin Howe, parallels Nick Adams, and Tom Randolph serves the same purposes as the companion who frequently accompanies Nick. Howe, who epitomizes American political innocence, early in the novel envisions the crumbling of all the evils in the world; the rest of the novel deals primarily with the crumbling of the illusions held by these young men from the provinces of the new world. After seeing wounded men for the first time, Howe exclaims, " 'God, it's so hideously stupid!' "; his companion, upon seeing a man with his sexual organs shot away, concurs: " 'Oh, God, it's too damned absurd! An arrangement for mutual suicide and no damned other thing . . .'." After discovering that the allies are guilty of as much atrocity as the "Huns," they, and others they meet, begin to see the war as solemnly inane, viciously stupid, and idiotic. Soon, they stop thinking of it as an engagement among nations representing different moral points of view; rather, it becomes the ultimate expression of a corrupt civilization, engineered somehow by a conspiracy of interests:

> "Think, man, think of all the oceans of lies through all the ages that must have been necessary to make this possible! Think of this new particular vintage of lies that has been so industriously pumped out of the press and the pulpit. Doesn't it stagger you?"

> Martin nodded.

There is a sense of national tragedy when, in a conversation among Howe, Randolph, and some Frenchmen, Dos Passos suggests that the United States has become involved in the conspiracy:

> "In exchange for all the quiet and the civilization and the beauty of ordered lives that Europeans gave up in going to the new world we gave them opportunity to earn luxury, and, infinitely more important, freedom from the past, that gangrened ghost of the past that is killing Europe to-day with its infection of hate and greed and murder."

> "America has turned traitor to all that, you see; that's the way we look at it. Now we're a military

nation, an organized pirate like France and England and Germany."

After discussing the loss of individual freedom within the context of an organized conspiracy concocted by industrial and political interest groups, they offer the toast, " 'To Revolution, to Anarchy, to the Socialist state . . .'." But, just as Hemingway has his revolutionist in the hands of the Swiss police and his Greek king living on in the garden of roses, so, too, Dos Passos offers little hope for change. All of the young men, who, somewhat drunkenly, discussed social amelioration and drank to change, end up destroyed or disenchanted.

In summing up Dos Passos' contribution to the tradition of the American military novel, it must be stated that he was the first novelist since Melville to use the military novel as a vehicle for social analysis and political statement. *First Encounter* and *Three Soldiers* may lack the sober objectivity of *Billy Budd,* but the conclusions Dos Passos draws are remarkably similar to Melville's. John Andrews and Billy meet similar fates at the hands of an organized society whose representative is the military structure. One killed, the other imprisoned, both are victims of a man-of-war world in which neither is able to live. Both are sympathetically drawn and their pathetic fates are reflections of lost illusions and ends to innocence. In his preface to the 1945 reissue of *First Encounter,* Dos Passos indirectly reveals that in Andrews and Howe he had projected the whole sense of shattered American ideals and naïveté. An older man, his own political views radically changed, he comments on the political discussions of the last pages of *First Encounter:*

> Reading it over I find the chapter scrappy and unsatisfactory, but I am letting it stand because it still expresses, in the language of the time, some of the enthusiasms and some of the hopes of young men already marked for slaughter in that year of enthusiasms and hopes beyond other years, the year of the October Revolution.
>
> It was this sanguine feeling that the future was a blank page to write on, focusing first about the speeches of Woodrow Wilson and then about the figure of Lenin, that made the end of the last war so different from the period we are now entering. Perhaps the disillusionments of the last quarter of a century have taught us that there are no short cuts to a decent ordering of human affairs, that the climb back out of the pit of savagery to a society of even approximate justice and freedom must necessarily be hard and slow.

Thomas Boyd's *Through the Wheat,* published two years after *Three Soldiers,* is inferior to its predecessor in almost all respects. Boyd takes some petulant pop-shots at the YMCA men but fails to create the sense that they are representative of a whole religious tradition. His hero, William Hicks, moves from the pastoral setting of a northern Michigan farmhouse through one horrifying experience after another until, finally, his soul numb, he walks with his platoon to probable death. He functions as a representative of all those who underwent the same process. Boyd does not develop him fully, however, and he is two-dimensional, flat, and conventional—like all other characters in the novel. For instance, little is revealed concerning his relationships with home, with women, or even with the other men in his unit. Near the end of the novel, Boyd has his hero comment on American involvement in Europe, and, in so doing, suggests that it spells an end to American innocence: " 'The point is, the French hate the En-

glish and the English hate the Americans and the Americans hate the Germans, and where the hell is it all goin' to end?' " That statement is about as profound as Boyd ever gets, and, all in all, the novel is not particularly distinguished. Leonard H. Nason's *Chevrons* is even less so, merely offering detailed depictions of some of the difficulties of army life in an effort to prove that war is not a very pleasant experience.

A number of American women wrote of the war with varying degrees of success. All are outside the mainstream of the World War I novel, primarily because of their general lack of intimate knowledge of the conflict. Edith Wharton's *A Son at the Front* is more concerned with psychological relations between father and son and with life in Paris than with the war itself, and Willa Cather's *One of Ours,* while more explicit on the subject of conflict, is really more concerned with the moral and cultural desolation of the American midwest. Mary Lee's *It's a Great War!* is a hodgepodge of experiences that detail the difficulties and joys of being an American nurse in Europe, but, except for the presentation of some of the brutally wounded, is hardly concerned with the war. Perhaps Mary Raymond Shipman Andrews epitomizes the worst of World War I writing, filling her novels with bathos and sentimentality.

In one of the stories of *In Our Time,* "Soldier's Home," Hemingway deals with the problems of the returned veteran's difficulty in readjusting to a value system that now seems out of step with his experience. The returned veterans of William Gilmore Simms and Hamlin Garland faced, primarily, problems of economic adjustment. Hemingway's protagonist, Krebs, who "went to the war from a Methodist college in Kansas," simply cannot readjust to the simple Christianity of the provincial midwest. In the war and the European experience he has discovered that he needs nothing that his former environment has to offer him: not marriage with one of the nice girls nor his father's bribe of the car nor his mother's sentimental love nor traditional Christian values. It is clear that he regards the beliefs of the culture as shams.

Laurence Stallings' *Plumes,* an excellent minor novel of social protest, also deals with the returned veteran but in a more traditional manner than Hemingway did. Richard Plume, wounded seven times, returns to his family filled with antagonism for the stupidity of war. His first words to his wife are, " 'God forgive me for my folly',", and he attacks even those he loves when they romanticize war. His problems are at least partially economic, returning home to outrageous rents, high prices, corrupt politics, and to a religion that ignores social justice. In short, he returns to a corrupt society enjoying a prosperity based on the war itself, a depiction of the American economic system common today among those concerned with the power of the Pentagon. *Plumes* is an unpretentious novel that expresses, in terms of a troubled and despairing returned American, an indictment of war and of American society. William Faulkner also deals with the situation of the returned veteran in an early and generally unappreciated work, *Soldier's Pay.*

Filled with echoes from Pater, Wilde and others, Faulkner's novel is as pretentious as Stalling's is not, but both indict a nation unappreciative of a soldier's sacrifice. While differing sharply concerning the book's artistic merit, Richard Chase, Joseph Warren Beach, and Alfred Kazin view it as a lost-generation novel, and William Van O'Connor [in his *The Tangled Fire of William Faulkner*] states one of its important themes as an expression of that generation: "Patriotism, the title implies, is meaningless in a world of selfishness and inevitable defeat." Donald Mahon, the returned veteran, has suffered such nearly total physical destruction that he is hardly more than a vegetable. Chase [in his *The American Novel and Its Tradition*] sees him as the first of Faulkner's doomed young men, but thinks that he is not fully created: ". . . he is so mortally wounded and so vaguely understood by the author that he is hardly more than an inanimate object." But it seems Faulkner's intention to present him, not as a character, but as the symbolic center of the novel—the symbol of a whole generation of American young men destroyed by the war.

As Hemingway so often does, Faulkner splits the novel's characters into two groups: those who have been touched by the war and violence and so understand the significance of Mahon, and those who have not had such experience and so lack understanding. Those who understand are Joe Gilligan, Margaret Powers, Emmy, and the Negro woman, Callie. Olga Vickery, in *The Novels of William Faulkner: A Critical Interpretation,* suggests that only those characters with direct experience of the war understand Mahon. Emmy is one of the exceptions to that rule. In fact, it is in her appreciation of his loss that Faulkner best emphasizes the theme of American innocence shattered by the war. She remembers her former lover as vital, innocent, guiltless, faun-like: " 'He wouldn't never have a hat or a coat, and his face was like—it was like he ought to live in the woods'." Also, her recollection of their love making reveals it as natural, uninhibited—full of youth, spontaneity, and life. Contrasted with Emmy is Mahon's fiancée, Cecily Saunders, who, as a type more fully realized in Temple Drake in *Sanctuary,* is superficial, incapable of compassion, and finally, as her elopement with George Farr indicates, interested only in her own sexual gratification. Cecily is Mahon's principal betrayer, but there are others. He has, of course, been betrayed by the whole cultural illusion that the United States entered the war to save the world for democracy; his father, a minister, betrays him in not recognizing his implied responsibility for his son's condition; and the townspeople betray him insofar as he merely becomes an amusement for them, the subject of their gossip.

As so frequently happens in Faulkner's work, a Dilsey-like Negro woman, existing outside the white man's Christian culture and a victim of it, sums up the central experience of the novel: " 'Donald, baby, look at me. Don't you know who dis is? Dis yo' Callie whut use ter put you ter bed, honey. Look here at me. Lawd, de white folks done ruint you, but nummine, yo' mammy gwine look after her baby'." "De white folks," with their European heritage, had made a war, and the destruction of Mahon, as a symbol of American youth and vitality, was the natural outcome of American involvement.

What Hemingway had accomplished in his psychological portrait of Krebs, Faulkner suggests in the symbolic destruction of Mahon. Mrs. Powers comments on its tragic significance: " 'That man that was wounded is dead and there is another person, a grown child. It's his apathy, his detachment, that's so terrible. He doesn't seem to care where he is nor what he does'." Whereas Hemingway left his story open-ended, however, Faulkner wishes to portray Mahon's complete defeat, and he does so, near the end of the novel, in Januarius Jones' seduction of Emmy. Faulkner somewhat romantically suggests that the gallant Mahon is dying and portrays in the Snopes-like Jones the ultimate victory of the pa-

tient and the cunning. The taps played for Mahon at the moment of the seduction seem to commemorate not only his personal death but also the death of a nation's youthful dreams.

> Emmy's sobbing died away: she knew no sensation save that of warmth and languorous contentment, emptiness, even when Jones raised her face and kissed her. "Come, Emmy," he said, raising her by the armpits. She rose obediently, leaning against him warm and empty, and he led her through the house and up the stairs to her room. Outside the window, afternoon became abruptly rain, without warning, with no flapping of pennons nor sound of trumpet to herald it.
>
> (The sun had gone, had been recalled as quickly as a usurer's note and the doves fell silent or went away. The Baptist dervish's Boy Scout lipped in his bugle, sounding taps.)

This sense of pointless and unredeemed destruction is also present in several of Faulkner's short stories. "Crevasse," "Victory," and "Ad Astra" conjure up reminiscences of Eliot's *The Waste Land* and Hemingway's *The Sun Also Rises,* particularly in their presentation of the dessicated landscape of war and war's effects upon the consciousness of those involved. In addition, the Subadar in "Ad Astra" seems to be in a line of disenchanted observers that runs from Hemingway's Count Mippipopolous to the old man in the brothel in *Catch-22.* In "All the Dead Pilots," Faulkner has a narrator maimed by the war relate the events surrounding a death as pointless as Mahon's: the death of John Sartoris—the death that precipitates the action of the first Yoknapatawpha novel, *Sartoris.* It is in the story "Turnabout," however, that Faulkner seems to voice his most pointed antagonism concerning the war. After hearing of the death of a brave and youthful English officer, the American Captain Bogard wishes while on a bombing run that he could kill all those responsible for the war. "Then his hand dropped and he zoomed, and he held the aeroplane so, in its wild snarl, his lips parted, his breath hissing, thinking: 'God! God! If they were all there—all the generals, the admirals, the presidents and the kings—theirs, ours—all of them'." This antagonism toward a structure regarded as responsible for the war will be further developed in Faulkner's final presentation of the conflict in the allegory of *A Fable.*

The hero of Dalton Trumbo's *Johnny Got His Gun* never makes it home, but Joe Bonham, left by the war faceless, limbless, without identity, emerges, like Mahon, as the ultimate product of war: the ruined innocent youth. Enclosed in bandages, capable only of conversations with himself, he attacks the same abstract words that Frederick Henry and John Andrews attacked, making a more forceful statement for pacifism than either of his predecessors had accomplished. One realizes how far one is from Cooper's romanticism when Trumbo has his hero speak about dying for a cause:

> There's nothing noble in death. What's noble about lying in the ground and rotting? What's noble about having your legs and arms blown off? What's noble about being an idiot? What's noble about being blind and deaf and dumb? What's noble about being dead? Because when you're dead mister it's all over. It's the end. You're less than a dog less than a rat less than a bee or an ant less than a white maggot crawling around on a dungheap. You're dead mister and you died for nothing.

In addition to its pacifism, *Johnny Got His Gun* is also the most class conscious of the World War I novels. Joe Bonham thinks of himself as one of "the little guys" who, throughout history, are victimized by those who control the economies and the politics of nations. He specifically links the United States to the Mediterranean past when he compares the American soldier with the slaves rowing on that sea, the slaves of Carthage and Rome, and the slaves who built the pyramids, and concludes that the only hope for social amelioration lies in class warfare and not in warfare among nations. He envisions himself as the perfect picture of the future and he hopes to serve as a warning to those who follow him, to prevent the powerful few from again causing war.

> To fight that war they would need men and if men saw the future they wouldn't fight. So they were masking the future they were keeping the future a soft quiet deadly secret. They knew that if all the little people all the little guys saw the future they would begin to ask questions. They would ask questions and they would find answers and they would say to the guys who wanted them to fight they would say you lying thieving sons-of-bitches we won't fight we won't be dead we will live we are the world we are the future and we will not let you butcher us no matter what you say no matter what speeches you make no matter what slogans you write. Remember it well we let we we are the world we are what makes it go round we make bread and cloth and guns we are the hub of the wheel and the spokes and the wheel itself without us you would be hungry naked worms and we will not die.

Johnny Got His Gun is not the best of the World War I novels, and Trumbo is frequently guilty of artistic and political oversimplification; yet, it deals forthrightly with those political considerations hinted at by Hemingway, dealt with generally by Dos Passos, and touched upon by Boyd, Faulkner, and Stallings: that an end to the constant of warfare in the western world lay in resistance to traditional economic and political structure.

John Dos Passos, in *Three Soldiers,* had partially initiated the tradition in American war novels of analyzing in detail various members of a single military unit. Two novelists in the thirties, William E. March Campbell and Hervey Allen, imitate that technique. Allen's *It Was Like This: Two Stories of the Great War* is the less successful of the two, containing a shocking scene or two of Americans enjoying the killing of Germans and a rather heavy-handed initiation of an American innocent named William Henry Virgin.

Campbell's *Company K* is an infinitely better novel, supplying an adequate array of points of view and capturing in vivid detail an entire unit's disenchantment with the war and its country's involvement in it. Contained in it is criticism of Christianity more profound than the petulance of Boyd and Allen. At one point, a captain orders his men to slaughter German prisoners, and, shortly thereafter, orders them to attend church services. In a comic aside, his YMCA representatives supply woman-impersonators rather than have American boys mix with French women. As in Heller's *Catch-22,* Campbell's men are at the mercy of experimenting doctors, and, like Melville, he presents military justice as cruel and expedient. Like Crane, he seems to conclude that all soldiers are prisoners, controlled by inhuman laws and absurd traditions. The more educated members of the company see the war as "brutal and degrading" and common soldiers as "pawns shoved about to serve the interests of others." Campbell's

Unknown Soldier is unknown because, lying on barbed wire with his entrails dripping out, he destroys his dog-tags, letters, and everything else that might identify him in order that his body would not be returned to the States and be fawned over by hypocrites. Those members of Company K who live through the war and return home meet defeat in one form or another, and Campbell makes clear that the war experience is ultimately responsible.

Thus, Campbell, like Hemingway, Dos Passos, Trumbo, and Stallings, uses a novel about the war as a vehicle of protest—a protest not directed at a specific political party or theory, but a protest against the hypocrisy of an entire culture, with particular emphasis upon Christian religious hypocrisy as underpinning all the others. Private Yancey, in *Company K,* conjectures that, "If the common soldiers of each army could get together by a river bank and talk things over calmly, no war could possibly last as long as a week."

Novelists were not alone in this naïve hope, but World War II waited in the wings to dispel it. From the vantage point of the post-World-War-II world, William Faulkner published in 1954 a retrospective novel, *A Fable,* imposing a Christ myth on the World War I experience, and, in effect, showing Campbell's Private Yancey what would happen should the common soldiers of opposing sides attempt to call an end to war. While the main thrust of the social criticism contained in the World War I novels was aimed at economic and religious traditions, particularly the hypocrisies of institutionalized Christianity, *A Fable,* like *Billy Budd,* suggests the ultimate victory of authority and tradition over innovation—in this case the innovation of trying to apply the pacifist social teachings of primitive Christianity. The obvious allegory of the corporal as Christ is often annoying, but, in its summing up of postwar disenchantment, the novel is often profound. The corporal's relationship with his father, the General, resembles Billy's relationship with Vere, and he is rejected for much the same reason as Vere rejects Billy.

Irving Malin comments [in his *William Faulkner: An Introduction*]: "The General admires the courage of his son, and he sympathizes with his desire to help people. But he feels that most people need the strength of authority to direct their actions. Like Mr. Compson, the General sees the folly and weakness of men, their motivation for wanting to be led. Thus he firmly believes that he is actually helping humanity, and he refuses to accept his son's philosophy." Peter Swiggart compares Vere and the Marshall, and in commenting on Faulkner's attitude toward the French military figure perhaps offers a parallel to Melville's attitude toward his Englishman:

> In complementary opposition to the idealistic Christ-figure is the French commander of the Allied armies, who understands and appreciates the Corporal's humanistic message, but nevertheless feels compelled to crucify him. Like Captain Vere in Melville's *Billy Budd,* the old Marshall is saddened by his awareness of incompatibility between personal human values and a corrupt human society. However, Faulkner's character acts not out of a sense of duty but out of his author's paradoxical conviction that the two forces are only superficially opposed, that the Corporal's crucifixion is the best way of causing his martyrdom and thus confirming the value of his mission.

Faulkner seems to say that, like Christ and Billy Budd, the

Corporal achieves religious transcendence but has little effect upon the actions of men and nations. [According to Irving Howe in his *William Faulkner: A Critical Study*], "A secret conference is arranged between the Allied and German generals, which decides that ordinary soldiers must never be allowed, in violation of all the rules, to end a war at their will." The powerful representative of authoritarianism and tradition, the Marshall, inevitably triumphs over the figure of change and innovation, the Corporal. Dos Passos, Trumbo, Campbell, and others, even in presenting the most destructive effects of war, offered their novels as testaments of horror, and, in so doing, expressed some hope for change. One feels that Faulkner would value them as representatives of the Corporal's message, but *A Fable* is testament that such hope is doomed to failure. In *Soldier's Pay* Faulkner dramatized Mahon as war's ultimate product, but by 1954 he knew that World War II and the small wars in its aftermath had produced a multitude of Mahons, and the United States was inextricably involved in the traditional alignments and realignments of European diplomacy and militarism. The novelists of World War II would not react to the country's participation with such naïveté, and would treat the war as, more or less, a normal expression of the culture. (pp. 103-28)

> *Wayne Charles Miller, "World War I and the Novel of Cultural Protest," in his* An Armed America, Its Face in Fiction: A History of the American Military Novel, *New York University Press, 1970, pp. 93-130.*

STANLEY COOPERMAN

[*Cooperman is an American poet and critic. In the following excerpt, he discusses the reactions to combat expressed in American novels of the First World War.*]

In Leonard Nason's *Sergeant Eadie* the protagonist wonders "what kind of a war was this anyway, with no enemy? He wanted to see some of them, to shoot off his pistol at them." Nason's book, in no way a novel of protest, reflects the fact that expectations of a "good fight" were basic to American military attitudes at the onset of World War I. Professional soldiers, even noncoms like Eadie, found all too suddenly that they had been "polishing their pistols" in vain; Eadie, indeed, finds that under his new military environment the chief task, even virtue, for a man is to "find a good, deep cellar." Certainly the impact of technological warfare was by no means confined to draftees and volunteers; the professional soldier no less than his amateur counterpart was disgusted by a war which rendered the facts of military life obsolete. Hence Urquhart, in [William March's] *Company K,* after "thirty years as a professional soldier" and after watching "the reactions of many men to pain, hunger, and death," takes back from France a bitterness equal to that of any disillusioned idealist, a bitterness resulting both from the shattering of the combat-as-a-proving-ground idea, and a close view of the politics within mass warfare. "There should be a law," Urquhart says, "in the name of humanity, making mandatory the execution of every soldier who has served on the front line and managed to escape death there."

The transitional nature of the American army (an essentially nineteenth-century establishment plunged, with an impact that shocked its own leaders, into a twentieth-century war environment) created moments of absurdity as well as horror, and both qualities proved to be major resources of the post-war novel. Dutch, for example, in Elliot Paul's *Impromptu,* is officially given the rank of "Horseshoer" and is humiliated when "a comrade with a talent for drawing made a cartoon of Dutch nailing a horseshoe on the Major's Dodge car." But only in training camp did such episodes seem amusing; in the front line, where officers and men alike were still expecting "horseshoes," death itself took on the element of absurdity. The reaction of many men was the laughter of a rictus.

In [John Dos Passos's *First Encounter,* 1945, first published as *One Man's Initiation,* 1920] the view of the war as an Alice-in-Wonderland situation, as a "solemn inanity" of both life and death, resembles the descriptions also to be found in virtually every novel of the war except those written for purposes of outright propaganda. So great was the gulf between military theory and practice (as between political rhetoric and reality), that a writer like Cummings was to give up direct protest altogether and use a deceptively casual, metaphoric mockery throughout *The Enormous Room* (itself a symbolic enactment of the Crusade): "Whistling joyously to myself," he writes, "I took three steps which brought me to the door end. The door was massively made, all of iron and steel. . . . It delighted me. The can excited my curiosity. . . . At the bottom reposefully lay a new human *t . . d.*"

The horror, however, cannot be underestimated, even—or especially—for those involved with a belief in war as an exercise in manhood. "We lay there like newly castrated sheep," says a soldier in *Company K*—a novel written by an author who had himself earned the Distinguished Service Cross. And Bayard Schindel, in *The Golden Pilgrimage,* typifies postwar attitudes toward mechanical combat, giving a vivid emotional portrait of the disgust aroused in a professional soldier by a war he could no longer respect:

> War had become the profession of the mechanic, a person in greasy overalls who merely worked the machines that killed better men. . . . It was a coward's way of making war, this crouching in sewer excavations and daring the other fellow, who is crouching in a similar excavation 200 yards away, to stick his head above the earth. . . . To hell with this machine war, he thought, this soulless grubbing in the dirt.

But the Uncle Toby complex died hard. Obsessed with the Winchester-on-the-wall frontier tradition, or with military romanticism personified by Teddy Roosevelt, Americans remained unperturbed by news of unparalleled casualties in Europe. Richard Plume, in [Laurence Stallings' novel *Plumes*], scion of a southern family with a history of military achievement dating back to the Revolutionary War ("there was not a coward among them"), is exposed to the martial rejoicing of his father, who—after congratulating his son upon enlisting—opens his own scrapbook: "There he was [as a member of the "Fulton Light Hussars"], white infantry cross-belts over a blue pouter's chest, epaulettes burnished, wide crimson sash bellied faultlessly and shako at the faintest angles. . . . He would give his soul to be with his boy and watch his face the first time Richard went 'over the top.' . . ."

What going "over the top" actually meant was a mystery to the vast majority of the American public, and it remained a mystery until returning veterans began writing books. Only then would a sense of World War I fighting be brought home dramatically to the American mind. For novelists like Edith Wharton (*A Son at the Front,* 1923), or Willa Cather (*One of*

Ours, 1922) had pictured the experience as something of a cross between the Alamo and Bunker Hill. That military officers on their way to France in 1917 had been under the same impression is indicated by the fact that the Germans often regarded the action of United States troops (the Marines at the Marne, for example) with a mixture of awe, hatred, and pity; German military commentators at the time, indeed, felt that such action could only be the result of total ignorance. Just as Hervey Allen describes [in *Toward the Flame*] the administrative chaos and poor liaison that heavily increased American casualties, so Thomas Boyd, in *Through the Wheat,* portrays the gradual wearing away of soldiers—even good soldiers like Hicks—under conditions of total attrition, with direct combat the exception rather than the rule. In Boyd's novel a visiting general addresses a battalion consisting mostly of replacements and proclaims with heavy rhetoric that "you" have shown that "you" cannot be beaten by the Hun. Hicks then remarks:

> "But it all seems so damned ridiculous. Take our going over the other day. A full battalion starting off and not even a fifth of them coming back. And what did they do? What did we do? We never even saw a German. They just laid up there and picked us off—direct hits with their artillery every time. . . . Think of being sent out to get killed, and the person who sends you not knowing where you're going. . . . It'd be all right if we could go up and clean things up with one big smash, but . . . you go up and come back, go up and come back, until you get knocked off. . . .
>
> "Where the hell is it all going to end? Gimme another drink."

Having begun his journey anxious for combat and proud of his "marksmanship badge," Hicks—like Irwin in *Impromptu*—finds battle in which "nobody knew what they were doing," and artillery barrages exploding "like bubbles bursting through the scum of a great cauldron." The similes used most often by World War I novelists to describe combat convey a mixture of inanity and sordidness, indignity and a sense of personal violation—like the castor oil torture perfected in World War II by Italian Fascists, who understood only too well the double death suffered by a man dripping away his life along with his bowels. It is this quality of personal violation by death which, again, accounts for the sense of physical or psychological emasculation so often evoked by the novelists.

If patriots found the nature of technological war difficult to imagine, they found the results impossible to stomach. "The wounds and scars of ancient warfare," L. L. Bernard points out in *War and Its Causes,* "were regarded as evidence of courage and therefore counted as badges of honor. But the disfigurements of modern warfare are looked upon with aversion, and their bearers are in large measure disqualified socially in the struggle for existence, their economic efficiency is weakened and their social acceptance diminished." Such "aversion" provides the dramatic unity of Stallings' *Plumes* and makes the ballroom scene in Faulkner's *Soldiers' Pay* so effective. "All your suffering," says Gary to Richard in the former novel, "comes to exactly the same thing that might have been gained from a fall under a freight train." And in *Company K,* Mrs. Steiner, determined to do her bit by helping a few brave boys, says to a nurse: "We want you to send soldiers wounded in action . . . but nothing gruesome, you understand: nothing really revolting or gruesome."

The impact of twentieth-century fire power on the American troops first exposed to it helped produce the combination of absurdity, protest, and numbness which were to become characteristics of the antihero in the post-World War I novel. American experience, indeed, was perhaps all the more violent because Americans lacked the expensive but thoroughgoing education provided by the early years of the war; the British and French soldiers who had suffered initial impact had already been consumed, and their replacements or survivors had, by 1917, some understanding of the machine to which their lives and deaths were being committed. Not so with the Americans, who had virtually no knowledge of the machine at all. "All the men disappeared; that is, the French did," Allen writes of a sudden artillery barrage. "The Yanks went wandering around like a plumbers' picnic until they had enough men killed off to get wise."

What Herbert Warren described as the "derelict rubbish" of the World War I battlefield ("death unredeemed, death with . . . no hint of heroism, none of heroic action, little even of heroic passion, just death, helpless, hopeless, pointing to nothing but decomposition, decay, disappearance, anéantissement, reduction of the fair frame of life to nothingness") received detailed testimony in the American war novels, even those novels—William Scanlon's *God Have Mercy on Us,* for example—which were not "protest" books as such. A collation of the more lurid descriptions—decapitations, castrations, remnants of uniforms and anatomy cascading over soldiers still hiding in their holes, pieces of the cook being blown into the very coffee he has just brewed—such details would be out of place in the present study. It must, however, be emphasized that the reaction to horror, indecency, squalor, chaos, and filth was especially violent in the work of American novelists precisely because of the more naïve expectation, and subsequent impact, of the American experience.

No less shocking than technological combat for American troops was trench strategy and a battle area which had taken on all the attributes of an open burial ground. The trenches running almost completely across Europe were, as Boyd remarks, "gigantic latrines built for monsters": lice, boredom, the stench of sewerage and unburied or half-buried corpses, trench rats, the thick, infested mud—these were in some ways even more shattering to initial expectations than machine fire power. Words like "putrefaction," "stench," "decay," "nausea," "infested" are reiterated in the war novels, and for good reason: one remembers Zorn [in Theodore Fredenburgh's *Soldiers March!*], a "good" soldier, tasting the Glories of Battle by vomiting into his gas mask and sitting with "the filthy stuff slopping about his mouth" all during a barrage. Fredenburgh describes the front line, where "patrols skirmished amid the putrefaction of the valley":

> On all sides lay great holes, half-filled with water. The chalky soil had been churned and rechurned until its vitals were spewed to the surface. Fragments of stained and rotten uniforms projected from the ground. The dirty bones of corpses reached despairingly from the soil that gave them no rest. . . .
>
> On the floor of the valley a sickly stream flowed. Its banks of yellow mud looked slimy and unclean in the sun. As far as the eye could reach the valley continued—a yellow, pestilent muck-heap.

It is small wonder that the very image of mountains could become for writers like Hemingway, Cummings, and Barbusse the symbol of something clean and fine.

Fredenburgh's description of the front line is echoed by other writers of fiction and nonfiction alike, who deal both with the "muck-heap" of trench warfare and the fact that casualties accumulated far beyond the capacities of medical sections to treat them, or burial details to put them away. Allen, for example, whose *Toward the Flame* is an explication rather than a protest, simply notes "the immense amount of decay all along the front . . . dead horses, dead men, the refuse, excrement and garbage of armies. The ground must have been literally alive with pus and decay germs. Scratch your hand, cut yourself while shaving, or get a little abrasion on your foot, and anything could happen." [Charles Yale] Harrison, in *Generals Die in Bed*, remembers most vividly the lice and trench rats "fat and sleek with their corpse-filled bellies"; Scanlon remembers half-decayed corpses being dug up by men deepening or repairing shelters; Dos Passos in *First Encounter* refers to the "gangrened soil" and "pulpy masses" of soldiers ("Have you ever seen a herd of cattle being driven to an abattoir?" asks the French aspirant.); and [Humphry] Cobb describes the survivors of trench warfare in a passage whose chief horror is its detailed indignity:

> "Look at their faces. See that sort of greyish tint to their skin? . . . Then look at some of those jaws. See how the lower jaw looks sort of loose, how it hangs down a bit? . . . Take a look at their eyes. They're open, but they have the look of not seeing much of anything. They're nearly all of them constipated, of course. . . .
>
> The Germans have all our trench latrines registered. And we've got theirs too. Now a soldier doesn't like to go to a place that's registered. What's more, he doesn't like to take his breeches down, because when his breeches are down, he can't jump or run. . . ."

And then, of course, there was the mud—an intrinsic part of a war in which protracted and concentrated fire power literally stripped topsoil from the earth. It is difficult to convey the sense of disgust which, the novelists insist, was produced by mud. It was a situation where (unlike World War II) not only was the rationale for operations often incomprehensible to officers and troops, but where futility was rivaled only by filth as a major characteristic of "battle." Allen describes troops "moving over the heavy mud like brown flies over fly-paper"; Harrison writes that "down a duckboard road what is left of the battalion dribbles toward the rear. We pass corpses stuck in the mud—walking wounded who became dizzy and fell into the black ooze and were drowned."

It is interesting to compare such accounts with those of Miss Cather, who in 1922 was able to describe trench war in a somewhat different light. Miss Cather's dugout is "clean"; the land, though bleak, is "quiet"; dawn comes up "saffron and silver"; even shell holes are delicately described as "opaque." The importance of Miss Cather's view of World War I combat, however, lies not in its own limitations, but rather in the fact that similar limitations have persisted ever since 1918 and have, indeed, through a burgeoning nostalgia abetted by the necessities of continuing world conflict, actually conditioned critical attitudes toward World War I fiction as a whole. Readers of Hemingway, for example, have often assumed a continuum of violence-in-the-north-woods to violence-in-war to violence-in-the-bull-ring; as recently as 1960

John Killinger, in *Hemingway and the Dead Gods*, could actually see Nick's war experience as a "moment of truth." That such assumptions are made is an indication of how completely the World War I impact has been blunted by time and a sense of continuing crisis. Hemingway, in his later career, was preoccupied with the formalization of death because his war experience showed him violence without truth, without will, and—perhaps most important—without virility. To understand his work, and the work of authors who found their own solutions in political protest or aesthetic retreat, the impact of World War I combat must be seen clearly for what it was.

Shortly before the battle of Waterloo, the Duke of Wellington is said to have remarked of his troops: "They are the scum of the earth, but by God, they can fight." While the remark is apocryphal, the reality behind it was not. The fact that Europe maintained such attitudes toward military service—"the aristocratic and professional concept"—is one reason why the military realities of World War I resulted in widespread demoralization among troops of all combatant powers. For in terms of army organization (if not in the sermons, political speeches, and journalism of ideological warfare), the "common sodjer" was indeed scum; his discipline, his life, and where necessary or convenient his death, were set in rigid patterns of bonded servitude. That such servitude rather than "service" existed must be remembered if the World War I literary protest is to be understood.

The nature of mass warfare, of course, merely reinforced notions of troop expendability. But even under the war of attrition, when divisions rather than companies became expendable, military leaders remained tragically unaware that the unparalleled manpower at their disposal was the result of an ideological revolution. A soldier was a soldier; "scum" remained scum; military codes perfected in the Foreign Legion or colonial labor battalions would obviously serve for the Western Front as well. For this reason the violently negative attitude of novelists toward the armies of World War I cannot be dismissed merely as adolescent protests. . . . (pp. 69-77)

In *Paths of Glory*, Humphry Cobb formulated one of the most dramatically effective indictments of military leadership in World War I. But despite the bitterness of his novel, Cobb understood the plight of army leaders caught in a technological situation they could not control and in a human situation they could not comprehend. Even as a villain General Assolant is not without a degree of personal integrity and military idealism. A veteran of many campaigns, possessed of a fierce pride in the fighting qualities of his men and the accuracy of his own judgment, Assolant vehemently opposes the suicidal attack on the impregnable "Pimple." And yet he is forced to capitulate: political rather than military considerations (an error in a communiqué already issued to the press) make the attack essential.

Even as he capitulates to political pressure, however, Assolant remains unchanged from the "fighting officer" he has been throughout his career—and this is the essential tragedy of the novel. For in dealing with the men under his command as though they were Foreign Legionnaires, Assolant is being true to the facts of his own military experience and untrue to the facts of a new military environment: "If those bastards won't face German guns, they will French ones!" he proclaims—a logical conclusion for a colonial army of social dregs, and a terrible miscalculation for a civilian army representing all elements of the population.

Assolant's determination to demand execution-for-example is a dramatization of military attitudes which had come to prevail in all combatant armies during World War I. That "professional" concepts of discipline, combined with mass warfare and technological casualties (shell shock, for example), resulted in enormous numbers of punitive executions or courts-martial is one reason why the military police emerge as such objects of hatred in all accounts of the war, including fictional ones. (pp. 78-9)

Soldiers were there to die; that was their function. When any plan miscarried—when any offensive or retreat failed to take place according to schedule (Caporetto, for example)—those soldiers who survived were by that very fact suspect. Since manpower was totally expendable and the objective was all important, military leaders tended to be concerned only with where and how men died rather than with the less relevant question of whether their deaths were necessary at all. Assolant is therefore reflecting a basic tenet of World War I military logic when he dismisses Dax's passionate defense of the 181st (that the men had already suffered more than 50 per cent casualties) by reminding him querulously that "the men had failed to advance. They should have gotten themselves killed outside the trenches instead of inside." Assolant's attitudes, indeed, are recapitulated in a [1961] novel of World War I, *Promenade in Champagne* by David Johnson. Far less rhetorical than Cobb's, Johnson's novel embodies a more subtle and powerful protest. Aiguillon, the narrator, assents to slaughter even while realizing its futility, defines military "honor" solely in terms of military death, and fails completely to understand the attitudes of civilian soldiers. It is almost as though Assolant, gentled by the years, is remembering his World War I experience:

> By 1917 it was quite impossible to turn an enemy's flank, for there were no flanks to be turned. The staffs of Europe's greatest armies were committed to bloody frontal assaults, of a kind which intelligent commanders had discarded a century before. One laid down one's barrage then, hoping that the enemy wire was sufficiently disarranged, launched one's infantry into the waste of shell holes. And by the time the enemy had laid down a counterbarrage and thrown in his reserves, all one had to show was a few kilometers of France and a pile of corpses.

It is this same military logic that ultimately convinces Frederic Henry (in *A Farewell to Arms*) that the war has deserted him; and after the Caporetto retreat punitive execution reduces whatever remains of military duty to a final absurdity. So too Cummings (who had volunteered for Norton-Harjes because of extravagant Francophilism and—at the time of his arrest—had been trying to arrange his own enlistment in Lafayette Escadrille) is educated into the meaning of World War I military death. First the Little Belgian tells him of English, French, Belgian, and German corpses dumped into the river to provide foundations for a bridge. Then the Little Belgian describes a bloody and indecisive battle:

> "We Belgians did not see any good reason for continuing. . . . But we continued. O indeed we continued. Do you know why?"
>
> I said that I was afraid I didn't.

> "Because in front of us we had *les obus allemands, en arrière les mitrailleuses françaises, toujours les mitrailleuses françaises, mon vieux*" ["German shells, and behind us French machine-guns, always French machine-guns, old chum"].

> *"Je ne comprend pas bien"* ["I don't really understand"]. I said in confusion, recalling all the highfalutin rigmarole which Americans believed—(little martyred Belgium protected by the Allies from the inroads of the aggressor, etc.)—"why should the French put machine-guns behind you?"

> "To keep us going forward. At times a company would drop its guns and turn to run. Pupupupupupupupup . . ." his short unlovely arm described gently the swinging of a *mitrailleuse* . . . "finish. The Belgian soldiers to the left and right of them took the hint. If they did not—pupupupupupupupup . . . O we went forward. Yes. *Vive le patriotisme.*"

So too Dos Passos' protagonists make similar discoveries [in his *1919*]:

> The poilus said la guerre was une saloperie and la victoire was une sale blague and asked eagerly if les americains knew anything about la revolution en Russie. . . . "Fellers," Fred Summers says before turning in, "this ain't a war; it's a goddamn madhouse. . . ."

> It rained all day and all night; all day and all night camions ground past the deep liquid putty of the roads carrying men and munitions to Verdun. Dick used to sit on his cot looking out through his door at the joggling mudspattered faces of the young soldiers going up for the attack, drunk and desperate and yelling a bas la guerre, mort au vaches, a bas la guerre. Once Steve came in suddenly, his face pale above the dripping poncho, his eyes snapping, and said in a low voice, "Now I know what the tumbrils were like in the Terror, that's what they are, tumbrils."

The fact that such revelations appear in the vast majority of post-World War I novels can be too easily dismissed; John Aldridge, for example, in *After the Lost Generation*, sees in these novels "the distillation of other men's despair." One must remember, however, that a romantic Francophilism (or, personified by Frederic Henry, an equally romantic love for Italy), had been a basic element of the bold journey itself. The high pitch of crusading idealism that had shaped American attitudes toward the war depended to a great extent upon *"La Belle France," "Classic Italy," "Our Anglo-Saxon Heritage,"* and various racial manifestoes pointing to the rescue of everything fine in European civilization from the menace of the Teutonic Beast. "Ever seen a French soldier yet that didn't have a photograph of a baby stowed away somewhere in his dirty uniform?" asks a soldier in Edith Wharton's *The Marne*. "*I* never have. I tell you, they're *white*. And they're fighting as only people can who feel that way about mothers and babies." Surely it was not necessary for Cummings to stand before French machine guns in order for him to be horrified at the uses to which they were put. (pp. 79-81)

There was, of course, more to shock American protagonists than disillusion with their allies. The spectatorial attitude so essential a quality in the postwar novel—the feeling of being a spectator at some heavy, unwieldy, often obscene and always death-orientated circus—had personal no less than abstract causes. Frederic Henry, for example, is himself under the sentence of death-through-absurdity, and refuses to remain quiescent under the sentence:

> You had lost your cars and your men as a floor-walker loses the stock of his department in a fire. There was, however, no insurance. You were out of it now. You had no more obligation. If they shot floorwalkers after a fire in a department store . . . then certainly the floorwalkers would not be expected to return when the store opened again for business. They might seek other employment; if there was any other employment and the police did not get them.

Other protagonists—Andrews, Methot, Harrison, Private Gordon (forced to butcher German prisoners), Zorn, Irwin—each in his own way suffers, and is broken or coarsened by a military environment which he never expected and which, in many ways, never expected him. (pp. 82-3)

We have already discussed the lack of preparation on the part of military leadership for the new war of attrition, trenches, and technology. This lack was later to be objectively analyzed by military experts and described by eye-witness accounts such as Alden Brooks's *As I Saw It* and Hervey Allen's *Toward the Flame.* Earlier commentators were bitter; Robert Herrick, for example, in 1920 reached the "inevitable conclusion" that "the military mind is ordinarily most incompetent . . . if mankind must have the sport of mass slaughter, the one thing to do at the outset of the war is to relegate all professional soldiers to subordinate administrative positions in the rear." Allen was to be quieter than Herrick, but no less firm in his portrait of officers who had "played at war like men in the textbooks" while others died; he offers, indeed, a reiteration of horrifying ignorance: "Each platoon was provided with its own rockets to signal artillery which, for the most part, none of us had the slightest idea how to use. No instructions were provided." One is reminded of the American attack in *Through the Wheat,* where tanks literally guide German shells to their human targets, and direct advance results in wholesale—and unnecessary—slaughter:

> A shell landed directly upon the moving front wave to the left of Hicks. An arm and a haversack foolishly rose in the air above the cloud of smoke. . . . Machine guns began. . . . More men fell. The front rank went on with huge gaps in it. On they stolidly marched.

> "Close in there, Hicks!" somebody yelled, and Hicks asked whether the men were not being killed quickly enough, without grouping them together more closely. They advanced to a point where they were enfiladed by the enemy's machine guns. As the four lines had become two, so now the two lines became one. But on they marched, preserving a line that could have passed the reviewing stand on dress parade.

It was not, however, in combat and organizational terms alone that the professional military establishment was unprepared for a civilian army. Like their European counterparts, American officers—commissioned and noncommissioned alike—regarded enlisted men as red-necks to be pounded into responsible soldiers only by "regular" discipline. Part of this country's historic schizophrenia toward war and armies (pacifism combined with militancy) was the conviction, often justified, that "joining up" was prima facie evidence of failure in responsible citizenship. Before World War I a man became a "regular" soldier—especially an infantry soldier—either because there was nothing else he could do, or because he had been involved in legal, economic, or social difficulties. Military life was a kennel in which a few gentlemen-professionals (officers) controlled the nation's watchdogs. Discipline was a leash.

Taken for granted so long as the kennel remained limited, the leash became intolerable when the civilian-soldier entered the closed circle of military life. Certainly American army discipline was not geared to a situation in which soldiering had become proof of enthusiasm rather than failure in citizenship. One must remember that the plight of the poor enlisted man was hardly mentioned, much less championed, before the war had begun; only when the rhetoric of the Great Crusade had settled did commentators like Herrick denounce "the military class" for claiming "the position of an autocrat with the wayward power of a God." The bitterness against army life, in other words, so vital a theme in the World War I novel of protest, was at least to some extent evoked by a rigid army environment, by a mass military establishment, and by the idealism of the Crusade itself.

In 1921 Francis Hackett remarked of John Andrews (one of the central triptych in Dos Passos' *Three Soldiers*) that "he brought to the army certain large assumptions of the American sort about justice and freedom and equality and consent. . . . He was the type of crusader who discovered in the American machine a school of intolerance, brutality and self-seeking violating everything he had ever been taught of equality and freedom and consent and all the other shibboleths of democracy. So long as he kept faith in these shibboleths . . . he was a sick soul, with the 'Y' men and the officers as the worst emetics of all." Hackett's remark is significant because he refers not only to the intolerance and brutality which, again, belonged to the nature of things in the military kennel; he also notes the "self-seeking" so intrinsic to survival in a closed military society—a factor in military disillusion that the postwar novelists were to dramatize repeatedly. "War is as mean as poor-farm soup and as petty as an old-maid's gossip," says Private Luston in *Company K;* the combination of wheedling, abasement, manipulation, informing, cheap cleverness, hypocrisy, and debased concentration on one's own appetites, all of which were part of a "regular sodjer's" equipment, later received almost universal testimony in the novels.

Sergeant Eadie the professional soldier no less than Mattock the opportunist is a master of intrigue and petty mechanism and reflects the philosophy of "take what you can get" basic to the military environment into which young Americans had been so rapidly plunged. The contrast, indeed, between the "Warriors of Christ" rhetoric and the sordid reality of army politics was to offer a major dramatic resource for writers in defining the impact of war upon their protagonists. Mattock profits by his environment; Andrews (his fate finally and irrevocably sealed when he forces himself to play Uncle Tom) is alienated by it; Cummings deserts it; Irwin and Fuselli are reduced by it; Zorn is coarsened by it. Each in his own way dramatizes the result of an obsolete military environment quite aside from the impact of technological combat.

Compounding the difficulty was the very naïveté of the civilian soldier, his essentially provincial background noted both by [Henry F. May in his *The End of American Innocence,* 1951] and by Alan Valentine (*1913: America between Two*

Worlds [1962]). Where the "regular" knew whoredom as a basic fact of military existence, for example, the Crusader was totally unprepared for it. In *Three Soldiers,* Dos Passos was able to see considerable irony in this situation: Fuselli, far from expecting whoredom, actually proposes marriage, contracting syphilis as a result of his "engagement." And punishment for Fuselli is precisely the same as for the five-hitch man—punishment, in other words, for a civilian soldier in a mass army sent to a European theater of operations, dealt out as though the offender were an old warhorse stationed at a backwater camp in Texas.

It was this lack of army flexibility that the novelists were to attack with particular vehemence. In one book it might be a man like Andrews arrested and held incommunicado for not having a school pass with him; in another, it might be a matter of "rest" camps where men were herded behind barbed wire like convicts and simply kept until the machine required their bodies; in another it might be military police arresting stragglers—or survivors—of front-line debacles; in still another it might be shell shock cases executed by their own officers. Such episodes must be read in view of the fact that the army itself too often persisted in regarding "sodjers" in the light of the Vera Cruz campaign. The continuation of such attitudes at the time of World War I may help explain Zorn's discovery, in *Soldiers March!*, of an unexpected military formula: men must be broken before they can be good soldiers; the army functions best when the individual is frightened of those above him and contemptuous of his subordinates.

It was a formula to which there were no objections after Vera Cruz, and to which there were violent objections, literary no less than historical, after World War I. The basic terms of the equation had changed; discipline accorded to watchdogs was not always efficacious when applied to white-collar workers, farm boys, musicians, teachers, small businessmen, young southerners with a local tradition of the masculine code (including the concept of the Intolerable Affront), or youngsters fresh out of a parental environment. Captain Powers, for example, in Faulkner's *Soldiers' Pay,* is killed by one of his own men; in *Three Soldiers,* Chrisfield (who kills an officer) cannot be secure in manhood until he acts to redeem it through violence, avenging insult by following a personal code; Dick Savage, discovering a pattern of pettiness, intellectual surveillance, and outright dishonesty, ultimately becomes what he most despises.

But traditional discipline was only one aspect of the kennel which caused difficulties in a civilian army. Watchdogs, after all, must be kept busy or they may get into mischief; when they cannot be kept busy they must be penned up or they may bite the little boy next door. The World War I novelists are unanimous in testifying to the demoralization produced by harshly ignominious fatigue duties and barbed-wire-and-mud "depots"—elements, again, whose theory of necessity belonged to stateside backwaters of army life, when the "sodjer" was considered, and was likely to be, a misfit cast up by a society in which he had no other place.

Hicks [in Thomas Boyd's *Through the Wheat*], for example, who is a good soldier and actually looks forward to combat, is disgusted by "working as a stevedore beside evil-odored blacks. . . . Soldiering with a shovel. A hell of a way to treat a white man." The indignity of "military" labor, indeed, is often defined by the novelists in terms of racial allusion—a reflection of the stereotypes so prevalent at the time of the Great Crusade, when songs like "The Coon Conscript" (an early Edison recording) were nationally popular. Irwin, who like Fuselli and Zorn sees the army as a means of earning rank and status, is—along with his comrades in the engineers—nauseated "at being used as floor-moppers for syphilitic blacks"; Chrisfield (a farm protagonist who makes an interesting contrast to Miss Cather's good-natured hired hands), despite his complete readiness to do whatever shooting is necessary, complains: "This ain't no sort of life for a man to be treated lak he was a nigger"; and Andrews, whose enlistment is a romantic military gesture, finds only "slavery" and ends—as he had begun—with another gesture, but this time "toward human freedom." One might almost say that Andrews, having set out as a Foreign Legionnaire, finds his true calling as an abolitionist.

The "slavery," of course, was accentuated by the very size of the Crusade itself; if the obsolete army environment was degrading to a civilian soldier, the sense of sheer mass—of being degraded by and for a machine—produced no less powerful an impact. One must remember that the military tradition, or rather the tradition of the civilian soldier in the United States, was still essentially a frontier tradition, what Archie Binns, in *The Laurels Are Cut Down* (1937), refers to as the "Winchester-on-the-wall" concept. Walter Millis remarks [in his *Arms and Men*] that the expectation of combat was still "we-uns against they-uns"; parallel to this was the consideration of soldiering—in general military terms, beyond that of combat alone—as a matter of personal action, personal status, personal identity. Americans were simply unprepared for new military necessities which reduced the soldier, as soldier, to "a cog in a great machine." The very enthusiasm of the Great Crusade, moreover, with its home-town parades, commencement speeches, and personal stature suddenly heaped on young men, only deepened the shock when these same young men discovered that their lives, deaths, rewards or punishments were not only arbitrary and often accidental, but also of no great concern to anyone but themselves.

The imagery of mass, of men no longer judged by their own good or evil, runs through the World War I novels accompanied by protest, as in Dos Passos' early novels; by a bitter, symbolic mockery, as in Cummings; by a benumbed understatement, as in *A Farewell to Arms* ("only 7,000 died of it in the army," Frederic Henry says of the cholera) and Harrison's *Generals Die in Bed;* or by a realization of absolute futility, in which motive no less than action is helpless. Hence Corporal Rose in *Company K* becomes a "hero" by being able to spot a tomato crate on the high seas; Frederic Henry is offered a medal for being attacked by a stray shell; Hicks—after fulfilling every duty as a good soldier—is denounced for cowardice and tossed out of the hospital when he is suffering from shell shock; the men of the 181st, in Cobb's novel, after acquitting themselves loyally in battle after battle, must face death-by-firing-squad via a lottery; Dick Savage does his hardest and most useful medical service after being branded as a political undesirable by the rear echelon at Paris; Lieutenant Dill, in [James Stevens's] *Mattock,* becomes a war "authority," while Captain Johnny Hard is ruined. Praise and blame, cowardice and bravery, loyalty and treachery become jumbled together like the pile of German, Austrian, French, Belgian, and American corpses heaped indiscriminately in Boyd's novel; hence Frederic Henry's dictum that everyone is broken, no matter who—or what—he is.

If mass gave to individuals like the rear-echelon officer in *1919* both power and security, and to men like Claude a sense of almost sexual fulfillment, for the war novelists as a group there was the sense of a blind thing being led to a slaughter—what René Fülöp Miller in *The Night of Time* was later (1949) to develop as his lemming symbol. In *Three Soldiers* marching troops are "lead" and their feet are "pistons"; in *Impromptu* the tramping soldiers become "hideous processions of empty boots"; Colonel Dax, in *Paths of Glory,* measures death by kilometers; Richard Plume, in Stallings' novel, wonders bitterly at "the kilowat hours of pain" produced by the war. "The enormity, the relentlessness and the ironic impersonality of the chaos in which he was shuttled overwhelmed Irwin once again," Elliot Paul writes:

> What malignant power was behind these grey, silent convoys, these night-faring troop trains, these wharves submerged with boxes, last hopes in red pantaloons, squareheads in field grey, railroad yards swarming with chanting Algerians? Wards full of quivering eyelids! Wards full of bare, brown buttocks. . . .
>
> All at once it seemed the moving file of telegraph poles was a Gargantuan tape measure. . . . How many feet? How many yards? How many miles of soldiers? What did an individual amount to? They were being measured by the mile for slaughter.
>
> [*Impromptu*]

Zorn, with his first glimpse of returning front-line soldiers, begins to understand the machine which is to reshape his own personality; it is this machine, operating beyond motive, beyond reason, and beyond cause, which becomes for Irwin too the final absurdity:

> The gun was detached, impersonal, obedient. Point it to the North and it shot into Germany, for the safety of the world. Wheel it in a semi-circle and it shot into France, for the Hun and the reign of terror. If the men who polished the gun wore olive caps like hickory nuts, the gun roared for the God of Hosts. If the cannon received its rations from the swarthy men with fezzes, it bellowed just as loud for Allah. . . .
>
> The hills and woods were neutral too. The trunks offered themselves as hitching posts for all passersby. The foliage sheltered uniforms of any colour. . . .
>
> The multiplication table was for everybody. All the artillery used the same figures, signs, tangents. . . .
>
> The men had all the worst of it. The men who saluted and cut their hair by orders, who ate when they could and worked when they could not avoid it, who marched in endless columns through heat and dust or the night and rain. The men had customs, obligations, consciences. They had flags. They grouped the letters of their alphabets differently. If they faced north, they were heroes and soldiers. If they faced south, they were barbarians and swine. They could not work impersonally for whoever fed them and rubbed them down. They had ideals which made it necessary to cut their throats if they got into the wrong woods.

The impact of "mud, smells, slops, vermin, insects," together with the debasement of "nigger" labor, kennel discipline, and the demoralizing anonymity of mass no less than technological warfare, was accentuated by the doses of propaganda which, as we have seen, preceded and followed America's of-

ficial entrance into the war. It was the contrast between civilian rhetoric and military realities that provided a major target for the novelists, a target most memorably attacked by the "Unknown Soldier" episodes of March's *Company K* and Dos Passos' *1919.* The propaganda, furthermore, continued in the army itself and, according to the testimony of the novelists (in addition to scholars), was often presented with a remarkable lack of perspective, in the midst of precisely those aspects of military life that the amateur soldier was to find so demoralizing. Zorn's company, for example, is given a rhetorical pep talk about the Crusade for Democracy immediately before being stuffed into cattle cars for transport ("Herded, jammed worse than cattle would be, cold, no provision for sleeping, no possible chance of lying down, no escape from sitting up . . ."). So too the moral and political rhetoric of the ubiquitous "Y" men created repugnance among troops returned to "rest" areas after combat; propaganda films and military speeches were hurled at men who were then marched off to mud-and-barbed-wire enclosures for days of heavy fatigue work.

The rhetoric of the Great Crusade, in other words, followed civilian soldiers to the army camp, followed them to France, followed them to the front line itself. While the American military machine was fumbling its way through a mass operation it never expected, while transport and supply difficulties created exhaustion among troops before they had even seen combat, the rhetoric continued. "That's what will survive you and me," Andrews says after a "Y" man finishes his performance. "By no stretch of his imagination could Irwin connect this conglomeration of mud, slops and salutes with Oliver Street," Elliot Paul's protagonist reflects after having his morale helped by a warriors-of-democracy, home-and-country speech. "Bull! Bull! Bull! Everything turned out to be bull if you tried to find out what the words really meant."

If postwar novelists were to indict the professional army man for failing to realize that he was not dealing with veterans of the Vera Cruz campaign, they were almost preoccupied with the amateur officer, who had his own role to play in creating the impact of army life upon the draftee or volunteer. The amateur officer of the war books (Lieutenant Fairbrother in *Company K,* the "new officers" in Scanlon's *God Have Mercy on Us*), no less than the civilian soldiers under him, in addition to being inadequately trained, found "regular" military etiquette quite alien to his expectations or experience. One alternative was to retreat from responsibility altogether, retaining—as the young officer in Nason's *Sergeant Eadie* retained—little more than the ability to delegate authority. The other was to out-military the military in rear-echelon "rest" camps, on troop marches, and in the combat environment itself. Officer jokes, of course, were common coin in the Second World War as they had been in the First. . . . The difference between the officer and enlisted man, however, was far greater in World War I, and it created problems more complicated—and in some ways more pernicious—than the humiliation of individuals like Andrews; the analysis of such problems was to be the subject of detailed irony and continuing bitterness in the World War I literary protest.

Unlike his professional counterpart, the amateur officer was insecure in his exalted position; it was Johnny Hard rather than Captain Matlock (ex-floorwalker in a department store) who understood when rules were to be bent, when the eye of military authority was to be closed. Allen remarks that the American army tended to view war as a "business enterprise." From the testimony of the war novels, his term is particularly applicable to civilian officers whose mannerisms were often those of an office supervisor in a roomful of recalcitrant typists. Not only did the businessmen-captains studiously apply all regulations, especially those pertaining to alcohol and sex, but—perhaps more important—they applied these regulations without fully realizing what the consequences for the enlisted man would actually be. In combat we have Captain Powers, in a "Shakespearean voice," ordering Hicks to "advance" upon a machine-gun post—or Lieutenant Fairbrother, who wraps himself with both dignity and rank and, despite the objections of his noncom, sends a group of men to their deaths by placing them in a totally vulnerable observation post. In rear areas, there is the maintenance of "discipline" by pompous dress inspections, insistence on all military protocol, and unreasonable "toughness" (Captain Matlock asserting his always doubtful authority by refusing passes). Appearance too was a vitally important matter for the civilian officer; in Scanlon's novel, for example, the fresh troops—never in combat—are selected for Paris leave: "The officers picked the men with the best-looking uniforms in order the make a showing in Paris. . . . We watched them ride away toward Paris. We fell in and hiked back toward the front." And in *Impromptu* there is Captain Anderson, who in civilian life "practiced law in a very large and very respectable office":

> The fact that he had been cheated out of prosecuting a court martial disappointed him, for he liked to write charges and declarations and affidavits. . . . From the first, he had taken his only prisoner very seriously. No other company in the regiment had a member in the guardhouse, and Captain Anderson felt a slight twinge of superiority as he passed Irwin, shoveling mud from the gutters, if there were any other commissioned officers present. The two armed guards, without ammunition, were always properly in evidence.

The combination of pettiness, incompetence, and ferocity-born-of-ignorance was further compounded by the fact that the amateur officers were very aware of political purity (and impurity). For one thing they—again, like the amateur ranks under them—had been deeply affected by the rhetoric of the Crusade: Captain Matlock, for example, repeating the usual atrocity stories, orders the execution of German soldiers as a demonstration both of his patriotism and martial firmness; ironically enough it is Sergeant Pilton, a professional, who is disgusted by the action. So too Dick Savage finds the most militant militarists among the rear-echelon patriots; it is they who are most shocked by his "cowardly" letters expressing doubts about the war and they who are most rhetorically extravagant in denouncing him for his lapse. And Cummings finds—in the "doughy" and highly moral Mister A.—a superior who not only cares for the moral and racial well-being of his charges ("stay away from those dirty Frenchmen"), but serves as political informer without the vaguest notion of the machinery he is setting in motion.

If the postwar novelists were to regard the civilian officers who carried the rhetoric of the Crusade into the army (indeed, into the combat environment itself) with particular loathing, they also remembered, with equal loathing, the role of these officers as political policemen. Historians, despite varying attitudes to the fact itself, are unanimous in pointing out that ideological surveillance was an inevitable corollary of the Crusade's ideological basis, hence the national preoc-

cupation, almost paranoia, regarding the evils of pacifism, socialism, anarchism, and what Wilson called "hyphenated Americanism"—all tossed into the same emotional hopper. "In the United States," Roland Bainton remarks, "the mood was a blend of hysterical nationalism and crusading idealism":

> American churchmen of all faiths were never so united with each other and with the mind of the country. This was a holy war. Jesus was dressed in khaki and portrayed sighting down a gun barrel. The Germans were Huns. To kill them was to purge the world of monsters. Nor was such action incompatible with love, because their deaths would restrain them from crime and transplant them to a better land. The Lord God of Battles was rolling up the hosts of Armageddon to destroy the great beast of the abyss that the New Jerusalem might descend from the sky.

The identification of nationalism with religion, of pacifism with blasphemy, had important results both in the development of Total Cause, and in the reaction against religion so marked in the postwar literature of protest. . . . The concept of Jesus in khaki, however, had significant results within the military environment itself; given the view of the war as a total struggle for democracy and Christianity, the pattern of assent demanded a demonstration of faith over and above mere works, any mere fulfillment of soldierly duties alone. The search for heresy, in other words, was not limited to the home front. "Think American!" became a military no less than civilian imperative, and postwar novelists were to dramatize this aspect of military life as a major breaking factor of the war experience.

In this connection the work of Arthur Train, one of the most widely read novelists of patriotism, is of special interest. Train, of course, was part of the wartime literary environment against which the later novelists were to react so violently; he typified the various concepts of war-as-proving-ground, religious cause, and racial invigoration (the view of combat as a cure for decadence). In *Earthquake,* published in 1918, Train recapitulates the full national rhetoric; more relevant to our purpose here, however, is the fact that he sees the army not only as a means for socio-religious assimilation, but also as a highly effective means of political decontamination. "I tell you when these fellows come out of the army," the narrator's son exclaims, "they will have a respect for the United States they'd never get in any other way. When Ikey and Abie go back to the East Side, if any greasy anarchist attempts to put anything over on them, Ikey and Abie will stand him up against the wall, and say . . . 'Uncle Sam's all right! Get out!' "

The earliest and perhaps the most violent attack upon thought control in the American armed forces is Upton Sinclair's *Jimmie Higgins* (1919). While the novel is window dressing for Sinclair's own ideological position, it effectively dramatizes the dilemma of American socialism (indeed, of international socialism as a movement) during the war years. The enthusiasm with which the Socialist movements greeted the Russian revolution during the closing months of the war was accompanied by a sharp intensification of political-police activity in the American army after bolshevism was added to anarchism as an ultimate political evil. Beaten to a senseless pulp in an army prison compound as an ideological criminal (after serving bravely and well as a soldier), Jimmy takes his place, modestly and obscurely, along with Faulkner's Mahon and Boyd's Hicks as an antihero of total withdrawal.

Unlike Sinclair, however, whose literary anger on occasion reaches absolute fury, most war novelists view the political policeman and informer as still another element of absurdity. Just as Martin Howe in *First Encounter* comes to see death itself—and the whole pompous international machinery of death—as a gigantic "circus," so Cummings, for example, reduces the ideological inspections of Mister A. and the French authorities to a subject of amusement, a comedy in which people suffer, of course, but one possessed of an irrationality so complete that only a sort of desperate laughter can do justice to it: hense Cummings' wild *non sequiturs,* puns, distorted syllogisms, and elaborate parodies (". . . the remarkable and demoralizing disclosure that President Poincaré had, the night before, been discovered in unequal hand to hand battle with a défaitistically-minded bed-bug." . . . *"Il n'y a plus d'heures—les gouvernement français les defend!"*). Hence too a whole series of absurd definitions for *La Ferté*—itself the basic symbol in Cummings' book for a world at war.

Although the war novels of protest, especially those of Dos Passos, Paul, and Binns, attack the ideological inspection which had extended from the home front to the army during the war (Eisenstein in *Three Soldiers* is court-martialed for "possible disloyal statements found in a letter addressed to friends at home"), the attack against the political informer reached in some ways its most effective statement in the work of James Stevens, whose *Mattock* is a novel of total satire—political, religious, and military. The alliance between Mattock himself and the flabby civilian officer Lieutenant Dill (who upon leaving the army makes a career of writing and lecturing on the Crusade to Conserve our Democratic Ideals) is portrayed with devastating detail; Stevens, for one thing, sustains his first-person dialect narrative remarkably well. Mattock's activities in discovering bolshevism, atheism, and various infringements of military regulations result in the demoralization of his company and the ruin of Captain Johnny Hard. The company's two sergeants make the final comment on this new war of ideological (as well as military) purity:

> Jeezus, oh, Jezus! What a war, Novak! What a war, Novak! Chris', the crap that's pulled—the snivelin' bastards that do dirt and call it good because it's right or righteous—yeah, let's make the world safe for the democrats—let's sweep hell from God's fair earth—let's pull all the old crap we can think of for the Glory of God—one hell of a God, I'll say, when I pipe the birds that's always rootin' for him! . . . Yeah, she's a great war; and the old army, boy, how she's growed; and the old USA. Jeezus, amen, what a noble Chrischun country it's come to be! Let's go, Novak. Let's be good Americans from now on. No Bolshevism for us! From now on we play the grand, new patriotic, religious, upliftin' American game of snoop, spy, frame up and stool. Yea, bo! Gimme a cigarette.

In commenting on an ideological situation in which facts have become drowned in rhetoric, truth made dependent upon political purpose, and words stripped of meaning, a protagonist in Binns' *The Laurels Are Cut Down* reflects that "on closer inspection, everything turns into something else." So too Frederic Henry says, "I was blown up while we were eating cheese"; Zorn, on morality, sees strength alone as the ultimate right and survival the only cause; soldiers in *Company K* are seen as "castrated sheep"; Henslow, in *Three Soldiers,*

advises Andrews to "tie a rock on your scruples . . . this is the Golden Age"; Irwin, in *Impromptu,* sees the world as a "multiplication table" and men as the merest digits in a machine arithmetic of death; Martin Howe, oppressed with the "tumbrils" carrying battle fodder to the front, calls for a counter-crusade to sweep away "all the lies"; Captain Sancy, while picking men for punitive execution in *Paths of Glory,* remarks that "the world is an open graveyard, getting perpetual care from the survivors who are living off it"; Summers, in *1919,* sees the Crusade as "a goddamn whorehouse." A combination of horror, dehumanization, numbness, and absurdity is the heritage that World War I novelists brought back from their broken world of combat and military glory. (pp. 83-97)

Stanley Cooperman, in his World War I and the American Novel, *The Johns Hopkins Press, 1967, 273 p.*

FRENCH LITERATURE OF WORLD WAR I

J. CRUICKSHANK

[*An Anglo-Irish educator and critic, Cruickshank is the author of several studies of French literature, including* Variations on Catastrophe: Some French Responses to the Great War *(1982). In the following excerpt, he discusses critical approaches to French World War I fiction and examines Adrien Bertrand's* L'appel du sol *and Henri Barbusse's* Le feu *as examples of traditional and pacifist war fiction.*]

There is much to be said for the view that the basic function of criticism is to understand and interpret rather than to classify. If such critical priorities are accepted, a good deal can be learned from the scrutiny of writers not generally regarded as outstandingly gifted or successful. It seems clear that the early Great War novelists come into this latter category. Novelists who responded immediately to the experience of mobilization and trench warfare did not, on the whole, produce artistically memorable writings. The few works of this time that are still read—Barbusse's *Le feu* (1916), Duhamel's *Vie des martyrs* (1917) or Dorgelès's *Les croix de bois* (1919)—are admired more as moral outcry than aesthetic achievement, more as documentation than art. Indeed, most of the thirty or so novels and collections of short stories published by 1919 have long been out of print. This fact may certainly be attributed in some measure not only to changes in literary taste but to the limited talents of these authors. Nevertheless, these writers also faced particular moral and technical difficulties which need to be stated, however briefly, before the attempt is made to sketch the broader critical problem of a legitimate and balanced approach to their work.

The basic difficulty was one of finding appropriate ways of articulating experiences which, at their worst, were totally horrifying and totally unfamiliar to the participants. The scale of the casualties, the nature of the killing and wounding, the increasing assault on human flesh by industrialized technology and machine-made ingenuity, the loss of personal identity and dignity in the names of discipline and military necessity—all these things were experienced and had to be absorbed not by a small professional army but by civilians suddenly up-

Henri Barbusse, the author of Le feu (Under Fire).

rooted by mobilization from normal life in villages and towns. The writers among them lacked an adequate rhetoric with which to express these unparalleled experiences. The traditional language of war writing was not only inadequate but inappropriate. It suggested high chivalry, the heroic trial of valour, a confidence in resounding moral absolutes. But these are precisely things which the Great War finally denied and destroyed. The phenomenon of industrialized and total war was one which required time and some detachment for its proper understanding and expression. Significantly, the most successful and admired novels of the war were almost all written in the 1920s and 1930s.

It can be argued that some of these later novels, because of their literary skill, lack the immediacy and also the authentic imperfection of less fully realized works of the 1914-18 period. The immediate pressure of their subject-matter urged the early war novelists in the direction of documentation and witness. It was a pressure that left only limited room for conscious craftsmanship. Most writers were forced, by the requirements of authentic testimony, into an indeterminate area on the borders of autobiography and fiction. A measure of generic definition was lost, but there were gains in terms of human conviction and a sense of actuality. However, while the experience of fighting on the Western Front provided immediate and dramatic material for some established and many aspiring writers, not all were anxious to appear in print while the holocaust was still taking place. A few even regarded their experiences as inappropriate material for literary treatment and kept silence. Those who did write fall into two main categories. Some, like Dorgelès, were reluctant to "ex-

ploit" their sufferings and those of their comrades. They published their work when the war ended. Dorgelès's *Les croix de bois* and Léon Werth's *Clavel soldat* both appeared in 1919. On the other hand there were writers who, for equally honourable reasons, sought publication as soon as possible in order to tell the truth to those at home and, in some cases, to counteract war propaganda. Barbusse's *Le feu* was published in 1916 and Duhamel's *Vie des martyrs* in 1917. None of these writers attempted to belittle the nightmare of the battlefield and each succeeded, in considerable measure, in the task of true testimony. The only writers who really emerge as failures are those who, through lack of moral imagination or for propagandist reasons, used a discredited heroic rhetoric to minimize the horror and disguise the folly. It is only right to add that this type of novel, exemplified by René Benjamin's *Gaspard* (1915), was mainly a product of the early months of the fighting. This was a period when, even for many honest witnesses, the true nature and significance of the war were still very unclear.

On the face of it the novel seems the most suitable literary form in which to give expression to the facts and conditions of war. As Holger Klein puts it [in *The First World War in Fiction*]: ". . . prose narrative, taking over in part the tradition of the great epics, is especially suited to the full re-creation of historical events and states of society. Moreover, as prose is the most frequently read genre of the modern era, this is the medium in which the war had its widest impact on the reading public." Nevertheless, these early war novels differed in emphasis from ordinary fiction in terms of their subject-matter and their aims. The more closely they dealt with the nature of the fighting in Flanders, the more they used what might be called ready-made material. The major facts were witnessed, not invented. They resembled the traditionally heavily autobiographical "first novel" of other writers and were in fact first novels in a number of cases. Again, their subject was a public and historical experience shared by thousands, and eventually millions, of their compatriots. Therefore, the more the war became central to these works, the more authenticity and actuality became required major aims. In other words there were limits, more strictly marked than in ordinary novels, to the extent to which truth could be modified or changed in the interests of art.

Two consequences affecting the form of these novels follow. One, resulting from the distinctive nature of their subject, is the repetition of certain incidents and scenes from novel to novel. Such set pieces as the baptism of fire, the infantry attack, the artillery barrage, or withdrawal from the front line recur on a number of occasions. These set pieces, in their turn, are given a common background of mud, rain, lice, barbed-wire, exhausted men, flooded trenches and ruined villages. Such repetition, if not aesthetically exciting, is some guarantee of truth. Again, a more significant feature, and one which must affect our critical approach, is the complex mixture of fact and fiction. It has already been pointed out that these books possess characteristics of both the war memoir and the novel (particularly when a first-person narrator is employed). It would therefore be pointless, even irrelevant, to follow the example of some commentators and apply to these works, in a rigidly normative way, those critical expectations which we bring to the analysis of ordinary novels. In fact, it is part of the interest of these narratives that they respond with what may be called generic flexibility to their subject-matter and their authors' purpose. They offer considerable justification of the present-day critical view that works should be appraised as "texts" and not in terms of strict fidelity to a particular genre. At the level of form, therefore, a strictly genre-based approach is inappropriate. (pp. 140-42)

There is perhaps a danger or an injustice in insisting too heavily on the artistic limitations of the early war novels. It is well to remember that *Le feu* and *Les croix de bois,* for instance, were highly praised by many writers and both have continued to be bought and read more than sixty years after their original publication. It may be that one clue to their persistent appeal lies in their successful use of the repetitive element mentioned above. In novel after novel we find a three-part sequence consisting of anticipation of battle, experience of battle, withdrawal from battle. This cycle of anticipation, action, withdrawal—a variation on departure, quest, return—is met many times and we know that it is deeply imprinted in the human spirit. At a formal level, then, a number of war novels contain a mythic structure which has pervaded Western literature in a multitude of versions from the travels of Odysseus and the quest of Orpheus to Dante's *Divine Comedy* and Bunyan's *Pilgrim's Progress.* Making a rather similar point in connection with English writing about the Great War, Paul Fussell [in his *The Great War and Modern Memory*] uses one of the many valuable insights to be found in Northrop Frye's *Anatomy of Criticism*: "As Frye reminds us, a standard 'quest' has three stages: first, 'the stage of the perilous journey and the preliminary minor adventures'; second, 'the crucial struggle, usually some kind of battle in which either the hero or his foe, or both, must die'; and third, 'the exaltation of the hero, who has clearly proved himself to be a hero even if he does not survive the conflict.' It is impossible not to be struck by the similarity between this conventional 'romance' pattern and the standard experience re-enacted and formalized in memoirs of the war." There is much truth in Fussell's comment. But it is important to note that the best of the early war novelists modified this "romance pattern" in markedly unromantic ways. Barbusse and Léon Werth probably took this tendency furthest. They transformed the crusade pursued by the hero into the chaos experienced by the victim—experienced in the mud and rain of Flanders. But whether the tone is patriotic or pacifist, complaisant or debunking, there exists a structure to which we appear to make an instinctive response.

The presence of mythic patterns in a work should not be taken as necessary evidence of literary sophistication. Indeed, in the case of these particular novels, the basic nature of the material—individual or collective experience of modern warfare—imposed a mythic structure independently of authorial intention. There is little evidence that they consciously exploited the cycle of anticipation, action, withdrawal. We are dealing, in general, with aesthetically innocent narratives. This is a further reason why so many of them have remained out of print. They appear naïve to readers of a more knowing age whose sensibilities are attuned to ironic and oblique modes of writing. Their episodic, anecdotal style seems crude and unformed in comparison with later techniques of crosscutting, counterpointing and general narrative control. And yet it may be argued, with some justification, that the relatively simple narrative techniques of a Bertrand or a Dorgelès, a Barbusse or a Werth, convey most accurately the preordained existence of the front-line soldier with its regular rhythm of fear, danger and boredom, set against a background of death and destruction.

As regards the subject-matter of these narratives, it is of course obvious that war, in common with love and death, has been a literary theme from the earliest times. Like love and death, too, it often served as a background or narrative framework against which quite other concerns were primarily explored. However, as Stanley Cooperman was one of the first to point out clearly, the early war novel broke with tradition under the pressure of a war which itself destroyed many precedents. With the spectacle of mass mechanized slaughter war ceased to be a narrative device and became a totally invasive narrative subject. [In his *World War I and the American Novel*] Cooperman says: "No longer one subordinate element among many contributing to a total aesthetic structure, environment—the war itself—became the chief protagonist; when this happened readers were left floundering in a situation where the traditional critical implements simply could not be applied." This shift of war to a position as central subject, together with its presentation as a form of mass martyrdom, demanded a moral response.

While these novels, then, were aesthetically innocent narratives, most of them also belong firmly to the literature of moral persuasion. The degree of persuasion naturally varies, but whether they are novels of honest witness and high traditionalist ideals, like Bertrand's *L'appel du sol,* or novels of honest outrage and left-wing values, like Barbusse's *Le feu,* they call for an ethical response. They work through direct emotional impact, not through subtle artistic effects. This is not to say that they are propagandist works, though no doubt Barbusse's book does come into this category. But it means, given the subject, that the moral stand they take will be judged, to a large extent, in terms of fidelity to the facts. The assumption is easily and naturally made that the moral message will derive its status and its strength from the fundamental truthfulness of the narrative.

Inevitably, then, these novels have given rise to a critical approach which has been broadly ethical. Their subject, particularly while the fighting continued, seemed to demand it; the authors themselves appeared to encourage it. Nevertheless, critical practice has proved neither clear nor simple. It is notoriously difficult to obtain agreement on moral criteria and these war narratives have not proved an exception. The convictions of critics and those of authors have clashed in a variety of ways. In general, the criteria in question have been the truthfulness of what is said and the passion with which it is expressed. Ideally, the truth and the passion should coincide, but in practice they often sort ill together. In the case of the early war novels—documents about the war and frequently denunciations of it—two forms of response arose. Some critics, concerned above all with documentary accuracy, admired only those novels which avoided shrillness, were not unsympathetic to the traditional virtues of the battlefield, and presented war as a natural, if cruel phenomenon. Other critics, chiefly sensitive to military mismanagement and the appalling sacrifice of human life, regarded novels of protest as alone worthy of attention, judging them according to the intensity of their denunciations. If the first group appeared to require a moderate account of unexampled violence, the second seemed to accept passion and unbalance as morally and artistically self-justifying.

While these contrasting critical approaches existed in some degree from the early days of the war, they became more clearly defined in the late 1920s and early 1930s. As the war began slowly to recede, and as technology and violence became seemingly inevitable features of modern society, there were those who experienced a measure of reconciliation with the fact of mechanized killing. Others, in the wake of a victory obtained at such enormous cost, contributed to a growing mood of pacifism and war repugnance. Critics seeking balance and restraint profited from the first of these attitudes. Those seeking an uncompromising denunciation of war profited from the second. The argument between these two sets of critics found what is perhaps its fullest and most precise form in the debate in America between Archibald MacLeish and Malcolm Cowley. The subject was *The First World War,* edited by Laurence Stallings, and it appeared in the *New Republic* during September and October 1933. MacLeish complained of the partiality and lack of balance in many war novels (he had in mind post-war as well as wartime novels). Too many, he asserted, concentrated on the futility and slaughter to the exclusion of the courage, the comradeship, the long periods of inactivity which also formed an integral part of the war experience. MacLeish's position implied that the role of literature is to explore and exhibit, not to preach and persuade. And it is true that the great works of art—*Hamlet* or *Middlemarch* or *The Brothers Karamazov*—contain the woven texture of human contradiction and complexity rather than the single thread of partisanship.

Cowley, in reply, defended partisanship in terms of the special, even unprecedented, nature of the Great War. A balanced, exploratory approach would have betrayed its character and placed it falsely in the continuing perspective of traditional warfare. Selectiveness and passionate commitment were necessary to convey the exceptional horror of trench warfare and mechanized killing. Cowley, and the novelists who felt like him, saw the war as absurdly pointless slaughter; MacLeish believed that the truth still demanded a recognition of heroism and generous sacrifice. This aspect of the debate was at least as much about terms as about facts.

While the writing of a novel of protest can be reconciled, at least in theory, with respect for the facts, some critics have been particularly sensitive to the distortions of fact, in the interests of propaganda or of art, which occur in novels of protest—and are by no means totally absent from "traditionalist" narratives. As recently as 1968 C. E. Carrington wrote of his own lengthy experience of the Great War: " . . . I never came across a glorification of war; I heard no bloodthirsty sermons by militant clergy; I remember no invocations of the joys of battle. . . . We were deadly serious about our assignment, without finding a necessity of often saying so, and there seemed no reason why we should not have fun when off duty, since we expected to die tomorrow." ["Some Soldiers" in *Promise of Greatness: The War of 1914-1918,* edited by G. A. Panichas]. This is some way from the war as Barbusse or Werth describe it. No doubt it is a very anglosaxon approach, phlegmatic and down-to-earth. But it also reminds us that if a writer were to confine himself to what he had actually experienced and seen with his own eyes, his account of the war might appear very limited and even positively unbalanced. The overall view of the individual was necessarily severely restricted. Referring to the sheer physical dimensions of the front, in terms of trenches and salients, Fussell writes of "a series of multiple parallel excavations running for 400 miles down through Belgium and France." He adds: "From the North Sea coast of Belgium the line wandered southward, bulging out to contain Ypres, then dropping down to protect Béthune, Arras, and Albert. It continued south in front of Montdidier, Compiègne, Soissons, Reims, Verdun, St. Mihiel, and Nancy, and finally attached

it southernmost end to the Swiss border at Beurnevisin, in Alsace. The top forty miles—the part north of Ypres—was held by the Belgians; the next ninety miles, down to the river Ancre, were British; the French held the rest, to the south."

This was a setting of such physical extent that the different types of terrain alone gave rise to a variety of war experiences. Also, it was so extensive that a total picture could not be obtained by a single individual. . . . For writers such as Barbusse, and indeed Dorgelès, the attempt to create an overall picture of the war necessarily meant an element of "invention" and an account of episodes which they themselves had not witnessed. In an apparently paradoxical way—one no doubt peculiar to art—the pursuit of a fuller "truth" meant the creation of "fictional" elements. This is something which J. Norton Cru criticized severely in 1930. Displaying a resolutely non-literary approach which demanded documentary realism and rejected the imaginative apprehension which art can provide, he complained of novelists who show their failure to understand war and their betrayal of it "en la découpant en chapitres de roman feuilleton" ["by cutting it up into chapters like a serial novel"]. He even hints at an unworthy playing to the gallery when he adds: "Cette trahison a d'autant plus de succès que le public y retrouve ses épisodes favoris" ["this treason has that much more success because the public finds there its favorite episodes"]. Cru's uncompromisingly documentary stand means that the war novel apparently favoured by MacLeish proves guilty of "l'erreur traditionaliste: l'héroïsme" ["the traditionalist fallacy: heroism"], while that defended by Cowley betrays "l'erreur pacifiste: la brute sanguinaire" ["the pacifist fallacy: the sanguinary brute"].

This division into traditionalist and pacifist fiction, although too categorical, makes general sense if we turn to specific novels. Also, a brief consideration of two novels in particular helps us to put into clearer focus the question of moral impact raised above. Adrien Bertrand's *L'appel du sol* and Henri Barbusse's *Le feu* both appeared in 1916 and were both awarded the Prix Goncourt. *L'appel du sol,* representing the more traditionalist view of war, is not widely known and copies are hard to come by. *Le feu,* an uncompromising denunciation of war, was greatly admired by Wilfred Owen and Siegfried Sassoon when they read it in 1917 in the Everyman translation. It sold extremely well and is the most famous novel of the 1914-1918 period.

Although the differences between them remain fundamental, Bertrand and Barbusse share some broad characteristics as war novelists. Both are preoccupied by the horror of trench warfare. Both are natural preachers and proselytisers pursuing a positive emotional effect. Their fictional characters (mostly officers in the case of Bertrand and other ranks in that of Barbusse) are immensely talkative. The conversations which result are a major means of conveying their "message" to their readers. Their descriptions of human suffering are vivid and harrowing, but the narrative element is fairly fragmentary. Rather than tell a story with a strong and distinctive linear form, they work with a series of scenes and episodes—almost set-pieces—which create something like a mosaic. However, in spite of such similarities, they have very different attitudes to the presentation of war and place their common experience in contrasting moral perspectives. Bertrand wrote from a humane and traditionalist position, showing a sympathetic—but certainly not uncritical— understanding of the classical military virtues of duty, discipline, honour, courage. Barbusse wrote from outside the military tradition as a civilian of strongly left-wing persuasion caught up in the horror of modern war. Bertrand opens a debate on war and the military experience whereas Barbusse insists on a single and exclusive interpretation of these events. Bertrand's novel is two-dimensional and seeks a measure of exploration. Barbusse's novel is one-dimensional and is concerned with demonstration and proof.

Bertrand, although the balance of his attitude is towards a conservative outlook, understands and articulates opposing viewpoints. He argues a case for military discipline and patriotism. His novel ends with the words: "Mais la France continue! . . ." ["But France continues! . . ."] But several of his characters also express a sceptical attitude towards military ideals. Acceptance and protest are juxtaposed to convey a sense of the moral complexity inherent in the Great War. On the side of acceptance we must place Bertrand's use of the traditional rhetoric of patriotism and war. Within the first six chapters we meet many predictable terms and phrases: *grandeur morale, acceptation résignée, obéissance passive, grand sacrifice, abnégation, mission rédemptrice, mourir pour son pays, ce que la Patrie attend, appel autoritaire du sol de France* ["moral grandeur, resigned acceptance, passive obedience, grand sacrifice, abnegation, redemptive mission, to die for one's country, that which the fatherland expects, commanding call of the French soil"], etc. Within the general tone created by this type of vocabulary the main characters (some of them regular soldiers) take a high moral view of both patriotic duty and military discipline. (pp. 142-48)

[Bertrand] is aware of those evils of exploitation which Barbusse denounces. But he conceives of a duty which overrides them and of an honour which can only be served by stoical acceptance. War is accepted clear-sightedly; it is not glorified. Stoicism is the attitude of . . . characters such as Vaissette, *ancien normalien* ["former student"] and *agrégé de philosophie* ["professor of philosophy"], who speaks of his "soumission aux lois mystérieuses du destin et de la raison" ["submission to the mysterious laws of destiny and reason"].

At the same time, Bertrand recognizes weaknesses in this position. Patriotism does not prevent him from showing the French army in a state of considerable confusion and disarray due to a lack of intelligent and responsible leadership. (pp. 148-49)

One of the ordinary soldiers, Rousset, puts the anti-war case succinctly when he exclaims: " . . . c'est pas la guerre, c'est la boucherie" [" . . . this is not war, this is butchery"]. This view is confirmed by the terrible deaths and maimings described. And in the course of the novel the main characters—Nicolaï, Vaissette, Fabre, de Quéré—are all killed, while Angielli loses his reason. The final moral impression is one of extreme confusion and tragedy. There is much that is horrific; there is much that compels admiration.

If Bertrand is ready to encourage discussion and debate, Barbusse is determined to carry conviction. This determination is reflected in his use of first-person narrative which allows direct contact with the reader. Frequent authorial interventions serve a similar purpose and leave the reader in no doubt as to how events must be interpreted. Indeed, there are moments when the final chapter reads like a *Pravda* editorial. Not least, by forsaking the dynamic relationships of linear plot for something approaching the cumulative, static, patterning of a mosaic, Barbusse (and Bertrand to some extent)

is able to repeat, and therefore emphasise, the moral points he wishes to make.

The first of these points is the outrageous horror of war as experienced by soldiers the majority of whom are "des civils déracinés" ["uprooted civilians"]. (p. 149)

Barbusse . . . preaches, through his fictional characters, an explicit anti-militarism. One of the soldiers (named Bertrand, as it happens) cries: "Honte à la gloire militaire, honte aux armées, honte au métier de soldat, qui change les hommes tour à tour en stupides victimes et en ignobles bourreaux. Oui, honte: c'est vrai, mais c'est trop vrai, c'est vrai dans l'éternité, pas encore pour nous" ["Shame on military glory, shame on armies, shame on the profession of soldiering, which changes men by turns into stupid victims and into ignoble executioners. Yes, shame: it is true, it is too true, it is true in eternity, not only for us"].

Towards the end of the novel the moral tone takes on an increasingly political character. War is interpreted as a particularly dramatic form of a continuing exploitation of the poor by the rich. . . . Finally, Barbusse sees the war as preparing revolution—"cette guerre, c'est comme la Révolution Française qui continue" ["this war, it is like the French Revolution continuing"]—and looks forward to "l'entente des démocraties, l'entente des immensités, la levée du peuple du monde, la foi brutalement simple" ["the entente of democracies, the entente of the major powers, the lifting of the people of the world, the brutally simple faith"].

It seems appropriate to end with a brief analysis of the effects likely to be achieved by these two very different presentations of war. One's first reaction is probably to say that *Le feu* makes the greater impact because of its anti-war militancy. Barbusse does not run the risk of confusing the reader with antithetical arguments or of undermining his desired effect by presenting a "human" picture of the slaughter. He works with such concepts as exploitation and class conflict. He interprets modern warfare as an intensification of capitalist evils. Nevertheless, history since 1918 has not confirmed Barbusse's message. It now seems naïve compared with that of Bertrand. Furthermore, the methods Barbusse uses to convey his message to the reader are open to considerable criticism. Kenneth Burke, in the course of his comments on the MacLeish/Cowley debate mentioned earlier, argues [in "War, Response and Contradiction" in his *The Philosophy of Literary Form*] that militant pacifism, fed by unrelievedly horrifying details of war, may prove an aesthetic basis for essentially warlike and violent reactions. He maintains that horror, repugnance and hatred can provide "the firmest basis upon which the 'heroism' of a new war could be erected." If Bertrand's approach is less positive, its subtle balance of opposites does not run the risk of creating a counter-violence. Barbusse's method, by contrast, with its fundamentally conflictual view of society, risks encouraging a counter-violence at variance with its anti-militaristic message. As Burke puts it: "Sunday-school texts have ever been considered by sophisticated moralists the essential stimulus to 'sin'—and I see no reason why the same fact should not apply to a Sunday-school simplification in dealing with the problems of war." The single thread of partisanship can all too easily prove self-defeating.

Finally, Burke argues that readers would have to respond in the direct and automatic manner of machines for the kind of persuasion used by Barbusse to have its intended effect. Fortunately, the widely canvassed machine model of human beings can be shown to be an illusion. Human stimulus and response, not least in the field of literature, are more complicated, more wayward, less predictable. In fact, *Le feu* has been frequently admired for its dramatic rendering of war. It has been much more rarely praised as a stimulus to pacifism. If it is true that "*contradictoriness of response* is basic to human psychology," *L'appel du sol* may turn out, a trifle ironically, to be the more potent pacifist document. (pp. 149-51)

J. Cruickshank, "Critical Approaches to Some Novels of the Great War," in Literature and Society: Studies in Nineteenth and Twentieth Century French Literature, Presented to R. J. North, edited by C. A. Burns, University of Birmingham, 1980, pp. 140-52.

ALBERT SCHINZ

[*In the following excerpt, Schinz presents an overview of French war-time drama.*]

The theater is one of the best means of influencing public opinion. Thus one might have expected that the theater would play a foremost part during the war. It seldom did.

The best war-plays, indeed, were written before 1914. There are especially two spy dramas: One is Lavedan's *Servir,* in two acts, given almost on the eve of the war, in 1913; a prophetic play truly. And the other is Kistemaeker's *La flambée* (known in English speaking countries under the title *The Spy*) which has more action, more spectacular drama in it, but which is not more deeply patriotic than *Servir.* To show how well, even before the war, some men in France had not only foreseen what was coming, but had well anticipated the courageous attitude of the French during the war, let us quote just one short passage from Lavedan's play.

Colonel Eulin discusses with Madame Eulin the military profession of their three sons, one of whom has just been reported killed in the colonies:

EULIN. The soldier is a man apart. I have often told you so. Accident is his opportunity, and catastrophe his glory. Every danger which threatens him is a privilege; every evil which befalls him makes him greater. Therefore if we are to rise to the level of those marks of honor, we are to train our sons to every loftier sentiment. Since we have sons who are above the crowd of ordinary mortals, let us, their parents, show ourselves worthy of them.

MADAME EULIN. How lightly you speak of the fate of your children.

EULIN. No, not lightly. But I must say that when I think of the possible death of some member of my family, it never strikes me as a calamity if I am sure that it will be beautiful.

MADAME EULIN. Parents know of no beautiful deaths of children.

EULIN. Some deaths are splendid . . . and they are necessary.

MADAME EULIN. Why necessary?

EULIN. To prevent ugly ones—or to redeem them. Be prouder; bear your grief with raised head. . . . What really matters is not that one should live or die, but that one should die well. If I should die of disease, you may mourn if you wish, but if I fall with a bullet through my forehead, I forbid you to show any grief.

From 1914 to 1915, attempts were made to echo on the stage, as in the other domains of literature, the indignation against Germany's barbarism. In Nozière's *Prière dans la nuit,* a loyal French woman of the invaded territory, who has married a naturalized German, discovers that she has given her love to a traitor, and she stabs him before he has time to do more harm. *La kommandantur,* by Fronson (the Belgian author of the famous *Mademoiselle Beulemans*) is a painful description of the conditions in Belgium under German rule; it presents the story of the return to Brussels of a German officer whose love had been spurned by a Belgian girl and who takes a cowardly vengeance by having the fiancé of the young woman shot; he also tries to force her; but she kills him. A third play of the same order is that of Soulié (1916), called *1914 à 1937:* a boy, an "enfant du crime," son of a French woman of Northern France and of a German soldier of the Great War, meets his father in 1937 and strangles him.

It soon became clear that the public did not care for such performances: one may bear to read about such things, but one does not like to see them acted. This kind of play, therefore, ceased to be produced; and it is worthy of note that the best one of them, though written in the earlier days of the war, was not acted until 1919, when a translation of it was presented at Springfield, Mass., and then in New York. We refer to Maeterlinck's *Le bourgmestre de Stilemonde.* Maeterlinck refrains from any jingoism and his restraint adds to the force of the play. The subject is the atrocious act of "the most humane of the German officers," who has the Burgomaster of Stilemonde shot under the pretext of reprisal, but probably with the purpose of terrorization. A German officer had been assassinated in the town, and the evidence clearly pointed to one of his own men who hated him, as author of the act. The Burgomaster is a splendid figure; he refuses to allow one of his gardeners who was plainly innocent to be shot; he also refuses the offers of others who want to die in his place, while the Germans just shrug their shoulders at what appears to them a ridiculous piece of sentimentality. The Burgomaster accepts his fate courageously, although in despair because he leaves behind a very young boy, and also a daughter who had married a German lieutenant. The latter had left Stilemonde on the eve of the war, but had returned to his adopted town at the head of his victorious soldiers; when he shows himself unable or unwilling to save his father-in-law, he is rejected with scorn by the wife.

Less unwelcome than the actual "atrocity plays" during the first winter of the war, was the dramatization of Maurice Barrès's *Colette Baudoche.* It may be due to the excellence of the play itself or to the fact that the good cause was upheld without gruesome scenes, or again to the fact that the problem of Alsace-Lorraine was too near the heart of all Frenchmen to be ignored on the stage . . . Paris seemed pleased to hear Colette make it so plain why, after forty years of annexation, there still could be no sympathy between the conquered and the conqueror.

Perhaps while waiting for more satisfactory war plays, the managers tried various revivals of former War-classics, like Corneille's *Horace,* Sardou's *Patrie,* Bornier's *La fille de Roland* (which had in 1875 stirred up France still depressed by the defeat of 1870); also the once very popular drama which had filled with enthusiasm the patriots of 1848, *Marceau, ou les enfants de la République;* and even the play from Dumas's lively novel *La jeunesse des mousquetaires.* Then also, Erkman-Chatrian's delightful Alsatian play *L'ami Fritz.* Sometimes they took up plays of the past which would offer a relaxation from the nervous tension, such as A. France's *Le crime de Sylvestre Bonnard,* Meilhac et Halévy's *Tricoche et Cacolet,* and the abundant and ever acceptable répertoire of Molière.

One of the most successful of these "reprises" was Kistemaeker's *La flambée.* In 1918, however, this author gave a new spy-play, *Un soir au front,* in which a rather interesting attempt was made to define the Honor of the French soldier as contrasted with the German Military Duty. But, while some situations are very strong, the play is encumbered with theoretical discussions which are clearly not what the public looks for in a war drama: A French woman has married a German who had been naturalized, and who, when the war broke out, had been forty years in the country. He was a captain of the French army; but almost immediately after the outbreak of hostilities he had been reported missing. He had passed into the German lines, but came back from time to time in his French uniform for the purpose of spying. One night his wife, who had returned to her dilapidated residence, now used as military quarters, met him—and guessed the truth. Although his behavior and person inspired her with scorn and horror, she asked an officer whose life she had saved, and who knew the situation, to spare the traitor for her sake. Her request is heeded; but nevertheless the spy does not escape his deserved fate.

Really only one play, written directly under the inspiration of the war and during the war, and written in the tradition of the French theater of the last forty years, achieved genuine success. This is Bernstein's *Elévation* (presented for the first time in June, 1917). The idea of the drama,—regeneration by the war of a man of purely worldly ideals—had already by that time been often discussed. And some critics seem to have been angry because they were stirred in spite of themselves by so commonplace a theme; yet they could not deny being moved. An idea, though not original, may none the less be beautiful; and the very fact that Bernstein succeeded in moving deeply with a trite theme, is a distinct testimony to the power of his art. *L'Elévation* was written in an hospital at Saloniki while the author was recovering from a wound;—he had served in the aviation corps.

The plays mentioned above were rather ambitious in so far as the authors seem to have aimed at writing regular, lasting plays on the ephemeral subject of the war. Such authors, who wrote in keeping well in mind that they were catering to a public laboring under very special conditions, succeeded better. There is really a good crop of what they call in French "pièces de circonstances" ["occasional plays"].

Some are written in a light and cheerful mood. Some are of the serious kind.

The following belong to the first group: *L'Impromptu du Paquetage,* in one act, a delicate sketch by Maurice Donnay. The stage represents an office for war-relief, to which come various callers from the humbler classes; they tell their touching and often heroic tales of self-sacrifice on the altar of the mother country . . . ; we may mention here, by the same author, *Le théâtre aux armées* (1917), a play to be performed before the soldiers at the front. Players are discussing which would be the best topic for such a representation, and this dis-

cussion quite naturally introduces many pleasant appreciations of the soldiers' virtues,—and the actors decide to go on the stage and present just that discussion; *Les deux gloires,* by Pierre Wolf (published for the first time in the *Annales,* July, 1916)—"les deux gloires" being the veteran of 1870-71, and the "Poilu" of 1914 (a pretty love episode is woven into the play); *Le Poilu,* Comédie-opérette, in two acts, by M. Hennequin and P. Veber, music by H. M. Jacquet—is a very bright and graceful vaudeville. A young soldier falls in love with his "marraine" ["correspondent"] just from reading the letters she sends to the trenches. He comes to Paris; complications arise; but all ends well.

Among the occasional plays in more serious mood, let us mention the following few: *Le gars,* a beautiful little dialogue in verse, by Zamacoïs, which came out first in *L'Illustration,* and then in the author's volume *L'Ineffaçable;* Paul Claudel, *La nuit de Noël de 1914:* it is a sort of one act mystery play, in verse, showing on the night commemorating the birth of the Divine Child, the murdered children of Belgium and Northern France who arrive in Paradise—from which place of delight they look down on the sufferings of the world. It is a moving indictment from the mouths of the innocents, recalling several concrete instances of German barbarity.

La vierge de Lutèce, by A. Villeroy represented at the Théâtre Sarah Bernhardt, June 29, 1915, is a dramatic presentation of the legend of Sainte Geneviève, the patron-saint of Paris who saved the city from the Huns in the fifth century. The allusions to the events of the Great War are clear to all: "Ils ne passeront pas!" ["They will not pass!"] exclaims Sainte Geneviève; "La civilisation, c'est moi!" ["I am civilization!"] says Attila; and when Actius, the commander of the army which defends Paris, gives his order of the day for the decisive battle, he does so in the words of Marshal Joffre's famous proclamation, on the 5th of September, 1914: "Le moment n'est plus de regarder en arrière. . . . Quiconque ne pourra plus avancer a l'ordre de garder le terrain conquis . . . il se fera tuer sans reculer d'un pas. . . ." ["It is no longer time to look backward. Whoever can go no further is ordered to guard the conquered territory . . . he will let himself be killed rather than retreat one step. . . ."] At the end, Sainte Geneviève is solemnly admonished by the Bishop Germain l'Auxerrois to "continuer à veiller sur la ville endormie" ["continue to watch over the sleeping village"].

Several plays were specially written for Sarah Bernhardt. We will mention only one: Eugène Moraud's very spectacular *Les cathédrales,* in fine verse (November, 1916). In a gray cloud, five nuns representing the cathedrals of five French regions are bemoaning the tragic events of the war. They are, Notre Dame de Paris, Saint Pol de Léon, Bourges, Amiens, Arles—and later are seen the two martyr cathedrals, Reims and Strassbourg. Maledictions and prophecies of divine punishments against the invaders are interpreted with all the passion at the command of Madame Sarah Bernhardt—who impersonates Strassbourg. There are other plays of that kind; such, for instance, as *L'Eternelle présence,* written by the poet André Dumas for the commemoration of the Battle of the Marne, at the Comédie Française, in 1917; or, as Lavedan and Zamacoïs's *Les sacrifices* (*Les Flandres, Noël, Reims, Poème dramatique en trois tableaux* [1918]); the first "tableau" is a picture of refugees fleeing before the invaders; the second, a Christmas in the trenches; and the third, a sort of monologue by the Rheims cathedral, evoking the memory of

Joan of Arc and of the heroic cohorts in horizon-blue uniform. The "poème" was not presented.

More ambitious than all the preceding plays—but still indisputably a "pièce de circonstance" is François Porché's *Les Butors et la Finette*. The author was already well known by a fine poem, *l'Arrêt sur la Marne*. The play—four acts, six tableaux, in verse—was presented for the first time on November 29, 1917, at the Théâtre Antoine, and created quite a sensation. It is an allegorical history of the war. The Miron family (this means the French people) are cultivating a beautiful garden for Princesse Finette (France), whose graceful kindness and genuineness of heart have been responsible for her blind confidence in the foreigner Buq, the superintendent of the domain, and a master spy. The Butors (the "Pigheaded" ones, as poetic a name as could be found for the Huns) invaded the domain just as every one was preparing for festivities. . . . During the war, the enemy proposes to Finette a luring but deceitful peace; but she has enough sense, and especially pride, to refuse. And finally François Miron, the impersonation of the chivalrous people of France, frees the country of the foe and becomes the lord of the fine lady. As to Buq, the traitor, he has paid with his life for his shameful and contemptible behavior. Victory has not been achieved without heavy sacrifices, but, free from the fear of invasion, Finette's people again set about cultivating the beautiful garden of France. (pp. 338-50)

[Another] attempt to abandon the realistic and the concrete, in favor of the ideal and the abstract, was made almost at the same time as Porché gave his *Les Butors et la Finette,* when the "Théâtre des Alliés" founded by M. Jean Billaud with the purpose of propaganda during and after the war, gave as its first production *Les epis rouges* by Emile Sicard, the Provençal poet. This work is an elaborately staged "Poème dramatique" in four acts, some parts of which are set to music. The author has aimed less at presenting regular scenes than tableaux representing the days of mobilization; women waiting with anguish for news of the front; a night of spectacular war display at Verdun, etc. And the characters are not so much individuals as abstractions: *the* mother, *the* betrothed, *the* ancestor, *the* warrior, etc. While *Les epis rouges* cannot be said to have been a failure, it certainly did not take the public by storm. (pp. 351-52)

This would be the place probably to say something about the theater in the trenches. Much interest has been shown for it; yet very scanty information is on hand. . . . It may be permitted, however, to doubt whether many of these occasional plays written by the soldiers will offer lasting literary value, and whether the study would not be rather of an historical or psychological value as showing the spirit that prevailed among the soldiers of the war. A few probably will be found worth preserving, as, for instance, the pretty little dialogue by Jean Suberville, caporal mitrailleur au 94° d'Infanterie, *Cyrano de Bergerac aux tranchées.* When it was printed, the little play was honored by a short "Lettre-Préface" by Edmond Rostand. Soldiers represented it on the "Théâtre Chantecler" of the "32° Corps d'armée" which gave 250 performances during thirteen months. Cyrano comes to our planet, in his fall almost pitching through the wings of "un papillon énorme qui passait," ["an enormous butterfly that was passing,"] and seeing very queer "gros hannetons aux bourdonnantes élîtres" (air torpedoes). In finding soldiers of France hiding in holes in the ground he is shocked terribly:

Le temps a-t-il changé les Français héroîques?

["Had time changed the heroic French?"]

To which the "Poilu" answers, well conscious that he has nothing to be ashamed of:

Ils sont ce qu'ils étaient, en étant plus pratiques!
Ce qui change, c'est la manière, pas l'élan!
Vous autres, vous faisiez la guerre en rigolant!
Ça ne durait qu'un an vos batailles gentilles!
Vos canons ne lançaient que des boules de quilles!
Puis quand vous reveniez dans vos nobles salons,
Les dames se haussaient au bout de leurs talons. . . .

• • • • •

Nous qui sommes vêtus de boue, admirez-nous!
Nous qui ne portons pas de plumet, mais des poux,

• • • • •

Je crois que nous valons encore nos aïeux;
Que, s'ils furent plus beaux, ils ne firent pas mieux. . . .

["They are what they were, being in addition practical!
What changed is the manner, not the enthusiasm!
You others, you made war by having a lark!
Your polite battles lasted but a year!
Your cannons shot nothing but bowling balls!
Then when you would return to your fine drawing rooms,
The ladies would raise themselves up on their heels. . . .

• • • • •

We who are clothed in mud, admire us!
We who do not wear plumes, but lice,

• • • • •

I believe that we are as good as our forebears;
That if they were more handsome, they did not shoot better. . . ."]

And Cyrano understands:

Et je te reconnais, France des mousquetaires,
Dans la France de ces Poilus!

["And I recognize you, France of the musketeers,
in the France of these Poilus!"]

We come now to a group of writers who borrowed materials from the war, but endeavored to remain entirely indifferent to the patriotic side of their plots. They are war-plays without the war spirit. They are not unpatriotic in purpose, merely a-patriotic. At the same time they are unpleasant—and if not atrocity plays, surely most of them are atrocious plays.

A good deal has been said about the unsettled state of moral standards during and after a war; and the question has been more than once asked, how far should the social obligations of normal times be considered binding? These plays are a few samples illustrating such preoccupations. *L'Amazone* (1915) by Bataille, is the painful story of a girl of the invaded provinces, who, having seen her whole family slaughtered, gets into a state of patriotic frenzy which in the milieu where she has taken refuge, proves to be contagious; she makes use of her womanly charms to induce the husband of her friend to join the army as volunteer; then, later, when she wants to marry another, the wife of the soldier maintains that she has no right to do so, since she is now morally bound to the man who went to war on her account; she accepts that view.

A somewhat analogous situation is sketched in Marcel L'Herbier's *L'enfant du mort* (1917). In André Couvreur's *Plus haut que l'amour* (1916), the heroine appears again as if completely at a loss when she has to decide on her line of conduct in love-affairs; she acts according to the inspiration of the moment, now ignoring the love of a man whom she knows to be worthy of her, now throwing herself away on a man who turns out to be a spy, and then finally taking refuge in the arms of the strong man who had protected her from the beginning. In Vernet et Delamarre's *L'autre combat,* a woman in a moment of self-sacrifice marries a blind soldier to whom she had been betrothed though she did not love him; she then betrays him; and finally she repents. . . . In 1917 the Comédie Française presented Francis de Croisset's *D'un jour à l'autre,* another keen study of a woman character during the war. This heroine hesitates whether to give her love to a fashionable *mondain* who has been divorced, to a business man who has grown rich through the war, or to a fascinating hero of aviation—she decides for the last, but only after long deliberation. (pp. 353-57)

Porto-Riche's gruesome drama, *Le marchand d'estampes* (1917), is the most powerful of those descriptions of normal moral lives which are shattered in consequence of the war: Aubertin was a quiet lover of art, selling engravings, leading a model life as husband and tradesman, in his little shop. Then he joins the colors. In the crude, natural, almost animal life of the trenches, his lower, bestial instincts are re-awakened and take the upper hand; so that, when he returns home, wounded, he falls in love (sensual love) at first sight, with a woman of the neighborhood (who is never seen on the stage). He retains, however, enough decency to realize the uncleanness of his passion, and to be profoundly unhappy about it. He does not want to do any wrong to the devoted companion of his life. She, too, is plunged in deep grief, and, finally, they both go together and throw themselves in the Seine,—he, so as not to be unfaithful to his wife, she, so as not to be separated from her husband.

Less gloomy—and more generously inspired—is Lauden-bach's *Le sacrifice* (1918); the author expresses the idea that war ought to reflect on the whole life of the soldier, making him chivalrous not only in his military activities but at all times. With all its loftiness of purpose, *Le sacrifice* is, after all, a "triangle play" of the trenches.

Having even more clearly the characteristics of a "triangle play" but one written by two skillful craftsmen of the stage, is *La veillée d'armes,* by Claude Farrère and Louis Népoty (1917). The scene is first on a small vessel, the *Alma,* a scouting cruiser. Captain Corlaix, 50 years of age, has a young wife of 23, Jeanne. She is a pretty woman, not bad at heart but made of the common clay, and she regards him as a father rather than a husband. She loves d'Ardelles, first lieutenant of the ship. There is a farewell dinner on board; they all expect war, and the men are eager to start. At 11 o'clock an order arrives, however, to remain for the present in Toulon, although war is now unavoidable. Jeanne and her sister must leave the boat, but Jeanne finds at the last minute some pretext—a lost vanity bag—to remain, and she spends the night in the room of d'Ardelles, expecting to leave by the 6 o'clock rowboat. But a counter order arrives, and the vessel sails. . . . In the morning, d'Ardelles finds with dismay that they are at sea, with the woman aboard. They are attacked by a German torpedo boat, which has used French code signals to lure the *Alma* to its destruction. The *Alma* is sinking. Corlaix is wounded; he thinks he is lost. D'Ardelles dies in trying to save Jeanne, and entrusts her to the care of his orderly. She succeeds in returning home, without any one except her sister suspecting what has happened to her. Corlaix also is saved and recovers. But then he is summoned before a court-martial to answer for the loss of his vessel. There is no witness to prove that the enemy used French signals; only two officers have survived, Corlaix himself, and Bramburg, a somewhat suspicious character, possibly a spy, who is in love with Jeanne but whom she hates. Under the pretext of amnesia, he declares himself unable to testify either way. Jeanne, in order to save Corlaix, intervenes. She has a means of forcing Bramburg to admit that he knows that the Germans used French signals:—of course, by doing this, she must own to the fact that she was on the vessel. Corlaix understands all; and,—rather as father and daughter now,—they shake hands and return home. *La veillée d'armes* is a strong drama, in which, however, the war has no essential part.

As the war proceeded, and its gloomiest days were succeeded by more hopeful ones, especially after the entrance of America, the theater ceased to be used as a means of inspiring the people. There are still plays recalling the war, of course, such as the humorous *Beulemans à Marseilles* (1918) in which Fronson revives his famous Belgian characters made up of pathos and joviality; or, as Jacques Richepin's "cocardier" ["jingoistic"] play, *La guerre et l'amour, Pièce héroïque, en quatre actes et en vers* (1918); or, such as Sacha Guitry's *L'Archevêque et son fils* (1918), in which the author seems to think that the war was made to give him material for witty but flippant stage effects, (the play reminds one somewhat of Mérimée's *Carosse du Saint Sacrement*). (pp. 357-61)

There is one play which will probably not be presented on the French stage for some time to come, but which may be mentioned as a curiosity, Romain Rolland's *Liluli* (1919). The pacifist of 1914 is anxious to show that he has not changed his views and is still willing to challenge the world that this war was absurd. He still refuses to draw any distinction between the Central Powers, who yielded to the folly of war because they wanted to do so, and the Allies, who waged war in order to exterminate the war spirit from the surface of the earth: *Any* war is folly! Liluli is the goddess of illusion, who persuades men, and especially youth, that war can be a noble thing. . . . When the curtain falls, this belief has brought about a formidable crash, and on a heap of ruins sits triumphantly Liluli, her tongue out and her finger to her nose. (p. 362)

Albert Schinz, "The Stage and the War," in his French Literature of the Great War, *D. Appleton and Company, 1920, pp. 338-62.*

WORLD WAR I LITERATURE AND MODERN HISTORY

CORRELLI BARNETT

[Barnett is an English military and political historian who spe-

cializes in twentieth-century subjects. Among his works about the First World War are The Swordbearers: Supreme Command in the First World War (1963) and The Great War (1980); he also served as co-author and historical consultant for the British Broadcasting Corporation's television series "The Great War," "The Lost Peace: 1918-1933," and "The Commanders." In the following excerpt from a lecture delivered before the Royal Society of Literature in April 1969, Barnett discusses the effect of war literature on British postwar foreign policy.]

In his excellent bibliography of war books published in 1930, Captain Cyril Falls listed some 690 titles. This number must surely have doubled by 1969. I have not read all these books. But I do not mean today to discuss official or regimental histories, or the grand memoirs, or any of the host of biographies and general historical studies. I mean to keep to personal reminiscences and novels. Of these Captain Falls lists nearly 200 titles. I haven't read more than a fraction of these either. Even more narrowly I intend to deal with those few British professional writers of distinction whose war books have made most impact on our national consciousness, and which have achieved a permanent place in our literature.

I shall exclude verse and writers who wrote only verse. From the point of view of a historian the verse adds little, if anything, in the way of information to the prose, mostly presenting similar subjects, though with greater intensity of feeling.

My purpose is historical. I hope therefore not to poach on the grounds of literary criticism so very ably covered by such critics as Bernard Bergonzi in his Heroes' Twilight. My concern will not be with the comparison of the literary merits or techniques of the books and their authors, but with the light they cast on British history in the twentieth century.

"A military historian's view of the Great War literature"— well, obviously the starting-point must be the value of the works as historical evidence about the operations and life of the British Army on the Western Front.

This value is two-fold. In the first place neither the memoirs of the grand people who ran the war, nor the official or regimental histories tell us what the Western Front was like. The reminiscences and the novels—the two often come to much the same thing—tell us just this—and do so with all the awareness, imaginative insight, and skill of writers of first-class talent. Books like Blunden's Undertones of War, or Williamson's Patriot's Progress, or Frederic Manning's Her Privates We enable us to see, smell, feel, and touch the reality of life and battle on the Western Front. I won't go into the details of billets, dug-outs, raids and patrols, rations, marches, and so on, because these after all form much of the substance of war literature, and are familiar to you. I would simply like to point out that, carefully weighed, this evidence is of the highest value to the historian, providing him with an intimate insight and understanding that otherwise he would lack, and cautioning him against a too abstract and intellectual approach to the subject. Curiously enough, however, one of the most famous works of war literature—Sassoon's Memoirs of an Infantry Officer—is less valuable than the books I have already mentioned, or, say, Charles Edmond's A Subaltern's War, for only a third of Sassoon's book deals with the Western Front.

In the second place, war literature is valuable as historical evidence about the army in France in a more specific way. It can tell us how the army was trained, how it functioned, its operational effectiveness, its human strengths and weaknesses. And once again it offers the reality of immediate and perceptive witness to supplement the dry, abstract accounts of these things in general histories. The professional writer in uniform was wonderfully placed to give posterity an outsider's inside view of the army of the 1914-18 era; small details as well as larger revelations.

We learn from Edmund Blunden's Undertones of War, for example, that in early 1916 British Very lights were not very good:

> . . . the effect was one of ejaculation rather than illumination, two or three deafening cartridges provided a thin whirl of sparks that died on their early way in to the sightless sky: meanwhile the Germans were sending up fine confident lights, which soared and sank in beautiful curves, or, suspended on parachutes, delayed their spiral fall and sought out all nooks and corners. The superiority of their flares was mortifying. . . .

Poor old British technology! It was better to buy German as long ago as 1916.

On the whole I find Blunden, however, too mannered and impressionistic in his descriptions to serve the historian well. I prefer for example Robert Graves's Goodbye to All That. He writes in a direct and factual and workmanlike way, less occupied with his aesthetic and moral responses than either Blunden, or, say, Sassoon. His approach is professional in a military as well as a literary sense.

Thus he tells us how second-lieutenants were trained in late 1914 in a regular, not a New Army or Territorial unit: "We . . . learned regimental history, drill, musketry, Boer War field tactics, military law and organisation, how to recognise bugle calls, and how to work a machine-gun, and how to conduct ourselves on formal occasions. We dug no trenches, handled no bombs, thought of the company, not of the platoon, still less of the section . . .".

Graves also casts light on the real professional state of even regular units in France by 1915. His battalion of the Welsh Regiment had only four time-serving N.C.O.s (i.e. not reservists), while only about fifty of the men had had more than two months' training. As for the Territorials, Graves records this 1915 opinion by a regular: "The Territorial battalion that used to relieve us were hopeless." And of Kitchener's New Army: "The general impression here is that the New Army divisions can't be of much military use."

Then again Graves describes the training camp at Harfleur in early 1916, when units were being prepared for the offensive on the Somme. In a fascinating passage he summarizes discussions in the Mess on all sorts of military topics, such as the relative fighting capacity of different divisions, and of men from different parts of the United Kingdom and the Empire. The Mess agreed that only a third of the army was dependable in all circumstances, another third middling, and the remainder "more or less untrustworthy." Does all this not cast light on the heavy British casualties to come on the Somme, while attacking a still highly trained German army, posted in very strong positions?

Graves also tells us that

> For the first three weeks (in the trenches), an officer was of little use in the front line; he did not know his way about, had not learned the rules of health

and safety, or grown accustomed to recognising degrees of danger. Between three weeks and four weeks he was at his best. . . . Then his usefulness gradually declined as neurasthenia developed. At six months he was still more or less all right; but, by nine months, unless he had been given a few weeks' rest . . . he usually became a drag on the other company officers. After a year or fifteen months he was often worse than useless.

Later on still, in 1916, Graves provides equally interesting reflections on the training of officer-cadets for three months in cadet-battalions. In his now experienced professional judgement, "The cadet-battalion system saved the army in France from becoming a rabble."

Yet it is not my main purpose today to explore Great War literature in this way as a repository of interesting military detail. I want to take a much broader historical view—by examining the impact of that literature on British history in the twentieth century.

The first point to note is the timing. Although there had been a spate of books about the war immediately after 1918, and a steady trickle of general works or novels throughout the 1920s—Mottram's *Spanish Farm* trilogy, for example, and Ford Madox Ford's four novels—the great bull market for personal trench reminiscences opened in 1927. In this year there were fifteen such books as against six in 1926. In 1928 there were twenty-one—in 1929 thirty-nine. Although the reviewers now began to argue that there was a glut of mud and blood, 1930 proved another boom year for trench horrors, and the market only subsided slowly afterwards. Essentially, however, it was the three years 1928-31 that produced the decisive impression on the public—1928, Blunden's *Undertones of War*, Sassoon's *Memoirs of a Fox-Hunting Man,* and Sheriff's *Journey's End* first staged; 1929, Aldington's *Death of a Hero,* Remarque's *All Quiet,* Grave's *Goodbye to All That,* Hemingway's *A Farewell to Arms;* 1930, Manning's *Her Privates We* and Sassoon's *Memoirs of an Infantry Officer;* 1931, Wilfred Owen's *Poems* in an edition by Edmund Blunden.

Why did the great flood come in 1928-30? There is evidence that the writers themselves were unable to express their terrible experiences before this. Aldington says: "I began the book almost immediately after the Armistice. . . . Then came demobilisation, and the effort of re-adjustment cost my manuscript its life. I threw it aside, and never picked it up again. The attempt was premature. Then, ten years later, almost day for day, I felt the impulse return, and began this book." Blunden even tried to write a war book before the war had ended, but he too completed little. Graves in the early 1920s made "several attempts during these years to rid myself of the poison of war memories by finishing my novel, but had to abandon it—ashamed at having distorted my material with a plot, and yet not sure enough to turn it back into undisguised history, as here."

Was the eventual timing of the great works of war literature due only to such personal psychological factors? Or was there some influence making for mental release in the general course of European affairs in the late twenties? Consider: Locarno, 1925; Germany admitted to the League of Nations, 1926; the Kellogg Pact renouncing war as an instrument of policy, 1928; the Young Plan settling reparations, and the beginning of the withdrawal of allied occupation forces from the Rhineland, 1929. And also 1928, death of Haig; 1929, death of Foch. Whether or not there was any connection, the

major works of war literature appeared exactly at the time when the Great War at last seemed to be dead and buried and part of history.

Yet before the war-book boom had spent itself, the entire European situation had changed, and another war became for the first time a real possibility again, if a distant one: 1930-33, the world slump; 1931, Japan exposed the League of Nations as a pious chapel meeting over Manchuria; in 1933 Hitler became Chancellor of Germany, left the disarmanent conference and then the League.

Thus the trench reminiscences began appearing in an epoch where they seemed the belated truth about an experience that now belonged completely to the past, but went on to appear in a new epoch where they had an immediate relevance to the present and future. What began as an epitaph ended as a warning. As a warning, the war books seemed to say that war was so terrible and futile that the British ought to keep out of another one at all costs. Thus war literature served as powerful ammunition for pacifists and appeasers of Hitler in the 1930s. The coincidence of the boom in trench reminiscences coming in 1928-30, that turning-point of the inter-war period—if it was a coincidence—could not have been historically more significant.

Now, despite great contrasts of style and personal response—between, say, the elegance of Blunden and the savagery of Aldington—the outstanding trench reminiscences tell much the same story and draw much the same moral. Their cumulative effect was—is—a generalized picture of idealism turning into sour disillusion, of the futility of the fighting on the Western Front, of the squalor of trench life, of the obscenity of death and mutilation on a modern battlefield, of the terrors of a great battle. Perhaps most of all the extinction of human individuality and life itself under the vast anonymous squashing boot of gunfire.

These trench reminiscences or novels will be so familiar to you that I will not pile up quotations to fill out this summary of the Great War as seen by soldier-writers. More important for my purpose . . . is to note that this picture of the war made an immense impact at the time, not only because there were so many war books, but because they were so avidly read. R. C. Sheriff's play *Journey's End* was reprinted thirteen times, for example, between January and October 1929, and had sold up to that date 45,000 copies. Blunden's *Undertones of War* was reprinted three times in one month—Manning's *Her Privates We* four times in a month.

What did the reviewers, as representatives of educated, indeed cultured opinion, make of these books? The *Sunday Times* wrote of Aldington's *Death of a Hero:* "The stupidity and humbug of those who 'made' the war, and the monstrous futility of the war itself; such is his theme . . .".

The *Daily Mirror* advised its more numerous readership: " . . . we commend the vituperative war novel as a useful reminder and sermon for those who are beginning to forget."

Victoria Sackville-West on the radio was rapturous about Sassoon's *Memoirs of an Infantry Officer.* "I daresay," she told her audience, "that Mr. Sassoon's manifesto of protest against the war—which comes at the end of the book—will stir many people to wish that they had had the moral courage to express the same sentiment." *Time and Tide* wrote of Sassoon's book that it had " . . . a quietness of judgement which does not disguise the deep indignation with which he saw men uselessly slaughtered . . .". The *Sunday Despatch* felt that "like Mr. Aldington, Mr. Sassoon leaves us with an abiding sense of the futility of the grim struggle . . . Both books, too, are in their full scope denunciations of the folly of war, more effective than many of the more direct phillipics of politicians and orators." Then again the *Daily Mirror:* " . . . we have his revulsion of feeling against the futility of the nightmare through which he and his fellow soldiers passed." Or, to give a fair spread of opinion, here is *The Tatler* on Henry Williamson's *Patriot's Progress:* "It leaves one angry—angry against war. It leaves one also angry against people who find in war anything finer than a supreme human disgrace."

"Stupidity and humbug," "monstrous futility," "useless slaughter," "deep indignation," "revulsion of feeling."— Such then was the general picture of the Great War that book reviewers—and presumably readers—got from the trench reminiscences. They took it to be the truth. It was of course true so far as it went. But was it the whole truth? Had the British army in general shared the war writer's retrospective agonizing? Did in fact the war writers—because they *were* writers and poets, and because also of their cultural and social background—did they serve up an untypical and unbalanced view of the war? And with the dire result that this unbalanced view was taken by British public opinion as the literal and complete truth. Did therefore the war writers do much and wrongly morally to disarm the British against Hitler? These are questions I would like to answer.

The war writers were indeed highly untypical people. With the exception of Manning and Rosenberg they came from the sheltered, well-off, upper or upper-middle classes. They had had an absurd upbringing at home and at their public schools which gave them no knowledge or understanding of the real world of their time, but instead a set of ludicrously romantic attitudes, most famously expressed in Rupert Brooke's excruciating poem "Now God Be Thanked." They were in fact the repositories of the liberalism and romanticism of Victorian England. They all lived at Howard's End, having delicate emotional responses to the aesthetic stimulus of landscape, and cherishing a knightly idealism.

Who would guess from Sassoon or Blunden or Graves that the landscape they loved in fact represented British agriculture in distress and decay? Who would guess from their work that Britain in 1914 was in fact an overwhelmingly urban and industrial country with profound social problems? That a third of the population lived in poverty?

The social, aesthetic, intellectual, and moral world in which the war writers lived before the war was in fact totally unreal—as artificial as the pastoral idylls of the French court before 1789.

Hence army and trench life—quite apart from the hazards and horrors of war itself—was their first introduction to the real world of struggle, discomfort, and hardship as most of mankind experienced it. We all know that much of the incidental detail in the trench literature is not connected with danger and death, but with such aspects as the following:

"Washing was a torment. They had three tubs of water between about forty of them a day. Since Winterbourne was a latecomer to the Battalion he had to wait until the others had finished. The water was cold and utterly filthy" (Aldington). Or the dug-outs:

"Each of the guttering candles had a halo round it. The smoke from them, and tobacco, and acrid fumes from the brazier, could not mask the stale smell of unwashed men, and serges into which had soaked and dried the sweat of months" (Manning). Not forgetting of course the ubiquitous rats. Then there were the pole latrines:

" . . . while they sat there they hunted and killed the lice on their bodies" (Manning).

To the war writers and their readers all this squalor was not the least unpleasant aspect of the Great War. Yet in fact nearly a third of the British population lived their entire lives in comparable conditions. Descriptions of contemporary British slums remarkably echo those of the trenches. Thus:

"Two rooms, seven inmates . . . Dirty flock bedding in livingroom placed on box and two chairs. Smell of room from dirt and bad air unbearable." Or: "Two Rooms. In the lower room the brick floor is in holes. Fireplace without grate in the bottom. Wooden floor of upper room has large holes admitting numbers of mice. Roof very defective, the rain falling through on to the bed in wet weather." Or: "There is no water supply in the house, the eight families having to share one water-tap with eight other families."

Compare a typical description of a trench with a yard in a slum. Here is Blunden:

"Under their floors of boards and slats, water swelled and stagnated, and an indescribable nocturnal smell, mortal, greenweedy, ratty accompanied the tramp of our boots to and fro."

And the slum:

"Large unpaved yard, full of holes. One ashpit and one closet is used by nine families . . . The smell from these places is simply horrible in hot or wet weather."

A no less prominent feature of trench reminiscence is the evocation of the dereliction and desolation of the trench zone—very much Blunden's and Sassoon's forte.

"The red-brick hollow of a station marked 'Cuinchy' told us that we were almost at our journey's end: other ruins of industrial buildings and machinery showed through the throbbing haze; the path became corrupt, and the canal dead and stagnant." Thus Blunden. Now Sassoon—but writing in fact about the outskirts of Liverpool:

" . . . the smoke-drifted munition works, the rubble of industrial suburbs, and the canal that crawled squalidly out into blighted and forbidding farm-lands." Let me add here a description of a Midlands town by Robert Blatchford that could almost be taken word for word as being the front-line:

" . . . a squalid, hideous place, ill-lighted and unpaved—the paths and roads heel-deep in mire. The houses are not homes—they have neither comfort nor beauty, but are mere shelters or sleeping pens . . . that sordid, odorous region."

Finally, to clinch this general comparison of trench squalor and the life of a third of the British nation, here is, firstly, Sassoon on returning to the Front:

"I was entering once again the veritable gloom and disaster of the thing called Armageddon . . . a dreadful place, a place of horror and desolation which no imagination could have invented. Also it was a place where a man of strong spirit might know himself utterly powerless."

And here is R. H. Sherard, an investigator of social conditions, on another place:

"I never set foot in Manchester without a shrinking at the heart, an instinctive and irrepressible feeling of pale terror. Is it on account of its almost perennial gloom? Is it because I am familiar with the dreadful squalor and surpassing misery of its slums?"

Then there are the dangers and hardships of trench life in the quiet times outside great battles—the patrols, raids, shelling, sniping, digging, carrying. Even here there are parallels with peacetime life as then lived by a large proportion of the population.

A chain works for example: " . . . I saw women making chain with babies sucking at their breasts. . . . I spoke to a married couple who had worked 120 hours in one week. . . . I saw heavy-chain strikers who were worn-out old men at thirty-five." Or, if it's a question of gas, take a Lancashire chemical works:

"The chemical men work amid foul odours and in intense heat—the temperature being often as high as 120 degrees. They sweat and toil in an atmosphere charged with biting acids, or deadly gases, or dense with particles of lime."

What I wonder would Sassoon and Co.—or ourselves—have made of four years of this? Clearly it lacks the concentrated, appalling impact of violence and death of the Somme or Third Ypres, but it is still a very long way away from Aunt Evelyn carrying her sweet-peas and roses "down to the drawing-room while the clock ticked slow, and the parrot whistled, and the cook chopped something on the kitchen table."

Now whereas the British industrial population had to cope with their squalor and hardships on their own scant and precarious resources, the troops in the trenches had the support—moral and material—of an immense organization, comradeship, regular food, medical care, canteens, sport, and even entertainment.

Thus it is hardly surprising that the rank and file did not take things so hard as the war writers. Many of them were in fact better off in the trenches than at home. The cheerfulness and stoicism of the troops, however, puzzled the war writers. Thus Sassoon: "It was queer how the men seemed to take their victimization for granted." Or Manning: "The strange thing was, that the greater the hardships they had to endure, for cold and wet bring all kinds of attendant miseries in their train, the less they grumbled. They became a lot quieter, and more reserved in themselves, and yet the estaminets would be swept by roaring storms of song." For the rank and file had been "victimized" all their lives—they had been servile parts of a great machine—another aspect of the war the writers hated—all their lives.

Thus I am arguing that a great deal of what the war writers took to be squalors and degradations peculiar to the war—and their equally upper-middle class reviewers and readers also so took—was in fact the common lot of many of their countrymen at all times. Therefore what came to be accepted as the objective truth about life in the trenches was only a highly subjective and untypical response of a sheltered minority. It is hard not to agree with Manning's working-class character Martlow, who says:

"Some of these beggars what come out 'ere now . . . 'ave never done anythin' they didn't want to do in their lives be-fore, and now they're up against something real nasty, they don't arf make a song about it."

Nevertheless there *are* the battles. Obviously no scenes of British industrial life, however dangerous, can parallel the Somme or Third Ypres. Nothing can diminish the crushing horror of such experiences, or invalidate such descriptions as that which opens Manning's *Her Privates We* or forms the climax of Williamson's *Patriot's Progress*. As John Bullock goes up to the line, the wounded come back past him:

> . . . men, single and in couples, shuffling past them, answering no questions. Tin hats on the backs of heads, no tin hats, tin hats with splinter-ragged sandbag-coverings; men without rifles, haggard, bloodshot-eyed, slouching past in loose file, slouching on anyhow, staggering under rifles and equipment, some jaws sagging, puttees coiled mud-balled around ankles, feet in shapeless mud boots swelled beyond feeling, men slouching on beyond fatigue and hope, on and on and on. G S waggons with loads of sleeping bodies. Stretcher-bearers plodding desperate-faced. Men slavering and rolling their bared-teeth heads, slobbering and blowing, blasting brightness behind their eye-balls, supported by listless cripples.

Or such cameos as Blunden's lance-corporal killed by a shell: " . . . gobbets of blackening flesh, the earth-wall sotted with blood, with flesh, the eye under the duckboard, the pulpy bone . . .".

Yet even with what, to us as well as them, must seem experiences beyond human powers to sustain, there is still a distinction between the objective fact of a battle and the subjective response. For example, read Sassoon's or even Graves's account of the Royal Welch Fusiliers' involvement in Loos or the Somme, with that written by Frank Richards, a long-service regular private in the same regiment. Things that stir Sassoon to savage indignation and hysterical horror and outrage, Frank Richards passes by with a laconic comment and a cynical wit. The endless casualties, the loss of friends, which is a constant refrain in the books of the war writers, weighing down their souls with a sense of loss and waste and futility and outrage, Frank Richards just accepts.

Here I think is another fundamentally important aspect of Great War literature—the sense of *outrage* the writers display, the moral indignation. This conveys the impression that there was compared with past wars something uniquely terrible about a Western Front battle and indeed the war itself—unique in the rate of casualties, and unique in that it became, in Sassoon's words, "undisguisedly mechanical and inhuman." The impression, though I think universally accepted by British public opinion, is historically a false one. The rates of casualties in Western Front battles in proportion to troops involved were much the same as in the great battles of the past. Napoleon, whom some wished could have commanded in 1914-18, lost 44,000 out of 100,000 at Aspern-Essling in 1809 in two days, and another 30,000 out of 175,000 at Wagram in a single day two months later. The total United Kingdom dead for all fronts in the Great War was less in proportion to national population than American losses in the Civil War. Nor were the battles of the past less horrible, less terrifying in their cruelty to the participants. This extract about a wounded man for example from a memoir of the retreat to Corunna equals any horror in the literature of the Great War:

It was impossible to distinguish a single feature (of a wounded man). The flesh of his cheeks and lips was hanging in collops, his nose was split, and his ears cut off. In addition to his wounds, it is probable that his limbs were frost-bitten, for it was quite horrible to see the manner in which he cowered near the fire, and raked the glowing embers towards him with his fingers.

(pp. 1-12)

As for the anonymous and machine-like quality of the Great War battles, here is a description of Chancellorsville in 1863:

"Why, we never saw any Rebels where we were: only smoke and bushes, and lots of our men tumbling about . . . wrang wr-r-rang all day, and the poor bleeding wounded streaming to the rear."

Even the permanency of the trenches was not novel; the American Civil War had ended in a year of "Somme-type" fighting round Richmond, while the Russo-Japanese War of 1904-5 was of course largely an affair of field fortification.

The war writers' evident belief that they were experiencing a historical novelty, and their deep sense of moral outrage, brings us back to the sheltered unrealism and idealism of late Victorian upbringing. They had never been taught, they had never read, anything about war as it really was. On the other hand, they had been indoctrinated with high romantic ideals of an absurdly unrealistic and impractical kind. They were—as were the British of the era generally—more emotional in their response to life than coldly analytical and sceptical. Even in the reviewers of 1928-30 one finds this desire to experience noble and uplifting emotions. Thus it was that the war writers joined up in the glow of an idealism perfectly expressed by Rupert Brooke's "Now God Be Thanked" verses. Of course real life and real human nature, to say nothing of real war, simply didn't come up to these Burne-Jones visions. All the war writers document the progress of their disillusion. But C. E. Montague in his book *Disenchanted* in 1922 was the first to do it, and perhaps does it best. Horror upon horrors! The Sergeant-Major accepts free drinks from trainees on a route march. A sergeant can be bribed for a cushy job or promotion. The officers aren't all Napoleons or Moltkes. The training is a muddle. And so on. Finally of course the war itself turns out to be like war, and not like Lady Butler's paintings or Newbolt's verse. And gradually it also dawns that the bright crusade for right and justice is just another episode in the European struggle for power.

And from high ideals thus callously trodden on by reality sprang the deep sense of outrage and indignation. Yet, although the war writers do not seem to see this, their disillusion is more a comment on themselves and on the absurdity of Victorian liberal idealism than on the war.

It is interesting to note by contrast the moral attitudes towards the war taken both by the British rank and file and by the local French peasants, few of whom had been brought up at Howard's End. Thus Manning records the effects of a headboy's-style moral pep-talk by an officer:

"They did not really pause to weigh the truth or falsity of his opinions, which were simply without meaning for them. They only reflected that gentlefolk lived in circumstances very different from their own, and could afford strange luxuries."

Or the soldiers' attitude to death, as recorded by Graves:

A corpse is lying on the fire-step waiting to be taken down to the grave-yard tonight. . . . His arm was stretched out stiff when they carried him in and laid him on the fire-step; it stretched right across the trench. His comrades joke as they push it out of the way to get by. "Out of the light, you old bastard! Do you own this bloody trench?" Or else they shake hands with him familiarly. "Put it there, Billy Boy." Of course, they're miners and accustomed to death.

A French woman who kept an estaminet, as recorded by Manning:

She was extraordinarily tranquil in her pessimism. . . . But all this pessimism was apparently for the course the war was taking; she was perfectly clear that the Hun had to be defeated. The world for her was ruined, that was irreparable; but justice must be done; and for her justice was apparently some divine law, working slowly and inexorably through all the confused bickerings of men . . . though she was a comparatively uneducated woman, her thought was clear, logical and hard. . . . There was in her some trace of that spirit which we had noticed among the older men in the ranks, a spirit which had ceased to hope for itself and yet was undefeated.

Elsewhere Manning's hero, Bourne, notes of the peasants near the line:

They would plough, sow, and wait for their harvest, taking the chance that battle might flow like lava over their fields very much as they took the chance of a wet season or a drought . . . their pessimism was equal to the occasion.

"C'est la guerre," they would say, with resignation that was almost apathy: for all sensible people know that war is one of the blind forces of nature, which can neither be foreseen nor controlled. Their attitude, in all its simplicity, was sane.

One must ask: which is the better equipment for life: this pessimistic acceptance of reality at its bleakest, or the optimistic idealism and romancing that the British war writers took to France?

It followed of course from outraged idealism that "they," the army, the staff, the generals, should cop it because the war, like in fact most human affairs, was often a hopeless muddle. Out of the failure of the military machine to work faultlessly, and of commanders to act with a perfect wisdom, understanding, tact, and inventive genius, came the legend of the army's general incompetence and of its generals' stupidity and callousness. There is Sassoon's wine-faced commander, who did for Harry and Jack with his plan of attack; there are the generals who issued reprimands about slack marching by tired men on bad roads. But what had the writers the right to expect of a military machine suddenly expanded to vast complication from a small, neglected and despised regular army? All the war writers take the immense administrative machine in France, and the regular supply of ammunition, stores, food, mail, and medical care absolutely for granted. Yet in fact it was an astonishing feat of rapid improvisation.

Now there is not time today to go into the whole complex question of whether or not Haig and his colleagues were callous fools. I simply want to note that the war writers show little sympathetic understanding of the real predicament of the men who, after a stagnant regimental life in peacetime, had to try to wage and win war on a vast scale.

And this brings me to another, and I think vital, point. It is understandable that such sympathetic understanding might not be forthcoming during the war. However, the war books appeared from 1928 onwards. They are, in fact, pondered, reflective views of the war. Yet there is no attempt to place personal experiences in the larger context of the war, as it was by then known through the histories and memoirs. There is no attempt to tackle the hard fundamental problems of the war, such as the German occupation of Belgium and northern France and its inescapable effect on allied policy, and indeed on the nature of a compromise peace.

Yet it is insoluble problems like these which determined the whole course and nature of the war—and of the writers' own personal sufferings. Could the war have been stopped? Were the endless offensives really unnecessary? Blunden for example says virtually nothing on these topics except that in early 1917 he "began to air his convictions that the war was useless and inhuman." Aldington's diagnosis of the causes of the war and determining factors of its continuance runs thus:

"But what were they really against? Who were their real enemies? He saw the answer with a flood of bitterness and clarity. Their enemies—the enemies of German and English alike—were the fools who had sent them to kill each other instead of help each other."

Ford Madox Ford was hardly more sophisticated in his analysis:

"These immense sacrifices, this ocean of mental sufferings, were all undergone to further the private vanities of men who amidst these hugenesses of landscapes and forces appeared pigmies!"

Graves simply tells us that by 1917 none of the writers in the army, including himself, "now believed in the war"—whatever that means.

Manning in a prefatory note believes that "War is waged by men; not by beasts, or by gods. To call it a crime against mankind is to miss at least half the significance; it is also the punishment of a crime."

Sassoon is content to re-create his pacifist *démarche* of 1917. His reconstruction of his first conversation with Massingham does his intellect and information no credit:

"It's only when one gets away from it [the war] that one begins to realize how stupid and wasteful it all is. What I feel is that if it's got to go on, there ought to be a jolly sound reason for it, and I can't help thinking that the troops are being done in the eye by the people in control."

Nor is his formal declaration about the war much more penetrating, although certainly more pompous: "I believe that this War, upon which I entered as a war of defence and liberation, has now become a war of aggression and conquest . . .". If, he goes on, British war aims had been stated " . . . the objects which actuated us would now be attainable by negotiation . . .".

Like his fellow writers, Sassoon has nothing to add by way of retrospective comment or comprehension of the larger political and strategic realities of the wartime dilemma.

Again, none seems to see any connection between the allies'

eventual victory in 1918 and the terrible battles that went before. How did they think the German army grew so weak?

It is fair, in my opinion, to accuse the authors of our war literature therefore of evading the really fundamental intellectual problems of the war, even when writing ten years afterwards with all the benefit of later information. They made no attempt to "place" and explain their own experiences in the light of these fundamental problems. They are content to express with enormous power and cumulative effect an emotional revulsion against war. And, as the reviews I quoted earlier show, they communicated to British opinion not enlightened and understanding about the causes and problems of war, simply this deep emotional revulsion against war, armies, and generals.

Now, in any period, in regard to any human problem, emotional revulsion is hardly a constructive approach. As it happened, the decade after the war books appeared turned out to be the decade of Hitler; and the British public's emotional revulsion against war made timely rearmament and resistance to Hitler's demands impossible—opened the way therefore to the eventual necessity of stopping him not by peaceful pressure, but actual force—i.e. another war. As the success of *Oh What a Lovely War* proves, emotional revulsion rather than candid and searching intellectual investigation is still the prevailing reaction to the Great War, and to the problem of war in general.

Let me now draw together the main threads of my argument and put forward a final and even more broad assessment of the effects of war literature on British history.

Firstly the war-writers themselves were highly untypical of the British people at large, being mostly upper-middle class poets and writers. Secondly, their idealistic upbringing meant that they took their war experiences much more hard than those with less sheltered backgrounds. Thirdly, they attributed, in their social ignorance, much to war that was true of peace as well. Fourthly, that as a consequence of all this, their books give an unbalanced and highly subjective impression of the war, the army, and its commanders. Finally, this unbalanced impression, because of their literary powers, was accepted in a generalized way by British educated opinion as "the truth" about the war.

And whence derives, in my view, the long-term and catastrophic effect of the war literature on British history. By the end of the 1920s the British had got into the habit of blaming all their troubles—perpetual high unemployment, the collapse of the export markets, social misery—on the war. C. E. Montague paved the way for this with his *Disenchantment,* written in 1922 when the post-war boom and the vision of a land fit for heroes to live in first collapsed. Later—today indeed—our general feebleness in diplomacy and industry since 1918 has been blamed on the allegedly crippling damage done to us in the Great War—the legend of the "Lost Generation" of brilliant young men.

The war literature of course exactly served—and serves—to bear out this national myth. Uncritical people got—and still have—the impression that our dead in the Great War numbered about a million—that in fact, to paraphrase Blunden, all our young men died round Ypres. It is widely accepted that the material and human damage done to us in the Great War was such as to legitimately explain our lack of will and energy ever since.

But the hard facts are otherwise. Since we are today discussing human experiences, I will pass over the material aspects, except to point out that no battles or demolitions were carried out on British territory, nor was part of this territory ever occupied, while the foreign investments sold to pay for the war were equal to less than two years' investment at the pre-war rate—a small fraction of the total.

It is in any case the question of the human loss that has made the deepest impression on the British mind.

The total United Kingdom dead for all fronts was in fact 744,000. Now it was the Western Front, which the war-writers evoked so powerfully, and which British public opinion came to think of as the grave of "the lost generation." In fact the United Kingdom losses on the Western Front were just over half a million—512,000. This is not much more than the losses suffered by Italy in three—not four years—of war—460,000.

To go back to the total national losses in dead. France lost out of a population roughly equal to that of Britain nearly twice as many dead—1,327,000. Take the Germans. If Britain had lost at the same rate per population as Germany, her dead would have numbered 1,200,000 instead of 744,000. Yet no one can say that Germany's will and energy were permanently impaired. And, as I said earlier, our losses were proportionately less than those of America in the Civil War. Yet post-1865 American history is hardly characterized by stagnation and loss of drive.

Thus in objective truth the Great War in no way inflicted crippling damage on British life. But—with catastrophic results for our subsequent history—the British, or particularly the British governing classes, thought—or chose to think—that it had. The war crippled Britain *psychologically,* and in no other way.

In this mistaken and disastrous national response, I submit that the authors of our war literature played a crucial, if unwitting role. (pp. 12-18)

> Correlli Barnett, *"A Military Historian's View of the Great War,"* in Essays by Divers Hands, *n.s Vol. XXXVI, 1970, pp. 1-18.*

HERBERT READ

[*Read was a prolific English poet, critic, and novelist. Several convictions are central to his discussions of literature, the foremost being his belief that art is a seminal force in individual and social development, and that a perfect society would be one in which work and art are one. In the following excerpt originally published in 1945, Read, who was decorated for distinguished service during the First World War, discusses the failure of literature about the war to deter succeeding generations from armed conflict.*]

Young writers who took part in the last war came back with one desire: to tell the truth about war, to expose its horrors, its inhumanity, its indignity. They knew that it was no good crying over spilt blood, no good trying to console themselves or their contemporaries. But at least they might warn the coming generations. "All a poet can do to-day is warn," wrote Wilfred Owen. "That is why the true Poets must be truthful."

It took a few years for a new generation to grow up and become war-conscious. In the meantime there was no public for war poetry or war stories. Between 1918 and 1928 it was almost impossible to publish anything realistic about war. Then came the reaction. It was slowly mounting when Remarque wrote *All Quiet on the Western Front.* Remarque, like Owen, wanted to warn the new generation. He did warn them; so did the film which was based on his book. So did scores of books that floated to success on the tide of *All Quiet,* which itself quickly became the best-selling novel of our time.

At first it looked as though the warning had taken effect. After the spate of anti-war literature, there was the famous debate at the Oxford Union at which an overwhelming majority of undergraduates declared that under no circumstances would they ever take up arms. The Peace Pledge Union sprang into existence and its membership reached hundreds of thousands.

It began to look as though our warning had taken effect, but from the beginning there was something specious about this youthful pacifism. It was based on a negation, whereas a true belief is always positive and affirmative. Further, this negation was the negation of an abstraction—war. War, thanks to the war books, was vivid enough to the imagination of these young men: it was a nightmare of senseless killing. But war acquires its reality from psychological and economic forces, and it is useless to protest against war unless at the same time there is some understanding of the workings of these primary forces and some attempt to control them.

But there was no such understanding. These forces gathered momentum and ten years after the publication of *All Quiet* we were at war again. Our books may have created a few extra conscientious objectors, but in their main purpose, the prevention of another war, they had failed.

In asking the reason for this failure it is easy to be wise after the event and say that our books were not good enough. It is said of *All Quiet,* for example, that it was sentimental. To some extent the criticism is true, but sentimentality was not, for effectiveness, a fault. The nearest parallel to *All Quiet* in the past is *Uncle Tom's Cabin.* That was a much more sentimental book than *All Quiet,* yet for that very reason it was largely instrumental in bringing about one of the greatest reforms in the history of mankind—the abolition of slavery. The abolition of war is no doubt a bigger problem, but if books are to play a part in its solution, they will be books at least as sentimental as *All Quiet.*

We must look for a deeper cause of this failure. I believe it can be found in that impulse which is loosely known as sadism, but which is surely something rather broader than that form of sexual perversion. Whatever we call it, there is no doubt that there exists in mankind a love of vicarious suffering and violence. From an early age we delight in stories of strife and bloodshed, and any attempt to eradicate this interest in children only seems to lead to compensatory complexes of a no less disagreeable nature. In writing our war books we were unwittingly ministering to this hidden lust. I have myself been struck by the fact that one and only one of my war poems has been extensively quoted in anthologies and reviews—a simple but very bitter and horrible poem called "The Happy Warrior." From a literary point of view I am sure it is by no means the best of my war poems, but it has had a terrible fascination for many people. It expresses in an extreme degree the horror of war, and it, and other poems and stories of the same kind, should have been an effective warning.

As it is, the suspicion now grows upon me that such writing was fuel to the inner flames of the war spirit. If we human beings have an irresistible urge to destruction, including an urge to self-destruction, then the imagination will feed ravenously on any vivid description of the process of destruction. War is not a spirit that can be exorcised by any form of incantation. It is an impulse that must be eradicated by a patient course of treatment.

That treatment will be partly social and partly psychological. That is to say, the necessary psychological treatment cannot take place in the present order of society, which does everything to perpetuate the impulses of competition and power. It can only take place in a society based on the impulses of mutual aid and service—an order of society where all the tendencies are against rivalry and the domination of groups or individuals. If these tendencies, which are by no means against the order of nature, could be established, then we might reasonably hope to eradicate the destructive impulse itself, and to provide adequate alternatives for the expenditure of the latent psychic energies of mankind.

I do not underestimate the power of propaganda, whether in the form of books or periodicals or the spoken word. Once it is in the hands of a single centralized authority, it can mould mass opinion to almost any kind of belief. It can do almost anything short of changing human nature. It cannot alter the basic instincts of men, and for that reason the uniformity it establishes remains insecure, a façade of stucco without any supporting wall. Human nature can only be changed by environment, genetics and other long-term physical factors. If we want to make mankind a more peace-loving animal, we must first create the right kind of social mould, the right kind of family life, the right kind of education; and all these things must be provided on a world scale, because peace must be universal.

We must continue to tell the truth about war, as about all things. But the telling must be a confession of shame and failure. After a second world war either we perish as a civilization or a new generation will create a new literature. Not a literature of reportage, of pride in experience, of vicarious suffering. But a literature of constructive imagination, of social idealism, of positive morality. To learn by experience—that is the method of the animal. In so far as we hope to be more than animals we must learn by what is greater than passive experience—by imaginative experiment. (pp. 72-6)

> Herbert Read, "The Failure of the War Books," in his A Coat of Many Colours: Occasional Essays, George Routledge & Sons, Ltd., 1945, pp. 72-6.

FURTHER READING

I. Anthologies

Brereton, Frederick, ed. *An Anthology of War Poems.* London: W. Collins Sons & Co., 1930, 191 p.
    Poetry in English, with an introduction by Edmund Blunden.

Brophy, John, and Partridge, Eric. *The Long Trail: What the British Soldier Sang and Said in The Great War of 1914-1918.* New York: London House & Maxwell, 1965, 239 p.
    Updated presentation of their *Songs and Slang of the British Soldier 1914-1918* (1930), including chants, marching songs, and a glossary of soldiers' slang.

Gardner, Brian, ed. *Up the Line to Death: The War Poets, 1914-1918.* London: Methuen & Co., 1964.
    Thematic arrangement of English poetry, with a foreword by Edmund Blunden.

Nichols, Robert, ed. *Anthology of War Poetry: 1914-1918.* London: Nicholson & Watson, 1943, 156 p.
    Includes English works introduced by a dialogue between Nichols and Julian Tennyson discussing the nature and value of war poetry.

Parsons, I. M., ed. *Men Who March Away: Poems of the First World War.* New York: Viking Press, 1965, 192 p.
    Thematic arrangement of English poetry, with an introduction by the editor.

Silkin, Jon, ed. *The Penguin Book of First World War Poetry.* Rev. ed. Harmondsworth, England: Penguin Books, 1979, 282 p.
    Works in English and translated works by Guillaume Apollinaire, René Arcos, Aleksandr Blok, Georg Heym, Osip Mandelstam, Eugenio Montale, Anton Schnack, August Stramm, Marina Tsvetaeva, Georg Trakl, Giuseppe Ungaretti, and others, with an introduction by the editor.

Tomlinson, Henry M., ed. *Best Short Stories of the War: An Anthology.* New York: Harper & Brothers, 1931, 826 p.
    Representative selection in English and in translation, including works by Richard Aldington, Henri Barbusse, Joseph Conrad, Roland Dorgèles, Georges Duhamel, Ernest Hemingway, J. P. Marquand, Somerset Maugham, André Maurois, R. H. Mottram, Leonard Nason, Erich Maria Remarque, Laurence Stallings, Fritz von Unruh, Georg van der Vring, Edith Wharton, and others.

II. Secondary Sources

Aichinger, Peter. "Part One: 1917-1939." In his *The American Soldier in Fiction, 1880-1963: A History of Attitudes toward Warfare and the Military Establishment,* pp. 3-29. Ames: Iowa State University Press, 1975.
    Discusses American war novels of the World War I era "in relation to historical, economic, and political events that accompanied or preceded their appearance."

Aldridge, John W. "Part I: The Lost Generation." In his *After the Lost Generation: A Critical Study of the Writers of Two Wars,* pp. 1-82. 1951. Reprint. New York: Arbor House, 1985.
    Focuses on John Dos Passos, F. Scott Fitzgerald, and Ernest Hemingway in an examination of the shattering effect that World War I had on writers who participated and assesses the influence of those authors on the generation that came of age during World War II.

Australian Literary Studies, Special Issue: Australian Literature and War 12, No. 2 (October 1985): 154-298.
    Includes thematic and historical surveys. Among works on World War I literature are: "Some Australian Women's Literary Responses to the Great War," by Jan Bassett, and "Australian Literature of the First World War," a checklist by J. T. Laird.

Baranski, Zygmunt G. "Italian Literature and the Great War: Soffici, Jahier, and Rebora." *Journal of European Studies* 10, No. 39 (September 1980): 155-77.

Considers the diverse attitudes toward World War I exhibited in the poetry of Ardengo Soffici, Piero Jahier, and Clemente Rebora.

Bate, Jonathan. "Arcadia and Armageddon: Three English Novelists and the First World War." *Etudes Anglaises* 39, No. 2 (April-June 1986): 150-62.
Discusses the contrasts between pastoral and anti-pastoral elements in Ford Madox Ford's *Parade's End*, R. H. Mottram's *The Spanish Farm Trilogy*, and the works of Virginia Woolf.

Bergonzi, Bernard. *Heroes' Twilight: A Study of the Literature of the Great War*. Rev. ed. London and Basingstoke: Macmillan, 1980, 241 p.
Combines history, biography, and textual analysis in a seminal study of English literature about the war.

Bonadeo, Alfredo. "War and Degradation: Gleanings from the Literature of the Great War." *Comparative Literature Studies* 21, No. 4 (Winter 1984): 409-33.
Examines degradation and dehumanization as the price paid for survival by soldiers in World War I as portrayed in the works of Robert Graves, T. E. Lawrence, Frederic Manning, Erich Maria Remarque, and Siegfried Sassoon.

Bowra, C. M. "Poetry and the First World War." In his *In General and Particular*, pp. 193-221. London: Weidenfeld and Nicolson, 1964.
Compares works by Guillaume Apollinaire, Aleksandr Blok, Karl Bröger, Walter Flex, Nikolai Gumilev, Thomas Hardy, Georg Heym, Rainer Maria Rilke, Georg Trakl, Giuseppe Ungaretti, and others.

Bridgwater, Patrick. *The German Poets of the First World War*. New York: St. Martin's Press, 1985, 209 p.
Examines the works of front-line poets writing between 1914 and 1918, including Anton Schnack, August Stramm, and Georg Trakl.

Buitenhuis, Peter. "Writers at War: Propaganda and Fiction in the Great War." *University of Toronto Quarterly* 45, No. 4 (Summer 1976): 277-94.
Traces the history of English propaganda writing during the war.

————. "American Literature of the Great War." *American Studies International* 23, No. 2 (October 1985): 79-86.
Bibliographical essay listing secondary sources.

Cadogan, Mary, and Craig, Patricia. *Women and Children First: The Fiction of Two World Wars*. London: Victor Gollancz, 1978, 301 p.
Includes several chapters on popular literature of World War I in a study "concerned with the experiences of British women and children in the two major wars of the twentieth century, as presented in contemporary and retrospective fiction."

Churchill, R. C. "War and the Poet's Responsibility." *The Nineteenth Century and After* 137, No. 818 (April 1945): 155-59.
Contrasts the patriotic view of war expressed in the poetry of Rupert Brooke with the tragic view adopted by Wilfred Owen, Isaac Rosenberg, and Siegfried Sassoon, among others.

Clarke, I. F. "Politics and the Pattern of the Next Great War, 1880-1914." In his *Voices Prophesying War: 1763-1984*, pp. 107-61. London: Oxford University Press, 1966.
Examines fantasy literature of the prewar era based on the idea of a future European war.

Cohen, J. M. "The Earth Is Hungry." *The Listener* 74, No. 1911 (11 November 1965): 753-55.
Retrospective overview of World War I poetry drawing on the works of Kurt Adler, Guillaume Apollinaire, Robert Graves, Wilfred Owen, Siegfried Sassoon, Ernst Stadler, Edward Thomas, and others to illustrate common themes among soldier-poets.

Cohen, Joseph. "The War Poet as Archetypal Spokesman." *Stand* 4, No. 3 (1960): 23-7.
Maintains that society's tendency to romanticize the lives of war poets is detrimental to our critical understanding of their works.

Costigan, Giovanni. "British Poetry of World War I." In *War: A Historical, Political, and Social Study*, edited by L. L. Farrar, Jr., pp. 247-51. Santa Barbara, Calif.: ABC-Clio, 1978.
Quotes from works by Rupert Brooke, Julian Grenfell, John McCrae, Wilfred Owen, Siegfried Sassoon, Charles Hamilton Sorley, and others in order to present the most significant attitudes toward the First World War expressed in English poetry.

Cowley, Malcolm. "The Other War." In his *A Second Flowering: Works and Days of the Lost Generation*, pp. 3-18. New York: Viking Press, 1956.
Recounts the responses of young American writers to World War I and traces the effect of their experiences on American writing in the decades that followed the war.

Crozier, Emmet. *American Reporters on the Western Front: 1914-1918*. New York: Oxford University Press, 1959, 299 p.
History of American journalists reporting on the Western Front. Crozier includes a register of American correspondents and a bibliography of their autobiographical works.

Cruickshank, John. "Saying the Unsayable: Problems of Expression in Great War Fiction." In *Mélanges de littérature française moderne offerts à Garnet Rees*, edited by Cedric E. Pickford, pp. 59-76. Abbeville, France: Librairie Minard, 1980.
Discusses technical difficulties, moral concerns, and language restrictions encountered by French writers attempting to portray their war experiences for readers.

————. *Variations on Catastrophe: Some French Responses to the Great War*. Oxford: Clarendon Press, 1982, 219 p.
Views French intellectual responses to World War I from the anticipation of war before 1914, through the experience of war (1914-1918), to an understanding of its significance (post-1918).

Daiches, David. "War Poetry—The Imagists—Post-War Satire—The Sitwells." In his *Poetry and the Modern World: A Study of Poetry in England between 1900 and 1939*, pp. 61-89. Chicago: University of Chicago Press, 1940.
Examines trends in English poetry during the World War I era. According to Daiches: "Just what the war of 1914-18 did to English poetry is very difficult to determine. . . . It probably helped to make the Georgians look out of date some years before they otherwise would have, though it is difficult to be certain of this. One specific and tangible result was that it killed off a great number of promising poets, chief among whom was Wilfred Owen."

Dickinson, Patric. "Poets of the First World War." *The Listener* 67, No. 1715 (8 February 1962): 259-60.
Reassesses the critical reputations of war poets Rupert Brooke, Wilfred Owen, and Isaac Rosenberg.

Enright, D. J. "The Literature of the First World War." In *The Pelican Guide to English Literature: The Modern Age*, Vol. 7, rev. ed., edited by Boris Ford, pp. 154-69. Harmondsworth, England: Penguin Books, 1964.
General introduction to the major writers and themes of English poetry of World War I.

Evans, B. Ifor. "War and the Writer." In his *English Literature between the Wars*, rev. ed., pp. 102-13. London: Methuen & Co., 1949.
Defines attitudes toward war expressed by writers of the World War I era, the "war books" period of the late 1920s, and the 1930s.

Falls, Cyril. *War Books: A Critical Guide*. London: Peter Davies, 1930, 318 p.

Guidebook to general histories, formation and unit chronicles, foreign histories, memoirs, and fiction.

———. *The Great War.* New York: G. P. Putnam's Sons, 1959, 447 p.

Chronological battle history of the war.

Fenton, Charles A. "A Literary Fracture of World War I." *American Quarterly* 12, No. 2, Part 1, (Summer 1960): 119-32.

Discusses the schism that occurred in American writing between the prewar literary establishment and the writers of the war generation.

Field, Frank. *Three French Writers and the Great War: Studies in the Rise of Communism and Fascism.* Cambridge: Cambridge University Press, 1975, 212 p.

General discussion of political trends in the World War I era, followed by assessments of the political development of three French novelists: "Henri Barbusse and Communism," "Drieu la Rochelle and Fascism," and "Georges Bernanos and the Kingdom of God."

Frierson, William C. "Diffusion, 1929-1940." In his *The English Novel in Transition: 1885-1940,* pp. 279-322. Norman: University of Oklahoma Press, 1942.

Maintains that war novels from 1929 through 1931 differ from those written soon after the war because, unlike the earlier works, they reveal "the gruesome details of the carnage. Equally distinctive is the fact that they sound a protest against inefficiency and waste—and . . . against war itself as a way of solving international problems."

Fussell, Paul. *The Great War and Modern Memory.* New York and London: Oxford University Press, 1975, 363 p.

Seminal literary study of the experiences of British infantry on the Western Front from 1914 to 1918. Fussell examines the literary means through which the war has been "remembered, conventionalized, and mythologized," focusing on the reciprocal process "by which life feeds materials to literature while literature returns the favor by conferring forms upon life."

Genno, Charles N., and Wetzel, Heinz, eds. *The First World War in German Narrative Prose.* Toronto: University of Toronto Press, 1980, 169 p.

Collection of essays discussing works by Alfred Döblin, Leonhard Frank, Hermann Hesse, Erich Maria Remarque, Carl Sternheim, Arnold Zweig, and others.

Genthe, Charles V. *American War Narratives, 1917-1918: A Study and Bibliography.* New York: David Lewis, 1969, 194 p.

Reveals the innocent and romantic attitudes toward the war held by many Americans through an examination of American war memoirs.

Gibson, R. "The First World War and the Literary Consciousness." In *French Literature and Its Background: The Twentieth Century,* Vol. 6, edited by John Cruickshank, pp. 56-72. London: Oxford University Press, 1970.

Surveys changing attitudes toward France, the military, and the church in French literature of the pre-war and war periods. According to Gibson, "[In France] bellicose patriotism was not the ideology which was most damaged by the First World War. The revelation of the savage forces just beneath the civilized surface of modern Europe provided a specially traumatic shock to those writers who at the turn of the century professed their optimistic belief in the essential goodness of Man."

Gillet, L. B. "Poets in the War." *North American Review* 209, No. 763 (June 1919): 822-36.

Discusses the development and output of poetry during the war. Gillet focuses on the lives and works of Rupert Brooke, Robert Graves, Julian Grenfell, Alan Seeger, and Charles Hamilton Sorley.

Gosse, Edmund. "Some Soldier Poets." In his *Some Diversions of a Man of Letters,* pp. 261-85. New York: Charles Scribner's Sons, 1920.

Surveys the war poetry of Maurice Baring, Rupert Brooke, Robert Graves, Julian Grenfell, Robert Nichols, and Siegfried Sassoon.

Hagboldt, Peter. "Ethical and Social Problems in the German War Novel." *The Journal of English and Germanic Philology* 32 (1933): 21-32.

Discusses significant themes and subjects in Werner Beumelburg's *Die Gruppe Bosemüller,* Rudolf G. Binding's *Aus dem Kriege,* Ernst Johannsen's *Vier von der Infanterie,* Egon Erwin Kisch's *Schreib das auf, Kisch!,* Karlheinz Lemke's *Niemandsland,* Erich Maria Remarque's *Im Westen nichts Neues* and *Der Weg zurück,* Ludwig Renn's *Krieg,* Peter Riss's *Stahlbad Anno 17,* Fritz von Unruh's *Opfergang,* and Arnold Zweig's *Der Streit um den Sergeanten Grischa.*

Hatcher, Harlan. "The War Generation." In his *Creating the Modern American Novel,* pp. 221-33. New York: Farrar & Rinehart, 1935.

Discusses the disillusionment of American authors who took part in the war and examines three novels representative of the anti-romantic attitude toward war that resulted: John Dos Passos's *Three Soldiers,* E. E. Cummings's *The Enormous Room,* and Thomas Boyd's *Through the Wheat.*

Hewett-Thayer, Harvey W. "The Novel of the Great War." In his *The Modern German Novel: A Series of Studies and Appreciations,* pp. 214-53. Boston: Marshall Jones Co., 1924.

Survey of German war fiction focusing on works by Otto Ernst, Leonhard Frank, Gustav Frenssen, Andreas Latzko, Fritz Lienhard, Heinrich Mann, Clara Viebig, and others.

Hibberd, Dominic, ed. *Poetry of the First World War: A Casebook.* London: Macmillan, 1981, 247 p.

Critical collection offering general and individual assessments of the major English poets of the First World War by such critics as Bernard Bergonzi, Winston Churchill, T. S. Eliot, Paul Fussell, Edmund Gosse, C. Day Lewis, John Middleton Murry, Jon Silkin, Dylan Thomas, Arthur Waugh, Virginia Woolf, and W. B. Yeats.

Higonnet, Margaret Randolph, et al., eds. *Behind the Lines: Gender and the Two World Wars.* New Haven and London: Yale University Press, 1987, 310 p.

Collection of essays first presented as papers at the Workshop on Women and War, Harvard University, Center for European Studies, January 1984. Among studies treating the literature of the World War I era are: "Vera Brittain's Testament(s)," by Lynne Layton and "Soldier's Heart: Literary Men, Literary Women, and the Great War," by Sandra M. Gilbert.

Hobsbaum, Philip. "The Road Not Taken." *The Listener* 66, No. 1704 (23 November 1961): 860, 863.

Suggests that had they not been killed during the war, Wilfred Owen, Isaac Rosenberg, and Edward Thomas would have greatly influenced the direction of modern English poetry.

Kazantzis, Judith. "Preface." In *Scars upon My Heart: Women's Poetry and Verse of the First World War,* edited by Catherine W. Reilly, pp. xv-xxiv. London: Virago, 1981.

Examines attitudes, themes, and subjects of women's poetry of World War I in an appreciative essay introducing an anthology that includes the works of Nora Bomford, Vera Brittain, Rose Macaulay, Charlotte Mew, Alice Meynell, Emily Orr, Sara Teasdale, Katharine Tynan, and others.

Klein, Holger, ed. *The First World War in Fiction: A Collection of Critical Essays.* New York: Barnes & Noble, 1977, 246 p.

Collection of essays on works by Henri Barbusse, E. E. Cummings, Roland Dorgèles, John Dos Passos, Jean Giono, Ernest Hemingway, Ernst Jünger, Erich Maria Remarque, Drieu la Rochelle, and others.

Knightley, Phillip. "The Last War: 1914-1918" and "Enter America: 1917-1918." In his *The First Casualty: From the Crimea to Vietnam: The War Correspondent as Hero, Propagandist, and Myth Maker*, pp. 79-112, pp. 113-36. New York and London: Harcourt Brace Jovanovich, 1975.

Examines information gathering, reporting, censorship, and propagandizing during World War I, while relating the exploits of several prominent journalists of the era who covered the Western Front.

Laird, J. T. "Australian Poetry of the First World War: A Survey." *Australian Literary Studies* 4 (1970): 241-50.

Discusses the literary responses of Australian popular versifiers, balladists, and poets, including William Baylebridge, Christopher Brennan, J. Le Gay Brereton, Leon Gellert, Frederic Manning, Harley Matthews, Vance Palmer, and Frank Wilmot.

————. "Australian Prose Literature of the First World War: A Survey." *Australian Literary Studies* 5, No. 2 (October 1971): 146-57.

Surveys Australian fiction and personal accounts of World War I, including William Baylebridge's short stories in *An Anzac Muster* (1921), John Lyons Gray's autobiography *Red Dust* (1931), Leonard Mann's novel *Flesh in Armour* (1932), Frederic Manning's *Her Privates We* (1930), and Harley Matthews's short story collection *Saints and Soldiers* (1918).

Lewis, Wyndham. "The War Writers." In his *Enemy Salvoes: Selected Literary Criticism*, edited by C. J. Fox, pp. 212-216. London: Vision Press, 1975.

Disagrees with Siegfried Sassoon, Erich Maria Remarque, and other war writers who placed blame for the horrible bloodbath of World War I on those in command and others of the preceding generation. Lewis finds the causes in "the intricacies of the power-game and the usurious economics associated with war-making."

Lost Generation Journal: Salute to Writers in the Ambulance Corps—World War I 5, No. 2 (Winter 1977-78): 1-25.

Includes essays about the war experiences of Harry Crosby, E. E. Cummings, Ernest Hemingway, and others.

McKenzie, Sister M. L. "Memories of the Great War: Graves, Sassoon, and Findley." *University of Toronto Quarterly* 55, No. 4 (Summer 1986): 395-411.

Assesses Timothy Findley's fictional treatment of World War I in *The Wars* (1977) by comparing the tone, action, and underlying attitudes presented by Findley with those found in the works of Robert Graves and Siegfried Sassoon.

McQueen, Humphrey. "Emu into Ostrich: Australian Literary Responses to the Great War." *Meanjin Quarterly* 35, No. 1 (April 1976): 78-87.

Examines the impact of the war on Australian social and economic progress and discusses attitudes toward the war expressed in works by Dowell O'Reilly, Furnley Maurice, Clarence Webster, Leonard Mann, and J. P. McKinney.

Melada, Ivan. "The Politics of Writers in the Trenches." *Dalhousie Review* 59, No. 2 (Summer 1979): 338-49.

Discusses the degree to which political consciousness colors works written about World War I by Richard Aldington, Henri Barbusse, Edmund Blunden, Ford Madox Ford, Robert Graves, Jaroslav Hašek, Rose Macaulay, Frederic Manning, Erich Maria Remarque, Siegfried Sassoon, R. C. Sherriff, and Arnold Zweig.

Moore, T. Sturge. *Some Soldier Poets.* London: Grant Richards, 1919, 147 p.

Includes individual essays on poets writing in English, including Richard Aldington, Rupert Brooke, Julian Grenfell, F. W. Harvey, Francis Ledwidge, Alan Seeger, Charles Hamilton Sorley, and Edward Thomas.

Panichas, George A., ed. *Promise of Greatness: The War of 1914-1918.* New York: John Day Company, 1968, 572 p.

Collection of essays, many by war veterans, on social, military, and literary topics, commemorating the fiftieth anniversary of the armistice. Among contributors are Correlli Barnett, Edmund Blunden, Vera Brittain, Roland Dorgèles, Cyril Falls, Maurice Genevoix, Robert Graves, L. P. Hartley, Frederick J. Hoffman, G. Wilson Knight, Sir Compton Mackenzie, R. H. Mottram, R. C. Sherriff, Vivian de Sola Pinto, and Alec Waugh.

Partridge, Eric. "The War Continues." *The Window* 1, No. 2 (April 1930): 62-85.

Examines German, French, and English novels and personal reminiscences published in 1929 and 1930.

Peacock, Ronald. "The Great War in German Lyrical Poetry, 1914-1918." *Proceedings of the Leeds Philosophical and Literary Society* 3, Part 4 (May 1934): 189-243.

Considers such topics as "The Development, 1914-1918," "Patriotism," "The Idealism of the Worker Poets," and "Stefan George."

Priestly, J. B. "Brief Interlude." In his *Literature and Western Man*, pp. 370-75. New York: Harper & Brothers, 1960.

Introduces the major writers of World War I and their contributions to literature. According to Priestly: "The strange world of the front line that these ex-combatant writers tried to describe . . . was the same for both sides; the hatred and monstrous nationalistic prejudices of politicians, editors, professors, and clergymen could not exist in it; all its inhabitants . . . were deep in conflict not with other men but with the gigantic machinery dealing out wounds and death, with heat and cold, hunger and thirst, and the dark madness of the age that had swept them into holes in the ground."

Rascoe, Burton. "What They Read during the Last War." *The Saturday Review of Literature*, New York 20 (23 September 1939): 3-4, 13, 14, 16.

Discusses propaganda and popular literature in America during World War I.

Ross, Robert H. "War and the Georgians." In his *The Georgian Revolt, 1910-1922: Rise and Fall of a Poetic Ideal*, pp. 139-65. Carbondale and Edwardsville: Southern Illinois University Press, 1965.

Literary history tracing the effect of the war on the Georgian movement. According to Ross, the decline of interest in the anthology *Georgian Poetry*, edited by Edward Marsh, "can be blamed directly or indirectly upon the war. . . . In 1912 and 1915 'Georgian' had implied vigor, revolt, and youth. After 1917 it was to imply retrenchment, escape, and enervation."

Rutherford, Andrew. "The Common Man as Hero: Literature of the Western Front." In his *The Literature of War: Five Studies in Heroic Virtue*, pp. 64-112. New York: Barnes & Noble, 1978.

Discusses sociological, historical, and military factors that sent "men of literary sensitivity and talent . . . who would never normally have thought of soldiering" to the Front and comments on their responses to the experience.

Sait, James F. "Charles Scribner's Sons and the Great War." *Princeton University Library Chronicle* 48, No. 2 (Winter 1987): 152-80.

Describes the literary and financial interests of publishers Charles Scribner's Sons in World War I.

Schröter, Klaus. "Chauvinism and Its Tradition: German Writers and the Outbreak of the First World War." *The Germanic Review* 43, No. 2 (March 1968): 120-35.

Discusses the private and public responses to the war expressed by older German writers, including Richard Dehmel, Gerhart Hauptmann, Stefan George, Hugo von Hofmannsthal, Robert Musil, Heinrich Mann, and Thomas Mann.

Skvor, Georges. "The First World War and Czech Literature." In

Canadian Slavonic Papers, Vol. 7, pp. 195-202. 1965. Reprint. Millwood, N.Y.: Kraus Reprint Co., 1976.

Considers the impact of the war on Czechoslovakian poetry, prose, and drama.

Škvor, Jiří. "Czech Literature and the First World War." In *Czechoslovakia Past and Present,* edited by Miloslav Rechcigl, Jr., pp. 962-71. The Hague and Paris: Mouton, 1968.

Examines such important themes and subjects in Czechoslovakian literature about World War I as patriotism, nationalism, German expansionism, humanism, Christian morality, and the conflict between individualism and collectivism.

Spender, Stephen. "English Poets and the War." In his *Love-Hate Relations: English and American Sensibilities,* pp. 177-88. New York: Random House, 1974.

Defines the motivation behind English war poetry as a fundamental love of English gentleness and the English countryside, an attitude much removed from the American view that the war was being fought to preserve such abstract ideals as democracy.

Stallworthy, Jon. *Poets of the First World War.* London: Oxford University Press, 1974, 31 p.

Biographical and critical sketches of Edmund Blunden, Rupert Brooke, Wilfred Owen, Isaac Rosenberg, Siegfried Sassoon, and Edward Thomas.

Stromberg, Roland N. "The Intellectuals and the Coming of War in 1914." *Journal of European Studies* 3, No. 2 (June 1973): 109-22.

Recalls the approval with which philosophers, historians, poets, and novelists on both sides greeted the declaration of war.

Taylor, Andrew. "A Blameless Boyhood: Australian Poetry about the Great War." *Westerly* 32, No. 2 (June 1987): 55-61.

Compares war poetry written during and immediately after the war to that written during the post-Vietnam era, when World War I emerged as an important subject in Australian literature and film.

Thompson, Eric. "Canadian Fiction of the Great War." *Canadian Literature,* No. 91 (Winter 1981): 81-96.

Discusses Canadian novels of the war, notably *All Else Is Folly: A Tale of War and Passion* (1929) by Peregrine Acland, *Generals Die in Bed* (1930) by Charles Yale Harrison, and *God's Sparrows* (1937) by Philip Child.

Tomlinson, H. M. "Authors and Soldiers." In his *Waiting for Daylight,* pp. 80-7. New York: Alfred A. Knopf, 1922.

Considers many war writers too tentative in recording their experiences. According to Tomlinson: "Is it not remarkable that soldiers who could face the shells with an excellent imitation of indifference should falter in their books, intimidated by the opinions of those who stayed at home? . . . [These authors] write in whispers, as it were, embarrassed by a knowledge which they would communicate, but fear they may not."

———. "War Books." *The Yale Review* 19, No. 3 (March 1930): 447-65.

Appreciative, informal essay describing the continuing interest in war books for those who participated in the war. Tomlinson praises the works of Edmund Blunden, Georges Duhamel, C. E. Montague, R. H. Mottram, Herbert Read, and others.

Walsh, Jeffrey. *American War Literature, 1914 to Vietnam.* New York: St. Martin's Press, 1982, 218 p.

Devotes three chapters to World War I literature: "Poetic Language: First World War," "Two Modernist War Novels," and "Radicalism: *Plumes* and *Three Soldiers.*"

West, Herbert Faulkner. "The Literature of War." In his *The Mind on the Wing: A Book for Readers and Collectors,* pp. 204-48. 1947. Reprint. Freeport, N.Y.: Books for Libraries Press, 1971.

Collector's survey of war literature of the twentieth century, calling T. E. Lawrence's *Seven Pillars of Wisdom* and Frederick Manning's *The Middle Parts of Fortune* the most important prose memoirs of the war.

Wilkinson, Clennell. "Recent War Books." *The London Mercury* 21, No. 123 (January 1930): 236-42.

Comments on Henri Barbusse's *Under Fire,* Edmund Blunden's *Undertones of War,* Robert Graves's *Goodbye to All That,* Compton Mackenzie's *Gallipoli Memories,* Erich Maria Remarque's *All Quiet on the Western Front,* and Henry Williamson's *The Wet Flanders Plain,* among others, in a discussion inspired by the revival of public interest in war books.

Wohl, Robert. *The Generation of 1914.* Cambridge, Mass.: Harvard University Press, 1979, 307 p.

Generational history arranged by nationality of the writers who came of age during World War I.

ISBN 0-8103-2416-4

90000